Encyclopedia of United States Army Insignia and Uniforms

Encyclopedia of United States Army Insignia and Uniforms

by William K. Emerson

University of Oklahoma Press
Norman and London

Library of Congress Cataloging-in-Publication Data

Emerson, William K., 1941–
Encyclopedia of United States Army insignia and uniforms / by William K. Emerson.
p. cm.
Includes bibliographical references and index.
ISBN 0–8061–2622–1 (alk. paper)
1. United States. Army—Insignia—Encyclopedias.
2. United States. Army—Uniforms—Encyclopedias.
I. Title.
UC533E432 1996
355.1′4′0973—dc20 95–45567
CIP

Text design by Cathy Carney Imboden.

The paper in this book meets the guidelines for permanence and durability of the Committee on Production Guidelines for Book Longevity of the Council on Library Resources, Inc. ∞

1 2 3 4 5 6 7 8 9 10

For My Parents,
Kary C. and Mary Rebecca Emerson

Contents

Tables

PREFACE

RESEARCHERS, HISTORIANS, collectors, dealers in old militaria, curators, and others interested in U.S. Army uniforms and insignia have lacked a comprehensive, documented reference. Years ago, J. Duncan Campbell started such a reference book, but ill health caused him to cease that work. After my second tour in Vietnam, I picked up the start Duncan had made. This book is the result.

The majority of this encyclopedia is devoted to branch insignia. Actual insignia are shown and associated histories are discussed. The goal of this work is to delineate insignia which people may encounter, either "in the flesh" or through photographs, written descriptions, or artwork.

Once most of the portion of this book that concerns insignia was completed, it became clear that uniforms—the things that display the insignia during their use—had to be covered. Uniforms are an essential part of the story of U.S. Army branch insignia. Coats, headgear, and even trousers, especially during the nineteenth century, often were an outward sign of the wearer's army occupation. Slowly, uniforms became more standardized, and the ornaments upon the coats and hats took on more importance. For this reason, it is worthwhile to examine the garments that carry the many branch insignia of the U.S. Army. The branch insignia portion of this book is intended to be complete, but the uniform part is essentially an overview. Many details are presented, but a few people may find it wanting in some minor aspects. One entire book has been written just on flight clothing of the Army Air Force during World War II. Repeating such information is unnecessary, but assembling diversified information is worthwhile.

WILLIAM K. EMERSON
Huntsville, Alabama

Acknowledgments

To show so many insignia required the cooperation of a great many people. Virtually all collectors and museums contacted generously opened their collections to examination and photography. Without this help, most of us would never be able to see so many treasures. My thanks go to the very many people who shared the results of their years of work.

Despite the large number of people involved, a few stand out. J. Duncan Campbell, of Harrisburg, Pennsylvania, started the project, as noted, and contributed some of his writings, especially on the early insignia. His encouragement to all involved with military insignia is well known, and he was extremely generous in sharing with me both his knowledge and his collection. Frank Storer, of the Detroit, Michigan, area, preformed extraordinarily as he took hundreds of photographs. Without them we would not be able to enjoy the sights of so many insignia. Both men served their country as U.S. Army Reserve officers and are now retired. Their interest in this project is reflected in their many positive contributions. Buddy D. Patterson; the Pennell Collection of the University of Kansas Libraries, with special thanks to Nicollette Bromberg; and Donald Kloster and Dan Stanton of the Military History Division, Smithsonian Institution, made substantial contributions. Without their help, the work could not have been done.

Photographs of uniforms or insignia, or the uniforms and insignia and artwork themselves, were loaned by Terry Avery, Leonard F. Ball, Paul Braddock, Michael F. Bremer, Sergeant H. H. Booker, Mike C. Bruun, Kevin Carroll, George Cress, Dr. B. F. Cooling, Dr. Charles H. Cureton, Brian Dunnigan, Eglin Air Force Base and Armaments Museum, Lieutenant Colonel James B. Emerson, Colonel Kary C. Emerson, 1st Battalion of the 3d U.S. Infantry, Fred Gaede, Anthony Gero, Colonel Charles Gill, Edward Gliniecki, Richard Graney, Stephen Henry, R. T. Huntington, The Institute of Heraldry, Lawrence Johnson, A. E. Kauffman, Dr. John Langellier, Mike McAfee, Minnesota Historical Society, J. Craig Nannos, George Nicholas, Jr., Donald Norton, Steven Osman, Ronn Palm, Dave Parham, Gary Poppleton, Presidio of San Francisco Museum and Ed Green, Lieutenant Colonel Frank Robertson, Gil Sanow, Smithsonian Institution, Shelby S. Stanton, Stefan Wesplowskie, Lieutenant Colonel Beatrice Whitomb, and James Wilson.

In addition, several organizations took special photographs and in some cases staff members gave most generously of their time to find the "right" illustration. These organizations include the Amon Carter Museum; Armed Forces Institute of Pathology; Arizona Historical Society; Association of the U.S. Army, especially Eric C. Ludvigsen; Bureau of Archives and History of New Jersey State Library; Custer Battlefield National Monument; Defense Audio Visual Agency; Denver Public Library; DOD Still Media Depository; Fort Benning Museum; Fort Bragg Museum; Fort Leavenworth Museum; Fort Mason (San Francisco, California) Museum; Fort Sill Museum; Kentucky Military Museum and Nicky Hughes; Library of Congress; Mackinac Island (Michigan) State Park Commission; Mount Vernon Ladies Association; National Air and Space Museum; National Library of Medicine; National Park Service; Office of the Army Chief of Staff; Office of the Sergeant Major of the Army; Office of the U.S. Army Surgeon General; Patton Museum of Cavalry and Armor; Pennsylvania Historical and Museum Commission; Rensselaer County (New York) Historical Society; Still Photo Division of the National Archives; the White House; U.S. Air Force; U.S. Army Chaplains School; U.S. Army Marksmanship Unit of Fort Benning; U.S. Army Natick Laboratories; U.S. Army Quartermaster Museum; U.S. Army Transportation Corps Museum; U.S. Military Academy Archives; U.S. Military Academy Band; U.S. Military Academy Museum and Mike McAfee; U.S. Military History Institute, including Michael Winey; and Washington and Lee University.

Many others, whose names appear throughout the photo credits and in the background files, provided valuable assistance. Without them, this book would have been less complete and less accurate. I gratefully acknowledge the assistance of all those who helped.

For those areas which lack either substance or accuracy, the author apologizes. For the wonderful assistance offered by so many, the author extends his thanks.

WILLIAM K. EMERSON
Huntsville, Alabama

SECTION I

SETTING THE STAGE

Chapter One

Introduction

ARMY UNIFORMS HAVE always represented the traditions of the wearer's skill and professionalism. From the Romans until the present, uniforms have changed with the fashions of the times but always have been much more than simply soldiers' clothing. Uniforms tell of the history of the service, display individual and organizational awards, and encourage pride in a soldier's unit though identification with fellow troops. The evolution of today's uniforms and insignia has been built on all these factors, along with the influence of contemporary clothing and the various duties performed by soldiers.

Military "uniforms" of Rome declined along with the empire. However, until the early fourteenth century, Roman civilian clothing fashions prevailed. Generally both men and women wore tunics and mantles until tailoring skills evolved and apparel began to conform more to the body's shape. Tailoring techniques developed rapidly, and by the end of the fourteenth century the whim of fashion was being felt. Styles changed rapidly, and clothes became "old fashioned" in a few years.

Medieval military "uniforms" (other than body protection) were confined to knights, who wore long, sleeveless tunics over chain-mail armor. A coat of arms on these tunics or the color of the cloth served to identify the otherwise disguised wearer. Thus, an insignia or a color, or both, became associated with military men and the garments used exclusively by them.

But how did uniforms, as we know them today, evolve? The school-child image of early New World settlers coming ashore wearing civilian clothing, organized as a temporary fighting force, and bearing rustic, somewhat ineffective firearms (at least by today's standards) could also characterize early-seventeenth-century armies overall. Likewise, one hundred years later the bright uniforms of professional French and British armies during the French and Indian Wars reflected changes in armies generally and in military clothing particularly. The actual transition from civilian garments to national uniforms occurred between 1660 and 1720.[1]

Uniformed men formed into standardized units typify today's armies, but in the early seventeenth century the very opposite was true. Gustavus II, King of Sweden, was instrumental in initiating that change. During the Thirty Years War he adopted firearms for the army and, through organizational innovation and reform, developed small-unit tactics, thus setting in motion the evolution leading to today's armies. Increased efficiency in tactics and the subsequent need for marching introduced formations and a number of junior leaders. Thus, the individual became subordinate to the unit. In the European religious wars of the sixteenth and seventeenth centuries, as in most previous conflicts since the fall of Rome, the majority of soldiers were employed part time. Eventually, however, leaders such as Gustavus II recognized the greater merit of full-time forces. The raising of new armies each campaign season was not cost effective, and changes in military requirements made standing armies a necessity. Starting with the Thirty Years War, major political leaders not only raised, paid, and partly housed these new permanent armies, but they also began to equip and clothe them uniformly.[2]

At the outset of the Thirty Years War, soldiers joined armies, fought battles, and died in their own clothes. Some early leaders may have organized and even inspired the troops, but kings did not furnish many standardized supplies such as uniformly matched clothing. One inevitable result of the seventeenth-century organization of armies was the adoption of uniform clothing for members. At first, regiments were attired in standard clothing, as initiated during the 1640s.[3] Soon, however, armies could be identified by uniforms. In France, during the last third of the seventeenth century, Louis XIV supplemented the regimental uniforms with some he supplied. In addition to increasing the organizational effectiveness of armies during the late seventeenth and early eighteenth centuries, uniforms had a psychological aspect. By presenting the image of total efficiency and invincibility, an army gained a key edge. Uniforms and the new linear tactics, coupled with extreme discipline, allowed the British, for example, to form the "thin red line" that was nearly impossible to defeat.

Until the seventeenth century regiments were raised by well-to-do members of society, and the soldiers owed loyalty to their immediate overlord. Whether the troops owed allegiance to the king or only to the immediate master, who may have been several layers down the social scale from the king, was the immediate question. By the seventeenth century in most European countries the ultimate loyalty was to the sovereign, but in some areas, most notably Germany, there was no true central authority until later. By accepting uniforms supplied by the king, troops acknowledged their indebtedness to the king. Through the introduction of army uniforms, everyone—civilians, soldiers, and kings—recognized who was responsible and responsive to the sovereign.

The military influence on dress was strongly felt in the mid-seventeenth-century European wars. Buff leather coats, introduced for protection, along with military sashes ("insignia" of the day) came into common use. It was this uniform as much as anything that set the soldier apart from his fellow countrymen. When military dress began to become standardized, styles were based on current fashions, but the clothing of the rank and file did not always change as rapidly as civilian dress. As uniforms evolved, trends were established and distinctive uniform characteristics were developed. Austrian infantry wore black hats and grey coats, Prussian regiments wore blue, and Swiss and Irish wore red.[4] These seventeenth- and eighteenth-century developments reflected the changes of the times.

Once uniforms became common, they began to fall victim to fashion trends. These predictable changes were just as regular as they are today and even more noticeable in men's clothing during the time when uniforms were being developed. This tendency continued well into the nineteenth century. Uniforms proved no exception. Eighteenth- and nineteenth-century military wear often closely followed civilian fashion. One example is the late-nineteenth-century shirt collar, which by 1890 was typically not turned down but was worn standing straight up. This single collar (as opposed to the double or turned-down collar) was not in use in 1880, and before World War I it was again out of fashion, even though, during the interim period, it saw wide use both in the army and in civilian life. Similarly, the three-cornered hats of the American Revolution were out of fashion by 1790, both within and out of the military. Sometimes civilian wear was patterned after military trends, such as the trench coat, which was born during World War I and survives with shoulder loops, belts, and various buckles today. Coats, trousers, and other apparel changed frequently simply because of styles until World War II, when the introduction of man-made fibers and other factors also began to influence apparel.

Near constant temperature levels resulting from modern heating, both in conveyances such as automobiles and in homes and businesses, increased mechanization, and frequent travel all affected twentieth-century clothing. This was also true of military clothing in the last half of the twentieth century, when soldiers became more specialized, more troops worked in vehicles even in a field environment, and an increasing number of soldiers worked indoors. These factors of changing working environments and of new artificial materials have worked to influence the latest uniform changes.

Similarly, American army members have, through their uniforms and appearance, reflected this nation's civilian clothing trends. For example, the dominance of Victorian England's fashions resulted in the helmets in the style of English horse guards and in the

Fig. 1-1.

Fig. 1-1. The ornate "gilded 1890s" are reflected in this lieutenant's dress uniform, which was worn through 1902. Gentlemen's dress clothing changed with the times, and these styles carried through to the army. Fifteen years after this uniform became obsolete, the army would be in France, fighting in mud-filled trenches.

gaudy uniforms of the U.S. Army from 1872 until 1903. Later, the sheer size of America and its twentieth-century growth as a world power allowed greater U.S. influence on more recent military fashions. The American movement to less formal dress and less concern about social status resulted in changes in other armies' clothing during the twentieth century. Between the world wars American civilians began to wear waist-length jackets with elastic at the waist and cuffs and with diagonal pockets at about elbow height. When armored forces were formed for World War II, U.S. soldiers adopted these jackets as uniforms. This typical "casual" American clothing became more common over time, both within the military and in the civilian community (Fig. 1-1).

While uniforms of the Regular Army reflected the general clothing of the times, the various state militia and volunteer units, and a few special organizations, strayed more from the conservative trends of the regular force. During the Civil War many units adopted more unusual colors or cuts in an effort to show their enthusiasm or special status. The best-known examples are the zouave units, which adopted the baggy trousers and short, open-front, collarless jackets derived from French uniforms. In addition, many state uniforms were similar to those of the Regular Army yet had added trim or other distinctions. The Civil War U.S. Sharpshooters wore green uniforms, and the Veteran Reserve Corps, consisting of partially disabled soldiers, wore sky blue uniforms during their existence from 1863 to 1865.

Color is the most notable distinctive feature of uniforms. If only one word is used to describe a uniform, most often it is color. In the twentieth century, color remained the one debated feature throughout the time. The new U.S. Navy built its uniform tradition upon the navy blue of the British Royal Navy uniform. Seamen valued their traditional white or navy blue uniform blouse with large square collar with such pride that when a revised, more modern uniform replaced the old style after the Vietnam War, popular demand soon forced the return of the traditional clothing.

The traditional U.S. Army uniform color was dark blue, the color that George Washington introduced during the Revolution. The dark blue coat was accompanied by light blue trousers for most troops. Blue was discarded as a field uniform in 1898, replaced by khaki. Olive drab became the color of another field uniform in 1902, and by World War I, blue uniforms were completely eliminated. The army used various shades of brown and tan during the first part of the twentieth century. After World War II the army leadership decided that there was no traditional uniform color and thus began to "build (a) uniform tradition with the adoption of the Army Green Uniform."[5] But by the end of the 1980s various professional journals were carrying letters to the editors calling for a return to the "traditional" olive drab or some color other than green—something with a tradition.

Chapter Two

The Changing U.S. Uniform

Fig. 2-1. *These 1905 soldiers on their way to clean stables wear frocks over their blue uniforms. Today's "fatigue" uniform comes from such clothing, which was used on fatigue duty. Today's clothing concept, based both on a plentiful supply and on different dress for different occasions, is a radical change from the past. Less than forty years after this picture was made, Life magazine showed the private in World War II with six different uniforms, and several other sets of military clothing existed.*

Not all uniforms that are supposed to be the same are truly similar. Some range widely from the prescribed, but usually this contradictory clothing ("nonuniform" uniforms) belonged to officers, at least in the nineteenth century. The federal government supplied the enlisted clothing it prescribed. The army had most enlisted mens' clothing made under its direct supervision through contracts. The terse phrase which appears

Fig. 2-1.

time and again in nineteenth-century regulations, "according to pattern," was adequate: soldiers wore what was provided by the army. Officers, in contrast, purchased their own uniforms and, until the twentieth century, often had them tailor-made. Nineteenth-century uniform regulations describe officers' uniforms in detail and were an attempt to cause uniformity; but individual preferences of both the officers and their tailors contributed to variations despite the regulations. During the twentieth century mass production techniques complicated the problem. Both officers' and enlisted men's uniforms appeared in regulations in detail, and large quantities of clothing were made. Changes could be affected easily.

Both dress and work uniforms were needed. In response to demands, uniforms for various purposes, with various titles assigned to them, evolved and became more specialized. The uniforms worn on campaign varied considerably over time. Fatigue clothing, used during dirty work such as stable duty, allowed the better uniform to be saved for parades, guard duty, and other occasions (Fig. 2-1). At times the fatigue uniform was worn on campaign, while in other periods what we might call the dress uniform was the normal attire. As the nineteenth century progressed, specially made clothing appeared, a result of new challenges such as the army's mission to explore Alaska and fight in the tropics and of industry's ability to effectively supply late-nineteenth- and twentieth-century troops economically (Fig. 2-2). Early in the twentieth century, specialized work uniforms such as those worn exclusively at artillery emplacements or in power generating stations appeared. For those soldiers prepared to fight a war in fixed stations, these were the counterparts of field uniforms.

Throughout history, the U.S. Army has changed uniforms frequently, and with the support of industrialization, expanded the variety of uniforms. At the beginning of World War I the army had several uniforms: full dress, dress, service, and various fatigue clothing. Both the World War I winter and summer uniforms were olive drab, the wearing of khaki having been discontinued in 1909 because of many problems in obtaining consistent shades over the years. Also during that war olive drab became used to the exclusion of the traditional blue, which until then had been the color of full dress uniforms; the army attempted to have one standard of dress for economic reasons. Olive drab served all of the time—for dress, garrison, and field. There was dissatisfaction with the "all-purpose" service uniform, however, and in 1928 the dress blue uniform was reinstated on an optional basis. The army, conservative by nature, found it hard to eliminate the previous attitude of formality. Troops even wore neckties in the field as late as World War II. Also during World War II the army introduced special combat clothing that would eventually leave the olive drab wool uniforms and the cotton khaki clothes, reintroduced in the 1930s, for wear in offices and as dress uniforms.

Uniforms may most easily be examined by cut and color of coat, but one must also remember the purpose of a particular uniform, which will explain why it and other styles may have seen use together on any given date. Before moving to the survey of each general style of coat, some additional

Fig. 2-2.

Fig. 2-2. *Specialized winter clothing, 1904. Increased capability of American industry allowed the army to provide a wider variety of uniforms tailored to specific climates and missions.*

background may be helpful: general comments on shoulder trim, buttons, sashes, insignia, and exceptions for musicians.

Fig. 2-3. *A pair of wings, 1808–14, worn by Captain Benjamin Burch of the Washington Artillery (a militia unit). These particular wings are more ornate than the enlisted versions. Wings buttoned on the shoulder near the neck, and the end with the bullion fringe conformed to the shoulder.*

Fig. 2-4. *An 1835-pattern sergeant majors' epaulette made of worsted (wool) materials.*

Fig. 2-5. *Captains' epaulettes of the 1851 pattern. The number indicates the regiment and the disk color the branch. For officers senior to captains the bullion fringe was larger in diameter (1/2 inch versus 1/4 inch) and longer (3 1/2 inches versus 2 1/2 inches), while lieutenants wore smaller bullion (1/8 inch in diameter and 2 1/2 inches long).*

Fig. 2-3.

Shoulder Ornaments

Military uniforms added many different kinds of trim on shoulders. Typically one or two different styles of devices went on the shoulders of various uniforms during a given period. Because of this overlapping, one name may represent more than one type of shoulder ornament. For clarification, in this chapter the following terminology will be used at some expense to historical accuracy:

Wings (Fig. 2-3) fit the curve of the shoulder and extended outward from the shoulder. Wings were worn from 1816 until 1832.[1]

Epaulettes (Figs. 2-4 through 2-6) were adopted for noncommissioned officers of the Continental Army in 1775 and expanded for officer wear in June 1780. They were used intermittently by enlisted men until 1854, by company- and field-grade officers until 1872, and by generals until 1917 (Fig. 2-7).[2]

Knots are the most diverse shoulder insignia, and the many names for them can cause confusion. The knots shown in Fig. 2-8 were used by company- and field-grade officers on dress uniforms, 1872–1903. The type shown in Fig. 2-9 was made from gold wire and used on various officers' mess and dress uniforms after 1902. These knots had rank insignia added between 1911 and 1938 (Fig. 2-10). From 1860 until 1872, light or mounted field artillery officers added "Russian" shoulder knots to their uniform. Rank insignia were added to the knots' center.[3]

Shoulder knots are different from sleeve

Fig. 2-4.

Fig. 2-5.

knots. The term *knot* is also used to describe a series of lacing decorations on the lower sleeve to indicate officers' ranks. These lower-sleeve knots were first used on overcoats and later on various mess, dress, and evening uniforms (Fig. 2-11).

Enlisted men also wore shoulder knots, some of which were similar in design to those of officers but of different materials. Fig. 2-12 shows an issued enlisted men's shoulder knot of the type worn by musicians from 1885 until the dress uniform was replaced by the 1902-design dress coat.[4] Gold cord 1/4 inch in diameter was used to make 1872–1903 officers' shoulder knots (the pad was branch-colored), while branch-colored worsted cords and pads made up enlisted band members' shoulder knots.[5] Many nineteenth- and early-twentieth-century militia organizations used shoulder knots, and those knots can be confusing if one tries to account for them as Regular Army insignia.

During the nineteenth century each branch usually added its own unique colored trim to many uniforms. In the twentieth century this evolved so that now these branch colors are normally used only on dress uniforms. In nineteenth century regulations, branch colors for officers included: artillery, red; cavalry, yellow; infantry, light blue or white (this branch changed back and forth between these two colors); and staff officers, dark blue. Such colors used by various branches are more complex than it may first appear. Beyond such generalizations as already made, the dates and location of the trim must be specified. At the end of the nineteenth century, for example, the branch trim used by enlisted men of the Corps of Engineers was red with white edging. Officers of the Corps did not adopt these colors until 1901, as they used dark blue on shoulder straps at that time, even though they previously used other colors as cap and hat trim. Enlisted men of the signal service used orange, then black and white, followed by orange and white, as their chevron colors, yet officers did not wear any of these colors as their shoulder straps were dark blue for many years. Before the Civil War, ordnance officers wore a pompon on their dress caps, with the "lower two-thirds buff, upper one-third crimson," yet at that same time their shoulder straps were dark blue. Even in the twentieth century when use of branch colors was more standard, ordnance officers have had two different sets of "branch colors": black

Fig. 2-6. *General Henry Leavenworth's epaulette, as worn on his 1832–35 coat. On this particular uniform the epaulette was held in place by a shoulder strap.*

Fig. 2-7. *Surgeon Richard H. Coolidge, who served from 1841 through 1865, wears epaulettes with gold fringe.*

Fig. 2-6.

Fig. 2-7.

Fig. 2-8. Officers wore shoulder knots of this design on dress uniforms between 1872 and 1903. The color of the cloth pad indicated branch.

Fig. 2-9. Knots such as this one, made from gold cord 1/4 inch in diameter, went on officers' full dress uniforms prescribed from 1907 to 1917 and on mess uniforms from 1902 to the present. Rank was added to these knots from 1911 until 1938.

Fig. 2-10. Captain William Mitchell, about 1912. A Signal Corps officer, Mitchell was detailed to the General Staff Corps, as is shown by the General Staff insignia on his shoulder knots. Captains' bars are on the shoulder knots, as prescribed between 1911 and 1938. The aiguillette on his left shoulder was used by selected branches until World War I. Before 1912 the aiguillette went on the right shoulder.

Fig. 2-11. Sleeve knots, or trefoils, were of this pattern for company- and field-grade officers. The number of narrow bands told the rank: none for second lieutenants; one for first lieutenants; two for captain, as shown in this picture; and so on. Branch insignia often were worn in the lower angle of the trefoils. This officer is Captain McGee of the 12th Cavalry, 1912.

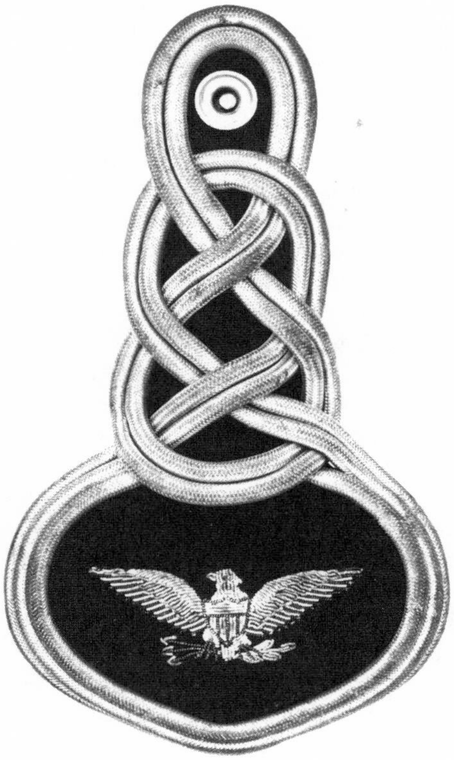

Fig. 2-8.

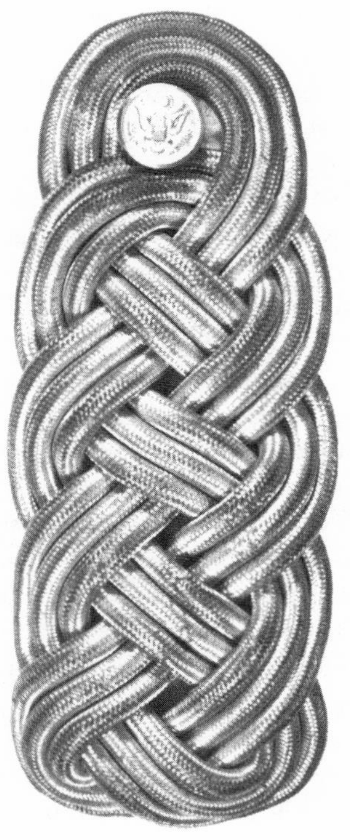

Fig. 2-9.

Fig. 2-10.

Fig. 2-11.

Fig. 2-12.

Fig. 2-14.

Fig. 2-15.

piped with scarlet before World War I, followed by crimson piped with yellow.

Shoulder Straps (Figs. 2-13 and 2-14) were worn by officers on most post-1832 nineteenth-century uniforms and on twentieth-century blue uniforms to show rank. The center, or field, was colored according to branch for field- and company-grade officers. Some nineteenth-century contemporary terminology may be confusing if caution is not exercised. In 1832 orders, privates were to wear "a strap" instead of epaulettes, but the device was actually an epaulette with very short fringe. By authority of General Order 36, June 1839, dragoon officers began to wear "shoulder straps," which were in the general shape of epaulettes without fringe, rather than the standard straps used by all officers up to that time (including dragoons since 1833). These shoulder straps were of blue cloth with gold lace edging and a gilt crescent enclosing the regimental number. Similarly, during the Spanish-American War the khaki field uniform blouse had "shoulder straps" that, in the terms used in this book, are known as shoulder loops.

Shoulder Loops (Fig. 2-15) are cloth, approximately 1 to $1\frac{1}{2}$ inches wide and usually 4 to 5 inches long, extending from shoulder seam to the base of the collar. These were either detachable or stitched into the shoulder seam. Shoulder loops, first introduced in the 1780s, were part of several late-nineteenth-century coats and some twentieth-century coats and shirts (Fig. 2-16). The shoulder loops were usually stitched into the shoulder seam, but occasionally they were detachable. They were often edged or completely colored according to branch until World War I. Between the world wars shoulder loops on shirts distinguished officers' from enlisted men's shirts.[6] Frequently metal insignia were pinned to the cloth shoulder loops, especially for officers' ranks. Use of insignia on shoulder loops expanded to enlisted personnel after World War II. In the

Fig. 2-12. *At first glance this may appear to be a militia member, but he is actually Musician John McCauley of the Regular Army, 1900. He has added branch-colored cloth aiguillettes and shoulder knots that were issued by the Quartermaster General's Department at the end of the nineteenth century in red for artillery and Corps of Engineer bands, in yellow for cavalry, and in white for infantry.*

Fig. 2-13. *Captain W. P. Chambliss, 5th U.S. Cavalry. His rank is shown by shoulder straps.*

Fig. 2-14. *Second Lieutenant Samuel B. Arnold, 1st Cavalry, 1898. Before World War I, second lieutenants were distinguished by shoulder straps without any other insignia. Straps measured $1\frac{3}{8}$ by 4 inches until 1912, when they became $1\frac{5}{8}$ by 4 inches. Post–World War II women's shoulder straps measured $1\frac{5}{8}$ by $3\frac{1}{2}$ inches.*

Fig. 2-15. *Colored shoulder loops on an 1899 coat.*

Fig. 2-13.

Fig. 2-16. Shoulder loops are usually made of the same material as the coat or shirt on which they appear. In this photograph of the 1902 enlisted men's coat, branch-colored cord edging has been added. The upper end of shoulder loops near the neck has always been fastened by a single button.

Fig. 2-17. A shoulder mark, introduced in the 1980s for officers and noncommissioned officers to wear on the green shirt and the black pullover sweater. Initially, officers' marks were green with a gold bar at the end, while enlisted men's marks were on plain black cloth. In 1990 generals switched to black marks, and in 1991 remaining officers changed to black backgrounds.

Fig. 2-16.

Fig. 2-18.

1980s shoulder loops began to hold cloth shoulder marks (Fig. 2-17) instead of the metal insignia. On the light green shirts and the black sweater, shoulder marks showed ranks of corporals and above.

Scales (Fig. 2-18) are brass shoulder ornaments worn in the nineteenth century by enlisted men to ward off saber blows. The general shape was that of the top of an epaulette. The army adopted scales for enlisted dragoons in 1833 and for all other enlisted men in 1854.[7] They were prescribed to be worn on coats and jackets until 1872, but in practice men usually did not wear them in the field.

Aiguillettes are braided, looped cords attached to one shoulder, with the free ends usually affixed to a coat button in such a manner that they hang in a partial loop. Gold cords were first prescribed for dragoon field-grade and regimental staff officers in 1833, but their use spread to the general staff (Adjutant General's, Inspector General's, Quartermaster's, Subsistence, Pay, and Medical Departments) and aides in 1839. Aiguillettes for regimental staff officers were made of gold and silver between 1839 and 1847. Senior regimental noncommissioned officers (NCOs) added aiguillettes to the right shoulder of their dress uniform in 1839.

Gold aiguillettes were not used between 1847 and 1872, after which they were worn on dress uniforms by aides, regimental adjutants, and members of the Adjutant General's Department, Inspector General's Department, and Records and Pension Office. These aiguillettes were attached to the right shoulder knot and to the top two right chest buttons (Fig. 2-19).

Fig. 2-19.

Fig. 2-17.

Regulations of 1912 changed the way men wore aiguillettes. Adjutants, aides, and members of several branches placed them on the left shoulder, but the chief of staff and aides to the president wore them on the right shoulder. After World War I only presidential aides wore aiguillettes with their dress uniforms, but in 1936 the cords had a brief pre–World War II revival only to be dropped and revived again in 1947 for aides and military attachés.

After World War II, two forms of the aiguillettes appeared: a dress version, with two braided cords and ferrule (metal tips) in a style reminiscent of the older version, and a new garrison version, which was used only with the service uniform. This new aiguillette consisted of a single section of braided cord with one ferrule. Ferrules, which were added to the hanging or loose end of aiguillettes and fourrageres, are metal tips about the size of a pencil and usually 2 1/2 to 3 inches long. Many ferrules are very ornate, while some made in the twentieth century are unadorned. Both styles are still worn today (Figs. 2-20 and 2-21).

Fourrageres were used during World War I by the French Army, which cited units for bravery equivalent to that required of individuals for the Croix de Guerre. When a unit received a second citation, unit members were awarded a green and red braided cord (fourragere) worn on the left shoulder. A fourth citation resulted in the fourragere's colors being changed to yellow and green. During World War II, France and Belgium awarded fourrageres and the Netherlands awarded an orange lanyard, and briefly during the Vietnam War some units received Vietnamese fourrageres.

Individual soldiers with the unit when it was cited wore the fourragere or lanyard, but the French fourragere was not only an individual but also a unit award. Once a unit received the fourragere, all members of the organization wore the cord. After World War I, men who wore the citation as an individual award (those who had been with the unit when the fourragere was earned), added a special distinctive mark. Frequently the distinctive marks worn on World War I fourrageres were small branch insignia. An example is shown in Fig. 2-22. These small, bright metal pins went on the knot above the fourragere's ferrule. Most units receiving insignia were of the 1st or 2nd divisions, and men of these divisions wore either a 3/8 inch-high numeral *1* or a star and Indian head (2d Division insignia) in a 1/2-inch circle in addition to the insignia of the smaller unit. The few units not in these two divisions wore just a small branch insignia. A list of the distinctive marks used on fourrageres is in Table 2-1.

Uniform Trim and Additions

Sashes of red cloth evidently were worn by officers on duty and assigned to troops by the 1790s. Regulations of 1821 called for red net sashes to be tied "with a knot in front of the right hip," although this was evidently the earlier practice. Use of sashes expanded in 1832, and the knots were to be placed on the left hip, with the pendant part to be one foot in length when tied. Generals added buff-

Fig. 2-18. *Mounted troops of the mid-nineteenth century wore metal scales on their jackets. These particular versions are for privates and corporals. Sergeants' scales had raised crescents below the metal straps as well as above. Higher-ranking noncommissioned officers had articulated scales with three rows of six rivets each.*

Fig. 2-19. *Brigadier General Arthur Murray wearing an aiguillette on the right shoulder of his full dress uniform in 1898.*

Fig. 2-20. *President and Mrs. Bush with various presidential aides. The army lieutenant colonel to the left of the president wears his full dress aiguillette on his right shoulder, a post-1912 practice reserved for White House aides.*

Fig. 2-20.

Fig. 2-21.

Fig. 2-21. In 1947 the army introduced new, simple, single-cord aiguillettes for generals' aides to wear on service uniforms. Major David H. Petraeus, aide to the chief of staff, is shown wearing his service aiguillette and special lapel insignia.

Fig. 2-22.

Fig. 2-22. Maj. Gen. Louis E. Hibbs, commander of the 63d Division during World War II, wears a fourragere with a 3/8-inch-high numeral 1 on the upper portion of the knot, and below that a small 5th Field Artillery device, showing that he was a member of the 5th Field Artillery Regiment, 1st Division, when the unit received the award during World War I.

Fig. 2-23.

Fig. 2-23. Captain Leonard Wood, 15th Regiment, Massachusetts Volunteer during the Civil War. By wearing his officer's red sash over his shoulder, he indicated he was serving as officer of the day.

Fig. 2-24.

Fig. 2-24. This general officer is wearing a post-1902 buff-colored sash, which was placed over the right shoulder by major generals but only around the waist by brigadier generals. He is wearing the insignia of his assignment on his epaulette, a practice only of officers assigned to the General Staff Corps after 1911.

colored silk sashes with bullion fringe; staff officers in dress uniforms and artillery, infantry, and ordnance officers all added a red silk net sash with gold bullion tassels. When the army formed the dragoons in 1833, these officers added a deep orange sash tied on the right hip and worn only with the dress uniform or when directed by the commanding officer. During the first half of the nineteenth century various branch officers wore sashes, while others did not, with the exact list changing over time.

Substantial changes occurred in 1851. The pendant portion could be as long as 18 inches, and the sash was tied behind the left hip. While generals continued to wear buff sashes, all branch officers except those of the Medical Department wore crimson silk net sashes. Medical Department officers wore green sashes, and senior noncommissioned officers wore red wool sashes. These were to be worn on all occasions except stable and fatigue duty. For the first time the officer of the day was directed to wear his sash from the right shoulder to the left hip, as a mark of his designation (Fig. 2-23). Officers' sashes varied in size and quality. Noncommissioned officers' sashes from 1851 to 1872 were 70 inches long and 5½ inches wide.

In 1872 the army directed that the use of sashes cease, with the exception of the buff

Table 2-1. *Combination of Distinctive Marks Worn on World War I French Fourrageres.*

Upper Insignia	Lower Insignia
2d Division device	None
2d Division device	Infantry
2d Division device	Infantry with 4 above
2d Division device	Infantry with 9 above
1st Division number	Infantry with 16 above
1st Division number	Infantry with 18 above
2d Division device	Infantry with 23 above
1st Division number	Infantry with 26 above
1st Division number	Infantry with 28 above
1st Division number	Infantry with M and G in horizontal angles and 1 above
1st Division number	Infantry with M and G in horizontal angles and 2 above
1st Division number	Infantry with M and G in horizontal angles and 3 above
2d Division device	Infantry with M and G in horizontal angles and 5 above
2d Division device	Field artillery
1st Division number	Field artillery with 5 above
1st Division number	Field artillery with 6 above
1st Division number	Field artillery with 7 above
2d Division device	Field artillery with 12 above
2d Division device	Field artillery with 15 above
2d Division device	Field artillery with 17 above
2d Division device	Field artillery with T and M in horizontal angles and 2 above
None	Aviation with 103
2d Division device	Medical
None	Medical with 539 above
None	Medical with 525 above
None	Medical with 546 above
2d Division device	Engineers
1st Division number	Engineers with 1 above
2d Division device	Engineers with 2 above
1st Division number	Signal Corps with 2 above
2d Division device	Signal Corps with 1 above
2d Division device	Quartermaster Corps
2d Division device	Ordnance
2d Division device	Adjutant General

sash for generals, which continued until 1917 (Fig. 2-24). In 1877 those above the grade of brigadier general were given the option of wearing their sash across the body, from the left shoulder to the right side. After 1902 brigadiers wore the buff sash around the waist and higher generals wore it across the body from right shoulder to left side. While the office of Chief of Artillery existed early in the twentieth century, that officer wore a distinctive red sash. With the action of the Mexican border and World War I, sashes, along with dress uniforms, disappeared.

Buttons were an easily available insignia early in the army's history. Each regiment had its own button. Such regimental buttons were often similar in the case of like units; rifle regiments had similar designs, as did infantry regiments until the war of 1812. Early nineteenth-century buttons were more than regimental devices; the general design could, and usually did, indicate branch. Army buttons evolved so that by 1821 each arm had a button whose central design was an eagle with a shield. On the shield was a branch initial, with the most common letters *A* for artillery, *C* for cavalry, *D* for dragoons, and *I* for infantry, as shown in Fig. 2-25. In 1854 enlisted men dropped the letters and went to the same design without any letter (a general service button), while officers continued to use branch-distinguishing buttons.

Early buttons usually matched the color of other metal insignia on a given uniform. Generally, until 1851 infantry had "white metal" (silver or pewter) buttons, and other branches wore "yellow" or brass trimmings, while after 1851 all buttons and metal insignia were yellow until dark or black metal insignia and buttons came into wide use in 1903 as a result of recent combat in the tropics.[8]

Beginning in the early nineteenth century many staff departments had buttons bearing designs peculiar to their organization. These were continued throughout the century, and as new branches, such as the Signal Corps, evolved, they often adopted a distinctive branch button. The army's general service button, adopted in 1902 and 1903 and in use today, takes its design from the Great Seal of the United States (Fig. 2-26), although versions with rims, lined backgrounds, and other details often have more precise dates of use.[9] Except for officers of the Corps of Engineers, this overall design replaced branch buttons in 1903.

Insignia Designs to show branch came into use with the 1851 standardization of uniforms, although several branches wore special devices on caps or on shoulder trim well before the Civil War. Engineer and ordnance soldiers wore the first collar insignia on their 1851 uniforms. Because Confederate officers placed rank on their collars, after the Civil War some Federal officers opposed placement of insignia on the coat collars, but this prejudice was finally overcome at the end of the nineteenth century. Today's army collar insignia trace their history to 1892 with the introduction of a dark blue sack coat (Fig. 2-27), designated "undress," for officers' daily wear. Line officers—infantry, cavalry, and artillery—wore silver regimental numbers on their coat collars. Since some staff departments lacked unique insignia, they began to adopt new branch devices. At first the 1892

Fig. 2-25.

Fig. 2-26.

Fig. 2-25. *The combat branches wore buttons of this general design from 1821 until 1902. The letter on the eagle's breast designated the soldier's branch. Enlisted men omitted the letter on the eagle's breast in 1854. This particular button was for a dragoon, as noted by the D. This button is 29/32 inch in diameter, but other sizes were also made.*

Fig. 2-26. *A general service button, first introduced in 1902 and still in use today. Several variations have been made, including an early design without the rim, changes in other details, various sizes, and various colors, but they all differ from the 1821–1902 design (Fig. 2-25) by their inclusion of the motto ribbon and the "glory" above the eagle's head. (Example 29/32 inch in diameter).*

Fig. 2-27.

Fig. 2-27. *Officers of the 25th Infantry. This coat, with frogging on the chest, was used between 1892 and 1895, as were the regimental numbers on the coats' collars. Branch insignia worn in the U.S. Army today trace their history to this period, as officers not assigned to combatant branches began to wear insignia of their service on this coat. The bearded individual wearing the hat and standing in the rear is the regiment's chaplain in his prescribed uniform.*

staff insignia were simply designs, such as the Corps of Engineers' castle, used previously elsewhere on the uniform. Other branches, however, formulated new designs for wear on the collar of the new coat. The Quartermaster General's Department had to develop an insignia, for example, since officers had worn the letters *QD* up to that time.

Fig. 2-29. *Officers' metal insignia made to look like embroidery were common at the end of the nineteenth century. These so-called etruscan insignia have occasionally been used throughout the twentieth century.*

Fig. 2-30. *An officers' smooth-finished insignia of the type commonly used during the Spanish-American War and later. Enlisted men's branch and US insignia that were not on 1-inch disks were always to be of this finish.*

Fig. 2-31. *Insignia of the Quartermaster Corps, adopted in 1895. The insignia was one of the first made like a piece of jewelry, with a detailed gold eagle, an enameled six-mule wagon wheel (with a red and white hub and a blue felloe), and silver sword blade.*

Fig. 2-28. *An officer in a coat first introduced in 1895. When worn after 1902, it was known as a dress coat. Infantry, cavalry, and artillery officers wore branch insignia on the collar after 1895.*

Between 1892 and 1895 staff departments adopted insignia for the standing-collar coat, so only the line did not have branch insignia for collars by 1895. This probably accounts for the adoption of crossed arms by the infantry, cavalry, and artillery in place of regimental number (Fig. 2-28). Of course the three arms had used crossed weapons as insignia before, so while collar or lapel insignia are generally descended from the 1892 officers' coat, the roots of some designs can be traced back further—some to the 1832 uniform change. Virtually all of the 1892–95 staff designs, plus those staff and arms devices from 1832, remain in use today with only slight modification.

Insignia Manufacture

The 1892–95 officers' sack coat collar insignia were the last to be widely embroidered, and even then it was cheaper to make some metal insignia that looked like embroidery. This imitation embroidery finish was called "etruscan," as opposed to the smooth finish. Two contrasting examples are shown in Figs. 2-29 and 2-30. Etruscan insignia had generally fallen into disuse by 1907, but some lasted into the 1930s, and a few persist today, of which the most notable is the Finance Corps' diamond.

A few staff insignia did not lend themselves to embroidery, however. The Quartermaster Department's design was very complex (Fig. 2-31), but it could be adopted because the technology of the time allowed such insignia to be made at a reasonable cost. Likewise, the Inspector General's Department and Corps of Engineers insignia could be produced with more faithful detail through the use of jewelry techniques than through embroidery, and ease of manufacture and attractiveness of the product increased the popularity of this type of insignia. With the 1898 adoption of the officers' khaki coat, metal insignia became universally adopted, and with the 1902 uniform changes, great quantities of pin-on, stamped metal insignia were used by enlisted men for the first time.

Cotton and bullion embroidered devices saw a revival during and after World War II. This embroidery (although now almost exclusively mass-produced machine embroidery) was widely seen on combat clothing before the 1950s. Since some twentieth-century insignia were hand-embroidered overseas, especially during the Vietnam War, variations abound and are impossible to fully catalog. They are clearly different from nineteenth-century insignia, but some late-twentieth-century dealers have reproduced many Civil War-style hand-embroidered insignia in an attempt, unfortunately, to defraud collectors and museums or for use by reenactment groups. As techniques of imitation become better and minor technical construction flaws are corrected, and as these insignia age, the spurious insignia will become harder to distinguish from the originals.

Musicians

Musicians have often worn uniforms that differ from the "standard" enlisted uniforms. Those soldiers who were band members or field musicians often were exempted from the usual rules and often wore distinctive uniforms and/or insignia, as do some even today. Because in the eighteenth and nineteenth centuries drum, fifes, and bugles were the only effective means of rapid communications with troops during the confusion of fighting, officers had to be able to find these key people on a battlefield quickly. Musicians were given distinctively colored coats to solve this problem.[10]

Until 1851, U.S. Army field musicians generally wore coats that were of a different color than those of other soldiers. Regular soldiers very early in the nineteenth century typically wore dark blue coats trimmed in red, while field musicians wore red coats trimmed in blue. When the various branches adopted different colors of trim, red remained the color of field musicians' coats. Between 1851 and 1902, field musicians' coats were of standard blue color but had additional branch-colored trim on the chest. One example is shown in Fig. 2-32. The army issued musicians' trousers with two branch-colored stripes, each one-half inch wide, between 1883 and 1917.[11] Each company-sized unit normally had two field musicians (these men were called trumpeters in the cavalry.)

By contrast, generally twelve to thirty musicians formed each regiment's band. (The number of band musicians varied over time.) Band members often added special ornamentation such as branch-colored shoulder knots and aiguillettes to the normal soldier's uniform.[12] Two examples are shown in Figs. 2-33 and 2-34. Before 1832 many band members wore white coats. The army limited band uniforms and the number of soldiers in the bands in that year, and generally after that time band members added different insignia and trim to their uniforms to distinguish them from field musicians rather than having totally different uniforms.[13] In 1885, General Order 104 expanded uniform trim allowances for all band musicians by prescribing mounted helmets (with plumes and cords), aiguillettes with shoulder knots, music pouches, and white linen trousers. An example of uniform additions from Fort Riley, Kansas, at the turn of the century is shown in Fig. 2-35. A few special bands had unique uniforms, and even today the Military Academy Band and the U.S. Army Band have distinctive uniforms (Fig. 2-36).

The unique uniforms and uniform trim used by field and band musicians must be taken into account for a comprehensive and accurate picture of uniforms. Besides this uniform trim, between the 1880s and the 1930s a small lyre was often the insignia

Fig. 2-32.

Fig. 2-32. *Three Civil War drummer boys of the 12th Infantry. The horizontal stripes in the shield shape on the chest were used by musicians from 1854 until 1872. From 1851 to 1854 branch-colored solid shields of the above shape were used. Before 1851 red coats distinguished field musicians.*

worn by band musicians, while a bugle or trumpet was a field musician's insignia from the last part of the nineteenth century until 1918. Further complicating the scene was the nonregulation use of many insignia by musicians (Figs. 2-37 and 2-38).[14]

Changes in Uniform Styles

Beginning in 1821, regulations described officers' uniforms but gave only very brief descriptions of enlisted men's uniforms. In 1902 regulations contained detailed descriptions of officers and enlisted men's uniforms, and uniforms were divided by occasion and named accordingly, such as full dress, dress, field service, and so on. Uniforms themselves differed in cut, and the trimmings and insignia varied among different uniforms. These practices continued until after World

Fig. 2-33.

Fig. 2-33. *A Regular Army band member, 1898. Three rows of buttons and gold shoulder knots and aiguillettes were nonregulation, although regimental commanders frequently authorized such changes.*

Fig. 2-35.

Fig. 2-35. *A 6th Cavalry Band member in his 1901 dress uniform. All members of this band added the baldric (sash), various cords and epaulettes, and the fur busby. The trim across the coat's chest was distinctive of band and field musicians, a carryover from the time when field musicians needed to stand out clearly on the battlefield so officers could find them to transmit orders using musical instruments.*

Fig. 2-34.

Fig. 2-34. *The 3d Cavalry Band in the 1880s. Most members have added two rows of buttons down their coat fronts and have added a variety of shoulder and breast cords.*

Fig. 2-36. *In 1968 the U.S. Army Band adopted its blue coat with yellow trim and high collar that carries a distinctive insignia. Such special uniforms are long rooted in military tradition. As on many earlier band uniforms, a shoulder cord has been added for decoration.*

Fig. 2-37. *These four band members should have lyres but no wreaths as their cap insignia. Wreaths were ordinarily used only by noncommissioned officers, and gold cap cords were for commissioned officers only.*

Fig. 2-38. *The 4th Cavalry Band members of 1904 wore officer-style dress coats with US insignia and a lyre on the collar, all strictly nonregulation.*

Fig. 2-36.

Fig. 2-38.

Fig. 2-37.

War II, when insignia and trim, instead of the actual cut of the clothing, came to indicate the difference between officers and enlisted personnel. In general, the army made changes in basic uniform styles every twenty to thirty years until World War II.

In the 1970s a subtle change started in army uniforms. The concept of prescribing and wearing of uniforms began to evolve, and the change was completed during the 1980s. A few years after the end of the Vietnam War, females could select from a wide range of uniforms, and all office personnel could choose on a daily basis their basic uniforms, complete with a choice of options. Mandatory dates of change from summer to winter uniforms and back disappeared. Each person could wear what he or she wanted, when he or she wanted.

Although women gained the flexibility to choose from a significantly greater number of uniforms than men had, men's flexibility of choice increased as well, and individuals of both sexes are now able to choose uniform components freely. Green shirts, for example, can be worn with various sweaters, plain, or with coats, and the shirts and some sweaters can be worn with or without a tie. Thus, for office and travel wear, the basic green uniform was made adaptable, just as civilian clothing could be worn in a variety of circumstances at the wearer's whim. A general summary of some of these options and the many frequent uniform changes for men and women after this fundamental change is shown in Table 2-2.

About This Book

The purpose of this encyclopedia is to allow detailed identification of branch insignia and general identification of the uniforms which carried these insignia. For this reason, chapters are generally arranged to allow identification of like objects. Insignia are grouped by branch and then by similar type, such as nineteenth-century enlisted men's cap insignia. Uniform components are likewise described in chapters based on similar garments. This arrangement has been made to assist those not familiar with these objects so that readers may find objects easily.

Various branch insignia are covered in the initial two-thirds of the book immediately following this chapter. The general styles of U.S. Army uniforms are discussed in the remaining sections. A simplified summary of the many coats used by men in the regular army is presented in Tables 2-3 through 2-6. The start and end dates of these tables indicate changes in contemporary regulations.

Table 2-2. Uniform Changes since 1975.

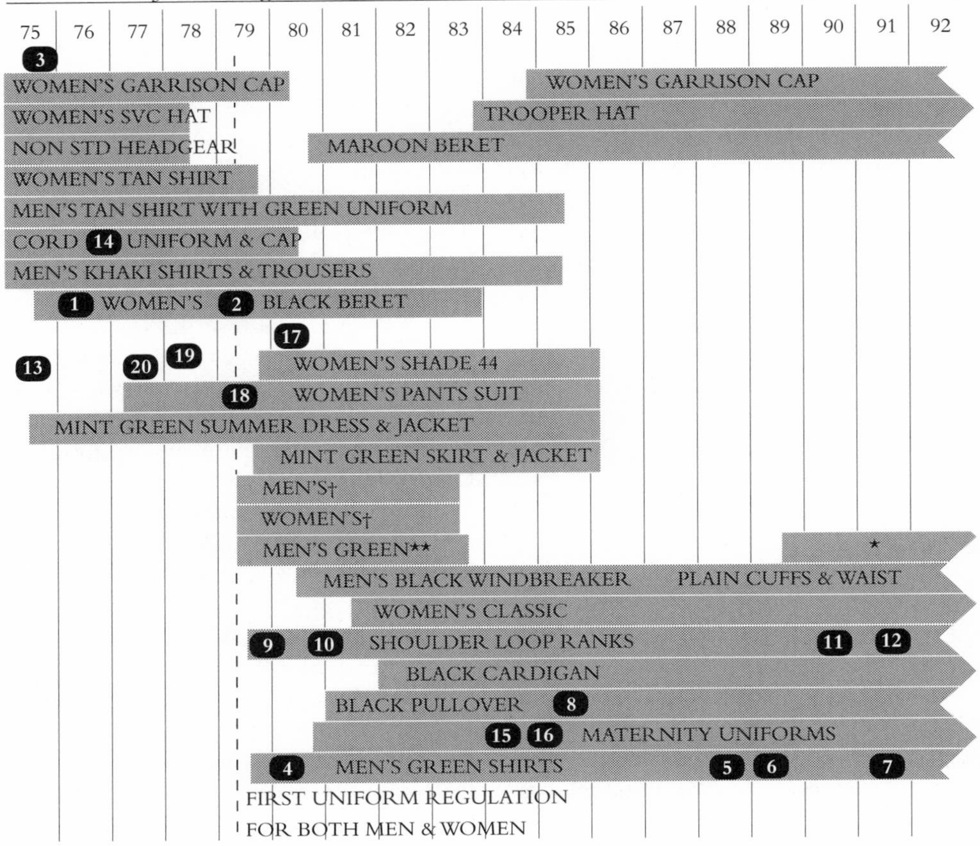

Notes: During the late 1970s and the early 1980s a large number of significant and frequent changes occurred in U.S. Army uniforms. These changes included the disappearance of some differences between women's and men's uniforms, the introduction and the withdrawal of several sweaters and jackets, many changes in women's headgear, and several short-lived women's uniforms. Hardly any uniform used in 1975 survived a dozen years unscathed. Diversity of and changes in military clothing began to more closely mirror those of civilian styles. These trends are shown in this table. Field clothing (fatigue and battle dress uniforms) and mess, dress, and evening uniforms are not included; however, these uniforms became equally complex, with frequent changes.
*Black windbreaker with elastic cuffs and waist.

1. Initial issue.
2. Required.
3. Wear with cord uniform.
4. Awards worn on shirt in tropics only.
5. Recruiters wear awards on shirts.
6. All personnel wear awards on shirts.
7. Pleated pockets introduced.
8. Distinctive insignia required on chest (previously optional).
9. Green background for officers.
10. NCOs introduced.
11. Black background for generals.
12. Black background for all officers.
13. Bright brass chevrons first worn.
14. Officers' rank placed on right collar.
15. Officers change collar insignia.
16. Officers add trouser stripes.
17. Single-weight green uniform approved.
18. Women in MP & airborne blouse pants like men.
19. Common method of insignia wear prescribed.
20. No seasonal change required for uniforms.

*Black windbreaker with elastic cuffs and waist.
†Green cardigan sweater.
**Windbreaker.

Table 2-3. *Officers' Coats Introduced between 1821 and 1902 (general dates of wear).*

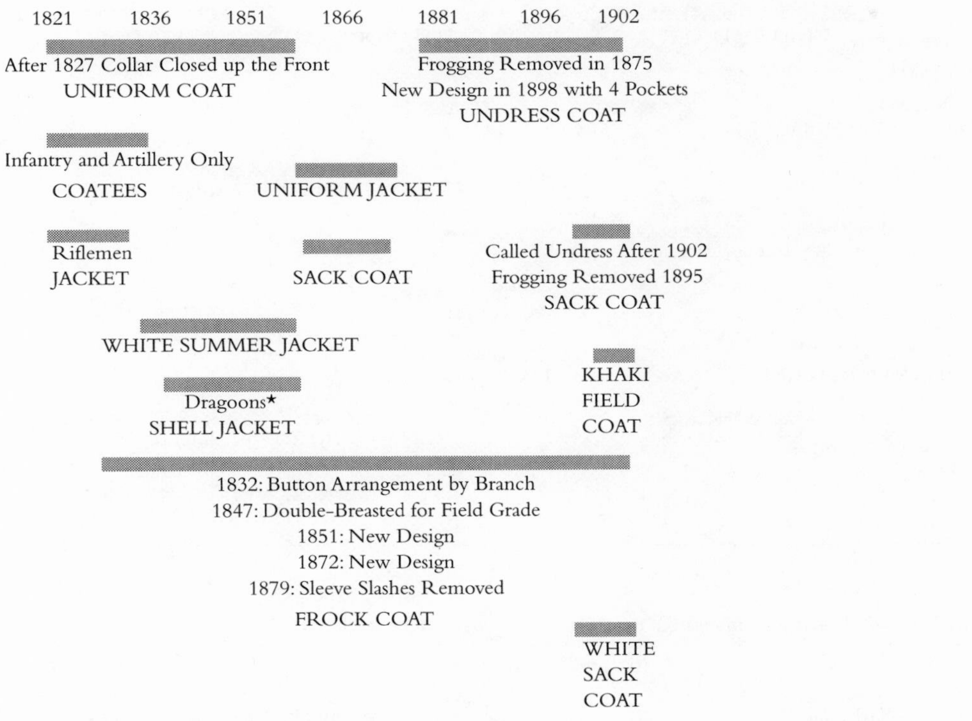

*Mounted riflemen and engineers added in 1846; horse artillery added in 1845.

Table 2-4. *Major Coat Versions for Officers, 1902–62 (general dates of wear).*

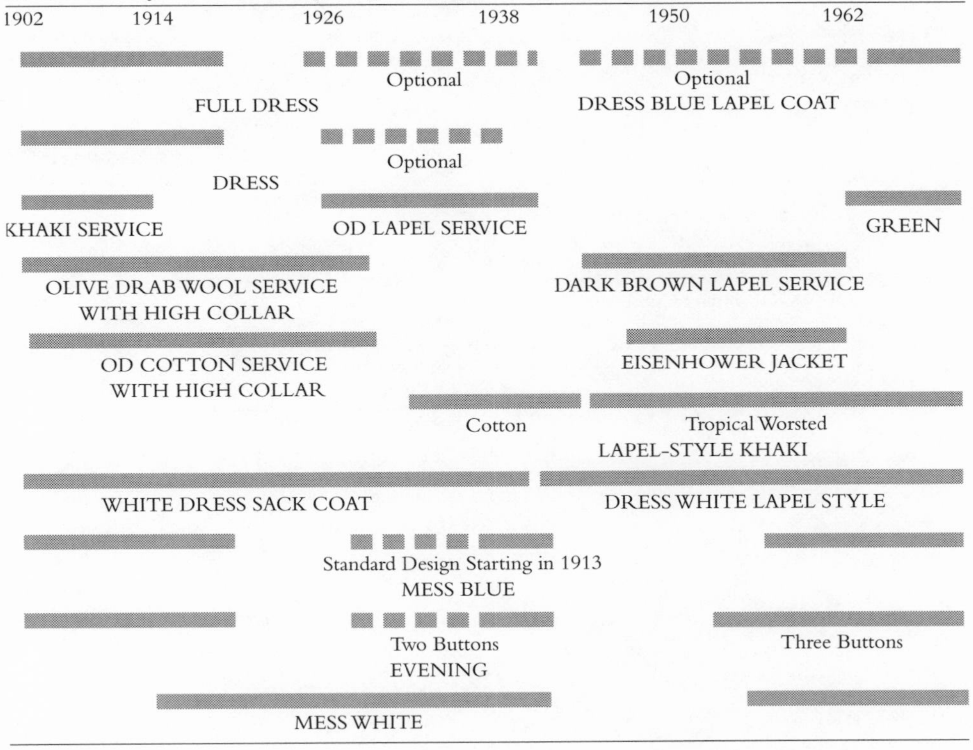

Table 2-5. *Enlisted Men's Coats Introduced between 1821 and 1902 (general dates of wear).*

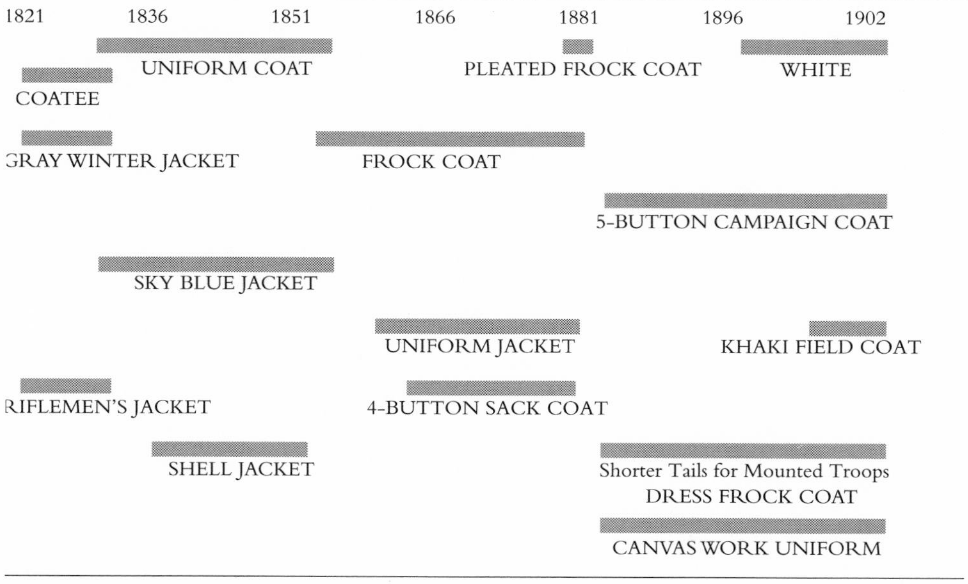

Table 2-6. *Enlisted Soldiers' Coats, 1902–62 (general dates of wear).*

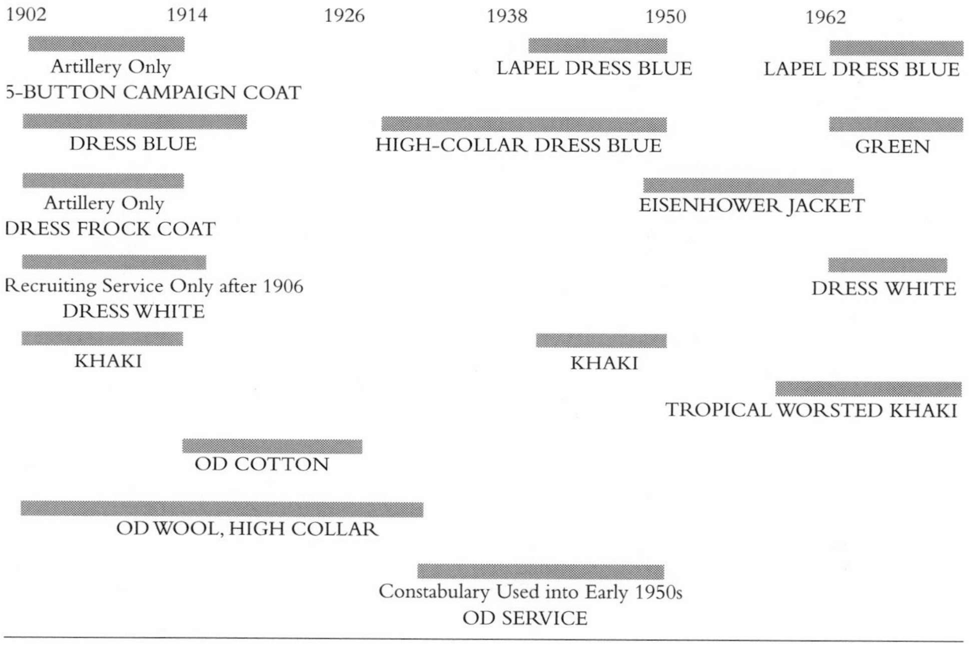

Chapter Three

Regular Army Uniforms and Insignia, 1782–1802

FROM THE END of the Revolution, for almost twenty years men of the U.S. Army were tossed by the tides of fortune of the young republic, and at times there was a question whether the army would survive. Indeed, the founding fathers wanted a citizen army, and the militia was thought by many as all the force that the infant nation needed. The development of Regular Army insignia parallels the growth of the military arm itself, and for both we have a starting point just about as close to zero as one can get.

In September 1783, shortly after the formal end of the Revolution, Congress allowed General George Washington to discharge those parts of the federal army that he deemed proper. After the British withdrew from New York, he retained about six hundred men to guard the various posts that held military supplies. During the spring of 1784, Congress renewed its inclusive debates of 1783 on the proper size of the army. The debate became one of state financial responsibilities and claims to western lands. As a compromise between the factions, on 2 June 1784, at the end of its session, Congress ordered the last existing regiment and battalion of artillery disbanded, except for twenty-five men to guard the stores at Fort Pitt, fifty-five men at West Point, and a proportional number of officers, with no one remaining above the rank of captain.[1] This scant force of eighty men and a handful of officers comprised the whole of the U.S. Army. Most were artillerymen.

The infantry regiment and artillery battalion ordered discharged in June 1784 were manned mainly by men from Massachusetts and New Hampshire, and this New England burden was at the heart of the controversy about who supported the army. With the 2 June discharge decree, Congress at the same time established quotas for Pennsylvania, Connecticut, New York, and New Jersey. The 700 new men were to guard the Northwest Territory against Indians urged on by the British. Army strength increased to a mixed regiment of eight companies of infantry and two of artillery, but there was no change of uniform. Recruits received infantry and artillery clothing regardless of the branch to which they were assigned. Size and availability evidently were the main criteria. On 20 October 1786, Congress authorized an additional 1,340 noncomissioned officers and privates, but despite the need of the republic's frontier, this modest goal was not achieved.[2] The total new force had uniforms similar in color and trim to those of the "late war."

In 1785 newly appointed General Josiah Harmar wrote to one officer, "I am sorry to observe that some of your men's coats are faced with white and some with red—I wish you to endeavor to procure a sufficiency of Scarlet, and alter the white in order that the Regiment may be in Uniform."[3] Despite attempts of this type, the army seems to have continued to wear a mixture of leftover Revolutionary War uniforms in an odd assortment of colors.

In an attempt to create standard appearance, Secretary of War Knox prescribed artillery uniforms on 30 January 1787:

> Hats cocked—yellow trimmings—coats blue scarlet lappells, cuffs and standing cape—length of the coat to reach the knee, Scarlet linings and yellow but-

> tons*—vests white with short flaps, three buttons on each pocket—overalls—cockades of black leather round with points four inches diameter—shoulder straps—blue, edges with red on both shoulders—feathers—black and red, tops to rise six inches above the brim of the hat—epauletts—the Officers, gold—the Majors 2, a single row of bullion—Captains 1 epaulette on the right shoulder, 2 rows of bullion—Lieuts.—1 epaulette on the left shoulder, 1 row of bullion—Sergt. 2 epaulettes, yellow worsted—Corporals 1 epauletts [*sic*] right shoulder—Swords saber form, yellow mounted, the Major 3 feet & capts and Subs [subalterns] 2½ feet—the uniform of the Music to be red, faced with blue.[4]

Knox also ordered that both the infantry and the artillery would wear the same type of white vests, except infantrymen would wear "white buttons" (made of pewter) and artillerymen would have "yellow buttons" (made of brass). Even so, in 1786 the department quartermaster at West Point, William Price, issued New Jersey infantry recruits yellow-bound artillery hats. He also issued these same infantrymen a mixture of uniform coats from the "old army."[5]

In January 1787 regulations prescribed similar epaulettes, "blue, edge with red," for both infantry and artillery. Cavalry, Rifle Corps and infantry officers' epaulettes were silver, and the colonel commandant had a double row of silver bullion on each epaulette; artillery officers wore gold. "Sergts Major, Quartermaster Sgt., drum and fife Major two silks and silver; Sergeants, two worsted—cpls., one right shoulder—Artillery, yellow, infantry coats, short fatigue coats, and drummer coats,"[6] thus indicating there was some movement toward uniformity.

The uniform of the army is again described in a letter to General Harmar from Secretary of War Knox dated 21 April 1788. Knox stated in part:

> With respect to cocked hats and long coats I have to observe—that long coats appear to me not to be proper for service on the frontiers as short one—overalls are conceived to be greatly preferable to breeches—but overalls and long coats and cocked hats are in my opinion an unseemly association—the few men who are in this town belonging to Captain Bradfords' company are judged to be most properly clothed for real service.
>
> It has been my desire that the American troops should have a characteristically national uniform, *Blending utility and appearance* (author's emphasis) together without implicitly following the customs of the Europeans—I have had the hope that something might be adopted in this respect, might evince a judgement of our own, I confess that the present uniform is very different from my wishes and judgement, yet long coats and cocked hats would not be parts of the uniform— I hope the time will arrive when a system of this kind may be adapted agreeable to troops and honorable to the nations.[7]

Between early 1785 and 1788, army clothing became more like the uniforms they were intended to be rather than simply something to cover a man's body.

During the period from the Revolution through the War of 1812, button designs were an essential insignia form. The Revolutionary War infantry wore solid, shanked, cast pewter buttons bearing devices such as a regimental number or the raised monogram letters *USA*. Officers of infantry wore more elaborate buttons of stamped tin, crimped over a bone or wood back, bearing the number or device of their regiment or having a large letter *S* in the monogram *USA*. The artillery buttons, made of thin brass, display such devices as a cannon in profile and a flag, or a small coehorn mortar.[8]

Early in the twentieth century a group of amateur historians representing the New York Historical Society went to the site of West Point's "Villefranche Barracks" of the Revolution and excavated an interesting series of buttons issued to troops organized by the various states. In addition to state buttons, they found several small pewter buttons bearing an embossed eagle with a scroll over its head bearing the word *Federal*.[9] These buttons very likely date from 1786, when the infantry separated into a regiment by

*This uniform is very similar to the artillery uniform described in October 1779 when Knox was artillery commander. At that time he called for blue uniforms "faced with scarlet; scarlet lining; yellow buttons; yellow-bound hats; coats edged with narrow lace or tape, and buttonholes bound with the same."

itself and the artillery was broken into four companies.

In 1786, Colonel Henry Jackson, who then directed recruiting in Massachusetts, wrote to General Knox suggesting that uniform buttons should display an eagle on the center with the regimental number.[10] The design of the eagle on the buttons introduced at that time closely resembles the eagle on the Massachusetts cents of 1787. Both the coins and the buttons were the product of the same men, Joseph Callendar and Jacob Perkins, who were associated with the Massachusetts mint. Two known specimens of the federal buttons are signed—one *Parki* for Jacob Perkins and the other *JC* for Joseph Callender, a Boston engraver.[11] Because these buttons are pewter, they are ascribed to infantry, as that branch wore buttons of white metal. Although it is possible that artillerymen wore these "federal" buttons, that is doubtful because the artillery normally was ascribed buttons with cannon or coehorn mortar patterns or of plain brass.

Writing to Alexander Hamilton on 26 November 1798, Major Thomas H. Cushing, the army inspector, forwarded his inspection returns for the 4th Infantry made in December 1797. His return states, "The materials of which it [the coat] is made are badly matched both in color and quality. It is not uncommon to find three or four shades of blue, and as many grades of cloth in the same Company; and the facings, cuffs and collars and linings are as various in quality on the outside. The Artillery Button is plain yellow; that of the Cavalry and Infantry bears the Emblem of an Eagle but its appearance is exactly that of lead, and it cannot be kept clean."[12] The root of these problems lay in the status of the fledgling national clothing industry and the lack of credit extended to the federal government.

During the period 1785–90, while the army struggled to establish presentable uniforms, a cloth or leather cockade was recognized as an easily made adornment for the hat or cap. On 1 July 1785, General Harmar wrote to Secretary Knox suggesting that the black-and-white cockade worn by the regiment could be changed with a view towards securing a "national one." Knox replied that the cockade should be black for both soldiers and officers, noting that light-colored cockades were impractical, while black leather ones presented a more respectable appearance when they were polished. In January 1787, regulations prescribed a standard cockade for artillery and infantry, "black leather, round, with points, four inches in diameter." Despite the intention that officers wear leather cockades, many officers used silk or other cloth cockades. General Harmar wore a three-colored cockade that still survives; it was made by forming individual silk loops into three concentric circles.[13]

As the new republic's settlements moved westward, Indian resentment of white encroachment grew, fomented by British agitation. Sporadic fighting developed, and the army received the chore of keeping peace on the frontier, which in turn necessitated annual increases in the military force until 1792, when the "Legion of the United States," composed of four sublegions, developed. Each sublegion contained one company of dragoons, one company of artillery, a battalion of infantry consisting of eight companies, and a four-company battalion of riflemen, totaling 1,346 officers and men.[14]

We find cockades mentioned in General Anthony Wayne's orders to the legion at Fort Greenville, Ohio, 25 December 1794, in preparation for a grand parade by the troops on New Year's Day, 1795, "when the Sub Legions will parade in perfect uniform with Plumes and other Distinctive Decorations, for which purpose the Adjutant General, will make out an estimate, and return of the necessary Materials; the Quarter Master Genl. will supply the Pay Masters with the same, the soonest Possible; He will also direct the saddlers to stamp out as many Cockades, in Addition to those now on hand, as will be sufficient to supply all the Troops now on the Ground."[15] These obviously leather cockades were probably of the type mentioned ten years earlier, made round with points.

Several examples exist of cockades with a slice removed from the bottom and a part added at the top, resembling a lady's folding fan; these are often called fan cockades. All known attributed fan cockades belonged to militiamen. Since the known Regular Army cockades are round, it is plausable to assume that federal forces used only round cockades and not fan cockades.[16] A militia fan cockade of the artillery with a slice out at the bottom is shown in Fig. 3-1.

In January 1799 orders specified that noncommissioned officers, musicians, and privates were to wear black leather cockades

Fig. 3-1.

Fig. 3-1. *A fan cockade with stamped brass eagle at the center worn by a Captain Maynard of the New York militia early in the nineteenth century.*

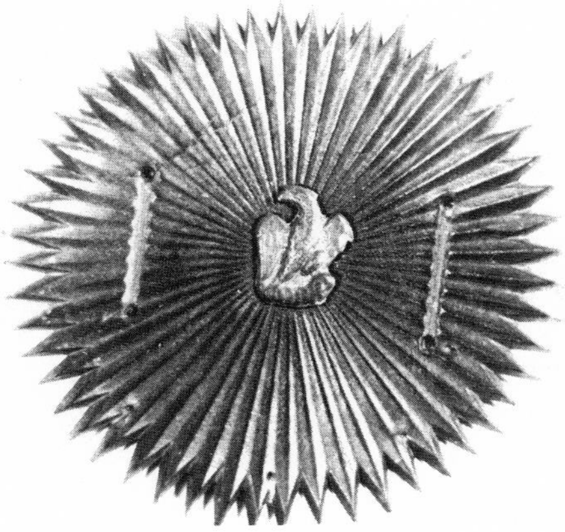

Fig. 3-2.

Fig. 3-2. *An artilleryman stationed at Mackinac Island, Michigan, dropped this cockade about 1802 during the building of a log blockhouse, where it remained until its discovery in the 1960s. The 4-inch-diameter cockade is round with points, as described in regulations for regular troops, with a brass eagle as used by the artillery.*

Fig. 3-3.

Fig. 3-3. *An infantry officers' silver-plated sword belt plate from the time of Wayne's legion, 1792–96. (2 23/32 inches wide)*

with a small white tin eagle in the center.[17] A 4-inch-diameter leather cockade with a brass eagle, made in perhaps 1802, is shown in Fig. 3-2. A regular-force officer serving at this time even wore his cockade when off duty as a "badge of his profession, and an acknowledgement that he receives the pay and is in the service of the United States." By July 1802 officers of the 1st Infantry Regiment were wearing a cockade "of black ribband and an eagle" on the cocked hats.[18] From these early cockades later eagles evolved, which are discussed in the chapter 8, "Eagle Insignia."

Other trim on headgear also could be modified to produce a uniform appearance. In September 1788, General Harmar ordered the white bindings to be removed from all hats and replaced with bearskin and scarlet bucktails. In orders to the legion, while at Pittsburgh on 11 September 1792, General Wayne prescribed distinctive marks for soldiers of each sublegion: "The first Sub-Legion white Binding on their Caps, with white plumes and Black hair. The Second Sub-Legion Red binding to their Caps, red plumes, with White hair. The third Sub-Legion Yellow binding to their Caps—Yellow plumes and black hair. The Fourth Sub-Legion Green binding to their Caps with Green Plumes and white hair." The following day Wayne's officers were instructed, "The officers will wear plain cock'd hats with no other distinctive marks, but the plumes of the respective sub-legions, except in actual service, when they will wear the same caps with the noncommissioned officers and privates of the respective Sub-Legions."[19]

Among others of the "Distinctive Decorations" for Wayne's legion which led to the adoption of insignia, we find mentioned in Fort Greenville orders of 26 June 1795: "The Commanding Officers of Corps, will cause the uniforms to be repaired, and the Hatts and Caps properly decorated: The acting Quarter Master will procure Bear Skins; for covering the Hatts and Caps."[20]

Preserved in Wayne's orders of 16 February 1796 is a description of the uniform of infantry officers of the legion: "The following Uniform for the Officers of Infantry is to be observed and adopted until otherwise regulated—Coats reaching to the knee and full trimmed—Scarlet lapels, Cuffs and

Standing Capes, White Buttons & trimmings, Lapels & Cape two Inches, and Cuffs three Inches wide—Vests and Breeches white. The former with short flaps and three Buttons, Black Stocks or Cravats, Cocked Hats; and full Boots with black tops."[21] (*Cape,* as used in this and many orders of the times, is a collar.)

The legion, with its four sublegions, was abolished on 31 October 1796 and reconstituted as four infantry regiments, two companies of light dragoons, and a corps of artillerists and engineers. The extent of change to uniforms is not precisely known, but it is possible there was no change other than perhaps in buttons. One change in buttons had taken place scarcely four years after the 1792 patterns came into being, and there may have been no change at all in 1796. This assumption is strengthened by the fact that there was a change in button pattern between two and four years later (1798–1800).[22]

Fig. 3-4.

Fig. 3-4. This engraved sword belt plate was made in 1799 for Captain Erasmus Babbitt, Jr. (2¼ inches wide)

In the eighteenth century soldiers carried swords variously on waist belts or on shoulder belts. During the American Revolution, officers most often wore their swords on shoulder belts slung diagonally across the body. The open belt buckled near the chest to adjust the height of the sword. Soon after 1768 the British army replaced the open buckle with a solid metal plate carrying two studs (like large nail heads) and a hook on the reverse side. The two round studs were permanently set through slits cut in one end of the leather belt, and the hook was passed through any one of several spaced holes near the other end of the belt to adjust the length. This arrangement gave the belt a neat appearance, with its excess overlap hidden on the underside of the plate. British officers in the American Revolution wore handsome sword belt plates of gold, silver, and silver on copper bearing elaborate engraved designs, and examples have been excavated at British Revolutionary War sites. Similar cast brass plates worn by British soldiers on their cross-belts, which carried the bayonet and cartridge box, usually bore a numeral or other design associated with their regiment. To what degree American officers wore ornamented sword belt plates during the American Revolution is unknown, and I know of no U.S. plates authenticated to the period 1776–83.

The oldest known officers' shoulder belt plate of the Regular Army (Fig. 3-3) is dated to the period 1792–95, when the Legion of the United States formed the army. Made of silver on copper with two round studs and a hook on its reverse, this die-struck oval plate shows the embossed eagle as first depicted in 1783 and particularly as it appears both on buttons worn at the time of President Washington's 1789 inaugural and on pewter buttons ascribed to the legion. The silver finish of the plate indicates that it was worn by the infantry, which used silver-colored buttons and trimmings.

The sword belt plate shown in Fig. 3-4 is precisely dated to the year 1799. Made of silver with engraved design, it has two studs and a hook brazed on its reverse, where the owner's name, E. Babbit (*sic*) is engraved. During the undeclared war with France, Erasmus Babbitt, Jr., was commissioned a captain in the newly formed 14th U.S. Infantry Regiment, which was raised in Massachusetts and attained about half strength. He served from 8 January 1799 to 15 June 1800.[23]

The size of Captain Babbitt's oval plate, 2¼ inches wide by 3 inches high, is given in General Orders, Headquarters, Greenville, Ohio, 26 June 1795, which additionally state that such plates shall be "ornamented with an Eagle, in gold or silver," to match the buttons. In a general order of 30 March 1800, the swords of all officers were "to be attached by a white shoulder belt 3 inches by 2½ inches, ornamented with an Eagle." Standing orders, published in July 1802, contain vague wording about sword belt plates and give no clue to their ornamentation: "The [sword] . . . to be worn with a white belt over the coat, with a Breast plate, such as has been established; as no others will be permitted to be worn."[24]

Included in the standing orders cited above for the 1st Regiment of Infantry there is a mention of gorgets. Gorgets were crescent-shaped metal ornaments, worn around the neck, that originally were a piece of armor that protected the junction of the helmet and the breastplate and that slowly evolved into symbolic plates worn on the breast to show rank or position. The July 1802 order dealing with officers' dress gorgets states: "when on duty they [officers] are to wear Sashes and Regimental Gorgets, the strings of the Gorget to be red ribband with small roses, the Gorgets to hang over the Cape [collar] of the coat, and the upper button of the coat, so that it may not be more than 2 inches from the Collar." In the paragraph headed "General Directions" a sentence reads, "Sashes, Regimental Gorgets and Breast plates may be procured by application to Colonel Hamtramck."[25] The size and ornamentation of these gorgets is presently unknown, but the "breast plate" could have been similar to that worn by Captain Erasmus Babbitt, illustrated earlier.

Section II

The Ground Soldier

Chapter Four

Riflemen

Riflemen, as differentiated from infantrymen, first appeared in the American Revolution. Their dress was most often the linen or fringed buckskin hunting jacket of the frontier, with hats or caps of wide variety. Military men divided over the combat effectiveness of riflemen in the late eighteenth century because the deadly accuracy of their weapons at ranges beyond those for muskets was offset by the fact that it took longer for them to load and fire, and the rifle could not use a bayonet.

"Rifles or Light Troops" are mentioned in General Orders of 1787; their dress included round hats covered with bearskin instead of the cocked hats of the infantry. The Legion of the United States (1792–96) established one battalion of riflemen of four companies each in the first two of the four sublegions. Its riflemen wore caps modified from cocked hats, with an upright front piece. The order books for General Anthony Wayne infer a dislike for riflemen. After the riflemen had altered both their hats and cartridge boxes in an unauthorized fashion while at Legionville near Pittsburgh, Wayne ordered them to turn in their rifles and perform fatigue duties before the campaign against the Indians on the frontier began.[1]

Not until 1808 did riflemen become a separate branch of the army. On 12 April 1808 an act of Congress expanding the army authorized several new branches, including the "Regiment of riflemen."[2] In addition to distinctive buttons with raised letters *RR,* riflemen added separate brass outline letters *USRR,* each one and one-quarter inches high, on their round caps, with the *US* over the *RR.*

Fig. 4-1.

Fig. 4-1. *This 1812 brass cap plate replaced the separate US over RR letters. (5³/64 inches wide)*

With the advent of tall caps and cap plates in 1812, the riflemen received a diamond-shaped brass plate bearing only the letters *R.R.* (Fig. 4-1). Sometime later that year or early in 1813 the plate was replaced by a brass diamond of the same size bearing an eagle and other embellishments (Fig. 4-2) more in keeping with the plates issued to other branches. On 10 February 1814, Congress authorized three additional regiments of riflemen, and on 17 March 1814 the army published general orders describing their uniform. Brass buttons were to "exhibit a bugle surrounded by stars, with the number of the regiment within the curve of the bulge," and their new cap plates were to have a "design similar to that of the buttons."[3] These 1814 brass cap plates were made without a number within the curve of the bugle

Fig. 4-2. The third style of cap insignia worn by riflemen was introduced during the War of 1812. (5¼ inches wide)

Fig. 4-3. A common design for riflemen's cap plates was introduced in 1814. These came plain, as in this case, and with a regimental number. (3³⁄₁₆ inches in diameter)

Fig. 4-4. The only cap plate worn by the 4th Regiment of Riflemen. (3³⁄₁₆ inches in diameter)

Fig. 4-5. The cut-out eagle and bugle horn were worn by the Rifle Regiment from 1818 until 1821. (3⁷⁄₁₆ inches maximum dimension)

Fig. 4-2.

(Fig. 4-3) and with the numbers *1, 2, 3,* or *4* within the center (Fig. 4-4).

The 1815 army reorganization eliminated the three wartime additional regiments of riflemen, reducing the branch to the old 1st Regiment, generally referred to as the Rifle

Fig. 4-3.

Fig. 4-4.

Regiment, until it, too, was abolished in 1821. Colonel Talbot Chambers, regimental commander, wrote to Commissary General of Purchases Calendar Irvine on 24 June 1817 requesting some changes in the uniform. The new cap plate, according to Chambers, was "a bugle suspended by an eagle, instead of the plate which is estimated too conspicuous." In August 1818 the regiment received this new brass plate, composed of an eagle from the old diamond plate and the open bugle horn also shown on that plate, enlarged to give the new insignia better proportion (Fig. 4-5).[4] The plate was worn until 1821.

In 1821 the rifle companies in each infantry regiment were to wear green pompons. Officers of rifle companies wore gold tassels and bullion, while enlisted men wore green worsted cords and tassels.[5] Riflemen are not further mentioned for many years until an 1846 act of Congress authorized the Regiment of Mounted Riflemen. This organization and its insignia are discussed with dragoons, mounted riflemen, and cavalry. The regiment of Voltigeurs and Foot Riflemen was authorized by Congress in 1847 for service in the Mexican War.[6] During their brief existence they wore no branch insignia, but they did have a distinctive arms branch button appropriately bearing the letter *V* on the eagle's shield. During the Civil War the army formed sharpshooter regiments and clothed the men in green uniforms. Some cap insignia bearing the letters *USSS* or *SS* are known, but the army never authorized unique insignia, and known specimens vary in design.

Fig. 4-5.

Chapter Five

Infantry

Infantry formed the bulk of America's eighteenth-century army. Some of the early infantry uniforms and insignia are discussed in chapter 3. A rather broad dividing line between the very early army and the later forces discussed in this chapter was drawn when Congress increased the army to two regiments and then subsequently converted the army into a legion. Congress added five regiments in 1808, then several more during the War of 1812.[1]

Cap Plates

Before identified patterns of the earliest cap plates worn by the early-nineteenth-century infantry are discussed, one undocumented plate should be mentioned because it may antedate all others. This thin, tin-dipped sheet iron plate (Fig. 5-1) bears only the embossed letters *USI*. Excavated at Sackets Harbor, New York, the plate came from an area garrisoned by regular infantrymen in September 1812, although a company of regular infantry had been sent there four years earlier. While the location of the 1808 encampment is presently unknown, it was in the same general vicinity.

Fig. 5-1.

Fig. 5-1. *This first infantry cap plate was probably used in 1811 and 1812 and bears the impressed letters US over I for U.S. Infantry, conforming to a scheme similar to that used by the Regiment of Riflemen (RR on a plate).*

How early is this plate? In 1808 the army procured separate outline letters *USRR, USLD,* and *USLA* for placement on leather caps worn by riflemen, light dragoons, and light artillery, respectively. Almost immediately the men complained that these letters did not clinch firmly to the caps, resulting in a slovenly appearance. The army had not issued such separate letters for infantry hats; however, by 1811 most infantrymen had been issued tall caps with sufficient space to exhibit such letters. If the earlier unsatisfactory experience with outline letters had made it advisable to change the form, the problem could have been solved by embossing the letters on a metal sheet. If this was the solution for the tall infantry cap, our excavated plate tentatively can be identified as a plate for U.S. infantry in 1811. Further substantiation of this conjecture is found in the first diamond-pattern cap plate for the Regiment of Riflemen, which bears only the embossed letters *RR*.

Uniform descriptions of 1812 prescribed plates for the tall, cylindrical, cloth-covered infantry caps to be "oblong, bearing the Name of the Corps and the Number of the Regiment." In February 1812, William Crumpton of Philadelphia submitted a bill for payment to the purveyor of public supplies for cap plates he had delivered for the 5th, 6th, 12th, and 15th infantry regiments. Less than six months after these plates were issued, the colonels commanding the 6th and

Fig. 5-2. *Several regiments used iron plates dipped in tin of this design during 1812. ($3\frac{21}{64}$ inches wide)*

Fig. 5-3. *Pewter cap plates of this style were made in late 1812. ($3\frac{5}{32}$ inches wide)*

Fig. 5-4. *Excavated specimen similar to that of Fig. 5-3 but with the word INFANTRY spelled out.*

Fig. 5-5. *This pewter cap plate follows the same general layout as the previous two but is unique in the details.*

Fig. 5-6. *Struck from the same die as artillery plates, this 21st Regiment version has the 2 only slightly visible.*

Fig. 5-2.

Fig. 5-3.

Fig. 5-4.

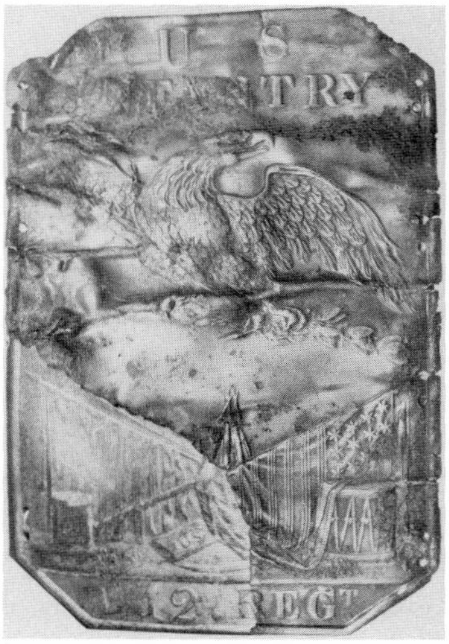

Fig. 5-5.

Fig. 5-6.

15th regiments complained about their quality. The new commissary general of purchases, Callendar Irvine, assured the commanders the plates would be replaced as soon as possible.[2] Fig. 5-2 is an excavated pattern of this 1812 infantry cap plate for the 15th Infantry Regiment. The lettering is impressed on a sheet of tin-dipped iron, and small holes are drilled along the sides to allow the plate to be sewn to the cap. The plate is oblong, bearing the name of the corps and the number of the regiment, precisely as written in the uniform description.

In November 1812, William Armitage, also of Philadelphia, contracted to make pewter cap plates for several infantry regiments, commencing with one for the 16th Infantry (Fig. 5-3).[3] A very similar plate, substituting the word *INFANTRY* for the abbreviated *INFANY* and without a regimental number (Fig. 5-4), was excavated at a War of 1812 encampment site.

A larger plate incorporating the same design elements, but with a distinctly different eagle and arrangement of flags and drum (Fig. 5-5), is marked for the 12th Infantry. Since this is not Armitage's die, it may be ascribed to his sole local competitor at that time, William Crumpton.[4]

In 1964 a surprisingly different infantry cap plate with the embossed *21Rt.* within an oval (Fig. 5-6) was excavated. This plate was lightly struck on a poor composition metal instead of quality pewter. A maker used this same die to strike brass plates bearing the words *1 Rt. Arty.* and *3 Rt. Arty.* within the oval (see Fig. 6-5 in chapter 6, "Artillery"). The 21st Infantry Regiment was constituted on 26 June 1812, and well before the year's end it had been recruited and uniformed.[5]

Fig. 5-7.

Fig. 5-8.

Fig. 5-9.

Fig. 5-7. *An excavated version of the 1814 infantry cap plate. (2¾ inches wide)*

Fig. 5-8. *A mint example of the plated copper 1814 cap plate.*

Fig. 5-9. *This 1814 plate had the excess material cut from around the central design before it was used on a cap or shoulder belt.*

Until additional research gives an exact date, we can not determine whether this plate was issued in late 1812 or early 1813. The same design, made in brass for artillery, is believed to have been issued in the first half of 1813.

National Archives records of the commissary general of purchases show in several instances that infantry regiments received blank plates without any number struck before the word *REGT,*[6] and several blank plates have been found on War of 1812 sites. Forty-four regiments authorized by Congress were organized.[7] The exact pattern and design of cap plates issued to each of these regiments may be unknown forever. The four infantry plate designs already described would have been sufficient for all regiments if proper numbers were substituted where appropriate on the plates or if blank plates were issued. But which style went to which regiments?

On 12 January 1814 Commissary General of Purchases Irvine wrote the secretary of war asking permission to replace current infantry plates with smaller ones. He sent the secretary a sample, stating, "It is lighter neater and will not cost half [the] price. The present plate covers the greater part of the front of the cap, is heavy in appearance, and adds much to the weight of the cap." On March 1, Irvine wrote again to the secretary of war, asking, "If the infantry-cap plate is decided upon, I will thank you to inform me what it is like." Probably the secretary of war had no decision at that time and wanted additional information, because on March 22 Irvine wrote to the military storekeeper in Philadelphia: "Inform me of the number of cap plates remaining in store, designating the kind and the no. of the regt. for which marked."[8]

The 1814 pattern, made of silvered copper (Fig. 5-7) is an excavated specimen. The same plate, not an excavated example, is shown in Fig. 5-8. The eagle in the upper portion of the plate has a representation of clouds beneath it. This same design on a pewter oval (Fig. 5-9) probably was worn as an ornamental crossbelt plate, and these plates may have been cut down from cap plates. Both excavated and nonexcavated specimens exist. Fig. 5-10, of silvered copper, has no clouds beneath the eagle. This example, excavated at Fort Atkinson, Nebraska, was probably struck after the War of 1812 and used until these plates became obsolete in 1821.

Brass cap eagles and chin straps made of overlapping metal scales were adopted for some infantry units in 1820–21 "because a sufficiently cheap and durable white metal . . . could not be procured." In December 1821 white metal trim returned for the infantry even though these changes were not reflected in either the 1821 or 1825 regulations.

Early Officers' Insignia

From 1800 until 1821 there was limited uniformity with regard to ornamented plates worn on officers' leather caps, shoulder belts, or waist belts. Officers were required to purchase these uniform trimmings, so many assumed the right to buy whatever they preferred. Although little is presently known about the designs on officers' insignia, all evidence confirms a lack of standardization. Excavated fragments suggest that some infantry officers wore cap plates of the same design as that of soldiers, but of better metal than pewter. A surviving 1814-pattern officers' cap and plate indicates that at least one officer wore the device shown in Fig. 5-11.[9] An excavated fragment of an officers' rectangular cap plate with scalloped corners bearing an unknown engraved device is shown in Fig. 5-12. This portion bears upper parts of the words *Regt. U.S. INFANTRY.*

Fig. 5-10.

Fig. 5-11.

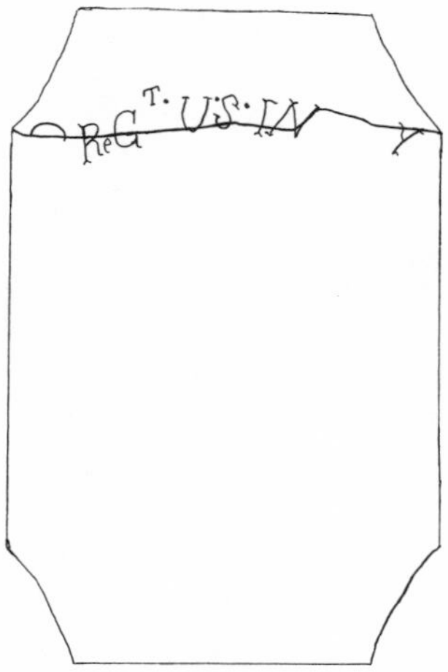

Fig. 5-12.

Fig. 5-13.

Fig. 5-14.

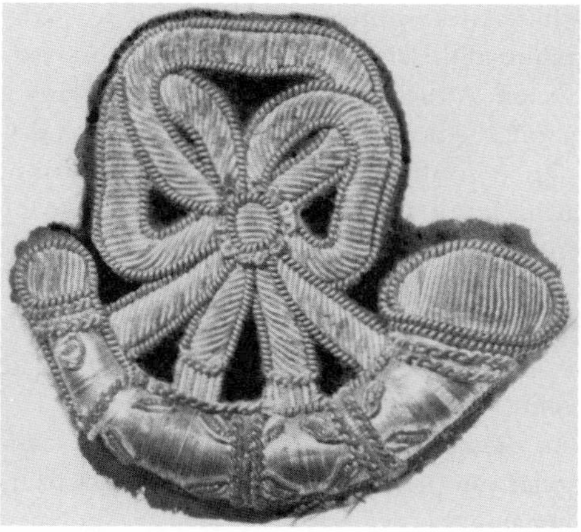

Fig. 5-15.

Fig. 5-16.

Fig. 5-10. *Clouds are missing from this silvered plate excavated at Fort Atkinson, Nebraska. (21$^{59}/_{64}$ inches wide)*

Fig. 5-11. *Officers wore better-quality cap plates than did soldiers. One such 1814 infantry example is shown.*

Fig. 5-12. *This drawing is a partial reconstruction of an infantry officers' cap plate. The top portion is the only fragment recovered, and some of the letters are reconstructed based on portions of the engraved words R(e)G^{T} U.S. IN(FANTR)Y, which can be seen on the original. The central design is not known.*

Fig. 5-13. *From 1821 through 1832, infantry soldiers wore eagles displaying cut-out regimental numbers.*

Fig. 5-14. *The initial 1832 pattern of embroidered silver bugle horns worn on infantry officers' coattails. Militia organizations frequently used such devices, and most embroidered bugle horns were made for state units.*

Fig. 5-15. *An open silver bugle horn, introduced in the mid-1840s for the coat skirts.*

Fig. 5-16. *The mate to the bugle horn shown in Fig. 5-15. While horns were made in pairs, they were usually not as lustrous as these. (Embroidery 2$^{27}/_{64}$ inches wide)*

From 1821 until 1832 the seven infantry regiments had no distinctive branch insignia. The 1821 bell-crowned leather cap for infantry was ornamented only with a pewter outline eagle with a 3-inch wingspread. The shield on the eagle's breast had the regimental number cut out of it, as shown in Fig. 5-13. In 1831 the price of the eagle was reduced from eight cents to five cents, although the exact changes are not now known. Men wore 5-inch-long pompons on the cap between 1821 and 1825—white for infantry and yellow for light infantry. All infantry enlisted men wore tassels and cords of white worsted material, while infantry officers wore silver tassels. The army changed enlisted pompons to white with red tops for light infantry in 1825, although the basic infantrymen continued to wear all-white 5-inch pompons.[10]

Coat Devices before the Civil War

Early regulations called for a lace-bound blue cloth diamond on the tails of coats, but General Order 50, Adjutant General's Office, dated 11 June 1832, prescribed a silver-embroidered bugle horn device for the skirts of infantry officers' dress coats. The 1832 pattern (Fig 5-14), with looped bugle, was worn until the mid-1840s, when larger open bugle horns replaced them (Figs. 5-15 and 5-16).[11]

Cap Ornaments, 1833–51

In 1833, caps for infantry officers and soldiers carried an outline eagle and below it a separate insignia of an open bugle horn. The eagle was made of gilt and the horn of silver-colored metal (Fig. 5-17). This device was worn with a regimental number.[12] The style and pattern of the horns are somewhat reminiscent of the earlier insignia of the Regiment of Riflemen. Somewhat reduced in size, these infantry insignia may have been worn in the 1840s or possibly used by non-regular volunteers. From about 1835 until 1850 several volunteer organizations wore the open horn device as an additional insignia on the rear of the tall cap of the period.

The year 1851 saw the traditional silver or white color for infantry trimmings replaced by the new "Saxony" blue and buttons and insignia changed to gilt or gold color. The cord that appeared with the open infantry bugle changed from a suspension cord to one wrapped around the reintroduced looped horn. The pattern of the cap also changed from its old tall, cylindrical form to a much smaller shako modeled after the French army cap of the period.[13]

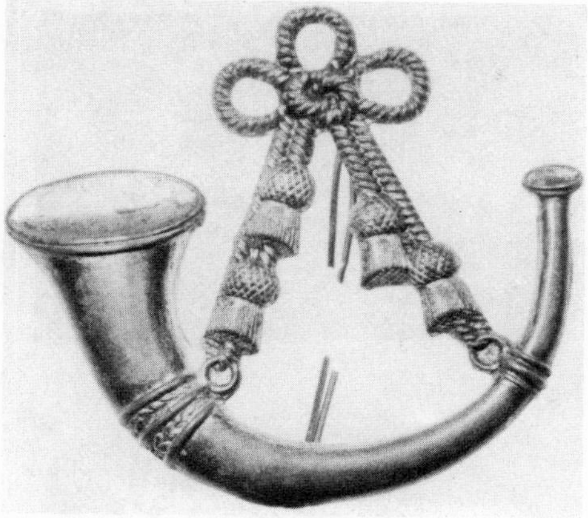

Fig. 5-17.

Fig. 5-17. This silver open bugle horn went below the eagle on the 1832–51 caps.

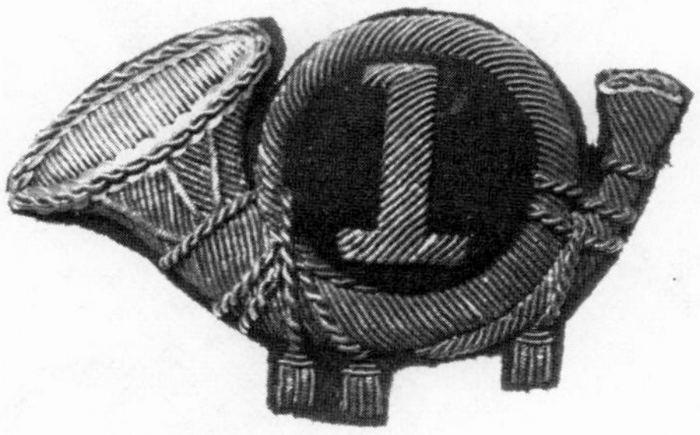

Fig. 5-18.

Fig. 5-18. Infantry abandoned silver as its distinctive color in 1851, and as a result, gold embroidered horns like this were worn after that change. This gold embroidered horn with silver number was made for an officer's 1851–72 forage cap.

Officers' Cap Insignia, 1851–72

Officers' caps carried a gold bullion–embroidered looped horn with a silver-embroidered regimental number within the bend (Fig. 5-18). The official drawings of June 1851 in the Horstmann Company publication show a horn like this with two tassels hanging close together and a third about an inch to the right. In addition, the drawing shows a row of sequins running the length of the horn's side.[14] The officers' forage cap insignia (Fig. 5-19) resembles the 1851 style but with a row of bullion stitching instead of sequins on the horn's side, although in practice most horns did not have any sequins other than those around the bugle's mouth.

An officers' insignia made in brass imitation embroidery (Fig. 5-20) has the beaded effect on the mouth of the bugle in an interpretation of round sequins shown on the War Department illustrations. The Civil War brought about many unofficial variations in

Fig. 5-19.

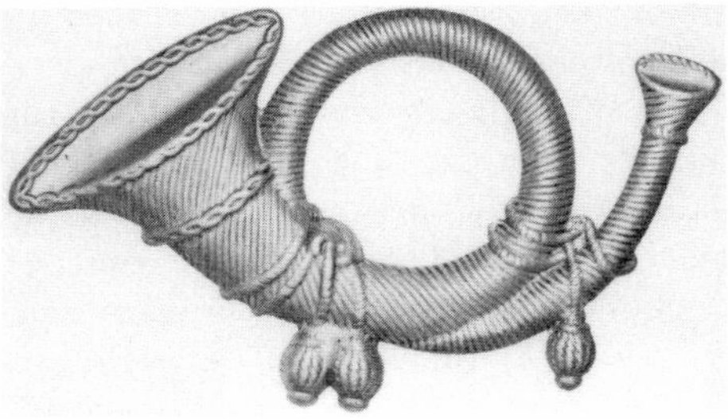

Fig. 5-20.

Fig. 5-21.

Fig. 5-23.

Fig. 5-24.

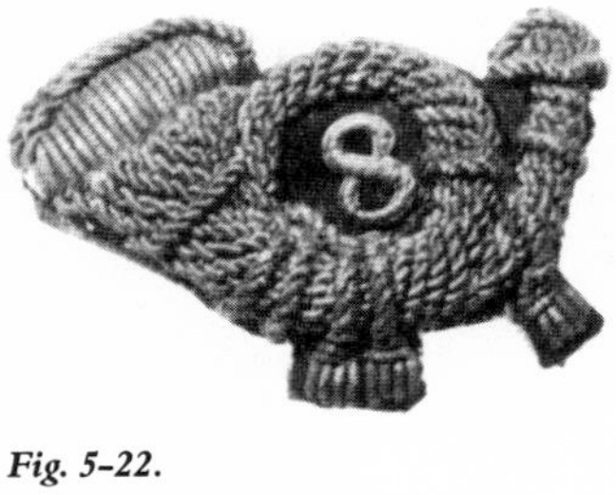

Fig. 5-22.

Fig. 5-19. *Many Civil War dealers carried stock insignia and added unit numbers, as was done in this case. (2 7/8 inches wide)*

Fig. 5-20. *Brass horns in imitation embroidery were an inexpensive insignia frequently sold during the Civil War. (3 inches wide)*

Fig. 5-21. *Officers from several state units designated as the 16th Infantry could have used this Civil War insignia. The attribution of a particular insignia to a specific unit is often difficult. (Embroidery 2 5/8 inches wide)*

Fig. 5-22. *A small, stock Civil War insignia with a metal 8 added.*

Fig. 5-23. *This smaller than usual cap insignia was probably made in a reduced size to fit the front of a low-crowned Civil War forage cap. (2 3/8 inches wide)*

Fig. 5-24. *The cap on the table shows that the open-loop 1840s infantry horn was still occasionally used during the Civil War.*

the basic looped horn insignia worn on forage caps. The embroidered style with a slight cloth border following the outline of the horn is a very common form (Fig. 5-21). Many were made of embroidery as "stock patterns," without regimental numbers, so the buyer could add the proper number later, and in some instances these insignia exist in quite small size (Fig. 5-22) or in at least a smaller than standard horn (Fig. 5-23). Many of these nonregulation insignia were probably made for militia organizations and can not be ascribed to the Regular Army unless documented. The cap of the volunteer officer shown in Fig. 5-24 carries an older straight horn with the number *95* above.

Officers' Hat Insignia, 1858–72

On 24 March 1858 the army prescribed a hat for all branches of the army, and on the front of the hat infantry officers wore the gold-embroidered looped bugle insignia placed on an oval background (Figs. 5-25 and 5-26). The design illustrated in Fig. 5-26 was for the 43d Infantry and was probably worn by an officer of some state regiment using these high numbers. Not until 1866 were regular regiments increased to forty-five, and that number was reduced again in 1869. The 1858 hat insignia differed from the 1851 cap insignia only in that for the first time the horn was to be on a "black velvet background" with a gilt edge tracing.[15]

An example of a hat once owned by a Civil War lieutenant from the 10th Michigan Infantry is shown in Fig. 5-27. Two non-standard-colored infantry insignia are shown in Figs. 5-28 and 5-29. Fig. 5-28 has a horn with a light blue center, and Fig. 5-29 shows a gilt bugle horn embroidered on a medium brown background, with a metal regimental number. A small hat insignia worn by an officer of the 17th Michigan is shown in Fig. 5-30. The regimental numbers on these officers' insignia, within the loop, were made of either smooth silver, metal imitation embroidery (etruscan), or the prescribed embroidered silver bullion. These oval hat insignia were worn until 1872.

Enlisted Men's Hat Insignia, 1858–72

The ornaments on infantry soldiers' hats were similar to the design for officers but larger and of stamped smooth brass. The looped bugle horn worn on the front of the hat was struck in smooth brass without cord or tassels (Fig. 5-31) and was to be worn with the company letter. In 1861 wording of the regulation changed to state that the enlisted men's insignia would correspond to the officers' but in brass, thus implying that the number was to go in the loop, yet within the same sentence the regulation specified that "the number of the regiment, five-eighths of an inch long, in brass, and the letter of the company, one inch, in brass, [would be] arranged

Fig. 5-25. *Officers' hat insignia were embroidered on oval backgrounds, as opposed to cap ornaments that were not required to have a gilt oval edge. (Embroidered oval $3\frac{9}{16}$ inches wide)*

Fig. 5-26. *A stock hat insignia with metal regimental numbers added.*

Fig. 5-27. *Lieutenant Nathan Levy of the 10th Michigan Infantry wore this low-crowned Civil War hat.*

Fig. 5-28. *This infantry oval has been tailored to minimize extra material around the insignia and has a light blue disk inside the horn's loop.*

Fig. 5-29. *Without a gilt edge, this oval brown background is typical of 1860s militia hat insignia. (Horn $2\frac{7}{8}$ inches wide)*

Fig. 5-30. *A smaller than regulation infantry had insignia. Usually officers wore embroidered insignia like this, but their use by enlisted militia units is a possibility. (Oval $2\frac{33}{64}$ inches wide)*

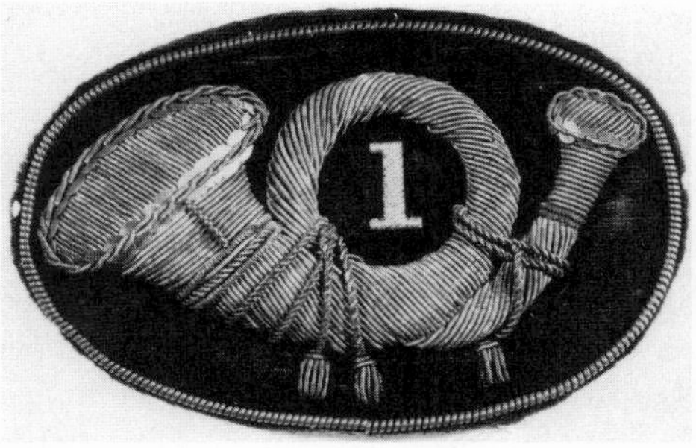

Fig. 5-25.

Fig. 5-26.

Fig. 5-27.

Fig. 5-28.

Fig. 5-29.

Fig. 5-30.

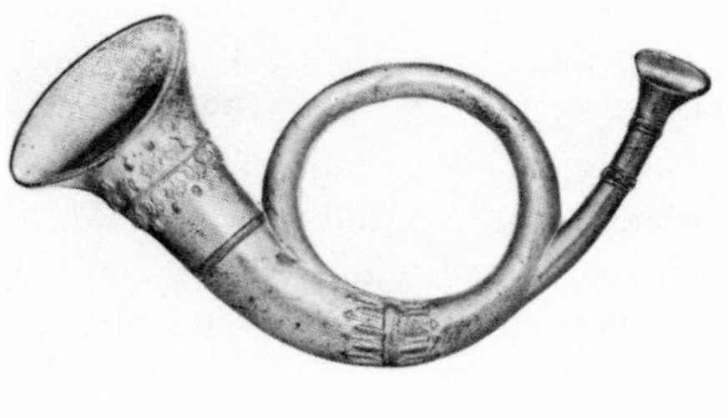

Fig. 5-31.

Fig. 5-33.

Fig. 5-34.

Fig. 5-35.

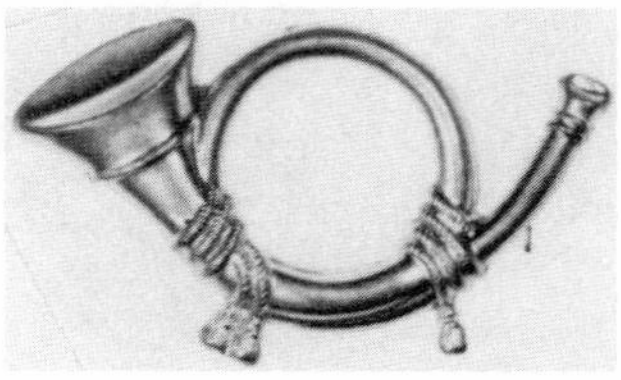

Fig. 5-32.

Fig. 5-36.

Fig. 5-31. *The stamped brass, issue Civil War infantry enlisted men's hat insignia. (3 17/32 inches wide)*

Fig. 5-32. *A smaller 1872–75 enlisted men's infantry cap insignia. The large surplus of these insignia, left after 1875, caused the quartermaster general to have them issued to field musicians (trumpeters) in infantry and artillery units until 1896. (2 5/32 inches wide)*

Fig. 5-33. *Stamped high-comb muskets were used from 1875 until 1896 as enlisted men's cap insignia. (2 13/32 inches wide)*

Fig. 5-34. *Struck from a die different from that used in Fig. 5-33 (compare the area around and above the trigger), this 1875–96 cap insignia was filled with lead on the reverse to hold a safety pin fastener and small wires which affixed the regimental number and company letter. (2 7/16 inches wide)*

Fig. 5-35. *A third die shows a different style of support wires used with the 1875 infantry enlisted men's cap insignia. (2 15/32 inches wide)*

Fig. 5-36. *Worn by James Grigsby in the late 1880s or early 1890s, this is a typical enlisted men's infantry cap with insignia from the later Indian Wars period.*

over the insignia."[16] Photographic evidence shows that most soldiers wore their regimental number inside the loop.

Enlisted Men's Cap Insignia, 1861–66

Throughout the Civil War, War Department regulations authorized only the "yellow metal letter" on cap fronts.[17] Civil War practices of the mainly volunteer units, however, included an enormous variety of nonregulation insignia. Hat insignia often found their way to the caps, as did regimental numbers. Many enlisted men's caps carried the issue stamped metal hat devices, but large numbers of men also wore the more elaborate officers' style bugle horns. Quite often the bummer's cap had all or some of the unauthorized insignia affixed to the top of the cap rather than to the front.

Enlisted Men's Cap Insignia, 1872–75

The War Department published new uniform regulations in 1872. For enlisted soldiers the 1872-pattern looped trumpet was struck in smooth brass, as shown in Fig. 5-32. The 1872 pattern, besides being smaller, is quickly identified by three loops of cords with the tassels next to them. The initial 1872 regulation was not clear about the insignia worn, but in 1873 the army specified the "badge of the corps" and company letter.[18] When the infantry adopted crossed muskets in 1875, field musicians continued to use the looped bugle ornament, and these are discussed further in the chapter on musicians' insignia.

Crossed Rifles on Caps

The crossed rifles replaced bugle horns for infantry insignia by General Orders 96, dated 19 November 1875, to conform with crossed cannons for artillery and crossed sabers for cavalry. In the first issue to soldiers the following year, the rifles were 2 5/8 inches long with short, stubby stocks having a very high comb. The badge is a hollow brass stamping with four round wire loops

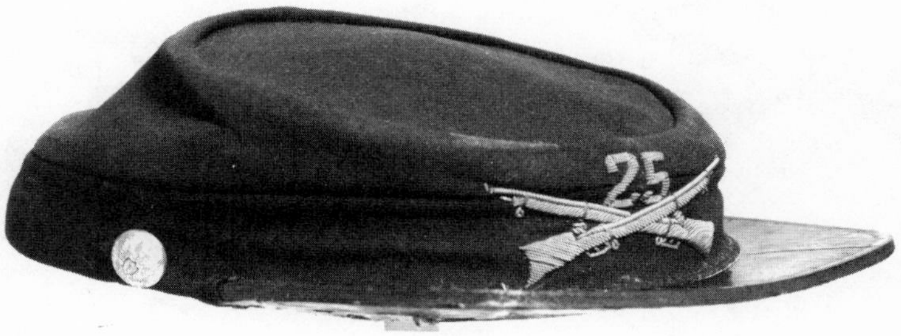

Fig. 5-37.

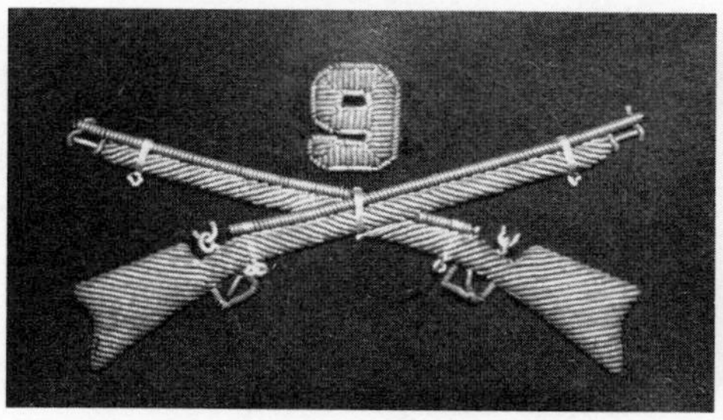

Fig. 5-38.

Fig. 5-39.

Fig. 5-40.

Fig. 5-41.

Fig. 5-37. *Officers' forage caps, 1875–95, carried gold-embroidered crossed muskets with a silver regimental number.*

Fig. 5-38. *A War Department sample officers' forage cap insignia, made about 1890. (Embroidery 3 inches wide)*

Fig. 5-39. *This insignia is probably a militia officer's forage cap ornament, about 1890.*

Fig. 5-40. *An 1896–1905 enlisted men's screw-back infantry cap insignia. (2 5/8 inches wide)*

Fig. 5-41. *A regimental noncommissioned staff cap insignia, 1896–1905. (2 5/8 inches wide)*

soldered on the back for fastening to the cap (Fig. 5-33). In some cases lead was added to the back to give more substance to the insignia, with a crude pin fastener imbedded during the same operation. These cap insignia also had small wires imbedded in the lead to hold the numbers and letters (Figs. 5-34 and 5-35), although initially enlisted soldiers wore both the regimental number and company letter as separate 1/2-inch-high pieces above the insignia, with the number closer to the muskets. In March 1876 the number of the regiment moved to the upper angle and the company letter to the lower angle.[19] An 1880s cap with the insignia is shown in Fig. 5-36.

Officers' forage cap insignia of 1876 had the rifles, 2 5/8 inches wide, embroidered in gold, with the regimental number embroidered in silver above (Figs. 5-37 and 5-38).[20] This same insignia is prescribed in General Orders 38, dated 28 March 1890, to be embroidered on blue cloth and to have "two gold rifles, crossed, without bayonets, barrel upward, with the number of the regiment, in silver, in upper angle." A similar militia design, shown in Fig. 5-39, is identified as such because the workmanship is not as fine as that of Figs. 5-37 and 5-38, which are known Regular Army insignia. All officers replaced branch cap devices with the national eagle in 1895.[21]

The enlisted men's crossed rifles insignia worn on forage caps went unchanged until 1896, when the Quartermaster General's Department introduced solid brass ornaments with threaded binding posts. The design changed slightly: the stocks were longer with a reduced comb, and the insignia had a much flatter appearance (Fig. 5-40). The noncommissioned staff wore muskets without any company letter (Fig. 5-41). Manufacturers firmly soldered these regimental numbers and company letters to the muskets, replacing the light attachment wires previously used.[22]

Fig. 5-42.

Fig. 5-43.

Fig. 5-44.

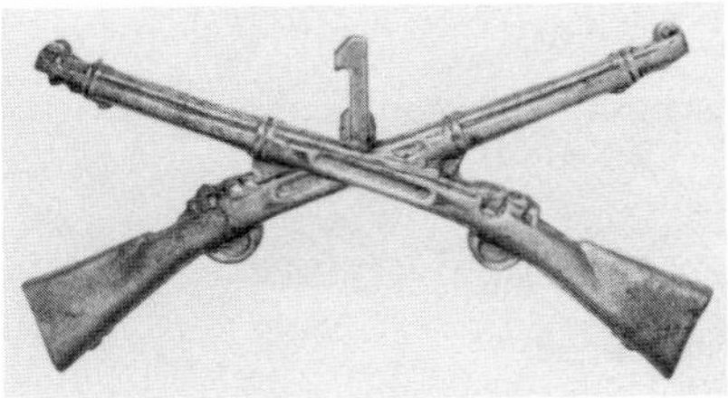

Fig. 5-45.

Fig. 5-46.

Fig. 5-47.

Fig. 5-48.

Fig. 5-49.

Fig. 5-42. *A bronze noncommissioned staff service cap insignia, 4th Infantry Regiment, 1905–18. (2 inches wide)*

Fig. 5-43. *Company members wore the company letter below, as in this cap ornament. ($1\frac{63}{64}$ inches wide)*

Fig. 5-44. *Machine gun companies were formed in 1916, thus dating this bronze cap ornament from then until early 1918. ($2\frac{1}{64}$ inches wide)*

Fig. 5-45. *A gilt 1905–17 dress cap insignia. ($1\frac{63}{64}$ inches wide)*

Fig. 5-46. *A standard enlisted men's infantry helmet eagle, 1881–1903. ($3\frac{3}{4}$ inches wide)*

Fig. 5-47. *A variation of the 1881–1903 helmet eagle. Besides less detail in the muskets, the area between the arrows is not pierced, and many lesser details are changed from Fig. 5-46.*

Fig. 5-48. *An infantry officers' helmet plate with the shield and muskets applied over the eagle. ($3\frac{35}{64}$ inches wide)*

Fig. 5-49. *This infantry officers' plate is an excellent example of die variations (compare it with Fig. 5-48.) The musket stock that goes over the arrows has been broken off.*

The army modernized the designs for most branch insignia in 1905, and the infantry's weapons were changed to bolt-action rifles on the insignia and were reduced to the overall size of 2 inches.[23] Examples of these 1905–18 cap ornaments are shown in

Fig. 5-50.

Fig. 5-50. An example of the infantry insignia brought into use on the 1895 sack coat. (Embroidery approximately 1 13/16 inches wide)

Fig. 5-51.

Fig. 5-51. A black mohair collar for the right side with embroidered insignia, 1895–1905.

Figs. 5-42 through 5-45. That of Fig. 5-42 was for the 4th Infantry noncommissioned staff to wear on the service cap. Those of Figs. 5-43 and 5-44 were for members of G Company, 7th Infantry, and for the machine-gun company of the 5th Infantry, respectively. Because machine-gun companies were not formed until 1916, this piece dates from late 1916 or from 1917. The 1st Infantry gilt insignia of Fig. 5-45 was made for the regimental noncommissioned staff to wear on the dress uniform.

Infantry Helmets

Uniform regulations of 7 January 1881 prescribed a dress helmet for all branches of the army except for staff and general officers, who continued to wear the chapeau. The enlisted infantrymen's helmet plate was struck on a thin piece of brass (Figs. 5-46 and 5-47) with a ½-inch white metal regimental number placed on the lower portion of the shield. For officers the plate was made of heavier metal in composite form. The center portion, consisting of the shield and crossed rifles, was a separate piece applied to the eagle background, with a separate silver regimental number on the shield (Figs. 5-48 and 5-49). The army stationed in the United States phased out these dress helmets in 1903 and 1904.[24]

Enlisted Men's Campaign Hat Insignia

The various styles of numbers and letters worn on service hats between 1899 and 1907 are described in chapter 10, "Numbers and Letters." Most infantrymen wore the metal regimental numbers above the company letter from 1899 until 1907; members of the regimental noncommissioned staff wore only the regimental number. Infantrymen indiscriminately used improper metal insignia, as well as various prescribed hat cords, on campaign hats during the latter part of the nineteenth century.

Officers' Collar Devices, 1895–1905

In April 1895 the army replaced infantry block regimental numbers on the 1892-style dark blue coat with gold crossed muskets. The embroidered gold or gilt crossed rifles, as the muskets were called in regulations, were 1 inch high, with gilt regimental numbers in the upper intersection (Fig. 5-50).[25] When officers had their coats made to order, the devices were frequently embroidered directly on the collar. Fig. 5-51 shows the right side of a collar with both the 19th Infantry insignia and the *US*. By the end of the Spanish-American War, etruscan metal insignia were in wide use (Figs. 5-52 and 5-53), and soon some men began to use smooth metal ornaments (Fig. 5-54).

Figs. 5-55 and 5-56 are patterns worn by officers of the 1st and 35th infantry regiments, the latter a militia unit. On the reverse sides these insignia have either short, straight wires to bend over and attach to the collar before adding the collar lining, or small loops by which the insignia can be sewn to the finished collar. These insignia also appear on the khaki authorized in the summer of 1898. At nearly the same time, the War Department directed state volunteer infantry officers to wear crossed rifles with state designations below (Fig. 5-57). A bronze device of the 1895–1905 pattern is shown in Fig. 5-58. Fig. 5-59 displays a common gilt insignia without regimental number that clearly shows the design that ended in early 1905.[26]

Officers' Insignia, 1905–23

In 1905 the infantry modified their insignia and adopted the then new slender Springfield rifles, Model 1903. The 1-inch-high 1905 patterns, in gilt and dull bronze for officers, shown in Figs. 5-60 and 5-61, are typical of the insignia used until 1923.[27] Both have sew-on loops on the back, and the gilt rifle even has a pierced trigger guard.

World War I brought about an unprecedented demand for military insignia. In addition to increased production by estab-

Fig. 5-52. *This etruscan insignia was stamped out of cheap, thin metal and has a safety pin–style fastener. (1 5/8 inches wide)*

Fig. 5-53. *A metal insignia nearly 1/10 inch thick, from about 1898. (1 5/8 inches wide)*

Fig. 5-54. *This 1903 photo shows an example of the smooth metal insignia that were then coming into widespread use.*

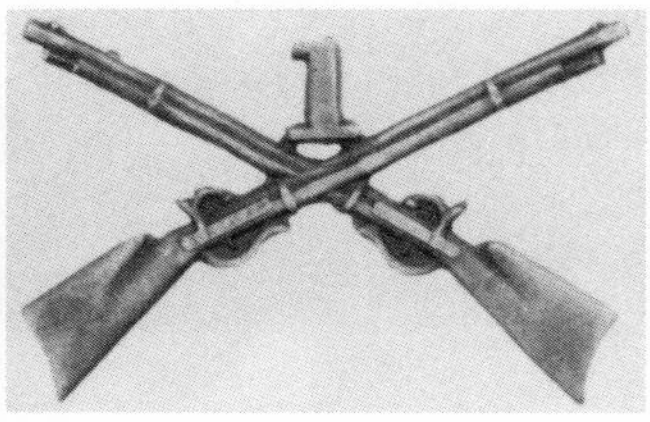

Fig. 5-55. *A smooth bronze 1st Infantry officers' insignia, 1895–1905. (1 37/64 inches wide)*

Fig. 5-56. *Gilt metal muskets, curved to fit on a coat collar. (1 1/2 inches wide)*

Fig. 5-57. *In June 1898 the War Department directed that "the abbreviation of the state" would appear below the crossed-arms insignia for militia. A resulting infantry officers' insignia is shown. (1 5/8 inches wide)*

Fig. 5-58. *Club-stock muskets of this type were replaced in 1905. Since bronze color was not worn until 1903, this insignia can be dated within the three years. (1 11/16 inches wide)*

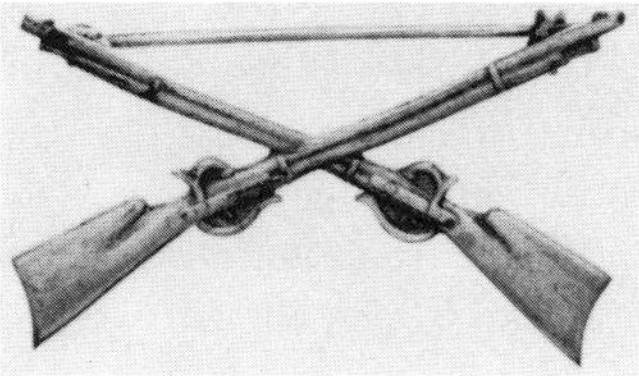

Fig. 5-59. *Although this design of gilt muskets was in use from 1895 until 1905, the pin back did not come into wide use initially. (1 5/8 inches wide)*

Fig. 5-60. *A gilt version of the 1905 infantry insignia, which brought in long, thin, bolt-action rifles. This particular piece has small holes drilled in the trigger guard forward of the trigger and was to be attached to the uniform by sew-on loops. It was made by Pasquale Company, San Francisco. (1 31/32 inches wide)*

Fig. 5-61. *The officers' "modernized" infantry collar insignia, prescribed in early 1905. (2 inches wide)*

Fig. 5-61.

Fig. 5-62.

Fig. 5-63.

Fig. 5-64.

Fig. 5-65.

Fig. 5-66.

Fig. 5-68.

Fig. 5-69.

lished firms, even heavy manufacturing companies entered the field, and in several cases jewelry companies added military insignia to their line of products. As also happened again later during World War II, not all manufacturers adhered strictly to regulations.[28] The first variant form is shown in Fig. 5-62, crossed Krag-Jorgensen rifles of the Spanish-American War period, with the left rifle incorrectly placed on top. At least one manufacturer designed his infantry insignia using the Lee navy rifle as his design (Fig. 5-63). A bronze 82d Infantry insignia, marked on the back *JESSOP SAN DIEGO CAL.*, and with unusually large numbers, is illustrated in Fig. 5-64.

The bolts are clearly visible on the model 1903 Springfield rifles used to make the 9th Infantry insignia shown in Fig. 5-65, which was fastened with one short screw post, just as an enlisted collar disk was fastened. The two French-made officers' bronze insignia shown in Fig. 5-66 and 5-67 are distinctly different from each other and the other previous designs.

Various officers' insignia were also made with nonregulation additions in the lower angle, such as the gilt insignia for members of the 69th New York Infantry, which became the 165th U.S. Infantry in federal service (Fig. 5-68). Officer insignia should not have been made with company designations, but two such bronze-colored nonregulation examples are illustrated in Figs. 5-69 and 5-70. The 45th Infantry (Philippine Scouts) insignia (Fig. 5-71) shows a proper gilt collar ornament of the pre-Depression period.

Officers' Shirt Insignia

Initially, officers' rank insignia went on the shirt collar when the shirt was the outer garment, but since second lieutenants had no rank insignia until World War I, those offi-

Fig. 5-62. *Rather than the proper Springfield 1903 rifles, this 3d Infantry insignia is made to depict Krag-Jorgensen rifles and has the incorrect weapon crossed over the other. ($1\frac{31}{32}$ inches wide)*

Fig. 5-63. *This variant World War I insignia is made with a shiny bronze finish and shows Lee rifles. ($1\frac{31}{32}$ inches wide)*

Fig. 5-64. *The 82d Infantry Regiment was organized in September 1918 and demobilized in February 1919 at Camp Kearny, California, thus dating and placing this insignia. It is marked on the back for a company located in San Diego. ($2\frac{1}{32}$ inches wide)*

Fig. 5-65. *This gilt 9th Infantry Regiment insignia has a short screw post, like that of an enlisted men's disk, as the method of collar attachment. (2 inches wide)*

Fig. 5-66. *These bronze rifles look more like sporting weapons than those made for the military. This piece was made in France for U.S. officers during World War I. ($1\frac{29}{32}$ inches wide)*

Fig. 5-67. *A common World War I infantry variation made in France. ($1\frac{23}{32}$ inches wide)*

Fig. 5-68. *A unique gilt interwar-period collar insignia showing both the federal (165th Infantry) and the state (69th New York) designations for this famous National Guard regiment. ($2\frac{1}{32}$ inches wide)*

Fig. 5-69. *A World War I infantry officers' insignia with unauthorized company designations. ($2\frac{1}{32}$ inches wide)*

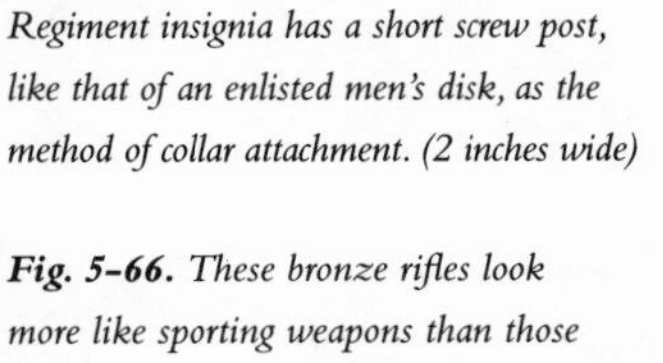

Fig. 5-67.

Fig. 5-70.

Fig. 5-71.

Fig. 5-72.

Fig. 5-73.

Fig. 5-74.

Fig. 5-75.

Fig. 5-76.

Fig. 5-77.

Fig. 5-79.

Fig. 5-78.

Fig. 5-80.

Fig. 5-81.

Fig. 5-70. *This officers' insignia's nonregulation company letter has no support bar. (2 inches wide)*

Fig. 5-71. *This 45th Infantry (Philippine Scouts) piece illustrates a correct 1923–26 gilt officers' insignia. (2 inches wide)*

Fig. 5-72. *Shirt collar insignia for one of the two Regular Army infantry regiments composed of black soldiers. ($1\frac{3}{20}$ inches wide)*

Fig. 5-73. *A typical bronze officers' shirt insignia, World War I ($1\frac{1}{16}$ inches wide).*

Fig. 5-74. *A World War I officers' shirt insignia. (1 inch wide)*

Fig. 5-75. *Very few shirt insignia had large regimental numbers and small rifles like this collar ornament. ($1\frac{1}{8}$ inches wide)*

Fig. 5-76. *This shirt insignia has small numbers that match the scale of the rifles. ($1\frac{3}{20}$ inches wide)*

Fig. 5-77. *After October 1923, gilt insignia like this were worn on shirt collars. ($1\frac{1}{8}$ inches wide)*

Fig. 5-78. *This gold 19th Infantry shirt collar ornament has miscolored rifle barrels because of poor soldering of the pin hinge and the catch on the reverse. ($1\frac{1}{8}$ inches wide)*

Fig. 5-79. *An unusual example of shirt collar insignia worn on a coat.*

Fig. 5-80. *Immediately after the Spanish American War, battalion and regimental staffs were formalized, which in turn led to staff insignia like this gilt adjutant's insignia, 1900–1905. Adjutants in both battalions and regiments wore the adjutant general staff device, but other staff devices were worn by regimental staff members only. ($1\frac{41}{64}$ inches wide)*

cers wore bronze branch insignia instead.[29] Often the shirt insignia came in a small size to fit onto the collar better (Figs. 5-72 and 5-73). These insignia continued through World War I in dull bronze finish in a variety of patterns: Figs. 5-74, 5-75, and 5-76. Gilt crossed rifles, made in the size to be worn on the shirt, are shown in Figs. 5-77 and 5-78. Occasionally these small insignia found their way onto coats, as exemplified by the colonel shown in Fig. 5-79.

Staff Devices

General Orders 63, 7 April 1899, stated, "The staff of a regiment consists of the adjutant, the quartermaster, and the commissary and they will be so designated." Almost a year and a half later this statement was the basis for a modification of insignia. General Orders 126, 4 October 1900, prescribed "regimental adjutants, quartermasters, and commissaries . . . and battalion adjutants . . . will wear in the lower angles of their insignia the devices (of gold or gilt metal) of the respective staff departments to which their duties correspond." A greater number of adjutant insignia exist because at the battalion level, as the founding order prescribed, only the adjutant wore the staff device. Illustrations of these initial staff insignia include Fig. 5-80 for the 1st Infantry adjutant, Fig. 5-81 for the 3rd Infantry quartermaster, and Fig. 5-82 for the commissary officer of the 27th Infantry Regiment. All of these staff insignia come in many variations from the basic insignia, such as the imitation embroidery shown in Fig. 5-83.

Fig. 5-81. *A 3d Infantry quartermaster's bronze collar device, 1900–1905. ($1\frac{21}{32}$ inches wide)*

Fig. 5-82.

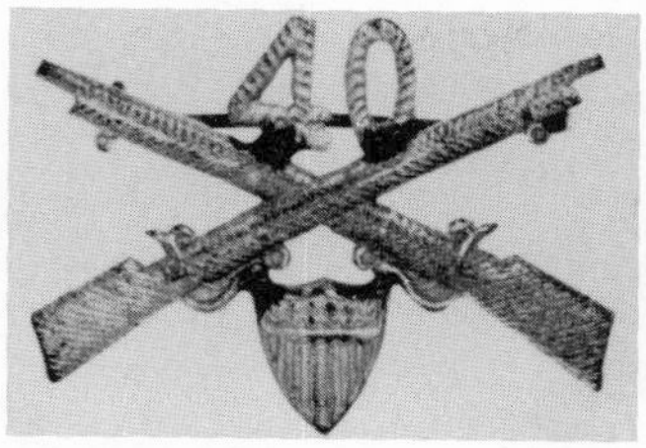

Fig. 5-83.

Fig. 5-84.

Fig. 5-85.

Fig. 5-86.

Fig. 5-87.

Fig. 5-88.

Fig. 5-89.

Fig. 5-90.

Fig. 5-82. *This 1900–1905 gilt infantry commissary insignia has wires on the back as attachment means. ($1\frac{21}{32}$ inches wide)*

Fig. 5-83. *An etruscan 40th Infantry adjutants' gilt insignia with a pin back. Because the adjutants at both battalion and regiment level wore the shield, this cannot be positively identified as an insignia for the regimental staff. ($1\frac{5}{8}$ inches wide)*

Fig. 5-84. *Medical staff devices like this were used only by some state units such as New York.*

Fig. 5-85. *In the case of inspectors of rifle practice (or positions of similar name), many state militias preceded the federal government in their establishment. Most states used square targets, like that shown, which were never adopted by the Regular Army. ($1\frac{21}{32}$ inches wide)*

Fig. 5-86. *High regimental numbers like that shown for the 65th New York Infantry's adjutant, when coupled with this club stock design used until 1905, may show that the insignia was intended for a state unit rather than the Regular Army. ($1\frac{5}{8}$ inches wide)*

Fig. 5-87. *A state unit's infantry quartermaster insignia. The insignia is marked on the back BRONZE. ($1\frac{43}{64}$ inches wide)*

Fig. 5-88. *The first staff insignia added to the original list of staff devices was for chaplains. This gilt 3d Infantry example has a silver cross below. ($1\frac{21}{32}$ inches wide)*

Fig. 5-89. *Gilt collar insignia for an adjutant in the 30th Infantry Regiment, 1905–17. ($1\frac{15}{16}$ inches wide)*

Fig. 5-90. *Bronze service uniform insignia for a 7th Infantry adjutant, 1905–23. ($1\frac{31}{32}$ inches wide)*

The insignia for a surgeon of the 4th New York National Guard Regiment, shown in Fig. 5-84, is typical of special staff devices used in 1902 by some members of state units but not by the federal forces. Other states also used square targets below the muskets (Fig. 5-85) or letters *IRP* to show an inspector of small arms or rifle practice, although some states did adopt the small ordnance flaming bomb. Since the Regular Army did not adopt the ordnance bomb as a staff device until 1914,[30] any pre-1905 rifles for the inspector of small arms practice are clearly militia, although unit numbers, such as for the 65th New York (Fig. 5-86) or the 47th Infantry (Fig. 5-87), may also indicate a state unit.

In July 1902 the War Department placed chaplains into standard officers' uniforms with branch insignia carrying a small cross below (Fig. 5-88). The chaplains' and other staff devices continued in 1905 under Springfield rifles: Fig. 5-89, in gilt, for the adjutant, 30th Infantry; Fig. 5-90 for the adjutant, 7th Infantry, in bronze for the service uniform; Fig. 5-91 for the commissary officer, 12th Infantry; Fig. 5-92 for a chaplain; Fig. 5-93 for an inspector of small arms practice, 22d Infantry; and Fig. 5-94 for a quartermaster. Commissary insignia disappeared after 1913 as a result of the absorption of the Commissary General's Department by the new Quartermaster Corps. Commissioned band leaders added lyres below their basic insignia in October 1918.[31]

Shirt insignia also came with staff devices, and these provide many variations, as shown for adjutants in Figs. 5-95, 5-96, and 5-97, the last in gilt. A gilt regimental quartermaster's insignia is shown in Fig. 5-98. During World War I manufacturers made extremely small shirt insignia for officers. The rifles

Fig. 5-91.

Fig. 5-92.

Fig. 5-93.

Fig. 5-94.

Fig. 5-95.

Fig. 5-96.

Fig. 5-99.

Fig. 5-97.

Fig. 5-98.

Fig. 5-91. *Commissary insignia came in pairs, with the cusps of the moon worn to the rear, making this 1905–13 bronze insignia for the right collar. ($1\frac{31}{32}$ inches wide)*

Fig. 5-92. *An infantry chaplain's insignia, 1905–14. In 1914 chaplains received their own branch insignia. ($1\frac{63}{64}$ inches wide)*

Fig. 5-93. *Inspectors of small arms practice in the infantry wore this bronze insignia from 1914 until 1923. (2 inches wide)*

Fig. 5-94. *Infantry regimental quartermaster insignia, 1905–23. ($1\frac{31}{32}$ inches wide)*

Fig. 5-95. *Shirt collar–sized infantry adjutant insignia, circa World War I. ($1\frac{3}{32}$ inches wide)*

Fig. 5-96. *This infantry adjutants' bronze shirt insignia has the shield only $\frac{3}{16}$ inch high. ($1\frac{1}{16}$ inches wide)*

Fig. 5-97. *The 7th New York Infantry adjutants' gilt shirt insignia. ($\frac{13}{16}$ inches wide)*

Fig. 5-98. *A 2d Infantry quartermaster's gilt shirt insignia. ($1\frac{3}{20}$ inches wide)*

Fig. 5-99. *This large gilt infantry collar insignia illustrates the design introduced in 1902 and worn until 1905 on the enlisted men's dress blue uniform. ($2\frac{3}{10}$ inches wide)*

Fig. 5-100. *Bronze infantry collar insignia of the 1902–1905 design for the enlisted men's service uniform. ($2\frac{3}{8}$ inches wide)*

shown in Fig. 5-97 are only $\frac{13}{16}$ inch long.

Army Regulation 600-40, 27 September 1921, continued shirt insignia "approximately $\frac{3}{4}$ the linear dimensions" of the coat insignia. These larger shirt insignia became the official size for the lapel coats in 1926. The army finally abolished all staff devices in October 1923.[32]

Enlisted Men's Outline Collar Insignia, 1902–17

With the new 1902 uniform came collar ornaments for enlisted men. On the dress coat soldiers placed large gilt muskets $2\frac{5}{8}$ inches long, with unit designation (Fig. 5-99). Service uniforms carried identical designs in bronze (Fig. 5-100). A set of bronze muskets of the 1902 pattern from the Smithsonian Institution collection, apparently made in the Far East, is for a noncommissioned staff member of the 27th Infantry Regiment (Fig. 5-101). General Order 197, 31 December 1904, prescribed smaller crossed Springfield rifle insignia with company letter and regimental number for enlisted soldiers' uniforms collars (Fig. 5-102 for Company K, 2d Infantry Regiment).[33] Regimental staff noncommissioned officers wore insignia similar to those of officers with

Fig. 5-100.

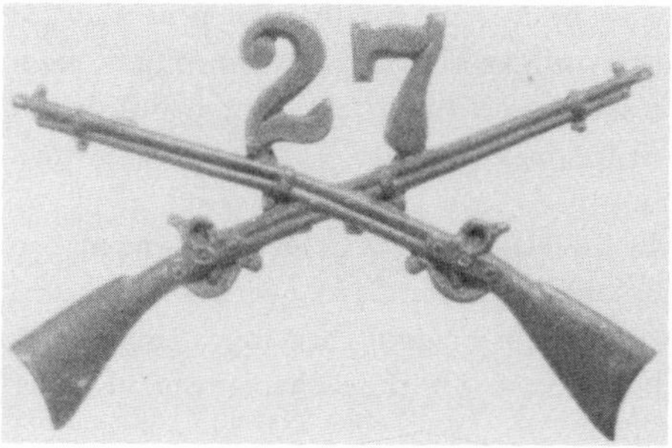

Fig. 5-101.

regimental numbers only. These styles continued until the army suspended the dress uniforms during World War I.

Before leaving outline collar insignia, it is worth noting a typical state insignia (Fig. 5-103) with a company letter but without a regimental or state number. In some states militia officers wore rifles with company letters like this or with both a unit number and company letters added, unlike the practice of Regular Army officers.

Enlisted Men's Bronze Disks

In 1907 the army proposed soldiers' collar insignia of a very different type for wear on the service uniform and finally implemented the 1-inch-diameter dull bronze disks on 1 July 1910 (Figs. 5-104 through 5-109).[34] Figs. 5-107, 5-108, and 5-109 are three examples for basic infantry: M Company, 36th Infantry; Supply Company, 119th Infantry; and B Company, 308th Infantry. The last two represent a federalized National Guard unit and a reserve or National Army regiment after 1917, respectively. Noncommissioned staff officers, such as color sergeants and sergeants major, wore only regimental numbers, as they were not members of any company until 1916; an example is shown in Fig. 5-110.

During World War I, to simplify supply procedures, just the company letter was added to the crossed rifles, because the regimental number moved to the *US* disk.[35] An example is shown Fig. 5-111 for an H company. Endless varieties of such insignia can be found; one example of an unauthorized insignia is shown in Fig. 5-112 for a supply company.

As a general rule, during World War I the War Department established infantry divisions numbered 1 through 25 in the Regular Army, numbered 26 through 75 in the National Guard, and numbered above 75 in the reserves, which were initially known as the National Army and made up of draftees. Regimental numbers 1 through 100 were for regulars, 101 through 300 for the National Guard, and 301 and upwards for reserves.[36]

Machine-Gun Units

One of the terrible killers of World War I was the machine gun; armies used this new weapon with grim efficiency. As is typical, a new weapon called for a new organization and consequently new insignia. The first pattern of disk for machine-gun companies had the letters *MG* below (Figs. 5-113 and 5-114). Only one machine-gun company

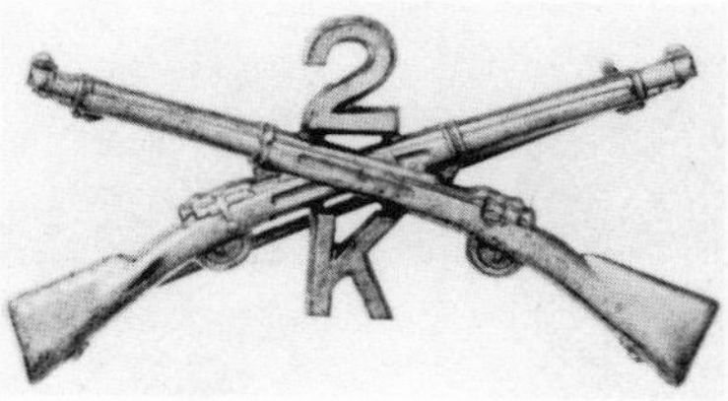

Fig. 5-102.

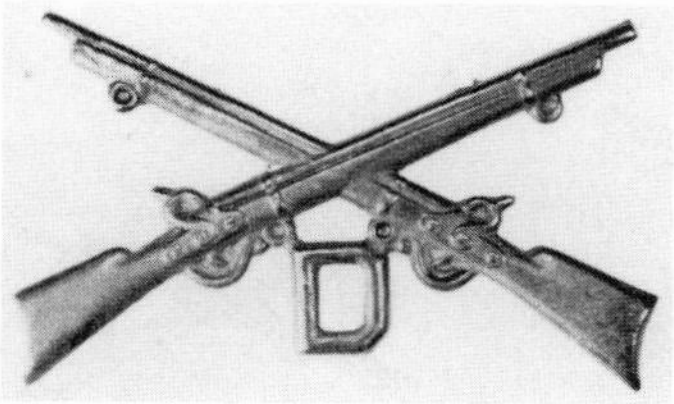

Fig. 5-103.

Fig. 5-104.

Fig. 5-105.

Fig. 5-106.

Fig. 5-107.

Fig. 5-108.

***Fig. 5-101.** The 27th Infantry served in the Philippines immediately after its organization in 1901. This bronze enlisted men's collar insignia for a regimental noncommissioned staff uniform was made overseas about 1902–1903.*

***Fig. 5-102.** In 1905 a smaller enlisted men's insignia showing bolt-action rifles came into use. The finish was gilt for dress uniforms and bronze for service uniforms. (2 inches wide)*

***Fig. 5-103.** Muskets in the style of 1902 with company letters below, like this insignia, were used by militia and not the Regular Army. (1 5/8 inches wide)*

***Fig. 5-104.** This World War I soldier wears a standard 1-inch-diameter enlisted service uniform collar insignia, used from 1910 through 1923.*

***Fig. 5-105.** Heavy rifles used on a bronze infantry disk, circa World War I. (1 inch in diameter)*

***Fig. 5-106.** Bronze disk with rifles crossed at a steeper angle than normal. Such variations show the insignia was made by a private firm not under War Department contract. (1 inch in diameter)*

***Fig. 5-107.** Small numbers and letters and a pebbled background make this bronze disk an unusual variation. (1 inch in diameter)*

***Fig. 5-108.** During World War I the War Department reserved numbers for infantry regiments 101 through 300 and divisions 26 through 75 to be assigned to the National Guard. Infantry regiments 101 through 104 were assigned to the 26th Division (four regiments to a division), 105 through 108 to the 27th Division, and so on. This insignia was for the 119th Infantry, a regiment in the 30th Division. (1 inch in diameter)* could be placed in an infantry regiment because of a National Defense Act limitation, so the army found it necessary to create separate machine-gun battalions. Enlisted men in machine-gun battalions placed the letters *MG* in the upper angle (Fig. 5-115), allowing space below to designate the company. Officers wore the letters *M* and *G* in the horizontal angles (Fig. 5-116). Fig. 5-117 shows the enlisted men's insignia for Company A of a machine-gun battalion organized with a headquarters and four machine-gun companies (A through D). A totally unauthorized disk with *MG* in the horizontal angles, similar to the officers' insignia, is shown in Fig. 5-118. The army rescinded infantry machine-gun battalion insignia in March 1921, because after 1920 the fourth company in each infantry regiment (companies D, H, and M) was designated a weapons company, and these units wore standard company letters instead of the *MG* below the rifles.[37]

In October 1917 the machine-gun insignia were shown in *National Geographic* magazine before they were announced in regulations, so the actual initial date of their use is difficult to determine. Fig. 5-119 shows the insignia for the adjutant of the 24th Machine Gun Battalion, with a letter, number, or device in each of the four angles formed by the crossed rifles. Gilt rifles with block *MG* letters added, and evidently worn unofficially in 1919 and 1920, are shown in Fig. 5-120. Two service insignia sized for wear on the shirt are illustrated in Figs. 5-121 and 5-122. An especially small gilt set of rifles with the letters *MG* soldered on top of the weapons is shown in Fig. 5-123. In 1921 the War Department eliminated the officers' machine-gun insignia.[38]

Fig. 5-109. *National Army divisions (starting with the 76th) incorporated regiments starting with the 301st, and both division and regimental numbers ran in sequence, four regiments to a division. The 308th Infantry (shown) was part of the 77th Division. (1 inch in diameter)*

Fig. 5-110. *Before 1916 the regimental noncommissioned staff wore the regimental number without company designation. (1 inch in diameter)*

Fig. 5-111. *Properly, after 1917 the regimental number went on the US disk (or variant) and the company letter went on the branch insignia. This disk could be used by an H company in any infantry regiment under this concept. (1 inch in diameter)*

Fig. 5-112. *Several nonregulation company abbreviations exist, such as this example for the Supply Company, 359th Infantry. (1 inch in diameter)*

Fig. 5-113. *Infantry regiments had one machine-gun company, and on their enlisted insignia the letters MG went below the rifles. (1 inch in diameter)*

Fig. 5-114. *The periods after the M and G on this disk were not regulation.*

Fig. 5-115. *Enlisted men of a machine-gun battalion had MG in the upper angle. Each World War I division had three machine-gun battalions. (1 inch in diameter)*

Fig. 5-117. *Machine-gun battalion disks exist with HQ, B, C, and D company letters below, besides the A shown. (1 inch in diameter)*

Fig. 5-118.

Fig. 5-116. *Machine-gun officers placed M and G in the horizontal angles of their insignia. (2 1/32 inches wide)*

Fig. 5-121.

Fig. 5-119.

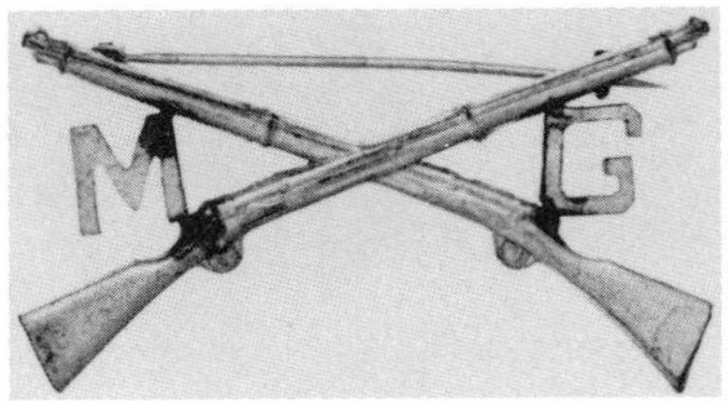

Fig. 5-120.

Fig. 5-122.

Fig. 5-123.

Fig. 5-124.

Fig. 5-126.

Fig. 5-125.

Fig. 5-127.

Fig. 5-118. *An enlisted men's World War I bronze disk with M and G letters improperly following the form of the officers' design.*

Fig. 5-119. *Adjutants were the only machine-gun battalion officers to have staff devices authorized. (2 inches wide)*

Fig. 5-120. *A machine-gun battalion gilt piece, probably worn in 1919 and 1920 when some returning citizen soldiers added bright buttons and insignia against regulations. ($1\frac{31}{32}$ inches wide)*

Fig. 5-121. *An officers' 1918 shirt insignia for the 305th Machine Gun Battalion. ($1\frac{3}{20}$ inches wide)*

Fig. 5-122. *Shirt insignia, adjutant, 22d Machine Gun Battalion. ($1\frac{9}{64}$ inches wide)*

Fig. 5-123. *Very small gilt shirt insignia with the machine-gun letters applied over the rifles. ($\frac{13}{16}$ inch wide)*

Fig. 5-124. *Officers' insignia, Puerto Rico Regiment. The provisional regiment was organized in 1899 and became the 65th U.S. Infantry in 1920. This particular insignia, because of the rifles' design, can be recognized as first worn in 1905. ($1\frac{31}{32}$ inches wide)*

Fig. 5-125. *A gilt enlisted men's collar insignia, Puerto Rico Provisional Regiment, 1902–1905. Similar bronze pieces went on the service uniform. ($2\frac{5}{16}$ inches wide)*

Fig. 5-126. *This private in the Puerto Rico Regiment wears a bronze service coat insignia on his hat and letters intended for his hat on his shirt collar.*

Fig. 5-127. *Between 1905 and 1917 enlisted members of the Puerto Rico Regiment wore gilt insignia of this design on the dress cap and uniform collar. (2 inches wide)*

Philippine and Puerto Rico Units

During March, April, and May 1899 the army recruited natives to form a provisional Puerto Rico Battalion of four hundred men, which was soon expanded to a provisional regiment of eight companies. Instead of a regimental number above crossed rifles, men wore the letters *PR*.[39] An officers' insignia for the Puerto Rico Regiment is shown in Fig. 5-124. Dress and service collar devices worn about 1902 are shown in Figs. 5-125 and 5-126. A post-1904 insignia is shown in Fig. 5-127. Cap ornaments used the same *PR* letters (Fig. 5-128).

The men of the Philippine Scouts used *P* instead of regimental numbers to indicate their organization, with companies numbered and that designation placed below the infantry insignia for enlisted soldiers (Fig. 5-129).[40] Although fifty-two separate Philippine Scouts companies existed in 1914, the Philippine Department renumbered and reorganized the companies into thirteen battalions, even though companies retained separate numbers, as did their insignia.[41] Fig. 5-130 shows an officer's service coat insignia from about 1903, and Fig. 5-131 illustrates a later but still pre–World War I collar insignia. For the first several years after formation of the Philippine Scouts the army did not allow scouts to wear dress uniforms, so the native troops initially wore only bronze insignia.[42] Bronze disks introduced in 1910 for the Puerto Rico Regiment had raised letters *PR* above the crossed rifles and the company letter below (Figs. 5-132, 5-133, and 5-134), and those for Philippine Scouts had *P* above the rifles (Fig. 5-135) and, where applicable, the number of the company below (Fig. 5-136).

Congress, in the 1920 National Defense Act, transferred the officers and men of the Puerto Rico Regiment to the Regular Army, and the War Department then designated the unit the 65th Infantry Regiment.[43] The Philippine Scouts, previously limited to infantry, were also authorized to be formed into branches and tactical units prescribed by the president, even though before World War I the 37th Infantry Company performed engineer duties.[44] With this change, standard regimental numbers were assigned to the scouts, such as the 57th Infantry (Philippine Scouts), which accounts for the elimination of the letter *P* above crossed rifles, although

Fig. 5-128.

Fig. 5-129.

Fig. 5-130.

Fig. 5-131.

Fig. 5-132.

Fig. 5-133.

Fig. 5-134.

Fig. 5-135.

Fig. 5-136.

Fig. 5-137.

Fig. 5-139.

Fig. 5-138.

Fig. 5-140.

Fig. 5-128. *A bronze cap insignia, Puerto Rico Regiment of Infantry, 1905–18. The same design was used on the service uniform as a collar insignia, 1905–10. (1 31/32 inches wide)*

Fig. 5-129. *Until 1921, Philippine Scouts enlisted men wore P above crossed rifles and the company number below. A bronze cap insignia for the 49th Company, used until 1918, is shown. (1 31/32 inches wide)*

Fig. 5-130. *Philippine Scouts officers were Americans, and this is a typical pre-1905 etruscan (imitation embroidered) collar insignia they used. (1 5/8 inches wide)*

Fig. 5-131. *An officers' service uniform insignia, 1905–23. (2 inches wide)*

Fig. 5-132. *Puerto Rico Regiment noncommissioned staff bronze disk for the service uniform, 1910–21. (1 inch in diameter)*

Fig. 5-133. *Company H, Puerto Rico Regiment. (1 inch in diameter)*

Fig. 5-134. *Supply Company enlisted men's collar ornament, Puerto Rico Regiment. (1 inch in diameter)*

Fig. 5-135. *A Philippine Scouts bronze collar insignia for the service uniform, 1910–21. (1 inch in diameter)*

Fig. 5-136. *Company numbers went in the lower angle of crossed rifles of the Philippine Scouts disks, 1910–21.*

Fig. 5-137. *United States Guards officers' gilt insignia, World War I. Since the guards used old dress uniforms instead of olive drab service clothing, some men wore gilt insignia instead of the bronze normally placed on the service uniforms. (2 inches wide)*

the units continued to exist.

Letters Other Than P and PR

The chief of the Militia Bureau controlled United States Guards after their establishment on 22 December 1917. U.S. Guards' uniforms consisted of "dress uniforms (and) blue kersey overcoats." Ultimately, the army formed forty-eight battalions, using officers and men who were too old for the draft or who could not serve overseas because of physical limitations. These units guarded shipyards, docks, railroad terminals, government stores and buildings, and the like, freeing twenty regiments of regular infantry and several coast artillery units for other service.[45] U.S. Guards officers wore crossed rifles with the gothic letters *USG* (Figs. 5-137 and 5-138). The same design on a round bronze disk (Fig. 5-139) was specified for enlisted men except in practice these usually had roman letters. U.S. Guards insignia were declared obsolete in August 1920.[46] Gilt U.S. Guards insignia (Fig. 5-137), including disks with company letters (Fig. 5-140), are common probably because guards wore blue uniforms. Officers and men should have worn the letters *USNA* or *US* to accompany the guards insignia, but two unique sets of *USG* letters are shown in Figs. 5-141 (gilt) and

Fig. 5-141.

Fig. 5-142.

Fig. 5-143.

Fig. 5-144.

Fig. 5-145.

Fig. 5-146.

Fig. 5-147.

5-142 (bronze), which one must presume were intended for U.S. Guards officers.

Some thirty-seven pioneer infantry regiments existed in World War I, but they were not numbered consecutively. In announcing pioneer infantry units, the army stated that they were specially trained and equipped to follow an attack and make immediate repairs and at the same time be prepared to fight as infantry.[47] The *Army and Navy Journal* for 2 February 1918 refers to their organization that month at Camp Wadsworth, South Carolina, and reports, "The collar device has not yet been announced. The general impression is that it will be 'crossed rifles, with a castle underneath.' It is presumed that the work of the Pioneer troops is to be mainly guarding depots, railroads, supplies and engineering work of different kinds" (in fact, U.S. Guards performed most of these duties). Change Number 3 to Special Regulation Number 42, dated 19 February 1918, prescribed, for pioneer infantry, "the letter P, one inch high, to be added at the intersection of the rifles." Some examples are shown: Fig. 5-143, made in France for the 5th Pioneer Infantry; Fig. 5-144 for the 60th Pioneer Infantry; Fig. 5-145 for the 12th Pioneer Infantry; and Fig. 5-146 for the 4th Pioneer Infantry. (The 801st through 816th regiments were formed with black personnel).[48] A 1919 portrait of a company commander of the 53d Pioneer Infantry, wearing his American Expeditionary Forces (AEF) uniform with insignia, is shown in Fig. 5-147.

Fig. 5-138. *A bronze U.S. Guards officers' collar insignia. (2 inches wide)*

Fig. 5-139. *A bronze enlisted men's U.S. Guards disk, 1918–20.*

Fig. 5-140. *Gilt U.S. Guards disks are more common than the bronze versions. This insignia has the company letter below. (1 inch in diameter)*

Fig. 5-141. *Some officers wore gilt U.S. Guards, National Army, letters like this with the infantry insignia.*

Fig. 5-142. *A nonregulation variation of officers' U.S. Guards collar letters.*

Fig. 5-143. *A large P over an infantry insignia was the collar device used by pioneer infantry officers. This insignia was made in France during World War I. ($1\frac{11}{32}$ inches in diameter)*

Fig. 5-144. *The official World War I historical order of battle lists pioneer infantry units under engineer troops. Officers for most of these units wore insignia of this design. The rifle and P are struck from one piece of metal. (2 inches wide)*

Fig. 5-145. *This applied P, although larger than other pioneer letters shown, is slightly more than $\frac{3}{4}$ inch high instead of the specified 1 inch.*

Fig. 5-146. *Made as one piece, this officers' pioneer infantry insignia not only has an unusually small P, but the letter is also set on an oval. ($1\frac{31}{32}$ inches wide)*

Fig. 5-147. *A company commander in the 53d Pioneer Infantry Regiment.*

Because the enlisted soldiers' disks could carry a *P* larger than the standard company letter, and the regulations failed to indicate the size of the enlisted letter, at least two different interpretations resulted: Figs. 5-148 and 5-149 with the letter *P* 1/4 inch high and Fig. 5-150 with the letter 3/8 inch high. Pioneer infantry insignia became obsolete in 1920, as did those of U.S. Guards.[49]

Fig. 5-148. *An enlisted World War I collar ornament for Company G, 55th Pioneer Infantry. (1 inch in diameter)*

Fig. 5-149. *This is a correct disk for the pioneer infantry, since the regimental number was to go on the US disk. (1 inch in diameter)*

Fig. 5-150. *An enlisted men's 1918 pioneer infantry service uniform collar insignia with a large P. (1 inch in diameter)*

Fig. 5-151. *Officer's depot brigade insignia with D and B (as shown) were not authorized by regulations. (1 31/32 inches wide)*

Fig. 5-152. *An officers' 1918 depot brigade collar insignia with sew-on loop attachments, an unusual feature for an insignia made so late. (2 inches wide)*

Fig. 5-153. *Enlisted men's depot brigade insignia were not authorized. This unofficial version evidently has both brigade and battalion numbers.*

Fig. 5-154. *An enlisted men's World War I disk for the 159th Depot Brigade.*

Fig. 5-155. *This depot brigade disk carries the same general design as the officers' insignia.*

Fig. 5-156. *Apparently enlisted men in the small company headquarters section wore disks like this during World War I.*

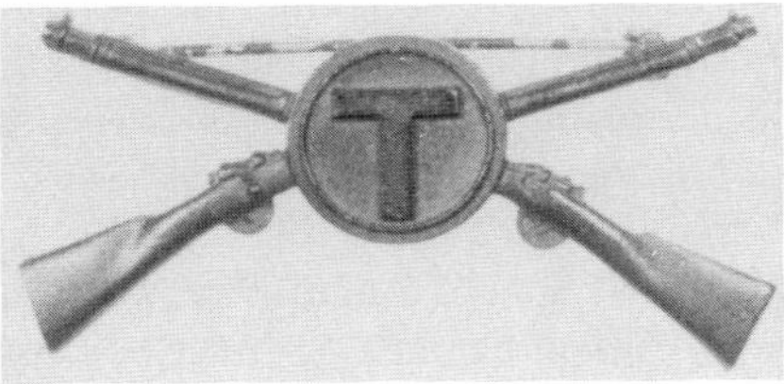

Fig. 5-157. *Infantry (tanks) insignia for officers, 1921–22. Several die variations exist for the T superimposed on crossed rifles. (2 1/16 inches wide)*

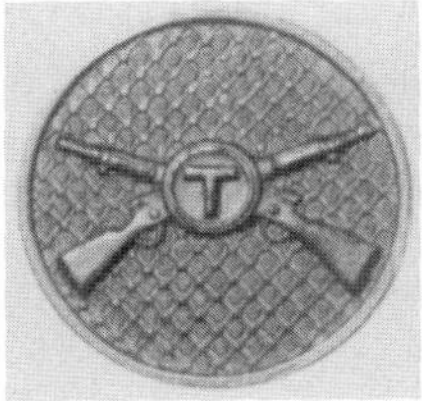

Fig. 5-158.

Fig. 5-159.

Members of some depot brigades wore the letters *DB* with their rifles, although the army never authorized any special insignia for depot brigades. Although depot brigades were originally part of tactical divisions, the army quickly made them separate units functioning as training units to supply replacements. Many officers physically unfit for overseas duty served in depot brigades. Depot brigades typically included receiving battalions, training battalions, and development battalions (to train men of less than average learning ability). Shown in Figs. 5-151 and 5-152 are officers' insignia for the 165th and 158th Depot Brigades, located at Camp Travis, Texas, and Camp Sherman, Ohio, respectively.[50] An enlisted men's disk showing both brigade and battalion designation is shown in Fig. 5-153, while Fig. 5-154 illustrates *DB* below and Fig. 5-155 shows an enlisted men's disk with the same design as that of officers' insignia.

Nonregulation insignia with the letters *HQ* above the crossed rifles exist for soldiers assigned to headquarters sections of different rifle companies. A soldier assigned to the headquarters of a B company wore the disk shown in Fig. 5-156.

Tanks in the Infantry

The National Defense Act of 4 June 1920

Fig. 5-160.

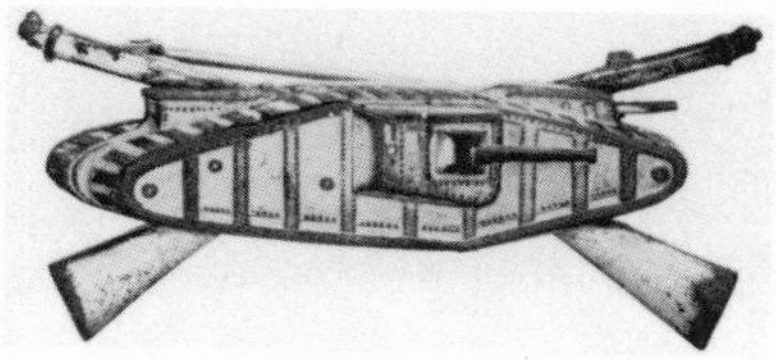

Fig. 5-161.

Fig. 5-162.

Fig. 5-164.

Fig. 5-163.

Fig. 5-158. *Bronze enlisted insignia for infantry (tanks), 1921–22, with the background of lines and shields. (1 inch in diameter)*

Fig. 5-159. *A gilt version of the design of Fig. 5-158, for infantry (tanks), made in preparation for a design switch to bright brass but rendered obsolete by the elimination of the T. (1 inch in diameter)*

Fig. 5-160. *Made from an old World War I tank insignia, this bronze piece is an early version of the 1922 infantry (tanks) insignia.*

Fig. 5-161. *A post-1923 officers' infantry (tanks) insignia with a tank applied separately. ($2\frac{1}{32}$ inches wide)*

Fig. 5-162. *Officers' infantry (tanks) gilt insignia made by applying a complete World War I Tank Corps insignia over rifles.*

Fig. 5-163. *Lieutenant Neal D. Franklin in 1928 wears the insignia shown in Fig. 5-161.*

Fig. 5-164. *Officers' infantry (tanks) insignia made from a single die for the standing collar. These insignia came in gilt and in bronze. ($1\frac{31}{32}$ inches wide)*

assigned tanks to the infantry. War Department Circular 72, published in March 1921, prescribed the 1-inch-high insignia for officers of the infantry tank service as "crossed rifles with the letter T in round center, all raised." Fig. 5-157 illustrates one of several die variations found today. The same design was worn by soldiers on their collar disks (Figs. 5-158 in dull bronze and 5-159 in gilt), which have a background of lines and small shields approved by the War Department on 2 September 1919. In November 1921, just eight months after the introduction of the *T* on the rifles, came a demand to make a more satisfactory insignia for the men assigned to tank units. Because the *T* insignia had just been made, the Quartermaster Corps delayed the change until March 1922, when the tank service insignia became "the infantry insignia with tank superimposed." (The official drawing shows that crossed muskets were actually prescribed the entire time, instead of the rifles called for in the regulations.)[51]

Fig. 5-160 is the 1922 insignia made in dull bronze with the side view of a small World War I tank.[52] A gilt insignia of the 1923 period, made by a different manufacturer, used such a large tank that it almost obscures the rifles (Fig. 5-161). These first two 1922 designs had the tanks cut out of the World War I Tank Corps insignia. An early gilt piece made about 1923 had the complete tank insignia applied (Fig. 5-162). Fig. 5-163 shows the infantry (tanks) insignia being worn on the new lapel coat in 1928. The general device with crossed muskets was executed with the entire design as an integral part of the die (Fig. 5-164, which shows a gilt insignia, although the same die was also used to make bronze pieces). These were made in pairs for standing-collar coats (Figs. 5-165 and 5-166).[53] In March 1926 the size was reduced to $\frac{3}{4}$ inch high for the lapel coat, the size previously allowed for shirts in 1923. With these smaller insignia the army directed infantry tank personnel to use only insignia with the tank facing to the observer's left (Figs. 5-167 and 5-168).[54] An infantry insignia with the tank applied in an earlier style is shown in Fig. 5-169, and Fig. 5-170 shows a tiny shirt collar insignia. Enlisted soldiers' disks are shown in Figs. 5-171, 5-172, and 5-173, the latter two typical of disks with unit designations.

The infantry tank insignia were worn but not authorized for a short period early in

Figs. 5-165 and 5-166. *A pair of infantry (tanks) gilt collar insignia. (Each 2 inches wide)*

Fig. 5-167. *One of several dies made for the shirt collar and the roll-lapel coat. Officially this insignia was eliminated in 1933, but it was commonly used until 1942. (1 15/32 inches wide)*

Fig. 5-168. *A yellow embroidered infantry (tanks) insignia for the World War II officers' coat. (1 7/16 inches wide)*

Fig. 5-169. *A small shirt collar insignia made with a World War I tank applied over small rifles. (1 1/8 inches wide)*

Fig. 5-170. *A tiny shirt collar insignia for officers, about 1925.*

Fig. 5-171. *An enlisted 1923–33 infantry (tanks) gilt disk. (1 inch in diameter)*

Fig. 5-172. *Between the world wars some tank companies were lettered as part of battalions. Enlisted men's insignia were of the type shown. (1 inch in diameter)*

Fig. 5-173. *In the 1930s infantry divisions included a tank company. An enlisted men's insignia is shown. (1 inch in diameter)*

Fig. 5-174. *The 66th Infantry (Light Tanks) was organized in 1932. This was a proper officers' insignia for tank units from 1933 until the introduction of the armored force insignia in 1942.*

Fig. 5-175. *A two-part infantry (tanks) collar insignia, made separable for cleaning, about 1940. (1 inch in diameter)*

Fig. 5-176. *A typical circa-1940 enlisted men's infantry coat collar insignia with unit number below. (1 inch in diameter)*

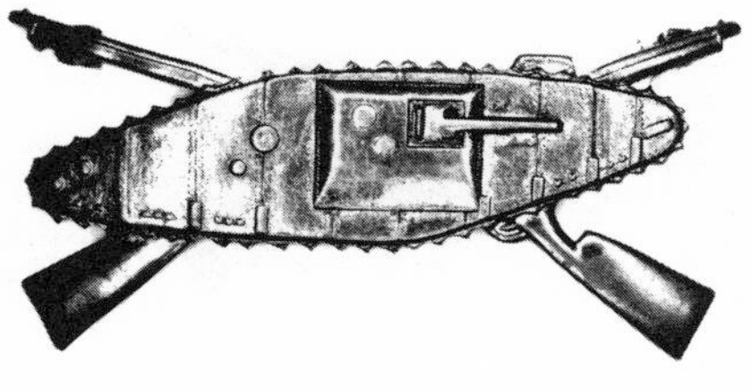

Fig. 5-165.

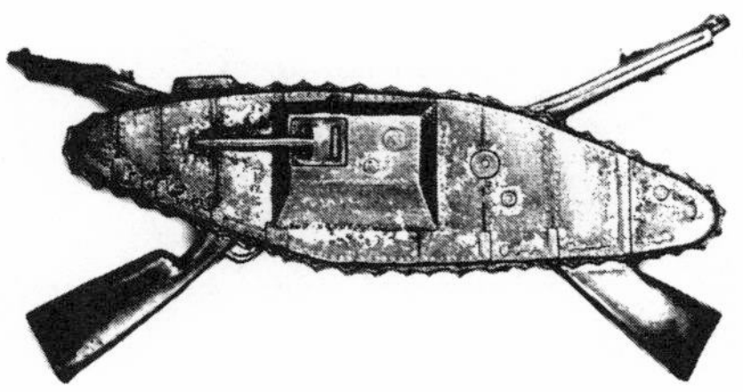

Fig. 5-166.

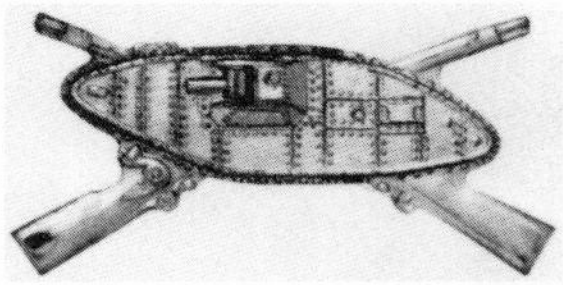

Fig. 5-167.

Fig. 5-168.

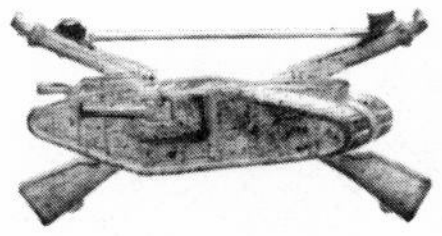

Fig. 5-169.

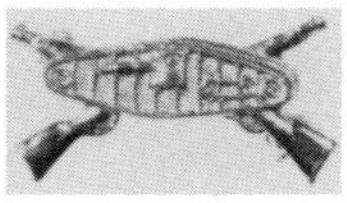

Fig. 5-170.

Fig. 5-174.

World War II in armored units. Change Number 2 to Army Regulation 600-35, dated 22 August 1933, abolished this insignia, and until 1942 infantry tank personnel had no special collar insignia. In that nine-year period tank personnel were identified only by their regimental numbers and unit titles (such as Fig. 5-174 for the 66th Infantry Regiment [Light Tanks]). Despite this change, many men wore the tank insignia during early World War II before the War Department prescribed the armored force insignia.[55] Typical enlisted disks are in Figs. 5-175 through 5-179; the last is actually made as one piece, despite its appearance. Men in some post–World War II units, such as the 42d Armored Infantry Battalion, stationed in Mainz, Germany, as part of the 2d Armored Division, wore the insignia as late as 1953 (Fig. 5-180).

Post–World War I Infantry Rifle Insignia

The gilt infantry insignia worn after World War I and until 1924 were characterized by heavier, thicker crossed Springfield rifles such as those illustrated in Fig. 5-181 for the 17th Infantry Regiment. In the mid-1920s and 1930s officers' shirts could carry small crossed rifles, although most officers used full-size collar ornaments. The prescribed shirt insignia's height was 3/4 inch and its length, 1 1/8 inches (Fig. 5-182).[56]

Officers' Muskets

In 1924 the War Department changed the Springfield rifle design to the conventional

Fig. 5-171.

Fig. 5-172.

Fig. 5-173.

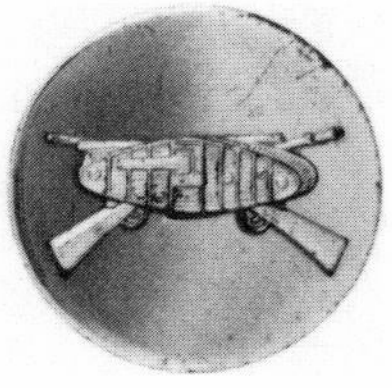

Fig. 5-175.

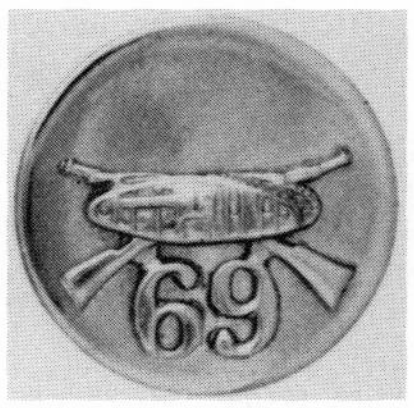

Fig. 5-176.

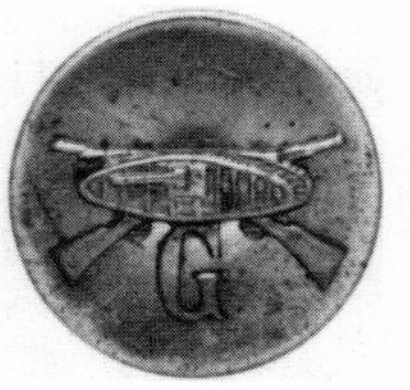

Fig. 5-177.

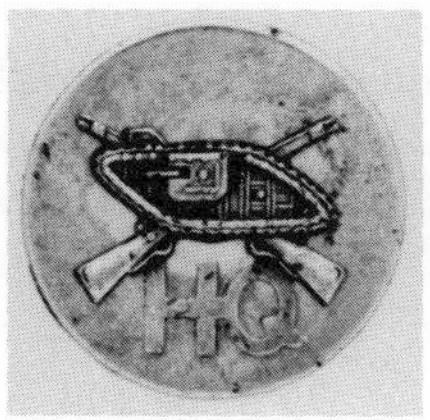

Fig. 5-178.

Fig. 5-179.

flintlock musket, symbolizing the weapon of the original U.S. infantry and eliminating the need to change the insignia pattern whenever the army adopted a new model of rifle. Various official drawings of the time, which began to show muskets, and notes on file indicate that the change was intended as early as October 1921. Shown in Fig. 5-183 is the 1923 master sketch of a musket, which the artist, Mr. A. DuBois, in an attached note called a rifle. The weapon was to be the 1795 Springfield Armory army musket. This wording adds to the confusion, since the official regulation of the time called for a rifle.[57] The War Department abolished bronze insignia in October 1923, but before it did, some manufacturers produced a few of these first flintlocks in dull bronze finish common to World War I—some perhaps as early as October 1921 (Fig. 5-184). These new patterns made in gilt with special fasteners used only in the Philippines are shown in Figs. 5-185 and 5-186, the latter for the 57th Infantry Regiment (Philippine Scouts). An unusual variant form is shown in Fig. 5-187, made in the Philippine Islands for an officer of the 31st Infantry Regiment, one of the regular regiments stationed there at the outbreak of World War II. Many of the Philippine-made insignia are marked on the back *CRISPULO ZAMORA,* the name of a Philippine insignia manufacturer. These 1-inch-high muskets were for the standing-collar coat. For wear on the olive drab shirt and the 1926 lapel coat, 3/4-inch-high muskets came into use (Fig. 5-188), although some were slightly smaller (Fig. 5-189).[58]

Enlisted Soldiers' Disks, Post–World War I and World War II

The design of the enlisted soldiers' disk insignia did not change following World War I, but the insignia issued in 1923 were gilt instead of dull bronze (Fig. 5-190). A great many variations exist in gilt disks of the first pattern, which show a background of dots or fine lines. According to regulations, these disks should not have been used, but probably insignia makers simply used old dies to make the gilt insignia such as those shown in Figs. 5-191 through 5-196. Enlisted men's infantry disks changed to a second pattern of background, crosshatched lines and small shields, in 1923 (Fig. 5-197 as issued and Fig. 5-198 with removable design). Most designs have crossed muskets and the various unit designation: Fig. 5-199 for an H company; Fig. 5-200 for a B company, that letter having been soldered to the disk, and Fig. 5-201 for a howitzer company, which had its insignia first authorized in October 1921. Band members wore a lyre below the crossed muskets (Fig. 5-202) between December 1927 and 1937, while enlisted men of battalion headquarters added the battalion number below instead of a company letter (Fig. 5-203).[59]

A new style of disk with the infantry device separate and removable to facilitate polishing and with a smooth backing is shown in Fig. 5-204. Soldiers could purchase these two-piece insignia by 1925, but the army did not authorized them for issue until September 1937 after supplies of the one-piece disks were exhausted. The 1920 howitzer company was replaced in 1939

Fig. 5-180.

Fig. 5-181.

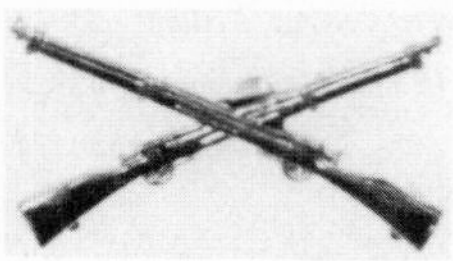

Fig. 5-182.

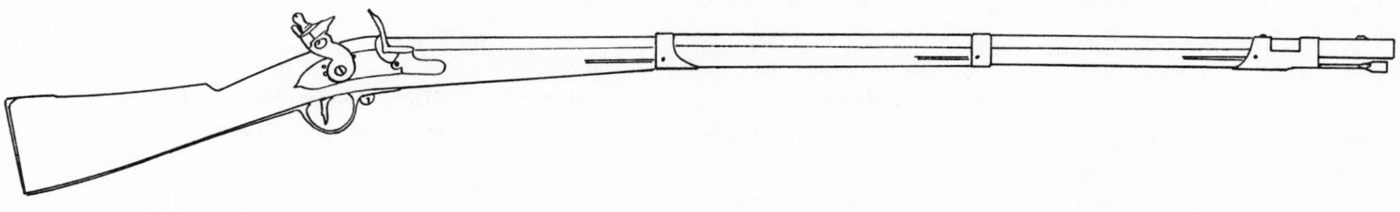

Fig. 5-183.

Fig. 5-177. *This privately made disk with company letter, with a screw-post back, was used from the late 1930s until 1942. (1 inch in diameter)*

Fig. 5-178. *This infantry (tanks) has the muskets crossed at a steeper angle than those of the three previous disks, and the tank is seen directly from the side, as the rear track surface is not visible. (63/64 inch in diameter)*

Fig. 5-179. *Except for the company designation, this disk is similar to the previous one, but the design was permanently affixed to a background with a raised edge.*

Fig. 5-180. *The 42d Armored Infantry Battalion was part of the 2d Armored Division that went to Germany in 1950, whereupon its officers wore this insignia, twenty years after it was officially rescinded. (1 1/2 inches wide)*

Fig. 5-181. *Gilt, heavy Springfield rifles like these were common on insignia after World War I and before 1924. (2 inches wide)*

Fig. 5-182. *An officers' shirt-collar gilt insignia, 1923–24. (1 1/8 inches wide)*

Fig. 5-183. *In 1923, Mr. A. DuBois of the Quartermaster Corps' heraldric section drew this musket, which became the basic design used in the 1924 infantry insignia.*

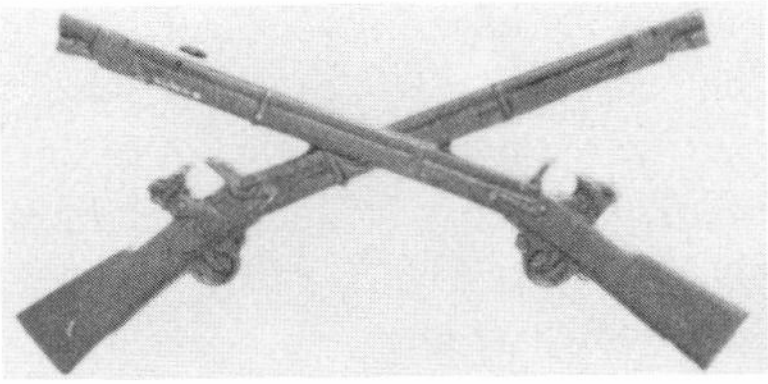

Fig. 5-184.

Fig. 5-185.

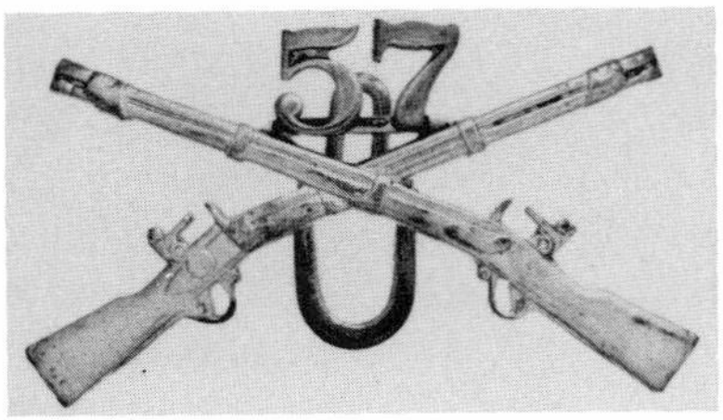

Fig. 5-186.

Fig. 5-187.

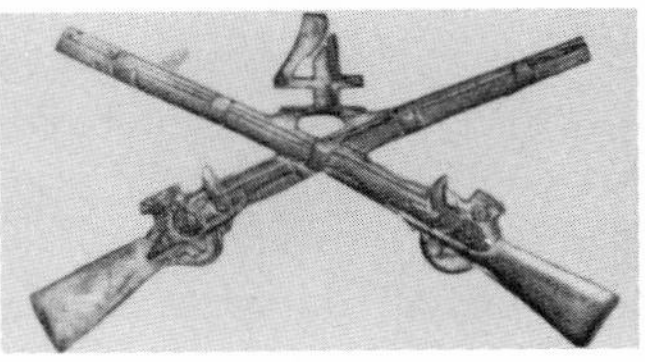

Fig. 5-188.

Fig. 5-189.

Fig. 5-190.

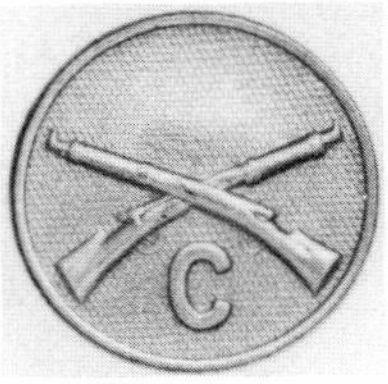

Fig. 5-191.

Fig. 5-192.

Fig. 5-193.

Fig. 5-194.

Fig. 5-195.

Fig. 5-196.

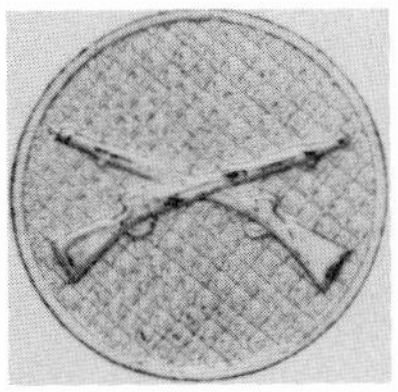

Fig. 5-197.

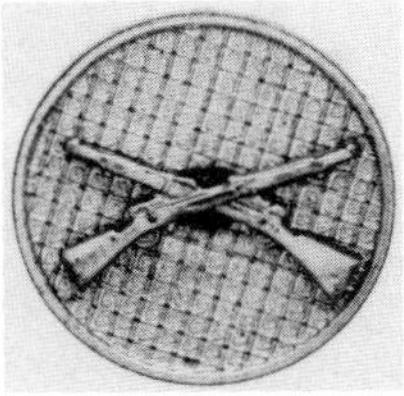

Fig. 5-198.

Fig. 5-184. *A pair of bronze musket insignia from about the 1922–24 period. (1 31/32 inches wide)*

Fig. 5-185. *These gilt muskets were made in the United States by the N. S. Meyer Company. The fastening device consists of two spring-loaded loops in the back center that could be inserted into a slot like a buttonhole and that then spread as shown to hold the muskets to the uniform. (1 15/16 inches wide)*

Fig. 5-186. *The 57th Infantry was a Philippine Scouts regiment, and this insignia has a typical fastener used in the Philippine Islands in the 1920s. (2 inches wide)*

Fig. 5-187. *The 31st Infantry was stationed on the Philippine Islands between the world wars when this officers' insignia was made.*

Fig. 5-188. *Crossed muskets 3/4 inch high were introduced in 1926 for shirts and for lapel-collar coats. (1 1/2 inches wide)*

Fig. 5-189. *Made between the world wars, this infantry insignia is slightly smaller than the size specified in 1926 and has the adjutant's staff device, which was obsolete before the muskets were prescribed. (1 7/16 inches wide)*

Fig. 5-190. *Although this looks like a World War I bronze disk, it is gilt and was made in the 1920s using a World War I die.*

Fig. 5-191. *An early gilt post–World War I enlisted men's collar device, about 1923, with a company letter.*

Fig. 5-192. *This 183d Infantry gilt disk has the number struck with the rifles, with the company letter subsequently added.*

Fig. 5-193. *Machine-gun companies were dissolved as a result of the 1920 National Defense Act. Perhaps such gilt insignia were worn after the 1918 armistice before bright disks were authorized.*

Fig. 5-194. *A machine-gun battalion gilt disk.*

Fig. 5-195. *This gilt disk with company letter above was probably made for a National Guard unit; it is not prescribed in Regular Army regulations. (1 inch in diameter)*

Fig. 5-196. *This gilt disk has sew-on loops for fastening. The unusual size of the company letter and its position indicate it was not intended for Regular Army forces. (1 inch in diameter)*

Fig. 5-197. *An official 1923 issue infantry disk with the background of lines and shields behind crossed rifles. (1 inch in diameter)*

Fig. 5-198. *Some early removable enlisted men's infantry coat collar ornaments still had the crossed rifles, but with the later background of lines and shields.*

Fig. 5-199. *An H company infantry disk, 1924–37. (1 inch in diameter)*

Fig. 5-199.

Fig. 5-200.

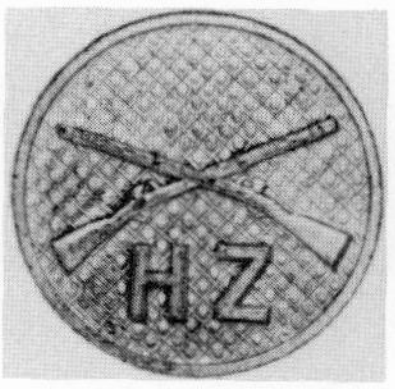

Fig. 5-201.

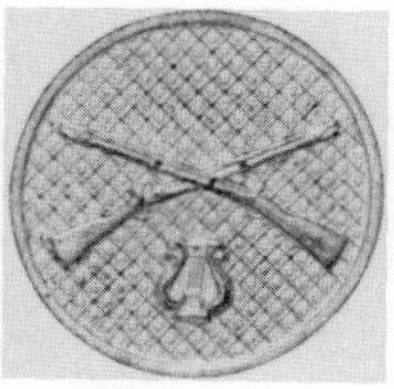

Fig. 5-202.

Fig. 5-203.

Fig. 5-204.

Fig. 5-205.

Fig. 5-206.

Fig. 5-207.

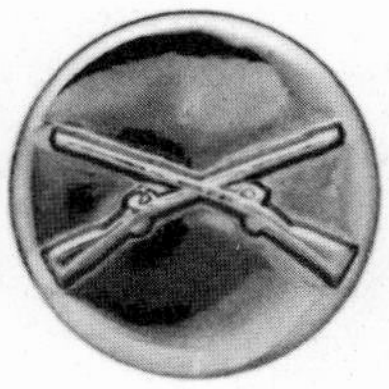

Fig. 5-208.

by an antitank company, which existed in infantry regiments until 1943.[60] This change led to the disk with *AT* below the muskets (Fig. 5-205), although sturdy separable disks with *HZ* and regimental numbers (Fig. 5-206) were worn by some soldiers. Also made before World War II was the machine-gun company disk shown in Fig. 5-207.

Disks of World War II and Later

When the 1940 draft brought a rapid increase to the army, the quartermaster general issued two-piece insignia to many draftees; the 1942 thin embossed brass stampings (Fig. 5-208) soon became common, however, because they could be produced quicker and cheaper. Privately made two-piece disks became common, both in high quality and in low quality with poorly executed designs (Figs. 5-209 and 5-210). Use of the stamped issue disks effectively ended widespread use of additions such as letters and numbers on enlisted soldiers' disks, although many troops did wear unit numbers and company letters on sturdy screw-back insignia (Figs. 5-211 through 5-214) purchased through private firms, even though the War Department clearly specified "insignia of the arm or service . . . without numerical or letter designation" in mid-1937.[61]

Enlisted soldiers' dome-shaped disks during and after the war included those shown in Fig. 5-215 for the 5th Infantry Regiment, Figs. 5-216 and 5-217 for airborne units, and six German-made pieces: Fig. 5-218 for L Company, 6th Infantry; Fig. 5-219 for the 16th Infantry Regimental Headquarters; Fig. 5-220 for the Service Company, 371st Infantry; Fig. 5-221 for the Heavy Mortar Company, 22d Infantry; Fig. 5-222 for the 5th Infantry; and Fig. 5-223 for the 18th Infantry. These last two are each made from one piece of metal and were manufactured shortly after World War II. Note that infantry disks were made virtually throughout the world; the one shown in Fig. 5-224 was made in India about 1944.

To enhance the prestige of infantrymen, in 1952 the Department of the Army authorized blue edging to be added to insignia for enlisted personnel assigned to infantry units.[62] A plastic edging disk (Fig. 5-225) and a metal disk with a blue enameled edge (Fig. 5-226) are typical examples. Nonstandard infantry disks include variations such as that in Fig. 5-227, which may have been used by a military school, as shown by the rays, like those on the Reserve Officers Training Corps torch insignia; gilt pebbled disks used by the Missouri State Guard during World War II (Fig. 5-228), resembling a 1920 piece; and a 1970s disk for the 3d Battalion of the 36th Infantry (Fig. 5-229).

World War II and Later Officers' Insignia

Officers of the 802d Tank Destroyer Battalion wore the muskets shown in Fig. 5-230 during World War II. Fig. 5-231 shows an insignia for a 804th Antitank unit. A 804th

5-200. *Occasionally company letters were added to enlisted disks instead of having them struck with the insignia itself, but this was not a common practice.*

Fig. 5-201. *HZ stood for howitzer company and was authorized for infantry regiments from 1920 until those companies were replaced by antitank companies in 1939.*

Fig. 5-202. *Regimental bands used lyres instead of company letters from 1927 until 1937. (1 inch in diameter)*

Fig. 5-203. *During the 1930s a 1, 2, or 3 below muskets indicated members of an infantry battalion headquarters.*

Fig. 5-204. *Smooth backgrounds were introduced with privately purchased disks. This example was made by Gaunt and has a raised edge similar to that of issue insignia with the background of lines and shields.*

Fig. 5-205. *Antitank companies existed from 1939 until 1943, and members frequently used AT letters on insignia.*

Fig. 5-206. *A 1942–43 howitzer company insignia, used by an element of the 93d Division, one of the two divisions manned by African American personnel.*

Fig. 5-207. *Federal machine-gun companies were replaced in 1920. Perhaps this disk was intended for a separate battalion or for a state guard or militia organization. (1 inch in diameter)*

Fig. 5-208. *Millions of these embossed brass enlisted men's infantry collar insignia were issued during and after World War II. The use of such construction saved brass, compared to the previous method of making separable enlisted men's insignia.*

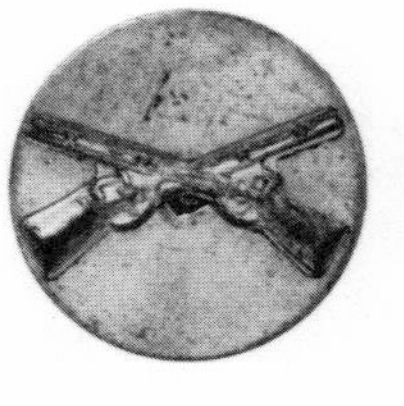

Fig. 5-209.

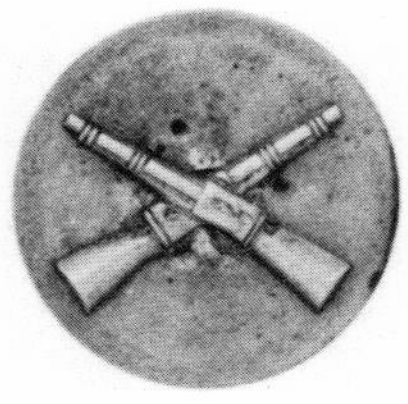

Fig. 5-210.

Fig. 5-211.

Fig. 5-212.

Fig. 5-213.

Fig. 5-214.

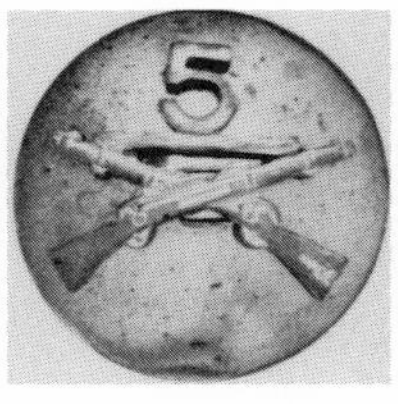

Fig. 5-215.

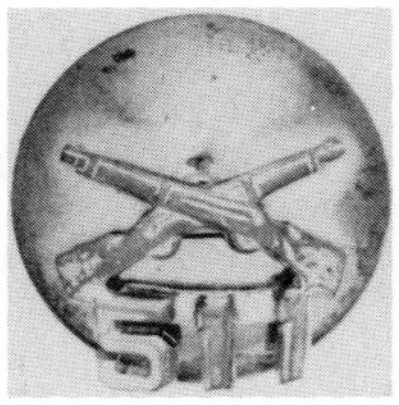

Fig. 5-216.

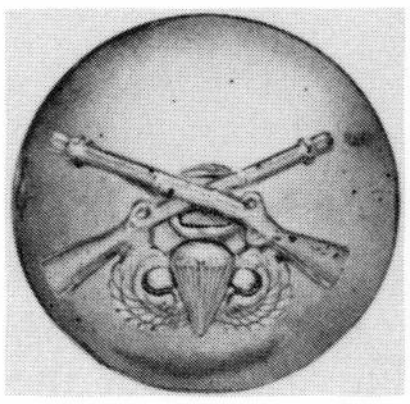

Fig. 5-217.

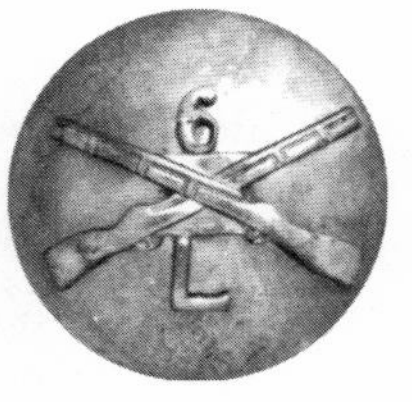

Fig. 5-218.

Fig. 5-219.

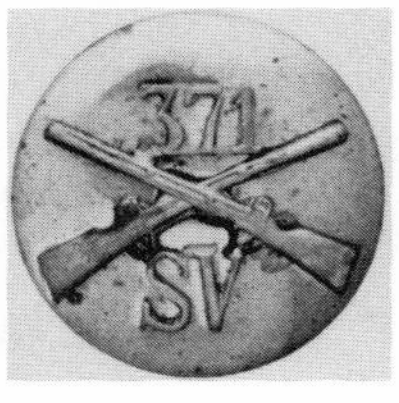

Fig. 5-220.

Fig. 5-221.

Fig. 5-222.

Fig. 5-223.

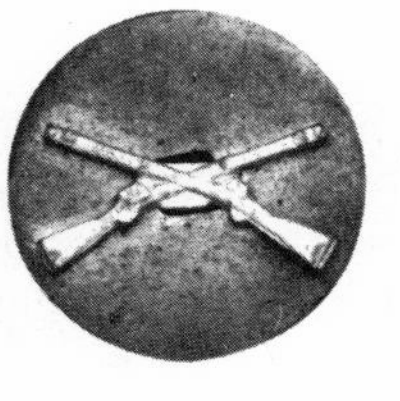

Fig. 5-224.

Fig. 5-225.

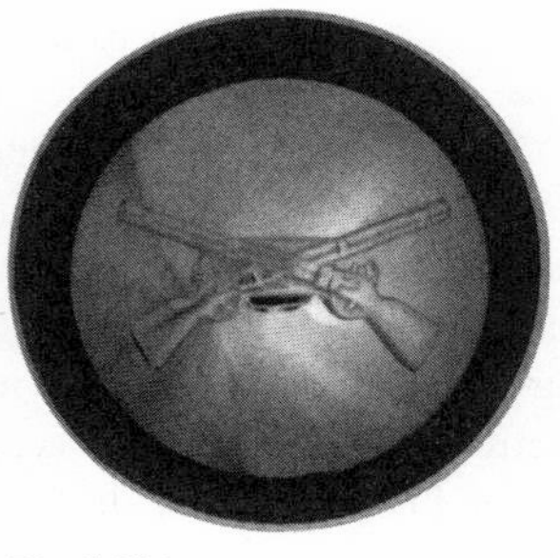

Fig. 5-226.

Fig. 5-209. *A crudely made World War II–period separable infantry disk. (1 inch in diameter)*

Fig. 5-210. *Poorly designed, this infantry insignia even lacks the triggers. (1 1/32 inches in diameter)*

Fig. 5-211. *This heavy, screw-back, two-piece insignia with company letter below is typical of those commonly made in the late 1930s and during World War II.*

Fig. 5-212. *A heavy separable disk with battalion number below.*

Fig. 5-213. *The 179th Infantry Regiment was a part of the 45th Division. Some of its members wore this disk that is slightly convex. (1 inch in diameter)*

Fig. 5-214. *For reasons now unknown, some 315th Infantry Regiment troops had their regimental number added below the rifles. The screw post that joins the design to the background is offset to center the overall insignia. (1 inch in diameter)*

Fig. 5-215. *A highly convex disk with a bar to support the 5. (1 inch in diameter)*

Fig. 5-216. *This parachute infantry regiment wore its number below, suspended on a bar. (1 inch in diameter)*

Fig. 5-217. *Army stores outside Fort Bragg, North Carolina, in the 1950s sold this silver-colored insignia that emphasizes the airborne nature of the Fort Bragg units.*

Fig. 5-218. *Both the size of the screw post and the small size of the unit designation on this slightly convex disk identify it as made in Germany.*

Fig. 5-219. *This disk was made in Germany for the 16th Infantry Regimental Headquarters Company.*

Fig. 5-220. *This Service Company, 371st Infantry Battalion insignia was made in Germany in the 1950s.*

Fig. 5-221. *This Heavy Mortar Battery, 22d Infantry Regiment disk was made during the 1950s.*

Fig. 5-222. *This insignia was made in Germany in 1945 or 1946 from a solid metal disk and has a small safety pin as the fastener. (1 1/64 inches in diameter)*

Fig. 5-223. *This disk was stamped from a piece of thin metal in Germany in 1945 or 1946 and has a thin screw-post fastener similar to that of U.S.-made insignia of World War II. (1 1/32 inches in diameter)*

Fig. 5-224. *Cast in India for U.S. troops in 1944, this disk is constructed like a U.S. separable screw-post disk. (61/64 inches in diameter)*

Fig. 5-225. *This B Company, 371st Infantry Battalion disk displays an issue plastic background trim authorized in 1952. (1 1/4 inches in diameter)*

Fig. 5-226. *This infantry-distinctive trim of a blue outer rim is enameled. (1 3/8 inches in diameter)*

Fig. 5-227. *The rays emanating from the center of this disk may indicate that it was for the Reserve Officers Training Corps, since ROTC disks had similar rays. (1 inch in diameter)*

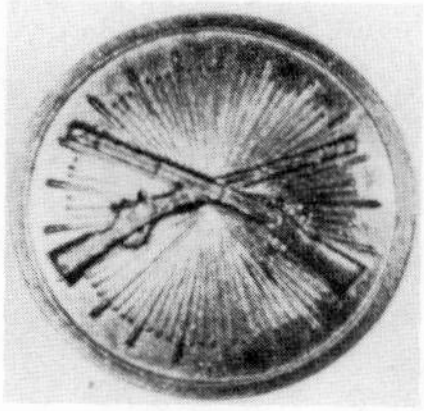

Fig. 5-227.

Fig. 5-228.

Fig. 5-229.

Fig. 5-230.

Fig. 5-231.

Fig. 5-232.

Fig. 5-233.

Fig. 5-234.

Fig. 5-235.

Fig. 5-236.

Fig. 5-237.

Fig. 5-228. *Looking like a 1920s disk, this gilt insignia was used by the Missouri State Guard during World War II. (1 inch in diameter)*

Fig. 5-229. *In the 1970s and 1980s some German-made insignia began to use numbers that looked more like those of U.S.-made insignia, as in this case. (1 inch in diameter)*

Fig. 5-230. *A U.S.-made insignia for the 802d Tank Destroyer Battalion, which served during World War II. (1 1/2 inches wide)*

Fig. 5-231. *This insignia was made overseas, but the 804th Tank Destroyer Battalion was not an element of the U.S. Army. The history of the insignia is a mystery.*

Fig. 5-232. *Antiaircraft units were normally artillery; but the AA with the infantry insignia questions that conventional wisdom. (1 9/16 inches wide)*

Fig. 5-233. *This officers' antitank insignia was for use early in World War II.*

Fig. 5-234. *Made of yellow cotton embroidery on khaki, this nonregulation antitank officers' insignia is a throwback to some World War I general designs when letters were placed in the side angles of crossed arms. (Embroidery 1 1/4 inches wide)*

Fig. 5-235. *World War II 187th Glider Infantry Regiment officers' insignia. (1 17/32 inches wide)*

Fig. 5-236. *World War II 3rd Regiment, Missouri State Guard officers' insignia.*

Fig. 5-237. *World War II Wisconsin State Guard officers' insignia. (1 1/2 inches wide)*

Tank Destroyer Battalion does not appear in U.S. Army records. Evidently made for light antiaircraft units is the insignia shown in Fig. 5-232. The antitank Company, 104th Infantry, perhaps wore the insignia shown in Fig. 5-233, while a more common cloth antitank piece is shown in Fig. 5-234. A typical World War II set of muskets is shown in Fig. 5-235 for the 187th Infantry Regiment. State guard examples often have initials added, as for the 3d Regiment, Missouri State Guard (Fig. 5-236) and for the Wisconsin State Guard (Fig. 5-237). A post–World War II insignia embroidered on a lightweight greenish tan cloth has a yellow design (Fig. 5-238).

After World War II some units stationed in Germany had unusual insignia made: Figs. 5-239 and 5-240 for 3d Battle Group, 6th Infantry; Fig. 5-241 for C Company, 371st Infantry; and Fig. 5-242 for members of the 2d Brigade, 8th Infantry Division. Battalion

Fig. 5-238.

Fig. 5-239.

Fig. 5-238. Yellow embroidered insignia on lightweight green cloth. (Embroidery approximately 1 5/8 inches wide)

Fig. 5-240.

Fig. 5-241.

Fig. 5-242.

Fig. 5-243.

Fig. 5-244.

Fig. 5-245.

Fig. 5-246.

Fig. 5-247.

Fig. 5-248.

Fig. 5-249.

***Fig. 5-239.** Worn in Berlin in the early 1960s, this insignia was for officers of Company A, 3d Battle Group, 6th Infantry.*

***Fig. 5-240.** Insignia of the Headquarters Company, 3d Battle Group, 6th Infantry, about 1961. (1 17/32 inches wide)*

***Fig. 5-241.** The 371st Armored Infantry Battalion was stationed in Bavaria, Germany, in 1955 when this insignia was locally made in Nuremberg. (1 17/32 inches wide)*

***Fig. 5-242.** This insignia was sold in Baumholder, Germany, in 1966 for officers of the 8th Infantry Division's 2d Brigade.*

***Fig. 5-243.** In the 1950s the historic regiments went through changes as battle groups and then battalions became the primary building blocks for divisions. To preserve historic lineages, the army designated these battle groups and battalions as part of regiments, although the regiment existed only on paper as the battle groups and then battalion formed. The Combat Arms Regimental System led to the widespread use of battalion and regimental numbers on insignia in the 1960s and 1970s, as in this example. (1 35/64 inches wide)*

***Fig. 5-244.** This insignia was made in Korea for officers of the 2d Battalion, 23d Infantry. (1 21/32 inches wide)*

***Fig. 5-245.** Insignia of the 3d Brigade, 2d Infantry Division, stationed in Korea. (1 21/32 inches wide)*

***Fig. 5-246.** Jet black 1970s metal insignia with regulation regimental number and the battalion number properly omitted. (1 29/64 inches wide)*

***Fig. 5-247.** Subdued (black) embroidered insignia for fatigue uniforms. (Embroidery 1 7/16 inches wide)*

***Fig. 5-248.** In this 1970s subdued example, the regimental and battalion numbers are reversed from the normal positions. Such changes occur depending on the unit and the members' preference. (1 29/64 inches wide)*

***Fig. 5-249.** Insignia for officers of the 92d Brigade. The HHC stands for Headquarters and Headquarters Company. (1 29/64 inches wide)*

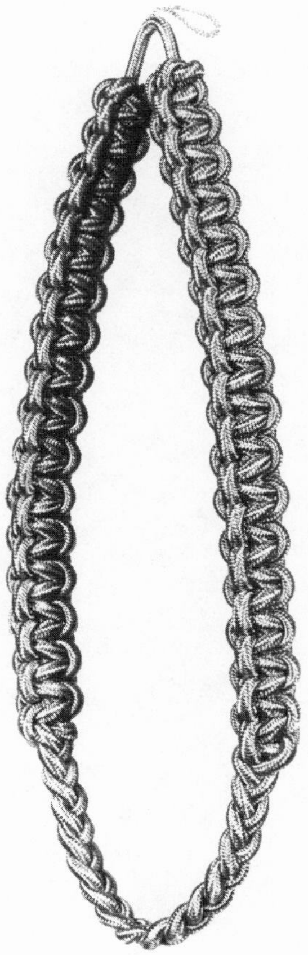

Fig. 5-250.

numbers also came into wide although unauthorized use. An example is shown in Fig. 5-243 for the 2d Battalion, 48th Infantry. A battalion insignia made in Korea, shown in Fig. 5-244, represents the 2d Battalion, 23d Infantry. A similar crudely made piece (Fig. 5-245) is for the 3d Brigade, 2d Division. In the 1970s and 1980s, infantry insignia came in subdued shade (Fig. 5-246). Some had battalion numbers (Fig. 5-247 for the 1st Battalion, 75th Infantry [Ranger] or Fig. 5-248 for the 1st Battalion, 342d Infantry). A gilt piece with nonregulation company designations is shown in Fig. 5-249.

Blue Shoulder Cord

With the esprit-de-corps blue trim added to enlisted infantry disks in 1952 came a special light blue shoulder cord. Composed of square braids (Fig. 5-250), this morale-boosting uniform addition was for wear by men assigned to infantry units.[63]

Fig. 5-250. *The square-braided cord authorized for infantry unit members in 1952. It is worn on the right shoulder, with the loop passing under the arm.*

Section III

Artillery

CHAPTER SIX

ARTILLERY

THE OLDEST INSIGNIA worn by artillery officers are shoulder belt plates beginning with those bearing the federal eagle and letters *USA* below, made in gilded brass. The silver counterpart of this plate, worn by officers of the Legion of 1792–96, is illustrated in Fig. 3-3. Orders of 26 June 1795 prescribed officers' belt plates to be "ornamented with an eagle . . . to match the color of the buttons."[1] No surviving artillery plate of this pattern is known, but it is also believed to have been similar to the contemporary plate illustrated in Fig. 3-3.

The oldest surviving artillery shoulder belt plate is cast brass, with its principal device an eagle on a cannon, but the total design includes flags seen only on buttons worn by artillery from 1802 to 1810. Just within the uppermost edge of the plate can be seen impressed letters *US,* and directly opposite, at the bottom edge, the impressed legend *1 REG.* The artisan who made it was by far a better brass puddler than an artist, because the entire cannon barrel is outside the wheel. This plate (Fig. 6-1) was recovered in a lake near an early-nineteenth-century U.S. artillery encampment site and has been eroded by lake surge. It is conservatively dated to 1808, and it may have been worn by a noncommissioned officer instead of an officer.

The 1813 artillery officers' uniform was generally the same as prescribed for the general staff except that artillery officers wore a blue cloth diamond bordered in gold lace as an ornament on each coat skirt until 1832.[2] It is not presently known whether or not officers of artillery wore cap plates identical to those of soldiers (between 1813 and 1821) or if they had better-quality plates of similar designs. Excavated plates of infantry officers from the same period show they wore engraved cap plates or plates of design identical to that of soldiers' plates, but on silver. Some evidence supports 1816 artillery officers' wearing black chapeaus with gold eagles on black cockades, but details are not clear.[3]

The 1821 regulations introduced various colors of pompons for caps. Company artillery officers wore five-inch-long yellow pompons, except for officers of the light artillery, who had white pompons with red tops. The material used in these 1821–25 officers' pompons is not clear today, although four years later worsted was specified. Similar-colored enlisted men's pompons were worsted. This lasted only four years. In 1825 light artillery colors changed to yellow pompons with red tops. In addition to pompons and cap plates, officers wore gold cap tassels and cords, while enlisted men wore tassels and cords of yellow worsted.[4]

Headquarters of the Army General Order 50 of 1832 prescribed several different devices to be embroidered on officers' coat skirts. For officers of artillery and ordnance the device was "a gold embroidered shell and flame"; an example is shown in Fig. 6-2.

EARLY ENLISTED MEN'S CAP INSIGNIA

United States artillerists of the early nineteenth century changed headgear or cap ornaments often. Enlisted artillerymen wore a *chapeau de bras* after the infantry abandoned the cocked hat in 1805. This hat was in turn replaced in 1808 by a leather cap which included blue feathers "tipt with red." The ornament used, if any, is not known. In 1813 the men received cylindrical caps and brass cap plates. In 1812, Congress added two regiments to the old regiment of artillerists. The second regiment received cylindrical caps bearing large and very distinctive cap plates

Fig. 6-1. *A noncommissioned officers' artillery belt plate, from about 1808, retrieved near Sackets Harbor, New York, in Lake Ontario. At the plate's bottom is the faint impression 1 REG, which was eroded by lake surge for over 140 years. ($2^{35}/_{64}$ inches wide)*

Fig. 6-2. *Artillery and ordnance officers wore a "gold embroidered shell and flame" on coat skirts after 1832. (Design $1^1/_8$ inches wide)*

with the basic design of six stacked cannonballs (Fig. 6-3). Later in 1812 the third regiment received its first pattern cap plates, ornamented with a cannon, large flag, and staff and with the embossed letters *ARTILLERY* and *US* above and *3 REG*T below (Fig. 6-4).[5]

In 1813 the three artillery regiments drew similar buttons for the first time. The button design was an elaborate script letter *A* with an oval below enclosing the regiment's number *1, 2,* or *3*.[6] Two incomplete cap plates have been found bearing an eagle design with oval below; one is marked *3 RT. ARTY* within an oval (Fig. 6-5), and the other is marked *1 RT. ARTY.* Having seen the numbers *1* and *3* and having examined inventories that list cap plates for all three regiments using an identical description, we can assume a cap plate for the 2d Regiment of Artillery, although to date there is no known example.

The artillery appears always to have been reorganizing, and in 1814 the army scrapped the three artillery regiments to form a Corps of Artillery with battalion-sized units, thus ending use of the 1813 buttons and cap plates after just one year.[7] Quartermasters issued new cap plates and buttons, both bearing almost identical designs. Brass buttons exhibited an eagle on a cannon, with cannonballs stacked under the gun's muzzle and the word *CORPS* below. The brass cap plate is rectangular with clipped corners, embossed with an eagle on a cannon standing on grassy ground and showing cannonballs stacked under the muzzle and a small raised oval above the eagle's head (Fig. 6-6). A slightly different design of the same cap plate substitutes a small oval in place of the grassy ground below the cannon (Fig. 6-7). This difference is not believed to be significant and perhaps is only a die sinker's desire for individuality, for we are sure more than one manufacturer made these plates. An excavated example of this plate with two ovals, now in the Field Artillery Museum at Fort Sill, Oklahoma, has two round studs and a hook brazed onto the reverse, indicating that men wore this shape and design as a shoulder belt plate as well as a cap plate. The more

Fig. 6-3.

Fig. 6-3. *The 2d Artillery Regiment's initial cap plate, introduced about 1812. (3 15/32 inches wide)*

Fig. 6-4.

Fig. 6-4. *In 1812, the newly formed 3d Artillery Regiment received cap plates like this with a flag and staff, a cannon, and stacked cannonballs. (3 9/64 inches wide)*

Fig. 6-5.

Fig. 6-5. *In 1813 the three artillery regiments all drew cap plates of this type, with the oval bearing the regimental number and RT. ARTY. (Maximum fragment width 2 19/20 inches wide)*

Fig. 6-6.

Fig. 6-6. *An 1814 Corps of Artillery cap plate. (2 9/16 inches wide)*

Fig. 6-7.

Fig. 6-7. *A variation of the 1814 Corps of Artillery cap plate, with a small oval replacing the grassy ground under the cannon. (2 5/8 inches wide)*

Fig. 6-8.

Fig. 6-8. *Shoulder belt plates often exhibited designs similar to those on helmet plates. This example was used until 1821. (2 9/20 inches wide)*

Fig. 6-9.

Fig. 6-10.

Fig. 6-9. *A light artillery cap plate from the time of the War of 1812. ($4\frac{13}{32}$ inches wide)*

Fig. 6-10. *This plate is identical to that of Fig. 6-9 except for the addition of SEMPER PARATUS in the wreath. ($4\frac{2}{5}$ inches wide)*

Fig. 6-11. *Design of the light artillery cap plate, 1814–21. An original is in the Essex Institute, Salem, Massachusetts.*

common oval shape for wear on shoulder belts (Fig. 6-8) continued until 1821.

Besides these identified plates, at least one other is known to exist, but its design has so far escaped detection. An 1819 inventory of obsolete artillery cap plates lists all of those thus far discussed and the light artillery plates, which will be discussed next, plus one other plate identified only as "round on top."[8] Because most of the time periods have been accounted for with specific designs, both in inventories and contracts as well as excavated examples, we must presume this plate with an unknown design was used for only a short time. Further research may unveil its design.

In addition to the three artillery regiments that became the Corps of Artillery in 1814, from 1808 until 1812 the army included a regiment of light artillery. The insignia for light artillery from 1808 until 1812 consisted of the four brass outline letters *USLA,* 1½ inches high, placed on the caps with the *US* above the *LA,* similar to those described for light dragoons in chapter 7. In 1812 the light artillery drew tall caps carrying large rectangular brass front plates with clipped corners. A known surviving example of the plate, shown in Fig. 6-5, has *LT. ARTY* within the oval. Perhaps the men initially used this plate; perhaps they wore another of the known plates. On the upper half of another plate is an embossed flying eagle with a laurel wreath of victory in its left talon and lightning bolts issuing from its right talon. The lower portion of the plate has a thin, wavy ribbon running from left to right and bearing the legend *LIGHT ARTILLERY* (Fig. 6-9). A second, revised plate is identical but has the words *SEMPER PARATUS* within the wreath (Fig. 6-10).[9]

In May 1814, after correspondence between the commissary general of purchases and the light artillery's deputy commander, the army issued a newly designed cap plate for the light artillery.[10] It was worn until light artillery was abolished in 1821. The principal design is composed of large intertwined letters *LA,* exactly as they appeared on contemporary buttons, on an irregularly shaped shield copied from a British cap plate. The upper portion of the plate shows an eagle with its head below reversed wings and a scroll in its beak bearing the legend *SEMPER PARATUS* (Fig. 6-11).

Lieutenant Colonel J. R. Fenwick, who commanded the Light Artillery Regiment from 1812 through 1814, never was able to bring his entire unit together throughout the War of 1812. His command garrisoned and fought in small units and detachments almost everywhere in New York state. Some of the men served as garrison artillery, but many fought as infantry. At the beginning of the war the longsuffering Colonel Fenwick took a large segment of his newly expanded unit to Sackets Harbor, New York. Callendar Irvine, commissary general of purchases, wrote to him at Greenbrush, New York, telling him that the distinctive uniforms for

Fig. 6-12. *An 1820s artillery eagle cap plate.*

Fig. 6-13. *Enlisted men's artillery cap insignia, 1834–51. (3 1/2 inches wide)*

Fig. 6-14. *Hat insignia, 1858 (Insignia 3 1/4 inches wide; cannons 3 1/2 inches long)*

Fig. 6-15. *Some Civil War volunteer organizations had crossed cannons of this style (2 3/4 inches wide)*

Fig. 6-16. *A common stamped nineteenth-century artillery insignia. While some men wore such insignia on Civil War forage caps, the authorized device was the battery letter. (2 3/10 inches wide)*

Fig. 6-17. *Officers' 1851-style artillery cap insignia. (2 11/16 inches wide)*

Fig. 6-18. *A stamped metal version of an officers' 1851 cap insignia. (2 5/8 inches wide)*

Fig. 6-12.

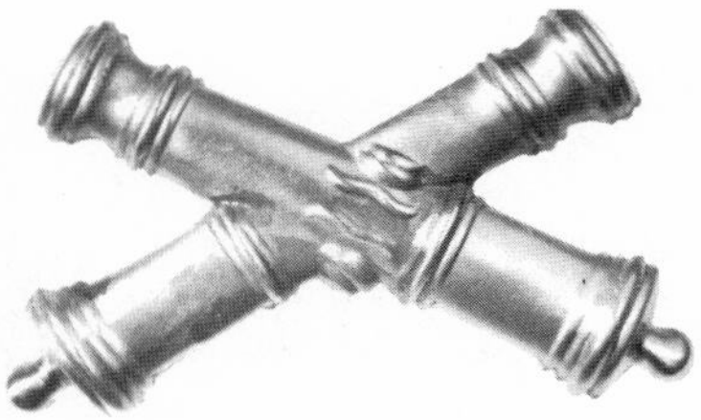

Fig. 6-13.

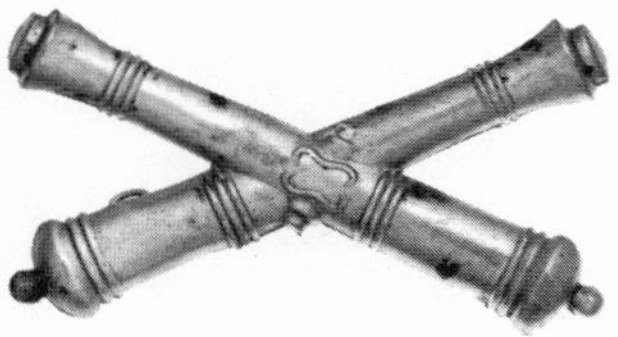

Fig. 6-14.

the light artillery had been sent to Sackets Harbor and that on his arrival there Fenwick could get the uniforms from the quartermaster and issue them to his regiment. When Colonel Fenwick arrived at Sackets Harbor, he learned that the harassed quartermaster already had issued all of the light artillery clothing to shivering militiamen of New York, who needed winter clothing. Fenwick wrote a vehement letter of protest about the incident directly to the secretary of war, but nothing could be done.[11]

In 1814, Irvine, who as commissary general of purchases had complete supervision of the design, manufacture, and procurement of army insignia, wrote Fenwick, then in New York, that an officer of the light artillery had dropped into Irvine's office wearing on his cap a plate with a design Irvine had never seen before (the intertwined letters *LA* previously described). The light artillery officer had assured Irvine that the cap plate was for the light artillery. In his letter to Fenwick, Irvine wrote, in effect, "Here is a drawing of the cap plate. It is lighter and neater than the ones presently worn. If you approve, we will have it made."[12]

Starting in 1820 artillerymen were authorized to wear bell-crowned caps carrying a 3-inch yellow eagle with the regimental number cut out of the shield on the eagle's breast (Fig. 6-12). In 1831 the price for these eagles dropped by half, perhaps because of a design alteration, although neither the reason for the price change nor any design change is now known.[13]

Enlisted Men's Cannons, 1834–72

Uniform regulations implemented in 1833 and 1834 prescribed for the first time "gilt . . . crossed cannons" to be worn beneath the outline eagle device on the tall, cylindrical cap (Fig. 6-13). These original crossed cannon insignia can be identified by their massive size and the blunt cannons. The army attached separate regimental numbers to these caps, which artillerymen wore until 1851, when a new cap with the branch shown by colored trim came into existence.[14]

The 1858 army enlisted artillery hat ornaments reintroduced yellow-metal crossed cannons, longer and thinner than the pre-1851 insignia (Fig. 6-14). A separate brass letter went above the intersection of the cannons. In addition to the crossed cannon insignia in front, the 1851 brass pompon eagle ornament held the side of the hat brim close to the crown.[15]

Fig. 6-15.

Fig. 6-16.

Fig. 6-17.

Fig. 6-18.

Fig. 6-19.

The popular forage cap of the Civil War period, introduced in 1858, first had branch-colored welts and a metal company letter. The colored welts soon disappeared, and although the War Department did not authorize crossed cannons on the cap,[16] many soldiers put the large hat cannons on the cap. The size of the hat insignia made it difficult to place the insignia on the front, so many enlisted artillerymen wore them on the top of the familiar "bummers'" cap, either with or without the separate brass ⅝-inch regimental numbers and 1-inch battery letters prescribed in the regulations. In 1865 a War Department quartermaster manual described the issue cannons in detail: each one 3½ inches long with a ⅝-inch-wide breech and ½-inch-wide muzzle, the cannons crossing at the trunnions.[17] A non-regulation stamped crossed cannon insignia, shown in Fig. 6-15, is typical of Civil War contractor-produced insignia.

Officers' Cap and Hat Devices

In response to the 1832 regulations, officers wore gilt metal crossed cannons likely similar to those shown in Fig. 6-13. Regulations of 1841 and 1847 describe the device simply as gilt "cross cannons and number of regiment."[18] A smaller cap insignia, quite possibly from before 1851, is shown in Fig. 6-16.

The lower band of the 1851 artillery officers' cap carried gold-embroidered crossed cannons (Fig. 6-17) or metal imitation embroidery cannons (Fig. 6-18), with a separate silver-embroidered regimental number above the intersection.[19] When designs of cannon change so little, it becomes necessary to examine the insignia closely to determine the method of manufacture, the type of fasteners, or, in the case of embroidery, the materials and methods used. Unfortunately, since World War II a flood of fake and reproduction embroidered crossed cannon insignia has appeared, and some of these copies have been used for book illustrations, giving them credibility.

Starting in 1858, the forage cap badge for artillery officers included the description: "with the number of the regiment, in silver, at the intersection of the crossed cannons."[20] This wording caused a small cloth disk to be added at the cannon juncture. Often makers added metal numbers over this red or black cloth disk rather than the more expensive embroidery. A Civil War cap with artillery insignia and number above the intersection is shown in Fig. 6-19. In the last half of the nineteenth century, many militia organizations wore plain crossed cannons with numbers above, and these may be confused with Regular Army insignia. Fig. 6-20 shows an officers' cap insignia made about 1890.

On the 1858 hat, officers were to wear crossed cannons with a silver number at the intersection, as on the cap, except the hat insignia was to be made on a dark velvet oval. Because the crossed cannons shown in Fig. 6-21 and 6-22 are without a number at the intersection but are on an oval velvet background, they are identified as militia or volunteer insignia for the tall 1858 hat, but in practice some regulars also wore these without the central number.

Fig. 6-19. *Famed Civil War photographer Mathew Brady captured this portrait showing an officer's artillery cap insignia with regimental number.*

Fig. 6-20. *From the Smithsonian Institution's collection of War Department samples, this forage cap insignia was made about 1890. ($12\frac{13}{16}$ inches wide)*

Fig. 6-21. *Officers' hat insignia, Civil War militia. (Embroidered oval 3½ inches wide)*

Fig. 6-22. *A variation of Civil War militia artillery insignia. (Embroidered oval $3\frac{11}{32}$ inches wide)*

Fig. 6-20.

Fig. 6-21.

Fig. 6-22.

Fig. 6-23.

Fig. 6-23. *The 1881–1901 foot artillery officers' helmet. After 1901 the artillery did not use regimental numbers on helmet plates.*

Fig. 6-24.

Fig. 6-24. *An officers' 1881 helmet eagle. The shield and cannons were stamped separately from the eagle and then applied. ($3\frac{5}{8}$ inches wide)*

Fig. 6-25.

Fig. 6-25. *Enlisted men's 1881 artillery helmet plate struck from a single piece of brass. ($3\frac{1}{2}$ inches wide)*

Fig. 6-26.

Fig. 6-26. *An 1872–81 enlisted men's dress cap.*

Fig. 6-27.

Fig. 6-27. *A stamped, crossed-cannon insignia, ca. 1885. ($1\frac{15}{16}$ inches wide)*

Helmet Plates

In 1872 light artillery units received a large eagle plate (see Fig. 73-2 in chapter 73). Nine years later the army issued all artillery units new helmets and helmet plates (Fig. 6-23). Officers' plates were made from two pieces of brass, with the cannons and shield, which composed the first piece, applied over the eagle itself, which made the second piece (Fig. 6-24). Enlisted men's plates were made from a single stamping but otherwise were of the same design (Fig. 6-25). Although the army issued field artillerymen new uniforms in 1903 and 1904, including caps to replace the helmets with helmet plates, coast artillery troops continued to wear these helmets and plates until 1912. The eagles' shields carried small silver regimental numbers until 1901, when separate companies and batteries replaced regiments. After the 1901 change the shield was "without number or device."[21]

Enlisted Men's Cap Insignia, Post–Civil War to 1900

The 1872 dress cap carried stamped metal cannons below an eagle (Fig. 6-26), as did the new 1872 smaller forage cap. On it enlisted artillerymen wore the cannons $1\frac{1}{8}$ inches long, as shown in Figs. 6-27 and 6-28, with the regimental number added in the upper angle and the battery letter in the lower angle. Thin stamped cannons with wire fasteners and later lead-filled stamped cannons with safety pin fasteners remained until the invention of more substantial screw-post fastening devices in 1896. The initial 1896–1900 screw-post artillery insignia was slightly convex, and an example is shown in Fig. 6-29 for O Battery, 6th Artillery Regiment. (All seven artillery regiments had N and O batteries in their organization at this time.)[22] Fig. 6-30 shows the later flat ornament with the 1896 screw post. Regimental noncommissioned staff members wore cannons with the regimental number above the cannons and without any battery letter (Fig. 6-31).

Reorganization and Enlisted Men's Cap Devices

Because of the major artillery reorganization in 1901 and its effect on enlisted men's insignia, it is appropriate to undertake a brief examination of artillery units. An act of Congress of 2 February 1901 constituted the Artillery Corps of the Army, to be comprised of the coast artillery and the field artillery, with a common chief. Congress organized the Artillery Corps with thirty field artillery batteries and 126 seacoast artillery companies. On 25 January 1907, Congress recognized the Russo-Japanese War experience and separated the two artilleries to form a Coast Artillery Corps and six field artillery regiments of two battalions each, with three batteries to a battalion. The chief of artillery remained as such until 1 July 1908, when he became chief of the Coast Artillery Corps.[23]

As an interesting historical sidelight, note that this type of reorganization happened once before almost a century earlier. Three 1814 artillery regiments were redesignated the Artillery Corps and organized into separate battalions, only to be reorganized again as regiments after seven years.[24]

Following the 1901 artillery reorganization, company and battery members wore their unit's number below the cannons (Fig. 6-32), while the noncommissioned staff wore plain cannons (Fig. 6-33). The army modernized most enlisted insignia in 1905, and thinner cannons resulted (Fig. 6-34). Company letters, as well as regimental numbers, appeared on the post-1907 field artillery regimental insignia, as shown in Fig. 6-35, while the noncommissioned staff insignia had only the regimental number above (Fig. 6-36). The army also introduced bronze devices for wear on the service cap in 1905, as previous enlisted men had worn only hats.[25] An example of a bronze cap insignia is shown in Fig. 6-37. Fig. 6-38 shows the bronze 1905–1907 insignia for men in either a 3d Battery or a 3d Company. Artillerymen of the West Point detachment wore the letters

Fig. 6-28. *A variation of the enlisted men's stamped metal artillery insignia. (1 29/32 inches wide)*

Fig. 6-29. *Battery O, 6th Artillery, enlisted men's cap insignia, 1896–1900, made with a screw-post fastener. The insignia is convex in overall shape, unlike insignia made just a couple of years later. It is interesting that some regiments included batteries N and O at the turn of the century.*

Fig. 6-30. *This style of cap insignia was flat instead of the previous convex shape. (1 13/16 inches wide)*

Fig. 6-31. *Cannon insignia of this design, with only a regimental number in the upper intersection, were worn by regimental staff noncommissioned officers from 1896 until 1901. (1 3/4 inches wide)*

Fig. 6-32. *This wide style of cannons with the battery number in the lower angle was used by soldiers between 1901 and 1905. (1 7/8 inches wide)*

Fig. 6-33. *Noncommissioned staff members wore plain cannons after 1901. The cannon design dates the insignia as made before 1905. (1 17/32 inches wide)*

Fig. 6-34. *These thinner cannons were introduced in 1905. The high number and the number's location in the lower angle indicates that it was made for the 137th Coast Artillery Company. (1 23/32 inches wide)*

Fig. 6-35. *After 1907 the field artillery reorganized into regiments, which caused this design of enlisted cannon insignia to be used with a regimental number above and a battery letter below. (1 3/4 inches wide)*

Fig. 6-36. *A gilt cap device, 1907–18, worn by field artillery regimental noncommissioned staff. The fastening nut and washer are visible behind the cannons' intersection. (1 7/10 inches wide)*

Fig. 6-37. *The bronze-colored version of the insignia shown in Fig. 6-36. Bronze cap insignia came into use with the 1905 introduction of khaki and olive drab service caps. (1 23/32 inches wide)*

Fig. 6-38. *Because of the artillery organization after the start of the twentieth century, this could have been worn in two different organizations: service cap insignia, 1905–1907, for a 3d Battery of field artillery, or service cap insignia, 1905–16, for a 3d Company of the Coast Artillery Corps. (1 25/32 inches wide)*

Fig. 6-39. *The proper U.S. Military Academy Detachment gilt insignia for the dress cap, 1910–17. (1 23/32 inches wide)*

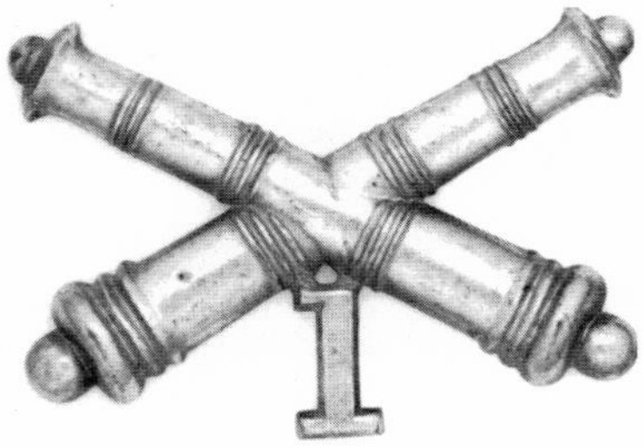

Fig. 6-32.

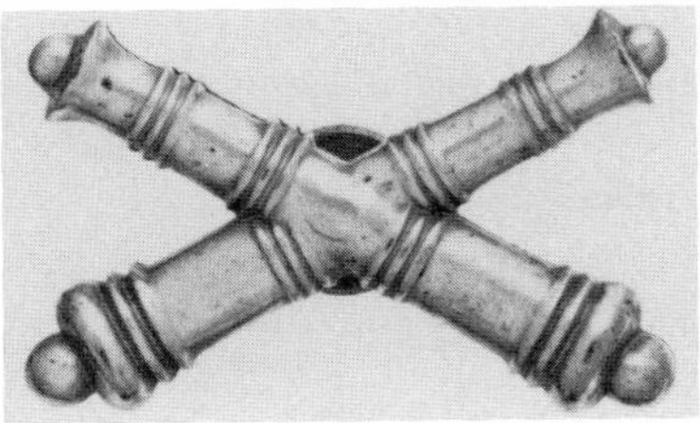

Fig. 6-33.

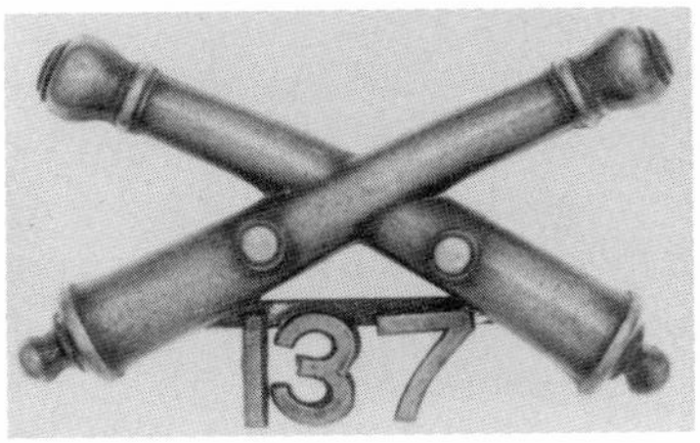

Fig. 6-34.

Fig. 6-35.

Fig. 6-36.

Fig. 6-37.

Fig. 6-38.

Fig. 6-39.

Fig. 6-40.

Fig. 6-41.

Fig. 6-42.

Fig. 6-43.

Fig. 6-44.

Fig. 6-45.

Fig. 6-40. *The Philadelphia Quartermaster Depot had cap insignia made with oversized letters and USMA instead of the proper MA. Apparently these were never issued. (1¾ inches wide)*

Fig. 6-41. *A gilt version of the unissued 1910 Military Academy artillery detachment cap ornament. (1 23/32 inches wide)*

Fig. 6-42. *Coast Artillery district noncommissioned officers wore this style of gilt cap device from 1907 until 1917. (1 29/32 inches wide)*

Fig. 6-43. *A bronze variation of the Coast Artillery Corps 1907–16 district noncommissioned officers' cap ornament with the wreath containing a supporting bar. (1 25/16 inches wide)*

Fig. 6-44. *Pin-backed, narrow bronze cannons with the battery number below were worn on field artillery campaign hats from 1905 to 1907. (1 49/64 inches wide)*

Fig. 6-45. *An 1895 officers' embroidered coat collar insignia. (Design 1¾ inches wide)*

Table 6-1. Authorized Campaign Hat Insignia for Artillery Enlisted Men, 1899–1907.

Device	Organization	Dates of Use
Brass regimental number above a brass letter	Artillery	1899–1901
Brass company or battery number	Artillery	1901–1902
Bronze company or battery number*†	Artillery	1902–1905
Bronze company number†	Coast Artillery	1905–1907
Bronze cannons with battery number below†	Field Artillery	1905–1907

*In practice many men continued to wear the earlier brass numbers, because the color change was not significant.
†Sergeants major wore plain crossed cannons.

MA above and *DET* below their cap cannons (Fig. 6-39). Early versions with *USMA* instead of the proper *MA* were made but never actually used; they are shown in Fig. 6-40 (bronze) and 6-41 (gilt).[26]

The Coast Artillery Corps further grouped companies into artillery districts, and these districts contained the noncommissioned staff. After 1907 the artillery noncommissioned officers wore crossed cannons in a wreath on their cap (Fig. 6-42 for dress, showing the more common construction style, and Fig. 6-43 for service wear, showing a bar to support the cannons).[27]

In July 1916 the Coast Artillery Corps quit using numbers *1* through *170* to designate coast artillery companies. Thereafter, units became "Fort Commands," and at each fort the companies were consecutively numbered "1st Company," "2d Company," and so on. Cap insignia of crossed cannons without any numbers resulted from the change.[28]

Enlisted Men's Hat Insignia

On the olive drab service (campaign) hat, artillerymen worn a variety of insignia. The numbers and letters are illustrated and discussed in detail in chapter 10, "Numbers and Letters," and are summarized in Table 6-1. These subtle changes reflect the greater and more important organizational changes taking place within the artillery between 1901 and 1907.

A 1905–1907 field artillery pin-back hat insignia is shown in Fig. 6-44. Sergeants major of the Artillery Corps wore plain bronze crossed cannons on their hats.[29]

Officers' Coat Collar Ornaments until 1902

From 1892 to 1895 artillery officers wore only silver-colored, block-shaped regimental numbers on their collars. A modified version of the undress sack coat, introduced in 1895, carried crossed cannons on each end of the collar, the regimental number being placed within a round medallion at the center. Used into 1901, these insignia were also worn on the collar of the 1898 khaki service uniform. After June 1898, volunteer officers added their state abbreviations in the lower angle below the cannons.[30]

The size illustrated in Fig. 6-45 is correct for the 1895 collar. It has the rectangular touchhole block not seen in earlier patterns of crossed cannons. Some 1895 artillery insignia did still have round touchholes, as shown in Fig. 6-46, but the round touchhole is more typical of older insignia. Late-nineteenth-century officers' collar insignia could be made of metal in etruscan (imitation embroidery) style. An etruscan officers' collar insignia for the 1895 undress coat is shown in Fig. 6-47 with the regimental number *5* on a black enamel medallion. Fig. 6-48 shows a different die with the regimental number *3,* and a larger number is shown in Fig. 6-49. These 1895 patterns lasted until July 1901.[31]

Fig. 6-46. *An officer with his US and 5th Artillery Regiment 1895–1901 insignia embroidered directly onto his coat collar.*

Fig. 6-47. *An etruscan (imitation embroidery) 5th Artillery Regiment insignia with black center medallion, as used by officers, 1895–1901. ($1\frac{17}{32}$ inches wide)*

Fig. 6-48. *A smooth metal 3d Artillery insignia, 1895–1901. It has a black center under the number and small loops on the back for sewing to the coat collar. ($1\frac{17}{32}$ inches wide)*

Fig. 6-49. *This smooth metal, gold-colored 2d Artillery officers' insignia has a red center instead of the more common black. ($1\frac{9}{16}$ inches wide)*

Fig. 6-50. *The artillery insignia carrying a bare red central oval dates this portrait to 1901–1903. This was the insignia for the new Artillery Corps, formed in mid-1901.*

Fig. 6-51. *This 1901–1903 Artillery Corps insignia is slightly less than the proper 1 inch high and has the red oval made from hard enamel. ($\frac{15}{16}$ inches high)*

Fig. 6-52. *A stamped brass Artillery Corps ornament with a medium red painted oval. ($1\frac{3}{10}$ inches wide)*

Fig. 6-53. *An Artillery Corps captain's shoulder knot, 1901–1903. The artillery insignia is embroidered directly onto the pad's background. (Knot $8\frac{1}{4}$ inches long)*

Fig. 6-54. *This major's shoulder knot has the artillery insignia embroidered separately and then applied to the pad. The 1901–1903 Artillery Corps was the only combatant branch that did not use a branch-colored pad with an embroidered regimental number.*

Fig. 6-46.

Fig. 6-50.

Fig. 6-47.

Fig. 6-48.

Fig. 6-49.

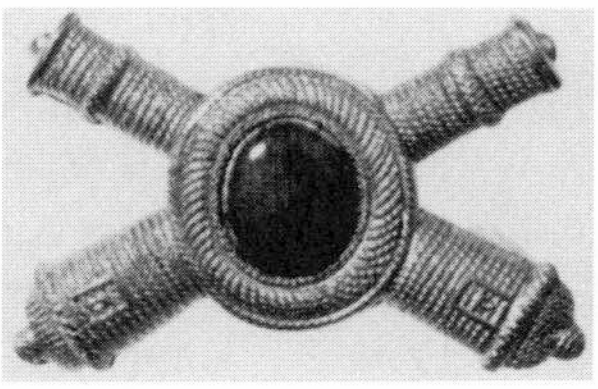

Fig. 6-51.

Fig. 6-52.

Fig. 6-53.

Fig. 6-54.

Fig. 6-55.

Fig. 6-56.

Fig. 6-57.

Fig. 6-55. *With the formation of the Coast Artillery Corps the new branch received short, stubby cannons with a projectile on a central red oval. The design was prescribed in 1902 and was worn by officers by mid-1903. (1 1/2 inches wide)*

Fig. 6-56. *A sterling silver etruscan Coast Artillery Corps insignia with a red enameled medallion. (1 27/50 inches wide)*

Fig. 6-57. *Selected officers added small staff-related insignia to their branch insignia starting in 1900, as did Captain Philip R. Ward, shown here, in 1902.*

There was much comment and speculation about a new insignia for the 1901 Artillery Corps in the two army papers of the time, the *Army and Navy Register* and the *Army and Navy Journal*. This culminated in illustrations of a series of "suggestions" sent to the *Army and Navy Journal* and published in the issue of 1 June 1901. None of the suggestions came close to the final design, but some had considerable merit. General Orders number 28, dated 25 July 1901, announced the new insignia for officers: "Artillery—two crossed cannon of present design, one inch high, of gold metal or gilt metal, or embroidered in gold, oval at the intersection having a plain scarlet center, according to pattern in the office of the Quartermaster General." The officer shown in Fig. 6-50 wears an example of this 1901 insignia. Fig. 6-51 shows one with a scarlet hard enamel center and of imitation embroidery. Fig. 6-52 has wires on the back to hold the thin, stamped metal cannons to the coat collar. The red oval is painted. From April 1901 until 1903, veterinarians wore this artillery insignia in silver.[32] In less than one year the 1902 uniform regulations called for a replacement artillery insignia.

Shoulder Knots

Until 1901, artillery officers wore the 1872 knots with a scarlet background and an embroidered regimental number. With the dissolution of the artillery regiments, the knots carried the new Artillery Corps insignia on a scarlet pad. Two examples are shown in Fig. 6-53 and 6-54; the first has the cannons and red oval embroidered directly onto the pad, while the second has a separately embroidered insignia added to the pad.

Coast Artillery Officers' Insignia, 1902–17

The 1902 Coast Artillery Corps insignia was the traditional crossed cannons with a "red oval . . . to exhibit an oblong projectile in gilt outline."[33] An example is shown in Fig. 6-55. Fig. 6-56 shows a metal insignia, worn on a dress coat cuff, made to resemble embroidery and with sew-on loops on the back for attaching.

For the khaki and olive drab service uniforms the insignia had a dull bronze finish. Small staff devices, first prescribed in October 1900 for placement in the lower angle of the cannons, indicated an officer's staff duties within his regiment.[34] The 1903 bronze insignia included Fig. 6-58 for adjutants, Fig. 6-59 for quartermasters, Fig. 6-60 for commissary officers, and Fig. 6-61 for chaplains. Similar insignia came for the dress uniform, with gilt finish and a red enamel oval (Figs. 6-57 and 6-62).

In 1905 the War Department modernized the crossed cannons, and more artistic long, slender cannons replaced the stubby cannons (Fig. 6-63). Typical staff officers' devices for the 1905 version of Coast Artillery Corps insignia include those shown in Fig. 6-64 for adjutants and in Fig. 6-65 for quartermasters. These staff insignia continued through World War I, with the addition of devices for small arms inspectors (Fig. 6-66) in 1914, and the War Department added a lyre in October 1918 for commissioned band leaders.[35]

Fig. 6-67 shows an insignia worn during World War I for the 6th Coast Artillery Provisional Regiment. Regiments had been disbanded with the creation of the Artillery Corps in 1901, but during 1917 and 1918 a

Fig. 6-58.

Fig. 6-59.

Fig. 6-60.

Fig. 6-61.

Fig. 6-62.

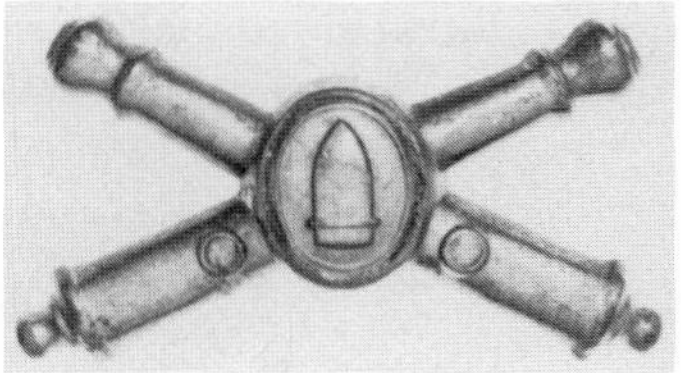

Fig. 6-63.

Fig. 6-64.

Fig. 6-65.

Fig. 6-66.

Fig. 6-58. *Bronze-colored 1903–1905 Coast Artillery Corps collar insignia for a district adjutant. (1 1/2 inches wide)*

Fig. 6-59. *Bronze 1903–1905 collar insignia for a Coast Artillery Corps district quartermaster officer. (1 1/2 inches wide)*

Fig. 6-60. *Bronze 1903–1905 collar insignia for a district commissary officer. (1 1/2 inches wide)*

Fig. 6-61. *Bronze 1903–1905 collar insignia for a district chaplain. (1 1/2 inches wide)*

Fig. 6-62. *A gilt Coast Artillery Corps quartermaster insignia with a blue enameled felloe (wheel edge) on the quartermaster emblem. (1 15/32 inches wide)*

Fig. 6-63. *In 1905 the War Department introduced officers' Coast Artillery Corps insignia with more slender cannons. (1 23/32 inches wide)*

Fig. 6-64. *A World War I example of a Coast Artillery Corps adjutants' collar device in bronze color. (1 3/4 inches wide)*

Fig. 6-65. *From the Smithsonian Institution's collection, a World War I Coast Artillery Corps quartermaster collar insignia. (1 23/32 inches wide)*

Fig. 6-66. *Insignia of inspectors of small arms practice, authorized in 1914. (1 3/4 inches wide)*

total of thirty-four heavy artillery regiments were organized, and men in those units wore coast artillery insignia with regimental numbers. The War Department assumed that American coastal cities would not be subject to attack by German ships because the enemy fleet was contained by Allied sea power. As a result coast artillery personnel assigned to major-caliber guns (all howitzers and mortars above 6-inch caliber, all 5-inch guns and upward organized as army artillery, and all trench mortar and antiaircraft units assigned to corps or army troops) were available for service overseas. Antiaircraft and trench mortar units added the letters *AA* and *TM* to the standard coast artillery bronze collar insignia.[36] A coast artillery insignia made in France in 1918 is shown in Fig. 6-68.

Warrant Officers' Army Mine Planter Service Insignia, 1920

Coastal defense included explosive mine fields sown in offshore waters at strategic places. A branch of the coast artillery, designated the Army Mine Planter Service, was charged with the responsibilities of various defensive measures, some of which are discussed below in the paragraphs on enlisted men's Army Mine Planter Service insignia. The army's first warrant officers joined the mine planter service in January 1920, and until the War Department created distinctive warrant officers' insignia, those men wore the insignia shown in Fig. 6-69 and described as, "a submarine mine . . . 1/2 inch high, . . . maneuvering ring up," placed at the lower angle of the coast artillery insignia. In November 1920 regulations called for warrant officers to remove these insignia and to wear no branch insignia, but no doubt the use of coast artillery insignia lingered for some time.[37] In addition, the warrant officers wore special sleeve devices described in chapter 43, which discusses warrant officer insignia.

Coast Artillery Officers' Insignia, 1920–51

The army authorized shirts as outer garments in 1924. Artillery officers' shirt insignia were to be 3/4 inch high (Fig. 6-70).[38] Officers assigned to regiments could wear the insignia with the regimental number above, as shown in Fig. 6-71 for the 74th Coast Artillery Regiment. An insignia denoting the quartermaster of a coast artillery regiment is shown in Fig. 6-72, with cannon 3/4 inch long. The same basic design with still smaller cannons is shown in Fig. 6-73. Many different shirt-sized insignia were made, and four examples are illustrated in Figs. 6-74 through 6-77, with the last piece marked *GAUNT LONDON* on the back.

After 1921 the army permitted gilt insignia with a red enamel oval for the white uniform, and after October 1923, for all uniforms. During the life of the standing-collar coat, it used 1-inch-high cannons.[39]

One of the new machines of war, the airplane, caused the organization not only of the Air Service but also of antiaircraft units. Officers serving with the antiaircraft service wore coast artillery insignia after May 1919. Many

Fig. 6-67.

Fig. 6-68.

Fig. 6-69.

Fig. 6-70.

Fig. 6-71.

Fig. 6-72.

Fig. 6-73.

Fig. 6-74.

Fig. 6-75.

Fig. 6-76.

Fig. 6-77.

***Fig. 6-67.** During World War I the Coast Artillery Corps formed provisional regiments. Officers in these heavy units added unit numbers above the insignia, as shown. (1 23/32 inches wide)*

***Fig. 6-68.** This French-made bronze Coast Artillery Corps insignia was struck from two separate pieces, with the central oval later applied to the cannons. (1 11/32 inches wide)*

***Fig. 6-69.** Warrant officers of the Army Mine Planter Service, January to November 1920, wore this bronze insignia with a 1/2-inch-high sea mine in the lower angle. (1 3/4 inches wide)*

***Fig. 6-70.** A Coast Artillery Corps bronze-colored insignia for the shirt collar during World War I. (1 3/32 inches wide)*

***Fig. 6-71.** This officers' bronze insignia for 74th Coast Artillery Regiment is marked on the back BRONZE B.B.&B. (for the firm of Bailey, Banks and Biddle). The 74th Coast Artillery was organized in June 1918, went overseas in September 1918, and returned in December 1918.*

***Fig. 6-72.** A 71st Coast Artillery Corps quartermaster's shirt collar insignia in a medium brown bronze. The 71st served in Massachusetts except for seven months overseas, July 1918–February 1919. (1 1/100 inches wide)*

***Fig. 6-73.** A small insignia for a coast artillery quartermaster. (27/32 inches wide)*

***Fig. 6-74.** Officers' shirt collar insignia in bronze color like this, less than 1 inch wide, were common during World War I. (13/16 inch wide)*

***Fig. 6-75.** This gilt-colored Coast Artillery Corps officers' shirt insignia, from about 1925, has the central red oval painted instead of the usual enamel. (27/64 inch wide)*

***Fig. 6-76.** An all-gilt Coast Artillery Corps insignia for shirts sold in southern Texas in the 1920s for the Gulf Coast defense officers. (23/64 inch wide)*

***Fig. 6-77.** This chocolate-colored shirt insignia is marked J. R. GAUNT LONDON on the reverse. (25/32 inch wide)*

officers added the letters *AA,* and the practice continued into the 1920s with gilt insignia such as that of Fig. 6-78 for the 212th Coast Artillery (AA), a National Guard unit that the army inducted into federal service on 10 February 1941 at Camp Stewart, Georgia.[40]

War Department Circular 15, 10 March 1926, specified the 3/4-inch-high crossed cannons, previously worn on the shirt, for the lapel coat. This insignia had a raised, red enamel center bearing a projectile, point up. Officers used this insignia until 1951,[41] but two common versions exist. The official 1936 drawing shows blunt cannons of the type shown in Fig. 6-79. In some cases, various coast artillery insignia were made with guns of the type specified for the field artillery, but with the oval and shell of the coast artillery (Fig. 6-80). Besides the length differences, both the muzzle and breech ends differ between the two official designs.[42] Several coast artillery insignia designs may be found, and samples are shown in Figs. 6-81 through 6-87. Coast artillery cloth insignia for the World War II period are shown in Figs. 6-88 and 6-89, the first design with long field guns and the oval not filled in, which allows the khaki cloth to show around the projectile, and a more proper design with the coast artillery guns and an embroidered red central oval on brown for the World War II coat.

Field Artillery Officers' Insignia, 1902–41

When the 1901 Artillery Corps split into the coast and field branches in 1902, the resulting branches placed unique devices at the cannon intersection: the coast artillery's well-known shell and the field artillery's less well recognized wheel.[43] A red oval carrying a gilt wheel went on the field artillery dress uniform cannons (Fig. 6-90), while the service uniform insignia used a bronze oval and wheel (Fig. 6-91), although Fig. 6-92 illustrates a variation with a bronze insignia and an enamel oval. The small staff devices previously added below the cannons continued: Fig. 6-93 for adjutant; Fig. 6-94 for quartermaster; Fig. 6-95 for commissary; and Fig. 6-96 for chaplain.

The modified design of the officers' insignia which appeared in 1905 replaced the blunt cannon with longer and more graceful

Fig. 6-78. *An outgrowth of aircraft as war machines was the birth of antiaircraft units. Both coast and field artillery initially had antiaircraft units, but this eventually became a Coast Artillery Corps function. This officers' gilt insignia was worn on the high-collar coat after 1923. (1 3/4 inches wide)*

Fig. 6-79. *This officers' Coast Artillery Corps insignia follows the official 1936 design of blunt cannons. (1 1/8 inches wide)*

Fig. 6-80. *In 1936 the army officially prescribed long, thin cannons of this design for the field artillery, while the cannons shown in Fig. 6-79 were for the Coast Artillery Corps. Because of the previous use of long field guns on many coast artillery insignia, manufacturers made lapel ornaments of this general style during World War II. Besides the distinguishing difference of the red oval and projectile for the coast artillery and the cannon lengths, both the muzzle and breech ends differ between the two types of cannons.*

Fig. 6-81. *This solid brass Coast Artillery Corps insignia did not have the red enamel added. Its back is marked B.B.&B., and it has four small sew-on loops. (1 3/4 inches wide)*

Fig. 6-82. *Stamped from heavy metal, this pin-back 63d Coast Artillery officers' piece is typical of those made in the 1920s. (1 3/4 inches wide)*

Fig. 6-83.

Fig. 6-84.

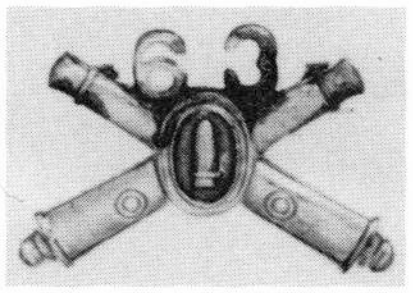

Fig. 6-85.

Fig. 6-86.

Fig. 6-87.

Fig. 6-88.

Fig. 6-89.

Fig. 6-90.

Fig. 6-91.

Fig. 6-92.

Fig. 6-93.

Fig. 6-94.

Fig. 6-95.

Fig. 6-96.

Fig. 6-83. *This is a common example of a World War II officers' clutch-back Coast Artillery Corps lapel insignia except that the red enamel is missing. Around the oval, on the reverse, is stamped a wreath and the words GEMSCO N.Y. ($1^{11}/_{32}$ inches wide)*

Fig. 6-84. *Probably worn in the 1930s on a shirt collar, this pin-back ornament displays the field artillery guns. ($1^{1}/_{16}$ inches wide)*

Fig. 6-85. *A 63d Coast Artillery (Anti-Aircraft) shirt insignia with enameled medallion. The unit was organized as a regiment in 1924. ($1^{1}/_{32}$ inches wide)*

Fig. 6-86. *Similar to the insignia shown in Fig. 6-84, this device has larger numbers. ($1^{3}/_{32}$ inches wide)*

Fig. 6-87. *The bar holding the unit number of this insignia is soldered to the medallion instead of the cannons.*

Fig. 6-88. *A World War II–period light yellow embroidered Coast Artillery Corps insignia on khaki. The background around the projectile is khaki, and not red as it should be. (Design $1^{3}/_{16}$ inches wide)*

Fig. 6-89. *A World War II yellow insignia with a red oval, embroidered on dark brown for an officer's coat. (Design $1^{3}/_{8}$ inches wide)*

Fig. 6-90. *The field artillery insignia prescribed in 1902 and used until 1905. Cannons and wheel are gilt, and the oval is red enamel. ($1^{15}/_{32}$ inches wide)*

Fig. 6-91. *A pin-back bronze version of the 1902–1905 field artillery officers' insignia. ($1^{15}/_{32}$ inches wide)*

Fig. 6-92. *This bronze field artillery insignia is marked STERLING on the back and affixed with four small loops. On the face the oval is enameled dark red, and the wheel and oval edge are gilt. ($1^{15}/_{32}$ inches wide)*

Fig. 6-93. *Adjutant, field artillery, 1903–1905. The bronze insignia was for wear on khaki and olive drab service or field uniforms. ($1^{15}/_{32}$ inches wide)*

Fig. 6-94. *Field artillery quartermasters' collar insignia, 1903–1905. ($1^{15}/_{32}$ inches wide)*

Fig. 6-95. *Field artillery commissary officers' collar insignia. This particular insignia was made in 1903. ($1^{15}/_{32}$ inches)*

Fig. 6-96. *Collar insignia for a chaplain assigned to the field artillery, 1903–1905. ($1^{15}/_{32}$ inches wide)*

Fig. 6-97.

Fig. 6-97. *A dress version of the "modernized" field artillery insignia introduced in early 1905. (1 3/4 inches wide)*

Fig. 6-98.

Fig. 6-98. *The service uniform insignia for field artillery, 1905–1907. (1 3/4 inches wide)*

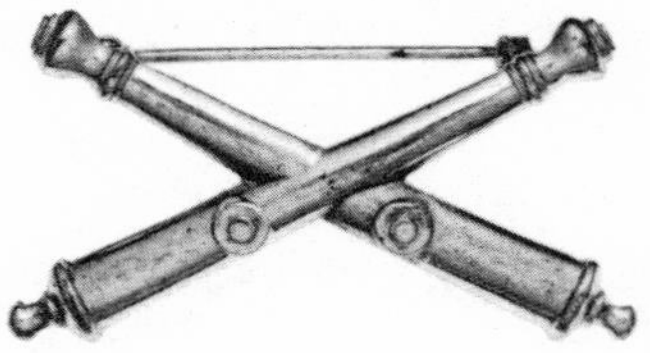

Fig. 6-99.

Fig. 6-99. *Plain gilt crossed field guns prescribed in April 1907 for field artillery officers. (1 23/32 inches wide)*

Fig. 6-100.

Fig. 6-100. *Bronze service insignia for the regimental quartermaster, 10th Field Artillery Regiment, 1907–1923.*

Fig. 6-101.

Fig. 6-101. *Adjutants' gilt insignia for the dark blue sack coat collar, 15th Field Artillery, 1907–17. (1 23/32 inches wide)*

Fig. 6-102.

Fig. 6-102. *Before veterinarians became part of the Medical Corps in 1916, those assigned to the field artillery after 1907 wore this style of bronze insignia. (1 23/32 inches wide)*

Fig. 6-103.

Fig. 6-103. *This 1930s field artillery adjutants' lapel insignia has the small shield enameled. (1 29/64 inches wide)*

Fig. 6-104.

Fig. 6-104. *A 1930s adjutants' lapel device in all gilt. (1 25/64 inches)*

Fig. 6-105.

Fig. 6-105. *Made in France during World War I, this field artillery officers' collar insignia has a shiny black finish. (1 11/32 inches wide)*

forms, as shown in Figs. 6-97 (dress) and 6-98 (service).[44] General Order 94, dated 20 April 1907, removed the wheel and caused the two long field guns to become the field artillery insignia (Fig. 6-99). The regimental number straddled the upper angle of the cannons when appropriate. On both bronze and gilt insignia, staff officers continued to add small devices to show duties within the regiment: Fig. 6-100 (in bronze) for quartermaster, 10th Field Artillery Regiment, and Fig. 6-101 (in gilt) for the adjutant, 15th Field Artillery Regiment. Between December 1902 and June 1916 field artillery veterinarians added a winged horseshoe in the lower angle of the crossed cannons (Fig. 6-102). October 1914 saw small arms inspectors add ordnance insignia as a staff device. After October 1918 commissioned band leaders wore a lyre below their cannons. Commissary devices disappeared in 1913, and chaplains switched from staff insignia to their own branch insignia in 1914. Other field artillery staff insignia were rescinded in the fall of 1923, although officers continued to wear them for several years.[45] An example used in the 40th Division (California National Guard) during the 1930s, with an enameled adjutant's shield, is shown in Fig. 6-103, while the more common all-gilt shield appears as Fig. 6-104.

Not all manufacturers during World War I conformed strictly to official patterns. An example of a variant form of field artillery officers' insignia, shown in Fig. 6-105, was made in France and has the typical fastener

Fig. 6-106.

Fig. 6-107.

Fig. 6-108.

Fig. 6-109.

Fig. 6-110.

Fig. 6-111.

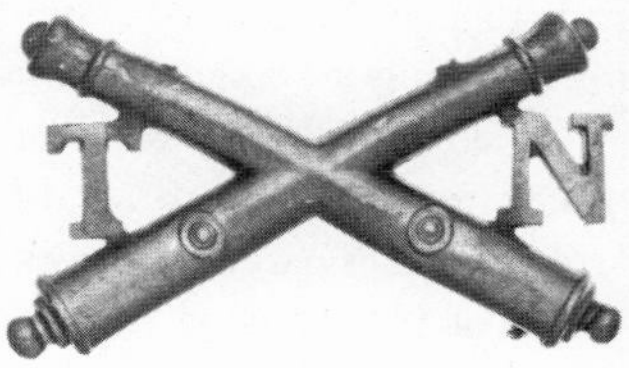

Fig. 6-112.

Fig. 6-113.

Fig. 6-106. *An oversized version of officers' World War I collar insignia, displaying unusual trunions. (1 5/8 inches wide)*

Fig. 6-107. *A World War I field artillery officers' insignia made with a brown finish and sewn to the standing collar through loops on the reverse. (1 21/32 inches)*

Fig. 6-108. *A common style of World War I field artillery insignia made in the United States and chemically treated to turn the finish black. (1 3/4 inches wide)*

Fig. 6-109. *World War I 9th Ammunition Train officers' collar insignia. (1 15/32 inches wide)*

Fig. 6-110. *An officers' ammunition train collar ornament with letters below, a variant not as common as that with the letters in side angles. (1 15/32 inches)*

Fig. 6-111. *Because ammunition trains were not the size of regiments, the only staff insignia that should exist for these units is that of the adjutant. (1 13/16 inches wide)*

Fig. 6-112. *The letters T and N also indicate trains. This ammunition train insignia originally had a unit number in the upper angle; it has since been broken off. (1 21/32 inches wide)*

Fig. 6-113. *Trench mortar units often added their letters to World War I insignia, as shown in this case. (1 21/32 inches wide)*

and surface finish from that country. Fig. 6-106 shows a World War I–period officers' insignia that is incorrect in both form and size. It is larger than the prescribed 1-inch-high cannons, and in design it resembles the Civil War pattern, with the large trunnions at the cannons' intersection. It is an example of one manufacturer's complete ignorance or disregard of insignia specifications. More common World War I insignia are shown in Figs. 6-107 and 6-108.

Some officers assigned to ammunition trains wore the field artillery insignia with letters *AT* added to the left and right of the cannons, as shown in Fig. 6-109 for the 9th Ammunition Train. A different pattern is shown in Fig. 6-110. Worn by Lieutenant Harry Barnhart, it has the letters *AT* below the cannons for the 103d Ammunition Train, a part of the 28th Division. Fig. 6-111 illustrates an adjutant's insignia for the 13th Ammunition Train. Fig. 6-112 shows the use of the letters *TN* to signify trains, and Fig. 6-113 illustrates an officers' trench mortar device.

Small shirt collar insignia, introduced before World War I, continued into the 1920s. Because their use was optional from 1919 until 1926, many officers wore full-sized insignia on shirts. In 1921 regulations authorized cannons 3/4 inch high for shirts, and the artillery chose this size (Fig. 6-114) for the 1926 lapel coat.[46] A smaller shirt-sized insignia, with cannons 7/8 inch long, is shown in Fig. 6-115. Smaller shirt collar insignia are shown in Figs. 6-116 and 6-117.

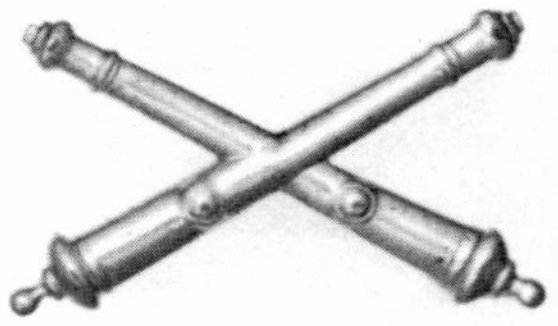

Fig. 6-114.

Fig. 6-115.

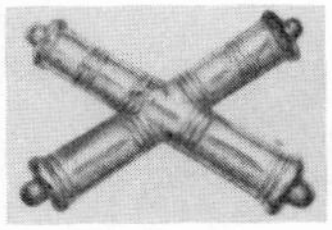

Fig. 6-116.

Fig. 6-117.

Fig. 6-118.

Fig. 6-119.

Fig. 6-120.

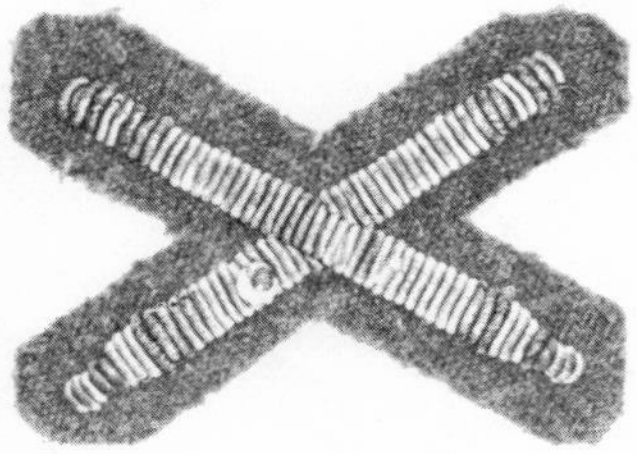

Fig. 6-121.

Fig. 6-114. *These gilt crossed field guns, 3/4 inch high, were prescribed by the War Department in the late 1920s for wear on an officer's shirt collar or on the lapel coat. (1 13/32 inches wide)*

Fig. 6-115. *A gilt shirt insignia, smaller than regulation, from about 1930. (1 3/32 inches wide)*

Fig. 6-116. *These gilt field artillery insignia display very small coastal cannons. (25/32 inches wide)*

Fig. 6-117. *An officers' shirt collar insignia, gold-colored, made using a die originally sunk during World War I for bronze collar pieces. (1 11/32 inches)*

Fig. 6-118. *The most common World War II field artillery officers' insignia, with unit numbers added. (1 11/32 inches wide)*

Fig. 6-119. *A World War II insignia that closely follows the 1936 official drawing. (1 7/16 inches wide)*

Fig. 6-120. *This bullion-embroidered field artillery insignia has cannons shaped more like bowling pins than field guns. (Design 1 9/32 inches wide)*

Fig. 6-121. *The materials show this insignia was embroidered in Germany after World War II for an Eisenhower jacket. (1 3/8 inches wide)*

Fig. 6-122. *This unit saw service intermittently from 1942 through 1957. Construction of the officers' lapel coat insignia indicates it was made in the United States, although such small numbers frequently indicate German manufacture. (1 23/64 inches wide)*

Fig. 6-123. *Made in Germany shortly after World War II, this insignia closely approximates the official War Department prewar design. (1 13/32 inches wide)*

Field Artillery Officers' Insignia, 1941–51

A new edition of Army Regulation 600-35, published in November 1941, called for "two crossed field guns 3/4 inch in height. When applicable the regimental number 1/4 inch in height in the upper angle." An example in Fig. 6-118 shows the most popular and usual form seen during World War II, but it does not follow the official drawings of insignia distributed to manufacturers by the War Department. The insignia that most clearly follows the official 1936 drawing, with blunt cannons, is shown in Fig. 6-119.[47] It was made by the American Emblem Company of Worcester, Massachusetts. An interesting World War II device worn by officers of the 606th Tank Destroyer Battalion, crossed cannons with the number *606* above and the letters *TD* below, is shown in chapter 10, "Numbers and Letters." Bullion insignia made about the time of World War II include those shown in Figs. 6-120 and 6-121.

Design variations continued after the war's end. A pattern from the 1950s with thin, short cannons is shown in Fig. 6-122. Dealers in Germany made many types of field artillery insignia. Usually these are distinguished by small regimental or battalion numbers. Two examples of German-made insignia are shown in Figs. 6-123 and 6-124. Another German-made piece has a battery designation, an addition normally reserved for enlisted men (Fig. 6-125). Fig. 6-126 shows a Korean-made pair of cannons with numerals for the 42d Artillery cast as part of the overall insignia. It is typical of U.S. insignia made in the Far East after World War II.

In the 1950s infantry regiments included a mortar battery, and artillery officers in some of these batteries wore special insignia. Some examples are shown in Fig. 6-127 for the 4th Infantry's Mortar Battery and Fig. 6-128 for the 504th Infantry's Mortar Battery.

The last pre-1957 officers' insignia is shown in Fig. 6-129. The letters *OBSR* and the number indicate that the cannons were made for the 235th Field Artillery Observation Battalion, which was formed as part of the Pennsylvania National Guard after World War II and served in Korea during the Korean War.

Consolidated Artillery

In 1950, Congress consolidated the coast artillery and the field artillery into the artillery, members of which wore the plain crossed cannons. The army added a missile to the historic crossed cannons of this con-

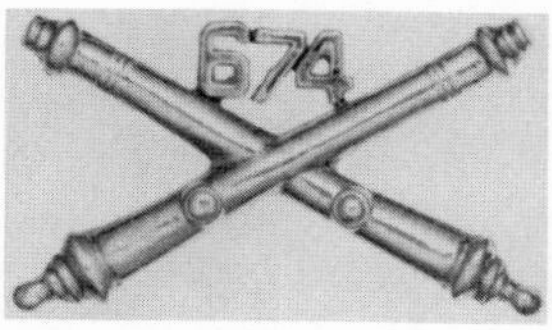

Fig. 6-122.

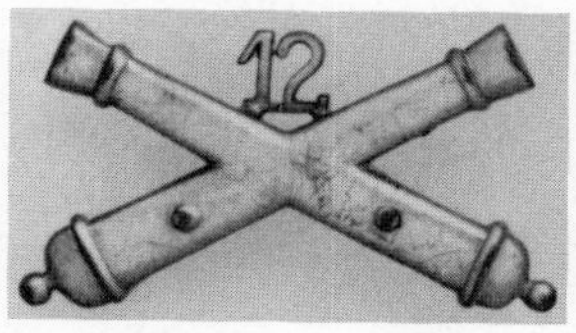

Fig. 6-123.

Fig. 6-124.

Fig. 6-125.

Fig. 6-126.

Fig. 6-127.

Fig. 6-128.

Fig. 6-129.

Fig. 6-131.

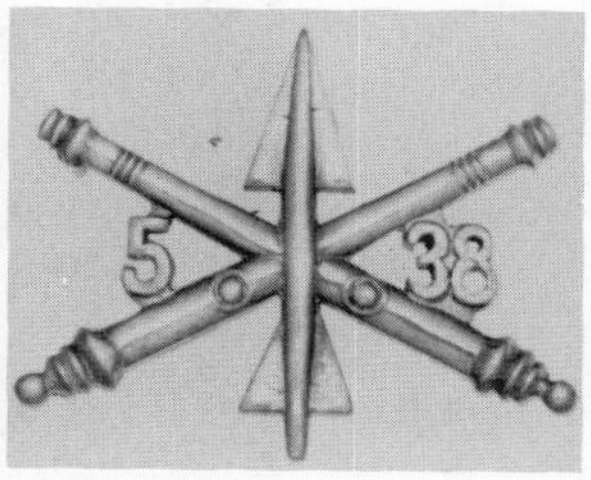

Fig. 6-132.

Fig. 6-133.

Fig. 6-130.

solidated artillery in early 1958 (Fig. 6-130).[48] Regulations did not initially authorize regimental numbers on this insignia, but almost immediately red numbers appeared at the intersection (Fig. 6-131).

Some units added designations in other ways, as did a Korean maker (Fig. 6-132). A German-made silver insignia with red enameled numbers applied directly to the curved cannon surfaces rather than to a recessed center is illustrated in Fig. 6-133.

Field Artillery Insignia, 1968 to the Present

In 1968 history again repeated itself. Just as twice before the two artillery branches had been joined and then split a few years later, so it was again. In 1968, Congress established the air defense artillery. This new branch continued to use the 1958 artillery insignia carrying the missile, while the reestablished field artillery continued to use plain crossed cannons.[49]

Fig. 6-124. *This German-made insignia resembles many made in the United States except that the unit numbers are smaller. (1 3/8 inches wide)*

Fig. 6-125. *A German-made officers' insignia with battery designation, a practice never sanctioned by regulations. Some German-made officers' insignia included company designations. (1 23/64 inches wide)*

Fig. 6-126. *A typical Korean-made U.S. officers' artillery insignia. (1 11/64 inches wide)*

Fig. 6-127. *Officers of the 4th Infantry Regiment's Mortar Battery wore this overseas-made artillery insignia in the 1950s. (1 21/32 inches wide)*

Fig. 6-128. *Insignia worn by an officer in the 504th Airborne Infantry Regiment's Mortar Battery in the 1950s. (1 3/8 inches wide)*

Fig. 6-129. *Insignia made for the 235th Field Artillery Observation Battalion officers. (1 1/2 inches wide)*

Fig. 6-130. *The 1958 artillery insignia. Air defense artillery used this same insignia when they later separated from the field artillery in 1968.*

Fig. 6-131. *Unit numbers of red enamel appeared with the introduction of the 1958 artillery insignia. (1 11/32 inches wide)*

Fig. 6-132. *Korean-made insignia for officers of the 5th Battalion, 38th Artillery. (1 29/64 inches wide)*

Fig. 6-133. *A silver-colored, German-made officers' artillery insignia from the early 1960s, with red unit numbers applied directly to the cannons. (1 3/8 inches wide)*

Fig. 6-134.

Fig. 6-135.

Fig. 6-136.

Fig. 6-137.

Fig. 6-138.

Fig. 6-139.

Fig. 6-140.

Fig. 6-141.

Fig. 6-134. *Officers' collar insignia of the 12th Artillery Group. Any addition other than the battalion or regimental number was not authorized. (1 11/32 inches wide)*

Fig. 6-135. *Insignia of the 2d Battalion, 162d Field Artillery. Use of battalion numbers for units formed under the Combined Arms Regimental System was common in the 1960s and 1970s but never authorized. (1 13/32 inches wide)*

Fig. 6-136. *A metal subdued field artillery insignia with the battalion number above and the regimental number below, a variation of the type of unit designation shown in Fig. 6-135. (1 13/32 inches wide)*

Fig. 6-137. *This subdued jungle fatigue shirt insignia was hand-embroidered in Vietnam during 1966. (Design 1 7/16 inches wide)*

Fig. 6-138. *A gilt insignia for artillery enlisted dress coats, first prescribed in 1902 and initially replaced in 1905. (1 13/16 inches wide)*

Fig. 6-139. *A bronze 9th Coast Artillery Company or 9th Field Artillery Battery enlisted men's service coat insignia, 1902–1905. (1 13/16 inches wide)*

Fig. 6-140. *This 2d Field Artillery Battery trumpeter of 1905 has removed the bronze finish from his collar insignia and shined them. The red cloth projectile on the trumpeter's sleeve shows the man was qualified as a first class gunner.*

Fig. 6-141. *A 1902–1905 enlisted artillery insignia with the black finish removed and polished. Men wore these insignia in 1905 and 1906 until the newer collar ornaments were made and distributed. (1 57/64 inches wide)*

Examples of three post-1968 field artillery insignia are shown in Figs. 6-134, 6-135, and 6-136. The Vietnam War introduced subdued (black) insignia, and one of the artillery insignia made by a Vietnamese native and worn by a colonel during the war is shown in Fig. 6-137.

Enlisted Men's Outline Collar Insignia

The artillery introduced wide, heavy cannons with company and battery numbers below in 1902 (Figs. 6-138 and 6-139). These gilt and bronze cannons are identical to the cap insignia except for the fastening devices. The Quartermaster Department produced many of the 1902–1904 bronze artillery insignia only to have the design modernized immediately in early 1905.[50] Although the Quartermaster General eventually sold a great number of these older devices as surplus, the army issued many, and the men polished the insignia, removing the bronze finish, as did the 2d Field Artillery Battery trumpeter in Fig. 6-140.

An example of such an insignia is shown in Fig. 6-141.

The "modernized" 1905 enlisted men's collar insignia with company and battery numbers is shown in gilt (Fig. 6-142) and in bronze (Fig. 6-143). As was usual, the noncommissioned staff did not wear company designations, so plain cannons designated coast artillery district staff members or (from 1905 through 1907) field artillery staff noncommissioned officers. When the field artillery reorganized into regiments in 1907, battery members switched to collar devices with numbers above and letter below (Fig. 6-144). Field artillery regimental noncommissioned staff members wore cannons with only the number above, as they wore cap insignia already described.[51] Bronze disks replaced the service uniform outline devices in 1910, but the gilt outline insignia remained with the dress uniform until World War I.

Fig. 6-144.

Fig. 6-142.

Fig. 6-143.

Bronze Disks

The 1910 change to bronze-colored disks simply transferred the existing designs to the 1-inch-diameter insignia. Coast artillery district staff noncommissioned officers wore plain cannons without numbers or letters, indicating that they did not belong to a company. Company members added their company number below (Fig. 6-145), while field artillery regimental noncommissioned staff members added the regiment's number above the cannons (Figs. 6-146 and 6-147). Field artillery battery members had the regimental number above and battery letter below (Figs. 6-148 and 6-149). In 1918 men were to wear only battery letters, the regimental designation being on the *US* disk (Fig. 6-150). It is interesting to note that quartermaster specifications called for two types of plain disks: those with cannons crossed high for the coast artillery (Fig. 6-151), and those with cannons crossed low for the field artillery (Fig. 6-152).[52]

Several noteworthy variations of artillery bronze disks occur. These include a disk made in Germany after World War I for occupation troops (Fig. 6-153), which used the older scheme of a regimental number and a battery letter with the cannons. Soldiers fixed this disk to the uniform by inserting two wires, fixed to the disk's back, through the collar grommet and then bend-

Fig. 6-142. *"Modernized" cannons in use about 1912. Gilt insignia of this type with unit number below were used by field artillery enlisted men between 1905 and 1907. Coast artillery companies used this style of collar insignia between 1905 and 1916.*

Fig. 6-143. *Worn on the collar of the service uniform until replaced by 1910 disk insignia, this is a typical bronze-colored coast artillery company device introduced in 1905. With a screw-post fastener, this design served as a cap ornament for coast artillery into World War I. (1 23/32 inches wide)*

Fig. 6-144. *After 1907 the field artillery returned to regimental organizations. This was reflected in enlisted men's insignia by the use of a regimental number in the upper intersection and a battery letter below. Field artillery gilt insignia of the 1905 "modernized" design, with numbers and letters, went on enlisted men's dress uniform caps and collars between 1907 and 1917.*

ing the wires over. The two wires can be seen protruding from under this black-painted gray metal disk. Enlisted men assigned to artillery trains sometimes wore a letter *T* in the cannons' upper angle (Fig. 6-154) or the letters *A* and *T* in the horizontal angles (Fig. 6-155) although the War Department did not authorize such additions. U.S. Military Academy Detachment members wore disks as shown in Fig. 6-156 until March 1921.[53] Two of the many unauthorized field artillery disk variations are shown in Figs. 6-157 and 6-158. The varieties that can be found are virtually endless and range from minor differences to the changes in cannon design and addition designations as shown.

In December 1917 coast artillery enlisted men switched from the plain cannons to those with a projectile at the center, the same design coast artillery officers had used since 1902 (Fig. 6-159). Generally the coast artillery remained organized as separate companies, but the AEF initially formed three regiments, the 6th, 7th, and 8th.[54] Examples of enlisted men's disks with the projectile in the center are shown in Fig. 6-160 for the 6th Regiment and Fig. 6-161 for an 8th Company.

During World War I the army formed both antiaircraft and trench mortar units and added the letters *AA* and *TM* to artillery insignia to distinguish men assigned to the new organizations. Medium trench mortar units came from the field artillery, and heavy units came from coast artillery organizations. Trench mortar disks, which the War Department authorized until March 1921, are shown in Figs. 6-162, 6-163, and 6-164. Antiaircraft insignia involving the letters *AA* (Figs. 6-165, 6-166, and 6-167) were rescinded in October 1923.[55]

One-Piece Gilt Disks

Initial post–World War I gilt disks came with the same stippled background as used on the older bronze pieces. This basic field artillery disk, in gilt, is shown in Fig. 6-168. Its coast artillery counterpart is shown in Fig. 6-169. Artillery disks had field artillery battery or coast artillery company letters below (Fig. 6-170) or, for battalion headquarters, the numbers *1, 2,* or *3* (Fig. 6-171). For other disks manufacturers added either a regiment or a battalion number above and a battery letter below (Fig. 6-172).

Most of the 1920s and 1930s gilt one-piece

Fig. 6-145.

Fig. 6-146.

Fig. 6-147.

Fig. 6-148.

Fig. 6-149.

Fig. 6-150.

Fig. 6-151.

Fig. 6-152.

Fig. 6-145. *A coast artillery bronze collar disk with company number below, adopted in 1910 for wear on the olive drab service coats. (1 inch in diameter)*

Fig. 6-146. *A 1910–17 field artillery disk worn by members of the regimental noncommissioned staff. (1 inch in diameter)*

Fig. 6-147. *A bronze collar disk for men of the 303d Field Artillery Regiment. (1 inch wide)*

Fig. 6-148. *World War I bronze-colored enlisted collar insignia for C Battery, 109th Field Artillery, part of the Pennsylvania National Guard. (1 inch in diameter)*

Fig. 6-149. *Insignia for a member of Headquarters Battery, 319th Field Artillery, 82d Division, during World War I. (1 inch in diameter)*

Fig. 6-150. *A 1918–23 field artillery bronze disk with battery letter below the crossed cannons. The regimental number was to go on the US collar disk. (1 inch in diameter)*

Fig. 6-151. *The quartermaster general's initial 1910 specification for enlisted men's collar disks called for Coast Artillery Corps ornaments to have the cannons crossed high to allow room for a company number below. This example is without the number added. (1 inch in diameter)*

Fig. 6-152. *The field artillery version of the disk specified in 1910 had the cannons lower than that for the coast artillery. (1 inch in diameter)*

Fig. 6-153. *Made in Germany for U.S. occupation troops, this disk is painted black. Two wires on the insignia back, to be put through a uniform collar grommet and then bent over to hold the insignia in place, extend from the back. (1 1/100 inches wide)*

Fig. 6-154. *The T is an unauthorized abbreviation for ammunition trains.*

Fig. 6-155. *Members of the National Army from New York's 77th Division wore this 302d Ammunition Train enlisted men's collar ornament. (1 inch in diameter)*

Fig. 6-156. *A U.S. Military Academy Field Artillery Detachment's enlisted men's bronze collar disk, 1910–21. (1 inch in diameter)*

Fig. 6-157. *A variation of a World War I enlisted men's field artillery collar disk.*

Fig. 6-158. *Improperly placed and nonstandard designs made this field artillery enlisted men's collar insignia unusual. (1 1/32 inches wide)*

Fig. 6-159. *Coast Artillery Corps soldiers of early World War I began to wear disks bearing the same design as that used by officers. (1 inch in diameter)*

Fig. 6-153.

Fig. 6-154.

Fig. 6-155.

Fig. 6-156.

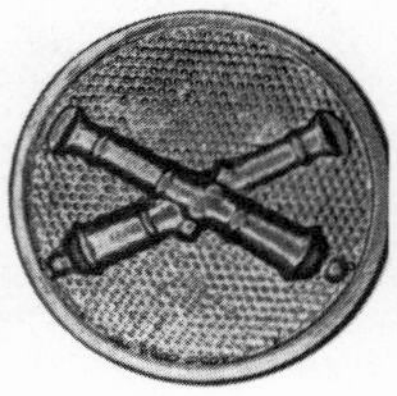
Fig. 6-157.

Fig. 6-158.

Fig. 6-159.

Fig. 6-160.

Fig. 6-161.

Fig. 6-162.

Fig. 6-163.

Fig. 6-164.

Fig. 6-165.

Fig. 6-166.

Fig. 6-167.

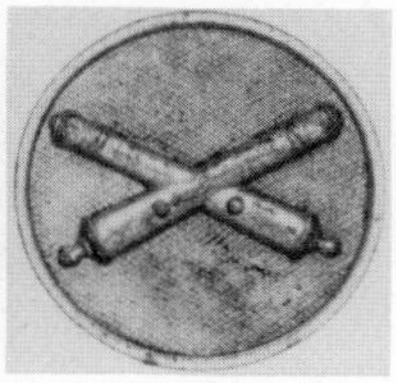
Fig. 6-168.

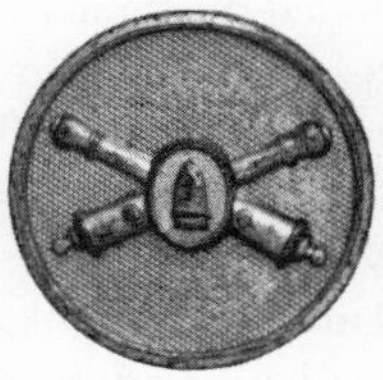
Fig. 6-169.

Fig. 6-170.

Fig. 6-171.

Fig. 6-172.

Fig. 6-160. *A 6th Regiment, Coast Artillery Corps enlisted men's collar insignia, used after World War I. (1 inch in diameter)*

Fig. 6-161. *An 8th Company, Coast Artillery Corps disk from about 1918. Regimental numbers were in the upper angle; company numbers were in lower angles.*

Fig. 6-162. *Enlisted men's collar insignia from 1918 for medium trench mortar units. (1 inch in diameter)*

Fig. 6-163. *World War I collar ornament for enlisted men of the 13th Medium Trench Mortar Battery. (1 inch in diameter)*

Fig. 6-164. *Heavy trench mortar batteries wore coast artillery insignia with TM. (1 inch in diameter)*

Fig. 6-165. *Bronze antiaircraft enlisted men's coat collar ornament with cannons crossed high.*

Fig. 6-166. *A field artillery enlisted men's collar insignia with AA (for antiaircraft), used from 1918 until 1923. (1 inch in diameter)*

Fig. 6-167. *Coast artillery antiaircraft unit men wore this style of bronze disk in the early 1920s. (1 inch in diameter)*

Fig. 6-168. *A field artillery enlisted men's collar insignia made with gilt finish and stippled background, used about 1923. (1 inch in diameter)*

Fig. 6-169. *A gilt enlisted men's coast artillery disk of the type initially used when bright insignia reappeared in 1923. (1 inch in diameter)*

Fig. 6-170. *Gilt-finished coast artillery disk, from about 1923, with battery letter below, made using a die with a stippled background. (1 inch in diameter)*

Fig. 6-171. *Numbers 1, 2, or 3 below the cannons on gilt disks of the 1920s through 1940s signified the battalion headquarters to which the enlisted wearer belonged. (1 inch in diameter)*

Fig. 6-172. *This gilt disk has both the regimental number and the battery letter applied. It was apparently made in the late 1920s using dies sunk about the time of World War I or shortly thereafter. (1 inch in diameter)*

Fig. 6-173.

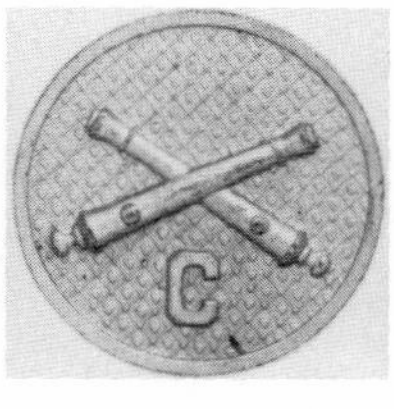

Fig. 6-174.

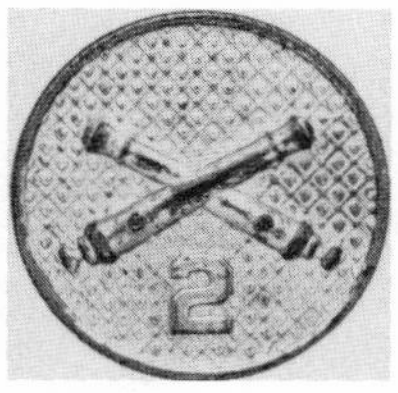

Fig. 6-175.

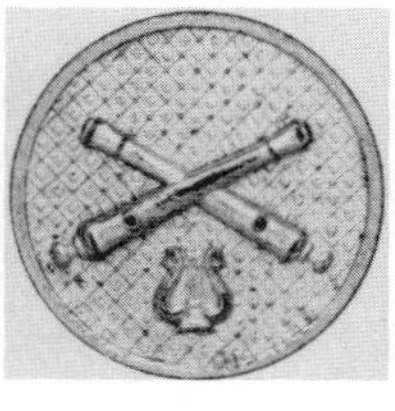

Fig. 6-176.

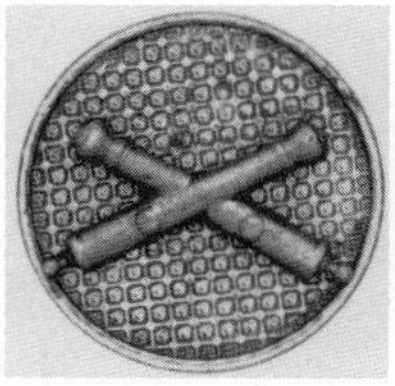

Fig. 6-177.

Fig. 6-178.

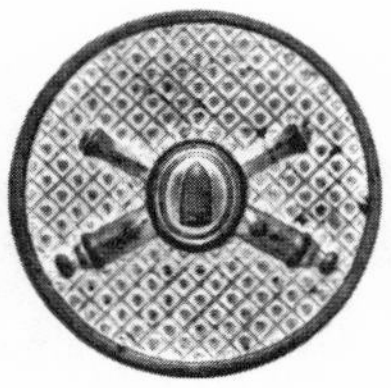

Fig. 6-179.

Fig. 6-180.

Fig. 6-181.

Fig. 6-182.

Fig. 6-183.

Fig. 6-184.

Fig. 6-173. *A 1923–37 gilt issue disk with the prescribed background of diagonal lines and small shields that replaced the fine stippling used earlier. (1 inch in diameter)*

Fig. 6-174. *An enlisted men's regulation 1930 gilt field artillery disk with battery letter below. (1 inch in diameter)*

Fig. 6-175. *An issue 1930 gilt field artillery enlisted men's collar disk with a battalion headquarters number below. (1 inch in diameter)*

Fig. 6-176. *Between 1927 and 1937, regimental band members wore a lyre below their cannons. (1 inch in diameter)*

Fig. 6-177. *This privately made disk has the cannons removable for cleaning. (1 inch in diameter)*

Fig. 6-178. *The 1923–37 coast artillery enlisted men's collar insignia in gilt. (1 inch in diameter)*

Fig. 6-179. *One of many variations of the gilt Coast Artillery Corps disks, authorized 1923–37. (1 inch in diameter)*

Fig. 6-180. *A coast artillery disk, from about 1930, with a battery letter below. (1 inch in diameter)*

Fig. 6-181. *Regimental headquarters battery enlisted men's collar insignia, Coast Artillery Corps, used in the late 1920s and the 1930s. (1 inch in diameter)*

Fig. 6-182. *Separately numbered coast artillery companies continued to show the company number below into 1924. This particular enlisted men's collar insignia has a light yellow finish that has partly worn off. (1 inch in diameter)*

Fig. 6-183. *Enlisted men's collar insignia for a 2d battalion antiaircraft regiment. (1 inch in diameter)*

Fig. 6-184. *Enlisted men's collar ornament for the service battery of an antiaircraft regiment, 1930s. The regimental number went on the US collar disk. (1 inch in diameter)*

Fig. 6-185. *Members of the Army Mine Planter Service wore a sea mine in the lower angle of the Coast Artillery Corps insignia, all on a disk like this. Bronze color was used until 1923, then gilt. (1 inch in diameter)*

Fig. 6-186. *An issue stamped World War II Army Mine Planter Service disk for enlisted men. (1 inch in diameter)*

Fig. 6-187. *This design, with heavy guns, was common in the 1930s on Coast Artillery Corps two-piece screw-back disks. (1 inch in diameter)*

Fig. 6-188. *A common variation of coast artillery two-piece screw-post disks is of this style, featuring thin, long field guns and a small central oval displaying a projectile. (1 inch in diameter)*

Fig. 6-189. *Headquarters and other battery designations like this were officially not to be worn after 1937, although in practice the government continued to issue them and the men certainly wore them. (1 inch in diameter)*

Fig. 6-190. *This 1930s commercially made two-piece enlisted men's collar ornament has the design higher than the center, which gives balance to the overall design when the battery letter is added. (1 inch in diameter)*

disks had the background of small shields and crosshatched lines. Fig. 6-173 shows the basic one-piece field artillery disk, while Figs. 6-174, 6-175, and 6-176 are versions with a battery letter, a battalion number, or (after 1927) a lyre used by regimental band members.[56] Some disks have a removable design (Fig. 6-177), which allowed it to be polished more easily, although the makers did not take care to align the center square hole and the rectangular keyway on the back of the crossed cannons. As a result, the background did not run perpendicular to the central design, as did that of the one-piece issue disks.

Coast artillery disks included the standard designs alone (Figs. 6-178 and 6-179) plus those for company organizations (Figs. 6-180 and 6-181). Separate numbered companies also had their disks, as shown in Fig. 6-182, as well as unauthorized antiaircraft unit disks (Fig. 6-183 for a 2d Battalion headquarters of an antiaircraft regiment and Fig. 6-184 for a service battery).

Fig. 6-185.

Fig. 6-186.

Army Mine Planter Service Disks

In August 1920 the secretary of war approved a special insignia for the Army Mine Planter Service.[57] The coast artillery supplemented harbor defenses with mines that soldiers on shore could electrically detonate. The Army Mine Planter Service stored mines ashore with many miles of control cables and used boats so that in an emergency the mines could be rapidly planted. Routine peacetime activities then included practicing the planting and retrieving of mines and the tieing of this system into the cannon defenses. Shown in Fig. 6-185 is the first enlisted men's bronze disk, which changed to gilt in 1923. The 1942 stamped disk (Fig. 6-186) lasted until the War Department rescinded the insignia in February 1947.[58]

Two-Piece Coast Artillery Disks

Starting in the late 1930s, and continuing through World War II, most coast artillery disks came in two parts. Many dies exist, but the two most common styles either have a large oval and shell at the center of sturdy guns possessing short muzzles and breech decorations, as shown in Fig. 6-187, or have a small shell and an extended design at both ends of thin guns (Fig. 6-188). Both versions, as well as other dies, come with battery designations, two of which are shown in Figs. 6-189 and 6-190. World War II disks also come with regimental or battalion numbers and with unit number and battery letter, as illustrated in Fig. 6-191.

The above insignia are all on flat disks, but the domed insignia come in greater varieties. Three examples are shown in Figs. 6-192, 6-193, and 6-194. A German-made piece, worn in 1948 and made for members of B Battery, 48th Anti-Aircraft Battalion, is illustrated in Fig. 6-195. Coast artillery disks disappeared from use in 1951, when, under 1950 congressional direction, the coast and field artilleries combined. By the time of the demise of the coast artillery, all remaining units had antiaircraft missions.[59]

Recent Crossed Cannons

One of the earliest two-piece disks was described earlier in this chapter and shown in Fig. 6-177. It is similar to the issue disk of the late 1920s and 1930s also discussed earlier, but its cannons are removable for easy cleaning. Most common separable disks, both flat and domed, come in many versions, such as those flat disks shown in Figs. 6-196 (made in Vietnam), 6-197 (made in Germany), and 6-198 (1st Battalion headquarters). Unusual markings are seen on disks for a regimental

Fig. 6-187.

Fig. 6-188.

Fig. 6-189.

Fig. 6-190.

Fig. 6-191.

Fig. 6-192.

Fig. 6-193.

Fig. 6-194.

Fig. 6-195.

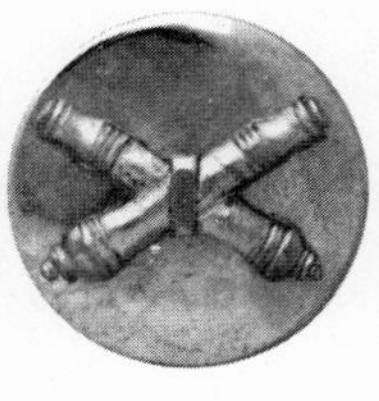

Fig. 6-196.

Fig. 6-197.

Fig. 6-198.

Fig. 6-191. *Probably made about 1937–41, this disk has the coast artillery insignia low to allow for the nonregulation but common practice of adding both the regimental number and the battery letter. (1 3/64 inches in diameter)*

Fig. 6-192. *This domed-shaped disk is typical of enlisted men's collar insignia made in 1945 and later. (1 inch in diameter)*

Fig. 6-193. *Domed enlisted men's insignia of a post–World War II antiaircraft artillery battalion. (1 1/64 inches in diameter)*

Fig. 6-194. *Silver-colored disk worn by members of the 80th Antiaircraft Artillery Battalion (Airborne), 82d Airborne Division. Initially comprised of African American personnel, the unit served at Fort Bragg from 1949 until 1958. (1 inch in diameter)*

Fig. 6-195. *Enlisted men's collar insignia made in Germany about 1948 for B Battery, 48th Antiaircraft Artillery Battalion. (1 inch in diameter)*

Fig. 6-196. *This disk, slightly smaller than regulation, was made in Vietnam about 1966 from very thin brass-colored sheet metal. (31/32 inch in diameter)*

Fig. 6-197. *Made in Germany, this insignia has the unit number and letter struck with the cannons. (1 3/64 inches in diameter)*

Fig. 6-198. *First Battalion Headquarters, Field Artillery insignia from about 1940. The insignia is screw-backed to go on the enlisted men's lapel coat. (1 inch in diameter)*

Fig. 6-199.

Fig. 6-200.

Fig. 6-201.

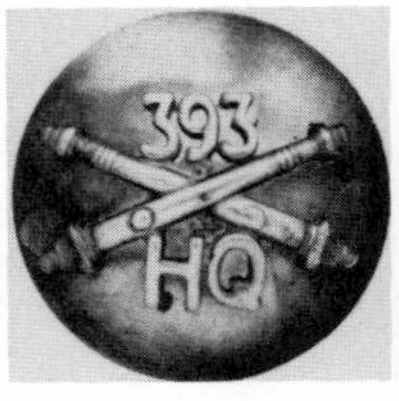

Fig. 6-202.

Fig. 6-203.

Fig. 6-204.

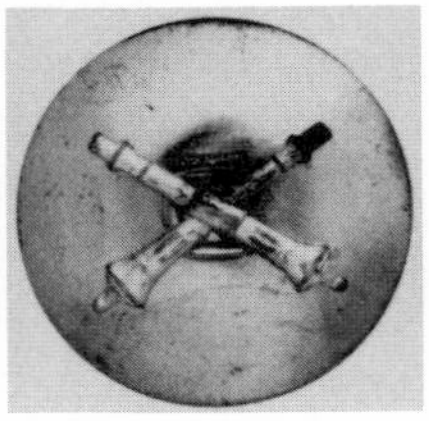

Fig. 6-205.

Fig. 6-206.

Fig. 6-207.

Fig. 6-208.

Fig. 6-209.

Fig. 6-210.

Fig. 6-211.

Fig. 6-212.

Fig. 6-213.

Fig. 6-199. *A nonregulation addition for field artillery regimental headquarters, from about 1940. (1 1/32 inches in diameter)*

Fig. 6-200. *Post–World War II nonregulation enlisted men's collar insignia for the 2d Field Artillery Group. (1 inch in diameter)*

Fig. 6-201. *Unit guidon regulations for 1938 called for CT to stand for combat trains. This may have been the basis for this 3d Field Artillery enlisted men's disk.*

Fig. 6-202. *A German-made domed (convex) field artillery enlisted men's disk. (1 inch in diameter)*

Fig. 6-203. *A 360th Field Artillery Battalion domed gilt disk, made for wear after the close of World War II. (1 1/32 inches diameter)*

Fig. 6-204. *Some airborne field artillery troops of the 82d Airborne Division wore these nonregulation silver-colored domed disks in the 1950s. (1 inch in diameter)*

Fig. 6-205. *Unusual cannons and a slightly domed background mark this German-made disk. (1 1/16 inches in diameter)*

Fig. 6-206. *Based on the infantry-distinctive blue trim of 1952, this silver domed disk was made with a red-painted edge as part of the overall background. The red trim for artillery was unauthorized. (1 11/32 inches in diameter)*

Fig. 6-207. *A two-piece domed disk with an impressed ring near the background edge. (31/32 inch in diameter)*

Fig. 6-208. *Plain block letters on disks made from thin metal were common early in World War II. (1 1/32 inches in diameter)*

Fig. 6-209. *World War II–period letters come not only in plain block style (Fig. 6-208) but also with serifs. (1 inch in diameter)*

Fig. 6-210. *The round 9 and its placement on a bar are two points that distinguish this World War II–period, two-piece flat enlisted men's collar insignia, which has the cannons lower than the center of the background. (1 3/64 inches in diameter)*

Fig. 6-211. *The 3 on this disk is of a block instead of a round style and is applied directly to the field guns. (1 inch in diameter)*

Fig. 6-212. *A 1970s disk made for the 2d Battalion, 19th Field Artillery, 1st Cavalry Division, Fort Hood, Texas. (1 inch in diameter)*

Fig. 6-213. *2 D HOW above 34 shows this disk was for the 2d Howitzer Battalion of the 34th Artillery. The 34th Artillery was part of the Combat Arms Regimental System. The howitzer distinction was probably made since the 1st Battalion, 34th Artillery was a missile unit. The large A below the cannons is the battery designation. These elaborate insignia additions were typically made to collar disks produced in Germany.*

Fig. 6-214. *An issue stamped brass disk from about 1960. When made, it was for the artillery, but by 1968 it was for the air defense artillery. (1 inch in diameter)*

Fig. 6-215. *A domed silver air defense enlisted men's collar insignia. (1 inch in diameter)*

headquarters (Fig. 6-199), for an artillery group (Fig. 6-200), and for combat trains of the 3d Field Artillery (Fig. 6-201), if one notes that wartime regulations called for the letters *CT* on artillery wartime guidons.[60]

Domed versions include a German-made insignia with unit number and battery designation (Fig. 6-202), a U.S.-made piece with battalion number below (Fig. 6-203), an insignia used by airborne units (Fig. 6-204), and a German-made ornament with unusual cannons (Fig. 6-205). A totally nonregulation insignia with a red enameled border, modeled after the blue-edged infantry disk prescribed in 1952, is shown in Fig. 6-206.[61] The disk shown in Fig. 6-207 has an indented ring near the edge, giving it an unusual appearance.

Besides cannon and background variations, the styles of letters and numbers show many changes, too. Block letters (Fig. 6-208) and letters with serifs (Fig. 6-209) are two common types. Numbers also are in block or round style, either on a bar (Fig. 6-210) or applied directly (Fig. 6-211).

When the army reestablished the field artillery in 1968, it once again used the crossed field guns.[62] In the 1970s, battalions formed the army's central building blocks through the Combat Arms Regimental System, and some units adopted insignia reflecting these designations, as shown by Fig. 6-212 for the 2d Battalion, 19th Field Artillery. In addition, cavalry and infantry regiments and battle groups contained some organic artillery batteries, which resulted in unusual insignia in some cases. An example made in Germany is shown in Fig. 6-213.

Cannons and Missile Disks

In 1957, when the army added a missile to traditional artillery cannons, disks came in one-piece and two-piece versions. The issue insignia is shown in Fig. 6-214, a domed version is illustrated in Fig. 6-215, and a two-piece disk made in Vietnam is in Fig. 6-216. The missile precluded using standard brass numbers or letters above and below the cannons, so makers placed small red numbers at the intersection in the style of officers' insignia (Figs. 6-217 and 6-218). In 1968, when the army separated the artillery into field artillery and air defense, the missile over crossed cannons remained for the air defense.[63]

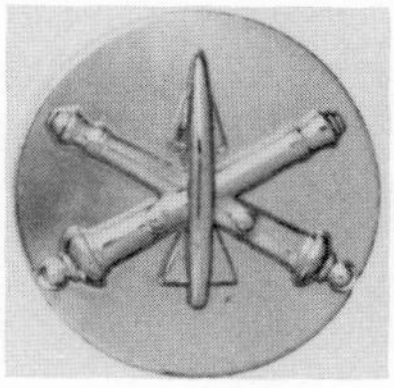

Fig. 6-214.

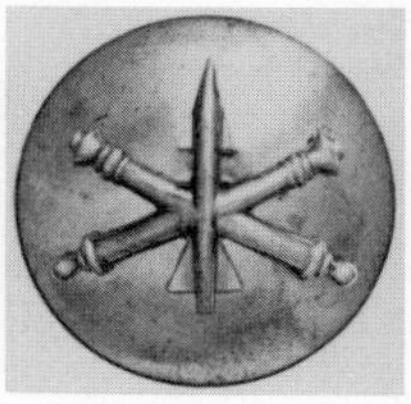

Fig. 6-215.

Fig. 6-216.

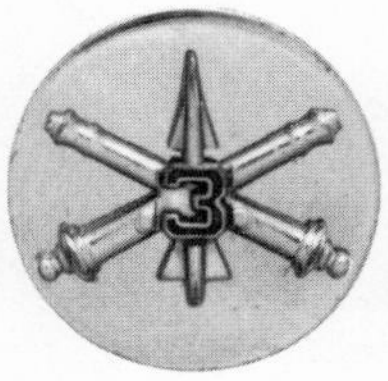

Fig. 6-217.

Fig. 6-218.

Fig. 6-216. *Made in Vietnam about 1967, this artillery disk was worn by a soldier on his khaki uniform during his trip home. (31/32 inch in diameter)*

Fig. 6-217. *This 3d Artillery enlisted men's collar insignia is of the type authorized by a Department of the Army circular, dated 31 October 1960, which allowed red enamel regimental numbers 3/16 inch high to be added on an optional basis. (1 inch in diameter)*

Fig. 6-218. *Two- and three-digit numbers required different dies so that the recessed center area to hold numbers was properly sized.*

Section IV

Horse-Mounted Men

CHAPTER SEVEN

CAVALRY, DRAGOONS, AND MOUNTED RIFLEMEN

EARLY IN AMERICAN history, military men used the words *horse* and *cavalry* interchangeably for units whose members served on horseback. Some U.S. cavalry actually were light cavalry, used for reconnaissance and screening, but most were truly dragoons, trained for fighting both on foot and on horseback. At the start of the American Revolution, very few horse units existed in fact, but by 1780 one thousand cavalrymen were serving in the Continental Army.

Cost limited the cavalry's growth during the Revolution, but after the war the funds required to support mounted men simply became prohibitive compared to those for foot troops. After George Washington released most soldiers, cavalry units ceased to exist until 1792, when the army formed a squadron of dragoons, which was immediately broken up, the unit serving as separate troops. This was typical of U.S. horse units until 1833: mounted organizations came and went, depending upon national and international tensions.[1] Because of the disjointed history of cavalry, there is no continuing evolution of its insignia. Cavalry insignia, like the cavalry itself, came and went until the army formed the Regiment of Dragoons (now the 1st Cavalry).

The terms *troop* and *company* are used in this chapter, but many devotees of the mounted arm react with horror when the word *company* is applied to a cavalry unit. The U.S. Army until the Civil War used *company* to designate units headed by captains; then a gradual change began. By the start of the twentieth century most cavalry units used the term *troop,* but during nearly half a century of transition it was not unusual for some cavalry regiment units to call themselves companies while other units in the same regiment called themselves troops.[2] During World War II and later the army organized some cavalry units as infantry but retained the historical cavalry designations. In these later-twentieth-century units the word *company* shows an infantry or (after the late 1970s) possibly a tank organization, while *troop* continues to show the cavalry function.

EARLY INSIGNIA

Dragoons became the first branch of the U.S. Army to have their own distinctive metal insignia. General Orders of 30 March 1800, described a device for helmets as "a brass front, with a mounted dragoon in the act of charging." The design may have been like that shown within the oval of Fig. 72-4 in chapter 72, "Men's Headgear through the Civil War." The insignia did not last long, for Congress soon disbanded dragoons as an economy measure.[3]

When horse soldiers returned to the army in 1808 as light dragoons, they ornamented their helmets or caps with the separately outlined, 2-inch-high letters *USLD,* with the *US* above the *LD,* and with blue feathers with white tips. To match their uniform trimmings these letters should have been of white metal, either silvered brass or pewter. Excavated examples, however, have been found in both pewter and in unsilvered brass. John B. McMaster mentions these letters: "It was about this time [1812] that the phrase Uncle Sam became popular. Just when or where it originated is not known. One story, believed in 1812, is that when a regiment of light dragoon was raised in 1808, the letters USLD on their caps were interpreted by some wag as *Uncle Sam's Lazy Dogs.* The contact of the militia with the regulars in 1812 gave the phrase greater currency, and it became popular. . . . The *American Daily Advertiser* of August 15, 1816, attributed the origin of 'Uncle Sam' to the letters USLD."[4] There are other stories about the origin of the character Uncle Sam, but the story concerning the light dragoons is the earliest reference yet found.

In 1973 some historians digging in an old trash pit discovered a cache of discarded 1808 cap letters at a site where no dragoons had been stationed after 1810. These letters are of cast brass with integrally cast pointed wires on the reverse for clinching to the caps (Fig. 7-1 and Fig. 10-1 in chapter 10, "Numbers and Letters"). The script letters may be older than the Roman letters, although there is no corroborative documentation.

Fig. 7-2 shows a die used to make the light dragoon cap plate worn during the War of 1812. The design follows the description of the 1800 pattern, reduced in size and placed inside a rectangular plate with clipped corners. Several known surviving 1812 helmets bear these original plates (Fig. 72-4 in chapter 72). In 1815, as part of the postwar reduction, the army disbanded the light dragoons, but the need for mounted troops along our western frontier resulted in the organization of a unit of mounted rangers in 1832. Apparently this small unit had no distinctive insignia or button, and the military disbanded it the following year.[5]

Militia and volunteer units of dragoons and cavalry continued to wear the "charging

Fig. 7-1. *Block letters used 1808–12 on the leather caps of the U.S. Light Dragoons. (Letter D 1 9/16 inches wide)*

Fig. 7-2. *The die used to make the 1812–15 light dragoon plates. The resulting insignia went on the leather helmet. Militia units continued to use insignia struck from this die long after the Regular Army had abandoned the insignia. (Oval 2 21/32 inches wide)*

Fig. 7-3. *When dragoons were formed in 1833, officers began to wear embroidered six-pointed stars. Initially the stars went on the tails of the coat, but after 1839 they went on the front of the officers' forage caps. The six-pointed star was a widely used general-purpose military insignia during the first half of the nineteenth century. (Embroidery 1 3/8 inches wide)*

Fig. 7-4. *Dragoons from 1833 until 1851 wore this type of dress cap with a gilt sunburst and silver Napoleonic eagle.*

Fig. 7-5.

Fig. 7-6.

Figs. 7-5 and 7-6. *Etruscan officers' crossed sabers (1851) for wear on the then-new shako. The difference is most noted by the way the hand guards end near the blade. (Fig. 7-5, 3 23/32 inches wide and slightly bowed and 3 28/32 inches wide if laid flat; Fig. 7-6, 3 9/16 inches wide)*

Fig. 7-7.

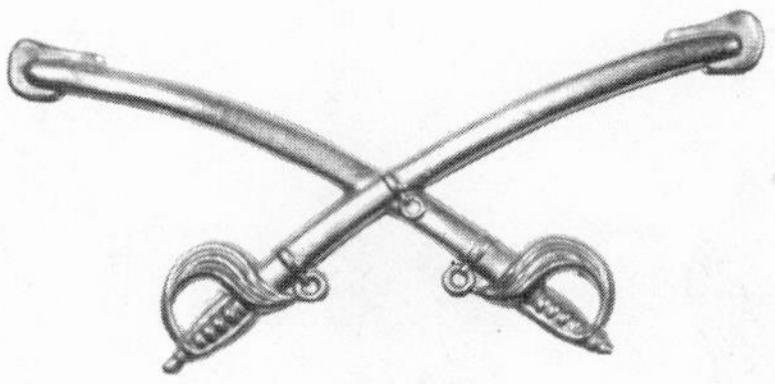

Fig. 7-9.

Fig. 7-8.

Fig. 7-7. *The 1858 officers' hat was ornamented with gilt crossed sabers on a velvet oval. This particular insignia has an imitation embroidered regimental number, although many officers' insignia were fully embroidered. During the Civil War the point at which the sabers crossed moved further from the hand guards than was the previous design. Hat insignia, as opposed to cap insignia, had gold tracing around the edge of the oval. (4 inches wide)*

Fig. 7-8. *An officers' 1858-pattern cavalry hat.*

Fig. 7-9. *An enlisted men's cap insignia ornament with the sabers crossed near the hand guards, as was common before the Civil War. (3 13/16 inches wide)*

dragoon" cap plate for more than twenty-five years after it became obsolete for regulars in 1815. In some cases the only change was to make the plate in plated brass instead of pewter, as worn by the Chester County Troop (Pennsylvania) about 1835 and the Rockbridge Dragoons of Lexington, Virginia, who purchased their caps and plates from Canfield Brothers & Company of Baltimore as late as 1860. Without some care, these and other early insignia may be mistakenly identified as Regular Army insignia.

Dragoon Insignia

In 1833, Congress authorized the Regiment of Dragoons to replace the mounted rangers that had been formed only one year earlier. The 1833 uniform description for dragoons included a gilt star to be embroidered on the officers' dress coat skirts. Officers also wore star insignia (Fig. 7-3), designed by Commander in Chief Alexander Macomb, as a forage cap ornament after 1839 and through the Mexican War.[6] Because militia widely used the six-pointed star as an all-purpose ornament throughout the nineteenth century, it is difficult to ascribe a given device to the Regular Army dragoons unless a precise history of the artifact is known.

On the tall, cylindrical, leather and felt dragoons' cap, officers and men wore a large, gilt, eight-pointed sunburst cap plate with a superimposed separate silver Napoleonic eagle, with wings reversed, standing on a modified wreath (Fig. 7-4). The gilt plate, buttons, and other uniform trimmings ended the earlier tradition of silver ornaments for dragoons. These same ornaments were also used by the 2d Regiment of Dragoons when they were organized in 1836. The army introduced gold-embroidered crossed sabers in 1851 for officers to wear on the lower front of the new dress shako.[7] Although regulations prescribed the new insignia to be embroidered, insignia of this design were also later made of gilt brass with the design stamped in imitation embroidery (Figs. 7-5 and 7-6). In these 1851 patterns, the sabers cross at the lower scabbard rings; the lower scabbard ring of the upper saber is at the intersection, and more of the saber is above the intersection than below.

By the time of the Civil War, the brass crossed sabers for enlisted soldiers (and some of those embroidered officers' pieces) showed four scabbard rings of the two crossed sabers. Photographs, 1851 drawings, and some surviving examples show that unlike the 1851 design, most Civil War saber insignia are crossed near the center. Embroidery is more difficult to pin down, and styles changed, but this crossing pattern appears to be generally consistent, although the 1851 style returned to some extent about 1890. Two gold-embroidered sabers, edge upward, on a black velvet background with silver regimental number in the upper angle were introduced for the front of the dragoon officers' 1858 army hat (Figs. 7-7 and 7-8). Gilt embroidery traced the oval edge of the insignia background. Enlisted men wore metal crossed sabers (Fig. 7-9) with a brass letter placed in the upper angle.[8]

Mounted Riflemen

When the War Department organized the Regiment of Mounted Riflemen in 1846, initial uniform regulations prescribed a most interesting officers' cap ornament, "A gold

Fig. 7-11.

Fig. 7-12.

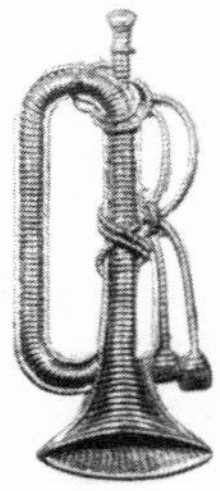

Fig. 7-13.

Fig. 7-14.

Fig. 7-15.

Fig. 7-10.

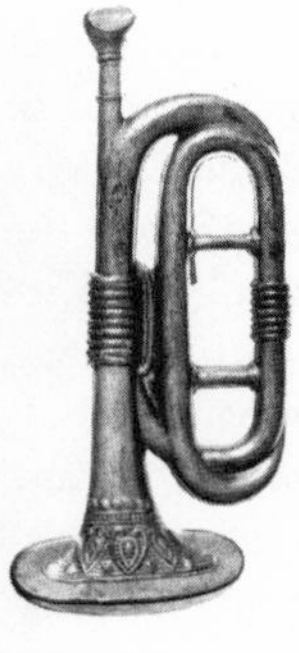

Fig. 7-16.

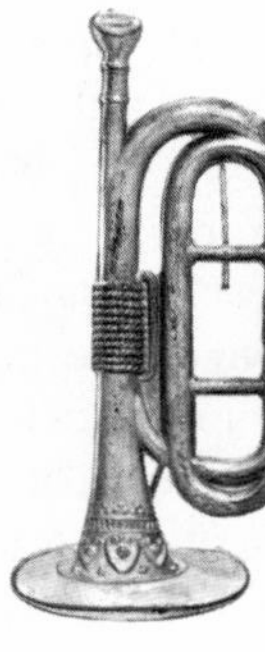

Fig. 7-17.

Fig. 7-10. *In 1850 officers of the recently formed Regiment of Mounted Riflemen adopted an upright trumpet as their cap insignia, and the army adopted this basic design as the 1858 hat insignia. Lieutenant Rodger Jones is shown in 1858 with his regulation hat insignia, including the regimental number inside the trumpet's bend.*

Figs. 7-11 and 7-12. *Cap insignia of the type worn by officers of the Regiment of Mounted Riflemen, 1851–61. Some militia units also wore these devices on their caps or hats. (Embroidery 15/16 and 27/32 inch wide, respectively)*

Fig. 7-13. *Etruscan brass was used by some mounted rifle officers. (1 inch wide)*

Fig. 7-14. *The trumpet was placed on a gilt-edged oval for hat insignia worn by officers of the Regiment of Mounted Riflemen. (Oval 2 3/16 inches wide)*

Fig. 7-15. *Smooth brass trumpets like this were worn by enlisted men of the Regiment of Mounted Riflemen. This pattern follows the Regular Army regulations and may have been made for that organization. (31/32 inch wide)*

embroidered spread eagle, with letter *R* in silver, on the shield." No surviving example of this insignia is presently known, although there is a photograph showing the eagle worn by Lieutenant George H. Gordon of Company I, Regiment of Mounted Riflemen. Early in 1850, officers' cap insignia changed to a "trumpet, embroidered in gold, with the number of the regiment, in silver, within the bend," although use of this device was not actually implemented until 1851. None of the several insignia today verified as original Regular Army include the number, although such insignia are known to have existed. An 1858 portrait of First Lieutenant Roger Jones (Fig. 7-10) clearly shows the hat and insignia with the number introduced that year. Figs. 7-11 and 7-12 are examples of the officers' cap insignia as usually worn. Fig. 7-13 is the same device struck in brass with the design in imitation embroidery to meet the requirements of the regulation and to withstand field use. The last change to the Mounted Riflemen officers' cap insignia came in 1858, when all officers' cap insignia for the arms were placed on oval backgrounds for wear on the 1858 hat (Fig. 7-14).[9]

In 1858 the army issued enlisted men the brass upright trumpet of smooth metal (Fig. 7-15). Figs. 7-16 and 7-17 show larger examples, in brass, with the trumpet coil on the opposite side. These devices may have been worn by volunteers or militia; however, several slightly damaged insignia of this pattern have been uncovered at a site occupied by the Regiment of Mounted Riflemen in 1858, proof that Regular Army soldiers wore them before the Civil War.[10] It is probable that some regimental members continued to wear the trumpet insignia after 1861, when Congress and the army redesignated the unit as the 3d Cavalry Regiment. Many of these brass trumpets were restruck in the 1960s and 1970s for collectors.

Officers' Cavalry Cap and Hat Insignia

Congress authorized the first two cavalry regiments in 1855. These were in addition to the two dragoon regiments and the one regiment of mounted riflemen already in existence. Officers placed only the regimental number on the unique cavalry hats from the introduction of the hats in 1855 through the next three years, since the hat itself was distinctive of the branch. When the entire army adopted a modified 1855 hat in 1858, both dragoons and cavalry officers used crossed sabers as a hat insignia. In March 1858 the army directed cavalry officers to wear crossed sabers with edges down on the hat (Fig. 7-18). Apparently this insignia was adopted because the dragoons already wore a logical insignia of crossed sabers with the edges up. By inversion of the device a distinction between the branches could be easily made. Three months after these instructions appeared, an amendment prescribed all crossed sabers to be worn with edges up, but dragoon officers would have their regimental number in the upper angle and cavalry officers in the lower angle (Fig. 7-19).[11]

When the army consolidated the horse branches in 1861, no new insignia were necessary. All of the newly designated cavalry officers would wear crossed sabers, edge up, with the new regimental number, in silver, above the intersection.[12] During the Civil War, officers used a wide variety of embroidered crossed sabers, including small embroidered devices (Figs. 7-20 through 7-23) that both officers and enlisted men wore on the tops or the fronts of their caps. When the army prescribed the new chasseur-pattern forage cap in 1872, officers wore crossed sabers of the type shown in Figs. 7-24 and 7-25 on the front of the forage cap until 1895.

Fig. 7-18.

Fig. 7-19.

Enlisted Dragoon and Cavalry Cap and Hat Devices, 1851–1917

Smooth brass crossed sabers with attaching wire loops on the back were prescribed in 1850 as enlisted men's cap insignia, but they were not actually worn. In 1851 men placed brass company letters on the cap front. As discussed in the section on officers' cavalry hat insignia, no new insignia came with the distinctive 1855 hat. Enlisted men wore the company letter alone on the front of the hat until 1858 (Fig. 7-26). Three years after the 1855 introduction, the entire army adopted a similar hat, and, as officers did, enlisted men then wore sabers but with the company letter rather than the regimental number. Regulations of 24 March 1858 prescribed "yellow metal crossed sabers, edges up, with the company letter in the upper angle of the sabers" for enlisted dragoons (Fig. 7-27). For the two cavalry regiments, enlisted soldiers wore the crossed sabers, edges down, with the company letter in the lower angle (Fig. 7-28).

Within three months the regulations were simplified, and all metal crossed sabers would thereafter be worn edges up, but the company letter would remain as before: dragoons above and cavalry below.[13]

The Civil War regulations did change placement of enlisted men's numbers and letters. Officially in 1861 both the number and letter went above the sabers, with the letter uppermost. Photographs show that in practice men usually wore either a letter

Fig. 7-20.

Fig. 7-21.

Fig. 7-22.

Figs. 7-16 and 7-17. *Two slightly different patterns of upright trumpets for mounted riflemen. The design differences are most easily seen in the decoration around the trumpets' bells. Even though there is a double loop on the wrong side of the trumpet, and the decorative cord is missing, these were worn by the Regiment of Mounted Riflemen just before the Civil War. They may also have been used by militia units, and the army may even have purchased stock pieces for the 1858 hat, thus accounting for the use of them by the Regular Army. The particular devices shown were probably restruck in the mid-twentieth century, because pointed wire fasteners instead of iron loops are on the back. (Bell of each horn 1 5/16 inches wide)*

Fig. 7-18. *Cavalry officers were to wear crossed sabers, with the edges down, on their hats for three months in 1858. (Oval 4 inches wide)*

Fig. 7-19. *After cavalry officers turned their crossed sabers with the cutting edges up in mid-1858, they placed their regimental number below the sabers, as did Colonel David Hunter of the 1st Cavalry Regiment, shown here. Dragoon officers wore the same insignia but with the regimental number above the crossed sabers.*

Fig. 7-20. *Typical cavalry cap insignia as used by some Civil War militia officers. (Embroidery 2 31/32 inches wide)*

Figs. 7-21 and 7-22. *Small embroidered cavalry cap insignia from the second half of the nineteenth century. Although officers usually wore embroidered insignia, these small stock pieces also may have been used by some enlisted men. (Embroidery 1 22/32 and 2 1/16 inches wide, respectively)*

Fig. 7-24.

Fig. 7-25.

Fig. 7-26.

Fig. 7-27.

Fig. 7-28.

Fig. 7-23.

Fig. 7-23. *Cavalry hat insignia with etruscan crossed sabers. (Oval 2 3/4 inches wide.)*

Fig. 7-24. *A 2d Cavalry officers' cap insignia, post–Civil War, from the Smithsonian Institution collection. (Embroidery 3 33/64 inches wide)*

Fig. 7-25. *Officers' forage cap insignia, post–Civil War, from the Duncan Campbell collection. (Embroidery 3 3/8 inches wide)*

Fig. 7-26. *The only known extant 1855–58 enlisted men's cavalry hat. Because the hat was distinctive for the branch during those three years, only the company letter was worn. Crossed sabers were added in 1858 when other branches adopted the wide-brimmed hat.*

Fig. 7-27. *From 1858 until 1861 enlisted dragoons wore metal crossed sabers (edges up) with the company letter above. (3 11/32 inches wide)*

Fig. 7-28. *For three months in 1858 cavalrymen wore metal sabers with the edges down and the company letter below; after that the sabers were turned with the edges up, but the letter remained below. The placement of letters was the only difference between cavalry and dragoon enlisted cap insignia from mid-1858 until the dragoons were redesignated in mid-1861. (3 11/32 inches wide)*

alone above the sabers, or, if both a company and a regimental designation were worn, one went above the sabers and the other below. Throughout the war, officers and enlisted men usually wore a wide variety of crossed sabers on the cap front. An example, Fig. 7-29, is a photograph of Sergeant Boston Corbett, the man who shot John Wilkes Booth. The sergeant is wearing small embroidered sabers, without any letter or number, on the cap top. Another cap worn by the same man in another photograph shows metal insignia with a company letter.[14]

Regulations of 1872 modified the forage cap, and enlisted men switched to "the badge of the corps or letter of the company." On June 25, 1873, the adjutant general corrected the enlisted men's insignia by prescribing the company letter in the upper angle of the sabers. In 1877 the cap insignia regulations further changed to add the regimental number above the intersection and the company letter below, as had been ordered for infantry the previous year. The men used some of these brass insignia with wire loops and separate brass letters and numbers, while other insignia came with both numbers and letters soldered to the sabers. In May 1876 the quartermaster general specified the sabers to be 3 inches in length.[15]

The 1896 introduction of a threaded screw-post fastening device brought a sturdier method of attaching the cavalry cap insignia, which was 2 3/8 inches wide. Men assigned to troops wore both the regimental number and the troop letter (Fig. 7-30), while the regimental noncommissioned staff cap insignia carried only the regimental number. In 1905 the army brought out smaller sabers in bronze (Fig. 7-31 for regimental staff and Fig. 7-32 for an A Troop member) for the service cap as well as smaller gilt ornaments for dress wear (Fig. 7-33). When Congress added supply, headquarters, and machine-gun troops to cavalry regiments in 1916, the Quartermaster Corps added the letters *S, HQ,* and *MG* in the lower angles for men in these new troops. Cavalrymen of the U.S. Military Academy Detachment wore the letters *MA* above and *DET* below the cavalry sabers (Fig. 7-34) after 1910, although the detachment had previously existed without any special insignia.[16]

Some mysterious cap ornaments, such as

Fig. 7-29.

Fig. 7-30.

Fig. 7-31.

Fig. 7-32.

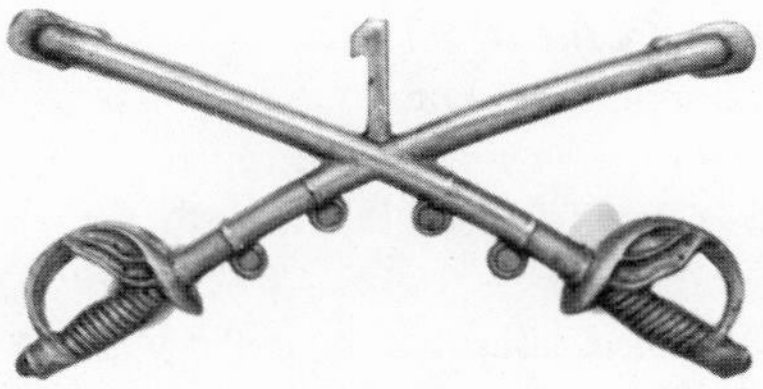

Fig. 7-33.

Fig. 7-34.

Fig. 7-29. *Sergeant Boston Corbett, who shot John Wilkes Booth. On the table is his cap, which carries an embroidered insignia on the top front that was typical of unauthorized insignia during the Civil War.*

Fig. 7-30. *An 1896–1905 enlisted cap insignia with screw-post fastener. This same arrangement with regimental number above and troop letter below was used from 1877. (2 7/16 inches wide)*

Figs. 7-31 and 7-32. *Small 1905 cavalry cap insignia. The bronze color was for use on the service uniform caps. The first piece was for members of the regimental noncommissioned staff, because there is no troop number below. (1 15/16 and 2 1/32 inches wide, respectively)*

Fig. 7-33. *Gold-plated cap insignia, for use with the dress uniform, worn by the noncommissioned officers of the regimental staff, such as the regimental sergeant major, the color sergeants, the regimental commissary sergeant, and (until 1916) the regimental supply sergeant. (1 15/16 inches wide)*

Fig. 7-34. *This cap insignia was prescribed in 1910 for cavalry members of the U.S. Military Academy Detachment. (1 15/16 inches wide)*

one with the letter *A* in the upper angle, which would seemingly eliminate it as a regular insignia, appear in federal documents; however, it is illustrated as a sample insignia in the 1915 quartermaster specification intended for use by manufacturers. It is probably intended for the New York National Guard, but why it is described in federal specifications remains a puzzle. As for other enlisted men's cap insignia, December 1917 regulations call for a bronze disk, 1 1/2 inches in diameter and bearing the coat of arms of the United States, to replace branch-specific insignia.[17]

Between 1899 and 1907 cavalrymen wore brass or bronze numbers and letters on their campaign hats to show their regiment and troop, as described in chapter 10, "Numbers and Letters."

Helmet Plates

Introduced for the cavalry and light artillery units in 1872, the English horse guards–style cloth-covered cork helmet carried an eagle looking to its right with an arched scroll bearing the motto *E PLURIBUS UNUM* over its head (Fig. 73-2 in chapter 73). In 1881 the army extended wear of the dress helmet to virtually the entire army and changed the eagle design. Officers' new helmet plates (Fig. 7-35) were made with the shield and crossed sabers as a separate piece applied to the eagle's breast, giving added depth to the plate. Enlisted soldiers wore the same design, but it was stamped in one piece from thin brass (Fig. 7-36). Both officers and men wore regimental numbers applied to the center of the shield. Because of many supply problems, during 1903 and early 1904 only the 1st, 5th, and 6th regiments and part of the 15th had replaced these helmets with dress caps, with the remaining units changing in late 1904 and 1905.[18]

Fig. 7-35. *An officers' 1881–1903 dress helmet insignia. For officers the piece with the shield and sabers was made separately and then applied to the eagle. Both officers and enlisted men were to wear regimental numbers on the shield, but officers' varied widely, since they bought their own. (3 3/4 inches wide)*

Fig. 7-36. *In 1881 enlisted men were issued helmet eagles with sabers, all made from one piece of brass. (4 1/4 inches wide)*

Fig. 7-37. *From 1895 until 1905, officers were to wear this type of heavy saber insignia, in gold color, on the 1895-pattern coat.*

Fig. 7-38. *Bronze insignia of this general pattern were worn on service uniforms from 1902 until 1905, when more delicate, thinner sabers were introduced. Officers actually continued to wear these heavy sabers for many years after the official change. (1 31/32 inches wide)*

Fig. 7-39. *Starting in 1900, regimental staff officers and squadron adjutants began to wear small staff devices below their crossed sabers. This officer's small shield below his branch insignia shows he was an adjutant.*

Fig. 7-40. *A 1903 bronze collar insignia for an adjutant of the 2d Cavalry. These sabers are of the pre-1905 design. (1 31/32 inches wide)*

Fig. 7-41. *Insignia for the 6th Cavalry Regiment's quartermaster, about 1903. (1 31/32 inches wide)*

Fig. 7-42. *Each cavalry regiment had one officer assigned as the unit's commissary officer. The insignia was a small crescent placed below the branch insignia. The quarter-moons were made in mirror-image pairs so they would be matched when placed on the collar. (1 31/32 inches wide)*

Fig. 7-35.

Fig. 7-36.

Officers' Collar Insignia to 1905

Although the 1892 sack coat introduced block-style regimental numbers on the collar, in 1895 the insignia were replaced by gold-embroidered crossed sabers with a small regimental number above.[19] These initial officers' crossed sabers for the collar were actually made three ways: in gold embroidery, in etruscan imitation embroidery, and in smooth metal. In some cases the regimental number was not part of the insignia but was separately applied to the collar, but most metal sabers bore the regimental number brazed above the intersection (Fig. 7-37). Heavy sabers of this first pattern also came in bronze (Fig. 7-38) for 1902 service coats.[20] For a short time in 1900, veterinarians of cavalry wore plain crossed sabers; these are discussed with veterinarian insignia in chapter 11.

In 1900 officers on regimental staff duties and squadron adjutants wore small devices in the lower angle of the insignia (Fig. 7-39). Initially only commissary officers, adjutants, and quartermasters wore these, but other staff devices were added later. The following are examples: Fig. 7-40, adjutant, 2d Cavalry; Fig. 7-41, quartermaster, 6th Cavalry; Fig. 7-42, commissary officer, 3d Cavalry; Fig. 7-43, chaplain, 13th Cavalry; and Fig. 7-44, veterinarian, 11th Cavalry. Regulations of 1898 also called for volunteer officers to wear state abbreviations in the lower angle of the sabers (Fig. 7-45).[21]

Officers' Collar Insignia After 1905

The army introduced thinner, slightly modified crossed sabers in 1905, although the overall height and width remained the same as before (Figs. 7-46 and 7-47). Officers contin-

Fig. 7-37.

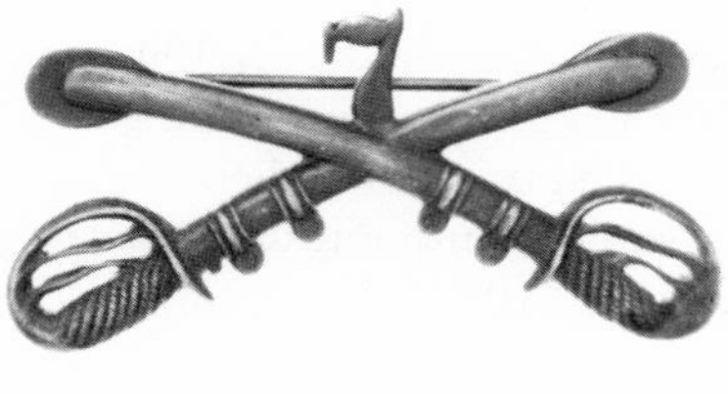

Fig. 7-38.

Fig. 7-39.

Fig. 7-40.

Fig. 7-41.

Fig. 7-42.

Fig. 7-43.

Fig. 7-44.

Fig. 7-45.

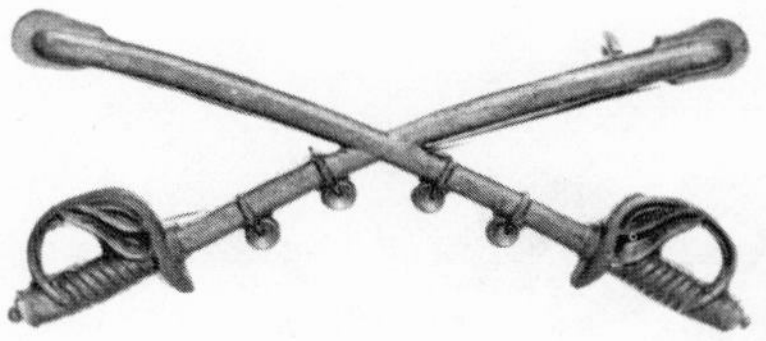

Fig. 7-46.

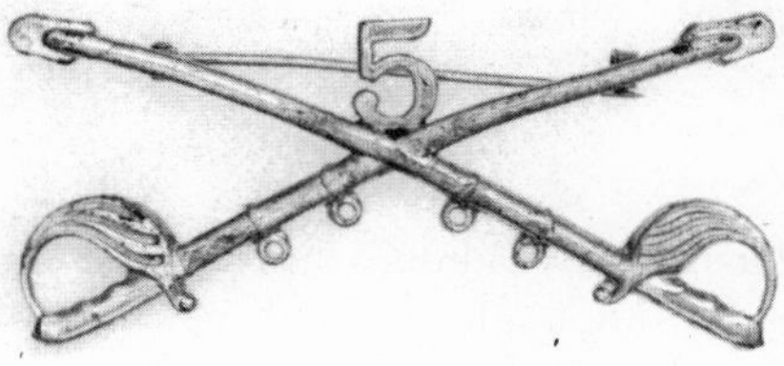

Fig. 7-48.

Fig. 7-47.

Fig. 7-43. *Between 1902 and 1914 chaplains wore small crosses as a staff device below the crossed arms. This insignia is for a chaplain of the 13th Cavalry. ($1\frac{31}{32}$ inches wide)*

Fig. 7-44. *From 1902 until 1916 veterinarians wore a winged horseshoe as a staff device. This example was made in 1903 and has a bronze finish. ($1\frac{31}{32}$ inches wide)*

Fig. 7-45. *State initials placed below sabers were introduced in 1898 and were used for several years. This example for Massachusetts was made after 1905.*

Fig. 7-46. *Officers' cavalry insignia of this "modern" design were introduced in 1905. This particular insignia is gilt.*

Fig. 7-47. *This officer of the 311th Cavalry Regiment wears bronze saber insignia with the unit number above in 1918.*

Fig. 7-48. *Most cavalry officers wore regimental numbers above their 1905-style sabers, like this example for the sack coat. ($2\frac{1}{32}$ inches wide)*

ued to add regimental numbers (Fig. 7-48) and, when appropriate, the small staff devices in the lower angle in both bronze (Fig. 7-49 for adjutant, 4th Cavalry) and gilt (Fig. 7-50 for quartermaster, 5th Cavalry). In 1914 inspectors of small arms practice began to wear small Ordnance Department insignia with sabers (Fig. 7-51). Commissioned band leaders received lyres 3/8 inch high below the crossed sabers in October 1918. The War Department rescinded all staff devices in 1923.[22]

After the start of the twentieth century, insignia manufacturers introduced smaller devices for shirt collars. Like the larger counterparts, they came in gilt (Fig. 7-52) and in bronze with various regimental numbers (Fig. 7-53) and with miniature devices in the lower angle to show staff functions within the regiment. The army sanctioned shirt insignia, initially recognized as regulation in 1919, "no less than 5/8 full size," while after 1923 these became, "3/4 the linear dimension of full size," and changed to gilt. Their use continued to 1926.[23] Examples are shown in

Fig. 7-49.

Fig. 7-50.

Figs. 7-49 and 7-50. *The thinner 1905 officers' cavalry collar insignia came with the various staff devices, as had the previous style. Fig. 7-49 is the insignia for the 4th Cavalry adjutant in bronze for the service uniform; Fig. 7-50 is the 5th Cavalry's quartermaster insignia for the sack coat. (Each 2 1/32 inches wide)*

Fig. 7-51.

Fig. 7-51. *Inspectors of small arms practice began to add small Ordnance Department insignia below their branch insignia in 1914. (2 inches wide)*

Fig. 7-52.

Fig. 7-53.

Figs. 7-52 and 7-53. *These bronze shirt collar insignia for cavalry officers were worn during World War I. (1 11/16 and 1 1/8 inches wide, respectively)*

Fig. 7-54.

Fig. 7-55.

Figs. 7-54 and 7-55. *Very small shirt insignia in both gilt and bronze, made about the time of World War I. The piece in Fig. 7-55, which is bronze, was made in France for American Expeditionary Forces officers. (25/32 and 13/16 inch wide, respectively)*

Fig. 7-56.

Fig. 7-56. *The War Department rescinded staff devices in 1923, but some officers continued to wear them into the 1930s. This example was probably made in the late 1920s or the 1930s. (1 1/2 inches wide)*

Fig. 7-57.

Fig. 7-57. *During the periods 1917–21 and 1924–28, officers assigned to machine-gun squadrons wore the letters M and G in the horizontal angles of crossed sabers. This gilt piece dates from the latter period. During 1921–24 the letters went in the upper angle.*

Fig. 7-58.

Fig. 7-58. *Shirt collar, gilt machine-gun squadron insignia, 1924–26. (1 9/64 inches wide)*

Fig. 7-59.

Figs. 7-54 and 7-55, the latter made in France during World War I. Some staff officers continued to use small staff devices, although they were not regulation, into the 1930s (Fig. 7-56).

Officers' Insignia with Letters

Machine-gun squadron officers initially wore letters *M* and *G* in the bronze insignia's horizontal angles (Fig. 7-57) in December 1917, while after October 1923 insignia changed to gilt. Between October 1921 and November 1924 regulations required the letters to be above the sabers, but the army returned to *M* and *G* in the horizontal angles in 1924. An example of the post-1924 gilt collar ornament is shown in Fig. 7-58 for the 56th Machine Gun Squadron. Sabers with *M* and *G* in the side angles became obsolete in December 1928.[24]

The letters *M* and *C* illustrated in Fig. 7-59 represent mechanized cavalry, and officers in the 52d Cavalry Brigade wore this particular insignia about 1932, even though the eleven-sixteenths-inch height came in during 1926. The size of cavalry insignia remained at one inch high and 2 3/8 inches wide after World War I for the standing-collar coat throughout the wearout period of the 1920s and 1930s.[25]

In March 1926 the War Department reduced the size of officers' insignia to 11/16 inch high (Figs. 7-60, 7-61, and 7-62) for use on the lapel coat and the shirt. This

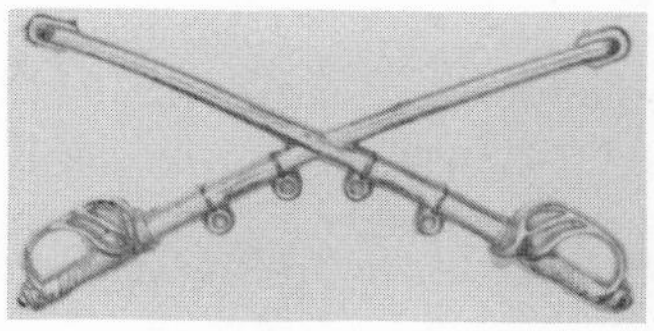

Fig. 7-60.

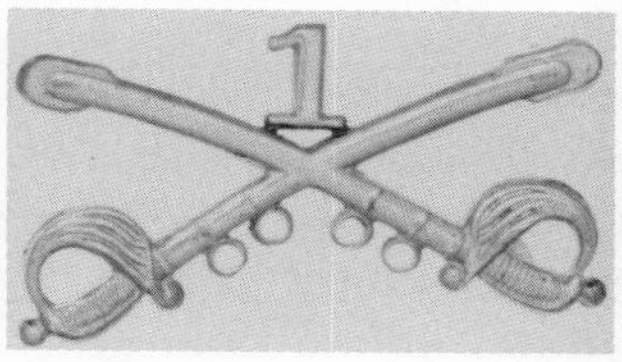

Fig. 7-61.

Fig. 7-62.

Fig. 7-63.

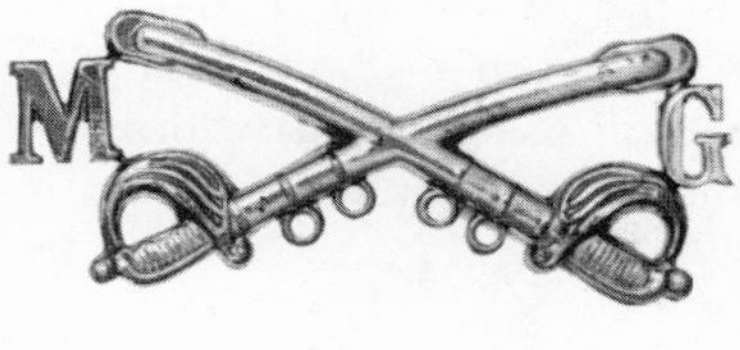

Fig. 7-64.

height has continued to the present. Armored car squadron officers used the letters *A* and *C* (Fig. 7-63) between December 1928 and 1941, and machine-gun squadron insignia came in 11/16 inch high between 1926 and December 1928 (Fig. 7-64). The official 1936 drawing shows the sabers 3/4 inch high and 1 5/8 inches long.[26]

Officers' Insignia after 1950

Congress combined the historic cavalry with the newer armor branch in 1950. In designating the branch, the official language stated, "the Armor shall be a continuation of the Cavalry."[27] The mission of cavalry units, whether performed on horseback, in tanks, or in aircraft, includes reconnaissance (finding the enemy), screening (shielding a flank from attack), and economy of force (replacing a larger unit and deceiving the enemy of this fact). Men in many modern cavalry units continued to wear crossed sabers during the 1950s and 1960s, although the regulations supporting the 1950 congressional act made such insignia unauthorized. The 1st Cavalry Division, dismounted and reorganized as infantry during World War II, generally retained cavalry designations, and the practice has continued today. In this way, old cavalry regiments continue to live, even if distorted by the army's various "regimental" systems that link battalion-sized units by a common designation. These units, organized as infantry until the end of the Vietnam War, carry "battalion" designations, while similar-sized units that function as cavalry carry "squadron" designations. Thus the 1st Battalion, 8th Cavalry title, used in Vietnam, shows that this historic cavalry unit was equipped as infantry, while the 1st Squadron, 9th Cavalry title shows that this cavalry unit still performed a cavalry mission. Before the battalion and battle group concept, cavalry regiments (organized as infantry) in Korea wore crossed sabers, as shown in Fig. 7-65 for the Service Company, 8th Cavalry, and the oversized insignia as shown in Fig. 7-66 for the 7th Cavalry.

In the post-1950 cavalry units, officers often added squadron or battalion numbers. (Fig. 7-67, made in Vietnam, was worn by pilots of the 1st Cavalry Division's cavalry squadron in Vietnam during 1967.) In response to field pressure, the army changed regulations and allowed men assigned to cavalry units to wear sabers legally after May 1972.[28] This authorization allowed subdued officers' saber insignia (Fig. 7-68) to be worn officially on fatigue clothing, although men had never really stopped wearing the sabers, despite regulations to the contrary. Even some units that retained a true regimental organization had officers who wore squadron numbers, as shown in Fig. 7-69 for the 3d Squadron, 11th Cavalry. Some interesting variations made and worn in the 1950s and 1960s are shown: Fig. 7-70 for

Fig. 7-59. *Officers of the 52d Mechanized Cavalry Brigade (Pennsylvania National Guard) wore this unofficial insignia in the early 1930s even though smaller sabers had been prescribed for shirts and the new lapel coats in 1926. (2 inches wide)*

Fig. 7-60. *Cavalry officers' insignia were made 11/16 inch high in 1926. (1 19/32 inches wide)*

Figs. 7-61 and 7-62. *Two variations of the cavalry insignia worn from 1926 to the present. These were made during the World War II era. (1 33/64 and 1 1/2 inches wide, respectively)*

Fig. 7-63. *Armored-car squadron officers added the letters A and C in the horizontal angles in the 1930s. (1 21/32 inches wide)*

Fig. 7-64. *With the smaller 1926 insignia came the previously authorized letters for machine-gun squadrons. (1 53/64 inches wide)*

Fig. 7-65. *In the 1950s the 1st Cavalry Division was stationed in Korea. Officers of the 8th Cavalry's Service Company wore this Korean-made insignia during that time. (1 17/32 inches wide)*

Fig. 7-66. *These oversized insignia, made in Korea for the 1st Cavalry Division's 7th Cavalry Regiment, have a short screw-post fastener and were probably made for wear on the front of the winter field cap. (2 25/64 inches wide)*

Fig. 7-65.

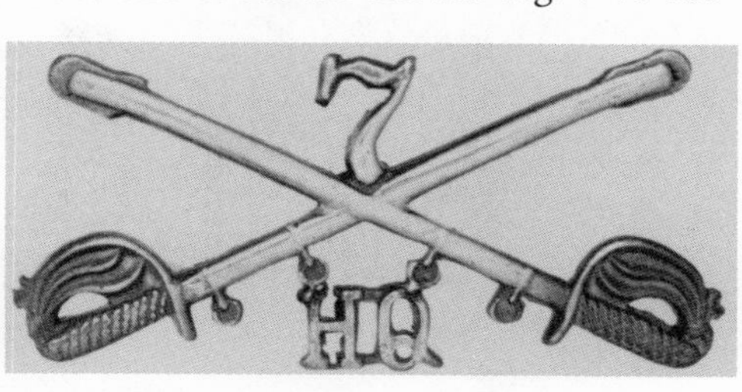

Fig. 7-66.

the 6th Cavalry Regiment, intended for wear on the fatigue uniform about 1966; Fig. 7-71, made in Germany for the 3d Squadron, 11th Armored Cavalry Regiment; and Fig. 7-72, made in Korea. Other unusual insignia made in Korea are shown in Figs. 7-73, 7-74, and 7-75 (the first two for units of the 1st Cavalry Division) and Figs. 7-76, 7-77, and 7-78, made in Germany. American-made insignia with interesting numbers and letters are shown in Figs. 7-79, 7-80, and 7-81. Cloth insignia come with battalion and squadron numbers (Figs. 7-82 and 7-83), as do exotic pieces such as the one shown in Fig. 7-84, which was made in Burma during World War II. An experimental unit, the Air Cavalry Combat Brigade, formed in the 1970s at Fort Hood, Texas, allowed officers to wear *ACCB* on their sabers (Fig. 7-85). The most interesting contemporary cavalry insignia was worn in the 1970s by members of the 113th Army Band, stationed at the U.S. Army Armor Center: the number *113* is above the sabers (Fig. 7-86).

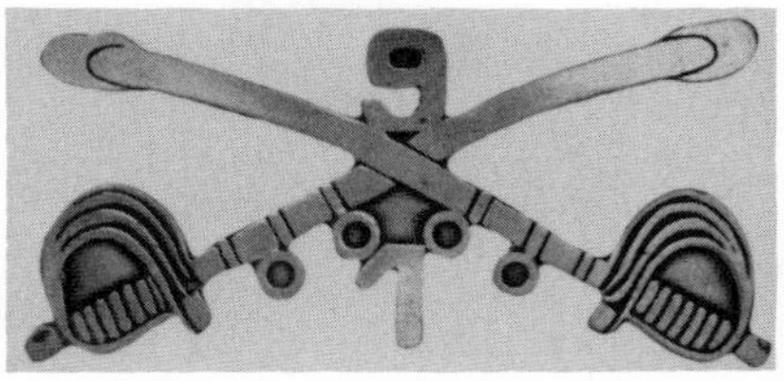

Fig. 7-67.

Fig. 7-67. *In Vietnam the 1st Squadron, 9th Cavalry was the 1st Cavalry Division's reconnaissance unit. Some officers wore this insignia made from thin sheet metal, commonly called "beer can" metal, since it was about the same thickness as those cans. Some pilots in this organization wore western-style hats adorned with this or U.S.-made comparable insignia. (2 1/64 inches wide)*

Fig. 7-68.

Fig. 7-68. *Cavalry officers' fatigue shirts often carried crossed sabers during the time that insignia was not authorized, 1951–72. Subdued insignia came into general use during the late 1960s.*

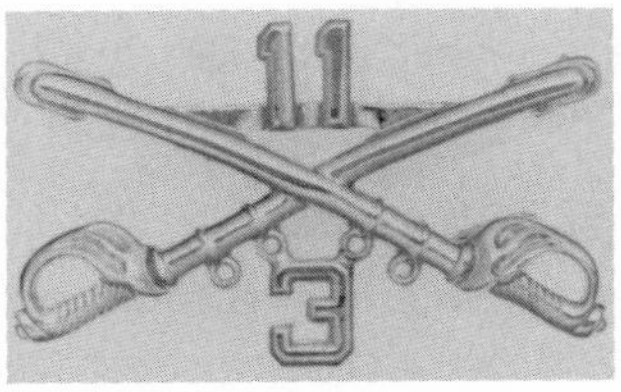

Fig. 7-69.

Fig. 7-69. *This insignia was worn in the late 1970s by officers of the 3d Squadron, 11th Cavalry while the unit was in Bad Hersfeld, Germany. Use of squadron numbers, while a common practice, was never allowed by regulations. (1 17/32 inches wide)*

Fig. 7-70.

Fig. 7-70. *A 6th Armored Cavalry Regiment officers' embroidered insignia for fatigue uniforms, 1966. This piece is unusual in that the cloth edge is stitched. (Design 1 45/64 inches wide)*

Fig. 7-71.

Fig. 7-71. *Made in Germany about 1977, this 3d Squadron, 11th Armored Cavalry Regiment insignia was embroidered on an olive drab strip that was usually used to make cloth name tags for the fatigue uniforms. (Design 1 5/8 inches wide)*

Fig. 7-72.

Fig. 7-72. *Brass cast insignia made in Korea in the late 1950s or early 1960s. CS stands for Combat Service Company, 12th Cavalry. (1 41/64 inches wide)*

Fig. 7-73.

Fig. 7-74.

Fig. 7-75.

Fig. 7-76.

Fig. 7-77.

Fig. 7-78.

Fig. 7-79.

Fig. 7-80.

Fig. 7-81.

Fig. 7-83.

Fig. 7-84.

Fig. 7-85.

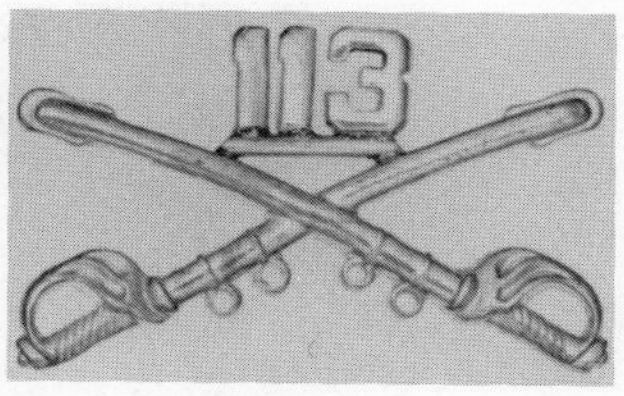

Fig. 7-86.

Figs. 7-73, 7-74, and 7-75. *Three officers' brass collar insignia made in Korea. The first two were made for elements of the 1st Cavalry Division, and the last, with a crudely made 2, was for part of the 7th Infantry Division. ($1\frac{39}{64}$, $1\frac{35}{64}$, and $1\frac{19}{32}$ inches wide, respectively)*

Fig. 7-76. *A German-made, silver-colored officers' insignia from the late 1970s. Most troops did not add their troop letter, as was done in this case ($1\frac{17}{32}$ inches wide)*

Figs. 7-77 and 7-78. *Subdued insignia made in Germany for armored cavalry regiments about 1970. The 2d Cavalry insignia has thin, delicate scabbards and grips. The embroidered 14th Cavalry piece is typical of officers' fatigue insignia made in Germany in the 1960s (Metal insignia $1\frac{17}{32}$ inches wide; embroidery $1\frac{35}{64}$ inches wide)*

Fig. 7-79. *The 3d Armored Cavalry Regiment was stationed at Fort Bliss, Texas, when this subdued insignia was made. While many companies and troops of the regiment did not add letters below, a few did, as shown by this insignia for the Tank Company of the 3d Squadron. ($1\frac{33}{64}$ inches wide)*

Fig. 7-80. *Some armor units wore cavalry insignia to show their heritage. The 1st Battalion, 142d Armor is such an example. This New York National Guard collar ornament is silver-colored. For some reason the battalion number was placed above and the regimental number below, in contrast to the standard practice. ($1\frac{33}{64}$ inches wide)*

Fig. 7-81. *This 3d Brigade insignia was intended for staff members of the 1st Cavalry Division about 1980. ($1\frac{1}{2}$ inches wide)*

Fig. 7-82. *Insignia made in Vietnam for an officer of the 1st Battalion, 8th Cavalry. During their tour in Vietnam, cavalry units organized as infantry carried battalion titles. (Design $1\frac{7}{16}$ inches wide)*

Fig. 7-83. *Organized in 1963, the 1st Squadron, 230th Cavalry Regiment was an element of the 30th Armored Division, with units stationed in Tennessee, Alabama, and Mississippi. This fatigue insignia was yellow-embroidered cotton. (Design $1\frac{15}{32}$ inches wide)*

Fig. 7-84. *Yellow, hand-embroidered cavalry insignia on khaki made in India during World War II for wear on khaki shirts. (Design $1\frac{19}{64}$ inches wide)*

Fig. 7-85. *The letters stand for the Air Cavalry Combat Brigade, which was an experimental unit formed in the 1970s at Fort Hood, Texas. ($1\frac{1}{2}$ inches wide)*

Fig. 7-86. *This insignia was not used by a cavalry unit, but by the 113th Army Band, which was stationed at Fort Knox, Kentucky. The band played at various Armor School functions, and the band members wore dark, nineteenth-century-style campaign hats with the sabers on the front. ($1\frac{33}{64}$ inches wide)*

The 1st Cavalry Division, converted to infantry in 1943, as previously noted, became an armor division in the 1970s. The division that fought in Vietnam as airmobile then became a tank unit, with the word *battalion* indicating armor units, and *squadron* still reserved for true cavalry units.

Outline Enlisted Men's Collar Insignia

The army added large gilt crossed sabers, 2 3/8 inches long, to the new 1902 enlisted dress uniform (Fig. 7-87). For the service uniform, these insignia were made in bronze. The neater, more modern 1905 insignia also were made in both bronze and gilt for the two uniform types. Except for the pin back, rather than the screw post, the collar insignia were identical to the cap devices. Troop members wore the regimental number in the upper angle and the troop letter below, while regimental noncommissioned staff officers wore only the regimental number. The familiar round bronze disks replaced bronze outline insignia in 1910, but the gilt outline insignia continued on the dress uniform until 1917.[29] Use of *MG, S, HQ* and *MA DET,* as discussed in the cap insignia section, also appeared on the outline collar insignia.

Collar Disks

Introduced in 1910, the enlisted men's bronze disks worn on the service coat collars were produced in great quantity during World War I. Some disk variations are shown, including those with troop letter below, with regimental number only, and with both regimental number and the troop letter (Figs. 7-88, 7-89, 7-90, and 7-91). The 2d Cavalry was the only U.S. cavalry regiment to receive a named campaign streamer

Fig. 7-87.

Fig. 7-87. *Large gilt crossed sabers with pin backs were added to the 1902 enlisted men's dress uniform collars. This same design and size, but in bronze, went on the olive drab and khaki service uniform collars. Two years later these gave way to smaller sabers, similar to the officers' style and size. As always, the normal enlisted men's insignia had the troop letter below except for the noncommissioned staff, which bore only the number. (2 11/32 inches wide)*

Fig. 7-88.

Fig. 7-88. *The cavalry enlisted men's collar insignia introduced for the service uniform in 1910 and used until after World War I. (1 inch wide)*

Fig. 7-89.

Fig. 7-89. *The plain regimental number above the sabers was used by the regimental noncommissioned staff. (1 inch wide)*

Fig. 7-90.

Fig. 7-90. *Although the sabers are crossed at a slightly greater angle than those of most insignia, this disk was probably made during World War I, when regimental numbers were moved to the US collar disks and the troop letter remained with the branch insignia. (1 1/64 inches in diameter)*

Fig. 7-91.

Fig. 7-91. *This disk shows the type of number and letter placement authorized until 1918 and in practice worn throughout the war by some units. (1 inch in diameter)*

Fig. 7-92.

Fig. 7-92. *This 2d Cavalry trooper wears the 1917-style collar insignia in this AEF photograph.*

Fig. 7-93.

Fig. 7-94.

Figs. 7-93 and 7-94. *Machine-gun squadrons had insignia with the MG above the sabers and sometimes with troop letters below. (1 1/64 inches and 1 inch in diameter respectively)*

Fig. 7-95.

Fig. 7-96.

during World War I, and one of these AEF troopers is shown in Fig. 7-92 wearing his collar disks. Machine-gun squadrons had the letters *MG* above (Figs. 7-93 and 7-94) to distinguish them from regimental machine-gun troops, whose letters went below (Fig. 7-95). Men in the U.S. Military Academy Detachment wore the disk with *MA DET* (Fig. 7-96) until 1921.[30]

Postwar gilt disks, made beginning in 1919, exist in several die variations, and some examples are shown in Figs. 7-97, 7-98, and 7-99. The proper background consisted of crosshatched lines and small shields (Figs. 7-100 through 7-103), which replaced the earlier light stippling. Economy forced cavalry regiments to inactivate several troops, so after 1923 only headquarters, service (previously supply), and A, B, C, E, F, and G troops remained active. In 1928 the War Department eliminated separate machine-gun troops and further reduced regiments so that only troops A, B, E, and the reintroduced regimental machine-gun troop formed each regiment. This reorganization caused the reuse of the letters *MG* below sabers for enlisted disks (Fig. 7-104). This situation generally continued until 1939, causing enlisted men's cavalry disks with less used troop letters to be scarce today. For ten years, starting in December 1927, members of regimental bands wore a small lyre below their crossed sabers (Fig. 7-105), and armored car squadron members wore *AC* in the horizontal angles after December 1928 (Fig. 7-106). In 1933 the *AC* moved to below the sabers for enlisted men's insignia (Fig. 7-107).[31]

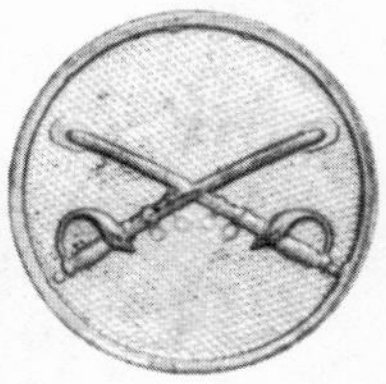

Fig. 7-97.

Fig. 7-98.

Fig. 7-99.

Fig. 7-100.

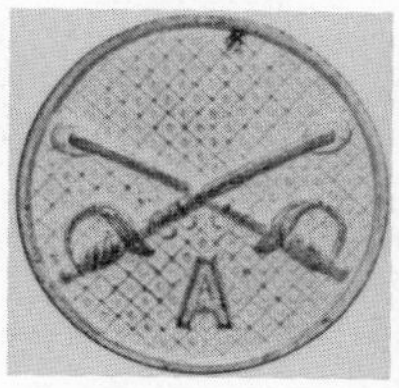

Fig. 7-101.

Fig. 7-102.

Fig. 7-103.

Fig. 7-104.

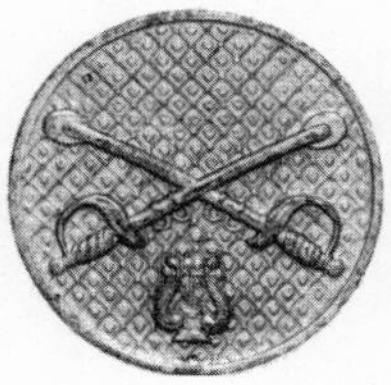

Fig. 7-105.

Fig. 7-106.

Fig. 7-107.

Fig. 7-95. *During World War I each regiment had one machine-gun troop, which was distinguished by the letters below crossed sabers. (1 inch in diameter)*

Fig. 7-96. *From 1910 until 1921 this insignia for cavalrymen of the U.S. Military Academy Detachment was authorized in regulations. (1 1/64 inches in diameter)*

Fig. 7-97. *A gilt disk used after 1923 but made from a die of World War I or earlier. The fine dotted background shown here changed to diagonal lines and small shields with the advent of bright collar insignia. (1 inch in diameter)*

Figs. 7-98 and 7-99. *Enlisted men's collar insignia with the stippled background and with various numbers and letters applied.*

Figs. 7-100 and 7-101. *Enlisted men's gilt collar insignia, with a background of diagonal lines and small shields, introduced in 1923 and used into the late 1930s. (Each 1 1/64 inches in diameter)*

Fig. 7-102. *Number 1, 2, or 3 below signified that the enlisted man was assigned to squadron headquarters. During the time these were in use the Regular Army did not have the 3d squadrons active, although some National Guard or reserve regiments may have had portions of all three squadrons. (1 1/64 inches in diameter)*

Fig. 7-103. *Various troop letters exist below the MG and sabers. Before the introduction of gilt enlisted men's insignia of this general style, the letters above would have indicated a machine-gun squadron, but such a combination was not regulation between the world wars, so this insignia awaits further research. (63/64 inches in diameter)*

Fig. 7-104. *Starting in 1928, because of further troop strength limitations, one regimental machine-gun troop was formed in each active regiment. This was their insignia. (1 1/64 inches in diameter)*

Fig. 7-105. *Regimental band members began to wear small lyres below crossed sabers. This continued until 1937. (1 1/32 inches wide)*

Fig. 7-106. *Armored car units added letters in the horizontal angles of their insignia starting in late 1928. This insignia is for an A Troop. (1 1/64 inches in diameter)*

Fig. 7-107. *In 1933 the armored car units moved their letters to below the crossed sabers. This insignia is an example of a separable disk. These insignia with a separable design were introduced by private manufacturers between the world wars. (1 1/64 inches in diameter)*

Two-Piece Disks

Two-piece disks, both neater in appearance and easier to clean, came into the army through private purchase at least twelve years before the Quartermaster Corps began to issue them in 1937.[32] A typical example of a 1930s privately purchased disk with a raised rim is shown in Fig. 7-108. Three of the many variations made before 1942 are shown in Figs. 7-109, 7-110, and 7-111. Although many of the first-year draftees received two-piece disks in 1940 and 1941, wartime metal shortages soon caused the change to a thin stamped disk crimped over a zinclike inner disk or over a thin steel strip (Fig. 7-112).[33]

Domed disks (Fig. 7-113) appeared in the last days of World War II and continued for more than a decade, but they were available only by private purchase on the part of the soldier. Many disks, both flat and domed,

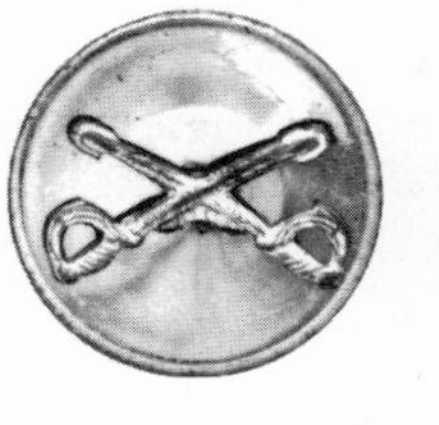

Fig. 7-108.

Fig. 7-109.

Fig. 7-110.

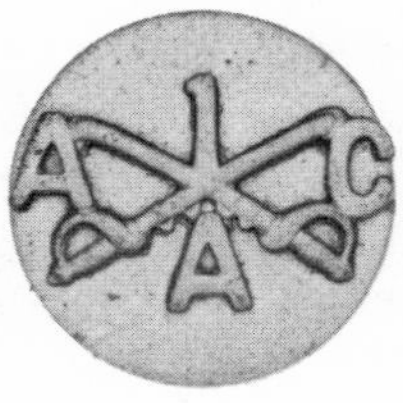

Fig. 7-111.

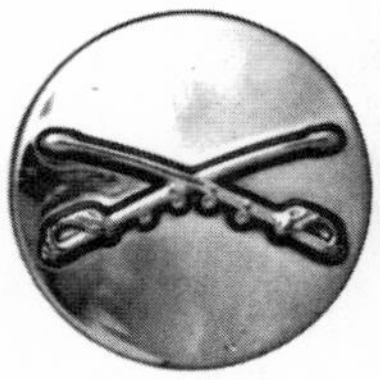

Fig. 7-112.

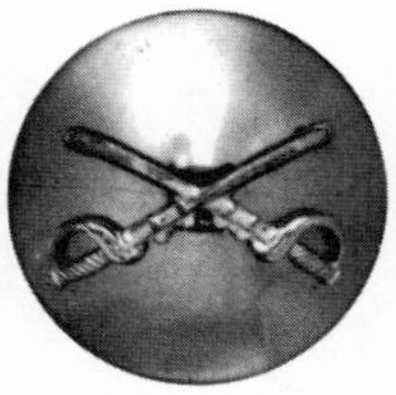

Fig. 7-113.

Fig. 7-114.

Fig. 7-115.

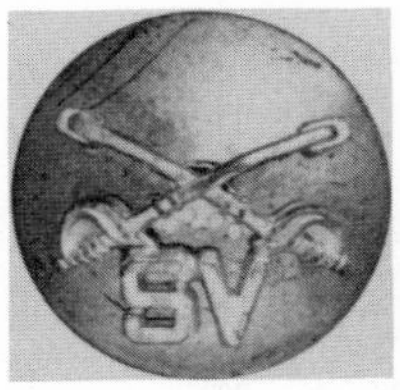

Fig. 7-116.

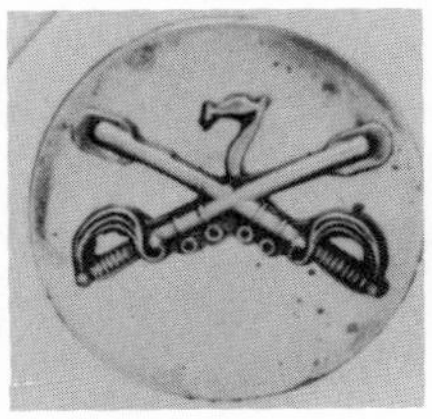

Fig. 7-117.

Fig. 7-118.

Fig. 7-119.

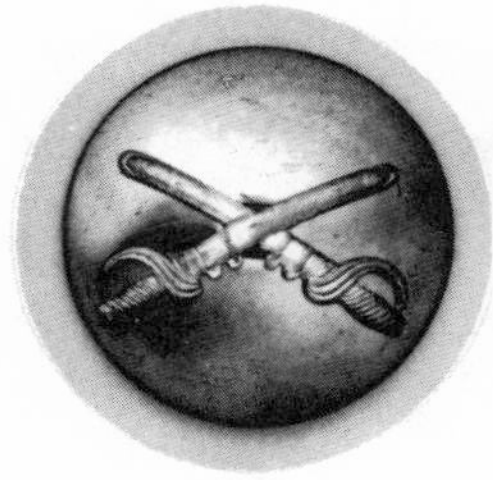

Fig. 7-120.

Fig. 7-121.

Fig. 7-108. *Probably made in about 1942, this disk with an edge is modeled after some insignia made in the 1930s. These enlisted men's insignia with removable designs came about because they were easy to shine. (1 inch in diameter)*

Fig. 7-109. *A two-piece enlisted men's collar insignia for a 1930s machine-gun troop. (1 inch in diameter)*

Fig. 7-110. *A typical screw-post enlisted men's collar insignia of the type made about 1940, with a troop letter below. (1 inch in diameter)*

Fig. 7-111. *A forerunner of the armored branch that was formed during World War II was the armored car squadrons. This two-piece disk was for A Troop, 1st Armored Car Squadron. (1 1/64 inches in diameter)*

Fig. 7-112. *Embossed World War II enlisted soldiers' collar insignia lasted until 1950, when the new armor branch was created. (1 inch in diameter)*

Fig. 7-113. *A domed or convex disk of the type commonly purchased by soldiers after World War II. (1 1/64 inches in diameter)*

Fig. 7-114. *The 1st Reconnaissance Troop was part of the 1st Infantry Division during World War II. This domed insignia was probably made immediately after the close of the war. (1 inch in diameter)*

Figs. 7-115 and 7-116. *Nonstandard abbreviations appeared on many insignia after 1945. That shown in Fig. 7-115 could have been used by any reconnaissance unit, while that in Fig. 7-116 was for a service troop. (Each 1 inch in diameter)*

Fig. 7-117. *Made in Korea for part of the 1st Cavalry Division, this enlisted troopers' collar insignia was for the 7th Cavalry when it was organized as infantry. (1 3/64 inches in diameter)*

Fig. 7-118. *A 5th Cavalry Regiment enlisted insignia for I Company. This domed insignia is silver in color and dates from about 1953–56. (1 inch in diameter)*

Fig. 7-119. *Worn at Fort Hood, Texas, in the late 1970s, this insignia is typical of those with nonregulation squadron or battalion numbers below that became more common for enlisted personnel during this period. (1 inch in diameter)*

Fig. 7-120. *Unauthorized yellow trim, like this plastic disk around the outer edge of the brass insignia, modeled after the prescribed infantry light blue trim, was introduced during the Korean War. Variations were made in a range of plastics and from enameled metal. (Yellow disk 1 5/16 inches in diameter)*

Fig. 7-121. *Evidently made about 1940–43 for antitank units, the AT below a cavalry insignia was never in regulations. (1 inch in diameter)*

bore special designations, as shown in Figs. 7-114, 7-115, and 7-116. Other postwar disks include one made in Korea (Fig. 7-117), one with a company designation (Fig. 7-118), and a post-Vietnam disk for the 1st Squadron, 9th Cavalry (Fig. 7-119).

For a time after 1952 some cavalry troopers wore yellow edges under their cavalry brass in a style similar to the infantry's blue trim (Fig. 7-120), but the yellow was never regulation. The final cavalry insignia may have been used by early members of tank destroyer units, since the *AT* (antitank) designation was not in standard cavalry units (Fig. 7-121).

Enlisted Men's Breast Insignia, 1901

Shown in Fig. 7-122 is a unique insignia, not authorized by regulations, but clearly worn by troopers of the 14th Cavalry at Fort Riley, Kansas, in 1901. This unofficial breast badge is a forerunner of both distinctive insignia and the collar insignia introduced for enlisted men in late 1902, both of which showed unit of assignment. While pride of one's unit has always been a soldier's characteristic, this particular insignia may indicate more. It may have been prompted by the growing U.S. Army, which increased the cavalry by 50 percent in 1901. The device precedes enlisted men's collar insignia by a full year and distinctive insignia by nearly a quarter of a century. The outline insignia, without details on the surface, was pinned to the five-button coat by a safety-pin fastener embedded on the insignia's reverse.

Fig. 7-122.

Fig. 7-122. *Private Charles H. Mark, B Troop, 14th Cavalry, in 1901 wearing an unauthorized breast badge. Such insignia may have been prompted by the growth of the U.S. Army (the cavalry was increased from ten to fifteen regiments that year). The next year the army prescribed collar insignia of this general configuration, which filled the need for soldiers to show their assignment.*

Section V

General Insignia

Chapter Eight

Eagle Insignia

DESPITE BENJAMIN FRANKLIN'S strong argument for the turkey as our national bird, on 20 June 1782 the U.S. Congress adopted the American bald eagle, which had emerged as a symbol during the American Revolution, as the principal device on the Great Seal of the United States.[1]

Eagles appeared as part of cap plate designs and on belt plates early in the United States as well as being used as a sole device. An eagle appears on the Society of Cincinnati badge, on coins, and on ship figureheads. In separate chapters eagles are discussed as part of other branch insignia (General Staff Corps and aides) and as branch insignia alone (unassigned and National Guard Bureau). Within this chapter eagles are considered as separate cap or hat devices and as a national symbol on the collar or shoulder loops. Very early eagles are briefly discussed and shown in chapter 3, "Regular Army Uniforms and Insignia, 1782–1802," and eagles appeared as a central design on many 1780–1830 infantry and cavalry cap plates.

Cockade Eagles before 1820

General George Washington labored on the organization of the army in 1798, looking into an endless number of questions and directing men throughout the United States to a variety of tasks. Washington queried Major Generals Hamilton and Pinckney in November, asking their thoughts on adding an eagle to the military hats' black cockade to distinguish the United States' cockade from all others, stating, "I have seen, and it appeared to have no bad effect, a small eagle (of pewter, tin, and in instances silver) fixed by way of a button in the center of a rose cockade."[2]

A month later Washington wrote in army regulations: "All persons belonging to the army to wear a black cockade, with small white eagle in the centre. The cockade of the Non Commissioned officers, musicians, and privates to be of leather with eagles of tin." In private correspondence in January 1799, Washington asked to receive four of these eagles "no larger than would cover a quarter of a dollar at most."[3] Surviving at Mount Vernon is a silver eagle worn by General Washington on a cockade (Fig. 8-1), evidently one of the four requested in 1799.

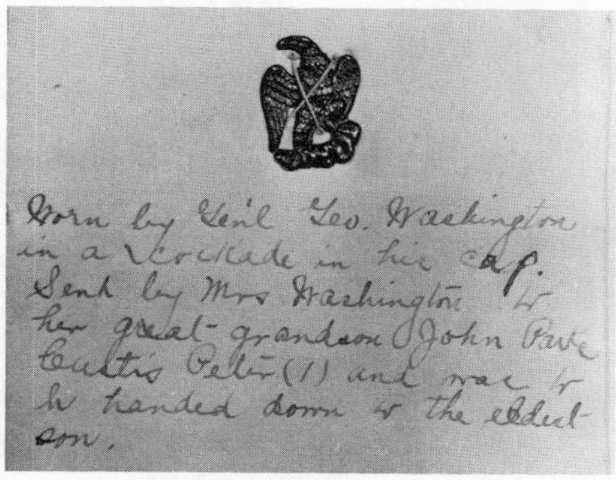

Fig. 8-1.

It would appear that metal eagles were always used with Regular Army cockades after 1799. On enlisted men's price lists of 1799 and later, eagles are always mentioned with cockades. Prices varied but generally ran from four and one-half cents to eight and one-half cents for the cockade and the eagle, but after 1798 the term *cockade* by itself is not used except in relation to a few officers such as doctors. Regulations of 1800, like those of 1799, call for a "small white eagle" on the cockade. The eagles pro-

Fig. 8-1. *One of the four original silver cockade eagles ordered by George Washington about a year before his death.*

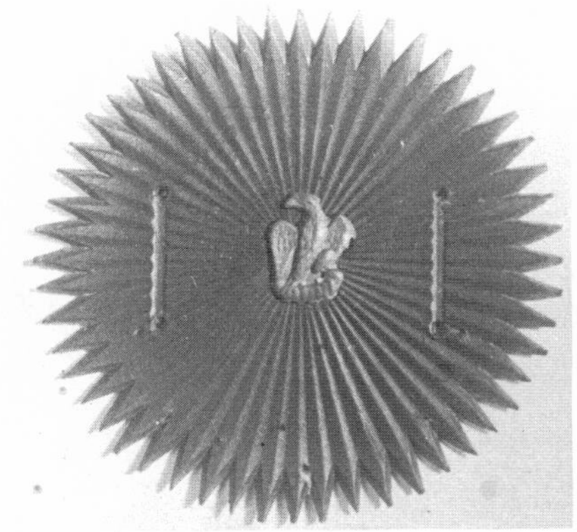

Fig. 8-2.

Fig. 8-2. *A 4-inch-diameter leather cockade with brass eagle, believed to have been used by Regular Army artillery troops in 1802 at Mackinac Island.*

cured for enlisted men in 1802 were tin for infantry to match their white trim and brass for the artillery to match their yellow trim.[4] Attributed to the artillery troops stationed at Mackinac Island, Michigan, in 1802, is the brass eagle and cockade shown in Fig. 8-2. In 1801, orders at Fort Johnston, North Carolina, prescribed officers to wear a cockade

Fig. 8-3.

Fig. 8-4.

Fig. 8-5.

Fig. 8-6.

Fig. 8-7.

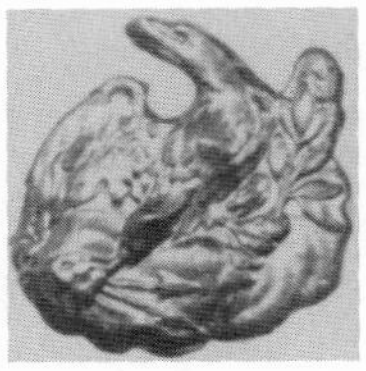

Fig. 8-8.

Fig. 8-9.

Fig. 8-10.

Fig. 8-3. *The navy's first cockade eagle, which was made by George Armitage of Philadelphia in 1799. (47/64 inch wide)*

Figs. 8-4 and 8-5. *Two early white metal (infantry) cockade eagles standing on clouds. This general style was evidently in infrequent use, at best, by the War of 1812. (19/32 and 5/8 inch wide, respectively)*

Figs. 8-6 through 8-10. *Five pewter cockade eagles excavated at War of 1812 encampment sites. In this second general style the clouds have become larger, and the arrows and olive branches have appeared, allowing the piece to be made more easily, without any cut-out areas. (15/16, 15/16, 7/8, 15/16, and 7/8 inch wide, respectively)*

at all times as "an acknowledgement that [they] receive the pay and [are] in the Service of the United States."[5]

Contracts show eagles and cockades very much in use until the 1821 uniform change, when they also became listed in commonly available regulations.

Besides the 1799–1802 eagles already mentioned, several other early cockade eagles exist, and although this book is about army insignia, it is worth mentioning the first U.S. Navy eagle, shown in Fig. 8-3. It is similar to the Washington eagle in size, design, and fastening means but is of a gilt metal, probably brass, and is marked with the initials *GA* on the clouds. This evidently is the insignia described in Claypoole's *American Daily Advertiser* for June 11, 1799:[6]

> Volunteer troops and companies who are not furnished with the uniform eagles, are informed that their officers or commissioners may be supplied with them in silver, gilt or plated, at the manufactory of George Armitage, in Race Street [Philadelphia] . . . ; likewise the eagle and anchor for the navy in gold or gilt, with a variety of fancy eagles and ornaments, which are sold at most shops in the city. . . .
>
> N.B.—the uniform eagles are marked G.A. in order that it may be known in the future; every true American ought to recollect it is adopted by George Washington.

Shown in Fig. 8-4 is an early army eagle on clouds, 7/8 inch high, of solid silver. This piece was probably made in 1799 or 1800, but it was not marked by the maker. The 1813 regulations call for a black leather cockade, 4½ inches in diameter, with gold eagle in the center for the general staff and artillery. Regulations of 1820 specified that officers and enlisted men were always to wear a black cockade with eagles of white metal for the infantry and of yellow metal for others.[7] Recent evidence indicates that on the 1813 leather cap, all branches wore yellow metal cockade eagles, either cut out as on the hat or on buttons in the center of the cockade, starting in 1817, while the artillery, which wore cocked hats, added a gilt button bearing an eagle on the cockade.

Excavations at War of 1812 sites have produced several pewter cockade eagles worn by infantry soldiers (Figs. 8-5 through 8-10).

The minor die differences in these indicate that more than one contractor made eagles, and records show that in 1818 alone at least three contractors delivered cockade eagles to the army. Lieutenant William Boyce wore the chapeau eagle shown in Fig. 8-11 in the late 1820s; it is one of the few positively dated early federal eagles.[8]

The eagle used from 1782 until about 1810, not on clouds, often was of a "frog leg" design instead of the more common fig. of today. With the long, scrawny neck, long legs, and wings that were usually upraised, the bird looked as if it had just been shot and hung by the neck awaiting the cooking pot.

Separate Eagles for Caps and Hats, 1820–51

Cockades and eagles continued to evolve in the 1800s. Orders of 1820 required officers always to wear a black cockade with yellow eagle, while enlisted men also wore yellow eagles on their caps. By 1821 regulations a gold eagle, 1 1/2 inches between wing tips on a 4 1/2-inch black cockade, ornamented officers' chapeaus.[9] These are perhaps the same insignia mentioned the previous year.

Several federal-style eagles are known to have been worn by militia, and most early eagles now encountered are probably those of militia. Fig. 8-12 shows a fan cockade with brass eagle that belonged to a U.S. Marine Corps officer, while Fig. 3-1 in chapter 3 shows a small, thin brass eagle, without arrows and olive branches, that was worn by a captain in the New York militia. Like many early eagles, this insignia was fastened to the cockade by stitches through small holes at the insignia's edge.

Later cockade eagles, both militia and federal, are more widely known than the earlier eagles. Three examples of these later insignia follow. The first (Fig. 8-13) is solid silver, 7/8 inch high and slightly more than an inch wide. Fig. 8-14 shows another small eagle of copper with silver plating and *E PLURIBUS UNUM* between the wings. A larger eagle, one and three-quarters inches wide of silver-plated copper with a button shank for fastening, is shown in Fig. 8-15. A smaller gilt eagle is shown in Fig. 8-16, while a larger silver eagle is illustrated in Fig. 8-17.

A new tall bell-crowned hat, introduced in 1821, had near the top an eagle, gilt for officers and brass for enlisted men, with the regimental number cut out of the shield center (Fig. 8-18). This 1821 outline eagle with the three-inch wingspan enjoyed a long life as a U.S. Army insignia through various modifications (Fig. 72-6 in chapter 72,

Fig. 8-11.

Fig. 8-11. This chapeau eagle was worn by a Regular Army officer in the 1820s.

Fig. 8-12.

Fig. 8-12. This federal-style eagle was worn by a U.S. Marine Corps officer. While the eagle itself could have been used by a Regular Army officer, the shape of the leather cockade rules this out. Militia units also wore cockades that were not round.

Fig. 8-13.

Fig. 8-14.

Fig. 8-13. A solid silver cockade eagle, estimated to postdate the War of 1812. (55/64 inch high)

Fig. 8-14. This silver-plated copper cockade eagle was to be sewn to a cap or hat. (1 1/4 inches wide)

Fig. 8-15.

Fig. 8-15. An infantry cap or hat eagle with a button shank fastener on the reverse. (1 25/32 inches wide)

Fig. 8-16.

Fig. 8-16. A gold-colored eagle believed to be for a cap or hat. (7/8 inch wide)

Fig. 8-18.

Fig. 8-19.

Fig. 8-20.

Fig. 8-21.

Fig. 8-17. *After this design was stamped into a sheet of silver, it was cut out by hand as shown by the straight cut lines around the olive branch. (1 5/8 inches wide)*

Fig. 8-18. *A cap eagle fragment, dug up at Fort Snelling, Minnesota, shows the cut-out number on the eagle's breast. This design was used from 1821 until the early 1830s. (Fragment 2 17/32 inches wide)*

Figs. 8-19, 8-20, and 8-21. *These three patterns of the 1832 cap eagles are similar to the 1821 design, with the omission of the cut-out regimental number. The first eagle (Fig. 8-19), silver-plated on copper, was stamped from a die and then trimmed by hand. In the other two, the maker trimmed the eagles by using a second cutting die after the design had been stamped. (3, 3, and 3 1/16 inches wide, respectively)*

Fig. 8-22. *The 1833–51 dragoon cap insignia of a silver eagle on a gilt background. (Sunburst 5 7/16 inches wide)*

"Men's Headgear through the Civil War"). In 1833 and 1834 a changed gilt eagle moved up several inches on the tall leather and felt caps to make room for the crossed cannon artillery insignia or for the silver infantry horn, as shown in Fig. 72-7. This eagle, prescribed in the 1832 regulations, also shared use with several militia units. After it was made obsolete in 1851 for the regulars, the militia continued to use the 1832-pattern eagle for several years following the Civil War.[10] Even high school bands adopted this design, and it is still used by some civilian organizations today. Three original 1832-pattern eagles are shown in Figs. 8-19, 8-20, and 8-21. Artillerymen placed a very similar eagle above the crossed cannons on the 1864 artillery cap, as shown in Fig. 72-8.[11]

The year 1832 also saw West Point instructors, chaplains, and civil staff (storekeepers) with a new "round hat" bearing a cockade and eagle, presumably the earlier type. This style lasted until 1851, when the eagles on cockades disappeared.[12]

The nation's mounted arm came and went during the republic's early years until the formation of the Regiment of Dragoons in 1833. These horse soldiers' cylindrical caps carried a Napoleonic style of silver eagle superimposed on a gilt star (Fig. 8-22) until the headgear was replaced by a cap in 1851. The eagle design itself continued in use by militia and commercial organizations for many years. On the forage cap, officers of the Reg-

Fig. 8-17.

Fig. 8-22.

Fig. 8-23.

Fig. 8-24.

Fig. 8-25.

Fig. 8-26.

Fig. 8-27.

Fig. 8-28.

Fig. 8-23. *An enlisted men's brass eagle for wear on the left side of the hat, introduced in 1858. This was the first eagle to be worn in brass by all branches. It is slightly convex. (Flat width nearly 2 inches; straight width $1\frac{7}{8}$ inches)*

Fig. 8-24. *Facing the opposite direction from the previous example, this hat eagle was intended to pin up the right side of the 1858 hat. ($1\frac{15}{16}$ inches wide)*

Fig. 8-25. *General U.S. Grant's hat eagle, a typical Civil War officers' hand-embroidered insignia. (Total oval width $2\frac{1}{16}$ inches)*

Fig. 8-26. *An unusually small officers' Civil War hat eagle. (Oval $1\frac{5}{8}$ inches wide)*

Fig. 8-27. *Slightly larger than most, this Civil War hat eagle faces to its left, indicating that it was made for the right side of the hat. (Oval $2\frac{5}{16}$ inches wide)*

Fig. 8-28. *An example of the 1872 enlisted men's cap eagle. ($1\frac{9}{16}$ inches wide)*

iment of Mounted Riflemen (formed in 1846) wore a gold-embroidered spread eagle with a silver *R* on the eagle's shield. No original specimens survive.[13]

Cap and Hat Insignia, 1851–1895

With the design of cloud and stars included, a new eagle came with the 1851 cap (Fig. 8-23). The eagle had a ribbon bearing *E PLURIBUS UNUM* on the area between the upraised wings. Both officers' embroidered and enlisted men's yellow metal insignia vary in size. The official 1865 metal eagle was to be 2 inches wide and $2\frac{1}{2}$ inches high, but actual Civil War sizes ranged from $1\frac{3}{4}$ to 2 inches wide and $2\frac{3}{8}$ to $2\frac{5}{8}$ inches high.[14] This same eagle design, placed on the side of the 1858 hats, held up part of the brim (note that Fig. 8-23 has a hook at the bottom). Most of these metal insignia were made with the eagle's head over its right wing, although a few were made in the reverse direction (Fig. 8-24). An example of an enlisted man's 1858 artillery hat with the metal eagle is shown in Fig. 72-14 chapter 72.

General U. S. Grant's embroidered eagle is shown in Fig. 8-25, while a smaller embroidered eagle is illustrated in Fig. 8-26. A slightly oversized eagle with sparse arrows and olive branch and facing the reverse direction is shown in Fig. 8-27.

The War Department in 1872 introduced a completely new uniform that included an enlisted men's dress cap with a branch insignia and a brass eagle of the type shown in Fig. 8-28. A ribbon held in the eagle's beak connected the tip of the arrow bundle and the olive branch. As before, officers' caps carried embroidered eagles instead of the metal insignia, and an example is illustrated in Fig. 73-1 in chapter 73, "Men's Headgear with Roots, 1872–1916."[15]

Chapeau Insignia after 1820

On the 1832 dress chapeau generals wore a 6-inch black silk cockade with a "silver

Fig. 8-29. An 1832–40 chapeau eagle. Generals wore a silver eagle, adding gold rays and twenty-four stars. Staff officers had a gold-colored eagle and motto only. (2 13/16 inches wide)

Fig. 8-30. Chapeau eagles from 1840 through 1917 were on a gold strap of this general shape. This particular insignia is for a Corps of Engineers chapeau from just before World War I. (Strap 2 1/8 inches wide)

Figs. 8-31 and 8-32. Two 1872–81 helmet eagles, restruck from original dies for collectors in the 1960s. (4 3/32 and 4 1/32 inches wide, respectively)

spread eagle." Gold rays emanated from the eagle, terminating in twenty-four silver stars. An example, worn by General Lawson, is shown in chapter 72. General staff officers wore a similar chapeau, eliminating the rays and stars and with a gilt instead of a silver eagle (Fig. 8-29).[16]

About 1840 a new chapeau insignia, characterized by a 2-inch-wide gold strap bearing an eagle, appeared.[17] The basic eagle and separate motto ribbon initially remained unchanged and were about 3 1/2 inches wide, but over time the design varied, if surviving samples and drawings are an adequate guide. Slowly the eagle shrank until it fit completely on the gold strap, as shown in Fig. 8-30. Precise dating during this evolution is difficult, since the regulations always use cryptic phrases such as, "according to pattern," or, "as adopted," but this final change in eagle sizes may have come about in the 1872 changes.

Fig. 8-29.

Fig. 8-30.

Other Eagles before 1895

Artillery and ordnance officers fastened their cloaks of 1832 at the collar with a gilt eagle and chain. General Order 36 of 1829, "with a view to economy, comfort and uniformity," directed officers to adopt a frock coat on which field-grade officers were to wear a gold or gilt cockade eagle on each side of the collar and company-grade officers were to wear an eagle on only one side. Two months later the army eliminated the eagle.[18]

Fig. 8-31.

Fig. 8-32.

Fig. 8-33.

Fig. 8-33. *A die for the 1872 helmet eagle. This is the only surviving die from which insignia have not been restruck after World War II. The die sinker's name, engraved on the steel block, is W. Eck. (Eagle 4 1/8 inches wide)*

Helmet Eagles

Mounted troops of 1872 received European horse guard–style helmets adorned with a large eagle and ribbon embossed *E PLURIBUS UNUM.*[19] This initial eagle design lasted nine years before being replaced by other designs. Restruck in the 1960s, these remade eagle insignia far outnumber surviving original devices. Twentieth-century dealers used at least two dies to remake this scarce eagle; insignia from these dies are shown in Figs. 8-31 and 8-32. An original 1872 die, not used in the twentieth century, is shown in Fig. 8-33. One reason for the current shortage of original 1872 eagles is that a large part of the surplus stock was modified by clipping off the motto scroll and then applying another device over the national shield, allowing state militias to use the resulting helmet plates.

Infantry, cavalry, and artillery personnel all received helmet eagles in 1881. These bore respective arms crossed under the national shield, which carried silver regimental numbers. Staff personnel wore the eagle and shield without any arms and with a small silver staff insignia in place of the regimental number (Fig. 8-34). Enlisted men were issued eagles stamped from one piece of brass, while officers' helmets carried a sturdier insignia with the shield or shield and arms as a separate piece applied over the basic eagle.[20] Fig. 8-35 is taken from an 1881 War Department document and shows the eagle and various staff overlays then in use. Fig. 8-36 shows a helmet worn by an infantry adjutant.

The 1901 artillery reorganization caused artillerymen to eliminate unit numbers. Since most artillery units used the helmet well into the twentieth century, this special

Fig. 8-34.

Fig. 8-34. *An 1881–1903 enlisted man's helmet with Medical Department insignia applied to the eagle. Mounted troops had branch-colored plumes instead of the spike on the top. Only the Medical Department had side buttons with a silver overlay, introduced in 1887 to replace the caduceus.*

Fig. 8-35.

Fig. 8-35. *A portion of the official 1881 illustration showing the parts of helmet insignia. On officers' insignia the shield and crossed arms were applied separately to the eagle, then the regimental number was added, as in this case for the 1st Cavalry. On the separate shields are the silver staff insignia then in use. See also Fig. 73.4.*

use of eagles without numbers lasted until 1912. During 1903 and 1904 soldiers other than artillery phased out the use of helmets and helmet insignia.[21] Examples of the combatant arms' 1881–1902 eagles are shown in Fig. 8-37 and in chapters associated with the various branches.

Officers' Cap Eagles

When officers received a new short, cylindrical cap in 1895, a gold-embroidered eagle (Fig. 73-6 in chapter 73, "Men's Headgear with Roots, 1872–1916") instead of the previous branch insignia adorned the front. This eagle can be easily distinguished since it is not from the Great Seal of the United States; the "glory" or the cloud with thirteen stars that usually is above the eagle's head is absent.[22] As officers replaced this 1895 eagle in 1902 and 1903, the current cap device came into use, although it was of smaller size and, at least initially, usually embroidered (Figs. 8-38 and 8-39).

In March 1902, Corps of Engineers officers received new uniforms including a visor cap with an embroidered arms of the United States, "edged with scarlet silk, excepting the

Fig. 8-36. *The adjutant of the 20th Infantry Regiment wearing the dress 1881–1902 helmet.*

Fig. 8-37. *This member of the newly formed 14th Cavalry Regiment is shown in 1901 holding his dress helmet, which bears the eagle superimposed over crossed sabers. Evidently because of the many new units formed at this time, there was a shortage of the small silver regimental numbers, for they have not been added to the eagle's shield.*

Figs. 8-38 and 8-39. *Officers' embroidered eagles of the design of the Great Seal of the United States were introduced for dress caps in 1902. (Designs 2⅞ and 2 5/32 inches wide, respectively)*

Fig. 8-40. *An officers' bronze-colored metal device of the type used on olive drab and khaki caps from 1902 through 1923. (1 29/32 inches wide)*

Fig. 8-36.

Fig. 8-38.

Fig. 8-37.

Fig. 8-39.

Fig. 8-40.

Fig. 8-41.

Fig. 8-42.

Fig. 8-43.

scroll and stars, arrows, and laurel branch." An all-gilt eagle "the coat of arms of the United States" became the cap insignia for other officers during 1903.[23]

Fig. 8-44.

Fig. 8-45.

The 1896 Quartermaster General's adoption of a screw-back enlisted men's cap insignia showed how officers' bronze metal eagles could be used as cap ornaments (Fig. 8-40). These bronze insignia ultimately lasted until 1923. The eagles came from many dies, one of which, made in England during World War I, is shown in Fig. 8-41. Gilt screw-post cap eagles, specifically introduced in November 1905 for the white cap, have been used ever since. Many of the 1930s eagles had clouds that were oval instead of round (Fig. 8-42). After World War II one New York company made oversized eagles (Fig. 8-43). It is worth noting that the official June 1936 drawing is followed closely in the piece shown in Fig. 8-44, with a variation shown in Fig. 8-45.[24]

Women's Cap and Hat Eagles

When the War Department formed the Women's Army Auxilliary Corps (WAAC) it was not formally part of the army, and con-

Fig. 8-41. *This bronze-colored officers' service cap insignia was made in England during World War I. The design is rather peculiar, and the fastening device is British, made of two loops with a long cotter pin passing through them. ($1\frac{27}{32}$ inches wide)*

Fig. 8-42. *A typical 1930s and early World War II officers' cap eagle with the glory (cloud and thirteen stars) an oval instead of round ($2\frac{11}{32}$ inches wide)*

Fig. 8-43. *A striking oversized cap insignia made by N. S. Meyer following World War II. ($2\frac{37}{64}$ inches wide)*

Fig. 8-44. *This officers' cap insignia closely follows the official design established in 1936 and still used today. ($2\frac{1}{4}$ inches wide)*

Fig. 8-45. *A variation of the officers' cap insignia made during World War II. ($2\frac{31}{64}$ inches wide)*

Fig. 8-46.

Fig. 8-47.

Fig. 8-46. Women's Army Auxiliary Corps (WAAC) officers' cap device, 1942 and early 1943. The popular name for the walking eagle insignia was, "the buzzard." Collectors' demands for this insignia caused it to be restruck in the 1980s. ($2\frac{13}{64}$ inches wide)

Fig. 8-47. The WAAC enlisted women's cap insignia. ($1\frac{1}{2}$ inches wide)

Fig. 8-48.

Fig. 8-49.

Fig. 8-48. This finely detailed WAAC officers' cap eagle was photographed by the War Department in 1942.

Fig. 8-49. At the time of the Korean War, Women's Army Corps (WAC) officers received small hat insignia like this in "antique bronze" color. This version has two clutch fasteners. ($1\frac{29}{64}$ inches wide)

Fig. 8-50. An enlisted WAC 1951 hat insignia. The eagle was the same size and color as that of women officers, with a ring added. ($1\frac{23}{32}$ inches wide)

Fig. 8-51. Women officers returned to gold-colored hat insignia of this size in the late 1950s. Like those of antique bronze, these came with a screw-post fastener, two tines and clutches, or a pin fastener. ($1\frac{1}{2}$ inches wide)

sequently, women could not wear U.S. Army insignia. Thus a "walking eagle" (Figs. 8-46 and 8-47) became the WAAC cap insignia. Nicknamed "the buzzard," this insignia was replaced by the army eagle a year later when the WAAC changed to the Women's Army Corps (WAC).[25] An unusual version of the WAAC eagle from official army files is illustrated in Fig. 8-48.

Starting in 1943, women wore the same cap ornaments as men until a taupe-colored uniform, peculiar to the WAC, was introduced in 1951. With the taupe uniform came cap ornaments in "antique bronze." Officers wore an eagle of the same design as that of male officers except for the size ($1\frac{1}{2}$ inches high) and color (Fig. 8-49). Enlisted women wore an antique bronze eagle the same size as that of enlisted men, but instead of being mounted on a disk, the eagle appeared within a thin ring (Fig. 8-50). When the army reintroduced the dress blue uniform in 1957, gold cap insignia (Figs. 8-51 and 8-52) were made for wear with the blue cap. These gilt insignia completely replaced the bronze pieces with the introduction of the army green hat starting in January 1960 and ending in 1964.[26]

Enlisted Men's Cap Eagles

Until World War I an enlisted man's regiment or staff duty determined his cap

Fig. 8-50.

Fig. 8-51.

Fig. 8-52.

Fig. 8-54.

Fig. 8-52. An enlisted women's hat insignia in a dark yellow, worn from 1960 to the present. (1 45/64 inches wide)

Fig. 8-53. Black-bronze enlisted men's cap insignia of this design were introduced during World War I so that use of a single insignia would simplify supply problems. These insignia were worn until 1923. (1 1/2 inches wide)

Fig. 8-54. Although the eagle on the 1 1/2-inch disk was introduced for wear in 1918, many enlisted men did not begin to wear it until after World War I. These two 1920 soldiers were assigned to the 2d Cavalry Regiment.

Figs. 8-55 and 8-56. Gilt enlisted men's cap insignia with a background of very fine horizontal lines. (1 1/2 and 1 29/32 inches wide, respectively)

insignia, and infantry, cavalry, and artillery troops wore the device of their arm with the unit number and letter. This taxed the army during the 1917 expansion, because the number of different units became so large that the army could not efficiently supply each company-sized unit with an insignia with the proper regimental and company designation. To eliminate this problem, the army staff directed all enlisted men to wear the national eagle on a disk 1 1/2 inches in diameter (Figs. 8-53 and 8-54). With the reintroduction of gilt insignia in 1923, enlisted men wore devices like those shown in Figs. 8-55 and 8-56 on a background of crosshatching prescribed to be forty-eight lines to the inch.[27]

The early-nineteenth-century frog leg–style eagle jumped forward to the 1920s and 1930s, although today no reason can be found for the change. Many enlisted men's cap ornaments from between the world wars had eagles with their legs and necks of this much older design (Fig. 8-57). Instead of a crosshatching of forty-eight lines to the inch or a fine pebbled background, new cap ornaments with lines and shields as a background, just like the background of collar ornaments, appeared (Fig. 8-58). Private firms began to make two-piece cap ornaments for ease of polishing. An early variation is shown in Fig. 8-59, on which the eagle is struck separately from the backing but the two pieces are permanently joined.

The market for privately made insignia expanded between the world wars, competing with issue items. While officers had always bought their own insignia, many companies sought to offer the new citizen soldiers better insignia than those supplied by the government. Examples of these privately made items are shown in Figs. 8-60 and 8-61, the latter two-piece device matching the official June 1936 design.[28]

Fig. 8-53.

Fig. 8-55.

Fig. 8-56.

Poorly made insignia also came onto the market in 1940 and 1941 in response to the demand of the greatly enlarged army. An extreme example of a piece made to try to meet the demands caused by a growing army is shown in Fig. 8-62. It is made from a poor-quality silver metal, and the head of a straight pin is visible near the top of the glory. On the reverse the pin is bent ninety degrees to hold the insignia to the cap. Because of metal shortages, plastic insignia, such as that shown in Fig. 8-63, also came into existence early in the war. It is made from a golden but not shiny plastic in a modern design.

To improve infantry esprit, in 1952 the Department of the Army authorized a blue plastic disk, $1\frac{3}{4}$ inches in diameter, to be worn behind the enlisted men's cap insignia (Fig. 8-64).[29] A nonissue heavy silver insignia with an enameled blue rim is shown in Fig. 8-65. Soldiers used these heavy, impressive-looking enameled devices in the 1950s, but by the 1960s generally only the disk with plastic backing was worn. Insignia makers produced many other branch-colored rims, although they were nonregulation. These range from thin colored plastic disks to multienameled pieces, such as the red-and-white enameled disk shown in Fig. 8-66 for Corps of Engineers troops, behind a bright gilt frog-leg cap insignia of plastic.

Fig. 8-57.

Fig. 8-57. *This 1930s gilt enlisted men's cap insignia displays a late-eighteenth-century "frog leg"–style eagle on a background of small dots. ($1\frac{31}{64}$ inches wide)*

Fig. 8-58.

Fig. 8-58. *An official early 1930s cap insignia with a background of lines and shields. ($1\frac{1}{2}$ inches wide)*

Fig. 8-59.

Fig. 8-59. *Privately made in the 1930s or 1940s, this piece has the design and rim cut from one piece of metal, with the edge then crimped over the backing disk like a button. ($1\frac{17}{32}$ inches wide)*

Fig. 8-60.

Fig. 8-61.

Figs. 8-60 and 8-61. *Two cap insignia with the design separable for easy cleaning. The backgrounds are slightly convex. Fig. 8-60 has a raised edge and was made by the N. S. Meyer Company. The overall design of Fig. 8-61 follows the official drawing and is the type issued from the 1950s to the present. (Each $1\frac{1}{2}$ inches wide)*

Fig. 8-62.

Fig. 8-62. *This insignia was made during the shortages of World War II from pot metal. The head of a straight-pin fastener is visible near the top of the eagle's cloud. ($1\frac{1}{2}$ inches wide)*

Fig. 8-63.

Fig. 8-63. *This gold-colored enlisted personnel's cap insignia was made from plastic during World War II. ($1\frac{7}{16}$ inches wide)*

Fig. 8-64.

Fig. 8-64. *This 1989 drill sergeant of the year wears a light blue plastic trim around his hat eagle, as first authorized in 1952 for members of infantry units.*

Fig. 8-65.

Fig. 8-66.

Fig. 8-65. The blue trim around this insignia is enameled, and the metal is silver in color. During the 1950s many soldiers privately bought such insignia to improve their uniforms. ($1\frac{63}{64}$ inches wide)

Fig. 8-66. Members of many branches added unofficial trim to their insignia, especially when on leave or away from their home station. This gold-colored plastic cap device has a red-and-white enameled metal ring added to signify engineers. (2 inches wide)

Fig. 8-67.

Fig. 8-68.

Fig. 8-69.

Figs. 8-67, 8-68, and 8-69. Three designs of the 1898–1902 officers' eagles worn on the khaki coats. These follow the official pattern. The last piece was worn in the Philippine Islands by Captain James Lee "Gentleman Jim" Cochrun, a well-known officer who became a lieutenant colonel during World War I. ($1\frac{1}{64}$, $1\frac{1}{64}$, and $1\frac{1}{32}$ inches wide, respectively)

Fig. 8-70.

Fig. 8-71.

Figs. 8-70 and 8-71. Two variations of the officers' 1989–1902 khaki coat eagles with wings upraised. These came in gilt for most officers and in silver for selected medical officers. ($1\frac{1}{8}$ and $1\frac{3}{16}$ inches wide, respectively)

Shoulder Loop Eagles, 1898–1903

On the 1898 khaki coat, officers below the grade of colonel wore an eagle one and one-fourth inches high on the shoulder loops. Colonels and generals wore the eagle on the coat collar, with only the rank on the shoulder loops. The common use of the letters *US* or *USV* on the khaki coat was not regulation. These eagles were gilt (Figs. 8-67, 8-68, and 8-69) until 1900, when acting assistant surgeons switched to silver eagles.[30] Some variations, such as those shown in Figs. 8-70 and 8-71, are considerably different from the prescribed design.

Many officers had the insignia embroidered on their shoulder loops, and the "wings up" variety of eagles was most popular. In 1898 and 1899 infantry trim was blue, thus dating the shoulder loop eagle shown in Fig. 8-72. Figs. 8-73 and 8-74 illustrate a pair made on white ribbed cotton, while the eagles on white wool in Figs. 8-75 and 8-76 do not even have a motto ribbon. Figs. 8-77 and 8-78 show eagles on red wool for artillery.

The December 1902 dress uniform regulations called for officers above the rank of captain to wear shoulder knots embroidered with a gold eagle, but before the required date of wear, July 1903, this provision was revoked.[31]

Collar Eagles, 1902–1905

With the new 1902-pattern officers' service coat came a "dull finished bronze" coat of arms (Figs. 8-79, 8-80, and 8-81) worn 1 inch from the collar edge. On the white and blue dress uniforms, the insignia were of gold or gilt metal (Fig. 8-82). Volunteer officers wore a letter *V* behind the eagle. A small bronze insignia for wear on the shirt collar is shown in Fig. 8-83. Such eagles replaced the previously worn *US* letters and proved unpopular with officers, as shown by the many letters to the editor in the popular *Army and Navy Register.* The commanding general of the Philippines complained in 1903 that the eagle was too large for the collar and suggested that if it was to be retained it should be moved to the shoulder loop. Complaints of this type eliminated the eagle as a collar device, and it was replaced during June 1905 by the letters *US* and *USV.*[32]

Fig. 8-72. *An infantry first lieutenant's 1898–99 shoulder loops with embroidered eagle for the khaki coat. (Eagle $1^{15}/_{32}$ inches wide)*

Figs. 8-73 and 8-74. *A pair of 1899–1902 white wool shoulder loops with eagles, less the E PLURIBUS UNUM ribbon. (Each eagle $1^{3}/_{8}$ inches wide)*

Figs. 8-75 and 8-76. *These second lieutenants' eagles are embroidered on a white ribbed cotton. ($1^{15}/_{32}$ and $1^{3}/_{8}$ inches wide, respectively)*

Figs. 8-77 and 8-78. *Two artillery shoulder loops showing different embroidery of the eagles and two basic shoulder loop shapes, with round and angular ends. ($1^{15}/_{32}$ and $1^{1}/_{2}$ inches wide, respectively)*

Fig. 8-72.

Fig. 8-73.

Fig. 8-74.

Fig. 8-75.

Fig. 8-76.

Fig. 8-77.

Fig. 8-78.

Epaulettes

Generals' full dress uniforms introduced in 1902 had epaulettes with "the coat of arms of the United States embroidered in gold." Shown in Fig. 8-84, these epaulettes lasted until dress uniforms were suspended during World War I, except that after 1911 those generals assigned to the General Staff Corps substituted the general staff insignia for the national eagle.[33]

Adapted Eagles

Because the national symbol was readily available and easily identified, innumerable organizations adapted army cap eagles. A few state guard examples are shown. Fig. 8-85 is for the Ohio State Guard during World War II, and Fig. 8-86 illustrates the Missouri State Guard officers' cap insignia. The insignia identified as the 31st New Jersey in Fig. 8-87 was used by a Spanish-American War veterans' organization, but like the preceding state insignia, it is a modification created by removing the glory and replacing it with a distinctive addition.

Reserve Officers Training Corps (ROTC) cadets also wore modified eagles. Many schools used the national symbol with *ROTC* above (Fig. 8-88 from the 1930s and Fig. 8-89 from the 1960s). Some schools had their unique insignia. Fig. 8-90 shows one change, for Rutgers College (now Rutgers University), and an insignia modified even more is shown in Fig. 8-91, while an unusual insignia from the Massachusetts Institute of Technology is shown in Fig. 8-92.

Fig. 8-79.

Fig. 8-80.

Fig. 8-81.

Figs. 8-79, 8-80, and 8-81. *Effective July 1903 and for two years thereafter, officers wore eagles of this type, instead of the letters US, on their collars. General Pershing selected the 1903–1905 collar eagle as his insignia when he became General of the Armies. (1 1/4, 1 1/16, and 1 5/64 inches wide, respectively)*

Fig. 8-82.

Fig. 8-82. *This general's aide wears a pair of the unpopular 1903–1905 collar eagles.*

Fig. 8-84.

Fig. 8-84. *From 1903 until 1917, generals wore this insignia in the crescent of their epaulette.*

Fig. 8-85.

Fig. 8-86.

Figs. 8-85 and 8-86. *Two World War II state guard officers' cap insignia. These are but two of many examples showing how state troops modified the federal cap insignia. (2 5/32 and 2 11/64 inches wide, respectively)*

Fig. 8-83.

Fig. 8-83. *A small eagle worn on the shirt collar, 1903–1905. (11/16 inch wide)*

Fig. 8-87. Many organizations not sanctioned by any state or federal government modified the officers' cap eagles. This example was for a New Jersey chapter of the United War Veterans and was made in the late 1920s or the 1930s. ($2\frac{1}{64}$ inches wide)

Fig. 8-87.

Fig. 8-88.

Fig. 8-89.

Fig. 8-90.

Figs. 8-88 and 8-89. *Two types of Reserve Officers Training Corps (ROTC) cap ornaments not recognized by the federal government but worn at many schools. (Each 2 inches wide)*

Figs. 8-90 and 8-91. *Rather than the insignia shown in Figs. 8-88 and 8-89, some schools adopted eagles with their school name. Such modifications were common. ($1\frac{7}{8}$ and $1\frac{15}{16}$ inches wide, respectively)*

Fig. 8-92. *By covering the shield on the eagle's breast, the Massachusetts Institute of Technology made an ROTC cap device that was a distinctive modification of the federal insignia. ($1\frac{15}{16}$ inches wide)*

Fig. 8-91.

Fig. 8-92.

Chapter Nine

The Letters *US* and State Insignia

It is not my intention here to debate the origin of the abbreviations U.S. or U.S.A., but a short history of the army's use of the letters *US* is instructive. During the American Revolution the Continental Army impressed the letters *US* on gun locks, cannon tubes, files, and other pieces of ordnance and equipment to identify them as property of the United States. On the only "insignia" of the period, soldiers' solid pewter buttons, there were three raised and interwined letters *USA*. Some officers wore thin metal button shells, crimped over bone or wood disks, bearing raised intertwined letters *USA* with the *S* considerably larger.[1]

By the year 1800 the letters had been shortened in general military usage from *USA* to *US*. In 1808 the army placed pewter buttons with raised letters *US* on fatigue clothing.[2] In that same year light dragoons, light artillery, and the Regiment of Riflemen ornamented their caps with four separate letters, placed two above and two below: *USLD, USLA,* and *USRR,* as illustrated in chapters 7 and 10.

Although the date is not known exactly, about 1819 the plain unornamented cross-belt plate for enlisted soldiers changed to one with the raised letters *US*. When the army issued noncommissioned officers short swords in 1833, all three patterns of the accompanying belt plates included raised letters *US* on one of the two round plates. Three years later these belt plates were changed to a single pattern with raised letters *US* as the sole device.[3]

Officers' Cap and Hat Insignia

Not until the 1851 uniform changes did the letters *US* become officers' uniform insignia as an ornament for cap bands. Described as a gold-embroidered wreath encircling silver old English letters *US,* this new device was worn by generals and staff officers, the latter including members of the Adjutant General's, Judge Advocate General's, Inspector General's, Quartermaster General's, Subsistence, Medical, and Pay Departments, and aides-de-camp. Fig. 9-1 closely follows the official drawing, while Fig. 9-2, for the same period, illustrates to what degree hand embroidery can vary. From 1851 to 1872 these *US* letters in a wreath usually were worn by general officers and by all officers of

Figs. 9-1 and 9-2. *Two variations of the 1851-pattern cap insignia for generals and staff officers. The first closely follows the pre–Civil War official drawings. (Wreaths 2 1/4 and 2 3/16 inches wide, respectively)*

Fig. 9-1.

Fig. 9-2.

Figs. 9-3, 9-4, 9-5, and 9-6. *Starting in 1858 these insignia were worn on the broad-brimmed hats of staff and general officers. They were to have an edge of gold around the background. ($2\frac{7}{16}$, $2\frac{9}{16}$, $2\frac{5}{8}$, and $2\frac{5}{8}$ inches wide, respectively)*

the general staff except ordnance officers. After the 1858 army-wide adoption of the so-called Hardee hat, use of the wreathed *US* became common, and chaplains added the insignia in 1864.[4] These insignia normally are made on velvet ovals with the edge traced in gold wire. Four versions are shown in Figs. 9-3 through 9-6. Dealers in insignia and antiques reproduced this type of device in the 1970s, and as these new insignia age, it will be hard to separate them from older, original pieces except by the richness of the true nineteenth-century embroidery and the dark blue or black velvet background, although some original Civil War pieces were cheaply made. By 1858 the background was black velvet, and use of that material continued for many years.

Between 1872 and 1895 general officers and a decreasing number of staff officers continued to wear the silver *US* in a gold wreath as many staff sections obtained branch devices. A late-nineteenth-century cap with insignia is shown in Fig. 9-7.

The popular forage cap of the Civil War often carried the *US* and wreath in the size for the large hat, but some staff officers wore much reduced insignia (Figs. 9-8, 9-9, and 9-10)—miniature insignia not authorized by regulations. These miniatures show a great variation in both the *US* letters and the wreath because of hand embroidery and small regard for regulations. The official illustration shows that the wreath was to be a laurel with berries, and generally a laurel wreath was used, although several other leaves also saw use, including palm. The smaller forage cap insignia just discussed often have indistinct wreaths in which the leaves are indistinguishable.

Photographs in the National Archives show that some general officers removed the letters *US* and substituted stars within the wreath to indicate their rank, and in other cases they reduced the size of the *US* and added small stars above the letters. An example is shown in Fig. 9-11. Occasionally photographs also illustrate Civil War–era wreathed *US* devices with an embroidered volunteer unit number below or in place of the letters.[5]

ENLISTED MEN'S CAP AND HAT INSIGNIA

Only officers wore the embroidered *US* insignia in a wreath; it had no counterpart for enlisted soldiers until sometime between

Fig. 9-3.

Fig. 9-4.

Fig. 9-5.

Fig. 9-6.

Fig. 9-7.

1856 and 1861, when hospital stewards began to wear a brass wreath enclosing the silver-colored metal *US* in Roman letters. Two examples of these wreaths, about $2\frac{1}{2}$ inches wide and $1\frac{1}{2}$ inches high, are in Figs. 9-12 and 9-13. Although the colors of the officers' and hospital stewards' hat devices are identical, it should be noted that the officers' insignia was embroidered and contained old English letters, while the enlisted men's ornament was metal with Roman letters. The metal enlisted men's *US* was replaced by the caduceus in a wreath in 1882.[6]

Officers' *US* Letters on Coat Collars

The next use of the letters *US* as uniform insignia did not come until after the 1892 army adopted the officers' standing-collar sack coat. A collar insignia consisting of gothic letters *US* "of suitable height" on either side of the collar front, followed by the proper branch insignia, was prescribed in

Fig. 9-11.

Fig. 9-8.

Fig. 9-9.

Fig. 9-10.

Fig. 9-7. *An example of an 1872–95 staff officer's cap. The number of officers using the old English* US *decreased during this time as the various staff departments adopted their own branch insignia.*

Figs. 9-8, 9-9, and 9-10. *Some staff officers used these smaller insignia during the Civil War rather than the prescribed larger size. Since 1960 both smaller and larger versions have been made for collectors and those who reenact battles. As these recently made insignia age and their true history is lost, it will become more difficult to separate them from original insignia such as those shown in the first ten figures. (Wreaths $1\frac{3}{8}$, $1\frac{5}{16}$, and $1\frac{3}{8}$ inches wide, respectively)*

Fig. 9-11. *This general has added a star above the* US *on his cap. Photographs indicate that this was a common addition.*

1895. These collar letters were of bullion embroidery, metal imitation embroidery, or smooth metal and were in gilt or gold except for those of the Corps of Engineers (and in 1901 some medical personnel), who wore silver so the letters would match the color of their branch insignia (Fig. 9-14).[7]

Generally, before 1903, *US* insignia were (1) embroidered as part of the coat collar, (2) imitation-embroidered letters 11/16 inch high with separate periods (Fig. 9-15), or (3) separate smooth metal letters and periods (Fig. 9-16). Most early letters were separate and fastened to the coat collar by inserting wires (soldered to the letter or

Fig. 9-12.

Fig. 9-13.

Figs. 9-12 and 9-13. *Brass wreaths enclosing silver Roman letters* US *were the cap insignia used by hospital stewards. These Civil War insignia lasted until 1882, when a caduceus replaced the* US. *(Each wreath 2 19/32 inches wide)*

Fig. 9-14.

Fig. 9-14. *With the introduction of the 1895 coat came the collar insignia* US. *The most common of the early insignia were either embroidered directly onto the collar or were separate letters and periods made from metal.*

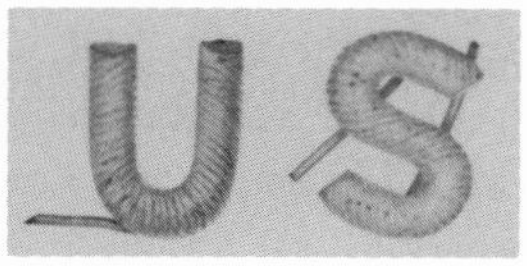

Fig. 9-15.

Fig. 9-15. *Imitation embroidered Regular Army collar letters of the type used from 1895 until about 1903. (Each letter 13/32 inch wide)*

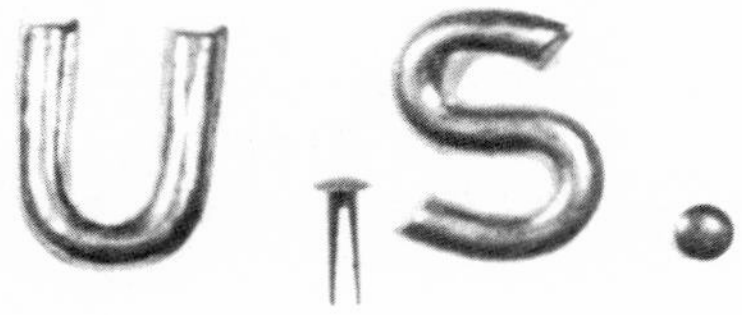

Fig. 9-16.

Fig. 9-16. *A set of the smooth letters introduced in 1895. These letters have small loops on the reverse by which they were sewed to the collar. Periods were made with one small sewing loop or were made with two tines that could be bent over once they were inserted through the collar. A side view of such a period is shown between the two letters.*

Fig. 9-17. *Some insignia were made by taking the separate letters and periods and soldering them to small metal stays, as in this example. In this case the resulting insignia was fastened to the collar with small wires. (1 5/32 inches wide)*

Fig. 9-18. *The initial technique of fastening separate pieces to make one insignia was used in this 1905 or later bronze-colored insignia. (1 inch wide)*

Fig. 9-19. *Separately made brass pieces, soldered together and affixed with a pin back, typical of those made in 1902. (1 5/32 inches wide)*

period back) through the collar. In other cases the letters or periods have small metal loops for sewing them to the collar. The next logical evolutionary step was to join the two letters and two periods with small bars underneath and then add attaching wires or sew-on loops to the composite insignia. An example is shown in Fig. 9-17. Army officers' insignia made the transition from separate to joined letters about the time of the Spanish-American War. Generally the pre-1902 one-piece devices were made by fastening the letters to parallel stays, with round periods placed after the letters. The square periods, first adopted in 1898, were used on those *US* insignia made from one piece of metal. The earlier practice was to solder each letter and period together, but it took a few years for one-piece *US* insignia to come into wide use. The older construction style lingered in some instances, as exemplified by the post-1905 bronze insignia shown in Fig. 9-18, with round periods and attaching wires. Another transition insignia, shown in Fig. 9-19, is a composite piece soldered together but with the more practical pin back.

After a two-year absence during which officers wore an eagle, the gothic *US* returned in June 1905.[8] The letters were 5/8 inch high with square periods. Examples are shown in Figs. 9-20 (gilt), 9-21 (bronze), 9-22 (bronze, made in France during World War I), and 9-23 (silver for engineers). On shirts some officers used 3/8-inch-high insignia in dull bronze as shown in Figs. 9-24 and 9-25, the latter made from separate letters soldered to stays.

Some personal preference was recognized in both size and style, since either embroidered or etruscan insignia were optional for officers' uniforms, and many early regulations stated the size was to be "of suitable height,"

Fig. 9-17.

Fig. 9-18.

Fig. 9-19.

Fig. 9-20.

Fig. 9-21.

Fig. 9-22.

Fig. 9-23.

Fig. 9-24.

Fig. 9-25.

Fig. 9-26.

Fig. 9-27.

Fig. 9-28.

Fig. 9-29.

Fig. 9-30.

Fig. 9-20. *Block* US *insignia in gilt for high-collar dress coats, used by enlisted men beginning in 1903 and by officers beginning in 1905. (1 13/64 inches wide)*

Fig. 9-21. *Bronze* US *insignia of prescribed size, with round periods and a supporting bar at the top between letters. (1 7/32 inches wide)*

Fig. 9-22. *While this insignia is of a common design worn by officers during World War I, the fastener shows it was made in France. (1 13/64 inches wide)*

Fig. 9-23. *Most post-1904* US *letters of this general style could be worn by either officers or enlisted men. This particular insignia is silver, which shows it was used only by Corps of Engineers Regular Army officers. (1 1/8 inches wide)*

Figs. 9-24 and 9-25. *Small bronze* US *insignia that Regular Army officers wore on shirt collars. The piece in Fig. 9-25 was made from separate letters soldered to two small strips. (25/32 and 19/32 inch wide, respectively)*

Fig. 9-26. *For a few years the army failed to specify a particular size of* US *insignia. This intermediate size selected by a vendor could fit neatly onto either shirt or coat collar. (1 3/32 inches wide)*

Fig. 9-27. *A* US *bronze insignia taller than normal. (29/32 inch wide)*

Fig. 9-28. *Officers were to wear this size of* US *on the lapel coat starting in 1926. (53/64 inch wide)*

Fig. 9-29. *A graduate of the Army School of Nursing wore this brass, slightly oversized insignia during the late 1920s and the 1930s. (13/16 inch wide)*

Fig. 9-30. *A typical variation of an officers' national insignia made before and during World War II. (61/64 inch wide)*

but then noted that 1/2 inch was "preferable."[9] In actual practice, officers wore metal letters almost exclusively by 1902, although some embroidered insignia survived. Several sizes are found today, although regulations called for an official height of 5/8 inch when a size was finally specified, and such variations are shown in Fig. 9-26, 1/2 inch high, and Fig. 9-27, 11/16 inch high.

War Department General Order 73 of 7 August 1918 made a major effort to consolidate the Regular Army, reserve, National Guard, and National Army forces. The War Department's intentions were clear: "This country has but one army—the United States Army. It includes all of the land forces in the service of the United States. . . . The insignia now prescribed for the Regular Army shall hereafter be worn by the United States Army." Although the plain *US* letters were to replace all previous variations, in practice the *USR, USNA,* and other variations discussed in the following sections continued until the army again called for them in 1919.[10]

New regulations of October 1921 prescribed 5/8-inch-high letters for the standing collar. White uniforms reintroduced the gilt *US,* but the bronze letters stayed until October 1923. The gilt *US,* 5/8 inch high, continued for the life of the high-collar coat into the late 1920s. Smaller variations exist as a result of the statement in regulations allowing shirt insignia to be "approximately 3/4 the linear dimensions" of standard insignia, and most are about 7/16 inch high. For use on the lapel or roll-collar coat in December 1926, smaller *US* letters, officially 7/16 inch high (Fig. 9-28), came into use.[11] Most officers wore slightly larger insignia, such as that shown in Fig. 9-29, worn by a nurse in the 1930s, or a similar example shown in Fig. 9-30.

Metal insignia would snag on parachute harness, so while most officers continued with metal insignia, pilots wore bullion-embroidered letters and flying cadets wore silk-embroidered insignia from 1926 until 1938, when cadets and Air Corps officers adopted metal letters. Sizes were 7/16 inch except for Air Corps officers' 5/16-inch insignia; even flying cadets wore the larger size (Fig. 9-31). In December 1928 National Guard aviation officers began to wear the larger metal *US,* while Regular Army Air Corps officers' letters remained embroidered in the smaller size. By the start of World War II the size and material differences had disappeared; all commissioned and warrant officers wore 7/16-inch-high *US.*[12]

Many officers wore embroidered *US* during and after World War II on an optional basis, although metal was prescribed until 1951, when embroidery again became optional. Four examples are shown in Figs. 9-32 through 9-35. When subdued insignia

Fig. 9-31.

Fig. 9-31. *This 1944 aviation cadet wears the* US *and Air Corps insignia.*

Fig. 9-32. *A bullion-embroidered* US *made during World War II. (Embroidery 7/8 inch wide)*

Figs. 9-33 and 9-34. *Yellow embroidered insignia for the shade 51 coat used during and after World War II. These two examples give some indication of the size of the insignia made during the 1940s. (Embroidery 27/32 inch and 15/64 inches wide, respectively)*

Fig. 9-35. *This officers'* US *is on a khaki cotton background. (Embroidery 59/64 inch wide)*

came in during the Vietnam War, they were worn by women officers on wool serge field coats.[13] These standard *US* letters were worn in ways not in regulations by West Point cadets and on fatigue uniforms by military intelligence agents.

The secretary of war authorized flying cadets special uniforms in March 1926. As has been noted, these cadets had special insignia which included silk-embroidered letters on the right collar of the coat and a silk Air Service insignia on the left collar.[14] Size was not specified. In December 1928 insignia changed so that cadets could wear the silk-embroidered 7/16-inch-high *US* on the slate blue coat collar, with the embroidered Air Corps device on the lapel (see Fig. 38-48 in chapter 38, "Aviation").

Enlisted Men's Outline US

With the 1902 change in enlisted uniforms, enlisted men started to wear the letters *US.* The bronze and gilt 1903 issue insignia both were made with separate letters and periods soldered onto two bronze strips, as shown in Fig. 9-19. The official construction clearly changed in 1905, and the *US* with square periods struck from one piece of metal, similar to those of Fig. 9-20, came into use.[15] In 1910 the bronze outline *US* letters were replaced by *US* on a 1-inch disk for service wear, but for blue uniforms men continued to wear the 1902 outline letters.

Enlisted Men's Disks Bearing *US*

An apparent minor change with far-reaching consequences occurred in 1910 when the War Department prescribed dull bronze disks, 1 inch in diameter, for service uniforms. Men wore two pairs of disks. One pair, with raised letters *US,* was worn with one disk on each side of the collar. Two disks with devices showing the branch of service were placed 1 inch to the rear of the *US* disks, as shown in Fig. 68-9 in chapter 68, "Early Khaki Uniforms." When the four disks were reduced to two in 1911, the disk on the right collar was to have the letters *US* (Fig. 9-36), and the one on the left the branch insignia.[16] Many variation of the *US* disks exist, since every soldier wore the letters. One such deviation from the regulation version is shown in Fig. 9-37. Note that from 1910 to 1917 the Army Service School Detachment members wore gilt collar disks, one bearing the cogged wheel with crossed hammer and quill pen and the other bearing the letters *US,* on the dress uniform. These insignia are further discussed in chapter 37, "Service School Detachments."

In December 1917 enlisted regulars started to wear a disk with the letters *US* reduced in size and with a regimental or battalion number added below, simplifying the issue of bronze disks to many numbered units. For example, a *US* with a *3* could be issued to the 3d Cavalry, 3d Infantry, 3d Signal Battalion, or any other 3d unit (Fig. 9-38). In actual practice such numbered disks had been made as early as August 1917.[17] Two interesting but unofficial disks with unit designation are shown in Figs. 9-39 and 9-40; they are evidently intended for use when veterans wore their uniforms in cere-

Fig. 9-32.

Fig. 9-33.

Fig. 9-34.

Fig. 9-35.

monies and parades. An unusual *US* collar disk made in Germany for the occupation army is shown in Fig. 9-41. It is more field grey than dull bronze, and its interior is hollow like that of a uniform button.

Shortly after World War I, all soldiers began wearing bright gilt disk insignia (Figs. 9-42, 9-43, and 9-44). When the army adopted roll-collar uniforms, soldiers wore the *US* disk on the right collar. The *US* disks of the 1920s and 1930s had letters 1/2 inch high and 3/4 inch wide, with a background of crosshatched lines and small shields (Figs. 9-45 and 9-46).[18] The 1940 draft swelled the army's ranks, and many units received two-piece insignia with the regimental or battalion number placed below the punctuated letters, as shown in Fig. 9-47. The large number indicates that it was intended for a federalized National Guard unit. A 1930s two-piece disk worn by a 7th regiment is shown in Fig. 9-48, and another variation made during World War II had the letters removable but the number firmly attached to the disk background (Fig. 9-49). The style most universally worn during World War II and still available was made with embossed letters on a thin brass stamping (Fig. 9-50), with letters 7/16 inch high. Some industrious merchants in Burma had enlisted insignia embroidered for U.S. servicemen stationed in the area. One result is shown in Fig. 9-51.

Metal shortage caused some plastic disks to be made during World War II. Two examples are illustrated in Figs. 9-52 and 9-53. That of Fig. 9-52 is made from painted clear plastic and affixed with a metal screw post. That of Fig. 9-53 has deep letters, in contrast to the slightly raised *US* of the previous example, and in addition is made from one piece of gold-colored plastic, including the fastening post.

Domed-shaped disks appearing at the close of World War II included gold and silver colors (Figs. 9-54 and 9-55, respectively), with the latter shown also made to include a buff enameled edge for unofficial use by Quartermaster Corps soldiers. Some soldiers preferred the silver or white gold insignia that could be polished with a soft, clean cloth. These domed disks also came with unit numbers below the letters (Fig. 9-56) and even with miniature airborne wings (Fig. 9-57). Formal use of the regimental numbers under the *US* ended in early 1947,[19] although in practice many men quit wearing them during World War II, while other units used them into the 1950s. The last *US*

Fig. 9-36.

Fig. 9-37.

Fig. 9-38.

Fig. 9-39.

Fig. 9-40.

Fig. 9-41.

Fig. 9-42.

Fig. 9-43.

Fig. 9-44.

Fig. 9-45.

Fig. 9-46.

Fig. 9-47.

Fig. 9-36. *A typical enlisted men's 1910–23 bronze "button insignia" worn on the right collar. (1 inch in diameter)*

Fig. 9-37. *A World War I enlisted men's insignia variation with only one round period. (1 inch in diameter)*

Fig. 9-38. *Beginning in 1917 and continuing through 1919, many units wore* US *disks like this with the unit number (usually for regiment or separate battalion) below. (1 inch in diameter)*

Fig. 9-39. *A unique and highly unauthorized enlisted men's collar disk with the unit designation around the edge.*

Fig. 9-40. *Some veterans bought these disks to replace lost insignia or just to show their service had been honorable. (1 1/64 inches wide)*

Fig. 9-41. *A grey metal enlisted men's insignia made in Germany for occupation forces. (1 inch in diameter)*

Figs. 9-42, 9-43, and 9-44. *Gilt enlisted men's* US *disks used after World War I and made from the dies intended for bronze insignia. (1 inch, 1 1/32 inches, and 1 1/64 inches in diameter, respectively)*

Fig. 9-45. *A 1924–36 official insignia made for issue by the army to enlisted men. (1 3/64 inches in diameter)*

Fig. 9-46. *While this type of 1924–36 gilt disk usually showed a regimental number, it could also indicate other assignments, including brigade and division headquarters. (1 inch in diameter)*

Fig. 9-47. *A screw-back, separable enlisted soldiers' insignia with regimental number below. This is typical of World War II* US *insignia. (1 inch in diameter)*

Fig. 9-48.

Fig. 9-49.

Fig. 9-50.

Fig. 9-51.

Fig. 9-52.

Fig. 9-53.

Fig. 9-54.

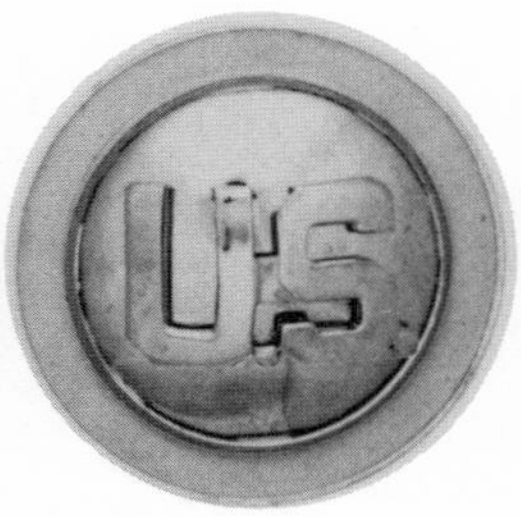

Fig. 9-55.

Fig. 9-56.

Fig. 9-57.

Fig. 9-58.

Fig. 9-59.

Figs. 9-48 and 9-49. *Variations of World War II enlisted soldiers' disks bearing unit numbers. (Each 1 inch in diameter)*

Fig. 9-50. *A stamped disk of the type first made in 1943. Most soldiers did not wear these but preferred to buy the separable insignia. (1 inch in diameter)*

Fig. 9-51. *A "disk" hand-embroidered in India during World War II. The design is yellow on a khaki background. (Embroidery 1 1/32 inches in diameter)*

Figs. 9-52 and 9-53. *To reduce metal shortages, some World War II insignia such as these were made of plastic. The disk in Fig. 9-52 was made from a clear plastic and painted gold on the bottom so the color showed through. The apparent surface flaws are caused by the paint flaking that has occurred over the years. The disk in Fig. 9-53 is made from a gold-colored plastic. (15/16 and 1 inch in diameter, respectively)*

Fig. 9-54. *A post–World War II domed (convex) disk. (1 inch in diameter)*

Fig. 9-55. *This silver-plated, domed insignia with a buff enameled edge (for the Quartermaster Corps) was made during or shortly after the close of the Korean War. The colored trim and the background disk were made as one piece. (1 23/64 inches wide)*

Figs. 9-56 and 9-57. *Two 1950s enlisted soldiers' insignia made for airborne units. (1 1/32 inches and 1 inch in diameter, respectively)*

Fig. 9-58. *A Vietnamese-made* US *disk from about 1968. (31/32 inch in diameter)*

Fig. 9-59. *A set of Spanish-American War collar letters for a volunteer force officer to wear on the sack coat.*

disk shown (Fig. 9-58) was made in Vietnam and was intended for wear by soldiers upon their departure when they wore khaki uniforms.

Starting in July 1918, recruits wore *US* disks on both sides of the collar, the left insignia being replaced by an appropriate branch insignia upon assignment after training. This practice has continued to the present, and for a period during World War II, wearing two *US* disks meant officially that the soldier was unassigned. During the first three years of World War II the War Department caused enlisted men to wear a pair of plain *US* insignia (no branch insignia) until their arrival at a replacement training center, whereupon one plain *US* was exchanged for an insignia of the appropriate arm or service. Then, "upon assignment to a numbered unit, the remaining insignia, U.S. plain, will be exchanged for collar insignia, U.S. with appropriate number."[20] During the 1947–51 period, when most enlisted personnel wore two pairs of disks, two *US* insignia on the collars and bare lapels indicated a training assignment, since replacement of the branch disks with *US* disks would have otherwise resulted in the wearing of four *US* disks.

Officers' *USV*

Volunteer officers wore letters *USV* on the collar of the 1895 sack coat, just as regular officers wore the letters *US* (Fig. 9-59). Fig. 9-60 shows the three separate letters, which usually were worn with separate periods. Khaki coats were specifically noted in regulations as not to have the *USV* letters, although many volunteers, including Teddy Roosevelt, did wear the letters on them (Fig. 9-61). Starting in 1903 and continuing until June 1905, the eagle from the Great Seal of the United States, followed by a *V,* replaced the *USV.* After June 1905 both officers and enlisted volunteers again wore *USV* block letters, in silver for Corps of Engineers officers and gilt for other officers and enlisted men, until the army eliminated dress uniforms during World War I.[21]

During World War I the army could not decide whether or not to distinguish nonregular officers by the use of some letters other than the *US.* Insignia for the National Guard, the National Army, and the regular forces were continuously mentioned, but volunteers received only occasional notice, since volunteer units did not serve in World War I. However, the army wanted to keep the volunteer insignia active, should volunteers later be required, and in May 1919 a new collar device appeared: the black block letters *US* with a small gilt *V* superimposed in the center (Fig. 9-62).[22]

Enlisted Men's *USV*

Enlisted volunteers wore gilt letters *USV* on the 1902 dress uniforms until 1917, with identical bronze block letters (Fig. 9-63) for service clothing. After the introduction of the "button insignia" (disks) in 1910, the official description called for "block letters with a square period after each letter."[23] Presumably this is the insignia shown in Fig. 9-64 with a large *S* flanked by slightly smaller letters *U* and *V* of a similar character, although in the bronze disks periods were normally omitted, as in this case.

In December 1917 the army prescribed the letters *US* with raised letter *V* in the center block (Fig. 9-64) and where appropriate the number below the letters. Shortly afterward this last design appeared on disks again, this time with a background of crosshatched lines and small shields (Figs. 9-65 and 9-66). The last date of authorized wear is not known, but a general staff memorandum dated 30 August 1920 lists the *US* with *V,* both with and without a number, as still intended for use. For dress uniforms the officer outline letters were prescribed in May 1919, but regulations fail to mention the design again, and volunteers subsequently disappeared from uniform regulations.[24]

Fig. 9-62.

Fig. 9-63.

Fig. 9-64.

Fig. 9-65.

Fig. 9-66.

Fig. 9-60.

Fig. 9-61.

Fig. 9-60. *A turn-of-the-century officer from Michigan wearing the* USV *insignia of a volunteer.*

Fig. 9-61. *Theodore Roosevelt in his uniform as colonel of the 1st U.S. Volunteer Cavalry (the Rough Riders). Roosevelt is wearing several incorrect insignia, including the* USV *collar letters, which should not have been worn on this uniform.*

Fig. 9-62. *Teddy Roosevelt and others who wanted to raise volunteer forces for World War I could not prevail over the War Department in 1917 and 1918, and volunteer units were not raised. Regulations intermittently continued to provide for volunteer insignia despite the immediate policy decisions, and this officers' collar piece was prescribed in March 1919. The* V *is gold-colored on a bronze* US. *($1\frac{13}{64}$ inches wide)*

Fig. 9-63. *Block letters for U.S. volunteers made in the 1902 style. If the nation had asked for volunteer units, both officers and enlisted men would have used these insignia. Similar gilt letters were prescribed for dress uniforms. ($1\frac{41}{64}$ inches wide)*

Fig. 9-64. *A volunteer enlisted men's bronze "button insignia" for the service uniform, 1910–17. (1 inch in diameter)*

Fig. 9-65. *An example of the enlisted volunteers' collar disk prescribed in December 1917.*

Fig. 9-66. *Like all enlisted volunteers' insignia on disks, this one was never worn, because volunteer units were not activated when disk insignia were used. This was the last version of volunteer force enlisted insignia that regulations prescribed.*

Officers' *USR*

The Reserve Corps is a twentieth-century development. Although reserve units predate the Revolutionary War, and the reserves today trace their history to 1908 with the formation of the Medical Reserve Corps, in reality most reserves were created by the 1916 National Defense Act. As a consequence, the block letters *USR* came into use then (Fig. 9-67 for nonengineers and Fig. 9-68 in silver for engineers). All reserve officers wore bronze insignia on the service uniform (Fig. 9-69), and consequently many variations appeared (Fig. 9-70 for one), especially during World War I.[25] Shirt-sized *USR* letters (Figs. 9-71, 9-72, and 9-73) were worn by some officers before and during World War I, while Fig. 9-74 shows a silver engineer's shirt insignia.

Enlisted men changed to *US* with a small *R* at the center in December 1917, but the officers' regulation insignia remained the triple letters. Despite this, makers produced and officers wore unauthorized designs (Fig. 9-75). A special investigation in June 1918 showed that even the Quartermaster Corps officers in charge of uniforms and insignia were wearing the nonregulation *US* with raised *R* at the center rather than the prescribed *USR*.[26] Typical unauthorized devices came with the letters *US* 5/8 inch high with gilt *R* in a box (Fig. 9-76) and 9/16 inch high with bronze *R* (Fig. 9-77). A similar smaller shirt insignia is illustrated in Fig. 9-78. A version for reserve

Fig. 9-67. *Most reserve forces were formed as a result of the 1916 Defense Act. This U.S. Reserve gilt collar insignia is for the dress uniform, 1916–17, and was for use by both officers and enlisted men. (1 3/4 inches wide)*

Fig. 9-68. *Corps of Engineers reserve officers wore silver* USR *insignia, like this one, on dress uniforms starting in 1916.*

Fig. 9-69. *The uniform and insignia tell that this is a World War I reserve medical doctor.*

Fig. 9-70. *An officer's standing-collar coat insignia for the service uniform, World War I. (1 13/16 inches wide)*

Figs. 9-71, 9-72, and 9-73. *Three variations of officers' shirt collar insignia, World War I U.S. Reserves. (1 5/16, 1 3/16, and 1 7/64 inches wide, respectively)*

Fig. 9-74. *A shirt collar insignia in silver for Corps of Engineers reserve officers. The use of dress insignia for shirts was not authorized during the same time as the* USR *device, so use of this piece cannot be documented. (1 1/8 inches wide)*

Figs. 9-75, 9-76, 9-77, 9-78, and 9-79. *Bronze* US *with superimposed* R *(for reserve). Although used during World War I, this style of insignia was not prescribed until after the war's close. (1 11/64 inches, 1 21/64 inches, 1 7/32 inches, 49/64 inch, and 1 5/32 inches wide, respectively)*

Fig. 9-80. *A 1919–22 officers' white uniform insignia, with gilt* US *and small central box with a black painted* R. *(1 5/16 inches wide)*

Fig. 9-67.

Fig. 9-68.

Fig. 9-69.

Fig. 9-70.

Fig. 9-71.

Fig. 9-72.

Fig. 9-73.

Fig. 9-74.

Fig. 9-75.

Fig. 9-76.

Fig. 9-78.

Fig. 9-77.

Fig. 9-79.

Fig. 9-80.

Fig. 9-82.

Fig. 9-83.

Fig. 9-84.

Fig. 9-85.

Fig. 9-86.

Fig. 9-87.

Fig. 9-91.

Fig. 9-92.

Fig. 9-88.

Fig. 9-89.

Fig. 9-90.

officers appeared with the outline gilt *R* directly superimposed on the *US* (Fig. 9-79).

Although War Department General Orders 73, 17 August 1918, abolished the special three letters *USR*, army officials evidently overlooked this in subsequent uniform changes. In any event, officers continued to wear *USR* and *US* with superimposed *R*. In May 1919 the army allowed gilt insignia for dress and white uniforms with either the raised *R* on a center block (Fig. 9-80) or a new pattern without the block (Fig. 9-81). Finally most *US* variations disappeared, but one remained in October 1921: a 5/8-inch-high *US* with 1/4-inch *R* superimposed.[27] Shirt-sized insignia (Fig. 9-82) also came in this postwar pattern.

In January 1922 the War Department abolished the officers' *US* insignia "with block R superimposed" and established the letters *US* for all reserve officers.[28] There has been no subsequent change in this policy.

Enlisted Men's *USR*

With the major introduction of reserves in 1916, the army prescribed even-sized gilt block letters for the enlisted dress uniforms. Disks with even-sized block letters (Figs. 9-83 and 9-84) as well as uneven script letters (Fig. 9-85) were used on service uniforms. In December 1917 the small *R* centered over the larger *US* was authorized, and also those bearing regimental numbers. Officially these disks were replaced in May 1918, but the small gilt *R* over the *US* on a bronze disk was revised in May 1919. The phase-out of this insignia is difficult to determine, since it was in use in October 1921, but by January 1922 only the officers' device is mentioned, although by October 1923 this disk was surely obsolete. Starting in 1923 the army introduced gilt disks, and because the enlisted *US* with *R* was by then nonregulation, gilt disks of the type illustrated in Fig. 9-86 should not exist, but probably some reservists wore them in the 1920s. Perhaps the last government-approved *US* with *R* is one with a background of lines and shields with a gilt *R* (Fig. 9-87).[29]

Officers' *USNA*

The World War I draft army was the National Army, as distinguished from the Regular Army or the federalized National Guard. Regulations stated that to distinguish the National Army " . . . the letters US as a base will have superimposed . . . the letters NA." Examples are shown in Figs. 9-88, 9-89, and 9-90 for coats and Figs. 9-91 and 9-92 for shirts. From mid-1917 until August 1918, gilt devices (Fig. 9-93) were authorized for dress uniforms (Corps of Engineers officers wore silver), although most men wore only service uniforms.[30]

Fig. 9-81. *A later version of the insignia shown in Fig. 9-80, but without the small central box. The plain superimposed letter* R *was typically used after the close of World War I. (1 21/64 inches wide)*

Fig. 9-82. *An all-gilt reserve officers' insignia for a shirt. The wearing of a small, nonbronze device does not fit into the scheme of garments and insignia finishes during the time such a design was used. It is probable that the insignia was made when brass insignia were in common use, after the design was obsolete. (49/64 inch wide)*

Figs. 9-83, 9-84, and 9-85. *Three styles of enlisted reserve collar disks, 1910–17. Many reservists were issued the* US *disks rather than the* USR.

Figs. 9-86 and 9-87. *Two gilt enlisted soldiers' insignia for reserves, after World War I.*

Figs. 9-88, 9-89, and 9-90. *Officers of the National Army (the drafted forces) of World War I wore coat collar insignia like these three bronze versions. These insignia were authorized from mid-1917 until 1918, but their use continued through the time draftees were discharged. The insignia of Fig. 9-90 was made from a shiny bronze metal. (1 1/64, 1 1/4, and 1 11/64 inches wide, respectively)*

Figs. 9-91 and 9-92. *Officers' bronze National Army shirt collar insignia. These come in many sizes and styles. (25/32 and 45/64 inch wide, respectively)*

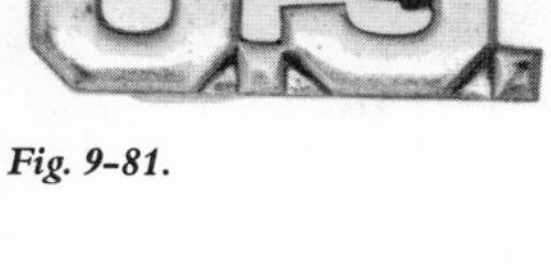

Fig. 9-81.

Enlisted Men's *USNA*

Enlisted men's 1-inch disk insignia created for the National Army differed from the officers' block letters. In July 1917 came the *USNA* monogram with large *NA* letters almost smothering the flanking *US* (Fig. 9-94). A similar insignia made from a different die with thin letters is shown in Fig. 9-95.[31] This concept gave enlisted men insignia not at all similar to the officers' counterpart, although the nonregulation enlisted men's disk shown in Fig. 9-96 has large block *US* with small *NA* between.

In some areas the sequence of insignia change during World War I becomes so confused that it is difficult to interpret and almost impossible to record. National Army devices fall into this category. For example, *National Geographic* magazine for October 1917 includes photographs of insignia not prescribed in regulations until more than seven months after its publication.[32] Examination of photographs of officers and soldiers in 1918 uniforms shows a majority are still wearing insignia patterns specified in 1917 that the War Department had changed one or more times. This can be partially accounted for by the fact that it was not always easy to purchase the newest patterns of branch insignia or *US* letter insignia. An equal reason was that soldiers enjoyed wearing obsolete patterns, which marked them as old-timers and veteran campaigners. They were in no hurry to rush out and buy the newest pattern.

Change one to Special Regulation 42, dated December 1917, prescribed the center block with *NA* for bronze *US* disks worn by the National Army (Fig. 9-97). This change was necessary to allow the use of regimental or battalion numbers below the *US* when appropriate.[33] These insignia were, however, manufactured well before December, for there are photographs of them in the October 1917 *National Geographic.* The disk shown in Fig. 9-98 was worn by the 301st regiments, battalions, or other units of the 76th Division. The *USNA* disk was also made in gilt metal after World War I (Fig. 9-99), although it was not prescribed in regulations. May 1918 directives ended the manufacture of National Army disks; supplies were to be issued until exhausted.[34] A mysterious disk is the gilt insignia shown in Fig. 9-100, which may have been intended for the National Army.

State Organizations in World War I

The various military organizations created during World War I caused a bewildering variety of insignia. It is important to remember the three types of state-associated units that were active during the World War I period so that some order may be given to the many insignia which were worn.

The best-known units were federally recognized National Guard organizations. Insignia associated with the federalized National Guard include the letters *US* and abbreviations for the appropriate state

Fig. 9-93.

Fig. 9-93. An officers' gilt National Army collar insignia from about World War I. Use of these insignia and the associated blue or white uniforms was infrequent during this time. (1 1/4 inches wide)

Fig. 9-94.

Fig. 9-95.

Figs. 9-94 and 9-95. One of the few times enlisted men's basic design differed from the officers' was with the July 1917 design for the National Army. Two versions are shown.

Fig. 9-96.

Fig. 9-96. A nonregulation enlisted men's collar disk for the National Army, the World War I draft army.

Fig. 9-97.

Fig. 9-98.

Figs. 9-97 and 9-98. Many men of the National Army (divisions numbered 76 and higher) wore insignia of one of these two types, with or without unit number.

Fig. 9-99.

Fig. 9-99. This unusual gilt National Army disk may have been used after the war's end to dress up a coat for the trip home.

Fig. 9-100.

Fig. 9-100. An all-gilt disk with large letters applied. Possible meanings for the letters include "National Army" or "N——Academy."

Fig. 9-101.

Fig. 9-101. An officers' National Guard insignia of the design specified in July 1917. (1 5/64 inches wide)

Fig. 9-102.

Fig. 9-102. This National Guard officers' insignia was made in England during World War I and has two large British-style fastening loops on the back. (1 5/32 inches wide)

Fig. 9-103.

Fig. 9-103. This shiny bronze National Guard officers' insignia has a separately made central box applied to the US. (1 3/16 inches wide)

or *NG* for both officers' and enlisted men's insignia. Not all National Guard units were federalized during World War I, and the National Guard organizations remaining under state control and jurisdiction of the Militia Bureau had the plain state letters as the basic insignia. This was the same insignia used by militia before 1916 or by federalized National Guard from late 1916 to mid-1917. When the National Guard was federalized during the Mexican border crisis of 1916 and the world wars, most states created other units under control of the governor to perform military duties in times of flood or other crisis. Because the National Guard could be called into federal service at any time, many states formed another organization that was fully under state control. Members of these supplemental units were not exempt from the federal draft, so a large part of these state forces was composed of men above draft age or men in critical occupations. Insignia for these organizations were required to be different from those of the various federal services, including the federalized National Guard, or from the National Guard left under state control. These state forces had various titles, including home guards, state guards, state militia, constabulary, and defense leagues.[35]

In some cases states continued to have state guards or state militias long after all of the National Guard had reverted to state control. Because of this close relationship and interchange of missions, the insignia of these units are intertwined. The National Guard devices involving the letters *US* will be addressed first, followed by insignia used by the National Guard without the abbreviation *US,* and finally by insignia of the state militias.

Officers' *USNG*

The large block letters *US* with the superimposed rectangle bearing *NG* was prescribed in July 1917. Three versions of this bronze insignia are shown in Figs. 9-101, 9-102, and 9-103. The first, with a pin back and black in color, is typical of World War I; the second has British loops for fastening; and the third is light brown with the *NG* box applied to a plain *US* although regulations prescribed these in gilt for the dress uniform, with the usual exception of the Corps of Engineers. Small shirt-sized bright bronze letters are shown in Fig. 9-104. Officially in August

Fig. 9-104.

Fig. 9-105.

Fig. 9-106.

Fig. 9-107.

Fig. 9-108.

Fig. 9-109.

Fig. 9-110.

1918 the standard letters *US* replaced this insignia, although officers continued to use the *USNG* design "while serviceable." Finally, the army eliminated the *NG* completely in May 1919, when regulations prescribed that state letters would be placed within the center blocks. A small nonregulation gilt insignia with black *NG* is shown in Fig. 9-105, which, judging from its fastener, was made in the 1930s. A totally unauthorized set of bronze letters is shown in Fig. 9-106.[36]

USNG on Disks

The state militias were formed into the National Guard of the various states in June 1916,[37] and National Guard enlisted men initially wore disks bearing state letters such as those illustrated in Figs. 9-107 and 9-108. Other state disks are shown in the section "State Letters before 1923," below. In 1917 the army also created disks carrying *USNG* monograms (Figs. 9-109 and 9-110) and block letters with unit numbers (Figs. 9-111 and 9-112). The history of these *USNG* insignia is identical to that of the *USNA* disks, including the phase-out starting in May 1918. Two gilt *USNG* disks, nonregula-

Fig. 9-104. *A National Guard officers' bronze shirt collar insignia, World War I. (45/64 inch wide)*

Fig. 9-105. *A nonregulation, small gilt insignia probably made in the 1930s. Instead of* NG, *state abbreviations were regulation at that time. (13/16 inch wide)*

Fig. 9-106. *U.S. National Guard letters of this style were never authorized. (2 11/32 inches wide)*

Figs. 9-107 and 9-108. *State letters on disks were worn by federalized enlisted National Guard members before the* USNG *disks (Figs. 9-109 and 9-110) were authorized.*

Figs. 9-109 and 9-110. *National Guard monogram insignia like these were regulation from the middle to the end of 1917, although issue to enlisted men of stocks on hand continued after then.*

tion in color and thus unexplainable, are shown in Figs. 9-113 and 9-114.

U.S. with State Letters for Officers

National Guard officers wore bronze *U.S.* letters 5/8 inch high with gilt state abbreviations 1/4 inch high from May 1919 until they were replaced by gilt insignia initially authorized for the white coat in October 1921 and for all uniforms in October 1923.[38] The large variety of *US* letters, combined with several styles of state abbreviations, makes a comprehensive catalog of all possible combinations

in Fig. 9-118, with the gilt letters for California on a dark bronze rectangle. Smaller, insignia, generally about 57/100 inch high, are shown in Figs. 9-119, 9-120, and 9-121. The first has separately applied letters soldered onto the *US*. A one-piece abbreviation is applied to the other two insignia by means of two small wires on the back of the letters; one hole in the *U* and one in the *S*, with the wires bent to retain the state initials. The *MD* of Fig. 9-121 is of note because the *M* is larger than the *D*.

When the October 1923 switch from bronze to gilt took place, the regulation-size

Fig. 9-111.

Fig. 9-112.

Fig. 9-113.

Fig. 9-114.

Figs. 9-111 and 9-112. *Enlisted National Guard members' insignia, about World War I. Unit numbers normally ran in the 100s and 200s.*

Fig. 9-113. *A gilt National Guard insignia. Use of this insignia can not be explained, since the design became obsolete at the end of 1917 and gilt disks were not prescribed until 1923.*

Fig. 9-114. *It is probable that this gilt disk was made in the late 1920s using old dies initially made for bronze insignia. When gilt disks became authorized, state abbreviations instead of* NG *should have gone on the block* US. *The 144th Infantry Regiment was with the Texas National Guard in the 1920s, although the insignia could have been used by members of other regiments or battalions numbered 144.*

Fig. 9-115.

Fig. 9-116.

Fig. 9-117.

Fig. 9-118.

Fig. 9-119.

Fig. 9-120.

Fig. 9-115. *National Guard officers wore this general style of insignia (bronze* US *and gilt state abbreviations) from May 1919 until October 1923. Two basic types exist: this style with the state letters applied directly to the* US, *and the state abbreviations on a small box which was in turn applied to the* US. *This particular piece was made in England by the J. R. Gaunt Company. (1 21/64 inches wide)*

Fig. 9-116. *Similar to the preceding insignia, this piece has the bars connecting the* ILL *letters acting as supports both to connect the state letters and to fasten the small overlay to the bronze* US. *(1 21/64 inches wide)*

Fig. 9-117. *J. R. Gaunt Company made this insignia. The entire design is made from one piece of metal, and the gold color in the* NY *was applied to the slightly raised letters. A tan color of bronze metal was used to make this insignia.*

very difficult to list. Actual size of the *US* varied from the official height, further making cataloging complicated. It is convenient to divide the state abbreviations into two general categories: (1) separately applied letters, and (2) state letters made as an integral part of the National Guard *US* device.

Made in England by J. R. Gaunt, Fig. 9-115 shows a 73/100-inch-high *US* with letters *NJ* applied. The period following the *N* acts like a bar to help support the state abbreviation. Bars connect the letters *ILL* on another English-made Gaunt piece, 72/100 inch high (Fig. 9-116). A third Gaunt insignia, 67/100 inch tall, has the letters and periods *N.Y.* cast as an integral design (Fig. 9-117). The background bearing the state letters is crosshatched, and the rectangle does not protrude from the overall insignia. A tan bronze was used to make this last insignia. A shiny black bronze was used to make the 65/100-inch-high ornament illustrated

Fig. 9-121.

US was 5/8 inch high with 1/4-inch state letters. Fig. 9-122 illustrates one such example for a Pennsylvania with the *PENN* applied by small wires to the *US* through two holes. More common are the less massive insignia about 65/100 inch high. This 65/100-inch size has abbreviations either in a box or individually applied. Those with a box may have the letters soldered on, as does that of Fig. 9-123 for Arizona, or formed by a stamped overlay, as shown in Fig. 9-124).

Gilt *US* for the National Guard also came approximately 0.57 inch high. Two examples are shown in Fig. 9-125 for Connecticut and Fig. 9-126 for Puerto Rico. In 1925, with the roll-collar coat, the insignia officially became 7/16 inch high, with the abbreviation

Fig. 9-122.

Fig. 9-123.

Fig. 9-124.

Fig. 9-125.

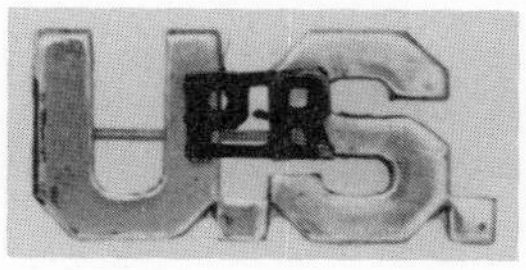

Fig. 9-126.

Fig. 9-127.

Fig. 9-128.

Fig. 9-129.

Fig. 9-130.

Fig. 9-131.

of the state name 3/16 inch high. A great many variations exist in this style; three examples are illustrated in Figs. 9-127, 9-128, and 9-129. Air Corps National Guard officers wore 5/16-inch-high metal *US* letters with state abbreviations between 1925 and 1938 (Figs. 9-130 and 9-131) even though regular Air Corps officers switched to bullion-embroidered *US* in 1928. Finally, state abbreviations on the *US* became obsolete in the spring of 1947, although since October 1940 National Guard personnel inducted into federal service had worn the plain *US*.[39]

Table 9-1 lists most of the War Department–approved state abbreviations. The exceptions are Washington, which initially used *WASH* until 1911 and then switched to *WN;* Arizona, which used *ARIZ* until 1926 and then *AZ;* Hawaii, which used *HAW* between 1926 and 1936 and then switched back to *TH* (for Territory of Hawaii), although in practice *HAW* was frequently used before 1926; and Utah, which used *UT* until 1926, when *UTAH* came into use. Alaska used no abbreviation until one was first specified in 1941. Because the Alaska National Guard was initially organized in 1939, and only members of the National Guard who were not on active duty wore the state letters, its insignia is the scarcest.[40]

US with State Letters on Disks

Regulations of 1919 directed enlisted men "of the Federally recognized National Guard" to wear bronze insignia with gilt state letters.[41] In some cases the regimental number appeared below the *US* and state letters, as in the bronze disk shown in Fig. 9-132.

Gilt disks also carried these schemes, as shown in Fig. 9-133, which included the unit number as well as the state. Figs. 9-134, 9-135, and 9-136 illustrate gilt disks for various states, the first with room to add a regimental number below and the last with the *VA* in separate letters soldered over the *US*. An unusual variation has the *US* and state completely separate, the *US* above the *CAL* (Fig. 9-137).

Fig. 9-118. *This 1919–23 officers' California National Guard insignia was made from a shiny, nearly black bronze metal. (15/16 inches wide)*

Fig. 9-119. *Although smaller than the preceding similar insignia, this one is also from about 1919–23. Each of the state letters was soldered directly to the base* US *instead of the more common practice of having a hole drilled into the* US *and then the state abbreviation, fixed with small wires, tied through the small holes. (1 11/64 inches wide)*

Figs. 9-120 and 9-121. *Two variations of 1919–23 officers' National Guard insignia. Note the two different sizes of letters used in the Maryland abbreviation. (Each 1 11/64 inches wide)*

Fig. 9-122. *National Guard officers were to wear brass* US *insignia with bronze letters applied on the high-collar coat beginning in October 1923. (1 21/64 inches wide)*

Fig. 9-123. *Although regulation in size, this insignia should have had the state letters in bronze instead of gilt. The individual letter s* ARIZ *were soldered to the central box, which was struck as part of the* US*. (1 5/16 inches wide)*

Fig. 9-124. *The brass* OR *(for Oregon) was stamped on a small rectangle, which was in turn applied to a rectangular box similar to that in Fig. 9-123, except for the smaller size. (1 5/16 inches wide)*

Fig. 9-125. *This post-1923 National Guard officers' gilt insignia has each letter painted black and applied separately. (1 3/16 inches wide)*

Fig. 9-126. *The* PR *(for Puerto Rico National Guard) is made from bronze and held to the brass* US *by means of small wires. Size indicates that the insignia was made for the standing-collar coat. (1 5/32 inches wide)*

Figs. 9-127 and 9-128. *Introduced for the roll-collar (lapel) coat was the* US *nominally 7/16 inch high with dark state abbreviation 3/16 inch high. These are the most common variations, with and without internal supporting bars. (Each 29/32 inch wide)*

Fig. 9-129. *The bronze rectangular box with raised letters for Montana complies with the general 1925–47 description of lapel coat and shirt collar insignia, although this variation is not as common as insignia with the abbreviations applied separately. (29/32 inch wide)*

Figs. 9-130 and 9-131. *Between 1925 and 1938, Air Corps National Guard officers were to wear* US *only 5/16 inch high, while other branches wore the 7/16-inch-high size. Properly the letters were to be dark, like the* MASS *shown here, although the all-gilt style shown by the Oklahoma insignia is somewhat more common. (Each 13/16 inch wide)*

Table 9-1. *State Abbreviations Approved by the War Department.*

State	Abbreviation	Notes
Alabama	ALA	
Arizona	ARIZ	Until 1926
	AZ	After 1926
Arkansas	ARK	
California	CAL	
Colorado	COLO	
Connecticut	CT	
Delaware	DEL	
Florida	FLA	
Georgia	GA	
Idaho	IDA	
Illinois	ILL	
Indiana	IND	
Iowa	IOWA	
Kansas	KAN	
Kentucky	KY	
Louisiana	LA	
Maine	ME	
Maryland	MD	
Massachusetts	MASS	
Michigan	MICH	
Minnesota	MINN	
Mississippi	MISS	
Missouri	MO	
Montana	MONT	
Nebraska	NEB	
Nevada	NEV	
New Hampshire	NH	
New Jersey	NJ	
New Mexico	NM	
New York	NY	
North Carolina	NC	
North Dakota	ND	
Ohio	OHIO	
Oklahoma	OK	
Oregon	OR	
Pennsylvania	PA	
Rhode Island	RI	
South Carolina	SC	
South Dakota	SD	
Tennessee	TENN	
Texas	TEX	
Utah	UT	Until 1926
	UTAH	After 1926
Vermont	VT	
Virginia	VA	
Washington	WASH	Until 1911
	WN	After 1911
West Virginia	WVA	
Wisconsin	WIS	
Wyoming	WYO	
Puerto Rico	PR	
Dist of Columbia	DC	
Hawaii	TH	For Territory of Hawaii, before 1926 and after 1936
	HAW	Between 1926 and 1936

Fig. 9-132.

Fig. 9-133.

Fig. 9-134.

Fig. 9-135.

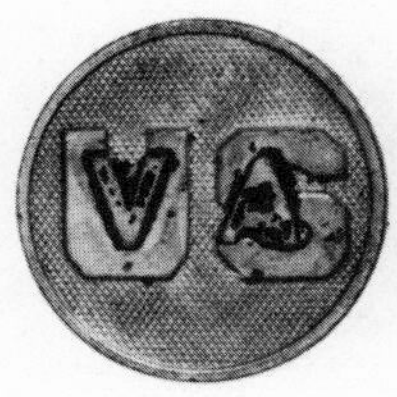

Fig. 9-136.

Fig. 9-137.

Fig. 9-138.

Fig. 9-139.

Fig. 9-132. *Federally recognized National Guard units had enlisted men wear bronze disks with gilt state abbreviations (and sometimes with the unit number below) from 1919 until 1923. While most disks are of the style with the background of lines and small shields, a few units had the background of light stippling as shown in this photograph.*

Fig. 9-133. *Although the background of this disk is the World War I pattern instead of that from the 1920s and 1930s, this gilt enlisted men's insignia otherwise meets the regulations of 1925. Compare it with the insignia shown in Fig. 9-114 for the same unit.*

Figs. 9-134, 9-135, and 9-136. *Three enlisted men's gilt National Guard insignia from the 1920s. The first has room for a unit number to be added, the second resembles some officers' abbreviations, since the letters are in a rectangle, and the third has had black painted letters soldered to a standard* US *disk, although a great deal of the paint has flaked off.*

Fig. 9-137. *An unusual insignia of a totally nonregulation design.*

Figs. 9-138 and 9-139. *Common designs of National Guard enlisted men's insignia prescribed for the 1923–36 period. These general patterns were still issued after they were replaced by the style shown in Figs. 9-142 through 9-146, below.*

Gilt disks with the second pattern of background (crosshatched lines and small shields) were widely worn in the late 1920s and the 1930s. These came in many combinations: *US* with only the state designation (Fig. 9-138) and *US* with the state and with the unit number (Fig. 9-139). Some early disks with a removable design are that of the 185th Regiment from California (Fig. 9-140) and the New York insignia shown in Fig. 9-141. These insignia could be disassembled by removing a nut on the back post, allowing the device to be cleaned.

Beginning in August 1937, two-piece disks with a smooth background became standard issue. These disks came in a wide variety of dies with state and unit designations (Figs. 9-142, 9-143, and 9-144) or with only the state abbreviations (Figs. 9-145 and 9-146). Starting in October 1940, National Guard personnel inducted into active service wore plain *US* disks, and in 1947 the state abbreviations officially ceased completely, although some units evidently used this concept during or after World War II, as shown by the domed disk in Fig. 9-147.[42]

State Letters before 1923

Before 1916 men in many militia units wore collar ornaments consisting of the state name or the state abbreviation, and the use of these is difficult to document without researching each state record from the Spanish-American War to 1916. One such example, shown in Fig. 9-148, shows a soldier from the 31st Michigan Infantry at the time of the Spanish-American War. Photographic evidence indicates that even colleges and universities had members of the local military training bodies wear state letters. Before the 1916 National Defense Act, officers in various state militias wore separate state letters on the 1890s high-collar sack coat. New York maintained a large militia, and as a result, *N* and *Y* are the most common separate letters, similar to the 1895 separate *U* and *S.* Occasionally a mixture of letter styles was used, although not by design. An example from a Wisconsin officer's uniform used three types of smooth letters (Fig. 9-149). In this case two of the letters probably were replaced at different times, resulting in all three different letter styles being used on one uniform.

Shortly after the introduction of separate letters, joined state letters of two basic styles came into use in both gilt and bronze: those with all letters the same size (Fig. 9-150), and those with letters of varying sizes (Fig. 9-151). Other examples of gilt insignia are shown in Figs. 9-152 and 9-153. A coast artilleryman is shown in Fig. 9-154 wearing *NY,* which is typical of the state abbreviations that were made from letters of the same size. Fig. 9-155 is another example of such letters in gilt. Bronze coat-size letters are illustrated in Fig. 9-156. For shirts, small bronze state abbreviations were made, as shown in Fig. 9-157. State letters exist in combination with nonregulation letters, such as those for the New Jersey Volunteers (Fig. 9-158).

The 1916 troubles with Mexico and the National Defense Act of that year caused many National Guard units to be called into federal service for use on the border. The question of what was the proper insignia for these men arose, since the *US* was for regular forces only, the *USV* for volunteers, and the *USR* for reserves. The newly formed National

Fig. 9-140.

Fig. 9-141.

Fig. 9-142.

Fig. 9-143.

Fig. 9-144.

Fig. 9-145.

Fig. 9-146.

Fig. 9-147.

Fig. 9-148.

Figs. 9-140 and 9-141. *These 1930s enlisted men's insignia have the designs separable for cleaning. The state abbreviations are also of the two basic types: on a rectangle and applied to the US separately.*

Figs. 9-142 and 9-143. *Enlisted men's disks of the type generally in use by National Guard units at the start of World War II. Although the size and relative location of the US vary, these both have the state abbreviations made with a single trace, as compared with that of Fig. 9-144.*

Fig. 9-144. *This pattern of National Guard disk with the state letters traced by a double line was in common use at the start of World War II.*

Figs. 9-145 and 9-146. *Two state disks from the late 1930s and early 1940s without unit numbers. Both have screw-post fasteners on the reverse and are of the variety with a flat background.*

Fig. 9-147. *A Kentucky National Guard enlisted soldiers' insignia made for the 149th Infantry Regiment probably between 1946, when the unit returned from the Pacific after World War II, and 1947, when this style of insignia was declared obsolete. The disk has a convex or domed background.*

Fig. 9-148. *Private Isaac Van Syckle, Company K, 31st Michigan Volunteer Infantry. Van Syckle enlisted on 24 June 1898 and wears MICH on his right collar and 31 on the left. Before 1916 use of state letters by either enlisted men or officers was not prescribed by the War Department, and thus use varied from state to state.*

Fig. 9-149. *These three letters, all of different styles, were used on a pre–World War I officer's dress uniform. The W is gilt and flat, the I is raised and of a different pattern, and the S is dark. The owner probably lost letters at different times and replaced them with whatever was available. All of the letters were fastened to the uniform by being sewn through small loops on the reverse.*

Figs. 9-150 and 9-151. *Gilt state letters. At the top of the A for Virginia can be seen a small loop used to sew the insignia to the garment. These two sew-on style state abbreviations are of the two general types commonly seen: those with all letters the same size, and those with two sizes made as one insignia.* ($1\frac{5}{32}$ *inches and* $\frac{7}{8}$ *inch wide, respectively)*

Figs. 9-152 and 9-153. *Two pin-back, gilt state letters, that of Fig. 9-152 with the letters and periods soldered to stays, as was often done about the time of the Spanish-American War and for a few years thereafter. The Iowa insignia of Fig. 9-153, while of similar construction, is more refined, using a square period like that of many later pieces; the supporting stays between the letters are not as wide nor as noticeable as the first construction.* ($1\frac{29}{64}$ *inches and* $\frac{45}{64}$ *inch wide, respectively)*

Fig. 9-149.

Fig. 9-150.

Fig. 9-151.

Fig. 9-152.

Fig. 9-153.

Fig. 9-154.

Fig. 9-154. A member of the New York Coast Artillery Corps' 22d Company sometime during the period 1910–16. This is a typical use of gilt metal letters before World War I, when the states often prescribed their abbreviations as collar insignia.

Fig. 9-155.

Fig. 9-155. C. E. Friend of the Kansas National Guard, 1910. Although the coat and trousers were similar to those of federal troops, the insignia were very different.

Fig. 9-156.

Fig. 9-156. Bronze state letters of this type could have been used by either enlisted men or officers of the National Guard before 1916, but from late 1916 until mid-1917 these were prescribed by the War Department as the insignia of federalized National Guard officers. (1 61/64 inches wide)

Fig. 9-157.

Fig. 9-157. Shirt-sized bronze state insignia from before World War I. (1 5/16 inches wide)

Guard did not fit into any of the above categories. An opinion by the War College Division of the General Staff Corps resulted in a December 1916 regulation change that prescribed the state abbreviation, up to four letters, to be the distinguishing device for National Guard members called into federal service.[43] These insignia came in letters of several styles. The previous militia outline letters would serve for officers, but disks were new. The most common are the letters formed to fit the disk (Fig. 9-159), uniform-size block letters without periods (Fig. 9-160), large letters struck from the same die as that for the disk, large applied letters with and without serifs (Figs. 9-161 and 9-162), small letters struck with the disk (Fig. 9-163), those with periods (Fig. 9-164) and those with uneven letters (Fig. 9-165). Disk insignia with state letters were made for all states, Hawaii, the District of Columbia, and Puerto Rico, although Nevada never organized National Guard units and other states had very small units that may never have worn these insignia. Some states are represented by two or even three abbreviations, which, when combined with the several design styles, make a formidable number of possible state disks. These state disks officially remained in use until the introduction of the *USNG* insignia in July 1917.

In 1918 the Militia Bureau became concerned about the legal implications of various state organizations' wearing of uniforms and insignia similar to those worn by federal forces.[44] State abbreviations, just in recent use, were still available. Because of the concerns and the availability of the letters, the War Department reinstituted use of state letters, this time to be worn by members of the National Guard not under federal control. In practice, some men who had worn the state letters before July 1917 as National Guard members continued to wear such insignia. Fig. 9-159 is such an example, showing in

Fig. 9-158.

Fig. 9-159.

Fig. 9-160.

Fig. 9-161.

Fig. 9-162.

Fig. 9-163.

Fig. 9-164.

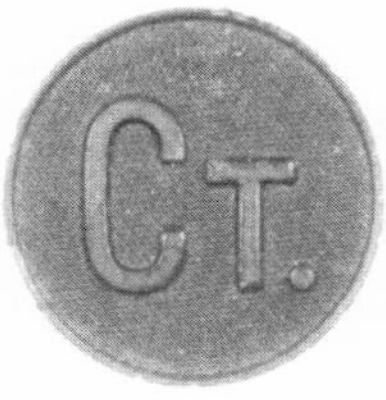

Fig. 9-165.

Fig. 9-166.

Fig. 9-167.

Fig. 9-158. *A gilt state insignia, not called for in national regulations. It could have been worn either by a volunteer unit or by veterans after discharge. (3 1/64 inches long)*

Fig. 9-159. *This late 1918 photo shows use of state letters on a disk being worn in an unofficial manner. Infantry insignia should have been worn in place of the* MASS. *The* US *insignia is on the other collar.*

Figs. 9-160, 9-161, 9-162, 9-163, 9-164, and 9-165. *As a result of the Mexican troubles of 1916 and the resulting federalization of many National Guard units, state letters on disks were instituted as the insignia of state troops called to active duty. These became obsolete in mid-1917 for federal troops, but for state units not in federal service they became the insignia in mid-1918. Shown are six different styles of enlisted men's collar insignia for National Guard troops on active duty, 1916–17, and nonfederal troops after mid-1918 to 1920. The* MD, *Fig. 9-161, has letters with serifs, while the insignia for Pennsylvania (Fig. 9-162) has flat block letters applied. The New Jersey piece (Fig. 9-164) is unusual in that it has periods, while the Connecticut insignia (Fig. 9-165) not only has a period but also follows the earlier design, sometimes used, with the second letter of an abbreviation smaller. The most common style letters are shown in Fig. 9-159.*

Fig. 9-166. *Enlisted men's collar insignia for the Oklahoma State Guard about World War I.*

Fig. 9-167. *Missouri had a greater variety of enlisted men's insignia for home guard units during World War I than did any other state. In this example the small central box contains HG, for Home Guard.*

late 1918 a Massachusetts disk that had been obsolete for over a year for men on active duty and had been returned to use for inactive soldiers.

In May 1918 the Militia Bureau established the policy that all officers of the National Guard not drafted into federal service would wear up to four letters on the coat collar, the letters "forming the authorized abbreviation of the name of the State, Territory, or the District of Columbia. . . . Letters to be 5/8 inch high, of Gothic design." Enlisted men also wore the same style of gilt insignia on dress coat collars, although the height of the letters was not specified. For enlisted men's bronze collar insignia, the same abbreviations of up to four letters were to be placed on a 1-inch-diameter bronze disk—the state letters on disks described above. Regulations called for the regimental or other unit number to go below the state letter when appropriate, although the author does not know of any surviving insignia of that kind.[45]

Abbreviations and Home Guards, World War I

Some states enlisted soldiers who wore abbreviations of their organizations such as insignia for the home or state guards. The Oklahoma State Guard and the Missouri Home Guard, for example, wore *OK SG* (Fig. 9-166) and *MO HG* (Fig. 9-167) during part of World War I. The 1918 Militia Bureau and War Department headquarters directed state units not constituted as National Guard organizations to use any collar and cap device except those resembling the insignia used by the army, navy, or Marine Corps.[46] Examples of these devices are shown for the balance of the chapter, although it is acknowledged that

Fig. 9-168.

Fig. 9-169.

Fig. 9-170.

Fig. 9-171.

Fig. 9-172.

Fig. 9-173.

Fig. 9-174.

Fig. 9-175.

Fig. 9-170. *A bronze state seal for Maine, of the type worn by many National Guard officers during the 1903–1905 period, when Regular Army officers wore the Great Seal of the United States. (1 1/8 inches wide)*

Fig. 9-171. *A gilt state seal for State of Washington officers. Like the insignia shown in Fig. 9-170, the dress versions of this one were generally used from 1903 until 1905. (1 11/32 inches wide)*

Figs. 9-172, 9-173, and 9-174. *Three examples of bronze disks bearing state seals. Various states used this type of insignia for home guards during World War I or for National Guard units before 1917. A few state insignia on enlisted men's collar disks also exist in gilt, such as those for Connecticut. (1 inch, 1 inch, and 1 5/64 inches wide, respectively)*

Fig. 9-175. *Rather than placing designs on a 1-inch disk, as did most states, Pennsylvania had enlisted insignia on keystones starting in 1908. The design on the keystone replaced the earlier practice of having a separate bronze keystone and separate ornament for arm or branch of service. This same type of insignia was worn by the Pennsylvania Reserve Militia about 1918–19. This is an example for the 8th Band. (1 5/32 inches wide)*

they may also have been authorized or used by other organizations.

Officers' State Collar Seals

When the 1902 U.S. Army adopted the eagle from the Great Seal of the United States for officers' collars, the War Department encouraged states to prescribe state seals as collar ornaments for militia officers. Between the Spanish-American War and World War I many states did comply and did authorize a variety of insignia other than state letters.[47] The most common device in either gilt or bronze is a small keystone (Fig. 9-168), worn for years by Pennsylvania officers. More complex insignia are shown in Figs. 9-169, 9-170, and 9-171. Some states had a variety of insignia, and Massachusetts is known to have had shields of two sizes, both with and without *MASS* or *MSG* (Massachusetts State Guard) below, in both gilt and bronze.

Enlisted Men's State Seals and Letters

While many militia officers wore the state insignia just described, after 1908 states began to adopt similar designs on 1-inch-diameter disks for enlisted men. In some cases the insignia were used by the militia before World War I or by state guards of that period. Some bronze disks bearing state seals are shown in Figs. 9-172, 9-173, and 9-174 for Connecticut, Virginia, and Vermont. Pennsylvania took a unique approach by placing the enlisted branch device on a keystone. Fig. 9-175 shows one such example for the 8th Pennsylvania Band. All branches are represented in this fashion, with field hospitals wearing gilt keystones. Missouri also had several collar ornament designs for home guards (Figs. 9-176 and 9-177).

Home guards wore a wide variety of insignia, including state seals, just discussed, as well as insignia bearing initials like those of the Wisconsin State Guard (Fig. 9-178) and a home guard insignia for general use (Fig. 9-179). A 1919 sample submitted to the War Department from the State of Washington is shown in Fig. 9-180; it bears the Washington design of three stars and two horizontal bars along with the state abbreviation.[48]

State Letters, 1930s and 1940s

During World War II, state guards were revived, and men in many of these units wore state letters. One example known to

Fig. 9-168. *One of the largest state militias was that of Pennsylvania, and from the late nineteenth century until 1917, National Guard officers wore small keystones like this gilt insignia. This particular insignia was again used for the Pennsylvania Reserve Militia from 1917 through 1919. These common insignia have a variety of fasteners, including two prongs similar to a heavy staple. Although this piece is gilt, the bronze is also frequently found, and examples of false embroidery and actual embroidery also exist. (45/64 inch wide)*

Fig. 9-169. *A small gilt Massachusetts officers' insignia from before World War I. These come in a slightly larger size and also have MSG (Massachusetts State Guard) below, as well as being without anything below. (49/64 inch wide)*

Fig. 9-176.

Fig. 9-177.

Fig. 9-178.

Fig. 9-179.

Fig. 9-180.

Fig. 9-181.

Fig. 9-182.

Fig. 9-183.

Fig. 9-184.

Fig. 9-185.

Fig. 9-186.

Fig. 9-187.

Fig. 9-188.

Figs. 9-176 and 9-177. *Two different enlisted men's collar insignia for the 3d Regiment, Missouri Home Guard, about World War I. (Disk $1\frac{17}{64}$ inches in diameter)*

Fig. 9-178. *Many initials in a wide range of shapes were used during World War I. This example is for the Wisconsin State Guard.*

Fig. 9-179. *This general-purpose enlisted insignia is for a home guard unit of the World War I era.*

Fig. 9-180. *An enlisted men's insignia used during late 1918 and 1919 by the State of Washington Home Guard. ($\frac{51}{64}$ inch wide)*

Fig. 9-181. *This particular insignia was used by an officer of the South Carolina State Guard during World War II. Many states prescribed brass state initials for their state guards during World War II, but other organizations also used this type of insignia, and caution must be exercised before identifying them as army. ($\frac{29}{32}$ inch wide)*

Fig. 9-182. *A gilt collar insignia for the Puerto Rico Home Guard, World War II. ($\frac{25}{32}$ inch wide)*

Fig. 9-183. *Officers' collar insignia, believed to be for the Nebraska State Guard, about World War II. ($1\frac{17}{64}$ inches wide)*

Figs. 9-184 and 9-185. *By the middle of World War II, most states had formed state guards, since other organizations had been declared improper. The Pennsylvania State Guard had these plastic insignia made in 1943 to help save metal for the war effort. There is no evidence they were ever worn. (Each $\frac{15}{16}$ inch wide)*

Fig. 9-186. *A large set of brass letters with the small black-enameled state guard abbreviation on the center. Despite the periods between the underlying letters, this insignia is believed to have been made for the Wisconsin State Guard during World War II. ($\frac{31}{32}$ inch wide)*

Fig. 9-187. *A World War II set of Utah State Guard letters. ($1\frac{9}{32}$ inches wide)*

Fig. 9-188. *An officer of the Utah State Guard wearing the insignia shown in Fig. 9-187.*

Fig. 9-189. *To replace federalized National Guard, many states organized various units before the initiation of state guards. One resulting insignia was for the Missouri Reserve Militia Force. ($\frac{59}{64}$ inch wide)*

Fig. 9-190. *A gilt enlisted men's collar insignia for the Missouri State Guard, World War II.*

Figs. 9-191 and 9-192. *The background for these World War II state guard insignia is more typical of pieces made in the 1930s.*

Fig. 9-193. *Enlisted soldiers' collar insignia for the 2d Regiment, New York State Guard. This insignia was made in 1944 or 1945.*

Fig. 9-194. *Made about 1942 for the New York State Guard, this insignia is made from plastic. ($1\frac{3}{64}$ inches wide)*

Fig. 9-195. *While this plastic disk was made for the New York State Guard, disks with plain numbers were also made for military schools, highway patrols, and other organizations that were not army units. ($1\frac{3}{64}$ inches wide)*

Fig. 9-196. *A silver-colored enlisted men's insignia made for a forerunner of a state guard, the Pennsylvania Reserve Defense Command. The insignia lasted until early 1943. Those with long screw posts were worn on the gray campaign hat used by the Pennsylvania Reserve Defense Corps. ($1\frac{1}{32}$ inches wide)*

Fig. 9-189.

Fig. 9-190.

Fig. 9-191.

Fig. 9-192.

Fig. 9-193.

Fig. 9-194.

Fig. 9-195.

Fig. 9-196.

Fig. 9-197.

Fig. 9-198.

Fig. 9-199.

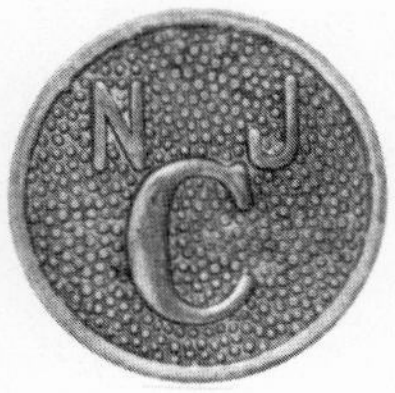

Fig. 9-200.

Fig. 9-197. *Many states initially established militia units using names other than state guards. This brass disk is an example for the California State Militia. (1 1/64 inches in diameter)*

Fig. 9-198. *A World War II insignia for the 1st Regiment, California State Guard. This insignia is stamped from a single piece of metal, but similar designs with the letters and number made separately for ease of polishing were made later in the war. (1 1/64 inches wide)*

Fig. 9-199. *Enlisted men's insignia for the 1st Regiment, Minnesota Defense Force, early World War II. The* MINN *is superimposed over large* D *and* F *(1 inch in diameter)*

Fig. 9-200. *Between 1935 and 1940, New Jersey had a battalion of black troops as part of its New Jersey Guard. Each company, the battalion headquarters, and a band had collar insignia of this type. (1 1/32 inches wide)*

have been worn by a South Carolina State Guard officer is illustrated in Fig. 9-181. This style of letters may also have been worn by other organizations, such as state police. World War II insignia used by Puerto Rico Home Guard officers is shown in Fig. 9-182, and Fig. 9-183 is believed to be the insignia for the Nebraska State Guard. Early World War II Pennsylvania State Guard insignia, made of plastic, are shown in Figs. 9-184 and 9-185. Wisconsin State Guard officers evidently used the insignia shown in Fig. 9-186. Utah State Guard officers used the insignia shown in Fig. 9-187, and an officer may be seen in Fig. 9-188 wearing the letters. Fig. 9-189 is for the Missouri Reserve Militia Force.

Although typically of a World War I or 1920s style, the disks shown in Fig. 9-190 for the Missouri State Guard and Fig. 9-191 for the Illinois State Guard were made during World War II. A 1930s-style *OHIO* disk, believed to have been intended for the Ohio State Guard, is illustrated in Fig. 9-192. Two-piece disks with state abbreviations were common during the 1940s and 1950s, and some had unit numbers, as shown in Fig. 9-193 for New York's 2d State Guard Regiment. Before this insignia, New York had used both metal and plastic disks of the type shown in Figs. 9-194 and 9-195. Fig. 9-196 shows a silver-colored piece used by the Pennsylvania Reserve Defense Command, a forerunner of the Pennsylvania State Guard. The California State Militia wore their initials (Fig. 9-197), and the California State Guard disks had the regimental number between the *SG* and *CAL,* as shown in Fig. 9-198 for the 1st Regiment. In Minnesota the state organization was called the defense force, and this was reflected in the enlisted insignia shown in Fig. 9-199.

Black New Jersey state troops formed the 1st Battalion, New Jersey Guard (note that *National* or *State* is not in the title), and each company had a disk of the type shown in Fig. 9-200 bearing the company letter. The letters *A* through *D, HQ,* and a band disk exist in this form. The 1st Battalion existed between 1935 and 1940 in various New

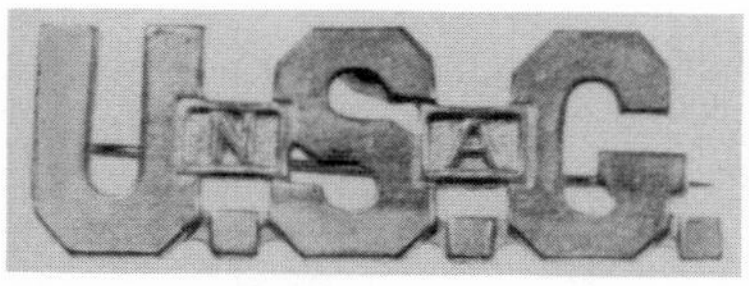

Fig. 9-201.

Fig. 9-202.

Fig. 9-201. *A nonregulation officers' insignia for the National Army's U.S. Guards. Because many of these units wore cast-off, obsolete dress blue uniforms, some men used gilt insignia.*

Fig. 9-202. *Some members of the wartime U.S. Guards had gilt cap insignia with the letters* USG, *which in some cases also had the National Army abbreviation added. Total enlisted strength of the U.S. Guards during World War I was approximately twenty-five thousand troops. (1 57/64 inches wide)*

Jersey cities. Company C (whose insignia is shown) drilled in Camden, New Jersey, until it and other companies formed the 1st Battalion, 372d Infantry.[49]

U.S.G. Letters

United States Guards are described in chapter 5, "Infantry," and officially U.S. Guards wore standard *US* letters. Various unique *USG* block letters do exist, one example of which is shown in Fig. 9-201. It is assumed that U.S. Guards officers wore these nonregulation collar ornaments. In addition, enlisted cap insignia wreaths exist for the U.S. Guards. These gilt wreaths contain either the letters *USG* or *USG* over *NA,* for National Army (Fig. 9-202).

Chapter Ten

Numbers and Letters

Officers and enlisted men used numbers and letters differently, and in the enlisted ranks there was a difference between company members and noncommissioned officers assigned to regimental staff positions. While most soldiers were enlisted into companies, the army assigned officers to a regiment. Because of this practice, officers wore only the regimental number. In no case did Regular Army regulations require officers to wear company letters on their uniforms or with their insignia. This practice means that Regular Army uniforms or insignia bearing company designations were for enlisted men. Even so, the absence of a company letter from an insignia, especially one from the early twentieth century, does not always mean the insignia was for an officer. Regimental noncommissioned officers may have been the intended wearers. For these men, the enlisted uniform and the absence of a company letter were the mark of the noncommissioned regimental staff. Although the Regular Army followed this practice, many state militia officers did wear company letters on insignia. After World War II a few units made officers' insignia with company letters, but these were often made in Germany and were never authorized. Except during the very early nineteenth century, numbers and letters normally indicated a soldier's regiment and company. Generally, enlisted men and noncommissioned officers in companies wore both the regimental number and the company letter, but at times during parts of the nineteenth century the company-level men wore just a company letter.

During the artillery reorganization of 1901 the army numbered company-sized units in both field artillery and coastal artillery. As a result of the 1907 artillery reorganization, the artillery included both numbered company units and numbered regiments that comprised lettered batteries. This 1907 practice continued for many years. The numbers and letters that were added to the basic artillery insignia, and their placement, reflected the peculiar problems caused by artillery reorganizations. This practice is discussed further in chapter 6, "Artillery."

Early Letters and Numbers on Caps

In 1808 the Regiment of Riflemen, the light dragoons, and the light artillery added separate outline letters (*USRR, USLD,* and *USLA*) to leather caps. In June 1808 the secretary of war specified the army use Roman letters 1½ inches high. For the artillery these were to be "of good brass, with good pliable brass tongues . . . at the price of 3 cents for each letter." Almost immediately after their issue in 1808, officers complained that these letters did not clinch firmly to the caps, resulting in a slovenly appearance. The secretary of war wrote that the letters "are clumsy and not attached sufficiently close to the leather."[1] Probably because of these unsatisfactory experiences, in 1811 the letters *USI* (for U.S. Infantry) were embossed on rectangular plates with clipped corners. The commissary general embossed *RR* (Regiment of Riflemen) on a diamond-shaped cap plate early the following year. These plates are illustrated in chapters 4, "Riflemen," and 5 "Infantry."

In March 1809 the purveyor of public supplies signed a contract that called for enough brass Roman letters to resupply the light artillery, light dragoons, and Regiment of Riflemen within three months. These letters cost five cents each, so it may be presumed that their quality had increased.[2] In 1973 a cache of discarded *USLD* Roman cap letters was found in a trash pit excavation at a site occupied by the U.S. Light Dragoons until 1810. They are 1 1/2 inches high, of cast brass, with integrally cast pointed wires on the reverse. They have been found in script letters (Fig. 10-1) and in block letters of the same style as the *USRR* letters in Fig. 10-2. The block letters exist for all three units, but the script letters are known only for the dragoons and riflemen. It is not known when these script letters were worn, given the 1808 and 1809 contracts. The script letters may have been worn first, since they are cheaper in appearance, and the Roman style initially called for may have been waived because the script letters present a more ornate appearance. We must await further research to solve the riddle of these script letters completely.

The 1825 forage cap was to be worn with white or yellow company letters for enlisted men and with regimental numbers for officers. These have been found in the "issue" style as well as various locally made patterns. These early letters were made with holes drilled in them so they could be sewn to the cap.

In 1832 the army introduced a unique folding leather cap with a company letter, "to be yellow in all cases," worn on the front. The leather cap was replaced in 1839 by a newer cloth version.[3] The 1839 cap itself is described as being "according to regulations," with no ornament described in regulations, although enlisted caps were issued with company letters that were again branch-colored: yellow or gilt for artillery and white or silver for infantry. An 1848 price list includes forage cap letters for dragoons, all artillery, infantrymen, and foot riflemen and

Fig. 10-1.

Fig. 10-1. Three of the four script letters worn on the leather caps of the U.S. Light Dragoons before and during the War of 1812. (Each letter approximately 1 1/2 inches high)

Fig. 10-2.

Fig. 10-2. A set of the block letters used by the U.S. Regiment of Riflemen on their caps (each letter approximately 1 1/2 inches high). Similar letters are known for the U.S. Light Artillery and for the U.S. Light Dragoons. The significance of the difference in style between the block letters and those in the script style is not known, although they may reflect two different purchases. The price of three cents for each letter was specified in June 1808, but in March 1809 the purveyor of public supplies signed a contract for letters for light artillery, light dragoons, and the Regiment of Riflemen at five cents each.

Fig. 10-3.

Fig. 10-4.

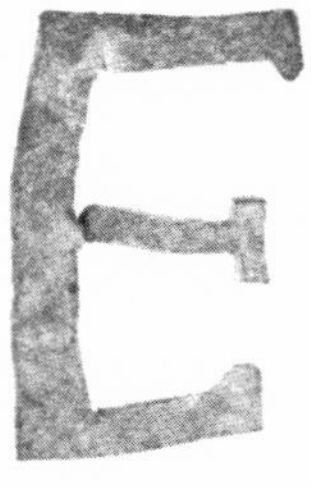

Fig. 10-5.

Fig. 10-6.

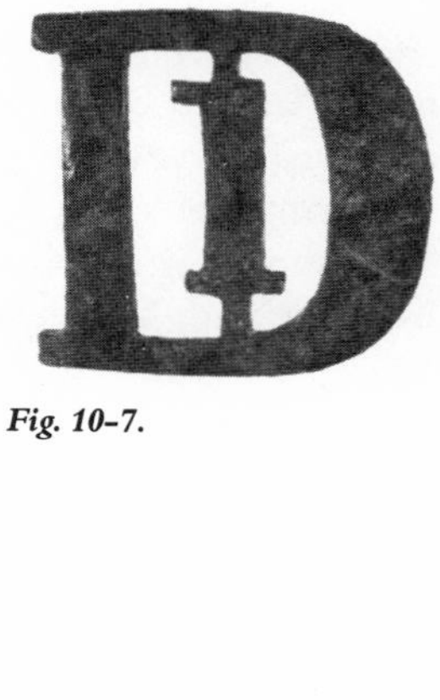

Fig. 10-7.

Figs. 10-3 through 10-7. Forage cap letters from the 1825–39 period. Fig. 10-3 shows an 1825–32 issue D. Fig. 10-4 shows an 1832–39 issue A made with a pierced tang on the reverse, which is slightly visible. Fig. 10-5 shows a cruder E, probably locally made between 1825 and 1832 and attached to the cap simply by thread looped around the letter's arms. The locally made combination number and letter devices were never official. Figs. 10-6 and 10-7 are a white metal G1 and a cast brass D1 recovered at Fort Snelling, Minnesota. Units represented by the last two insignia were stationed at Fort Snelling for rather short times, thus allowing dating of the pieces. Company G, 1st Infantry, was stationed at the post between May 1836 and June 1837 and again from September 1841 through September 1845. Company D of the 1st Infantry stayed at Fort Snelling between May 1834 and July 1837, only to return in September 1841 to remain until September 1848. (27/32 inch, 1 9/64 inches, 31/32 inch, 1 1/8 inches, and 1 19/64 inches wide, respectively) voltigeurs at four cents and for mounted riflemen at five cents each. The reason for the price difference is not now known, although it has been established that riflemen received artillery letters in 1846.[4] Several specimens of various post-1825 letters have been excavated at Fort Snelling, Minnesota, and in many cases the insignia can be rather precisely dated because of the various units that came and went at the frontier post. Some of these 1825–51 cap ornaments are shown in Figs. 10-3 through 10-7.

For the enlisted artillery, infantry, rifle, and dragoon soldiers, the 1851 uniform regulations eliminated the branch insignia on the dress caps and the letters on the rather flat-topped forage caps. The new dress caps carried 1-inch brass company letters below the eagle. An example is shown in Fig. 72-13 in chapter 72, "Men's Headgear through the Civil War." These letters lasted until 1859, and it is likely the same pattern of 1-inch-high letters carried through to 1872.[5]

The method of attaching letters to enlisted caps varied over time. The 1825–32 forage cap letters had holes to allow them to be sewn to a cap. From 1832 to 1851 it is probable that the letters were made so they could be easily removed. For these later letters a cut was made in the cap and the tab on the letter's reverse inserted into the cut. A leather thong or small peg could then be inserted into the hole in the tab to hold the insignia in place. Letters or numbers after 1851 had iron loops soldered to the reverse which allowed the numbers to be held on with a thong. Some later letters or numbers had two or three thin wires soldered to the back of the brass letter. The ends of the wires were often cut on a diagonal to form a point that allowed the wire to be inserted through the cap material.

Separate Numbers and Letters Worn with Cap or Hat Device

Regulations of 1832 describe a cylindrical infantry and artillery officers' beaver cap with leather top. The enlisted men's version was similar but was made of heavy felted wool. Ornaments for this cap included an eagle, a branch device, and a metal regimental number approximately 1 inch high. The color was not specified until 1839, when infantry wore silver and artillery, gilt.[6] These ornaments continued until 1851, when a new cap with only a company letter and eagle appeared.

Soldiers used a great variety of company letters during the Civil War, not only because of the immense size of the army and the resulting supply problems, but also because volunteers comprised most of the units. These nonregular organizations often outfitted themselves with locally procured uniforms and insignia, including letters to form various named units' initials. This multiple use of letters is one reason manufacturers produced all letters, *A* through *Z,* during the Civil War. A regulation brass letter is shown in Fig. 10-8; these also came in silver color. Another common Civil War–style letter is in Fig. 10-9. Regulations called for the company letters to be worn alone on the forage cap, but in practice men often added branch insignia and wore them with numbers and/or letters.[7]

The 1-inch-high Civil War letters proved to be too large for the 1872 forage cap, and the army sold the old letters at auctions in

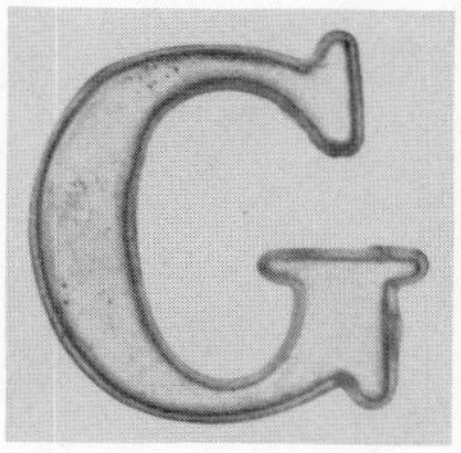

Fig. 10-8. *A regulation brass letter prescribed for Civil War forage caps. (1 1/64 inches wide)*

Fig. 10-9. *A common style of letter used by soldiers on their caps during the Civil War. (23/32 inch wide)*

Fig. 10-10. *Lead-filled letters of this type were issued by the U.S. Army after the 1872 uniform change and until the 1896 cap insignia had the letters brazed directly to the insignia. (17/32 inch wide)*

1872. The quartermaster general introduced 1/2-inch-high letters (Fig. 10-10) and issued them until 1896, when a new manufacturing technique made the separately applied letters obsolete. This initial change to the 1/2-inch-high size is recorded in Quartermaster Department letters and was actually accomplished in 1873, despite publication of a specification in May 1876 calling for 5/8-inch-high letters and numbers.[8]

The regulation Civil War numbers worn with the 1-inch-high letters were 5/8 inch high. The numbers, like the letters, usually had small iron loops on the reverse for fastening to the cap.

Separate Letters Worn Alone on Caps

Regulations required enlisted men to wear only a company letter, 5/8 inch high, on the 1851 dress cap and the 1858 forage cap (used until 1872), although during the Civil War men usually wore branch insignia and regimental numbers besides the company letter. When the army changed the enlisted cap design in 1872, regulations required the

Fig. 10-11. The style of numbers and letters worn on the campaign hat, 1899–1902. These were made of bright brass. (3/8 and 1/2 inch wide, respectively)

Fig. 10-12. These 14th Cavalry troopers in 1901 have bright brass regimental numbers and troop letters on their hats.

Fig. 10-11.

Fig. 10-12.

"badge of corps or letter of company of yellow metal [to be] worn in front." This proved to be a typographical error ("or" for "and") and was corrected next year, before the depot issued the new half-inch letters. Records show that the quartermaster general issued both branch devices and letters together.[9]

Numbers and Letters Worn Alone on Hats

On the 1855 cavalry hats, enlisted personnel wore their company letter and officers wore the regimental number. The hat itself was distinctive of the branch. This was the last authorized use of lone *hat* numbers or letters (but not *cap* numbers or letters) without branch devices until the last year of the nineteenth century. The quartermaster general modified the 1855 hat in 1858 and then issued it for all branches, with insignia to note the wearer's branch.[10]

In early 1899, the commanding officer of the 2d Cavalry Regiment wrote to the War Department asking the authority for "the very common practice of wearing crossed sabers & c. on the hat." During staff routings of the letter in Washington, the quartermaster general indorsed the request by writing, "It is suggested for consideration that a hat cord for each arm of service be adopted, and if thought necessary, the number of the regiment in brass." After further staff action, artillery, infantry, and cavalry began to wear regimental numbers and company letters, with the engineers wearing only their company letter, since an engineer regiment did not then exist. Between 1901 and 1905 the artillery wore the company or battery designation only. (See chapter 6, "Artillery," for a further discussion of this topic for that branch.) The numbers and letters initially prescribed differed from the forage cap and dress coat collar numbers previously worn. The pattern of numbers varied slightly: a little thinner and hollow. These initial numbers (Fig. 10-11) and letters (Fig. 10-12)

Fig. 10-13.

Fig. 10-14.

Fig. 10-15.

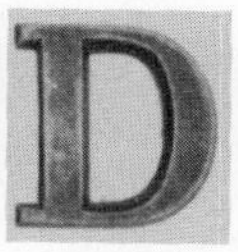
Fig. 10-16.

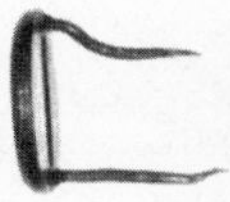
Fig. 10-17.

Fig. 10-18.

Fig. 10-19.

were made from number 28 sheet metal.[11]

In line with the dull camouflage look brought about by the 1902 uniform regulations, hat numbers and letters changed to a dull-finished bronze. These 1/2-inch-high bronze insignia (Figs. 10-13 and 10-14) also came in 28-gauge metal with thin-flexible attaching wires, just like the previous brass numbers. The quartermaster general's staff sought more substantial devices, and a third set of numbers and letters came into use in mid-1903. Still of the same general design and in dull bronze (Figs. 10-15 and 10-16), these were of a heavier metal, making the entire letter or number solid, about 1/16 inch

Fig. 10-20.

thick (17 gauge). Thicker, stronger, and less flexible fastening prongs accompanied this new design (Fig. 10-17).[12]

In December 1904 came a fourth style of numbers and letters: plain block letters slightly taller than previous styles (Figs. 10-18 and 10-19). Numbers were 17/32 inch high and letters were 9/16 inch tall. Both were made from a thicker metal (14 gauge), with the previous heavy fastening prong.[13] A person can not usually bend the thick attaching wires at a sharp angle near the insignia but must gradually curve the wire so the base of the wire remains perpendicular to the insignia. The solder used with these heavy fastening wires allows the prongs to break away from the insignia when pressure is applied to the wire's tip. The men complained of the breakage, and these poorly designed devices were never popular because of this fault.

From 1899 through early 1901 the army issued letters *A* through *O* (less *J*), because artillery regiments contained *N* and *O* batteries. Later the army issued letters to include *P, R,* and *S* (for Philippines, Puerto Rico, Recruiting Service, and prison guards). A 1901 Philadelphia Depot inventory shows hat letters *W* and *V* also in stock, although the reason for them is not known to me.[14]

Experiments conducted by the 20th Infantry in May 1907 eventually led to the 1910 adaptation of the enlisted men's collar disks. During the tests the 20th Infantry commander suggested that hat numbers and letters be discarded. The War Department published the change almost immediately.

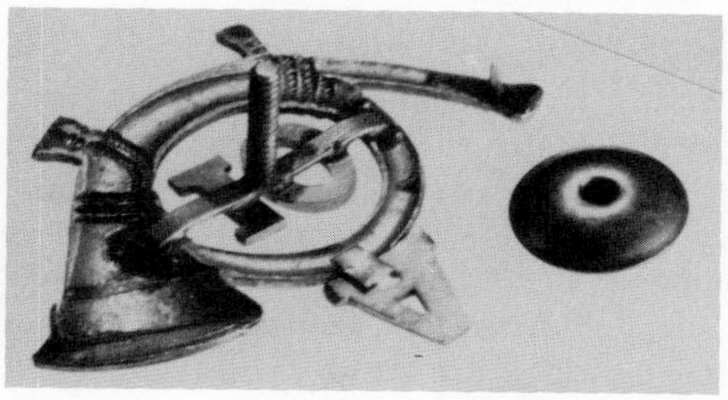
Fig. 10-21.

This left branch-colored cords as the only hat insignia. Bronze hat devices for field artillery and staff continued in use for a short time, "to be issued until exhausted," but an August 1907 general order on uniform changes officially rescinded all hat numbers and letters.[15]

Integrated Numbers and Letters on Cap and Hat Insignia

During the Indian Wars the army made some lead-filled enlisted cap ornaments with unit numbers and letters soldered to the basic branch insignia. Wires inserted into the back of letters and numbers held the composite piece together (Fig. 10-20). In 1896 the quartermaster general introduced a new manufacturing process for cap insignia. A screw post held the insignia to the cap, and one or two short needle points kept the piece from rotating (Fig. 10-21). Besides the new fastening device, 1/2-inch-high numbers and letters were brazed directly to the heavier insignia.

Figs. 10-13 and 10-14. *In 1902 the campaign hat numbers and letters were changed to bronze color but were otherwise identical to the previous style. (3/8 and 31/64 inch wide, respectively)*

Figs. 10-15 and 10-16. *Heavier than the 1902 numbers and letters but still of the same general design and bronze color, these campaign hat numbers were replaced in 1905. (13/32 and 33/64 inch wide, respectively)*

Fig. 10-17. *This side view shows fastening wires of the type adopted in 1905 for hat numbers and letters. These heavy, pointed wires broke off easily, and the soldiers complained of this problem.*

Figs. 10-18 and 10-19. *Block letters, made from 1905 through 1907, were the last of the separate campaign hat numbers and letters issued. Use of the regimental number and company letter on the campaign hat was ended in 1907, because soldiers wore collar insignia showing assigned units. (13/32 and 29/32 inch wide, respectively)*

Fig. 10-20. *Cap insignia of the early 1890s had the unit designations added when the insignia were filled with lead. The lead held not only the numbers and letters but also the safety pin fastener.*

Fig. 10-21. *The quartermaster general prescribed screw-post fasteners for forage caps in 1896. Small needle points like those at the bugle's mouthpiece and opposite edge kept the insignia from rotating.*

Figs. 10-22 and 10-23. *After 1896 the unit numbers and letters either were fastened to cap insignia by means of a small bar, as shown on the artillery insignia of Fig. 10-22, or they were brazed directly to the device, as seen on the engineers insignia of Fig. 10-23.*

Fig. 10-24. *A regimental brass letter of the style used from 1851 until 1858 on the enlisted men's coat. This example was dug at Fort Snelling, Minnesota. (37/64 inch wide)*

Fig. 10-25. *This illustration, from the 1851 regulations, shows placement of the 1-inch-high regimental numbers of the type shown in Fig. 10-24. The central V is the front collar opening.*

Fig. 10-26. *From 1872 until 1885 enlisted men wore regimental numbers of this type on the dress coat collar. (3/8 inch wide)*

Fig. 10-27. *From 1832 until 1851 officers wore their regimental numbers on epaulettes like this.*

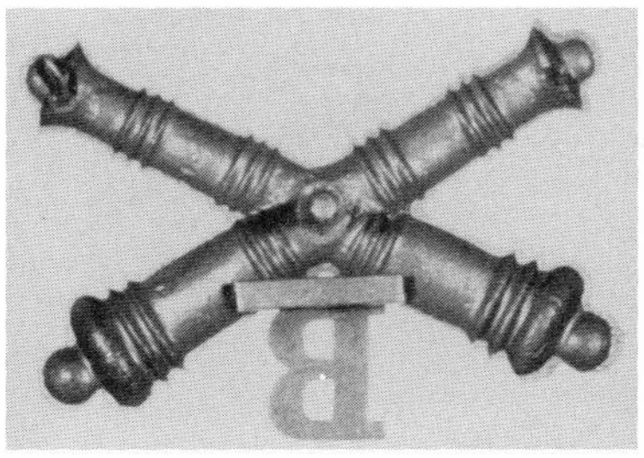

Fig. 10-22.

Fig. 10-23.

Fig. 10-24.

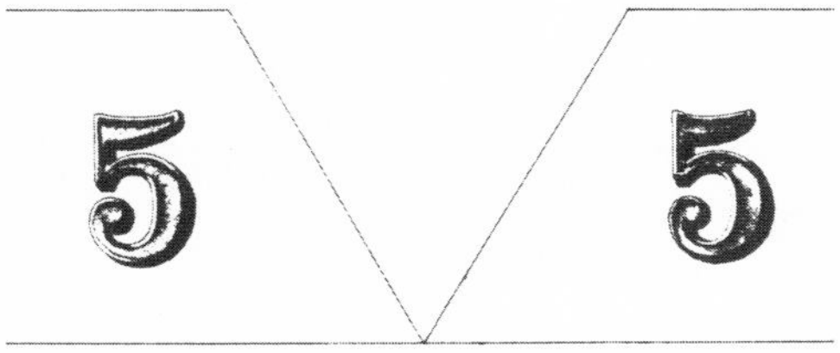

Fig. 10-25.

Fig. 10-26.

I believe that about 1901 a slightly heavier metal came into use for cap insignia, resulting in still more substantial devices. Sometimes letters and numbers were fixed directly to the basic device by means of a small, thin metal plate (Fig. 10-22), while at other times the additions went directly on the branch insignia (Fig. 10-23).[16]

The army introduced smaller branch insignia in 1905, with modernized cannon, rifles, and sabres depicted, among other changes. Smaller numbers and letters (5/16 inch high) came into use with these newer ornaments. Although the army directed a change to letters 1/4 inch high in 1908, it did not actually make the switch from 5/16-inch letters except in the case of the U.S. Military Academy Detachment.[17]

Enlisted Men's Coat Numbers

The 1851 uniform regulations called for enlisted men to wear a regimental number "in yellow metal one inch long" (Fig. 10-24) near the front of each collar (Fig. 10-25). An 1858 change eliminated this regimental number. On the 1872 dress coat collar, enlisted men wore 1/2-inch-high regimental numbers made from sheet brass (Fig. 10-26). In 1883, Colonel McCook, commander of the 6th Infantry, recommended that these regimental numbers be eliminated so the coat collars would remain clean. Shortly thereafter, in 1885, the army changed the dress coat. Because of McCook's and others' complaints about the breakage of the numbers and the soiling of coat collars, the army changed its policy and did not allow numbers on the new coat. The Quartermaster General's Department authorized plain white coats for enlisted men in extreme southern latitudes and in January 1900 added yellow metal regimental numbers on the collar. Records show the Philadelphia Depot did issue brass regimental numbers for wear on these coats, but the coat was phased out in 1903.[18]

Numbers on Epaulettes and Shoulder Knots

The 1832 infantry and artillery dress uniforms introduced officers' epaulettes with bullion numbers (Fig. 10-27). Infantry silver epaulettes

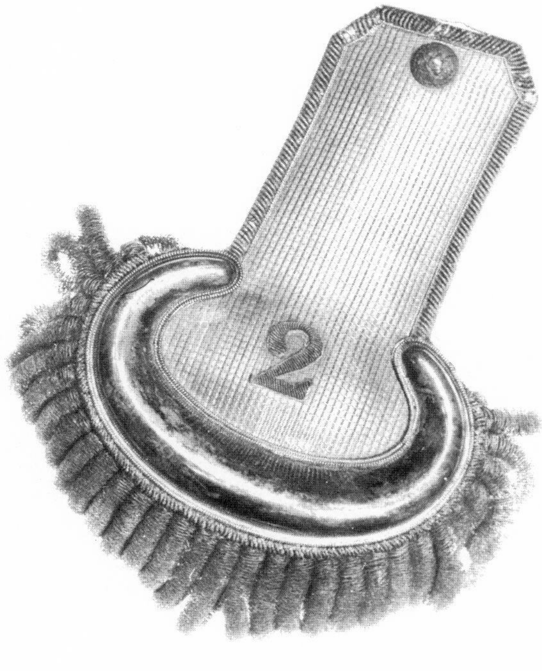

Fig. 10-27.

carried gilt numbers, while those for artillery officers were gilt with silver numbers. The army changed uniforms in 1851, and by 1855 the several branches (artillery, infantry, riflemen, cavalry, and dragoons) were distinguished by color. On the 1851-pattern epaulettes, gold-embroidered regimental numbers went onto a silver-bordered, branch-colored velvet disk (Fig. 10-28).[19]

In 1872 the shoulder knot came into existence for dress wear. Officers of combat arms wore the embroidered regimental number on a branch-colored knot pad. Two knots are illustrated in Figs. 10-29 and 10-30, which show knots for a colonel of the 3d Cavalry Regiment and for a first lieutenant of the 2d Infantry Regiment, respectively. Shoulder knots became obsolete in 1903.[20]

Numbers and Letters Added to Insignia on Disks

From 1910 through 1917, soldiers in the infantry, field artillery, and cavalry wore numbers and letters on their branch collar disks to indicate regiment and company, battery, or troop (Fig. 10-31). Prison guards, disciplinary barracks guards, recruiting district soldiers, and band members added only the unit number. From 1910 to 1916 engineers had only the company letter on their disk, but after engineer regiments were formed in 1916, both numbers and letters went onto disks. The "company letter" also began to include *HQ, MG,* and *S* for men in headquarters, machine-gun units, and supply units. To simplify the supply system, in December 1917 the Quartermaster Corps made a change so that only the company letters went on the branch collar disk (Fig. 10-32). At the same time, regimental numbers moved to the *US* disk (Fig. 10-33). Before the 1917 change, each company of each regiment needed a distinct collar disk because of the combinations of numbers and letters. The members of Company A, 1st Infantry, wore *1* above the *A* on crossed rifles, while members of Company A, 2d Infantry, wore *2* above *A* on their infantry disks. The intent of the December 1917 change was to make it possible for the A Company members of any regiment to wear the same insignia: crossed weapons with an *A*. This officially remained in effect until 1937, when company letters were to be omitted.[21] The 1917 change allowed all men in regiments with the same number (1st Cavalry, 1st Infantry, 1st Artillery) to wear the *US* disk with the regiment's number added, which also eased supply problems. Authorization for regimental numbers on *US* disks went out in 1947. Some units unofficially added both numbers and letters to branch insignia after 1937, and the unauthorized practice still continues.

Fig. 10-28.

Fig. 10-28. Starting in 1851 officers had their regimental numbers on epaulettes like these. The disk under the embroidered number was colored according to branch.

Fig. 10-29.

Fig. 10-29. Regimental colonels had their unit's number above the eagle on their 1872–1902 shoulder knots, as this 3d Cavalry example shows.

(For only numbers on disks, see Fig. 9-195.)

Between the world wars the army authorized enlisted men's disks to carry letters *A* through *M* (less *J*) in addition to *S* for service company, *HQ* for regimental and separate battalion headquarters, *HZ* for infantry howitzer companies, *MG* after 1929 for cavalry machine-gun troops (although the 1920 National Defense Act had abolished machine-gun companies), and *AC* after 1933 for cavalry armored car squadrons (Fig. 10-34). Men in battalion headquarters replaced the company letters with the battalion numbers (*1, 2,* or *3*) on their branch disk (Fig. 10-35).[22]

During and after World War II, some soldiers, especially occupation troops, began to use nonregulation company abbreviations. Examples include the Tank Company in the 6th Cavalry Squadron (Fig. 10-36) and 1st Howitzer Battery, 6th Armored Cavalry Regiment (Fig. 10-37).

Knot and Epaulette Letters

Regulations prescribed various old English letters for wear on epaulettes and shoulder knots during the nineteenth century (Figs. 10-38 and 10-39).[23] These letters and their dates of use are shown in Table 10-1.

Numbers on Officers' Collar Insignia

From 1895 until World War II, where regimental organizations existed (e.g., infantry, cavalry, and artillery) officers usually wore their regimental number as part of their branch insignia. During World War II, many officers transferred among regiments with such frequency that they often wore only the basic branch insignia without number. Starting in December 1940, the War Department directed officers not assigned to a regiment to wear their branch insignia without a unit number. This was a definite change from the World War I concept, by which officers continued to wear their regimental designation when on special assignment.[24]

After the formation of the Depart-

Fig. 10-30.

Fig. 10-30. *The background color indicated the branch, and the large gilt number told the regiment on the 1872–1902 shoulder knots.*

Fig. 10-31.

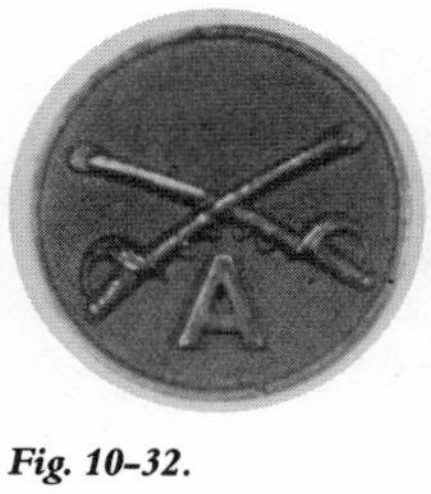

Fig. 10-32.

Fig. 10-33.

Fig. 10-31. *From 1910 through 1917 enlisted men were to wear bronze disks with the regimental and company designations, as shown in this example. This meant that there was a different insignia for each company-sized unit.*

Fig. 10-32. *In 1918 the army issued disks with just the company letters (regimental number omitted) to ease supply problems. With this scheme, all company-sized units with the same letter designation from the same branch could wear the same disk.*

Fig. 10-33. *With the 1918 change shown in Fig. 10-32, the unit number moved to the US disk, so, for example, any unit with the designation 1st could wear this disk.*

Fig. 10-34.

Fig. 10-35.

Fig. 10-36.

Fig. 10-37.

Fig. 10-34. *During the 1920s and 1930s the army prescribed several letters besides those for companies. This example for the armored car squadrons has A and C in the horizontal angles.*

Fig. 10-35. *The battalion number instead of the company letter showed one of the three battalion headquarters in a regiment. This 2d Battalion insignia from an infantry regiment was made in the 1930s.*

Figs. 10-36 and 10-37. *After World War II, enlisted personnel collar insignia began to carry many nonregulation unit designations. These two examples were made in Germany. That of Fig. 10-36 is for the Tank Company, 6th Cavalry, while it was a part of the constabulary. That of Fig. 10-37 is for the 1st Squadron's Howitzer Battery, 6th Cavalry Regiment.*

ment of the Army in 1947, it allowed use of regimental and separate battalion numbers on an optional basis. Officers in battalions organized under the Combat Arms Regimental System (CARS) often wear both battalion and regimental numbers on their branch insignia (Fig. 10-40), even though the battalion designation is nonregulation. In addition, other unofficial additions occasionally appear, such as that for the 606th Tank Destroyer Battalion shown in Fig. 10-41 and for the 7th Cavalry honor guard shown in Fig. 10-42. Regulations published after World War II did not address the topic of regimental and battalion numbers until 1956, when armor, artillery, infantry, and engineers regimental or battalion numbers became optional on branch insignia. In 1966 the army added military police, medical, chemical, intelligence, ordnance, quartermaster, signal, and trans-

Fig. 10-38. *An 1851–72 epaulette for a Pay Department officer. Old English letters of this general style were used by many staff departments on epaulettes until 1872.*

Fig. 10-39. *From 1872 until 1890, several staff department officers wore shoulder knots that carried old English department initials, such as this Medical Department knot.*

Table 10-1. *Nineteenth-Century Letters Used on Officers' Shoulder Insignia.*

Letters	**Branch**	**Authorized Dates of Use**
SS	Signal Service	1872–88
PD	Pay Department	1847–90
OD	Ordnance Department*	1872
MS	Medical Service	1847–72
MD	Medical Department	1872–90
AD	Adjutant General's Department*	1872
QD	Quartermaster's Department	1872–90
SD	Subsistence Department	1872–90
JA	Judge Advocate General's Dept.	1872–90
ID	Inspector General's Department	1872–90
EC	Corps of Engineers*	1872

*Probably never worn.

Fig. 10-38.

Fig. 10-39.

Fig. 10-40.

Fig. 10-41.

Fig. 10-42.

Fig. 10-43.

Fig. 10-46.

Fig. 10-47.

Fig. 10-45.

Fig. 10-40. *An officers' subdued collar insignia from the 1980s for use on battle dress shirts. While the regimental number above the sabers was allowed by regulations, the squadron number below was not. (1 1/2 inches wide)*

Fig. 10-41. *During World War II and the following years officers often added unauthorized letters to standard insignia. This piece, from the World War II 606th Tank Destroyer Battalion, is one such example. (1 3/8 inches wide)*

Fig. 10-42. *This Korean-made insignia from the 1950s or 1960s is a fine example of an addition besides a unit number. (1 9/16 inches wide)*

Fig. 10-43. *An example of the silver-colored numbers used on the 1892–95 officers' sack coat by infantry, cavalry, and artillery officers. (9/16 inch wide; sack coat numbers generally 45/64 to 49/64 inch high)*

Fig. 10-44. *The official drawings of the block regimental numbers, 1892–95, for officers. At the end of the 1890s these nominally 3/4-inch-high numbers were also applied on officers' helmet plates.*

Fig. 10-45. *George Custer's dress helmet with the 7th Cavalry regimental number on the eagle's breast. This style of helmet and eagle was introduced in 1872 and lasted until 1881.*

Fig. 10-46. *A silver regimental number issued to enlisted men in the 1880s and 1890s. This style of number, made from sheet German silver, was placed on helmet plates. (11/32 inch wide)*

portation units to the list of units allowed to use battalion numbers. In 1983 the chief of staff directed the formation of "paper" regiments to stabilize personnel assignments. Although those units were not regiments in a traditional sense, the new policy was a partial departure from the 1950s CARS and an attempt to return to the older concept. The idea was for officers to serve troop assignments in a very limited number of battalions—just those of their "regiment." Officers in these regiments were encouraged to wear their regimental designation during all assignments.[25]

Numbers Only on Officers' Collars

When the army introduced the 1892 sack coat, infantry, artillery, and cavalry officers placed three-quarters-inch-high silver-embroidered or metal block-style regimental numbers (Fig. 10-43) on the collar. Examples are shown in Fig. 2-27 in chapter 2. The official shapes of the numbers are shown in Fig. 10-44. In 1895 crossed arms with reg-

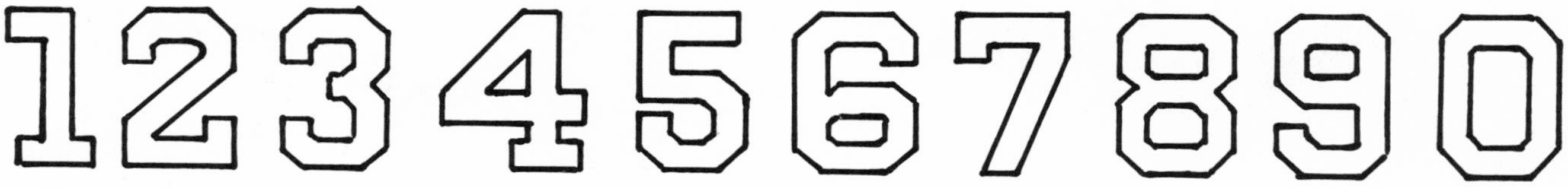

Fig. 10-44.

imental numbers attached replaced these block collar numbers.[26]

Helmet Plate Numbers

Regulations and specifications do not mention the addition of regimental numbers on the 1872 helmet plate. Characteristically, one would expect such a designation to be used, since the regiment was the basic army unit, and surviving examples and official photographs show that officers and enlisted men did added regimental numbers to the plate. An example worn by the ill-fated George Custer is shown in Fig. 10-45. When the army switched to the 1881 helmet plate, a War Department order called for one-half-inch-high silver numbers on the national shield. One of these numbers, made about 1900, is illustrated in Fig. 10-46. Initially the Quartermaster General's Department used joined numbers, and an example from the Quartermaster General's 1881 report is illustrated in Fig. 10-47.[27] Officers usually purchased their own uniforms; consequently, officers' helmet numbers vary considerably.

T on Disks

Division supply organizations of World War I were known as division trains. In August 1917 a 3/4-inch-high *T* on a 1-inch disk became the collar device for enlisted men in division trains. In the American Expeditionary Forces, enlisted men of division and corps ammunitions trains attached to the First Army or Second Army artillery wore *T* on the left collar and a *US* with the trains number on the right collar. In May 1919 the *T* disk changed title and was worn by men in "Headquarters of Trains and the Ammunition Trains." The War Department abolished the *T* insignia in March 1921.[28]

Two bronze disks are shown in Figs. 10-48 and 10-49. A gilt disk, possibly worn after World War I but certainly unauthorized, is in Fig. 10-50. Some organizations, perhaps National Guard trains, wore the disks between the world wars, as shown by the two-piece disk in Fig. 10-51, which was of the type popular in the 1930s, many years after the War Department withdrew authorization.

S on Disks

Mr. A. E. DuBois designed a plain *S* for service company enlisted men. Authorized in March 1921, it was the first insignia with a background containing crosshatched lines approximately 1/16 inch apart. The open spaces between the lines soon carried the small shields common during the 1930s. The company letter *S* below the branch device replaced the 3/4 inch block *S* in October 1921.[29] Despite this change, the block letter persisted. Several gilt variations exist (Figs. 10-52 and 10-53).

HQ on Disks

Men assigned to division and higher headquarters wore the letters *HQ* beginning in 1924. The issue gilt *HQ* had a background of lines and small shields (Fig. 10-54). Many styles of this insignia exist, including one with the official background and removable letters (Fig. 10-55). One interesting variation was that worn by personnel assigned to the headquarters of the 93d Division, with the number *93* below the *HQ* (Fig. 10-56). Two-piece disks exist with both round and square

Fig. 10-48.

Fig. 10-49.

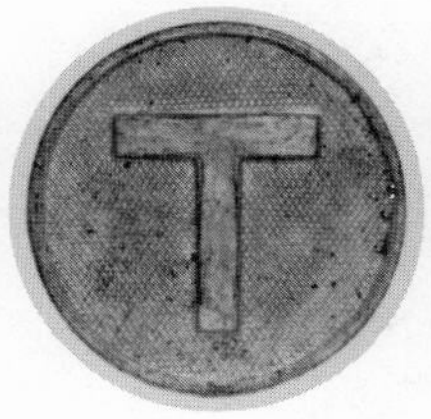
Fig. 10-50.

Fig. 10-51.

Fig. 10-52.

Fig. 10-53.

Fig. 10-54.

Fig. 10-55.

Fig. 10-47. *This illustration was initially published by the quartermaster general to show the official 1881 helmet insignia. This example shows two joined numbers, which are scarce today.*

Figs. 10-48 and 10-49. *Two examples of supply train insignia used in World War I by enlisted men. Letters such as these Ts frequently composed some branch insignia during World War I.*

Fig. 10-50. *This one-piece gilt disk was never regulation, but a few examples are known.*

Fig. 10-51. *A two-piece supply train disk, in gilt. This particular example was sold in Texas during and after World War I.*

Fig. 10-52. *Service company members were prescribed this insignia only during 1921. Because of the short life of this piece, most that were made survived to be sold as surplus.*

Fig. 10-53. *A nonregulation, two-piece gilt service company disk. Use of this block letter, declared obsolete in 1921, shows how letters persisted as insignia after World War I.*

Fig. 10-54. *Those men who served in division, corps, and army headquarters wore this insignia. This particular version is of the official pattern that was issued by the army after the insignia's inception in 1924.*

Fig. 10-55. *A gilt collar disk with removable design for men assigned to division and higher headquarters. Enlisted soldiers' insignia which allowed the background to be separated from the central design first became popular in the 1930s, although they were first worn in the 1920s.*

Table 10-2. Collar Insignia for Enlisted Men in Headquarters, 1930s.

Unit	Right Collar Device	Left Collar Device
Battalion	*US* with regimental number below	Insignia of arm or service with battalion number below
Regiment	*US* with regimental number below	Insignia of arm or service with *HQ* below
Brigade	*US* with brigade number below	Insignia of arm or service
Division	*US*	*HQ*
Corps	*US*	*HQ*
Army	*US*	*HQ*
General Headquarters	*US*	*HQ*

Qs and also with domed variations (Figs. 10-57 through 10-60). Use of the *HQ* disk is shown in Table 10-2.[30]

Officers' *HQ*

The U.S. Army did not authorize officers to wear the *HQ* letters separately as did enlisted men. Also, bronze insignia had just become obsolete when the enlisted men's *HQ* disk insignia came into being. Despite these facts, officers' *HQ* bronze letters are known (Fig. 10-61). These have large staple-style fasteners and may be of foreign origin, although they are commonly found in the United States.

H, *HDQ*, and *GHQ* on Disks

The thirteenth change to the Uniform Specifications of 1913, published on 14 August 1917, authorized a bronze disk with the capital letter *H* (Figs. 10-62 and 10-63) to be worn by division headquarters detachments and military police. In May 1919 the War Department prescribed the *H* for enlisted men at brigade and higher headquarters. The *H* became obsolete in the spring of 1921, and in 1924 *HQ* disks filled the need. A gilt *H* disk also exists (Fig. 10-64), possibly for National Guard use, although between 1921 and 1924 nothing was authorized and the *H* may have been used.[31]

Men assigned to the AEF General Headquarters wore their own special insignia after February 1918: the letters *GHQ* (Fig. 10-65). The AEF General Headquarters, officially formed in January 1918, continued to function after the war's end. The headquarters returned to the United States aboard the S. S. *Leviathan* in September 1919. Because the GHQ operated in the United States, some men wore the disk in the United States. The army declared the disk obsolete in August 1920 when the AEF General Headquarters disbanded in Washington, D.C.[32] *HDQ* disks, perhaps an unauthorized version of the *GHQ*, are known to exist (Fig. 10-66).

Fig. 10-56.

Fig. 10-57.

Fig. 10-58.

Fig. 10-59.

Fig. 10-60.

Fig. 10-61.

Fig. 10-62.

Fig. 10-63.

Fig. 10-56. *Made after World War I in New York City for the men who served in the headquarters of the 93d Division, this insignia has the letters and the unit number soldered to a gilt disk with the pre-1920s background. Regulations did not provide the use of numbers, as shown in this example.*

Fig. 10-57. *This is the most common version of the headquarters disk. It has a round Q, a flat, separable background, and a screw-post fastener.*

Fig. 10-58. *The shorter letters and a square Q distinguish this insignia from that of Fig. 10-57.*

Figs. 10-59 and 10-60. *Enlisted soldiers' collar insignia with a domed background can be documented by these disks. The HQ was not prescribed by the start of World War II, although no doubt some men continued to wear such insignia. The disk in Fig. 10-59 has a slight dome and a screw-post fastener. The disk of Fig. 10-60 is finished in silver and has a high domed (convex) background.*

Fig. 10-61. *A set of bronze letters that some people subscribe to officers of division headquarters. Such insignia were never regulation in the U.S. Army, and the insignia have a staple fastener instead of the normal pin fastener. (1 1/64 inches wide)*

Figs. 10-62 and 10-63. *From 1913 until 1921 various headquarters troops wore dark bronze insignia like these. Gilt versions exist, but they cannot be explained, since the design became obsolete in 1921, and gilt disks were not prescribed until 1923.*

HZ on Disks

Howitzer companies were a part of infantry regiments after World War I. In actuality, they were simply mortar companies instead of true howitzer units. Their purpose, however, was to place more firepower at the disposal of an infantry regiment commander. The capital letters *HZ* were proposed as insignia in early 1921, and the army established the disk in March 1921. The Quartermaster Corps actually designed the piece after establishment of the insignia concept, and the first pieces were made in the fall of 1921. Fig. 10-67 is an example of the bronze disk initially established. No sooner had the army made these insignia than an October 1921 regulation revision eliminated them in favor of crossed muskets with *HZ* below.[33] Even so, men wore the letters for some time. Fig. 10-68 shows a post-1923 gilt disk.

MG Letters

World War I caused the army to establish infantry machine-gun companies and battalions and cavalry machine-gun troops and squadrons. Unit insignia were crossed rifles or sabers with the letters *MG* above for battalions or squadrons or below for companies and troops. Several organizations such as the recruiting service and disciplinary guards, wore only initials at this time. I assume some manufacturers learned of the new machine-gun units and made the letters into an insignia. This would account for pieces of the type shown in Fig. 10-69. Some post-1923 gilt disks are known (Fig. 10-70), although their use is not documented. Officers' bronze insignia with a staple fastener also are known (Fig. 10-71), although the intended use of these pieces is not known.

Fig. 10-65.

Fig. 10-65. Men assigned to the AEF General Headquarters from February 1918 until August 1920 were to wear collar insignia of this type.

Fig. 10-66.

Fig. 10-66. An unauthorized World War I bronze collar disk for enlisted soldiers assigned to headquarters.

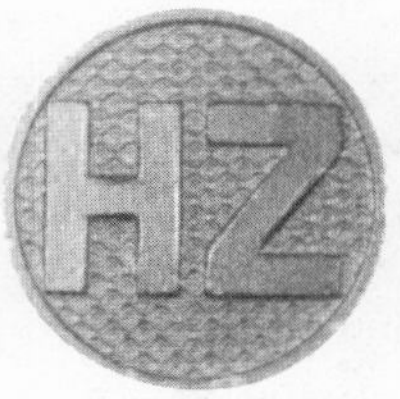

Fig. 10-67.

Fig. 10-67. Designed, produced, and declared obsolete all during 1921, this bronze howitzer company insignia was replaced by crossed rifles or muskets with small letters HZ below.

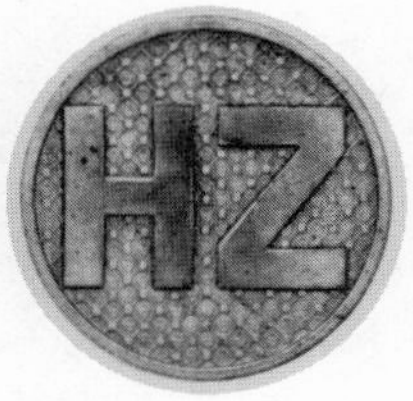

Fig. 10-68.

Fig. 10-68. This howitzer company disk should never have been made in gilt, but such versions are found today. The reason for the insignia in the dress form has not been discovered.

Fig. 10-64.

Fig. 10-64. Sergeant John Walker at Fort Riley, Kansas, in 1918. He wears a 1-inch disk bearing the letter H.

Fig. 10-69.

Fig. 10-70.

Figs. 10-69 and 10-70. Letters which formed initials were commonly used as insignia during the World War I period, and it must be assumed that these bronze and gilt enlisted disks were made for machine-gun units. Crossed rifles or sabers with small MG letters were the proper insignia until 1920, when distinctive designed insignia disappeared for machine-gun units.

Vietnam-Era *OCS*, *WOC*, and *NCOC*

In October 1963 the brass letters *OCS* (Fig. 10-72) replaced the OCS pocket patch introduced during World War II for students at officer candidate schools. Candidates wore the block letters, 7/16 inch by 1 7/32 inches, in place of other collar insignia on the green coat collar, on shirts, and on the overseas and fatigue caps.[34] After introduction of subdued ornamentation for fatigue uniforms, the letters came in black metal (Fig. 10-73) and black embroidery (Fig. 10-74). Various branches had officer candidate schools, and these schools established three or four "classes" or levels of proficiency to establish seniority among students. In 1965, for example, the Fort Benning "senior" class was noted by blue trim on the cap (Fig. 10-75) and blue shoulder marks (Fig. 10-76).

After the army established a special warrant officer candidate school to train heli-

Fig. 10-71.

Fig. 10-72.

Fig. 10-73.

Fig. 10-74.

Fig. 10-78.

Fig. 10-71. *U.S. officers were never prescribed letters like these, but some people believe they were worn either separately or below crossed rifles or sabers. There is no documentation to show that insignia of this type, with the staple-back fasteners, were used by American officers. (1 1/32 inches wide)*

Figs. 10-72, 10-73, and 10-74. *Insignia for officer candidate school members. The gilt metal version (Fig. 10-72) was introduced in the early 1960s. Subdued metal (Fig. 10-73) and embroidered cloth (Fig. 10-74) came along in the late 1960s. (Brass letters 1 7/32 inches wide)*

Fig. 10-75. *At various army posts local additions such as this light blue cloth disk, which was added to the cap by the upperclassmen and worn under the regulation letters, were added to officer candidate school insignia.*

Fig. 10-76. *A companion piece to the OCS cap disk (Fig. 10-70) is this blue cloth shoulder strap, which was pinned to the uniform shoulder strap by the distinctive insignia bearing the motto FOLLOW ME.*

Figs. 10-77 and 10-78. *Warrant officer candidates wore block letters like these, starting with the establishment of WOC schools during the Vietnam War. The metal letters are made in brass for the green service uniform and in subdued (black) for fatigue or battle dress clothing. (Metal letters 1 19/64 inches wide)*

Fig. 10-77.

copter pilots, the candidates received block *WOC* letters (Figs. 10-77 and 10-78) measuring 7/16 by 1 13/32 inches. Pilot warrant officer candidates wore the *WOC* while at Fort Wolters, Texas, and Fort Rucker, Alabama. In the 1980s the army changed the direct appointment system for warrant officers and had those noncommissioned officers aspiring to warrant officer rank attend special candidate schools. While attending these schools students wore the *WOC* insignia.[35]

Fig. 10-76.

To alleviate a shortage of junior noncommissioned officers during the Vietnam War, the Department of the Army established infantry, artillery, and armor noncommissioned officer candidate schools and prescribed *NCOC* insignia for wear by the students. The schools provided the students with additional leadership training, and upon graduation, the soldiers became sergeants. Noncommissioned officer candidates wore letters of the same type prescribed for warrant and officer candidates (Fig. 10-79), in both subdued and dress, except for the infantry NCOC school at Fort Benning, Georgia. At the infantry school, students wore a silver metal insignia, with dark blue enamel, bearing the *NCOC* monogram (Fig. 10-80). Although the insignia looks like a distinctive insignia, it was worn as a collar insignia.

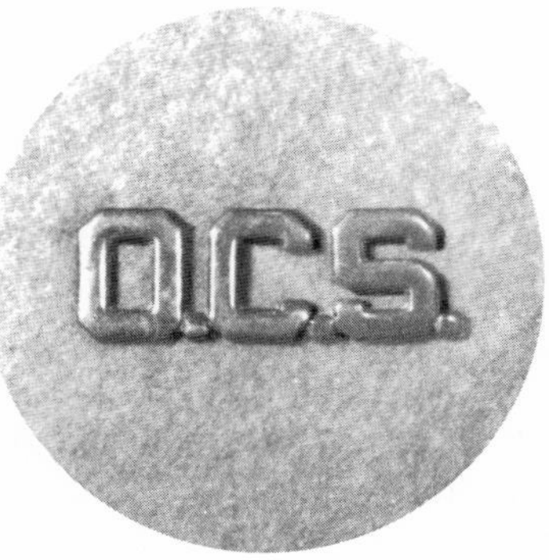

Fig. 10-75.

U.S. Military Academy Preparatory School

The army established a school to provide training for selected personnel before their appointments to the U.S. Military Academy. It was known as the U.S. Military Academy Preparatory School, and its students wore standard enlisted uniforms and insignia for many years. In the 1960s students began to wear block letters *USMAPS* (Fig. 10-81) as collar insignia. This practice followed the trend shown by the use of *OCS* and other collar letters. These letters are thinner but of the same height as the other late-twentieth-century letters previously discussed.

GHQ Added to Officers' Branch Insignia

Through World War I the army continued to recognize the regiment as the principal combat unit, and infantry, cavalry, and field artillery officers thought of themselves as members of a regiment. The crossed arms of the appropriate service were worn with the regimental number above. As a result of the World War I experience, officers serving on brigade, division, and higher staffs wore the

Fig. 10-79.

Fig. 10-81.

Fig. 10-80.

Fig. 10-82b.

Fig. 10-82a.

Fig. 10-82c.

Fig. 10-82d.

Fig. 10-82e.

Fig. 10-79. *During the Vietnam War the army established schools that would make new soldiers into sergeants. Men assigned to these noncommissioned officer candidate schools wore block letters such as these. Such insignia come in both bright and subdued metal. Neither was authorized by the Department of the Army.* *($1\frac{45}{64}$ inches wide)*

Fig. 10-80. *Insignia of the type shown in Fig. 10-74 were worn at most army posts except the Infantry School at Fort Benning. There, members of the noncommissioned officer candidate school wore this blue enameled insignia bearing the silver NCOC monogram.* *($\frac{23}{32}$ inch wide)*

Fig. 10-81. *Probably during the early 1960s students at the U.S. Military Academy Preparatory School began to wear these thin block letters on their green uniform lapels. Their use has never been sanctioned by regulations.*

Fig. 10-82. *A large display of World War I and post–World War I insignia was photographed shortly after the war's close. Several staff officers' devices are shown in the photo. Some extracts are reproduced: The small ordnance insignia worn with the rifles, sabers, and Corps of Engineers insignia were for inspectors of small arms practice. The small lyres added to the insignia in the bottom row were for commissioned band leaders.*

unit number, such as the brigade designation, on their insignia. The number, regimental or higher, was part of the recognized insignia. But what of the officers serving at the General Headquarters? Without a number to designate the headquarters, these officers wore either their previous number of the branch or an insignia without any number. To correct this problem, in August 1933 the army authorized officers assigned to General Headquarters to wear the letters *GHQ* in the upper angle of the crossed arms.[36] This provision disappeared in November 1941.

Officers' Staff Devices

Between 1899 and 1923, selected regimental and battalion staff officers wore small devices added to their basic branch insignia. For the infantry, cavalry, and various artillery insignia, the staff device went in the lower angle of the crossed arms, while for the engineers the device went above the castle's center turret. While these staff devices are discussed with the various branch insignia, they are summarized in Table 10-3. The accompanying photographs (Fig. 10-82) show extracts from an official display of 1920 insignia, including the various staff devices then in use.

Table 10-3. *Officers' Staff Devices, 1899–1923.*

Staff Position	Dates of Use
Adjutant	1899–1923
Commissary	1899–1913
Quartermaster	1899–1923
Chaplain	1903–14
Veterinarian	1903–16
Small arms inspector	1914–23
Commissioned band leader	1918–23

Table 10-4. *Chapters Associated with Letters Not Described in Chapter 10.*

Letters	Chapter No. and Title
US (and variants), *USR, USV, USNA,* and *USNG*	9. The Letters *US* and State Insignia
USS	24. Indian Scouts and First Special Forces
QMD	37. Service School Detachments
PG, DBG, DB	25. Prison Guards
RS	34. Recruiting Service
PC	27. Philippine Constabulary
MP	44. Provost Marshal and Military Police
USG	5. Infantry (Section "U.S. Guards")

Women's Airforce Service Pilots

In the spring of 1943, when the Women's Army Corps legislation began to take shape, the chief of the air staff proposed that some of the new WAC recruits become pilots to help in the ferrying of planes. In June 1943, Jacqueline Cochran was appointed director of women pilots. Miss Cochran, however, was opposed to making women pilots members of the WAC. This opposition caused the War Department to reverse its previous position. Instead of joining the WAC, women pilots became Women's Airforce Service Pilots (WASP) and served as civilian employees, although they were subject to military regulations. A June 1944 congressional attempt to bring the WASP into the army failed and ultimately resulted in the group's December 1944 deactivation.[37] WASP uniforms carried block letters *WASP* (Fig. 10-83) on the collar (Fig. 10-84). Some women's coat lapels included Army Air Force winged propellers, but other than a small eagle worn on the beret and their distinctive wings, the women did not have unique insignia.

Other Letters

Many branch insignia consist of letters not listed in this chapter. Because several such letters evolved to, or became connected with, other devices, these letters are discussed elsewhere. The letters and their associated chapters are summarized in Table 10-4.

Other insignia, such as that shown in Fig. 10-85, may be associated with military schools, Reserve Officers Training Corps, police, fire, or military organizations such as state guards or wartime militia. Remember, many insignia other than those of the Regular Army exist.

Fig. 10-83.

Fig. 10-83. *Letters worn on the jacket lapels by members of the Women's Airforce Service Pilots. ($1^{9}/_{64}$ inches wide)*

Fig. 10-84.

Fig. 10-84. *A member of the World War II Women's Airforce Service Pilots in the uniform of that organization.*

Fig. 10-85.

Fig. 10-85. *Insignia such as this one, worn at a military school, may not be associated with the Regular Army even though they may be similar to prescribed pieces in general appearance.*

Section VI

Medical

Chapter Eleven

Medical Department

Since the start of the American army in 1775, the service has had physicians, but the assignment of doctors and the structure of the Medical Department was never consistent in the eighteenth and early nineteenth centuries. Even determining a satisfactory date for the origin of the Medical Department is difficult, because the army virtually disbanded after the Revolution, and regimental surgeons were not authorized again until 1789. Medical departments formed and disbanded as war threats came and went. The army enrolled two surgeons and twenty-five mates in March 1802 and established the Office of the Surgeon General in 1813. Congress officially founded the Medical Department in 1818 by appointing the Surgeon General to have central authority over medical officers.[1] The current Medical Department descends from these humble origins.

Rank titles given to physicians varied from those used by other officers. That practice, coupled with the use of civilian doctors in some capacities, makes following the early history of the Medical Department difficult. Also, in the twentieth century Congress created various corps within the Medical Department. Distinguishing among these corps can be confusing for someone who is not aware of the differences, for example, between the Medical Reserve Corps and the Medical Officers' Reserve Corps or between the Army Medical Specialists Corps and the Medical Service Corps.

The Medical Department has grown from simply physicians to personnel of many varied skills and talents and has changed by dividing, combining, and expanding various functions. The name itself was changed to the Army Medical Service in 1950, but for historical reasons it was retitled the Army Medical Department in 1968.[2] The subelements within the department, such as the Dental Corps and Medical Corps, are properly known as corps.

Early Officers' Uniforms

Physicians, surgeons, apothecary generals, hospital surgeons, and mates of 1813 wore black uniforms with the standing collar bearing an embroidered star within 1/2 inch of the front edge and "pocket flaps, and buttons placed across the cuffs, four to each, and covered buttons . . . , of the color of the coat." Regulations of 1821 and 1825 simple describe medical officers' coats as "corresponding to that of the general staff, except in the collar and cuffs, which will be of black silk velvet. No embroidery is allowed them."[3]

The Medical Department introduced special dark blue double-breasted coats with black velvet standing collars in 1832. Two rows of ten equally spaced buttons, 4 inches apart at the top and 2 1/2 inches apart at the bottom, ran down the coat. Two gold-embroidered buttonholes on each side of the collar designated the surgeon general. Surgeons' uniforms were identical except only one gold-embroidered buttonhole appeared on each collar, while assistant surgeons' coats had no collar ornamentation. Many staff officers wore aiguillettes, as did medical officers from 1832 until 1851.[4]

Epaulettes and Knots

Another distinctive uniform adopted by the Medical Department in October 1840 was a dark blue double-breasted coat with the black velvet collar embroidered at each end with a

Fig. 11-1. *A medical officer's uniform coat as prescribed in October 1840. Cuffs and collar were black velvet with gold-embroidered laurel leaves. The coat itself was dark blue. Epaulettes went on the coat.*

Fig. 11-2. *A gold-embroidered laurel wreath enclosing old English letters MS (Medical Service), as used on pre-1872 epaulettes.*

Fig. 11-3. *With the new 1851 uniform came epaulettes of this design, used until 1872. The strap is gilt, while the embroidery, metal crescent, and bullion (fringe) are silver.*

Fig. 11-1.

Fig. 11-2.

With the introduction of the new 1851 uniform, medical officers adopted the standard staff officers' garb. A gold-embroidered laurel wreath enclosed the silver old English letters *MS* on the epaulette pad, as shown in Fig. 11-2.[6] A full epaulette is illustrated in Fig. 11-3.

In 1872, letters *MD* for Medical Department replaced the Medical Service initials with the new shoulder knots (Fig. 11-4). A militia example from the Smithsonian collection is shown in Fig. 11-5. The initials *MD* continued until October 1890, when a

gold laurel branch 5 inches long and a gold ring of laurel leaves. Three-inch-deep black velvet cuffs were similarly embroidered (Fig. 11-1). The gold fringe on the epaulette (or "bullion of the epaulette") distinguished rank as listed in Table 11-1. Examples of epaulettes with different diameter bullion are shown in Figs. 2-5, 2-6, 2-7, 10-28, and 10-38.

The surgeon general also wore a solid silver colonel's eagle on the epaulette strap. A gold laurel wreath enclosed silver-embroidered old English letters *MS* for all medical officers' epaulette pads except those of surgeons, whose silver and gold bullion embroidery was reversed.[5]

Fig. 11-3.

Table 11-1. *Medical Rank as Shown by 1840 Epaulettes.*

Rank	Bullion Fringe	Strap Color
Surgeon General	½ × 3½ inches	Gold
Surgeon	½ × 3½ inches	Silver
Asst. Surgeon over five years	¼ × 2½ inches	Gold
Asst. Surgeon under five years	⅛ × 2½ inches	Gold

gold-embroidered shield, as shown in Fig. 11-6, became the branch device.[7] A 1-inch-high gilt-embroidered Maltese cross replaced the shield in 1896 (Fig. 11-7) before knots became obsolete in 1902. All staff colonels, including doctors, were to wear a silver branch device on the knot's strap between the pad and the upper fastener after 1899, according to regulations.[8] Some Civil War surgeons wore rank straps with the Old English *MS*, as shown in Fig. 11-8.

Fig. 11-5.

Fig. 11-4.

***Fig. 11-4.** MD, for Medical, Department, replaced the MS in 1872 when the shoulder knot was introduced. This 1872–90 knot used a nonstandard gold cord.*

***Fig. 11-5.** A militia medical department knot about 1880. The light color and the unit number were not used by the Regular Army.*

***Fig. 11-6.** From 1890 until 1896 doctors wore this design of Medical Department knot with a gold-embroidered shield.*

***Fig. 11-7.** Between 1896 and 1902 doctors wore shoulder knots with a 1-inch-high Maltese cross, as shown on this lieutenant colonel's insignia.*

Fig. 11-6.

Fig. 11-7.

Officers' Cap and Hat Insignia

From 1821 until 1840, Medical Department officers wore cocked hats similar to those of a general but with a black loop and cockade for decoration. In 1840 doctors added gilt tassels to the hat.[9]

On the 1851 dress cap, medical officers wore colored pompons, the top part green and the lower part buff. The insignia, a silver *US* embroidered with a gilt wreath, (see chapter 9) was the same for generals and their staffs.[10] smooth metal insignia made for the New York militia appears as Fig. 11-14.

The Medical Department adopted a 1-inch-high gilt caduceus, Fig. 11-15, as its insignia in 1902. For the service uniform, officers wore the device in bronze (Fig. 11-16).[13] The caduceus, two serpents intertwined on a winged staff, was carried by Mercury, the god of commerce. Shortly after the surgeon general announced the caduceus as the medical insignia, critics said it was not appropriate, even though the caduceus had been used intermittently as various US Army insignia, starting with the chevrons for hospital stewards in 1851. The debate was important because it was apparent to all of the officers that the insignia was to become the device for the expanding Medical Department. The critics were unhappy with the caduceus as the medical insignia, and

Fig. 11-8. Regulations did not prescribe the letters MS, yet during the Civil War many surgeons wore shoulder straps like these.

Fig. 11-8.

Fig. 11-9.

Fig. 11-9. Some medical officers of the 1860s wore cap and hat insignia with the letters MS instead of the proper US. The narrow gold oval was often a gold laurel wreath.

Fig. 11-10. Between 1892 and 1896 doctors wore this style of gold shield on the collar of the new sack coat. (1 1/8 inch wide)

Fig. 11-11. A first lieutenant and doctor wearing a typical uniform and insignia used between 1896 and 1902.

Fig. 11-12. An embroidered Medical Department Maltese cross on a section of black mohair collar braid used on the 1895 sack coat. (Design 25/32 inch wide)

Because doctors' epaulettes carried a laurel wreath enclosing the old English letters *MS*, during the Civil War some medical officers wore hat and cap devices based on the epaulette letters, substituting *MS* for the proper *US*.[11] An example with the MS in an oval instead of the wreath is shown in Fig. 11-9. After the Civil War and until 1895, medical officers wore the chapeau instead of the dress cap or dress helmet and were given no distinctive mark for their headgear.

Doctors' Collar Insignia

Doctors wore a gold shield (Fig. 11-10) on the 1892 sack coat until 1896, when an embroidered 3/4-inch-high gilt Maltese cross became the medical insignia (Figs. 11-11 and 11-12).[12] The establishing general order also allowed the cross to be made of metal resembling embroidery, (Fig. 11-13). A similar

Fig. 11-11.

Fig. 11-10.

Fig. 11-12.

they stated that the single serpent looped about a staff was properly associated with Aesculapius, the Greek god of healing.

The *Army and Navy Register* of 28 June 1902 noted the argument about the appropriate insignia. Giving the badge an unusual interpretation, the editor wrote of the caduceus: "The rod represents power, the serpents stand for wisdom and the two wings imply dilligence and activity, qualities which are undoubtedly possessed by our Medical officers. The design, however, does not lend itself easily to a Corps emblem." The dispute over the appropriateness of a caduceus continued for many years but never flared into raging controversy.

In 1924 the April issue of *The Military Surgeon* printed a review of an article by one Maurice Boigey in the *Presse Medicale* in which Boigey stated, "There is nothing in history to justify the use of the caduceus as the emblem of the physician . . . [and] it is most unfortunate that the 'confusion' exists." In the July issue of *The Military Surgeon* an anonymous rebuttal appeared in a letter to the editor. The writer stated a brilliant case that seems to have died in obscurity:

> The late Col. J. Van Rensselaer Hoff, of the Medical Corps, was a member of the board that selected this emblem, if he was not the one who was chiefly instrumental in its adoption. . . . Colonel Hoff was far too scholarly and intelligent a man to commit the blunder of 'confusing' the caduceus with the serpent staff of Aesculapius. The sign of Mercury was deliberately adopted, as I have heard him state, because it was the emblem of the merchant and hence the the emblem of the noncombatant. (Author's note: Hermes is actually the Greek god; Mercury was the Roman name. The writer evidently misquoted Colonel Hoff, or Colonel Hoff was not as knowledgeable as you may be lead to believe.) That [the] emblem of the merchant should also be that of the noncombatant arose from the fact that during the period when piracy prevailed in the Mediterranean, in junctures when it was necessary for a vessel to proclaim its nature, it was customary for a merchant vessel to indicate its noncombatant status by flying a flag which bore the emblem of Mercury, the God of the Merchant. The caduceus, in our use of it, is not distinctively the emblem of the physician, but the emblem of the whole Medical Department. The enlisted men of the medical department outnumber the physicians of that department. Besides the ambulance wagons, many vehicles are employed in field service in war which are not distinctively medical, but which are used for medical purposes. Both the enlisted men and the vehicles of the department (not to mention many other objects), should bear some sign of their neutralization for protection. It seemed to Colonel Hoff and to the board that the Geneva cross, which in addition to its use as an emblem of neutrality is also the emblem of the Swiss Republic, there might well be substituted an emblem which is not the emblem of a foreign country, and the caduceus was selected, as the emblem which for many ages has served to indicate the noncombatant. Since the only class of noncombatants, besides chaplains, which is permitted in the field during war is the medical department, the sign is in a very particular way "connected with the healing art." Whether or not the caduceus is the most appropriate emblem is a question which is not here discussed, but there is no doubt that the selection of it instead of the staff of Aesculapius was not made through ignorance, but in

Fig. 11-13.

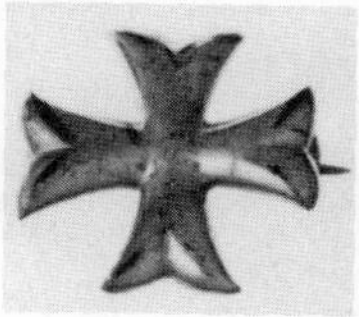

Fig. 11-14.

Fig. 11-15.

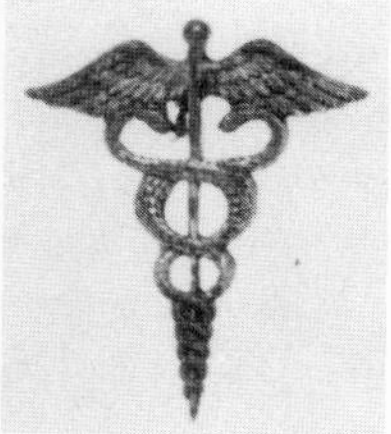

Fig. 11-16.

Fig. 11-13. *A metal, imitation embroidery insignia, 1896–1902, with wire loop fasteners. (3/4 inch wide)*

Fig. 11-14. *Various militia organizations, including that of New York, used a smooth Maltese cross for the medical department insignia. (13/16 inch wide)*

Fig. 11-15. *In 1902 the Medical Department adopted as its insignia a caduceus, the winged staff carried by Mercury in Roman mythology. For the dress coat, the 1-inch-high caduceus was gilt, as in this example worn by Doctor Van Poole in 1903.*

Fig. 11-16. *On the service uniform doctors wore a bronze caduceus, nominally 1 inch high. The device was selected by Colonel J. Van Rensselaer Hoff in 1902 based on ancient use of the emblem by merchant ships to distinguish them from pirates. In this context, the caduceus was the sign of a noncombatant. This particular insignia has two small loops by which it was sewn to the collar. (13/23 inch high and 29/32 inch wide)* the light of knowledge of ancient usages which very possibly was superior to that of the critic.

The army influence in selecting the caduceus carried over to civilian physicians in the early twentieth century, and many civilian medical personnel still use the caduceus as a symbol. Since World War II, many doctors have begun to display the Aesculapian staff. When the U.S. Air Force created new medical insignia, it adopted the staff of Aesculapius, with a single serpent, as the device for medical personnel.

Two bronze World War I caducei worn by officers are shown in Figs. 11-17 and 11-18. Small bronze shirt ornaments are shown in Figs. 11-19 and 11-20, and a gilt shirt device is shown in Fig. 11-21. These basic insignia continued into the 1930s with several artistic variations being made by different insignia companies. During the 1930s the Quartermaster Corps established official designs by making large drawings of each authorized insignia. Previously, most caducei had short

Fig. 11-17.

Fig. 11-18.

__Figs. 11-17 and 11-18.__ Two coat-sized caducei used during and after World War I by doctors. These examples point out some of the difference that typically exist. Both are of a light brown color, as opposed to the black color of the piece in Fig. 11-16. The shape of the wings is quite different in the two, with the one on the left (Fig. 11-17) having very straight and long wings compared to those of Fig. 11-18. The number of open or pierced areas differs between the two also. (1 1/32 inches and 57/64 inch wide, respectively)

Fig. 11-19.

Fig. 11-20.

__Figs. 11-19 and 11-20.__ Two shirt-sized bronze caducei. Fig. 11-19 has a shiny finish. These designs also exist in gilt for wear after 1923. (Each 5/8 inch wide)

Fig. 11-21.

__Fig. 11-21.__ A diminutive gilt caduceus for wear on the shirt collar. These very small insignia were often worn during and after World War I. (29/64 inch wide)

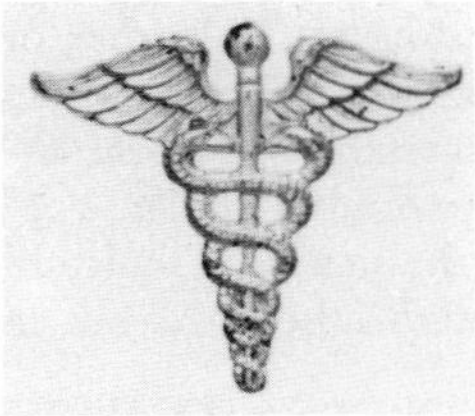

Fig. 11-22.

__Fig. 11-22.__ A brass Medical Department insignia, made about the time of World War II, that conforms to the official pattern adopted in 1936. (1 11/64 inch wide)

Fig. 11-23.

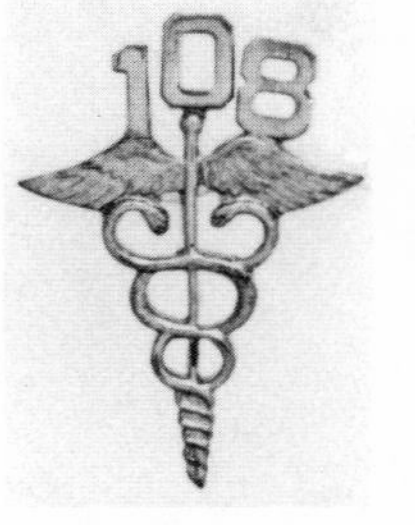

Fig. 11-24.

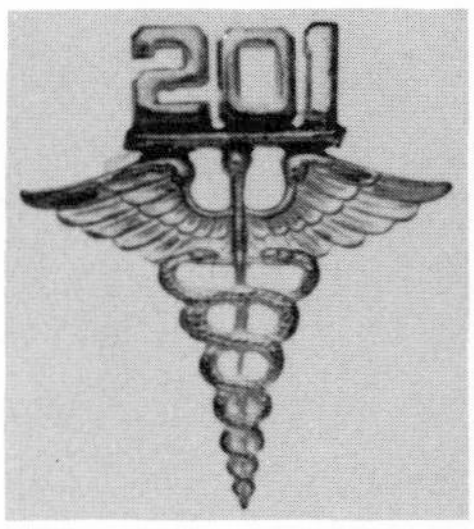

Fig. 11-25.

__Figs. 11-23, 11-24, and 11-25.__ Various doctors' branch insignia with unit numbers. Dates of use are the 1930s, World War II, and the 1980s. (31/32 inch, 15/16 inch, and 1 11/64 inches wide, respectively)

Fig. 11-26.

__Fig. 11-26.__ Major Irwin B. March, flight surgeon at Selfridge Field, Michigan, in the 1930s. While aviators were authorized to wear overseas caps with branch insignia at that time, other officers were not. Evidently Major March adopted the insignia style worn by the aviators, adapting it to fit his personal situation.

Fig. 11-27.

Fig. 11-28.

Fig. 11-29.

wings, although some companies made insignia with longer and straighter wings. In 1936 an "official" design replaced these many variations; an example is shown in Fig. 11-22.[14] Despite this, many companies continue to stamp insignia from their older dies, which generally had shorter wings.

A few medical units added numbers to the caduceus. In the 1930s the 102d Battalion placed a bronze number across the center of the device (Fig. 11-23). More common are World War II and later insignia with numbers added above the caduceus, as illustrated in Figs. 11-24 and 11-25. During the Vietnam War subdued collar insignia of black metal or black embroidery came into use for wear on fatigue uniforms.

Air Corps officers of the 1930s wore overseas caps carrying the branch insignia. Fig. 11-26 shows a 1937 flight surgeon assigned to Selfridge Field, Michigan, wearing the Air Corps cap but with the medical insignia indicating he is a doctor, not a pilot.

Medical Reserve

Congress established the Medical Reserve Corps in April 1908. Officers of this corps wore a gilt caduceus bearing a bronze monogram *RC* three-eighths inch high (Fig. 11-27). On service uniforms the men wore a bronze caduceus with gilt letters (Figs. 11-28 and 11-29). Because of a congressional act of 3 June 1916, the corps went out of existence on 3 June 1917, replaced by the Medical Officers' Reserve Corps. Although the army did not authorize an insignia for this new corps, I believe these doctors used the caduceus with *R* (Figs. 11-30 and 11-31), because most of the old Medical Reserve Corps physicians simply switched to the Medical Officers' Reserve Corps. Some collectors believe the *R* stands for roentgenologist (an early x-ray specialist), but there is no evidence to support this theory, and the reserve corps change is certainly plausible. It is worth noting that the entire U.S. Army Reserve system dates from 23 April 1908, when Congress established this corps.[15]

Acting Assistant Surgeons and Contract Surgeons

In the 1880s and early 1890s Congress allowed the secretary of war to employ up to fifty acting assistant surgeons, who were commonly called "contract surgeons." These men had no uniforms or insignia, and eventually authorization for their employment was withdrawn. Congress reintroduced the term "assistant surgeons" in May 1898 by allowing fifteen in the army. These men obtained special uniforms and insignia in July 1898 when the secretary of war prescribed the Medical Corps uniform stripped of "all marks and insignia of rank." A month later the War Department also initially permitted acting assistant surgeons to wear the uniform of assistant surgeons with the rank of first lieutenants and ornaments of silver instead of gold.[16]

Also in May 1898 Congress provided "that in emergencies the Surgeon General . . . may appointment as many contract surgeons as may be necessary." This resulted in the assignment of more than 650 contract surgeons during the Spanish-American War. No special uniform was specified; presumably the surgeons wore standard medical clothing, because they had acting ranks of lieutenant colonel and below. Civilian physicians remaining under contract with the army to supplement the Medical Corps after the Spanish-American War received military uniforms in 1901 of "an Assistant Surgeon with the rank of first lieutenant, the shoulder straps and ornaments to be silver instead of gold." Contract surgeons had no full dress uniforms, but starting in 1902 they wore a silver caduceus on the dress blue and dress white uniforms and a bronze caduceus on the service uniform. Instead of the U.S. coat of arms (1903–1905) or the letters *US* (after 1905) worn by regular army officers, contract surgeons wore the 1/2-inch-high block letters *CS* in silver (Fig. 11-32) or bronze (Fig. 11-33) to match the caduceus (Fig. 11-34). Contract surgeons also eliminated shoulder straps showing rank in 1902.[17]

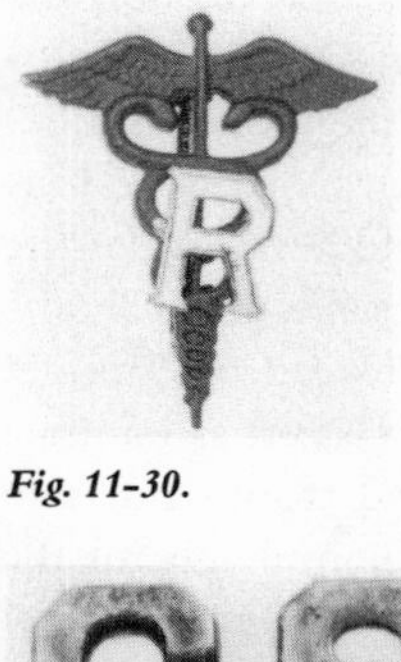

Fig. 11-30.

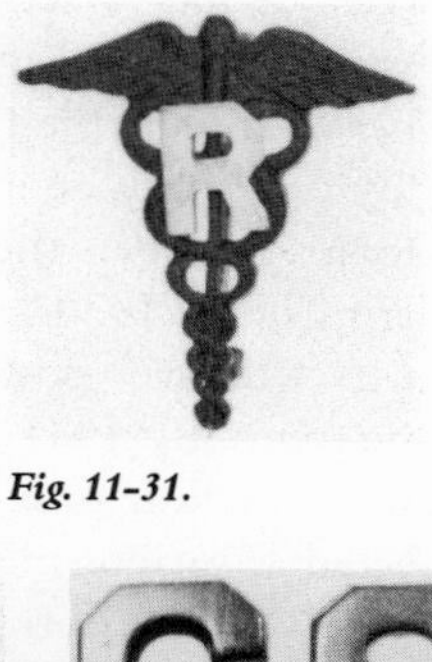

Fig. 11-31.

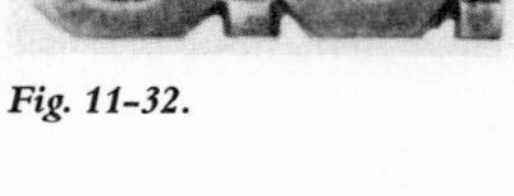

Fig. 11-32.

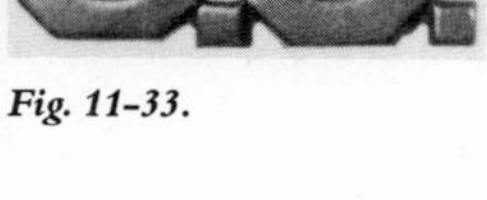

Fig. 11-33.

Fig. 11-27. *The U.S. Army Reserves trace their founding to the Medical Reserve Corps, established in April 1908. Corps members wore this type of insignia with a gilt medical insignia and bronze RC monogram. The insignia became obsolete in June 1917 when the corps went out of existence. (57/64 inch wide)*

Fig. 11-28. *A Medical Reserve Corps insignia for the service uniform, with bronze medical insignia and gilt monogram. (1 5/64 inches wide)*

Fig. 11-29. *Captain H. H. Walker, 1917, wearing a bronze caduceus with gilt Medical Reserve Corps RC monogram.*

Figs. 11-30 and 11-31. *Unauthorized insignia believed to have been worn by members of the Medical Officers' Reserve Corps, successor to the Medical Reserve Corps. Members of the Medical Reserve Corps became members of the Medical Officers' Reserve Corps in 1917. (29/32 inch and 1 1/64 inches wide, respectively)*

Fig. 11-32. *Silver letters worn by contract surgeons, 1902–1908, instead of the gilt national eagle (1902–1905) or gilt US (1905–1908) on dress uniforms. (1 15/64 inches)*

Fig. 11-33. *For service uniforms, contract surgeons used bronze letters with an accompanying bronze caduceus. (1 3/8 inches wide)*

With the creation of the Medical Reserve Corps in 1908, contract surgeons were virtually eliminated after a peak strength of slightly less than two hundred men. The number of contract surgeons greatly increased during World War I, and some of those men probably felt a need for a uniform to show their connection with the armed forces. Contract surgeons finally received special uniforms in July 1918, with the insignia a 1-inch-high bronze caduceus carrying a superimposed gilt *CS* monogram.[18] This two-letter monogram on a caduceus (Figs. 11-35, 11-36, 11-37) persisted after most of the other medical branches switched to only one letter on a caduceus after the close of the war.

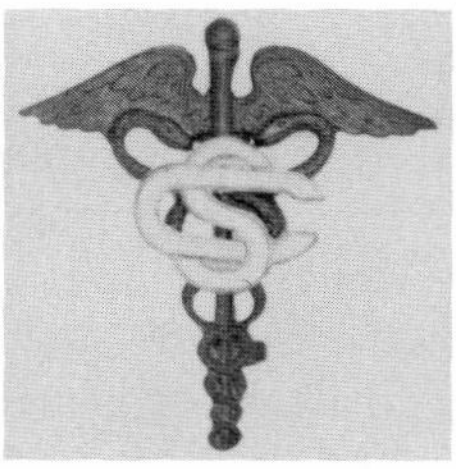

Fig. 11-34. *A silver caduceus worn by contract surgeons with the accompanying letters CS on dress uniforms. (49/64 inch wide)*

Figs. 11-35, 11-36, and 11-37. *Contract surgeons wore a bronze caduceus with gilt CS monogram from mid-1918 until 1920. These three versions are typical of insignia from World War I. Fig. 11-35 is a French-made insignia with the tops of the wings comparatively straight. Fig. 11-36 is an insignia with a screw-post fastener, which can be partly seen where the wings join the staff, and Fig. 11-37 shows a letter C that is totally curved instead of having a straight top and bottom. (1 3/64 inches, 7/8 inch, and 15/16 inch wide, respectively)*

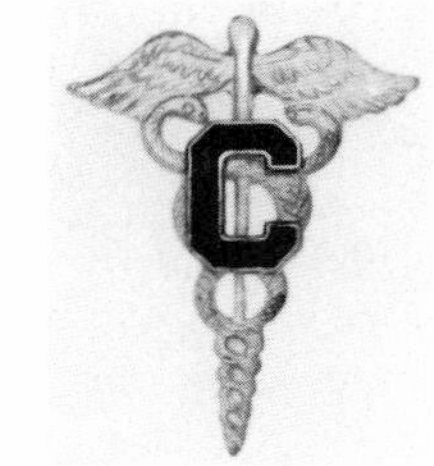
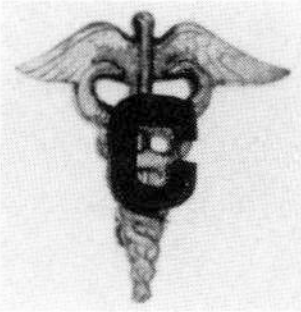

Fig. 11-38. *A post-1920 contract surgeons' insignia with a brown letter, as prescribed until World War II. The design of the basic caduceus dates the insignia from after 1936. (1 5/32 inches wide)*

Fig. 11-39. *The die made in the 1930s was used to stamp this contract surgeons' insignia with a black, block letter. (57/64 inch wide)*

Fig. 11-40. *This example is a typical small gilt caduceus with a bronze metal letter worn in the late 1920s by contract surgeons on shirts. (51/64 inch wide)*

Fig. 11-41. *A contract surgeons' insignia, as officially prescribed, with gilt caduceus and 3/8-inch-high black C. (1 11/64 inches wide)*

Fig. 11-42. *Dental surgeons wore 1/2-inch-high silver block DS letters on dress and white uniforms starting in 1902. (1 3/16 inches wide)*

In September 1920 army regulations prescribed a single letter for all parts of the Medical Department. Contract surgeons received a *C* on the caduceus, although the older *CS* monogram continued to be authorized "as long as serviceable." By the time the army published Regulation 600-35 in October 1921, only the *C* was mentioned. Probably few, if any, contract surgeons wore uniforms between the world wars, since the army of the 1930s used reserve medical officers wherever possible instead of contract surgeons. By 1941, men classed as contract surgeons not only served troops but also acted as various medical consultants for the massive war effort. Early wartime contract surgeons wore the same clothing as commissioned officers, less the rank insignia and *US* collar insignia. The lapel ornament was still the caduceus with brown *C* (Fig. 11-38), although after late 1942 contract surgeons added first lieutenant rank insignia. A 1930 contract surgeon coat insignia with the common but unauthorized black letter is shown in Fig. 11-39, and a shirt collar insignia is illustrated in Fig. 11-40. Provisions for this medical insignia disappeared from regulations in 1956, although as late as 1960 the government still sold the insignia with a black letter *C* (Fig. 11-41).[19]

Dental Corps Officers

Congress first allowed the army to enroll thirty contract dental surgeons in February 1901. Given uniforms in April 1901, contract dental surgeons initially wore a silver caduceus on the collar and *DS* in silver-embroidered block letters between the first lieutenant bars on the shoulder straps. Later changes omitted the unique straps and placed the silver block *DS* letters (Fig. 11-42) on the collar with the silver caduceus for the dress and white uniforms. On the service coat surgeons wore collar ornaments of the same design in bronze. A set of the 1/2-inch-high bronze letters is shown in Fig. 11-43. It should be noted that these early dentists wore *DS* instead of the *US* worn by the regular army officers (Fig. 11-44). Because of congressional limits, few dental surgeons actually saw service; in 1908 only thirty-one were in service.[20]

Acting dental surgeons adopted a gilt monogram *DS* superimposed upon a silver caduceus (Fig. 11-45) in 1911 for wear on

Fig. 11-44.

Fig. 11-44. A dental surgeon, Dr. Tignor, in service uniform about 1906.

Fig. 11-42.

Fig. 11-43.

Fig. 11-43. Bronze insignia for a dental surgeon's service uniform, 1902–11, with the letters replacing the normal US used by commissioned officers. (1 1/32 inches wide)

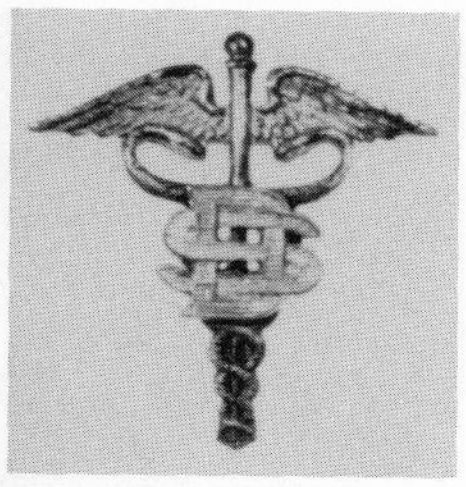

Fig. 11-45.

Fig. 11-45. Acting dental surgeons adopted a silver caduceus with gilt DS monogram in December 1911 and used the insignia until 1916. (1 1/32 inches wide)

all uniforms, still without the usual accompanying letters *US*. A nonregulation gilt caduceus with bronze *DS* is shown in Fig. 11-46. Congress abolished the grade of acting dental surgeon in December 1916, and the insignia disappeared. With the 1916 change, dental surgeons took a gilt caduceus with a bronze *DC* monogram, accompanied by the letters *US*, for both the dress blue and white uniforms. On the service coat dentists wore a bronze caduceus with a gilt monogram, Fig. 11-47. The comparable shirt insignia is shown in Fig. 11-48.[21]

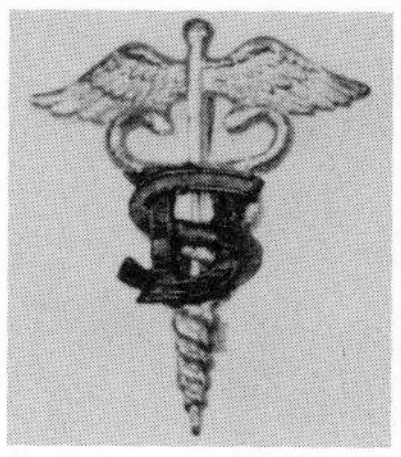

Fig. 11-46.

Fig. 11-46. A nonregulation gilt caduceus with bronze DS monogram. It is not known if this insignia was worn by acting dental surgeons, despite its incorrect color, or if a dental surgeon wore it rather than the proper DC monogram. (7/8 inch wide)

Fig. 11-47.

Fig. 11-47. Between December 1911 and December 1917, dental surgeons wore a medical insignia with a Dental Corps (DC) monogram. This service uniform insignia example has unusually narrow wings. (1 inch wide)

Fig. 11-49.

Fig. 11-49. Starting in December 1917, dentists were to wear the bronze caduceus with a single gilt D. (57/64 inch wide)

Fig. 11-50.

Fig. 11-50. A dental surgeon's insignia, made in France for the American Expeditionary Forces (AEF). The letter was struck with the basic insignia, and after it was chemically treated to make it dark, the face of the letter was buffed off, showing the bright metal. (1 1/64 inches wide)

In December 1917 dentists switched to a gilt *D* on a bronze caduceus as shown in Figs. 11-49 and 11-50, the latter made in France in 1918. Fig. 11-51 shows a World War I dentist, complete with collar insignia, at work. With the reappearance of white dress uniforms shortly after the close of World War I came a gilt caduceus with a bronze *D* (Fig. 11-52).[22] Smaller shirt insignia in both gilt and bronze from between the world wars are shown in Figs. 11-53 through 11-56. World War II and later ornaments are illustrated in Figs. 11-57 and 11-58, the latter having been made since 1970 and bearing a medical battalion designation.

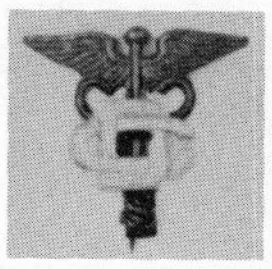

Fig. 11-48.

Fig. 11-48. Another standing coat collar insignia for dentists, 1911–17.

Veterinary Corps

Shortly after the Spanish-American War, veterinarians classified as civilian employees joined cavalry and field artillery regiments. In 1901 veterinarians wore the uniforms of either cavalry or artillery second lieutenants but without any shoulder straps of rank. Veterinarians wore crossed silver cannons or sabers, according to branch, on the collar and a silver *US* with a silver eagle on the field uniform straps. General Order 81, dated 17 July 1902, called for the silver *US* to be replaced by *VS*, but this probably did not see wide use, as the army did not require the insignia until mid-1903. Before this change was effective, the War Department changed devices in December 1902: for the dress uniform a gilt cavalry or gilt artillery device with a silver horse's winged and shod foot in the lower angle, or for the service uniform a similar design in bronze. A cavalry example is shown in Fig. 11-59. A 1902 change precluded veterinarians

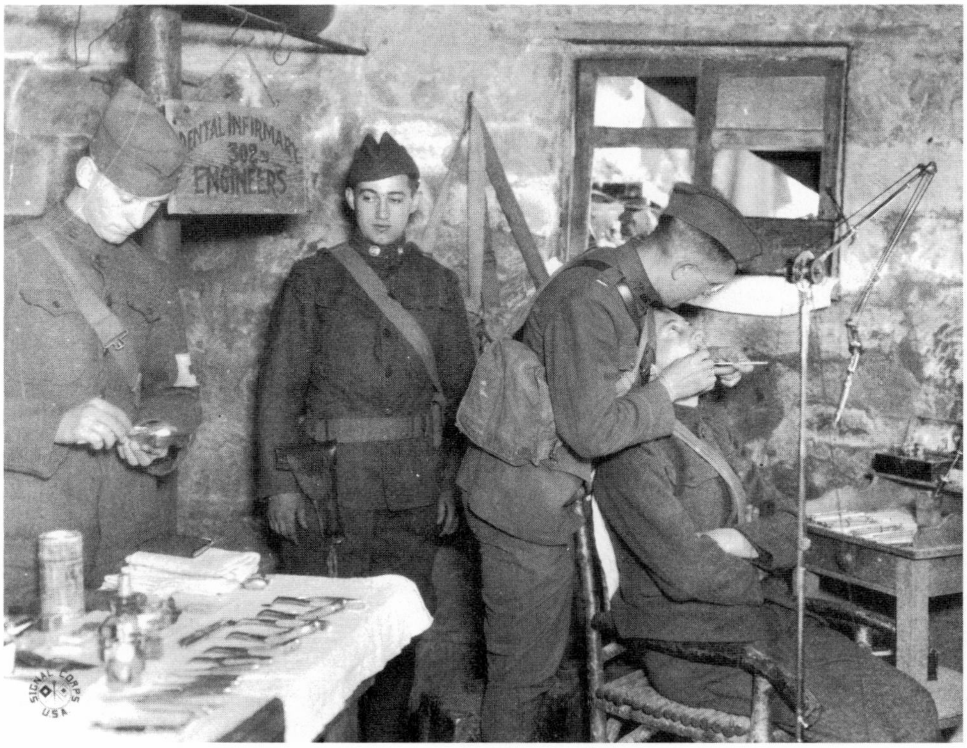

Fig. 11-51.

Fig. 11-51. A dentist at work in France during World War I.

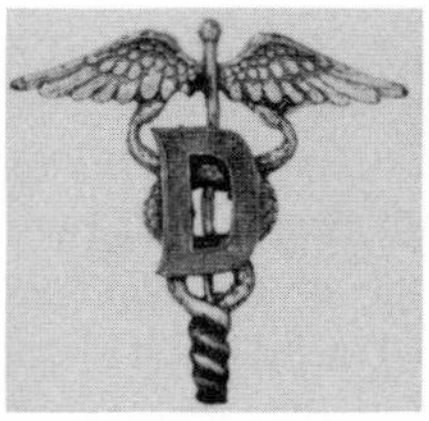

Fig. 11-52.

Fig. 11-53.

Fig. 11-54.

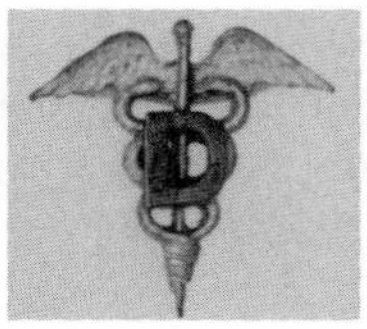

Fig. 11-55.

Fig. 11-56.

Fig. 11-52. For the white uniform after World War I the army introduced a gilt caduceus with a bronze D. (1 1/64 inches wide)

Figs. 11-53 and 11-54. Small World War I insignia for dentists' shirt collars. These were worn from 1918 through 1923. (51/64 and 5/8 inch wide, respectively)

Figs. 11-55 and 11-56. Starting in 1923 and for several years thereafter, Dental Corps shirt insignia were gilt with a bronze letter, as shown on the left, but many letters were actually black as in Fig. 11-56. (25/32 and 41/64 inch wide, respectively)

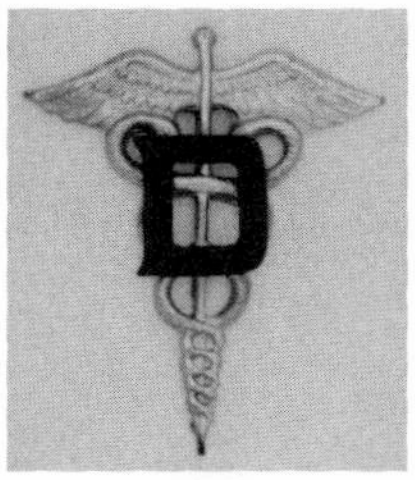

Fig. 11-57.

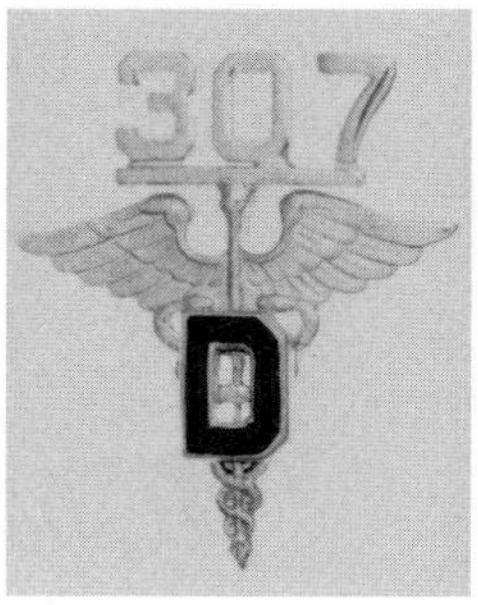

Fig. 11-58.

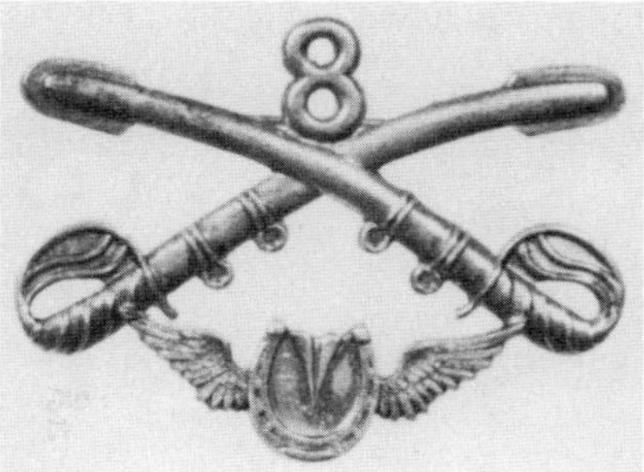

Fig. 11-59.

Fig. 11-57. Probably made during World War II, this clutch-back gilt insignia has a very dark bronze letter attached to the caduceus with a single brad. (29/32 inch wide)

Fig. 11-58. Made in the late 1970s, this dental insignia carries a unit number, an uncommon practice. (1 11/64 inches wide)

Fig. 11-59. In December 1902 the War Department prescribed a horse's winged and shod foot to be worn by veterinarians in the lower angle of either cavalry or field artillery insignia. Insignia of this general description were used until the formation of a Veterinary Corps in 1916. Veterinarians joined the army by an act of March 2, 1901. (1 15/16 inches wide)

from wearing rank and the coat of arms or the letters *US* (Fig. 11-60). The service uniform, with one of several versions of bronze artillery insignia, is shown in Fig. 11-61. The many changes of cavalry sabers and of artillery cannons is covered in chapters 6 and 7. It is important to note that these combat arms insignia did change during the times veterinarians wore them. Not only was the winged horseshoe worn under cavalry or artillery insignia, but as shown in Fig. 11-62, the device was also worn alone; certainly that was non-regulation.[23]

Congress established the Veterinary Corps as part of the Medical Department in 1916, and by the end of 1916 veterinarians changed to the gold caduceus with bronze intertwined letters *VC* (Fig. 11-63). Service

Fig. 11-60.

Fig. 11-61.

Fig. 11-62.

Fig. 11-63.

Fig. 11-64.

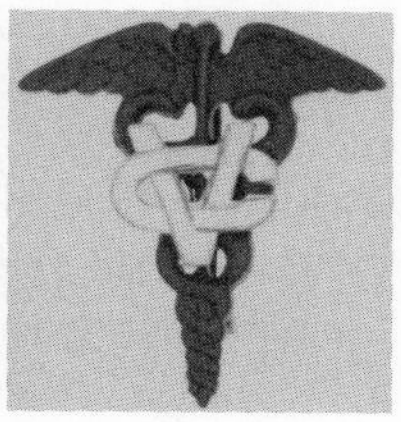

Fig. 11-65.

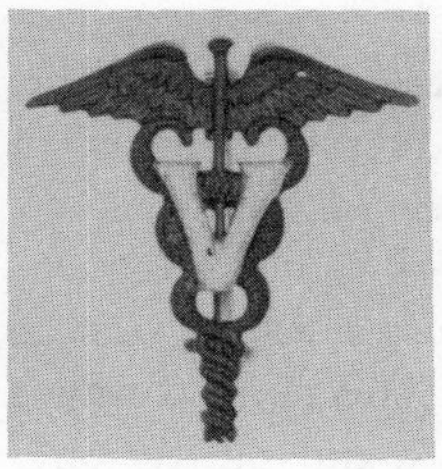

Fig. 11-66.

Fig. 11-67.

uniforms bore similar bronze insignia with gilt letters (Figs. 11-64 and 11-65). The letter *V* became the superimposed device in December 1917 (Fig. 11-66, made in London, and Fig. 11-67, made in Paris). Two versions of bronze shirt ornaments are shown in Figs. 11-68 and 11-69.[24]

The War Department prescribed gilt insignia with bronze *V* in September 1920 for the white uniform.[25] Fig. 11-70 shows

Fig. 11-60. *Dr. Jewell, a veterinarian, shown in 1911 in a dress coat. As in the case of dental surgeons and other skilled medical personnel who were not doctors, the US insignia were not worn.*

Fig. 11-61. *Field artillery veterinarian Norton in field uniform with bronze insignia in 1904.*

Fig. 11-62. *Nonregulation insignia used before World War I. The winged horseshoe alone was never prescribed, but it was made and worn by some officers. The caduceus was not prescribed until 1916.*

Fig. 11-63. *For less than a year, beginning in December 1916, members of the Veterinary Corps wore a gilt caduceus with bronze VC monogram. (1 3/32 inches wide)*

Figs. 11-64 and 11-65. *Two versions of service uniform insignia for the Veterinary Corps, prescribed until December 1917. (1 1/32 inches and 31/32 inch wide, respectively)*

Fig. 11-66. *This light bronze, beautifully detailed, late World War I insignia was made by the J. R. Gaunt Company, London. (1 inch wide)*

Fig. 11-67. *A French-made insignia with the letter struck as a part of the caduceus. This piece was made by a firm in Paris for the AEF during World War I. (1 inch wide)*

Fig. 11-68.

Fig. 11-69.

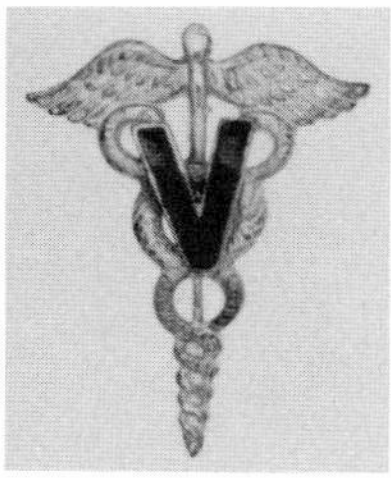

Fig. 11-70.

Figs. 11-68 and 11-69. *Medium-sized and small veterinarians' insignia made during World War I for shirts. (27/32 and 5/8 inch wide)*

Fig. 11-70. *In the 1930s, for a reason now lost, some veterinary insignia were made with a red letter, like this piece with a bright red enameled V. (57/64 inch wide)*

Fig. 11-71.

Fig. 11-71. *A machine-embroidered, cotton collar insignia made during World War II with a red letter instead of the prescribed black. (Design 1 1/16 inch wide)*

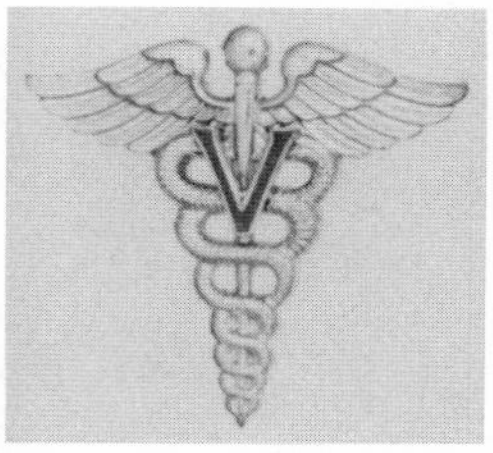

Fig. 11-72.

Fig. 11-72. *A World War II Veterinary Corps insignia with a smaller than normal letter of brown enamel. (1 5/32 inches wide)*

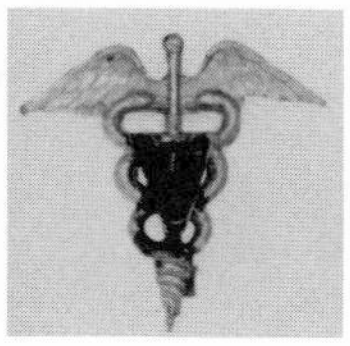

Fig. 11-73.

Fig. 11-73. *This pin-backed shirt collar insignia from the mid- or late 1920s has the metal letter painted black. (25/32 inch wide)*

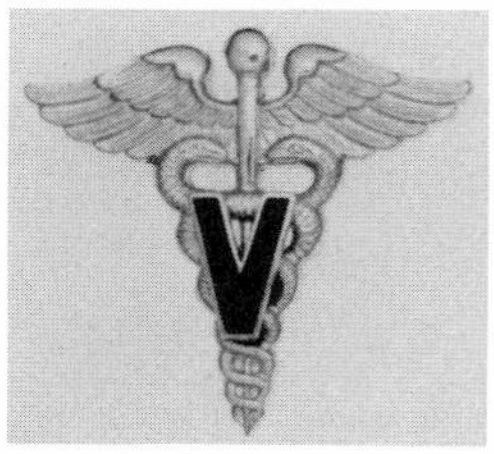

Fig. 11-74.

Fig. 11-74. *A current insignia worn by veterinarians, with a black enameled letter. (1 11/64 inches wide)*

an unauthorized but evidently widely worn red enamel *V* on a caduceus. A similar World War II khaki cloth device in Fig. 11-71 also has a red letter. An insignia with a smaller than normal *V* is shown in Fig. 11-72, and a 1920s shirt-sized insignia is illustrated in Fig. 11-73. The current insignia is in Fig. 11-74.

Nurse Corps

At the onset of the Spanish-American War, Congress authorized the surgeon general to appoint women nurses under contract. Slightly over 1,500 nurses signed contracts, and the maximum on duty at any given time though 1901 was 1,158. This number subsequently dropped rapidly, and shortly only about sixty nurses served the army.[26]

It is interesting that these early nurses, while members of the army, were neither enlisted nor commissioned. The uniforms of these Spanish-American War nurses were civilian clothing with a red enameled, modified cross of Saint John on the left collar. An example of the insignia is shown in Fig. 11-75, and the insignia in use is shown in Fig. 11-76. A June 1899 circular stated, "Each nurse will provide herself with the prescribed nurses' uniform of army blue and white." Congress permanently authorized women nurses on 2 February 1901. At that time women received a gilt-edged green cross (Fig. 11-77), similar to the red one it replaced, "to be pinned on the left side of the collar."[27]

This cross lasted until 1907, when nurses began wearing on the left collar a gilt caduceus bearing the white monogram *ANC*, which stood for Army Nurse Corps.[28] An example is shown in Fig. 11-78.

Before World War I nurses had only the indoor uniform with gilt caduceus bearing the white monogram; they had no special outdoor clothing. When nurses received orders for Europe in 1917, the need for recognizable outdoor clothing resulted in a May 1917 approval of a blue serge outdoor uniform shown in Fig. 79-3 in chapter 79, "Women's Uniforms through World War II." Initially the army told nurses to wear the bronze letters *US* and a bronze caduceus on this uniform, but the secretary of war changed the branch insignia to a bronze caduceus with gilt monogram, as shown in Figs. 11-79 and 11-80.[29]

During World War I the American Red Cross (ARC) worked closely with the army to supply nurses. Those ARC nurses who joined the army wore a red cross on the cap to signify their previous qualification (Fig. 11-81). The ARC also supplied all army nurses with red-lined dark blue capes, because

Fig. 11-75.

Fig. 11-76.

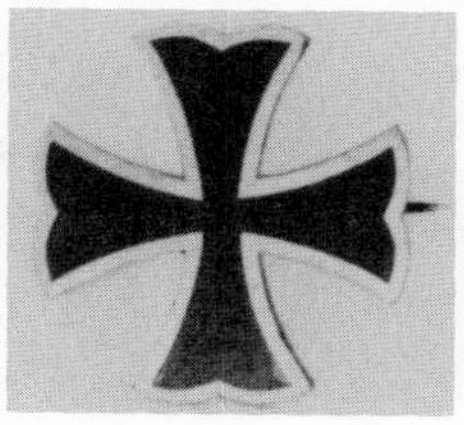

Fig. 11-77.

Fig. 11-78.

Fig. 11-79.

Fig. 11-80.

the government did not issue that piece of clothing until January 1919.[30]

Besides nurses, the American Red Cross supplied many other personnel during World War I, and the ARC published *American Red Cross Uniforms* on 28 February 1918 to describe uniforms for foreign service workers other than nurses and doctors. Uniforms of gray whipcord were made up of a single-breasted, four-button sack tunic with lapels and a pleated shirt plus a gray cloth hat and the letters *US* on the shoulder straps. Sleeve markings indicated grade or rank in the following system:

- Grade One: A 3/4-inch-wide blue band with two silver metal stars 1 inch above the band and with a Greek cross of red cloth 1 inch above the stars.
- Grade Two: Same as grade one, but with only one star.
- Grade Three: Five bands of blue cloth, each 3/8 inch wide and 2 1/2 inches long replacing the star in grade two.
- Grade Four: Same as grade three but with four blue bands.
- Grade Five: Same as grade three but with three blue bands (Fig. 11-82).
- Grade Six: Same as grade three but with two blue bands.
- Grade Seven: Same as grade three but with one blue band.

In addition, distinctively colored ties, collar trim, and hat bands showed a Red Cross worker's service, as described in Table 11-2.[31]

New insignia for Army nurses, introduced in 1920, carried just the letter *N*. For the white army uniform a gilt caduceus had a bronze letter, and for other uniforms a bronze caduceus had a gilt letter (Fig. 11-83). Because nurses wore white letters on the gilt 1907–20 caduceus, some manufacturers made the new device with the single letter in white, a widespread practice which continued into World War II (Fig. 11-84). An early 1930s caduceus with a red letter is illustrated in Fig. 11-85. Caducei with wider wings came into existence after 1936, and these have continued to the present.[32] A current caduceus with a post–World War II black enamel *N* is shown in Fig. 11-86. This design continues as the

Fig. 11-75. *A U.S. Army nurse of the Spanish-American War. On her collar she wears a red cross of the type shown in Fig. 11-76.*

Fig. 11-76. *A bright red–enameled modified cross of Saint John was the first insignia used by contract nurses. Over a thousand women wore this insignia, although it is not common today.*

Fig. 11-77. *Congress permanently authorized women nurses in 1901. Simultaneously the army prescribed this green cross, which was to be worn on the left collar. (15/16 inch wide)*

Fig. 11-78. *Starting in 1907, nurses replaced the green cross with a gilt caduceus bearing a white enameled Army Nurse Corps (ANC) monogram. (29/32 inch wide)*

Figs. 11-79 and 11-80. *U.S.-made (Fig. 11-79) and French-made nurses' insignia from World War I. These were worn on the first outdoor uniforms for nurses, since nurses were not prescribed any official clothing except those worn on wards until they had to go overseas. The light-colored but dull-finished monogram with pierced areas is held to the caduceus of Fig. 11-79 with two pins. The French-made letters of Fig. 11-80 are affixed with one pin. (1 1/32 and 1 3/64 inches wide, respectively)*

Table 11-2. American Red Cross Service Colors.

Service	Color Trim
National Headquarters	Royal blue
Military relief	Horizon blue
Civilian relief	Dark red
Development	Bottle green
Clerks	Tan
Chauffeurs	Peacock green
Delegates to meet transportation	Wine
Automobile services	White

Fig. 11-81. *This 1918 U.S. Army nurse in a ward uniform with cape wears the Army Nurse Corps caduceus on the cape collar. The red cross on her cap indicates that before she joined the Nurse Corps the American Red Cross had recognized her as a nurse.*

Fig. 11-82. *This World War I American Red Cross officer is of the fifth grade, shown by the three bars on his sleeve. He wears an army officer's uniform coat instead of the regulation lapel style.*

Fig. 11-83. *In the 1920s nurses wore a gilt caduceus with a bronze letter N, like this piece, which was worn by a woman who entered the army after graduating from the Army School of Nursing. (1 inch wide)*

Fig. 11-84. *During the 1920s through the early 1940s some nurses wore insignia with nonregulation white letters, possibly because of the influence of the 1907 design with the white ANC monogram. (1 1/16 inches wide)*

Fig. 11-85. *From the 1930s, this narrow-winged caduceus has a red-enameled N. (7/8 inch wide)*

Fig. 11-86. *A Nurse Corps insignia used during or after World War II. The design conforms to the official drawing. (29/32 inch wide)*

nursing insignia. Fig. 11-87 shows a hand-embroidered example made in Vietnam in 1967, with the *N* outlined in white.

A totally unauthorized "antique bronze" device with a dark red *N* is shown in Fig. 11-88. This was probably made about 1950 when the Women's Army Corps introduced insignia of this color and a manufacturer evidently believed all women would switch to antique bronze. Also not called for in regulations, but common in collections, is a silver caduceus with brown enamel *N*.

Army School of Nursing

World War I found the U.S. Army hospitals poorly staffed and practicing obsolete nursing

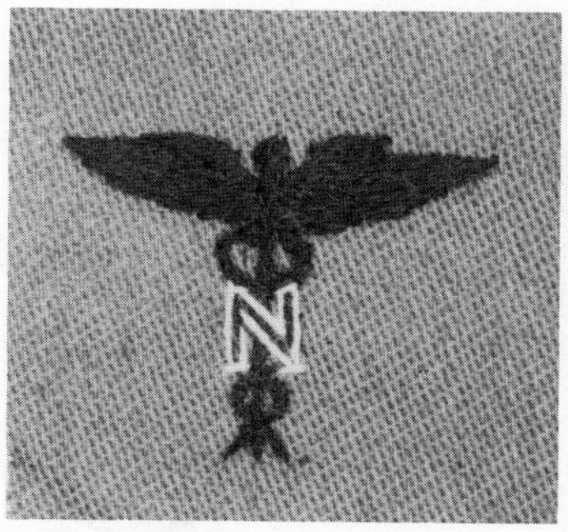

Fig. 11-87.

techniques. A study released in March 1918 recommended the founding of a nursing school to correct the deficiencies. In May 1918 the secretary of war approved the founding of the Army School of Nursing. The first students went to Camp Wadsworth, near Spartansburg, South Carolina, and Camp Devens, Massachusetts, while later students arrived at Walter Reed in August. Throughout the fall of 1918 the surgeon general established schools at a total of thirty-two military hospitals in the United States. By December 1918 there were 1,578 female students, classified as civilian employees, on duty at the schools. Students wore blue nurse uniforms with white collar and cuffs and a black four-in-hand tie.[33]

The dean of the Army School of Nursing, Annie Goodrich, entered into correspondence with the insignia makers Bailey, Banks and Biddle Company for submission of a design. In September 1918 the adjutant general approved a concept submitted by Dean Goodrich as a result of her correspondence with the jewelry firm and announced the attractive design in regulations of October 1918. An early school badge made by Bailey, Banks and Biddle is shown in Fig. 11-89. As a sidelight, this type of caduceus, with the leading edge of the wings made in a smooth downward slope and a narrow gap for the staff between the wing "shoulders," is distinctively made by Bailey, Banks and Biddle. Other caducei made by this firm are shown elsewhere in this chapter and are identical in design. An unusual variation of the nursing school insignia, with the lamp too high on the caduceus, is shown in Fig. 11-90. Women wore bronze ornaments on each collar of the outdoor uniform with the bronze *US*. On the indoor uniform the lamp and caduceus were worn on the left collar only.[34]

After the 1918 armistice the surgeon general consolidated those hospitals with students, and many students quit the army schools. Finally, in the summer of 1921 the first 404 students graduated from Walter Reed Hospital, and 108 graduated from Letterman Hospital. In the fall of 1923, coincidental with the introduction of gilt collar devices with the bronze lamp as shown in Fig. 11-91, the school was further consolidated at Walter Reed Hospital. In uniform regulations the bronze *US* and branch insignia continued to be authorized for wear on the outdoor uniform (although in practice outdoor uniforms were not used after 1921), even though the rest of the army discarded bronze insignia in 1923.[35]

In 1931 War Department officials decided to close the school. The class of 1932 and advanced members of the 1933 class graduated in 1932, and other students transferred to civilian schools, thus ending the use of the collar insignia.[36]

Fig. 11-88.

Fig. 11-89.

Fig. 11-90.

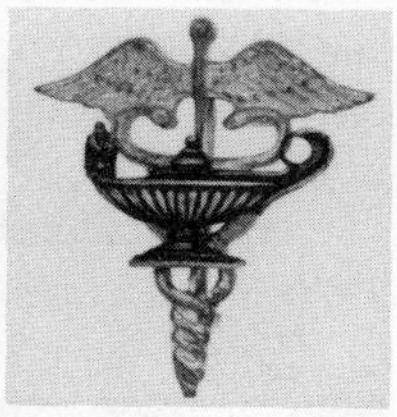

Fig. 11-91.

Training Unit

Various medical training camps opened across the United States during 1917 and 1918. One of the major training units established Camp Crane, near Allentown, Pennsylvania, in May 1917. This camp initially mobilized recruits for the Ambulance Service, and after the spring of 1918 it provided trained medical units of all types.[37] Officers of the training unit at Camp Crane wore the insignia shown in Fig. 11-92, which consists

Fig. 11-87. *Hand-embroidered in Vietnam, this black caduceus has the letter traced in white to make it stand out. (Design 1 3/8 inches wide)*

Fig. 11-88. *In the 1950s members of the Women's Army Corps wore buttons and hat insignia that were "antique bronze" in color. Evidently this antique bronze caduceus with brown letter was improperly made at that time, since nurses were never authorized insignia of this color. (1 3/16 inch wide)*

Fig. 11-89. *An Army School of Nursing bronze-colored insignia with a gilt lamp made by the Bailey, Banks and Biddle Company. (1 1/64 inches wide)*

Fig. 11-90. *A bronze nursing school insignia with the lamp too high. (7/8 inch wide)*

Fig. 11-91. *A gilt Army School of Nursing insignia worn by a 1932 graduate, the year the school closed. (49/64 inch wide)*

Fig. 11-92. *Training unit officers at Camp Crane, Pennsylvania, wore this nonregulation insignia during World War I. (1 inch wide)*

Fig. 11-92.

Fig. 11-93.

Fig. 11-94.

Fig. 11-95.

Fig. 11-96.

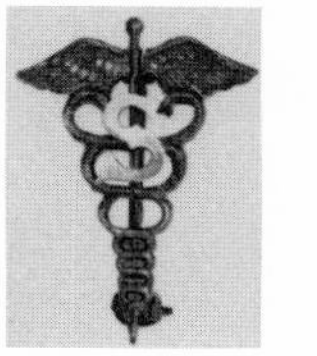

Fig. 11-97.

Fig. 11-98.

Fig. 11-93. *Although insignia of this type were officially designated for contract surgeons, some Sanitary Corps officers wore them in 1917 and early 1918 because the monogram could be interpreted as SC. (1 3/64 inches wide)*

Fig. 11-94. *Approved as the Sanitary Corps insignia in December 1917 was a bronze caduceus with gilt S. This sparsely feathered caduceus has a plain gilt letter soldered to the face. (63/64 inch wide)*

Fig. 11-95. *An ornate, slender S used by Sanitary Corps officers until 1921. (15/16 inch wide)*

Fig. 11-96. *This light bronze caduceus displays a thick letter decorated with horizontal lines. (1 5/64 inches wide)*

Fig. 11-97. *A petite, brown bronze caduceus with an ornate slender letter worn on shirts by Sanitary Corps officers during World War I. (5/8 inch wide)*

Fig. 11-98. *The caduceus used during World War I with a plain S is similar in design to that used during the 1930s. Its bronze color was not used after 1921. (26/32 inch wide)*

Fig. 11-99. *An officer of the Sanitary Corps, World War I, wearing his branch insignia.*

of the bronze letters *T* and *U* added on each wing of the caduceus.

Sanitary Corps and Specialists

Authorized by Congress on 18 May 1917, the Sanitary Corps included men who were sanitary engineers, chemists, lab technicians, mess officers, and others who possessed special knowledge required by the Medical Department. At first some sanitary officers unofficially wore a gilt *SC* monogram on a bronze caduceus (Fig. 11-93), although later contract surgeons also wore these, since the *SC* monogram could stand for either Sanitary Corps or contract surgeon. In December 1917, sanitary officers finally received an approved insignia: a caduceus with gilt *S*, as shown in Figs. 11-94, 11-95, and 11-96. Two bronze shirt devices are shown in Figs. 11-97 and 11-98.[38] A 1919 portrait of a sanitary officer wearing the caduceus with *S* is shown in Fig. 11-99.

Congress abolished the Sanitary Corps in 1920, and it ceased to exist on 31 December

Fig. 11-99.

1921, but it was reestablished as a reserve activity in 1923. A 1920s and 1930s coat insignia is illustrated in Fig. 11-100, and two shirt collar ornaments are shown in Figs. 11-101 and 11-102. The Sanitary Corps expanded after 1939 as officers came to duty in response to the president's emergency declaration. Sanitary Corps personnel often took over administrative duties from medical officers. From a cursory glance at Sanitary Corps titles, one might think the Medical Administrative Corps handled all such functions, but the Medical Administrative Corps was composed of specialists, and the World War II Sanitary Corps contained many administrative officers.[39]

The officer shown in Fig. 11-103 wears the insignia of the Sanitary Corps. Fig. 11-104 has a nonregulation black enamel block letter. Sanitary Corps personnel replaced the caduceus bearing the *S* with the new Medical Service Corps insignia in December 1947. The army brought the caduceus with *S* back from retirement in 1956 and gave it to members of the Army Medical Specialist Corps. This occurred when the army allowed men to receive commissions in what had previously been the Women's Medical Specialist Corps.[40] This corps now includes physical therapists, occupational therapists, and dietitians. A current subdued metal insignia is shown in Fig. 11-105.

Ambulance Corps

Unique in U.S. Army history is the origin of the U.S. Ambulance Service, for it had the distinction of being the first organization assembled by the U.S. Congress as part of a

Fig. 11-100.

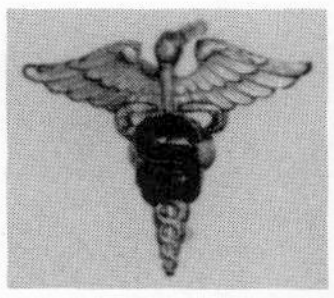

Fig. 11-101.

Fig. 11-102.

Fig. 11-103.

foreign army. In 1915 a group of American volunteers, primarily college students, formed the American Field Service to drive ambulances at the front. This service then became part of the French army.

With the entry of the United States into the war, the French government arranged for the American Field Service to become the U.S. Army Ambulance Service and for many of the units to continue to serve the French forces. Congress initially authorized an ambulance service in June 1917, and the president incorporated it into the Medical Department with an authorization of 214 officers.[41]

The army delayed some time before deciding what insignia would be worn by Ambulance Corps members. One early device is shown in Fig. 11-106 with the monogram *AS*. Although not authorized by regulations, apparently a gilt *AC* monogram on a caduceus was also in unofficial use by the fall of 1917. In December 1917 several medical branches changed from two or three letters to a single letter on a caduceus; the ambulance personnel switched to the *A*.[42] Three World War I–period caducei

Fig. 11-104.

Fig. 11-105.

with *A*s are shown in Figs. 11-107, 11-108, and 11-109; the first two were made in France. American Field Service uniforms and insignia varied, but three common badges exist, as sketched in Figs. 11-110 through 11-112. The American Field Service again organized and drove ambulances during World War II, but it kept its identity separate from that of the U.S. Army.

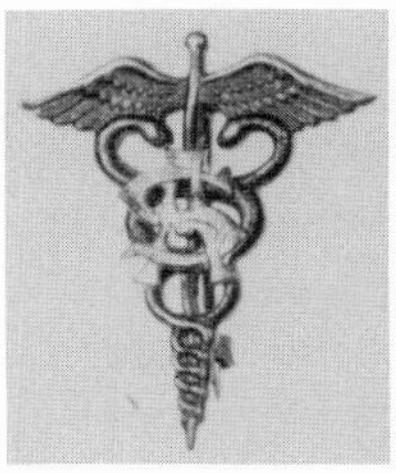

Fig. 11-106.

Fig. 11-107.

Fig. 11-108.

Fig. 11-109.

Medical Administrative Corps

Members of the Medical Administrative Corps began to wear the caduceus with the *A* in October 1921 after the end of the Ambulance Corps.[43] Shirt-sized insignia from the 1920s are illustrated in Figs. 11-113 and 11-114. Although the army used the same insignia design throughout World War II, in the 1920s and 1930s the corps itself changed.

In 1923, Congress limited the corps to seventy-two officers. Only pharmacy officers joined the Medical Administrative Corps after 1936, and the branch was further limited to sixteen Regular Army officers. After the 1939 armed forces expansion, a great many officers of several skills wore

Fig. 11-100. *A gilt Sanitary Corps insignia with a bronze enameled letter as used by reserve officers from 1923 to 1939. Corps members came to active duty in 1939 at the call of President Roosevelt. The Sanitary Corps was dissolved in 1947. ($1\frac{1}{32}$ inches wide)*

Figs. 11-101 and 11-102. *Two shirt collar insignia in miniature as prescribed in the late 1920s and used into the 1930s. That of Fig. 11-101 has a clutch back with the S painted, while the one of Fig. 11-102 has the letter made from a black metal. ($\frac{3}{4}$ and $\frac{37}{64}$ inch wide, respectively)*

Fig. 11-103. *Captain Joseph Gilbert of the Sanitary Corps, December 1941.*

Fig. 11-104. *This caduceus has small threaded screw posts and a black-enameled block S. ($\frac{15}{16}$ inch wide)*

Fig. 11-105. *The Army reintroduced the caduceus with an S in 1956 for the Army Medical Specialist Corps (AMSC). This is a subdued (black) metal AMSC insignia introduced during the Vietnam War and worn by dietitians, occupational therapists, and physical therapists. ($1\frac{3}{16}$ inches wide)*

Fig. 11-106. *An early ambulance service collar insignia with the typical 1917 intertwined letters, in this case AS. ($\frac{57}{64}$ inch wide)*

Figs. 11-107, 11-108, and 11-109. *Starting in December 1917 the ambulance service changed to a caduceus with the single letter A. The insignia are Fig. 11-107, a French-made piece with the letter struck as part of the overall design; Fig. 11-108, a brown metal caduceus made in France with an applied gilt letter; and Fig. 11-109, a black metal insignia, made in the United States, with an ornate A. (1 inch, $1\frac{3}{64}$ inches, and $\frac{29}{32}$ inch wide, respectively)*

Fig. 11-110.

Fig. 11-111.

Fig. 11-112.

Fig. 11-113.

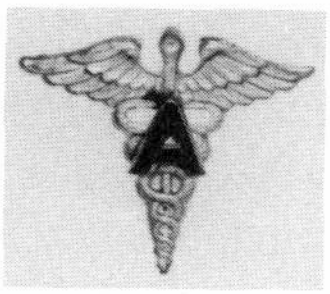

Fig. 11-114.

Fig. 11-115.

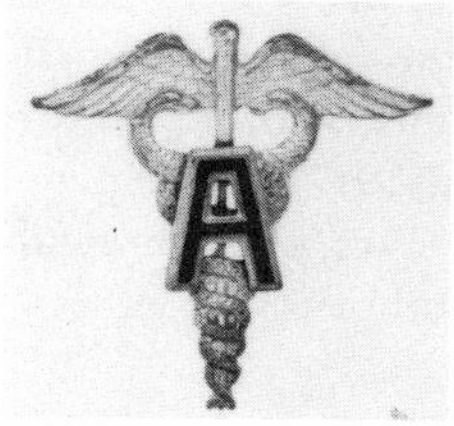

Fig. 11-116.

Fig. 11-117.

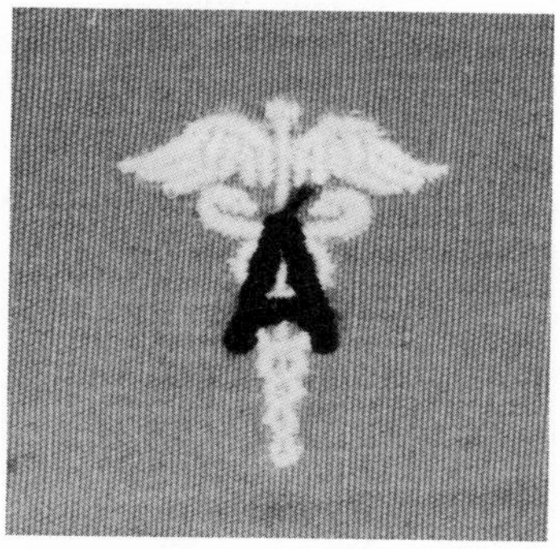

Fig. 11-118.

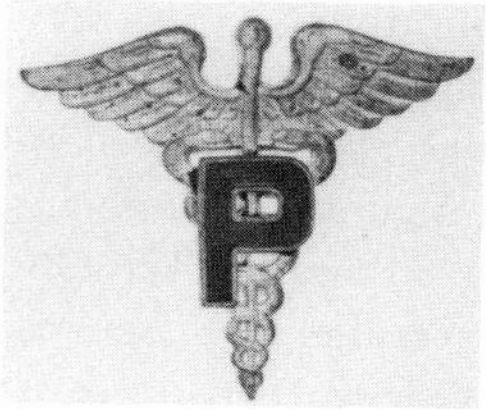

Fig. 11-119.

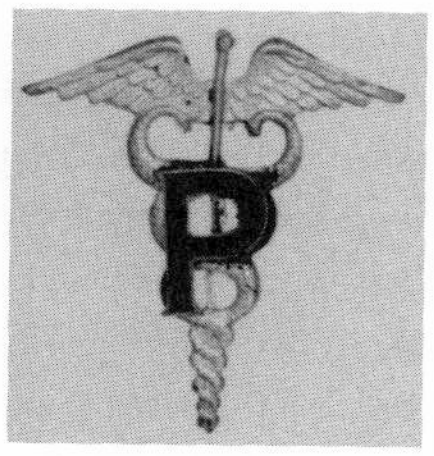

Fig. 11-120.

Figs. 11-110, 11-111, and 11-112. *The American Field Service provided ambulances and drivers before America entered World War I. Three insignia used by this organization are shown in these sketches.*

Fig. 11-113. *A shirt collar insignia with the A held in place by two small brads. This ornament was used by the Ambulance Corps through 1920, but in 1921 it became the insignia of the Administrative Corps. (13/16 inch wide)*

Fig. 11-114. *A diminutive gilt shirt collar insignia with clutch fasteners, probably made in the late 1930s for a pharmacist in the Administrative Corps. (3/4 inch wide)*

Fig. 11-115. *Second Lieutenant Zoltan Fozessery of the Administrative Corps, July 1942. Corps members were officers with special skills such as sanitary engineering or microbiology.*

Fig. 11-116. *A nonregulation block A used by an Administrative Corps member during World War II. (1 1/32 inches wide)*

Fig. 11-117. *This Administrative Corps insignia has both the caduceus and the letter in bright brass. (29/32 inch wide)*

Fig. 11-118. *A medium green cloth was used as the background material for this World War II machine-embroidered insignia. (Design 1 5/64 inches wide)*

Fig. 11-119. *A regulation Pharmacy Corps insignia, 1943–47, with a brown, 3/8-inch-high letter on a 1-inch-high caduceus. (1 5/32 inches wide)*

Fig. 11-120. *Black enameled letters were commonly used on medical insignia during World War II, as was this piece. Peak strength of the Pharmacy Corps was seventy officers. (63/64 inch wide)*

the administrative insignia, since Congress and the War Department lifted restrictions on the number of men and their skills in the corps. The Medical Service Corps device finally replaced the insignia in late 1947. From 1921 through 1947, black letters commonly appeared on the gilt caducei even though regulations called for brown or bronze letters (Figs. 11-115 and 11-116). A gilt caduceus with a gilt letter is shown in Fig. 11-117 and an embroidered yellow and black device on green cloth is shown in Fig. 11-118.[44]

Pharmacy

Pharmacists originally served as members of the Medical Administrative Corps, both as officers and enlisted men. Pharmacists transferred from the Medical Administrative Corps to the Pharmacy Corps after creation of a pharmacy branch, with an authorized strength of seventy-two officers, on 12 July 1943. (Actual peak strength was seventy officers in April 1945.) Regulations between August 1943 and mid-1947 called for Pharmacy Corps members to wear a brown *P* on their caduceus (Fig. 11-119). Pharmacy Corps members transferred to the Medical Service Corps and began to wear that insignia in 1947 as a result of an August 1947 congressional action.[45] A common but unauthorized version of the 1943–47 insignia with a black *P* is illustrated in Fig. 11-120.

Hospital Dietitians

During the Spanish-American War the surgeon general employed a few nurses as "dietists" but prescribed no special uniforms or insignia. These few employees did not continue with the army after the release of troops called up for the war effort. At the outset of World War I, the secretary of war began to appoint women dietitians, and several of them served overseas. It was not clear whether they were nurses or civilians. The army itself was not sure at times. The chief dietitian worked in the office of the superintendent of the Army Nurse Corps, but the Red Cross, closely allied with the army, classified dietitians as civilians if the woman was not a nurse in her own right.[46]

World War I women serving as dietitians wore special uniforms and insignia. For indoor wear they wore a white dress with a bronze caduceus bearing a *D* (Fig. 11-121).[47] The outdoor uniforms included a gray suit with the same caduceus and *D* and with the letters *US*. During the war the dietitians' uniform changed, but the insignia, later adopted by dentists, continued. A World War I dietitian, Mary Pascoe, is shown in Fig. 11-122 wearing the uniform in 1919.

Dietitians were civil servants between the world wars. They wore uniforms similar to nurses' with the addition of blue velvet ribbons on the cap. The head dietitian (allowed in departments having more than three dietitians) wore a 1/2-inch wide ribbon, while other Dietitians added a band 3/8 inch wide. Regulations did not specify a special cap ribbon for the chief dietitian, who was stationed at Walter Reed General Hospital, although she may have worn one.[48]

Selected civilian personnel serving with the Medical Department continued to wear special uniforms similar to nurse's until 1942. With the start of World War II dietitians serving outside the United States received word of a new medium blue uniform. It came with coats and skirts in two weights: one for summer and another for winter. Navy blue flat rayon stripes added to the sleeves showed the dietitian's grade, although the establishing circular letter did not specify the number of stripes or grades. The letter did note that the wearer should "allow 3/16 inch between stripes." On the collar, hospital dietitians wore plain one-half-inch-high block letters *HD*. The circular called for the letters to be "in thermal setting plastic brass metal covered," but the all-metal type shown in Fig. 11-123 is more common. For the white duty uniform, the white cap continued to carry a 3/8- or 1/2-inch-wide royal blue velvet headband.[49] Fig, 11-124 shows Lenna F. Cooper, supervisor of World War I dietitians, wearing her 1918 uniform, and Helen C. Burns, 1942 supervisor of dietitians, wearing the 1942 uniform, including four sleeve stripes to indicate her rank.

In December 1942, Congress allowed women dietitians to join the Medical Department, and as a result, women could wear the standard army women's uniforms with their own insignia. In March 1943 the War Department prescribed a caduceus carrying the two separate 1/4-inch-high letters *HD*. Several styles of this insignia exist, with

Fig. 11-121. *On the gray outdoor and the white indoor uniforms dietitians of World War I used a caduceus with a gilt D, the same insignia used by dentists. (7/8 inch wide)*

Fig. 11-122. *Gray travel uniform worn by Mary Pascoe, who served as a dietitian overseas during World War I.*

Fig. 11-123. *In 1942, before dietitians were members of the army, those women who were to accompany the army overseas wore 1/2-inch-high block letters as their insignia. These pin-back letters are struck from one piece of brass. (59/64 inch wide)*

Fig. 11-122.

Fig. 11-121.

Fig. 11-123.

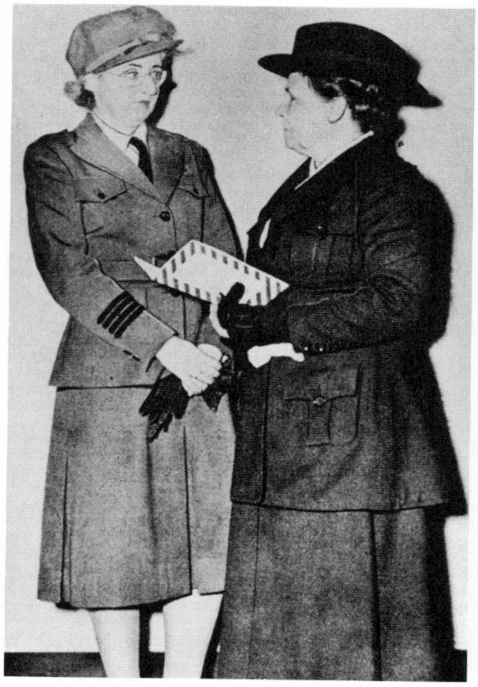

Fig. 11-124.

Fig. 11-127.

Fig. 11-124. World War I (right) and early World War II (left) dietitians' uniforms. Helen C. Burns, supervisor of dietitians in 1942, meets Lenna F. Cooper, supervisor of dietitians in 1918.

Figs. 11-125 and 11-126. The War Department prescribed two letters, each 1/4 inch high, for hospital dietitians in March 1943. Fig. 11-125 meets the regulations in that its letters are brown, in this case enameled, while the letters of Fig. 11-126, with serifs, are painted black. (1 1/8 and 1 11/64 inches wide, respectively)

Fig. 11-127. Hope Gray, a reconstruction aide on Ward 7, American Expeditionary Forces Base Hospital Nine, in France. At her neck she wears the letters US instead of the prescribed RA.

Fig. 11-128. A World War I caduceus worn by reconstruction aides (physical therapists) in 1918. (29/32 inch wide)

Fig. 11-129. Bronze block letters worn by World War I reconstruction aides. (1 1/8 inches wide)

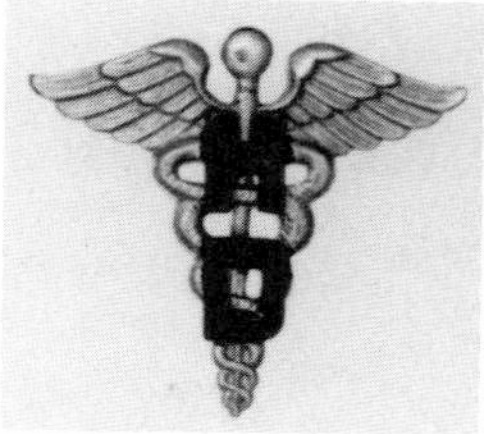

Fig. 11-125.

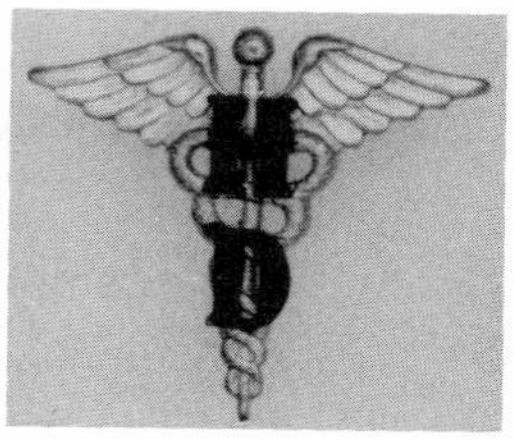

Fig. 11-126.

the letters in black and in brown enamel as well as painted. Two examples are shown in Figs. 11-125 and 11-126. Between December 1942, when dietitians joined the army, and March 1943, when the army specified the *H* over *D*, women wore the plain caduceus of doctors. The *HD* caduceus, rescinded in 1947, was replaced when dietitians became members of the Women's Medical Specialist Corps.[50]

Physical and Occupational Therapists, World War I

The Army Medical Department employed approximately eight hundred physical therapists during World War I. Most therapists, called reconstruction aides after December 1917, were civilian women, but a few enlisted men attended "physiotherapy aides" school, and a Medical Corps officer served as section chief. Civilian aides wore a blue one-piece dress with white cuffs and collar. Caps indicated rank or position. The chief physical therapist's cap was completely white, while other therapists wore a blue organdy cap with a white band.[51] Street uniforms consisted of a two-piece dark gray suit with maroon and white braid on the sleeves. A reconstruction aide is shown in Fig. 11-127 wearing a World War I outdoor uniform. Reconstruction aides wore a bronze caduceus with a gilt *RA* monogram (Fig. 11-128) and also a set of plain bronze letters *RA* (Fig. 11-129). Between the world wars, physical therapists continued to wear the long uniforms designed during World War I, complete with the blue and white or all white cap and a hemline within 12 inches of the floor. The surgeon general repeated the uniform description as late as December 1941.[52]

Fig. 11-130 shows an army dietitian (*right*) and a physical therapist at Walter Reed Hospital in 1941. Physical therapy students wore this dark blue uniform with white collar and

Fig. 11-128.

Fig. 11-129.

Fig. 11-130.

cuffs, popularly known as the "blue bago," during World War II. The uniform required thirteen safety pins and a daily pressing, according to one veteran, and evidently in a modest concession to more modern styles the hem went up 3 inches to 15 inches above the floor. Although the blue bago was without insignia, it was a distinctive uniform—so much so that when President Harding held a reception at Walter Reed Hospital, the therapists wore it while male officers wore their dress blue uniforms.[53]

Physical Therapists and Dental Hygienists, World War II

Congress in December 1942 provided that physical therapists could be members of the Medical Department. As a result, between March 1943 and December 1947 physical therapists wore caducei with the two separate one-fourth-inch-high brown letters *PT*. Several styles of letters exist, including brown and black enameled and black painted ones. Examples are shown in Figs. 11-131 and 11-132. Women physical therapists transferred to the Women's Medical Specialist Corps in 1947.[54]

Before Congress acted in late 1942, the surgeon general hired civilians and placed them in special uniforms similar to World War I clothing. The early branch members wore plain medical caducei and later 1/2-inch-high block letters *PTA* (for physical therapy assistant) or *DH* (for dental hygienist). Ultimately the dental hygienists became enlisted women in the Medical Department, and the physical therapists received commissions and branch insignia. The army closely controlled the rank given to these women, despite the army's wartime strength. Only one dietitian and one physical therapist received the grade of major.[55]

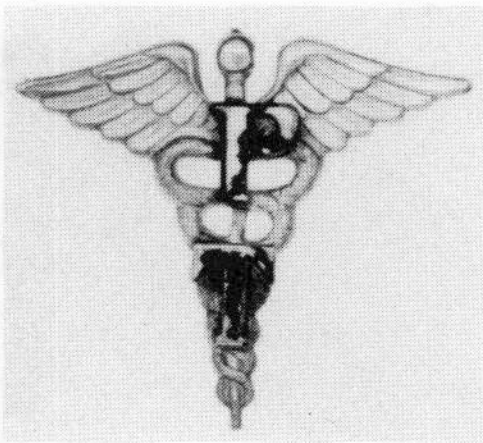

Fig. 11-131.

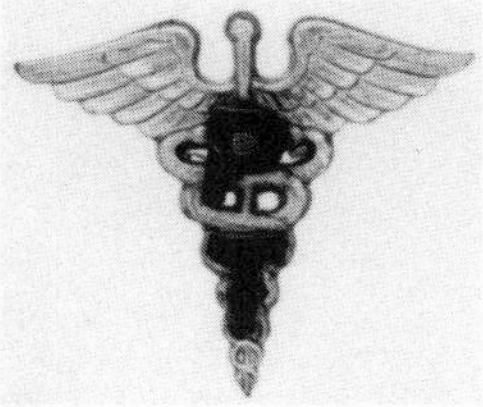

Fig. 11-132.

Medical Service Corps and Women's Medical Specialist Corps

The army eliminated three insignia—Administrative Corps, Sanitary Corps, and Pharmacy—in mid-1947, following Congress's establishment of the Medical Service Corps. The new Department of the Army in December 1947 selected a silver caduceus with the black monogram *MS* as the corps' device (Fig. 11-133).[56] Two variations are shown in Figs. 11-134 and 11-135. The first has a battalion number and the second is an unauthorized gilt caduceus with small gilt letters *MS* in the style previously used by dietitians and therapists. A bullion-embroidered insignia for a khaki coat is illustrated in Fig. 11-136, while a 1960s Vietnamese-made piece is illustrated in Fig. 11-137.

At the same time the army formed the Medical Service Corps, hospital dietitians, physical therapists, and occupational therapists joined to make the Women's Med-

Fig. 11-133.

Fig. 11-134.

Fig. 11-130. *After the close of World War I and into 1943, both dietitians and physical therapists employed by the War Department wore distinctive uniforms. This 1941 photograph shows the physiotherapy uniform (left), nicknamed the "blue bago" because some of the young women thought it looked like a blue bag, and the dietitian uniform (right). A blue velvet cap ribbon indicated the wearer's grade: 1/2 inch wide for head dietitians and 3/8 wide for others.*

Figs. 11-131 and 11-132. *Physical therapists received these insignia in 1943, when they became members of the army, and wore them until 1947. Fig. 11-131 has black-painted letters, and Fig. 11-132 has brown-enameled block letters. (1 9/64 and 1 7/64 inches wide, respectively)*

Fig. 11-133. *Medical Service Corps insignia, established with the corps in 1947. Not since before World War I had the army used a silver caduceus. The monogram is black enamel. (1 11/64 inches wide)*

Fig. 11-134. *Medical Service Corps insignia with a battalion number above. Previous members of the Administrative, Sanitary, and Pharmacy corps wore MSC insignia. (1 9/64 inch wide)*

Fig. 11-135. *A nonregulation gilt caduceus with gilt individual letters. This may have been an early Medical Service Corps insignia made about 1947. (1 3/16 inches wide)*

Fig. 11-136. *Hand-embroidered bullion Medical Service Corps insignia for the officers' tan coat. (Design 1 1/4 inches wide)*

Fig. 11-137. *Made in Vietnam, this insignia has a bright green S, while the rest of the design is black. (Design 1 9/32 inches wide)*

Figs. 11-138, 11-139, and 11-140. *Women who served as dietitians and therapists became members of the Women's Medical Service Corps in 1947. A silver caduceus with black WS monogram was the corps' insignia. These three examples were used from 1947 until 1957; with the caduceus of Fig. 11-140 in nonregulation gilt instead of the proper silver. (1 inch, 1 5/32 inches, and 1 3/16 inches wide, respectively)*

Figs. 11-141 and 11-142. *Civil War cap insignia for hospital stewards. The brass wreath was 1 1/4 inches high and the silver letters 1/2 inch high. (2 23/32 and 2 25/32 inches wide, respectively)*

Fig. 11-135.

Fig. 11-136.

Fig. 11-137.

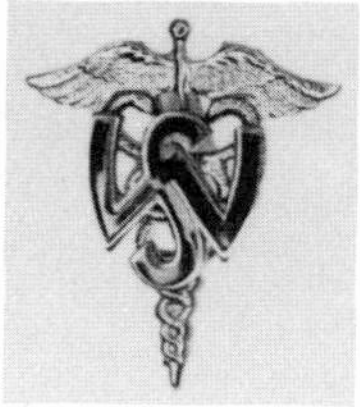

Fig. 11-138.

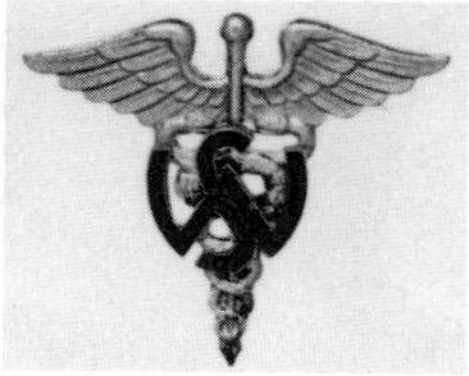

Fig. 11-139

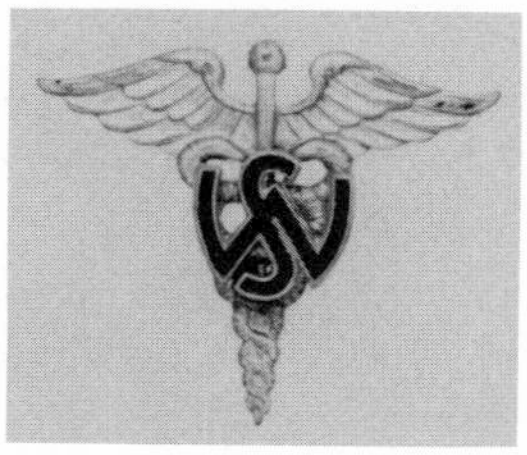

Fig. 11-140.

Fig. 11-141.

Fig. 11-142.

ical Specialist Corps. This corps lasted until women transferred to the Army Medical Specialist Corps in 1956 and 1957. An interesting note on the 1947 insignia is that the Medical Service Corps device could be made into the Women's Medical Specialist Corps insignia simply by applying the monogram upside down, thus eliminating the need for new dies.[57] Three examples are shown in Figs. 11-138, 11-139, and 11-140, the last being a nonregulation gilt insignia.

Letter Colors

The dramatic change in insignia color from bronze to gilt in October 1923 stated in part, "elements superimposed on insignia will . . . be of bronze metal." Since before this change insignia had been "bronze" (black in color), most soldiers of the time would have assumed the letters would be of black metal. In more common usage however, "bronze" denoted a brown metal, and in December 1926 the superimposed letters were to be "of bronze finish or brown enamel." This description remained in regulations until October 1951, when black letters were prescribed.[58]

Why then, are black enamel letters the predominate style on insignia made in the 1930s and 1940s? While the answer is not certain, it is probably because of the pre-1923 connotation of "bronze" being equated with "black." As enameled insignia became more common, many manufacturers switched to enamel without consulting the regulations, and this resulted in the use of black letters until the Department of the Army finally made the official color change in 1951. During World War II some insignia makers used brown enameled letters, but they are not as common as the black enamel or paint.

Enlisted Men's Cap Insignia

Hospital stewards first wore special chevrons in 1851, but regulations do not mention a distinctive metal cap ornament until 1861. Before 1861 the regulations are vague, although hospital stewards may have worn the metal Roman letters *US* within a brass wreath as early as 1857. No specification initially noted insignia size, but evidently the wreath was about 1 1/4 inches high and 2 inches wide with separate silver letters 1/2 inch high (Figs. 11-141 and 11-142). In January 1882 a silver caduceus replaced the letters *US* within the brass wreath (Fig. 11-143).[59]

Congress created the grades of acting hospital steward and privates of the Hospital Corps in 1887. As a result of this action, and the general international movement towards the red cross as a symbol of humanitarian efforts, in 1887 the army began to issue hospital stewards cap insignia of a silver Geneva cross within a silver wreath (Fig. 11-144) and acting hospital stewards and privates a plain silver cross. When the quartermaster general adopted the screw-post cap insignia in 1896, the same designs continued, but in more substantial form (Fig. 11-145 is for hospital stewards and Fig. 11-146 for other enlisted men). Collectors today still find New York militia gilt Geneva crosses with a screw post similar to the insignia in Fig. 11-146. A Maltese cross replaced the Geneva cross in February 1901 (Figs. 11-147, 11-148, 11-149).[60]

The caduceus replaced the Maltese cross in 1902, the same year hospital stewards were retitled sergeants first class, Hospital Corps. On caps these men wore a screw-post silver caduceus within a brass wreath 2 5/8 inches wide (Figs. 11-150 and 11-151). Lower enlisted ranks wore only a caduceus 15/16 inch wide and 1 inch high. The 1904 Army Uniform Board reduced the wreath for the sergeant first class to 1 1/4 inches high in 1905 (Fig. 11-152). On the service caps, bronze insignia of identical design came into use in 1905 for senior noncommissioned officers (Figs. 11-153 and 11-154), while other enlisted personnel wore plain bronze caducei (Fig. 11-155) until 1918.[61]

Enlisted Men's Hat Insignia

From 1857 to 1872 hospital stewards wore a silver *US* within a gilt wreath on the hat (Figs. 11-141 and 11-142). A buff and green hat cord with tassle ends was added in 1858. In 1899 the army introduced colored hat cords with acorn-shaped ends, and hospital personnel wore maroon and white intermixed cords until 1920, when the medics switched to maroon cords with white acorns. In addition to hat cords, between 1905 and 1907 enlisted personnel wore a bronze caduceus on the front of the campaign hat.[62] Between the authorized dates of these two types of hat insignia, (the *US* in a wreath and a bronze caduceus) many soldiers wore unauthorized insignia on hats, as did the medical soldiers in Fig. 11-156.

Helmet Insignia

All enlisted hospital personnel used a silver caduceus (Fig. 11-157) as an overlay on the helmet eagle from 1881 until 1887, when the Geneva cross (Fig. 11-158) became the medical insignia. This insignia lasted until

Fig. 11-143.

Fig. 11-144.

Fig. 11-145.

Fig. 11-148.

Fig. 11-143. *The 1882 enlisted men's cap insignia with separate silver caduceus and brass wreath. (2 47/64 inches wide)*

Fig. 11-144. *Hospital stewards switched to a silver wreath and separate silver cross in 1887 for their cap insignia. (2 47/64 inches wide)*

Fig. 11-145. *An 1896–1901 hospital stewards' forage cap ornament made from German silver, with screw back. (2 11/16 inches wide)*

Fig. 11-146. *Medical enlisted men other than hospital stewards wore silver Geneva crosses on their forage caps. The wire back was used from 1887 until 1896, when the screw back was introduced. (57/64 inch wide)*

Fig. 11-147. *A silver-colored enlisted men's medical cap insignia, 1901–1902. (7/8 inch wide)*

Fig. 11-148. *Medical Department noncommissioned officers wore a silver Maltese cross in a gilt wreath in 1901 and 1902. (2 25/64 inches wide)*

Fig. 11-146.

Fig. 11-147.

1896, when the Hospital Corps discontinued dress uniforms.[63]

Enlisted Men's Collar Ornaments before 1902

Despite some regulations to the contrary, hospital stewards wore no insignia on their coat collars until 30 November 1881, when they adopted a silver caduceus.[64] The 1885 dress coat eliminated enlisted staff collar insignia, but in 1887 Congress created the rank of acting hospital steward and the War Department stated acting hospital steward uniforms would include a cloth red cross on each side of the collar. Hospital Corps enlisted men quit wearing dress uniforms in 1896;[65] consequently, there were no enlisted medical collar insignia except for the 1900 to 1902 white duck coats used on ward duty.[66] The gilt pin-back collar insignia for this white work uniform is shown in Fig. 11-159. This insignia is common in collections today because the army ordered ten thousand of them in 1901 and, shortly after delivery by the Horstmann Company, suspended their use.[67]

Fig. 11-149. The private first class of the Hospital Corps (right) in 1902 models the forage cap with insignia.

Figs. 11-150 and 11-151. Sergeants first class of the Hospital Corps wore these cap insignia from late 1902 or early 1903 until 1905. (2 19/32 and 2 5/8 inches wide, respectively)

Fig. 11-152. Dress cap insignia with silver caduceus and gilt wreath for noncommissioned officers, 1905–17. (1 27/32 inches wide)

Figs. 11-153 and 11-154. Bronze cap insignia for the service uniforms of Medical Corps noncommissioned officers, sergeants first class and above. (1 29/32 and 1 15/16 inches wide, respectively)

Fig. 11-149.

Enlisted Men's Collar Insignia, 1902–23

Enlisted medical personnel adopted the Maltese cross insignia in February 1901. The next year the army introduced collar insignia for general wear on the blue dress uniform. Four months after the adjutant general published the December 1902 uniform regulations, the surgeon general changed the enlisted men's medical insignia to a caduceus of the same design as that for officers, making the Mal-

Fig. 11-150.

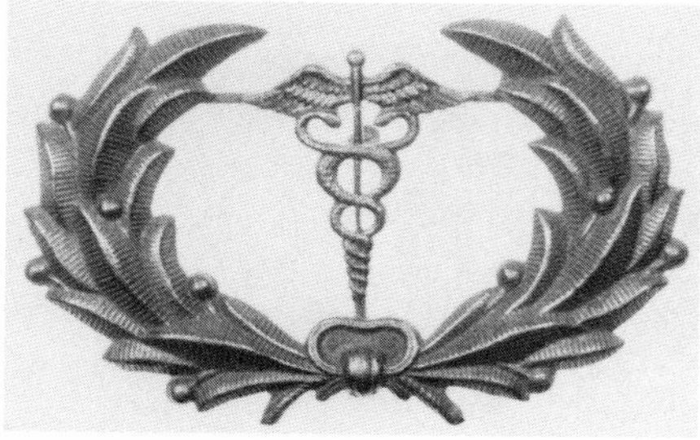

Fig. 11-151.

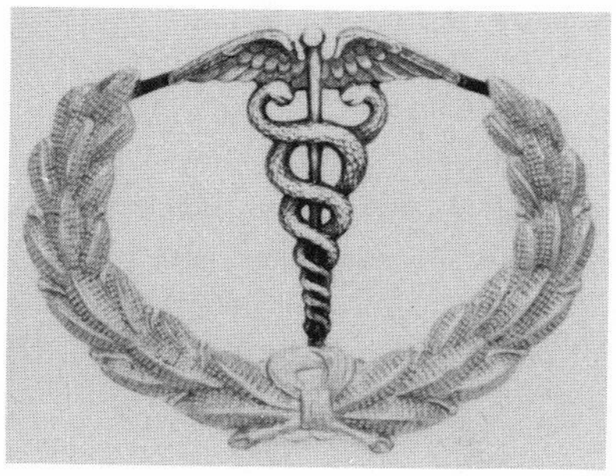

Fig. 11-152.

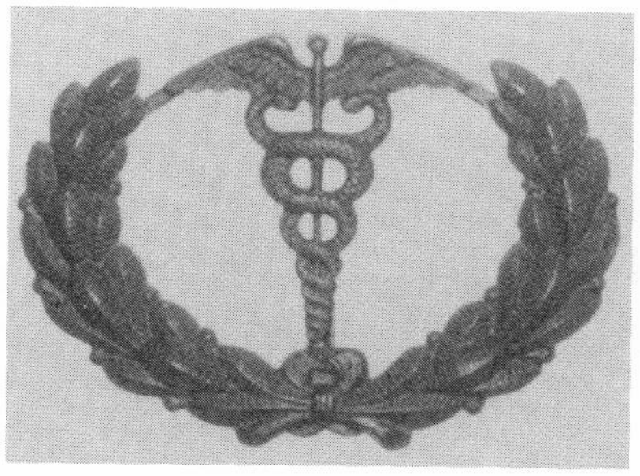

Fig. 11-153.

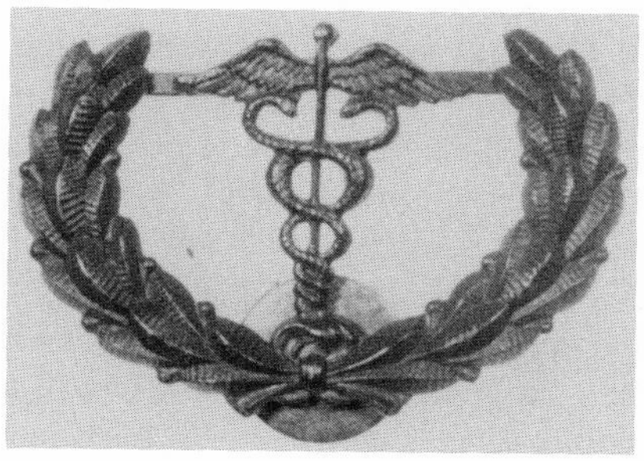

Fig. 11-154.

Fig. 11-155.

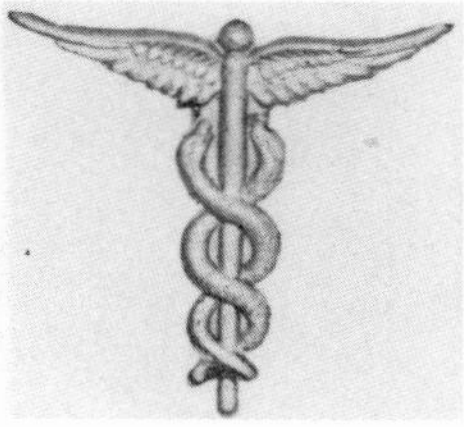

Fig. 11-157.

Fig. 11-158.

Fig. 11-159.

Fig. 11-156.

Fig. 11-155. *Bronze-colored service cap insignia worn by sergeants and below, 1902–18. (55/64 inch wide)*

Fig. 11-156. *Members of a local dispensary in their summer khaki uniforms, 1902. Wear of insignia on hats was common but not authorized in regulations.*

Fig. 11-157. *An enlisted men's helmet overlay in German silver, 1881–87. (27/32 inch wide)*

Fig. 11-158. *In 1887 the silver caduceus was replaced by the Geneva cross as a helmet overlay. (1 1/8 inches wide)*

Fig. 11-159. *A gilt, pin-back collar insignia used by enlisted medical men on the white uniform in 1901 and 1902. These insignia are common today, because the army ordered over ten thousand of them in 1901 and made the insignia obsolete in 1902 when it adopted the caduceus. (7/8 inch wide)*

Figs. 11-160 and 11-161. *After wearing the same collar insignia as officers from 1902 until 1910, enlisted medical soldiers switched to bronze disks. These two examples show some of the many variations made. (Each 1 inch in diameter)*

tese cross obsolete. Although the army had a stock of the gilt Maltese crosses for the white duck ward coats, men probably did not wear the gilt cross on the blue 1902 coat because of the short time the cross was authorized and because of the difficulty experienced by the quartermaster depot in making enough of the new 1902 coats. The 1902 amended regulations called for all enlisted medical personnel, noncommissioned officers and privates alike, to wear the 1-inch-high caduceus: gilt on dress coats and bronze on service coats. The gilt insignia survived until World War I, but as with all enlisted insignia, disks replaced bronze outline devices in 1910.[68]

Enlisted men continued to use the 1910-type bronze disks (Figs. 11-160, 11-161, and 11-162) until October 1923. Although all enlisted medical personnel should have used the same design of bronze disk on service uniforms, some men in the sanitary and veterinary service wore disks carrying a design similar to that of officers (Figs. 11-163 and 11-164). These ornaments may have been produced because of the special provisions for slightly less than four thousand enlisted men in the Sanitary Corps and an October 1917 authorization of sixteen enlisted men for each four hundred animals in the service. An official 1919 recruiting booklet shows enlisted medical disks with *D* for dental assistants, and

Fig. 11-160.

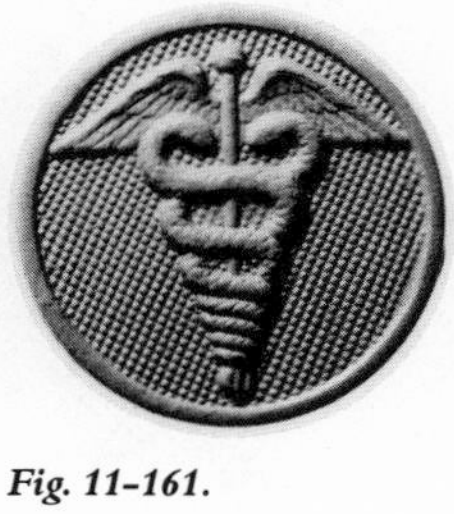

Fig. 11-161.

Fig. 11-162. *Private L. A. Helms of the Medical Corps, 1917.*

Fig. 11-163. *An unauthorized enlisted men's collar disk used during World War I by men assigned to sanitary units. (1 1/32 inches in diameter)*

Fig. 11-164. *Enlisted men assigned to the Veterinary Corps should have worn the plain caduceus instead of this style with a V. (1 1/32 inches in diameter)*

Fig. 11-165. *Enlisted men's disks were not authorized to have unit numbers added during World War I, but some with numbers were nevertheless made, like this one for the 105th Ambulance Company. (1 1/64 inches in diameter)*

Fig. 11-166. *This gilt enlisted men's collar disk was made shortly after World War I from a die originally made for bronze service disks. (1 1/64 inches in diameter)*

Fig. 11-167. *A gilt Medical Department enlisted men's collar insignia, with a background of lines and small shields, used from 1923 into the late 1930s. (1 1/64 inches in diameter)*

Fig. 11-168. *Never authorized, this disk with the small lyre just inside the rim at the bottom was evidently used by the medical band stationed at Carlisle Barracks in the 1930s. (1 1/32 inches in diameter)*

Fig. 11-169. *Privately made in the 1930s, this insignia is typical of those used to introduce the concept of separable insignia. (1 1/32 inches in diameter)*

Figs. 11-170, 11-171, and 11-172. *Late 1930s and 1940s enlisted men's medical insignia. Fig. 11-170 is a two-piece flat disk with a screw-post fastener, Fig. 11-171 is a two-piece insignia made in India about 1944, and Fig. 11-172 is a gilt domed disk from the late 1940s. (1, 15/16, and 1 inch in diameter, respectively)*

Fig. 11-173. *The medical unit of New York's 27th Division had insignia with its brass number on the upper part of the caduceus in the late 1930s. (1 1/32 inches in diameter)*

Fig. 11-174. *Made in Germany after World War II, this disk is silver-plated with a domed back. (63/64 inch in diameter)*

Fig. 11-162.

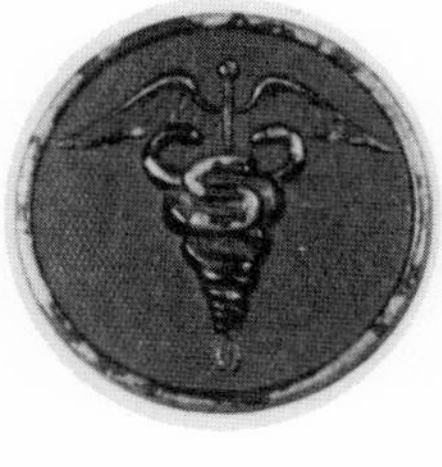

Fig. 11-163.

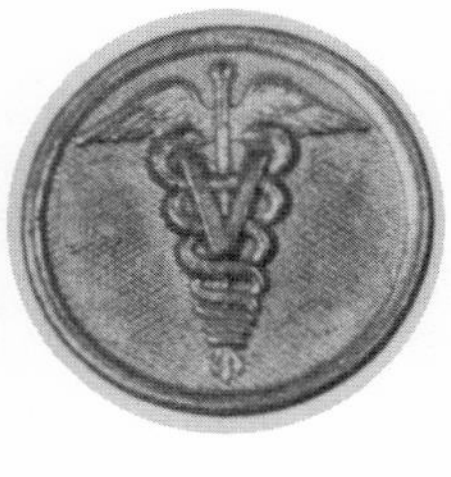

Fig. 11-164.

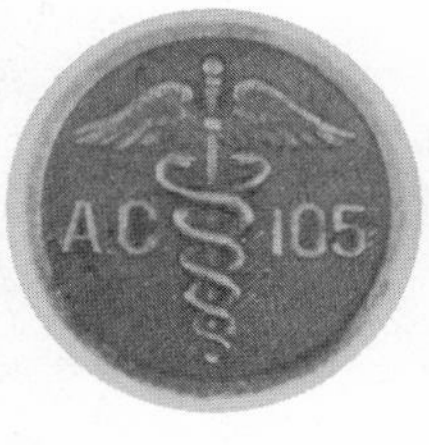

Fig. 11-165.

Fig. 11-166.

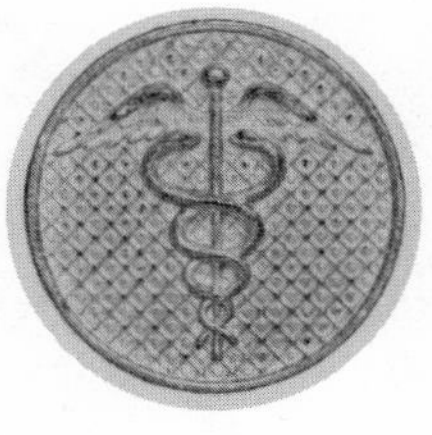

Fig. 11-167.

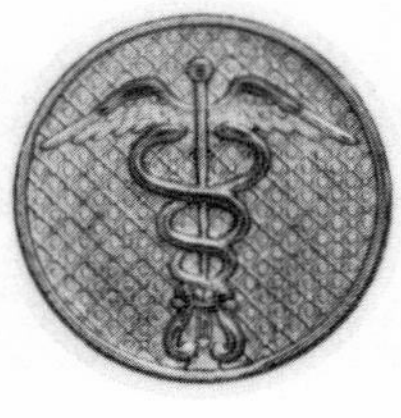

Fig. 11-168.

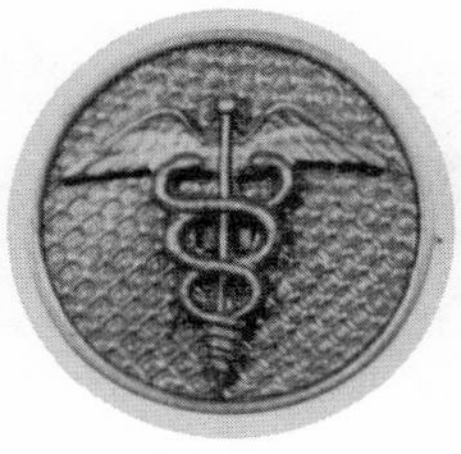

Fig. 11-169.

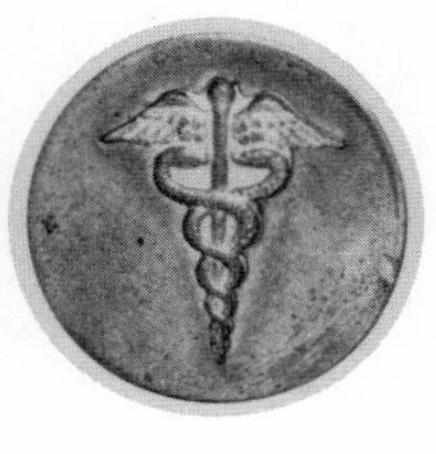

Fig. 11-170.

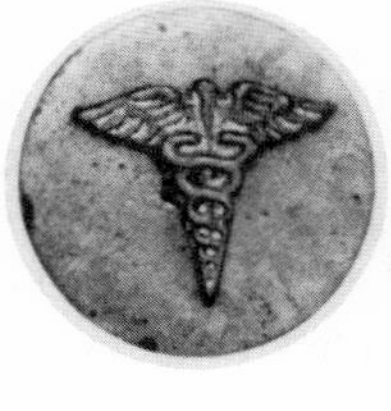

Fig. 11-171.

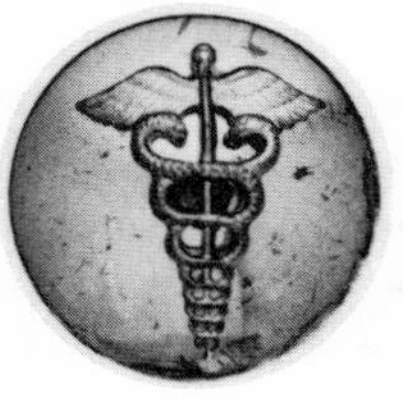

Fig. 11-172.

Fig. 11-173.

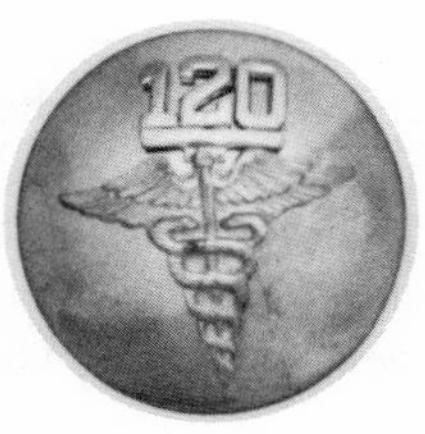

Fig. 11-174.

Fig. 11-175.

Fig. 11-176.

Fig. 11-177.

Fig. 11-178.

Fig. 11-179.

Fig. 11-180.

Fig. 11-181.

Fig. 11-182.

V for the enlisted force of the Veterinary Corps, further lending support to the belief the army issued some disk insignia with letters.[69] Several enlisted men's disk variations exist, including the disk for the 105th Ambulance Company shown in Fig. 11-165.

Collar Disks after 1923

Some gilt insignia worn shortly after World War I, such as that shown in Fig. 11-166, lasted only a short time and were made using dies for bronze disks with the stippled background. Soon after the war, however, the official background changed to a pattern of crosshatched lines and small shields, as shown in Fig. 11-167. In December 1927 the War Department authorized regimental band members to wear a small lyre below the basic insignia.[70] Fig. 11-168 shows an insignia with this lyre, which is assumed to be for the army's medical school band at Carlisle Barracks, Pennsylvania, during the 1930s.

A two-piece disk with the background of lines and shields is shown in Fig. 11-169. The two-piece disks that became common during World War II came in several styles, three of which are shown in Figs. 11-170, 11-171, and 11-172, the second having been made in India about 1944 and the last a domed disk. In some cases disks include battalion numbers, as shown in Figs. 11-173, 11-174, and 11-175. Some personnel wore collar devices with appropriate letters to show their assignment even though the War Department never approved such insignia. Examples are two flat pieces shown in Figs. 11-176 and 11-177 and two domed pieces in Figs. 11-178 and 11-179. A hand-embroidered "disk" from the China-Burma-India theater is shown in Fig. 11-180.

Unaccountable Medical Insignia

Several 1-inch-high caducei exist with various unexplained letters added. Most, if not all, were made in Europe. Some insignia may be attributed to foreign armies, but their similarity to U.S. collar devices is striking, and some undoubtedly were made for Americans.

A medical insignia with a white *F* (Fig. 11-181) has conventional tines and clutches and looks like a U.S. Army insignia. Immediately the question arises whether it might have been intended for female personnel. The unusual color of the letter supports the theory, because white has been exclusively used by medical women. Another possible women's insignia is shown in Fig. 11-182. Made in Germany, the silver caduceus carries the black enameled letters *FM*. This insignia obviously is similar to the 1947 Women's Medical Specialist Corps insignia, and possibly the *FM* was intended to stand for female medical specialists or some such organization. Until contact is made with a person associated with the manufacture of these insignia, their intended use remains clouded.

Fig. 11-175. *A gilt domed disk used by the 11th Airborne Division's medical battalion in the 1950s. (1 1/64 inches in diameter)*

Figs. 11-176 and 11-177. *These flat disks with unauthorized letters added were made in the 1950s and 1960s for enlisted personnel assigned to veterinary and dental duties. The veterinary insignia (Fig. 11-176) is brass, and the dental insignia (Fig. 11-177) is silver-plated. (1 and 1 1/32 inches in diameter, respectively)*

Figs. 11-178 and 11-179. *Gilt domed disk variations. Note the style differences of the letters from those shown in Figs. 11-176 and 11-177. (1 1/32 inches and 1 inch in diameter, respectively)*

Fig. 11-180. *Hand-embroidered insignia on khaki cotton made in the China-Burma-India theater during World War II. (Design 1 1/32 inches in diameter)*

Fig. 11-181. *An unknown insignia with a white letter F. Perhaps it was intended for some type of female medical personnel. (1 7/32 inches wide)*

Fig. 11-182. *Made in Germany, this silver caduceus has a black FM monogram, possible for members of the Women's Medical Service Corps. (1 3/16 inches wide)*

Section VII

Engineers

Chapter Twelve

Engineers

The Corps of Engineers' triple-turreted castle and unique *ESSAYONS* buttons are among the oldest U.S. Army insignia still in use. Because of the age of these devices, it is worth looking at early engineers history and then at the history of these insignia.

On 16 June 1775, the Continental Congress prescribed "a chief engineer for the Army in a separate department and two assistants under him." On 11 March 1779, Congress created the engineers branch in a resolution which stated that "the Engineers in the service of the United States shall be formed into a Corps and styled the Corps of Engineers." The many engineers serving in the Revolutionary army were trained officers from other countries; however, with the drastic 1783 postwar reduction of the army, the Corps of Engineers disappeared and did not return until 9 May 1794, when Congress created a Corps of Artillerists and Engineers by expanding the existing artillery. Although no insignia appeared at that time, officers' buttons are known that bear the device of a cannon standing on grassy ground with a stack of cannonballs under the muzzle, inscribed with raised letters above and below the cannon, *1.st Reg.t* and *USA&E.* A similar button is known with the legend *2.nd Reg.t* and *USA&E.* These buttons are ascribed to the period 1794 to 1802.[1]

The Corps of Engineers separated from the artillery on 16 March 1802, when Congress empowered the president to "organize and establish a Corps of Engineers . . . [which] shall be stationed at West Point in the state of New York and shall constitute a Military Academy."[2] By at least a dozen years later the unique Corps of Engineers buttons were in use. They have not substantially changed since (Fig. 12-1).

Shortly after the founding of the corps in 1802, it was given the job of constructing various harbor defenses. Perhaps because of this special work, or perhaps in an effort to set the elite apart, Colonel Jonathan Williams, chief of engineers, designed a special engineers uniform in 1807. General George Ramsey, writing about his days as a cadet, described the academy superintendent, Captain Alden Partridge: "His [uniform] was that of the Corps of Engineers with the embroidered collar and cuffs and the Essayons buttons."[3] This description is of the period 1814 (when Ramsey entered West Point) to 1817 (when Partridge left). What was this special uniform with embroidered collar and cuffs? Perhaps it is the one established by Colonel Williams in 1807.

Just a few years before and after the tantalizingly brief period of Partridge's uniform, both the 1813 and 1820 regulations contain the cryptic statement that Corps of Engineers officers "will wear the uniform already established for that corps."[4] Regulations of 1821 prescribe a single-breasted, ten-button dark blue coat with button holes of "blue twist." The high-standing black silk velvet collar was to be "embroidered with a sprig of laurel encircling a star. The cuffs of black velvet, three and a half inches wide, to be indented, within one and one-half inch of the edge, with three buttons lengthwise on each sleeve, at equal distances, the lower button to be placed on the centre of the indentation . . . of the cuff."[5] Is this the uniform that Partridge wore with embroidered cuffs and collar several years before? It is certainly reasonable to assume so.

In 1832 the collar embroidery was changed to "an embroidered wreath of laurel and palm crossed at the bottom, encircling a

Fig. 12-1. *Corps of Engineers officers still wear buttons of this unique design, which includes the corps' motto, "Essayons," a bastion with embrasures surrounded by water, and a rising sun. The design evidently alludes to the early Corps of Engineers work, which included the building of fortifications to guard U.S. harbors. (This button is $^{31}/_{32}$ inch wide, although several sizes exist.)*

Fig. 12-2.

Fig. 12-2. An example of the 1832–47 Topographical Engineers officers' coat, which was distinguished by the gold oak leaves and acorns on the collar and cuffs.

Fig. 12-3.

Fig. 12-3. This moth-eaten gold-embroidered cap device for the Topographical Engineers was owned by Alexander Macomb, an engineer who later became the general in chief of the U.S. Army. (Design 2 13/16 inches wide)

Fig. 12-4.

Fig. 12-4. This 1851 drawing of the Topographical Engineers officers' cap insignia represents the same design that General Macomb established in 1839 and that is shown in Fig. 12-3. The gold shield with stars became the symbol of the Topographical Engineers.

star; all in gold."[6] I know of no surviving examples of this or the earlier embroidered collars, but the design of a laurel branch and a palm branch crossed, introduced with this uniform, followed for many years.

Early Enlisted Men's Uniforms

By an act of 28 February 1803, Congress allowed the enlistment of eighteen men and one artificer in the Corps of Engineers. Chief of Engineers Lieutenant Colonel Williams designed a special uniform for the men. The initial cocked hat was from the artillery, with yellow worsted edging. It carried a cockade and a yellow worsted loop running from the cockade down the side. In 1807 the hat changed to a cylindrical one, with yellow trim and a cockade and plume on the side. The dark blue coat had eight artillery buttons down the front and had a black collar and black 4-inch cuffs. Each buttonhole had 4 inches of lace extending from the sides. These few enlisted engineer troops were not carried forward when Congress reorganized the army in March 1821. Only officers comprised the corps until the Mexican War again caused the formation of engineer troops.[7]

Topographical Engineers

Created in 1813 were positions for eight topographical engineers and eight assistant engineers. Topographical engineers, a special corps composed of only officers, were responsible for exploration and mapping the American West. Until 1832 only different buttons distinguished the topographical engineers from other engineer officers.[8]

The War Department prescribed special uniforms for topographical officers in 1832. The new Corps of Topographical Engineers uniform was single-breasted with one row of ten buttons, similar to other staff coats of the time but with a standing collar, cuffs, turnback tails, and pleats near the hips ornamented with oak leaves and acorns in gold embroidery. The same general concept of gold oak leaf ornamentation continued with the 1839 uniform change, which introduced a double-breasted coat carrying ten buttons in each row, with the rows 4 inches apart. This coat had collar, cuffs, and slashed flaps on the rear hips, as shown in Fig. 12-2. In addition, in a unique move, rank was indicated by "galloons of gold lace, half an inch wide, placed diagonally and entirely across the upper side of the sleeve just above the cuffs and below the elbow." Field-grade officers wore four such lace bars, captains three, first lieutenants two, and second lieutenants one, while recent Military Academy graduates attached to the corps while awaiting appointment had no galloons.[9] This uniform lasted until 1847.

Congress ordered "that the Corps of Topographical Engineers shall be organized and increased" in July 1838. The army commander, Major General Macomb, designed a gold shield as the officers' cap insignia in April 1839. Three stars appeared on the top half of the shield, and from the bottom a gold wreath of oak leaves encircled the shield. An insignia owned by Macomb, with a moth-eaten background, is shown in Fig. 12-3. Fig. 12-4 shows the illustration that appeared in the 1851 regulations. A similar insignia, with thirteen stars on the shield, went onto the coat skirt (Fig. 12-5).[10]

Why did Macomb select a shield with three stars for the cap? Although I have no conclusive proof, it is possible to speculate that Macomb was trying to memorialize George Washington. Washington was a surveyor on the frontier, as were the topographical engineers, and Washington's coat of arms consisted of a white shield bearing three red stars across the top and two red stripes on the bottom. War of 1812 lead seals used on army bales to prevent tampering had the shield with three stars, and this design would have been familiar to Macomb. Although the use of the Washington coat of arms as the basis for the topographical insignia is not proven, it is a plausible explanation that still awaits a firm solution through research.

Topographical engineers' epaulettes carried a gold-embroidered shield and, just below the shield, the old English letters *TE* in silver metal, except for majors, who wore yellow letters on the silver epaulette lace (Fig. 12-6).[11] Regrettably, in 1863 legislation consolidated the Corps of Topographical Engineers with the Corps of Engineers, thus eliminating this most elite branch, although certainly the Corps of Engineers

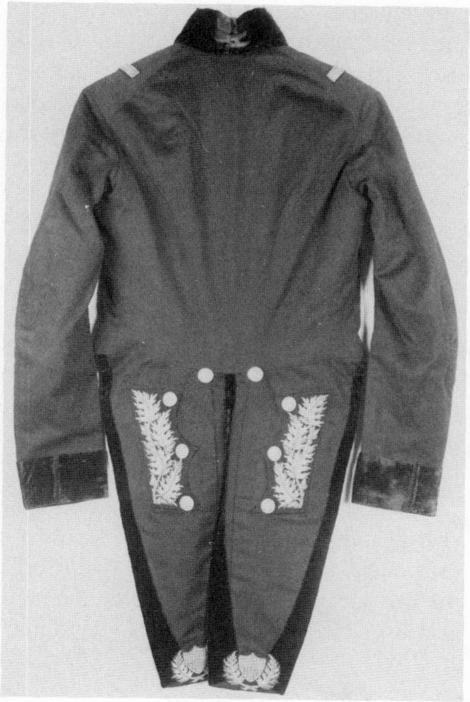

Fig. 12-5.

Fig. 12-5. *An 1851 Topographical Engineers' officers' coat. On the tails are crossed oak branches enclosing a gold shield with thrirteen stars.*

Fig. 12-6. *These nonregulation shoulder insignia, similar to epaulettes but without any fringe, were worn in the 1840s. Proper epaulettes were of this shape with fringe attached to the gold crescent, but the oak-leaf wreath should have been replaced by the old English letters TE. The shoulder insignia shown are from the West Point Museum.*

Fig. 12-6.

Fig. 12-7. *An 1872–1902 shoulder knot for a Corps of Engineers colonel. The pad background was dark blue and the castle was silver.*

Fig. 12-8. *Corps of Engineers officers below the grade of colonel had shoulder knots with large castles in the center of the pad, as shown in this sample.*

inherited the elite designation.[12] With the end of the Corps of Topographical Engineers the shield bearing stars and stripes disappeared until the Adjutant General's Department later revised the general design concept.

Epaulettes and Knots, Corps of Engineers

Initially, engineer officers wore epaulettes prescribed for members of the general staff. In February 1840, shortly after the topographical engineers introduced epaulettes with the old English letters *TE* below the shield, other engineer officers received epaulettes adorned with a silver turreted castle about $1\frac{3}{4}$ inches wide.[13] It is assumed that these triple-turreted castles were of metal.

A new shoulder knot, first described in December 1872, showed a silver metal castle $1\frac{2}{5}$ inches long and $\frac{9}{10}$ inch high to be worn with the new uniform. The original 1872 regulation stated that the knot would have the old English letters *EC*, but probably very few, if any, of these knots with *EC* letters were made because of the quickness of the change and because the castle had been worn previously (Figs. 12-7 and 12-8). Until 1902 the pad background was dark blue, the same as that of staff officers. With the adoption of new dress uniforms by the Corps of Engineers in March 1902, the knots changed to a red background with a narrow white inner border, the only branch to have a two-colored knot pad (Fig. 12-9). Generals in the Corps of Engineers wore epaulettes instead of knots, but from 1872 until 1899 no special device was prescribed. In November 1899 the chief of engineers was directed to wear metal castles on the epaulette straps.[14]

Officers' Cap and Hat Devices

In early 1839 Major General Alexander Macomb designed for the cap a six-pointed star enclosed in a gold-embroidered laurel and palm wreath; the design probably was based on the 1832 coat collar decoration. It is not known if the insignia was used, but one must assume that this regulation was followed. The familiar turreted castle was evidently designed in the fall of 1839 and sent to a die sinker in early 1840. The army prescribed the officers' insignia in February 1840.[15] The officers' caps were to have a black velvet band with a gold-embroidered wreath of laurel and palm around the castle. A design example with a metal castle, actually owned by Macomb, from the Smithsonian Institution collection is shown in Fig. 12-10.

Fig. 12-7.

Fig. 12-8.

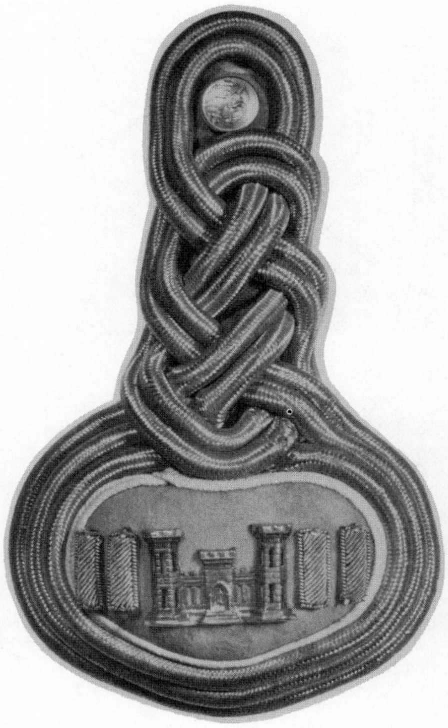

Fig. 12-9.

Fig. 12-10.

Fig. 12-11.

Fig. 12-12.

Fig. 12-13.

Fig. 12-9. The Corps of Engineers was the only branch to have a two-color shoulder knot when in March 1902 the corps changed to a red pad with white edging. Within a year a uniform change made the knots obsolete.

Fig. 12-10. General Alexander Macomb's example of the 1840 Corps of Engineers forage cap insignia, which exhibited crossed laurel and palm branches and a silver metal castle. (Wreath 2 7/8 inches wide)

Fig. 12-11. On the 1858 hat, officers wore their branch insignia on an oval with a narrow gold tracing. This example was owned by Robert E. Lee. The central design of a metal castle is very similar to that of the 1840 cap insignia.

Fig. 12-12. This Civil War officer is distinguished as a member of the Corps of Engineers by his cap insignia. Placement of the headgear on the table was hardly accidental.

Fig. 12-13. This Civil War–style cap ornament has an embroidered castle as opposed to the earlier metal versions, and the laurel and palm branches are not as richly embroidered as those shown in Fig. 12-12. These features, plus the fact that this particular device was never used, lead some collectors to believe the insignia was made late in the Civil War. (Wreath 2 1/2 inches wide)

In 1842 the castle design appeared in larger size in silver metal on caps of U.S. Military Academy cadets. The castle in the laurel and palm wreath appeared on officers' belt plates the previous year.[16]

Engineer officers' forage caps, discussed above, were for service wear. For dress occasions, engineers wore chapeaus similar to these of the general staff until 1851. In 1851 the cap with engineers' insignia became the dress headgear, replacing the chapeau.[17] Robert E. Lee's cap insignia is shown in Fig. 12-11. A typical Civil War Corps of Engineers officer with his hat is shown in Fig. 12-12. Of the various wreaths used on officers' caps, only the engineers' wreath was not symmetrical, as it used two different types of branches, the palm branch being on the right, as viewed (Fig. 12-13).

Although uniform regulations of 1861 again prescribed the wreath of laurel and palm around the silver metal castle,[18] some Civil War officers' cap insignia were made like the staff officers' wreathed *US* insignia, substituting a silver castle for the letters (Fig.

Fig. 12-14.

Fig. 12-14. A standard wreath of the type used to enclose a staff officer's letters US shows that this insignia was probably made from a stock wreath with the castle added. (Wreath 2 15/16 inches wide)

Fig. 12-15.

Fig. 12-15. Large brass castles like this one were worn on shakos by Military Academy cadets after 1842 and by enlisted engineer soldiers after 1846. The insignia became obsolete in 1851, when a dress cap with a smaller insignia was introduced.

Fig. 12-16.

Fig. 12-16. This die, used to make the large shako insignia (1842–51), was in the collection of the Stokes-Kirk store of Philadelphia for many years.

Fig. 12-17.

Fig. 12-17. This brass castle was worn by enlisted men on the 1851 dress cap, the forage cap used during the Civil War, and the 1858 hat. The width was 1 5/8 inches until a slight change during the Civil War made the insignia 1 1/2 inches wide. Such a slight change may have been the result of a change by the U.S. Quartermaster Department from one supplier to another. (1 13/16 inches wide)

12-14). It is presumed that some volunteer units used stock all-laurel wreaths simply because the use of stock wreaths was a common practice. An attributed 1872-style cap with a nonregulation wreath of this type is shown in Fig. 72-13 of chapter 72, despite the fact that the official badge for the chasseur-pattern cap remained the same as that prescribed in 1851.[19] After over one-half century, this device was finally replaced in 1895 by the gold eagle prescribed for all officers.

Enlisted Men's Cap and Hat Insignia

Congress authorized enlisted engineer soldiers for the first time since the close of the War of 1812 when it allowed a "company of Sappers, Miners, and Pontoniers" in 1846. The enlisted men's "Schako" insignia was to be a large "yellow eagle over a castle like that worn by the Cadets." An example is shown in Fig. 12-15, and an original die is shown in Fig. 12-16. A die sinker's note on the lid of the box containing one of the original dies stated, "The castle on the forage cap of engineer soldiers is to be like this, but yellow. The door and windows pierced through showing the cloth." The front of the enlisted men's forage cap then carried a smaller "yellow castle." This use of a cap insignia by enlisted men was unique to engineers and ordnance men; the other branches wore only company letters. The castle for the "uniform cap" or "schako" cost thirty-two cents, while at the same time the forage cap castle cost thirty-five cents. The reason for the difference is not known and is hard to explain, especially since the more expensive castle was smaller.[20]

Although most enlisted men's 1851–54 caps carried colored cap bands, the Corps of Engineers caps had only a colored welt of the style adopted throughout the army in 1854 and a yellow metal castle 1 5/8 inches wide by 1 1/4 inches high.[21] This device (Fig. 12-17), stamped from sheet brass, had the windows cut out. It was worn essentially unchanged on the 1851 cap, the 1858 hat, and the Civil War forage cap, although men added a separate one-inch-high letter above the turret during the Civil War. A group of Civil War engineer soldiers is shown in Fig. 12-18. By the end of the Civil War, the castle had become one-eighth inch narrower than the 1851 design and was to have "two iron wire loops" for fasteners.[22] The earlier fasteners were not specified but were probably the same.

It should be noted that between 1846 and 1861 only one Corps of Engineers company existed in the Regular Army. Then with the start of the Civil War, four companies comprised the enlisted strength of the corps. Engineers subsequently formed a five-company battalion in 1866, and between then and 1901 the number of men in the battalion varied. Congress finally authorized twelve companies in 1901, and this number continued until the National Defense Act of 1916, which expanded the corps to several regiments.

Fig. 12-18.

Fig. 12-18. *Civil War Corps of Engineers troops wearing the castle insignia. One soldier in the second row has his fastened to his shirt front.*

Introduced with the new 1872 uniform was a yellow metal "badge of the corps" for engineer troops. In a special one-page change to the regulation in December 1872, a brass wreath with the silver Roman letters *CE* was prescribed. These insignia may not actually have been made, because in June 1873 a brass castle with the company letter above was again specified. In 1876 the size increased to 1¾ by 1⅞ inches.[23] Fig. 12-19 shows some of the 2d Volunteer Engineers of the Spanish-American War wearing the castle and unit number.

In 1896 a screw-back castle, 1¾ inches wide and 1⅛ inches high (Fig. 12-20) was introduced. This insignia came in both thick (0.050 inch) and thin (0.014 inch) metals, with solid (Fig. 12-20) and pierced (Fig. 12-21) windows. Castles without company letters were intended for the noncommissioned staff, while those with letters (Fig. 12-22) were for men in companies. Large bronze castles (Fig. 12-23) were made for olive drab caps introduced with the service uniform in 1905, although officially smaller cap insignia came into use with the introduction of bronze-colored insignia.[24]

Reduced in size to 1¼ inches wide in 1905 (Fig. 12-24), the castle came in gilt for dress uniforms, with and without company letters, as before. The Quartermaster General's Department made similar insignia in bronze for the service uniform (Figs. 12-25 and 12-26). The height of the side towers was 13/16 inch, and, for just 1905, the width of the battlement above the door was 9/16 inch; this latter measurement was reduced to 7/16 inch in December 1905. Until 1916 the army's Corps of Engineers troops consisted of twelve companies, *A* through *M*, less *J*, so there was no regimental designation. Between 1905 and 1916 the only other cap ornament used by engineer soldiers was the insignia, introduced in 1910 and worn by West Point detachment members, which bore the letters *MA* and *DET.*[25] Field and band musicians of the engineers had unique cap insignia that carried castles on the bugle

Fig. 12-19.

Fig. 12-19. *Spanish-American War members of the 2d Volunteer Engineer Regiment wear cap insignia on their hats, a practice that was not authorized but was widely followed in the late nineteenth century.*

Fig. 12-20.

Fig. 12-20. *Gilt-colored 1896–1905 enlisted men's cap insignia with a screw-post fastener. This particular version came with the windows solid. (1 13/16 inches wide)*

Fig. 12-21.

Fig. 12-21. *The noncommissioned staff of the engineer battalions wore cap insignia of this type without any company letter above. This 1896–1905 cap device has both pierced windows and cut-out bastions, unlike the one shown in Fig. 12-20. (1 11/16 inches wide)*

Fig. 12-22.

Fig. 12-22. *A large brass 1896–1905 cap ornament with company letter. Men in the twelve engineer companies wore insignia with only the letter, because there was no Corps of Engineers regimental organization until 1916. A smaller device of same design was introduced in 1905. (1 39/64 inches wide)*

Fig. 12-23.

Fig. 12-23. *Olive drab bill caps were first prescribed in late December 1904 for wear with wool service uniforms. With the new caps came dark bronze-colored insignia. Although the size of the engineer castle was reduced when the wool caps came in, with the introduction of dark-colored cap insignia the Quartermaster Department treated some existing larger pieces with a chemical solution to turn them the appropriate dark color. (1 3/4 inches wide)*

or lyre faces. These are described in chapters 13 and 14.

Engineer regiments formed in 1916 as a result of the major army expansion. The resulting cap devices had regimental numbers above the center turret with the company letter on the castle face. Men of the regimental staff and the regimental band wore just the number above the turret from 1916 until they were phased out in 1918, replaced by the eagle from the national seal on a 1½-inch-diameter disk.[26]

On the campaign hat the plain company letter was worn between 1899 and 1907, as described in chapter 10, "Numbers and Letters," with a red and white intermixed hat cord.[27]

Officers' Collar Insignia

Introduced with the 1892 officers' sack coat were silver castles for the collar. The insignia illustrated in the 10 June 1893 issue of the *Army and Navy Register* shows the castle ¾ inch high with the notation "embroidered in silver," but these castles were soon made only in metal. In 1895 the

Fig. 12-24.

Fig. 12-25.

Fig. 12-26.

Fig. 12-27.

Fig. 12-30.

Fig. 12-28.

Fig. 12-29.

Fig. 12-24. *From 1905 until 1918, Corps of Engineers soldiers wore this size of cap device. This gilt color was worn on dress caps. The company letter indicates it was used by a company member between 1905, when the small castles were introduced, and 1916, when regiments were formed. ($1\frac{9}{32}$ inches wide)*

Fig. 12-25. *A bronze cap device for service (field) wear by a company member, 1905–16. ($1\frac{1}{4}$ inches wide)*

Fig. 12-26. *Regimental noncommissioned staff members of the 1905–16 period wore castle cap insignia like this without any company or regimental designation. ($1\frac{21}{64}$ inches wide)*

Fig. 12-27. *This silver-embroidered castle and US were for the 1893 sack coat collar. The castle followed the design that had been standard for many years.*

Fig. 12-28. *This embroidered castle's size ($\frac{3}{4}$ inch high) indicates it may have been made about 1893, when officers' collar insignia were introduced, but the simply made door may also point to a piece, smaller than regulation, made during the hasty buildup of the Spanish-American War.*

Fig. 12-29. *Silver castles were used from 1893 for Corps of Engineers officers. This larger 1-inch-high castle conforms to the size prescribed in 1895.*

Fig. 12-30. *Metal castles in etruscan style (made to look like imitation embroidery) were common for many years. This silver castle with darkened windows could have been used anytime from the 1890s until the 1920s.*

size of the triple-turreted castle was changed to 1 inch high. Two 1890s embroidered collar insignia are shown in Figs. 12-27 and 12-28; both are $1\frac{1}{8}$ inches long and almost $\frac{7}{8}$ inch high, but they have different doors. The difference in size of those shown here from that required in 1893 is less than $\frac{1}{16}$ inch, and these are probably some of the original insignia. Fig. 12-29 is $1\frac{1}{2}$ inches long and 1 inch high, as called for in 1895. After 1895 many collar insignia were of metal made to look like embroidery (Figs. 12-30 and 12-31). In July 1895 engineer insignia, and the *US* worn with them, were to be of "metal or embroidery" in silver.[28]

General Order 126, 1900, prescribed small insignia to be added to branch insignia to indicate an officer's staff duties. Because the Corps of Engineers was organized only into battalions, these staff insignia consisted initially of only the adjutant and the quartermaster. Examples are shown in Figs. 12-32 and 12-33. Fig. 12-34 shows a bronze insignia for the khaki service uniform. A $\frac{3}{4}$-inch-high ordnance bomb (Fig. 12-35) was added in 1914 for the inspector or assistant inspector of small arms practice in organized militia. These staff devices were rescinded in October 1923.[29]

When the khaki service uniform was first introduced in 1898, the then current silver branch insignia was prescribed for the collar, but imitation embroidery began to be dropped (Figs. 12-36 and 12-37).[30] After 1901 the collar insignia for the khaki uniform was 1 inch high and of dull finished bronze. These same bronze insignia lasted through World War I, and the colonel shown in Fig. 12-38 wears a typical 1918 uniform for the American Expeditionary Forces. For wear on shirt collars, small castles (Fig. 12-39) were made in bronze. Early coat castles were close to 1 inch in height, but by the end of World War I and into the early 1920s many were actually closer to $\frac{7}{8}$ inch high, as shown in Figs. 12-40 and 12-41.

When the bronze insignia were phased out in October 1923, Corps of Engineers officers returned to silver castles (Fig. 12-42) on coats and shirts (Fig. 12-43). In February 1924 the secretary of war directed the engineer insignia be changed to gilt, which was accomplished the following November. War

Fig. 12-31.

Fig. 12-32.

Fig. 12-33.

Fig. 12-34.

Fig. 12-35.

Fig. 12-36.

Fig. 12-37.

Fig. 12-31. *Small loops on the back of this silver castle allowed it to be sewn to an officer's uniform. Pierced or open windows of this type have been used by officers intermittently since metal collar insignia were introduced. (1 1/4 inches wide)*

Figs. 12-32 and 12-33. *Starting in 1900, engineer battalion adjutants and quartermasters added gilt staff devices of this style to their silver castles. Staff devices officially lasted until 1923. (Each 1 1/4 inches wide)*

Figs. 12-34 and 12-35. *Bronze castles and staff devices were used by Corps of Engineers officers on service uniforms. The ordnance insignia came into use in 1914 for inspectors or assistant inspectors of small arms practice in organized militia. (1 1/4 and 1 5/16 inches wide, respectively)*

Figs. 12-36 and 12-37. *Pre–World War I silver castles for dress uniforms, with plain metal designs instead of imitation embroidery. Officers' silver castles lasted until 1924. The distortion in the castle sides was caused by cutting out the windows in the thick metal. (1 7/32 and 1 23/64 inches wide, respectively)*

Fig. 12-38. *A 1918 Corps of Engineers colonel wearing bronze-colored shirt collar insignia.*

Department Circular 15, March 1926, shrank the gilt castles to 11/16 inch high for shirts and roll collar coats, while the standing-collar coats continued to carry nominal 1-inch-high gilt castles[31] (Fig. 12-44, which has loops for sewing to the coat). Figs. 12-45 and 12-46 show 11/16-inch-high castles in imitation embroidery. The latter insignia has black-painted windows to give the appearance they are cut out. Use of staff devices died hard, as evidenced by the small imitation embroidery castle shown in Fig. 12-47; its gilt color should preclude it from having the adjutant's addition. The interwar period also saw a revival of the imitation embroidery style, as exemplified in Figs. 12-48 and 12-49.

During World War II and afterwards engineer officers wore castles about 11/16 inch high, like those of 1926. Samples include those shown in Figs. 12-50, 12-51, and 12-52, the first having been made in Germany after World War II, the second in Korea, and the last in the United States, with a horizontal piece made as part of the insignia so only the numbers had to be added to the bar. A typical 1950s embroidered insignia is shown in Fig. 12-53. An unusually small foreign-made castle with integral

Fig. 12-38.

Fig. 12-39.

Fig. 12-40.

Fig. 12-41.

Fig. 12-43.

Fig. 12-42.

Fig. 12-44.

Fig. 12-45.

Fig. 12-46.

Fig. 12-47.

Fig. 12-48.

Fig. 12-49.

unit numbers is shown in Fig. 12-54. Subdued metal insignia adopted during the Vietnam War also have numbers and even nonregulation company letters (Fig. 12-55).

Helmet Insignia

Enlisted men in the Corps of Engineers wore the 1881 dress helmet with a small silver castle (Fig. 12-57) on the staff helmet eagle.[32] The 1902-pattern dress cap replaced the spiked helmet for the Corps of Engineers in 1903 and 1904.

Outline Enlisted Men's Collar Insignia

New 1851 regulations prescribed enlisted men's collar ornaments for Corps of Engineers troops (Fig. 12-58). This "castle of yellow metal," 1 5/8 by 1 1/4 inches, the same as for the cap, was worn on each side of the standing collar until 1858. The soldier of questionable neatness shown in Fig. 12-59 is wearing some of the pre–Civil War Corps of Engineers insignia used by the lone company then authorized. Brass castles 1 inch by 5/8 inch with loops on the reverse were worn on the 1872–85 coat collar, and these were evidently the same design as that of the helmet overlay. Troops of January 1900 in "extreme southern latitudes" received a gilt

Fig. 12-39. *An officers' small bronze-colored castle for wear on shirt collars during the World War I period. (29/32 inch wide)*

Figs. 12-40 and 12-41. *Some Corps of Engineers insignia were smaller than the prescribed 1 inch high, like these examples. The thin metal used in some insignia like these, made distortion of the castle and windows a problem. (Each 1 1/4 inches wide)*

Fig. 12-42. *For several months in 1923 and 1924 officers were to wear silver insignia like this on the post–World War I high-collar coat. After that time the corps changed to gilt insignia. (1 17/64 inches wide)*

Fig. 12-43. *A small shirt collar insignia in silver. Insignia of this size and color would have been worn in 1923 and 1924, according to regulations, although the 1923 switch to silver was not accomplished immediately by all officers. (51/64 inch wide)*

Fig. 12-44. *Officers' gilt castles, 1 inch high, were for the high-collar coat after February 1924. This particular insignia has four small sewing loops on the back. (1 9/32 inches wide)*

Figs. 12-45 and 12-46. *In March 1926 a smaller insignia was introduced for the lapel collar coat. That shown in Fig. 12-45 has the regimental number for the New York National Guard regiment of the 27th Division. The second piece has the windows painted black to resemble the earlier cut-out windows used in some insignia, and also shows the older practice of imitation embroidery. (Each 31/32 inches wide)*

Fig. 12-47. *This insignia is gilt, a color introduced for Corps of Engineers officers in 1924, yet the adjutant's staff device should not have been worn after 1923. A member of the Pennsylvania National Guard's 28th Division probably wore the insignia in the late 1920s. The use of special insignia, such as staff devices, often survived in practice several years after a change of regulations. (61/64 inch wide)*

Figs. 12-48 and 12-49. *The fasteners on these insignia, as well as the gold color, show they were made in the 1920s for the high-collar service coat. (1 13/64 and 1 1/4 inches wide, respectively)*

Fig. 12-50.

Fig. 12-51.

Fig. 12-52.

Fig. 12-54.

Fig. 12-53.

Fig. 12-56.

Fig. 12-55.

Fig. 12-57.

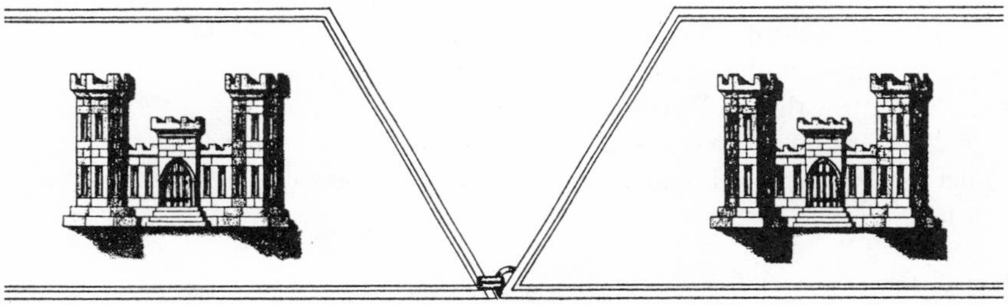

Fig. 12-58.

Fig. 12-50. *The 11/16-inch-high castle was introduced in 1926 for officers' lapel coats. This particular insignia was made in Germany after World War II for occupation forces. (1 1/16 inches wide)*

Fig. 12-51. *This insignia was made in Korea in the 1950s or early 1960s for officers of the 1st Cavalry Division. (1 inch wide)*

Fig. 12-52. *In the 1970s some insignia makers produced castles of this style with the battalion number on a bar instead of the center turret. (1 9/64 inches wide)*

Fig. 12-53. *Between World War II and Vietnam, officers usually wore yellow embroidered insignia on their fatigue uniforms. Some units added their numbers, as was done here. (Design 1 3/32 inches wide)*

Fig. 12-54. *Made overseas, this smaller than regulation insignia also had the unit number made as part of the insignia instead of having the number added later, as was the case with most collar ornaments. (13/16 inch wide)*

Fig. 12-55. *During the Vietnam War the army introduced black metal insignia for officers' fatigue uniforms, and this practice continued with the battle dress uniforms. While the unit numbers could properly be added above the castle, the company letter was strictly nonregulation. (1 1/8 inches wide)*

Fig. 12-56. *Major Frank W. Gano in the late 1930s wearing insignia of the 3d Engineers.*

Fig. 12-57. *The 1881–1903 enlisted men's Corps of Engineers helmets carried these silver-colored overlays on the eagles' shields. (7/8 inch wide)*

castle (Fig. 12-60) of the same design as the helmet overlay but with a pin back for wear on the collar of the white duck coat.[33]

With the introduction of the 1902 enlisted men's collar insignia for dress and service uniforms, engineers wore gilt castles 1 1/8 inches high (Figs. 12-61, 12-62, and 12-63). Smaller ornaments came into use in 1905, as shown in Fig. 12-64 for the dress uniform, with identical insignia of bronze on the khaki and olive drab service uniforms. The castle worn by the U.S. Military Academy Detachment had *MA* above the center turret and *DET* across the face (Fig. 12-65).[34]

Starting in mid-1916, the regimental number was placed above the center turret, and for company members the company letter went on the castle face, just as on the cap insignia; like the cap insignia, these devices are not common today.

Bronze Collar Disks

Typical enlisted men's bronze disk insignia worn from 1910 through 1916 and again from 1918 through 1923 are shown in Figs. 12-66 and 12-67. *MA* and *DET* for the U.S. Military Academy Detachment (Fig. 12-68) saw use until March 1921. After the Corps of

Fig. 12-59.

Fig. 12-62.

Fig. 12-65.

Fig. 12-66.

Fig. 12-67.

Fig. 12-68.

Fig. 12-60.

Fig. 12-61.

Fig. 12-63.

Fig. 12-64.

Fig. 12-58. *Enlisted men's dress uniform coat collars as shown in the 1851 uniform regulations. The castles were to be $1\frac{5}{8}$ by $1\frac{1}{4}$ inches.*

Fig. 12-59. *This pre–Civil War Corps of Engineers soldier is wearing branch insignia on his dress uniform collar.*

Fig. 12-60. *Gilt, pin-back insignia of the same design as that for the 1881 helmet overlays were used from 1900 to 1903 for the collars of the white duck coats. ($\frac{7}{8}$ inch wide)*

Fig. 12-61. *Large pin-back gilt castles without company letter were worn on dress uniform collars in 1903 and 1904 by recruits and by members of the battalion noncommissioned staff. ($1\frac{45}{64}$ inches wide)*

Fig. 12-62. *Corporal Dipple of the Corps of Engineers L Company in dress uniform with pre-1905 collar insignia. The photograph was taken in 1906.*

Fig. 12-63. *The large size of this insignia dates its period of manufacture as 1903 or 1904. The pin back indicates that it was for wear on the collar, and the company letter above the turret shows that it was intended for members of G company. ($1\frac{11}{16}$ inches wide)*

Fig. 12-64. *The smaller castle was introduced in 1905 for wear on enlisted men's uniform collars. Gilt insignia went on the dress uniform, as before, and bronze castles were introduced for wear on service coats. ($1\frac{9}{32}$ inches wide)*

Fig. 12-65. *Beginning in 1910, enlisted men in the U.S. Military Academy Corps of Engineers Detachment began to wear these unique collar insignia. ($1\frac{9}{32}$ inches wide)*

Fig. 12-66. *A bronze disk of the style worn on enlisted men's service uniforms from 1910 until 1923.*

Fig. 12-67. *Except for a period between 1916 and 1918, regulations called for bronze disks to have company designations of the type shown, with the letter above the center turret.*

Fig. 12-68. *A bronze disk for the U.S. Military Academy Detachment service uniform, as worn from 1910 until 1921.*

Fig. 12-69.

Fig. 12-70.

Fig. 12-71.

Fig. 12-72.

Fig. 12-73.

Fig. 12-74.

Fig. 12-75.

Fig. 12-76.

Fig. 12-77.

Fig. 12-78.

Fig. 12-79.

Fig. 12-80.

Fig. 12-81.

Fig. 12-82.

Fig. 12-83.

Fig. 12-84.

Fig. 12-85.

Figs. 12-69 and 12-70. *Between the time the army formed engineer regiments in 1916 and until a change of insignia occurred in 1918, unit designations were to be as shown, although use of this style of numbers and letters continued after the official cutoff date. The placement of number and letter was also used by battalions, as shown in Fig. 12-70, since the 9th Engineers was a mounted battalion reorganized and redesignated in 1918.*

Figs. 12-71 and 12-72. *Common but unauthorized placement of unit designations on World War I Corps of Engineers disks.*

Fig. 12-73. *Nonregulation use of company letters on the castle face probably came about during World War I when the unit number was to go on the US disk.*

Fig. 12-74. *T (for trains) was never prescribed by the War Department, but some unit members wore such insignia.*

Figs. 12-75 and 12-76. *Gilt disks for wear after 1923. Backgrounds of this type were not prescribed by the government for gilt insignia.*

Figs. 12-77 and 12-78. *Gilt disks of the style issued from 1923 until 1938. Company and battalion headquarters designations went above the center turret.*

Fig. 12-79. *For ten years starting in 1927, band members were to wear a lyre instead of a company or battalion designation. Very few Corps of Engineers band musicians were authorized during this period, making original disks hard to find today.*

Fig. 12-80. *A typical screw-post, two-piece Corps of Engineers enlisted men's collar insignia used during World War II.*

Figs. 12-81 and 12-82. *Typical 1940s two-piece disks with company designations above and below the castles. The addition of company letters above the center turret was most common, as in Fig. 12-82, for headquarters companies. The HS in Fig. 12-81 stands for headquarters and service company. (Each $1^{1}/_{32}$ inches in diameter)*

Fig. 12-83. *A domed disk of the type popular in the 1950s. This particular silver-colored insignia incorporates the old idea of pierced windows in the two towers. ($1^{3}/_{64}$ inches in diameter)*

Figs. 12-84 and 12-85. *These two gilt, domed disks were intended for wear by airborne troops at Fort Bragg, North Carolina. (Each $1^{3}/_{64}$ inches in diameter)*

Fig. 12-86.

Fig. 12-87.

Fig. 12-88.

Fig. 12-89.

Fig. 12-90.

Engineers formed regiments in 1916, the regimental number was added above the castle and the company letter moved to the face, as illustrated in Figs. 12-69 and 12-70.[35] The most common variation of this placement is with the regimental number below the castle and with the company letter in its original location above the center turret. An unusual example, with a number smaller than usual, is shown in Fig. 12-71, and the more frequent version is shown in Fig. 12-72. Similar disks with company letters on the face but without numbers exist (Fig. 12-73), although they are nonregulation. Some members of World War I engineer trains added a nonregulation *T*, as shown in Fig. 12-74.

Gilt Collar Disks

Many examples of the post-1923 gilt disk exist with the pebbled background (Figs. 12-75 and 12-76) and the regulation cross-hatched background (Figs. 12-77 and 12-78). After 1927 a lyre replaced the company letter or battalion number for regimental band members (Fig. 12-79).[36] In the 1930s and 1940s enlisted engineers purchased privately made two-piece disks (Fig. 12-80), many with company letters (Fig. 12-81 for a headquarters and service company and Fig. 12-82 for a headquarters and headquarters company).

Other two-piece insignia include the five domed disks shown in Figs. 12-83 through 12-87, the first, with pierced windows, produced in the United States and the last made in Germany after World War II. Flat two-piece disks also came with company and battalion designations (Fig. 12-88 for the 58th Engineer Company stationed in Fulda, Germany, for many years). Fig. 12-89, a U.S.-made disk, shows a castle lower than normal to allow room for the addition of unit numbers above. The insignia of Fig. 12-90 is a disk made in India about 1944 for use by U.S. troops in the China, Burma, India Theater.

Fig. 12-91.

Nonregulation red and white enamel edges exist for both the cap (Fig. 8-66 in chapter 8, "Eagle Insignia") and collar insignia (Fig. 12-91), and these evidently date from about 1952, when the infantry received a blue edging.

Figs. 12-86 and 12-87. *Both of these silver-colored, domed disks with unit numbers were made in Germany in the 1950s. The 485 number is much smaller than the 61. The latter (Fig. 12-87) was applied to a bar, which was not a common practice. (1 inch and 1 1/16 inches in diameter, respectively)*

Fig. 12-88. *Separate engineer companies were numbered, as was the 58th Engineers. The company supported the 14th Armored Cavalry Regiment and later the 11th Armored Cavalry Regiment, stationed in Fulda, Germany. The brass disk was made in Germany and is of the flat design. (1 1/32 inches in diameter)*

Fig. 12-89. *This particular castle was placed lower than that on most disks to allow room for the unit number. The insignia was made in the United States. (1 1/32 inches in diameter)*

Fig. 12-90. *This crudely cast insignia was made for U.S. troops in the India-Burma region near the end of World War II. (1 1/16 inches in diameter)*

Fig. 12-91. *The insignia edging is in red and white enamel. Use of the Corps of Engineers colors in such an unauthorized manner was probably modeled on the blue edging given to infantry troops in 1952. (1 7/16 inches in diameter)*

Section VIII

Musicians' Insignia

Chapter Thirteen

Lyres

Band members, the real dandies of the army during the Victorian era, had extra uniform trim, aiguillettes, and other adornments on gaudy uniforms. The ubiquitous lyre became the standard insignia, and it is still used today by band members. Militia bands spruced up their uniforms from the many styles of stock lyre insignia sold by nineteenth-century outfitters, while regulations allowed Regular Army regimental commanders to spend unit funds on special accoutrements for each regiment's band, as discussed and illustrated in chapter 2.

A unit's commander influenced the band's prominence. The 7th Cavalry Band apparently played "Garry Owen," an Irish drinking song, on every possible occasion, even during the field campaigns of the 1870s and 1880s. In other regiments' histories the band is scarcely mentioned, and photographs show that many bands did not wear even the authorized uniform additions. In 1851, for example, bands could have "such additions in ornaments as [the commander] may judge proper."[1] Turn-of-the-century photographs show that many band leaders wore fully embroidered lyres in wreaths. Because of these options, it is impossible now to know all of the ornaments used, but probably many commercial insignia appeared on army band uniforms.

Band musicians and field musicians were different, and this is not now always appreciated. Band musicians formed the regimental band and played various instruments, while field musicians, at least after the Civil War, played only bugles or trumpets to signal men as directed by officers. Each company had two field musicians, while the sizes of bands varied over time. In 1851 a regimental band had one sergeant and sixteen privates selected from various companies.[2] Band musicians used lyres as distinctive ornaments, in contrast to field musicians, who wore branch insignia or bugle devices.

Fig. 13-1.

Fig. 13-2.

Fig. 13-1. The lyre introduced in 1887. Musicians used the wire fasteners to place this silver-colored insignia on the flap of the music pouch. This same design was evidently worn on caps. (7/8 inch wide)

Fig. 13-2. A post-1896 band musician's insignia for the forage cap. Regulations did not call for the gilt regimental number on the lyre's face. (55/64 inch wide)

Cap, Hat, and Helmet Insignia

In the twenty years after the Civil War, the War Department stocked and issued available commercial lyre insignia for wear on caps and helmets. After considerable deliberations, the secretary of war allowed white lyres "for caps and helmets" in 1885. In 1887 the Quartermaster General's Department issued specifications for music pouches, including a new style of lyre (Fig. 13-1) that was to be added to the pouch flap. This lyre may have been the cap or hat ornament introduced in 1885. With the introduction of screw-backed cap devices in 1896, the Philadelphia Depot made a silver 1½-inch cap lyre of this design. Gilt regimental numbers also were placed on the center of these lyres (Fig. 13-2), although 1897 specifications did not list this practice.[3]

Beginning in 1885, band musicians placed a small silver lyre on the 1881 helmet shield (Fig. 13-3). The brass helmet eagle, to which the lyre was applied, carried crossed arms according to the arm of service, such as sabers for cavalry.[4] The same small silver lyre was simultaneously authorized for use on forage caps, although many subsequent nineteenth-century regulations are inconsistent concerning band musicians' insignia. Many soldiers added wreaths around the cap lyre (Fig. 13-4), as did Sergeant James Grigsby, a member of the 25th Infantry during the 1890s.[5] Another stock piece, made with the 1887 lyre, is shown in Fig. 13-5.

PR to represent the Philippine and Puerto Rico regiment bands (Fig. 13-10). In 1906 the recruiting service bands added *RS*, with numbers, on their lyres, and prison guard band members wore the lyre with *PG* (Fig. 13-11). In 1914 prison guards were retitled disciplinary barracks guards, and their band members wore *DB* on the lyre face after 1916.[6]

Fig. 13-12 shows a nonregulation cap device used by band members between 1903 and 1905. The piece can be identified by the screw back (introduced in 1896) and large wreath (replaced in 1905). The style of the 1903 lyre, combined with the large wreath, dates the piece. Senior noncommissioned officers other than those of infantry, cavalry, engineers, and field artillery had cap ornaments which included wreaths. Photographs show that some bands wore lyres in wreaths, both embroidered and in metal. In some cases principal musicians and chief musicians, members of the regimental noncommissioned staff, wore such insignia rather than crossed rifles or other proper cap ornament.[7]

Fig. 13-4.

Fig. 13-5.

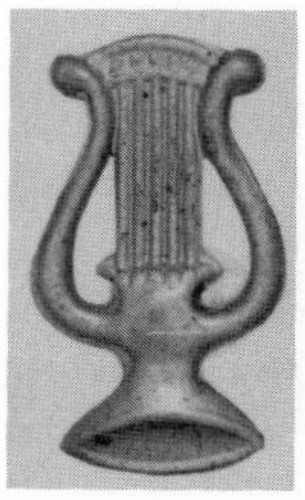

Fig. 13-3.

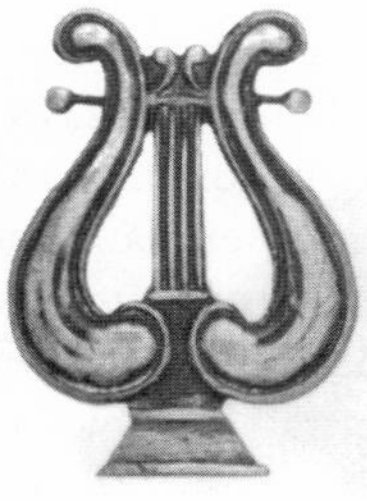

Fig. 13-6.

Fig. 13-7.

Fig. 13-8.

Fig. 13-9.

Fig. 13-10.

Fig. 13-11.

Fig. 13-3. *The 1885 silver lyre which went on the helmet eagle. This same insignia was also prescribed for the forage cap. (21/32 inch wide)*

Fig. 13-4. *A nonregulation cap insignia used in the 1890s. The insignia is from the Smithsonian Institution collection and consists of a standard silver helmet overlay lyre and a stock, stamped brass noncommissioned officers' wreath. The piece is held together with wire, and the back is filled with lead. It was fastened to the cap by a large safety pin. This was worn by Sergeant James Grigsby of the 25th Infantry during the 1890s. (2 11/16 inches wide)*

Fig. 13-5. *An unofficial cap insignia made before 1896, with wire fasteners on the back. (2 11/16 inches wide)*

Fig. 13-6. *The 1903-style cap lyre. (29/32 inch wide)*

Fig. 13-7. *Corps of Engineers band musicians wore silver lyres with gilt castles, like this cap insignia, on dress uniforms from 1903 until 1916. (57/64 inch wide)*

Fig. 13-8. *In 1903 and 1904 the band members for cavalry, infantry, and artillery wore silver lyres with a large gilt number above, like this insignia, on dress uniforms. (7/8 inch wide)*

Cap Lyres, 1901–17

For caps, a simpler screw-back silver lyre was worn in 1903 (Fig. 13-6). Engineer band musicians wore a gold castle on the face of a silver lyre (Fig. 13-7) until 1916, when Congress allowed more than one Corps of Engineers regiment. Gold regimental numbers were placed above the silver lyre for other than engineer bands (Fig. 13-8) until December 1904, when the number, reduced in size, moved to the center of the lyre (Fig. 13-9). The army also introduced bronze lyres in December 1904 (the same design as that shown in Fig. 13-9) as well as the letters *P* and

Fig. 13-12.

Fig. 13-13.

Fig. 13-14.

Fig. 13-15.

Fig. 13-16.

Fig. 13-17.

Another unauthorized and unexplained bronze cap insignia from 1905 to 1917 is shown in Fig. 13-13.

SPECIAL BAND HEADGEAR DEVICES

In 1910, all members of the West Point Band received a silver lyre with gilt letters *MA* (for Military Academy) within a gilt wreath (Fig. 13-14), the design still used by the U.S. Military Academy Band.[8] A variation is shown in Fig. 13-15. A large silver lyre in a wreath, with *USMA* above, appears on the band's shakos (Fig. 13-16). The 1904-style wreath also appeared after World War II as the cap insignia for the U.S. Army Field Band (Fig. 13-17), but it was superceded in 1974 by the standard enlisted men's cap ornament.

General John Pershing formed the U.S. Army Band when he became chief of staff in 1921. Band members' caps carried a large silver lyre with an eagle in a ring on the center (Fig. 13-18). Lasting only from June 1924 until May 1927, this large lyre was replaced by a special two-piece cap device, "capable of being burnished," that in 1937 became the standard cap insignia for all band enlisted men. The change from the original large lyre and small eagle was made at the request of the band commander, who stated that the original insignia was "cumbersome, of poor material, and . . . impossible to keep bright." The two-piece 1927 insignia was a commercial emblem, made and promoted by the N. S. Meyer Company. This is but one example of a basic government design being improved by a commercial firm and then becoming the government standard.[9]

In 1943 the U.S. Army Band received still another new cap insignia: a gilt lyre with

Fig. 13-9. *In 1905 regimental numbers were reduced in size and moved to the lyre's face. (7/8 inch wide)*

Fig. 13-10. *Cap insignia for band musicians of the Puerto Rico Regiment. (7/8 inch wide)*

Fig. 13-11. *Recruiting Service bands added the district number below the RS. (7/8 inch wide)*

Fig. 13-12. *A noncommissioned officers' nonregulation cap insignia, 1903–1905. (2 39/64 inches wide)*

Fig. 13-13. *A nonregulation cap insignia with bronze finish for the service cap, 1905–18. (1 29/32 inches wide)*

Fig. 13-14. *Military Academy Band members began to wear a silver lyre with a gilt wreath and letters MA in 1910. The insignia is still used. (1 15/16 inches wide)*

Fig. 13-15. *A variation on the U.S. Military Academy Band cap insignia. (1 5/8 inches wide)*

Fig. 13-16. *An all silver-colored insignia worn by Military Academy Band members on the shako. (3 3/8 inches wide)*

Fig. 13-17. *In the 1950s and 1960s Army Field Band members wore the 1905-style gilt wreath with a gilt pentagon as the central design. (1 7/8 inches wide)*

large letters *US*, all in a gilt wreath.[10] Several versions of this design exist. An early insignia has two bars tying the lyre top to the wreath (Fig. 13-19), while two 1960s insignia have the *US* high (Fig. 13-20) and low (Fig. 13-21) on the lyre, with the letters removable for polishing. With a new dress blue uniform and red cap introduced in 1968 came the present U.S. Army Band cap insignia (Fig. 13-22), which replaced the World War II lyre in a wreath.

Evidently used by the 16th Coast Artillery band in the 1920s or 1930s, the cap insignia, $1\frac{1}{2}$ inches in diameter, shown in Fig. 13-23 may be construed as an authorized insignia within the provisions allowing band mem-

Fig. 13-18. *The U.S. Army Band's cap insignia from 1924 until 1927. The commanding officer complained that this insignia was, "impossible to keep bright." ($1\frac{13}{16}$ inches wide)*

Figs. 13-19, 13-20, and 13-21. *Three versions of the 1943–68 U.S. Army Band cap insignia.*

Fig. 13-22. *The all-gilt cap insignia for the U.S. Army Band, first worn in 1968. ($1\frac{23}{32}$ inches wide)*

Fig. 13-23. *Some bands in the 1930s added nonregulation cap insignia. This 16th Coast Artillery piece is a typical example. ($1\frac{31}{64}$ inches wide)*

Fig. 13-24. *Bands in the 1950s stationed in Germany occasionally wore special cap devices. This gilt example is for the 3d Armored Division's Combat Command A. ($1\frac{13}{16}$ inches wide)*

Fig. 13-25. *A silver, German-made cap insignia. Fig. 13-26 shows use of these insignia in the early 1950s. The insignia also exists in gilt. ($2\frac{3}{8}$ inches wide)*

Fig. 13-19.

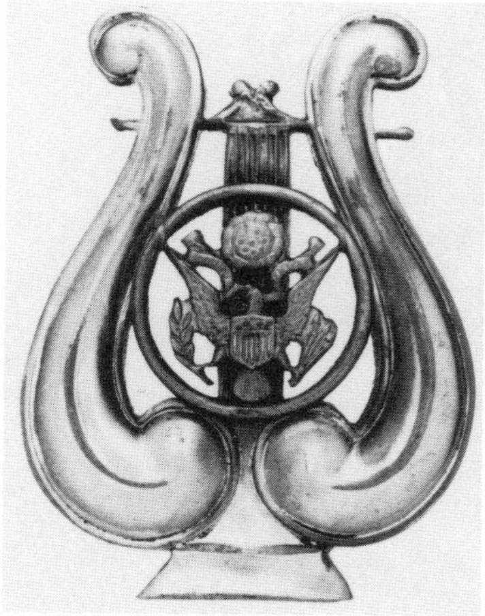

Fig. 13-18.

Fig. 13-20.

Fig. 13-21.

Fig. 13-22.

Fig. 13-23.

Fig. 13-24.

Fig. 13-25.

Fig. 13-26.

Fig. 13-26. *Shortly after the end of World War II, this segregated band adopted officer-style uniforms, totally nonregulation trim, officer-style US letters for the collar, and, for the enlisted men, a cap insignia consisting of a lyre in a wreath.*

bers additional ornaments that a commander "deemed proper."[11] This nineteenth-century heritage was loosely interpreted by many commanders in Germany after World War II. Special lyres appeared, including one in a wreath with *CCA* above (Fig. 13-24) for Combat Command A, 3d Armored Division. This command was not even authorized a band, since the division headquarters was responsible for all musicians. Even the existence of the men in the organization was nonregulation. A 1950s lyre in a wreath, made in Germany, also was popular (Fig. 13-25). A band with extra uniform trim and this cap device is shown in Fig. 13-26.

Fig. 13-27.

Cut-Out Collar Insignia

As with other branch insignia, the army brought in gilt and bronze ornaments in 1902 (Fig. 13-27). Engineer band members wore a gilt castle on their lyre faces (Fig. 13-28), while infantry, cavalry, and artillery band members had the number above the lyre. The number moved to the lyre face (Fig. 13-29 for dress and Fig. 13-30 in bronze) in 1905 to reduce the insignia height, because the tall piece gouged band members' necks. At this time the Puerto Rico Regiment Band began to wear *PR* on the lyre (Fig. 13-31), and a similar *P* was used by Philippine band troops in bronze only, since they had only the service uniform. The band for the army prison wore *PG* (later replaced by *DBG*), and recruiting service bands added *RS* to their lyres (Fig. 13-32). A gilt lyre with

Fig. 13-28.

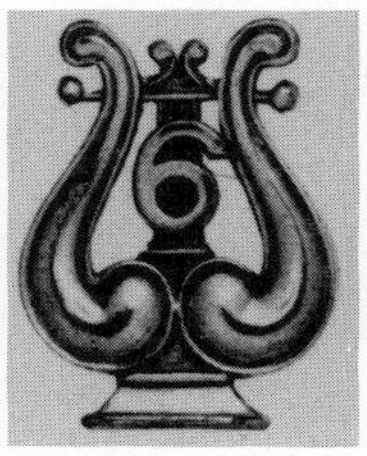

Fig. 13-29.

Fig. 13-30.

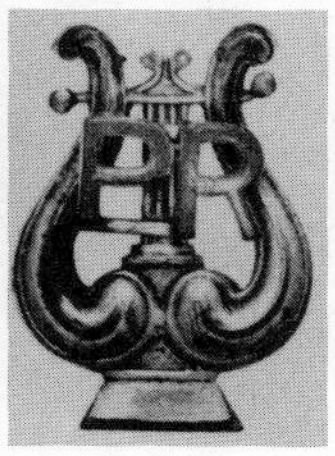

Fig. 13-31.

Fig. 13-27. *Collar insignia for regimental bands, 1903–1905. The design is similar to that shown in Fig. 13-9 except that for the collar the entire design was in gilt. (7/8 inch wide)*

Fig. 13-28. *The collar insignia for the Corps of Engineers Band, 1903–16. Although the design is similar to that shown in Fig. 13-8, the insignia is all gilt. (59/64 inch wide)*

Fig. 13-29. *An example of a regimental band members' collar insignia. The dress version, in gilt, lasted until World War I. (7/8 inch wide)*

Fig. 13-30. *An enlisted men's service coat insignia, 1905–10, for a member of the 29th Infantry Regiment Band. The finish is bronze, indicating that the insignia was intended for field use on the service coat. The fastener is a pin so it could be fixed to the collar. The same design, but with a screw-post fastener, would have gone on the service cap during the 1905–18 period. (55/64 inch wide)*

Fig. 13-31. *The gilt lyre and pin fastener show this is a collar insignia for the enlisted men's dress blue uniform, 1905–17. The PR stands for the Puerto Rico Regiment of Infantry. (7/8 inch wide)*

Fig. 13-32.

Fig. 13-33.

Fig. 13-35.

Fig. 13-36.

Fig. 13-32. *A bronze collar insignia for the 7th Recruiting Service District, 1906–10. (7/8 inch wide)*

Fig. 13-33. *Introduced in 1910 for the U.S. Military Academy Band, this style of all-gilt collar insignia is still worn on the special dress uniforms worn by the West Point band. (1 29/64 inches wide)*

Fig. 13-34.

Fig. 13-34. *This soldier wears a uniform unique to the U.S. Military Academy Band. The white trim comes from the fact that the band was previously organized as an infantry band, and infantry trim at that time was white. The US insignia and gilt lyre with MA are holdovers from the 1902-pattern dress uniform.*

Figs. 13-35 and 13-36. *U.S. Army Band enlisted men's collar insignia, 1926–68. Fig. 13-35 has a screw-post fastener on the back, which allows the US to be removed for cleaning. These were introduced in the 1920s. The lyre in Fig. 13-36 has the letters soldered further up the face and has clutch fasteners. (57/64 and 29/32 inch wide, respectively)*

Fig. 13-37.

Fig. 13-37. *A member of the U.S. Army Band in the 1920s wearing the band's unique insignia modeled after those previously used on the dress blue uniform.*

Fig. 13-38.

Fig. 13-38. *The sergeant on the right is the same member of the U.S. Army Band as shown in Fig. 13-37. This photograph was taken more than fifteen years later than that of Fig. 13-37. It shows how the unique lapel insignia were worn on the service uniform.*

MA came in during 1910 for the U.S. Military Academy Band (Fig. 13-33), which the band continues to wear on dress uniforms today, along with officer-style letters *US*, a holdover from the pre–World War I era (Fig. 13-34).[12]

In 1926 the U.S. Army Band began to wear a lyre 1 3/16 inches high with the 3/8-inch-high letters *US* superimposed on it (Figs. 13-35 and 13-36). Some came with removable letters *US*, while others have the letters brazed to the lyre. This style appeared on all uniforms until 1947. Fig. 13-37 shows a 1920s band member with the lyre collar piece and a pre-1926 lyre in a wreath on his cap. This same musician is shown in Fig. 13-38, during World War II, wearing the lyre on the lapels and the standard enlisted men's cap device. For the 1948–52 period, U.S. Army Band members wore yellow dress uniforms and blue uniforms with the lapel lyres

Fig. 13-39.

Fig. 13-40.

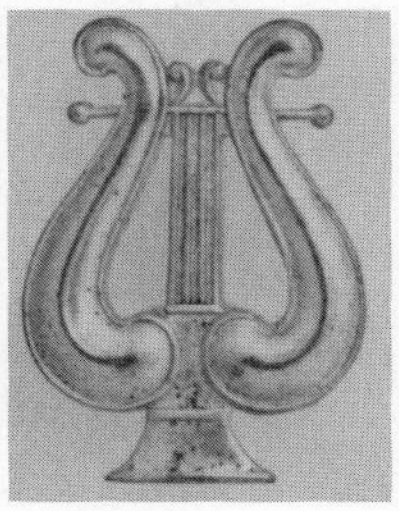

Fig. 13-42.

Fig. 13-41.

Fig. 13-39. *For four years, starting in 1948, the U.S. Army Band had yellow coats and trousers with yellow stripes (left and right). The enlisted man in the center (third from left) wears a dress lapel coat with the lyres on the lapels but a bare collar. The officer (second from left) has his standard uniform shoulder loops trimmed with special cord to note his association with the band.*

Fig. 13-40. *This insignia, first worn by the U.S. Army Band in 1968, is used as a distinctive insignia on the shoulder loops of the green uniforms, but on the special dress uniforms it is used as a collar insignia. The two branches that are formed like a lyre around the outer edge are of gold-colored metal, while the rest of the insignia is enameled. (1 inch wide)*

Fig. 13-41. *A member of the U.S. Army Band wearing the ceremonial uniform introduced in 1968. The enameled insignia shown in Fig. 13-40 is worn on the standing collar. Only miniature medals are worn with this uniform.*

Fig. 13-42. *This lyre, made for high school and college bands, was used by some army bands after World War II. (57/64 inch wide)*

(Fig. 13-39). For dress uniforms the band members used the lyre until 1968, when a new, distinctive style of insignia (Fig. 13-40) came into use (Fig. 13-41).[13]

The plain outline lyre still survives today as an additional, nonregulation insignia. Several bands wore a commercially available lyre (Fig. 13-42) in the 1960s and 1970s, and this practice will no doubt continue.

Bronze Enlisted Men's Disks

The lyre on a nominal 1-inch-diameter disk came into general use for band musicians in 1910 (Fig. 13-43). In many instances, band numbers were added to the lyre face. The numerical designation represented either the band number for artillery or the regimental number for cavalry and infantry (Fig. 13-44). Special bands wore the initials or other device of their parent organization instead of the number, as in the cases of the Philippine

Fig. 13-43.

Fig. 13-44.

Fig. 13-45.

Fig. 13-46.

Fig. 13-47.

Fig. 13-48.

Fig. 13-49.

Fig. 13-50.

Fig. 13-51.

Fig. 13-52.

Fig. 13-53.

Fig. 13-54.

Fig. 13-55.

Fig. 13-56.

Fig. 13-57.

Fig. 13-58.

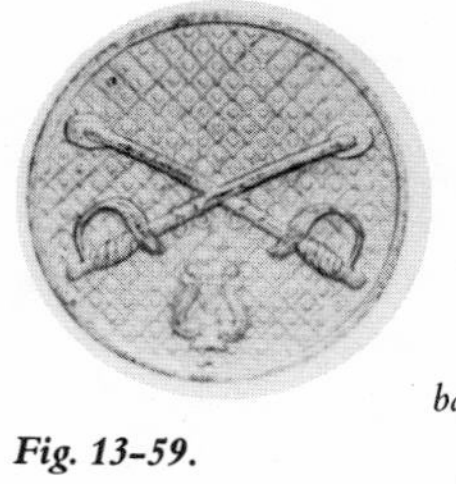

Fig. 13-59.

Fig. 13-43. *An example of enlisted band members' 1910–23 collar insignia in bronze color. (1 inch in diameter)*

Fig. 13-44. *Numbered artillery bands and bands with numbered regiments (infantry, cavalry, and later field artillery) placed their unit designation on the lyre face, as in this example. (1 inch in diameter)*

Figs. 13-45 and 13-46. *Enlisted men's collar insignia for the Philippine and Puerto Rico regiment bands, 1910–21. (Each 1 inch in diameter)*

Fig. 13-47. *Corps of Engineers Band enlisted men's bronze collar disk, 1910–16. (1 1/64 inch in diameter)*

Figs. 13-48 and 13-49. *Enlisted men's collar insignia for members of the Recruiting Service bands. The number, when used, indicated the recruiting districts. (1 1/32 inches and 1 inch in diameter, respectively)*

Fig. 13-50. *Bronze collar disk for the U.S. Military Academy Band. (1 1/32 inches in diameter)*

Fig. 13-51. *A gilt enlisted men's collar disk with the earlier, stippled background. After World War I, when gilt insignia were reintroduced, the lyre insignia like this was not authorized, although many soldiers assigned to bands wore it. (1 1/64 inches in diameter)*

Fig. 13-52. *Another unauthorized gilt band disk, this one with the background of crosshatched lines and small shields. The back has a small needle point added near the disk's edge to keep it from turning. This construction style indicates that it was probably made for a state unit or for a military school. (1 1/32 inches wide)*

Fig. 13-53. *This two-piece gilt disk, made in the 1930s, had the lyre struck separately, yet the central design came from an earlier die for which the checkered background was prescribed. Behind the lyre can be seen the lines and small shields called for by the regulations. (1 1/64 inches wide)*

Fig. 13-54. *Marked on the back, A E Co., UTICA, NY, this insignia was made for the New York State Guard during World War II. (1 1/16 inches in diameter)*

Fig. 13-55. *This brass nonregulation 1930s–World War II disk has a screw-post back. (1 inch in diameter)*

Figs. 13-56, 13-57, and 13-58 (left to right). *Domed post–World War II disks were never approved by regulation. That of Fig. 13-56 is silver-colored and was made in the United States. That of Fig. 13-57, also silver, was made in Germany, while that of Fig. 13-58 is brass-colored. (1 1/32 inches, 1 inch, and 1 1/32 inches wide, respectively)*

Fig. 13-59. *The regulation use of a lyre on enlisted men's insignia after World War I was in place of a company, troop, or battery letter.*

Regiment Band (Fig. 13-45), the Puerto Rico Regiment Band (Fig. 13-46), the Corps of Engineers band (Fig. 13-47), the Recruiting Service bands (Figs. 13-48 and 13-49), and the Military Academy Band (Fig. 13-50). All of these additions, except for numbers, were declared obsolete in March 1921, although stocks on hand could be used until exhausted.[14]

Gilt Enlisted Men's Disks

One may search post-1921 regulations in vain, trying to find authorization for lyres as primary enlisted men's insignia. Musicians, always having their special accoutrements, perhaps found it difficult to wear conventional branch insignia. A multitude of gilt disks bearing lyres exist. It is immaterial whether the troops demanded the insignia and the manufacturers dutifully complied (a doubtful situation), or the makers provided the insignia in hopes of making money through increased sales, with a wink at the regulations or a nod at the statement, "Commanding officers may provide . . . additional ornaments as they may deem proper."[15] Whatever the reason, some band members wore disks bearing a lyre design. The earliest gilt disk was struck using dies initially made for bronze insignia (Fig. 13-51), as noted by the fine dotted background. During the late 1920s and 1930s, lyres on backgrounds of crosshatched lines and small shields appeared (Fig. 13-52). During the transition to separable disks with a smooth background, the insignia shown in Fig. 13-53 came into use. This lyre was made from an earlier die; the checkered background is still visible within the lyre's arms. Some state guards or militia organizations organized during World War II had bands whose members wore the lyre on a disk. An example is shown in Fig. 13-54. Disks of World War II and later come in profusion of designs (Figs. 13-55 through 13-58), in both domed and flat versions. By the 1960s use of these nonregulation insignia had virtually ended, since band members were assigned to the Adjutant General Corps, and the number of bands in the army decreased.

Lyres as Insignia Additions

Commissioned leaders of infantry, artillery, cavalry, and Corps of Engineers bands wore small lyres with their large basic branch insignia between 1918 and 1923. Some are shown in Fig. 10-82 in chapter 10 "Numbers and letters." Enlisted band members added small lyres below their normal branch insignia in December 1927.[16] One example, for cavalry, is shown in Fig. 13-59. Infantry, coast artillery, engineers, and field artillery also were authorized these insignia, and medical disks with the lyre addition are known. These are illustrated in the chapters on the respective branches.

Chapter Fourteen

Bugles, Horns, and Trumpets

Fig. 14-1. With the initiation of screw-post enlisted men's cap insignia and the parallel upgrading of materials, field musicians finally received an insignia made expressly for them. Regimental and company designations were brazed to the field musicians' bugle insignia, like this 1896–1902 example. (2 1/8 inches wide)

Fig. 14-2. Starting in 1901, artillery field musicians wore their company or battery number in the center of their cap insignia. (2 inches wide)

THROUGH THE DIN of the eighteenth- and nineteenth-century battlefield, commanders communicated with their troops by the use of trumpets or bugles. Because of this, such devices often served as early infantry insignia. Many U.S. Infantry insignia before 1875 consisted of either open or looped bugle horns, as illustrated in chapter 5. Riflemen, as opposed to infantrymen, formed separate organizations until 1821. Riflemen's insignia often included bugle horns, as described in chapter 4. Buglers or trumpeters, the field musicians who translated an officer's commands into brief tunes all could understand, adopted cap devices of the infantry horn at the start of the last quarter of the nineteenth century.

Trumpets and bugles were used in the American Revolution, and by the War of 1812 these instruments were commonly used by rifle troops and dragoons as a means of announcing orders. A trumpet is generally a brass tube of constant thickness for two-thirds of its length, with the last third formed into a bell. In the military this instrument was used by the cavalry. A bugle, on the other hand, used by dismounted units, is formed by an ever increasing cone throughout its entire length. Bugles usually are of one of two shapes: a slightly curved horn that could have been made in the shape of an animal's horn, or a looped horn. U.S. forces have used both designs as insignia.

Field Musicians' Looped Bugle Horns

In 1875 the infantry changed insignia from a looped bugle horn to crossed muskets. Because the Quartermaster Department had many of the pre-1875 infantry horns in stock, field and band musicians initially were issued these horns. Early in 1877 the regulations called for the regimental numbers to be placed in the horns' centers, with the company letter above. Each infantry company or artillery battery included two field musicians who gave the bugle calls. The field musicians wore the looped horns, although cavalry trumpeters still wore crossed sabers at that time. Band musicians, soldiers who were members of regimental bands, received lyre insignia in 1885. When the quartermaster general introduced the screw-post cap ornament fastening device in 1896, the Philadelphia Depot made horns of thicker metal (Fig. 14-1), with both the regimental number and the company letter brazed to the insignia. In 1901, the depot began to manufacture this type of insignia, with only a

Fig. 14-1.

Fig. 14-2.

Fig. 14-3.

Fig. 14-4.

Fig. 14-5.

Fig. 14-6.

Fig. 14-7.

Fig. 14-8.

Fig. 14-9.

Fig. 14-10.

Figs. 14-3 and 14-4. *In 1905 straight trumpets like these bronze service cap ornaments replaced the previous curved bugle insignia. That of Fig. 14-3 is for cavalry and infantry regiments and field artillery regiments after 1907. That of Fig. 14-4, with just the company number, was used by the coast artillery until 1916 and by the field artillery until 1907. (Each 2 3/32 inches wide)*

Fig. 14-5. *A Puerto Rico Infantry Regiment bronze-colored cap insignia for one of the two field musicians in Company D. (2 3/23 inches wide)*

Fig. 14-6. *Before 1916 field musicians in engineers regiments had gilt trumpets with silver castles as cap insignia. (2 3/32 inches wide)*

Fig. 14-7. *A service cap insignia for an engineers regiment's field musician, but without the usual company letter. (2 1/8 inches wide)*

Fig. 14-8. *Starting in 1910, U.S. Military Academy field musicians received unique cap insignia like this one. (2 9/64 inches wide)*

Fig. 14-9. *Recruiting Service District field musicians had their own cap insignia starting in 1906. Recruiting district numbers ran from 1 through 25. (2 3/32 inches wide)*

Fig. 14-10. *Prison Guard companies, numbered from 1 through 4, had this type of cap insignia from 1906 through 1916. (2 1/8 inches wide)*

number in the loop, for artillery company and battery field musicians (Fig. 14-2). Changes of 1902 included placing a silver castle on the horn's center for Corps of Engineers field musicians, the initial use of looped horns by cavalry trumpeters, who had previously worn crossed sabers, and the exchange of location of regimental number and company letter. This last change carried through introduction of the straight trumpet, as discussed below, but more importantly, this number placement can date a cap device. The 1896–1902 bugles have the regimental number in the loop and the company letter above (except for the Puerto Rico Regiment). Those looped horns made in 1903 and 1904 have the company, troop, or battery designation within the center (Corps of Engineers excepted) and the regimental number, when appropriate, above the horn's center. Puerto Rico Regiment field musicians also began to use the letters *PR* above the bugle horn.[1]

Straight Trumpets

Straight trumpets with the regimental number centered above and the company letter on the coil (Fig. 14-3) were introduced during 1905. Those artillery musicians assigned to separate companies or batteries wore the unit number on the coil (Fig. 14-4). After 1907 the field artillery trumpeters used the standard regimental designations. In 1916 coast artillery field musicians began to wear plain trumpets without numbers. Just as with the previous looped horn, Philippines and Puerto Rican musicians used the letters *P* or *PR* to distinguish their units (Fig. 14-5). Engineer field musicians wore the castle with company letter (Figs. 14-6 and 14-7) until 1916, when these men switched to the standard number and letter scheme.[2]

The letters *MA DET* denoted the U.S. Military Academy Detachment field musicians (Fig. 14-8) from 1910 to 1918. Trumpeters for the Recruiting Service, prison guards, and disciplinary barracks guards, respectively, wore *RS* from 1906 to 1918 (Fig. 14-9), *PG* from

1906 to 1916 (Fig. 14-10), and *DBG* from 1916 to 1918 above the trumpet coil, with the unit number on the coil.[3]

A photograph taken about 1906 shows field musicians at Fort Riley, Kansas, wearing various cap and hat insignia, including both the pre- and post-1905 trumpets (Fig. 14-11). Fig. 14-12 shows field musicians in khaki uniforms in the early 20th century, with cap insignia incorrectly worn on their hats.

Fig. 14-11. *Field artillery field musicians, 1906. The men on the far left in the front row and second from the left and on the far right in the back row wear cap insignia made obsolete over a year before. The musician on the far left in the rear row wears the correct new cap insignia. The two men with crossed cannons are wearing the improper ornaments. The two musicians in olive drab uniforms, front row, center, have the correct bronze numbers on their campaign hats.*

Fig. 14-12. *Field musicians in 1904 at Fort Riley, Kansas, wearing cap insignia on campaign hats.*

Fig. 14-11.

Fig. 14-12.

Section IX

Other Branch Insignia with Roots before the Civil War

Chapter Fifteen

Adjutant General

After the army disbanded in 1783, there was no authorized adjutant general, although on 31 October 1784 an ensign was appointed adjutant. He served until 1791. Between 1792 and 1796 Congress allowed one "Adjutant and Inspector," and in 1798 it created a separate adjutant general. The Adjutant General's Department, established by the act of 3 March 1813, continued until Congress changed the title to Adjutant General's Corps in 1950.[1]

Between 1821 and 1830 unit adjutants were "designated by an arc of gold or silver fringe . . . connecting the extreme points of the chevrons" officers then wore. The adjutant general's staff members began to wear white hat plumes in 1839, whereas previously most staff department members wore a yellow plume. This yellow plume had represented not only members of the Adjutant General's Department, but also inspector generals and aides and officers attached to the general in chief. Before 1851, officers detailed to the Adjutant General's Department wore only the hat plume to single them out from other staff officers. On the 1851 cap men of the Adjutant General's Department and regimental adjutants wore a round pompon, the upper one-third white and the lower two-thirds buff. With the post–Civil War regulations, the Adjutant General's Department members began to wear distinctive branch insignia, which they have continued to wear since that time.[2]

Shoulder Knots and Epaulettes

Adjutants, inspector generals, and aides wore a gold aiguillette attached to the right shoulder knot after 1872. The sweeping 1872 changes included old English letters *AD* (which stood for Adjutant General's Department) embroidered on the new-style shoulder knots. The ink was scarcely dry on the October order when the army eliminated the letters and substituted a solid silver shield, 1 2/5 inches by 9/10 inch. In June 1873, in another quick change, the shield was changed to "[the] pattern in the Adjutant General's office." The proper dimensions were not mentioned. Because of these initial rapid changes, few, if any, adjutants probably wore the letters and the first size of shield.[3]

From 1872 through 1902 the adjutant general himself wore general officers' epaulettes, and in August 1899 he added "a solid shield of silver" between the star and the fastening button.[4] On shoulder knots the assistant adjutant general, with the rank of colonel, wore his silver shield on the gold knot lace between the pad and the fastening button. Fig. 15-1 shows a knot worn by lieutenant colonels typical of the 1873–1902 design.

Cap and Hat Ornament

In December 1872 a silver metal shield within an embroidered wreath replaced the previous general staff silver *US* in a gilt wreath as the forage cap ornament.[5] This remained the cap and hat insignia until all officers began to wear the national eagle in 1895.

Officers' Collar Devices

On the 1892 sack coat, the embroidered silver shield became the collar insignia for members of the Adjutant General's Department, although the shield soon changed to one of gold-colored metal in 1895 (Fig. 15-2). Some gold ornaments worn between 1895 and 1923 were of lesser height, although some (Fig. 15-3) are gilt shirt collar insignia. The army introduced bronze adju-

Fig. 15-1.

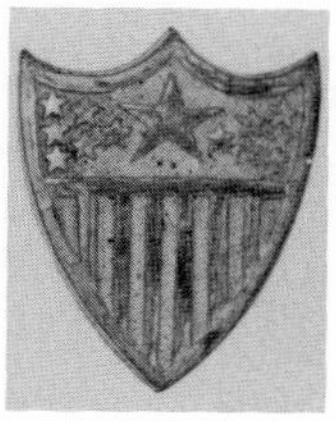

Fig. 15-2.

Fig. 15-3.

Fig. 15-5.

Fig. 15-4.

Fig. 15-6.

Fig. 15-7.

Fig. 15-8.

Fig. 15-9.

Fig. 15-10.

Fig. 15-11.

Fig. 15-12.

Fig. 15-13.

Fig. 15-1. *A typical shoulder knot for a lieutenant colonel of the Adjutant General's Department, 1873–1903. The pad is dark blue, and the metal shield silver. The assistant adjutant general (a colonel) wore his metal shield on the gold lace knot between the button and the pad. (Approximately 4 inches wide)*

Fig. 15-2. *Gold-colored shields of this type were worn by members of the Adjutant General's Department between 1895 and 1923. This particular insignia has sew-on loops on the reverse. Similar designs, but in bronze, went on the service uniforms. (25/32 inch wide)*

Fig. 15-3. *A small gold-colored adjutant general insignia before 1923. (43/64 inch wide)*

Fig. 15-4. *Produced in France for World War I American Expeditionary Forces members, this bronze insignia was for members of the Adjutant General's Department. (15/16 inch wide)*

Fig. 15-5. *This small, bronze-colored shirt collar insignia was sold in San Antonio, Texas, for Adjutant General's Department members who trained in the state during and immediately after World War I. (7/16 inch wide)*

Fig. 15-6. *Enameled adjutant general insignia appeared in 1923. This early version has gilt stars on a blue field, plus red and white stripes. (49/64 inch wide)*

Fig. 15-7. *A properly sized 1924 shirt collar insignia. (5/8 inch wide)*

Fig. 15-8. *Small shirt collar insignia of this size and style were worn by some officers in the 1920s and 1930s. (7/16 inch wide)*

Fig. 15-9. *A typical World War II and later adjutant general insignia. The stars are white enamel. (53/64 inch wide)*

Fig. 15-10. *This insignia was made in India during World War II for U.S. officers. (51/64 inch wide)*

Fig. 15-11. *In 1966 the army changed the insignia for Adjutant General's Corps officers so that the stars and some stripes were of a brushed aluminum (silver) color. Blue and red remained as before. (53/64 inch wide)*

Fig. 15-12. *The sides do not turn in near the top, and the stripes are not symmetrical on this unusual adjutant general insignia embroidered on khaki for a World War II shirt. From the collection in the Smithsonian Institution. (Design 7/8 inch wide)*

Fig. 15-13. *During the Vietnam War the army reintroduced dark colors like this subdued metal insignia for fatigue shirts. (13/16 inch wide)*

Fig. 15-14.

Fig. 15-15.

Fig. 15-14. Adjutant general of the U.S. Army in 1966, Major General Kenneth G. Wickham. He wears the older insignia with the white enameled stripes and stars that became obsolete the next year.

Fig. 15-15. Major General Allan K. Carrell, adjutant general for Kentucky. State adjutant generals wore insignia of the Adjutant General's Department to show their assignment.

Fig. 15-16.

Fig. 15-17.

Figs. 15-16 and 15-17. During 1919 and 1920 some clerks assigned to Adjutant General's Department duties were issued bronze disks of this design. Until mid–World War II no other enlisted personnel wore adjutant general insignia. (Each 1 inch in diameter)

tant general insignia in 1902 for field wear. These were worn until 1923.[6] A World War I French-made piece is shown in Fig. 15-4 and a bronze shirt-sized insignia is illustrated in Fig. 15-5.

The army expanded the use of enameled insignia in 1923. One result was new adjutant general collar insignia (Fig. 15-6) 1 inch high. The correct 1924 shirt-sized insignia is illustrated in Fig. 15-7. A smaller than authorized shirt insignia is shown in Fig. 15-8. The 1-inch-high collar insignia remained the regulation size for the lapel coat in 1926. An insignia of World War II and later is shown in Fig. 15-9, and a piece made in India is 1944 or 1945 is shown in Fig. 15-10. In 1966 the army introduced a silver-colored shield with blue and red enamel (Fig. 15-11), although service members could wear the older design with white stars and stripes until the end of 1967.[7]

Officers began to wear embroidered cloth insignia on uniforms during World War II. One such device, for a khaki uniform, is in Fig. 15-12. On fatigue clothing soldiers began to wear subdued insignia (Fig. 15-13) early in the Vietnam War, replacing colored insignia, either metal or cloth, on the work uniforms.

Enlisted Soldiers' Disks

Only officers comprised the Adjutant General's Department until World War I. Those enlisted clerks the army required wore *GHQ* on branch disks until 1919, when the quartermaster general introduced enlisted men's adjutant general disks. Fig. 15-16 shows a World War I bronze disk made by Bailey, Banks and Biddle Company. Another variation is in Fig. 15-17. The National Defense Act of 1920 provided only for officers in the Adjutant General's Department, so the army eliminated enlisted men's adjutant general insignia until World War II.[8]

In World War II, the army reintroduced adjutant general disks. The Adjutant General's Department did not assign enlisted men to its branch until late 1943, when about eight thousand soldiers finally joined a nearly equal number of officers.[9] Initially enlisted adjutant general troops were members of all bands except the division bands. In late 1944 and early 1945 other personnel began to wear adjutant general insignia, including replacement companies and postal troops.[10] Common enlisted troops' disks include stamped versions (Fig. 15-18), domed disks (Figs. 15-19 and 15-20), and flat two-piece disks (Fig. 15-21).

Other Officer Insignia

As noted in Chapter 2, "The Changing U.S. Uniform," officers assigned to the Adjutant General's Department between 1902 and 1912 wore aiguillettes on their right shoulder. The major shown in Fig. 15-22 (his rank is shown by sleeve knots) wears the adjutant general's insignia on his sleeves, inside the knots.

Fig. 15-18. *It was not until December 1943 that World War II enlisted personnel began to wear Adjutant General's Department insignia. The first enlisted men assigned to the department were band members. Later, postal clerks and others began to wear insignia like this embossed disk, issued starting in 1943. (1 inch in diameter)*

Figs. 15-19 and 15-20. *After World War II many soldiers began to wear Adjutant General's Corps insignia, especially privately purchased pieces like these two with convex backgrounds. That of Fig. 15-19, with a large shield, is silver; the other is brass. A great number of design variations exist for enlisted men's insignia. (Each 1 inch in diameter)*

Fig. 15-21. *A brass separable disk with a flat background, made in the 1960s. This piece is typical of enlisted men's insignia made into the 1990s. (1 inch in diameter)*

Fig. 15-22. *This early-twentieth-century officer was a member of the Adjutant General's Department. On the 1902-pattern dress uniform he wears the adjutant general insignia on his lower sleeve. Members of the Adjutant General's Department also wore aiguillettes, as shown.*

Chapter Sixteen

Ordnance Corps

The grenade, or "shell and flame," currently worn by the Ordnance Corps is one of the world's oldest known military ornaments. The grenade device has been traced back as far as 1704 as a sign used to designate grenadiers, selected soldiers who threw baseball-sized, round, hollow iron bombs after lighting a fuse which then burned through a small hole to the powder charge inside. By the time of the American Revolution, British, French, and German troops wore the grenade insignia.

In December 1832 infantry and artillery soldiers adopted a new leather dress cap, which several branches ultimately used until 1851. A pompon was inserted at the front of the crown above the cap insignia, and its metal base, or "tulip," as it was called, was covered by the outline of a grenade. These grenade insignia, shown in the top fronts of the caps in Figs. 72-7 and 72-8 of chapter 72 and in the sketches in Fig. 16-1, are not the insignia of the Ordnance Department, since

Fig. 16-1. Soldiers of the 1830s and 1840s wore tall caps adorned with pompons. The metal pompon holders were in the form of a flaming shell or grenade. This plate, taken from Scott's Tactics *of 1840, shows the flaming grenade at the top of the caps above the eagle. Many branches, including infantry and artillery, used this cap ornament. It was not until after the use of the shell and flame in this manner, which continued until 1851, that the historic insignia became used primarily by the Ordnance Department.*

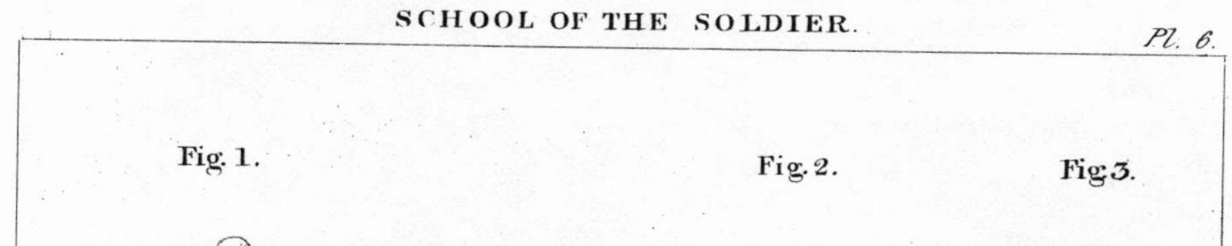

Fig. 16-1.

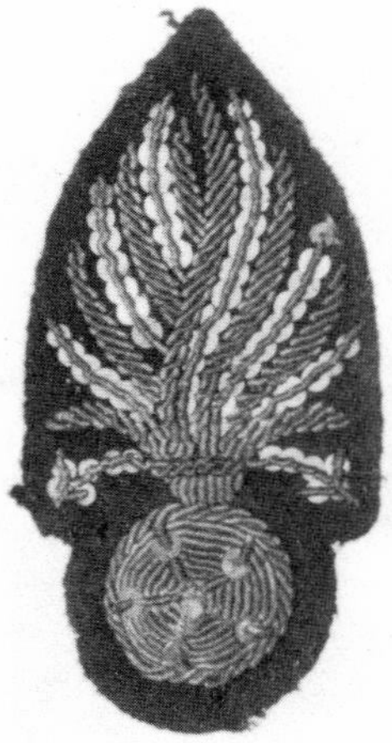

Fig. 16-2.

Fig. 16-2. A typical gold-embroidered nineteenth-century shell and flame. Such devices went on the tails of officers' 1832 coats, but they were widely used by militia units and quasi-military organizations later. Virtually all devices found today were made for other than Regular Army use after the Civil War.

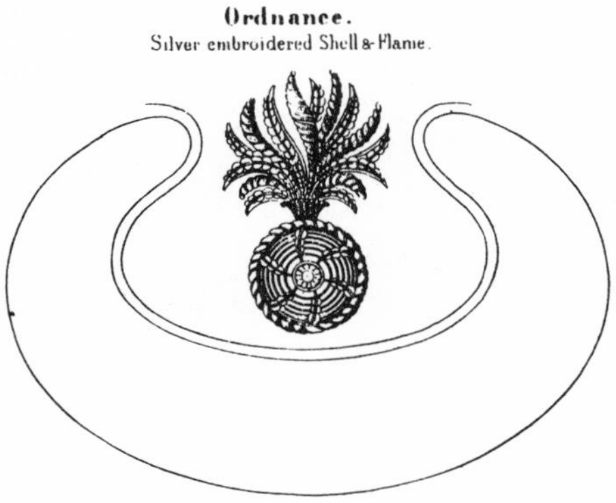

Fig. 16-3.

Fig. 16-3. This drawing, taken from the 1851 regulations, shows the use of a silver-embroidered shell and flame as an ordnance officers' insignia in the center of the epaulette. The metal "quarter moon" is the metallic part of the epaulette as seen from above.

Fig. 16-5.

Fig. 16-5. A center device for an Ordnance Department knot, 1872–1903. The flames used for this lieutenant colonels' knot are very different from those shown in Fig. 16-4.

Fig. 16-4.

Fig. 16-4. Between 1872 and 1903 ordnance officers wore shoulder knots bearing the shell and flame. This captains' insignia is from the Smithsonian Institution collection.

all of the men who wore these caps used this ornament.[1]

All ordnance responsibilities in the new American army fell within the province of the artillery until Congress established the Ordnance Department on 14 May 1812. No distinctive insignia is known from this period, although the artillery-style uniform had distinctive buttons "of appropriate type." After the major 1821 army reorganization, the artillery and ordnance again combined, thus abolishing the separate ordnance branch, although 1821 and 1825 regulations stated that "enlisted men of ordnance will wear artillery uniforms." This indicated that while the branches were combined, the functions (and the men performing the functions) remained separate.[2]

Established on 5 April 1832, the Ordnance Department changed title in 1950 to the Ordnance Corps, which then continued until 1 August 1962, when the chief of ordnance and the corps were replaced by the Army Materiel Command. Personnel in ordnance jobs still use the Ordnance Corps insignia, although there is truly no longer a corps.[3]

The War Department called for officers' insignia in June 1832 and appointed the first thirty ordnance sergeants in April 1833 from sergeants of the line with at least eight years' army service. With the reestablishment of the corps in 1832, ordnance officers and noncommissioned officers wore the artillery uniform but with no red trim.[4]

Officers' Early Insignia

Regulations of 1813 specified that the commissary general of ordnance was to embroider false buttonholes on the collar of an otherwise standard general staff uniform. Other than this exception, between 1813 and 1821 ordnance officers simply wore general staff clothing. Uniform regulations in General Order 50, June 1832, prescribed for ordnance and artillery officers "a gold embroidered shell and flame" (Fig. 16-2) to be placed on the skirts of the coat; otherwise ordnance officers used the artillery uniform with the omission of the red trim.[5]

Epaulettes and Knots

In 1851 a silver-embroidered shell and flame (Fig. 16-3) was placed in the crescent of epaulettes. It was used until 1872. With this 1851 change the flaming bomb became the exclusive property of the Ordnance Department. Regulations of 1872 called for the letters *OD* on the shoulder knots, but in December 1872 this was changed back to a silver-embroidered shell and flame, $1\frac{2}{5}$ inches by $\frac{9}{10}$ inch (Fig. 16-4). The center of another knot with a variation in the ordnance insignia is shown in Fig. 16-5. For colonels the insignia was on the fastening strap of the knots, while lower officers' insignia were in the center of the knot pad. The general who served as the chief of ordnance added a silver-embroidered flaming bomb to his epaulette straps in August 1899, while previously the straps had been bare. These knots and epaulettes lasted until the army phased out the nineteenth-century-style uniforms in 1903.[6]

Officers' Cap and Hat Insignia

Before 1851, ordnance officers wore the chapeau for dress occasions and forage caps for service use, evidently without special ordnance insignia. On the 1851 cap, ordnance officers wore a gold-embroidered shell and flame on the lower cap band (Fig. 16-6). The cap had a round pompon, the lower two-thirds buff and the top one-third crimson, as shown in Fig. 16-7 by the officer on the left. When the army adopted the Hardee hat in 1858, ordnance officers added to the hat from the gold-embroidered insignia on an oval background of black vel-

Fig. 16-6.

Fig. 16-6. Drawing from the 1851 regulations showing the insignia to be placed on the front of ordnance officers' caps.

Fig. 16-7.

Fig. 16-7. Major Alfred Mordecai, left, of the Ordnance Department, and Major Richard Delafield, right, of the Corps of Engineers, in 1851 uniforms. The flaming grenade on Major Mordecai's cap front is just visible.

Fig. 16-8.

Fig. 16-9.

Fig. 16-10.

Fig. 16-11.

Fig. 16-13.

Fig. 16-12.

Fig. 16-8. *An ordnance officers' forage cap device, 1872–95, from the Smithsonian Institution collection. (Embroidery approximately 2 inches high and $1\frac{1}{2}$ inches wide)*

Fig. 16-9. *Enlisted men's 1851–72 Ordnance Department cap and hat insignia, made of brass. ($1\frac{11}{16}$ inches wide)*

Fig. 16-10. *Stamped brass enlisted men's cap insignia, 1873–96. ($1\frac{3}{8}$ inches wide)*

Fig. 16-11. *An 1897–1905 ordnance screw-back gilt cap insignia. Slightly varying sizes were called for in detailed quartermaster specifications during this period. ($\frac{31}{32}$ inch wide and $1\frac{29}{64}$ inches high)*

Fig. 16-12. *Between 1903 and 1905 men in the grade of ordnance sergeant wore a silver ordnance insignia in a large gilt wreath. Sergeants of ordnance and lower grades continued to wear the insignia shown in Fig. 16-11. ($2\frac{5}{8}$ inches wide)*

Fig. 16-13. *On the dress blue 1905 cap ordnance noncommissioned officers wore this style of insignia, made with a gilt wreath enclosing a silver shell and flame. ($1\frac{31}{32}$ inches wide)*

vet. This insignia lasted until 1872, when the officers' dress cap insignia appeared, evidently without any special background and about $1\frac{5}{8}$ inches high (Fig. 16-8).[7]

Because many volunteer military organizations and civil and fraternal groups adopted the flaming bomb for its historic and universal design, many old embroidered devices may today be mistaken for officers' cap or coattail insignia. This common and frequent late-nineteenth-century use should cause collectors to assume that unattributed old embroidered flaming bomb insignia were not Regular Army pieces.

Enlisted Men's Cap and Hat Insignia

When the major 1851 uniform revision abolished the tall leather and felt dress caps, the shell and flame device became the sole property of the Ordnance Department, except for the 1864–72 light artillery dress cap. As noted previously, ordnance men shared the artillery insignia. On the 1832 cap, ordnance enlisted men wore the eagle and crossed cannons of the artillery.[8]

On the lower band of the 1851 dress cap, enlisted soldiers of the Ordnance Department wore a brass outline grenade with a broad flame (Fig. 16-9). The cap itself had a crimson welt on the upper welt of the lower band, where the combat branches initially wore solid-colored bands. The William H. Horstmann-illustrated regulations of 1851 and surviving insignia indicate that these shells and flames were slightly over $2\frac{1}{4}$ inches high.[9] The insignia went essentially unchanged through the Civil War period, with soldiers wearing the brass insignia on the front or top of the forage cap.

In December 1872 the brass shell and flame were to be replaced by a brass wreath enclosing the silver letters *OD*, but in June 1873 the army corrected this apparent error by calling out a trim insignia $1\frac{5}{8}$ inches high with a flame $1\frac{1}{8}$ inches wide (Fig. 16-10).[10] Soldiers wore this cap insignia until 1897, when the screw-back ornaments came into use with a 1-inch-wide flame.

The forage cap insignia was reduced slightly in 1897 to a 3/4-inch-diameter shell with a flame 7/8 inch tall and 1 inch wide for all noncommissioned officers and privates, and for the first time the Quartermaster Department had the ornaments made of solid metal (Fig. 16-11) instead of a hollow stamping. Ordnance sergeants began to wear a 1-inch-high silver flaming grenade in a gilt wreath 2 5/8 inches wide (Fig. 16-12) starting in 1903, while other noncommissioned officers, including sergeants of ordnance and corporals of ordnance, continued to wear the plain gilt flaming shell, which was 1 inch wide and 1 5/8 inches high. In 1905 the noncommissioned officers' insignia changed to a 1-inch-high silver device in a gilt wreath 1 7/8 inches wide (Fig. 16-13) for the blue dress uniform. Similar devices (Figs. 16-14 and 16-15) came in bronze for wear with the service cap. Lower-ranking enlisted men continued to wear the shell and flame without a wreath, and the insignia was reduced to 1-inch high in 1905. Fig. 16-16 snows an example for the service cap.[11]

Between 1905 and 1907 the War Department authorized enlisted ordnance personnel to wear a 1-inch-high bronze pin-back insignia on the front of the campaign hat.[12]

Helmet Insignia

In 1881 helmets became the new dress headgear for all soldiers and for most officers. Ordnance soldiers' helmets' included a small German silver ordnance insignia (Fig. 16-17) superimposed on the center of the large eagle device.[13]

Officers' Collar Insignia

On the 1892 coat collar ordnance officers wore the silver-embroidered flaming grenade, 1 inch high; some manufacturers made the device with an etruscan finish. In 1902 the collar insignia worn with the khaki and olive drab uniforms were dull bronze, 1 inch high. This size and style generally continued for over twenty years.[14] A version made in England during World War I is illustrated in Fig. 16-18. Officers' shirt-sized insignia are of the same design, but often only 1/2 inch high (Figs. 16-19 and 16-20).

Army regulations of 1926 specified that all officers' insignia would be 1 inch high.[15] Most insignia had stylized flames, although others with spreading flames were still in use. Also worn in the 1920s was the shirt insignia shown in Fig. 16-21.

Various die patterns made between the 1920s and the present include Fig. 16-22 with the older spreading flames, Fig. 16-23 with seven stylized flames, and Fig. 16-24 with the 1936 official design of four flames, each with engraved details.[16] Use of fatigue uniforms

Fig. 16-14.

Fig. 16-15.

Figs. 16-14 and 16-15. *Two versions of the service cap insignia worn from 1905 through 1917 by ordnance noncommissioned officers. Both are in the darkened bronze color, the first in a deep brown and the second, without the crossbar in the wreath, in a light brown color. (1 31/32 and 1 25/32 inches wide, respectively)*

Fig. 16-16. *Enlisted men's ordnance cap insignia, used from 1905 through mid–World War I. (21/32 inch wide)*

Fig. 16-17. *Ordnance Department soldiers wore small silver shells and flames on their helmet eagles between 1881 and 1903. (49/64 inch wide)*

Fig. 16-18. *A bronze Ordnance Department insignia for the service uniform, about World War I. This light brown piece is marked on the reverse, "Made in England." (5/8 inch wide)*

Fig. 16-19.

Fig. 16-20.

Figs. 16-19 and 16-20. *Diminutive ordnance insignia for officers' World War I shirt collars. (29/64 and 1/2 inch wide, respectively)*

Fig. 16-21. *A late 1920s or early 1930s shirt collar insignia for ordnance officers. (11/16 inch wide)*

Fig. 16-22. *Wide flaring flames realistically representing the fire of an escaping gas under pressure were commonly used by ordnance officers in the 1930s and 1940s. (11/16 inch wide)*

Fig. 16-23. *A Ordnance Department officers' insignia with seven stylized flames. (15/32 inch wide)*

Fig. 16-24. *This officers' insignia corresponds with the official 1936 version in that it has four stylized flames and is 1 inch high and slightly under 1/2 inch wide. (29/64 inch wide)*

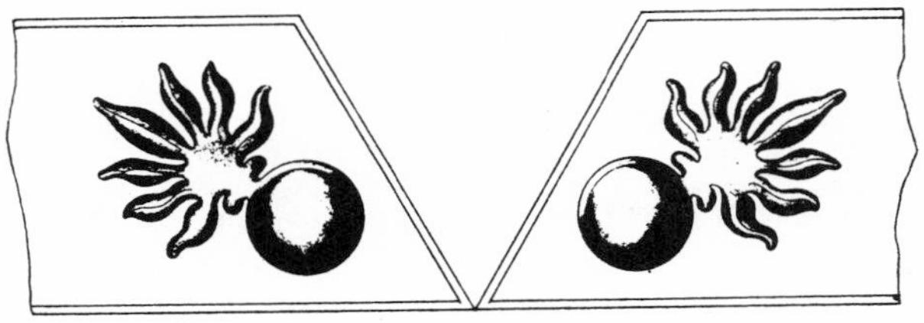

Fig. 16-25.

Fig. 16-26.

Fig. 16-27.

Fig. 16-28.

Fig. 16-29.

Fig. 16-30.

Fig. 16-31.

Fig. 16-32.

Fig. 16-33.

Fig. 16-34.

Fig. 16-35.

Fig. 16-36.

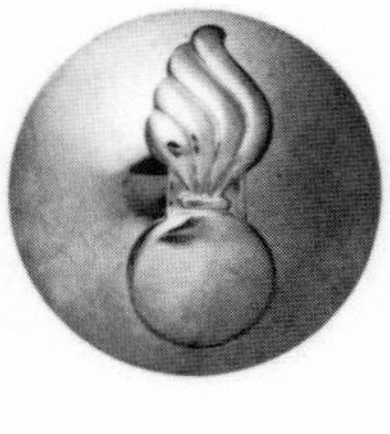

Fig. 16-37.

Fig. 16-25. *Illustration from the 1851 regulations showing how enlisted men of the Ordnance Department were to wear the 2 1/4-inch-high brass grenade on their dress coat collars. The actual insignia was the same as that used on the caps, as shown in Fig. 16-9.*

Fig. 16-26. *A small gilt, pin-back collar insignia made for wear from 1900 until 1903 on the white duck summer coats of Ordnance Department soldiers. The design was the same as that used on the 1881–1903 helmet overlays. (49/64 inch wide)*

Fig. 16-27. *Enlisted soldiers were issued this type of gilt insignia for the collar of dress uniforms from 1903 until 1917. Similar pieces, but in dark colors, went on the service uniforms from 1903 until 1910. (21/32 inch wide)*

Figs. 16-28 and 16-29. *Two variations of 1910–23 bronze collar disks used by enlisted men of the Ordnance Department. Many designs with different styles of flames exist. (Each 1 inch in diameter)*

Fig. 16-30. *A gilt enlisted men's collar insignia made in 1923 or later. The die used was originally intended for the pebbled background that became obsolete in about 1921. (1 inch in diameter)*

Fig. 16-31. *Made in France, this enlisted men's Ordnance Department insignia has a pin back and was painted a gold color over the original "bronze" paint. (1 1/64 inches in diameter)*

Fig. 16-32. *An issue 1930s-style enlisted men's collar insignia with gilt finish. (1 inch in diameter)*

Fig. 16-33. *A screw-backed disk with a separable design for the lapel coat. (1 1/32 inches in diameter)*

Fig. 16-34. *Stamped from a single sheet of brass during World War II, this insignia conforms to the official government design. (1 inch in diameter)*

Fig. 16-35. *Yellow embroidered enlisted men's insignia made on khaki cloth in the China-Burma-India Theater during World War II. (Design 1 1/16 inches in diameter)*

Fig. 16-36. *Screw-backed enlisted soldiers' insignia for the 103d Ordnance Maintenance Company. (63/64 inch in diameter)*

Fig. 16-37. *This Ordnance Department insignia for enlisted personnel was made with a silver-colored finish and with a domed-shaped background, as was popular for several years after World War II. (1 inch in diameter)*

caused yellow-embroidered insignia to appear after World War II, and after 1966 cloth and metal subdued insignia came into use, replacing those of yellow color.

Outline Enlisted Men's Collar Insignia

Yellow metal shell and flame insignia, $2\frac{1}{4}$ inches high—the same size as used on the cap—came with the high standing collar of the 1851 uniform coat (Fig. 16-25). On the 1872 dress uniform, ordnance men wore smaller yellow metal corps devices on the crimson-trimmed standing collars. It is believed that these 1872 insignia were the same as those specified in 1876 to be 1 inch high with flames $\frac{3}{4}$ inch wide. With the 1885 dress uniform revision, collar ornaments temporarily disappeared.[17]

A small gilt insignia made in the same die used for the helmet overlay was made for wear on the white duck clothing in January 1900, and the army bought six hundred of these insignia (Fig. 16-26). Soldiers' 1902 collar insignia were 1 inch high, the same as those of officers, and consequently this device was not reduced in 1904 when the army "modernized" many branch insignia. Fig. 16-27 shows the insignia for the dress uniform, which was identical in design to the one for the service coat.[18]

Enlisted Men's Collar Disks

Two 1910 disks are shown in Figs. 16-28 and 16-29. Soon after World War I soldiers were issued these insignia in gilt (Fig. 16-30). Variations include one made in France (Fig. 16-31) as well as the design of the late 1920s to 1937 with the background of lines and shields (Fig. 16-32). A World War II–era separable disk is shown in Fig. 16-33, while a 1942-design stamped disk is shown in Fig. 16-34. An embroidered enlisted men's collar insignia, made in India during World War II and intended for the khaki shirt, is illustrated in Fig. 16-35, while a metal disk with unit number of early World War II is shown in Fig. 16-36. Also made during and after World War II were dome-shaped disks, as shown in Fig. 16-37, including those with unit numbers or other additions (Fig. 16-38). The last disk is one made in Vietnam in about 1968 for departing troops to wear on their khaki shirts (Fig. 16-39).

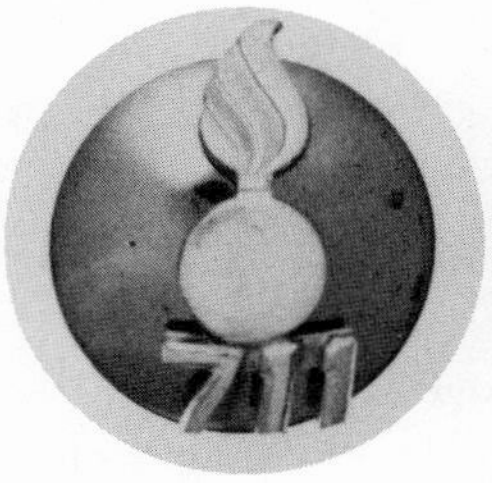

Fig. 16-38. *Some members of the 11th Airborne Division's Ordnance Company wore this insignia with dome background after World War II. The screw post that holds the shell and flame snug against the domed background has been applied to the center of the shell to allow room for the unit number, which in turn caused the overall design to extend above the disk. ($1\frac{1}{64}$ inches in diameter)*

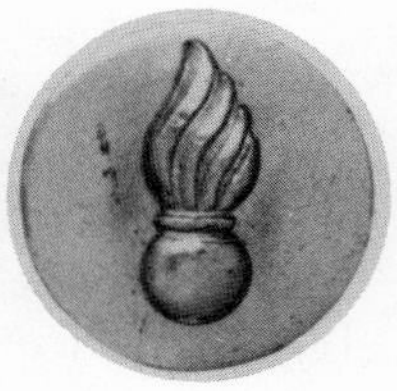

Fig. 16-39. *This brass insignia, made in Vietnam, was purchased by a soldier to wear home on the khaki shirt collar. Despite the crude design and construction, the design is separable from the background like that of most insignia of the time. ($\frac{61}{64}$ inch in diameter)*

JUDGE ADVOCATE GENERAL

Fig. 17-1. *An 1890–1903 dress uniform shoulder knot for a Judge Advocate General's Department lieutenant colonel. The crossed sword and pen over a wreath were the first truly uniquely designed judge advocate general's insignia, as shoulder knots from 1872 until 1890 simply had the old English letters JA.*

Fig. 17-2. *Starting in 1893, judge advocate officers wore gold-embroidered insignia on the 1892-pattern dark sack coat. This insignia has the sword and pen reversed from the standard design. (Design 1¾ inches wide)*

Fig. 17-3. *A design made entirely in the imitation embroidery style with four small loops on the reverse for sewing to the coat collar. (1 9/16 inches wide)*

THE OFFICE OF Judge Advocate of the Army is deemed to have been created on 29 July 1775. Congress, in 1812, authorized two judge advocates, but that office was discontinued in 1821. Congress again allowed a Judge Advocate of the Army in 1849, although the lone judge advocate was an Ordnance Department captain. The judge advocate general (JAG) and a group of judge advocates came into being during the Civil War, and the organization became the Judge Advocate General's Department in 1884. The various judge advocate officers did not have special uniforms or insignia until 1872.[1]

In 1820 the general staff uniform, without an eagle on the chapeau cockade, distinguished the JAG and other selected officers. This uniform lasted only one year, when regulations directed judge advocates to wear civilian clothes only. The 1851 judge advocates wore the standard staff uniform with a white pompon on the cap as a distinguishing mark.[2]

SHOULDER KNOTS AND EPAULETTES

Dress shoulder knots with the old English letters *JA* designated judge advocate officers on the 1872 staff officers' uniforms. In 1890 the insignia changed to "a sword and pen crossed and wreathed, according to pattern, embroidered in silver on the cloth of the pad (except for a Colonel . . . who will wear the device made of solid silver on the knot midway between the upper fastening and the pad)." From November 1899 through 1903 the JAG wore a solid silver branch device on

Fig. 17-1.

Fig. 17-2.

Fig. 17-3.

Fig. 17-4.

Fig. 17-5.

Fig. 17-6.

Fig. 17-7.

Fig. 17-8.

Fig. 17-9.

Fig. 17-10.

Fig. 17-11.

Fig. 17-4. *A gilt insignia similar to that of Fig. 17-3 but with the more common pin back and smooth sword blade and pen quill. (1 11/16 inches wide)*

Fig. 17-5. *The area enclosed by the horizontal angles of the pen and sword and the wreath are of a smooth, solid brass. (1 19/32 inches wide)*

Fig. 17-6. *The judge advocate general's representative at the U.S. Military Academy about 1924. The officer has gold-colored branch insignia, but his US insignia are still the darker bronze color, just declared obsolete.*

Figs. 17-7 and 17-8. *Two World War I Judge Advocate General's Department insignia for the service coat. That of Fig. 17-8 has the sword and pen applied over the wreath and was made by the Bailey, Banks and Biddle Company. (Each 1 5/8 inches wide)*

Fig. 17-9. *A French firm produced this variation in a shiny bronze color during World War I. (1 13/64 inches wide)*

Figs. 17-10 and 17-11. *Two small gilt shirt collar insignia. (Fig. 17-11 53/64 inch wide)*

Figs. 17-12 and 17-13. *Bronze shirt collar ornaments, that of Fig. 17-12 was made in London during World War I. (7/8 and 51/64 inch wide, respectively)*

Fig. 17-14. *A 1920s gilt shirt collar insignia with a screw-post back made by the Blackington Company. (29/32 inch wide)*

the epaulette straps, just as colonels had on the knot straps. An example of an 1890s lieutenant colonels' knot is shown in Fig. 17-1.[3]

Officers' Large Insignia

Gold-embroidered insignia (Fig. 17-2; note that the design is reversed) went on the 1893 sack coat collar. The first metal patterns were stamped to look like embroidery variations (Fig. 17-3) and came into use almost concurrently with the embroidered insignia, and by 1902 the War Department authorized these metal ornaments (Figs. 17-4, 17-5, and 17-6). The prescribed 1-inch-high devices also came in bronze, and many variations of both colors exist, with examples shown in Figs. 17-7, 17-8, and 17-9, the last having been made in France.[4]

Shirt Insignia

Small devices for the pre-1924 shirt collar came in gilt (Figs. 17-10 and 17-11) and in bronze (Figs. 17-12 and 17-13). A gilt variation showing a screw-post back, with the nut visible inside the wreath, is shown in Fig. 17-14. These insignia are all smaller than the later regulation shirt collar devices, 11/16 inch high, introduced in 1926 for both the shirt and lapel coat.[5]

Insignia, 1924

For one year judge advocates had a different insignia: golden scales balanced on the point of a 1-inch-high silver sword with a gold grip. A silver ribbon completed the design, which was approved in February 1924 and introduced in late 1924. Two examples are shown in Figs. 17-15 and 17-16. The design also was made 3/4 inch high for the shirt (Fig. 17-17). The immediate reaction of JAG

Fig. 17-12.

Fig. 17-13.

Fig. 17-14.

Fig. 17-15.

Fig. 17-16.

Fig. 17-17.

Fig. 17-18.

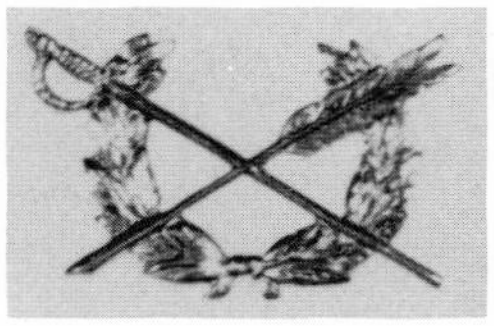

Fig. 17-19.

Fig. 17-20.

Figs. 17-15 and 17-16. *In 1924 judge advocates received new insignia. These insignia are for the standing coat collar. The scales (two pans and the balance beam) are gilt, as is the sword grip. The sword blade and decorative ribbons are silver. The piece in Fig. 17-15 has only the sword blade in very shiny silver, while that in Fig. 17-16, made by N. S. Meyer, has all the silver parts shiny. (Each 1 3/32 inches wide)*

Fig. 17-17. *A 1924 judge advocate general insignia for the shirt collar. (27/32 inch wide)*

Fig. 17-18. *A lapel coat and shirt insignia introduced for shirts in 1926. (1 11/64 inches wide)*

Fig. 17-19. *In the 1930s this shirt collar insignia was slightly smaller than required by regulations, yet it was larger than pre-1926 shirt collar ornaments. (1 1/16 inches wide)*

Fig. 17-20. *A 1940s insignia with a heavy pen and sword struck separately and applied over a wreath. (1 3/8 inches wide)*

Figs. 17-21 and 17-22. *Two versions of 1918–20 bronze disks for enlisted men assigned to the Judge Advocate General's Department. (Each 1 inch in diameter)*

Figs. 17-23 and 17-24. *Post-1968 issue insignia for enlisted legal clerks. The first design is separable from the background, while the latter has the design embossed directly on the disk. (Each 1 inch in diameter)*

Fig. 17-25. *In the 1950s and 1960s some legal clerks unofficially wore insignia like this one, which has a domed (convex) background. (1 1/64 inches in diameter)*

officers to the new insignia ranged from open hostility to ridicule, and the officers were almost unanimous in their opinion that the new device was no improvement. Because of the reaction, the adjutant general rescinded the insignia in December 1924, although regulations were not changed until 1926, when the older design of a wreathed pen and sword was revised and made 11/16 inch high.[6]

Insignia, 1926 to the Present

The 11/16-inch-high wreathed quill pen and sword insignia comes in several variations (Figs. 17-18 and 17-19 are examples). The insignia shown in Fig. 17-20 was made with the pen and sword as a separate piece, overlaying the wreath, and was made during World War II. The insignia design has remained unchanged to the present. Congress established the branch's name as the Judge Advocate General's Corps in 1948.[7]

Enlisted Personnel Disks

Bronze enlisted men's insignia of the type shown in Figs. 17-21 and 17-22 were not authorized initially during World War I, but on 22 March 1918 the War Department allowed special enlisted men in the Judge Advocate General's Department "for the period of the existing emergency," and by the end of 1919, sixty-one men were assigned to the office of the JAG. The army authorized the bronze disks from May 1918 through March 1920, but by June 1920, Congress restricted members of the department to officers.[8]

In February 1968 enlisted personnel assigned to staff judge advocate offices were allowed to wear the all gold-colored design on a disk, as shown in Figs. 17-23 and 17-24.[9] Before 1968 some legal clerks wore domed disks such as that shown in Fig. 17-25, although these collar insignia were not regulation.

Fig. 17-21.

Fig. 17-22.

Fig. 17-23.

Fig. 17-24.

Fig. 17-25.

Chapter Eighteen

Quartermasters

As Bill Mauldin pointed out, the quartermaster was a hewer of wood and hauler of water, a counter of buttons and sorter of socks with a rather safe existence. Despite having the "inside track" on uniforms, generally members of the Quartermaster Department (after 1912 the Quartermaster Corps) did not distinguish themselves with truly unique uniforms.

At the end of the Revolutionary War, Congress reduced the army severely and eliminated all quartermasters. A congressional increase from thirteen hundred to twenty-two hundred men on 3 March 1791 included one of four general staff officers assigned as the army's quartermaster. Lawmakers again increased quartermaster strength a year later, and on 1 June 1796, John Wilkins was appointed quartermaster general with rank of major general, a rise from his previous grade of lieutenant colonel. Organization of the Quartermaster General's Department occurred under the Act of 28 March 1812, and in March 1813 a commissary general of purchases came into being along with nine deputy commissaries and six assistant commissaries.[1]

The staff of the commissary general of purchases was never adequate, which caused the supply responsibilities for cap plates and other accouterments, as well as uniforms themselves, to pass back and forth between the quartermaster general and the commissary general of purchases. Military storekeepers supplemented quartermaster officers, and these men, civil servants of the times, wore uniforms discussed with clothing of the general staff.

In 1842 the quartermaster general assumed all supply functions from the commissary general of purchases, and Congress removed most military storekeepers. Only officers constituted the quartermaster staff until Congress authorized eighty post quartermaster sergeants in 1884. The two-hundred-man army general service detachment at West Point was included as part of the Quartermaster General's Department from 1891 until 1909. Insignia peculiar to this last group is in the chapter on the army service detachments.[2]

The Quartermaster General's Department, the Pay Department, and post commissary sergeants united to form the Quartermaster Corps, effective 1 November 1912, as a result of a rider attached to the Army Appropriations Act of 1912. Quartermaster responsibilities, besides purchase of supplies other than food, included transportation of personnel and equipment by water, rail, wagon, and stage; the purchase, repair, and operation of vessels; and the maintenance of wharves. When the need for troop transport ships arose during the Spanish-American War, the army considered this an expansion of quartermaster activities and established both the Army Transport Service and the Harbor Boat Service. Because of the unique uniforms and insignia of these two organizations, a separate chapter is devoted to them (chapter 36). The Quartermaster Corps temporarily relinquished transportation duties during World War I, and in early 1943 this function was permanently transferred to the new Transportation Corps. The insignia for the World War I Transportation Corps and the Motor Transport Service, and for the more recent Transportation Corps, are in chapter 42.[3]

Early Insignia

Until 1872 staff officers of the Quartermaster General's Department generally wore the general staff uniforms. Light blue plumes on the general staff hats distinguished the quar-

Figs. 18-1 and 18-2. Late-nineteenth-century Quartermaster Department officers used the old English letters QD, because there was no real branch insignia for the quartermasters. These pads were made for militia officers to add to their epaulette crescents. (2 15/16 inches wide)

Fig. 18-3. A typical German silver helmet overlay used by quartermaster sergeants, 1884–1903. (1 1/16 inches wide)

Fig. 18-4. A post quartermaster sergeant in dress uniform, late 1890s. The chevron and helmet overlay, as well as the buff trim, indicate the sergeant's branch.

Fig. 18-1.

Fig. 18-2.

Fig. 18-3.

termaster general and his staff between 1832 and 1851. For the 1851 dress hats, men of the Quartermaster Department and regimental quartermasters wore a pompon, the lower two-thirds buff and the top one-third light blue. These officers wore the silver *US* within a gilt wreath on hats and caps.[4]

Old English letters *QD* on the 1872 uniform shoulder knots distinguished Quartermaster Department officers from 1872 until 1891, when a solid dark blue pad knot without branch insignia or letters came into use. Presumably the militia epaulette pads shown in Figs. 18-1 and 18-2 were inspired by these 1872 Regular Army knots. In 1895, quartermaster officers placed an "enameled" design on the knots. Regulation wording almost immediately changed this to a platinum (the sword blade), enameled (the wheel hub and felloe), and gilt insignia identical to the collar device and made in pairs to face forward. These lasted until knots went out of use in 1903.[5]

Helmet Overlays

After years of appeals by the quartermaster general, Congress established the grade of post quartermaster sergeant in 1884. These noncommissioned officers wore a silver crossed key and pen on the 1885 staff helmet eagle until the helmets were replaced in the 1903–1904 period.[6] Fig. 18-3 shows the helmet overlay, and Fig. 18-4 shows a post quartermaster sergeant wearing the device on his helmet.

Cap Ornaments

Post quartermaster sergeants placed a gilt key and pen similar to the helmet overlay on forage caps from 1885 to 1888. Between 1881 and 1896 the silver helmet overlay was worn on the forage cap, surrounded by "a wreath of dead or unburnished gilt metal" (Fig. 18-5). In 1896 the design was consolidated into a more substantial insignia (Fig. 18-6), and the key and pen finally disappeared in 1903 in favor of a more complex design involving a wagon wheel, the national eagle, and a crossed sword and key (Fig. 18-7).[7] The 1903 cap ornament had a silver central design and bar in a gilt wreath. The dress cap insignia used by post quartermaster sergeants, with the smaller 1905 wreath, is shown in Fig. 18-8, and a variation is shown in Fig. 18-9. For service wear the cap insignia was of bronze-colored metal. Two designs are shown (Figs. 18-10 and 18-11), with the first the

Fig. 18-4.

issue piece and the second slightly different because the eagle, but not the key and sword, is reversed and the center support bar is omitted.

Between 1903 and 1910, caps of U.S. Military Academy Detachment members bore a plain gilt quartermaster insignia (Fig. 18-12). This same ornament, and the comparable bronze service piece (Fig. 18-13), became the insignia used by junior enlisted men in the Quartermaster Corps after 1912.[8] For reasons now unknown, the army made both cap devices with the designs reversed as well as forward, as shown in Figs. 18-14 and 18-15.

Hat Insignia

Between 1905 and 1907, post quartermaster sergeants wore a pin-backed bronze quartermaster insignia, identical to that in Fig. 18-13, on the campaign hat. In addition, enlisted quartermaster personnel wore a solid buff hat cord from the introduction of cords in 1899 until cords went out of use during World War II.[9]

Early Officers' Gilt Collar Insignia

In November 1895, officers in the Quartermaster General's Department received the insignia shown in Figs. 18-16 and 18-17. The design has a gilt eagle holding a six-mule-wagon wheel. The wheel has thirteen spokes, a red and white hub, and a blue felloe (the outer edge of the wheel) carrying thir-

Fig. 18-5.

Fig. 18-6.

Fig. 18-7.

Fig. 18-8.

Fig. 18-9.

Fig. 18-10.

Fig. 18-11.

Fig. 18-5. *This gilt wreath enclosed the silver insignia shown in Fig. 18-3, and the entire device went on the noncommissioned officers' forage cap, 1888–96. The same design had been used from 1885 until 1888, except that the wreath then was silver. (1 39/64 inches wide)*

Fig. 18-6. *A screw-backed, one-piece post quartermaster sergeants' cap insignia, 1896–1903, with a silver key and pen and gilt wreath. (2 5/8 inches wide)*

Fig. 18-7. *Used only two years, starting in 1903, this cap insignia with the eagle, wheel, key, and sword was for post quartermaster sergeants. (2 5/8 inches wide)*

Figs. 18-8 and 18-9. *Such dress cap insignia, 1905–18, were worn by post quartermaster sergeants until 1913, when they were adopted by noncommissioned officers of the newly formed Quartermaster Corps. (1 55/64 and 1 13/16 inches wide, respectively)*

Figs. 18-10 and 18-11. *Service cap insignia, introduced in 1905. Besides the obvious omission of the central supporting bar, the design of Fig. 18-11 also has the eagle facing in the opposite direction, although the key and sword are not reversed. (1 7/8 and 1 13/16 inches wide, respectively)*

teen gilt stars. Over the wheel a sword and key are crossed; the sword blade is of silver.[10] These devices often came in pairs, although sometimes only the eagles faced the front, while at other times the sword and key were also reversed. Many dies exist, and the variations are virtually endless.

Enlisted Men's Cut-Out Collar Devices

Starting in early 1900, post quartermaster sergeants wore the gilt crossed key and pen on the collars of white duck coats (Fig. 18-18). After 1902, enlisted men's dress and service insignia were the same as those for officers, except that the enlisted men's dress device was all gilt, the enamel and silver being changed to gilt (Fig. 18-19). For service wear the entire design was executed in bronze (Fig. 18-20), thus the enlisted insignia was identical to the service cap device except that the pin-back fastener replaced the screw post.[11]

Officers' Bronze Coat Insignia

Officers' service uniforms in 1902 carried bronze insignia, often made in pairs (Figs. 18-21 and 18-22).[12] During World War I a multitude of designs were made, and a few examples are shown in Figs. 18-23 through 18-28. The first pair (Figs. 18-23 and 18-24) are mirror images, while Figs. 18-25 and 18-26 simply have the eagles facing inward. Even the firm of Tiffany and Company made Quartermaster Corps ornaments, as shown in Figs. 18-27 and 18-28.

Shirt and Staff Insignia

Quartermaster officers of World War I and before wore very small bronze shirt collar insignia (Fig. 18-29), although slightly larger shirt ornaments were common during that war. Two bronze examples made in England are shown in Figs. 18-30 and 18-31. Gilt insignia worn in the 1920s are in shown in Figs. 18-32 and 18-33. Regimental quartermasters could also place the insignia in the lower angles of infantry, artillery, or cavalry insignia. One such example is shown in Fig. 18-34. Other examples are pictured in chapters concerning the basic branch insignia.

Women in World War I

In August 1918, Major General James G. Harbord, commanding general of Services of Supply, American Expeditionary Forces, formally requested a women's service corps of five thousand stenographers, typists, and gen-

Fig. 18-12.

Fig. 18-13.

Figs. 18-12 and 18-13. *A pair of gilt and bronze cap insignia. These were used by the U.S. Military Academy Detachment from 1903 until 1910 and by junior enlisted men of the Quartermaster Corps after 1912. (Each 1 inch wide)*

Fig. 18-14.

Fig. 18-15.

Figs. 18-14 and 18-15. *Cap insignia similar to those shown in Figs. 18-12 and 18-13, but with the eagles reversed. The bronze design, made with a pin back, was worn by post quartermaster sergeants on the campaign hat during the 1905–1907 period. (63/64 inch and 1 1/64 inches wide, respectively)*

Fig. 18-16.

Fig. 18-17.

Figs. 18-16 and 18-17. *A pair of officers' collar insignia introduced in late 1895. With a red and white wheel hub and a blue wheel felloe bearing thirteen stars, this device was the most colorful branch insignia. The basic design was made by Captain Oscar F. Long in 1895 at the request of Quartermaster General Batchelder. (Each 31/32 inch wide)*

Fig. 18-18.

Fig. 18-18. *Similar to the helmet overlay, but made in gilt and with a pin back, this insignia was for the collar of the white summer coat used by post quartermaster sergeants, 1900–1903. (1 3/32 inches wide)*

Fig. 18-19.

Fig. 18-19. *All-gilt collar insignia like this one were introduced for enlisted personnel with the 1902-pattern coat.*

Fig. 18-20.

Fig. 18-20. *Enlisted men's collar insignia for the service coat, 1903–10. (1 inch wide)*

Fig. 18-21.

Fig. 18-22.

Figs. 18-21 and 18-22. *A typical pair of Quartermaster Corps officers' standing-collar insignia, with only the eagles facing forward on opposite sides of the collar. (Each 1 inch wide)*

Fig. 18-23.

Fig. 18-24.

Fig. 18-25.

Fig. 18-26.

Fig. 18-27.

Fig. 18-28.

Fig. 18-29.

Fig. 18-30.

Fig. 18-31.

Fig. 18-32.

Fig. 18-33.

Fig. 18-34.

eral office employees be established in order to release men for military duties. This plan was not approved, but as the need for women clerks continued, several army service chiefs decided in the summer of 1918 to hire women stenographers and typists individually by contract, and the quartermaster general hired them both stateside and overseas. Women assigned overseas had to be between twenty-five and thirty-five years old and to pass a medical examination. They wore a uniform purchased with their own funds.[13] An example of one such uniform, with insignia, is shown in Fig. 18-35.

Bronze Disks

A great many variations of enlisted men's subdued disks of the World War I period exist. Two examples are shown in Figs. 18-36 and 18-37, from which one can see that these even come with the key and sword crossed in reverse. During World War I the army organized stevedore regiments, composed primarily of African American troops. These units later transfered to the Transportation Corps and Corps of Engineers, but while still assigned to the Quartermaster Corps, men in some of these organizations received insignia with company letters on the face (Fig. 18-38), although regulations did not authorize this addition.[14]

Gilt Disks

Early gilt disks come in several variations (Figs. 18-39 and 18-40), including those with the eagle's head reversed as well as the sword and key crossed in reverse. The background of crosshatched lines and shields, introduced in the 1920s, initially had the Quartermaster Corps disks with the flying eagle with its head on its wing (Fig. 18-41). Eagles on the later disks were usually more erect, the head upright between the wings.

National Guard quartermaster units often had letters and numbers on their disks before 1936. After 1923 and before 1936, cavalry brigades and divisions were supported by wagon companies and pack trains, each individually numbered. An infantry division's support came from quartermaster trains that included motor transport companies, wagon companies, and motor repair sections, with each of these units also individually numbered, while division special troops included a numbered motorcycle company. The army formed quartermaster regiments in 1936 and put all of these units, including motorcycle companies, into one regiment for each division, with the companies carrying letters.[15]

Figs. 18-23 and 18-24. *Made in a shiny bronze, this pair of officers' standing-collar insignia have the key and sword reversed as well as the eagles facing forward. (Each 1 1/16 inches wide)*

Figs. 18-25 and 18-26. *Similar in general design to the pair shown in Figs. 18-21 and 18-22, this pair was struck in much more detail, and the wings are higher. The metal is a dark tan color. (Each 1 1/16 inch wide)*

Figs. 18-27 and 18-28. *This magnificent pair of World War I officers' Quartermaster Corps insignia was made by Tiffany and Company. The metal is unusual in that it is nearly a yellow color bronze. Even the letters US can be read on the swords, just below the hilt. (Each 1 1/8 inches wide)*

Fig. 18-29. *A common shirt collar insignia in bronze is from World War I. (45/64 inch wide)*

Figs. 18-30 and 18-31. *These two bronze insignia were both made in England during World War I for U.S. officers' shirts. (Each 3/4 inch wide)*

Fig. 18-32. *This post-1923 gilt officers' shirt insignia does not have the area between the spokes pierced, and although the eagle faces the proper direction, the key and sword are reversed. (47/64 inch wide)*

Fig. 18-33. *This officers' gilt shirt insignia has the eagle facing the "wrong" direction, but the key and sword are correctly crossed. (49/64 inch wide)*

Fig. 18-34. *Combat regiments had one officer appointed as the quartermaster, and that officer added a small quartermaster insignia in the lower angle of his branch insignia, as done with this insignia for the 104th Cavalry Regiment. (1 15/16 inches wide)*

Fig. 18-35. *Not only does the officer wear a Quartermaster Corps insignia on the uniform collar, but so does his secretary. Use of insignia by women was not prescribed in regulations.*

Figs. 18-36 and 18-37. *A pair of matching enlisted men's disks, about 1910. (Each 1 inch in diameter)*

Fig. 18-38. *Unauthorized disks with company letters on the face were issued by the U.S. Army during World War I to members of stevedore regiments. (1 inch in diameter)*

Figs. 18-39 and 18-40. *Two typical gilt disks from the mid-1920s. (1 inch and 1 1/64 inches in diameter, respectively)*

Fig. 18-41. *An issue enlisted men's collar insignia of the late 1920s and early 1930s. (1 1/64 inches in diameter)*

Fig. 18-42. *Collar disk for the 106th Motor Transport Company, 1930s. After the demise of the World War I Motor Transport Corps in 1920, the Quartermaster Corps assumed transportation functions. (1 1/32 inches in diameter)*

Fig. 18-43. *Some divisions had motorcycle companies active between the world wars, and members of those companies added their unit number and the letters MC below. (1 1/64 inches in diameter)*

Fig. 18-44. *Cavalry divisions and brigades had wagon companies assigned, and members of those companies wore disks with the letter W. (1 1/64 inches in diameter)*

Fig. 18-45. *An enlisted men's two-piece disk that closely follows the 1936 official design. (1 inch in diameter)*

Figs. 18-46, 18-47, and 18-48. *Three examples of World War II enlisted men's collar insignia which depart considerably from the approved design. (1 inch, 1 inch, and 1 1/32 inches in diameter, respectively)*

Fig. 18-49. *Made of olive drab plastic, this modified Quartermaster Corps insignia was evidently an effort to conserve metal during World War II. (1 inch in diameter)*

Figs. 18-50 and 18-51. *Two post–World War II disks, the first (Fig. 18-50) in silver and showing an early design with the eagle's head on its wing, and the other (Fig. 18-51) in gilt that generally follows the proper design. Both disks are domed. (1 1/64 inches and 31/32 inch in diameter, respectively)*

Fig. 18-35.

Fig. 18-36.

Fig. 18-37.

Fig. 18-38.

Fig. 18-39.

Fig. 18-40.

Fig. 18-41.

Fig. 18-42.

Fig. 18-43.

Fig. 18-44.

Fig. 18-45.

Fig. 18-46.

Fig. 18-47.

Fig. 18-48.

Fig. 18-49.

Fig. 18-50.

Fig. 18-51.

Fig. 18-52.

Fig. 18-53.

Fig. 18-54.

Fig. 18-55.

Fig. 18-52. *This regulation central design is in silver but is on a domed background and has an unauthorized buff enamel edge. This type of branch-colored edging was popular late in the Korean War and immediately afterward. (1 23/64 inches in diameter)*

Fig. 18-53. *Just like the World War I nonregulation disks, this post–World War II disk had the company letter added to the wheel. (1 1/32 inches in diameter)*

Figs. 18-54 and 18-55. *Two officers' lapel coat insignia, designed in the 1930s. These were worn into World War II. (Each 49/64 inch wide)*

Fig. 18-56. *A Quartermaster Corps officers' insignia that follows the official 1936 design. The most obvious feature is the upright posture of the eagle. (7/8 inch wide)*

Fig. 18-56.

With this information available, we may surmise that numbered quartermaster disks from before 1936 exist for prefixes of suffixes *MT, W, MR, MC,* and *P* or *PT*. For example, men of the 106th Motor Transport Company (Brooklyn, New York, National Guard) wore the insignia shown in Fig. 18-42 with *106MT* below. Fig. 18-43 shows *119MC* below for the 119th Motorcycle Company, stationed in New Jersey. Fig. 18-44 shows *126W* for the 126th Wagon Company, a part of the 38th Division Quartermaster Train (Kentucky National Guard).[16]

Typical two-piece flat disks of World War II come in many variations, such as flat disks with the eagle's head erect (Figs. 18-45 and 18-46). Earlier designs show the flying eagle with its head on its wing, and, like the initial 1902 enlisted men's design that the army had reversed, the World War II pieces also come with this feature (Fig. 18-47) or with just the key and sword crossed backwards (Fig. 18-48). An interesting attempt to save metal during the early days of World War II resulted in the olive drab plastic insignia shown in Fig. 18-49, although a wreath instead of a wheel was used and can not now be explained. Domed disks came into existence at the close of World War II. Quartermaster Corps examples are shown in figs. 18-50, 18-51, and 18-52, the first with the older flying eagle design and the last with an unauthorized buff-colored enameled edge added. Fig. 18-53 has a company letter affixed directly to the front. This disk follows the 1918 stevedores' practice of covering part of the design, necessitated by a lack of clear space.

Officers' Gilt Coat Insignia, 1921–Present

For the 1921 white uniform, the only enamel on the 1-inch-high insignia was the blue felloe, although no doubt most officers wore the older pre–World War I, fully enameled insignia. Regulations of 1923 list the colors as "the felloe of the wheel to be of blue enamel, hub center red, edged with white." Regulations after November 1924 called for these 1-inch-high standing-collar ornaments to be made in pairs so the eagle would face forward.[17]

Starting in 1926, quartermaster insignia were 3/4 inch high for the lapel coat. Between the world wars, pairs continued to be made, although the army officially abandoned paired insignia for all but standing collars in March 1926.[18]

Examples of these 1930s lapel coat insignia are shown in Figs. 18-54 and 18-55. The official 1936 design raised the eagle's head, making (officially) the insignia look as it does today. An example is shown in Fig. 18-56. Between 1936 and World War II, mess blue uniforms were to carry insignia made in pairs, so it is reasonable to assume that the post-1936 design with an erect eagle comes in pairs.[19] During the 1930s and World War II, units occasionally added numbers. One such example is shown in Fig. 18-57 for the 511th Quartermaster Company. Shortly after World War II an insignia with straight eagle's wings, reminiscent of the Nazi style, was made in Germany for sale to occupying troops (Fig. 18-58).

Typical cloth insignia, made in quantity during World War II, are shown in Figs. 18-59 and 18-60. That of Fig. 18-59 is large in all yellow stitching except for the felloe and the white hub. That of Fig. 18-60 is a small insignia in "natural" colors. Vietnam-era subdued cloth insignia are shown in Figs. 18-61, 18-62, and 18-63. That shown in Fig. 18-61 was made in Germany with the felloe of dark blue, and the ones in Figs. 18-62 and 18-63 were hand-made in Vietnam about 1967.

Fig. 18-57. During World War II some units added unit numbers, as in this example. In divisions, quartermaster companies were numbered. (53/64 inch wide)

Fig. 18-58. This unusual eagle, with straight wings reminiscent of the Nazi eagle, was made in Germany. (57/64 inch wide)

Figs. 18-59 and 18-60. Widely different in size, these two World War II embroidered officers' insignia have the main design in yellow, the wheel felloe in blue, and the hub in white with a red center. (Designs 1 15/32 and 1 1/16 inches wide)

Fig. 18-61. A nearly subdued insignia made in Germany in the 1970s. The wheel felloe is blue and the hub is white on an otherwise black insignia. (Design 1 1/8 inches wide)

Figs. 18-62 and 18-63. Typical hand-embroidered subdued insignia made in Vietnam during the war. The dashes around the wheel are in green. (Designs 1 1/8 and 1 1/4 inches wide, respectively)

Fig. 18-64. Major General Hugh Mackintosh, October 1957, wearing quartermaster branch insignia on his coat lapels to show his position as quartermaster general.

Fig. 18-57.

Fig. 18-58.

Fig. 18-59.

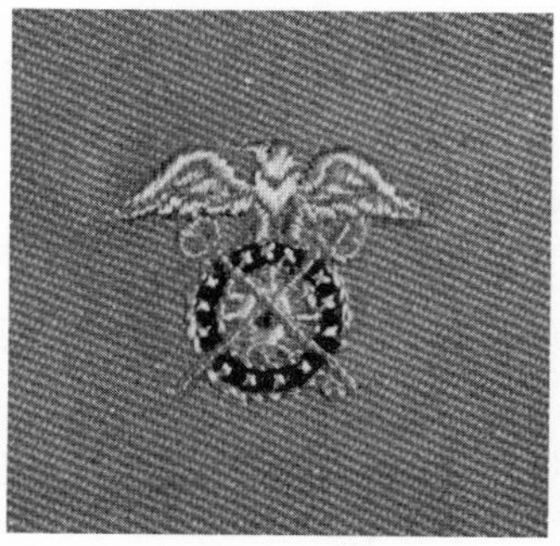

Fig. 18-60.

Fig. 18-61.

Fig. 18-62.

Fig. 18-63.

Fig. 18-64.

Chapter Nineteen

Commissary or Subsistence

Although the term *commissary* is now most often associated with food, in the first half of the nineteenth century the army had two different staff officers with *commissary* in their titles: the commissary general and the commissary general of purchases. Callender Irvine became the first commissary general of purchases in 1812, and as such he was responsible for "all arms, military stores, clothing, and generally all articles of supply." In 1842 the Quartermaster Department combined with the office of the commissary general of purchases, eliminating the latter.[1]

From 1821 until 1912, the commissary general, or commissary of subsistence, as he was sometimes known, with his staff supplied the army's food. In 1858 the Commissary General's Department was retitled the Subsistence Department, and in 1912 Congress merged that department with the Quartermaster General's Department and the Pay Department to form the Quartermaster Corps. The legislative branch first authorized commissary sergeants in 1873 (retitled post commissary sergeants in 1893), and these men were the only enlisted personnel assigned to the Commissary Department per se, even though during the period from 1867 to 1870 regimental commissary sergeants, not part of the Commissary Department, were part of regimental noncommissioned staffs.[2]

Regimental and battalion commissary officers and regimental and battalion commissary sergeants were members of infantry, cavalry, and artillery regiments and engineer battalions from 1899 until 1913. These men, as members of those arms, had no commissary-related insignia other than special chevrons for the sergeants and officers' small crescents added to their basic branch collar insignia. These officers' insignia are shown in the chapters for the infantry, cavalry, artillery, and the Corps of Engineers.

Officers' Cap and Hat Devices

In 1820 the army directed "commissaries" to wear the cockade with eagle on the chapeau but otherwise to wear the general staff uniform. Distinctive plumes came about in 1832, with the commissary general of subsistence and his staff officers wearing a general staff hat including an 8-inch-high plume, half blue and half white. On the 1851 cap subsistence officers wore the staff officers' *US* letters in a wreath, and for dress wear they added a pompon with the top one-third in royal blue and the bottom two-thirds buff. Commissary officers wore the general staff cap and hat insignia until 1895, when the eagle came into universal use.[3]

Helmet Plates

Commissary sergeants, numbering at times as many as two hundred, applied a silver crescent to the enlisted men's staff helmet shield between 1881 and 1902. When the insignia was properly placed, a horizontal line could be drawn between the crescent points, as shown in Fig. 19-1.[4]

Enlisted Men's Cap and Hat Insignia

Shortly after Congress established the grade of commissary sergeant in March 1873, a large silver crescent (Fig. 19-2) became the insignia these new men were to wear on the cap. Initial regulations specified that the imaginary line connecting the points be vertical, with the distance between points 1⅝ inches, although the illustrated 1882 reg-

Fig. 19-1. *Commissary sergeants wore silver crescents, like this one, on their 1881–1903 helmet eagles and on dress coat collars from 1881 to 1884. (31/32 inch wide, point to point)*

Fig. 19-2. *From 1873 to 1889 commissary sergeants wore this type of large insignia on their caps. Some wore the crescent with the points to the side and some with the points up. (61/64 inch wide)*

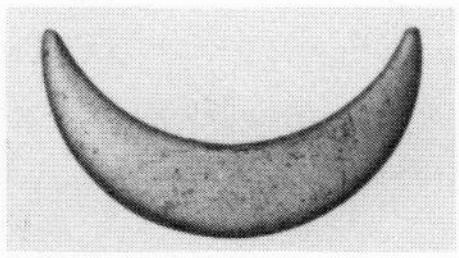

Fig. 19-1.

Fig. 19-2.

Fig. 19-3.

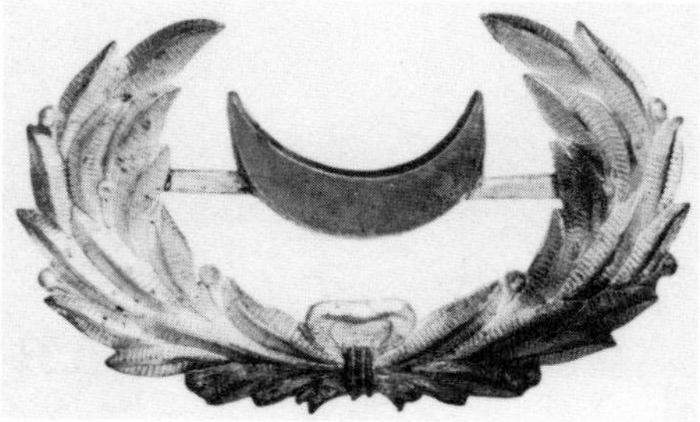

Fig. 19-4.

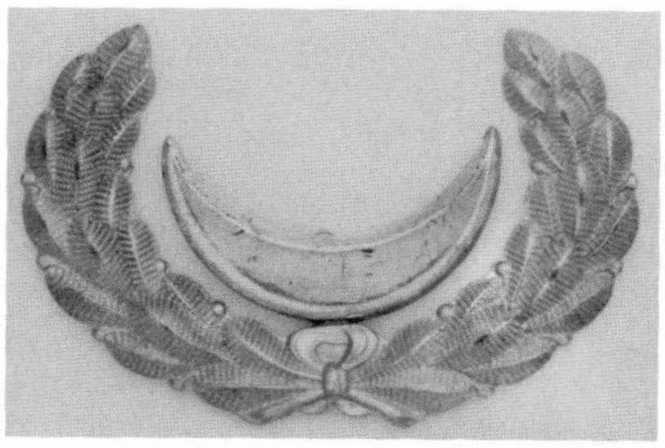

Fig. 19-5.

Fig. 19-6.

Fig. 19-7.

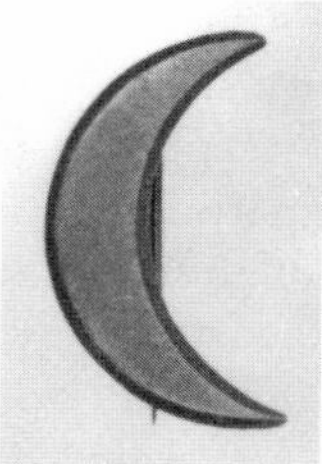

Fig. 19-8.

Fig. 19-9.

Fig. 19-3. *Post commissary sergeants wore a brass wreath enclosing a separate silver crescent as cap insignia from 1889 until 1896.*

Fig. 19-4. *A one-piece brass and silver-colored, screw-back cap insignia for post commissary sergeants, 1896–1905. (2 51/64 inches wide)*

Fig. 19-5. *An example of a 1905–13 post commissary sergeants' dress cap insignia. (1 15/16 inches wide)*

Figs. 19-6 and 19-7. *Two service cap insignia, in all-bronze color, for post commissary sergeants, 1905–13. (1 7/8 and 1 29/32 inches wide, respectively)*

Fig. 19-8. *This insignia was worn two ways: during 1905–1907 on the campaign hat, and during 1902–10 on the enlisted men's service uniform coat collar. (19/32 inch wide)*

Fig. 19-9. *Subsistence Department officers wore epaulettes of this general type on full dress uniforms until 1872. This view is from directly above, thus hiding the bullion fringe.*

ulations show the crescent points up, 90 degrees from the description in the text. In 1889 a smaller silver crescent, evidently 1 inch long, came into being. It was placed in a gilt wreath (Fig. 19-3). From 1896 until 1905, post commissary sergeants used a more substantial device with the new screw post, as shown in Fig. 19-4. Smaller wreaths 1 15/16 inches wide replaced the older insignia from 1905 until 1913 (Fig. 19-5 for dress and Figs. 19-6 and 19-7 for service caps). Post commissary sergeants transferred to the Quartermaster Corps in 1912, but the men could continue to wear the commissary insignia as long as they were servicable. From 1905 until 1907 the army authorized post commissary sergeants to wear a bronze crescent (Fig. 19-8) on the campaign hat, although this had been the general practice before 1905.[5]

Shoulder Knots and Epaulettes

Subsistence officers wore shoulder knots with the old English letters *SD* (for Subsistence Department) on the dress uniforms from 1872 through 1891 (Fig. 19-9), after which they switched to plain dark blue knots used by commissary, quartermaster, and

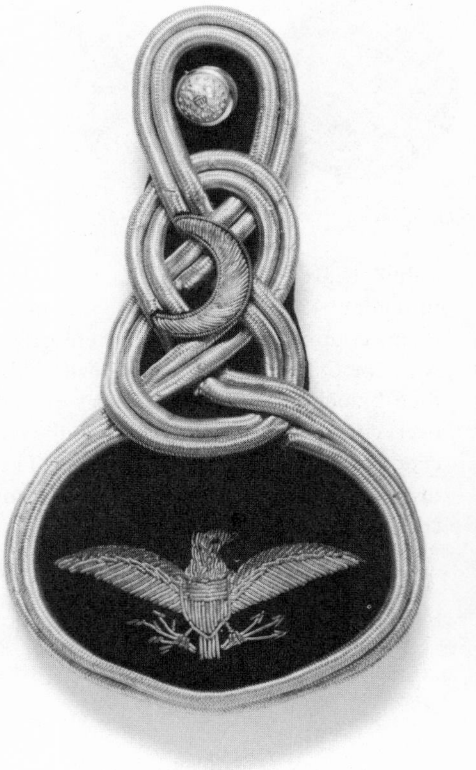

Fig. 19-10.

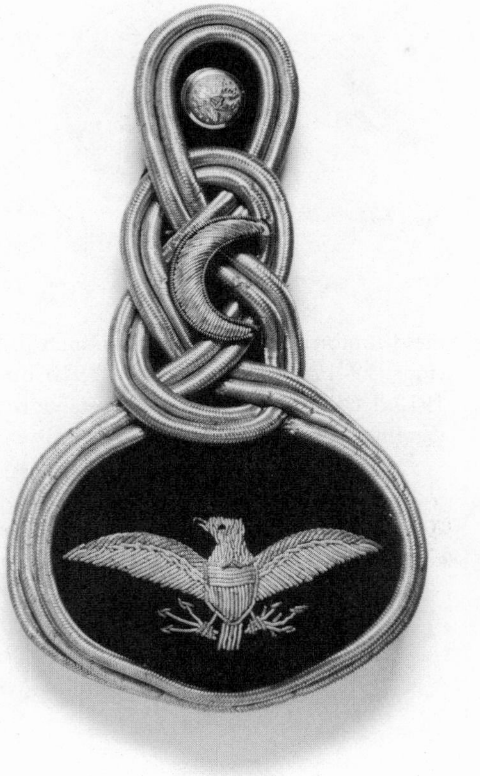

Fig. 19-11.

Figs. 19-10 and 19-11. *A pair of Subsistence Department colonels' shoulder knots, about 1901. The pad bearing the eagle is on dark blue cloth. The silver crescent on the upper knot was added after the Spanish-American War. The eagles faced the wearer's front, with the crescents pointed to the rear.*

Figs. 19-12 and 19-13. *Subsistence officers wore small crescents on their coat collars, 1895–1913. Like these examples, the insignia came in imitation embroidery and in smooth finish. (3/8 inch wide)*

Fig. 19-14. *A bronze collar insignia for a post commissary sergeant's service uniform, used until 1913. (9/16 inch wide)*

Fig. 19-15. *This style of gilt, pin-backed insignia was worn by post commissary sergeants on the white coats, 1900–13, and on the dress coats, 1903–13. (9/16 inch wide)*

finance officers.[6] Major General Nelson Miles, while he was army commander, added a silver crescent, 1 inch between points, to the epaulette of the commissary general and to other officers' shoulder knots. The insignia, either embroidered or made of silver to represent embroidery, was placed on the straps between the fastening button and the brigadier general's star or, for subsistence colonels, just above the epaulette pad on the gold cord knots, as shown in Figs. 19-10 and 19-11. Lieutenant colonels, majors, and captains placed the crescent on the pad center in the same manner as did members of other branches. All wore the cusps to the rear, making the epaulettes come in matched pairs.

Fig. 19-12.

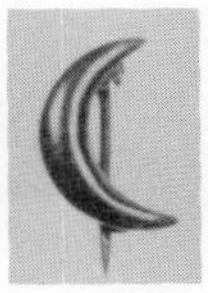

Fig. 19-13.

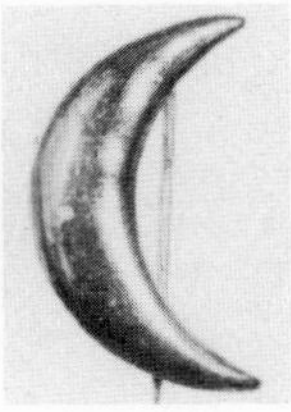

Fig. 19-14.

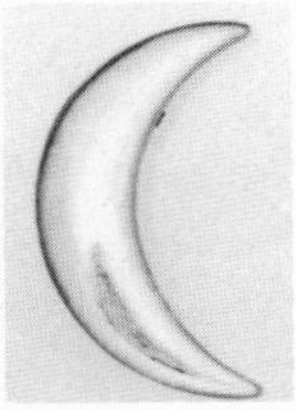

Fig. 19-15.

Officers' Coat Collar Ornaments

In February 1896 a small 1/2-inch silver crescent came into being for the collar of the new sack coat. The insignia, worn in pairs with the cusps to the rear, could be either real or imitation embroidery (Fig. 19-12). In 1902 these ornaments also started to be made in smooth metal, in both silver and bronze (Fig. 19-13). When the Subsistence Department became one of the elements of the Quartermaster Corps in 1912, commissary collar insignia became obsolete.[8]

Cut-Out Enlisted Men's Collar Insignia

Commissary sergeants wore 1-inch "white metal" crescents, the same as those of the helmet overlay (Fig. 19-1) on dress coat collars until the introduction of the newer style of dress coat in 1884. From 1902 through 1913, commissary sergeants used gilt crescents, 1 1/8 inches high (Figs. 19-14 and 19-15), on the dress uniform coats. Until replaced by disks in 1910, bronze crescents were worn on the olive drab and khaki field uniforms (Fig. 19-16).[9]

Fig. 19-16.

Fig. 19-17.

Fig. 19-18.

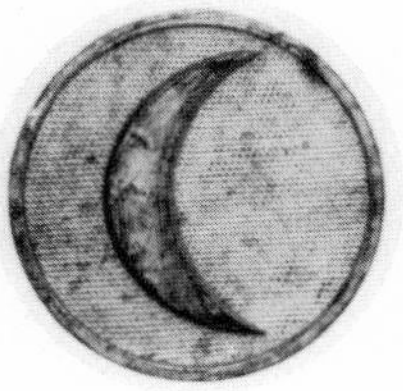

Fig. 19-19.

Fig. 19-16. *A smaller than regulation, bronze-colored enlisted men's service coat insignia. (15/32 inch wide)*

Figs. 19-17 and 19-18. *Two examples of bronze service uniform collar disks for post commissary sergeants, 1910–13 (Each 1 inch in diameter)*

Fig. 19-19. *Gilt disks bearing a subsistence insignia, like this one, were not used by the Regular Army. (1 1/64 inch in diameter)*

Collar Disks

Field uniforms carried bronze 1-inch disks (Figs. 19-17 and 19-18) from 1910 until 1913.[10] Gilt disks (Fig. 19-19) exist, but they were not described in army regulations.

Officers' Staff Insignia

Commissary staff officers of infantry, cavalry, and artillery regiments added small crescents below their branch insignia from 1899 through 1913, and although the title of battalion commissary remained, these officers wore the Quartermaster Corps device below their branch insignia, while Corps of Engineers commissary staff officers wore the crescent above the castle's center turret. These insignia are illustrated in the chapters concerned with the basic branch.

Chapter Twenty

Chaplains

Nineteenth-century arrangements for providing army chaplains varied. Usually chaplains served a post instead of a particular unit, although the army assigned chaplains to some regiments, especially the black units, after the Civil War. Regulations of 1820 describe chaplains' uniforms as those of the general staff except that the chapeau cockade was less the usual eagle. The following year, new regulations specifically directed chaplains and a few others to have no uniform, thus making civilian garb the chaplains' "uniform." This remained the case until 11 June 1832, when orders from the adjutant general stated that the West Point chaplain would wear "citizen's dress with the Corps of Engineers button, round hat and black cockade with gold eagle." An 1839 order added an engineers' forage cap and an optional engineers' frock coat.[1]

Fig. 20-1.

Fig. 20-1. Chaplain William H. McCormick, 1st Regiment, New Jersey Volunteer Infantry, in a regulation Civil War chaplains' uniform. The prescribed black coat had nine buttons down the front. The cross on the breast is a corps badge and is not a chaplains' insignia.

General Order Number 102, dated 25 November 1861, described the Civil War uniforms for chaplains shown in Fig. 20-1: "The uniform for chaplains of the army will be of plain black frock coat, with standing collar, and one row of nine black buttons; plain black pantaloons; black felt hat, or army forage cap, without ornament. On occasions of ceremony, a plain chapeau de bras may be worn."

In August 1864 the army directed that the chaplains' single-breasted nine-button black frock coat be modified by adding "herring bone" around the button holes. With this change chaplains could wear the hat or cap, as they desired, with the headgear bearing the letters *US* in a wreath as worn by general staff and general officers. This combination of black uniform and standard army headgear continued until 1884. Officers' overcoat sleeve braid was not worn by chaplains by virtue of General Order Number 92, 1872. Circular Number 1, 1884, changed chaplains' uniforms to the "undress for the officers" and eliminated the staff chapeau as headgear. These early uniforms distinguished chaplains, so no insignia was required. Civil War photographs show some volunteer unit chaplains wearing small Latin crosses on their collars, a practice whose origin cannot be readily traced today.[2]

Insignia, 1880–1914

In February 1880, the War Department established the first unique chaplains' insignia for the black coat, a "shoulder strap of black

Fig. 20-2. Chaplains received their first insignia in the form of a unique shoulder strap bearing a shepherd's crook in February 1880. It lasted until May 1888. (Strap approximately 1 9/16 by 4 3/8 inches)

Fig. 20-3. Chaplain Edward A. Horton in a chaplains' uniform of 1882.

Fig. 20-4. A chaplains' 1898 shoulder strap. The cross was silver on a black velvet background, with a gold bullion edge. (Strap approximately 1 3/4 by 4 3/8 inches)

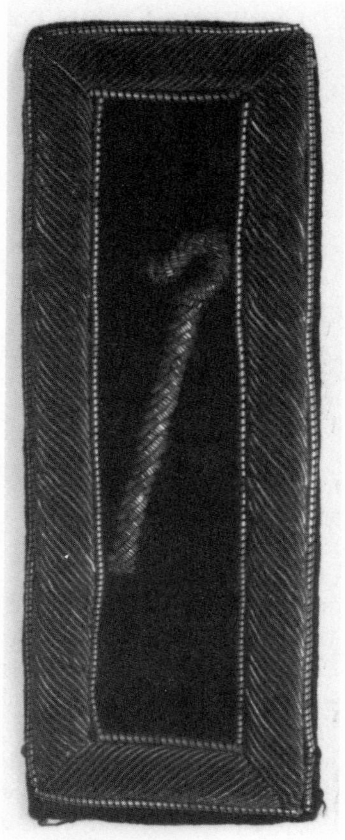

Fig. 20-2.

Fig. 20-3.

Fig. 20-4.

velvet, with a shepherd's crook of frosted silver on the center of the strap" (Fig. 20-2). The army considered the special black coat with shoulder straps an "undress" uniform, but the War Department did not require chaplains to have any dress uniform. In 1888 the army changed the black coat designation so that it was considered both full dress and undress, as, in fact, it had been (Fig. 20-3). Officials reinstituted chaplains' shoulder straps in May 1898 so that instead of a crook, they carried a silver cross (Fig. 20-4).[3]

By 1900 chaplains wore many different uniforms. Regulations allowed three coat styles: (1) the Civil War–style frock coat with nine buttons, (2) a plain black double-breasted frock coat with falling collar and two rows of seven buttons, or (3) a plain black falling-collar sack coat with one row of five buttons. In practice chaplains also wore the standard officers' sack coat, as shown in Fig. 20-5. The plain black coat with a black hat, similar to the olive drab hat used by other officers, with a gold and black silk interwined cord was considered full dress in the 1902 regulations.[4]

For the new 1902 dress uniform, chaplains wore the standard sack coat with branch insignia reflecting their assignment. For

Fig. 20-5.

branch insignia they wore infantry, cavalry, coast artillery, or field artillery branch insignia with a small cross below. An example is shown in Fig. 20-6. Instead of rank insignia chaplains continued to wear a plain metal Latin cross on the shoulder loops of the khaki and white uniforms. After 1907 these crosses were to be bronze for the service uniform (Fig. 20-7) and silver for the white coat (Fig. 20-8).[5]

Insignia, 1914–26

In 1914 chaplains began to wear the plain silver cross as a branch insignia (Fig. 20-9), discarding combat arms insignia with a small cross below. Chaplains were always to wear their new insignia in silver, even on the field uniforms when other officers wore bronze insignia, but bronze crosses saw wide use (Figs. 20-10 and 20-11).[6]

Early in 1918, chaplains reverted to the pre-1914 practice of wearing a silver cross on the shoulder straps instead of rank insignia (Fig. 20-12). An insignia made in France with a narrow engraved edge is shown in Fig. 20-13. A bronze cross, again replacing rank insignia, appeared on shirt collars in May 1918, and as with other branches, standard-size insignia (Fig. 20-14) were worn as well as small crosses (Fig. 20-15).[7]

From May 1918 until 1926 crosses replaced rank insignia on chaplains' uni-

Fig. 20-6.

Fig. 20-9.

Fig. 20-10.

Fig. 20-7.

Fig. 20-8.

Fig. 20-11.

Fig. 20-5. *Chaplain Dickson, 1901, wearing the 1895 coat with special chaplains' shoulder straps. Chaplains began to wear collar insignia on this coat in 1903.*

Fig. 20-6. *Between 1902 and 1914, regulations called for chaplains to wear small crosses below infantry, cavalry, and various artillery insignia. This example, made in 1903, was for the 8th Cavalry Regiment's chaplain. ($1\frac{31}{32}$ inches wide)*

Figs. 20-7 and 20-8. *When commissioned officers began to wear metal rank insignia on the shoulder straps, chaplains adopted metal crosses instead of rank insignia. Silver crosses were used on all uniforms until 1907, when the bronze version was adopted. ($1\frac{3}{64}$ inches and $\frac{25}{32}$ inch wide, respectively)*

Fig. 20-9. *This pin-backed silver cross is typical of early branch insignia adopted in 1914 for chaplains. In that year chaplains began to wear branch and rank insignia like those of commissioned officers. This style of cross was reintroduced in 1926 as a branch insignia after a temporary change in the way chaplains wore insignia during World War I. ($\frac{41}{64}$ inch wide)*

Fig. 20-10. *Chaplains were to wear silver crosses on all uniforms, but many men actually wore bronze insignia like this example. ($\frac{21}{32}$ inch wide)*

Fig. 20-11. *A chaplain in the United States early in World War I. The rank insignia on his shoulder would soon disappear as a result of General Pershing's insistence that chaplains' ranks hindered their ministry to soldiers.*

Fig. 20-12. This 1918 American Expeditionary Forces chaplain differs from his 1917 counterpart in that the overseas cap with silver cross has replaced the campaign hat, crosses have appeared on the center of the shoulder loops (replacing rank insignia), and a Sam Browne belt has been added.

Fig. 20-13. A bronze cross made in France for the AEF. (3/4 inch wide)

Figs. 20-14 and 20-15. Two typical chaplains' crosses of the type worn on shirt collars during and after World War I. (21/32 and 1/2 inch wide, respectively)

Fig. 20-16. A post–World War II chaplains' silver-colored insignia. (5/8 inch wide)

Fig. 20-17. Jewish chaplains wore this style of branch insignia from World War I until World War II. This particular all silver-colored insignia has the center of the star cut out. Between the World Wars all Jewish chaplains were reservists. (21/32 inch wide)

Fig. 20-18. A 1970s Jewish chaplains' insignia with a dark silver recessed area, which allows the design to be highlighted. (37/64 inch wide)

Fig. 20-19. Hebrew characters appeared on the Jewish chaplains' insignia, replacing the Roman numerals, in 1981.

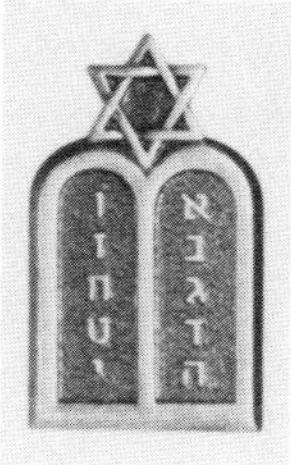

Fig. 20-19.

Fig. 20-12.

Fig. 20-15.

Fig. 20-13.

Fig. 20-14.

Fig. 20-16.

Fig. 20-17.

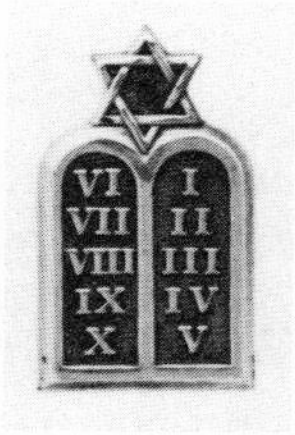

Fig. 20-18.

forms, including the insignia worn on the sleeves of officers' overcoats.[8]

Christian Chaplains after 1926

In March 1926 the 125 chaplains on active duty began to wear rank insignia, so the cross moved to the coat lapel as devices for other branches had done. According to regulations, crosses have not changed since 1926, although Christian chaplains have worn both large and small crosses on various uniforms, and the Quartermaster Corps has sold both large and small sizes. Interestingly, the army sometimes listed these two sizes of crosses under rank insignia and not as branch ornaments. The wider insignia, used from World War II to the present, is shown in Fig. 20-16.[9]

Jewish Chaplains

Federal law prevented Jews from official appointment as chaplains until July 1862, although some Jewish men served as chaplains during 1862 before the law was passed. Rabbis became chaplains during World War I because a large number of Jews served in the army. In August 1918, Jewish chaplains received tablets of law and a star of David as an insignia because Jewish chaplains considered the cross offensive as the insignia for rabbis. For a short time when the secretary of war authorized omission of branch insignia for Jewish chaplains, the War Department allowed a shepherd's crook for all chaplains. Great opposition to the crook arose from those chaplains already in the service, resulting in suspension of the order, and after a short delay the army granted a separate collar insignia for Jewish chaplains.[10]

Like the Christian chaplains' insignia, the tablets and star have changed little. A 1930s-style insignia with hollow star is shown in Fig. 20-17, but if a rabbi of the period actually wore the device, he was a reservist; between 1918 and 1940 no Jewish chaplain served on full-time active duty. A post–World War II insignia with a dark recessed finish is shown in Fig. 20-18. At the chief of chaplains' request, the Institute of Heraldry changed the Jewish chaplains' insignia to show Hebrew characters in late 1981, and Jewish chaplains were required to wear the insignia by 1 January 1983 (Fig. 20-19).[11]

Chaplains' Assistants

Army regulations from the 1920s allowed chaplains' assistants to help perform various duties, but it was not until World War II that the army began to provide assistants as a mat-

Fig. 20-20

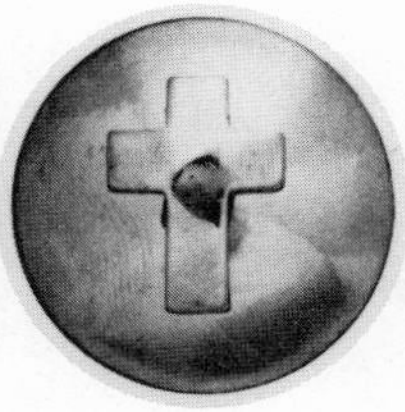

Fig. 20-21.

Fig. 20-22.

Fig. 20-23.

ter of course. Although special insignia were not authorized, some assistants wore insignia of the types shown in Figs. 20-20, 20-21, and 20-22. These men, technically clerk typists during World War II, wrestled portable field organs into and out of muddy jeep trailers, typed bulletin stencils, taught Sunday schools, and performed a wide variety of other tasks. After World War II chaplains' assistants were to wear adjutant general insignia until November 1984, when, after a two-year study, the vice chief of staff finally approved a unique enlisted assistants' insignia different from the officers' counterpart. The design is of a chapel, with its doors open, held in two hands, which symbolize the religious support provided to both the chapel and to religious programs (Fig. 20-23).[12]

Rank

During most of the Civil War the government generally recognized chaplains as service members and officers but failed to clarify any position of rank. Congress changed this in April 1864 when it established the "rank of chaplain without command." This was later changed to the assimilated rank of captain, that is, they were treated like captains, without a captain's authority. Again, this carefully crafted position was upset in 1904 when chaplains who had served ten years were promoted to major. Chaplains began to wear rank insignia in 1914, but this, too, was short-lived.[13]

Between 1918 and 1926 chaplains again quit wearing rank insignia. This change had its roots in the beliefs of General Pershing and Bishop Charles Brent, the chief of chaplains in the AEF. Pershing and Brent thought military rank stood in the way of good relations between chaplains and soldiers and recommended that chaplains have no rank. General Pershing believed that a successful chaplain depended upon his personality instead of his rank, and he believed it so much that he really thought chaplains were truly not soldiers. Accordingly, in 1918 the army directed chaplains to remove rank insignia and to wear the chaplains' insignia instead of rank insignia. Chaplains in Europe generally complied with the change; what could they do with the AEF commander in their immediate midst? In the United States the order was not widely followed. At the chaplains' school officials relieved three senior chaplains for leading protests against removal of rank insignia. In 1926 the first chief of chaplains, Col. John T. Axton, was successful in his efforts to have the army restore chaplains' rank insignia.[14] Chaplains have worn rank insignia ever since, although at some times the rank insignia on the cap was replaced by the chaplains' insignia.

Insignia of the Late Twentieth Century

In the 1990s the U.S. Army recognized that some soldiers needed other than traditional western Christian and Jewish chaplains. In 1990 the Armed Forces Chaplains Board took action to have the first Buddhist chaplain appointed, and the army was directed to develop an insignia for Buddhist chaplains. This was completed in August 1990 when the Institute of Heraldry prescribed a silver-colored *dharma cakra*, an eight-spoked wheel representative of religious observances. Details of the 1-inch-diameter wheel included ornate spokes and center. A copy of the official design is shown in Fig. 20-24.[15]

Muslims in the U.S. armed forces did not have any chaplains until the end of the twentieth century. The army's office of the chief of chaplains requested an insignia for chaplains of the Muslim faith on 14 December 1992. The Department of the Army approved the request in January 1993, and the resulting design was a silver crescent (Fig. 20-25).[16]

Figs. 20-20, 20-21, and 20-22. *During and after World War II chaplains' assistants wore a variety of nonregulation collar insignia, such as these. The disk in Fig. 20-20 is of the separable variety with a cross that has the edge traced by a line to make the design stand out. The convex disk of Fig. 20-21 bearing the plain-edged cross is silver, as is the Jewish chaplains' assistants' insignia in Fig. 20-22. Enlisted personnel who helped chaplains should have worn Adjutant General Corps insignia after World War II until the official enlisted insignia was introduced. (1 inch, 1 1/64 inches, and 1 1/32 inches in diameter, respectively)*

Fig. 20-23. *Chaplains' assistants were to wear this insignia starting in 1984. The design consists of a pair of stylized hands providing support to a chapel with open doors.*

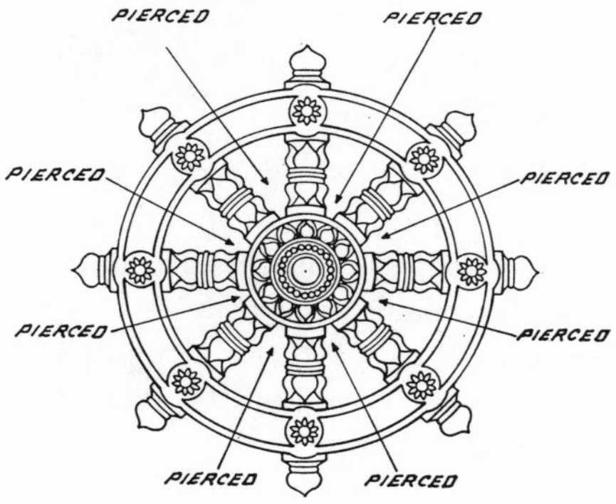

Fig. 20-24.

Fig. 20-25.

Fig. 20-24. *Insignia for Buddhist chaplains, approved in 1990. The silver 1-inch-high insignia is an eight-spoked wheel, the dharma cakra.*

Fig. 20-25. *Approved in January 1993, this design, executed in silver, is the insignia for Muslim chaplains. (1 inch high)*

Chapter Twenty-One

Inspector General

Initially the small U.S. Army combined the offices of inspector general and adjutant general, and even this combined office occasionally disappeared. The army formed Inspector General's Department under provisions of an Act of March 13, 1813. From time to time, inspector general are mentioned in uniform regulations from 1813 onward.[1]

Officers of the department wore general staff uniforms from 1813 until 1893. In 1832 the War Department further authorized inspector generals aiguillettes on the right shoulder. In 1839 members of the department started to use distinctive trim: a green 8-inch swan feather for the hat. Previously, inspectors wore the yellow hat feather of the general staff. The 1851 inspectors' caps carried pompons with the top one-third scarlet and the lower two-thirds buff. Other than these brief distinctions, inspectors used no distinguishing ornaments, although by 1872 aides and members of the Inspector General's and the Adjutant General's departments wore aiguillettes. Between 1872 and 1888, shoulder knots carried the old English letters *ID*, which stood for Inspector General's Department. Plain shoulder knots without any branch insignia saw use from 1888 until 1890.[2]

Officers' Gilt Devices

In 1890 officers began to wear a "solid gold or gilt sword and fasces, crossed and wreathed." Officers wore this insignia within a gold wreath on the forage cap (Fig. 21-1), on the shoulder knot pad (Fig. 21-2), and, after 1893, on the sack coat collar (Fig. 21-3). Lieutenant colonels and below wore shoulder knots of the type shown in Fig. 21-2, with a metal device on the knot pad. Full colonels wore knots with the branch device on the bullion cords between the pad and the button. Between 1900 and 1903 the inspector general added a metal branch device to his epaulette strap, midway between the fastening

Fig. 21-1.

Fig. 21-1. From the Smithsonian Institution collection, an Inspector General's Department forage cap insignia, 1890–95. Before 1890 officers assigned to the Inspector General's Department wore the staff officers' US in a wreath. (Wreath approximately 2 1/2 inches wide)

Fig. 21-2.

Fig. 21-2. Between 1890 and 1903 Inspector General's Department members wore shoulder knots bearing a "gold or gilt" metal insignia. (Metal insignia 1 1/8 inch wide)

Fig. 21-3.

Fig. 21-4.

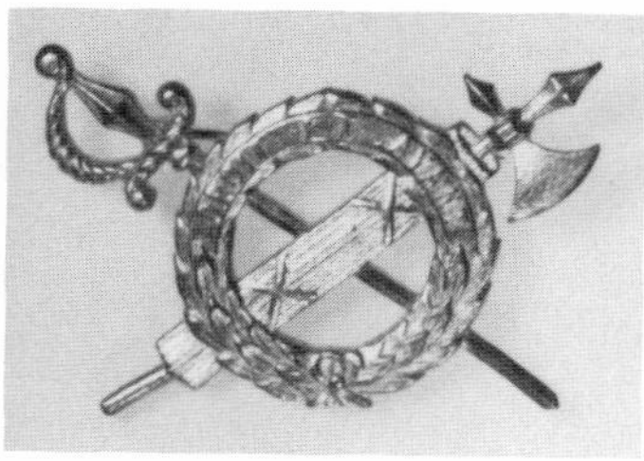

Fig. 21-5.

Fig. 21-6.

Fig. 21-7.

Fig. 21-8.

Fig. 21-9.

Fig. 21-10.

Fig. 21-3. *An embroidered collar insignia introduced in 1893 for the 1892-pattern sack coat. (Design approximately 1 3/16 inches wide)*

Fig. 21-4. *Imitation embroidery was popular between 1893 and World War I. This example has four loops on the reverse so it could be sewn to the coat. (1 9/16 inches wide)*

Fig. 21-5. *Sword grips like this and those previously shown with a diamond shape usually predate the more realistically shaped grips. This is an early-twentieth-century gilt, pin-back Inspector General's Department collar insignia. (1 9/16 inches wide)*

Figs. 21-6 and 21-7. *Very large standing-collar dress coat insignia used before World War I. (1 9/16 and 1 7/16 inches wide, respectively)*

Fig. 21-8. *J. J. Astor as a member of the Spanish-American War Inspector General's Department. The coat collar, cuffs, and shoulder loops were dark blue for a staff officer.*

Figs. 21-9 and 21-10. *World War I and earlier bronze collar insignia. Like the gilt pieces, these came with sword grips in both diamond and conventional shapes. (1 21/32 and 1 5/8 inches wide, respectively)*

Fig. 21-11. *A bronze World War I collar insignia, made in France. Rather than spell out the motto, which was usually on the upper part of the wreath, the die sinker used a series of vertical lines. (1 5/32 inches wide)*

Figs. 21-12 and 21-13. *Bronze shirt collar insignia, about World War I. (49/64 and 63/64 inch wide, respectively)*

and the star. Correspondence shows that although regulations required an embroidered insignia of a crossed sword and fasces with a wreath bearing the motto "Droit et Avant," men mainly used gold metal insignia.[3] An example in imitation embroidery (etruscan finish) is shown in Fig. 21-4. Most of these early metal insignia have a diamond-shaped sword grip, although not all were in imitation embroidery (Fig. 21-5). Later insignia have a realistic sword guard and grip (Figs. 21-6 and 21-7). John J. Astor is shown in Fig. 21-8, wearing the proper department insignia but incorrect *USV*.

Officers' Bronze Insignia

Turn-of-the-century regulations specified officers' high-collar coat insignia to be one inch high, and during World War I, regulations allowed smaller shirt collar insignia.[4] These were made with both types of sword grips (Figs. 21-9 and 21-10). Instead of a Latin motto, only vertical marks were placed on the wreath of a smaller device (Fig. 21-11) made in France during World War I. Shirt collar insignia also came in bronze during the World War I period (Figs. 21-12 and 21-13).

Fig. 21-11.

Fig. 21-12.

Fig. 21-13.

Fig. 21-14.

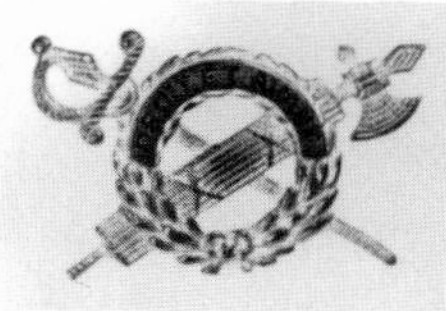

Fig. 21-15.

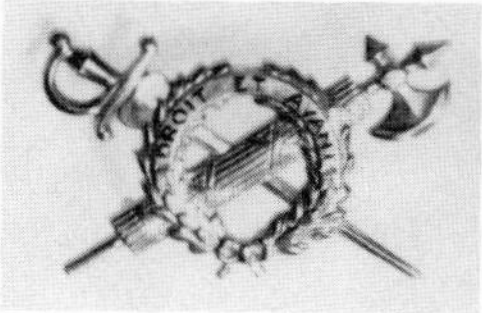

Fig. 21-16.

Fig. 21-17.

Fig. 21-18.

Fig. 21-19.

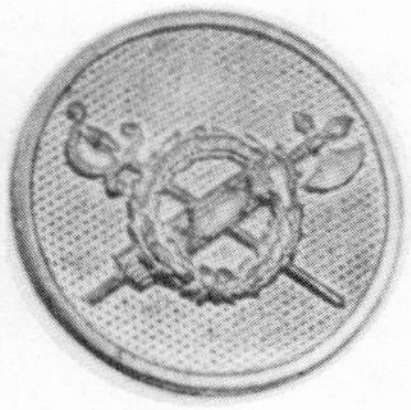

Fig. 21-20.

Officers' Post–World War I Gilt Insignia

The army changed the motto to blue enamel in November 1924; thus, a 1-inch-high insignia with enamel is from the postwar period (Fig. 21-14). Small shirt insignia, 3/4 inch high, were introduced after World War I. These smaller insignia made the transition to the present collar ornaments in March 1926 (Fig. 21-15). The official June 1936 design restored the diamond-gripped sword, with an overall height of 3/4 inch (Fig. 21-16).[5] An oversized and modernized insignia, made during World War II, with an applied circle instead of the wreath, by a New York City dealer, is shown in Fig. 21-17. Major General Andrew Anderson is shown in Fig. 21-18, wearing typical post World War II inspector general insignia.

Enlisted Staff Insignia

Except for a short period after World War I, the army did not allow enlisted personnel detailed to assist inspector generals to wear disks with the inspectors' device until mid-1976. The bronze post–World War I insignia, introduced in May 1919, is shown in Fig. 21-19. An early 1920s nonregulation gilt disk is shown in Fig. 21-20. The official cessation of the enlisted inspectors' disk is not known, but it was still being issued in the fall of 1920. By 1921 enlisted men had quit wearing the insignia, since by mid-1921 the National Defense Act of 1920 had taken effect, and only officers were authorized as inspectors.[6]

In June 1976, the army chief of staff authorized the approximately 370 enlisted personnel serving in inspector generals' offices to wear a disk version of the insignia. Before that time, enlisted personnel assigned inspector duties wore branch unassigned or MOS-related insignia.[7] (MOS stands for military occupation speciality, and is an alphanumeric code used as a short title for various army jobs.)

Fig. 21-14. *Before 1924 the motto "Droit et Avant" was made with raised letters. In that year blue enamel words, as in this example, were first prescribed. This large size went out with the standing-collar coat. (1 5/8 inches wide)*

Figs. 21-15 and 21-16. *Lapel coat and shirt collar insignia of the general size prescribed in March 1926. The first, in imitation embroidery, is slightly smaller than the norm. In June 1936 the Quartermaster Corps officially revived the diamond-gripped sword and introduced an S-shaped guard. The standard width was 1 1/8 inches wide. Various minor design variations have continued to the present. During the 1960s the army again replaced the diamond-shaped grip with a more realistic one. (1 inch and 1 11/64 inches wide, respectively)*

Fig. 21-17. *An oversized, clutch-back officers' insignia made during World War II by the Luxenberg Company, which made high-quality uniforms and insignia. (1 3/8 inches wide)*

Fig. 21-18. *Major General Andrew H. Anderson, assistant inspector general of the U.S. Army, 1981, wearing typical insignia for those detailed to the office of the inspector general.*

Fig. 21-19. *Starting in mid-1919 and continuing for one to one and one-half years, the army issued enlisted Inspector General's Department Insignia for the few soldiers assigned to work with officers of the department. (1 inch in diameter)*

Fig. 21-20. *A nonregulation gilt disk insignia from after World War I. (1 inch in diameter)*

Chapter Twenty-Two

Pay and Finance

Fig. 22-1. From 1841 through 1872 Pay Department officers used the letters PD on their epaulettes.

Fig. 22-2. An example of 1841–51 Pay Department epaulettes.

THE 1820 ARMY paymasters wore the general staff uniform, with the exception that the chapeau had only the cockade, omitting the small eagle normally applied to the cockade center. Evidently neither the paymasters nor other officers liked this arrangement, and the following year uniform regulations stated that paymasters would not wear any uniforms. The paymaster general and paymasters began to wear the standard army uniform, with wings, in 1825. Introduced in 1832 was a dark blue double-breasted coat bearing two rows of ten buttons each. The standing collar and the skirt linings were blue, the staff color. Two gold-embroidered blind buttonholes decorated each side of the paymaster general's collar, while paymasters had one blind buttonhole. Paymasters of 1832 also wore general staff cocked hats, except for the ornamentation, which was limited to a cockade and gilt eagle.[1]

Modified in 1841, the dark blue collar carried a 5-inch gold-embroidered laurel branch. The outer edges of the coat collar carried an embroidered "gold vine of laurel leaves." The 3-inch-deep cuffs also had similar laurel and vine embroidery. Another 1841 addition was epaulettes. Within the epaulette crescent was a gold laurel wreath with the old English *PD* (Figs. 22-1 and 22-2). The paymaster general also wore a silver metal eagle on the epaulette strap to show his rank as a colonel. The coiled bullion fringe was 1/2 inch in diameter and 3 1/2 inches long, while paymasters wore silver bullion of the same size. Pay department officers generally wore staff uniforms between 1851 and 1872, with the silver old English *PD* on the epaulettes. From 1872 until 1891, when plain dark blue knots came into use, pay officers' knots carried the same letters.[2]

Officers' sack coats, introduced in 1892, created a need for special branch insignia. Selected in 1896 was a gilt metal, imitation embroidery blind buttonhole 1 inch long

Fig. 22-1.

Fig. 22-2.

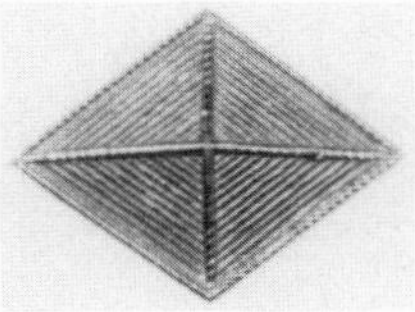

Fig. 22-3.

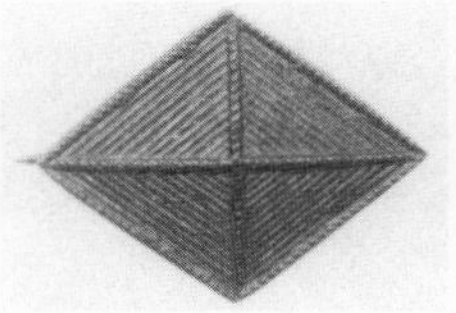

Fig. 22-4.

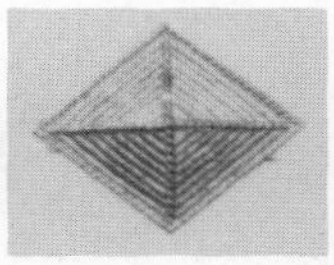

Fig. 22-5.

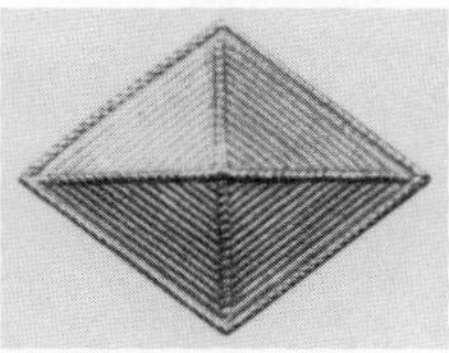

Fig. 22-6.

Fig. 22-7.

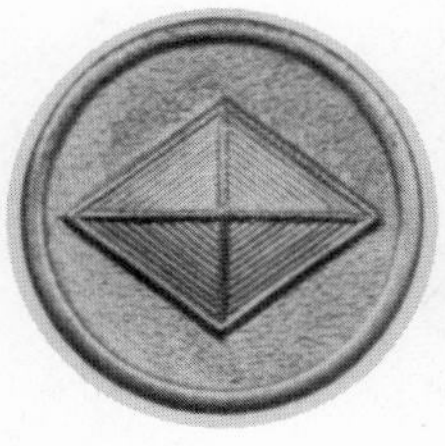

Fig. 22-8.

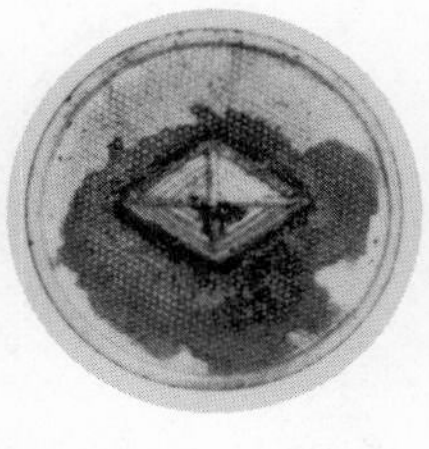

Fig. 22-9.

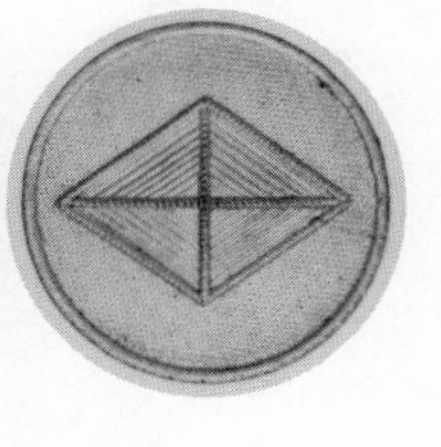

Fig. 22-10.

Fig. 22-11.

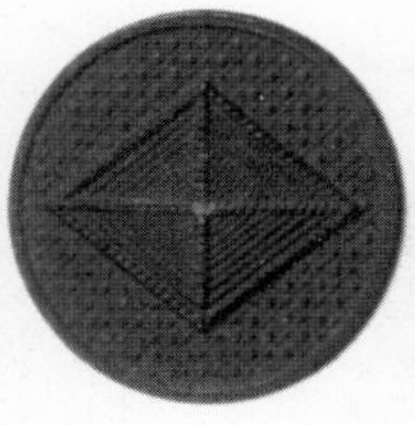

Fig. 22-12.

and 3/4 inch high (Fig. 22-3). Evidently its basis was the 1832–41 paymasters' blind buttonhole. If one takes a regular buttonhole and pulls on each side of the opening, it makes a diamond shape. This may be the reason for the shape adopted in 1896. In the late 1890s the paymaster general wore a silver blind buttonhole on the epaulette strap, while the assistant paymaster general (a colonel) wore a silver blind buttonhole on the shoulder knot strap. Other pay officers used a silver insignia on the shoulder knot pad. In 1912 the Pay, Quartermaster General's, and Commissary departments merged to form the Quartermaster Corps.[3]

Officers' Insignia after 1920

In June 1920, Congress separated the pay responsibilities from the Quartermaster Corps and formed the Finance Department, with an authorization of up to 142 officers. For a branch insignia the War Department revived the old Pay Department device, discarded in 1912. A subdued bronze insignia, 1 inch by 3/4 inch (Fig. 22-4) went on the coat collar. A smaller piece went on the shirt collar (Fig. 22-5). In 1923, gilt insignia returned for service wear (Fig. 22-6). This device has continued to the present in the 1 inch by 3/4 inch size. Congress retitled the Finance Department the Finance Corps in 1950.[4]

Enlisted Staff Insignia

Enlisted finance clerks began to wear the finance insignia in 1920 when Congress authorized nine hundred enlisted men for the new Finance Department.[5] Men stationed in Germany with the occupation forces had the disks shown in Figs. 22-7 and 22-8 made. That of Fig. 22-7 is grey metal painted black, and that of Fig. 22-8 is gilt. Both were made like a button and have the back marked "EXTRA FEIN." Gilt Finance Department disks made in the United States are shown in Figs. 22-9 and 22-10. The piece in Fig. 22-9 was made by a diamond soldered to a plain disk, in response to the limited demand caused by the nine hundred soldiers. The small number did not make it worthwhile for several makers to cut new dies. An early U.S.-made bronze disk for wartime wear is shown in Fig. 22-11, and the more common pattern of background in wartime bronze is shown in Fig. 22-12. This second pattern also exists in gilt (Fig. 22-13). World War II and later flat insignia are shown in Figs. 22-14 and 22-15, and domed disks are shown in Figs. 22-16 and 22-17.

Fig. 22-3. *An 1896–1913 gilt Pay Department officers' coat collar insignia. (1 1/32 inches wide)*

Fig. 22-4. *A bronze etruscan (imitation embroidered) officers' collar device, worn by Pay Department officers from 1902 until 1913 and by Finance Department officers after 1920 until 1923. (1 1/16 inches wide)*

Fig. 22-5. *A gilt shirt collar insignia for Finance Department officers used from 1923 into the 1930s. (45/64 inch wide)*

Fig. 22-6. *Lapel coats carried the same size of insignia as the high-collar coats. This nominal 1 inch by 3/4 inch insignia is still worn today. (1 1/64 inches wide)*

Figs. 22-7 and 22-8. *Bronze and gilt enlisted clerks' collar insignia for the Finance Department, both made in Germany after 1920.*

Fig. 22-9. *This early 1920s gilt enlisted clerks' disk has the diamond soldered to a plain background. The dark irregular area resulted from the flow of the solder flux a half century ago. (1 inch in diameter)*

Fig. 22-10. *A properly sized gilt enlisted men's Finance Department insignia from the mid-1920s. (1 inch in diameter)*

Figs. 22-11 and 22-12. *Bronze finance collar disks made with the second style of background. Fig. 22-11 has a "netted" background, while Fig. 22-12 has a prescribed background of lines and shields. (Each 1 inch in diameter)*

Fig. 22-13.

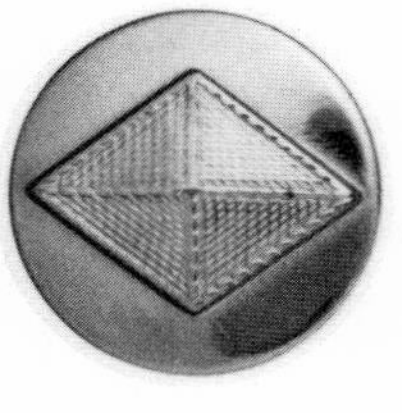

Fig. 22-14.

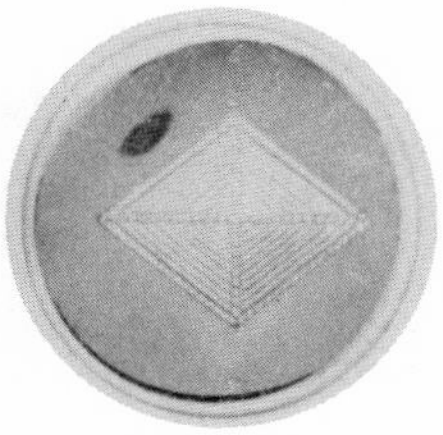

Fig. 22-15.

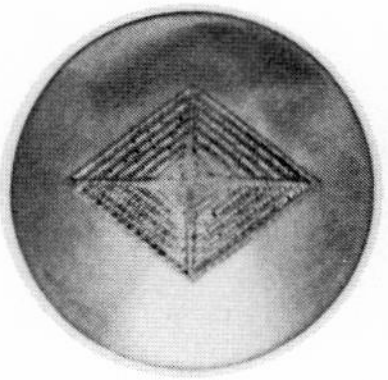

Fig. 22-16.

Fig. 22-17.

Fig. 22-13. *An official-pattern 1930s Finance Department collar insignia. (1 inch in diameter)*

Fig. 22-14. *Embossed disks similar to this one were introduced during World War II and issued into the 1970s. (1 inch in diameter)*

Fig. 22-15. *A silver-plated separable Finance Corps enlisted clerks' insignia with a flat background. ($1\frac{1}{32}$ inches in diameter)*

Figs. 22-16 and 22-17. *These two silver convex enlisted clerks' insignia show some of the variations in the post–World War II collar disks. (1 inch and $1\frac{1}{32}$ inches in diameter, respectively)*

Section X

Branch Insignia with Histories from the Civil War to 1910

Chapter Twenty-Three

Signal Corps

Born of the great deadly conflict now called the Civil War, the Signal Corps comprised an elite and separate group within the army for many years. Charged with providing the rapid transmission of messages, it was soon saddled with observations, including reporting the weather. During the 1870s and 1880s the Signal Corps formed a national weather service until the weather recording and reporting function, with the requisite men, was transferred to the Department of Commerce to form the National Weather Service.

The Signal Corps had several other unique functions, including the establishment of communications in Alaska, a new territory with few cities and a forbidding climate. Signal Corps troops in that remote part of the world wore special clothing during the arctic exploration that was part of their work. Even early military aircraft belonged to the Signal Corps until well into World War I, when the flyers separated to form the Air Service.

These factors, and others, resulted in a diversity of Signal Corps clothing and insignia, which, coupled with the fact that the history of the early uniforms is not clearly outlined in normal regulations and orders, makes a precise history difficult. There are two reasons records are now hard to find. First, the Signal Corps had few personnel. The small circle of men learned of the prescribed uniform and changes to it by direct contact with other signalmen. Second, the Signal Corps sometimes published its own orders, including uniform information, or used letters instead of general orders. These letters or orders circulated only in limited Signal Corps channels, and few are preserved today.[1]

Congress initially authorized one signal officer on 21 June 1860 as part of the army staff and organized the Signal Corps as a branch by the Act of 3 March 1863. The first signal officer was Assistant Surgeon Albert Myer, appointed to the position of chief signal officer as a staff major. The accoutrements of signal soldiers between 1860 and 1889 are something of a mystery, awaiting further keys to unlock our knowledge. A little is known about the early days, including the initial establishment of the first known distinctive Signal Corps insignia, a chevron, over a year after the founding of the corps. The Signal Corps controlled its own uniforms until 1891, when the Quartermaster General's Department began to treat the corps like other branches.[2]

Officers' Cap Ornaments

In July 1864 the Signal Bureau chief specified the cap insignia for signal officers: "A gold embroidered wreath on [a] black velvet ground, encircling crossed signal flag, with lighted torch and supported by the letters US in silver, old English characters, color of flags are red with white center, the other white with red center; size of flag three eights of an inch square, size of center are one eight of an inch square, length of staff one and one sixteenth inches."[3]

The following month, four dozen of these cap ornaments were ordered for the officers of the Signal Corps. They may not have been the first distinctive insignia worn by Signal Corps officers, but they are the earliest such devices recorded.[4]

Regulations of 1872 assigned all staff officers, including those of the Signal Service, the cap insignia of silver *US* in a gold wreath,

Fig. 23-1.

Fig. 23-2.

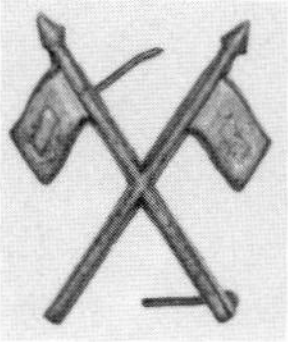

Fig. 23-3.

Fig. 23-4.

Fig. 23-5.

Fig. 23-6.

Fig. 23-1. *A Signal Corps officers' forage cap device from the Smithsonian Institution collection. It is believed that this device was made about 1892–95. (Wreath 2 7/16 inches wide)*

Fig. 23-2. *This Signal Corps officers' cap insignia is on the more common oval background. (Wreath 2 3/8 inches wide)*

Fig. 23-3. *The first-pattern helmet overlay, crossed flags without a torch, was used by enlisted men of the Signal Corps. This German silver insignia went on the 1881-pattern helmet eagle and was used until 1885. (27/64 inch wide)*

Fig. 23-4. *To the drooping crossed flags for helmets, enlisted men in 1885 added a torch, and usually the flags were square, as in this example. (1 3/32 inches wide)*

Fig. 23-5. *Signal Corps officers initially added this large device on the 1881 pattern helmet eagle. Like infantry, cavalry, and artillery officers, early Signal Corps officers added their branch insignia and the shield to the 1881-pattern helmet eagle. This short-lived insignia was not mentioned in regulations published armywide. (2 15/16 inches wide)*

Fig. 23-6. *A first lieutenants' Signal Corps shoulder knot used through 1902. The insignia was silver and gold and apparently was in use by at least 1884, although it may have been introduced as early as December 1872. This particular piece was probably made at the end of the 1890s.*

although it is possible that signal officers actually continued to wear crossed flags, with or without a torch, in a wreath. One Civil War veteran is known to have used a wreath enclosing crossed flags in the 1880s, so this cap or hat device without a torch was certainly made. General Orders 86 of 1878 called out a forage cap insignia, "according to the pattern deposited in the office of the Chief Signal Officer." It is assumed that this device is the one later described in 1884, consisting of gold-embroidered flags and a torch in a wreath (Figs. 23-1 and 23-2). This device lasted until 1895.[5]

Helmet Insignia

Signal troops, along with cavalry soldiers, wore English horse guard–style helmets from 1872 until 1881, then with the revised 1881 helmet the signalmen wore an overlay of crossed silver signal flags (Fig. 23-3) until 1885, when a new overlay with a torch and two flags (Fig. 23-4) came into use.[6]

Signal Corps officers began to wear a special gilt helmet ornament in June 1884 (Fig. 23-5), although it is not known how long the insignia lasted, since shortly after the introduction of this device the army moved the authority to prescribe signal uniforms to the quartermaster general, who authorized only the small silver overlay on the standard helmet eagle.[7] The large insignia was not mentioned in regulations.

Shoulder Knots and Epaulettes

Regulations of 1872 specified embroidered old English letters *SS* for Signal Service officers' knots. Six years later the insignia was "according to pattern," but in April 1884 the adjutant general published a general order making a change to "two crossed flags and a torch, according to pattern," effective 1 July 1884. One may assume the signal device was, starting in 1884, gold and silver instead of gold alone, since later orders called for epaulette insignia of gold and silver "according to pattern."[8] These continued through 1902. A complete Signal Corps first lieutenants' knot is shown in Fig. 23-6, and a second lieutenants' knot center is shown in Fig. 23-7, illustrating two different Signal Corps insignia.

Fig. 23-7.

From May 1900 through 1903 the chief signal officer added an embroidered gold and silver signal device to the epaulette straps worn on his dress uniform.[9]

ENLISTED MEN'S CAP AND HAT INSIGNIA

Photographic evidence shows that some enlisted signalmen wore crossed flags on their caps during the Civil War, but the pictures do not lead us to the dates of use. In July 1864 enlisted men were to wear on both hats and caps "crossed signal flags of yellow metal, length of staff one and one-fourth inches, size of flags seven sixteenths of an inch." In the 1880s a Civil War Signal Corps veteran, J. Willard Brown, wrote a corps history in which many Signal Corps personnel appear in postage-stamp-sized photographs. While some of the pictures were obviously taken after the Civil War, one does show a young man wearing a low-crowned, straight-brimed hat bearing large crossed signal flags. Because of the youthful appearance of the soldier, it is probable that his likeness was captured during the Civil War. The crossed flags themselves are on staffs perhaps 3 inches long and may be of metal, since no background required for embroidery is apparent.[10]

In recent years, evidence has emerged to indicate that a completely different cap device saw Civil War use. The insignia, shown in Fig. 23-8, is 2 inches high and 2¼ inches wide with the letters *US* and stars in silver, with the flags and insignia edge in gold, and with red silk centers in the flags. Evidently some sort of cap ornament continued until 1882, and perhaps longer, since in 1882 enlisted men were expressly forbidden by the chief signal officer to wear cap insignia, although this may have meant that the dress helmet was to be worn. In December 1887 enlisted men finally received the crossed flags and a vertical torch in a wreath for wear on the forage cap.[11]

Fig. 23-8.

Fig. 23-9.

A special uniform prescribed in February 1889 for men of the Signal Corps included a cap device "of crossed flags and torch embroidered on dark blue cloth, in silk and bullion, in high relief, attached to the front of the cap." This unusual embroidered insignia was replaced in 1891 by the common noncommissioned officers' metal cap device of the helmet overlay within a stamped brass wreath. Screw-post fastening devices, introduced in 1896 to replace the earlier wire backs, created a new cap insignia (Fig. 23-9). After the start of the Spanish-American War the army formed the first signal companies, with the Regular Army companies lettered

Fig. 23-7. *This is the center of an 1872–1902 Signal Corps second lieutenants' shoulder knot (the same basic insignia shown in Fig. 23-6, except for the rank). This pad was embroidered about 1890, and only the flags and flame have both silver and gold, while the previous insignia had the spear tips and the upper part of the torch in silver as well.*

Fig. 23-8. *This embroidered cap device is unusual in that it was used by an enlisted man. The small size of the Signal Corps and its exclusive status may account for the use of embroidered insignia by enlisted men. The use of metal crossed flags during the Civil War is documented, but genuine examples are unknown.*

Fig. 23-9. *An 1896–1905 Signal Corps cap insignia. The number above was introduced for volunteer companies during the Spanish-American War. Regular Army companies were lettered during the time large wreaths were used. Until 1901 all men wore this insignia; then it became the property of noncommissioned officers only. (2 15/32 inches wide)* and the volunteer companies numbered. The difference should be noted, because in some cases designations appear as part of the insignia, as shown in Fig. 23-9. Initially, all signal soldiers wore this gold wreath with silver crossed flags and torch, but in 1901 the War Department directed those men who were not noncommissioned officers to remove the gilt wreath from around the signal insignia (Fig. 23-10). The privates' cap ornament changed further when the flags and torch became all gilt in 1903.[12]

A smaller gilt wreath around the silver signal device (Fig. 23-11) was introduced in 1905 for noncommissioned officers except for master signal electricians. As with the previous insignia, the Regular Army pieces bore no unit designations, and for service uniforms the Quartermaster General's Department made bronze-colored insignia.[13] Fig. 23-12 shows one such bronze insignia for privates.

Fig. 23-10. *Privates' cap insignia for the Signal Corps were, like this example, silver from 1901 until 1903, when the plain flags and torch were made in all gilt. (1 9/32 inches wide)*

Fig. 23-11. *A silver-centered insignia with a small gilt wreath date this noncommissioned officers' Signal Corps insignia as the type used from 1905 until 1917. The same design, in bronze, was used with the service uniform until 1918. (1 29/32 inches wide)*

Fig. 23-12. *Signal Corps bronze cap insignia for the enlisted men's service uniform. (1 3/32 inches wide)*

Fig. 23-13. *A turn-of-the-century officers' collar insignia. One flag is gold with a silver center and the other is silver with a gold center. The balance of the insignia is in gold. Small loops on the back are slightly visible at the ends of the flagstaffs. The number indicates that the insignia was made for a state organization instead of the Regular Army. (1 13/64 inches wide)*

Fig. 23-14. *An officers' insignia in imitation embroidery, from about 1900. This particular device is bronze, although this same design exists in gold and silver. (1 1/4 inches wide)*

Fig. 23-15. *A common World War I bronze collar insignia. (1 15/64 inches wide)*

Fig. 23-16. *This World War I officers' collar insignia was made in England and has a tan finish instead of black. (1 7/32 inches wide)*

Between 1905 and 1907 men of the Signal Corps wore bronze signal insignia, of the same design as shown in Fig. 23-12 but with a pin back, on the front of the campaign hat in addition to the branch-colored hat cords. Between 1899 and 1902 the Signal Corps used black cords with tassels on the ends; after 1902 it used orange and white cords with acorn-shaped ends.[14]

Officers' Collar Insignia, 1893–1921

On the 1893 sack coat collar, signal officers wore embroidered flags and a torch in gilt and silver; the front flag was silver with a gold center. Fig. 23-13 shows an example of metal insignia, with colored silver and gold flags, made for New York's 1st Signal Company. The Spanish-American War saw the use of all gold-colored flags and torch on the service uniform, but by 1900 the silver and gold were again prescribed before the corps again reverted to all gilt in 1912.[15]

Bronze devices were introduced in 1902. In some cases manufacturers used older imitation embroidery dies, as reflected in Fig. 23-14, to make bronze insignia. More common are bronze insignia such as those shown in Figs. 23-15 and 23-16, the latter made overseas during World War I.

Initially the Air Service was part of the Signal Corps, and during 1917 and early 1918 some aviators wore signal devices with small wings superimposed on Signal Corps collar devices. Because of their relation to aviation history, these ornaments are discussed with Air Corps insignia in chapter 38.

Shirt Insignia

Examples of early-twentieth-century bronze insignia are shown in Figs. 23-17, 23-18, 23-19, and 23-20, and all-gilt insignia are illustrated in Figs. 23-21 and 23-22. Small enameled shirt insignia with red and white flags, first used in March 1926, are shown in Figs. 23-23 and 23-24.[16]

Officers' Insignia, 1921–Present

The army introduced 1-inch-high all-gilt signal insignia for the white uniforms in October 1921 and for the service uniform two years later. Enameled insignia with red and white flags replaced the gilt ones in March 1926. Officially, after 1926 the 7/8-inch-high insignia were for the lapel coat and the shirt and the 1-inch-high insignia were to be worn on the standing-collar coat. After the 1926 change, regulations called for the 7/8-inch size to be made with the wearer's right flag red with a white center. For the 1-inch size the flags came in pairs so the white flag would be worn to the front. Quartermaster drawings of 1936 show the 7/8-inch insignia with the note that the device would have the flags enameled in pairs for the sleeves of the blue mess uniform. Examples of 7/8-inch-high insignia with the proper and improper crossed flags are shown in Figs. 23-25 and 23-26, respectively.[17]

Shortly after World War II the collar ornament illustrated in Fig. 23-27 was made in Germany for officers of the 13th Signal Battalion. A more common style of insignia with unit number is shown in Fig. 23-28. The 1967 army switch to subdued insignia resulted in an embroidered insignia made about 1970 in Germany with the red portion

Fig. 23-17.

Fig. 23-18.

Fig. 23-19.

Fig. 23-20.

Fig. 23-21.

Fig. 23-22.

Fig. 23-23.

Fig. 23-24.

Fig. 23-25.

Fig. 23-17. *Two Signal Corps officers in late 1918. The collar insignia are clearly visible on the officer on the left. The officer on the right is wearing an experimental helmet.*

Figs. 23-18, 23-19, and 23-20. *Not only did designs vary, but so did size, as exemplified by these three shirt collar officers' insignia. (13/16, 51/64 and 23/32 inch wide, respectively)*

Figs. 23-21 and 23-22. *Two post–World War I all-gilt insignia for use on shirts until 1926. (45/64 and 27/32 inch wide, respectively)*

Figs. 23-23 and 23-24. *A pair of shirt collar insignia introduced in 1926. These are smaller than regulation size. The matched pair of flags were commonly made only on the larger insignia. (Each 23/32 inch wide)*

Fig. 23-25. *This insignia is the size prescribed for the lapel coat before World War II. The white flag on the observer's left, as in this example, shows the proper enameling. (15/16 inch wide)*

Fig. 23-26.

Fig. 23-27.

Fig. 23-28.

Fig. 23-29.

Fig. 23-30.

Fig. 23-31.

Fig. 23-32.

Fig. 23-33.

Fig. 23-34.

Fig. 23-35.

Fig. 23-36.

Fig. 23-37.

Fig. 23-38.

Fig. 23-26. *During the 1930s some Signal Corps insignia were made with the flags in pairs. As a result, some insignia have the red and white enamel reversed from the normal case, as shown. (31/32 inch wide)*

Fig. 23-27. *Made in Germany after World War II, this 13th Signal Battalion insignia has the number on an arc and the spaces between the lower staffs and the flags solid. (1 15/64 inches wide)*

Fig. 23-28. *Several Signal Corps units had numbers added directly to the torch top. This style of construction is typical of insignia made in the United States. (1 1/4 inches wide)*

Fig. 23-29. *In this German-made subdued insignia, the red color remains, with all other color in black. (Design 1 9/32 inches wide)*

Fig. 23-30. *This Vietnamese-made subdued insignia was worn during 1966–67. Both flags have a red center, with the balance of the device embroidered in black. (Design 1 3/32 inches wide)*

Fig. 23-31. *The 1900–1902 enlisted men's white coat collar insignia made in a gold-colored metal. (1 3/32 inches wide)*

Fig. 23-32. *From 1903 until 1917, enlisted men wore this type of branch device on the collar of their dress blue uniform. (1 7/32 inches wide)*

Figs. 23-33 and 23-34. *Enlisted signalers' bronze disk insignia like these come in numerous variations. (Each 1 inch in diameter)*

Fig. 23-35. *A gilt post-1923 collar insignia struck from an early die with a stippled or pebbled background, originally made before World War I. (1 inch in diameter)*

Fig. 23-36. *Of the issue, gold-colored branch disks used between the world wars, this Signal Corps design is somewhat more difficult to locate. (1 1/64 inches in diameter)*

Figs. 23-37 and 23-38. *Two of many designs for enlisted men's two-piece, separable flat disks. (Each 1 3/64 inches in diameter)*

Fig. 23-39.

Fig. 23-40.

Fig. 23-41.

Fig. 23-42.

Fig. 23-43.

Fig. 23-44.

Fig. 23-45.

Fig. 23-46.

Fig. 23-39. *A stamped issue disk with an orange plastic edging. The use of any colored trim other than blue for infantry was not authorized. ($1\frac{1}{4}$ inches in diameter)*

Fig. 23-40. *This enlisted men's disk has a screw post for fastening to the lapel coat. It was made in India during World War II. ($\frac{61}{64}$ inch in diameter)*

Figs. 23-41 and 23-42. *Two brass-colored domed disks made after World War II. (Each $1\frac{1}{32}$ in diameter)*

Fig. 23-43. *This silver-plated insignia has the background domed and the center of the two flags cut out. (1 inch in diameter)*

Fig. 23-44. *This disk was made in the late 1970s for the 1st Cavalry Division's 13th Signal Battalion. (1 inch in diameter)*

Fig. 23-45. *This yellow gold–plated disk was made in Germany. ($\frac{63}{64}$ inch in diameter)*

Fig. 23-46. *This disk was made in Vietnam for soldiers to wear on their khaki uniforms upon their return to the United States. The background material for the brass disk is especially thin and may bend easily. ($\frac{15}{16}$ inch wide)*

of the flags in color and the rest of the insignia in the prescribed black (Fig. 23-29). A device embroidered in Vietnam is shown in Fig. 23-30.

Enlisted Signalers' Collar Insignia

Between 1872 and 1885 men of several small branches wore their staff department insignia, although the Signal Corps did not do so, despite regulations. During 1900–1902, when men in southern areas were authorized to wear white duck coats with the "device of the corps in yellow metal" on the collar, the Signal Corps insignia were of the same die as the helmet overlay (Fig. 23-31). With the 1902 uniform regulations, Signal Corps enlisted men began to wear 1-inch-tall gilt (Figs. 23-32) and bronze (Fig. 23-15) collar ornaments.[18]

Bronze disks, introduced in 1910 and worn until 1923, exist in many variations, including those shown in Figs. 23-33 and 23-34. Two unusual signal disks exist either with three lightning bolts or with a telephone pole in place of the torch. Both were struck for collectors in the 1970s. Gilt disks (Figs. 23-35 and 23-36) replaced the bronze disks in the 1920s and in turn were replaced by the screw-post, two-piece disks (Figs. 23-37 and 23-38) in the 1930s. Some Signal Corps enlisted men wore an unauthorized orange trim around their disks in the 1950s, as illustrated in Fig. 23-39, which shows the stamped, thin metal disk issued during most of World War II.

Variations of disks used during and after World War II include one made in India (Fig. 23-40), two domed disks popular in the 1950s (Figs. 23-41 and 23-42), and a domed disk with the flag centers pierced (Fig. 23-43). Insignia from the 1970s include one with a unit number (Fig. 23-44) as finally authorized in September 1966, a disk made in Germany (Fig. 23-45), and one made in Vietnam (Fig. 23-46).

Shoulder Belts

With the new 1902 regulations came a unique branch symbol. Officers of the Signal Corps added, for full dress, "a shoulder belt . . . with field glasses attached." The belt, worn over one shoulder, was all gold lace for field-grade officers, or was of four stripes of gold lace interwoven with black for company-grade officers. On the small black leather field glasses pouch was an eagle and Signal Corps device. Captain Billy Mitchell is shown wearing one of these shoulder belts in Fig. 2-10 of chapter 2, although his belt has five gold stripes instead of the regulation four.[19]

INDIAN SCOUTS AND FIRST SPECIAL SERVICE FORCE

Fig. 24-1. Indian Scouts, 1891, in the special uniform prescribed from 1890 until 1903. Chevrons were white with red piping. Cords were white with some red intermixed on a special low-crowned hat carrying a silver-colored insignia.

BY ACT OF 28 JULY 1866, Congress authorized the Army to have a Corps of Indian Scouts. Until that time, Indians employed as scouts and guides were not actually soldiers but were simply considered employees. The history of Indians employed by the U.S. Army is a long one. Indians aided American troops in the Revolution, during the War of 1812, and in many lesser skirmishes. Indians fought on both sides in the Civil War, with at least one serving as a general. In 1891 the War Department manned some cavalry troops and infantry companies with Indians. These men served as regular troops and wore standard uniforms, and they were not Indian Scouts.[1]

The 1866 scouts wore castoff and obsolete uniforms. This practice continued until 1890, when special uniforms and insignia were prescribed. First Lieutenant Edward Casey, commander of the Indian Scouts troop at Fort Keough, Montana, wrote the secretary of war in June 1890 to propose a special Indian Scouts uniform. War Department Circular 10, dated 15 August 1890, authorized a unique Indian Scouts uniform and described it virtually unchanged from that envisioned by Lieutenant Casey. The specially designed service uniform is shown in Fig. 24-1. It included a black felt fatigue hat with a 3½-inch brim and a 3½-inch crown. A white hat cord with a red strand intermixed decorated the hat, along with a special hat ornament. The standard dark blue shirt was modified to have a deeper collar "to hold a neck-handkerchief."[2]

One truly different article was the overcoat. Casey designed it with lots of room to fit over all accoutrements. It was long (within 10 inches of the ground) and slit well up the rear to allow comfortable seating on a saddle, and it had a pointed hood. A surviving example from the Fort Sill Museum collection is shown in Fig. 24-2.[3]

Fig. 24-1.

Fig. 24-2.

Fig. 24-2. An Indian Scouts overcoat, as prescribed in 1890. The pointed hood is distinctive of the coat given Indian Scouts, as other soldiers' coat hoods were more rounded. Scouts overcoats lacked capes and had covered slits on each side so the men could easily reach revolvers and ammunition.

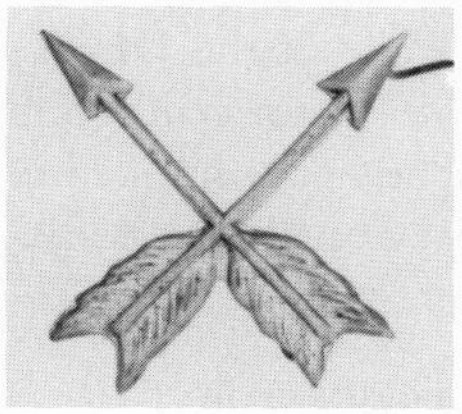

Fig. 24-3.

Fig. 24-3. The silver-colored helmet overlay used by Indian Scouts with their dress uniforms. (61/64 inch wide)

Scout dress uniforms were generally similar to standard uniforms, with chevrons, trouser stripes, and other trim of white with red trim.[4] When the Army changed uniforms during the 1902–1905 period, scouts also changed patterns, with white and red trim remaining.

Helmet and Hat Insignia

From 1890 until early in the twentieth century, regulations called for Indian Scouts to wear silver-colored crossed arrows (Fig. 24-3) on the dress uniform's brass helmet plate. The Quartermaster Depot initially stocked this insignia, but by 1900 it had issued all of its initial purchases.[5]

Lieutenant Casey recommended "two arrows crossed, to be made of nickel or of some white metal, three inches in height, the letters USS in the intersection" as the ornament for the special black hat. Shown in Fig. 24-4 is the Indian Scouts hat ornament as depicted in the Office of the Quartermaster General Specification Number 318, dated 10

Fig. 24-4.

Fig. 24-4. U.S. Scouts hat insignia. These silver-colored insignia were reproduced in the 1960s. I know of no complete original insignia. This illustration is from the Quartermaster General's Department's specification published in 1892 for insignia makers.

Fig. 24-5.

Fig. 24-5. With the introduction of bronze-colored hat numbers and letters in 1902 came these block letters for the Indian Scouts. Only the U.S. Scouts had joined letters on hats. This same insignia was for wear on the service uniform collar instead of the US and branch insignia worn by other enlisted men from 1903 until 1910. (1 21/32 inches wide)

March 1892. The Philadelphia Depot issued several hundred of these ornaments and in November 1900 placed another order for 323, at a cost of fifteen cents each. In the 1960s a partial original insignia was used to made a die and restrike copies of this fatigue hat insignia. I know of no complete original hat devices of this type, even though the Philadelphia Depot had 275 in stock in March 1901.[6]

Prescribed in 1902 were the plain block letters *USS*, which stands for United States Scouts (Fig. 24-5). Scouts wore these on the collar of service uniforms and on the campaign hat after 1902 (Fig. 24-6). The authorization for this special hat insignia was withdrawn in 1907 when the army removed all campaign hat metal insignia.[7]

Collar Insignia

Scouts also wore the bronze *USS* hat letters on the service uniform collars until the army introduced collar disks in 1910. At that time the army placed *USS* letters on bronze disks (Fig. 24-7). This insignia is unusual because it replaced both the branch and *US* disks.[8]

In 1902, officers in the Quartermaster General's Department decided not to issue the scouts new dress uniforms, but to give them service uniforms only. Specifications of 1915 call for gilt *USS* letters on the collar in the same design as that of the older bronze. It is doubtful that these letters were made, because no evidence has been found that the Quartermaster Department later issued dress uniforms requiring the gilt letters.[9]

In March 1921, Indian Scouts became members of the Detached Enlisted Men's List (DEML), but instead of giving them the

Fig. 24-6. These two Indian Scouts noncommissioned officers wear the bronze block USS letters on their hats.

Fig. 24-7. With the introduction of disk insignia for enlisted service wear in 1910 came this piece for the Indian Scouts. (1 inch in diameter)

Fig. 24-8. After World War I the army replaced the USS disks with those bearing crossed arrows, like this one. (1 inch in diameter)

Fig. 24-9. First Special Service Force officers' insignia, 1942–44. These were restruck in the 1970s using the original dies. (1 37/64 inches wide)

Fig. 24-6.

eagle from the U.S. great seal, as was done for other DEML members, the army prescribed crossed arrows for the left collar (Fig. 24-8). Few scouts actually wore this disk, for in 1922 only twenty-three men were eligible. With the introduction of the crossed arrows, the *USS* disappeared completely, because the *US* disk came to be worn on the right collar.[10]

During the 1920s and 1930s regulations specified continued use of the crossed arrows. In practice, scouts served as a labor force, assisting carpenters, plumbers, or others. Photographs show that after the 1920s scouts wore whatever insignia was available, including plain *US* disks, various pre–World War I insignia, or the eagle of the DEML. Indian Scouts faded into history, although one Apache scout detachment continued to perform military duties until it was disbanded in 1947.[11]

Fig. 24-7.

Fig. 24-8.

Fig. 24-9.

First Special Service Force

Early in World War II the British desired to form a special unit for action behind enemy lines, with the idea that snow, an obstacle in much of Europe during the winter, would hinder enemy pursuit. If an allied unit were specially equipped and trained for snow operations, it could play an important role in the war effort. Eventually such an organization appeared: the First Special Service Force. This unit contained both U.S. and Canadian personnel. Because of the force's special mission, war planners created a totally new table of organization for it and therefore decided that it was actually a separate arm. Officers for the new unit came from all branches, and indeed, its chief was a coast artilleryman. Operational plans for deployment of the force changed it to an assault force in 1942, and the tables of organization called for weapons similar to those of infantry units. Even so, the War Department authorized a special branch insignia in October 1942, and it inherited the insignia of the Indian Scouts: two crossed arrows.[12]

First Special Service Force personnel were reassigned to conventional units in December 1944, and the army disbanded the unit in January 1945. The insignia disappeared from regulations in 1947. In 1952 the army reactivated the unit and assigned it to the Special Forces. Personnel assigned to the Special Forces wore other branch insignia until the end of 1984, when enlisted men were again issued the historic crossed arrows.[13]

First Special Service Force Insignia

Fig. 24-9 shows one example of the original 1942–44 collar ornament with 1-inch arrows.[14] In the mid-1970s an insignia company restruck the design using original dies. When the army introduced the Special Forces in the 1950s, one manufacturer evidently believed the crossed arrows would be used again and created a new die, from which the device shown in Fig. 24-10 was stamped. In addition, at least one company made embroidered, gold-colored crossed arrows for wear on the fatigue uniform (Fig. 24-11).

In 1942 the enlisted men of the First Special Service Force began to wear crossed arrows. Most common is the one-piece, stamped, issues disk shown in Fig. 24-12. Less common is the two-piece, screw-back version shown in Fig. 24-13. A third, flat disk was struck from new dies in the 1960s (Fig. 24-14), although a domed version is also known (Fig. 24-15). Both Canadians and U.S. soldiers who made up the unit wore U.S.-style insignia, but instead of the usual *US* disk, Canadians wore disks with the word *CANADA*.

In addition to collar insignia, First Special Service Force members adopted a red, white, and blue shoulder cord shown in Fig. 24-16 as distinctive of the branch. The cord, worn by both U.S. and Canadian troops, was braided, and each end was buttoned to the cloth shoulder loop. Since both ends were fixed, the cord is of a simpler design than a fourragere.[15]

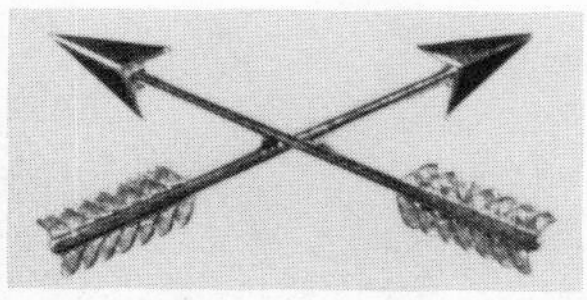

Fig. 24-10.

Fig. 24-11.

Fig. 24-12.

Fig. 24-13.

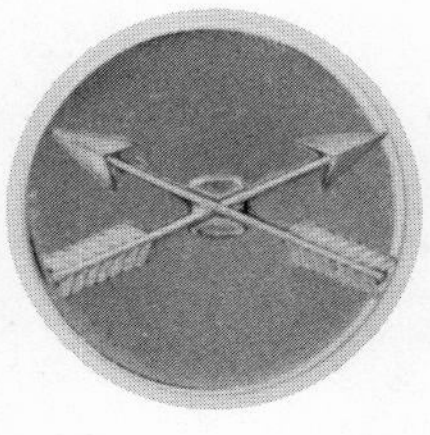

Fig. 24-14.

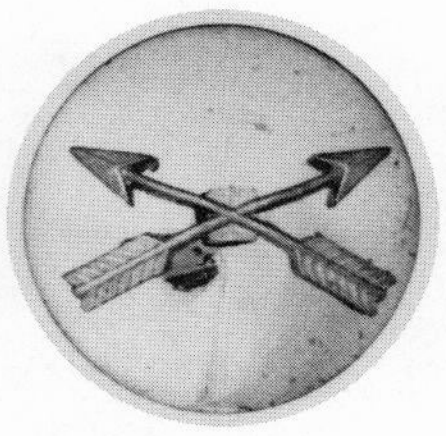

Fig. 24-15.

Special Operations

In February 1984 the J. F. Kennedy Special Warfare Center proposed that the crossed arrow insignia disk be revived for about three thousand men assigned to "special operations," since special operations enlisted men then wore a variety of branch insignia. The army chief of staff approved the request in July 1984. Officers in such assignments later began to wear crossed arrows made in black subdued metal and cloth as well as the bright brass.[16]

Fig. 24-10. *The die for this insignia was made in the 1950s when the Special Forces (the "Green Berets") were organized. When officers began to wear special operations insignia in the late 1980s, the collar insignia were of this style and were made in both subdued black metal and in bright brass. ($1\frac{25}{64}$ inches wide)*

Fig. 24-11. *With the organization of the Special Forces in 1953, some insignia makers believed the World War II insignia of crossed arrows would be authorized. In anticipation of that action, some manufacturers made embroidered insignia like this for the fatigue uniform. (Design $1\frac{17}{32}$ inches wide)*

Fig. 24-12. *An issue, stamped, First Special Service Force enlisted men's collar insignia of World War II. (1 inch in diameter)*

Fig. 24-13. *An early screw-post, separable enlisted men's disk from the 1942–early 1943 period. (1 inch in diameter)*

Fig. 24-14. *In the 1950s or early 1960s a jewelry manufacturer made a new die from which this insignia was struck. With the 1984 army decision to revive the branch, the die was probably used to make insignia again. (1 inch in diameter)*

Fig. 24-15. *The history of this disk is unknown. The background is slightly domed, and it was made at least before the mid-1960s. ($1\frac{1}{32}$ inches in diameter)*

Fig. 24-16. An original red, white, and blue shoulder cord worn by some members of the First Special Service Force during World War II.

Fig. 24-16.

Chapter Twenty-Five

Prison Guards

Only enlisted personnel served as prison guards. Under the pre-World War I regimental concept, officers stationed at the Fort Leavenworth army prison (and later Alcatraz) were detailed from regimental assignments. In 1913 the army formed special infantry units known as disciplinary companies and battalions to retrain minor offenders. Prisoner members of such organizations wore obsolete service uniforms "without facings or ornaments." Noncommissioned officers from the prison guard served as sergeants in disciplinary units until the guards were absorbed by the new Military Police Corps in 1922.[1] Insignia for the Provost Marshal's Department and the Military Police Corps are discussed in chapter 44.

Cap Insignia

By authorization of a special War Department letter, the military prison guards at Fort Leavenworth began to wear the silver letters *PG* within a silver wreath on the forage cap in 1882. One hundred twenty-five men composed the 1882 guard force, but only ninety-nine served in 1893. Congress directed that the military prison be turned over to the Department of Justice on 1 July 1895, thus ending use of this army cap insignia.[2]

The prison was returned to the army in 1906, and the Quartermaster General's Department specified a cap insignia of a gilt wreath 1 5/16 inches high containing the silver letter *PG*. Also made in bronze for service wear, that insignia can be found with just the letters (Fig. 25-1) and with *PG* above company numbers. Prison guards were retitled Disciplinary Barracks Guards in 1915, and regulations had *DBG* replace the *PG* in cap wreaths, both with and without company numbers. Despite this 1915 change, guards apparently continued to wear the letters *PG* until 1916, when a request from San Francisco for the new *DBG* insignia caused personnel at the Philadelphia Depot to admit that the *DBG* insignia had never been issued. Further correspondence ensued, and a decision was made to use the letters *DB* for the band and the noncommissioned staff, since they were not guards, and the letters *DBG* only for members of the guard companies.[3]

Hat Insignia

Prison guards' campaign hats during 1906 and 1907 carried the bronze letters *PG* above the bronze company numbers, as described in chapter 10, "Numbers and Letters."[4]

Dress Collar Insignia

Dress blue uniform collar insignia consisted of gilt wreaths with the silver letters *PG*, *DBG*, and *DB* similar to the cap ornaments. Like the cap insignia, these letters came with and without company numbers; however, the wreath around the collar insignia was of slightly different design from that used on the cap and was only 1 1/16 inches high.[5]

Bronze Collar Insignia

From 1906 until 1910, prison guards wore bronze wreaths with the letters *PG* on the service uniform collars (Fig. 25-1). With the introduction of the 1-inch bronze disks in 1910, the plain letters with company numbers (*1* through *4*) below came into use. Examples of the disks with and without company numbers are shown in Figs. 25-2 and 25-3.[6]

In 1916 bronze disks with the letters *DBG* and *DB* replaced those bearing *PG*. These disks came with and without numbers and with the letters in an arc arrangement as well

Fig. 25-1.

Fig. 25-2.

Fig. 25-3.

Fig. 25-4.

Fig. 25-5.

Fig. 25-6.

Fig. 25-7.

Fig. 25-8.

Fig. 25-9.

Fig. 25-1. *Prison guard service cap insignia in bronze, 1906–1916, for noncommissioned officers. Similar insignia with numbers 1 through 4 below were used by company members. For dress uniforms the wreath was gilt with silver numbers and letters. ($1\frac{27}{32}$ inches wide)*

Figs. 25-2 and 25-3. *Enlisted men's service uniform collar insignia, 1910–16. That of Fig. 25-2 is for members of the 2d Prison Guard Company, and the other has space for a company number to be added.*

Figs. 25-4 and 25-5. *Starting in 1916, disciplinary barracks noncommissioned officers and band members wore these disks, either with or without company numbers.*

Figs. 25-6, 25-7, and 25-8. *Guards in the disciplinary barracks companies wore DBG disks beginning in 1916. These three insignia show some of the various letter and number arrangements.*

Fig. 25-9. *A privately made disciplinary barracks guard collar insignia, from about World War I.*

as a straight line. These various combinations are illustrated in Figs. 25-4 through 25-8. By mid-May 1919 only the *DBG* was in use by guards and band members, without any company numbers added.[7] A commercially made *DBG* disk is shown in Fig. 25-9.

Gilt Collar Disks

Although never authorized, gilt *DB* and *DBG* disks are known to exist.

Chapter Twenty-Six

Bureau of Insular Affairs

After the United States won new possessions in the Spanish-American War, the question of territorial administration arose. Several early and diversified approaches were tried, but finally Congress and the president selected the War Department to administer those islands under U.S. control. A few select officers were detailed to the Division of Customs and Insular Affairs when it was established in December 1899. The Division of Insular Affairs, as it was renamed in December 1900, became the Bureau of Insular Affairs in July 1902. The bureau supervised and maintained pre–World War I liaison with governments of Cuba (1898–1902 and 1906–1909), Puerto Rico (1898–1900 and 1909–17), and the Philippines (after 1898), and after World War I it involved itself with other possessions. Initially, Colonel Clarence Edwards was the bureau chief, although later a general officer headed the bureau, with two to four additional assistant officers. After 1920 Congress limited the Bureau of Insular Affairs to two assistants and the chief.[1]

The chief of the Bureau of Insular Affairs received a special collar insignia in late 1902: a winged bundle of seven arrows. Evidently this device came about after Colonel Edwards had to wear his uniform to the White House on New Year's Day and had no prescribed insignia. In December 1902 Colonel Edwards wrote Major General Young, president of the uniform board:

> General Order No. 81, AGO, of this year was dated July 17th 1902, and therefore there are no orders governing the uniform for [a chief of insular affairs]. . . . Attention is invited to page 84 of the report of the Secretary of War for 1901, in which the Secretary states that the duties and functions of this Office on the insular side are analogous to those performed by the Adjutant General upon the Military. It is therefore assumed that the uniform of this rank should correspond to the rank of Colonel and Adjutant General, with the aiguillettes only differing from an Adjutant General's uniform in corps device. The rough sketch of such a proposed device is herewith submitted.[2]

Since the December 1902 regulations, as well as the 1904 regulations, specified insignia only for the chief, the other officers must have continued to wear their original branch insignia. Later, all of the officers detailed to the Bureau of Insular Affairs were authorized to wear the insignia.[3]

Gilt insignia for the dress blue and white uniforms had the area between the arrows pierced (Fig. 26-1) or solid (Fig. 26-2). Service uniforms carried the same devices in bronze, as shown in Figs. 26-3 and 26-4. A

Fig. 26-1.

Fig. 26-2.

Fig. 26-3.

Fig. 26-1. *A gilt collar insignia for the Bureau of Insular Affairs, 1903–36. The space between the arrows is solid. (43/64 inch wide)*

Fig. 26-2. *A bronze version of the first design for the Bureau of Insular Affairs. (43/64 inch wide)*

Fig. 26-3. *A gilt insignia for the Bureau of Insular Affairs, with the upper area between the arrows pierced. This insignia was worn by a member of the bureau from 1933 to 1936. (21/32 inch wide)*

Fig. 26-4. A chief of the Bureau of Insular Affairs wearing his bureau's unusual insignia. Generals assigned as department or bureau chiefs wore branch insignia, unlike other generals.

Fig. 26-5. The second design of Bureau of Insular Affairs insignia, used from 1936 until 1939. This design was restruck for collectors in 1987 using original dies. The backs of the remade insignia have two tines for clutches, just like some of the original 1936 insignia, but there are no hallmarks on the new pieces. (1 1/8 inches wide)

Fig. 26-4.

modern version of the winged bundle of arrows (Fig. 26-5) was specified in 1936 and was used until the Department of the Interior assumed the bureau's functions on 1 July 1939.[4]

Fig. 26-5.

Chapter Twenty-Seven

Philippine Constabulary

By presidential direction the military commander of the Philippines turned the Philippine government over to civil authorities on July 4, 1901. Because a military force was still needed, and because civil officials could not command U.S. Army units, a Philippine Constabulary was formed on August 8, 1901. Officers of the constabulary came from the Regular Army, volunteers, and other sources; by the end of 1901, a total of 180 officers were commissioned. Initially this police force was known as the Insular Constabulary, although the name was soon changed to the Philippine Constabulary. By 1905 the overall force was one hundred companies, with the normal strength of 2 officers and fifty men in each company.[1]

A unique khaki uniform with red piping distinguished the Philippine Constabulary, whose enlisted members usually were natives. The constabulary slowly enrolled more native Filipinos, and in early 1936 the constabulary became part of the Philippine Army. Although Philippine Constabulary members were not part of the U.S. Army, the early insignia are discussed here because some officers served in the constabulary on detail from the U.S. Army.[2]

In 1922 the officers' insignia changed, and by that time only four regular army officers were still on detail to the constabulary. This convenient cutoff date is used here, although the Philippine Constabulary still exists. The history of the Philippine Constabulary insignia is not now completely known, and until more research fills this void, the following represents a summary of the facts currently available.[3]

Officers' Collar Insignia

The first "branch" insignia consisted of the letters *IC*, for Insular Constabulary, within a wreath. This short-lived insignia must have existed from the initial formation in August 1901, for in just a few months a known change occurred: the letters *PC* appeared in a wreath. An example is shown in Fig. 27-1.[4]

Fig. 27-1.

***Fig. 27-1.** A bronze-colored collar insignia made in the Philippines for Philippine Constabulary officers, 1902–1905. This insignia evidently continued as an enlisted men's headgear insignia, as shown in Fig. 27-6. This replaced the initial similar design that included the IC (Insular Constabulary) monogram. (1 21/64 inches wide)*

A third and more common collar ornament appeared in 1905, although the army did not publish the authorization until May 1907. The insignia (Fig. 27-2) was for "Chief and assistant chiefs, Philippine Constabulary and other officers detailed for duty therewith.—The coat of arms of the Philippines less the crest, in gold or gilt metal with the letters 'P.C.' superimposed in silver." In the field, officers wore this insignia on the khaki shirt, centered and 1 inch above the left pocket seam. This insignia lasted until June 1922, when the insignia became an eagle bearing a Philippine coat of arms and the letters *PC*. As in the U.S. Army, constabulary officers wore bronze insignia on field uniforms.[5]

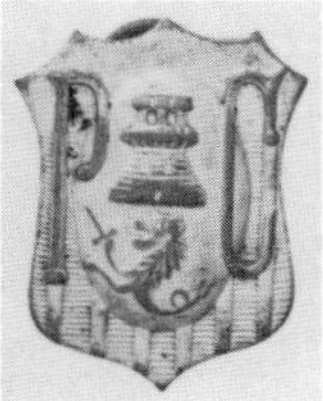

Fig. 27-2.

***Fig. 27-2.** Officers' 1905–22 collar insignia. The gold shield was to have the large PC letters silvered, but often the entire insignia remained all gold in color. The design is that of the Philippine coat of arms (adopted in 1905), with the addition of the letters. (13/16 inch wide)*

Special corps collar insignia, similar to those of the U.S. Army, existed in the constabulary. Medical officers wore a gilt cross from October 1903 to May 1908, when it was changed to a caduceus. It is reasonable to assume that both the medical cross and the caduceus were identical to those used by the Regular Army, because very few doctors

Fig. 27-3.

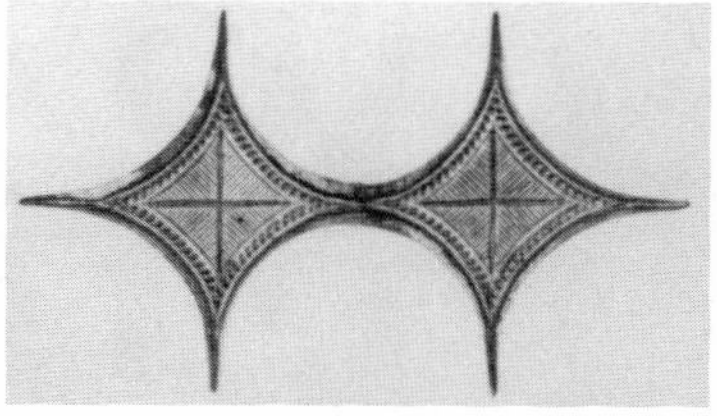

Fig. 27-4.

Fig. 27-5.

Fig. 27-3. *Officers' cap insignia, 1907–22.*

Fig. 27-4. *Silver diamonds "with concave sides" were used for various ranks at times during 1907–11. This insignia was worn by Captain James Lee Cochrun, who was a constabulary lieutenant from 1909 to 1913 and captain from 1913 to 1914. "Gentleman Jim" was well known and wrote about the constabulary in popular literature just before World War I.*

Fig. 27-5. *A bronze enlisted men's pin-backed collar insignia for Philippine Constabulary members. It was probably worn from about 1910 until the early 1920s. The back is marked CRISPULO ZAMORA MADE IN P.I. (1 17/64 inches in diameter)*

Fig. 27-6. *A company of Ifugao soldiers of the Philippine Constabulary, February 1912. The third lieutenant has bare red shoulder straps and an officers' cap and hat insignia. The barefoot soldiers evidently wear a PC monogram in a wreath on their turbans.*

joined the constabulary. In 1918 doctors switched to the caduceus "in addition to the collar ornament of the line," and dental officers added *DC* to the caduceus.[6]

Officers' Cap Insignia

Initially the cap insignia was the small eagle worn on the 1898 khaki uniform shoulder straps by U.S. officers. The eagle shown in Fig. 8-69 of chapter 8 was worn by an officer of the Philippine Constabulary in 1906 and 1907. A unique design of an eagle with the outspread wings above the shield, of the same type as that worn on the collar (Fig. 27-3), replaced this first cap device in October 1907. This second cap ornament was replaced in October 1922 at the same time as the collar insignia.[7]

Officers' Rank Insignia

With the founding of the constabulary, the authorities deliberately decided not to adopt military rank titles. Instead, unique positions were established, including such titles as chief, assistant chief, senior inspector, inspector, third class inspector, and the like. In December 1902 the constabulary added standard military titles to the ranks, so third lieutenant and fourth class inspector became a single title, just as first class inspectors became first class inspectors and captains. By 1907, military ranks existed exclusively, the original "inspectors" titles having been dropped.[8]

Fig. 27-6.

At first, red shoulder straps, similar to navy shoulder boards, indicated rank, with one through four gilt bands for third lieutenants through captains. Perhaps silver bands indicated rank above captain. Until January 1906 small eagles were worn on the shoulder straps above the rank loops. The rank insignia themselves also began a long evolution. In the fall of 1906, captains wore four "gold bars," which may still have been the initial four gold stripes on the shoulder boards. In September 1906, lieutenant colonels switched to "a silver lozenge" when two grades of major were established. Assistant directors (majors) wore the insignia "previously prescribed for majors," while senior inspectors (majors) wore four gold bars, the bar nearest the edge of the collar twice the width of the other three bars. By this time a switch to metal rank insignia must have been made. A January 1907 order revoked this short-lived system and clearly spelled out field-grade rank insignia: lieutenant colonels and assistant directors, two connected silver lozenges; majors and assistant directors, two connected gold lozenges; and the executive inspector, the superintendent of the information division, and the majors and senior inspectors, one gold lozenge.[9]

Some new rank insignia came about in November 1907, evidently coinciding with the switch to standard military titles, although I know of no details of the insignia. Apparently, captains began to use two concave lozenges (Fig. 27-4) in 1907, because a January 1909 change notes that "the present rank insignia for first lieutenants are abolished and there are adopted in lieu thereof single silver lozenges with concave sides of the same pattern and size as the lozenges composing the captain's [sic] insignia." In October 1911 the constabulary began to use standard U.S. Army insignia, with third and second lieutenants wearing the same insignia. Just earlier, in May 1911, officers' shirts (as an outer garment) began to carry rank insignia on the collars, with the *PC* ornament still worn above the left pocket.[10]

Enlisted Men's Collar Devices

It is reasonable to assume that enlisted men's "branch" insignia somewhat paralleled officers' and therefore to believe that the plain block monogram *IP* appeared as the initial collar ornament. A blurred photograph of a native private, taken about 1903, appears to show a bronze block *PC* monogram on the khaki collar.[11] Enlisted men's insignia are shown in 1904 and 1905 price lists at thirteen cents.[12]

The 1904 and 1905 price lists also show "white metal crosses" for enlisted men, evidently medical troops, and lyres for band members.[13] The Regular Army had several plans to introduce bronze disks for enlisted men's insignia between 1907 and 1910. Evidently the constabulary switched to the bronze disk shown in Fig. 27-5 during this interval. The pin-back insignia is marked *ZAMORA, MADE IN P.I.* This design, struck in gilt color, continued into the 1930s, although the date of the change from bronze to gilt is unknown.

Enlisted Men's Cap, Hat, and Fez Devices

The initial headgear insignia is believed to have been similar, if not identical, to that worn by constabulary officers: *IP* or *PC* in a wreath. A *PC* monogram, barely recognizable, appears in the early photograph mentioned above and may be the pin-backed, bronze-colored insignia, made in the Philippine Islands, shown in Fig. 27-1. Photographs indicate that the wreathed monogram lasted until the start of World War I, and apparently it was not replaced until the 1922 insignia change.[14]

Figs. 27-6 through 27-9 show characteristic insignia worn by various members of the Philippine Constabulary from 1901 to 1912.

Fig. 27-7.

Fig. 27-7. *Philippine Constabulary officers in 1904. They wear stiffened red shoulder loops with an eagle and various rank devices.*

Fig. 27-8. *Lieutenant Colonel Rafael Crame about 1908. As a general, Crame became the first Filipino chief of the constabulary in 1917.*

Fig. 27-9. *A Philippine Constabulary unit, Cavite Province, 1901. The two officers seated in chairs have narrow cord braid down their trousers legs.*

Fig. 27-8.

Fig. 27-9.

Chapter Twenty-Eight

Electricians

Congress added the grade of electrician to the Coast Artillery Corps in 1899. These men, among the most skilled in the army, received seventy-five dollars a month, the army's highest for noncommissioned officers. The chief of artillery appointed electricians directly from civilian life, and these men did not have to rise through the ranks. Most electricians had college training and were specialists, the counterpart of today's warrant officers.[1]

Additional electrician grades were established in the coast artillery in the early 1900s, and in 1904 the Signal Corps added master signal electricians. The lower-ranking electricians of various grades wore insignia of their branch, but master signal electricians, master electricians, and electrician sergeants wore special electrician insignia, the design consisting of five lightning bolts coming from a central source.[2]

Cap Insignia

Created with the electrician's grade was a new cap ornament of a silver five-forked lightning bolt within a gold wreath (Fig. 28-1). A smaller insignia (Fig. 28-2 in gilt and Fig. 28-3 in bronze) replaced the first device in 1905. As the army added additional ranks, master signal electricians, master electricians, and electrician sergeants all wore this cap device.[3]

Helmet Insignia

Electricians added a silver five-forked lightning bolt on the eagle's shield of the 1895–1903 helmet in 1899.[4]

Hat Insignia

The three senior electricians wore bronze lightning bolts (Fig. 28-4) on the campaign hat between 1905 and 1907.[5]

Collar Insignia

Made from the dies originally used for the helmet overlay, the small gilt pin-backed col-

Fig. 28-1. *Cap insignia for electrician sergeants, 1899–1905. (1 39/64 inches wide)*

Fig. 28-2. *Electrician sergeants' and master signal electricians' dress cap insignia, 1905–17. (1 7/8 inches wide)*

Fig. 28-3. *Service cap insignia in bronze color for the various electrician noncommissioned officers, 1905–18. (1 29/32 inches wide)*

Fig. 28-4.

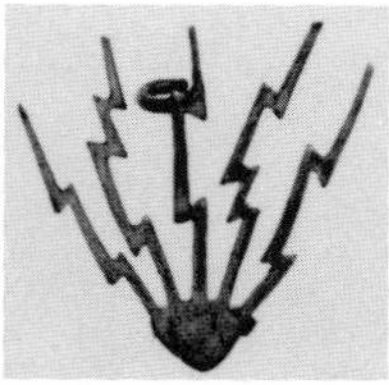

Fig. 28-5.

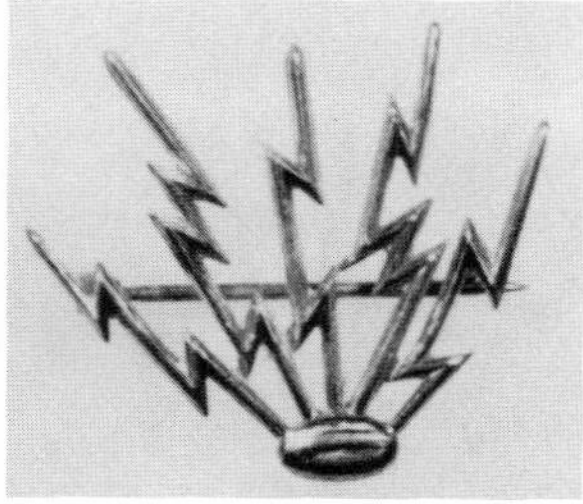

Fig. 28-6.

Fig. 28-7.

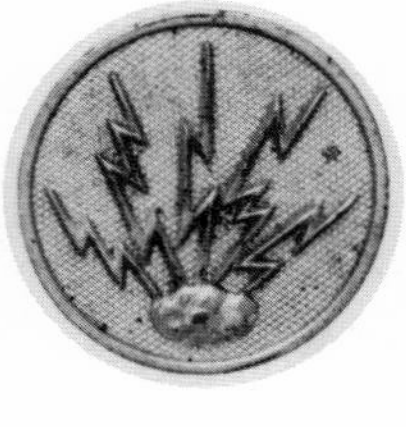

Fig. 28-8.

Fig. 28-4. *Bronze insignia for the campaign hats of electrician noncommissioned officers, 1905–1907. ($1\,^{15}/_{32}$ inches wide)*

Fig. 28-5. *Gold-colored collar insignia for the 1900 white duck coat, the same size as the silver overlay used on the helmet. ($^{31}/_{32}$ inch wide)*

Fig. 28-6. *These five large lightning bolts were made in both gold and black color as enlisted men's collar insignia starting in 1902. ($1\,^{13}/_{32}$ inches wide)*

Fig. 28-7. *A bronze disk used by various electrician noncommissioned officers from 1910 until after World War I. (1 inch in diameter)*

Fig. 28-8. *Gilt disks like this were not authorized in regulations but evidently were worn by some electrical or signal personnel in the 1920s. (1 inch in diameter)*

lar insignia shown in Fig. 28-5 was for wear on the 1900 white duck coat collar. The device has no design in the metal itself, since the early ornament consisted exclusively of the outline. In early 1903, large gilt and bronze lightning bolts (Fig. 28-6) were made as collar insignia. Disks (Fig. 28-7) replaced bronze outline lightning bolts in 1910, while the outline dress insignia lasted until World War I. The Quartermaster Corps issued disks with lightning bolts not only to electrician sergeants of various grades, but also during World War I to radio sergeants. This latter practice was not authorized according to uniform regulations, although the Quartermaster Corps did, through letters, allow this practice to continue until June 1919. Gilt disks of identical design exist (Fig. 28-8), but their use by Regular Army troops is questionable.[6]

Chapter Twenty-Nine

U.S. Military Academy Professors

When West Point is mentioned, most people think of tall, athletic, and handsome cadets, of great gray stone buildings as immovable as mountains, and of the emerald green grassy parade field known as "the Plains." If one really considers West Point though, one realizes that the faculty are the key element of the academy. Professors have long been associated with West Point, and in regulations of 1832, "Professors, Teachers, and their assistants, not of the Line of the Army, including the Sword Master" were to wear "citizens' dress with buttons of the Corps of Engineers, round hat and black cockade with gold eagle."[1] Thus, some teachers began to wear unique uniforms. The tradition that has evolved is for professors to wear miniature West Point insignia as a branch device on uniform coat lapels. The vast majority of instructors at West Point are army personnel assigned to teach for three years (from the "Line of the Army"), while only a few of the faculty are permanent professors who wear this special insignia.

Few descriptions of early professors' uniforms have survived. However, since West Point was an engineering school, the initial instructors were associated with that branch, and a professor's uniform from about 1817 is described in chapter 12, "Engineers." Presumably, this was the typical uniform until the 1832 regulations appeared. The next mention of unique clothing was in 1839, when the coat description for professors, teachers, assistants, and the sword master became "plain, blue cloth, with buttons of the corps of engineers." The round hat with military insignia remained, but forage caps also were allowed, the "same as for engineers." West Point's riding master was added to the list of specially uniformed faculty in 1847.[2]

After 1872 regulations allowed professors and other select instructors such as the sword master to wear modified army uniforms until the 1902 uniform change. After 1902 they wore standard army clothing with small U.S. Military Academy insignia as collar ornaments. In October 1921 the insignia was limited to "professors and assistant professors, United States Military Academy," but it was expanded to its previous scope again in October 1923, when it was given to "permanent professors, master of the sword, and civilian instructors, United States Military Academy."[3]

Before 1923 the academy insignia faced to the observer's left, as illustrated in Fig. 29-1, a professors' bronze device. Fig. 29-2 is a similar gilt insignia. In 1923 the insignia was changed to face the other direction, as shown in Fig. 29-3, and in November 1924 insignia

Fig. 29-1.

Fig. 29-2.

Fig. 29-3.

Fig. 29-1. *The U.S. Military Academy insignia designed by three academy professors in 1898 and adopted as the insignia of permanent professors with the 1902 uniform regulations. The insignia shown is in bronze color for the 1902–23 service uniform. (1 5/32 inches wide)*

Fig. 29-2. *A gilt version of the permanent professors' insignia, U.S. Military Academy, worn from 1902 until 1923. (1 5/32 inches wide)*

Fig. 29-3. *The West Point permanent professors' insignia was reversed in 1923 to conform to rules of heraldry. This is a revised insignia used in the 1920s. (1 7/32 inches wide)*

were made in pairs, to face forward.[4]

In December 1926 smaller shirt collar insignia, 3/4 inch high, were made regulation, although before that time shirt collar insignia had been made (Fig. 29-4). Today's design (Fig. 29-5) is very similar to that first adopted, except for the direction the design faces.

Not only are professors' insignia unique, but so is their retirement policy. Most professors are colonels and serve at West Point for many years. A special law allows any permanent professor below general officer grade "whose service has been long and distinguished" to be retired in the grade of brigadier general (Fig. 29-6).[5]

Fig. 29-4. *A 1923 shirt collar insignia for U.S. Military Academy professors. (61/64 inch wide)*

Fig. 29-5. *A brass collar insignia typical of that worn by permanent professors in the 1980s. (17/32 inches wide)*

Fig. 29-6. *A war veteran and professor of the U.S. Military Academy, about 1925.*

Section XI

General Staffs

CHAPTER THIRTY

NINETEENTH-CENTURY GENERAL STAFF

THE TERM *general staff*, as used in the U.S. Army, has a different meaning for each of two distinct eras: the nineteenth century and the twentieth century. The nineteenth-century term applied to officers serving as staff members of a department other than infantry, cavalry, artillery, dragoons, or other arm. These departments served under the secretary of war and did not answer to the senior general commanding the army. By the end of the nineteenth century, they included the Judge Advocate General's, Inspector General's, Adjutant General's, Quartermaster General's, and Subsistence and Pay departments. Although responsible for the entire army, the older staff was not centralized and did not conduct overall army planning; each bureau went its own way. Even in uniform regulations the general staff did not fully coordinate. Often regulations describe "general staff uniforms" and then list various branch distinctive uniforms. However, by the second half of the nineteenth century, dark blue was the trim used by all these officers.

With Secretary of War Root's army modernization shortly after the Spanish-American War, the army formed the General Staff Corps, a temporary grouping of officers who "prepared plans for the national defense and for the mobilization of the military forces in time of war . . . to assist the Secretary of War."[1] Later the term *general staff* included those men who directly served on a general's staff and assisted him in administration, intelligence, operations, and supply. These General Staff Corps officers could be detailed from any branch. Members of this twentieth-century group are discussed in the next chapter, along with their insignia, the national eagle on a general's star.

GENERAL STAFF OF 1813

Early-nineteenth-century regulations generally listed all of the staff departments together. The detailed May 1813 general staff uniform description was as follows:

> The coat—single breasted, with ten buttons, and button holes worked with blue twist, in front, five inches long at the top and three at the bottom. The standing coat collar to rise to the tip of the ear, which will determine its width. The cuffs, not less than three and a half nor more than four inches wide. The skirts faced with blue, the bottom of each not more than seven, nor less than three and a half, inches wide; the length to reach to the bend of the knee. The bottom of the breast and two hip buttons to range.
>
> 1. On the collar one blind button hole, five inches long, with a button on each side.
>
> 2. The blind holes on each side of the front, in the herring-bone form, to be in the same direction with the collar, from the top to the bottom.
>
> 3. Blind holes (in the like form) to proceed from four buttons, placed lengthwise, on each skirt. A gilt star, on the center of the bottom, two inches from the edge.
>
> 4. The cuffs, to be indented with one and a half inch of the edge, with four buttons lengthwise on each sleeve, and holes to the three upper buttons, corresponding with the indentions of the cuff, on the centre of which is to be inserted the lower button.
>
> 5. All general officers will be permitted to embroider the button holes. The Commissary General of Ordnance, the Adju-

tants, Inspectors, and Quartermasters General, and the Commissary General of Purchases, will be permited to embroider the button holes of the collar only.

Vests, breaches, and pantaloons—White (or buff for general officers)—blue pantaloons may be worn in the winter, and nankeen in the summer. Vests single breasted, without pocket flaps.

1. Breaches, or pantaloons, with four buttons on the knee, and gilt buckles.

2. High military boots and gilt spurs.

Black stock—of leather or silk.

Chapeaux—of the following form: the fan not less than six and a half, nor more than nine inches high in the rear, nor less than fifteen, nor more than seventeen and a half inches from point to point, bound round the edge with black binding half inch wide.

1. Button and loop, black.

2. Cockade, the same, four and a half inches diameter, with a gold eagle in the centre.

Swords—Yellow mounted, with a black, or yellow, gripe. For the officers of the Adjutant, Inspector, and Quartermaster General's departments, sabres; for all others, straight swords.

Waist belts—of black leather. No sashes.

Epaulettes—of gold; according to rank.

Note.—Officers of the Corps of Engineers will wear the uniform already established for that corps.

The dress of the hospital staff will conform, as to fashion, to the uniform of the staff, except that they will wear pocket flaps, and buttons placed across the cuffs, four to each, and covered buttons in all instances, of the color of the coat, (black).

Officers of the line appointed to a staff station, which confers no additional rank, will wear the uniform of their rank in the line, with high boots and spurs.[2]

An example of a general staff coat from about 1813 is shown in Fig. 30-1.

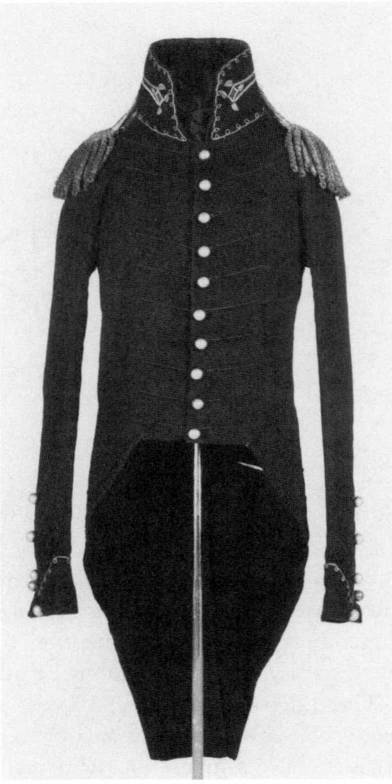

Fig. 30-1.

Fig. 30-1. *Andrew Jackson's coat, in the style used from 1813 until 1821. The trim across the front is in dark blue.*

1820s

General staff uniforms for the 1820s varied little from the 1813 pattern, but in 1821 and later the maximum skirt width was to be between 5 and 3½ inches, and the embroidery of buttonholes was changed. In 1820 some staff officers were allowed to embroider buttonholes on the collar and cuffs, but in 1821 and 1825 the regulations allowed generals to have all buttonholes embroidered, whereas general staff officers were limited to embroidered collar buttonholes. Chaplains, judge advocates, commissaries of purchases, storekeepers, and paymasters had no prescribed uniform in 1821, although in 1825 paymasters returned to uniforms. It is interesting to note that the coat and coatee tails of general staff officers carried an embroidered gilt star, while infantry and artillery officers' coattails had a blue diamond.[3] An example of an 1820s staff officers' coat is shown in Fig. 30-2.

1832

Three staff coats were introduced during 1832: new dress and undress coats and a frock coat. Dress coats were dark blue with one row of nine buttons down the front and 3½-inch-deep blue cuffs. The skirts, as before, extended to the bend in the knee and retained the gilt star, but the skirt linings changed from blue to buff. The front 4 inches of the standing collar was buff, with the remainder blue (Fig. 30-3). The undress coat was identical to the dress coat, except the buff trim was omitted. The frock coat was plain, made from dark blue cloth.[4]

The hat changed completely. It carried a 6-inch black silk cockade with 11-inch-long gold loops and a gold spread eagle. Hat plumes, made from swan feathers, varied with the officers. The adjutant general, inspector general, aides, and officers attached to the general-in-chief wore an 8-inch yellow plume. Aides and officers attached to other major generals had an 8-inch swan feather plume, the top half white and the lower half black. Aides and officers attached to brigadier generals wore an 8-inch plume, the top half red and the lower half white. All quartermaster officers had a light blue swan feather, while subsistence officers had the same except that the lower 4 inches were white.[5]

The hat of the commissary general of purchases had no feathers, and the general wore a unique dark blue double-breasted coat, ten buttons to each row. The standing collar was blue, each side bearing two gold-embroidered buttonholes. To distinguish this officer from the paymaster general, who wore a similar coat, the tails were lined with buff cloth.[6]

Other staff officers' 1832 uniforms are described in the chapters on the pay and medical departments and the Corps of Engineers. The Corps of Engineers, it should be noted, had two uniforms: one for topographical engineers and one for other corps members. General staff officers also wore on the right shoulder an aiguillette consisting of "twisted gold cord with gilt engraved tags."[7]

Insignia, 1839

With only minor changes, the general staff uniforms of 1839 remained similar to those of 1832. The skirt bottoms bore the same type of star previously used, but regulations were becoming more precise, as exemplified by the dimensions: "a gold embroidered star on buff cloth, three and a half inches in diameter by three inches, the longest point perpendicular." Aides wore their regimental uniforms with their special hat plume and aiguillette marking them as aides. Aides and other officers attached to generals continued to wear hat plumes the same color as that of the general they served; however, the staff plume was shortened to 7 inches. The color of some staff hat plumes was changed in 1839 as follows: adjutant general's staff, white; inspector general's staff, green; quartermaster's staff, light blue; and subsistence, top half light blue, lower half white.[8]

The commissary general of purchases, military storekeepers, and ordnance storekeepers were called civil staff and were given uniforms that were a cross between the general staff and civilian dress. Regulations described the entire uniform simply:

> Coat—plain, of blue cloth.
>
> Button—of the department to which the officers respectively belong; if of no particular arm, the General Staff button.
>
> Trousers—plain blue for winter, and plain white or cotton for summer.
>
> Round hat, black cockade, and yellow eagle.
>
> Sword and belt—same as for Pay Department.
>
> Frock coat—Same as the general Staff; single breasted; buttons of department; without straps.[9]

Those storekeeper uniforms had eliminated hat insignia by 1851, but otherwise they remained similar to the above description until 1888, when Congress virtually eliminated storekeepers.[10]

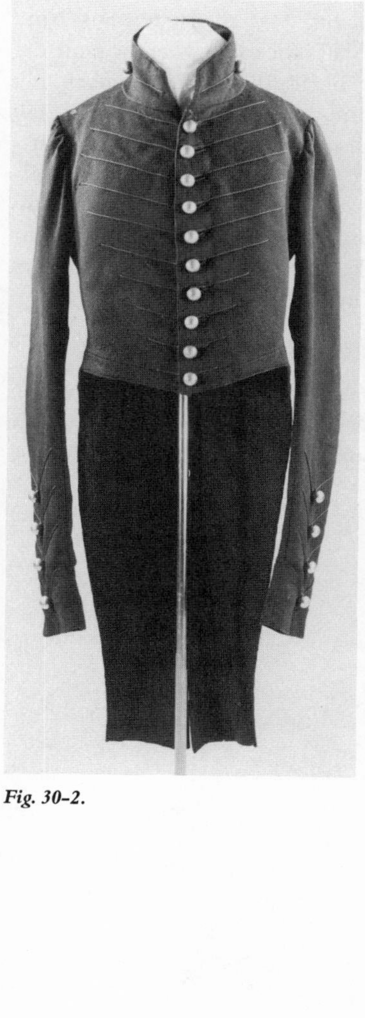

Fig. 30-2.

Fig. 30-3.

Fig. 30-2. *An 1821-pattern staff coat. The waist seam was introduced into fashions about 1820. The collar is also lower, following fashions in civilian clothing some years after the War of 1812.*

Fig. 30-3. *This staff officer's uniform of the 1832 pattern was a dramatic style change from the general staff uniforms of the previous twenty years. While the 1813 coat may to the untrained eye appear similar to the 1821 version, the 1821 version had a noticeably lower collar and skirts cut separately. The 1832 change included not only a new cut, but also a switch to buff trim. With the 1851 uniforms staff officers wore the same patterns as other officers.*

Table 30-1. Officers' Pompon Colors, 1851.

Department	Upper Two-thirds	Lower One-third
Adjutant General's	Buff	White
Inspector General's	Buff	Scarlet
Quartermaster's	Buff	Light blue
Subsistence	Buff	Royal blue
Judge Advocate's	White	White

INSIGNIA, 1841–1851

Despite the previous use of buttons and their placement as one of the distinctive features on nineteenth-century uniforms, officers of the general staff were allowed to have "eight to ten buttons placed at equal distances, according to the length of the waist." In addition, colonels, lieutenant colonels, and majors could, at their option, wear a double-breasted coat. In other respects the 1832 staff dress coat remained unchanged until 1851. Aides and officers assigned to selected departments (Adjutant General's, Inspector General's, Quartermaster General's, Subsistence, Pay, and Medical departments) wore aiguillettes on the right shoulder.[11]

INSIGNIA, 1851

The army introduced new uniforms in 1851, completely revising the old uniforms. Officers of equal rank received identical uniforms, except for accoutrements and epaulettes. Staff officers all wore the same cap device as generals, the *US* in a wreath, but colored pompons showed the general staff department. In addition to the War Department staff, regimental adjutants and quartermasters also wore the colored pompons described in Table 30-1. Uniforms for military storekeepers generally continued as before, but without hat insignia.[12]

INSIGNIA, 1858 AND LATER

By General Order Number 3, 24 March 1858, the War Department authorized a new hat, commonly called the Hardee hat, for the army, as described in chapter 72. On this new hat officers of the Adjutant General's, Inspector General's, Quartermaster's, Subsistence, Medical, and Pay departments, and the judge advocate, wore the *US* in a wreath. The 1847 cocked hat became optional for generals and field-grade officers, but the use of distinctively colored plumes stopped, and all staff officers wore three black ostrich feathers.

Officers "of the General Staff, and Staff Corps" were permitted the option of wearing a light French chapeau of the 1847 design. On it, generals and field-grade officers wore three feathers, and company-grade officers wore two.[13] Distinctive epaulettes, described in the appropriate branch chapters and in chapter 10, "Numbers and Letters," distinguished staff departments. Generally staff officers wore dark blue shoulder knots, and several branches continued to wear the *US* cap ornaments. Instead of the 1881–1903 helmets, staff officers wore the chapeau with dress uniforms.

With the introduction of the 1893 sack coat, each staff branch developed its distinctive collar insignia. Because of the change to a standard uniform and the adoption of branch collar insignia by all officers, the nineteenth-century term *general staff* was replaced by reference to each branch. The evolutionary elimination of "general staff" allowed the second, and current, meaning of the term to come into use. With the reorganization following the Spanish-American War, Congress established the General Staff Corps effective 15 August 1903.

Chapter Thirty-One

General Staff Corps

After the War of 1812, Secretary of War John C. Calhoun established the basic concept that was to govern the operation of the War Department and the U.S. Army until 1903: the various army staff departments were to answer to the secretary of war, and each department was to receive appropriations directly from Congress. Although army units reported to the commanding general, he had much less authority than one today might expect of such a senior officer. In any event, the "general in chief" did not control the various staff officers.

The Spanish-American War revealed the problems associated with the many independent staff departments, among them inefficiency because of a lack of an agency to conduct overall planning. Elihu Root became secretary of war in 1899 and proposed to create a chief of staff position to assist in the control of the various departments and to conduct overall planning. By an Act of 14 February 1903, Congress created the General Staff Corps including the Chief of Staff. The following year the army announced an insignia for officers detailed to the general staff. This device consisted of a general's silver star, 1 1/4 inches high, with a 3/4-inch coat of arms superimposed (Fig. 31-1). A bronze insignia known to have been made in 1904 is shown in Fig. 31-2. In April 1911, orders required the general officers serving on the general staff to remove the U.S. coat of arms from the dress uniform epaulette crescent and to use the general staff insignia instead. An example is shown in Fig. 2-24 in chapter 2, "The Changing U.S. Uniform."[2]

In creating the General Staff Corps, Congress placed many limitations on the size and use of general staff officers. The authorized number grew until 1916, when Congress allowed a total of fifty-five men, with not more than half in Washington, D.C. The 1917 ceiling was eighty-eight general staff officers in addition to the chief of staff and four generals serving as assistant chiefs of staff. During World War I Congress and the president suspended this limitation.[3]

Many officers at division and higher level wore the general staff insignia. Several insignia variations exist, especially in the size of the eagle (Figs. 31-3 and 31-4). Some general staff members wore small shirt collar ornaments (Fig. 31-5). In October 1921 the U.S. Army revised the white uniform, along with the silver, gold, and enameled insignia (Fig. 31-6). After October 1923, general staff members wore these 1 1/4-inch-high dress insignia on the service uniform, and three-quarters size insignia on shirts. When the army introduced the lapel collar coat in March 1926, the smaller insignia was worn (Fig. 31-7). An

Fig. 31-1. *A pre–World War I General Staff Corps insignia. The design is a national eagle on a general's star. (1 15/64 inches wide)*

Fig. 31-2. *Made in 1904, this bronze General Staff Corps collar insignia was typical of service uniform insignia used until 1923. (1 21/64 inches wide)*

Figs. 31-3 and 31-4. *World War I General Staff Corps high-collar coat insignia. (1 7/32 and 1 3/32 inches wide, respectively)*

Fig. 31-5. *This small shirt insignia was made during World War I. (5/8 inch wide)*

Fig. 31-1.

Fig. 31-2.

Fig. 31-3.

Fig. 31-4.

Fig. 31-5.

insignia from the 1920s that is smaller than regulation is shown in Fig. 31-8. The one-inch height, specified for shirts and lapel coats in December 1926, has continued.[4]

CUFF BRAID

Effective in June 1905, officers detailed to the general staff wore a 1/2-inch-wide black stripe 3 inches from the lower edge of the service coat sleeves (Fig. 31-9). Shortly afterwards, all other commissioned officers began to wear brown cuff braid on their sleeves. During World War I many officers wore the general staff collar insignia, but only the eighty-eight members provided for by congressional action wore the black braid until July 1918, when division and higher commanders became eligible to appoint general staff officers "for the existing emergency." For the war's duration, all general staff officers wore the black sleeve braid. This black band around coat sleeves continued until 1941 to distinguish those officers assigned to the general staff (Fig. 31-10).[5] An example of the braid on a World War I overcoat sleeve is shown in Fig. 31-11. The black braid caused the major's rank knot to be raised above the cuff. Other commissioned officers did not wear a special 1/2-inch-wide stripe on the overcoat, and their rank knots rested on the bottom of the sleeve. War Department Circular 266, 11 October 1921, rescinded the general staff overcoat sleeve braid.

Fig. 31-6. A screw-back fastener on this star with the small eagle was of the type revised for the white uniform after World War I. (1 7/64 inches wide)

Fig. 31-7. In 1926 the army introduced this size of General Staff Corps insignia for the shirt collar. This was the size subsequently adopted for the lapel coat, and it is still worn today. (59/64 inch wide)

Fig. 31-8. Unofficially many officers continued to wear smaller-than-regulation insignia like this on shirts in the 1920s. (11/16 inch wide)

Fig. 31-9. Captain Harry C. Hale of the 20th Infantry Regiment was as one of the original officers detailed to the General Staff Corps. Besides the General Staff Corps insignia inside his lower sleeve rank knots, he wears gold wire cord aiguillettes, which were used only by officers of the General Staff Corps, the Adjutant General's and Inspector General's departments, aides to general officers, and adjutants. The photograph was taken in June 1906.

Fig. 31-10. Members of the General Staff Corps wore black sleeve braid on their khaki and olive drab uniforms until the eve of World War II. This major, assigned to a division general staff in Hawaii during the mid-1930s, has the black braid and General Staff Corps lapel insignia.

Fig. 31-11. On the overcoat sleeve General Staff Corps officers wore a black 1/2-inch-wide sleeve band with their rank knots above the band. Other officers had their rank knots resting on the sleeve end.

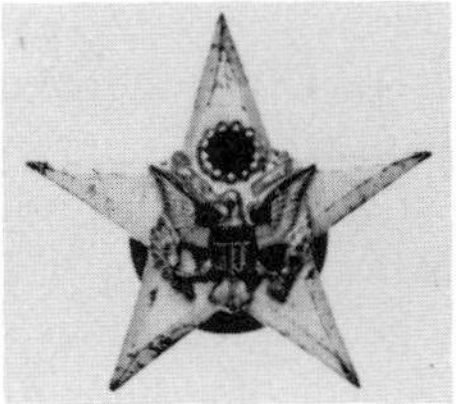

Fig. 31-6.

Fig. 31-7.

Fig. 31-8.

Fig. 31-9.

Fig. 31-10.

Fig. 31-11.

Fig. 31-12.

Fig. 31-12. A General Staff Corps armband of the type worn in Europe during World War I. The background colors indicated the wearer's assignment. In this case, solid red signified a division General Staff Corps position.

Fig. 31-13. This armband, equally divided into red above and white below, shows assignment to an army headquarters in the AEF.

Figs. 31-14 and 31-15. Miniature armbands had small clips on the back so they could be affixed to the front of the coat. Use of these small insignia made the wearer less noticeable in the trenches. (Designs 3/4 inch long; overall length of device in Fig. 31-13, 4 3/16 inches)

Armbands

During World War I the army introduced various armbands to be worn on the left arm between the elbow and the shoulder. Some of these armbands included special ones for general staff members, "to insure their free circulation when moving about." The colors of these silk, 3-inch-wide armbands designated the level of general staff assignment. An embroidered general staff device went in the center. An example of a division headquarters armband is shown in Fig. 31-12. An AEF officer is shown in Fig. 31-13 wearing an army headquarters armband. The armband colors were general headquarters, red, white, and blue; army headquarters, red and white; corps headquarters, white and blue; and division headquarters, red.

For wear in the trenches, general staff members clipped a 4-inch-long miniature of the armband to the coat front above the second button. Two examples of these small insignia are shown in Figs. 31-14 and 31-15

Fig. 31-13.

Fig. 31-14.

Fig. 31-15.

Fig. 31-16.

Fig. 31-18.

Fig. 31-17.

Fig. 31-19.

Fig. 31-20.

Fig. 31-16. *A World War II General Staff Corps armband. While the red, white, and blue color scheme remained from World War I, the eagle was replaced by a more easily made set of initials.*

Fig. 31-17. *Two general staff badges issued to those completing a year on the War Department General Staff or Department of the Army General Staff. The 3-inch diameter is for chiefs of staff and former chiefs of staff, while the 2-inch-diameter badge is for all others.*

Fig. 31-18. *Colored General Staff Corps fatigue insignia, used until the late 1960s. (Design 1 3/16 inches wide)*

Fig. 31-19. *This subdued insignia was made in Japan for U.S. troops in Vietnam. (1 7/32 inches wide)*

Fig. 31-20. *A partially subdued collar insignia, handmade in Vietnam for a U.S. General Staff Corps officer. The star is black, but the eagle from the Great Seal of the United States is sewn with colored thread. The use of semisubdued insignia was common in the first two years when they were introduced during the Vietnam War.*

for corps and for division headquarters. During World War II the letters *GSC* replaced the General Staff Corps insignia on wool armbands that used the same colors developed during World War I (Fig. 31-16).[6]

Badge

General Douglas MacArthur, while chief of staff, introduced a special identification badge for officers who served on the War Department staff. The chief of staff wore a badge 3 inches in diameter, and other officers wore a 2-inch badge (Fig. 31-17). From the badge's introduction in 1933 until early 1937 the chief of staff wore his badge on the left coat pocket above the waist, while other officers wore it on the right side. After a January 1937 change, all general staff badges were worn on the right upper coat pocket. In 1979, the sergeant major of the army and a few other selected senior noncommissioned officers became eligible for the badge. By the early 1980s authorization for wear of the badge had been expanded so that approximately twelve hundred personnel were eligible to qualify for permanent wear of the badge, which occurred after a year's service on the army general staff. In June 1985 the chief of staff, General John A. Wickham, Jr., changed the badge's name to the Army Staff Identification Badge and authorized another two hundred officer positions in the army's special staff sections (offices of the chief of chaplains, the adjutant general, and others) to become eligible for the badge.[7]

Insignia of World War II and Later

Manufacturers produced cloth collar insignia for general staff to wear on khaki uniforms during World War II, but they were not widely used. In the 1950s and 1960s many officers wore cloth branch devices on fatigue clothing (Fig. 31-18). During the Vietnam War these insignia changed from bright colors to subdued. One such device, made in Japan about 1966 for troops in Vietnam, has the eagle in purple instead of the proper brown (Fig. 31-19). A subdued insignia made in Vietnam is shown in Fig. 31-20.

Section XII

Other Detailed Branches

Chapter Thirty-Two

Aides-de-Camp

On 27 May 1778, Congress passed certain resolutions in connection with the establishment of the "American Army," including the resolutions that "two Aids-de-camp [*sic*] be allowed to each major general," thus formally beginning the use of aides.[1] Aides have always been special officers singled out to assist senior commanders. The aides to generals or to the president were, and are, distinguished by additions to the uniform, most common of which was an aiguillette (a braided gold cord) worn around one shoulder.

In June 1780, aides were distinguished from other officers by a green feather in the hat; George Washington's own aides were to wear feathers of green and white. Regulations of 1821 and 1825 stated that officers "doing duty as Aides-de-Camp are allowed to wear the staff uniform and the epaulettes according to their rank." In 1832 aides wore the general staff uniform, which included the initial use of aiguillettes, and staff officer hats with the addition of a plume identical to that of the general being served. These 8-inch-tall plumes were of different colors for the major general commanding, other major generals, and brigadier generals. Aides kept the same colors in 1839, but the plume was to be 1 inch shorter than the general's. With the 1851 cap, colored pompons replaced plumes, and aides wore buff pompons as a mark of their position. With the 1872 uniform change only the aiguillettes distinguished aides.[2]

Collar Insignia, 1902–23

Howard Chandler Christy created a special collar insignia in 1902 that has generally remained unchanged: a gilt eagle with wings reversed holding a shield bearing thirteen red and white enameled stripes. On the shield a blue chief bears stars corresponding in number to the rank of the general whom the aide serves. A convenient means of cataloging aides' insignia is by noting the designs and colors of the stars. Many of the insignia were made with the eagles in pairs to face forward, although the practice was not prescribed in regulations after 1941.[3]

Early dress insignia for aides to brigadier and lieutenant generals are shown in Figs. 32-1 and 32-2. The stars are in gold, with their variations being styled as thin-armed (Fig. 32-1) and broad-armed (Fig. 32-2). Both styles come in pairs. Figs. 32-3 and 32-4 show some service uniform bronze insignia for major generals' and lieutenant generals' aides for wear on the standing coat collar and on the shirt collar, respectively. Die variations are shown in Figs. 32-5 and

Fig. 32-1. *One of the first insignia for aides-de-camp to brigadier generals. It was introduced in 1902. Gold stars were used until World War I. (1 3/32 inches wide)*

Fig. 32-2. *Like the rank insignia worn by lieutenant generals of the time, this device for aides-de-camp has the center star larger than the other two. These stars have wide arms as opposed to the thin arms shown in Fig. 32-1. (1 1/32 inches wide)*

Fig. 32-3. *A bronze insignia for aides to lieutenant generals, for the service uniform. (1 5/64 inches wide)*

Fig. 32-4. *Shirt collar insignia for service wear by aides to major generals. (23/32 inch wide)*

Fig. 32-1.

Fig. 32-2.

Fig. 32-3.

Fig. 32-4.

32-6, with the insignia shown in Fig. 32-6 having been made in France. Fig. 32-7 shows an insignia similar to that of Fig. 32-1 but made in bronze color. Although a bronze insignia for an aide to a full general (four stars) is known, Pershing's aides evidently did not wear this device during World War I, for a photograph taken in May 1918 shows the American Expeditionary Forces commander's aide wearing a major general's aide insignia.[4]

Insignia, 1923–45

The army reintroduced enameled insignia for the white uniform from 1921 until October 1923. Late in 1923 enameled insignia became prescribed for the service uniform, replacing the bronze. Stars at that time changed from gilt to white enamel, although the size remained as before: a 1/2-inch-high eagle and a 3/4-inch-high shield. The most common variety of aides' insignia of this type is shown in figs. 32-8 and 32-9. Although army regulations specified white stars after 1924, Marine Corps aides' insignia had gold stars. On the Marine insignia the appropriate number of stars was applied to the chief of the shield after it was stamped by the die, in contrast to the common army practice of making the stars at the same time as the rest of the insignia. Evidently army officers also used the Marine Corps insignia. Both the shirt size (Figs. 32-10 and 32-11) and the coat size were initially made in pairs with from one to four stars. After 1926, regulations called for shirt insignia to be 15/16 inch high and all eagles to face to dexter (right).[5]

Some interwar shields are highly curved, while others are flat. Very small enameled insignia (Figs. 32-12 and 32-13) were used into the 1930s. The most common of these are without stars, although the normal design with stars is also found (Fig. 32-14). The reason behind the aides' insignia without stars is not known, but these curious designs exist in the large size also (Fig. 32-15). At first glance, this last 1930s insignia appears to have the eagle's wings covering the shield corners, but upon close inspection one can see in the die work that the wings do not extend to the surface of the shield, making the shield look as if the corners were clipped and the wings are resting in the notches. This design exists with both the gold stars (Fig. 32-16) and in large and small sizes with white stars (Figs. 32-17 and 32-18). With the 1926 change to the lapel coat, the standing-collar insignia, 1 1/4 inch high, made the transition to the

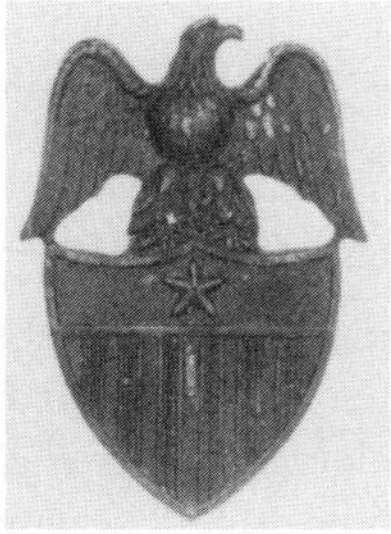

Fig. 32-5.

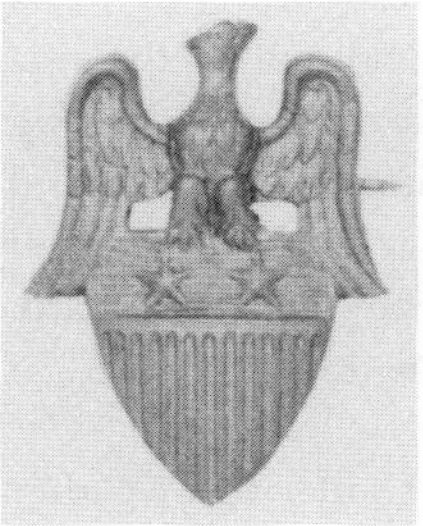

Fig. 32-6.

Fig. 32-7.

__Figs. 32-5, 32-6, and 32-7.__ Variations of aides' insignia. The insignia of Fig. 32-6 was made in France during World War I. (29/32 inch, 61/64 inch, and 1 3/32 inches wide, respectively)

Fig. 32-8.

Fig. 32-9.

__Figs. 32-8 and 32-9.__ A matched pair of insignia for aides to major generals. The white stars were used after World War I. (Each 1 3/64 inches wide)

Fig. 32-10.

Fig. 32-11.

__Figs. 32-10 and 32-11.__ Between the world wars aides' insignia with gold applied stars were made for U.S. Marine Corps officers, but they were also worn by army officers. This pair was for the shirt collar. (Each 11/16 inch wide)

Fig. 32-12.

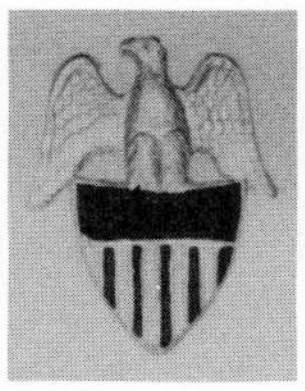

Fig. 32-13.

__Figs. 32-12 and 32-13.__ The most common small aides-de-camp insignia are these, without any stars, made between the world wars. (Each 41/64 inch wide)

Fig. 32-14.

__Fig. 32-14.__ Similar in size to the previous devices, shirt collar insignia were also made to support brigadier generals through generals, as was this one, for lieutenant generals' aides, made during the emergency period before World War II. (41/64 inch wide)

__Fig. 32-15.__ A large aides' coat insignia, without any stars, from the 1930s. (59/64 inch wide)

Fig. 32-15.

Fig. 32-16.

Fig. 32-17.

Fig. 32-18.

Fig. 32-19.

Fig. 32-20.

Fig. 32-21.

Fig. 32-22.

lapel without a size change, and the insignia remained in pairs.[6]

In 1936 these earlier insignia started to be replaced by the design shown in Fig. 32-19.[7] This 1936 style is slightly smaller than previous insignia. It lasted into the mid-1970s. Eagles vary somewhat in these insignia, and differences in the breast feathers are the easiest way to distinguish between dies. Another variation is in the size of the stars (Fig. 32-20).

Senior Aides, 1945–63

With the advent of the five-star rank in 1945 came a new design for the aide to the general of the army, as shown in Fig. 32-21. The field is blue with a ring of five white stars. Shortly after the end of World War II the insignia shown in Fig. 32-22 became that for the aide to the president. Bearing the basic aide design without any stars on the chief, the device includes an annulet with forty-eight blue stars. This insignia, first worn in July 1946, was replaced by that shown in Fig. 32-23 in May 1953. The aide to the president wore a blue shield and white stars; the vice-presidential aide had a white shield and blue stars (Fig. 32-24).[8]

Some U.S. officers wear foreign-made insignia, and one example is shown in Fig. 32-25, which was made in Germany for occupation troops after World War II and is a smaller insignia (31/32 inch high) than normal (1 1/4 inches high). Also made overseas, the insignia in Fig. 32-26 has the top of the shield nearly straight. The aide's device shown in Fig. 32-27, made in pairs in England during World War II, has the stars applied so that one die could be used for all aides up to the rank shown.

Fig. 32-23.

After the creation of the Department of Defense in 1947, the army designed insignia for their officers serving as aides to various

Fig. 32-16. *This 1930s lapel coat device for aides to major generals has gold stars and is convex. (29/32 inch wide)*

Fig. 32-17. *Besides having white stars, this aides' insignia differs from the previous one in the way the eagle faces. Between the world wars aides-de-camp insignia were often made in pairs so that the eagle would face to the wearer's front. (15/16 inch wide)*

Fig. 32-18. *For many years after World War I the chief of staff was the only general above the grade of major general, thus dating this insignia from 1939 or later. Sized to fit onto a shirt collar, it was probably made based on some late 1920s designs. (23/32 inch wide)*

Figs. 32-19 and 32-20. *Insignia of this general size and design were first made in 1936. The primary distinguishing features are the size of the stars and the pattern of the eagle's breast feathers. White enameled stripes were used until 1972. (53/64 and 27/32 inch wide, respectively)*

Fig. 32-21. *Following the creation of the rank of General of the Army came the companion aides' insignia, which had five white stars on a blue shield. (51/64 inch wide)*

Fig. 32-22. *Made by the Bailey, Banks and Biddle Company, this is the 1946–53 insignia for aides to the president. (1 7/64 inches wide)*

Fig. 32-23. *Since 1953 presidential aides have worn the standard design of an eagle above a shield, but with a blue shield bearing thirteen white stars. Only White House aides wear aiguillettes on the right shoulder, a practice dating from 1912. Single-cord aiguillettes like this were introduced in 1947 for everyday wear.*

Fig. 32-24. *Insignia of aides to the vice president, a white shield with blue stars. (55/64 inch wide)*

Figs. 32-25, 32-26, and 32-27. *Three foreign-made insignia for aides, made in Germany, Korea, and England. The first is smaller than those from the United States. The last was made with the eagles facing in pairs for all general grades. (41/64, 25/32, and 29/32 inch wide, respectively)*

Figs. 32-28, 32-29, and 32-30. *Insignia for aides to the secretary of defense (blue shield), secretary of the army (red shield), and under secretary of the army (white shield). (55/64, 53/64, and 7/8 inch wide, respectively)*

Figs. 32-31 and 32-32. *Insignia for aides to the army chief of staff. That of Fig. 32-31 is for dress and service uniforms and has a red and white shield. That of Fig. 32-32, for the fatigue uniform, has a black design on a brown shield. (7/8 and 25/32 inch wide, respectively)*

Fig. 32-33. *A typical 1950s and 1960s embroidered colored insignia for aides' fatigue uniforms. (Design 3/4 inch wide)*

Figs. 32-34 and 32-35. *Aides' insignia, hand-embroidered in Vietnam. (Designs 7/8 and 23/32 inch wide, respectively)*

Fig. 32-36. *A Korean-made aides' insignia from the 1970s. (Design 29/32 inch wide)*

Fig. 32-24.

Fig. 32-25.

Fig. 32-26.

Fig. 32-27.

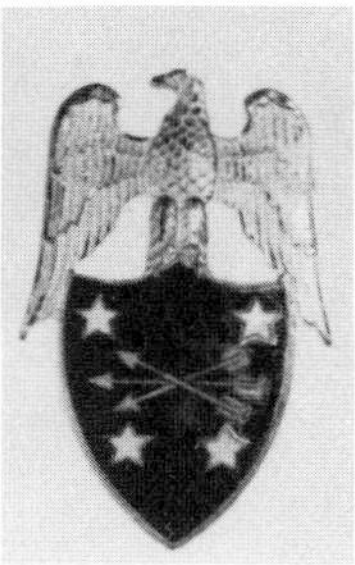

Fig. 32-28.

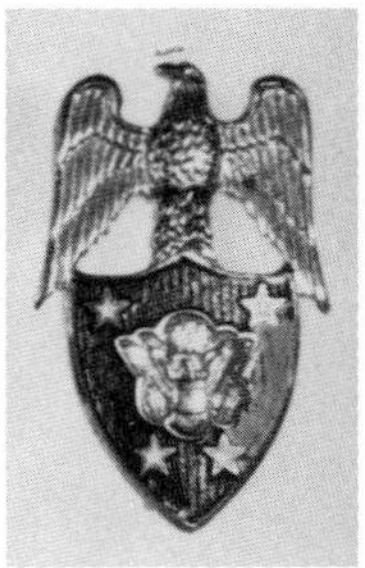

Fig. 32-29.

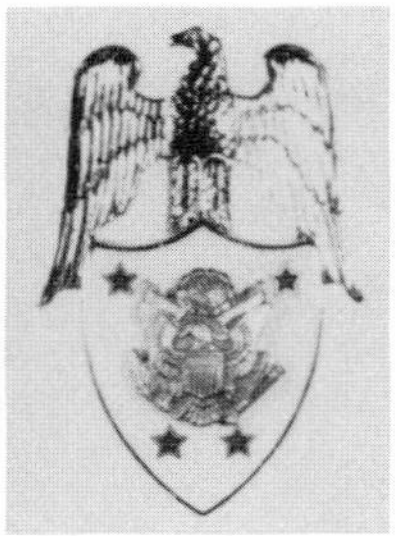

Fig. 32-30.

Fig. 32-31.

Fig. 32-32.

Fig. 32-33.

Fig. 32-34.

Fig. 32-35.

Fig. 32-36.

civilian secretaries. These insignia each bear unique designs on the shield. A blue field bearing the design from the flag of the secretary of defense (Fig. 32-28) was given to the secretary's army aide. The aides to the secretary of the army had a design on red (Fig. 32-29). In February 1963 the aide to the under secretary of the army was authorized the same design (Fig. 32-30) on a white shield. Although the last insignia has been made and may have been used at first, during the 1970s no person was assigned as the aide to the under secretary. Several variations exist for the last two designs, the most obvious being differences in the dies and three variations in the red enamel: transparent, opaque shiny, and opaque flat. Aides to the chief of staff were given special insignia (Fig. 32-31) in the fall of 1963. An example of U.S.-made cloth insignia intended for this aide is shown in Fig. 32-32.[9]

Design and Material Changes after World War II

Fig. 32-33 shows a cloth insignia of the type that became common for fatigue wear after World War II. Early in the Vietnam War, before subdued insignia became common, a Vietnamese woman hand-sewed the insignia shown in Fig. 32-34. Fig. 32-35 shows a subdued, Vietnamese-made, hand-embroidered piece. Fig. 32-36 illustrates an insignia made in Korea for an aide to a U.S. brigadier general. Although all aides' insignia are now authorized to be made in subdued cloth and metal, at least until the mid-1970s only aides to military officers wore such insignia, there being little need for officers assigned as aides to high civilians to wear field uniforms. When the need for subdued insignia arose, aides to civilians normally wore general staff insignia or the dress aides' devices, although in 1971 the army spelled out the subdued colorations in both cloth and metal. Two examples are shown in Figs. 32-37 and 32-38. It is interesting to note that all metal subdued aides' insignia are to be black, except for the insignia for the aide to the under secretary of the army, which was brown.[10]

The army changed the design of aide insignia in 1972. Instead of white enamel, brushed aluminum formed the lighter stripes and the stars. One of these new insignia, which had a mandatory wear date of 1 January 1972, is shown in Fig. 32-39.[11]

In 1977 the Institute of Heraldry designed an insignia for the army aide to the chairman of the Joint Chiefs of Staff, based on an army Uniform Board approval of 4 May. The design (Fig. 32-40) has a diagonally divided shield, the upper part blue and the lower part white, with a gold-colored eagle.[12]

National Guard

Governors' aides in various National Guard units have unique insignia. Two early bronze examples are shown in Fig. 32-41 for New Jersey and Fig. 32-42 for Connecticut. Similar dress designs are shown in Fig. 32-43 for New Jersey and Fig. 32-44 for Maryland.

Figs. 32-37 and 32-38. *Subdued U.S.-made insignia for aides to the president and aides to the secretary of defense. (Designs 13/16 inch wide)*

Fig. 32-39. *Starting in 1972, aides' insignia were to have aluminum-colored stars and stripes instead of the earlier white enamel. (51/64 inch wide)*

Fig. 32-40. *Insignia for army aides to the chairman of the Joint Chiefs of Staff. (7/8 inch wide)*

Figs. 32-41, 32-42, 32-43, and 32-44. *Insignia for aides to governors were used by National Guard officers. Components from state seals often comprised the design either on the chief, as shown by three plows of New Jersey (Figs. 32-41 and 32-43), or of the entire shield, as shown for Connecticut (Fig. 32-42) and Maryland (Fig. 32-44). (1 1/16 inches, 1 1/32 inches, 1 5/64 inches, and 1 inch wide, respectively)*

Fig. 32-37.

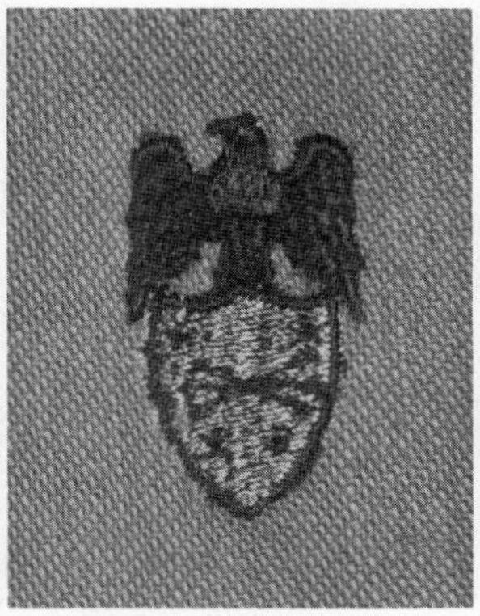

Fig. 32-38.

Fig. 32-39.

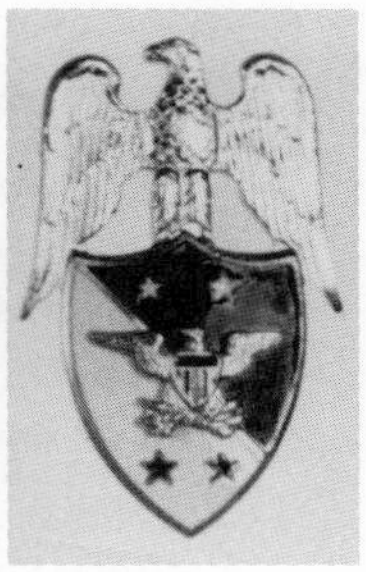

Fig. 32-40.

Fig. 32-41.

Fig. 32-42.

Fig. 32-43.

Fig. 32-44.

Fig. 32-45. Many National Guard aides added the state name to the insignia. This general style is the most common modification to the aides' insignia. (1 inch wide)

Fig. 32-46. The letters ING on the eagle's breast could stand for Illinois or Indiana National Guard, and the C in C for commander in chief. (3/4 inch wide)

Fig. 32-47. Captain C. B. Lee, aide to the army chief of staff, in July 1937. He wears aiguillettes made from gold cords with two "pencil" tips. This style is still worn on dress uniforms, and a simplified version of the type shown in Fig. 32-23 came into existence for service uniforms in 1947.

Fig. 32-48. Designed in mid-1987, this is the configuration of the insignia for the aide to the vice chief of staff. Like the insignia for the aide to the chief of staff, the shield is red and white.

Fig. 32-49. Insignia for the army's aide to the vice chairman of the Joint Chiefs of Staff. The center stripe is in blue, and the outer ones are white.

Fig. 32-45.

Fig. 32-46.

Fig. 32-48.

Fig. 32-49.

Fig. 32-47.

The most common insignia style has the state's initials or title on the chief, as for Iowa in Fig. 32-45, although the device in Fig. 32-46 is assumed to have been made for the commander in chief of the Indiana or Illinois National Guard.

AIGUILLETTES

Aides, along with other selected officers, began to wear gold aiguillettes attached to the right shoulder with the 1872 uniforms. They were worn until 1912, when aides to the president of the United States wore aiguillettes on the right shoulder and all other aides wore their aiguillettes on the left shoulder. This distinction has continued. Initially, aides wore aiguillettes only on dress and full dress uniforms. On service uniforms aides were distinguished only by the collar insignia discussed in this chapter.[13]

After World War I only presidential aides wore aiguillettes with their dress blue and white uniforms.[14] When the blue uniforms were revived for all officers in 1936, all aides again adopted the gold cords for their blue uniforms. Between the world wars, regulations did not prescribe aiguillettes for service uniforms. Despite this lack of formal authorization, some aides wore aiguillettes at that time, as in Fig. 32-47, which shows Captain C. B. Lee as aide to the chief of staff in 1937. During World War II aides did not wear aiguillettes, but in 1947 the Department of the Army reinstituted the cords. This included for the service uniform a new, simpler version, which consisted of a single cord, as shown in chapter 2, "The Changing U.S. Uniform."[15]

ADDITIONS, 1987

After ten years without any additional aides' insignia, the army added two new designs in 1987. In June 1987 the director of the U.S. Army's Institute of Heraldry received a telephone call from an officer on Lieutenant General Brown's staff, shortly after the general had been designated as the next vice chief of staff and selected for promotion to full general. The general wanted his aide to wear a unique insignia, and he requested that the Institute of Heraldry start development of such an insignia immediately. Colonel Gerald Luchino of the Institute of Heraldry, accordingly presented the first pair of insignia to the new vice chief of staff on the morning of 7 October 1987, and the general pinned them on his aide, Major Randal M. Tieszen.[16]

The insignia developed is shown in Fig. 32-48. Similar to the insignia for the aide to the chief of staff, it consists of four stars on a red and white background, with a General Staff Corps device in the center, the difference being that the red and white background is quartered instead of being cut diagonally. As with other officers' collar insignia of the time, it was also made in subdued embroidered cloth. The design itself was approved on 24 June 1987.[17]

On 26 June 1987, two days after approval of the collar ornament for the army vice chief of staff, the Institute of Heraldry's director approved an insignia for the aide to the vice chairman to the Joint Chiefs of Staff. This design is shown in Fig. 32-49.[18] Evidently the cause of this insignia was the creation of the insignia for the aide to the army vice chief of staff. It was only logical that the similar position in the Department of Defense have an insignia.

Chapter Thirty-Three

Records and Pension Office

Fig. 33-1. Embroidered Records and Pension Office insignia for the 1895 sack coat collar. The trefoil is silver, and the wreath is gold.

Fig. 33-2. A gold and silver Records and Pension Office insignia, 1899–1904. (1 11/32 inches wide)

Fig. 33-3. For the service uniform the few members of the Records and Pension Office wore a bronze insignia like this. The bronze insignia was used only in 1903 and early 1904. (1 11/32 inches wide)

The adjutant general organized the Records and Pension Office in 1889 but prescribed no special insignia until August 1892, when shoulder knots for the "Chief of the Records and Pension Office" were specified to be the same as those for the officers of the Adjutant General's Department, omitting the shield. The shoulder knots had a plain, dark blue pad bearing only the rank device, and the uniform included a gold wire aiguillette. In March 1899 the office chief became a brigadier general, and Congress allowed an assistant chief in the grade of major. At the same time, the War Department gave the assistant chief a uniform as previously described for the chief: that of the Adjutant General's Department, but without the shield insignia on the shoulder knots.[1]

Fig. 33-1.

The army established a striking insignia for the Records and Pension Office in April 1899: a "silver trefoil within and partly upon a gold wreath" (Fig. 33-1). This design was not only for the major's shoulder knots and the general's epaulette straps, but also for the collars of the dark blue sack coat and the khaki coat.[2] The metal dress insignia with silver trefoil in gilt is shown in Fig. 33-2, and the service piece in bronze for the khaki uniform is shown in Fig. 33-3.

Congress directed that the Records and Pension Office combine with the Military Secretary's Department in April 1904, and thereafter the members of the department wore the adjutant general's shield, thus abolishing the Records and Pension Office insignia.[3]

Fig. 33-2.

Fig. 33-3.

Chapter Thirty-Four

Recruiting Service

Nineteenth-century noncommissioned officers detailed from their regiments to recruiting duty continued to wear their regimental insignia. In September 1906 the army established twenty-five recruiting districts, and the sergeants and corporals assigned to those districts began to wear the letters *RS* in a wreath instead of the regimental branch insignia. Cap insignia wreaths with the *RS* were $1\frac{5}{8}$ inches high. Usually the number of the recruiting district or recruiting company was included below the letters, although today the ornaments without any numbers, used by sergeants major, are common. These insignia came in bronze (Figs. 34-1 and 34-2) and with silver letters and numbers in a gilt wreath (Fig. 34-3).[1]

Dress uniform collar insignia were of a design similar to the cap ornaments, but with the wreath more open at the top and $\frac{1}{4}$ inch shorter than the cap insignia (Fig. 34-4).[2] The 1910 bronze disks came with just the letters (Fig. 34-5) or with the *RS* and the district number (Fig. 34-6). A commercially made variation with script letters is shown in Fig. 34-7.

Fig. 34-1.

A bronze Recruiting Service cap insignia without unit number. These were made to be worn by sergeants major, but corporals and sergeants may also have used them. ($1\frac{27}{32}$ inches wide)

Fig. 34-2.

Twenty-five recruiting districts (also known at times as companies) were reflected in numbered insignia such as this bronze cap ornament. ($1\frac{53}{64}$ inches wide)

Fig. 34-3.

For dress blue and dress white uniforms Recruiting Service personnel wore cap insignia of gold wreaths. The parallel stays, letters, and numbers were silver. ($1\frac{7}{8}$ inches wide)

Fig. 34-4.

A Recruiting Service collar insignia for dress uniforms. The wreath was not as high as that for the cap ornament of similar design. The narrow center "bar" is the pin fastener that runs behind the central design. ($1\frac{27}{32}$ inches wide)

Fig. 34-5.

For sergeants major and for general issue, army regulations of 1910–21 prescribed service uniform insignia with plain block letters.

Fig. 34-6.

A typical enlisted men's 1910–21 collar insignia that includes a Recruiting Service district number.

Fig. 34-7.

Some privately made enlisted men's collar disks had stylized letters. This particular piece is gold-colored, indicating that it may have been intended for wear after 1923 (when bright insignia returned), even though the design was officially declared obsolete as of 1921. This design also exists in bronze.

Recruiting Service band members wore lyres with the letters *RS* or with *RS* and the district number superimposed.[3] Field musicians or trumpeters wore cap insignia of the straight trumpet with the same additions, as discussed in chapter 13 and 14 on musicians' insignia.

Usually dress blue or special white uniforms were worn by Recruiting Service noncommissioned officers, but even so, in 1906 and 1907 these men were prescribed the bronze letters *RS* and the district number on the campaign hat front, whenever it was worn.[4] Fig. 34-8 shows the uniform of the Recruiting Service before World War I.

The War Department abolished all special insignia for the Recruiting Service in March 1921.[5]

Fig. 34-8.

Fig. 34-8. *This private was assigned to the Recruiting Service just before World War I. He wears infantry cord edge trim on the coat, along with an infantry breast cord.*

Chapter Thirty-Five

Chief of Staff and Assistant Chiefs of Staff

AT THE URGING of Secretary of War Elihu Root, Congress provided for an army chief of staff and for members of the army's General Staff Corps by Act of 14 February 1903. In creating the General Staff Corps, however, Congress greatly limited the number of officers who could be detailed to the corps.[1] With the 1916 expansion of the army, these limitations necessitated the adoption of a new insignia for officers detailed as a chief of staff or an assistant chief of staff but who were not members of the General Staff Corps. The chief of staff for a National Guard division, for example, needed a distinguishing insignia but could not use the device of the General Staff Corps.

The army staff recommended a new collar insignia in November 1916 for officers of National Guard and regular divisions, and higher commands, who were not of the General Staff Corps. The reasoning of the War Department officials is most interesting:

> Analyzing the insignia of the General Staff Corps, it is at once seen that the national coat of arms could not be used for a national guard division. The plain star itself would be desirable if there were not danger of confusing it with the insignia of rank of general officers. Hence, it is recommended that for the Chief of Staff there be adopted a six-pointed (instead of a five pointed) star, $1\frac{1}{2}$ inches in diameter, and that for further individuality, this star be hollow, i.e., be made of material $\frac{1}{6}$ inch wide.[2]

Announced as the insignia in December 1916 was a hollow six-pointed star, $1\frac{1}{4}$ inches in diameter, with the width of the metal $\frac{1}{6}$ inch.[3] Two bronze versions are shown in Figs. 35-1 and 35-2. A gilt insignia that could have been worn on the white or blue uniform in early 1917 is illustrated in Fig. 35-3. Small bronze shirt collar ornaments (Fig. 35-4) were also made.

In May 1917 Congress gave the president authority to enlarge the army as necessary for the world war, and this action ended the need for the insignia, which was rescinded in December 1917, although the devices continued to be included in some commercial catalogs into the 1920s.[4]

Fig. 35-1. *In late 1916 and in 1917 a few officers who were not members of the General Staff Corps, but who were assigned general staff duties in tactical units such as divisions, wore hollow six-pointed stars like this bronze example. ($1\frac{3}{32}$ inches wide)*

Fig. 35-2. *This version does not follow the official design in that the metal is $\frac{1}{8}$ inch wide instead of the prescribed $\frac{1}{6}$ inch. ($1\frac{1}{8}$ inches wide)*

Fig. 35-3. *Officially designated for the chief of staff and assistant chief of staff, this gilt insignia would have been used only from December 1916 until April 1917 on dress uniforms. It was probably worn on very few uniforms because of both the short time of authorization and the limited number of officers who qualified to wear it. ($1\frac{3}{32}$ inches wide)*

Fig. 35-4. *A small chief of staff and assistant chief of staff insignia for the shirt collar. ($\frac{37}{64}$ inch wide)*

Fig. 35-1.

Fig. 35-2.

Fig. 35-3.

Fig. 35-4.

Section XIII

The Army's Navy

Chapter Thirty-Six

Army Transport Service and Harbor Boat Service

THE U.S. NAVY sailed into Guantanamo and Manila bays in 1898, establishing the United States as a world power. The sea service, however, was geared to fighting, not to supporting the army on distant shores. The army clearly had a problem providing supplies and support services to its forces across the ocean, and it had to solve its own problem. The army previously had used boats during support of western explorations and in the Civil War, but those efforts had been made only with shallow-water fleets.

At the outbreak of the war with Spain, the United States did not have under its control a single ship designated for passenger or freight service in the Atlantic or the Pacific, although the government did own several harbor boats and ferries operating around the ports of New York and San Francisco and in the Gulf of Mexico. The demands of the U.S. commitment in Cuba, Puerto Rico, the Philippines, Hawaii, China, and elsewhere required several ships to support the army. The Army Transport Service (ATS) grew to fulfill that demand. A companion service to the ATS, the Harbor Boat Service (HBS), evolved from the ferry boats and other small craft in 1904, when the army finally organized it and gave it official status.[1]

Both the ATS and the HBS had special and unique uniforms and insignia until 1944, when the Transportation Corps dropped the two organizational titles and reorganized seagoing personnel as marine personnel of the Transportation Corps, with assignment to transport, interisland, or harbor service. In 1949 the organization of the new Military Sea Transport Service ended the half-century of army control of some ships, although a July 1917 agreement between the army and the navy that had placed all troop ships under the navy for the duration of World War I had earlier interrupted this fifty-year span.[2]

To understand the uniforms and insignia described in this chapter, the reader needs to be aware that some crew members of an ATS ship were army personnel, some (during World War II) were navy personnel, and some were civilians operating under contract with the army. Normally the administrative personnel were military, while the ships' crews were civilians.[3] Because civilians formed the bulk of a ship's permanent personnel, they evidently influenced the military on board. Few men wore uniforms. On some occasions the army specified special uniforms and insignia for ATS and HBS members, but apparently most ships' captains did not put a high priority on enforcement of uniform regulations. The majority of evidence is that seagoing military members and contract crews did not follow the requirements for insignia and uniforms.

While the Quartermaster Corps controlled most ships used for transporting soldiers, supplies, and animals, a few vessels did have responsibilities to other branches. Ships used for laying deep sea cable, while supplied and maintained by the Quartermaster Corps, came under the operational control of the Signal Corps. The HBS operated a large fleet of small vessels for the transport of troops, passengers, freight, baggage, ammunition, and supplies between army posts and neighboring cities as well as for support of the Coast Artillery Corps. These coast artillery boats pulled targets, served as dispatch vessels, and planted mines. Between 1917 and 1919 the U.S. Navy took control of the ATS, as noted above, and the army supplied few men to the

Fig. 36-1. During World War I the U.S. Navy took control of Army Transport Service ships, but ATS shore personnel continued to be army members. In this photograph of World War I ATS members, the man on the right in the rear wears a two-colored armband with the letters ATS. The significance of the armband during this period has been lost.

Fig. 36-1.

ATS in that time, but some dock personnel wore armbands like that shown in Fig. 36-1.[4]

In early 1943 the Quartermaster Corps ships were transferred to the newly formed Transportation Corps, becoming part of the Water Division. They remained there until the new Department of Defense merged the Army Transport Service and the Naval Transport Service to form the U.S. Military Sea Transport Service (MSTS) in October 1949. This organization was later renamed the Military Sealift Command in August 1970.[5] ATS and HBS uniforms and insignia after 1949 are not discussed because those organizations were no longer part of the army.

Army Transport Service

Initial ATS uniform regulations of 1899 prescribed various ship markings as well as uniforms and insignia and required each ship to carry uniforms and insignia for sale to officers and crew. The 1899 officers' blouse described in these regulations was a single-breasted, standing-collar, navy blue coat very similar to that adopted by army officers in 1895. Insignia, however, were very different. Stripes on the lower sleeve showed rank in the navy style (these ranks will be discussed later because they are insignia unique to the ATS). Regulations also authorized a similar white coat without any collar devices. With the blue coat officers could wear either blue or white trousers, while with the white coat only white trousers were proper. Officers wore the letters *USAT* on the front of the collar, followed by one of the insignia listed in Table 36-1.[6] Examples of this uniform, with insignia, are shown in Fig. 36-2.

ATS Officers' Insignia, 1912–30

The Army Transport Service regulations published by the quartermaster general in 1912 prescribed both blue and white uniforms for officers and men, and also khaki clothing for those personnel engaged in Philippine interisland service. Officers' rank insignia remained of the same type as those of 1899, and collar devices did not radically change. The letters *ATS* became an integral part of each insignia, however, replacing the separate letters *USAT*. Gold devices added silver letters, and the chief steward's silver crescent added gold letters.[7] These 1912 collar ornaments are shown in Table 36-2.

ATS Officers' Changes, 1930

In 1930 the quartermaster general revised the 1912 circular on ATS and HBS uniforms and insignia. Although some changes can be noted between the 1912 and 1930 directives,

Table 36-1. *Officers' Collar Insignia Worn with USAT Letters, 1899.*

Device	Worn By
Gold propeller and star	Superintending engineering
Gold propeller	Assistant superintending engineering Engineering officers
Gold anchor and star	Marine superintendents
Gold anchor	Assistant marine superintendents Chief stevedore Assistant chief stevedore Port steward All line officers Clerks on piers
Two crossed gold pens	Clerks on transports
Silver crescent	Chief steward

Fig. 36-2.

Fig. 36-2. *U.S. Army Transport Service officers about 1900. Either white or dark blue trousers could be worn with the dark blue coat, which bore the gold-embroidered letters U.S.A.T. (U.S. Army Transport) and another insignia on the collar. Rank was shown by sleeve bands similar to those used in the navy except for their black color.*

Table 36-2. *Officers' Collar Insignia, Army Transport Service, 1912–30.*

Device	Worn By	Device	Worn By
 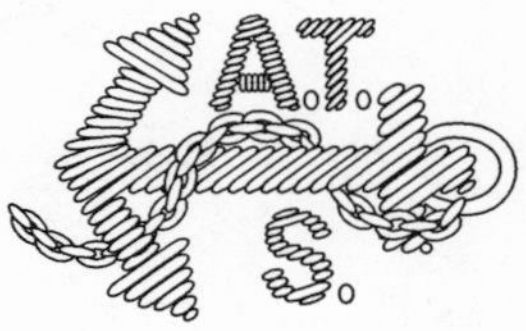	Marine superintendent		Engineer officer
 	Superintending engineer	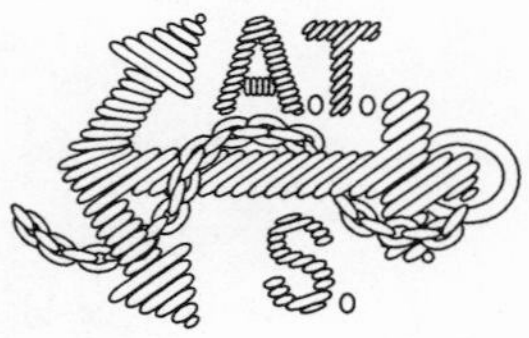	Deck officers, chief and assistant stevedore, port steward, clerks on pier
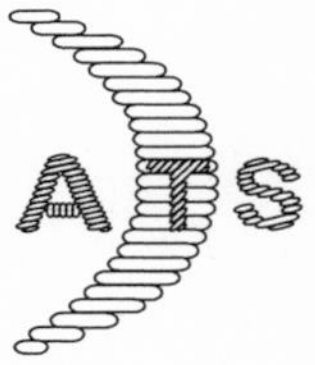	Chief steward	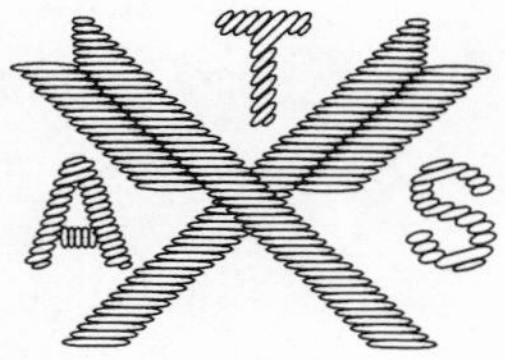	Clerks on transports

Fig. 36-3.

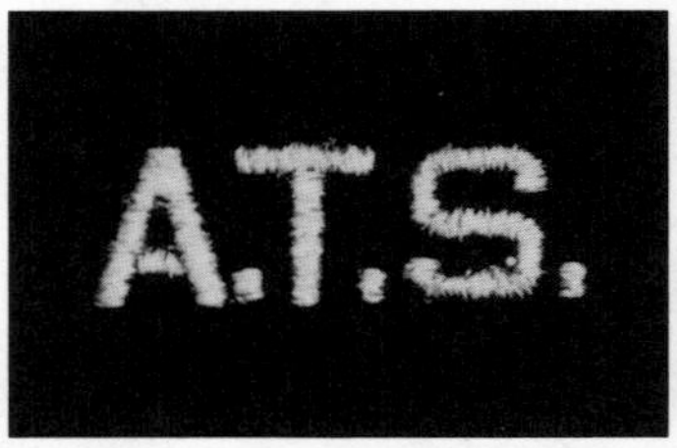

Fig. 36-4.

Fig. 36-5.

Fig. 36-3. *Metal block A.T.S. letters of the type commonly made during World War II. This design was prescribed first in 1930. Silver letters were for stewards and associated personnel, and gold for all others. (1 1/4 inches wide)*

Figs. 36-4 and 36-5. *The two styles of embroidered letters used during the World War II period. That of Fig. 36-4 is made with fine silver wire, and that of Fig. 36-5 uses the wider gold wire that required hand stitching. (Letters 1 11/32 and 1 9/32 inches wide, respectively).*

Fig. 36-6. *After 1930 only senior ATS officers wore this lapel insignia with a blue wheel rim and gold-colored metal. Users were marine superintendents and superintending engineers. (1 1/4 inches wide)*

there are many similarities, including the provision of khaki uniforms for vessels engaged in Hawaiian and Philippine interisland service.[8] Some U.S. Army photographs show these new uniforms in 1929, a year before the announcements in regulations. Because of these similarities, it is reasonable to assume that most if not all people in the affected organizations, especially officers, continued to use the 1912-style insignia until almost 1930, despite the substantial gap in documentation.

Regulation collar insignia changed in 1930 along with the official switch from the standing-collar coat to the lapel coat. On the collar, above the lapel notch, men were to wear one of three devices: steward's department members had silver block *ATS* letters 7/16 inch high; ships' officers, clerks, and quartermaster agents were to have identical letters, but in gold color (Figs. 36-3, 36-4, and 36-5); and the marine superintendent and superintending engineer wore the gilt *ATS* letters superimposed "on and over a ship's

Fig. 36-6.

Table 36-3. *Army Transport Service Officer-Style Lapel Insignia, 1930–49.*

Device	Worn By	Dates
Gold fouled anchor, 1 inch high	Marine superintendent	1930–44
	Asst. marine superintendent	1930–44
	Master	1930–44
	Chief stevedore	1930–44
	Asst. chief stevedore	1930–44
	All deck officers	1930–49
Five gold lightning rays	Radiomen (see Figs. 36-9 to 36-11)	1933–44
Gold three-bladed propeller, 1 inch in diameter	Superintending engineer	1930–44
	Asst. superintending engineer	1930–44
	All engineering officers	1930–49
	Associate superintending engineer	1942–44
Silver crescent, 1 inch	Stewards	1930–44
Gilt crescent, 1 inch	Steward officers	1945–49
Quartermaster device, 3/4 inch high	Quartermaster agents	1930–42
Two gold crossed quill pens, 1 inch high	Clerks (see Fig. 36-12),	1930–44
	Administrative officers	1945–49
Transportation Corps device	Transportation agents	1942–44

Fig. 36-7.

Fig. 36-7. *Regulations called for a change in uniforms and insignia in 1930, and evidently this change actually started in 1929. These officers wear the new ATS uniform with the old insignia on their lapels, but the captain, in the center, wears one of the new insignia on his collar. He does not wear the prescribed ATS letters.*

Fig. 36-8. *An ATS steward in 1930 wearing the new-style uniform. His insignia are not according to regulation; the silver letters ATS should be on the collar and not on the cap.*

steering wheel, 1 1/3 inches in diameter, with 13 spokes, handles, and 13 stars on a blue enameled rim" (Fig. 36-6). Several insignia could appear on the lapel below the collar insignia, as listed in Table 36-3. These are illustrated in the authoritative National Geographic Society publication of 1944, and they are common in collections.[9]

Unusual events, still unexplained, occurred during the 1930 transition. One 1929 shipboard photograph shows the "1930" lapel coat.[10] Several 1931 photographs of the new lapel coat show men using the old 1912–30 insignia with the *ATS* letters integral to the design and not separate. These older insignia should have gone out with the standing-collar coat, and new insignia should have come into use. In the 1931 photographs, no one wore the "new" separate *ATS* letters on the collar. In Fig. 36-7 the captain wears his insignia vertically on his collar, but all others wear the anchor and integral *ATS* on the lapel, some with the anchor pointing out and others with the anchor pointing in. Fig. 36-8, a photograph of a steward in this series, shows the 1930–44 lapel devices but does not include the prescribed *ATS* collar letters. The army could write regulations, but it had a hard time enforcing them. The writers in Washington evidently did not understand shipboard conditions, and War Department staff officers did not convince ships' captains to change their ways. With the World War II expansion of the armed forces, uniforms and proper insignia appeared. Examples shown in Figs. 36-9 through 36-12 are typical lapel insignia.

Transportation Corps Marine Service, 1944–49

Modern warfare, with its complex weapons, depends on the timely delivery of many pieces at key locations when required. In World War II, as during World War I, the army discovered that no single branch was

Fig. 36-8.

fully coordinating all transportation. The Quartermaster Corps had transportation responsibilities between the world wars, but the demands of the worldwide conflict overwhelmed the corps, and a new branch dedicated to transportation came on the scene: the Transportation Corps.

With the creation of the new branch, the ATS and HBS were transferred to the Transportation Corps. ATS and HBS insignia changed somewhat, but the 1930 concept of collar devices remained until 1944. Although regulations concerning the 1944 change have

Figs. 36-9 and 36-10. *ATS insignia of the style typically used in the 1930s and during World War II. These particular pieces were for a radioman. The metal insignia of Fig. 36-10 was similar to the insignia used by electricians about 1900. (Embroidered device $1\frac{5}{8}$ inches wide; metal lightning bolts $1\frac{3}{8}$ inches wide)*

Fig. 36-11. *A late World War II radiomen's insignia. ($1\frac{1}{32}$ inches wide)*

Fig. 36-12. *Lapel insignia for clerks (1930–44). The title was changed to administrative officer near the end of World War II (1945–49). ($1\frac{1}{16}$ inches wide)*

Fig. 36-13. *Late in World War II most ATS officers wore naval uniforms without any collar or lapel insignia. Shown is Captain Stefan Wesplowske, commander of U.S. Army Transport (USAT) Ganandor, 1944–45. Above the stripes on his sleeve is the Transportation Corps insignia.*

Fig. 36-14. *Rechristening of the USAT Acorn Knot as the USAT Sergeant George Keathley at San Francisco. Sergeant Keathley's mother holds his photograph, while his wife holds a citation. The ATS captain on the left is the ship's master. This March 1949 photograph shows the uniforms and insignia which became obsolete later that year. The anchor on the lapel shows that the captain is a deck officer.*

Fig. 36-9.

Fig. 36-11.

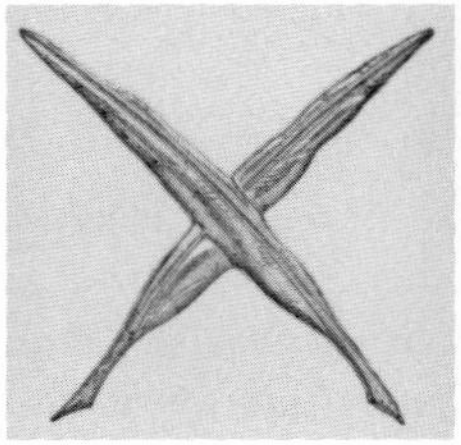

Fig. 36-12.

Fig. 36-13.

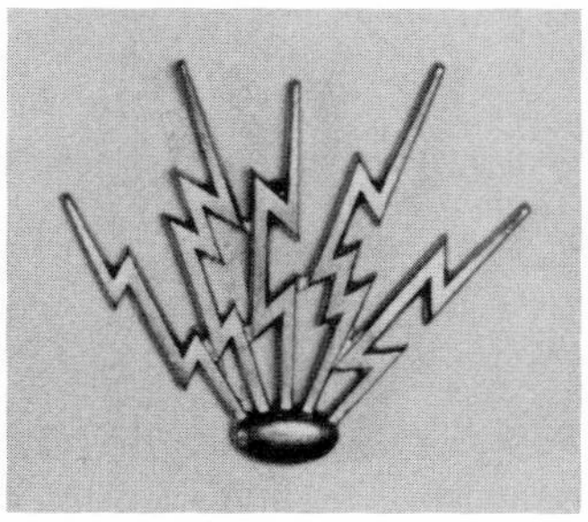

Fig. 36-10.

Fig. 36-14.

Table 36-4. *Officers' Lapel Insignia, Transportation Corps Marine Personnel, 1945–49.*

Device	Worn By
A gold fouled anchor, 1 inch high	All deck officers (example in Fig. 36-14)
A gold three-bladed propeller, 1 1/8 inches in diameter	All engineering officers (example in Fig. 36-16)
Two gold quill pens, crossed, 1 inch high	All administrative officers (example in Fig. 36-12)
A gold crescent, 1 inch high	All steward officers

not yet been located, photographs show that collar insignia disappeared in 1944 (Fig. 36-13). In August 1945 the army's Transportation Corps changed the uniforms associated with what had been the ATS and HBS. Actually, more than the uniforms changed. Instead of two services, the War Department switched to a concept of marine personnel with a single uniform and three pay scales, and ATS and HBS personnel became civilian Transportation Corps marine service employees.[11]

Examples of some officers' uniforms used from 1945 or 1946 until 1949 are shown in Figs. 36-14, 36-15, and 36-16. On the collar, ships' officers wore 7/16-inch-high gilt block letters, either embroidered (Fig. 36-17) or metal (Fig. 36-18). Stewards wore silver letters *TC* (Fig. 36-19). One of the lapel insignia listed in Table 36-4 went 1/2 inch below the collar notch. Photographs show a wide variance in what officers actually wore, and the uniform mixture shows that officers could and did wear any naval-looking uniform and insignia. A 1945 example is illustrated in Fig. 36-20. New cap insignia, described in the following section, also came into use, as did new rank insignia, until the new MSTS, founded in 1949, finally replaced these army ship employees.

Harbor Boat Service

Before the organization of the HBS some six years after the Spanish-American War, civilian contract crews manned government vessels. In 1903 the Quartermaster's Department

Fig. 36-15. *ATS Captain Pumphrey in his post–World War II uniform along with the master-at-arms of the USAT Admiral Sims, January 1947. While the ship's captain is in the correct uniform, the master-at-arms wears only his regulation cap along with khaki clothing without any collar insignia.*

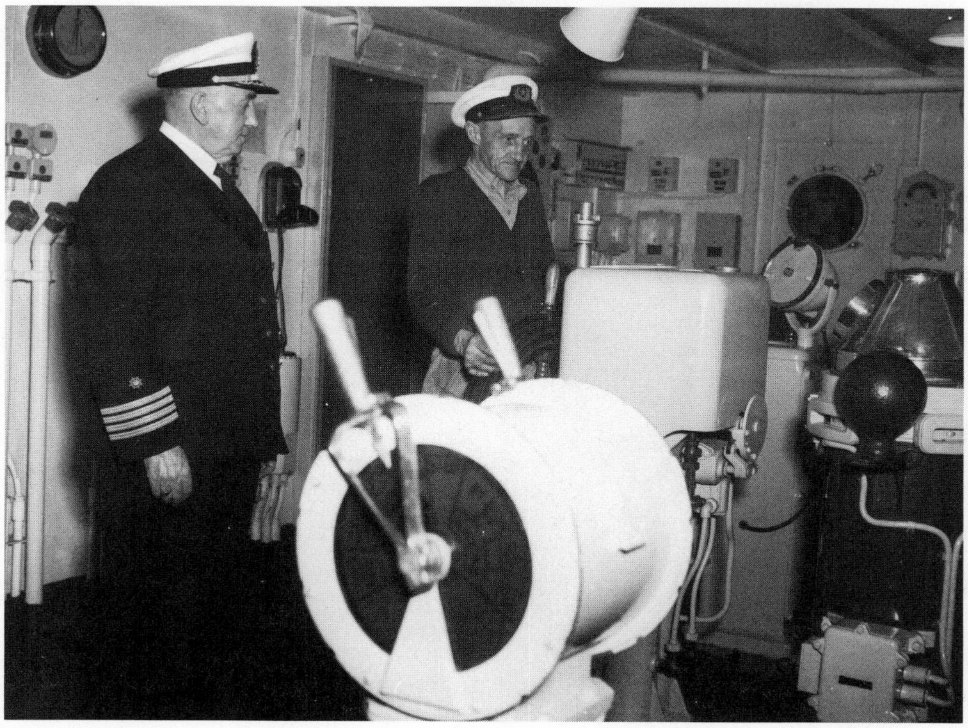

Fig. 36-15.

Table 36-5. *Harbor Boat Service Officers' Ranks, 1912.*

Device	Worn By
Two stripes and a fouled anchor	Master
One stripe and a fouled anchor	First mate or pilot
A fouled anchor	Second mate
Two stripes and a three-bladed propeller	Chief engineer
One stripe and a three-bladed propeller	Assistant engineer

Fig. 36-16. *Engineering officer aboard an army transport in early 1949. The Transportation Corps insignia on the sleeve above the gold rank bands on the cuff show the person is a member of the ATS, while the three-bladed propeller on the lapel indicates engineering duty.*

Fig. 36-17. *The letters T.C. (Transportation Corps) were prescribed at the close of World War II for both officers and petty officers. Commissioned officers typically used embroidered insignia. (1 3/16 inches wide)*

Figs. 36-18 and 36-19. *Gilt and silver letters introduced at the close of World War II. Stewards wore the silver, and all others the gold. Note that the silver letters are joined at the top and have clutches for fastening. Both construction styles are common in both colors. Petty officers wore these on the right khaki shirt collar point. (57/64 and 15/16 inches wide, respectively)*

Fig. 36-20. *The ensign on the left is a member of the ATS, while the officer on the right is from the Coast Guard. By the end of World War II, any nautical uniform was apparently in use within the ATS.*

contained fifty-three such boats, including seven ferry boats, one serving New York City. The organization of the HBS in 1904 marked a gradual and orderly increase in service, including replacement of old boats with newer, more efficient ones.[12]

The HBS received uniform and insignia regulations in September 1904. The uniforms themselves were generally the same type as those of the ATS, but apparently men wore no insignia except cap devices and enlisted rank chevrons. Regulations of 1912 first fully described HBS uniforms.[13] I do not know if officers used rank insignia between 1904 and 1912, but it is reasonable to presume that these early ranks are identical to those of 1912. The 1912 officers' ranks, embroidered on the lower coat sleeves, are shown in Table 36-5.

The 1929–31 ATS uniform modernization included changes to HBS clothing and insignia. Officers' ranks, still worn on the coat sleeves, changed to those listed in Table 36-6. Collar insignia omitted the *ATS* letters that had been introduced for the larger service, but below the bare collars the lapels did carry one of the two devices listed in Table 36-7.[14]

Fig. 36-16.

Fig. 36-17.

Fig. 36-18.

Fig. 36-19.

Fig. 36-20.

Table 36-6. Harbor Boat Service Officers' Ranks, 1930.

Device	Worn By
Two ½-inch bands, ¼ inch apart	Master or chief engineer
One ½-inch band	Mate, pilot, or assistant engineer

Table 36-7. Harbor Boat Service Officers' Lapel Insignia, 1930.

Device	Worn By
Gold 1-inch fouled anchor	Master, mate, or pilot
Gold three-bladed propeller, 1 inch in diameter	Chief engineer or asst. chief engineer

Fig. 36-21. An ATS captain with the pre-1933 sleeve rank insignia. When the ATS omitted these cuff bands, they were replaced by navy-style shoulder boards.

Figs. 36-22 and 36-23. About 1944, ATS officers placed Transportation Corps insignia on their lower sleeves just above the rank bands. (embroidery each 1 1/16 inches wide)

Fig. 36-24. A 1933–44 ATS shoulder insignia, used to show both rank and department. The widths and number of bands indicated rank, while red between the bands was used by engineers, light blue was for transportation agents, and a lack of special color specified deck officers.

ATS Officers' Rank

Between 1899 and 1933 officers' coats showed rank by means of sleeve braid (Fig. 36-21). The navy blue coats carried black sleeve braid, usually with a gold five-pointed navy-style star above, while the khaki coat used khaki stripes without any star. The white coat showed no rank insignia. A summary of the regulation sleeve braid is in Table 36-8 and includes that used after 1933.

Most of the officers' black sleeve braid disappeared in May 1933, replaced by more nautical looking devices, including shoulder boards that regulations called "shoulder insignia." These insignia, 5½ inches long and of dark blue cloth, indicated both rank and duty. Gold bands showed the rank, while colors between the bands indicated the department. Light blue showed that the wearer was a transportation agent, while red was worn by the men of the engineering department. The absence of a special color indicated deck officers.[15] An example of the engineering department shoulder insignia is shown in Fig. 36-24. These shoulder boards were replaced by other boards under the 1944 marine personnel regulations. Another change, evidently in 1945, caused ATS officers to switch to

Fig. 36-21.

Fig. 36-24.

Fig. 36-22.

Fig. 36-23.

shoulder boards of U.S. Navy style, with the Transportation Corps emblem as the corps device (Fig. 36-25).

Between 1945 and 1949, Transportation Corps marine personnel were graded into three pay scales: transport, inter island, and harbor. Rank distinction was by color of the stripes. Transport scale ranks were shown by

Table 36-8. *Army Transport Service Officers' Sleeve Stripes (black or gold if not otherwise noted).*

Device	Worn By	Dates of Use
Four stripes 1/2 inch wide, 1/4 inch apart, and star above	Marine superintendent	1899–1930
	Superintending engineering	1899–1930
	Asst. marine superintending	1899–1930
	Asst. superintending engineering	1899–1930
	Master of transports	1899–1930
	Chief engineer	1912–30
One stripe 1 3/4 inches wide and one stripe 1/2 inch wide	Marine superintendent	1942–44
	Superintending engineer	1942–44
One stripe 1 3/4 inches wide	Marine superintendent	1930–42
	Superintending engineer	1930–42
	Associate marine superintendent	1942–44
	Associate superintending engeer	1942–44
Four stripes 1/2 inch wide, 1/4 inch apart	Chief engineer	1899–1912, 1930–44
	Chief stevedore	1899–1938
	Asst. chief stevedore	1899–1938
	Port steward	1899–1938
	Asst. marine superintendent	1930–44
	Asst. superintending engineer	1930–44
	Master	1930–44
	Quartermaster agent	1930–34
Three stripes 1/2 inch wide, 1/4 inch apart, and star above	First officers	1899–1930
	First engineers	1899–1930
Three stripes 1/2 inch wide, and one stripe 1/4 inch wide, 1/4 inch apart	Chief officer	1938–44
	Staff engineer	1942–44
Three stripes 1/2 inch wide, 1/4 inch apart	First officer	1930–44
	First asst. engineer	1930–44
	Quartermaster clerks on transports	1930–33
	Chief steward	1930–44
	Quartermaster agent	1934–42
	Transportation agent	1942–44
Two stripes 1/2 inch wide, and star above	Second officers	1899–1930
	Second engineers	1899–1930
Two stripes 1/2 inch wide	Quartermaster clerk (senior)	1934–42
	Second officer	1930–44
	Second asst. engineer	1930–44
	Freight clerk on transport	1930–33
	Second steward	1930–44
	Second cabin steward	1930–33
	Transport clerk (senior)	1942–44
	Electrical engineer	1942–44
One stripe 1/2 inch wide, and star above	Third officer	1899–1930
	Third engineer	1899–1930
One stripe 1/2 inch wide	Third asst. engineer	1930–44
	Third officer	1930–44
	Third assistant officer	1930–33
	Third steward	1930–44
	Quartermaster clerk (junior)	1934–42
	Transport clerk (junior)	1942–44

***Table 36-8.** Army Transport Service Officers' Sleeve Stripes (black or gold if not otherwise noted).* continued

Device	Worn By	Dates of Use
One stripe 1/4 inch wide	Fourth officer	1930–38
	Junior third asst. engineer	1930–33, 1942–44
	Junior engineer	1933–42
	Junior third officer	1942–44
	Junior officer	1938–42
Star	Fourth officer	1899–1930
	Fourth engineer	1899–1930

NOTE: In addition to the rank braid, between 1930 and 1933 a square made from 1/2-inch braid, with a 1/2-inch hollow center, went on the upper sleeve stripe of licensed officers as shown in Fig. 36-21 (WD, AR 30-1180, 1 Oct. 1930, par. 2b[6]). Photographs show that officers switched to a gold-embroidered Transportation Corps insignia on the coat cuff, above sleeve marks in the style of the U.S. Navy, about 1944 or 1945. One such example is in Fig. 36-13, with two insignia shown in Figs. 36-22 and 36-23.

all gold stripes. Inter island scale ranks had the lowest stripe of lustrous black lace with other stripes of gold, while harbor scale ranks had all stripes of lustrous black lace. These Transportation Corps marine officers' ranks are shown in Table 36-9.

ATS and HBS Officers' Cap Insignia

Both officers and petty officers wore cap devices. The original 1899 officers' device, illustrated in Fig. 36-26, was a "U.S. Army silver spread eagle, surmounting two crossed anchors in gold." While regulations illustrate only the embroidered piece, the wording allowed for gilt metal also. A new cap insignia came with the 1930 regulations: a gilt eagle, 1 2/3 inches high, with a colored shield (Figs. 36-27 through 36-30).[16]

The 1904 HBS cap device consisted of a vertical gold-plated metal anchor, 1 3/4 inches high, with an enameled Quartermaster's Department device on the center (Fig. 36-31). This remained the HBS officers' cap insignia until 1942, when the ATS ornament officially replaced the anchor.[17] Examples of this device for the overseas cap are shown in Figs. 36-32 and 36-33.

A more nautical insignia was introduced in August 1945. The metal insignia was to be made with a red shield covered by the Transportation Corps device (Fig. 36-34), although most actually have a gilt shield, as shown in Figs. 36-35 and 36-36.[18]

Fig. 36-25.

***Fig. 36-25.** Officers wore shoulder boards like those of the U.S. Navy with a Transportation Corps insignia, like this one, from 1944 until 1949.*

Fig. 36-26.

***Fig. 36-26.** An original 1899–1930 officers' ATS cap insignia. (Eagle 2 inches wide)*

Fig. 36-27.

***Fig. 36-27.** Starting in 1930, ATS officers' cap insignia were to add a red, white, and blue shield. This metal version was made late in World War II. (2 13/64 inches wide)*

Figs. 36-28 and 36-29. *Typical World War II ATS officers' cap devices. That of Fig. 36-28 was made from a fine gold thread, and that of Fig. 36-29 was made from a heavy silver wire. Steward officers wore silver cap ornaments. Both thicknesses of wire were used to make both colors of insignia. (Eagles 2 9/32 and 2 7/16 inches wide, respectively)*

Chief Petty Officers' Uniforms and Cap Devices, 1899–1930

Chief petty officers wore a gold-embroidered cap wreath with various center devices until 1930. These are summarized in Table 36-10, and examples are shown in Figs. 36-37 through 36-43. For all petty officers of 1899 except stewards, the coats, either white or blue, were double-breasted with a roll collar and five gilt buttons on each side. Stewards wore silver buttons. Navy blue seamen's trousers went with the double-breasted coats.[19]

Chief Petty Officers after 1930

Chief petty officers wore the same style of uniform after 1930 as before. In 1945 chief petty officers began to wear the officer-style *TC* block letters on the coat collars. A 1947 example is shown in Fig. 36-44, although the two chief petty officers also have

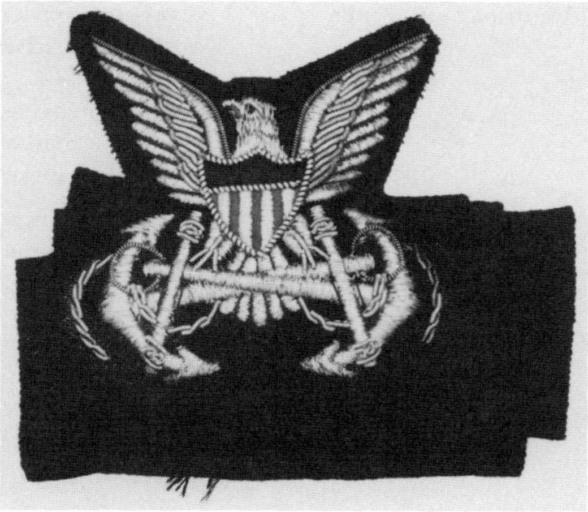

Fig. 36-28.

Table 36-9. *Officers' Rank Insignia, Transportation Corps Marine Personnel, 1945–49.*

Transport Scale				Inter Island Scale			Harbor Scale		
Assim. Army Rank	**Title**	**Salary**	***No. of Stripes**	**Title**	**Salary**	***No. of Stripes**	**Title**	**Salary**	***No. of Stripes**
				DECK DEPARTMENT					
Col.	Master	$5486	4						
Lt. Col.	Chief Officer	3731	3½	Master (IS)	$4988	4	Master (HS)	$4190 & up	3
Major	1st Officer	3199	3	Chief Officer (IS)	3392	3½	Chief Officer (HS)	3150–4189	2½
Capt.	2nd Officer	2818	2	1st Officer (IS)	2909	3	1st Officer (HS)	2735–3149	2
1st Lt.	3rd Officer	2420	1	2nd Officer (IS)	2562	2	2nd Officer (HS)	2381–2734	2
2nd Lt.	Jr. 3rd Officer	2057	½	3rd Officer (IS)	2200	1	3rd Officer (HS)	2035–2380	1
Warrant				Jr. 3rd Officer (IS)	1870	½	Jr. 3rd Officer (HS)	Below 2035	½
				ENGINE DEPARTMENT					
Col.	Chief Engineer	$4955	4						
Lt. Col.	Staff Engineer	3731	3½	Chief Engineer (IS)	$4505	4	Chief Engineer (HS)	$4190 & Up	3
Major	1st Asst. Engineer	3199	3	Staff Engineer (IS)	3392	3½	Staff Engineer (HS)	3150–4189	2½
Capt.	2nd Asst. Engineer	2818	2	1st Asst. Engr. (IS)	2909	3	1st Asst. Engr. (HS)	2735–3149	2
1st Lt.	3rd Asst. Engineer	2420	1	2nd Asst. Engr. (IS)	2562	2	2nd Asst. Engr. (HS)	2381–2734	1½
2nd Lt.	Jr. 3rd Asst. Engr.	2057	½	3rd Asst. Engr. (IS)	2200	1	3rd Asst. Engr. (HS)	2035–2380	1
Warrant				Jr. 3rd Asst. Engr. (IS)	1870	½	Jr. 3rd Asst. Engr. (HS)	Below 2035	½
				ADMINISTRATIVE DEPARTMENT					
Major	Ship Trans. Agent	$3210	3						
1st Lt.	Ship Trans. Clerk	2517	1	Ship Trans. Agent (IS)	$2919	2			
2nd Lt.	Asst. Ship Trans. Clerk	2217	½	Ship Trans. Clerk (IS)	2289	1			
				STEWARD'S DEPARTMENT					
Major	Chief Steward	$2979	3						
Captain	2nd Steward	2709–2978	2	Chief Steward (IS)	$2709	2	Chief Steward (HS)	$2709	1
1st Lt.	3rd Steward	2200–2708	1	2nd Steward (IS)	2200–2708	1	2nd Steward (HS)	2200–2708	½

*NOTES:

1. ¼ inch above top stripe, a ¾-inch embroidered Transportation Corps device (Figs. 36-14 and 36-22).
2. Shoulder tabs, as shown in Fig. 36-25, were worn on khaki and white coats and on overcoats.
3. Sleeve of blue uniform coats carry rank stripes, as shown in Figs. 36-14, 36-15, and 36-16.
4. Transport Scale ranks are all gold stripes.
5. Inter Island Scale ranks have the lowest stripe of lustrous black lace and the remaining stripes of gold.
6. Harbor Scale ranks have all stripes of lustrous black lace.

Table 36-10. *Embroidered Army Transport Service Petty Officers' Cap Devices, 1898–1930.*

Device* (within wreath)	Worn By	Dates	Figure Number
Crossed anchors	Boatswain	1899–1930	36-37
Crossed axes	Carpenter	1899–1930	36-38
Crossed guns	Gunner	1899–1930	36-39
Ship's wheel (silver)	Second steward	1899–1908	
Crescent (silver)	Second steward	1908–30	36-40
Star	Master-at-arms	1899–1930	36-41
	Asst. master-at-arms	1899–1930	
WATCHMAN	Watchman	1899–1930	
BAGGAGE MASTER	Baggagemaster	1899–1930	36-42
Propeller	Chief machinist	1899–1930	36-43
	Machinist	1899–1930	
	Refrigerator mechanic	1899–1930	
	Asst. refrigerator mechanic	1899–1930	
	Deck engineer	1899–1930	
	Electrician	1899–1930	
	Plumber	1899–1930	
	Boilermaker	1899–1930	
	Water tender	1912–30	
2nd CABIN STEWARD	Second cabin steward	1912–30	
3rd STEWARD	Third steward	1912–30	
4th STEWARD	Fourth steward	1912–30	
COM'S'Y STOREKEEPER	Commissary storekeeper	1912–30	
YEOMAN	Yeoman	1912–30	
PORTER	Porter	1912–30	
BARBER	Barber	1912–30	

*Gold color if not otherwise noted.

the Transportation Corps insignia on the lower sleeve, which is not specified in the post–World War II marine personnel regulations. Also authorized in 1945 was the use of department insignia on coats and shirts by chief petty officers. The two chief petty officers shown in Fig. 36-44 should have department insignia on the coat lapels below the *TC*

Fig. 36-29.

Fig. 36-30. *HBS officers, as well as those of the ATS, used the same cap insignia after 1942. This piece was used on the Pacific Coast during World War II.*

Fig. 36-31. *From 1904 until 1942, HBS officers used this cap insignia. (1 inch wide)*

Fig. 36-32.

Fig. 36-33.

Figs. 36-32 and 36-33. *Starting in World War II, ATS and HBS officers could wear khaki uniforms with matching overseas caps. These small insignia were to go on the caps. (1 13/64 inches and 7/8 inch wide, respectively)*

Fig. 36-34. *Starting in August 1945, ATS officers were to wear cap insignia like this one, with a red enameled shield bearing the Transportation Corps device. ($2^{25}/_{64}$ inches wide)*

Figs. 36-35 and 36-36. *These are basically all-gilt U.S. Navy cap insignia with a Transportation Corps insignia added. These expediently made pieces should have had an all-red shield. ($2^{13}/_{32}$ and $2^{33}/_{64}$ inches wide, respectively)*

Fig. 36-37. *ATS petty officers' cap insignia for boatswains, 1899–1930.*

Table 36-11. *Chief Petty Officers' Department Devices, 1945–49.*

Device	Worn By
BAGGAGE MASTER	Baggageman-embalmer
Two 1-inch crossed anchors	Boatswain
Two 1-inch crossed hand axes	Carpenter
Three-bladed propeller, $1^1/_8$ inches in diameter	Machinist Refrigerating engineer Deck engineer Chief electrician Plumber Boilermaker
Two crossed 1-inch batons	Master-at-arms
1-inch crescent	Steward Chief cook Chief baker
Two crossed 1-inch keys	Storekeeper
CLERK	Transportation clerk
Wheel with thirteen spokes, handles, and stars on blue rim, $1^1/_8$ inch in diameter	Wheelman
YEOMAN	Yeoman

Fig. 36-34.

Fig. 36-36.

Fig. 36-35.

Fig. 36-37.

letters. On khaki shirts, the *TC* went on the right collar and the department insignia on the left.[20] A complete 1945–49 listing of these department insignia is in Table 36-11, and two examples are shown in Figs. 36-45 and 36-46.

Metal cap devices, of the same design as the embroidered insignia, were specified in 1930. Table 36-12 lists the design that was placed within a gold-colored wreath, 1 3/4 inches high and 2 3/8 inches long, supported on gold-colored crossbars.[21] The official drawing of these insignia states that the metal ornament was to be three-fourths size for use on the World War II overseas cap, although regulations did not list this provision. In many cases cap devices constituted a chief petty officer's only "uniform," since, as already noted, many ships did not enforce

Table 36-12. *Metal Army Transport Service Chief Petty Officers' Cap Devices, 1930–49.*

Device (within wreath)	Worn By	Dates	Figure Number
Crossed anchors	Boatswain	1930–49	36-47
Crossed guns	Gunner	1930–45	36-48
COMMISSARY STOREKEEPER	Commissary storekeeper	1930–33	36-49
Crossed axes	Carpenter	1930–49	36-50
Crossed batons	Master-at-arms Asst. master-at-arms	1930–49 1930–45	36-51
Propeller	Chief machinist Machinist Refrigerating engineer Asst. refrigerating engineer Deck engineer Electrician Asst. electrician Plumber Boilermaker Water tender Asst. deck engineer Chief electrician Asst. machinist Asst. plumber	1930–42 1930–49 1930–49 1930–45 1930–49 1930–42 1930–45 1930–49 1930–49 1930–45 1942–45 1942–49 1942–45 1942–45	36-52
BAGGAGEMASTER	Baggage master Baggageman-embalmer	1930–45 1945–49	36-53
WATCHMAN	Watchman	1930–45	36-54
YEOMAN	Yeoman	1930–49	36-55
PORTER	Porter	1930–45	36-56
BARBER	Barber	1930–45	36-57
STORE KEEPER	Storekeeper	1933–45	36-58
Ship's wheel with thirteen stars on a blue rim	Wheelman	1933–49	36-59
ASSISTANT STOREKEEPER	Asst. storekeeper	1942–45	
Crescent	Steward Chief cook Chief baker	1945–49 1945–49 1945–49	
Crossed Keys	Storekeeper	1945–49	
CLERK	Transportation clerk	1945–49	
Plain wreath with no central design	Oiler Bath steward	1942–45 1942–45	

uniform regulations. Fig. 36-15 shows a 1947 photograph of a chief petty officer wearing a cap device officially obsolete nearly twenty years. Several proper cap insignia are shown in Figs. 36-47 through 36-59.

One nonregulation cap insignia is a gold-colored anchor with the Transportation Corps device superimposed. The two similar insignia from which it descends are the previously discussed HBS officers' cap device (a

Fig. 36-38. *ATS petty officers' cap insignia for carpenters, 1899–1930.*

Fig. 36-39. *ATS petty officers' cap insignia for gunners, 1899–1930.*

Fig. 36-40. *ATS petty officers' cap insignia for second stewards, 1908–30.*

Fig. 36-41. *ATS petty officers' cap insignia for masters-at-arms or assistant masters-at-arms, 1899–1930.*

Fig. 36-42. *ATS petty officers' cap insignia for baggagemasters, 1899–1930.*

Fig. 36-43. *ATS cap insignia for a variety of petty officers, 1899–1930. Those who wore this design included various machinists and machanics.*

Fig. 36-44. *Post–World War II petty officers with the new Transportation Corps insignia. The man on the left should have branch insignia on his lapels below the letters TC which appear on his collar. A Transportation Corps device is on his lower sleeve.*

Fig. 36-38.

Fig. 36-39.

Fig. 36-40.

Fig. 36-41.

Fig. 36-42.

Fig. 36-43.

Fig. 36-44.

gold anchor with the Quartermaster Corps device) and the U.S. Navy chief petty officers' cap ornament (a gold fouled anchor with silver *USN*). This post-1942 army insignia, obviously associated with the sea, may have been worn by some petty officers of the ATS or HBS, because commissioned officers already had a more substantial insignia. Examples for the visor and overseas caps are in shown Figs. 36-60 and 36-61.

More closely related to official insignia are the devices shown in Figs. 36-62, 36-63, and 36-64. The last consists of a stock embroidered wreath with the central design consisting of a brass insignia taken from a separable enlisted men's collar disk.

World War II saw the manufacture of many commercial stock cap insignia embroidered in naval style, and today they may be mistaken for regulation ATS pieces. An example is shown in Fig. 36-65, but the difference is evi-

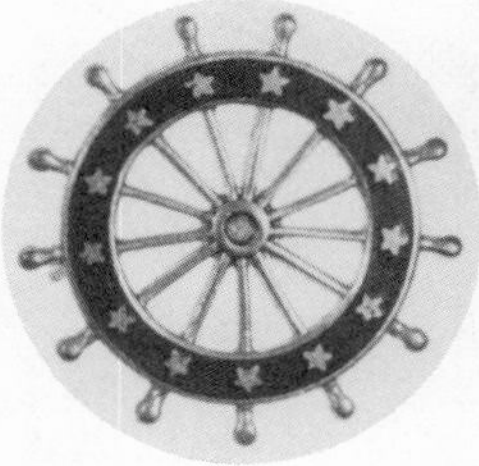

Fig. 36-45.

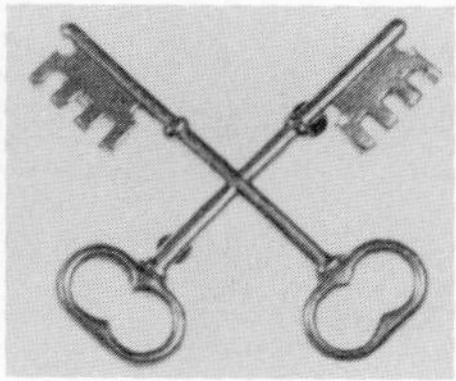

Fig. 36-46.

Fig. 36-47.

Fig. 36-48.

Fig. 36-49.

Fig. 36-50.

Fig. 36-51.

Fig. 36-52.

Fig. 36-45. *Lapel insignia of wheelmen, 1945–49. ($1\frac{3}{16}$ inches wide)*

Fig. 36-46. *Lapel insignia of storekeepers, 1945–49. ($1\frac{3}{32}$ inches wide)*

Fig. 36-47. *Cap insignia for boatswains, 1930–49. This large size was worn on the bill cap, but similar insignia two-thirds this size went on overseas caps. ($2\frac{3}{8}$ inches wide)*

Fig. 36-48. *Cap insignia for gunners, 1930–45.*

Fig. 36-49. *Cap insignia for commissary storekeepers. The prescribed design was to have the two words spelled out, and it was to be used from 1930 to 1933, but the insignia shown was made during World War II.*

Fig. 36-50. *Cap insignia for carpenters, 1930–49.*

Fig. 36-51. *Cap insignia for masters-at-arms, 1930–49, and for assistant masters-at-arms, 1930–45.*

Fig. 36-52. *A wide variety of mechanical personnel wore this cap insignia during various dates between 1930 and 1949.*

Fig. 36-53. *Cap insignia for baggage masters, whose title was changed to baggageman-embalmer in 1945, although the insignia did not change.*

Figs. 36-54 through 36-58. *Various cap insignia used by the ATS during World War II. Some of the insignia made at the close of the war had the words on the parallel bars applied over the wreath instead of under the wreath, as in these examples.*

Fig. 36-59. *Cap insignia for wheelmen, 1933–49. The wheel's rim was enameled in dark blue.*

Figs. 36-60 and 36-61. *Nonregulation cap insignia made during World War II and modeled after the pre-1942 HBS device. The smaller insignia (Fig. 36-61) was for the overseas cap. ($1\frac{3}{32}$ inches and $\frac{49}{64}$ inch wide, respectively)*

Fig. 36-53.

Fig. 36-54.

Fig. 36-55.

Fig. 36-56.

Fig. 36-57.

Fig. 36-58.

Fig. 36-59.

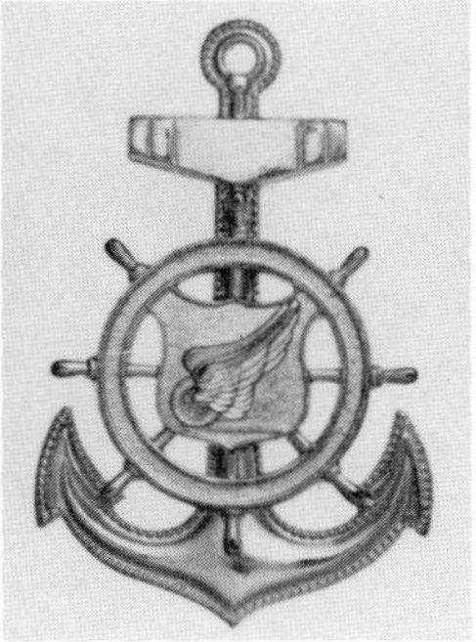

Fig. 36-60.

Fig. 36-61.

Fig. 36-62.

Fig. 36-63.

Figs. 36-62 and 36-63. *Unofficial cap insignia of this type were widely worn by ATS petty officers during and after World War II. (Wreaths $2\frac{9}{16}$ and $2\frac{25}{32}$ inches wide, respectively)*

dent when it is compared with the proper wreaths shown in Figs. 36-37 through 36-43.

Enlisted Men's Uniforms and Insignia, ATS and HBS

Seamen of the ATS and HBS wore traditional navy-style seamen's jumpers with long, square collars and, under the collar, a black neckerchief. Through 1942 the large collars carried stars, but evidently Transportation Corps school personnel switched to ship's wheels in 1943 and then to the Transportation Corps device to show the ATS affiliation and to distinguish the uniform from the navy's. Photographs of enlisted ATS men in uniform are scarce and so have provided little of what has been learned. Regulations of 1945 describe sailors' uniforms: a blue jumper decorated in each corner of the collar with a $\frac{3}{4}$-inch white embroidered Transportation Corps device, and a white jumper with a blue embroidered insignia. During World War II the ATS also authorized khaki shirts, and in 1945 seamen were to wear the block *TC* letters, the same design as those of officers and petty officers, but the letters were to be worn on both shirt collars.[22]

For enlisted men the 1899 cap was of the navy style, of dark blue cloth, flat on top, with a crown that extended over the vertical sides. Around the side the men wore a special cap ribbon that ended in a bow on the

Fig. 36-64.

Fig. 36-64. *An enlisted men's collar disk was taken apart and the Transportation Corps insignia was fastened to a stock embroidered cap wreath to make this nonregulation ATS or HBS cap insignia. (Wreath $2\frac{23}{32}$ inches wide)*

Fig. 36-65.

Fig. 36-65. *Standard nautical cap insignia of this type may be mistaken for ATS or HBS insignia. These were often used by commercial maritime petty officers and may occasionally have been used by ATS or HBS members. ($2\frac{5}{8}$ inches wide)*

Fig. 36-66.

Fig. 36-66. *Until World War II, crew members of U.S. Army transports wore cap ribbons bearing their ship's name, like this example. (Letters $\frac{1}{2}$ inch high)*

Fig. 36-67. This early World War II armband continued the interwar practice in which armbands were heavily used in and around ports to identify key personnel to the many passengers. The buff background indicates that this armband was made while the ATS was still part of the Quartermaster Corps, before the advent of the Transportation Corps.

Fig. 36-67.

left. Enlisted men's cap ribbons through 1930 were black silk, 1½ inches wide, with the letters *USAT* and the ship's name in ½-inch-high gold woven letters (Fig. 36-66). Members of the HBS wore a cap ribbon with the ship's name and a Quartermaster Corps insignia at each end. During early World War II, apparently three sets of letters came into use with the cap ribbons, all following the navy's wartime lead and eliminating the ship's names: *TC, ATS,* and *US ARMY.* This was in contravention of the 1930 and 1942 regulations prescribing "a white tape or braid, ½ inch in width, around brim, ½ inch from edge" and the 1945 requirement calling for a band "set with a *TC* cap ribbon and bow."[23]

Armbands

Armbands, or brassards, as shown in this chapter's first illustration, were common in the ATS. Throughout the 1920s and through 1947 regulations prescribed a multitude of armbands for personnel associated with the ATS so that passengers could readily identify men performing selected duties or personnel in authority.[24] Besides the regulation armbands, ATS men created additional ones, such as that shown in Fig. 36-67, which predates the Transportation Corps, since the cloth is a Quartermaster Corps buff with navy blue letters.

Section XIV

Branch Insignia Developed Between 1910 and 1945

Chapter Thirty-Seven

Service School Detachments

By a congressional act of 1890, the artillery detachment then serving at West Point changed to the Army General Service Detachment in the Quartermaster's Department. This was the army's first special school detachment. At other army schools, before 1909 the army simply stationed support troops at the site and retained the men on regimental rolls. In 1909, Congress authorized each of the schools to have special detachments. The men in the detachments no longer belonged to regiments, but instead formed the Army Service Schools Detachments, except for the support soldiers at the U.S. Military Academy, whose unit was renamed Service Detachment, USMA.[1]

Starting in 1900 the Army General Service Department wore various quartermaster-related cap insignia. Initially the men wore silver *QMD* letters in a gilt wreath (Fig. 37-1), a device first proposed in 1894. In 1900 the Philadelphia Quartermaster Depot ordered 500 letters *QMD* in wreaths. This insignia lasted until 1903, when the Quartermaster's Department design (Fig. 37-2) became the cap insignia. The three years in which the *QMD* was used allowed issue of about 100 of the 492 ornaments actually delivered.[2]

The Army Service Detachment, USMA, contained wagoners, librarians, brick masons, and others required to assist at the military academy, while the Army Service Schools Detachments comprised troops who performed instructional or instructional support duties at a school of their speciality. In 1910 enlisted men of both organizations received special insignia consisting of a hammer crossed with a quill pen, all encircled by a cogged wheel. The bronze or gilt design went on a disk 1½ inches in diameter for the cap (Figs. 37-3 and 37-4) and on a 1-inch-diameter disk for the collar (Figs. 37-5 and 37-6). The circular shape was the reason the quartermaster general selected this design, because from

Fig. 37-1.

Fig. 37-2.

Fig. 37-3.

Fig. 37-4.

Fig. 37-1. *A West Point Army Service Detachment cap insignia, 1900–1903. The silver letters are in a gilt wreath. (2 39/64 inches wide)*

Fig. 37-2. *Between 1903 and 1910, members of the U.S. Military Academy service detachment wore Quartermaster's Department insignia, like this one, since the Quartermaster General's Department controlled the organization during that period. (1 1/32 inches wide)*

Figs. 37-3 and 37-4. *Cap insignia, 1910–18, for members of the Army Service Detachment, USMA, and of the Army Service Schools Detachments. The gilt disk was for the dress cap, and the bronze for the service cap. (Each 1½ inches wide)*

Fig. 37-5.

Fig. 37-6.

Fig. 37-7.

Fig. 37-8.

Fig. 37-9.

Fig. 37-5. *A bronze service uniform collar insignia prescribed in 1910. (1 inch in diameter)*

Fig. 37-6. *Only members of Army Service Schools Detachments wore gilt disks before World War I. This example could have been worn by detachment members at several schools, including Fort Leavenworth, Fort Riley, Fort Monroe, and the U.S. Military Academy. A gilt US disk accompanied this insignia on the dress uniform.*

Fig. 37-7. *At least one private firm made this nonregulation enlisted men's collar insignia, without the gear, about the time of World War I.*

Fig. 37-8. *Although they were not in regulations after 1921, gilt insignia exist with the background of lines and small shields. These may have been worn at West Point or at one or more of the service schools in the late 1920s.*

Fig. 37-9. *The detachment at West Point, about 1904, with officers. The large cap wreaths contain the letters QMD shown in Fig. 37-1.*

Fig. 37-10. *A sergeant of the Army Service Schools detachment (colored) with his wife, 1911. The disk shape of the cap and collar ornaments were distinctive of the Army Service Schools Detachments.*

Fig. 37-11. *The sergeant major of the Army Service Schools Detachment, Fort Riley, Kansas, 1916. He wears on his collar and cap the bronze insignia of the crossed hammer and quill pen inside a cogwheel.*

a distance a detachment member could be easily identified by the round insignia outline on his cap.[3]

For a consistent appearance on the dress uniform, service school detachments members wore the letters *US* on a gilt disk instead of the usual outline letters. Only service school detachments soldiers wore the gilt *US* disks until 1923, when all soldiers switched to gilt disks. Some editions of regulations called for school insignia to be a crossed hammer and quill pen; consequently, some makers produced the device without the cogwheel (Fig. 37-7). The army rescinded the service school insignia in 1921, but evidently West Point support personnel continued to wear theirs, as gilt disk insignia exist with the background of crosshatched lines and small shields (Fig. 37-8).[4]

Fig. 37-10.

Fig. 37-11.

Note that the army stationed other special groups at West Point, including artillery, cavalry, and engineer detachments and trumpeters. These men were administratively separate from the Army Service Detachment, USMA, as was the USMA Band, which also had its own insignia. Neither the Army Service Detachment, USMA, nor the Army Service Schools Detachments insignia were made for officers. Figs. 37-9, 37-10, and 37-11 show insignia worn by various service detachments personnel.

Chapter Thirty-Eight

Aviation

INITIALLY, ARMY AVIATION personnel served as part of the Signal Corps. Pilots and mechanics split off during World War I and formed a separate branch, the Air Service, which the National Defense Act of 1920 formally established as a part of the Regular Army. The branch title changed to the Air Corps in 1926 and to the Army Air Force in 1942.[1]

Officers' Insignia to 1920

From 1 August 1907 until publication of Special Regulations Number 41, 15 August 1917, personnel assigned or attached to the aviation section of the Signal Corps had no special insignia other than the pilot's badge. Uniforms and insignia for those assigned to the aviation section were identical to others in the same branch of service; the few officers and soldiers attached from other army branches for training purposes wore insignia of their assigned branch.

In an 18 April 1918 request, the AEF chief of the Air Service sent a letter to the AEF commander in chief requesting authorization of a sketched insignia for "Air Service, Overseas." General John J. Pershing approved the request on 27 April 1918. Another document, dated 2 May 1918, also from the AEF chief of the Air Service, is headed, "New Insignia for the Air Service" and includes a large drawing of the insignia. At the bottom is a notation by General Benjamin Foulois: "Notify all sections and stations of the Air Service." The insignia resulting from these April and May actions are shown in several variations.[2]

Fig. 38-4.

Fig. 38-4. This pilot's uniform is unusual in that he wears a campaign hat overseas during 1918. Most troops overseas wore the trench or overseas cap adopted from the various allied armies. On this aviator's collar is the first Air Service insignia.

Fig. 38-1.

Fig. 38-1. The first aviation branch insignia for members who were assigned to the "Air Service, Overseas." The officers' insignia were authorized from April to July 1918, but the official approval was probably in recognition of insignia already in use. The winged globe is silver superimposed on a bronze Signal Corps insignia. (1 13/64 inches wide)

Fig. 38-2.

Fig. 38-2. One of several variants of the Overseas Air Service insignia. (1 7/32 inches wide)

Fig. 38-3.

Fig. 38-3. This gold Signal Corps insignia and silver winged globe is baffling. It may have been worn on the dress white uniform, use of which was not suspended during World War I.

Fig. 38-5.

Besides these large insignia for the standing collar, both designs, with and without the globe, were made in the smaller shirt sizes, as shown in Figs. 38-9 and 38-10.

On 29 May 1918 the Air Service separated from the parent Signal Corps and adopted an attractive design representing the new-found ability to fly. The basic design served the army aviation branch until the formation of a separate service in 1947, and then it was reintroduced in 1983. July 1918 regulation changes announced the new Air Service branch insignia as "a pair of wings, with a vertical silver propeller, the height of the device . . . to be 1 inch.[3]" The most common design is of the type shown in Fig. 38-11, although military tailors and uniform companies in France and England sold variations of the insignia made in those countries. A pattern made in England (Fig. 38-12) features broad tan wings instead of dull bronze ones. Fig. 38-13 shows a IX Corps pilot wearing this type of insignia. Those insignia made in France are unique in both wing style and in the S-curved propeller (Fig. 38-14). The insignia made in small shirt sizes are shown in Figs. 38-15 ($1\frac{1}{4}$ inches wide) and 38-16 (1 inch wide).

Fig. 38-6.

Fig. 38-7.

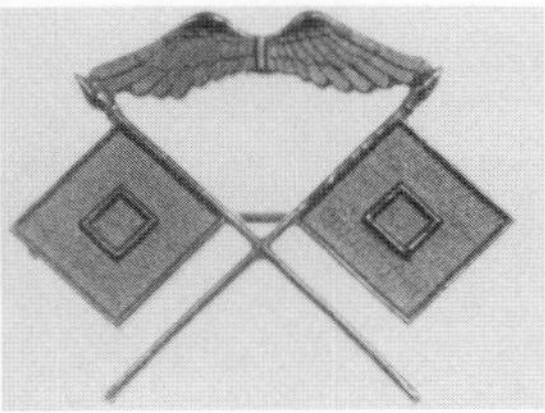

Fig. 38-8.

Fig. 38-9.

Fig. 38-10.

Fig. 38-11.

Fig. 38-12.

The first of these is a Signal Corps officers' collar insignia superimposed by a small silver winged world globe (Fig. 38-1). A variant pattern, with a smaller silver winged globe, also exists (Fig. 38-2). A totally unexplained piece, shown in Fig. 38-3, has a gilt Signal Corps insignia and a silver overlay. These and many other variations were used by pilots, as shown in Figs. 38-4 and 38-5.

Widely used variations include the wings only, leaving off the globe. Figs. 38-6 and 38-7 show small silver wings superimposed on the signal flags and torch. The most unusual variation is shown in Fig. 38-8, which omits the center torch and adds dull bronze wings between the upper flagstaffs.

Fig. 38-5. *Aviators led the movement toward more comfortable lapel coats. This 1918 pilot wears a British coat, shirt, and tie with U.S. insignia. The pilot's wings on the overseas cap were another unauthorized liberty.*

Fig. 38-6. *Instead of the winged globe, many early aviation insignia carried only the silver wings. ($1\frac{15}{64}$ inches wide)*

Fig. 38-7. *Not only are the wings on this insignia of an unusual shape, but they also are placed very high on the Signal Corps flags. ($1\frac{13}{64}$ inches wide)*

Fig. 38-8. *This insignia with the missing torch and bronze wings may have been made for a pre–World War I state aviation organization, although its unauthorized use by Regular Army personnel can not be ruled out.*

Fig. 38-9. *A shirt-sized Overseas Air Service insignia of the prescribed design.*

Fig. 38-10. *A shirt-sized insignia with only the silver wings instead of the globe and wings. ($\frac{27}{32}$ inch wide)*

Fig. 38-11. *Starting in July 1918, the newly formed Air Service adopted a silver propeller and bronze wings. ($1\frac{23}{32}$ inches wide)*

Fig. 38-12. *An English-made U.S. Air Service insignia with light brown wings and short silver propeller.*

Fig. 38-13.

Fig. 38-14.

Fig. 38-15.

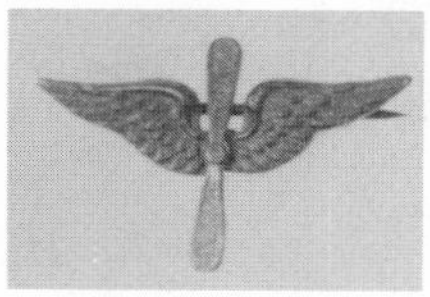

Fig. 38-16.

Fig. 38-13. *The pilot on the right is wearing a collar insignia similar to, if not identical to, that shown in Fig. 38-12.*

Fig. 38-14. *This insignia was made in France for AEF pilots. (1 3/4 inches wide)*

Figs. 38-15 and 38-16. *Shirt collar insignia for the Air Service, 1918–23. (Fig. 38-16, 1 1/64 inches wide)*

Fig. 38-17. *New York's 1st Aero Squadron may have had this bronze insignia for its enlisted men. (1 inch in diameter)*

Fig. 38-18. *Although the officers' design was approved, the enlisted men's version was never allowed by regulation. This insignia is all bronze in color. (1 inch in diameter)*

Fig. 38-19. *Another unusual enlisted men's insignia is this one with the number 1 near the top. These disks were remade for collectors in the 1980s. (1 1/64 inches in diameter)*

Fig. 38-20. *The four-bladed propeller was used on cloth insignia for enlisted men in certain aviation assignments, but it was never prescribed for collar insignia. (1 1/8 inches in diameter)*

Figs. 38-21 and 38-22. *U.S.-made enlisted men's collar insignia came with either a bronze or a silver propeller, although only the bronze one was regulation. (Each 1 inch in diameter)*

Fig. 38-23. *This common World War I enlisted men's collar insignia with stubby wings has an applied silver propeller. (61/64 inch in diameter)*

Fig. 38-24. *A French-made enlisted men's Air Service insignia. (1 1/64 inches in diameter)*

Bronze Disks

The regulation 1-inch bronze collar disk for the Signal Corps had shown crossed signal flags with an upright burning torch at the center. Some pre–July 1918 nonregulation disks for the Air Service exist based on the Signal Corps insignia. The first (Fig. 38-17) has the number *1* and wings and may represent New York's 1st Aero Squadron, while Fig. 38-18 shows the approved officers' design adapted in a nonregulation way to a bronze disk. No reference has yet been found describing the 1-inch disk shown in Fig. 38-19, but the device of a four-bladed propeller with wings on either side seems to identify it as a collar insignia for enlisted aviators. The small number *1* on the disk shows that this unique piece may also have been made for the New York National Guard before World War I, but its true history must await further research. The last early nonauthorized design is on a slightly oversized disk and consists of a four-bladed propeller, the same design worn by World War I enlisted aviation ground personnel as a sleeve insignia (Fig. 38-20).

The new wing and propeller device replaced the Signal Corps insignia on sol-

Fig. 38-17.

Fig. 38-18.

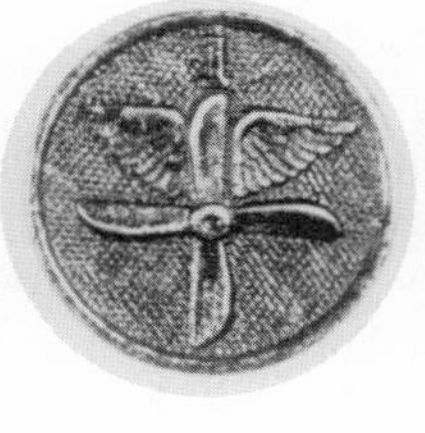

Fig. 38-19.

Fig. 38-20.

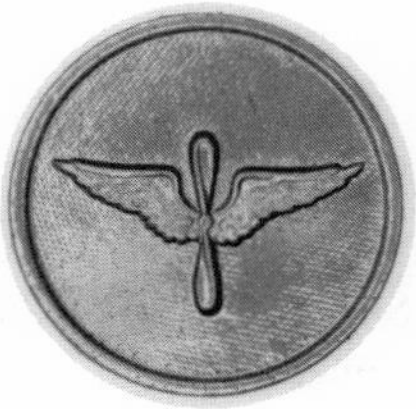

Fig. 38-21.

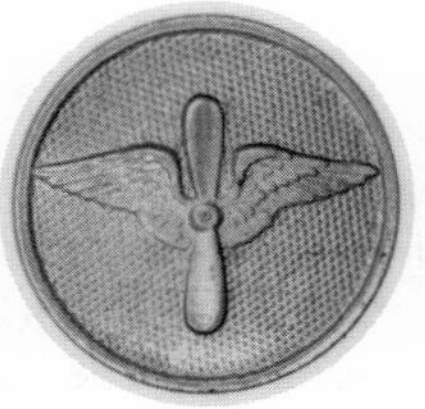

Fig. 38-22.

Fig. 38-23.

Fig. 38-24.

diers' disks, and the design continued to be the insignia for, consecutively, the Air Service, the Army Air Corps, and the Army Air Forces. While many variations of World War I patterns exist, only five are illustrated. A silver propeller was commonly applied or painted (Figs. 38-21 and 38-22), following the precedent of the officers' device, but the bronze propeller was specifically called for by October 1921.[4] The insignia shown in Fig. 38-23, with a silver propeller, was made overseas in an unknown country, while the disk shown in Fig. 38-24, with a bronze propeller, is known to have been purchased in Paris. A U.S.-made disk with a bronze propeller is shown in Fig. 38-25.

Enlisted Men's Cap Insignia

The wreathed Air Service branch insignia shown in Fig. 38-26 conforms to noncommissioned officers' cap insignia described from 1904 through 1917. However, the army discarded all such insignia in December 1917, a full six months before the wing and propeller device came into existence. This insignia must have been made sometime after July 1918, but the army never returned to wearing this pattern—at least not officially. To further complicate the situation, a photograph is known of Air Service noncommissioned officers assigned to the airship *Roma* in 1921 wearing this insignia on their visored service caps. These same men are wearing the 1917 sleeve insignia for enlisted aviators, which is clearly incorrect for their assignment.[5] All this can best be explained by stating that uniform regulations were not strictly enforced, especially for men assigned to "special" units like the *Roma* crew.

Gilt Disks

Not until after World War I were enlisted men's disks made in bright gilt metal. For that reason the gilt disk shown in Fig. 38-27 is incorrect in both color and design. As authorized in bronze, the winged world globe was

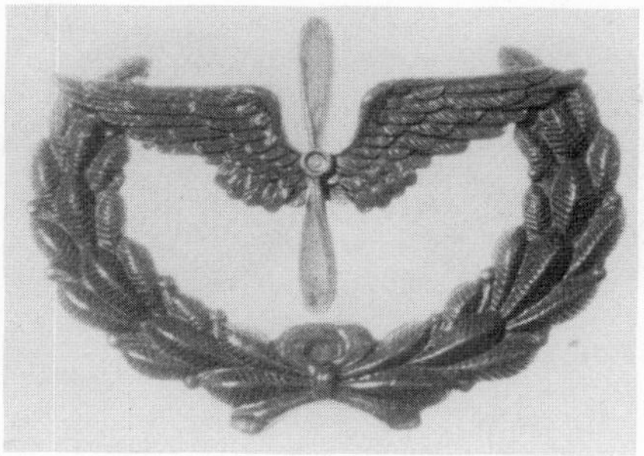

Fig. 38-26.

superimposed on the flags, not above them. To date we do not know anything about the manufacture or use of this disk. In 1924 the Air Service began issuing the enlisted men's collar disks in bright metal.[6] A standard example, identical to wartime issues except that it is bright gilt, is shown in Fig. 38-28. Soldiers stripped many older disks of bronze paint and scoured, buffed, and polished them for reuse, so many disks are now found in a reddish coppery color. As worn by most men about 1925, the disks had an applied or painted silver propeller. Most of the bright gilt disks issued after the war had the background of small shields issued in the interwar period (Fig. 38-29).

In the late 1930s the aviation branch began to use two-piece disks that could be taken apart for cleaning; however, such disks had been available for private purchase as early as 1925, when the new lapel collar coat replaced the old high collar of World War I. The earliest of these two-piece insignia has a raised rim around the edge (Fig. 38-30) not found on most disks. In 1940, when the initial draftees entered the army, most received the two-piece disks without the rim (Fig. 38-31). Soon however, wartime metal shortages became a factor, and insignia became embossed on thin brass or lapped over zinc forms or over a steel strip, with clutch fasteners (Fig. 38-32). A separable Air Corps insignia made in Mexico for U.S. soldiers stationed in Texas is shown in Fig. 38-33.

Fig. 38-25. *This U.S.-made collar insignia is all bronze and follows the intended design closely. (1 inch in diameter)*

Fig. 38-26. *Although this cap insignia was not in regulations, some post–World War I enlisted men wore it in the early 1920s. I know of only one authentic piece. In the 1980s these insignia were remade for collectors. (2 3/64 inches wide)*

Fig. 38-27. *Several of these gilt insignia are known, but their history is unclear, since gilt disks did not come into use until 1923, five years after the Signal Corps and aviation functions had separated. (31/32 inch in diameter)*

Fig. 38-28. *A 1923 or later enlisted men's collar insignia (so noted because it is gilt) made using a die produced during World War I with the finely stippled background. (1 1/64 inches in diameter)*

Fig. 38-29. *Enlisted men's gilt insignia issued between the world wars. (1 1/64 inches in diameter)*

Fig. 38-30. *Made in the 1930s by a private firm, this disk with a separable design has a raised edge. (1 inch in diameter)*

Fig. 38-25.

Fig. 38-27.

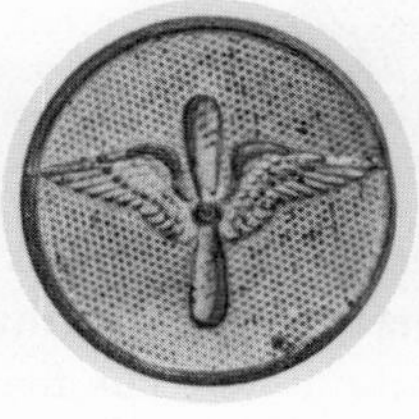

Fig. 38-28.

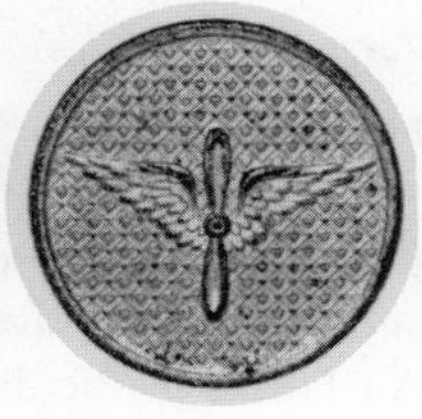

Fig. 38-29.

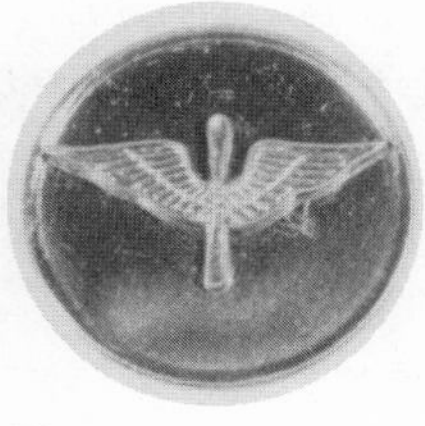

Fig. 38-30.

Fig. 38-31.

Fig. 38-32.

Fig. 38-33.

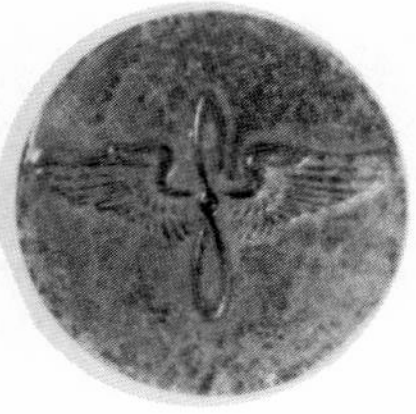

Fig. 38-34.

Fig. 38-35.

Fig. 38-36.

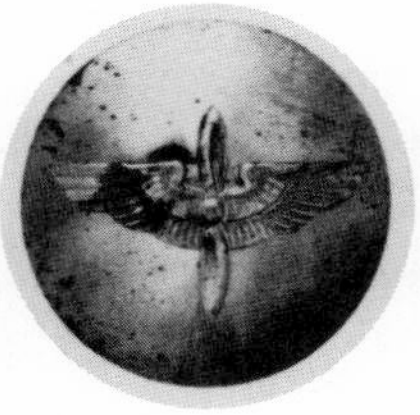

Fig. 38-37.

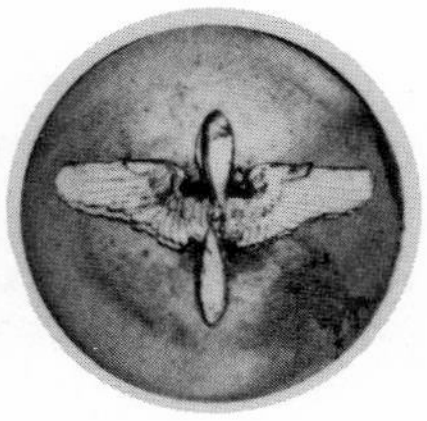

Fig. 38-38.

Fig. 38-39.

Fig. 38-40.

Fig. 38-41.

Fig. 38-42.

Fig. 38-43.

Fig. 38-31. *An issue Air Corps enlisted collar insignia from about 1940. (1 inch in diameter)*

Fig. 38-32. *Metal shortages forced the army to issue enlisted insignia embossed in thin sheet brass, like this example. (1 inch in diameter)*

Fig. 38-33. *This World War II Air Corps insignia is stamped "Made in Mexico" on the reverse. It has a screw post and is of the type with the design separable from the background disk. ($1\frac{1}{32}$ inches in diameter)*

Fig. 38-34. *To save metal, this insignia was made from transparent plastic and painted underneath, allowing the yellow paint to show through. The cracking and chipping is a result of the age of the paint. ($\frac{61}{64}$ inch in diameter)*

Fig. 38-35. *This yellow plastic separable disk is totally devoid of metal. Even the fastening nut on the back is plastic. ($\frac{63}{64}$ inch in diameter)*

Fig. 38-36. *The background of this Army Air Forces enlisted collar insignia is slightly convex. It was made by the Gemsco Company at the close of World War II. ($1\frac{1}{64}$ inches in diameter)*

Figs. 38-37 and 38-38. *With the separation of the U.S. Air Force in 1947, the use of Army Air Forces insignia like these, with a highly convex background, came to an end. These were probably first made about 1944 or 1945. (Each 1 inch in diameter)*

Plastic came into use during World War II as another way to save metal, and two Army Air Forces plastic disks are shown. The first (Fig. 38-34) is one piece with a metal screw-post fastener. Its original yellow paint, applied to transparent plastic, has cracked and chipped because of its age. The second plastic disk (Fig. 38-35) closely follows the concept used in metal disks in that the design is made separable from the background and the plastic is colored throughout. Enlisted men's disks of the latter type worn by Army Air Forces members are of two pieces and can be either slightly domed (Fig. 38-36) or highly domed (Figs. 38-37 and 38-38).

Officers' Insignia, 1921–47

Beginning in October 1921, officers wore a 1-inch silver propeller and bronze wings on the service uniform and a silver propeller with gilt wings on the white uniform (Fig. 38-39). In October 1925 the Quartermaster Corps reduced the wingspread (Fig. 38-40). While regulations authorized many officers to wear smaller insignia on shirts, Circular 42 of 1925 excepted Air Service officers and directed them to wear wings with a $\frac{3}{4}$-inch propeller, but even so, some officers wore smaller gilt devices on shirts (Fig. 38-41). In December 1926 army regulations called for a $\frac{3}{4}$-inch-high insignia for shirts and lapel

Fig. 38-44.

coats and the older 1-inch-high insignia for the standing collar coat.[7]

In 1925 only aviation officers received the new lapel or roll collar coat. Secretary of War Dwight F. Davis detailed the reasons for this decision in a press release of 5 December 1925, explaining that he deemed the change "essential due to the nature of the duties of Air Service Officers." The October 1925 circular that implemented the change stated that Air Service officers would wear embroidered *US* letters on the lapel of the service coat above the branch insignia. The changeover from high collar uniforms to the new lapel collar by the soon-to-be Air Corps created a unique lapel insignia: the letters *US*, 5/16 inch high, 1/8 inch above the wing and propeller. Confusion resulted when Circular 3, 1926, pointed out that the *US* went on the collar (the part above the lapel notch) and the Air Service device went on the lapel (the part below the notch, separating the collar from the lapel). This was the case for all but Air Corps officers, and regulations of 1926 correctly described the combined embroidered *US* and Air Corps insignia (Figs. 38-42 and 38-43). Regulation 600-40 of June 1931 again described in detail this combined Air Corps device on the coat lapel. The embroidery was originally intended to eliminate metal insignia that might snag on parachute harness, but in 1929 National Guard aviators switched to metal insignia, leaving bullion for the Regular Army Air Corps officers.[8]

In the 1930s the quartermaster general intended for officers to wear metal collar insignia on the cotton uniform and embroidered insignia on the wool uniform. This practice is shown in Fig. 38-44. Officers of 1940 are shown in Fig. 38-45, some with the 1925 *US* and Air Corps combined insignia, and some with the standard insignia arrangement. In March 1938 Air Corps officers switched to the same insignia arrangement as that of other officers. Two portraits showing the placement before and after 1938 are in Figs. 38-46 and 38-47. Fig. 38-48 shows the cloth insignia of a cadet. The *US* is on the collar and the winged propeller is on the lapel, as discussed in the following section, and the officer wears the combined insignia, embroidered in cotton, on the lapel.[9]

A Quartermaster Corps drawing of June 1936 modernized and formalized the Air Corps insignia. An example of this design is shown by the collar insignia in Fig. 38-49. Despite the change, on the 1938 mess uniform many officers wore the large, older design, as shown in Fig. 38-50. On khaki shirts some World War II aviators wore cloth embroidered insignia. An example of an

Fig. 38-39. *Officers began to wear gilt wings and a silver propeller on the high collar coat in 1923, although the same insignia had been authorized for the white uniform since 1921. These were too large for the lapel coat introduced in 1925. (1 11/16 inches wide)*

Fig. 38-40. *This insignia of gilt wings and silver propeller is typical of the insignia used by Air Corps officers. Metal insignia of this type were not commonly used on the coat, since most officers used embroidered insignia. This was the proper insignia for the shirt collar. (1 13/64 inches wide)*

Fig. 38-41. *Use of small insignia persisted into the 1920s, despite regulations calling for shirts to carry Air Corps insignia 3/4 inch high. This insignia of gilt wings and silver propeller probably was not used much past the early 1930s.*

Fig. 38-42. *Regular Army Air Corps officers wore this combination embroidered insignia on the winter service coat lapel from 1926 to 1938. (Wings approximately 1 3/16 inches wide)*

Fig. 38-43. *During the late 1920s, Air Corps officers wore this type of embroidered insignia on the summer cotton khaki coat. These were replaced by metal insignia in the early 1930s. (Wings approximately 1 13/32 inches wide)*

Fig. 38-44. *These Air Corps officers display the insignia as the army intended them to be worn by Regular Army aviators in the 1930s. The combination embroidered US and winged propeller went on the winter coat lapels, while the metal insignia, placed the same as other officers wore them, went on the summer coat. Starting in 1929, National Guard aviators were to wear metal insignia on both summer and winter uniforms.*

insignia handmade in the Far East is shown in Fig. 38-51. The Air Corps, redesignated the Army Air Forces in 1942, used embroidered insignia until early World War II, when use of embroidery gradually faded away. During World War II, flight officers, a grade equivalent to warrant officers, wore the Air Corps device as their collar insignia. When Congress

Fig. 38-45. *Some of these Air Corps officers in 1940 wear the old pre-1938 insignia arrangement, while others wear the then current style with the US on the coat collars.*

Fig. 38-46. *Lieutenant Frank P. O'Neil, 1938, wearing the unique Air Corps insignia arrangement.*

Fig. 38-47. *A flying officer assigned to Selfridge Field, Michigan, in 1938, Captain Carl B. Squires is shown here wearing the insignia placed as prescribed that year.*

Fig. 38-45.

Fig. 38-46.

Fig. 38-47.

Fig. 38-48.

Fig. 38-48. A tactical officer in summer uniform, wearing cotton embroidered insignia, inspects the room of an aviation cadet in 1936. The officer is wearing the older arrangement of insignia on the khaki coat. The cadet is wearing his special slate blue uniform with cotton embroidered US and Air Corps insignia.

formed the U.S. Air Force in 1947, the new service dropped army collar insignia.[10]

Cap and Hat Insignia

When the Air Corps first received the field cap (the "overseas cap" of World War I) for "use in flying missions" in 1925, officers wore it with a 1-inch-high Air Service branch insignia, although the collar insignia was reduced to 3/4 inch high at that same time. The cap itself had piping of ultramarine blue with golden orange threads. Flying cadets wore the cap with colored trim on the curtain, but without insignia, until 1 December 1928, when cadets added insignia. The insignia was placed with the tip of the wing 1 inch from the cap's front and the propeller tip 1/2 inch from the cap bottom. Two examples for the 1930s are shown in Figs. 38-52 and 38-53, illustrating both the khaki and the olive drab wool caps. Unit distinctive insignia officially went on enlisted men's caps at the end of 1937, and officers switched to rank insignia.[11]

Cadet Insignia

Flying cadets of World War I were set apart only by "a white pique hat band, one and one-half inches wide, to be worn on the service cap and the service hat." Several cadets with the white bands are shown in Arkansas during 1918 in Fig. 38-54. The uniform regulations of 27 September 1921 again prescribed their uniform to be the same as that of Air Service enlisted soldiers, with a white hat band now reduced to 1 inch wide.[12]

In March 1926 the army authorized flying cadets the *US* insignia embroidered in silk for the right collar and silk-embroidered Air Service insignia on the left side.[13] Change 1 to AR 600-35, 1 December 1928, included the first appearance of a section in uniform regulations for flying cadets, wedged in as paragraph 13 1/2. This section is important because it announced the army cadet slate blue uniform that would be worn for the next twelve years. The collar and lapel insignia were "U.S.

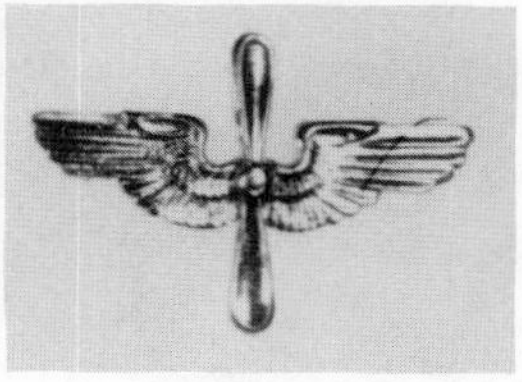

Fig. 38-49.

Fig. 38-49. The Air Corps officers' insignia "modernized" in 1936 and worn until 1947. (15/32 inches wide)

Fig. 38-50.

Fig. 38-50. A 1938 Air Corps officer in the new mess uniform. His branch insignia is on the lower sleeve in the first lieutenant's rank knot.

Fig. 38-51.

Fig. 38-51. These yellow wings and white propeller were hand-embroidered in India during World War II for an Army Air Forces officer's shirt. (Wings approximately 1 13/64 inches wide)

Fig. 38-52. Starting in 1925, aviators began to wear the field cap when flying. Officers wore a large, 1-inch-high metal insignia on the cap's side. The cap trim was blue and orange, the Air Corps colors. Colored piping for officers continued until just before the start of World War II. The khaki shirt collar has the prescribed metal insignia.

Fig. 38-53. Captain Leo Dawson wears an embroidered Air Corps insignia on his winter cap. The winged propeller used by Air Corps officers on caps was replaced by rank insignia at the end of 1937 as a result of the increased use of the field cap by mechanized personnel.

Fig. 38-54. White cap bands, 1½ inches wide, distinguished World War I flying cadets.

Fig. 38-52.

Fig. 38-53.

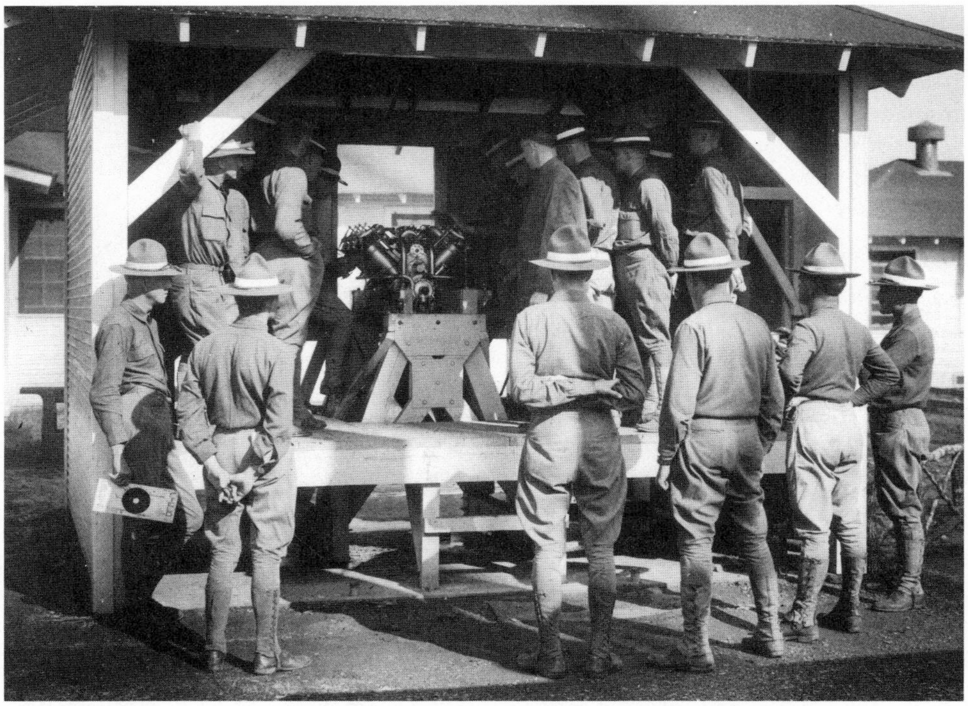

Fig. 38-54.

embroidered in block letters seven-sixteenths inch high" (Fig. 38-48). The insignia for the field (overseas) cap was "the regulation Air Corps embroidered insignia" with the 1-inch propeller discussed above.

War Department Circular 14, 16 March 1938, changed flying cadets' insignia to metal. This revived the 1925–37 officers' pin-back metal cap device with 1-inch propeller (Fig. 38-55). This 1-inch height distinguishes the cap insignia, because the metal lapel insignia was identical to officers', with a ¾-inch-high propeller. Some photographs show aviation cadets (as they were designated on 5 July 1939) wearing black disks on overseas caps, the disk embroidered with a white propeller

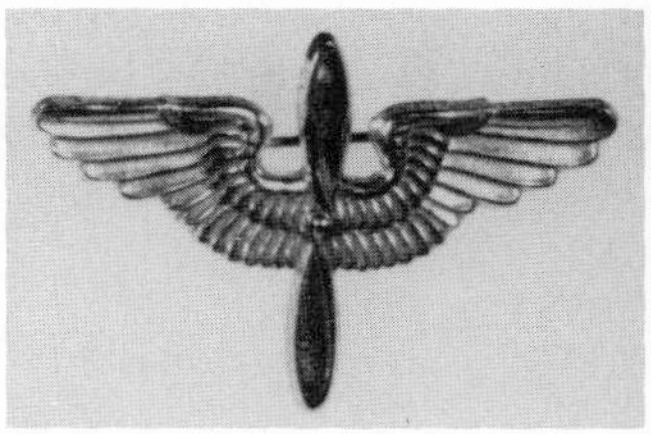

Fig. 38-55.

Fig. 38-56.

Fig. 38-57.

Fig. 38-58.

and yellow wings (Fig. 38-56).[14] The visor cap insignia (Fig. 38-57) of gold-colored wings, 3 inches tip to tip, and a 2-inch silver propeller also became very familiar to thousands of cadets between December 1928, when the insignia first appeared, and 1947, when the air force separated from the army. The cadets shown in Fig. 38-58 wear both types of uniforms and insignia. The new cadets, in khaki and with cloth cap insignia, are escorted by senior cadets wearing the slate blue uniforms and visor caps.

Revision, 1983

The Army Air Forces ended in 1947 with the formation of the U.S. Air Force as a separate armed force. Pilots remaining in the army flew light observation air-

Fig. 38-55. *Initially this pin-back, 1-inch-high Air Corps insignia was worn by officers on their field or overseas caps from 1925 until 1937. It returned in 1938 as the cap insignia for aviation cadets. This size and the pin back set it apart from coat or shirt insignia, which were only 3/4 inch high. (1 1/2 inches wide)*

Fig. 38-56. *At some locations, aviation cadets wore this type of insignia on their field caps. The background disk is black, the wings yellow, and the propeller white. (Disk approximately 2 1/32 inches wide; wings approximately 1 1/16 inches wide)*

Fig. 38-57. *Aviation cadet insignia for the visor cap, 1928–47. The silver propeller was made separately and was fixed to the gold-colored wings by the threaded post that held the insignia to the cap. (3 3/64 inches wide)*

Fig. 38-58. *New aviation cadets, in their khaki uniforms, being marched to their barracks by upperclassmen in the older slate blue uniforms.*

Fig. 38-59.

Fig. 38-59. *In 1983 the army established a new aviation branch for its pilots. For the branch insignia a slightly redesigned but familiar device appeared; the difference between the new and old insignia was only in the slightly pointed wings of the new ones. This is the officers' insignia; the enlisted version was all gold and on the standard 1-inch-diameter circular background. (1 1/4 inches wide)*

craft and, later, helicopters. Use of helicopters greatly increased during the Vietnam War, and once again aviators were an important part of the army. Although many pilots belonged to the Transportation Corps, a number of other branches included aviators in their ranks. In the 1970s most army warrant officers flew helicopters. Secretary of the Army John Marsh approved formation of an aviation branch in April 1983, and in August 1983 the chief of staff revived the winged propeller as the new branch's insignia.[15] The new design (Fig. 38-59) was very similar to that used before 1947, with a minor change to make the wing tips slightly more pointed.

Chapter Thirty-Nine

Tank Corps, Tank Destroyer Forces, and Armor

During World War I two U.S. tank organizations developed in parallel—one as part of the American Expeditionary Forces (AEF) in France and the other in the United States as part of the National Army. On December 22, 1917, General Pershing appointed Colonel Samuel Rockenback as chief of the Tank Corps, AEF. Four tank battalions of the AEF Tank Corps eventually saw combat before war's end.[1]

Simultaneously with the organization of overseas units, the War Department formed in the United States the Tank Service, National Army, which did not have any direct command relationship with the Tank Corps, AEF. The War Department organized the Tank Service, National Army, as part of the Corps of Engineers in February 1918. The first unit was formed at Camp Colt (Gettysburg), Pennsylvania, as the 65th Engineer Regiment, and the Tank Corps, National Army, absorbed it on 22 March 1918 when that corps took over from the Tank Service, National Army. Upon the return of the AEF General Headquarters to the United States in August 1919, the AEF Tank Corps and the National Army Tank Corps combined, and Brigadier General Rockenback became the first chief. The history of the two tank corps and their formation often causes confusion today, especially since the National Defense Act of 4 June 1920 abolished the Tank Corps and assigned tank units to the infantry, although the cavalry was later allowed to form armored car units.[2]

In December 1917 army regulations described the first insignia for the army's newest combatant arm, the Tank Corps, as "a conventionalized tank, one inch high, with the number of the regiment attached to the bottom."[3] Fig. 39-1 is an example of this insignia without the number. No example of the insignia with a number below has ever been seen. Several manufacturers also made the original Tank Corps insignia in a reduced size for the shirt collar (Figs. 39-2 and 39-3). A matching 1-inch-diameter bronze disk for enlisted soldiers is shown in Fig. 39-4. Enlisted men's disks of this type were restruck in the 1970s using original dies and are more common than the genuine insignia.

Most people did not readily understand this artistically attractive 1917 design. It showed the front view of a French tank with armor plate and large rivets, with an enclosure for three cannons and two additional cannons sticking out of the sides, all topped by a small turret. This first pattern did not last long. On the last day of February 1918, Colonel Rockenback requested General Pershing to formally approve the insignia armywide. General Pershing approved this new collar device on 19 April 1918 and published the orders in May 1918. For offi-

Fig. 39-1. *This front view of a French tank did not clearly and quickly convey that the wearer was an officer in the Tank Corps. This bronze insignia for the standing-collar coat was used from late 1917 through early 1918. (1 15/16 inches wide)*

Figs. 39-2 and 39-3. *Branch insignia sized for the shirt collar in the first design for the Tank Corps. These are the most common designs for this size of the insignia. (15/16 and 31/32 inch wide, respectively)*

Fig. 39-4. *In the 1970s enlisted soldiers' disks like this for the first Tank Corps were reproduced for collectors. (1 inch in diameter)*

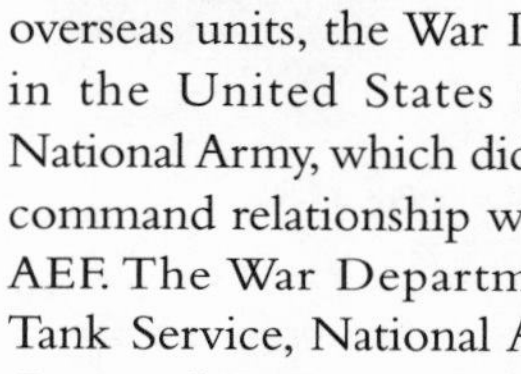

Fig. 39-1.

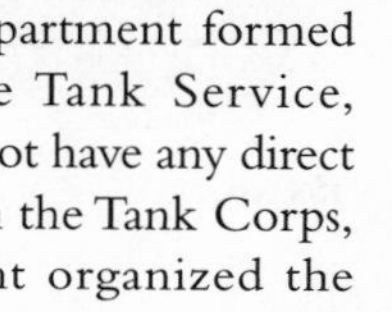

Fig. 39-2.

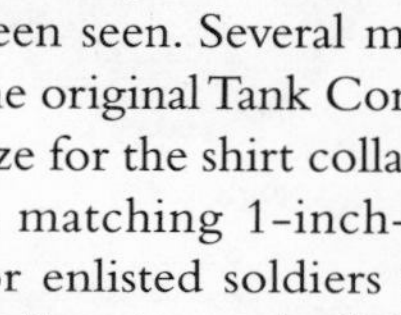

Fig. 39-3.

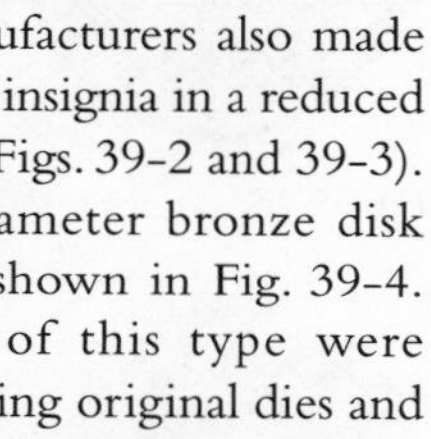

Fig. 39-4.

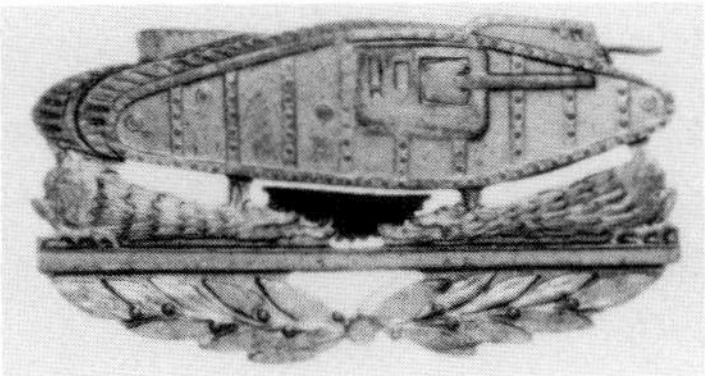

Fig. 39-5.

Fig. 39-6.

Figs. 39-5 and 39-6. This matching pair of officers' Tank Corps insignia has a short screw post (the nut slightly visible just under the center of each tank) and was made in a shiny bronze finish. (Each 1 25/32 inches wide)

Fig. 39-7.

Fig. 39-8.

Fig. 39-7. One example of a variation of the World War I Tank Corps insignia used after May 1918. (1 53/64 inches wide)

Fig. 39-8. This gilt Tank Corps insignia was made in France, evidently after the end of World War I. (1 13/16 inches wide)

Fig. 39-9.

Fig. 39-10.

Fig. 39-11.

Fig. 39-12.

Figs. 39-9 and 39-10. A matching pair of officers' shirt collar bronze insignia from 1918. (1 inch wide)

Fig. 39-11. Shirt collar insignia came in many die variations; this one is nearly circular. (7/8 inch wide)

Fig. 39-12. A medium-sized Tank Corps insignia. This particular insignia had the bronze finish cleaned off to show the copper color underneath. (1 5/32 inch wide)

Fig. 39-13.

Fig. 39-14.

Fig. 39-15.

Fig. 39-17.

Figs. 39-13 and 39-14. Two variations of the second Tank Corps insignia for enlisted men. (Each 1 inch in diameter)

Fig. 39-15. A gilt enlisted men's disk, evidently used in the 1920s when the tanks were part of the infantry yet separate tank companies existed. (1 inch in diameter)

Fig. 39-16.

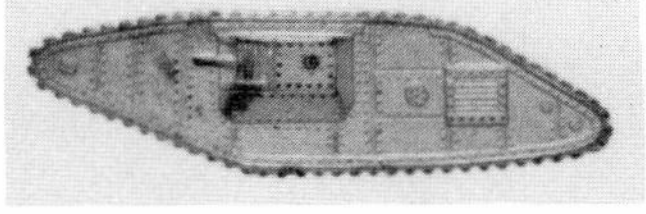

Fig. 39-18.

Fig. 39-16. Between 1940 and 1942 officers assigned to the new armored force were officially to wear either cavalry or infantry insignia, yet some wore this insignia of an M-3 tank. (59/64 inch wide)

Fig. 39-17. An unauthorized enlisted men's insignia of the early armored force. (1 inch in diameter)

cers it was to be a "wreath surmounted by two dragons supporting a tank, guns pointed to the front. The device is to be one inch in height."[4]

Figs. 39-5 and 39-6 illustrate a pair of these 1918 tank insignia in black metal with screw backs. An additional officers' insignia made from a different die and in an orange brown metal is illustrated in Fig. 39-7. A French-made gilt ornament is shown in Fig. 39-8. A smaller matching pair of shirt-sized insignia 1 inch long and 5/8 inch high are shown in Figs. 39-9 and 39-10. The smallest size made for shirt wear is shown in Fig. 39-11. Fig. 39-12 shows still another version struck by a different manufacturer.

The army also prescribed a bronze enlisted men's disk in May 1918. Two examples are shown in Figs. 39-13 and 39-14. Obsolete insignia die slowly, and if a market is available, manufacturers will act to fill the need. After World War I, tank personnel continued to wear the obsolete designs in the post-1923 gilt metal (Fig. 39-15). We do not know how long men wore these, but a gilt disk is shown in a 1925 manufacturer's catalog.[5]

The insignia worn from 1921 through 1942 are included in the chapter 5, "Infantry," while insignia for cavalry armored car squadrons and mechanized cavalry are identified in chapter 7, "Cavalry, Dragoons, and Mounted Riflemen."

World War II

The War Department created an armored force as a separate arm in July 1940 but prescribed no new insignia for this arm until February 1942. The lack of armor force insignia between 1940 and 1942 caused some officers to wear the pre-1933 infantry tanks insignia. In spite of a large buildup of forces during this time, armor men had no insignia showing their new method of war-

Fig. 39-19.

Fig. 39-20.

Fig. 39-21.

Fig. 39-22.

Fig. 39-23.

fare. Early in 1942 the chief of the armored force requested that the army provide a distinctive branch color (green piped with white), a distinctive branch insignia, and special shoulder patches. The adjutant general disapproved the request and described the following system of insignia wear: cavalry sabers would be used by the headquarters of the armored force; by armored corps, division, and brigade headquarters; and by reconnaissance battalions and light armored regiments. Infantry muskets were to be used by tank groups, tank battalions, and medium armored regiments.[6]

Fig. 39-16 illustrates an officers' insignia of a three-quarters view of an M-3 tank. The enlisted men's counterpart is shown in Fig. 39-17. Evidently made about the time of America's entry into World War II, both devices are crudely made and typical of the quality of some insignia produced early in the war. The insignia were evidently made for wear by early armor force personnel before the 1942 introduction of the Mark VIII tank insignia.

Finally, in early 1942 the Quartermaster Corps selected as the insignia for the armored force a side view of America's giant Mark VIII tank of World War I. Officers' insignia were to be $1\frac{1}{4}$ inches long and of the design shown in Fig. 39-18. During World War II some regiments and battalions added their unit number above the tank (Figs. 39-19, 39-20, and 39-21). Post–World War II German-made insignia are shown in Figs. 39-23 through 39-25, with the first of these a variation of the basic design. A collar device from the late 1940s embroidered in bullion is shown in Fig. 39-26.

Although the Mark VIII tank insignia were not authorized for wear after 1951, some tank units in Germany wore them, as did the 2d Battalion, 68th Armor in 1966–67 and the 3d Battalion, 33d Armor. The latter unit became known as the Pickle Battalion in reference to the outline of the old Mark VIII, which somewhat resembles a pickle. A 1970s German-made subdued piece for an officers' fatigue shirt is shown in Fig. 39-27.

The enlisted men's disks were described by regulations throughout World War II as the insignia for "Armored Center and Units." The title changed to "Armor" in February 1947.[7] Examples of these disks from World War II to the 1960s came in many designs (Figs. 39-28 through 39-31). A German-made insignia with unit number is illustrated in Fig. 39-32. U.S.-made armor insignia also sometimes had numbers above (Fig. 39-33) or letters below (Figs. 39-34 and 39-35).

Consolidation, 1951

In January 1951 the Army Congressional Act of 1950 consolidated armor and cavalry into one branch. The act stated, "The Armor shall be a continuation of the Cavalry."[8] Selected for the new insignia was a design combining

Fig. 39-24.

Fig. 39-25.

Fig. 39-18. *An official officers' insignia of the armored force, announced in February 1942. ($1\frac{19}{32}$ inches wide)*

Figs. 39-19, 39-20, and 39-21. *Three examples of World War II or later officers' insignia with unit numbers above. All three units represent some of the diverse heritage of the armored force from the cavalry, from the infantry, from the National Guard, and from the Regular army. The "11th" insignia (Fig. 39-19) could be for the 11th Armored Regiment, formed from the 11th Cavalry in 1942, or for the 11th Tank Battalion, formed from the 11th Regiment in 1943. The 143d Tank Battalion (Fig. 19-20) was organized in 1949. The 67th Armor (Fig. 39-21) is a historic regiment, originally organized as infantry and an early tank regiment that was part of the 2d Armored Division during World War II. ($1\frac{9}{16}$, $1\frac{35}{64}$, and $1\frac{9}{16}$ inches wide, respectively)*

Fig. 39-22. *This insignia was made by L. G. Balfour, a U.S. jewelry firm. ($1\frac{39}{64}$ inches wide)*

Fig. 39-23. *This German-made piece has the unit number struck as part of the basic insignia, instead of being added later, and a thin screw post typical of some German insignia. ($1\frac{39}{64}$ inches wide)*

Fig. 39-24. *Made in 1965 for officers of the 2d Battalion, 68th Armor, stationed in Baumholder, West Germany, these insignia were used on the dress blue uniforms. ($1\frac{19}{32}$ inches wide)*

Fig. 39-25. *The 3d Battalion, 33d Armor retained its ties to the World War II armored force by keeping its old-style insignia, just as many of the cavalry units did in the 1960s and 1970s. This insignia was made locally in Germany, near the unit's station. ($1\frac{19}{32}$ inches wide)*

crossed sabers and an M-26 tank in front view (Fig. 39-36). One firm made an early officers' insignia by superimposing the tank over the older crossed sabers (Figs. 39-37 and 39-38). In this way the maker not only produced an attractive design, but also used a supply of obsolete cavalry insignia. Another variation made in a single die is shown in Fig. 39-39. Many separate battalions added numbers above or below the armor insignia (Figs. 39-40 through 39-43) in the 1950s. Also, flexible battalions formed under the Combat Arms Regimental System as parts of regiments had special insignia made in the 1960s and 1970s. For example, the 1st Battalion, 68th Armor had the battalion number below with the regimental designation above (Fig. 39-43). Fig. 39-44 shows a German-made example with the battalion and

Fig. 39-26. *Gilt-embroidered armored force insignia of the type worn on service coats by some officers after World War II. (Design 1⅝ inches wide)*

Fig. 39-27. *An officers' subdued insignia made in Germany during 1977 on a strip ordinarily used to embroider fatigue uniform names tags. (1[11]/16 inches wide)*

Figs. 39-28, 39-29, 39-30, and 39-31. *Four examples of the 1942–50 armored force enlisted personnel insignia. (1 1/32 inches, 1 inch, 1 inch, and 1 inch in diameter, respectively)*

Fig. 39-32. *Like its officers' counterpart shown in Fig. 39-23, this enlisted men's insignia has the number stamped out with the basic design. (1 1/16 inches wide)*

Fig. 39-33. *Enlisted tankers' insignia for the 351st Heavy Tank Battalion, which was active from 1949 until 1952. (1 inch in diameter)*

Figs. 39-34 and 39-35. *Company designations were applied to domed-shaped disks (Fig. 39-34) and to flat disks (Fig. 39-35), and styles of letters also varied. (1 1/32 inches and 1 inch in diameter)*

Fig. 39-36. *This 1951 commander of the 24th Constabulary Squadron wears on his collar the newly approved insignia for armor.*

Fig. 39-37. *This 1951 insignia was the continuation of cavalry insignia, just as was the branch itself, as prescribed by Congress in 1950. A cavalry insignia had a front view of the M-26 tank added directly over the crossed sabers. (1 9/16 inches wide)*

Fig. 39-38. *Rear view of the insignia shown in Fig. 39-37.*

Fig. 39-39. *German-made armor insignia like this are common because a large number of American tank units were stationed in Germany to counter Warsaw Pact forces. (1 15/32 inches wide)*

Fig. 39-40. *Officers' insignia of the 894th Tank Battalion, which was active at Fort Knox (home of the armor school) from 1954 until 1958. (1 19/32 inches wide)*

Fig. 39-41. *The 710th Tank Battalion not only was composed of African American personnel in 1950, but it also was assigned to the 11th Airborne Division. (1 9/16 inches wide)*

Fig. 39-26.

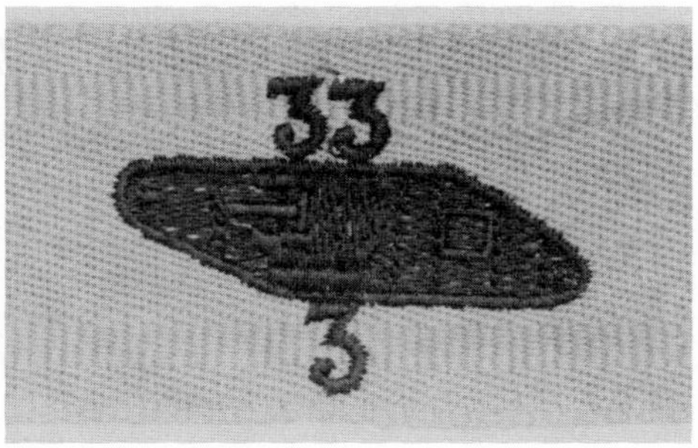

Fig. 39-27.

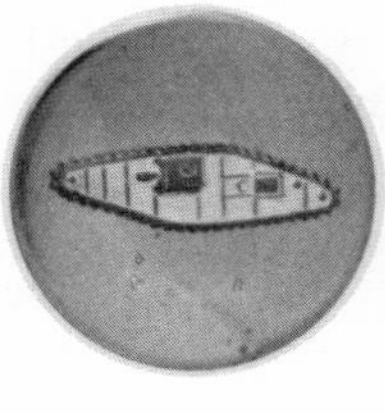

Fig. 39-28.

Fig. 39-29.

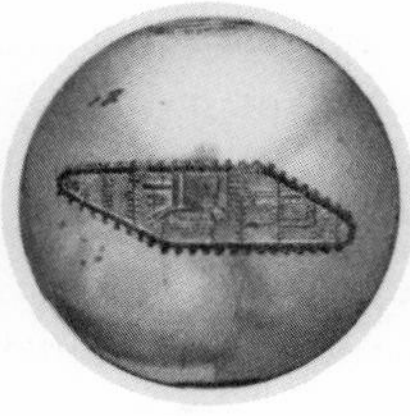

Fig. 39-30.

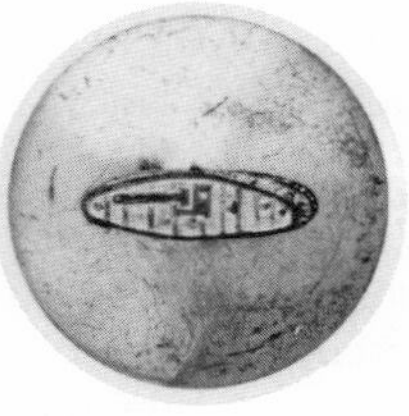

Fig. 39-31.

Fig. 39-32.

Fig. 39-33.

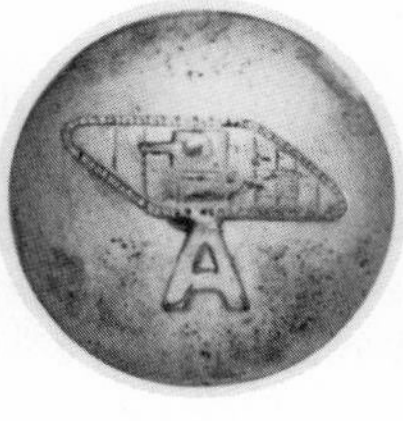

Fig. 39-34.

Fig. 39-35.

Fig. 39-36.

Fig. 39-37.

Fig. 39-38.

Fig. 39-39.

Fig. 39-40.

Fig. 39-41.

Fig. 39-45.

Fig. 39-42.

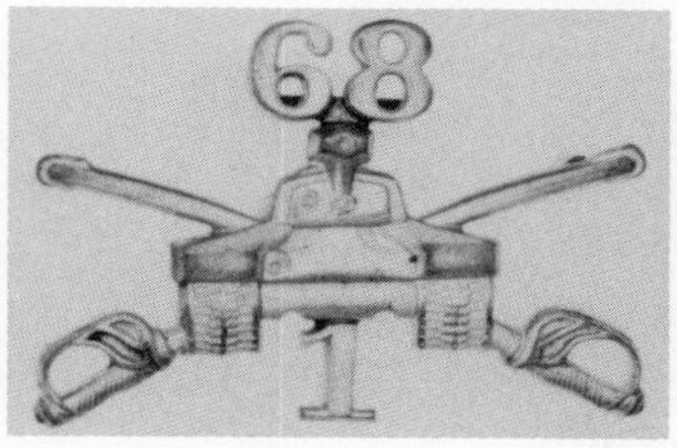

Fig. 39-43.

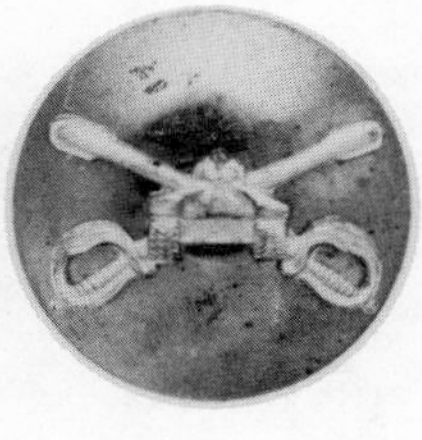

Fig. 39-46.

Fig. 39-44.

Fig. 39-47.

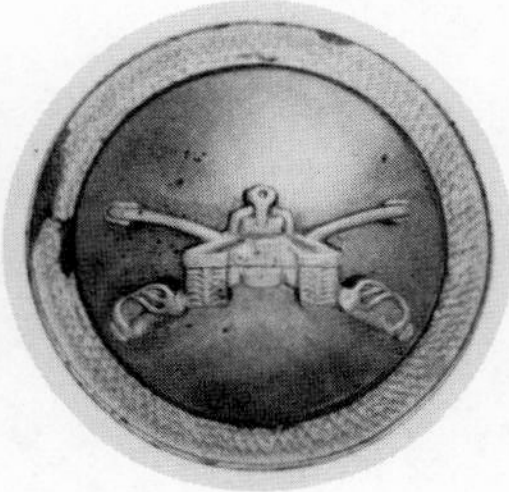

Fig. 39-48.

Fig. 39-42. *Regulation insignia for battalions assigned to the 34th Armor under the Combat Arms Regimental System. ($1\frac{37}{64}$ inches wide)*

Fig. 39-43. *Made in the United States for a battalion stationed in West Germany, this insignia with the proper regimental number above the tank has been supplemented by an unauthorized battalion number below. ($1\frac{19}{32}$ inches wide)*

Fig. 39-44. *An example of a regimental number placed improperly below the tank and an unauthorized battalion number added above on a German-made insignia. ($1\frac{17}{32}$ inches wide)*

Figs. 39-45, 39-46, and 39-47. *Three enlisted tankers' collar insignia for the 1951 armor branch: a U.S.-made flat disk, a German-made disk with a slight dome shape to the background, and a German-made piece with a high-domed backing. Design, sizes, details, and the angles of the sabers distinguish these, which are but a few examples of the many die variations produced for the tank forces from the time of the Korean War through the Vietnamese War. (1 inch, $1\frac{1}{16}$ inches, and $1\frac{1}{32}$ inches wide, respectively)*

Fig. 39-48. *With the official introduction of light blue edging for infantry insignia in 1952, some armor troops also began to wear similar trim. One such example is shown here with the transparent yellow enamel made as an integral part of the circular background. ($1\frac{1}{4}$ inches wide)*

regimental designations reversed from the normal practice.

The post-1950 armor enlisted disks show as many variations as do the officers' insignia (Figs. 39-45, 39-46, and 39-47). Fig. 39-48 shows a domed disk with a nonregulation yellow enameled edge. Disks with unit designations are shown in Figs. 39-49 and 39-50.

Some forces in Germany formed the constabulary in 1946. Cavalry and armor units primarily made up the constabulary, and these had some unique designations. Constabulary squadrons consisted of a headquarters and service troop, three reconnaissance troops, and two mechanized troops. Three such squadrons, a tank troop, and a regimental headquarters troop (which included a horse and motorcycle platoon) formed a regiment.[9] This accounts for some nonstandard abbreviations found on some enlisted soldiers' collar insignia worn from 1946 to 1952 in Germany. Men in the Tank Troop of the 6th Armored Cavalry Regiment wore the disks shown in Fig. 39-51.

Only the cavalry maintained some true regiments after 1957,[10] which again explains some insignia from that time with older or unusual designations added. Units assigned to Germany often added designations such as those shown in Figs. 39-52, 39-53, and 39-54, since the increased cost for the unit marking was very slight. Some interesting officers' insignia are those shown in Figs. 39-56 from Korea, 39-57 through 39-59 from Germany, and 39-60 from the United States.

Tank Destroyer Forces

As a counter to Axis tank forces, the U.S. Army formed the Tank Destroyer Forces in

Fig. 39-49.

Fig. 39-50.

Fig. 39-51.

Fig. 39-52.

Fig. 39-53.

Fig. 39-54.

Fig. 39-55.

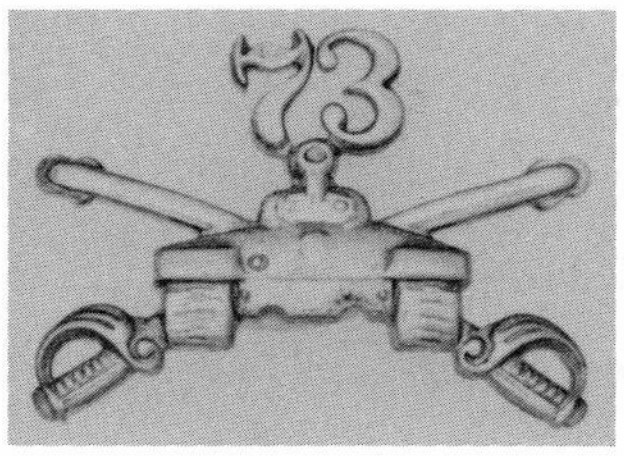

Fig. 39-56.

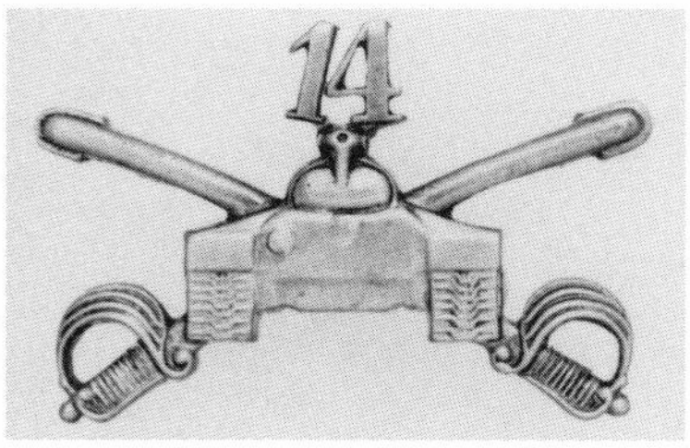

Fig. 39-57.

Fig. 39-58.

Fig. 39-59.

Fig. 39-60.

Fig. 39-61.

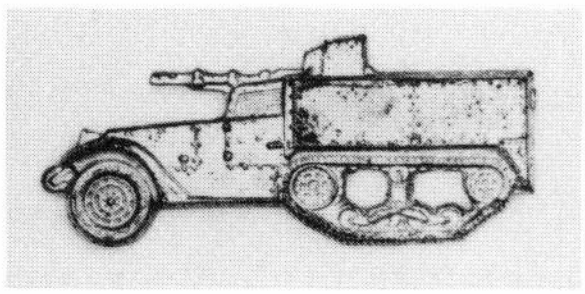

Fig. 39-62.

Figs. 39-49 and 39-50. *Typical unit numbers worn by enlisted tankers in the 1950s and 1960s. The 2d Cavalry disk was made in Germany, and the 44th Tank Battalion was part of the 82d Airborne Division from 1950 until 1957. (1 inch and 1 1/32 inches wide, respectively)*

Fig. 39-51. *Insignia for enlisted men of Tank Troop, 6th Armored Cavalry, of the 1950s. (1 1/64 inches wide)*

Figs. 39-52 and 39-53. *Two German-made disks with small regimental numbers and company or troop letters from the 1950s. The 3d Cavalry disk is flat, while the 15th Reconnaissance Battalion insignia has a domed background. (1 1/64 inches and 1 inch wide, respectively)*

Figs. 39-54 and 39-55. *Many units stationed in West Germany added unit designations in addition to the numbers. (1 1/32 and 1 1/16 inches wide, respectively)*

Fig. 39-56. *The 73d Armor was stationed in Korea for many years, which indicates where this foreign-made insignia was produced. (1 7/16 inches wide)*

Figs. 39-57 and 39-58. *The 14th Armored Cavalry Regiment was stationed on the border of East Germany and West Germany, where the oversized officers' insignia of Fig. 39-57 was made. The 8th Reconnaissance Battalion likewise had its insignia (Fig. 39-58) made in West Germany. (1 3/4 and 1 33/64 inches wide, respectively)*

Fig. 39-59. *This subdued officers' fatigue shirt collar insignia was made in Germany in the late 1960s and could have been used within several divisions stationed there. (Design 1 1/2 inches wide)*

1941. The War Department announced no insignia for this new branch until March 1943, when it selected an M-3 half-track mounting a 75-mm gun, 1/2 inch high.[11] A great many variations in officers' insignia exist. Two original examples are shown in Figs. 39-61 and 39-62, the main differences being in details of the road wheels inside the track and the length of the gun tube. Both have the area inside the track pierced, as called for in regulations. An insignia made in England by the J. R. Gaunt firm is

Fig. 39-63.

Fig. 39-64.

Fig. 39-65.

Fig. 39-66.

Fig. 39-67.

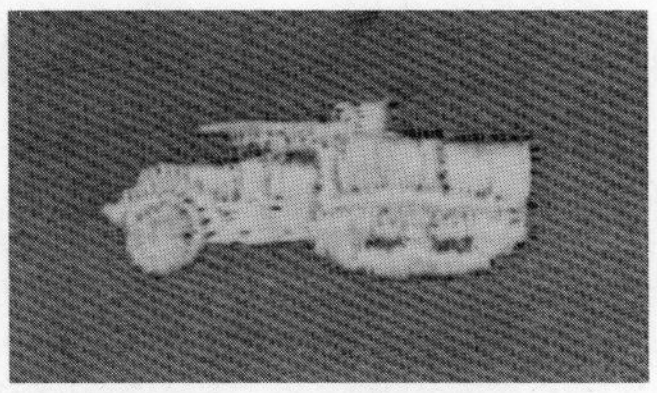

Fig. 39-68.

Fig. 39-69.

Fig. 39-70.

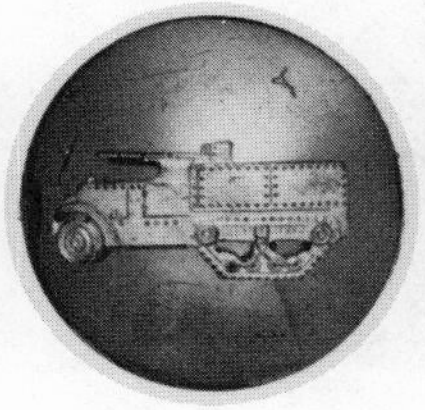

Fig. 39-71.

Fig. 39-72.

Fig. 39-60. *Unusual in that its insignia was made in the United States with designations added, the 31st Medium Tank Battalion was active only from 1950 through 1953. (1 1/2 inches wide)*

Figs. 39-61 and 39-62. *Two examples of officers' insignia for the Tank Destroyer Forces. This World War II branch was not authorized insignia until March 1943. The design differences can most easily be seen by examining the area around the supporting wheels inside the tracks. (Each 1 5/32 inches wide)*

Fig. 39-63. *This English-made World War II officers' insignia has the area inside the tracks solid instead of cut out as mentioned in the uniform regulations of the time. (1 1/4 inches wide)*

Fig. 39-64. *The 899th Tank Destroyer Battalion saw service in North Africa, Italy, and central Europe until it was deactivated in 1945. Authentic Tank Destroyer Forces insignia with unit numbers and those facing "reversed" like this are scarce. (1 5/32 inches wide)*

shown in Fig. 39-63 and can be distinguished by the solid area inside the tracks. One unusual insignia has the half-track facing the wrong way and has a unit number (Fig. 39-64). The concept of facing pairs, displayed in part by this piece, was evidently the inspiration for the two ornaments shown in Figs. 39-65 and 39-66, which were struck for collectors about 1982. There is no evidence to show that these particular insignia, which are without any back marks and are of slightly thinner metal than is seen in authentic insignia, were used during World War II. One must suppose that these were to represent to collectors "rare" insignia somewhat akin to the 1920s shirt collar devices. Fig. 39-68 shows a yellow embroidered insignia for wear on an officers' khaki shirt.

Issued enlisted men's disks are made in one piece (Fig. 39-69), while two-piece variations with an open area inside the tracks are shown in Figs. 39-70 and 39-71 and with a solid tracked area in Fig. 39-72. The army rescinded Tank Destroyer Forces insignia during February 1947 because it had redesignated, de-activated, or disbanded tank destroyer units at the end of the war.[13] A World War II veteran shows his tank

Figs. 39-65 and 39-66. *A pair of Tank Destroyer Forces insignia made for collectors in the early 1980s. These are made from thin metal and do not have any marks on the back. (Each approximately 1 5/32 inches wide)*

Fig. 39-67. *A fake "small, shirt sized" insignia made for collectors over thirty years after the end of World War II. (7/8 inch wide)*

Fig. 39-68. *Yellow embroidered insignia on khaki for the summer shirt or coat. (Design 1 1/8 inches wide)*

Fig. 39-69. *This insignia, made by the Quartermaster Corps during the World War II period, is an enlisted men's collar device for the Tank Destroyer Forces. (1 inch in diameter)*

Figs. 39-70 and 39-71. *Both of these commercial enlisted men's insignia have the area within the track pierced. The disk in Fig. 39-70 is flat, and that of Fig. 39-71 is domed. (1 inch and 1 1/16 inches in diameter, respectively)*

Fig. 39-72. *The stamping detail on this disk is not as crisp as that of the previous two insignia, and this domed disk has a solid area within the tracks. (1 inch in diameter)*

Fig. 39-73.

Fig. 39-73. *This officer wears tank destroyer insignia on his jacket at the end of World War II.*

Fig. 39-74.

Fig. 37-74. *The 813th Tank Destroyer Battalion was formed in 1941 before any unique insignia were available. Perhaps the enlisted men assigned to the unit wore this insignia. (1 inch in diameter)*

destroyer lapel insignia in a 1945 photograph taken in Czechoslovakia (Fig. 39-73).

Antitank battalions were formed during the second half of 1941, primarily as artillery units, although some infantry antitank battalions existed. Crossed musket and crossed cannon insignia continued until the half-track design was introduced. Not everyone wanted to follow these regulations. What did these men of the Tank Destroyer Forces wear before their new insignia was approved in early 1943? Perhaps enlisted men wore the insignia shown in Fig. 39-74.

Chapter Forty

Chemical Corps

An innovation of modern warfare has been the use of poison gas, first employed by the Germans in the second battle at Ypres in 1915. When the United States entered World War I two years later, the army had no unified chemical service. The Ordnance Department was charged with the manufacture of gas shells, the Medical Department was responsible for gas defense, and the Corps of Engineers provided personnel and material to conduct gas operations. The army needed an agency to coordinate and direct the new chemical effort. An American Expeditionary Forces (AEF) Gas Service was authorized by AEF General Orders Number 31, dated 3 September 1917, in an effort to unify chemical weapons employment. The chief of the AEF Gas Service was charged with the conduct of all gas and flame service. On 28 June 1918, the Gas Service, AEF, became the Chemical Warfare Service, AEF. In the United States the Chemical Warfare Service (CWS) was established in June 1918, replacing the 1917 ad-hoc organization of the Chemical Service Section, which had been formed in the United States to consolidate activities. The CWS became a part of the Regular Army in 1920, and its name was changed to the Chemical Corps after World War II.[1]

Fig. 40-1.

Officers' Bronze Collar Ornaments

In December 1917 the newly established Chemical Service Section received, as a collar insignia, "a benzol ring superimposed in the center of crossed retorts; the device to be 3/4 inch high" (see Figs. 40-1, 40-2, and 40-3). The CWS used the Chemical Service Section insignia beginning in June 1918, and the following month the 1st Gas Regiment was established using men from the 30th Engineer Regiment.[2] A few officers may have worn the Chemical Warfare Service insignia with a *1* above, as shown in Fig. 40-4. This addition of the number apparently occurred after the war's end, since

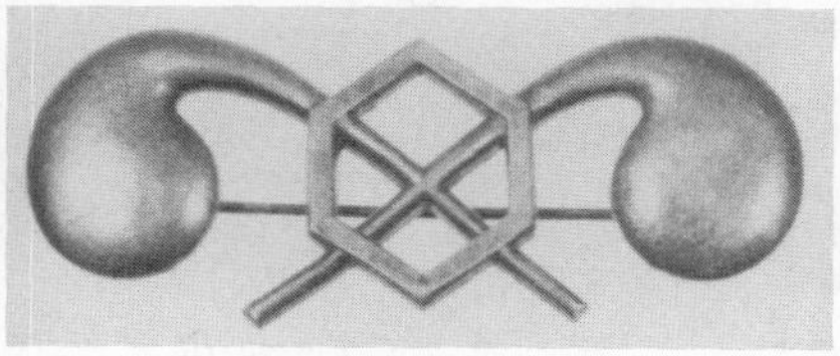

Fig. 40-2.

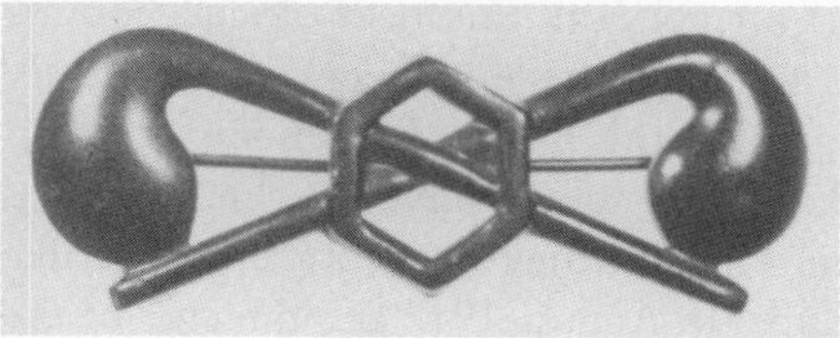

Fig. 40-3.

Fig. 40-1. *Brigadier General Amos A. Fries wearing insignia of the Chemical Warfare Service. Fries received his second star and became chief of the CWS on 1 July 1920. His blue and yellow shoulder patch is of the AEFCWS.*

Fig. 40-2. *One of the many bronze insignia used by officers of the Chemical Service Section and the Chemical Warfare Service during World War I. (2 1/32 inches wide)*

Fig. 40-3. *Very long stems distinguish this version of the bronze-colored CWS officers' insignia, made during World War I. (2 1/16 inches wide)*

Fig. 40-4.

Fig. 40-5.

Fig. 40-6.

Fig. 40-7.

Fig. 40-8.

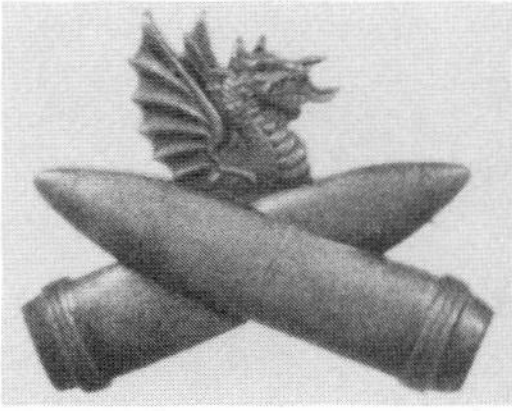

Fig. 40-9.

Fig. 40-10.

Fig. 40-4. *The 1st Gas Regiment was the only numbered chemical regiment organized during World War I. It was organized from the 30th Engineer Regiment. (1 15/32 inches wide)*

Fig. 40-5. *This AEF officer, identified only as Major Urban, is wearing the Gas Service insignia.*

Fig. 40-6. *In this end-of-war scene, the officer on the left is wearing the CWS insignia, while the officer on the right still has the Gas Service insignia.*

Figs. 40-7 and 40-8. *Right and left mates of the Gas Service insignia. (1 9/32 inches wide)*

Figs. 40-9 and 40-10. *A pair of Gas Service insignia made so the shells do not have a center band like that of the previous pair. A few Gas Service insignia were remade for collectors in the 1970s using the lost wax process, and others were struck from dies in the 1980s.*

most former 30th Engineer officers continued to wear the engineers' castle while assigned to the 1st Gas Regiment.

The men who delivered the chemical munitions felt they needed a more warlike insignia. In August 1918 the director of the CWS stated, "The overseas section, which includes the division gas officers and the gas and flame troops, desire an insignia a little more warlike than that of the old chemical service section." Proposed as the insignia was a dragon's head above crossed gas shells. The War Department disapproved the adoption of the new gas service insignia. However, before this opinion was known to the AEF, the army in Europe assumed that the request would be approved, and the proposed insignia was made and sold through the AEF quartermaster's office.[3] An officer is shown in Fig. 40-5 wearing this collar ornament. In Fig. 40-6, one officer is seen wearing a Gas Service insignia while his office mate is wearing a CWS insignia. The Gas Service insignia were made in pairs, and at least two dies exist, as shown in Figs. 40-7 through 40-10. These insignia were reproduced in the 1980s.

Officers' Gilt Collar Insignia

Congress designated the CWS a permanent branch of the army on 1 July 1920. From that

Fig. 40-11.

Fig. 40-12.

Fig. 40-13.

Fig. 40-16.

Fig. 40-14.

Fig. 40-15.

Fig. 40-11. *An all-gilt 1923–24 CWS insignia for the standing-collar olive drab uniform. (21/32 inch wide)*

Fig. 40-12. *A post November 1924 insignia with the blue enamel benzine ring added. (1 3/5 inches wide)*

Fig. 40-13. *Chemical insignia this small were still being sold in the 1960s for wear on the lapel coat, although such sizes did not conform to official drawings. (13/16 inch wide)*

Fig. 40-14. *The army's quartermaster sales stores stocked this style of insignia in the 1960s. (1 9/32 inches wide)*

Fig. 40-15. *Lieutenant Colonel Henry C. Hall, of the office of the chief of the CWS, in August 1943. Colonel Hall wears embroidered chemical insignia on his tropical worsted coat.*

Fig. 40-16. *A few CWS units added numbers above their insignia, as in this 1940s example. (1 3/16 inches wide)*

time until October 1923, assigned officers wore an insignia with a 3/4-inch-high benzol ring, the entire device being dull bronze for the service uniform or with an all-gilt finish, as shown in Fig. 40-11, for the white uniform. From October 1923 until November 1924 the insignia was all gilt for all of the uniforms. In November 1924 the army modified the insignia by inlaying blue enamel on the six-sided benzene ring and specifying the entire insignia length as 1 3/4 inches. An example is illustrated in Fig. 40-12.[4]

Chemical Warfare Service insignia that were actually worn varied a great deal. Although official sizes changed, many pieces exist in totally unauthorized dimensions and are impossible to document. A March 1926 circular called for the new lapel coat to carry insignia measuring 3/4 inch by 1 3/8 inches, the same size that was previously used on the high-collar uniform. In December 1926 a new edition of Army Regulation 600-35 changed the lapel device to the approximate size prescribed for the shirt in 1921: 1/2 inch high and 1 3/16 inches long.[5] This last dimension later caused problems, because all regulations between 1951 and late 1963 gave the size as 13/16 inch. A specific change in September 1963 restored the intended 1 3/16-inch measurement. Because of this error, some manufacturers produced and sold small officers' insignia in the 1950s and 1960s. Examples of the 13/16-inch and 1 1/4-inch widths are shown in Figs. 40-13 and 40-14.

A World War II CWS officer, wearing embroidered insignia, is shown in Fig. 40-15. A few chemical units added numbers above the benzene ring, as shown in the piece in Fig. 40-16, which came in the common 1 3/16-inch width.

In the January 1975 regulations, no Chemical Corps insignia was listed, for reasons that will be discussed shortly. Later in 1975 the listing reappeared with the size at 1 13/16 inches, where it has remained. The CWS title was changed to the Chemical Corps in February 1947.[6] Hand-embroidered officers' insignia made in Vietnam during the war there are shown in Figs. 40-17 and 40-18.

Enlisted Men's Disks

At least one original bronze enlisted men's collar insignia is known to exist for the Gas Service (Fig. 40-19). During the 1980s several of these were remade for collectors. A bronze disk for the CWS is shown in Fig. 40-20. Bronze disks with the background of lines and small shields were made a few years after World War I and occasionally have the company letter below, as shown in Fig. 40-21.

An interesting insignia, shown in Fig. 40-22, is a disk for the Field Test Section, Gas Service Division, CWS. This small unit, stationed on Long Island during World War I, tested various gas masks. Some people may

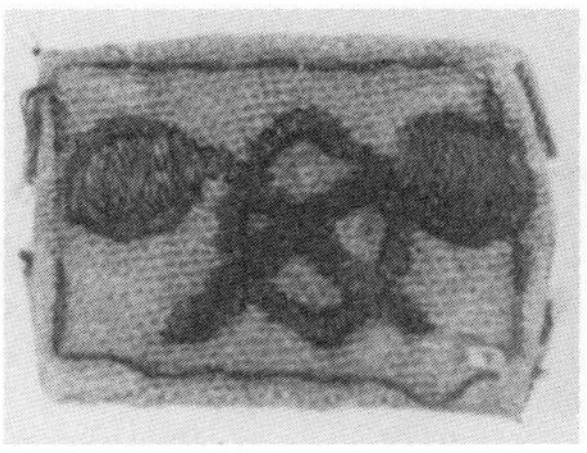

Fig. 40-17.

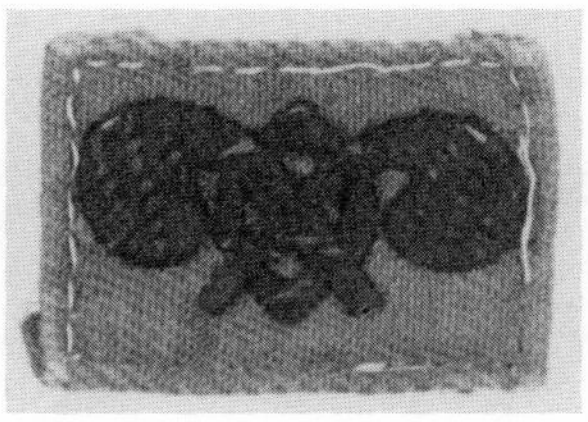

Fig. 40-18.

consider the disk a commemorative or memorial device or a civilian work badge instead of a true military insignia. It is said to have been worn by the two hundred enlisted men in the unit, but the officers' device, if any, is not known. The manufacturing date of the piece has not been determined, and it may have been made after the war's end. Clearly, the designation "Chemical Warfare Service" around the edge and the CWS insignia in the lower portion of the scene clearly place the design after June 1918.[7]

With the return to gilt insignia enlisted men wore disks of the type shown in Fig. 40-23. When enlisted men's insignia with checkered backgrounds appeared throughout the army after World War I, the chemical disk of the type shown in Fig. 40-24 and the ornaments with company letters (Fig. 40-25) came into use. In the mid-1920s the first two-piece disks with the design removable for polishing appeared (Fig. 40-26), and in 1943 thin stamped brass insignia came into use.[8] A 1944 or 1945 insignia made in the Far East is shown in Fig. 40-27. Two-piece domed disks (Figs. 40-28 and 40-29) were made during and after World War II. The first has the area

Fig. 40-19.

Fig. 40-20.

Fig. 40-21.

Fig. 40-22.

Fig. 40-23.

Fig. 40-24.

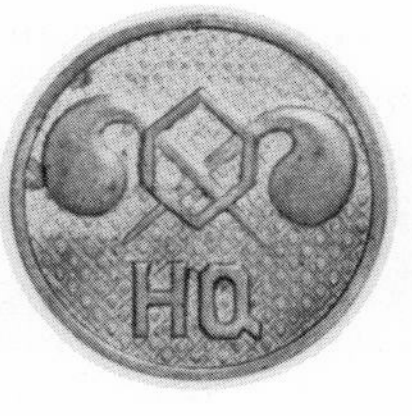

Fig. 40-25.

Fig. 40-26.

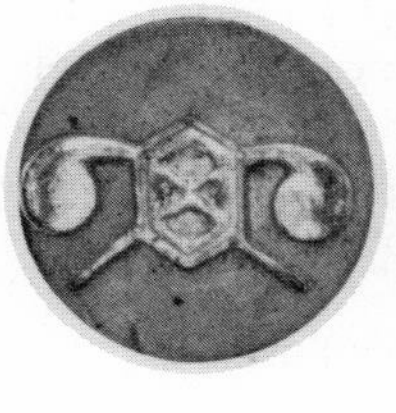

Fig. 40-27.

Fig. 40-28.

Fig. 40-29.

Fig. 40-17. *A machine-embroidered subdued Chemical Corps insignia, made and worn in Vietnam in 1967. (Design 1 5/16 inches wide)*

Fig. 40-18. *This 1967 insignia was hand-stitched in Vietnam. (Design 1 1/4 inches wide)*

Fig. 40-19. *An enlisted men's disk for the Gas Service. This was probably intended for men of the 1st Gas Regiment, as the dragon's head prevented placement of the number above, where regimental numbers normally are located. In the 1980s some of these disks were remade for collectors. (1 inch in diameter)*

Fig. 40-20. *The approved World War I CWS disk. (1 inch in diameter)*

Fig. 40-21. *A bronze disk with service company letter below, made about 1923 and incorporating the second style of disk background, crosshatched lines and small shields. The letter S is the most common of the letters found on disks of this design. (1 inch in diameter)*

Fig. 40-22. *A disk made for a World War I field test unit. Some people consider this type of device a memorial insignia for veterans instead of a true insignia. (1 inch in diameter)*

Fig. 40-23. *A gilt disk made using a die originally intended for bronze World War I insignia. (1 inch in diameter)*

Fig. 40-24. *An issue gilt disk, 1923–37, for the CWS. (1 inch in diameter)*

Fig. 40-25. *Between the world wars the army had few men in the CWS, thus making most company-designated disks scarce. Because all units had headquarters companies, this is the most common of the company disks. (1 inch in diameter)*

Fig. 40-26. *A two-piece disk made during World War II for CWS members. (1 inch in diameter)*

Fig. 40-27. *A disk made in India during World War II for U.S. CWS troops. (15/16 inch in diameter)*

Fig. 40-28. *A typical domed disk made in the 1950s. The area inside the benzine ring is cut out. (1 inch in diameter)*

Fig. 40-29. *This domed CWS disk has a solid area inside the center, and the benzine ring is simply impressed into the metal. (1 inch in diameter)*

within the benzine ring cut out, and the other has a solid center.

Insignia after the Vietnam War

During the later period of the Vietnam War and the subsequent antimilitary feeling in the United States, most citizens and many soldiers believed that the army's Chemical Corps was dissolved in response to an army request to the Ninety-third Congress. It was thought that the army intended to make Chemical Corps activities part of the ordnance branch's responsibilities. However, there was no disbanding of the Chemical Corps and little consolidation of activities. Although many Chemical Corps enlisted men became part of the Ordnance Corps, the separate Chemical Corps school closed, Chemical Corps insignia disappeared from regulations, and the corps shrank, it did not disappear. Within three years of the request to dissolve the corps, however, the army stated, "Circumstances have changed since the decision to disestablish the Chemical Corps was originally made."[9] Because Congress had never dissolved the corps, the army was then able to expand the existing Chemical Corps to correct its needs. With this 1976 action all discussions ended concerning the demise of the Chemical Corps.

Chapter Forty-One

Interpreters and Intelligence

During World War I the U.S. Army formed both a Corps of Interpreters and a Corps of Intelligence Police. These two organizations later supplied personnel to the Military Intelligence Reserve Corps, which existed from 1920 until 1963. The current intelligence branch was organized in February 1963.

World War I Officer Interpreters' Insignia

The *National Geographic* magazine of October 1917 shows the officer interpreters' insignia as the letters *INT* in a wreath. This follows the general World War I pattern of an abbreviation in a wreath as a branch insignia. The magazine is the first record I can find of this or of the enlisted men's device, since regulations did not announce the insignia until December 1917.[1]

Officers assigned to the Corps of Interpreters wore bronze insignia of the type shown in Fig. 41-1. Fig. 41-2 shows a device made in France, and Fig. 41-3 shows one with a smaller, more delicate wreath and letters, part of the Smithsonian Institution collection. Apparently made for wear after the close of hostilities is the gilt piece shown in Fig. 41-4. A most unusual example, shown in Fig. 41-5, is a bronze wreath, of the type worn on the enlisted men's cap before 1918, with the letters *INT*. Although the device is large, it was clearly intended for the collar, because it has four sew-on loops on the reverse. All of these devices existed only for a short time; the War Department rescinded them in March 1921.[2]

Bronze IP and INT Disks

Members of the Corps of Intelligence Police wore bronze disks bearing the letters *IP* (Figs. 41-6 and 41-7), while interpreters wore the letters *INT* as their collar devices (Fig. 41-8). During the latter half of 1920

Fig. 41-1. *The most typical officers' bronze-colored collar insignia for the Corps of Interpreters, 1917–21. (1 1/4 inches wide)*

Fig. 41-2. *A French-made World War I Corps of Interpreters collar insignia. (17/32 inches wide)*

Fig. 41-3. *Small letters suspended on tiny wires are a part of this unique insignia. As in the other insignia shown in Figs. 41-1, 41-2, and 41-4, the dark center line behind the letters INT is the pin used to fasten the device to the collar. (1 1/4 inches wide)*

Fig. 41-4. *An officers' insignia of the World War I design, but executed in gilt. (1 1/4 inches wide)*

Fig. 41-5. *Made like an enlisted men's cap insignia, this device was evidently intended for an officer's collar, since this piece has small loops that were typically used on some officers' collar insignia. (1 15/16 inches wide)*

Fig. 41-6.

Fig. 41-7.

Fig. 41-8.

Fig. 41-9.

Fig. 41-10.

Fig. 41-11.

Fig. 41-12.

Fig. 41-13.

Fig. 41-14.

Fig. 41-15.

Fig. 41-16.

and early in 1921 the army phased out these disks, which were originally authorized in late December 1917. Authorized army strength into the 1920s included thirty intelligence police sergeants.[3]

Officers' Collar Insignia after 1924

After World War I the War Department organized Military Intelligence Reserve Corps personnel into one branch and in November 1924 prescribed a new insignia: a 1-inch-high, gilt metal eared shield bearing a sphinx (Fig. 41-9).[4] Some manufacturers made these insignia with part of the background cut out around the sphinx (Figs. 41-10 and 41-11). The large shields, made in facing pairs (Figs. 41-12 and 41-13), were worn only until the army prescribed the lapel coat. The small 3/4-inch-high shirt size usually faced only one way.

Military intelligence reserve officers wore shirt-sized insignia (Figs. 41-14 and 41-15) on the 1926 lapel coat. Regulations specified that these insignia all should be made to face one way. As reserve personnel, few intelligence officers went on active duty. They wore the insignia until 1940 and the pre–World War II buildup. Early in 1942 the War Department discontinued the insignia and directed intelligence officers to wear "insignia of the unit with which [they] are serving" or to wear infantry insignia. In mid-1946 the criteria changed so that an officer would wear the military intelligence reserve insignia except when his commanding officer "deemed [it] desirable" to wear some other branch device.[5]

The army changed the title of the Military Intelligence Reserve Corps in 1959 to Army Intelligence, U.S. Army Reserve (USAR). With the title change the regulations again noted that among officers only reservists wore the insignia. If officers went on extended active duty, they wore the branch insignia "in which they are detailed."[6] A large cloth insignia for a fatigue uniform of the 1950s and early 1960s is shown in Fig. 41-16.

In February 1963 the army replaced the original insignia with a new design after it had combined Army Intelligence, USAR, and Army Security, USAR, and expanded the branch as part of the regular army. The branch was called Intelligence and Security. The insignia of the new branch, retitled Military Intelligence in February 1968, is shown

Fig. 41-6. *The most common of the enlisted men's collar disks for the Corps of Intelligence Police. (1 inch in diameter)*

Fig. 41-7. *Periods were not authorized for the letters IP, but in this version they were applied with matching block letters. (1 inch in diameter)*

Fig. 41-8. *World War I enlisted men's collar insignia for members of the Corps of Interpreters. (1 inch in diameter)*

Fig. 41-9. *A 1924 officers' gilt insignia for the standing-collar coat. This insignia has sew-on loops as the fastening method. The sphinx and raised ribs are bright gold color, while the background is a dull gilt. (1 1/16 inches wide)*

Figs. 41-10 and 41-11. *The cut-out area around the sphinx was not called for in regulations, but at least two different pairs of dies for these insignia exist. (Each 1 1/8 inches wide)*

Figs. 41-12 and 41-13. *A pair of the 1924 officers' insignia. The large, standing-collar insignia were usually made in pairs and worn with the sphinx facing to the front. (Each 1 1/32 inches wide)*

Figs. 41-14 and 41-15. *Two versions of the 1926–63 officers' Military Intelligence Reserve Corps insignia made for the shirt and lapel coat. (Each 13/16 inch wide)*

Fig. 41-16. *Slightly oversized, this yellow embroidered officers' insignia was for the fatigue uniform. (Design 1 5/16 inches wide)*

Fig. 41-17.

Fig. 41-18.

Fig. 41-19.

Fig. 41-20.

Fig. 41-21.

Fig. 41-22.

Fig. 41-23.

Fig. 41-24.

Fig. 41-25.

Fig. 41-17. *The branch called Intelligence and Security was introduced in 1962 and was given this insignia in 1963. The branch was retitled Military Intelligence in 1968. This insignia consists of several elements, including a sun, a rose, and a dagger. The gold-colored sun has four straight and four wavy rays. (This is the symbol of Helios, god of the sun, and in addition the four straight rays allude to the four main compass points and the army's worldwide mission.) The gold, partially concealed dagger symbolizes the aggressive and protective requirements as well as the physical dangers inherent in the mission, and the rose with dark blue petals is an ancient symbol of secrecy. (1 3/32 inches wide)*

Fig. 41-18. *A Japanese-made U.S. Army military intelligence insignia with a light yellow central design and a black rose. (Design 1 7/32 inches wide)*

Fig. 41-19. *This Vietnamese-made officers' insignia is embroidered in black except for the five central V's, representing the rose petals, which were embroidered in light blue. (Design 1 1/16 inches wide)*

Fig. 41-20. *Army-issue insignia for enlisted personnel in the Military Intelligence USAR. The insignia was first introduced in 1958. (1 inch in diameter)*

Fig. 41-21. *A two-piece, separable insignia for enlisted military intelligence personnel. These were worn well before they were sanctioned by regulations in 1958. (1 inch in diameter)*

Figs. 41-22 and 41-23. *Two domed disks made for military intelligence reserve enlisted personnel in the late 1940s and 1950s. (1 inch and 1 1/32 inches in diameter, respectively)*

Fig. 41-24. *An issue 1970s two-piece insignia for military intelligence enlisted personnel. (1 inch in diameter)*

Fig. 41-25. *This domed-shaped insignia shows that that style of background was still being made in the early 1960s. (1 1/32 inches wide)*

in Fig. 41-17. Cloth versions are shown in Figs. 41-18 and 41-19; the first was made in Japan, the latter in Vietnam.[7]

Enlisted Personnel Collar Insignia

The army first authorized enlisted intelligence soldiers' insignia in 1958.[8] Initially the army issued one-piece disks of the type shown in Fig. 41-20. Some unofficial versions, both domed and flat, are shown in Figs. 41-21, 41-22, and 41-23. Two-piece disks are made in several different dies and in both silver- and gilt-colored metal. The 1963 design also is made in flat (Fig. 41-24) and domed (Fig. 41-25) versions.

Chapter Forty-Two

Transportation

During the rapid expansion of the army in 1917, the various branches bought motor vehicles at an alarming rate, giving no attention to potential problems of maintenance or the possibility of standardization. Branches often failed even to consider the intended use of the vehicle. To unify this purchasing effort the War Department assigned responsibility for motor vehicle procurement to the Transportation Division, Quartermaster Corps, with the mission of centralizing purchases of all motor vehicles, providing parts and men necessary for maintenance, and supplying certain drivers. General Orders 75, 15 August 1918, eased the burden on the Quartermaster Corps when the War Department created a Motor Transport Corps separate from the then Motor Transport Service of the Quartermaster Corps, as the Transportation Division had been retitled in April 1918. The new corps took control of assignment, organization, and technical training of motor transport personnel.[1]

Although the Motor Transport Corps controlled motor vehicles, the War Department needed another branch to regulate all of the diverse transportation systems, principally the rail network. An early act of the AEF had been to form a transportation department in September 1917, and in the United States the army organized a series of offices to do the same thing. On November 12, 1918, the AEF formed the Transportation Corps, and in March 1919 the War Department established the Transportation Service. Congress allowed both the Motor Transport Corps and the Transportation Service to be disbanded in June 1920, and the Quartermaster Corps assumed transportation functions until the middle of World War II. The current Transportation Corps was formed in July 1942.[2]

The Quartermaster Corps and the later Transportation Corps furnished boat and ship transportation. The specific insignia associated with maritime transportation are discussed in chapter 36, "Army Transport Service and Harbor Boat Service."

Motor Transport Corps

A contemporary eight-spoked truck wheel, with Mercury's winged hat superimposed at the center, became the branch insignia for the Motor Transport Corps in September 1918. The tire was silver on the officers' insignia, and these silver-edged bronze collar insignia usually came in facing pairs (Figs. 42-1 and 42-2). Two styles made in France for the AEF vary from the more common designs. The pair shown in Figs. 42-3 and 42-4 are heavy and of light bronze color, with the silver square tire edge just showing.

Figs. 42-1 and 42-2. *A pair of officers' Motor Transport Corps standing coat collar insignia. These are bronze in color, with an applied silver rim representing the tire. (Each 1 1/16 inches in diameter)*

Figs. 42-3 and 42-4. *This pair of officers' insignia, made in France, features a light brown metal and a square-edged silver tire. (1 inch in diameter)*

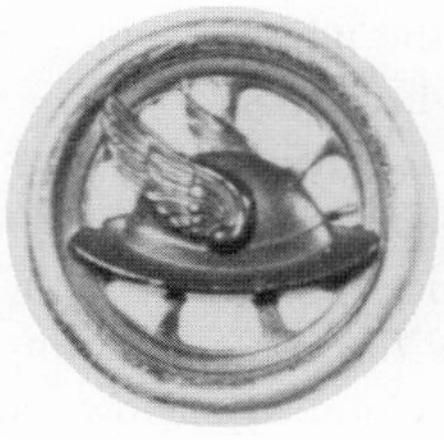

Fig. 42-1.

Fig. 42-2.

Fig. 42-3.

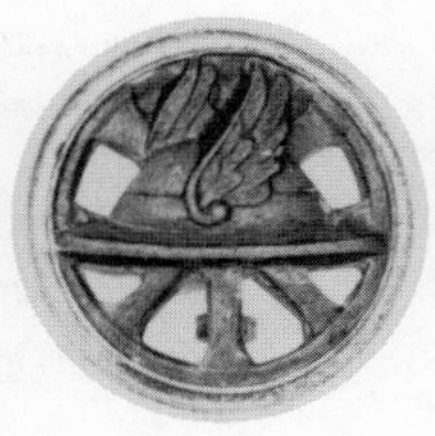

Fig. 42-4.

Fig. 42-5.

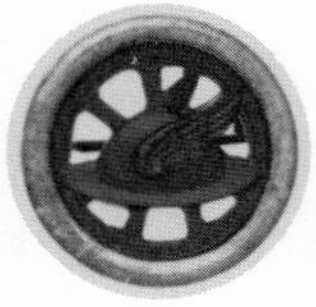

Fig. 42-6.

Fig. 42-7.

Fig. 42-8.

Fig. 42-9.

Fig. 42-10.

Fig. 42-11.

Fig. 42-12.

Fig. 42-13.

Fig. 42-14.

Fig. 42-15.

Fig. 42-16.

Fig. 42-5. *An attractive insignia with Mercury's helmet made from a separate piece and applied to the wheel. (1 5/16 inches in diameter)*

Fig. 42-6. *Shirt-sized Motor Transport Corps officers' bronze insignia. (49/65 inch in diameter)*

Fig. 42-7. *Gilt Motor Transport Corps designs were never authorized, because the branch was disbanded shortly after World War I, yet this insignia is gilt with a silver tire. This is a coat-sized piece (1 3/32 inches in diameter.*

Fig. 42-8. *An officers' gilt-colored shirt collar insignia. (49/64 inch in diameter)*

Fig. 42-9. *An enlisted men's bronze collar disk. This particular tire is smooth, a common design. (1 inch in diameter)*

Fig. 42-10. *A few enlisted men's insignia not only had a rough tire but also displayed an air valve stem for the wheel, as does this piece. (1 inch in diameter)*

Fig. 42-11. *Made in Germany in 1919 for Army of Occupation members, this hollow disk was originally painted flat black. (1 inch in diameter)*

Fig. 42-12. *This enlisted men's collar insignia was evidently made after the close of World War I, because it is gilt. Some soldiers wore such improperly colored devices to add some color to their uniforms. (1 inch in diameter)*

Fig. 42-13. *In the 1930s motor truck companies were assigned to the Quartermaster Corps, and some units adopted insignia like this, with the number and type of unit. (1 inch in diameter)*

Figs. 42-14 and 42-15. *A pair of officers' insignia for the World War I Transportation Corps. These differ from the enlisted men's versions only in that the officers' pieces were pierced. (1 1/64 inches and 1 inch wide, respectively)*

Figs. 42-16 and 42-17. *These World War I enlisted men's Transportation Corps insignia were worn only in 1919 and 1920. (1 inch in diameter)*

Fig. 42-18. *An officers' small World War II insignia. The design incorporated the World War I design, the outline of a federal highway marker, and a ship's wheel, all showing the major means of transportation. (25/32 inch wide)*

Fig. 42-19. *This World War II insignia had the winged wheel applied separately. (1 1/64 inches in diameter)*

Fig. 42-20. *The Luxemburg Company made this attractive but oversized officers' insignia. (1 5/32 inches wide)*

Fig. 42-5 is a more artistic design, with the hat made separately and brazed to the wheel, allowing the hat to project in relief some distance from the wheel. Officers also wore small insignia (Fig. 42-6). The Motor Transport Corps disbanded before dress insignia returned to general use, so the gilt insignia for the coat in Fig. 42-7 and for the shirt in Fig. 42-8 were never authorized. Strength of the corps at the armistice was 1,135 officers and 26,957 enlisted men.[3]

The solid bronze enlisted men's disk bears the same design as the officers' insignia except that the tire is not silver (Fig. 42-9). Two variations are shown in Figs. 42-10 and 42-11; the first has a rough tread on the tire, and the latter, made in Germany about 1920, has the hat facing the wrong way. A nonregulation gilt disk is shown in Fig. 42-12. All Motor Transport Corps insignia were "abolished" in March 1921, although the insignia could be used until exhausted "where applicable."[4]

In the small postwar Regular Army, truck companies became a part of the Quartermaster Corps.[5] Authorized gilt disks of the 1930s had legends like *110 MT,* indicating the 110th Motor Truck Company, below the Quartermaster Corps device (Fig. 42-13).

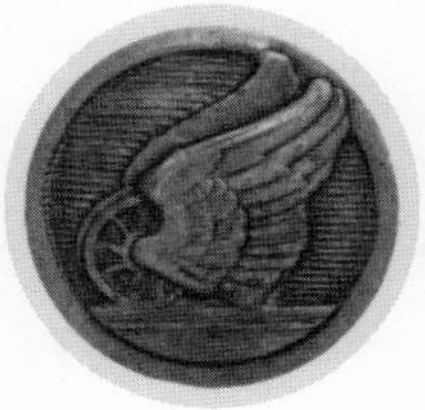

Fig. 42-17.

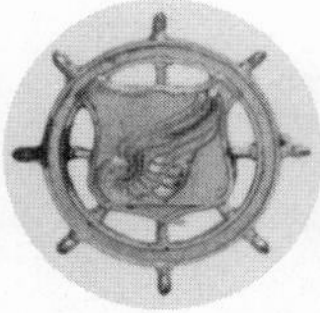

Fig. 42-18.

Fig. 42-19.

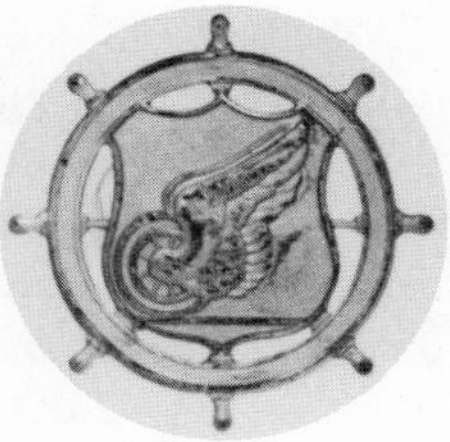

Fig. 42-20.

Fig. 42-21.

Fig. 42-22.

Fig. 42-23.

Fig. 42-24.

Fig. 42-25.

Fig. 42-26.

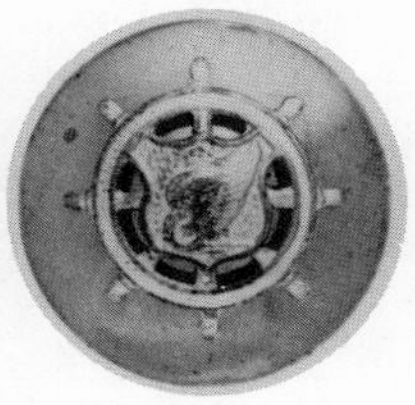

Fig. 42-27.

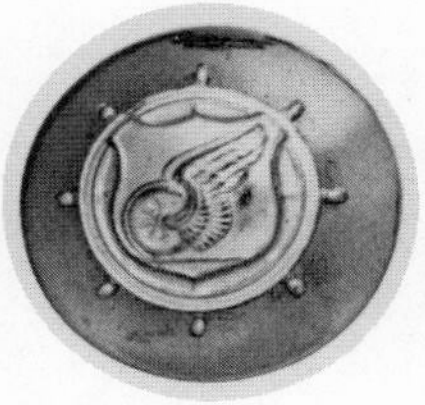

Fig. 42-28.

Fig. 42-21. *Yellow embroidered World War II–period insignia on khaki cloth. (Design $1\frac{3}{8}$ inches wide)*

Fig. 42-22. *Unit numbers were first authorized in 1966, although some were worn well before that time. This particular insignia was made in Germany for U.S. officers stationed there. ($1\frac{1}{64}$ inches wide)*

Fig. 42-23. *A woman from the highlands of Vietnam hand-embroidered this particular insignia on lightweight cloth for use on jungle fatigues. (Design $1\frac{3}{32}$ inches wide)*

Fig. 42-24. *A World War II enlisted men's disk of the style with the design embossed on thin metal. (1 inch in diameter)*

Figs. 42-25, 42-26, 42-27, and 42-28. *Disk insignia, all with the background domed in the style popular in the 1950s. The first three designs all have the area between the shield and the wheel rim pierced, although the design details and size vary widely. ($1\frac{3}{64}$ inches, $1\frac{1}{32}$ inches, 1 inch, and 1 inch in diameter, respectively)*

Other examples are shown in chapter 18, "Quartermasters."

Transportation Corps, World War I

A winged railway wheel on a section of track, all enclosed in a circle, became the branch insignia of the Transportation Corps in World War I. Officers' devices came in facing pairs, as shown in Figs. 42-14 and 42-15. The wheels faced front on each side of the collar. Enlisted men's disks, worn until mid-1920, bore the same design (Figs. 42-16 and 42-17). Peak strength, reached in January 1919, was 1,935 officers and 58,353 men.[6]

Transportation Corps, World War II and Later

In World War II the Quartermaster Corps selected for the Transportation Corps an insignia design representing the rail, sea, and highway responsibilities of the new branch. The basic shape is that of a ship's wheel with a superimposed shield in the shape of a federal highway marker. Upon the shield is the winged railway wheel used as the Transportation Corps insignia after World War I.[7]

Officers' insignia came in many sizes and styles, although the device was supposed to be, according to regulations, 1 inch high. Four samples of insignia that were used are shown (Figs. 42-18 through 42-21). The standard design has not changed since it was first announced in regulations of February 1943. As of September 1966, Transportation Corps battalions were permitted to add numbers to their basic branch insignia (Fig. 42-22). Fig. 42-23 shows a subdued insignia made in Vietnam for wear on fatigue uniforms.[8]

Enlisted soldiers' disks come in a wide variety of design styles. Fig. 42-24 is the one-piece issue disk first specified for production on 5 January 1943,[9] a full month before the design was announced in regulations. Domed disks, shown in the remaining photographs, display wide variations. Figs. 42-25, 42-26, and 42-27 all have pierced areas between the shield and the ship's wheel. Figs. 42-28 and

42-29 have the design stamped from one nonpierced piece of metal, and the latter disk has the unit number on the face, a most unusual position. A flat pierced disk with the design off-center and shrunk to accommodate the unit number in its proper place is shown in Fig. 42-30.

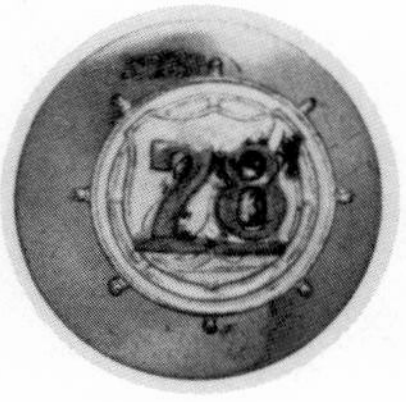

Fig. 42-29.

Fig. 42-30.

Fig. 42-29. *A unit number on the face on a Transportation Corps disk made with a slight dome shape. (1 inch in diameter)*

Fig. 42-30. *To allow room for a unit number, this insignia's central design was made smaller than usual and placed lower on the standard circular background. (1 inch in diameter)*

Chapter Forty-Three

Field Clerks and Warrant Officers

Veterans of the two world wars will agree with the wit who altered Napoleon's maxim to fit the twentieth century: "The army that moves on its stomach slides on paper." If one particular year in army history could be singled out as the beginning of the "paperwork era," 1917 is a strong candidate. Two factors, men and machines, brought that era about. The men were draftees and volunteers who swelled the ranks of the army to more than two million men overseas by the time of the 1918 armistice; the machines were typewriters, by then in common use throughout the army.

To cope with the increasing paperwork and administrative duties, the army added civilian headquarters clerks in 1896. An act of Congress of 29 August 1916 transferred all of these War Department headquarters clerks out of civil service status and made them a part of the army, but without any designation of rank, by stating, "Hereafter, headquarters clerks shall be known as field clerks." Also specified were field clerks, Quartermaster Corps—civilians who had previously been known as pay clerks.[1]

Collar Disks

When some clerks began to go overseas in 1917, a uniform was required, because the clerks would be located in a war zone with troops. In July 1917 the insignia specified were disks with the letters *US* and with crossed quill pens,[2] as shown in Figs. 43-1 and 43-2. Although the army rescinded authority for these disks very quickly, some were made in France. However, it is doubtful that the insignia were manufactured while they were still authorized. It is likely that the Quartermaster Corps ordered these disks inadvertently along with many authorized insignia sometime in 1918.

Officer-Style Collar Insignia for Field Clerks

As forerunners of warrant officers, field clerks were similar to commissioned officers, although they were not entitled to salutes from enlisted men.[3] The round disk in the style of enlisted men's insignia irked them, so before the first change to Special Regulation Number 41 was published in December 1917, the clerks found relief in American Expeditionary Forces (AEF) General Order Number 50, 27 October 1917. By that order, army field clerks were to have a miniature of Adjutant General's Department insignia below the crossed quill pens; field clerks, Quartermaster Corps, were to have a miniature of the quartermaster device below the pens. Both types of clerks were to wear officers' uniforms with no rank insignia and without the usual cuff braid on the officers' brown service coat but with the officers' *US* letters or variations.[4] Insignia described in this order were outline forms as worn by officers, not round disks. Change number one to Special Regulation Number 41, 29 December 1917, repeated the AEF order and confirmed it thoughout the army.

Army field clerks' bronze insignia come in several sizes for the coat (Figs. 43-3, 43-4, and 43-5) and the shirt (Figs. 43-6 and 43-7). Examples of Quartermaster Corps field clerks'

Fig. 43-1. *Field clerks traced their existence to 1896, but they had no uniforms or insignia until they were ordered overseas in 1917. Crossed quill pens on a disk became their initial collar insignia. (1 inch in diameter)*

Fig. 43-2. *This field clerks' disk was made in France for the AEF. (1 inch in diameter)*

Fig. 43-3. *Army field clerks received insignia that were not on enlisted men's disks in late October 1917. The crossed quill pens with the Adjutant General's Department shield below were for army field clerks. This particular insignia is in bronze. ($1^{17}/_{32}$ inches wide)*

Fig. 43-1.

Fig. 43-3.

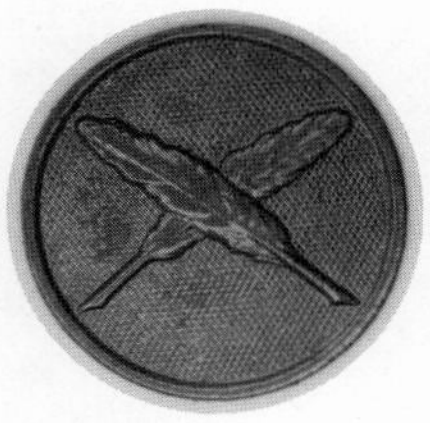

Fig. 43-2.

Fig. 43-4.

Fig. 43-4. Army field clerks' insignia with the feathers ending above the point where the pens cross. (1 17/32 inches wide)

Fig. 43-5.

Fig. 43-5. A variation of an army field clerks' insignia in bronze color. (1 17/32 inches wide)

Fig. 43-6.

Fig. 43-6. Shirt collar insignia for army field clerks. (21/32 inch wide)

Fig. 43-7.

Fig. 43-7. A variation of a shirt collar insignia made for army field clerks. (1 inch wide)

Fig. 43-8.

Fig. 43-8. In late 1917 field clerks, Quartermaster Corps, began to wear crossed pens with a Quartermaster Corps insignia below instead of the shield used by army field clerks. (1 5/8 inches wide)

Fig. 43-9.

Fig. 43-9. A variation of the insignia for field clerks, Quartermaster Corps. (1 5/8 inches wide)

insignia are shown in Figs. 43-8 and 43-9. An unusual shirt collar–sized example made overseas is shown in Fig. 43-10. Although not prescribed in regulations, plain quill pens were worn by some clerks. Some of them, both for the coat and for the shirt, are illustrated in Figs. 43-11, 43-12, and 43-13.

In the 1921 regulations the insignia height was 1 inch, with bright brass for the white uniform and bronze for the service coat. The Quartermaster Corps and Adjutant General's Department devices in the lower angle were 3/8 inch high. With the total return to bright brass insignia in 1923, both types of clerks wore the gilt ornaments. Figs. 43-14 and 43-15 show standard-sized ornaments, while Fig. 43-16 illustrates a shirt-sized insignia in gilt. A gilt insignia of unknown history, with the *4* in the lower angle of the pens, is shown in Fig. 43-17. Shirt collar devices were three-fourths the standing coat collar size, and this smaller size became that worn on lapel coats in 1926.[5]

After June 1920 no more field clerks were appointed, the clerical duties being assumed by warrant officers, after a peak strength of nearly thirty-five hundred field clerks. The last field clerk collar insignia, authorized in late 1924, had a 1-inch-high adjutant general's shield or quartermasters' device behind the intersection of two quill pens 3/4 inch high. Insignia of this type are shown in Figs. 43-18, 43-19, and 43-20. Quartermaster Corps field clerks wore their insignia in pairs, the eagle's head facing forward. For the few remaining field clerks, in 1926 the insignia were reduced to 3/4 inch high when worn on the lapel coat. The regulations called for the eagle's head to face right for field clerks of the Quartermaster Corps, although in practice they came in pairs despite specific instructions to the contrary. Thus, the smaller size exists with the eagle facing left (Fig. 43-21).[6]

Field Clerks' Cap Devices

In March 1921 special cap ornaments of plain crossed pens were described for all field clerks, although the chief of staff did not approve the exact design until May 1921. Initially all service uniform caps had bronze pens, although in late 1921 gilt insignia for white uniforms came into use. In mid-1924 the insignia changed to the devices shown in Figs. 43-22 and 43-23, the army field clerks having the shield behind the pens and their quartermaster counterparts having the Quartermaster Corps device behind the pens. Fig. 43-24 illustrates an unauthorized screw-back cap insignia with the branch device below the crossed pens.[7]

Introduction of Warrant Officers

Before 1916 both men and women were employed at the various posts as clerks under the civil service rules. In 1916 a blanket law

Fig. 43-10.

Fig. 43-11.

Fig. 43-12.

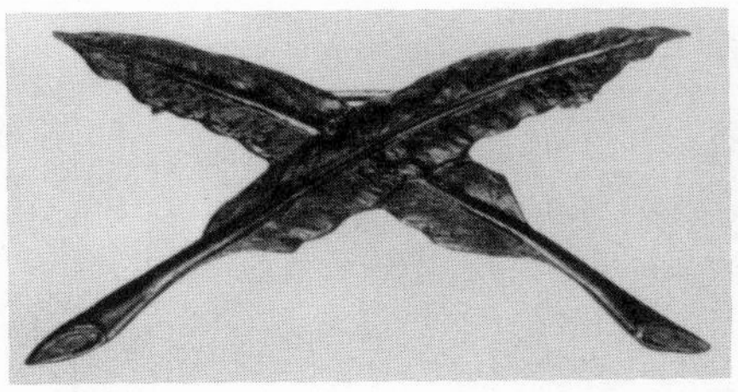

Fig. 43-13.

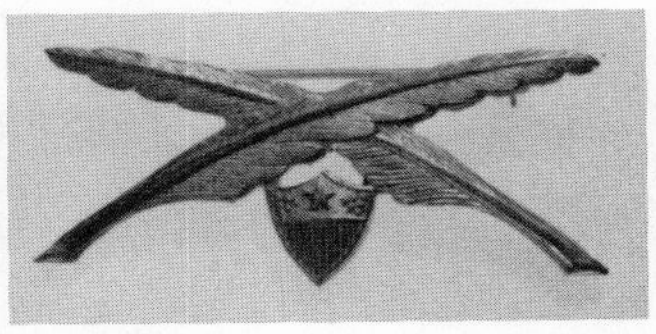

Fig. 43-14.

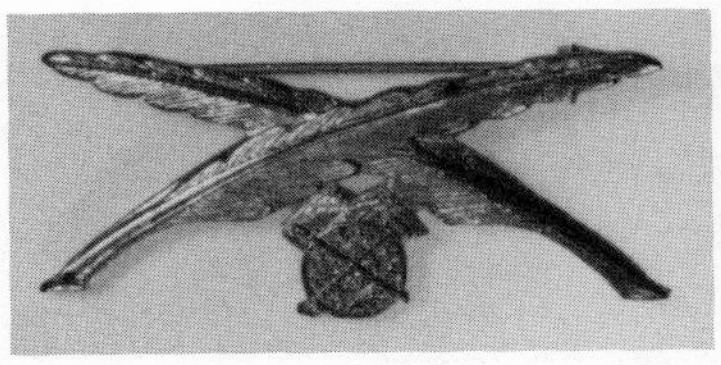

Fig. 43-15.

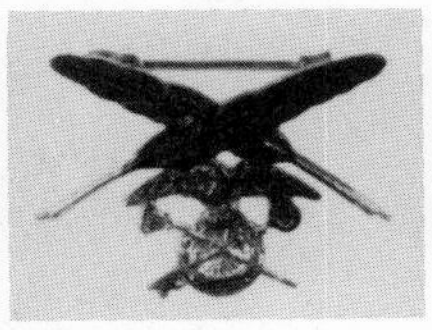

Fig. 43-16.

Fig. 43-17.

Fig. 43-18.

Fig. 43-19.

was passed which, as already noted, provided that clerks were to become army field clerks. The law did not provide for any special qualifications, nor did it contain any limits as to who might be appointed, other than that they be headquarters clerks. It took every headquarters clerk, regardless of sex or age, who was then employed. By various rulings and statutes they were given military status, which lasted until 1926.

Following World War I it was quite clear that the army would thereafter require specialists to perform field clerks' duties, but the army wisely decided to make a fresh start in a parallel direction. The solution came in June 1920 with an act of Congress creating warrant officers, who received presidential warrants instead of presidential commissions. When the army established warrant officers, it did not abolish field clerks until 1926, when most remaining field clerks transferred to warrant officer status. The handwriting was on the wall in October 1925, when Congress passed a law to phase out field clerks, and then in December 1925, Congress failed to pass appropriations to continue field clerks in service.

Field clerks were retained on active duty until 27 April 1926, when the president signed a bill that provided for field clerks then on active service to be given the rank, pay, and allowances of warrant officers in the Regular Army. This blanket law did not require any qualifications or place any restriction on appointments, and accordingly the army received its first two women warrant officers: Jean Doble, on duty at the IX Corps area headquarters in San Francisco, and Olive Hoskins, on duty at the VII Corps area headquarters in Omaha. Both women each then had approximately twenty years' service.[8] It would be World War II before the army would again receive women warrant officers.

Fig. 43-10. *This bronze-colored shirt insignia has the pens crossed at a much steeper angle than most insignia, and the Quartermaster Corps insignia is superimposed on top of the lower portion of the pens instead of being placed in the lower angle. (21/32 inch wide)*

Fig. 43-11. *Plain crossed pens such as this were not authorized for collar insignia, but they were commonly used during World War I. (1 9/16 inches wide)*

Fig. 43-12. *This smaller set of quill pens may have been worn on either shirt or coat collars. These officer-style plain quill pens were never authorized. (1 5/32 inches wide)*

Fig. 43-13. *This set of crossed bronze pens is unusually large, even for the World War I period. (1 27/32 inches wide)*

Fig. 43-14. *A gilt 1921–24 insignia of the design intended for the standing coat collar of army field clerks. (1 3/4 inches wide)*

Fig. 43-15. *Standing-collar gilt insignia for field clerks, Quartermaster Corps, 1921–24. (1 3/4 inches wide)*

Fig. 43-16. *Gilt shirt collar insignia, 1923–24.*

Fig. 43-17. *This very small gilt crossed quill pen insignia is for a field clerk, but the number 4 is a mystery. (11/16 inch wide)*

Figs. 43-18 and 43-19. *A matched pair of gilt insignia for the standing-collar coat, 1924–26, for field clerks, Quartermaster Corps. (Each 1 3/4 inches wide)*

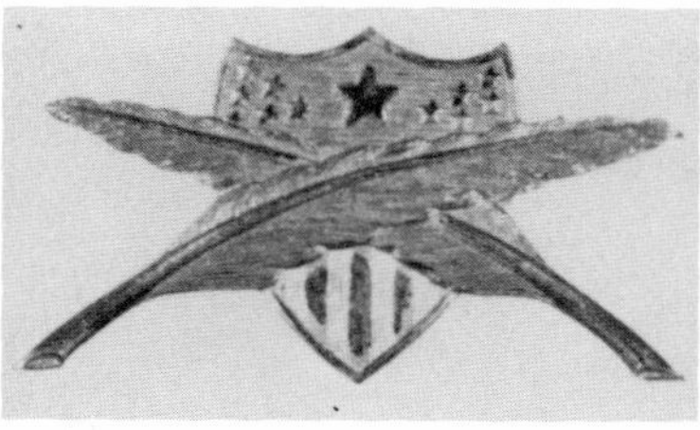

Fig. 43-20.

Fig. 43-21.

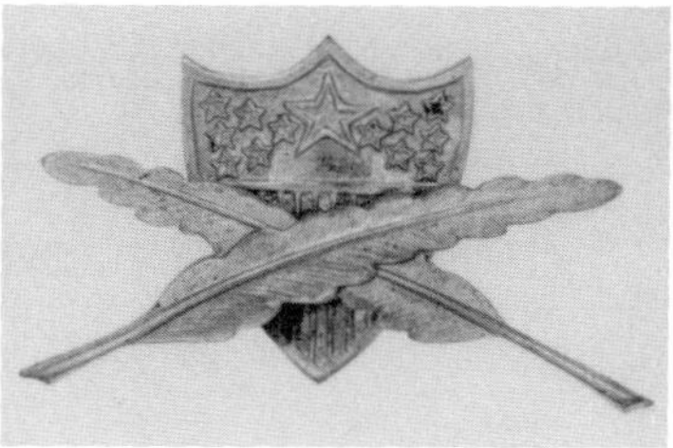

Fig. 43-22.

Fig. 43-23.

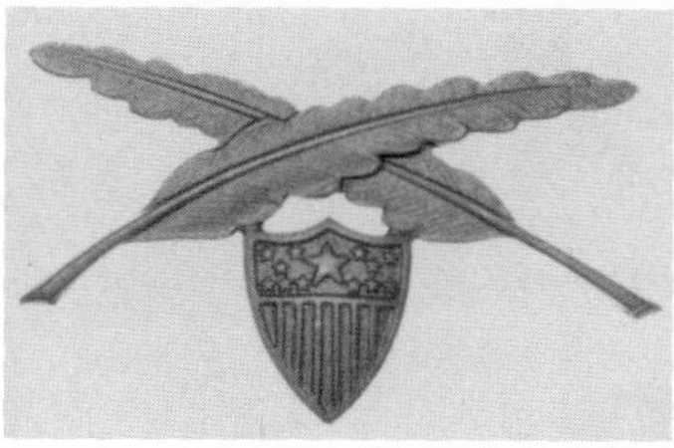

Fig. 43-24.

Fig. 43-25.

Fig. 43-26.

Fig. 43-27.

Fig. 43-20. *Gilt insignia, 1924–26, for the standing-collar coat for army field clerks. (1 13/16 inches wide)*

Fig. 43-21. *Shirt and lapel coat insignia, 1924–26, for field clerks, Quartermaster Corps. (1 25/32 inches wide)*

Fig. 43-22. *Army field clerks' cap ornament, in gilt, 1924–26. The pens were made separately and applied to the shield. (1 7/10 inches wide)*

Fig. 43-23. *A cap insignia for field clerks, Quartermaster Corps, the counterpart of the insignia shown in Fig. 43-22. (1 43/64 inches wide)*

Fig. 43-24. *A nonregulation bronze-colored cap device for army field clerks. (1 43/64 inches wide)*

Fig. 43-25. *The initial cap insignia, in bronze color, for warrant officers, introduced in March 1921. (2 11/64 inches wide)*

Fig. 43-26. *A 1970s warrant officers' cap insignia. (2 3/64 inches wide)*

Fig. 43-27. *Made in Germany in the 1950s, this warrant officers' cap ornament has the wreath pierced like that of the initial 1921 bronze version. (2 3/64 inches wide)*

Warrant Officers' Cap Insignia

Warrant officers initially wore enlisted men's cap devices before the design of a special cap ornament for their exclusive use in 1921. From March 1921 until 1923 warrant officers wore a black metal eagle, 1 1/2 inches high, grasping two arrows and seated in a wreath, as shown in Fig. 43-25, the design having been created by the Fine Arts Commission. A 1960s gilt insignia is shown in Fig. 43-26, while Fig. 43-27 shows a German-made 1950s piece, and an interesting but unauthorized silver insignia is shown in Fig. 43-28. During World War II, flight officers, a special rank for pilot warrant officers, also wore this design of cap device, although these men wore the Air Corps lapel insignia. Except for color, the warrant officers' cap insignia has remained unchanged since its introduction in 1921.[9]

Sleeve Insignia

A large device for warrant officers to wear on overcoat sleeves, embroidered in yellow on olive drab cloth, is shown in Fig. 43-29. Similar devices were prescribed and worn by both types of field clerks.[10]

Fig. 43-28.

Fig. 43-29.

Fig. 43-28. A warrant officers' cap insignia made in the Far East. (2 1/8 inches wide)

Fig. 43-29. Warrant officers wore this insignia on their lower overcoat sleeve in the 1920s and 1930s. (Design 2 5/32 inches wide)

Fig. 43-30. "Deck" warrant officers in the Army Mine Planter Service wore anchors like this, either embroidered in white (as shown) or in olive drab to match the uniform, on their lower sleeves.

Fig. 43-31. Service coat lower sleeve propeller for "engineer" warrant officers in the Army Mine Planter Service, 1921–51. (Design 7/8 inch wide)

The most unusual warrant officers' insignia are the embroidered lower sleeve disks worn by Army Mine Planter Service warrant officers. The device, either an anchor, as shown in Fig. 43-30, or a three-bladed ship's propeller, Fig. 43-31, along with bands of cuff braid indicated rank. White coats had disks and stripes of white, and the service coats had the identical insignia in brown. All other warrant officers wore four bands on the sleeves from 1921 until 1941, when white uniforms were suspended.[11]

In 1922, Congress directed the army to discharge all but forty warrant officers in the Army Mine Planter Service and not to increase the force above that number. These officers remained at low strength until 1951, when the distinctive sleeve braid disappeared with the abolition of the Coast Artillery Corps. However, one new sleeve insignia for a second assistant engineer did appear in 1941 in response to an October 1940 law that increased the number of mine planter personnel and also created that new grade.[12] A summary of the insignia with dates of wear is shown in Table 43-1.

Warrant Officers' Collar Insignia

The first warrant officers joined the coast artillery in January 1920. Between January and November 1920 these men wore on their collars a bronze coast artillery insignia with a sea mine in the lower intersection. This device is illustrated and discussed in chapter 6, "Artillery." Between November 1920 and March 1921 warrant officers wore only the *US* without any branch insignia on their collars.[13]

A unique branch insignia was established by War Department Circular 72, dated 16 March 1921. Large bronze insignia 1 inch high (Fig. 43-32) went on the standing coat collar, while smaller ornaments, 3/4 inch high according to regulations, went on shirt collars. A smaller-than-regulation bronze shirt device is shown in Fig. 43-33. Gilt insignia replaced bronze ones in 1923 and were made in pairs from 1924 until 1926. For the new

Fig. 43-30.

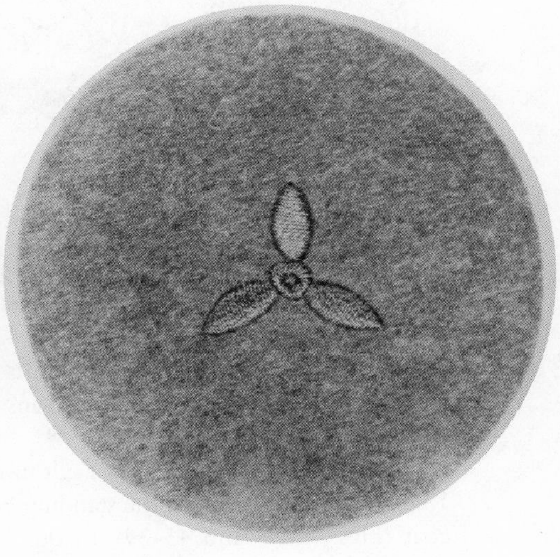

Fig. 43-31.

Table 43-1. *Army Mine Planter Service Warrant Officer Sleeve Insignia.*

Title	Year of Wear	Sleeve Insignia
Master	1921–51	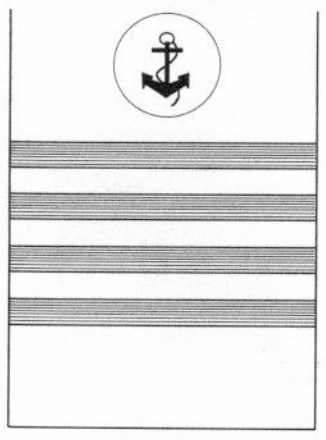
Chief Engineer	1921–51	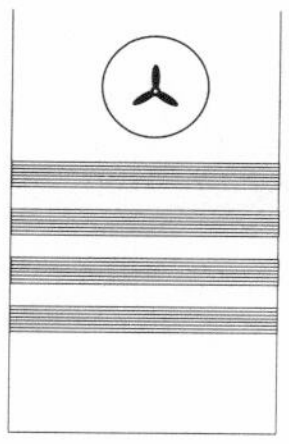
First Mate	1921–51	
Asst. Engineer	1921–51	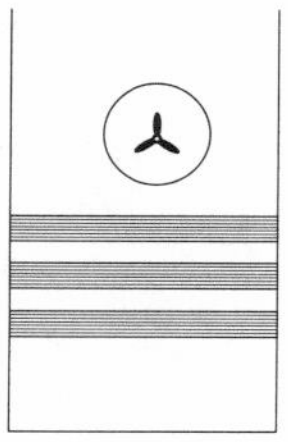
Second Mate	1921–51	
Second Asst. Engineer	1941–51	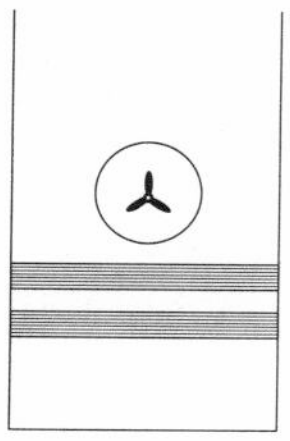

Fig. 43-32. *The bronze warrant officers' coat collar insignia, prescribed in November 1921. (1 3/8 inches wide)*

Fig. 43-33. *A miniature bronze insignia for the shirt collar, 1921–23. (13/32 inch wide)*

Figs. 43-34 and 43-35. *A pair of lapel coat warrant officers' insignia with the features more indistinct than those of most insignia. (Each 1 1/16 inches wide)*

Fig. 43-36. *Made from two pieces of brass, this warrant officers' insignia has the insignia seated in a truly separate wreath. (1 1/16 inches wide)*

Fig. 43-32.

Fig. 43-33.

Fig. 43-34.

Fig. 43-35.

Fig. 43-36.

1926 lapel coat men wore shirt-sized (3/4-inch-high) ornaments with the eagles' heads facing right. Figs. 43-34 and 43-35 show a typical pair. This basic design is currently worn, although some variations may be found (Figs. 43-36 and 43-37).[14]

During the late 1920s pairs of gilt insignia 1 inch high continued on the standing-collar coat (Figs. 43-38 and 43-39). In the 1920s and 1930s the army appointed few warrant officers other than those assigned as band leaders, Army Mine Planter Service personnel, and a few other skilled specialists. During the Depression some warrant officer positions were virtually impossible to fill because of the special skills required. The 1930s chief of the Air Corps lamented almost each year that the Air Corps could not obtain enough warrant officers. As soon as a highly qualified enlisted man received his warrant,

Fig. 43-37.

Fig. 43-38.

Fig. 43-39.

Fig. 43-40.

Fig. 43-41.

another skilled warrant officer retired, and the training required for Air Corps warrant officers was hard to find. Not counting the seven warrant officer band leaders, the Air Corps had twenty-eight warrant officers in 1931, and three years later the corps lost two of them by retirement.[15]

Throughout the Depression warrant officers composed a very small part of the army. A major change occurred in 1941, when the president increased the number of warrant officers, expanded the powers and duties of warrant officers, and brought in men to formerly vacant fields. The final large growth occurred during the Vietnam War, when thousands of warrant officer pilots, as well as men in other skills, were required for the mass introduction of the helicopter. Special warrant officer candidate schools were created to train the many pilots required. A cloth insignia made in Southeast Asia for warrant officers during the Vietnam War is shown in Fig. 43-40, while Fig. 43-41 shows a hand-made cloth insignia from the Far East to be worn on the khaki uniform.

Fig. 43-37. *A 1960s warrant officers' bright brass collar insignia. (1 1/16 inches wide)*

Figs. 43-38 and 43-39. *Gilt warrant officers' eagles for the standing-collar coat. These orange-colored brass pin-backed insignia were made in England and imported into the United States. (1 23/64 inches wide)*

Fig. 43-40. *Handmade in Vietnam, this warrant officers' insignia was purchased in 1967 in the local village adjacent to the headquarters of the 1st Cavalry Division (Airmobile). (1 3/8 inches wide)*

Fig. 43-41. *This insignia was embroidered on a khaki background in the Far East. (1 1/4 inches wide)*

CHAPTER FORTY-FOUR

PROVOST MARSHAL AND MILITARY POLICE

Fig. 44-1. This bronze wreath with silver letters became the collar insignia of the Provost Marshal General's Department in January 1919. It was used only in the United States. (1¼ inches wide)

Fig. 44-2. Enlisted men assigned to the Provost Marshal General's Department in the United States wore bronze disks of this style. (1 inch in diameter)

A PROVOST MARSHAL GENERAL was appointed in September 1862, and the office was discontinued in August 1866. While the office existed, it enforced draft laws, apprehended deserters, arrested disloyal persons, and performed other federal military police (MP) duties. The position of provost marshal remained vacant from 1866 until May 1917. The World War I Provost Marshal General's Department functioned primarily to induct men into military service, from registration to their initial arrival at camp. Civilians comprised the vast majority of personnel in the Provost Marshal General's Department, with only 192 commissioned officers assigned as of 31 October 1918. Initially all officers were from the Judge Advocate General's Office, and they wore the JAG insignia. Despite the small number of men involved, in January 1919 the War Department prescribed for officers of the Provost Marshal General's Department the silver letters *PM* in a 1-inch wreath, as shown in Fig. 44-1. The Provost Marshal General's Department discontinued activities on 15 July 1919, and the army rescinded the insignia in March 1921.[1]

In the AEF in France, the provost marshal general functioned as commander of MPs and had charge of prisoners, traffic control, and enforcement of regulations, much as one would expect of a provost marshal today. Like many branches, this one started with several reorganizations. Initially the AEF provost marshal general, appointed 20 July 1917, was a General Headquarters staff member at Paris, and the entire staff consisted of one additional officer and eleven enlisted men. Addition of movement control to the duties in August 1917 caused an expansion in the office. Combat units, such as divisions, formed their own MP units, which were not connected with the AEF Provost Marshal General's Department initially. However, in late 1918, when a former chief of the Philippine Constabulary came to France as the provost marshal general, the AEF brought all unit MPs under the technical supervision of the newly formed Military Police Service, a part of the AEF Provost Marshal General's Department. Under the new provost marshal general's direction the department reorganized, and a distinct Military Police Corps became established as a part of it.[2]

Provost Marshal General's Department enlisted men wore a bronze disk (Fig. 44-2) bearing the letters *PM* after January 1919. Although the War Department General Staff declared the disk obsolete in August 1920, the regulations of 1921 stated that these disks would be worn until stocks were exhausted.[3]

MILITARY POLICE, WORLD WAR I

Army field service regulations established before World War I provided for MPs using men assigned to a division, with a distinctive armband bearing the letters *MP*. Initially the only distinguishing insignia was the field service device, a "blue brassard on the left arm half way between the elbow and shoulder, bearing the letters 'M.P.' in white" (Fig. 44-3). In July 1918 the AEF formed "a specific force to be known as the Military

Fig. 44-1.

Fig. 44-2.

Fig. 44-3.

Fig. 44-3. Made from blue denim and embroidered with white stitching, the MP armband was the only insignia used by World War I MPs until July 1918. (Letters 2 3/8 inches high)

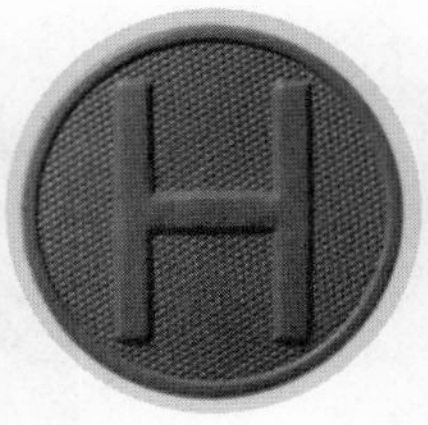

Fig. 44-4.

Fig. 44-4. Established in August 1917, the H on a disk was worn by enlisted men assigned to division headquarters detachments and MPs. (1 inch in diameter)

Fig. 44-5.

Fig. 44-5. This nonregulation disk was probably used by division MPs, who were also identified by red cloth tabs on their collars. (1 inch in diameter)

Fig. 44-6.

Fig. 44-6. Bronze disks bearing block letters were common during World War I, but those for MPs, like this one, were not regulation. Gilt disks struck from this die also exist, and these perhaps saw use in the 1920s. (1 inch in diameter)

Fig. 44-7.

Fig. 44-7. Periods following letters were not common and did not follow the usual scheme of block letters on disks. (1 inch in diameter)

Police Corps,"[4] although insignia were not described. This changed in early September when a general order prescribed red cloth collar tabs for members of the Military Police Corps:

> 2. For officers, a strip of scarlet cloth, 2 inches long and 1–1 1/4 inches wide, rounded at the corners, sewn on the collar lengthwise 1 inch from each end of the collar and midway between the upper and lower edges of collar, with regulation bronze metal letters "U.S." superimposed on center.
>
> 3. For enlisted men, a strip of scarlet cloth, 2 inches long and 1–1 1/4 inches wide, rounded at the corners, sewn on the collar lengthwise 1 inch from each end of the collar and midway between the upper and lower edges of collar with regulation button insignia "U.S." superimposed on center.[5]

Fig. 44-8.

Fig. 44-8. This 1918 soldier has the block letters MP on the right collar disk.

For divisions in the United States, the War Department prescribed in August 1917 the letter *H* on a bronze disk (Fig. 44-4) for wear by division headquarters detachments and by military police. The infantry device with *MP* below (Fig. 44-5) was made during World War I, although it was not authorized. Also not in regulations were the block letters *MP*, which exist in both bronze and gilt. Three examples are shown (Figs. 44-6, 44-7, and 44-8). The War Department established the *PM* disk in January 1919, and some AEF MPs may have worn it, because the AEF's Military Police Corps was part of the Provost Marshal General's Department.[6]

Officers' Military Police Insignia

The War Department selected crossed Model 1806 Harper's Ferry pistols for the Corps of Military Police insignia in October 1921, although the design was not published until April 1922. During World War I the army had used crossed automatic pistols for a marksmanship insignia, and the results looked like carpenters' squares and could not be easily recognized. This may account for the use of the older model pistols. Fig. 44-9 is the bronze insignia 1.70 inches wide, used only until 1923, when a gilt insignia, Fig. 44-10, became the authorized device. The army specified gilt pistols from 1921 onward

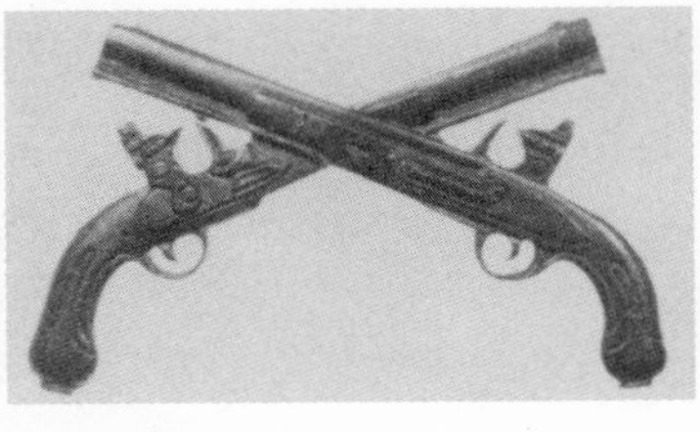

Fig. 44-9.

Fig. 44-9. The bronze 1922–23 officers' MP insignia for the high-collar service uniform. (1 23/32 inches wide)

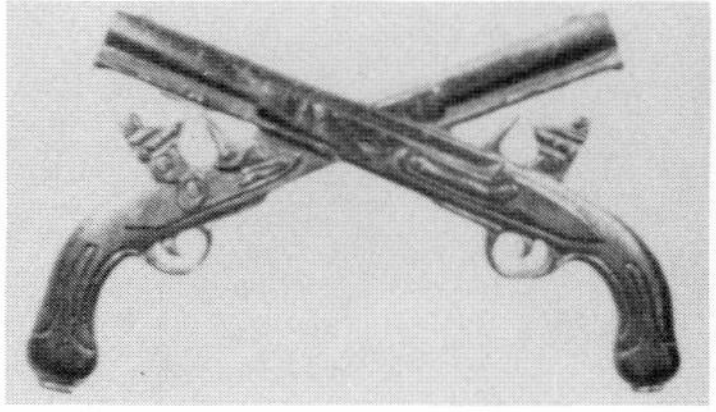

Fig. 44-10.

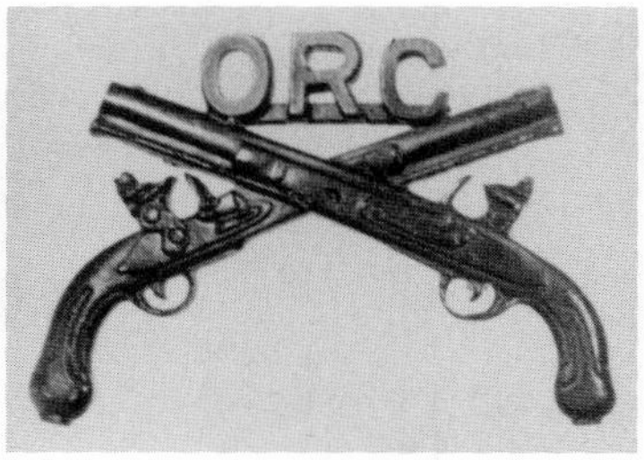

Fig. 44-11.

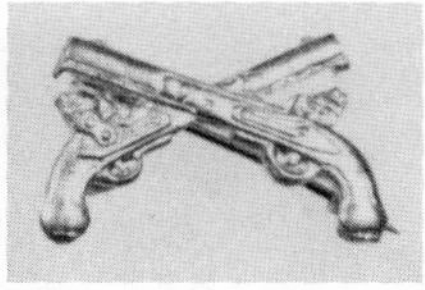

Fig. 44-12.

Fig. 44-13.

Fig. 44-14.

Fig. 44-15.

Fig. 44-16.

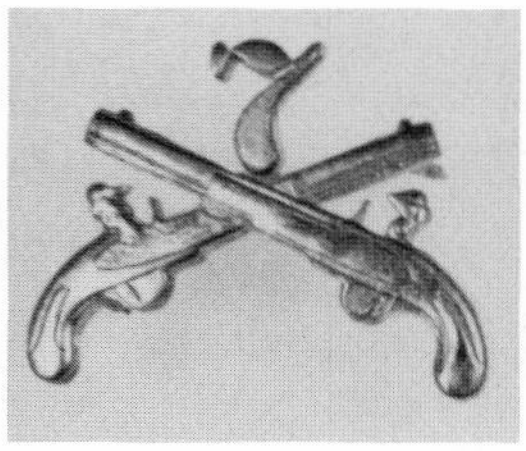

Fig. 44-17.

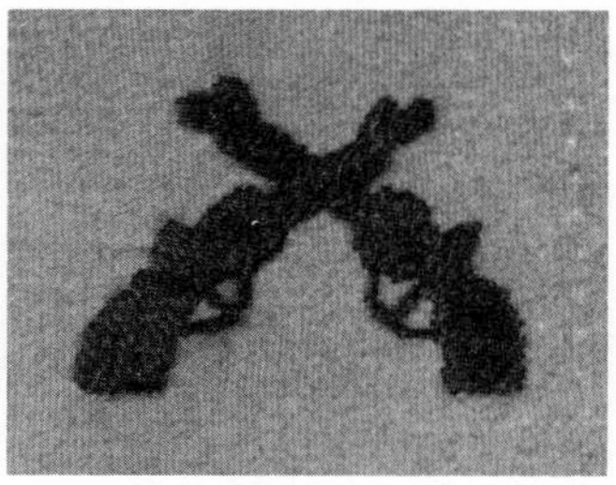

Fig. 44-18.

Fig. 44-10. *Gilt-colored Harper's Ferry Model 1806 pistols for officers standing-collar coats, for use after 1923. ($1\frac{23}{32}$ inches wide)*

Fig. 44-11. *Some Organized Reserve Corps members added letters showing their components, as was done with this scarce bronze insignia. ($1\frac{23}{32}$ inches wide)*

Fig. 44-12. *Small MP insignia like this were worn by officers on shirt collars during the 1920s. ($\frac{15}{16}$ inch wide)*

Fig. 44-13. *A common machine-embroidered Corps of Military Police insignia from World War II for the officers' winter blouse. (Design $1\frac{1}{32}$ inches wide)*

Fig. 44-14. *Officers in many MP companies and battalions added unit numbers to their branch insignia during and after World War II. ($1\frac{1}{4}$ inches wide)*

Fig. 44-15. *Made in Germany, this 793d Military Police Battalion insignia has a silver-colored finish. ($1\frac{11}{32}$ inches wide)*

Fig. 44-16. *Korean-made brass crossed pistols with a small unit number stamped with the insignia. ($1\frac{9}{32}$ inches wide)*

Fig. 44-17. *This Military Police Corps Officers' insignia with the oversized number was made in Korea during the 1960s. ($1\frac{5}{16}$ inches wide)*

Fig. 44-18. *A hand-embroidered MP insignia made in 1967 for wear on jungle fatigues in Southeast Asia. (Design $1\frac{9}{32}$ inches wide)*

Fig. 44-19. *A 1930s issue, enlisted military policemen's collar disk. (1 inch in diameter)*

for white uniforms. Members of the Organized Reserve Corps wore *ORC* above the pistols (Fig. 44-11). A shirt ornament worn in the early 1920s is shown in Fig. 44-12. Regulations of 1926 called for standing-collar coats to carry pistols 1 inch high, while lapel coats and shirts used $\frac{3}{4}$-inch-high pistols.[7]

During World War II, MP insignia were embroidered on various types of cloth. An example for the officers' winter coat is shown in Fig. 44-13. Some companies and battalions added numbers, as shown in Figs. 44-14 and 44-15, the latter made in Germany. The insignia shown in Fig. 44-16 was made in Korea with small numbers, while that of Fig. 44-17 is from the same country but with large numbers. A cloth subdued insignia, handmade in Vietnam, is shown in Fig. 44-18. In 1950, Congress changed the official title from Corps of Military Police to Military Police Corps.[8]

Enlisted MP Disks after World War I

Not many men served as MPs between the world wars, but the Regular Army did have a few units, and the members wore the crossed pistols on their insignia. During the early 1920s the divisional MP and headquarters elements were consolidated to form a single unit called Headquarters and Military Police Company, Division. This unit included one platoon of MPs. Within the Regular Army the 1st, 2d, 3d, Hawaiian, and Philippine divisions had such units. In other Regular Army divisions the units were inactive until 1939 or 1940, when each division activated an MP platoon.[9] The official organization date of the current Military Police Corps is 26 September 1941.

The National Guard had some MP platoons and companies between the world wars. Army reserve MP units existed only on paper. With the 1939 armed forces expansion, several nondivisional MP units became active. A 1930s gilt disk with a crosshatched background used by both the Regular Army and the National Guard is shown in Fig. 44-19. A disk of the same period used by Chicago, Illinois, members of the 33d Division's MP Company (a National Guard unit)

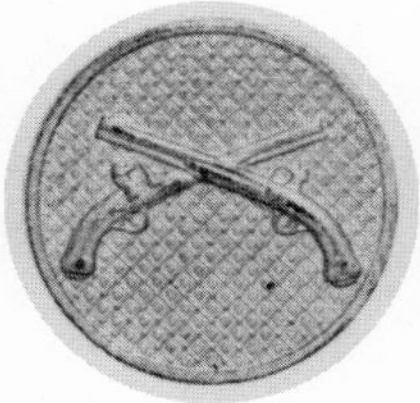

Fig. 44-19.

Fig. 44-20.

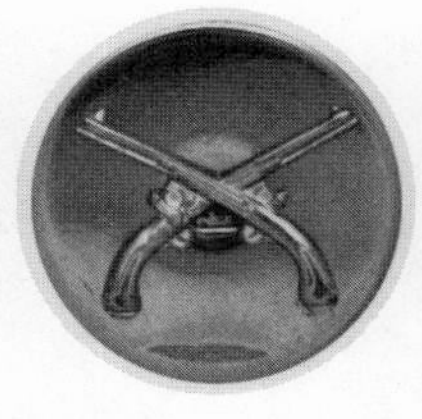

Fig. 44-21.

Fig. 44-22.

Fig. 44-23.

Fig. 44-24.

Fig. 44-25.

Fig. 44-26.

Fig. 44-27.

Fig. 44-28.

Fig. 44-29.

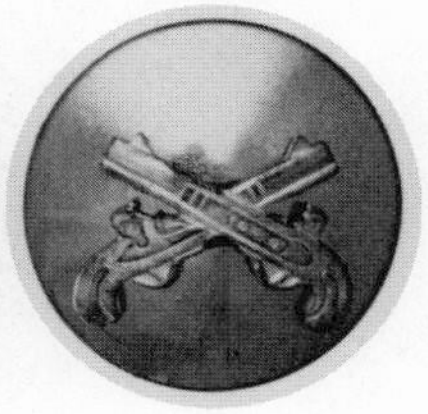

Fig. 44-30.

Fig. 44-20. *Some 1930s MP units added their numbers to collar insignia. This example was made for the MP platoon in the 33d Division, Illinois National Guard. (1 1/64 inches in diameter)*

Fig. 44-21. *A screw-post MP insignia for enlisted men, from about 1940, with slender pistols separable from the background. (1 inch in diameter)*

Fig. 44-22. *During World War II many poor-quality insignia like this were produced. (1 1/16 inches in diameter)*

Fig. 44-23. *An MP collar disk, made during World War II, embossed to save metal. (1 inch in diameter)*

Fig. 44-24. *A German-made flat disk collar insignia, silver in color. Some units added the letters HP, for highway patrol, or MP, as in this case. (63/64 inch in diameter)*

is shown in Fig. 44-20.[10] With the emergency buildup a wide variety of MP disks came into existence, ranging from excellent, detailed designs (Fig. 44-21) to crude pot metal insignia (Fig. 44-22). Fig. 44-23 shows the one-piece issue insignia made during and after World War II.

Some MP units in Germany after World War II were designated as highway patrol. The insignia shown in Figs. 44-24, 44-25, and 44-26 are typical of disks made in Germany during that period. The green enamel edge shown on the disk in Fig. 44-27 is an unauthorized addition to an enlisted MPs' disk.

Fig. 44-28, with the numbers made as an integral part of the pistols, is typical of ornaments made in Korea. Ornaments made in the United States are shown in Figs. 44-29 and 44-30, the first on a flat disk with both pistol butts and unit numbers extending over the disk edge, and the latter a plain dome-shaped disk popular in the 1950s. Unit designations were also placed below the pistols on both domed and flat disks (Figs. 44-31, 44-32, and 44-33). The last piece was struck from a metal slug in Germany immediately after World War II and has a safety pin fastener. After February 1965, enlisted Military Police Corps disks added battalion numbers

Fig. 44-25. *Made for the same battalion as the insignia shown in Fig. 44-24, this enlisted military policemen's collar insignia is of brass and was formed in a high dome. (1 inch in diameter)*

Fig. 44-26. *While most German-made insignia added small numbers and letters, as exemplified in the two previous insignia, some insignia manufacturers used a large addition. This insignia is silver in color. (1 inch in diameter)*

Fig. 44-27. *After the 1952 introduction of a narrow blue edge around infantry disks, manufacturers made similar trim in nonregulation colors, like this green trim for enlisted MPs. (1 5/16 inches in diameter)*

Fig. 44-28. *These Korean-made crossed pistols show the design details nicely. (1 1/64 inches in diameter)*

Fig. 44-29. *On this insignia, made in the United States, the unit number and the pistol butts are almost squeezed onto the disk, but some of the edges overhang the circular background. (1 1/32 inches in diameter)*

Fig. 44-30. *A common domed disk made in the 1950s. (1 inch in diameter)*

Fig. 44-31.

Fig. 44-32.

Fig. 44-33.

Fig. 44-34.

Figs. 44-31 (left) and 44-32. *Company designations were commonly adapted to domed (Company D) and flat (Company A) disks. (Each 1 inch in diameter)*

Fig. 44-33. *Made in Germany shortly after the end of World War II, this stamped flat disk has a safety pin back. (1 1/64 inches wide)*

Fig. 44-34. *The history of this disk is not certain, but probably some MPs wore such disks during the 1939–41 period of army expansion, before the crossed pistols were specified as enlisted MP insignia. (1 inch in diameter)*

below the pistols, according to official drawings, although regulations did not so describe the location.[11] The last insignia (Fig. 44-34) is also a two-piece disk of a type perhaps used between the wars, since it carries the letters *MP*, although the actual use of such a device is not documented.

Chapter Forty-Five

Unassigned, Army Specialists, and Administrative Reserve

DURING THE World War I expansion of the army, some officers entered on duty with special skills not applicable to traditional branches. These men were considered "detailed, detached, and unassigned officers." Selected in February 1918 as an insignia for those officers was the federal coat of arms on a disk 3/4 inches in diameter. Although the original device was actually made, as shown in Fig. 45-1, because of its similarity to enlisted men's disks it was quickly changed. In July 1918 the insignia was enlarged to a 3/4-inch-high eagle in a pierced ring 7/8 inch in diameter. Later regulations amended the diameter of the ring to 1 inch. An example of a 1921 bronze 1-inch-diameter insignia is shown in Fig. 45-2, and a gilt device is shown in Fig. 45-3. A smaller coat of arms, 9/16 inch high within a 3/4-inch ring, was prescribed for shirts in 1924 and for lapel coat collars in March 1926 (Fig. 45-4).[1]

The designation of unassigned officers changed to "Officers not members of an Arm or Service" in August 1933 and then to "Officers not members of an arm or service, Special Reserve," in November 1941. During April 1943 the designation again changed to "Officers and Warrant Officers not members of and not on duty with an arm or service; special reserve," although the reference to warrant officers was an error and three months later was rescinded. The title in February 1947 became Staff and Administrative Reserve.[2]

Many people find it hard to imagine an army officer not associated with one of the many arms or services. The "unassigned" insignia were worn by those specially skilled officers appointed from civilian life, such as attachés and military government specialists. Provisions for use of the insignia stated that nonmedical officers "appointed from civilian life" would wear the specialist reserve insignia during the initial ninety-day period of active duty. Upon completion of "an appropriate training course" and the ninety days, and if they were considered qualified, the officers could wear branch devices. For officers not formally detailed to a branch, the eagle in a ring continued to be used.[3] An officer wearing the insignia just before World War II is shown in Fig. 45-5.

The officers' eagle in a ring was rescinded in June 1948 and replaced by a design encompassing an open book, a sword, and a laurel wreath (Fig. 45-6). This new design, designated for Staff Specialists, USAR from 1950 until 1979, was worn by officers not on extended active duty. In 1979 the in title became Staff Specialists, Army National Guard/U.S. Army Reserve. A post–World War II revision to the National Defense Act, published in 1949, outlined those men who

Fig. 45-1. *The original February 1918 insignia for officers detailed, detached, or unassigned. This uninspired insignia was changed in part because of the recommendation from Bailey, Banks and Biddle Company that the insignia might be confused with an enlisted men's collar disk. (13/16 inch in diameter)*

Fig. 45-2. *A 1921–24 bronze collar insignia for officers unassigned to a branch. The 1918–21 design was similar, differing in that it was only 7/8 inch in diameter. (1 1/32 inches in diameter)*

Fig. 45-3. *A gilt insignia for the shirt and the lapel coat for officers "unassigned to a branch" during the interwar period. (7/8 inch in diameter)*

Fig. 45-4. *Smaller than allowed by regulations, this insignia was made in the late 1920s for the shirt collar. (11/16 inch in diameter)*

Fig. 45-1.

Fig. 45-2.

Fig. 45-3.

Fig. 45-4.

Fig. 45-5. *Major Dwight Garrison, a public relations specialist assigned to the Ordnance Department in mid-1941, wears the insignia for men "not members of an arm or service."*

Fig. 45-6. *This design for staff specialists reserve replaced the eagle in the ring in 1948. It is still worn today under the title Staff Specialists, ARNG/USAR. The finish on this insignia is a frosted gilt that was not meant to be polished. This design exists for officers only. ($1\frac{11}{32}$ inches wide)*

Fig. 45-7. *A subdued metal staff specialists' insignia for the fatigue uniform. ($1\frac{3}{8}$ inches wide)*

Fig. 45-8. *From the 1950s, this yellow machine-embroidered insignia is on olive green fatigue material. ($1\frac{21}{64}$ inches wide)*

Fig. 45-9. *This initial 1921 design for the Detached Enlisted Men's List (DEML) was made with the eagle separate and then applied to the background. (1 inch in diameter)*

Fig. 45-10. *A 1921–24 bronze collar disk for the DEML. (1 inch in diameter)*

Fig. 45-11. *Bronze DEML insignia with the second type of background (crosshatched lines and small shields), as used about 1923 and 1924. (1 inch in diameter)*

Figs. 45-12 and 45-13. *Two versions of the gilt DEML insignia worn in the 1930s. These insignia are of the style issued by the Quartermaster Corps. (1 inch in diameter)*

Fig. 45-14. *This crudely made eagle with a screw-post back for the DEML was probably made about 1940. (1 inch in diameter)*

Fig. 45-5

Fig. 45-6.

Fig. 45-7.

Fig. 45-9.

Fig. 45-10.

Fig. 45-8.

Fig. 45-11.

Fig. 45-12.

Fig. 45-13.

Fig. 45-14.

Fig. 45-15.

Fig. 45-16.

could be reserve and National Guard staff specialists: public information officers, men in selected special service fields, civil affairs specialists, historians, and educators. Subdued metal and yellow embroidered cloth insignia for fatigue clothing are shown in Figs. 45-7 and 45-8, respectively.

Unassigned Enlisted Personnel

After World War I, selected enlisted men were placed on the Detached Enlisted Men's List (DEML). This list was a catch-all for men with various duties, such as prison guards and recruiters, who previously had been recognized with a variety of insignia. In March 1921 men on the list, except for Indian Scouts, wore bronze disks with the eagle (Figs. 45-9 and 45-10), and the insignia was simply known as the device for the DEML.[5] Later the army introduced these disks with the background of lines and small shields in both bronze (Fig. 45-11) and gilt (Figs. 45-12 and 45-13). Two-piece flat disks used in the 1930s and 1940s are in Figs. 45-14 and

Fig. 45-17.

Fig. 45-18.

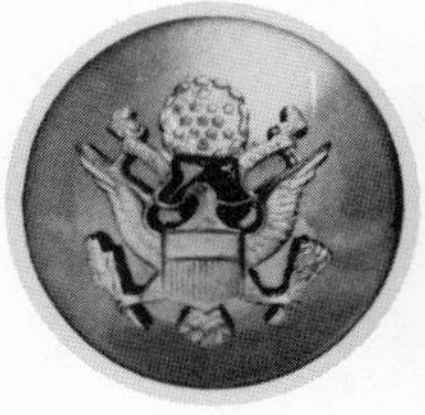

Fig. 45-19.

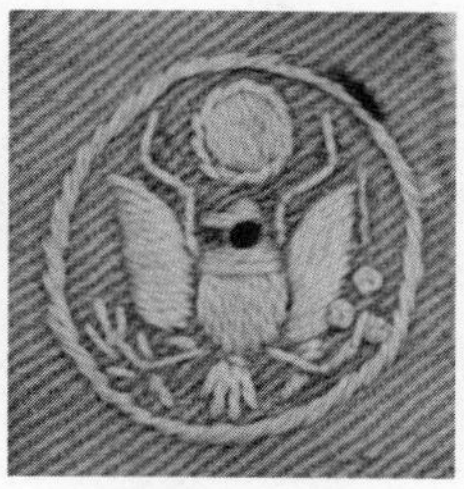

Fig. 45-20.

45-15. A stamped, one-piece insignia is shown in Fig. 45-16. Soldiers in the 1940s and 1950s began to buy domed disks of the types shown in Figs. 45-17, 45-18, and 45-19; the first of these was made by adding a backing to an officers' 3/4-inch-diameter device. The insignia shown in Fig. 45-20 was hand-embroidered in India during 1944 or 1945 so that men could sew the eagle onto khaki shirt collars.

In February 1947 the title of soldiers on the DEML was changed to Staff and Administrative Reserve and then in 1951 to the title Army Specialist. By 1956 those enlisted soldiers were classified as Unassigned to Branch, and the insignia was worn by any soldier not having "appropriate branch insignia." Regulations listed examples of these enlisted personnel, such as those assigned for duty with a general staff section or those in a psychological warfare unit.[6]

In June 1976 the chief of staff established a policy that all command sergeants major would wear the eagle insignia, and he redesignated the insignia as Branch Immaterial. At that same time all other enlisted soldiers were directed to wear branch insignia according to the soldier's basic job (or, as the army calls it, Military Occupation Specialty [MOS]), leaving the Branch Immaterial device exclusively to command sergeants major.[7]

Fig. 45-15. *Heavy brass and a well-made design with a screw-post back are characteristics of this DEML insignia. (1 inch in diameter)*

Fig. 45-16. *An issue post–World War II insignia that was first designated for the DEML; then for Staff and Administrative Reserve; then for Army Specialists, Unassigned to Branch; and finally for Branch Immaterial. (1 inch in diameter)*

Fig. 45-17. *An officers' World War II "unassigned" insignia adapted to a domed enlisted men's disk. (1 inch in diameter)*

Figs. 45-18 and 45-19. *Two domed disks, showing different degrees of stamping details and designs. (Each 1 inch in diameter)*

Fig. 45-20. *Hand-embroidered DEML insignia produced in India during World War II. (1 inch in diameter)*

WORLD WAR I ARMY SERVICE CORPS

Fig. 46-1.

Fig. 46-2.

Fig. 46-1. *A French-made officers' Army Service Corps insignia. These were unique in that officers placed them on their shoulder loops instead of their collars. (1 1/64 inches wide)*

Fig. 46-2. *Enlisted men's Army Service Corps collar disks of this type were made in France. (1 inch in diameter)*

AS THE AMERICAN Expeditionary Forces (AEF) expanded in France during World War I, dozens of special activities became necessary to support the burgeoning army. Many of these diversified functions, such as administrative labor companies, depot labor companies, laundry units, printing companies, and guard companies, did not fit neatly into any established branch of the peacetime army. The need to organize these many new activities into one coherent group came to the attention of General Pershing. After various cables between AEF headquarters and the War Department during May, June, and July 1918, the AEF received authorization for a corps on 23 July 1918, and the AEF Services of Supply organized the Army Service Corps on 22 August 1918 with an authorized strength of 100,000 enlisted men and 1,500 officers. The actual maximum strength was reached in March 1919 at 1,170 officers and 25,943 men.[1]

As the Army Service Corps existed only in Europe as part of the AEF Services of Supply, its insignia were not described in War Department orders. AEF General Headquarters approved a small shield on a cogged wheel as the Army Service Corps insignia in December 1918. Officers' overseas cap cords, authorized in November 1918, were steel gray with blue threads. The officers' branch insignia consisted of a 1-inch-diameter cogwheel with eight spokes and sixteen teeth and a 1/3-inch-high bronze shield over the wheel's hub.[2]

Officers detached for service with the Army Service Corps came from many different branches, and they continued to wear their original collar insignia. To show their Army Service Corps detail they placed the Army Service Corps insignia on the shoulder loop, centered between the upper button and the rank insignia, as distinctive insignia would be placed after the war. An officers' insignia is shown in Fig. 46-1. The enlisted soldiers' collar disk, worn like all other enlisted men's collar insignia of branch, is shown in Fig. 46-2.

Chapter Forty-Seven

Postal and Courier Service, World War I

The armistice and subsequent peace brought about a little-known, unique insignia. U.S. delegates to the peace conference required information and data concerning enemy countries that could be used as a basis for negotiation and agreement, so the army dispatched missions to Berlin and Vienna. In order that these missions might function and report quickly to the Paris Commission to Negotiate Peace, some rapid method of communications, both confidential and reliable, had to be established. The war had disrupted all previously existing communication agencies, and even if it had been possible to fully reestablish them quickly, information of a secret or confidential nature could not have been sent through commercial channels.

During the war the War Department had established regular transatlantic courier service and had maintained confidential communications between Washington and Pershing's headquarters. Shortly after the armistice, Major Amos J. Peaslee, who was in charge of communications at Tours, transferred to Paris, where he organized and operated a courier service of U.S. officers for the benefit of the American peace commission. From this modest beginning the Courier Service of the American Expeditionary Forces (AEF) Postal Express Service grew. Little by little, the Courier Service extended its operation until its members traveled by rail, boat, air, automobile, and foot among the capitals and important cities of the entire continent.[1]

Was the "running greyhound" insignia used by the Courier Service alone or by the AEF Postal Express Service? Neither the officers' (Fig. 47-1) nor the enlisted men's (Fig. 47-2) collar insignia are mentioned in any regulations or orders found to date. The Courier Service symbol was a running greyhound, so there is a basis for accepting at least the officers' insignia as that of the Courier Service of the Military Postal Express Service.

Members of the 1918 AEF Postal Agency wore a red-bordered gray cloth disk with the letters *PA* in red, centered in the circle, showing that the person belonged to the U.S. Postal Agency. No other insignia was prescribed except that all men wore the officers' letters *US*. The AEF established the Military Postal Express Service by AEF General Order 72 in May 1918, and the War Department confirmed this action in August 1918. At the close of the war a staff member of the Military Postal Express Service sent a letter to the United States, expressing an "urgent need for some distinctive insignia for the Courier Service" and suggesting that officers acting as couriers "wear on the left breast an insignia in the form of a silver greyhound embroidered in silver 2–1/2" long and 3/4" high."[2]

Fig. 47-1. *The fastener on this scarce running greyhound insignia indicates that it was made in France. Exactly who wore this branch device has not been determined. It may have been used by officers of the Courier Service or of the Military Postal Express Service. Regardless, the question remains, Was it worn on the collar (very likely if used by officers of the courier service) or on the shoulder loops as in the case of the insignia of the Army Service Corps of World War I? Evidence supports the belief that it went on the collar instead of other branch insignia. (2 inches wide)*

Fig. 47-2. *The enlisted men's postal service insignia was made in France. (1 inch in diameter)*

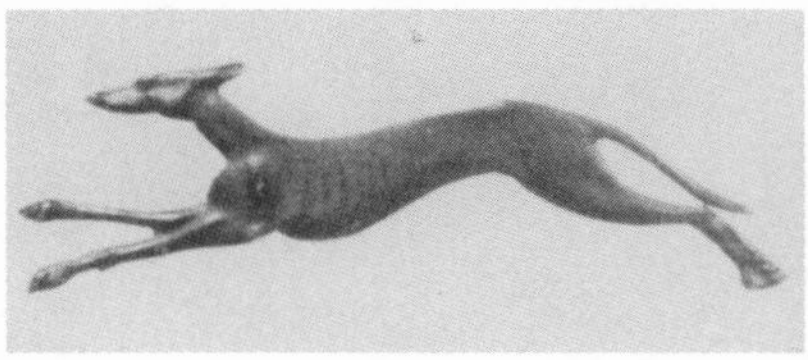

Fig. 47-1.

Fig. 47-2.

Major Amos J. Peaslee sent a follow-up request from Paris in January 1919, stating, "Any minor change regarding the location of the insignia would make little difference to us here. The principal point is to have something as quickly as possible." General Peyton C. March, chief of staff, disapproved the January 1919 request. In April 1919 the men in France again submitted a request, stating that since January 1919 shoulder insignia had been worn consisting "of a silver dog embroidered on a blue background, with officers of the courier service exclusively wearing the device with a gold border. Enlisted men wore a white cotton dog on a blue background without any border."[3]

While there is no mention of collar insignia in any of the records found, it is apparent some were made without War Department authorization in 1919. Because both the officers' piece and the enlisted men's disk were made in France, it is believed that the disk was for the Military Postal Express Service and the officers' insignia for the Courier Service.

Chapter Forty-Eight

National Guard Bureau

Congress established the Bureau of Militia Affairs in March 1911, then retitled it the Militia Bureau following passage of the June 1916 National Defense Act. On 15 January 1933 the current name, the National Guard Bureau, was established, although no change of insignia occurred. In practice, few officers were assigned to the bureau, and even during World War I the maximum strength was thirteen officers in Washington, D.C.[1]

Officers' Collar Insignia

Officers detailed to the Militia Bureau wore branch insignia designed by Anthony de Francisci in 1921. The insignia consisted of the American bald eagle with wings reversed, bearing two crossed fasces on the breast. These insignia were usually made in pairs so that the eagles would face forward. An example of the 1921 bronze coat-sized insignia, 1 inch high, is shown in Fig. 48-1. Gilt collar ornaments worn on the 1921 white uniforms and on all high-collar uniforms after October 1923 are shown in Figs. 48-2 and 48-3. Shirt-sized devices should have been 3/4 inch high and are shown in Figs. 48-5 and 48-6.[2]

The 3/4-inch-high shirt insignia came into use on the lapel coat in March 1926 (Figs. 48-7 and 48-8). These interesting insignia have the fasces separately applied. Another 1926 change was the requirement that the eagle face to its right for the lapel coat insignia (3/4 inch high), but this rule was widely ignored, and in the 1930s the Quartermaster Corps still sold 3/4-inch-high devices with the eagles facing left and right. The official 1936 drawing has the note, "blue uniform insignia to be worn in pairs."[3]

The World War II insignia retained the same design but with reduced quality of workmanship, probably because of exigencies of the war (Fig. 48-9). Officers, both in the National Guard and in the regular force, wore the device from 1922 through World War II if (1) the officer served in the Office of the National Guard Bureau in Washington, D.C.; (2) the officer was in charge of National Guard affairs at a corps headquarters; or (3) the officer was an instructor detailed to the National Guard.[4]

This practice changed after World War II, and only a few National Guard officers in each state wore the insignia, as did officers in the bureau headquarters in Washington (Fig. 48-10). In 1977 officers in Washington stopped wearing this device, replacing it with the General Staff Corps insignia.[5] Fig. 48-11 shows a subdued insignia made in the 1970s for wear on fatigue clothing.

On 22 October 1984 the chief of the National Guard Bureau ordered officers

Fig. 48-1. *Designed in 1921 by Anthony de Francisci, this is an example of the first bronze collar insignia worn by officers assigned to the Militia Bureau. (1 5/32 inches wide)*

Figs. 48-2 and 48-3. *Rolled in gold with pin backs, this pair of officers' Militia Bureau insignia were for the white uniform and, after 1923, for all coats. (Each 1 11/64 inches wide)*

Fig. 48-1.

Fig. 48-2.

Fig. 48-3.

Fig. 48-4.

Fig. 48-5.

Fig. 48-6.

Fig. 48-7.

Fig. 48-8.

Fig. 48-9.

Fig. 48-10.

Fig. 48-11.

Fig. 48-12.

Fig. 48-13.

Fig. 48-14.

Fig. 48-15.

Fig. 48-4. *Militia Bureau chiefs, unlike other general officers, wore branch insignia. This 1924 chief of the Militia Bureau wears brass buttons, insignia, and metal fixtures.*

Fig. 48-5. *A 1923–26 gilt shirt collar insignia for officers. (13/16 inch wide)*

Fig. 48-6. *Despite the short time that small shirt-sized insignia were worn, such insignia from several dies exist. Besides facing the opposite direction from the insignia shown in Fig. 48-5, this eagle's neck and head are different, as is the lower wing just above the fasces. (13/16 inch wide)*

Figs. 48-7 and 48-8. *This pair of National Guard Bureau insignia from the 1930s was the prescribed size for the lapel coat and the shirt collar. The crossed fasces were applied separately to the eagle's chest. (29/32 inch wide)*

Fig. 48-9. *This officers' insignia could have been worn from the late 1930s to the present. (59/64 inch wide)*

Fig. 48-10. *A 1970s subdued insignia for an officer to wear on fatigue shirts. (7/8 inch wide)*

Fig. 48-11. *Made like older insignia, this current piece has the fasces made separately and applied to the eagle. (7/8 inch wide)*

Fig. 48-12. *Major General Francis S. Greenlief, February 1965, wearing National Guard Bureau insignia while serving as chief of the bureau.*

Fig. 48-13. *An issue enlisted men's National Guard Bureau insignia from the 1930s. (1 inch in diameter)*

Fig. 48-14. *Commercially made in the 1930s, this enlisted men's collar insignia has the design separable from the background so it could be polished easily. (1 inch in diameter)*

Fig. 48-15. *A screw-back, two-piece disk, probably made in the late 1930s or early 1940s. (1 inch in diameter)*

assigned to field operating activities and National Guard Bureau officers who were not on the Department of the Army staff to wear the bureau's insignia. In addition to these officers, each state's officer assigned as the U.S. property and fiscal officer, plus other selected officers prescribed by the chief of the National Guard Bureau, wore the insignia.[6]

Enlisted Men's Collar Insignia

It is not clear whether enlisted men wore the Militia Bureau disks from September 1921 until 1924, when it is known that the army detailed men to the bureau. During the 1920s and early 1930s enlisted men wore disks of the type shown in Figs. 48-13 and 48-14, and typical disks for the late 1930s are shown in Figs. 48-15 and 48-16. An early bronze disk made for wartime use is shown in Fig. 48-17.

Enlisted men continued to wear the National Guard Bureau disk until 1951, when its use was suspended.[7]

Fig. 48-16.

Fig. 48-17.

Fig. 48-16. *This large National Guard Bureau eagle has clutch fasteners. Enlisted soldiers' National Guard Bureau insignia were obsolete by 1951. (1 inch in diameter)*

Fig. 48-17. *Regulations called for bronze disks for wartime use, which accounts for this enlisted men's collar ornament. Just before World War II this provision was dropped, and thus the dark National Guard Bureau insignia were never worn. (1 inch in diameter)*

Chapter Forty-Nine

World War II Army Specialist Corps

Fig. 49-1. The gray plastic service cap insignia for the 1942 Army Specialist Corps. (2 1/4 inches wide)

Fig. 49-2. The distinctively styled, gray-colored US worn by Army Specialist Corps members. (1 11/64 inches wide)

Fig. 49-3. Instead of a branch insignia, Army Specialist Corps members wore these silver letters. (1 21/32 inches wide)

Fig. 49-4. An Army Specialist Corps uniform, used from July to December 1942. Only the buttons and insignia made it different from the standard army uniforms then in use.

Less than three months after the attack on Pearl Harbor, the president established a corps of uniformed civilians known as the Army Specialist Corps. This corps consisted of technical, professional, scientific, and administrative personnel who could assist the army without actually joining the service. Appointments were without regard to normal civil service regulations so that Army Specialist Corps personnel could immediately release military men for combat, further train scientific and professional persons, or serve as either part-time or full-time consultants to the War Department.[1]

Officers were appointed with equivalent army rank or as specialists equivalent to enlisted grades. Until the War Department prescribed a corps uniform, Army Specialist Corps members wore the woolen or cotton army service uniform with no insignia other than a cloth noncombatant emblem midway between the left shoulder and the elbow (see Fig. 57-24). In July 1942, Chief of Staff General George C. Marshall authorized a distinctive uniform for the corps: a standard army uniform with silver gray plastic buttons and with gray plastic insignia. A silver gray plastic eagle, 2 inches high, became the cap insignia (Fig. 49-1). On the coat and shirt officers placed the gray block letters *US* (Fig. 49-2) and *ASC* (Fig. 49-3), the *ASC* letters replacing the corps device. Specialists used

Fig. 49-2.

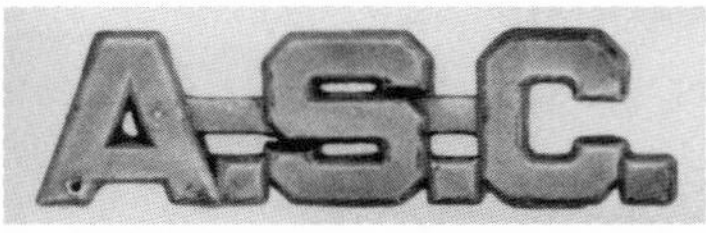

Fig. 49-3.

Fig. 49-1.

Fig. 49-4.

the same insignia, but these men did not wear any collar insignia on the shirt.[2]

With the establishment of a distinctive uniform, normal military courtesies, respects, and obligations practiced between army officers and enlisted men became the rule within the corps and between members of the corps and army personnel. Officers' grade insignia became the same as those used in the army (Fig. 49-4), and specialists adopted standard chevrons, corporal through master sergeant, with the addition of a tab of silver gray cloth bearing the burgundy letters *ASC* placed 1/2 inch below the chevrons.[3]

Shortly after the introduction of the uniform, William O. Hotchkiss, acting director general of the Army Specialist Corps, approved a new collar device designed by Arthur E. DuBois and directed that the device, a small eagle with *ASC* superimposed, be produced. All of this was for naught, because in the fall of 1942 the War Department stopped all appointments to the Army Specialist Corps. Applications not acted upon by 4 November 1942 were returned to the individual seeking appointment, and those officers not requesting appointment in the army by 1 December 1942 were discharged on 31 December 1942.[4]

CHAPTER FIFTY

WOMEN'S ARMY CORPS

Fig. 50-1. An officers' Women's Army Auxiliary Corps (WAAC) and Women's Army Corps (WAC) collar insignia. (23/32 inch wide)

Fig. 50-2. Quartermaster Corps–issued enlisted women's branch insignia for the WAAC and WAC. (1 inch in diameter)

Fig. 50-3. Many minor variations of the WAC insignia exist, but this officers' piece is especially interesting because it was made in an antique bronze color that the army authorized for the cap ornament color briefly in the 1950s. (11/16 inch wide)

Fig. 50-4. A 1950s enlisted women's collar insignia with a domed background. (1 inch in diameter)

WITHOUT COMPLETE OFFICIAL approval, women accompanied the American army in various campaigns as early as the Revolution. Certainly most American school children know of "Molly Pitcher" (Mary Ludwig Hays), who accompanied her artillery gunner husband at the Battle of Monmouth. Women were involved in many aspects of the Civil War, and some women even fought in that great conflict, besides serving as nurses. During wars in the twentieth century the army planned and executed a variety of programs in which women worked both with and within the military, freeing men to serve in combat. During World War II women joined the army proper for the first time as soldiers.

Women's official participation in the army can be traced to the Spanish-American War, with congressional authorization for contract nurses. In 1901 a law was passed allowing nurses to join the army and to hold relative ranks. These early army medical women received their own insignia, which are discussed in chapter 11, "Medical Department," and the uniforms of the various women are described and illustrated in chapter 75 and section XXII.

World War I saw the initial use of women in army uniforms. During that war the Signal Corps employed several hundred uniformed American women in France as telephone operators ("hello girls," as they were commonly known). Other branches employed women, and one from the Quartermaster's Corps is shown in chapter 18 wearing a special uniform. These women, however, were not members of the army proper but were contract personnel. Although the World War I War Department considered bringing women into the army, the end of the war earlier than had been anticipated terminated any efforts to use women in the army as replacements for men.[1]

Women's social status limited them to the medical field as far as the army was concerned, and even medical women were not given full military rank until 1944. The Women's Army Auxiliary Corps (WAAC) was formed in May 1942 as a supplement to the army but did not become part of the force itself until July 1943, when the president signed a bill admitting women into the army as members of the Women's Army Corps (WAC). Congress abolished the WAC as a component of the army in 1978. Those women in the army at that time transferred to various branches, and they acquired the same status as men except in direct combat fields, which were still restricted to men.[2]

Fig. 50-1.

Fig. 50-2.

Fig. 50-3.

Fig. 50-4.

WAAC and WAC Headgear Insignia

Fig. 50-5.

A walking eagle became the unique WAAC cap insignia in 1942, but it was discarded in 1943 when newly inducted WAC members adopted standard army insignia. Both the officers' and enlisted women's headgear ornaments are shown and discussed in chapter 8, "Eagle Insignia." In addition, some are illustrated in use in Figs. 75-5, 79-12, and 79-13.

WAAC and WAC Collar Insignia

The War Department envisioned WAAC members performing an expansive range of duties, so selection of a pertinent symbol was difficult. After extensive study the Heraldric Section of the Office of the Quartermaster General created the design eventually adopted: the helmeted head of the Greek goddess Pallas Athene. Athene was the goddess of handicrafts, the industries of peace, and the arts of war as well as a goddess of storms and battle and the goddess who taught enjoyment of peace.[3] The insignia (Fig. 50-1 for officers and Fig. 50-2 for enlisted women) remained unchanged throughout WAAC and WAC history. Fig. 50-3 shows an officers' version made about 1950 in antique bronze, a color then prescribed for WAC cap devices and buttons but not for collar insignia. Variations of enlisted women's collar insignia are shown in Figs. 50-4 and 50-5.

Because the WAC was, by legislation, a component of the army like the reserves or the Regular Army, rather than a branch such as the infantry or Quartermaster Corps, it became the only component to have its own insignia. The Army Air Force and the World War II technical services desired members of the WAC to wear their branch insignia to show the duty the women performed, while the combat arms of infantry, cavalry, armor, and artillery strongly opposed such a practice, although some jobs filled by WAC members normally would have entitled them to wear such insignia. This difference of opinion within the War Department caused initial regulations to be vague about which WAC members could wear non-WAC branch insignia. By 1945 regulations prohibited women from wearing the insignia of infantry, armor, and artillery.[4] As described in Section XXII, "Women's Uniforms," insignia were not always worn in the same manner as men. Fig. 50-6 shows Mary Clarke wearing WAC insignia on her green coat.

Fig. 50-6.

Fig. 50-5. *This version of Pallas Athene, the Greek goddess, gives some indication of how much the designs can vary from the insignia shown in Figs. 50-2 and 50-4. (1 inch in diameter)*

Fig. 50-6. *Because of the small lapels on many women's uniforms, after the Korean War WAC officers wore their insignia as enlisted women did, with the US on the wearer's right collar tip and the WAC insignia on the left. Shown is Brigadier General Mary Clarke, one of the few WACs to rise to the general officer ranks.*

Chapter Fifty-One

Office of Strategic Services

Fig. 51-1. This gilt spearhead is in high relief on a black background surrounded by a steep gilt edge. This insignia was the property of an OSS officer. ($^{31}/_{32}$ inch wide)

Fig. 51-2. An enlisted men's disk supposedly worn by OSS personnel. (1 inch in diameter)

Figs. 51-3 and 51-4. Both of these insignia were made in Germany and were reproduced for collectors in the 1950s and again in the late 1970s. ($1^{7}/_{32}$ and $1^{9}/_{32}$ inches wide, respectively)

The insignia illustrated in Fig. 51-1 is considered by many collectors to be the distinctive insignia (commonly called a crest) worn by personnel assigned to the Office of Strategic Services (OSS). However, this insignia apparently was intended for wear on the uniform coat lapel as a branch device for officers of the OSS. According to notes uncovered by one researcher, General William Donovan, chief of the OSS, requested permission in 1943 for OSS personnel to wear a collar device as well as a distinctive shoulder patch. Initially the quartermaster general denied the request, but General Donovan personally pursued his case, and in June 1943 he obtained approval for the insignia. Although the OSS and its activities were not publicized, one must assume Donovan thought that the organization and its exploits would become commonly known and that its men would need some sort of recognition. The new insignia received no publicity at that time, because both Donovan's request and the subsequent approval were classified confidential. By the time the documents were declassified, the OSS had been disbanded.[1]

Fig. 51-1.

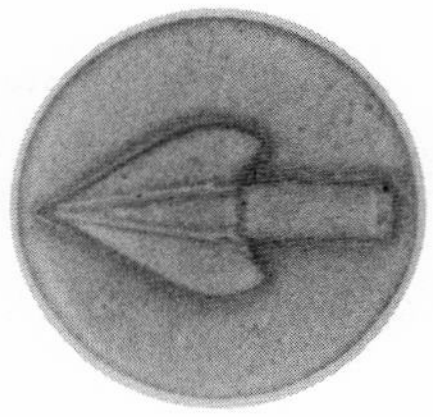

Fig. 51-2.

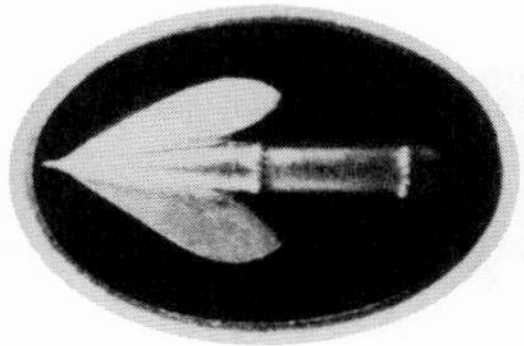

Fig. 51-3.

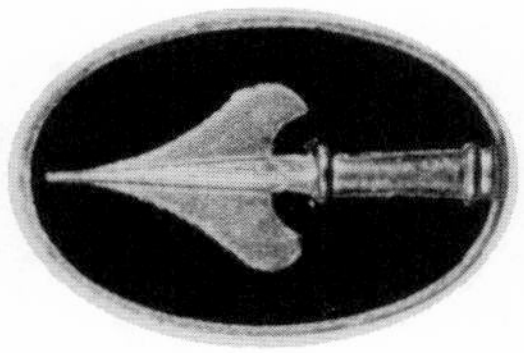

Fig. 51-4.

The officers' insignia is a black oval with a gilt edge and a gilt spearhead of the type used on the tips of flagstaffs carried by color guards on parade. It was worn with the tip to the observer's left. An insignia known to have come from an OSS officer is shown in Fig. 51-1. The enlisted men's all-brass disk, Fig. 51-2, closely resembles conventional branch insignia. It is known that examples of the officers' insignia were made for collectors in the 1970s from German dies initially made immediately after World War II. One of these pieces is shown in Fig. 51-3. Another German-made OSS officers' insignia is shown in Fig. 51-4. Both of the last two insignia have typical German screw-back fasteners.

Section XV

Post–World War II Insignia

Chapter Fifty-Two

Special Services

The War Department established the office of the chief of Special Services Division in the adjutant general's office on 22 July 1940. The division was responsible for morale and sports within the army. After various moves during World War II, the Special Services Division became a separate administrative service in June 1946. The three jousting lances upon a green-enameled wreath made up the collar insignia design announced for Special Services in July 1947. Only officers had an official insignia (Fig. 52-1). The green wreath symbolizes the honors and awards granted winners, while the three lances represent the three divisions of special services, the lance itself standing for military sport or recreation. A device smaller than regulation size, made in Germany, is shown in Fig. 52-2. The army did not authorize enlisted men insignia, but in Germany some disks were made (Fig. 52-3) in all-brass and all-silver colors with enameled leaves (Fig. 52-4). On 28 February 1950 the army abolished the Special Services Division.[1]

Fig. 52-1.

Fig. 52-2.

Fig. 52-3.

Fig. 52-4.

Fig. 52-1. *An example of an officers' official Special Services Division insignia. It is of gold-colored metal, with the leaves of the wreath in medium green. The branch, established in 1947, was responsible for recreation activities in the army. (1 1/64 inches wide)*

Fig. 52-2. *Made in Germany about 1948, this insignia is undersized and has transparent green enamel. Special Services Division, as a branch, disappeared in early 1950. (7/8 inch wide)*

Figs. 52-3 and 52-4. *Enlisted men were not specified Special Services insignia, although such insignia, as shown in these examples, were made in Germany. That of Fig. 52-3 is all metal, while that of Fig. 52-4 has the wreath in green. (1 inch in diameter)*

Chapter Fifty-Three

Army Security

The Army Reorganization Act of 1950 created several fields of intelligence for U.S. Army personnel. As a result of the new law, one such office established was the Army Security Agency, which monitored electronic transmissions and conducted "eavesdropping." The Army Security Agency desired a special insignia for personnel in the U.S. Army Reserves assigned to that agency.

Fig. 53-1.

Fig. 53-1. *Officers' insignia for Army Security, U.S. Army Reserves. This insignia was introduced in 1956. (1 1/64 inches wide)*

Crossed keys and a lightning bolt were established as the insignia for Army Security, U.S. Army Reserves (USAR), in February 1954, and announced in regulations in September 1956. Illustrated are an officer's device (Fig. 53-1), two flat enlisted men's disks (Figs. 53-2 and 53-3), and two domed disks (Figs. 53-4 and 53-5). These insignia were rescinded in February 1963 when the branch was combined with Army Intelligence, USAR, and replaced by the intelligence insignia (see chapter 41).[1]

Reserve officers and enlisted personnel on inactive status wore the Army Security insignia while on duty for training. When on extended active duty, personnel wore the branch insignia in which they were detailed.[2]

Fig. 53-2.

Fig. 53-3.

Fig. 53-4.

Fig. 53-5.

Fig. 53-2. *Enlisted men's disks for Army Security came in a wide range of design details. This one is on a flat background and has the design completely cut out. (1 1/64 inches in diameter)*

Fig. 53-3. *This collar disk has the design stamped into a single piece of metal. The holes in the key handles are solid. (1 1/32 inches in diameter)*

Fig. 53-4. *A collar disk with dome-shaped background and a detailed, cut-out design. (1 inch in diameter)*

Fig. 53-5. *A silver-colored domed disk. The separable design has solid key handles. (1 1/32 inches in diameter)*

CHAPTER FIFTY-FOUR

CIVIL AFFAIRS

THE U.S. ARMY acquired some experience in foreign government administration as a result of the Spanish-American War. Puerto Rico, Cuba, the Philippines, and China all served as places for army officers to learn about foreign governments. The Bureau of Insular Affairs, established shortly after the 1898 war with Spain, helped administer U.S. possessions, and in a historical sense it might be considered the forerunner of the later civil affairs branch.

Fig. 54-1.

Fig. 54-2.

The army dealt with civil governments again during World War I and its aftermath, although the War Department did not form a branch of specialists. Politicians served in the army during and after World Wars I and II, and many World War I veterans had become leaders by World War II. These factors made the World War II military leaders sensitive to political and governmental issues in occupied countries.

During World War II some army officers performed civil affairs duties and helped to run local governments. Personnel assigned to perform civil affairs and military government functions received no special training but relied on their civilian experience, which often had been previous association as politicians with various government functions at local, state, or national level. The Army Special Staff organized the Civil Affairs Division on 1 March 1943. After various moves and title changes it was designated as the Civil Affairs and Military Government Division. For a while after World War II, civil affairs officers were members of the Staff Specialist Reserve section, wearing the "unassigned" insignia (see chapter 45).[1]

The Department of the Army finally recognized the potential need for government specialists in 1955 by establishing a new branch of the army for reserve personnel: Civil Affairs/Military Government. This organization was in part a result of a 1954 Department of the Army initiative designed to emphasize both reserve activities and civil affairs. In 1956 the army selected as the collar insignia for the fledgling branch a torch of liberty superimposed over a globe. Crossed in front of this design are a sword and a scroll.[2]

Officers' metal insignia are shown in Figs. 54-1 and 54-2, and a 1950s cloth fatigue uniform insignia is shown in Fig. 54-3. An enlisted one-piece stamped insignia was first authorized in 1959 (Fig. 54-4), although

Fig. 54-3.

Fig. 54-1. *Officers' insignia for Civil Affairs/Military Government. The Department of the Army established the branch in 1955 and the insignia the following year. This particular insignia has a shiny brass finish. (51/64 inch wide)*

Fig. 54-2. *A common variation of an officers' insignia for Civil Affairs, U.S. Army Reserve (USAR), as the organization was retitled in 1959. The old gold–anodized finish precluded shining the insignia. (3/4 inch wide)*

Fig. 54-3. *Yellow embroidered officers' insignia used until about 1967 on the fatigue uniform. During the Vietnam War and later, Civil Affairs, insignia were made in black for wear on field clothing. (Design 1 inch in diameter)*

Fig. 54-4.

Fig. 54-5.

Fig. 54-6.

Fig. 54-4. *An army issue, embossed enlisted men's collar insignia for Civil Affairs, USAR. (1 inch in diameter)*

Fig. 54-5. *A flat, separable enlisted men's insignia used by army reserve members of Civil Affairs, USAR. (1 inch in diameter)*

Fig. 54-6. *Commercially made Civil Affairs, USAR, insignia with the background of a convex shape. These were popular in the 1950s but by the 1960s were not widely worn. (1 1/32 inches in diameter)*

many men wore a two-piece disk (Fig. 54-5) or a domed disk (Fig. 54-6). In 1959 the army retitled the branch Civil Affairs, U.S. Army Reserve (USAR).[3]

Initially only reserve personnel wore the insignia, since those soldiers on extended active duty were to wear the insignia of a detailed branch, but in January 1971 regulations were changed to allow personnel on active duty with civil affairs units to wear the insignia. The Department of the Army later reversed this policy and allowed only reserve soldiers to wear the insignia.[4]

Chapter Fifty-Five

Sergeant Major of the Army

The army clearly identified its senior enlisted man and the chief of staff's advisor on enlisted matters when William O. Wooldridge became the first Sergeant Major of the Army in 1966. General Harold K. Johnson, while army chief of staff, established the position of Sergeant Major of the Army as a result of a recommendation made to him by army sergeants major during their 1965 conference. On 4 July 1966 the army formally established the position, and on 11 July 1966 Sergeant Wooldridge was sworn in at Washington, D.C. The function of the Sergeant Major of the Army is to provide a direct line of communication between enlisted personnel in the field and the top army echelon. Although the men in this position have had various and diversified careers, the common denominator for all of them is that they have all been combat arms sergeants major of armor, artillery, infantry, or combat engineers.[1]

Fig. 55-1.

The designation of such a noncommissioned officer is historically equivalent to creating a rank, and in July 1966 the chief of staff personally pinned on Sergeant Wooldridge a unique collar insignia to distinguish his position. Instead of one *US* disk and one branch insignia, the Sergeant Major of the Army wears both disks of an enameled shield based on the army chief of staff's flag and aide's insignia, as shown in Fig. 55-1.[2]

This use of two identical disks occurred despite army regulations, which classified the unique Sergeant Major of the Army insignia as a branch insignia. According to the regulations from 1966 until 1984, the Sergeant Major of the Army device should have been worn only in place of the branch insignia and not in place of the *US* device. This practice continued into the 1980s, although the governing regulations were never changed, as some Sergeants Major of the Army wanted. Other Sergeants Major of the Army used the device like a distinctive insignia by placing it on the garrison cap, a practice which was finally placed in regulations. An example of the insignia is shown in Fig. 55-2. Later in the 1980s the Sergeant Major of the Army was finally given a unique insignia for service caps, a coat of arms of the United States within a wreath $1\frac{15}{16}$ inches high.[3]

Fig. 55-1. *Sergeant Major of the Army Glen Morrell, 1983. The Sergeant Major of the Army is distinguished by his chevron bearing two stars and by his unique collar devices. The chief of staff of the army established the position of Sergeant Major of the Army in 1966, and it has been continually occupied since that time.*

Fig. 55-2. *A collar insignia used by the Sergeant Major of the Army. The shield is diagonally divided red and white, with white and red stars and a gold eagle and star. This is the only enlisted men's collar insignia that is not all brass.*

Fig. 55-2.

Chapter Fifty-Six

New Branches for the 1990s

Fig. 56-1. Design for the so-called distinctive collar insignia for soldiers of the public affairs career field, as approved by the army chief of staff in October 1989.

Fig. 56-2. The enlisted personnel collar insignia for psychological operations, as designed and approved at the end of 1990.

After the end of the Cold War, even with armed forces reductions the army added new collar insignia. Chaplains of various religions were approved and their new insignia introduced. These have been described in chapter 20, "Chaplains." In other cases the army created new collar insignia that represented, in historical context, new branches.

Fig. 56-1.

Public Affairs

In 1989 the Department of the Army took a historic step when it approved a collar insignia just for enlisted men assigned to public affairs duty. Although the Sergeant Major of the Army had unique insignia, and specialists and later sergeants major had worn the eagle from the Great Seal of the United States, there had been no other collar insignia for enlisted men that did not have an officers' counterpart.

Before World War II the army authorized several enlisted men's collar insignia for which there were not officers' counterparts. The last of these were those worn by members of the Army Mine Planter Service, although prison guards, disciplinary barracks guards, Indian Scouts, and other enlisted men had earlier worn devices for which there was no similar officers' insignia.

In January 1989 the chief of public affairs, Brigadier General Pat Brady, requested that the deputy chief of staff for personnel support the development and approval of a distinctive collar insignia for soldiers assigned to the public affairs field. At that time soldiers in public affairs wore either Signal Corps or Adjutant General's insignia, depending upon their assignment, but new personnel rules were coming into effect, and General Brady felt that these historic insignia would be inappropriate.[1]

On 18 October 1989 the chief of staff of the army, with the concurrence of the sergeant major of the army, approved the insignia concept shown in Fig. 56-1. Symbolism of the insignia included the quill pen and lightning flash to show the printed and electronic media. The sword represented the "indispensable role information plays on the battlefield; and that public affairs professionals are, above all else, soldiers."[2]

Psychological Operations

In September 1990 the commanding general of the U.S. Army's John F. Kennedy Special Warfare Center requested a new, unique collar insignia for enlisted personnel assigned to the career field of psychological operations. The Institute of Heraldry accordingly designed the insignia shown in Fig. 56-2, which was approved in November 1990. The following month the U.S. Army approved

Fig. 56-2.

wear of the insignia.[3]

In the 1980s and 1990s the Institute of Heraldry used the Trojan horse on shoulder patches and distinctive insignia associated with psychological operations to show an unconventional approach to warfare, since the knight in chess can jump over other figures and thus make a nondirect approach. The sword with the blade of lightning was first used on the shoulder patch of the 1st Signal Brigade during the Vietnam War. Lightning became another popular component used in designs during the 1980s, thus making this design typical of those created in that period. Like the public affairs insignia created in 1989, this insignia had no direct officers' counterpart.

Section XVI

Other Insignia

Chapter Fifty-Seven

Other Branch Insignia

Besides the branch insignia previously described, soldiers wore other devices much as they wore official branch cap or lapel ornaments. A few of these insignia are illustrated in this chapter.

Crossed Skis

During World War II the U.S. Army formed the 10th Mountain Division, with the fighting elements composed of three regiments of ski troops instead of standard infantry units. Although the proper branch insignia was crossed muskets, some 10th Mountain Division soldiers in the three infantry regiments and one reconnaissance troop of the division wore crossed skis, often with a small *US*, eagle, or regimental number placed over or under the skis' intersection. Examples of such insignia are shown in Figs. 57-1 through 57-5. Officers and some enlisted men wore the ski insignia above the left pocket, although a larger insignia intended for wear like a badge is shown in Fig. 57-6.[1] Many enlisted men wore the ornaments on the cap (Figs. 57-7 and 57-8).

Crossed Musket and Sabre

Large bronze insignia of this style are known to have been worn by private military school students before 1923, but the use of an insignia with a crossed rifle or musket and sabre by troops inducted into federal service has not been established. Gemsco Company of New York City during World War II or later made insignia of this design (Fig. 57-9), although the intended use of the device can not be firmly established.

Tank and Muskets

Possibly intended as an armored infantry device, the insignia in Fig. 57-10 is made with a small screw post and may be of foreign origin.

Medical Insignia with Unusual Letters

U.S. medical insignia with unauthorized letters superimposed, including *F, O, M,* and *WF,* are shown in chapter 11, "Medical Department." The intent of such devices is not known.

Fig. 57-1.

Fig. 57-2.

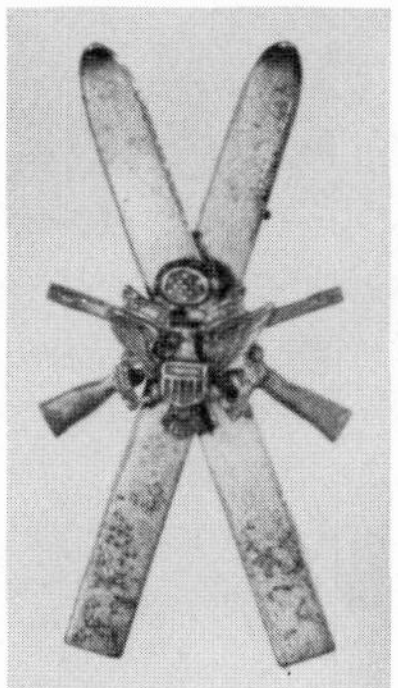

Fig. 57-3.

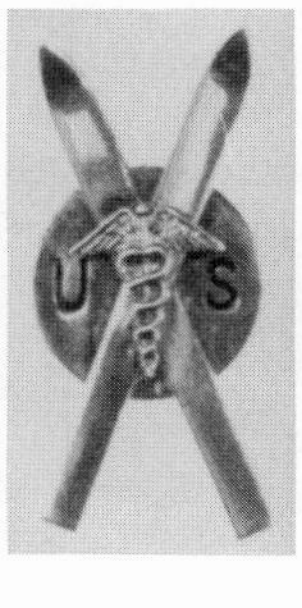

Fig. 57-4.

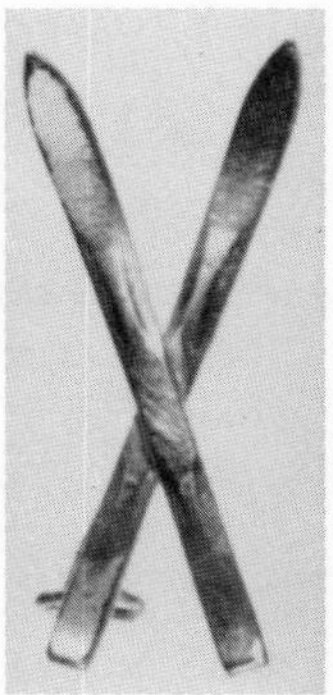

Fig. 57-5.

Fig. 57-1. *Crossed skis insignia worn by some members of the 10th Mountain Division during World War II. Such insignia were most often used like distinctive insignia. (US letters 29/32 inch wide)*

Fig. 57-2. *Insignia consisting of crossed silver-colored skis were worn by those men who had received ski training. Such training was limited to those personnel assigned to the three infantry regiments and the reconnaissance troop of the 10th Mountain Division. The number on the brass US is for the 85th Infantry Regiment. (29/32 inch wide)*

Fig. 57-3. *A military ski pin that could have been worn by members of any of the 10th Mountain Division ski regiments during World War II. (25/32 inch wide)*

Fig. 57-4. *Some medical personnel assigned to the three infantry ski regiments wore sterling silver pins like this one. (19/32 inch wide)*

Fig. 57-5. *These plain crossed skis originally could have been made for a woman to wear, but they were adopted by a member of the 10th Mountain Division. (21/32 inch wide)*

Fig. 57-6.

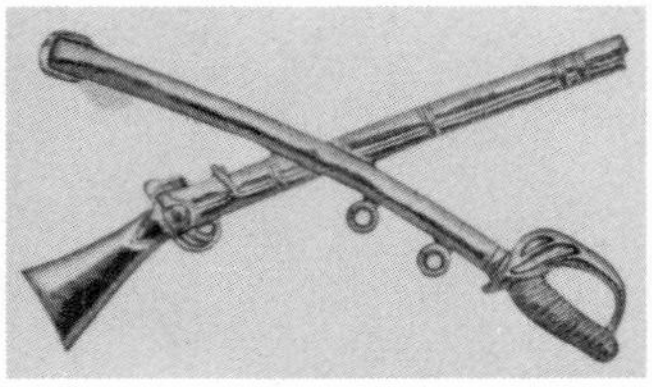

Fig. 57-9.

Fig. 57-7.

Fig. 57-8.

Fig. 57-10.

Fig. 57-11.

Fig. 57-12.

Fig. 57-6. *Officers and some enlisted men wore their ski pins over their pocket like a badge. This large silver pin with brass eagle and crossed rifles was worn in that manner. (2 1/2 inches wide)*

Fig. 57-7. *A 1943 portrait of Sergeant George W. Gundel of the 10th Mountain Division, who is wearing a ski pin like a distinctive insignia on his cap.*

Fig. 57-8. *Another version of the crossed skis worn by Sergeant Dillon Snell of the 10th Mountain Division, 1943.*

Fig. 57-9. *This crossed musket and saber was made during or immediately after World War II, but the design is much older. Similar designs were used by some military schools at the time of World War I. The U.S. Army never sanctioned the wear of this device. (1 9/16 inches wide)*

Fig. 57-10. *Similar to the 1951 design of the armor branch, this insignia has crossed muskets instead of crossed sabers. Who used this insignia is not known, but it may have been made for an armored infantry battalion during the Korean War. (1 23/64 inches wide)*

Fig. 57-11. *Cap device for civilian instructors at the army's flight school in Fort Rucker, Alabama, from 1956 until 1969. (1 51/64 inches wide)*

Fig. 57-12. *Gilt disks with a torch were prescribed for members of the Reserve Officer Training Corps, but this piece, from between the world wars, varied from the prescribed design in that the letters were added. (1 inch in diameter)*

Tanks

A three-quarters view of an M-3 tank, used as both officers' and enlisted men's insignia, is included in chapter 39, "Tank Corps, Tank Destroyer Force, and Armor."

Army Aviation Instructors' Insignia

Civilian aviation instructors wore unique bottle green uniforms from 1956 to 1969 at the army's flight school in Alabama.[2] For wear on the cap, army regulations specified an eagle on a gauntlet (Fig. 57-11). During World War II, civilian instructors employed by the Civil Aeronautics Agency wore a variety of insignia, but none were described in army regulations. The use of many such unofficial devices occurred when the army contracted with several civilian flight instructor schools for the training of aviation cadets.

School Insignia

Congress, in the 1916 National Defense Act, created the Reserve Officers Training Corps

(ROTC), thus introducing to the army cadets supported by the federal system other than those from West Point. In addition, at the close of World War I the army formed the Student Army Training Corps, with its own insignia.[3] Examples of insignia associated with these organizations are in Figs. 57-12 through 57-15.

Schools too small to be authorized an ROTC organization could form a branch of the National Defense Cadet Corps, whose members wore a lamp on a disk (Figs. 57-16, 57-17, and 57-18).[4] Many schools made insignia showing school association or an organization in the school. Examples are illustrated in Figs. 57-19, 57-20, and 57-21.

A complete listing of all military school insignia is far too long to be included in this book, and a separate volume the size of this work would be required to contain it.

Corps of Engineers Boat Personnel Insignia

In 1969 the corps of engineers established a policy that civilian officers serving on dredges, tow boats, and ships more than sixty-five feet long would wear a khaki cap with black visor and a special insignia. This cap ornament is shown in Fig. 57-22 and is composed of a dark silver-colored castle and silver eagle with a gold-colored anchor.[5]

Equipment Markers

Web gear was marked with thin, stamped, bronze-colored identification disks that may be mistaken for insignia. These equipment markers were embossed with *US* on the upper quarter, and the bottom half carried an appropriate branch insignia. On a narrow strip between the *US* letters and the insignia was stamped the regimental number, company letter, and the number of the man. For example, a stamping of *37 E 28* on an infantry marker would indicate the 37th Infantry Regiment, Company E, twenty-eighth man.

An example of a new equipment marker, not stamped with a unit or man's number, is shown in Fig. 57-23. Three triangular prongs extend from the edge of the marker, and these prongs were inserted into the web gear and bent over a washer placed on the opposite side of the canvas. When the prongs were bent over this plain disk, the marker was held in place. Although an infantry marker is shown, these disks were made for all branches that formed units, such as field artillery, chemical, and aviation units.

Insignia of Civilians with the U.S. Army

Throughout the history of the U.S. Army,

Fig. 57-13.

Fig. 57-14.

Fig. 57-15.

Fig. 57-16.

Fig. 55-17.

Fig. 57-18.

Fig. 57-19.

Fig. 57-20.

Fig. 57-21.

Fig. 57-13. *Prescribed ROTC cap insignia were to be a wreath enclosing the letters ROTC. Patterns of wreath and letters vary widely. ($1\frac{27}{32}$ inches wide)*

Fig. 57-14. *The Student Army Training Corps existed from August to December 1918. Members wore a variety of insignia bearing the letters SATC. These block letters were similar to officers' US devices. ($2\frac{3}{16}$ inches wide)*

Fig. 57-15. *The approved ROTC collar insignia, introduced in 1916 and still used. The torch is the torch of knowledge taken from the Statue of Liberty. (1 inch in diameter)*

Figs. 57-16, 57-17, and 57-18. *Insignia of the National Defense Cadet Corps. NDCC units were formed by schools too small to be authorized ROTC units but that still wanted to provide some standardized military training. The first collar disk is of the separable type so that the lamp may be removed for easy cleaning.*

Figs. 57-19, 57-20, and 57-21. *High schools and colleges often provided members of their military training units with collar insignia designed exclusively for their institution. The insignia in Fig. 57-19, for the New Mexico Military Institute, has a removable unit number. The form bearing the number is enameled red and black. Both of the other insignia were struck from a single die.*

Fig. 57-22.

Fig. 57-22. Cap insignia for Corps of Engineers civilian officers serving on selected boats and ships. The eagle and castle are of a silver color, and the anchor is brass. (2 25/32 inches wide)

civilian employees have accompanied the army in wars. Until the Spanish-American War these personnel wore complete civilian clothing. In 1898, however, the army put nurses, veterinarians, and other civilian personnel in uniform. In World War I the Young Men's Christian Association (YMCA) and similar morale organizations, as well as the American Red Cross, placed civilians in uniform with the troops. It was during that war that special uniforms and insignia became common for civilians.

Fig. 57-23.

Fig. 57-23. A bronze-colored infantry equipment marker, introduced in 1919 and used only two or three years. A man's unit number could be stamped on the blank strip. Three prongs on the reverse allowed the insignia to be fastened to web gear, and the disk served to identify the owner. These disks were made for the following branches: Air Service, Finance Department, Chemical Warfare Service, infantry, cavalry, field artillery, coast artillery, Ordnance Department, Signal Corps, Corps of Engineers, Quartermaster Corps, and Medical Department. Miscellaneous units had a similar disk but without any insignia other than the US. (1 inch in diameter)

The YMCA was the largest contributor of World War I civilians. Men in the YMCA usually wore officer-style uniforms with the bronze letters *YMCA* on the collar. The American Library Association, the Jewish Welfare Board, and other groups also supplied support personnel during World War I. Their insignia, like the YMCA's, were not prescribed by the U.S. Army, although in 1919 some support organizations received special lapel coats with insignia prescribed for various activities.

The American Red Cross uniformed support personnel for World War II. Service club hostesses received special uniforms during World War II, as did other personnel who worked with soldiers. These people and others such as newspaper correspondents, however, were not War Department employees who were likely to be confused for soldiers. The army needed certain specially skilled civilian employees to accompany troops into combat zones.

Personnel recognized by the War Department as civilian employees working as part of the forces of the army received sleeve insignia during World War II. Initially the

Fig. 57-24.

Fig. 57-24. The basic sleeve insignia design introduced during World War II for War Department civilians to wear on uniforms. Initially the insignia was 3 1/2 inches on each side. This sleeve brassard was the sole prescribed insignia to be added to uniforms, according to regulations.

Fig. 57-25.

Fig. 57-25. War Department civilian insignia changed to khaki rectangles, 2 1/2 inches by 3 inches, by the end of World War II. Often the title of the civilian skill was added as shown. On these embroidered cloth patches the triangle was blue, with khaki US letters.

Fig. 57-26.

Fig. 57-26. A war crimes interpreter is seated (right) in this June 1946 trial in Germany. On his lapels are blue cloth triangles, point down, with khaki-colored letters US in the center. The design is similar to the central design shown in Fig. 57-25 except for the direction of the triangle's point. These lapel insignia were also made in metal and painted.

insignia was a dark blue square, 4½ inches on a side, enclosing a white triangle, point up, carrying the letters *US*.[6] This insignia was later modified so that noncombatant civilians would wear the white triangle while civilian combatants would wear the same design with a red triangle in the center. These sleeve insignia eventually became tan or brown rectangles 2½ inches by 3 inches bearing a blue triangle with tan or brown letters *US*. On the last devices at times the title of the wearer's special skill was embroidered above and/or below the point-up triangle. Examples are shown in Figs. 57-24 and 57-25. Noncombatants later wore the patches on overseas caps and on the left pocket.[7] During and after World War II civilian employees who wore the above emblems also wore special cloth lapel insignia not described in regulations. These were blue triangles, worn point down, bearing the letters *US*. An example is shown in Fig. 57-26.

Section XVII

Nineteenth-Century Coats

Chapter Fifty-Eight

Uniform Coats and Coatees

Yesteryear's fashion standards and ideas of comfort are not like today's. Early-nineteenth-century officers' coats shown in contemporary oil paintings exhibit a wide variety of extremely high standing collars (Fig. 58-1), and the rapid evolution of these fashions over about forty years is of interest.

During the Revolutionary War, men's coats had a "cape" that had no stand or rising portion but simply laid flat on the neck seam. Shortly after the end of the Revolution, some standing cloth began to creep up coat collars, resulting in a standing-falling collar like that of today's shirts. In the 1790s that collar evolved into a standing collar, which grew to the highest extreme about 1810. These collars were set lower and more widely into the coat body, permitting additional layers of shirt collars underneath. At the same time, the shoulder seam became cut further into the coat body, which was especially noticeable at the top of the shoulder. Because of the collar and shoulder seam construction, only a small portion of the coat body went between the collar and the sleeve. A War of 1812 coatee with a typically high collar is shown in Fig. 58-2. In 1821 the coat shoulder line came back to the natural shoulder width, then in 1827 military uniform collar styles and coat cut changed to so-called Prussian collars, which fastened all the way up and were limited in height by the wearer's chin (Fig. 58-3).

Rich embroidery and lace often embellished the high collars, cuffs, and tails of the uniform coat, and the epaulettes or wings for

Fig. 58-1.

Fig. 58-2.

Fig. 58-1. *Lieutenant Boyce, U.S. Infantry, in the 1820s. His very high coat collar, extending to the bottom of his ear, was typical of coats worn in the very early part of the nineteenth century. Such high collars could only be used with a V-shaped front opening. Wings are on Boyce's shoulders.*

Fig. 58-2. *Infantry coatee of Captain John E. Wool, who entered the U.S. Army as a captain of the 13th Infantry in April 1812 and was promoted to major in April 1813. This garment is made from dark blue wool, with red collar and cuffs and silver trim. Captains wore a single epaulette on their right shoulder and a silver-trimmed cloth loop on the left. The silver buttons carry an eagle with USI (U.S. Infantry) above and 13REGt below. Wool later became a general and received the thanks of Congress for his distinguished service in that rank during the Mexican War.*

Fig. 58-3. Robert E. Lee as a captain of the Corps of Engineers. Prussian collars (ones that closed completely up the front) were standard after 1827.

Fig. 58-4. A musicians' 1821–32 coatee. This short-tailed wool garment carried wings (used by all enlisted men) at the shoulder seam and worsted lace on the coat front (used by musicians only).

Fig. 58-3.

Fig. 58-4.

officers were trimmed in gold or silver. On many uniforms officers' collars were virtually covered with gold or silver lace. The staff departments all adopted distinctive uniform coats that were different from the infantry and artillery versions and that further varied by rank. Overall, these tailed coats closed down the front and were form-fitting to the waist, where they cut back sharply, with just two long tails remaining that went to about the back of the knees. By 1821 the top of the skirts narrowed noticeably.

Early-nineteenth-century styles dictated that gentlemen's sleeves were worn almost down the back of the hand, well beyond the wrist. These uniform coats usually had branch-colored trim, cuff trim known as slashes, and a great many buttons down the front, arranged in one to three rows. Buttons, with metallic lace (for officers) or cloth trim (for enlisted men) often appeared on the coat cuffs. Enlisted men's cloth trim was of worsted wool binding tape, while in 1832 the noncommissioned staff (that is, the sergeant major and chief musician) had Prussian (metallic) lace trim.

Short-tailed coats, called coatees, were used intermittently through 1832. Comparative length was a consideration of fashions, and other than a physical measurement of the relative height from the knee (which was done in some regulations), there is no easily identified point when coats became coatees. Enlisted men often wore coatees, while officers frequently wore full-tailed uniform coats, although from 1821 until 1832 artillery and infantry officers wore coatees similar in tail length to the enlisted men's version. After 1832 enlisted men adopted a full-tailed uniform coat.[1] (Fig. 58-4 shows an 1821–32 coatee with wings.)

The army last prescribed single-breasted blue coatees in the 1825 regulations. These coatees had 4-inch-high standing collars that carried two blind buttonholes trimmed in worsted binding: white for infantry and yellow for artillery. Enlisted men of ordnance wore artillery uniforms. Ten buttons closed the front, and round cuffs 3 inches wide had four buttons around the upper edge, 1 inch apart. On the short tails blue braid ran down the skirt to the tips, which each carried a blue cloth diamond "bound round with lace or braid like that of the collar." Soldiers wore wool worsted wings trimmed in the branch color on coatee shoulders. The coatee served as a general-purpose coat and was one of the garments worn on campaign and for many garrison duties, and it was the usual coat on parade. Musicians wore scarlet coats instead of the blue worn by other soldiers, while noncommissioned officers during the 1820s were distinguished by chevrons and the better quality of material used to make their coats.[2]

Having examined these shorter-tailed garments, let us now turn to full-tailed coats, first officers' and then enlisted men's. Officers wore full-length uniform coats reaching to the knees at the time of Wayne's Legion (1790s), and often these garments were exclusively worn by officers. In 1813 the army prescribed them for officers, while enlisted men wore coatees with shorter tails.[3] Most tailed coats were for dress wear, but in 1817 the army introduced an undress version for off-duty wear by light infantry and light artillery officers, and this provision was made universal in 1821. Essentially the off-duty coat was similar to the field-grade officers' dress coat, with epaulettes instead of wings.

Uniform changes of 1832 marked a new trend: colored trim or facings noted branch, and the current concept of officers' and enlisted men's rank insignia came into use. Some contrasting features of 1821–34 officers' uniform coats and coatees are generalized in Tables 58-1 and 58-2.

Placement of buttons formed various subgroups of uniform coats. During part of the nineteenth century, while uniform coats were still in vogue, company-grade officers often had single-breasted coats, while other officers wore double-breasted versions. Generals arranged their buttons by rank: brigadier generals by twos and major generals by threes. Fig. 58-5 shows Major General Edmond Gaines in an 1840 uniform, with the generals' embroidered collar and the coat buttons in groups of three. Fig. 58-6 shows a Civil War brigadier general with his coat buttons arranged by twos.

Major General Alexander Macomb, longtime army commander, modified officers' uniforms in 1839. General officers' uniform coats could "be embroidered with oak leaves in gold, in which case the collar and cuffs will be of blue cloth instead of buff." Corps of Engineers officers were to have embroidered on the collar a wreath of laurel and palm encircling a gold star.[4] Other minor changes were made, according to branch, until tailed coats went out with the new uniforms of 1851.

From 1832 until 1851 dismounted enlisted troops wore uniform coats as dress uniforms. The coattails (the coats were sometimes called "claw-hammer" coats because of the shape of these tails) usually carried buttons, lace, or special ornaments, and the tails were turned back to show the branch-colored facings. This is an example of a functional article evolving to a dress form and finally solely to a decorative ornament. The long skirts of coats before and during the Revolutionary War were functional in that soldiers could use them for warmth when seated or sleeping in the field. These large tails were hooked back somewhat out of the

Fig. 58-5. Major General Edmund P. Gaines in one of the earliest dress uniforms to be photographed (General Gaines died in 1849). The general's rank is indicated by the buttons grouped by threes. His coat is unusual for its collar embroidery (authorized in 1839) and its embellished shoulder straps that were devoid of rank insignia.

Fig. 58-6. Buttons arranged by twos signified a brigadier general. The practice of generals grouping their buttons on uniforms persisted on dress uniforms until the start of World War II. During the Civil War officers were allowed to wear their rank insignia directly on their coat rather than on the shoulder straps.

Fig. 58-5.

Fig. 58-6.

Table 58-1. Officers' Coatees, 1821–32.

Assignment	Buttons	Collar Trim
Artillery	Single row of ten buttons	Two blind buttonholes of yellow lace
Infantry	Single row of ten buttons	Two blind buttonholes of white lace

Table 58-2. Officers' Coats, 1821–39.

Assignment	1821	1832 Dress	1832 Undress
Staff	Single row of ten buttons; one blind buttonhole on collar end	Single row of nine buttons; front 4 inches of collar buff	Single row of nine buttons; plain blue collar
Engineers	Single row of ten buttons; black silk velvet collar embroidered with sprig of laurel around star		
Topographical		Single row of ten buttons; blue collar with gold-embroidered oak leaves and acorn	Same as dress
Medical	Single row of ten buttons; black silk velvet collar	Two rows of ten buttons each; gold-embroidered buttonholes on black velvet collar	Same as dress
Pay		Two rows of ten buttons each. Gold-embroidered buttonholes on blue collar	Same as dress
Generals	Single row of ten buttons	Double-breasted;* buff collar	Double-breasted;* blue collar
Infantry	Single row of ten buttons; two white blind buttonholes on collar†	Double-breasted, ten buttons per row; two loops on white-trimmed collar‡	
Artillery	Single row of ten buttons; two yellow blind buttonholes on collar	Double-breasted, ten buttons per row; two loops on yellow-trimmed collar‡	
Ordnance		Double-breasted, ten buttons per row; two loops on untrimmed collar‡	
		1833 DRESS	*1833 UNDRESS*
Dragoons		Two rows of ten buttons each; two loops on yellow collar	Two rows of nine buttons each; single button on collar

NOTE: Buttons will vary by branch; epaulettes vary by grade and sometimes by branch.
*The major general commanding: nine buttons per row, evenly spaced. Other major generals: nine buttons per row, grouped by threes. Brigadier generals: ten buttons per row, grouped by twos.
†Field grade only. Company officers allowed to wear similar uniform when off duty.
‡The "loops" on the collar and cuffs were double stripes of bullion lace, with a button inside each loop. Rank distinctions on cuffs were as follows:

Field grade—Four loops and buttons on sleeve.
Captain—Three loops and buttons on sleeve.
Subalterns—Two loops and buttons on sleeve.

Fig. 58-7.

Fig. 58-8.

Fig. 58-7. *Long tails evolved during the eighteenth and early nineteenth centuries until they were a major decorative part of the coat. This militia coat has wide colored trim around the tail and a gold lace diamond—all without any particular significance.*

Fig. 58-8. *Henry Leavenworth's coat of the 1832 pattern. Fashions caused tails to narrow over time; George Washington's tails of forty years before were very unfashionable by Leavenworth's time. The six-pointed stars and various diamonds were typical tail trim until 1832, when a standardized set of insignia appeared: bugle horns for infantry, flaming bombs for artillery and ordnance, stars for some staff officers, and oak leaves for topographical engineers. Wool's coatee in Fig. 58-2 has diamonds on the tails.*

way when marching (Fig. 58-7). By 1800 all of the turn-backs on tails were permanently stitched back in place. Lace trim (or, after 1832, insignia) could be placed where the inside lining color showed the most and where the tail had been hooked back on itself (Fig. 58-8). Thus, the lace trim, insignia, lining color, and length of a once functional part evolved to a style of dress.

In 1832 the adjutant general announced, "The President having directed that the facings worn by the revolutionary army be restored," then introduced new patterns of dark blue dress coats. For the noncommissioned staff (sergeant major, quartermaster sergeant, and chief musician), the coat was double-breasted with ten buttons in each row. Company noncommissioned officers' and privates' coats were single-breasted with nine buttons down the front. Dress coats all had on the collar double stripes of trim called loops or blind buttonholes, with each loop terminated by a button. Two such stripes, 4½ inches long, decorated each end of the collar. (The 1821 coats had two similar blind buttonholes, but the lengths had not been specified.) Cuffs were trimmed white for infantry and, after 1832, red for artillery.[5]

Dress coat variations came about with rank. The slashed sleeve flaps were 6½ inches long and varied from 2¼ inches to 2⅛ inches wide. On the flaps were small loops, the number of loops indicating rank group.[6] A summary of those groups is presented in Table 58-3.

The 1832 uniform coat continued essentially unchanged for infantry and artillery until 1851 (Fig. 58-9). When engineer sol-

Fig. 58-9.

Fig. 58-9. *Captain Lucian Bonepart Webster, Battery C, 1st Artillery, in a dress uniform of the 1839–51 pattern. Rank was shown not only by the epaulettes, but also by the gilt bullion loops on the sleeves: two for subalterns, three for captains, and four for field grades. Several branches besides the artillery wore double-breasted coats with ten buttons per row. Captain Webster's sash and sword belt cover his bottom buttons.*

diers joined the army in 1846, they were clothed in a variation very similar to the artillery version of the 1832 coat, but with a small pocket added on the right side for carrying percussion caps, the collar in black cotton velvet with a single loop and button, and black cotton velvet cuffs.[7]

Table 58-3. *Enlisted Men's Uniform Coat Differences, 1832.*

	Noncommissioned			
	Staff	**Sergeant**	**Corporal**	**Private**
Loops on slashed sleeve flaps	4	3	2	2
Skirt length above knee (inches)	3½	7	7	7
Buttons	Two rows of ten each	One row of nine	One row of nine	One row of nine
Epaulettes	Gold fringe 2½ inches long, ½ inch in dia.*	Worsted fringe, 2½ inches long, ¼ inch in dia.	Worsted fringe, 2½ inches long ⅛ inch in dia.	Extremely short worsted fringe

*Changed to "worsted bullion" with metal crescent about 1835. See Fig. 2-4, chapter 2, "The Changing U.S. Uniform."

(WD, General Regulations . . . , 1841, pp. 389–93; WD, General Regulations . . . , 1847, pp. 201–202; Peterson, "American Army Epaulettes, 1814–1872," *MC&H,* March 1951, pp. 6, 8, and 9; *Uniform or Dress of the Army of the United States,* 1837, pp. 31–32; HQA, AGO, GO 18, 4 June 1832, p. 3).

Chapter Fifty-Nine

Frock Coats

Frock coats had a fitted chest with skirts all of the way around, extending between mid-thigh and the knee. In contemporary civilian terms the frock coat was often called a skirted coat. This coat developed in the 1730s in England as an alternative to a more formal coat. Distinguished by a turned down collar and ordinary cloth, it was initially for working men. Gentlemen adopted it because of its comfort, and it finally became commonly known as a frock coat, rather than the previous term, "*frock,*" by the start of the nineteenth century. In civilian life the coat was out of fashion by 1900. The frock coat came into use by the U.S. Army in 1829 and lasted until 1902, with a gradual reduction in the skirt length and fullness during that time until it evolved into a uniform coat that just covered the wearer's hips. Only officers wore these coats before 1851, and although both officers and enlisted men wore frock coats after that date, their coats were of a significantly different pattern. The 1829 frock coat carried only a lace strap on one shoulder instead of epaulettes—one on the left for lieutenants and one on the right for captains.

Officers' Frock Coats before 1872

"With a view to economy, comfort and uniformity," the War Department introduced officers' frock coats in May 1829. The single-breasted blue coat had ten buttons which closed the front and was to be worn "on such occasions, and on such duties as the regulations or usage . . . do not require an officer to be in full dress."[1] An example is shown in Fig. 59-1.

In 1832 the button pattern for the blue frock coat switched to that also used for uniform coats, with the major general commanding wearing nine buttons per row in double-breasted fashion. Other major generals wore the same but with the buttons grouped by threes. Brigadier generals wore ten buttons per row grouped by twos in each of two rows. Staff officers and engineers wore one row of nine buttons. Topographical engineers, artillery, ordnance, and infantry officers wore one row of ten buttons. In 1839 frock coats for artillery, ordnance, infantry, and dragoon officers were changed to have between eight and ten buttons, "depending on the size of the officer." Early photographs showing these coats from the Mexican War are in Figs. 59-2 and 59-3. Medical officers changed to a double-breasted frock coat in 1840.[2]

A metamorphosis began in 1847 when field-grade officers of the line were allowed to wear double-breasted frock coats, while

Fig. 59-2.

Fig. 59-1. An officer in an 1832 frock coat. The skirt was cut square and extended nearly to the knee. No insignia were on the coat other than the shoulder straps.

Fig. 59-2. Colonel Hamtramck of Virginia volunteers during the Mexican War. He wears a frock coat very similar if not identical to those of the Regular Army. On the chest is a small nonregulation pocket.

Fig. 59-1.

company officers had to retain the single-breasted version. This optional button placement set the stage for the 1851 regulations, which required the distinction.[3]

Initially, officers' 1851 frock coats could be worn with epaulettes or shoulder straps, but during the Civil War the exigencies of the service necessitated a change which allowed only rank insignia on the shoulders. Otherwise the coats were devoid of officers' marks except for buttons. Company-grade officers and enlisted men had single-breasted coats with nine buttons, as shown in Fig. 59-4. Field-grade officers wore coats with two rows of seven buttons each, evenly spaced, and as before on other uniforms, generals grouped buttons by rank.[4]

In general the 1851 dark blue officers' frock coats had skirts that extended "from two-thirds to three-fourths of the distance from the top of the hip to the bend in the knee," thus hanging longer than the wearer's hands. The standing collars opened at the coat's front instead of the previously popular Prussian collar that was higher and that hooked straight up the front. Cuffs were 2½ inches deep with three small buttons at the underseam.[5]

Enlisted Men's Frock Coats

Enlisted men's frock coats differed in design from the various officers' versions. They were first cited in General Order 2, dated 13 February 1850, although the order was

Fig. 59-3.

Fig. 59-3. An unknown captain from the Mexican War wearing his ten-button frock coat. Around his waist is a red sash.

Fig. 59-4.

Fig. 59-4. For many officers, company-grade coats were single-breasted like this one, while higher-ranking officers after 1847 had double-breasted garments. The epaulettes were used on formal occasions, with shoulder straps replacing them for ordinary duty.

Fig. 59-5.

Fig. 59-5. Enlisted men during the Civil War wore nine-button frock coats of this style, which essentially had been introduced in 1851. Shortly after the coats were issued, changes were made to modify some of the piping, epaulettes were replaced by shoulder scales, and metal collar devices were omitted.

revoked. They were then prescribed and introduced in 1851 and soon became well established. Changes dominated their early use. This coat was an attempt to establish a single uniform following the Mexican War. The color of the cuffs and collars initially showed the branch of service, but an 1854 modification left only the top edges with colored piping, as engineer troops had initially done in 1851.[6] Men wore regimental numbers (or branch insignia for engineers and ordnance troops) on the 1851 frock coat collars and epaulettes.

After 1854, when mounted men changed to jackets, brass scales replaced the epaulettes, and four years later collar devices were dropped for all enlisted personnel.[7] During 1854–55, the army issued some of the enlisted men's frock coats in a chasseur pattern, which had a pleated skirt. By 1858 coat skirts returned to the straight cut. Thus transformed to the coat shown in Fig. 59-5, these uniforms saw some campaign use during the Civil War, especially early in the conflict. Numerous versions existed during the Civil War, especially among the volunteers and militia units. Some included coats with the cuff piping parallel to the sleeve end, instead of the inverted V, and coats with no trim at all.

One Civil War inheritance was the enormous stock of material procured for the volunteer army and left for the much smaller regular force. These stocks dominated postwar supply decisions. It would be seven years after the war's close before new uniforms could be introduced. Finally, in 1872 the army prescribed a new uniform with a changed frock coat.

Enlisted arm or service distinction in 1872 was by branch-colored trim on the collar front, coattails, and shoulder loops. Sleeve trim changed from the Civil War pattern of branch-colored piping on the cuff to colored slashed flaps carrying three buttons. Dress coat skirts for mounted men were shorter than those for unmounted soldiers. Metal regimental numbers reappeared on enlisted men's collars, as did some staff insignia (Fig. 59-6).[8]

The army modified the dress coat in 1885. The most obvious shifts in enlisted men's coats were in the collar, modified so that the branch color went all the way around the wearer's neck, and in the elimination of the regimental number or staff insignia, which had tarnished the collars. Another change was the removal of belt loops from the sides of the coat. Nearly coinciding with these changes was the original introduction of more ornate gold lace chevrons for dress coats in 1884. As a result, coats of 1872–84 carried only cloth chevrons, and coats worn between 1885 and 1902 were to have gold lace chevrons. An 1885–1902 coat is illustrated in Fig. 59-7. The coats' replacements were prescribed in 1902, but most units did not receive the new shorter-style coats until 1905. Many coast artillery companies wore the 1885-pattern coat until 1909 or 1910.[9]

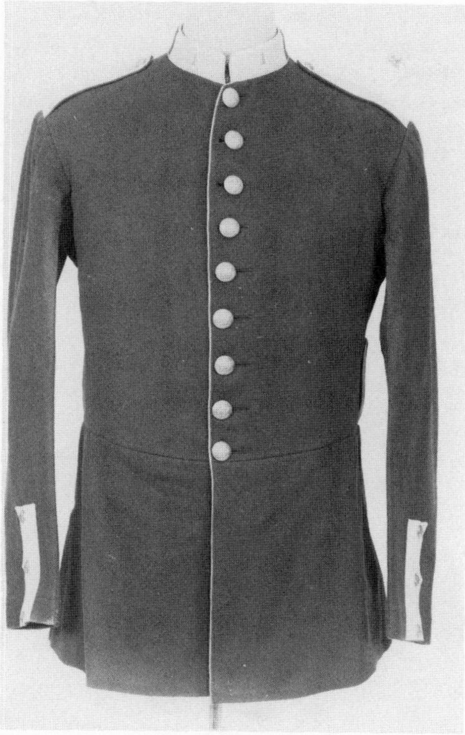

Fig. 59-6.

Fig. 59-6. *Enlisted men's dress coats introduced in 1872 had collars that were branch colored only on the first 4 inches and that carried regimental numbers. One of the side loops eliminated in 1885 can be seen on the coat's left side. The skirts in 1872 were shorter than those on earlier coats in response to changing styles.*

Table 59-1 provides a brief summary of the regulation enlisted men's dress frock coats worn between 1851 and 1902.

Officers' Frock Coats, 1872–1902

These coats were also of a new pattern, with collars lower than those on the older coats. Shoulder knots of a new style, and universally worn by all company- and field-grade officers for the first time, displayed an officer's arm or service and his rank. For infantry, cavalry, and, before 1901, artillery,

Fig. 59-7. A post commissary sergeant of the 1890s. Enlisted men's dress coats were modified in 1885 to this style. Branch was shown by a completely colored collar, shoulder loops, cuff flaps, and the background behind the chevron bars. The branch color in the case of commissary sergeants was gray. Helmet insignia and trouser stripes also indicated branch.

Fig. 59-8. Lieutenant Taylor of the 1st Artillery wearing his double-breasted dress coat introduced in 1872. The double rows of lace and the buttons on the cuffs were eliminated in 1879. Company-grade officers wore two such sleeve marks, while field grades wore three.

Table 59-1. *Enlisted Men's Dress Frock Coats.*

Initial Authorization Date	Collar Facing	Cuff Buttons	Shape of Cuff Trim	Collar Devices
1851	Full*	2	Full-color inverted V shape*	Regimental number or engineer or ordnance insignia
1854	Welt	2	Welt in inverted V shape	Regimental number or engineer or ordnance insignia
1858	Welt	2	Welt in inverted V shape	None (see Fig. 59-5)
1872	4 inches	3	Slashed flap	Regimental number or staff insignia (see Fig. 59-6)
1885	Full	3	Slashed flap	None (see Fig. 59-7)

*For engineer soldiers and ordnance sergeants the cuffs were of the inverted V-shaped welt.

Fig. 59-7.

Fig. 59-8.

the embroidered regimental number and color of the central pad told the wearer's unit. For other officers a branch insignia (usually on dark blue) or a dark blue pad with only rank insignia indicated a staff assignment.[10]

Placement and number of buttons are the easiest method of noting the 1872 pattern change. Field-grade officers had nine buttons in each of two rows, while company-grade officers wore seven buttons in a row. Above the sleeve ends officers wore vertical double rows of gold braid, three for field grade and two for company grade (Figs. 59-8 and 59-9). These sleeve marks disappeared in 1879, and thus modified, these coats lasted until they were replaced by an entirely new dress coat prescribed in 1902, although some alterations took place in 1885.[11]

Civil War Sharpshooters

During the Civil War the army formed the 1st and 2d regiments of sharpshooters, commonly called Berdan's Sharpshooters after

Fig. 59-9.

Colonel Hiram Berdan, commander of the 1st Regiment. The regiments' uniforms consisted of a dark green frock coat, a cap with black plume, light blue trousers (later exchanged for ones in green), and leather leggings.

Fig. 59-9. *A late-nineteenth-century major's dress coat in the field-grade, double-breasted style. The lack of vertical lace and buttons on the cuffs indicate it was worn after 1879.*

CHAPTER SIXTY

SACK, CAMPAIGN, AND 1898 FIELD COATS

Fig. 60-1. A Civil War four-button sack coat.

Fig. 60-2. Second Lieutenant Baker of the 13th Infantry in an officers' 1872–75 field coat with the distinctive mohair herringbone pattern extending from the buttons.

IN 1857 THE ARMY designed a sack coat that some today would describe as a service and campaign uniform. Made especially for fatigue work, it represented a new uniform concept, because the army had not previously provided a coat solely for such duty. This loose-fitting coat was cut straight, with a square skirt that ended generally halfway between the hips and the waist. It had only three vertical seams and was without a waist seam. The sack coat was the first coat made from flannel instead of wool like other coats, and this cheaper material reflected the nature of the duty expected of the garment. The only pocket was on the inside left. The coat closed with four buttons. Officers often wore their similar garments stylishly long. These sack coats were widely used during the Civil War and lasted until 1872 (Fig. 60-1). No enlisted branch or rank distinction was made on this coat except by chevrons.[1]

OFFICERS' UNDRESS COAT, 1872

In 1872 the quartermaster general prescribed an officers' dark blue five-button undress coat for field use. This sack coat had a falling collar and 1/4-inch-wide black braid extending 6 inches from each button and terminating in herringbone loops (Fig. 60-2). This coat was replaced by the 1875 officers' coat, which was identical but without the herringbone trim (Fig. 60-3). The five-button officers' sack coat added three small buttons to each cuff in early 1885.[2]

Fig. 60-1.

Fig. 60-2.

Campaign Coats

Enlisted men began to wear a five-button dark blue sack coat in 1874 as a replacement for the four-button sack coat and the pleated 1872 blouse (Fig. 60-4). The coat was cut straight down from the shoulders, without any fitting at the waist. Each cuff carried two small buttons and branch-colored cord in an inverted V shape. Branch distinction on the coat itself was by collar and cuff edging. The colored trimmings were removed in 1883, leaving branch designation on the coat only by chevrons (Fig. 60-5). In 1884 an additional button was added to each cuff, so each lower sleeve carried three buttons.[3]

Troops wore the five-button blouse for work in garrison and during field campaigns. This popular and widely used coat was replaced in 1903 and 1904 by all except coast artillery troops and recruits. New recruits stopped receiving the coat in early 1908, and

Fig. 60-3.

Fig. 60-5.

Fig. 60-4.

Fig. 60-3. *1st Lieutenant William Bixby of the Corps of Engineers in an officers' 1875 coat.*

Fig. 60-4. *The 3d Cavalry trooper standing at the right rear is wearing one of the pleated 1872–74 field blouses. As shown by this photograph, there was scarcely much uniformity when on campaign until the late 1880s.*

Fig. 60-5. *This Spanish-American War veteran wears the five-button campaign coat that proved very popular from about 1875 until after the start of the twentieth century.*

Fig. 60-6. Officers of the 21st infantry wearing the 1892-pattern sack coat. Distinctive features of the coat are the horizontal frogging on the front, black braid on the sleeve, and the block regimental numbers on the collar. This coat was regulation between 1892 and 1895.

Fig. 60-7. Lieutenant and Mrs. Barry in 1899. Several army and department marksmanship awards and a gold distinguished rifleman's badge are rare additions to his 1895-pattern sack coat, which was renamed a dress coat in 1902. This was the first coat to have infantry, cavalry and artillery collar insignia.

Fig. 60-6.

Coast Artillery Corps soldiers finally depleted the last army stocks in 1911. During this extended period of obsolescence, other soldiers wore the coat off-duty.[4]

Officers' Dark Blue Sack Coats, 1892 and 1895

The army brought forth what was to be a transitional design when it introduced a new dark blue "undress" coat for officers in 1892. Trimmed along the edges and front with 2-inch-wide black mohair braid, it also had a series of narrow braid stripes (frogging) on the chest and sleeves until that braid was removed in 1895. The initial design with frogging is shown in Fig. 60-6, and the 1895 version is in Fig. 60-7. As noted in earlier chapters, it was on this coat that officers originally wore branch insignia. Many basic branch insignia designs still in use were created for this coat. The same 1895 change that removed the frogging from the coats' chest removed the large silver block regimental numbers worn by infantry, cavalry, and artillery officers and added the letters *US* to the collar.[5]

Fig. 60-7.

The origin of these two transitional coats may be in 1878. Colonel Nelson Miles, commander of the 5th Infantry, was appointed to head a board charged with examining the army's equipment. Board officers were "selected by reason of their special fitness and their large experience with the wants of troops in actual service." One recommendation of the group was the adoption of an officers' sack coat ornamented with heavy black silk braid and with insignia on the collar. Army commander General Sherman noted in public, "No marked change in existing pattern [of the uniform] will now be sanctioned . . . . The familiar ornaments . . . must not be altered." This widely distributed rejection must have stung the ambitious Miles, and he

Fig. 60-8.

***Fig. 60-8.** The officer seated with the white helmet and walking cane wears the four-pocket blue field blouse introduced in May 1898. It was not widely worn, and several variations existed.*

probably waited in silence for a better time. Miles became a major general in 1890, two years after Sherman died. An influential officer destined to become commander of the army in 1895, Miles probably dusted off the concept presented to General Sherman many years before. The 1892 coat has its roots in the 1878–79 equipment board, and the uniform change Sherman did not want was simply postponed.[6]

Size of the early collar insignia worn on the 1892 coats varied. Adjutant General Office Circular 7, dated 14 May 1894, specified that branch insignia were to be 3/4 inch high. An early 1900 regulation change specified infantry, cavalry, and artillery collar insignia to be 1 inch high.[7] Despite these and other clear statements of insignia size, officers wore collar ornaments of various dimensions through the turn of the century, and there is no guide to allow us to easily determine when a particular collar device saw use.

After the 1902 uniform change, this coat continued for company- and field-grade officers under the title "dress coat." Under various regulation clauses that allowed the continued use of old uniforms as long as they were serviceable, these coats were worn by some officers into the 1930s.[8]

Field Coat, 1898

In 1898 the army introduced not only the well-known khaki coat, but also new blue field blouses with a falling collar and four pockets. These roll-collar coats were for wear "on marches, fatigue duty, and ordinary wear." Officers added shoulder straps and collar insignia on the roll-collar blue field blouse in the same manner that they had worn them on the 1895 standing-collar blouse.[9]

These four-pocket coats came in a double-breasted version with grouped buttons for generals and a single-breasted style for other officers (Fig. 60-8). The skirt just covered the wearer's hips. Starting in 1902, olive drab and khaki coats replaced this five-button blue sack coat, and for all except troops in China and the Philippines, the change was well under way by 1905.[10]

NINETEENTH-CENTURY JACKETS

Fig. 61-1. The original 1833 dragoon jacket had trim not only on the front of the standing collar, but also on the cuffs, collar top and bottom, jacket bottom, and back, as shown. This trim was evidently one of the reasons for the higher cost of the dragoon jacket compared to the price of other jackets. The two small cylindrical pieces at the small of the back, called bolsters or pillows, gave some relief from the saber belt that cut into the wearer's back. Bolsters remained a part of jackets through the Civil War.

LIGHT TROOPS often wore approximately waist-length jackets instead of coats or coatees at the time of War of 1812. Jackets, at one time called sleeved waistcoats, are close-fitting upper garments that end at the waist much like a vest with sleeves. In the early nineteenth century, troops wore jackets during some garrison work and on some campaigns. Because these jackets were not described in regulations and were functional garments that were used until they wore out, little is commonly known about them today.

These early jackets were either dress, as in the case of dragoons, or undress uniforms. The jackets of light dragoons (formed in 1808) were dark blue trimmed in blue and white, with the typical contemporary high collar and three rows of white buttons down the front. Space prohibits detailed description of all early jackets, but as a general rule winter wool jackets had branch trim, while the summer drilling (lightweight) jackets were usually made from cotton or occasionally linen and were not trimmed. Before 1818 these undress jackets, as they were also called, came only in gray kersey (wool). Between 1818 and 1821 the army added summer jackets made of cotton. Trimming for winter consisted of binding and fifteen small buttons.[1]

It should be noted that the early history of jacket collars was the same as that discussed in chapter 58, "Uniform Coats and Coatees." As was the case with coats, the jackets' shoulder lines came back to the natural width in 1821.

Regulations of 1821 called for riflemen to wear green jackets. The collar, body, back, seams, cuffs, and welts of these green jackets were trimmed in black worsted. The standing collar had two blind buttonholes terminating in crow's-feet with a button at the upper end of each blind hole. Officers' jackets were to use black silk braid at the collar, seams, cuffs, and crow's-feet. Three rows of nine buttons each went down the front, and cuffs 3½ inches wide carried three buttons. Men were to wear worsted black wings on these jackets. The Rifle Regiment was disbanded in 1821, but rifle companies formed part of infantry regiments. It is not clear if the rifle jacket was ever made or issued after 1821, although it was again described in the 1825 edition of *General Regulations.*[2]

It is probable that the rifle companies in the regiments never wore the green uniforms, and the descriptions in the 1821 and

Fig. 61-1.

1825 regulations simply stated the earlier rifle regiment's clothing. Rifle companies were disbanded about 1830. Beginning in the 1820s, sergeants' winter drilling jackets cost more than privates' because of the increased quality of their cloth. Ten-button "sky blue" wool jackets replaced those of gray in 1832, but branch trim remained the same. Officers were authorized white cotton or linen jackets for summer wear starting in 1832. Cut like the enlisted men's versions, they had the waist formed with slight downward points front and rear.[3]

So-called shell jackets are simply military jackets with branch-colored trim. Dragoons, added to the army in 1833, evidently received summer cotton shell jackets similar to those previously issued to other troops except for the design details and a change to twelve buttons. Dragoon blue woolen shell jackets cost over 50 percent more than unmounted troops' woolen jackets, evidently because of increased use of trim down the back seams, an improved design, and the better quality of cloth (Fig. 61-1). The dragoon summer shell jacket cost a few cents more than the infantry and artillery drilling jackets, and again one may presume that increase is a result of increased quality.[4]

Although regulations normally describe officers' uniforms in detail, an exception to the usual guidance came with the dragoon jacket: officers were allowed to wear a gold-trimmed blue cloth jacket "corresponding to that of the men" in the winter. For summer use, dragoon officers had white jackets. In 1839 officers of infantry and artillery joined those of dragoons when the War Department permitted them to wear jackets according to seasons: white in summer and light blue in winter.[5] Randy Steffen, in his book *The Horse Soldiers*, reports that officers' blue jackets had slanting chest pockets covered with pointed flaps.

Only the "undress" uniform (a shell jacket) was prescribed for the Regiment of Mounted Riflemen from their formation in 1846 until after the Mexican War. Enlisted engineers, likewise formed during the Mexican War, had dark blue shell jackets with trim of yellow lace and black cotton velvet, like the uniform coat, and with the right pocket covered by a flap. The engineers' white summer jacket was similar to the artillery's except for the pocket flap and the buttons.[6] Artists recorded some officers in

Fig. 61-2.

Fig. 61-2. *Infantryman in a shell jacket, about 1845. This 1840s jacket ended at the waist and was not popular because it rode up above the waist. Jackets were worn by all troops during the Mexican War and later until replaced by frock coats in 1851.*

the Mexican War wearing blue shell jackets with white trousers during the summer, but during wartime practicality ruled instead of parade ground guidelines.

Note that similar styles of jackets had different names and minor construction changes. The "roundabout" jacket popular in the 1820s was followed by the shell jacket and then the uniform jacket of 1854. Today many people interchange the names shell jacket and uniform jacket, but historically the blue wool shell jacket came first. Shell jackets (Fig. 61-2) came just to the waist and were not popular because they rode up over the wearer's waist, though the trousers that completed the uniform were quite high-waisted. Full-skirted coats authorized for enlisted men in 1851 by regulation replaced the shell jackets,[7] although in actuality these functional jackets may have continued, especially for the mounted troops. Several minor changes, such as the cuff depth, occurred throughout the life of the jackets, although in the field these changes were considered really distinctive.

The second jacket (Fig. 61-3) properly called a uniform jacket, was officially introduced in 1854 for mounted troops. This jacket should have extended about 2 inches below the waist, but during the Civil War these enlisted men's jackets actually varied from ending at the waist to running down as low as 5 inches below the waist.[8] The jacket had twelve buttons and was trimmed with

3/8-inch-wide branch-colored worsted lace. In general, the trim was around the edges of the 2½-inch-high collar and down the jacket front and around the bottom, plus two loops on the collar, the two curving back seams, and above the cuffs. Shoulder scales were called for, but men commonly omitted them in the field.

Civil War photographs of jackets that do not meet regulations are frequently found. These can be explained in several ways. Unscrupulous manufacturers took advantage of the government during the Civil War and produced some jackets that did not meet army standards, accounting for jackets, for example, with only one false buttonhole on the collar or with more or fewer than the two regulation buttons on the cuffs. Many soldiers individually modified their jackets, and some state units had their own distinctive designs. The army ceased issuing uniform jackets with the introduction of new clothing in 1872.[9]

Often overlooked by students of military clothing is the fact that from 1851 to 1872, officers serving with mounted units were allowed to wear an untrimmed dark blue jacket. Buttons were in one or two rows according to rank, the same pattern as on frock coats. Additionally, rank and branch were shown by shoulder straps.[10] This undress coat replaced officers' jackets after 1872.

During the Civil War, in 1863, the army formed the Invalid Corps. Renamed more appropriately the Veteran Reserve Corps in 1864, members received sky blue kersey uniforms with dark blue trim. The jacket for the Veteran Reserve Corps was similar to the standard Civil War jacket design except that the skirt was a few inches longer, it had cloth shoulder loops (trimmed in dark blue), it did not have bolsters or pads for the small of the back, and it fastened with eleven buttons.[11]

Fig. 61-3.

Fig. 61-3. *The 1864 light artillery uniform, including the Civil War uniform jacket. Uniform jackets extended a few inches below the waist to correct the problem of riding up in the 1851 shell jacket. This uniform jacket was introduced in 1854 to replace frock coats for mounted troops.*

Chapter Sixty-Two

Other Nineteenth-Century Coats

Chapter two, "The Changing U. S. Uniform," pointed out that especially in the nineteenth century regulations did not fully describe some uniforms, or in some cases, even mention special clothing. This chapter briefly describes some of the mid-nineteenth-century coats not covered elsewhere in this book. The heavy use of volunteers and the many unique uniforms worn by these volunteers accounts for many of these uniforms.

Body Coats, 1851–72

In 1851 army regulations authorized officers to wear, on an optional basis, a plain, dark blue uniform coat called a body coat. The only "insignia" on these coats were the normal branch or department buttons. With this nondress coat, which continued until 1872, officers could wear white, buff, or blue vests, also with branch or department buttons.[1] These vague guidelines opened even wider the great design of officers' uniforms, and accordingly there was a wide range in the patterns of dark blue coats and vests.

Special Civil War Uniforms

During the Civil War a tremendous variety of uniforms saw use. Some were supplied by the federal government, while states furnished some of the clothing used during the 1861–65 war. Uniforms unlike Regular Army uniforms were specified for the Veteran Reserve Corps, sharpshooter regiments, and various state volunteer units, including Zouaves.

Wounded veterans could enlist in the Veteran Reserve Corps, initially known as the Invalid Corps when it was formed in 1863. In March 1864 the organization received the more appropriate name. Uniforms were made from sky blue cloth with dark blue trim and included both a jacket and a frock coat, worn with standard light blue trousers (Figs. 62-1 and 62-2).

Two regiments of sharpshooters formed during the Civil War wore green frock coats trimmed in emerald green and green caps with a black plume. Initially their trousers were the standard light blue, but later the army supplied matching dark green trousers. High leather leggings completed this unique uniform. The insignia used on the cap apparently was a set of initials *SS* or *US SS*.

Fig. 62-1.

Fig. 62-1. *A second lieutenant of the Veteran Reserve Corps in a light blue frock coat trimmed in dark blue. The Veteran Reserve Corps was for disabled men who wished to continue their service to the Union during the Civil War. This officer had lost his left hand and lower arm yet continued to serve in this organization.*

Fig. 62-2. A private in the late Civil War period wearing a jacket of the Veteran Reserve Corps. No special insignia set this organization apart; its light blue uniforms, trimmed in dark blue, did that. Shoulder straps were part of this jacket, unlike the standard dark blue uniform.

Fig. 62-3. During the Civil War a great many Zouave units wore highly trimmed, collarless, waist-length jackets with baggy trousers. Details of such uniforms varied with the units, but this is a typical example. These uniforms were loosely based on the clothing of French colonial troops from North Africa.

Fig. 62-2.

Fig. 62-3.

Volunteer units comprised most of the Civil War Union Army. Especially early in the war, companies or regiments adopted uniforms as the units or commanders saw fit. Accordingly, uniforms came in a wide range of colors and styles. Although blue was the most common color, red, gray, and other colors appeared as well. Even on uniforms which were the same as those of Regular Army troops, some men wore nonregular cap insignia or chevrons. The most unusual uniforms were those of Zouaves.

Typically, Zouave clothing consisted of a highly decorated, collarless, waist-length jacket worn open over a vest or shirt. On the jacket front and sleeves were various decorative trims made from braid which was often of a contrasting color. Trousers were cut full with baggy legs. Headgear for zouaves included a wide range of caps, including turbans, stocking caps with tassels, and fezes. Zouave uniforms were loosely based on clothing used by French colonial troops in North Africa and were popularized by drill teams just before the Civil War (Fig. 62-3).

Section XVIII

Uniforms Span the Centuries

Chapter Sixty-Three

Trousers

Breeches cut for civilian horseback riding usually matched the civilian coat color, but by the end of the eighteenth century gentlemen had adopted tight trousers that required a pliable yet firm material. Buckskin or doeskin came into use by some upper-class gentlemen and by some military officers. During the Revolutionary War and into the nineteenth century, snug-fitting lower garments called overalls replaced breeches and gaiters (leggings), although enlisted men wore breeches and gaiters at times into the nineteenth century. For enlisted men these overalls were of various colors, especially during the shortages of the War of 1812, but normally they were white in the summer. Breeches continued for officers' dress through the start of the War of 1812.

By the start of the nineteenth century, pantaloons, which today we would call trousers, had come into common use. These were normally white in the summer and grey (for enlisted men) or blue (for officers) in the winter. The riflemen's green 1820s uniforms had matching green pantaloons. Stripes made of flat pieces of material were often added over the pants leg seams, but at times soldiers added welts (round cordage usually inserted into the seam) during the nineteenth century.

Enlisted men's military trouser stripes or welts were added in 1832. Stripes were used on some trousers worn for service and dress until 1902, when they became worn exclusively for dress. When trouser stripes were used, they were colored to indicate branch assignment for both officers and enlisted men until World War II. Some trouser stripes also showed rank (corporal, sergeant, or officer). After World War II, dress blue and army green uniforms carried stripes down the legs, while other uniforms did not, but these stripes were without regard to branch and merely served as uniform trim or to show officer status.

Trousers, 1821–51

Enlisted men's trousers prescribed in 1821 were of gray wool for winter service and white wool for parades, with white cotton worn in the summer. For dress, staff officers wore buff wool, medical officers wore blue wool, and other officers wore white for parade and blue for service. Pre-1832 officers' winter trousers had colored trim down the outer leg seams. From 1832 until 1851, summer trousers for all ranks were white without any trim, while winter trousers were either dark blue or light blue with various stripes. Enlisted men's first branch-colored stripes, 1½ inches wide, appeared in 1832 on their sky-blue winter trousers. Colors were red for artillery, dark blue for ordnance, and white for infantry. Summer white trousers remained without any trouser stripes, the same as for officers.[1]

With the 1833 formation of the Regiment of Dragoons, trouser stripes became more diverse. Dragoon field-grade officers and the adjutant had two stripes of gold lace on each outer leg seam of the dress trousers, with a space between them (Fig. 63-1). Company-grade officers wore two ¾-inch-wide yellow cloth stripes with ¼ inch between. Enlisted men's rank was also shown on the trousers. Sergeants had double yellow stripes like those of the company-grade officers, and corporals and privates had a single ¾-inch-wide stripe. Mounted riflemen followed this same pattern in 1846, except that their single stripes were "of black cloth . . . the outer seam edged with yellow cord." Engineer soldiers of 1846 adopted a different scheme: sergeants wore a black stripe 1½ inches wide, while corporals and privates had a black welt.[2] During the 1840s and 1850s civilian trousers were often made with braid along the legs. Whether this style came from the military is not known, but certainly within the army trouser trim was in wide use by all branches.

Trousers, 1851–1902

In 1851 uniform regulations eliminated white summer trousers. Wool became standard for year-round wear, with light blue for regimental officers and enlisted men and dark blue for the staff and generals. During 1858–61 trousers were dark blue. Mounted trousers were reinforced inside the legs and seat, and had straps that buttoned under the instep to hold the trousers down. During the 1854–58 period, pleats were added to issue trousers, making them fuller.

Officers' trouser trimmings were ⅛-inch welts, as shown in Fig. 63-2, buff for staff or with regimental colors: artillery, scarlet; infantry, dark blue (changed to "saxony blue" in 1854); riflemen, green; and dragoons, orange. Enlisted men also had ⅛-inch-diameter cord in the same colors; in addition, engineer troops had yellow and ordnance men had crimson. Because a colored welt indicated a company- or field-grade officers' assignment, either to the staff or to a regiment, the lack of a welt, or plain dark blue trousers, showed that the wearer was a general. Officers who were part of the cavalry branch formed in 1855 wore yellow welts. Four years before the Civil War, enlisted men were directed to remove their trouser stripes. In 1861 trousers and the stripes were again revised as shown in Table 63-1.[3]

The 1872 regulations revised the trouser stripe scheme again. Regimental officers went to branch-colored stripes, 1½ inches wide, still on light blue trousers. Enlisted men initially wore light blue trousers, and noncommissioned officers wore branch-colored stripes (Fig. 63-3), as outlined in Tables 63-2 and 63-3. From the 1870s through the 1890s the army reintroduced white, untrimmed trousers for both officers and enlisted men to wear in hot climates during the summer, though the extent of use varied over time.

Dress Uniforms after 1902

After the Spanish-American War the army reorganized, expanded, and modernized. Part

Fig. 63-1. Dragoon officers of 1833 adopted double gold stripes down their trousers. This was an initial attempt to distinguish rank and branch by trouser trim.

Fig. 63-2. Two Civil War colonels. The seated officer is evidently assigned to a staff, because he wears narrow buff trim on his trousers. The trim down the other officer's leg is barely visible because it did not contrast with his dark trousers. The frequent switching between dark and light trousers just before the start of and during the Civil War resulted in many men wearing nonregulation trouser colors.

of this change resulted in new uniforms, which the army described in 1902 for wear in 1903. Despite this change of uniforms, dress trouser stripes continued to be dictated by rank and branch. As new branches were created, members received new colors for trim. Noncommissioned officers above corporal all went to stripes 1¼ inches wide, while corporals retained ½-inch-wide stripes. Band musicians, field musicians, and cavalry trumpeters also kept their scheme of two ½-inch-wide stripes (Fig. 63-4). Offi-

Table 63-1. *Regulation Trousers, 1851–72.*

Duty/Branch	Dates	Trouser Color	Stripe Colors
General staff and	1851–58	Dark blue	⅛-inch buff welt
Staff Corps officers*	1858–72	Dark blue	⅛-gold cord
Ordnance officers	June 1858–1872	Dark blue	None
Dragoon officers	1851–58	Sky blue	⅛-inch orange welt
	1858–Aug. 1861	Dark blue	⅛-inch orange welt
Cavalry officers	1855–58	Sky blue	⅛-inch yellow welt
	1858–Dec. 1861	Dark blue	⅛-inch yellow welt
	Dec. 1861–1872	Sky blue	⅛-inch yellow welt
Mounted Riflemen officers	1851–58	Sky blue	⅛-inch emerald or medium green welt
	1858–Aug. 1861	Dark blue	⅛-inch emerald green welt
Artillery officers	1851–58	Sky blue	⅛-inch scarlet welt
	1858–Dec. 1861	Dark blue	⅛-inch scarlet welt
	Dec. 1861–1872	Sky blue	⅛-inch scarlet welt
Infantry officers	1851–58	Sky blue	⅛-inch dark blue welt
	1858–Dec. 1861	Dark blue	⅛-inch sky blue welt
	Dec. 1861–1872	Sky blue	⅛-dark blue welt
All enlisted men	1851–54	Sky blue	⅛-inch welt
			Artillery scarlet
			Infantry saxony blue
	(1854 only)		*Infantry* sky blue
			Riflemen medium green
			Dragoons orange
			Engineers yellow
			Ordnance crimson
Sergeants	1858–Mar. 1861	Dark blue	1½ inches, branch-colored
(except light artillery)	Mar.–Dec. 1861	Dark blue	1½ inches, branch-colored
	Dec. 1861–1872	Sky blue	1½ inches, branch-colored
Light arty. sergeants	Mar.–Dec. 1861	Sky blue	1½ inches, scarlet
Ordnance sergeants	1851–Dec. 1861	Dark blue	1½ inches, crimson
	Dec. 1861–1872	Sky blue	1½ inches, crimson
Hospital stewards	1857–58	Sky blue	⅛ inch crimson welt
	1858–Dec. 1861	Dark blue	1½ inches, crimson
Corporals	1858–Mar. 1861	Dark blue	½ inch stripe
(except light artillery)	Mar.–Dec. 1861	Dark blue	½ inch stripe
	Dec. 1861–1872	Sky blue	½ inch stripe
Light arty. corporals	Mar.–Dec. 1861	Light blue	½ inch scarlet stripe
Enlisted men (not NCOs)	1854–58 Dec. 1861–1872	Sky blue	None
	1858–Dec. 1861	Dark blue	None

*Includes ordnance officers until June 1858. Regulations indicate ordnance officers may have switched to a gold cord in December 1861, but apparently most ordnance officers continued to wear trousers without stripes.

Table 63-2. *Regulation Dress Noncommissioned Officers' Trousers, 1872–1902.*

Branch	Dates	Trouser Color	Stripe Colors
Infantry	1872–84	Light blue	Dark blue
	1884–1902	Light blue	White
Artillery	1872–1902	Light blue	Red
Cavalry	1872–1902	Light blue	Yellow
Engineers	1872–94	Light blue	Scarlet with white edge
	1894–1902	Dark blue	Scarlet with white edge
Hospital stewards	1872–88	Light blue	Green
Hospital Corps	1888–94	Dark blue	Green with white edge
	1894–1902	Light blue	Green*
Post commissary sgt.	1873–1902	Light blue	Gray
Signal Service	1872–89	Light blue	Orange
Signal Corps	1889–1902	Light blue	Black
Post quartermaster sgt.	1884–1902	Light blue	Buff
Ordnance	1872–1902	Light blue	Crimson
Indian Scouts	1890–1902	Light blue	White with red edge
Electrician sgt.	1899–1902	Light blue	Scarlet
USMA Detachment	1890–1902	Light blue	Buff

*All enlisted men of the Hospital Corps wore stripes; hospital stewards' were 1 1/4 inches wide; acting hospital stewards', 1 inch wide; and privates', 1/2 inch wide.

Table 63-3. *Trouser Stripe Width, 1872–1902.*

Rank	Stripe Width
Regimental officers	1 1/2 inches
Ordnance sergeants; hospital stewards; post quartermaster sergeants; commissary sergeants; electrician sergeants	1 1/4 inches
Other sergeants; acting hospital stewards	1 inch
Corporals; privates of Hospital Corps; lance corporals with renewed appointments	1/2 inch
Musicians*	Two, 1/2 -inch stripes, 1/4 inch apart

*First prescribed by General Order 58, 31 July 1883.

cers of cavalry, artillery, and infantry wore branch-colored stripes 1 1/2 inches wide, while those of the Corps of Engineers added an extra 1/4 inch. In 1938 all company- and field-grade officers adopted a new scheme for the colored stripes of dress uniforms: 1 1/2 inches wide for services that had a single color and 1 3/4 inches wide for branches with two colors (1 1/2-inch-wide stripes with 1/8 inch trim on each edge).[4]

Breeches became widely accepted as part of service uniforms, and during the late 1930s trousers and shoes replaced breeches and boots or shoes and leggings. With the dismounting of all troops during World War II, breeches were finally discarded.[5]

After World War II, when the army reintroduced dress blue uniforms, all officers adopted gold-colored stripes on their dress blue trousers, and enlisted men wore plain trousers without stripes. Generals added two narrow gold stripes on their traditional dark blue trousers. Other officers added a single wide stripe on their light blue trousers.

Green Uniforms

When the army introduced green uniforms in the mid-1950s, officers added black mohair stripes to their trousers. Warrant, company- and field-grade officers had a single stripe 1 1/2 inches wide, while generals had two 1/2-inch-wide stripes 1/2 inch apart (Fig. 63-5).[6]

Fig. 63-3.

Fig. 63-5.

Fig. 63-4.

Fig. 63-3. *Sergeant Blake of the 4th U.S. Artillery Band, 1901. His trouser stripes tell something of his assignments. Their red color is for artillery, and their 1½ inches' width is for the rank of sergeant. The gold cap band, the collar insignia, and the coat were not issue, but they were worn by all of this band's members.*

Fig. 63-4. *Most militia organizations followed the Regular Army's practice for trouser stripes. Musicians had two narrow stripes, as does the musician standing on right. Corporals wore a single stripe, as does the seated man on the right. Sergeants and above wore a wide stripe (seated, left).*

Fig. 63-5. *This 1991 photograph shows a general (left) wearing the army green trousers introduced in the late 1950s, with two ½-inch-wide stripes on each leg. The colonel (right) wears a single wide stripe, as did all officers other than generals. The green grousers are the only twentieth-century nondress uniform to distinguish rank group by trouser stripe design.*

WORK AND FATIGUE CLOTHING

Fig. 64-1. Three small metal buttons and a lack of pockets distinguished the 1879-pattern cavalry stable frock coat.

Fig. 64-2. The prisoner on the right is wearing one of the brown fatigue uniforms used army-wide in the late nineteenth century by dismounted soldiers.

THE U.S. ARMY usually did not describe enlisted work uniforms in regulations, because the fatigue or work uniforms were: (1) issued to the men, (2) were well known to army members, and (3) the manner in which the uniforms were worn was not much concern to officers. The general practice of little or no information in regulations continued until after World War II, when uniform regulations became more voluminous and the fatigue uniforms became worn more in public and thus the uniforms' appearances became a point of interest for commanders.

EARLY WORK CLOTHING

Various stable or fatigue frocks had been supplied to mounted soldiers even before the Mexican War, but they were not described in quartermaster publications until 1879, when the army adopted light canvas or unbleached drilling sack frock coats for troops. This gave noncommissioned officers and men a suitable uniform to wear over other clothes when working in and around stables and on other dirty duty. The coat had no pockets, closed up the front with three metal suspender buttons, and had a standing collar 2 1/4 inches wide (Fig. 64-1).[1]

Fig. 64-1.

For once, economy acted in the soldiers' favor when, in 1884, the army took surplus shelter tents and made them into clothing for dismounted men to wear as work uniforms. These work garments were the counterparts of mounted men's stable frocks. The uniforms were made from 6- and later 7- and 8-ounce cotton duck and were died brown. The coats were single-breasted, in sack style, with a falling collar, six India rubber (later black bone) buttons, and two breast pockets. Matching canvas trousers with a bib front had slanting top pockets, a watch pocket, and one or two hip pockets (Fig. 64-2).[2]

Minor changes were made in the uniform in 1903 and 1904, and by 1904 it was prescribed for all men. The government evidently continued to issue those stable frocks on hand until about 1912, when the supply was nearly exhausted and mounted men started to receive the brown fatigue clothing. These brown canvas coats still buttoned up the front with six buttons, but now they had one small breast pocket and two larger ones on the lower coat front. Brown canvas fatigues began to be phased out in 1908 for

Fig. 64-2.

Fig. 64-3.

Fig. 64-3. A farriers' class shows a wide range of work uniforms just before World War I. The bib overalls were part of the brown canvas fatigue clothing. The pullover coats were the blue denim first introduced in 1908.

Fig. 64-4. A 1940 comparison of old and new work uniforms. The army initially saw the herringbone twill (HBT) version simply as a new cut of a work suit with a change in cloth, and not as the combat uniform it soon became.

coast artillery troops and were replaced by blue denim work uniforms.[3]

Blue Denim

In April 1908 the army introduced a new jumper-style work uniform for the Coast Artillery Corps. The entire uniform consisted of a soft-brimmed hat, a pullover shirt or jumper with three buttons down the front, and trousers, all made from blue denim. This first denim jumper had two large pockets with flaps on the lower front and a similar smaller one on the left chest. Signal Corps men who worked on telephone and telegraph lines, aviation mechanics (who were then part of the Signal Corps), quartermaster men "whose classification calls for manual labor," and others began to wear blue denim as well. In June 1909 the uniform was prescribed for all soldiers (Fig. 64-3). The army issued several versions of denim work clothing during and after World War I, including some made in brown (1918–19). An example of this last clothing is shown in Fig. 66-3, chapter 66, "Light Outer Garments."[4]

Fig. 64-4.

Used for over thirty years, the blue denim was generally discarded in 1941 after several pattern changes. The pullover shirt of 1910 had been temporarily replaced by a four-button coat in late 1917 and early 1918, but the pullover style returned in July 1918. In 1940 a coat-style shirt with five metal buttons was prescribed (Fig. 64-4). Use of the denim work clothing was phased out beginning in May 1941 in favor of a new herringbone twill (HBT) olive drab fatigue uniform, although during World War II mine planter

Fig. 64-5. Armored crewmen training at Fort Knox, Kentucky, in 1942 wear one-piece HBT overalls introduced for the mechanized force crews and mechanics. HBT cloth and metal buttons on work uniforms continued into the early 1950s.

Fig. 64-6. An HBT work shirt, as developed during World War II. The "burst of glory" metal buttons had thirteen stars as exhibited on the Great Seal of the United States. Various versions of the shirts were made, including some with gas flaps on the sleeves that could be tightened to help keep out chemical agents. Most units wore patches on the left shoulder, as on other uniforms, but the 2d Armored Division wore their patch above the pockets, as shown here.

Fig. 64-5.

servicemen and some aviation crash crews continued to wear the blue denim.[5]

Work Uniform Names

The names associated with the work clothing that developed during and after World War II are revealing. The blue denim work clothing was replaced by HBT "work uniforms," by which title they were known well into the 1950s. The work uniforms were to be worn whenever clothes might become soiled (fatigue duty) or during drill, combat, and simulated combat. The title officially became "utility cotton work uniforms" in 1952, and this name was used into the 1970s in regulations, even though the common name used by troops was "fatigues," which, as we have seen, was rooted in the uniform's development.[6]

By the middle of World War II the concept of these work uniforms, with an associated field jacket, was well established. The army used them, modifying them several times, into the 1980s, when camouflage clothing, called battle dress uniforms (BDU), replaced them. For service in the tropics, including Vietnam, special lightweight fatigues, with a revised four-pocket shirt, were developed under the common name of "jungle fatigues."

Identification on Fatigues

New insignia in the form of cloth tapes bearing the wearer's last name and *U.S. ARMY* came about for the work clothing. Black, woven "distinguishing insignia" 4 1/2 inches long and 7/8 inch high, bearing yellow block letters *U.S. ARMY*, were added above the upper left pocket on various

Fig. 64-6.

Fig. 64-7.

Fig. 64-7. *In a few instances U.S. Army troops wore camouflage fatigues during World War II, as shown by these engineers shortly after the Normandy invasion.*

pieces of field clothing in October 1953.[7] Many units had previously prescribed similar white strips of cloth, carrying the wearer's last name, over the right pocket, and this ultimately became prescribed army-wide, but not before a few units called for branch-colored name tags or placement of the name tags above the left pocket.

Fatigues, World War II and Later

Generally the early fatigue uniforms were made from a greenish HBT material with metal buttons. Two-piece HBT work uniforms (shirt and trousers) came into wide use without much notice in regulations from the time they were issued. Officially the shirt was termed a "jacket, Herringbone twill," and it existed in several versions that are of no real consequence, although it is worth pointing out that the initial 1941 jacket/shirt had box-pleated pockets, sleeves that were slit at the wrists with one or two buttons, and a bi-swing back that allowed wide movements in the back and shoulders. The late 1942 and subsequent World War II shirts were made more simply and cheaply with more easily constructed pockets and sleeves, and the two buttons found at the waist of the 1941 version were omitted.

The denim one-piece work suits worn by Air Corps personnel, mechanics, and similar troops until 1933 were replaced by olive drab HBT coveralls just before the start of World War II. Armored force crewmen and mechanics had one-piece work suits, including 1941–43 versions with bi-swing backs, throughout the World War II period (Fig. 64-5).[8]

During World War II a basic change in attitude took place toward fatigue uniforms. Before that war soldiers had worn fatigues as work uniforms to keep other uniforms clean. During the war, fatigues became combat uniforms.

Fatigues were issued as summer combat clothing starting in 1942 in the Southwest Pacific. For some jungle operations the quartermaster general introduced camouflaged HBTs, which saw limited use, but overall the one-color fatigues were most common. In 1944 and 1945 the jungle combat clothing changed to solid olive drab poplin, and in 1952 standard fatigues began to be made from a newer cotton sateen (Figs. 64-6 and 64-7).[9] This dual use of fatigue clothing as both a work uniform and a combat uniform caused a blurring of the previous distinctions between the two types of apparel. Note that most World War II fatigue clothing went to the Pacific theater because, for the most part, the soldiers there needed tropical garments, while in Europe the wool service uniform generally persisted. A few units wore camouflage fatigue uniforms in Europe in the summer of 1944, but that was an exception.

This change in the use of fatigues continued after World II as the cotton uniforms became normal wear in many garrison situations. As soldiers began to wear fatigue uniforms as everyday clothing, badges and other insignia began to appear on fatigues.

Officers' and enlisted men's fatigues were not distinguished by cut during World War II. Distinction was by insignia. Officers began to wear insignia on this clothing in 1943 in the same way that insignia were worn on other shirts, but starting in the 1950s such devices were usually embroidered on small pieces of cloth were sewn to the collar.[10]

The Vietnam War caused two immediate changes in the wearing of insignia. The first change was the introduction of subdued

Fig. 64-8.

Fig. 64-8. *Balloon cloth one-piece uniform as used by 1940 airborne troops. All pockets were closed with zippers. The only insignia were rank insignia, worn in the usual manner, and small leather strips, embossed with the wearer's name, place on the left chest.*

Fig. 64-9.

Fig. 64-9. *Two-piece airborne uniforms replaced the balloon cloth overalls in 1941. The two chest pockets slanted opposite those of the balloon cloth version. With four large cargo pockets on the jacket and two on the trousers, this cut of clothing formed the model for jungle fatigues, which became widely worn in Vietnam.*

Fig. 64-10.

Fig. 64-10. *The winter field uniform composed of green wool trousers and shirt. In places like Korea and parts of Europe, this was the primary uniform during the winter months.*

Fig. 64-11.

Fig. 64-11. *Details of a winter wool shirt like that shown in Fig. 64-10. The subdued cloth insignia indicates that the shirt was used after the late 1960s. Officers wore rank on the right collar tip and branch on the left. After the introduction of black metal chevrons, they went on enlisted troops' field uniform collars which previously had been bare.*

ornamentation, which became essential in the short combat ranges of the Vietnam jungle. Fatigue uniform insignia became black and brown. Cloth name and *U.S. Army* strips changed to match the uniform and had black lettering. This transition became official when the U.S. Army in Vietnam authorized green and black insignia in March 1965. In July 1966 the Department of the Army authorized subdued insignia worldwide.[11] The second change came about when men began to roll up their fatigue sleeves, covering noncommissioned officers' chevrons. As a result, they began to use small metal enlisted men's rank insignia pinned to the shirt collar; eventually those collar insignia became embroidered.

Variants

Other uniforms related to fatigues also were brought out. During World War II special parachutists' clothing was designed and issued. Examples are shown in Figs. 64-8 and 64-9. Since the 1950s army aviators have had a variety of special flight clothing, including aviation jackets. The basic heavily zippered flight overalls had insignia placed as on standard fatigue uniforms, except that some flight personnel wore a leather rectangle bearing the aviator's name, rank, and aviation badge on one side of the chest. During the Vietnam War flame-retardant Nomex uniforms were adopted for aircrew members. These brown uniforms had a shirt generally cut like the conventional fatigue shirt, but the matching trousers had cargo pockets placed to be more accessible when the wearer was seated. Also in the 1950s the army brought out a special olive green wool field uniform for winter wear (Figs. 64-10 and 64-11), and in some places troops wore these uniforms instead of the cotton fatigues.

Under a variety of conditions men also modified fatigue shirts. In some units officers added shoulder loops, and occasionally in hot climates like that of Vietnam, men modified them to be short-sleeved. In 1977, "wash and wear" material became the cloth for utility (fatigue) uniforms (Fig. 64-12), although that material had been tested since 1973 and commercially available several years before. The new material eliminated the need for soldiers to starch their field uniforms in garrison. In the mid-1970s armored vehicle crewmen received one-piece overalls of new design, as production and wear of the HBT overalls had been suspended in the 1950s.

Fig. 64-12.

Fig. 64-12. Officially called "men's durable press utility uniform, shade Olive Green 507," these were commonly called "wash-and-wear" fatigues. The army made small improvements in these and the previous versions, which required starching, with changes in the shape of pocket flaps and cuffs.

The best-known field uniforms were the jungle fatigues worn in the Vietnam War. Tropical fatigues, made of lightweight material, included a lightweight shirt, officially known as a hot weather coat, with four large cargo pockets, two on the chest and two starting at the waist. The shirt came with the chest pockets slanted and with either covered or exposed buttons. Three basic versions were made: with exposed buttons, with covered buttons but with shoulder loops, and with covered buttons without shoulder loops (Figs. 64-13 through 64-17). The *U.S. ARMY* and name strips were to be worn parallel to the ground, but they were frequently slanted to be parallel to the slanted chest pockets. The accompanying trousers

Fig. 64-13.

Fig. 64-13. Brigadier General Willard Pearson (right) and Major General Stanley Larsen in 1966. Both officers wear jungle fatigue uniforms with exposed buttons and colored insignia.

had large cargo pockets like those of the early HBT work trousers, but with drawstrings at the leg bottoms to allow soldiers to blouse them over boots.

In 1984 the army allowed issue of lightweight jungle fatigues again. The four large shirt cargo pockets proved popular with the troops and led to the revision of the cut of nontropical fatigues when the army introduced battle dress uniforms (BDUs) in woodland and desert camouflage colors in the early 1980s. The resulting BDUs were cut like the jungle fatigues of Vietnam (Fig. 64-18) but in a heavier material. The heavier fatigues showed themselves to be impractical in hot climates like that of Grenada, and a lightweight version of the same style was then adopted for hot climates in 1986.[12]

In Vietnam, U.S. soldiers wore a great many unofficial camouflage fatigue uniforms. The most common were called tigerstripes because of their sharp-edged pattern, which included large black stripes, usually edged with a light green, intermixed with narrow light green stripes on a darker green. These fatigues were cut like standard utility uniforms instead of the jungle (hot weather) pattern. Additionally, some elite units wore Vietnamese camouflage fatigues and vari-

Fig. 64-14.

Fig. 64-14. *Details of one of the early jungle fatigue shirts (officially called a hot-weather coat) with exposed buttons and bright insignia. These were typically worn in Vietnam into 1966.*

Fig. 64-15.

Fig. 64-15. *A jungle fatigue coat with straight pockets and rectangular pocket flaps.*

Fig. 64-16.

Fig. 64-16. *A typical jungle fatigue coat of the late Vietnam War. Insignia were black, pockets were slanted, and the name and U.S. ARMY strips were parallel to the ground.*

Fig. 64-17.

Fig. 64-17. *Brigadier General Elmer R. Ochs in late 1970. The insignia were embroidered directly on the hot-weather coat, with the name and U.S. ARMY slanted parallel to the pocket tops.*

Fig. 64–18.

Fig. 64–19.

Fig. 64–18. *Battle dress uniform shirt of the type introduced in the early 1980s. These shirts were cut like the Vietnam War's jungle fatigues, but the pockets were not slanted. Enlisted personnel wore black metal chevrons on the collars, and officers wore subdued branch and rank.*

Fig. 64–19. *This World War II technician wears one of the 1941 field jackets with six buttons and slash pockets. The overall design was based on civilian outdoor clothing. This style of jacket came in five sizes, weighed about half as much as the wool coat it replaced, and was water-repellent.*

Fig. 64–20. *Officers in 1943-model field jackets. The basic pattern is still used by the army.*

ous experimental patterns as well as jungle clothing in a four-color pattern devised by the U.S. Army's Engineering Research and Development Lab in 1948. This last uniform was introduced in late 1967 and in 1968.[13]

Jackets

Design details varied over the years, but the jackets worn with World War II and later fatigues, known as field jackets, were wind-resistant and water-repellent coats. Many versions exist. The first one, introduced in 1940 and 1941, had six or seven buttons, depending on the coat's length, which was just to the waist, and two slash pockets (Fig. 64-19). A redesigned 1943 jacket was longer and corrected many of the style's problems. This overall style, shown in Fig. 64-20, has basically continued despite many minor improvements. These changes include modifications allowing for use of a button-in liner in 1950 and changes to a zipper front, a drawstring at the bottom, and snaps on the pocket flaps in 1951. One of the most significant changes was made in 1966 when the traditional collar was modified to have rounded collar tips and an integral zippered hood. Enlisted men wore chevrons but no branch insignia on these jackets, but, as on the fatigue

Fig. 64–20.

and special field clothing, shoulder patches and often distinctive insignia showed the wearer's organization.[14]

Waist-length jackets, functional in cramped vehicle compartments, were adopted to go with various World War II and later fatigue uniforms. Armor crews called such garments tanker jackets, and they were often privately purchased and are worn even today by some men. In aviation units they were usually called flight jackets. Flight jackets varied in color and material, and those introduced with the Nomex uniforms were of brown fire-retardant material to match the basic flight uniforms. Examples are shown in chapter 66, "Light Outer Garments."

Chapter Sixty-Five

Greatcoats, Overcoats, and Cloaks

The second seminole war began in Florida when Brevet Major Dade's command was attacked in December 1835 by Indians. The weather was cold, and the troops, believing they were in a peaceful area, had their capes fully buttoned over their greatcoats so that when they were attacked, their arm movements were inhibited.

While heavy outer coats have always been worn during cold weather, the U.S. Army blithely failed to mention them in various uniform regulations until the Mexican War, when the coats began to rate a few sentences.[1] An 1819 internal memo shows that greatcoats of that time were made from 3½ yards of wool kersey and were fastened with six large buttons, with the cape closed with three small buttons. Samples of early greatcoats are scarce, but it is clear that the mounted arms such as dragoons had a special pattern that lent itself to wear while mounted on horseback.

Fig. 65-1.

Fig. 65-1. *A Pennsylvania infantry officer wearing an 1851-style officers' overcoat and cape.*

With the introduction of olive drab in 1902 came matching overcoats, and with an increased industrial base, a wider range of coat styles became available, which allowed proliferation of various cold and wet weather gear. Enlisted men and officers wore different styles of overcoats in the nineteenth century and from after World War I until the introduction of a green overcoat in the late 1960s, although in the 1950s the "officers'" overcoat was optional for off-duty enlisted men, and officers could wear the "enlisted men's" coat in the field.[2]

Nineteenth-Century Greatcoats

The nineteenth-century enlisted men's greatcoats were made from very heavy light blue wool cloth, although during the Civil War the Federal army initially purchased heavy overcoats of several dark colors for issue to militia units. Buttons were according to branch. Attached under the collar was a cape, which was at times lined according to branch. These capes could be buttoned up the front to provide an extra layer of material around the shoulders and arms. Mounted men's coats were double-breasted, with six pairs of buttons, and were slit up the back, which allowed the skirts to cover a mounted soldier's legs. In contrast, Civil War foot soldiers wore a single-breasted coat with five buttons.

Capes for the mounted men were long, coming nearly down to the cuffs, whereas for their unmounted companions, the capes extended only down to the elbow. Civil War capes were sewn into the coat, but even so, some men removed them. Photographic evidence shows that during the Civil War mounted and unmounted men received the two patterns of coats indiscriminately; thus, some infantrymen wore the mounted men's pattern and some cavalrymen wore the infantry styles.[3] Photographs show that during the Civil War, branch trim was not applied to overcoats.

These Civil War coats lasted past the war's end. In 1872 the mounted men's style, with seven pairs of buttons, became worn by all branches. The double-breasted style varied slightly over time, with five pairs of buttons prescribed in 1880 and later, in the 1880s, six pairs.

"Cloak" was the regulation term used to describe an officers' cold weather garment during the first half of the nineteenth century. The heavy cloaks were lined with blue, buff, white, or red according to the wearer's branch or department. Dragoon officers, unlike officers of other branches, wore blue gray, double-breasted overcoats like those of their men. Regulations of 1841 and 1847 describe cloaks for artillery, ordnance, and infantry officers as being fastened with a gilt eagle and chain clasp ornament.[4]

New overcoats were prescribed for officers in 1851. They were dark blue, virtually black, and closed with double-breasted frogs. An example of this 1851 overcoat is shown in Fig. 65-1, although many photographs show that officers wore a range of styles and colors during the Civil War. By at least 1851 mounted officers, like mounted enlisted men, wore longer coats than did their unmounted counterparts. Various minor changes were made to both the officers' and enlisted men's coats until 1902. For example, enlisted men adapted a single version of their coat for both mounted and unmounted men in 1872, and the number of buttons

Fig. 65-2. *The officers' dark blue overcoat, as revised in 1875, when frogging on the sides was eliminated. Previously, black trim decorated the side above the waist and under the wearer's arm. Rank was indicated on the lower sleeve by black mohair knots. Several minor variations, including a removable hood, which the army introduced in 1884, were used until olive drab came into use in 1902.*

Fig. 65-2.

Fig. 65-3.

Fig. 65-4.

was changed (Figs. 65-2, 65-3, and 65-4). Supply shortages forced the 1872 decision to be delayed, and General Order 67 of June 1873 provided that the older single-breasted overcoat could be issued to and worn by all enlisted men.[5]

Trim on various nineteenth-century overcoats was not extensive, being limited to colored cape linings and rank devices. Enlisted men wore branched-colored chevrons on the lower sleeves of overcoats, since the capes would have covered the chevrons if they had been worn on the upper sleeves as on other coats. Officers had sleeve knots of black braid to show rank, and "on campaign" they could wear enlisted men's light blue overcoats with officers' sleeve rank knots (Fig. 65-5). One result of a special board convened late in 1878 and in session for over half a year was the addition of colored cape linings for enlisted men.[6]

Greatcoats of the Western Frontier

Civil War–style greatcoats were issued to enlisted men and purchased by officers. By 1880 the Civil War mounted men's overcoat was reduced to five pairs of buttons. On the western frontier the army began to issue buffalo-skin overcoats for wear during very cold weather, as prompted by an 1868 medical report suggesting improvements in army uniforms and reinforced by a board of officers appointed in 1875 to study various quartermaster problems. While a variety of fur coats were used in early 1876, by the fall of 1876 buffalo-skin coats were being issued (Fig. 65-6). Officers could purchase these coats, but for the common soldier they remained government property and were issued for temporary wear. Muskrat caps with flaps that could be fastened up or, in very cold weather, worn down over the ears and tied under the wearer's chin; heavy mittens; and buffalo overshoes usually accompanied the buffalo coat.[7]

With the demise of the buffalo, the army adopted heavy canvas coats as replacements in 1879. These were double-breasted and made of brown cotton duck lined with

Fig. 65-3. An officer just before the Spanish-American War, with the cape attached to his overcoat. Like previous models, this coat had a slit in the side so the saber could be worn outside the coat.

Fig. 65-4. It was a cold day in Anniston, Alabama, when this soldier had his photograph taken in 1898. The overcoat had seven sets of hooks and eyes under the collar to allow a cape to be fastened at the wearer's option.

Fig. 65-5. Overcoat sleeve knots used by officers from 1872 to 1902. The generals' knots were replaced in 1902 by stripes worn parallel to the coat cuff. Second lieutenants' sleeves were plain until World War I, at which time they adopted a knot made of a single brown strip of braid. All other commissioned officers wore black overcoat sleeve trim.

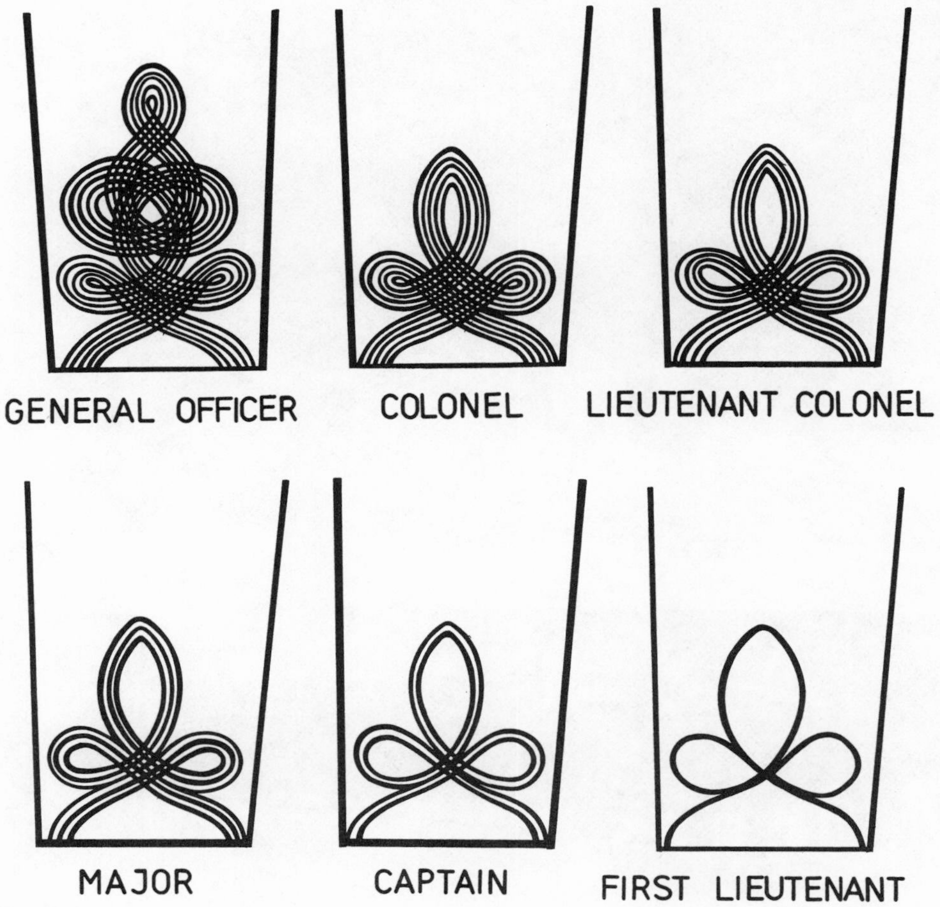

Fig. 65-5.

blanket wool. Various versions of blanket-lined overcoats, which for the most part remained army property instead of being given to soldiers, were worn into the twentieth century.[8]

With the revolutionary 1902 uniform regulations came several changes besides the new olive drab color. Officers and enlisted men adopted overcoats of the same general design and cut. The coat was double-breasted with a hood, although this was not an innovation for the army, because some officers had previously added hoods. Like previous versions, the new coat had a side slit to allow the saber to hang outside the coat while the belt remained under the coat. It was also slit up the back for use on horseback. Initially, buttons were of vegetable ivory or horn, but for enlisted men they were changed to bronze in 1905 (Figs. 65-7 and 65-8). Chaplain's coats were of identical cut but were black. As World War I approached, the detachable hood fell into disuse (Figs. 65-9 and 65-10). As if marking an end to the western frontier, in 1907 the Quartermaster Corps issued dark blue woolen, short, double-breasted mackinaw coats and matching "mackinaw trousers" for troops stationed on the last frontier, Alaska.[9]

War Department Circular 10 of August 1890 established a unique overcoat for Indian Scouts. It was slit up the back for horseback use, was especially heavy, and had a pointed hood. It lacked a cape, but it had a high col-

Fig. 65-6. *Guard mount for the 5th Infantry. Both the band and the guards wear buffalo-skin overcoats introduced in the 1870s.*

Fig. 65-7. *Men of the 2d Artillery Battery, 1906, wear the 1902-style overcoat made with five pairs of buttons. Removable capes, lined in branch colors, could be fastened to this coat. The men also wear muskrat winter caps and mittens and arctic overshoes.*

Fig. 65-7.

Fig. 65-6.

Fig. 65-8.

Fig. 65-8. *A military funeral, 1904. The men wear overcoats with red-lined capes and muskrat mittens. The chaplain, with his back to the camera, is wearing a black overcoat as prescribed in 1902 regulations.*

Fig. 65-9.

Fig. 65-9. *When the weather was not severe, officers could wear a cape as an outer garment, as this lieutenant did in the 1890s. Only officers wore capes, which became the outer garment with the dress uniform starting in 1902. Capes were lined with the branch color. Capes are still authorized but not widely worn.*

Fig. 65-10.

Fig. 65-10. *First Lieutenant Elliott, 1908, wearing the olive drab overcoat with cape. His rank is shown by the knot composed of one strip of black braid. At that time officers' buttons were usually made of horn instead of metal ones displaying the eagle, but enlisted men switched to these metal buttons in 1905, and this officer must have followed suit.*

lar under the hood that buttoned with a flap across the front (Figs. 65-11 and 65-12). The overcoat pattern itself was distinctive of the Indian Scouts.

Insignia on Overcoats

Insignia became more diversified with the 1902 overcoats. Enlisted men continued to wear only chevrons on overcoats, but officers added more trim than before. Company- and field-grade officers continued to use the rank knots, shown in Fig. 65-5, that had seen service for many years. A bronze-colored branch insignia was now inserted, however, in the lower opening of the sleeve knot, and it continued until 1912. During World War I, when rank insignia were introduced for second lieutenants, the junior officers began to wear a single knot of brown braid on their overcoat, identical in design to the first lieutenants' black braid. Overcoat sleeve knots for company- and field-grade officers remained until 1926.[10]

Until 1902 generals' sleeves had been decorated with a "double knot" composed of five narrow strips of braid applied in a more complex pattern, but in that year generals adopted a new scheme for overcoats. A black band $1\frac{1}{4}$ inches wide was placed with the lower edge $2\frac{1}{2}$ inches above the end of the sleeve. Above this band a parallel black band $\frac{1}{2}$ inch wide was applied, and in the $1\frac{1}{2}$ inches between the two mohair bands went bronze stars 1 inch high to show rank. This pattern of a wide black band below a narrow black band continued on generals'

Fig. 65-11. Indian Scouts received a special overcoat starting in 1890. It had a pointed hood and omitted the capes used by other troops. Unlike light-colored coats worn by other soldiers, this overcoat was of dark material. Deliberately large, it had an adjusting buckle across the back. On each side were horizontal slits covered with flaps so that the scouts would have ready access to their revolvers and ammunition.

Fig. 65-12. Double-breasted Indian Scouts' overcoats had a high collar with an extra fastening flap that covered the wearer's chin and an adjustable drawstring in the hood.

Fig. 65-13. Lieutenant General Bullard (center), Second Army commander, in January 1919. The general's overcoat has the pair of black sleeve stripes introduced in 1902 for general officers. Silver stars were worn by generals on their overcoats between the end of 1912 and 1926.

Fig. 65-11.

Fig. 65-12.

olive drab overcoats until after World War II. Stars on the sleeves became silver in 1912 (Fig. 65-13), and they were dropped from the sleeves altogether in 1926, when they were moved to the shoulder loops.[11]

Between the world wars, warrant officers wore one of two general types of insignia on their overcoat sleeves: those in the Army Mine Planter Service wore two, three, or four narrow bands (depending upon rank) with either an embroidered anchor or a ship's propeller, while warrant officers not part of the Coast Artillery Corps wore an eagle seated in a wreath, the warrant officer insignia.[12] An example is shown in chapter 43, "Field Clerks and Warrant Officers."

Overcoats of World War I and Later

Starting with the expansion of the army for World War I, a great many outer coats came into widespread service. Before the war, aviators received a special coat, and soon motorcycle riders and others had special clothing.[13] Special aviation clothing developed to satisfy the needs of high-altitude

Fig. 65-13.

Fig. 65-14.

Fig. 65-14. *The captain on the left wears the roll-collar short overcoat permitted as of 1917. Regulations only required that it be double-breasted, have a 6-inch roll collar, and have two outside lower pockets. Second from the left, the major wears a trench coat, which was not mentioned in regulations but nevertheless was widely worn by officers and made popular during World War I.*

and open-cockpit flying is beyond the scope of this overview.

Short coats, or mackinaws, became standard for many ground troops. Officers were allowed a short, double-breasted sheepskin coat for field wear, while enlisted men were issued mackinaws.[14] Officers and men bought coats of widely varying lengths and styles, so by the end of the war coats of virtually every description were in use (Figs. 65-14 through 65-19).

After the close of World War I the army tried to tighten uniform regulations, and short overcoats disappeared as a result. During the mid-1920s revised uniform regulations included officers' overcoats in two varieties. The first was an optional short, double-breasted version with a smooth shawl collar, three sets of buttons, and a belt that used two additional buttons. This generally described the short overcoat widely used during World War I. The second coat was a long, double-breasted, olive drab wool model with three pairs of buttons. Unlike the World War I version, it had a notched lapel and shoulder loops. For Air Corps officers, between 1926 and 1941 the coat had horizontally opening patch pockets, while other coats had vertically opening, inside-hung pockets. During 1943 it was declared obsolete. Enlisted men's coats did not change greatly between the world wars. In 1927 a lapel version was introduced, but the phase-in period took eight years (Fig. 65-20). During the 1930s many of the World War I–style overcoats were issued to enlisted men in transit status to ensure that they had overcoats.[15]

During World War II, as during World War I, a large variety of coats was introduced for

Fig. 65-15.

Fig. 65-15. *An enlisted man of the 13th U.S. Cavalry in 1917, wearing a short overcoat similar to the enlisted men's mackinaw authorized in December 1917. Use of such short overcoats was influenced by officers, as shown in Fig. 65-14, as well as the practicality of a short coat on horseback. During World War I the Quartermaster Corps issued mackinaws to some troops.*

Fig. 65-16. This group of soldiers had their photograph taken at Fort Riley, Kansas, in 1917. The length of overcoats varied widely from the prescribed "8 to 10 inches below the knee." Note the button-down cuff tabs (on the second, third, and fifth men from the left), which were used on the overcoats made early in World War I.

Fig. 65-17. The armed guard wears an overcoat of the style adopted during World War I. The most noticeable distinction is the lack of a tab on the cuff. The captain wears a trench coat with various buckles and strips, a style still popular today.

Fig. 65-16.

various climatic conditions and to accommodate an enormous range of jobs. Some of these coats included various models of mackinaws, which were made in several versions during World War II in an attempt to find a satisfactory coat; trench coats, which at that time were lined with wool and made from water-repellent poplin; and an assortment of arctic parkas and ski coats. Mackinaws, introduced well before World War I, were not well received by military commanders for a variety of reasons, but nevertheless, several olive drab versions, some made from canvas and certain versions with belts, were introduced during World War II. These World War II mackinaws, one of which is shown in Fig. 65-21, usually carried shoulder patches and chevrons.[16]

Other heavy parkas and the like usually carried no insignia. During World War II the army adopted pile material as a substitute for fur and used pile extensively from then on for nonaviation personnel. Pile-lined parka overcoats (with both attached and detachable hoods) came into use, and a number of styles saw service, including white reversible ones and styles of various lengths.[17]

Officers ended World War II with an entirely different set of coats than those with which they started it. Generally, by the war's end officers wore two varieties of overcoats. The first was the double-breasted short coat with notched lapel. The 1943 version was without a belt, unlike the 1926 coat, which was still in use at the start of World War II. This short coat, including the special sleeve trim used by general officers,

Fig. 65-17.

Fig. 65-18.

Fig. 65-18. *Two French officers, on the left, joined several American aviators of the Siberian Expeditionary Forces for this photograph. Under harsh winter conditions and wartime exigencies, virtually any heavy coat that approximated olive drab in color was pressed into service.*

Fig. 65-19.

Fig. 65-19. *Officers at the Mounted Service School, 1921. The fourth seated officer from the left is a member of the General Staff Corps, as shown by his rank sleeve knot resting on a black band encircling the sleeve. Each small gold-colored chevron worn on the lower left sleeve represents six months' overseas service during World War I.*

is shown in Fig. 65-22. It became obsolete in July 1952. The second coat was a long, olive green (olive drab shade number two) field coat to which a removable hood could be added. It had two diagonal pockets, just below the belt, covered with pointed flaps; five pairs of buttons to close the coat; and shoulder loops.[18]

Postwar uniform plans included a new overcoat, which was the last of the new articles to be announced in mid-1949. It was a long, grey (shade 79) woolen trench coat with a buttoning yoke on the right front shoulder and a detachable matching cloth belt (Fig. 65-23).[19] This trench coat served as the primary overcoat until the introduction of the green wool overcoat during the late 1960s. Thus, the first ten years' use of the green uniform was accomplished by either the officers' grey overcoat or the enlisted men's long, olive green field overcoat (Fig. 65-24).

Fig. 65-20. Enlisted men entered World War II with this style of overcoat. Adopted in 1927 and phased in between then and 1935, it was modified in 1939 to include a looser fitting back to make it more functional in combat. Except for emergency issue in Europe during the winter of 1944–45, overcoats were not worn in combat by U.S. troops. For winter combat wear soldiers actually wore field and Eisenhower jackets and mackinaws. Metal shortages necessitated that the brass overcoat buttons be replaced by plastic ones during World War II.

Fig. 65-21. A technician fourth grade checks communications lines in front of a demolished pillbox in the Huertgen Forest early in 1945. He wears one of many styles of mackinaws made during World War II. This common style had a wool lining made from blanket material and a canvas outer shell. These were the only heavy winter coats that were to carry chevrons and shoulder patches.

Fig. 65-22. This 1943 photograph shows Major General Sherman Miles (left), wearing the new design of general officers' short overcoat with notched lapel, vertical pockets, and a belt only in the back, presenting a medal to Brigadier General Daniel Noce, who wears the older roll-collar coat with buttoned belt. Only general officers wore black cuff trim on their overcoats during and after World War II.

Fig. 65-20.

Fig. 65-21.

Fig. 65-22.

Fig. 65-23.

Fig. 65-24.

Fig. 65-23. *An officers' gray trench coat worn during the 1950s and most of the 1960s.*

Fig. 65-24. *Enlisted men of the Korean War–Vietnam War period wore this style of poplin field overcoat. During the Vietnam War this overcoat was replaced by a green wool version worn by both enlisted men and officers.*

Chapter Sixty-Six

Light Outer Garments

Many miscellaneous outer garments are included in this chapter, including raincoats and ponchos, rain suits, jerkins, sweaters, and twentieth-century waist-length jackets. Not all of this type of clothing carried insignia, but it is useful to mention them both for completeness and to acknowledge a lack of insignia on some of this clothing. Some clothing that might fit in this chapter is covered elsewhere, since it better fits that other section. Field jackets are discussed in Chapter 64, "Work and Fatigue Clothing," and the common uniform coats are in Section XVII, "Nineteenth-Century Coats" and Section XIX, "Coats Used in the Twentieth Century."

Rain Garments

Starting in 1855 dragoons received raincoats (called talmas in contemporary regulations), and these were later extended to some other mounted troops.[1] During the Civil War most troops, including mounted troops, were issued ponchos after talmas fell into disfavor. From then into the next century officers and men wore privately purchased raincoats on an optional basis, although frequently all enlisted men should have worn ponchos, according to regulations. At first raincoats were usually rubber, later they were of rubberized material, and in the twentieth century they were often olive green or drab. At the time of World War I they were known at times as slickers. Insignia were not worn on them.

The Quartermaster Corps issued raincoats for mounted cavalry and artillery troops for the first time in 1908.[2] According to this pattern, used during World War I, enlisted soldiers' raincoats had metal buckles of the style used on overshoes. As in the case of overcoats, several versions of raincoats for both mounted and unmounted men existed. The mounted troops' patterns accommodated wear on horseback and were more voluminous, with a box pleat up the back, ending just above the waist, and sometimes with two sets of fasteners to allow for tight or loose adjustment. A patch pocket with a flap was on the right, and some versions had a flap and slit on the left to accommodate a saber. The unmounted soldiers' version had a slit in the pocket to allow access to the trousers, a yoke or capelike piece across the back, and no box pleat.

Several versions of both mounted and unmounted soldiers' raincoats, including designs made in 1935 and 1938, were issued between the world wars to enlisted men. These later designs retained the large collars of the World War I raincoats but adopted buttons instead of the galoshes-style fasteners. The 1938 model had pouchlike pockets. During World War II raincoats of a cleaner, simpler design came into use, and the differences between the mounted and unmounted styles disappeared. These 1940s raincoats were made from a matte material instead of the earlier natural rubber surface.[3]

Officers could continue to purchase raincoats of a commercial pattern that were "of an appropriate color" until 1959, although the outer shell of the long field overcoat was also intended to serve as an officers' raincoat. In 1955 the army introduced a new taupe raincoat of cotton coated on both sides with synthetic rubber and with no between-shoulders vent. Soldiers complained that this version was too "steamy," because the material held air, and sweat could not evaporate. The official taupe raincoat became obsolete in mid-1971, replaced by a green version starting in 1964.[4]

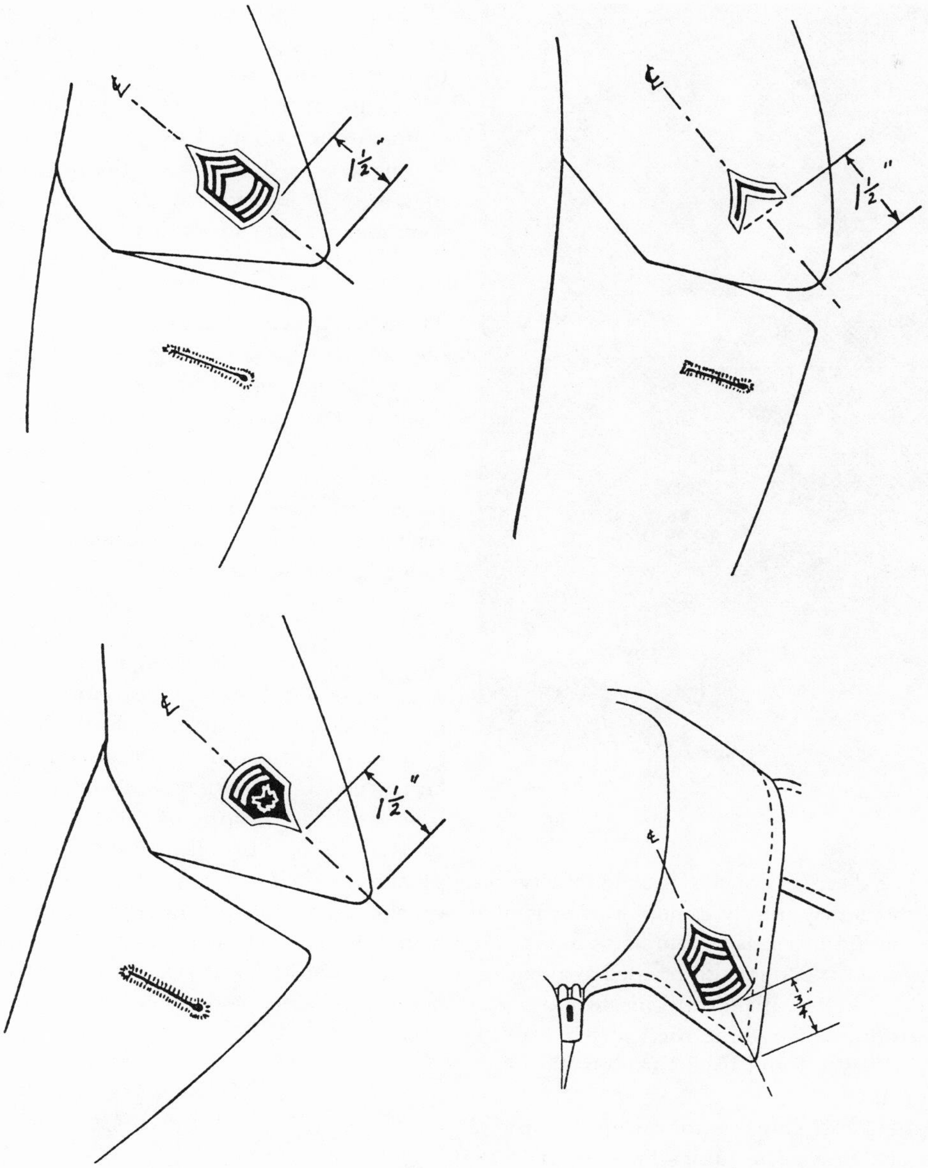

Fig. 66-1.

***Fig. 66-1.** Many lightweight garments used in the 1960s, including raincoats, windbreakers, and overcoats, did not carry any metal insignia other than officers' rank. In late 1967 the Department of the Army approved black metal chevrons for enlisted personnel to wear on the collar tips of fatigue uniforms and other garments. These black metal chevrons caused recognition problems, so in 1971 white plastic backings were placed behind the black rank pins on uniforms other than fatigue shirts and field jackets. These, and the subsequent bright brass chevrons, went on collars as shown, bisecting the collar tip.*

Enlisted soldiers wore all of these various raincoats without insignia, but officers added rank on the end of the shoulder straps. During the Vietnam War the army introduced the small black metal chevrons for field clothing, and troops added the enlisted rank insignia to raincoat collars. Between 1971 and 1975 white plastic backgrounds went behind the small black rank devices so that the insignia would stand out (Fig. 66-1). In February 1975 the army authorized bright brass insignia for use on overcoats, raincoats, and windbreakers.

A new outer coat was finally introduced at the end of 1978 when the army gave male soldiers a combination overcoat and raincoat. Like many outer garments introduced at that time and later, it was black. It included a zip-out liner that allowed the wearer to use it only as a raincoat in warmer weather. The women's version of this garment preceded the men's. On all raincoats, officers wore metal rank insignia on the shoulder loops, while enlisted personnel displayed the small metal rank chevrons on the lapels.[5]

The usual wet-weather gear used by soldiers in the field was the poncho, a rectangular waterproof sheet with a hole in the center so it could be worn over the head. Ponchos saw wide use during the Civil War,

Fig. 66-2. Soldiers wore special rain suits or wet weather gear of various styles for many years, starting with turn-of-the-century oilskin clothing used on mine planting boats associated with harbor defense. Widespread use of armored vehicles and amphibious operations during World War II caused adoption of olive drab, waterproof overalls and pullover jackets. The army adopted them from the navy, and the only markings on this clothing used by the army, until the adoption of this style of wet weather gear in the 1960s, was the previous owners' USN.

Fig. 66-3. A light tank in the rear of the 28th Division, Bouresville, France, 25 October 1918. The officer and the sergeant on the left wear leather jerkins. Some men decorated their jerkins with drawings, especially after the armistice.

Fig. 66-4. Army troops received sweaters before World War I, but except for enlisted chevrons, after World War I sweaters carried no insignia until the introduction of black pullover sweaters in 1981. These sweaters carried shoulder marks showing ranks and on the right chest a black plastic name tag and distinctive insignia.

Fig. 66-2.

as noted earlier. Ponchos issued in the twentieth century usually came with an integral hood and often had grommets around the edge so they could also be used as a tent or other shelter. Black oilskin clothing was introduced for some men just before World War I and used through World War II.[6]

In 1942 some amphibious troops received navy rain suits, which consisted of a short pullover-style jacket with integral hood and bib-style overalls.[7] The army issued these rain suits, complete with U.S. Navy markings, as late as the mid-1960s to armored force troops. During the Vietnam War lighter-weight rain suits without markings were issued (Fig. 66-2). No insignia were used on ponchos or rain suits.

Jerkins

These sleeveless garments made of leather or of wool saw wide service during World War I. Many photographs of troops in Europe show them wearing this garment when working. No insignia were to be worn on them, but after the close of the war shoulder patches occasionally were sewed to the chest. Surplus leather jerkins were issued to enlisted men up to the start of World War II (Fig. 66-3).[8]

Sweaters

Most people usually do not visualize sweaters as a part of a military "image," but sweaters have been a part of army uniforms in this century, and on two occasions insignia have been added to the sweaters. For cold-weather field use only, troops of 1911 received sweaters for wear over flannel shirts. On the sweaters enlisted men wore chevrons, but as on the shirts of the time, there were no branch insignia. During World War I other sweaters appeared, and aviators and motorcycle messengers wore special sweaters but

Fig. 66-3.

Fig. 66-4.

Fig. 66-5.

Fig. 66-5. World War II armored force men wearing lined, winter-weight jackets especially made for armored crewmen. They also wear matching special "field trousers." On the jacket the commander (top center, squatting) wears chevrons and a shoulder patch in the same manner as on other uniforms. In some armor units men sewed "shoulder" patches to the left chest.

without insignia, sweater chevrons having been eliminated in 1917.[9]

Sweaters subsequently prescribed were worn without insignia until 1981, when the black pullover sweater was adopted. Officers and noncommissioned officers began to wear cloth shoulder marks on that sweater to show rank (Fig. 66-4).[10]

Crew Jackets

Jackets of various styles were introduced during World War II. After Hitler's blitzkreig, the United States seriously expanded its minuscule armored force, and for use in tanks the army introduced armored force winter uniforms. Winter armored force combat jackets, trousers, and helmets were first issued during the winter of 1941–42.[11] Examples are shown in Figs. 66-5 and 66-6.

The jackets in particular were popular. After the war the armored force jacket was rescinded, but many soldiers privately purchased these so-called "tankers' jackets," and as such these commercial versions survived into the 1980s, when specialized combat vehicle crew uniforms were reintroduced. Armored force jackets were waist-length, with knit elastic at the bottom and around the cuffs. They were designed to prevent any loose material from catching on protruding pieces of metal inside the fighting compartment. Insignia were of the same type and placement as on field jackets, except that frequently tank crew members wore "shoulder" patches on the left chest instead of the shoulder.

Aviation personnel had a wide range of flight jackets and intermediate-weight jackets. Many flight versions were made of leather, and most of them were lined, while the intermediate-weight jackets were normally cloth. A good number of the designs incorporated elastic cuffs and waists like those of the armored force jackets, although some, especially the heavier versions, had straight cuffs and waists.

Leather aviation jackets originated before World War I and reached the peak of their popularity during World War II. During most of that time the army had few rules for wearing insignia on these jackets. This hole in regulations allowed for some of the most colorful insignia of World War II. Many officers wore rank insignia on the shoulder loops of the jackets. Beyond this, jackets carried shoulder patches, including printed versions of the Army Air Force patch, as well as American flags on the sleeve just below the shoulder seam. Unique to aviation jackets were large, colorful squadron patches, usually painted on leather or heavily

Fig. 66-6.

Fig. 66-6. Three members of the 15th Cavalry Reconnaissance Squadron in front of their armored car in Germany in March 1945. All three men wear armor crew member jackets, which continued to be used unofficially into the late 1970s, when the army again began to issue "tankers' jackets." The man on the right wears an armored crewmen's helmet.

Fig. 66-7.

Fig. 66-7. *These two fighter pilots wear typical leather flight jackets, but they have applied their insignia differently. The captain on the left has a minimum of insignia: only his large squadron patch on the jacket front. His rank and branch are on his shirt collar. The captain on the right has a leather name tag with his name in three languages above his squadron patch, rank on the jacket shoulder loops, and shoulder patches on each upper sleeve. A wide range of leather flying jackets and insignia combinations were commonly used during World War II.*

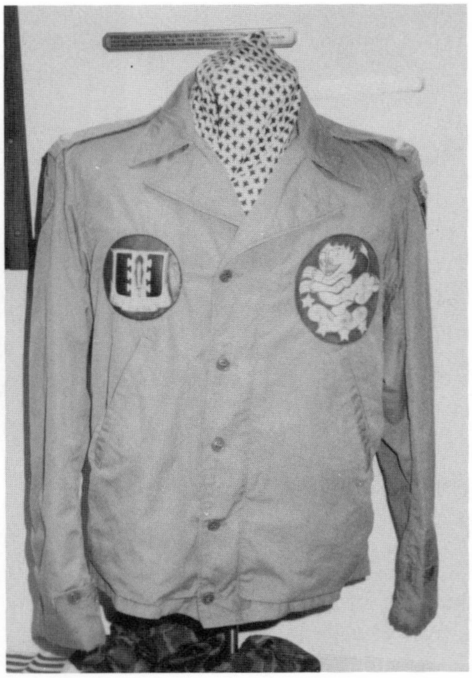

Fig. 66-8.

Fig. 66-8. *Army Air Force crew members of World War II often added more than one large unit patch to their flight jackets. This example is a cloth 1941 field jacket used in the Far East. It has a patch of the China, Burma, India Theater on the left shoulder, a Tenth Air Force patch on the right shoulder, lieutenants' bars, and two flying unit patches.*

Fig. 66-9.

Fig. 66-9. *Army aviators continued the practice, almost as old as flight itself, of wearing jackets, because such clothing was very functional in cramped cockpits. This flight jacket, worn in Vietnam, continues the tradition of displaying large, colorful unit patches on the chest.*

embroidered, worn on the left chest. Examples of leather jackets are shown in Fig. 38-52 of chapter 38, "Aviation," and in Fig. 66-7, while a cloth field jacket converted to a makeshift light jacket with various insignia is shown in Fig. 66-8. In the Far East, some 14th Air Force members wore so-called "blood chits" or "escape flags" on the back or inside their leather jackets. These multilingual devices offered a reward for the return of downed airmen and included a Chinese Nationalist flag.

After World War II, with the advent of the separate U.S. Air Force, army aviators went their own way. Flying needs caused these light aircraft pilots and crewmen to again adopt cloth jackets with elastic at waist and cuffs. Insignia were the same as those used on field clothing. An exception was that aviators could wear a small leather rectangle embossed with their name, rank, and aviator wings, and when this was done, usually shoulder patches and other insignia were not worn. A carryover from the World War II Army Air Force tradition was the use of large cloth aviation patches on the chest of these flight jackets (Fig. 66-9).

WINDBREAKERS

The army introduced lightweight green windbreakers for optional use in 1971 as part of the changes made in the 1970s and early 1980s that historically can be viewed as an introduction of new uniforms that normally occurs every twenty to thirty years.[12] The army was right on historical schedule, since the green uniform had come into service in the mid-1950s. The windbreaker replaced the field jacket in some circumstances. Cooks and medical personnel who wore special white short-sleeved work uniforms indoors had used field jackets in inclement weather. At some locations soldiers also wore field jackets with khaki uniforms during cool weather. The new windbreaker replaced the field jacket under these circumstances. When green shirts and trousers replaced the khaki shirts and trousers during the late 1970s, windbreakers (and soon the black pullover sweaters already described) were the prescribed outer garments.

The color of the first green windbreaker was ill-conceived. The army immediately moved to many black outer garments, and the green windbreaker could only be used until the end of September 1983. Almost immediately a black windbreaker was authorized, and it continued until 30 September 1993.[13]

Windbreakers officially could be worn by officers and enlisted troops with the army tan uniform, the various army green shirts when worn as outer garments, and with white food service and hospital clothing. Both were slightly longer than the wearer's waist, with the black version cut slightly longer to prevent the jacket from riding up to the belt. Diagonal slash pockets were just above the waist, and both jackets had lapel collars and shoulder loops. Only bright-colored metal rank insignia went on officers' windbreaker shoulder loops. Enlisted personnel wore metal chevrons on the collar, as on the raincoats: black metal chevrons with white plastic backing from 1971 until that style was replaced by bright metal chevrons in 1975. The jacket was to be worn zippered at least three-fourths of the way up (Fig. 66-10).

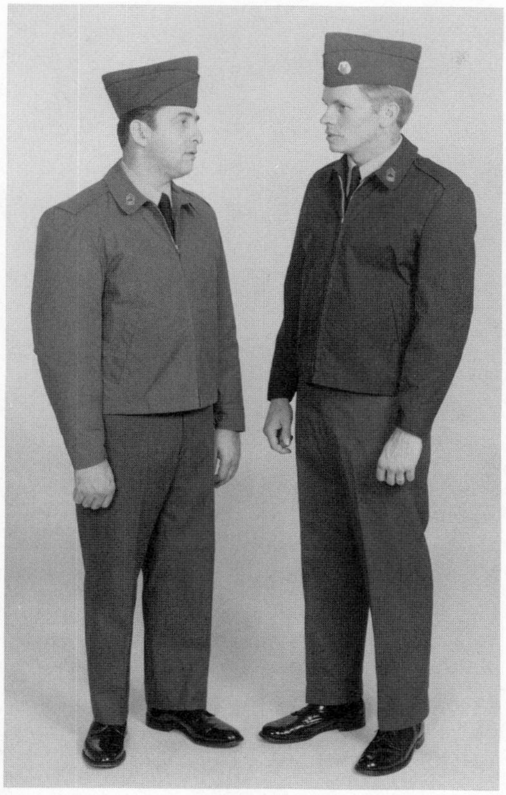

Fig. 66-10.

Fig. 66-10. *Two army windbreakers used in 1980. The one on the left is the green model, which became obsolete in 1983. It was slightly shorter at the waist than the black model (right), which would be worn until 1993. Officers wore rank insignia on the shoulder loops, while enlisted men used small metal chevrons on the collar tips. In 1975 the bright brass chevrons shown replaced the black metal versions introduced during the Vietnam War.*

In late 1989 the army changed windbreaker styles and brought out two versions: one for enlisted personnel and another for officers. The officers' windbreaker had a knit collar, cuffs, and waistband. Rank went on the shoulder loops. The enlisted troops' version also had knit cuffs and waistband, but it had a lapel collar for placement of the pin-on, bright metal chevrons. Black remained the color.[14]

Chapter Sixty-Seven

Shirts

Shirts had been worn for years, yet regulations scarcely mention them, because coats were always to be worn over them. Shirts were not to carry insignia until the late nineteenth century. The style of shirts is not often considered by military collectors, reenactors, and movie costumers today, yet styles changed along with insignia and insignia placement.

Nineteenth-Century Shirts

Contemporary nineteenth-century accounts often tell of rough-looking soldiers wearing outdoorsmen's shirts as part of their uniform. Although soldiers frequently wore shirts as outer garments on the western frontier, the generals in Washington did not intend for troops to use these shirts as part of the formal uniform any more than underwear or socks were a significant part of the uniform. Early shirts are thus not described in regulations.

A brief overview of shirts may be helpful before discussing the insignia and their relationship to shirts. From the end of the War of 1812 through the Mexican War, privates and sergeants were issued both cotton and flannel shirts of a single size. The pullover style shirts had a simple rectangular collar with a single button at the neck and a single button at the cuff. Shirt material changed to flannel in the early 1850s, although the style did not change, and during the Civil War several types of shirt were issued, although according to the Woodhull report the army had three official types: white flannel, blue gray flannel, and knit. (This report, published by the Surgeon General in 1868, was a digest of medical officers' and "professional men's" opinion on army uniforms.) Wear of shirts as outer garments was confined to work details in hot weather. Some officers added shoulder straps to their shirts when on the frontier on campaign, but there was no uniformity and often no other attempt to place insignia on them.

Insignia began to creep into use with shirts on the post–Civil War frontier. In 1881 the then-current enlisted men's gray flannel shirt was replaced by a new dark blue "overshirt" that was piped with branch-colored cord around the lower collar edge and the upper cuff. For the first year (January 1881 to February 1882) these shirts had gilt buttons. No other insignia went on the shirts. Sergeants and corporals were distinguished only by their trouser stripes, because they did not wear chevrons on shirts. In 1883 the branch braid was ordered removed, in part because of fading onto the dark blue shirt material. The new blue shirts were of the pullover pattern, were closed with three hard rubber buttons, and had a buttoned pocket on each breast. This dark blue shirt is shown in Fig. 77-1 of chapter 77, "White Uniforms."[1]

The Spanish-American War prodded the army into some decisions and official action on the shirt "problem." Finally the army specifically allowed the wearing of shirts without coats in the field, as had actually been done for many years, and in July 1898 a ruling by the secretary of war permitted officers to place rank on their shirt collars. Noncommissioned officers added the nearly 1-foot-wide chevrons to shirts worn as outer garments, and this practice eventually led in 1901 to smaller chevrons made specifically for shirts. Dark blue wool was not a comfortable summer shirt material in the heat of the American West or in the tropics, and finally in

Fig. 67-1.

1902 chambray (woven blue and white cotton) became the standard cloth, although khaki shirts were first made in 1900. Cut similar to the previous dark blue models, chambray and later olive drab shirts were of the pullover style (Figs. 67-1 and 67-2). After experimenting with various shirts such as woolen khaki ones in the Philippines in 1901 and 1902, olive drab shirts replaced chambray blue between 1902 and 1907.[2]

Olive Drab Shirts

Olive drab shirts were of the pullover style, a holdover from the previous century. Although civilian shirts were of the coat style, the army hesitated to change. In 1924 officers' shirts added shoulder loops to prevent the Sam Browne belt from slipping off the shoulder. This distinguishing feature separates officers' post–World War I shirts from the enlisted men's. After World War I and until 1938 soldiers could not officially wear shirts as outer garments except as prescribed by the local commander, although after 1934 all men in the Panama Canal Department had been allowed to do so. This meant that men wore shirts as outer garments on post and in the field.[3]

A change in cut occurred in 1934, when the quartermaster general introduced enlisted men's shirts that buttoned completely up the front. These coat-style shirts eliminated the need for the wearer to put them on over his head and represented a significant evolution in clothing (Fig. 67-3). Whatever other changes might occur, such as material, color, or sleeve length, subsequent shirts were always to be of this design. With this change the army authorized khaki cotton shirts to replace olive drab cotton shirts, leaving olive drab shirts to be of wool.[4]

The incongruity of wearing a necktie as part of a combat uniform was not apparent

Fig. 67-2.

Fig. 67-1. *First Lieutenant W. J. Riley, 1907. This is a typical officers' olive drab field uniform used early in the twentieth century. All military shirts of the period were of the pullover style, but there conformity ends. Shoulder loops were not prescribed. Regulations of 1902 called for officers to wear rank insignia on shirt collars. Civilian social customs dictated ties with shirts for gentlemen, and this practice carried over into the army.*

Fig. 67-2. *Officers on the Mexican border before World War I. There were no neckties for this group. Even so, their collars, carrying rank insignia, are buttoned. These are regulation shirts and have pocket flaps and reinforced elbows, unlike Lieutenant Riley's shirt shown in Fig. 67-1. Only the officer on the far right wears his collar insignia in accordance with regulations.*

Fig. 67-3. Lieutenant R. T. Huntington of the 16th Infantry during the period of President Roosevelt's limited emergency before World War II. He wears an olive drab wool shirt as a field uniform, with US insignia on the right collar and an infantry insignia on the left collar. Rank is on the cloth shoulder loops, as on coats. Officers' shirts were the only ones to have cloth shoulder loops until well after World War II. Enlisted men received coat-style shirts instead of the pullover style in 1934.

Fig. 67-4. U.S. Constabulary troops in Fulda, Germany, about 1949. Left to right: a master sergeant in winter shirt and trousers with special leather belt and helmet liner worn by the Constabulary; General I. D. White, commanding general, in an Eisenhower jacket; and Captain Charles A. Gill, also in the winter wool shirt and trousers but without the special Constabulary accoutrement. Insignia placement had changed after World War II, so officers' rank went on the right collar. Branch insignia remained on the left collar, and the shoulder loop now held distinctive insignia.

Fig. 67-5. Khaki uniforms in use, September 1945. The master sergeant (left) and the private (center) wear shirts without collar insignia and without cloth shoulder loops, as was proper at that time. The shirt of the officer (right) has both of these features. The Liscum Bowl they are examining was made from ninety pounds of silver in Yokohama shortly after the Boxer Rebellion, when the Chinese government donated the silver to the 9th Infantry. The bowl is named for the regiment's commander during the Boxer Rebellion, who was killed in combat.

Fig. 67-3.

Fig. 67-4.

to early-twentieth-century soldiers. Pershing is often pictured in Mexico during 1916 wearing a necktie. World War I did not see men wear shirts as outer garments in Europe, but the use of neckties continued well into World War II. General Patton and others enforced the wear of neckties during wartime in some units. Even after World War II men often continued to wear a necktie as part of the field uniform or for a more formal activity when the coat was inappropriate. This was a holdover from turn-of-the-century formality. When used in these circumstances, after World War II the tie was tucked into the shirt front between the second and third buttons (Figs. 67-3 and 67-4). Tucking the tie into khaki shirts continued until 1966.

Shirts after World War II

Men in some units frequently did not wear ties with their shirts. A 1945 example is shown in Fig. 67-5. After World War II many soldiers frequently wore shirts, especially khaki ones, as outer garments without ties.

Several changes in shirts occurred after World War II besides the introduction of new colors and materials. Enlisted men's shirts gained shoulder loops in 1949. Short-sleeved khaki shirts were authorized in 1956, and their collars laid flat. Until that time, shirt collars remained generally upright even when the neck button was not fastened. When long-sleeved cotton khaki and army tan tropical worsted shirts became obsolete as outer garments in 1966, the army authorized men to modify the long-sleeved shirts to short-sleeved versions.[5]

Uniform changes resulted in the final elimination of branch insignia on shirt collars after the end of the Vietnam War, when the green uniform totally replaced khaki. With the tropical worsted (TW) coat abandoned in 1968, long-sleeved TW shirts, which had been worn by many officers instead of cotton khaki, became obsolete. Only TW short-sleeved shirts remained (used with TW trousers), and they were worn in the same way as short-sleeved khaki uniforms. In addition to the cotton khaki uniforms, the army brought out a durable-press version known as shade 445. All three uniforms that included short-sleeved khaki-colored shirts (cotton khaki, TW, and shade 445) continued until they were totally replaced by the green uniforms when the khaki wearout period ended in September 1985.[6]

Note that with the short-sleeved shirt introduced in 1956 came khaki shorts and tan knee socks, which comprised the abbreviated cotton uniform. Shorts were phased out in the 1960s, leaving just the short-sleeved shirt, as noted (Fig. 67-6). Short-sleeved khaki shirts were authorized with long khaki trousers in 1959, and by the summer of 1966 the long-sleeved cotton khaki shirt was obsolete, replaced by the short-sleeved version.

The short-sleeved shirts came in two basic styles. First was the style with pleats down the pockets and with slightly scalloped pocket flaps. A later versions had flat pockets and flaps that were straight across the bottom but with clipped corners.

Initially the army green uniform was not worn without the coat, but in 1978 the army approved a green shirt to replace the tan one, and this changed the uniform concept. The new green shirts came in both long- and short-sleeved versions, and while the tie and coat combination could be worn with both shirts, they could also serve as outer garments without the coat. The short-sleeved shirt could be worn without the tie, although the long-sleeved shirt had to be accompanied by the necktie. On both green shirts officers wore rank on cloth shoulder marks, and enlisted personnel initially placed small metal rank insignia on their collars. No branch insignia were used. First wear of the shirts army-wide was in 1979 (Fig. 67-7). In December 1988 the chief of staff approved wear of awards and decorations on recruiters' greens shirts, and the following month this practice was expanded to all troops.[7]

Insignia on Shirts

Insignia worn on shirts have a history of size and placement that is often not fully appreciated, especially because the small shirt collars eventually influenced the size of insignia worn on the lapel coats. The combination and placement of rank insignia, letters *US* (and variants), and branch insignia have varied on shirts throughout the twentieth century. From 1898 until 1916 officers' metal

Fig. 67-5.

Fig. 67-6.

Fig. 67-7.

Fig. 67-6. *The 1956 regulation illustration of the abbreviated cotton khaki uniform. On these shirts, the collar laid flat against the shirt body instead of standing up. Similar shorts with knee socks had been worn during World War II at various Caribbean stations.*

Fig. 67-7. *Green shirts worn by enlisted personnel in the early 1980s, with and without ties. Branch insignia completely disappeared from enlisted soldiers' shirts when the green uniform finally caused the phase-out of khaki-colored uniforms. Shirts made of a slightly heavier material and with pleated pockets were approved in 1990, and these appeared in 1991.*

rank insignia were placed on the shirt collar, although in 1914 second lieutenants, having no rank insignia at that time, wore bronze insignia of their arm or service.[8]

In 1916 branch and *US* insignia appeared. Three 1917 regulation examples are shown in Figs. 67-8, 67-9, and 67-10. On the small shirt collars then in use, the coat-sized insignia were too large to fit neatly. As a consequence, use of miniature insignia made expressly for wear on shirt collars became widespread before World War I. The War Department finally recognized this common practice and the solution of putting undersized insignia on small collars. In October 1918 the army allowed diminutive shirt collar devices and eliminated the *US* insignia.[9]

Fig. 67-8.

Fig. 67-8. *Congress, with the 1916 National Defense Act, brought major changes to the National Guard and the reserves, which in turn caused changes in the shirt collar insignia. Shown is the placement for a line brigadier general. For a staff general such as the quartermaster general, the star on the left collar would have been replaced by the appropriate staff insignia. Full-sized insignia initially designed for the larger coat collar were used in this photograph.*

Fig. 67-9.

Fig. 67-9. *From 1916 until 1923, company- and field-grade officers wore rank (first lieutenant), component (reserves), and branch (Medical Corps) in this manner. All insignia shown are of the small size made especially for shirts.*

The exact size of these insignia varied widely until the 1920s, despite army attempts to specify proper dimensions. Regulations of October 1921, for example, stated that the officers' collar insignia for olive drab shirts "may be of small size, approximately 3/4 the linear dimensions of the full size." Regulations of 1924 and later clearly called out the size for shirt collar insignia, which became the same size as the insignia for the new lapel coat for most branches after 1926. In 1924 rank insignia moved to the new shoulder loops, and the branch insignia and *US* remained on the collar, but in August 1942 the rank replaced the *US* on the right collar, leaving the branch on the left. This practice continued on fatigue shirts and is the pattern on them to this time.[10]

Enlisted men's shirts and their collar insignia also varied over time. In December 1916 the War Department prescribed bronze collar disks on the olive drab shirts, worn as on the coat (Fig. 67-11). By regulation, enlisted men's shirts carried disks until the mid-1920s, when their use was again restricted to the service coat (Fig. 67-12).[11]

It was not until 1947 that enlisted troops' collar insignia, with fastening tines on the reverse, returned to the shirt. In the interim, enlisted men wore bare collars. An example from World War II is shown in Fig. 67-13.

Fig. 67-10.

Fig. 67-10. *In late 1916 and early 1917 National Guard troops wore state abbreviations to show their component instead of the USR or US used by regulars or reserves.*

Men put *US* disks on the right and branch insignia on the left, with the vertical line of the disk parallel to the front collar edge (Fig. 67-14). This same placement continued even when the necktie became optional. Initially the insignia remained placed the same with the reference to the front collar edge, so when the collar was worn open, insignia were tilted about 90 degrees to 100 degrees in relation to the horizon. Finally, in 1975 enlisted soldiers' collar insignia were rotated to the positions shown in Fig. 67-15.[12]

Note that it was not until June 1938, when War Department circular number 32 was published, that service ribbons could be worn on shirts. This initial authorization was for khaki shirts only, while the olive drab service shirt, like overcoats and field clothing, remained without ribbons or badges.

White Shirts

White shirts have been authorized for dress wear during the twentieth century, starting

Fig. 67-11.

with optional use at the end of 1926 with the new lapel service coat. At that time the War Department authorized white shirts and black neckties for off-duty wear by enlisted men. This ruling was widened in 1931 so that when directed, enlisted men wore white shirts on duty. This practice continued until 1936.[13]

Officers began to wear white shirts with the lapel coat, "at official or social functions, when out of quarters after retreat, or whenever ordered," and the white shirt could also be worn when not under arms.[14] Because of this provision, many officers wore the white shirt with the olive drab and khaki lapel coats between the world wars.

Fig. 67-13.

With the dress blue and white lapel coats men also wore white shirts, and after the introduction of the army green uniform in the 1950s, enlisted men in some units wore white shirts on formal occasions until this practice was sanctioned army-wide in 1975.[15]

Cooks and bakers wore various white uniforms that were not mentioned in regula-

Fig. 67-12.

Fig. 67-11. *A World War I private wearing his shirt with bronze-colored collar disks, as called for after October 1918.*

Fig. 67-12. *This unit had the men wearing collar insignia on their shirts in field training during the late 1920s. Note that the troops are wearing neckties tucked into the shirt front in this field environment.*

Fig. 67-13. *A World War II technician 5th grade. Enlisted men wore no collar insignia on the shirt, which was without shoulder loops. The necktie was tucked into the shirt between the second and third buttons. This practice continued whenever the long-sleeved khaki shirt was used with a necktie.*

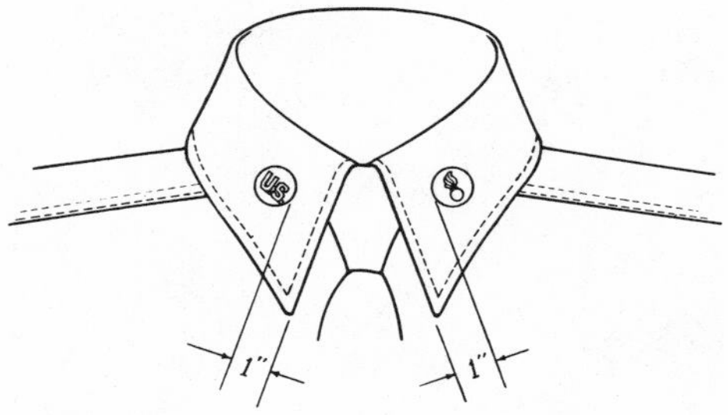

Fig. 67-14.

Fig. 67-14. *Insignia placement on the collar of the shirt for enlisted personnel, as introduced in 1947.*

tions until after World War II. Even as late as the 1970s regulations were usually silent on this clothing, which consisted of white short-sleeved shirts and white trousers. During this period mess sergeants often wore chevrons on the sleeves of their white work shirts. In 1975 white work uniforms for medical and food service personnel were prescribed to carry rank insignia on the collar, like other shirts: bright metal rank and branch for officers and subdued metal chevrons for enlisted soldiers' uniforms.[16]

Fig. 67-15.

Fig. 67-15. *This drill sergeant wears a durable-press tan (shade 445) summer uniform, which was authorized until 1986. The collar insignia were rotated in 1975 so that the horizontal axes were parallel to the ground, while previously the insignia's vertical axes were parallel to the inside collar edge, as were those of officers' insignia.*

Section XIX

Coats Used in the Twentieth Century

Chapter Sixty-Eight

Early Khaki Uniforms

The army introduced an officers' khaki cotton uniform in May 1898.[1] Called a "field service uniform," it was the first uniform for which the army had used the word *field* in its title. Significantly, the intended use of the uniform shows the increased sophistication of the army. Its use was soon extended to enlisted men, and it supplemented the blue field uniform. In general the various versions of coats were slightly fitted, with a standing or standing-falling collar, five yellow metal buttons, and four patch pockets with buttoned flaps, two on the chest and two at the waist. The coat was short, just covering the hips (Fig. 68-1).

During several years many variations of the khaki field service uniform were made. The Spanish-American War and subsequent military activities accelerated demands, and the Quartermaster's Department could not enforce a standard design or even a uniform color. Because of these problems, the many minor variations in issue coats cannot be easily documented today. Perhaps the easiest way to easily distinguish versions is to note the shape of the pocket flaps. Officers' khaki clothing varied even more widely (Figs. 68-2 and 68-3).

Initially the cuffs, pocket flaps, and shoulder loops were trimmed in branch colors

Fig. 68-1. *Off to the local town, these soldiers wear two of many khaki uniform pattern variations introduced during and immediately after the Spanish-American War. For a few years at the turn of the century, shirt collars were worn stylishly high. Note that the private (left) is wearing striped shirt cuffs.*

Fig. 68-2. *An official army photograph of an infantry officers' 1899 khaki coat with white shoulder loops. The insignia are properly placed, which was often not the case for volunteer units. The pocket flaps are unusual in that they are rather pointed.*

Fig. 68-1.

Fig. 68-2.

(Fig. 68-4), but this caused supply problems, because not only sizes but also branch needs had to be considered when the coats were ordered. In August 1898, three months after initial introduction of the coat, specifications for its trim changed so that in most cases only shoulder loops (called shoulder straps in the contemporary regulations) showed branch. Officers' colors were the usual for artillery and cavalry, with dark blue for generals and the staff corps. Infantry had light blue in 1898 and 1899 and then switched to white. For enlisted men the colors were more varied, as listed in Table 68-1. Chevrons also indicated arm or service. After 1902, khaki loops replaced the colored versions (Figs. 68-5 and 68-6).[2]

The khaki tropical field uniforms were used in Cuba, Puerto Rico, and the Philippines almost immediately, as well as at southern posts in the United States. Besides being a cooler color and fabric, the khaki uniform was an initial move towards concealment, a result of the development of better rifles and smokeless powder. Several changes to the uniforms were not described in quartermaster specifications, and the many variants included standing, falling, and standing-falling collars. Paperwork finally caught up with practices when a standing-falling collar was called for in December 1902 regulations and subsequently described in 1903 specifications.[3]

Khaki service coats lasted until June 1912, when olive drab became the sole color for field use. This is one of the few cases in which the wearout period did not last long. Even in the Philippine Islands, where almost every-

Fig. 68-3.

Fig. 68-3. *Artillery officers of the Spanish-American War wearing khaki coats. The many different minor variations are most easily seen in the pockets and pocket flaps.*

Fig. 68-4.

Fig. 68-4. *An early 1898 branch-trimmed khaki coat. The pointed cuffs protrude just above this artilleryman's gauntlets. Coat collars were often higher than this example. Many soldiers wore the cap insignia on the hat, as did this soldier. This hat insignia is for the blue-colored bill cap introduced in 1895. Properly, the hat carried only unit numbers and letters besides the hat cord.*

Fig. 68-5.

Fig. 68-5. *An 1898-style khaki coat being worn in 1904 with khaki-colored shoulder loops.*

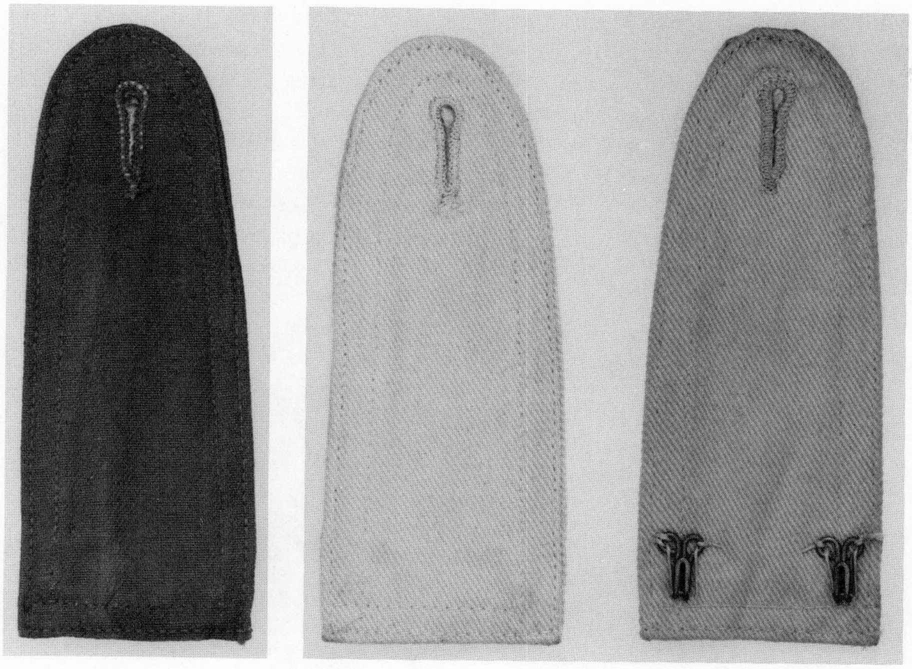

Fig. 68-6.

Fig. 68-6. *Enlisted men's colored shoulder loops for the 1898 khaki coat. Left to right: artillery red; infantry white, and cavalry yellow, turned over to show the two hooks used to fasten the loop to the coat.*

thing else arrived and departed last, khaki was declared obsolete at the end of 1912.[4]

Insignia on Khaki Uniforms

Only officers wore collar insignia on khaki coats, and during the coats' initial months these insignia were either embroidered or metal in many variations, although the army quickly prescribed metal. Brief statements in regulations did little to stifle the overnight warriors of the Spanish-American War. No letters *US* or *USV* were to be worn on the coat collar, but a great many commissioned men disregarded this provision, most notably Teddy Roosevelt, as shown in Fig. 9-61 in chapter 9, "The Letters *US* and State Insignia." Officers below the rank of colonel were to wear rank insignia on their shoulder loop at one-third the distance from the shoulder seam to the collar; midway between this rank insignia and the collar went a U.S. coat of arms (Fig. 68-7). For colonels and generals only, the rank alone went on the shoulder; the coat of arms was placed on each side of the collar near the throat. If these men wore branch insignia, they were placed behind the eagles (Fig. 68-8).[5]

The various enlisted men's insignia that evolved between 1902 and 1912 affected the coat collars, and they are discussed in chapter 69, "Olive Drab Standing-Collar Coats," but a brief summary of the insignia used on the khaki enlisted men's coats is useful at this point. The large-sized bronze-colored collar insignia used by enlisted men in 1902 went on this coat. Various changes were made later

Table 68-1. *Shoulder Loop Colors for Enlisted Men, 1898-Style Khaki Coat.*

Used By	Colors
Infantry (1898–99)	Light blue
Infantry (1899–1902)	White
Cavalry	Yellow
Artillery	Red
Engineers	Red with white edge
Post quartermaster sergeant	White with buff edge
Post commissary sergeant	White with gray edge
Ordnance	Crimson with white edge
Electrician sergeant	Red
Signal Corps	Black with white edge
Hospital Corps	Emerald green

to the 1902-style khaki coats themselves, but insignia were greatly modified. In 1904–1905 smaller bronze insignia replaced the large ones, in 1910 the designs were placed on two pairs of disks, and in 1912 men switched to single disks. Fig. 68-9 shows the 13th Cavalry Band in 1911 during the transition to disk insignia, with band members wearing both styles of insignia on the khaki coats.[6]

Bronze buttons, first introduced in 1902, distinguish successors to the 1898 coat. Officers wore bronze-colored *US* letters and branch insignia placed in the same manner as on the 1895 sack coats and on the olive drab wool coat with standing-falling collar also brought in at the same time.[7]

Fig. 68-7. *Lieutenant colonels and below wore the 1898–1902 eagle insignia on shoulder loops along with rank insignia.*

Fig. 68-8. *Colonels and generals were to wear insignia on the khaki coats, as did this regimental commander in 1902.*

Fig. 68-9. *Regulations called for two pairs of disks on enlisted men's service uniforms between 1910 and 1912. Although many men in this picture have switched to this pattern, a few still wear the previous plain US or lyre collar devices. The large bellows pockets are typical of post-1904 enlisted men's coats, while khaki-colored high-collar uniforms were last issued in 1911.*

Chapter Sixty-Nine

Olive Drab Standing-Collar Coats

The need for camouflage and concealment was conclusively proven to the army during the Spanish-American War. Although the War Department introduced a summer khaki uniform in 1898, soldiers still had only blue clothing for moderate and cold climates. As a result of the war, the quartermaster general conducted experiments at West Point to determine which uniforms would best provide: (1) durability and strength, (2) warmth with least weight, and (3) inconspicuousness.

Wool Coats with Standing and Standing-Falling Collars

Olive drab wool was selected for winter wear to best meet the quartermaster general's criteria. Initial use of this cloth was in the winter service uniform required for wear by officers in 1903. Issue of the new enlisted men's uniforms was severely limited during 1903–1904 as the Philadelphia Depot began production slowly, and most troops actually received their first olive drab wool coats after 1904.[1]

Several variations of this versatile coat were ultimately worn. The 1902 enlisted men's coat had a standing-falling collar and four patch pockets: two on the chest and two starting at the waist. All branches wore this coat, which underwent several modifications, including one in August 1911, when the quartermaster general approved a change to a full standing collar. It was with these pure standing-collar coats that the U.S. Army entered World War I (Fig. 69-1).[2]

Men's military styles moved towards a more spartan, leaner look during the period between the Spanish-American War and World War I. As a result, the service coat began to evolve to a more form-fitting garment that by 1911 had a simple standing collar and pockets that were mere vestiges of their former selves and that certainly were no longer functional in the field. Table 69-1 and Figs. 69-2 through 69-6 summarize the principal enlisted men's coat designs.

One inescapable problem frequently mentioned in these pages is especially troublesome with olive drab wool coats. Several versions were constantly in use at any given time. In a photograph Fig. 69-7 of new troops at Fort Riley, Kansas, in 1908, some troops wear the old five-button nineteenth-century campaign coat that was still issued to recruits, others have the 1902 dress blue uniform with bright collar insignia and still others have the

Fig. 69-1.

Fig. 69-1. *A typical World War I woolen enlisted men's uniform, with the US disk on the right collar and the branch disk, in this case the Air Service, on the left.*

Fig. 69-2. The soldier on the right in the front row wears the first-pattern olive drab uniform, called out in 1902 regulations and detailed in 1903 specifications. The flat chest pockets with pleats down the front distinguish this coat.

olive drab coats with standing-falling collars and new bronze-colored insignia. The frequent changes in cut, coupled with the sudden increase of coats needed during World War I, which in turn caused several sequential changes in techniques of production, made for a myriad of coat designs.

Officers' olive drab wool uniforms of this period generally follow the evolution of enlisted men's coats, although the quality of cloth was considerably better (Fig. 69-8). Materials varied widely, especially after World War I, when whipcord became the predominant cloth in officers' coats. The earliest version of the officers' olive drab coat, adopted in 1902, had a low, turned-down collar, shoulder loops, four flat patch pockets, and plain cuffs. This coat differed from the enlisted men's

Table 69-1. *Versions of the Government-Issued Olive Drab Wool Standing-Collar Coat.*

Year Prescribed	Distinguishing Features
1903	Top pockets have two pleats down center and are sewn flat; bronze buttons; low standing-falling collar (Fig. 69-2).
1904	Similar to 1903 but with four choke bellows pockets; pointed cuffs sewn to sleeve (Fig. 69-3).
1907	More pronounced stand to the standing-falling collar (Fig. 69-4).
1909	Two sewn grommet holes on each side of collar for new bronze "button" insignia (Fig. 69-5).
1911	Straight standing collar; single grommet on each end of collar; no cuffs on sleeves; patch pockets (Fig. 69-1).
1918	All pockets concealed (Fig. 69-6). The 1911 model continued to be made at the same time.
1920	Patch pockets return.
1924	Smooth, whipcordlike material; brass buttons (initially introduced in 1923); long skirts; hooks for leather garrison belt.

NOTE: Changes noted by year: 1903—WD, OQMG, Specification 609; 1904—WD, *Annual Report of the Quartermaster General*, 1904, p. 7; 1907—WD, OQMG, Specification 879; 1909—WD, OQMG, Specification 1049; 1911—WD, *Annual Report of the Quartermaster General*, 1911, p. 30; WD, OQMG, Specification 1126; 1918—Erna Risch, *Quartermaster Support of the Army: A History of the Corps, 1775–1939*, p. 683; 1923—WD, Changes 9, AR 600-35, 16 Oct. 1923; 1924—WD, AR 600-35, 25 Nov. 1924, par. 5a(1).

Fig. 69-2.

version, which had pleated chest pockets initially. The officers' coat featured the new rimless general service buttons, five down the front and one on each pocket flap. Later versions, adopted starting in 1904, were similar but had choke bellows pockets and a somewhat higher "standing-falling" collar.

It was on the olive drab wool service coats and their khaki summer companions that officers' cuff braid first appeared. Starting in June 1905, General Staff Corps officers added a ½-inch-wide black cuff braid 3 inches above the end of the coat sleeve. Two years later all other commissioned officers added a similar stripe in brown (Fig. 69-9).[3] Such bands may not appear in early photographs of these coats.

Unauthorized deviations to various officers' coats occurred frequently. As a practical matter, olive drab coats replaced blue and white dress uniforms early in 1917; thus, an officer's best coat was his service coat. During World War I allied officers influenced Americans, and many U.S. officers altered their coats so that the fit and length varied considerably from the regulation versions. Also during the war, U.S. officers in Europe wore Sam Browne belts with this coat, and after the war this style of belt was adopted

Fig. 69-3.

Fig. 69-4.

Fig. 69-5.

Fig. 69-3. *The 1904 olive drab coat, with low falling collar and four bellows pockets.*

Fig. 69-4. *Corporal Joseph Laskey wears his field artillery first-class gunner badge on his 1907 coat, which was similar to the 1904 version but with a higher collar.*

Fig. 69-5. *The Mounted Service School attracted a cross-section of soldiers from throughout the army. Although all the uniforms shown are generally the same, details of collar and pocket construction vary. A wide range of leggings help to emphasize the general similarity yet diverse uniforms caused by personal preferences and the army's frequent design changes. The soldier on the lowest step and the two leftmost soldiers on the second step up all wear the 1909 coat with grommets for two pairs of bronze collar disks.*

army-wide (Fig. 69-10). The 1923 uniform change that converted buttons and insignia to gilt also lengthened the officers' coats slightly and required two previously optional waistline hooks for the Sam Browne belt. The official postwar coat was to be semi-tailored, with some slight flair at the waist and skirts just covering the hips. The lower (fifth) button was placed to be just below the newly adopted leather belt.[4]

With the introduction of the new 1902 olive drab wool and khaki coats, the army simultaneously introduced enlisted men's dark bronze cut-out branch insignia, as already noted in sections on other coats. But why did the size change just two years later? In his annual report, the commander in the Philippine Islands complained that the collar insignia were too large. Perhaps this complaint caused the January 1904, 15th Cavalry test of smaller collar devices, which the War Department approved for enlisted men in late 1904.[5]

The army prescribed and began to make collar disks for enlisted men's uniforms in

Fig. 69-6. During World War I some coats were made with the pockets hung inside instead of the prewar and postwar patch pockets.

Fig. 69-7. The plethora of uniforms used after 1902 is dramatically portrayed in the 1908 exposure of newly assigned cavalry and artillery soldiers.

Fig. 69-8. This second lieutenant's 1908 olive drab coat, while somewhat similar to enlisted men's coats, was of better quality wool and had 1/2-inch-wide braid on the lower sleeve.

Fig. 69-9. An officers' olive drab wool coat with gilt buttons and insignia as worn after 1923. After learning of British regimental badges during World War I, General Pershing allowed U.S. Army units to adopt distinctive insignia, which in most cases were small enameled insignia worn by officers on the shoulder loops.

Fig. 69-6.

Fig. 69-7.

Fig. 69-8.

Fig. 69-9.

1907 because of dissatisfaction with the outline ornaments, which caught and snagged on brush and thus were commonly lost or bent in field service. However, after this initial work the quartermaster general delayed the first issue of the insignia until the summer of 1910. Originally, soldiers wore two pairs of disks on the standing collar: a disk bearing the letters *US* went on each side of the collar near the front opening, and behind each *US* disk was worn a disk bearing the branch insignia with regimental number and company letter. In late 1911 the army changed regulations so that only two disks were worn: the *US* disk on the right and the branch disk on the left.[6]

Officers' insignia likewise underwent transformations. The 1903–1905 eagle from the Great Seal of the United States, replaced in June 1905 by the *US* letters or variants such as *USR*, came into use with the olive drab uniforms. To the rear of the national device went a branch insignia, placed as on the 1895 blue coat. Although gilt insignia were suspended along with dress uniforms during World War I, almost immediately after the end of the war a few men began to wear bright brass buttons and insignia on the olive drab coat, despite regulations to the contrary. In 1923 the army eliminated bronze insignia, bringing gilt trimmings into exclusive use, although bronze ornaments were still prescribed for wartime.[7]

In 1926 a roll-collar (lapel) coat replaced the standing-collar uniform that had seen service in World War I. On 31 December 1927 the official wear-out period for the standing-collar uniform ended, and the new roll collar supposedly became mandatory. The harried quartermaster general, without adequate funds for new coats and still with a supply of older garments, could not comply with the requirement. Many units did not receive the new design uniforms until 1930 or later, which coincided with the publication of the official clothing specification, although many men modified the old high-collar coats to the new lapel versions.[8]

Cotton High-Collar Coats

Khaki proved unsatisfactory as a color for summer uniforms as a result of color variations caused by the fugitive dye. These problems led to a temporary end of khaki in 1910, when the army introduced an olive drab cotton uniform cut like the winter

Fig. 69-10. *General Pershing (left) and other former American Expeditionary Forces officers in 1922. All wear the recently authorized Sam Browne belts. Enlisted men also received leather garrison belts after the Great War. Lighter shades of officers' trousers can be noted, a trend that grew as the time after World War I increased.*

Fig. 69-10.

wool version. Other than the cotton material and the lack of lining, the coat was similar to the ones of olive drab wool.[9] These coats lasted into the 1920s, but during the transition to the lapel coats, the Quartermaster Corps reintroduced khaki, no doubt believing that the earlier technical problems had been solved.

Insignia for this coat were those common to the times. Enlisted men wore disks—*US* on the right and branch insignia on the left—first in bronze and later in gilt, with distinctive insignia added as they were introduced after World War I.[10]

At the time of the introduction of olive drab cotton uniforms, the army had an enormous supply of khaki chevrons, and the army singlemindedly acted to eliminate the surplus by directing that khaki chevrons be worn on the olive drab coat. As the various khaki rank insignia were used up, the army replaced them with olive drab. After World War I the unpopular practice of using obsolete chevrons continued, so the 1920 chevron style with olive drab bars on a navy blue background did not immediately apply. Officers' insignia for this dark cotton coat similarly paralleled those for the wool service coat. Two of the enlisted men's version, one from before World War I and one from after, are illustrated in Figs. 69-11 and 69-12.[11]

Modifications

The many pattern changes made to olive drab coats often caused men to modify older coats in their possession so that their coat more closely followed the current style. The member of the Mounted Service School Detachment shown in Fig. 69-13 wears a coat of the pattern made between 1904 and 1907. This coat can be dated by the pointed cuffs and the bellows pockets. The soldier

Fig. 69-11.

Fig. 69-11. *This first sergeant wears an olive drab cotton uniform just before World War I. Such uniforms replaced similar khaki-colored uniforms in 1910.*

Fig. 69-12.

Fig. 69-12. *A post-1924 enlisted men's olive drab coat made of cotton. These were worn well into the late 1920s by some soldiers.*

Fig. 69-13.

Fig. 69-13. *Private Lawrence of the Mounted Service School Detachment, 1912, wears a 1904–1907 coat with bellows-style pockets, modified so that the collar stands up in the then-current pattern.*

has modified the falling collar, however, with small hooks to make the collar stand up. The single disk on each end of the collar shows that the photograph was made about 1912 or later. The World War I and later standing-collar coats left when lapel-style coats came into use in the 1920s were modified to lapel styles. Some of them are shown in chapter 70, "Service Coats with Lapels."

CHAPTER SEVENTY

SERVICE COATS WITH LAPELS

Fig. 70-1. This Civil War colonel wears an early lapel coat with his rank insignia directly on the civilian garment. Such civilian influences were felt by the army.

Fig. 70-2. A few U.S. World War I pilots wore British-style lapel coats like this one. The profound British influence hastened the army's change to lapel coats, which occurred in the late 1920s.

EVEN THOUGH the coat style has proven popular, it came to the army slowly. Lapel coats had been in common civilian use for some time during the second half of the nineteenth century, but uniforms retained standing collars (Fig. 70-1). After America's entry into World War I, many U.S. officers became familiar with the more modern roll-collar uniform coats of the British. Many American officers favored the comfortable pattern, and a few pilots even wore them (Fig. 70-2), although officially only paramilitary organizations adopted the notched lapel uniform coats: the American Red Cross, the American Library Association, the Jewish Welfare Board, and the like (Fig. 70-3).[1]

OLIVE DRAB SERVICE COAT

After that tantalizing look at a more comfortable and stylish coat, Air Service officers finally led the army into a new uniform. The army prescribed the lapel coat in 1925 for Air Service officers and in 1926 for all other personnel.[2] These olive-colored wool, lapel service coats have four bright brass buttons closing the front and skirts covering the wearer's hips (Fig. 70-4 and Fig. 71-1 in chapter 71, "Insignia for Lapel Coats"). Since this coat's introduction it has remained the general cut used by the army, despite subsequent changes such as additions or omissions of cloth or leather belts and many color and material changes.

The first 1925 officers' lapel coat was of a green-tinted olive drab that could be made from several materials, including cotton, gabardine, serge, barathea, and whipcord. It was somewhat similar to the high-collar coat in that it had four pockets: two pleated patch breast pockets and two concealed hung

Fig. 70-1.

Fig. 70-2.

Fig. 70-3.

Fig. 70-3. Volunteer organization members, such as these Knights of Columbus secretaries, started to wear lapel coats during World War I. Bronze insignia were KC or K of C. Hat cords were black.

Fig. 70-4. The Air Service olive drab lapel coat, introduced in 1925.

lower pockets, and the skirt remained at crotch length with only a slight flare at the hips (Fig. 70-5).[3] The enlisted men's version was similar, but the construction was slightly different, with the collar lapel notch being the easiest way to distinguish them. Other subtle differences were in the body seams and materials besides the insignia types and placement. Enlisted men's insignia of the period had screw posts on the reverse, thus requiring that grommets to be added to the collars (and, if distinctive insignia were to be used, to the coat lapels). Units added these grommets at their local station if they had distinctive insignia. For summer wear, until the khaki tan came back into use in the 1930s, replacing the olive drab color, coats of identical cut and color were to be used but with cotton as the material. (Figs. 70-6, 70-7, and 70-8).

Fig. 70-4.

Changes, World War II

Just before and during World War II enlisted men's coat changes came at a rapid rate. The Quartermaster Corps made several modifications that resulted in slightly different coat patterns too detailed for this overview. The blouse was still considered a service coat to be worn in the field. This concept resulted in some changes as the pace of the national emergency quickened, although many small changes were to make the coat more attractive. A bi-swing back, which included side pleats near the shoulders, was a modification introduced in January 1940 to make the snug-fitting service coat more suitable for combat (Fig. 70-9). Soldiers were to wear the coat in the field, but early in the war the coat

Fig. 70-5. A 1930s officers' coat showing the brass hooks at the waist to hold the Sam Browne belt.

Fig. 70-6. Members of Company A, 125th Infantry (Michigan National Guard) in 1930. Two noncommissioned officers wear the high-collar coat, with brass buttons but otherwise similar to the World War I garments, while the other two have converted their high-collar coats to the newer lapel style.

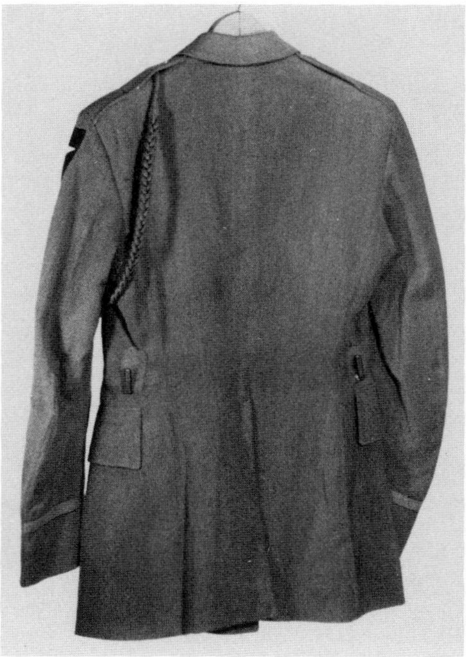

Fig. 70-5.

was relegated to dress and off-duty wear, as field and fatigue clothing was introduced for combat. As a result, in mid-1942 the army eliminated the bi-swing back in favor of the previous standard cut, and the pockets were modified to be decorative only, instead of being designed primarily for carrying objects in the field. In late 1943, issue of the enlisted men's coat ceased, and in November 1944 it became "limited standard," replaced by the Eisenhower jacket.[4]

The enlisted men's olive drab coat was revived as a special uniform for the U.S. Constabulary, part of the army of occupation in Germany, after World War II. On May 1, 1946, the constabulary was formed as a special unit to enforce occupation rules, and several U.S. Army units were assigned to this force. Besides specially painted helmet liners, the men wore leather belts, of the type issued to military police, and the older coats. This unique apparel set them apart from other U.S. soldiers in Germany. Scarves of the yellow branch color were worn at the neck to further distinguish there men. A first sergeant in the constabulary uniform is shown in Fig. 70-10.

Besides the changes in cut such as the bi-swing back, officers' uniforms also underwent color changes. The green-tinted officers' coat was replaced during 1941 by a dark brown blouse made from elastique, although catalogs from the 1930s list officers' coats "in darker OD shades," showing the gradual but unofficial darkening of the coats. The new official color was called olive drab (dark shade), which later became known as shade 51. This new uniform was also called "pinks and greens" with the "pink" color coming from the pinkish gray trouser color (officially known as drab number 54).[5]

As with the model it replaced, the officers' dark brown coat had four large bright buttons down the front and branch insignia on the lapels. For all but Army Air Force (AAF) officers, two brass belt hooks were at the waist by the elbows to support a leather Sam Browne belt. AAF officers were to have 2-inch-wide sewn-in cloth belts without buckles (Fig. 70-11). In November 1942 the brass hooks became optional, and the Sam Browne belt was replaced by a cloth belt for all but AAF officers, although in practice some AAF officers wore the belt with buckle. With this change the lower brass button was replaced by a dark plastic one that the belt covered. Post–World War II officers' coats all had a full cloth belt that, at the wearer's option, could be sewn down around the baseline or be fully detachable. In the latter case two 9/16-inch cloth belt loops were placed at the side seams.[6]

The contrasting color between officers' service coats and their trousers had started over twenty years before. By the end of World War I some officers were wearing stylish lighter-colored breeches, and by November 1924 this practice was officially acknowledged when regulations noted, "Commissioned officers may wear breeches of Bedford cord or similar material, slightly lighter in color than the service coat."[7] Many

Fig. 70-6.

photographs of the 1920s and 1930s show the common practice of officers wearing lighter-colored breeches (Fig. 70-12), which ultimately led to the "pinks and greens."

During the time of these officers' coats, the sleeve bands introduced in 1905 and 1907 changed. Initially only commissioned officers wore the olive drab ½-inch-wide band with the lower edge 3 inches from the sleeve end. Warrant officers and enlisted men who had been commissioned during World War I wore a similar band in green (Fig. 70-13). In April 1945 this provision was extended to include World War II commissioned service. All commissioned and warrant officers adopted olive drab braid, and green braid disappeared from mention in regulations in 1949.[8]

The pinks and greens lasted until the late 1950s, when the army phased in the army green uniform, although during the time of the olive drab coats, similarly cut khaki uniforms were worn by officers and enlisted men.

Khaki Lapel Coats

In a persistent search for cool, lightweight clothing for tropical wear, the army returned again to khaki in 1929, replacing the olive drab cotton that had been introduced in 1911. Enlisted men stationed in hot climates received roll-collar coats of the type shown in Fig. 70-14. The coat was cut similar to the enlisted men's olive drab lapel coat introduced in the 1920s, and it included cloth shoulder loops, plain cuffs, four rectangular pocket flaps, and gilt buttons. Insignia placement was the same as that on the olive drab wool version. At overseas tropical stations, most notably the Philippines, some men wore locally made khaki uniforms that varied slightly from the official cut. The army

Fig. 70-7. *A high-collar coat made over into the "new" lapel style. Most soldiers converted at least one coat to the new pattern in the early 1930s.*

Fig. 70-8. *Officers in hot locales such as the Philippines and Hawaii wore olive drab cotton lapel coats in the 1930s. Other than the material, the coats were identical to the olive drab wool versions.*

Fig. 70-9. *These two views of the olive drab coat show the bi-swing back, with side pleats down the rear shoulder seam.*

Fig. 70-7.

Fig. 70-8.

Fig. 70-9a.

Fig. 70-9b.

Fig. 70-10. This first sergeant, assigned to the U.S. Constabulary in Germany about 1948, wears the early World War II enlisted men's coat. The Constabulary wore the olive drab coat after the war as a dress uniform.

Fig. 70-11. This aviation cadet wears the aviation officers' olive drab shade 51 coat. During World War II this coat came with either a cloth belt with metal buckle, used by all but the Army Air Force, or a sewn-down belt without any buckle, as in this example. Upon graduation the cadet changed his coat by adding lieutenants' bars to his shoulder loops and commissioned officers' braid to his sleeve. Aviation cadets switched to this type of standard uniform instead of their previous slate blue uniforms immediately after Pearl Harbor. Blue braid, designating aviation cadets, went around the olive drab dark-shade cap and was replaced by olive drab wool braid upon graduation.

Fig. 70-12. Lieutenant Colonels Crowel and Spicer of the 125th Infantry about 1932. Lighter-colored trousers were at the individual officer's option in the 1930s, resulting in a wide range of trouser colors.

Fig. 70-10.

ceased issue of the khaki coat in March 1938 and allowed men in hot climates to wear a khaki shirt with tie as an off-post uniform.[9]

The officers' 1930s khaki coat was cut like the olive drab wool version until 1942, when the War Department authorized an optional tropical worsted tan coat for commissioned and warrant officers for summer wear. This new 1942 tan coat was similar to the recently introduced dark shade 51 coat: single-breasted and semiform-fitting and with four brass buttons but without a belt. Two upper patch pockets had a box pleat on a vertical line; the lower two pockets were inside hung with outer flaps. Sleeves carried a 1/2-inch khaki braid (green for warrant officers who had previously been commissioned) with the lower edge 3 inches from the sleeve end (Fig. 70-15). These coats became optional for enlisted men in 1951. Officially called a "summer semidress and dress" coat, and later an "army tan" coat, the uniform commonly known as TWs, for tropical worsted, was widely replaced by khaki shirts and by the green uniforms in the late 1950s and early 1960s, becoming completely obsolete in July 1968 as it was replaced by the lightweight AG 344 green uniform.[10]

Lapel Jackets

During World War II the army designed an amazingly popular jacket that was copied by some police forces, bus drivers, and other uniformed civilians; that made the transition to the U.S. Air Force upon the formation of

Fig. 70-11.

Fig. 70-12.

Fig. 70-13.

that service; and that was used until the mid-1950s. U.S. soldiers wore wool olive drab Eisenhower jackets of two major versions, although several minor variations existed, especially for officers. Before addressing the assorted jacket styles, it is worth examining how the army adopted a new jacket in wartime that essentially ended up as an "undress" uniform.

The genesis of the Eisenhower jacket lies in a concept that the quartermaster general had retained for many years and that we have seen throughout: service and field uniforms were one and the same. The army adopted a "battle" jacket for wear in the field that could also be worn in garrison. The result was a waist-length, olive drab wool garment initially known as a wool field jacket and commonly called the Eisenhower jacket after the general who wore it frequently. The design was influenced by both the British battle dress and by the beginnings of the principle of layered clothing. Soldiers often wore it instead of the service coat in rear areas because of its neat appearance.[11]

Fig. 70-14.

Fig. 70-15.

Fig. 70-13. *Effective April 1920, noncommissioned officers and warrant officers who had previously been commissioned began to wear olive green cuff bands. An example is the warrant officer in the front row, third from the right, who wears green cuff braid while his companions on either side do not. Note the variety of collar and lapel insignia placement among the enlisted men in the two rear rows.*

Fig. 70-14. *Enlisted men in the tropics and at some mainland posts wore khaki lapel coats in the 1930s. This private first class was assigned to the Philippines in the late 1930s. Distinctive insignia for his unit appear on the campaign hat and on the lapels.*

Fig. 70-15. *In this 1962 photograph, Colonel K. C. Emerson wears the tropical worsted uniform, which was cut much like the World War II olive drab coat except for the lack of a cloth belt.*

Fig. 70-16.

Fig. 70-17.

Fig. 70-18.

Fig. 70-19.

Fig. 70-16. *The first-pattern Eisenhower jacket is easily distinguished by the black metal waist adjustment buckles, a seam that ran down the center of the back, and, as is apparent in this photograph, cuffs that button. This was the first lapel garment that was of identical design for officers and enlisted men. Lieutenant Hank Johnson is shown, in 1945, without the normal collar insignia.*

Fig. 70-17. *General George C. Marshall on the Normandy beach in 1944. His jacket is similar to the standard Eisenhower version with concealed buttons, but it is one of the many variations, which included diagonal pockets and false chest pockets.*

Fig. 70-18. *Jackets converted from the shade 51 coat were common after World War II. This version is interesting in that the old brass buttons on the pockets and the shoulder loops have been left.*

Fig. 70-19. *During World War II the U.S. Army had several styles of uniforms made overseas. The label inside this particular jacket states that the "officers service coat" was made in conformance to USAETO Specification 1185B in 1943. The peculiar sewn-in belt, 4 3/4 inches wide, fastened under the right arm with a brass buckle.*

Although the jacket came in various designs, they all had common features. The waist-length jacket had a very wide collar and a neck opening that could be closed in cold weather, like the field jacket it was designed to be. All front buttons were concealed, including those on the two chest pocket flaps. A waistband with blackened steel buckles allowed adjustment on the sides, and brown buttons adjusted the banded cuffs. An example of the basic version is shown in Fig. 70-16. During World War II the War Department brought out several similar styles, some made overseas and others for special purposes. One example was designated the B-13 flight jacket and was for wear by aircrews (Fig. 70-17). It resembled the basic Eisenhower jacket, but it had two slanted openings by the pockets to allow better use of a parachute harness.[12]

Two more radical jackets were primarily used by officers. One was made of khaki-colored material and another from shade 51 material, the same as that of service coats. Initially officers' jackets could be made from either olive drab wool, like that of the enlisted men's version, or shade 51 material. Thus, basic jackets were made in 1944 using shade 51 materials. The army had some made in England.[13]

"Pinks and greens" service coats converted into jackets also saw wide use. Many officers

Fig. 70-20.

Fig. 70-20. A wide variety of jackets appear in this 1947 photograph. Front row, left to right: a jacket made from a shade 51 coat and worn with olive drab trousers that were properly worn with the issue Eisenhower jacket, a European-made jacket with slash pockets and made from shade 51 material, the standard shade 51 coat, and a custom-made jacket with the proper "pink" trousers.

had purchased several of the olive drab (dark shade) service coats, but the introduction and wide use of the Eisenhower jacket caused them to want the jackets as additional uniforms. In 1943 and 1944 the army sanctioned conversion of the coats to jackets. Local tailors usually made the changes, so there were a multitude of styles. Examples are shown in Figs. 70-18, 70-19, and 70-20. Typically the bright buttons on the shoulder loops were covered, although some, like the ones illustrated in Figs. 70-18 and 70-19, retained the bright buttons. Often the cuffs were converted to button like the cuffs of the official jacket. Wear of these converted jackets was suspended in 1951 with the issue of the second standard pattern of Eisenhower jacket, covered below.[14]

As the summer of 1945 developed and peace was declared in Europe, the many men in the large U.S. Army looked at the previous summer's khaki uniforms and at the new Eisenhower jackets. The two uniform concepts merged into a tan waist-length jacket (Fig. 70-21). Some men had unauthorized tan jackets made even in 1944 and early 1945, and finally in September 1945 the War Department recognized the practice by allowing officers to wear such clothing, although commanders could "neither require the purchase nor the wearing" of them. These jackets were to be cut like the olive drab wool shade 33 jackets, with only the cloth differing. Only officers could wear these initially, but in April 1947 the army relented and allowed enlisted men also to wear them. Tan jackets became obsolete in 1951.[15]

Fig. 70-21.

Fig. 70-21. A typical privately tailored tan jacket, from about 1945. Such jackets were allowed by regulations from mid-1945 until 1951, although they evidently were worn well before the end of World War II.

The Pentagon prescribed a newer version of the winter service coat, as the Eisenhower jacket was then officially called, in 1950. The cut was generally similar to that of the original Eisenhower jacket. The angle between the collar and the lapel was wider, and the fly front covered four dark plastic buttons, as opposed to the original version's five buttons. The back was cut from a single piece of cloth, eliminating the seam that before had run down the back. The waistband had buttons instead of metal buckles, and the sleeves

Fig. 70-22. The second-pattern Eisenhower jacket was officially called a "winter service coat." The straight sleeves without any buttons and the buttons (instead of metal buckles) at the waist above each hip joint distinguish this olive drab wool jacket. Like the earlier version, the buttons were concealed with a fly front.

Fig. 70-23. This National Guard sergeant major wears the green uniform introduced in the mid-1950s.

Fig. 70-22.

Fig. 70-23.

were straight at the ends, without buttons (Fig. 70-22).[16] The switch to the army green uniform in the late 1950s ended wear of the Eisenhower jacket.

Army Green Uniforms

The army carefully implemented a grand strategy for the introduction of the army green uniform during the 1950s. Dissatisfaction was not with the jacket design, but with the olive drab color. Even so, the cut was changed at the same time. A special board appointed to study uniforms after World War II concluded that the dual-use uniform, worn both in the field and in garrison, was impractical. Henceforth the army would have two separate uniforms: one for field wear and one for garrison wear. The latter was to be the green uniform.[17]

Having suffered from the sporadic availability of the new lapel coat thirty years before, the many versions of the World War II service coat, and the Eisenhower field jacket that became a service coat, the Quartermaster Corps planned the green uniform more carefully. An officers' green service cap was phased in almost immediately after the Korean War. Although it was initially worn with the "pinks and greens," it brought the first piece of the green uniform into use. Enlisted specialists' chevrons that were first worn on the olive drab Eisenhower jacket were made with a green background and gold designs, the color scheme for the new green uniform, and black shoes became standard.

Initially, two uniforms were introduced, although they were cut identically. Heavy wool serge, between fourteen and eighteen ounces, was for enlisted men (and optionally for officers), while most officers had their uniforms made from heavy wool elastique. Green uniforms became available through the quartermaster supply system in September 1956 and became mandatory in September 1961.[18] The khaki or tropical worsted uniforms remained for summer wear, and the green replaced only the winter uniforms. In 1965 a lightweight green uniform (AG 344) satisfactory for summer wear was first sold by the army's clothing sales stores. The cut was identical to that of the heavier uniform. As other materials became popular in the civilian market, some of them were adopted for uniforms, including knits and a wide range of cloth weights. The basic green uniform is illustrated in Fig. 70-23.

At the end of 1989 the army announced minor changes to the green uniform. A slightly darker green came into use to better highlight the light green shirt. At the same time, slight tailoring changes were introduced, including minor narrowing of the lapels and a reduction in the waist by 1 inch when compared to the proportion of the previous coat's shoulder sizes.[19]

Chapter Seventy-One

Insignia for Lapel Coats

Following World War I, when General Pershing became army chief of staff, he instituted several uniform innovations inspired primarily by the British. Besides the addition of the Sam Browne belt for officers and the leather garrison belt for enlisted men, insignia changed. One idea was the adoption of distinctive badges or other uniform trim by each regiment, since it was more economical to add an insignia to a uniform than to have truly unique regimental clothing. In the small army before 1916, Regular Army officers of one arm or service knew one another and knew the various regiments. In the expanded army this was not true, so emblems that might preserve some of the "old army" spirit were sought.

The army's initial concept was for each regiment or smaller numbered unit to have a uniform addition to set it apart from all others.[1] Some of the first units adopted a small bronze or enameled badge that enlisted men wore on the standing collar behind the branch and *US* disks. An example is shown in Fig. 69-12 in chapter 69, "Olive Drab Standing-Collar Coats." Other units, however, followed Pershing's intent more closely. The 9th Infantry was the only unit to select a special belt buckle for the garrison belt, the 2d Infantry wore a blue square with two red arrows on one cuff, the 3d Infantry added a black strap with buff strips to encircle a shoulder, and the 4th Infantry chose a red and green band around the shoulder loop. When the army switched to the roll-collar coat, these new distinctive insignia influenced the placement of the *US* and branch disks.

In January 1943 the army quit approving distinctive insignia for new units in an effort to save metal and because of the large influx of requests that could not be handled. Because of the wartime army expansion and this policy, many men wore coats with collar disks but no distinctive insignia, resulting in bare lapels. The army resumed official approval of distinctive insignia in 1947, although in practice many units had distinctive insignia manufactured for them in 1945 or 1946—blatant but innocent challenges to Washington.[2]

Enlisted Men's Branch Insignia

How did these distinctive insignia fit into the overall scheme with other insignia, especially branch devices? Enlisted men wore two disks on roll-collar coats, one on each side of the collar, a carryover from the style of the high-collar service uniforms. The lapels remained bare, as shown in Fig. 71-1, in the late 1920s. For those few units whose distinctive insignia consisted of their coat of arms or crest, the insignia went on the collar above the disks (Fig. 71-2), following the high-collar concept of the unit insignia being behind the

Fig. 71-1. *The enlisted men's olive drab lapel coat introduced in the late 1920s and worn well into World War II.*

Fig. 71-2. *Philippine Division soldiers in the 1930s wearing their distinctive insignia above their collar insignia on khaki uniforms.*

Fig. 71-2.

Fig. 71-1.

Fig. 71-3. In this 1941 picture the men are ready to go to the field wearing their wool service uniforms. Insignia include distinctive insignia, commonly known as "unit crests," on the coat lapels.

Fig. 71-4. Before and during World War II enlisted men wore their distinctive insignia on the service coat lapels, tilted to be parallel to the crease formed by the collar and lapel. The US and branch disks went on the wearer's right and left collar, respectively, with the horizontal axis of their designs parallel to the horizon.

Fig. 71-5. Starting in 1947, enlisted personnel wore pairs of US disks on the collar and pairs of branch insignia on the lapels, similar to the scheme used by officers.

Fig. 71-3.

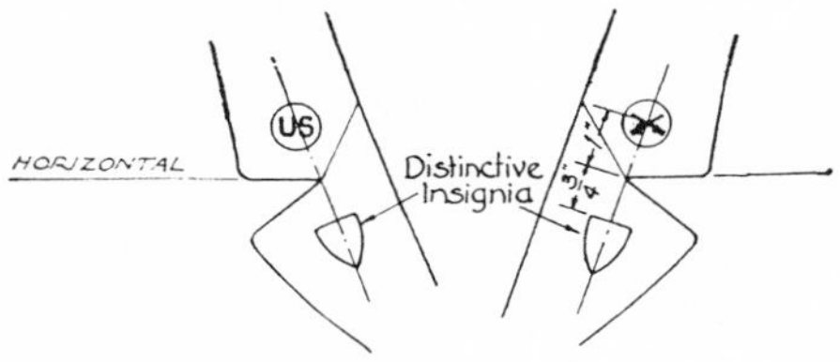

Fig. 71-4.

branch disks. In 1928 the army realized that most units would adopt small metal distinctive insignia based on their coats of arms, so the War Department instituted a policy that such unit-distinctive insignia would go on the lapel below the collar disks, where they fit better (Figs. 71-3 and 71-4).[3]

Almost immediately after the wartime ban on new distinctive insignia was lifted in 1947, the placement of collar and distinctive insignia changed. Officers had worn distinctive insignia on their shoulder loops, because their branch insignia went on the lapels. The 1947 change moved the enlisted men's insignia to the same positions as those used by officers. The distinctive insignia went to the shoulder loops, the *US* disks (worn in pairs as in the original 1910–12 introductory period) went on the collar, and branch disks (also in pairs) went on the lapels. An example is shown in Fig. 71-5. This overall effort to remove the clothing differences between officers and enlisted men also included the

Fig. 71-5.

addition of shoulder loops to enlisted men's shirts, making them like those of officers. In October 1951 the army dropped the disk pairs and reverted to the earlier practice of having the *US* disk on the right collar and the branch disk on the left, but the distinctive insignia stayed on the shoulder loops, thus leaving the lapels bare. This practice has continued (Fig. 71-6).[4]

Officers' Insignia on Lapel Coats

Current officers' and enlisted men's uniforms are cut the same, with the distinction between the two being made with insignia and trim. This is a new phenomenon that has come about recently. It is worth looking at how officers wore their insignia on twentieth-century coats that were somewhat similar to enlisted men's. Some dating can be accomplished simply by insignia placement or by the trim, and those details should not be overlooked. Such points of distinction include sleeve braid and the configuration of lapels and collars.

On the 1905 khaki and wool service coats, General Staff Corps officers added 1/2-inch-wide black braid, and in 1907 other officers added brown braid, as previously mentioned. This narrow strip of cloth grew to 3/4 inch wide and has remained so for commissioned officers on most semidress coats since then, the Eisenhower jacket being the notable exception. Generals' black sleeve braid on the army green coat is 1 1/2 inches wide, the first time in the twentieth century that a rank distinction by sleeve bands has been made on other than dress coats.[5]

Dress blue uniforms after the turn of the century introduced stripes, in gold or in gold and branch colors, parallel to and usually 4 inches above coat cuffs. Mess blue and white and usually dress white coats of this century also followed suit, with the bottom of the braid edge 3 inches above the end of the sleeve.

In addition to cuff braid, the shape of lapels and collars distinguished officers' coats from enlisted men's from the initial introduction of the lapel coat until the early 1950s. The 1926–44 enlisted men's service coat exhibited a notch of approximately 30 degrees between the collar and the lapel, while the comparable officers' coat had a narrow slit, with the lapel top nearly parallel to the collar bottom (Figs. 71-4 and 71-8).[6]

The colonel shown in Fig. 71-7 wears the *US* letters on the collar and the branch insignia (cavalry in this case) on the lapels. Exact placement of officers' insignia on the lapel coat has varied slightly over time, but the general location has remained unchanged. The initial pattern with the *US* on the collar (above the notch) and the branch below on the lapels is also shown in Fig. 71-8.[7]

Both officers' and enlisted men's Eisenhower jacket collars and lapels had a narrow angle between then, similar to that of officers' service coats, but the collar tip overhung the lapel. The slit separating the collar and lapels ran perpendicular to the folded inside lapel edge on enlisted men's coats (Figs. 71-6 and 71-9). Insignia went on the Eisenhower jacket lapels and collars in a manner generally

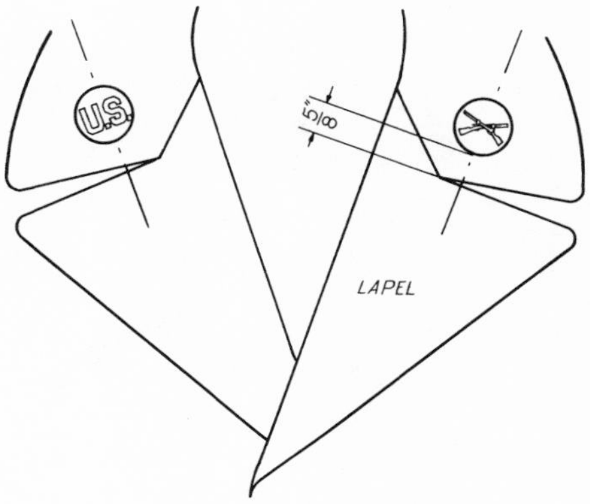

Fig. 71-6.

Fig. 71-7.

Fig. 71-6. *By the end of 1951 the army ceased its experiment of having enlisted men wear pairs of US and pairs of branch insignia and reverted to the practice of having single insignia. This shows placement on the Eisenhower jacket as illustrated in contemporary regulations.*

Fig. 71-7. *Proper collar insignia placement for officers, 1940. The angle of the notch between the lapel and the collar was very slight on the officers' coat, while it was about 30 degrees on the enlisted men's.*

similar to that of the service coat, but with the insignia slightly tilted so that the vertical line of the insignia was parallel to the inside roll of the lapel. This ultimately caused the 1951 change in lapel coat insignia placement shown in Fig. 71-10.[8]

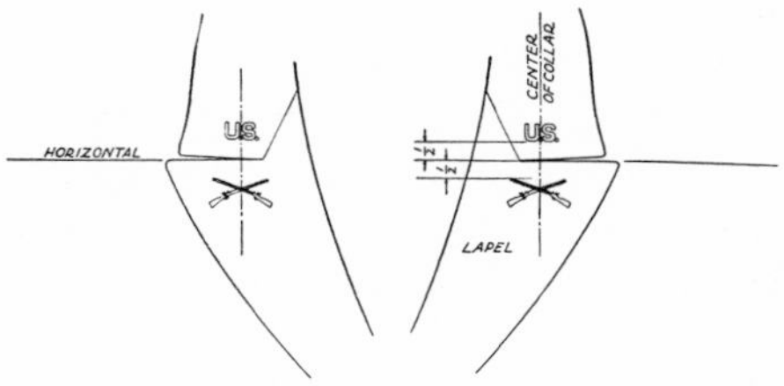

Fig. 71-8.

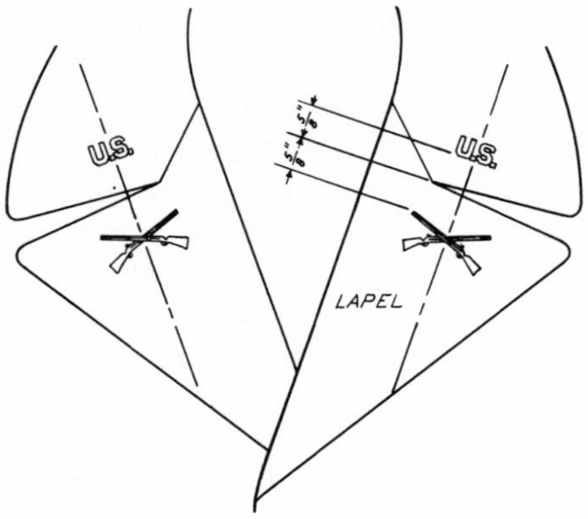

Fig. 71-9.

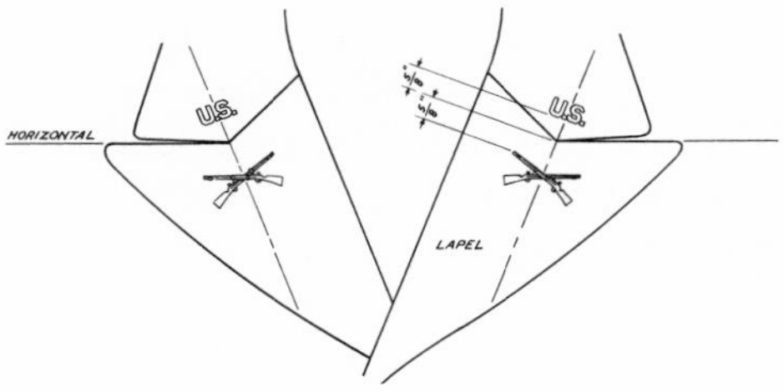

Fig. 71-10.

Fig. 71-8. *Regulation illustrations for proper officers' lapel coat insignia placement, 1930s, with the axis of the insignia vertical.*

Fig. 71-9. *Officers' insignia placement for the Eisenhower jacket.*

Fig. 71-10. *Illustration from army regulations for officers' lapel coat insignia after the 1950s. The insignia axes were first tilted on the Eisenhower jacket, and this practice carried over to the coat.*

Section XX

Headgear

Chapter Seventy-Two

Men's Headgear through the Civil War

Military head coverings were originally worn to protect the head from weather and from blows. Headgear quickly became decorative and an essential part of military uniforms. Almost immediately with the adoption of uniforms, military organizations began the practice of intermixing various headgear with coats and trousers. Thus, a specific cap or hat could be used with a variety of coats and trousers, and with one coat more than one hat or cap could be worn. It remains so in the military today. (The reader should note that hats have a brim, whereas caps do not, although they may have a bill. The difference is carried throughout this book.)

Chapeaus

American school children readily recognize the colonial three-cornered cocked hat, the common headgear of the American Revolution. As a practical matter, this popular hat, introduced in England in its general shape about 1690, continued in military use just through the end of the revolutionary period. The turned-up brim helped prevent the hat from being taken off by the wind and from getting in the way of drawing a sword. By about the time George Washington became president, the tricorn with three sides turned up had evolved into a hat with two sides folded up, called the *chapeau de bras.* That hat was the first of several seen in the next 150 years, and at that time it was rigid. The crown, taller rear fan, and shorter front fan had little give or flexibility.

Army uniform regulations of January 1787 described cocked hats for both officers and enlisted men, with infantry using white trim and artillery, yellow. This is the first known case of the post-Revolutionary army using white cloth and silver-colored metal for infantry and yellow cloth and brass or yellow-colored metal for artillery. Worn on the hats, adorned with feathers, were cockades of black leather, "round, with points, four inches diameter . . . the feathers to rise six inches above the brim of the hat." Feathers worn by the artillery were black with red tips; those for the 1st, 2d, and 3d infantry regiments were red, black, and white, respectively.[1]

Officers of the general staff and the engineers received chapeaus in 1800. Gradually, the practice evolved so that plumes worn on the chapeaus identified rank and assignment. Although in May 1813 generals were directed to "wear cocked hats without feathers," several plume variations, of gradually decreasing height, were used until 1832, when a new chapeau variation was introduced. Distinction among generals, general staff, and engineers was made by colors of drooping swan feathers fixed at the hat's peak. An example of an 1820 officers' chapeau is shown in Fig. 72-1.[2]

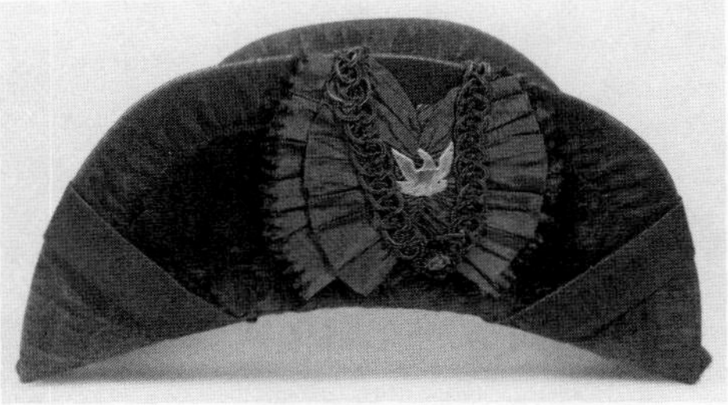

Fig. 72-1.

Fig. 72-1. *A black beaver chapeau worn by William Boyce, an 1822 U.S. Military Academy graduate. The chapeau is 17 inches from point to point, carries a brass eagle $1^3/_8$ by $1^1/_8$ inches, and was made by Thomas Lindsay of Philadelphia.*

Until 1840 the turned-up brim, now purely decorative, still conformed to an arc, so from the front the chapeau actually looked like a hat with the front and back turned up, as, in fact, it was. In 1840 a new chapeau form came into existence

(Fig. 72-2). The front and back chapeau ends actually formed points, and the brim was modified so that it was taller near the crown. The hat was more flexible and could be more easily folded flat and carried under the arm, in continuation of the gentlemanly practice that started with the tricorn. After a brief interruption, the army again authorized the chapeau for dress wear in 1858 and 1859 for field- and general-grade officers. An 1859 example with different insignia from the 1840 example is shown in Fig. 72-3. Generally, staff officers could wear the chapeau until World War I, although officially its use was allowed until shortly before World War II.[3] Often students of military uniforms fail to realize how long this hat, prescribed immediately after the Revolution, lasted, even though the hat and insignia evolved and changed throughout the period.

Fig. 72-2. *An 1840 chapeau, with the points formed more distinctly than those of the earlier style of chapeau. The officer is Brigadier General Thomas Lawson, who became surgeon general in 1836 and was breveted a brigadier general in the Mexican War. The eagle is surrounded by thirteen stars.*

Fig. 72-2.

Leather Helmets

Another early headgear common at the close of the Revolution was the leather helmet. Popular with mounted troops, the helmet, for a man on horseback, offered some protection from tree limbs or a fall as well as some ability to deflect a sword blow. Periodically unmounted branches adopted the helmet, especially in the militia, perhaps because of its smart appearance, but for unmounted troops it did not see much service.

It is quite possible that leather headgear was worn during the period of General Anthony Wayne's legion, but its exact form is presently unknown, and it probably was not a helmet but a cap. The artillery of 1794 had helmets with red plumes, but they were worn only a short time. Dragoons, authorized helmets in 1800, wore them until the end of the War of 1812.[4]

It may be that the first helmet insignia was an oval brass plate picturing "a mounted dragoon in the act of charging," although this is not certain. In 1808 the letters *USLD* (for U.S. Light Dragoons) replaced the plate on a similar helmet. Light dragoons added blue feathers with white tips to "leather caps or helmets" in 1808. From 1812 until 1815 (when dragoons were disbanded) the charging dragoon design of 1800 was worn, with

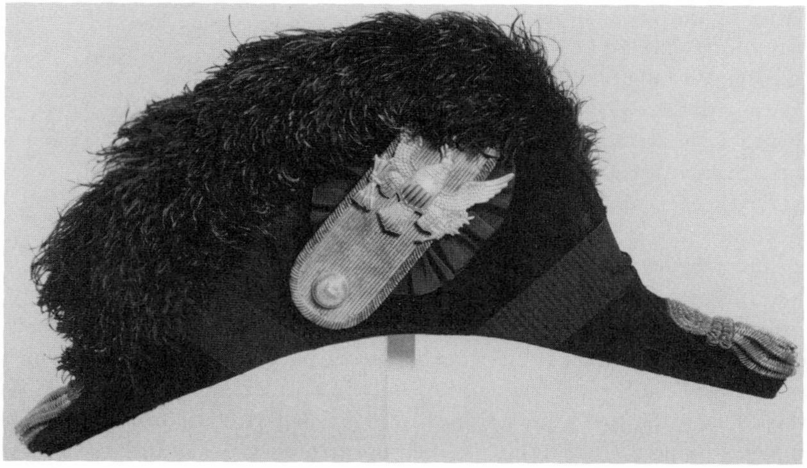

Fig. 72-3. *The 1859-style chapeau with eagle insignia, worn by Major General George McClellan, commander of Union forces early in the Civil War. The chapeau was made by the Warnock Company, New York City. The eagle and the separate ribbon bearing E. Pluribus Unum remained as on earlier chapeaus but were applied to a bullion strip. Later chapeaus were similar but with smaller eagles.*

Fig. 72-3.

the plate reduced in size and the design placed within a rectangular pewter plate with clipped corners, as shown in Fig. 72-4.[5]

A new uniform, introduced for the artillery in 1808, included a leather cap instead of hat, with "blue feather, tipt with red." This same 1808 order prescribed for the Rifle Regiment, "light leather caps, with green feathers, tipt with black."[6] Although discarded by regular forces before the current cavalry arm came into existence in 1833, the leather helmet persisted well into the nineteenth century in some militia organizations.

Cylindrical and Bell-Crowned Caps

While the light dragoons were wearing helmets, between 1811 and 1815 the infantry wore cylindrical caps—a felt version from 1811 until 1813 and then leather ones. Because of the 1813 cap's durability and popularity, all branches of the Regular Army adopted it by 1816, with various plates worn on the front (Fig. 72-5).[7] These caps were generally copied from the British, who wore similar caps in the War of 1812. Slightly different versions were worn by American artillery and infantry during that war, although the felt caps lasted into 1814 in some units. In some cases cap plates were not applied, but according to research by Fredrick Gaede, some had a white painted stripe around the front of the crown, evidently with or without use of a cap plate. Other trim included a colored pompon and a small leather cockade worn on the side, the cockade ornamented with either a small cut-out eagle or a button, this distinction varying over time.

The bell-crown cap replaced the cylindrical cap in 1821. All enlisted men and company officers serving with troops wore this leather headgear, as shown in Fig. 72-6. The cap was ornamented with white metal for infantry and yellow brass for other branches. A 3-inch-wide outline eagle displaying a shield with a cut-out regimental number went on the cap. Pompons ornamented the front: yellow for artillery, white with red tops for light artillery, and white for infantry, except light infantry was yellow and rifle companies green.[8] While this headgear did not significantly change form, its insignia did change. Previously the insignia design had been struck in a single piece, often rectangular, and included a very detailed design.

The various plates worn on these caps span a wide spectrum of designs and are shown in chapters 4, 5, and 6. From a distance, however, only the rectangular shape used on most plates was apparent. These early-nineteenth-century plates evolved from a single plate to a "set" of insignia: an eagle and a branch device. Each of the two pieces of the "set" was individually struck. This was the first time the eagle was a separate insignia on a cap.

After the bell-crowned cap, a straight cylindrical cap came into use in 1832 and

Fig. 72-4. A cavalry helmet of the style worn between 1812 and 1815, bearing a plate showing "a mounted dragoon in the act of charging."

Fig. 72-5. A so-called tombstone cap, so named because the front rose above the cap's top. This style was copied from the British during the War of 1812. The "scales" or chin strap, are incorrect for this cap. This strap and the side buttons may be a later addition.

Fig. 72-4.

Fig. 72-5.

Fig. 72-6.

Fig. 72-6. *A bell-crowned cap adopted in 1821 and used until 1832. A pompon was attached at the top front of the cap, while the cut-out number on the eagle's shield indicated the regiment.*

Fig. 72-7.

Fig. 72-7. *Infantry and artillery soldiers wore this style of cylindrical cap starting in 1832. For the artillery, cannons replaced the infantry horn. The "tulip" above the eagle held a plume and did not signify a branch.*

1833 for all but dragoon soldiers. These caps, one of which is shown in Fig. 72-7, were ornamented with a separate infantry or artillery device below an outline eagle and with plumes (either cock feathers or horse hair) at the cap's top front, secured by a "tulip" or plume holder ornamented with a flaming bomb.[9] Although the cap would have been recognized by a soldier from just thirty years before, the insignia concept had drastically changed.

With the establishment of dragoons in 1833, the army created a dress cap with a distinctive insignia. Of generally the same cut as the infantry and artillery dress cap, the dragoon headgear was slightly narrower at the top than at the base, and it had only one major ornament and a cord attached to the wearer's cap.[10] This cap, with metal insignia, is shown in Fig. 7-4 of chapter 7.

The last of the cylindrical caps came into use during the Civil War. In 1864 light or horse-drawn artillery received a distinctive cap, ornamented with crossed cannons and an eagle, as shown in Fig. 72-8.[11] It replaced the "old pattern cap," but it is not now clear if that was the 1833 cap or not. The European horse guard–style helmet replaced the 1864 headgear eight years later.

Forage Caps, 1825–95

Forage caps were practical from a soldier's standpoint, since they took up little room (always a soldier's concern), offered some head protection, and could be maintained easily. Because they were not objects that were to be used on parade, they were simple, with a minimum of insignia. On the cloth forage cap used from 1825 until 1832 (Fig. 72-9), officers wore their regimental number, while enlisted men wore their company letter. These numbers and letters were white for infantry and yellow for other branches.[12]

The army changed from cloth to leather forage caps in 1832, only to revive the cloth in 1839. The 1839 design lasted, in three versions, until 1851. One model is shown in Fig. 72-10 and another in Fig. 72-11. Distinctive branch trim or insignia were not officially authorized, other than the enlisted engineers' castle and the mounted riflemen officers' "gold embroidered spread eagle with the letter *R* in silver on the shield," but it is known that branch-colored stripes often went around the headband of these caps.[13] Examples of some insignia worn on this cap are discussed in various branch chapters and shown in Fig. 72-11.

Again, the army officially eliminated this functional headgear in 1851, only to have it return in modified form in 1858. Initially the 1858 forage cap for enlisted men was prescribed to have a branch-colored welt around the crown, as described in General Order 13, dated 30 November 1858, but this idea was short-lived, and by the Civil War the cap was a solid dark blue (Fig. 72-12). A change in the cap's size took place in 1872, when uniform regulations of that year introduced a chasseur pattern.[14] In general appearance it was a shorter Civil War forage cap with a slanting round top and squared leather visor. In its new form it held its shape rigidly, whereas the taller Civil War versions had sides that easily collapsed. Comparisons of the caps used before and after 1872, with insignia, can be seen in Figs. 72-12 and 72-13.

Fig. 72-8. *The 1864 light artillery dress cap with red wool worsted cords. The tulip held a red horsehair plume.*

Fig. 72-9. *The first pattern of cloth forage cap, used for seven years starting in 1825. Officers wore their regimental number on the front, while enlisted men had company letters. This cap was replaced by a leather version, which also lasted seven years.*

Fig. 72-10. *Three different versions of this cloth forage cap were used between 1839 and 1851. During the Mexican War it was very popular. Regulations did not provide for any infantry, cavalry, dragoons, or artillery enlisted men's insignia, but it is known that branch-colored cloth was often added around the headband.*

By regulations, enlisted men ornamented their forage caps with metal insignia, and officers used embroidered devices. Only the company letter had been authorized before 1872, although during the Civil War men placed a good many nonregulation branch devices on the cap fronts and tops. In 1872 the company letter or branch insignia was specified, although this was a typographical error, and the choice was unintentional. The War Department changed regulations in 1873 so that the company letter was worn with the branch insignia. In 1877 the regimental number was added above the rifles, cannons, or sabers and the letter was moved to below the crossed arms. Caps of this design continued until 1895, when a new visor cap replaced the Indian Wars' forage cap.[15]

Army Dress Caps, 1851–95

Although in 1850 the War Department authorized a new officers' cap, "nearly the pattern of the present forage cap," ornamented with branch insignia and a new enlisted men's cap with a "gig" (creased) top so that it would fold like the 1832 leather forage cap design, the army did not fully place the regulation in force. If this cap had been widely issued, it would have introduced a cloth cap of the 1832–39 form. This was one of several 1850 uniform changes that were published and withdrawn.[16]

The cap pattern changed in 1851 from its old tall, cylindrical form to a much smaller kepi shako modeled after the French army cap of the period, wider at the bottom than the top. The cap was fitted with a colored pompon and had a wide colored band around the base to show the soldier's branch. Ordnance and engineer soldiers had a thin

Fig. 72-11.

__Fig. 72-11.__ This Mexican War photo, taken about 1847, is believed to show Colonel Jones Withers. He wears a gold-embroidered looped horn for infantry on his forage cap.

Fig. 72-12.

__Fig. 72-12.__ Major Thomas B. Griffits of the Massachusetts Volunteers wore this forage cap with an infantry insignia during the Civil War. High crowns of this type were described in regulations until 1872. Enlisted men's caps were to carry metal insignia and a strap (just above the brim) with a single metal buckle. Also known as "bummers' caps," the early versions had flat bills; those made late in the Civil War were curved.

Fig. 72-13.

__Fig. 72-13.__ Militia officer Gilbert Thomson owned this late-nineteenth-century forage cap of the 1872–95 pattern. The wreath around the engineers' castle is not in accordance with regulations, because one branch of the wreath should be of palm and the other of laurel, not completely of laurel like this one. Before early 1884, officers wore leather chin straps as shown on the cap in Fig. 72-12. During January and February 1884 officers were to provide themselves with gold straps such as the one shown here.

Fig. 72-14.

__Fig. 72-14.__ An 1851 enlisted men's dress cap. In 1854 the wide colored band was eliminated, replaced by a narrow colored welt that traced the previous upper edge of the band. Branch distinction was also shown by the colored pompon.

welt instead of a wide band. A brass eagle, representing the arms of the United States, went on the front, with enlisted men wearing a brass company letter below the eagle and officers wearing embroidered branch insignia (Fig. 72-14). In 1854 the army modified the cap by eliminating the colored bands used by combat troops and adding a branch-colored narrow welt, tracing the upper edge of where the band had been, just as the 1851 engineer and ordnance troops had done.[17]

Hats replaced these caps in 1858 and 1859. Without the stiffener, insignia, and pompon, hats were to serve as forage caps. This concept did not prove practical, and the forage cap returned in 1858, as already noted.

Hats, 1855–72

In 1855 the two new cavalry regiments received a new hat, commonly called a Hardee hat after William Hardee. This hat proved popular, and the War Department, on 2 March 1858, prescribed a modified hat for all branches (Fig. 72-15). During the life of the hat, regulations prescribed various rules about which side was to be turned up. In practice men often pinned up neither side with the regulation eagle that was made of metal for enlisted men and embroidery for officers. Enlisted men's hat fronts carried a brass ornament indicative of the wearer's branch, while officers wore gold-embroidered branch insignia on oval backgrounds. This use of yellow metal and gold embroidery marks a departure from the previous practice of the use of silver-colored metal to represent infantry and gold or yellow for other branches.[18]

During the Civil War many variations of the dress hat existed, usually without the feathers on the side required by regulations, as men adopted it for field use. Also during that war soldiers often used civilian hats similar to the 1858 hat, but lighter in weight and often allowing for ventilation, with insignia added. Most common was a hat with a low crown and a straight brim not turned up at all.

Fig. 72-15.

Fig. 72-15. *Although regulations called for troops of different branches to pin up one side or the other of the 1858 hat, in practice this rule was often ignored. The decorative feathers were not commonly worn. Enlisted men wore branch-colored hat cords with tassels, while officers wore gold and black intermixed cords with acorn ends. The edge of the brim of officers' hats was bound, while that of enlisted men's versions was stitched.*

Chapter Seventy-Three

Men's Headgear with Roots from 1872 to 1916

Fig. 73-1. This officers' 1872 dress cap is distinguished by the embroidered insignia, because enlisted men wore stamped brass insignia. The cavalry did not adopt this cap, as mounted troops began to wear a black felt helmet in 1872.

Fig. 73-2. A contemporary photograph of the helmet introduced in 1872 for cavalry, light artillery, and signal troops. This model had neither plume nor spike on the top, and the eagle had a ribbon that extended in an arc above its head.

Uniform regulations of 1872 created an entire new set of U.S. Army uniforms. Between 1872 and the end of the nineteenth century, the army introduced some of the headgear that for many people still have romantic links to the "old army": campaign hats and English horse guards' helmets. The former is still used today, while the latter is now often viewed as a gaudy uniform component of a bygone era. While other headgear came and went during this time, the service cap, or billed cap still used by the military, is another survivor that was introduced before World War I. On it enlisted men wore a huge range of insignia until the exigencies of World War I caused a radical switch to a single insignia design for enlisted men.

Dress Caps, 1872–81

The army introduced a complete set of new headgear in 1872, although generally the forage cap was simply made with a lower crown. One new uniform part was a dress cap that looked something like a stiffened Civil War forage cap, as shown in Fig. 73-1, with a new style of eagle and smaller branch insignia than had been previously used. Officers' insignia were embroidered, while the enlisted men's versions were stamped metal.[1]

Helmets

In 1872 mounted troops received a black felt dress helmet (Fig. 73-2). Although today many people believe the helmet came from French or German influence, records show that it was modeled after the English horse guards' helmets. Both cavalry and light artillery wore identical 1872 helmet plates with a brass regimental number 1½ inches high on the lower portion of the shield. Signal Corps troops also used the helmet, but these helmets carried no number, because that corps was not organized into numbered units at that time.[2]

Uniform regulations of 7 January 1881 expanded the use of modified black helmets to all branches except staff and general officers (Fig. 73-3). This move had been recom-

Fig. 73-1.

Fig. 73-2.

mended first in 1879, but General Sherman delayed the change for two years. Those officers without a helmet (except chaplains) wore the chapeau. Officers wore black wool cloth or felt, while the enlisted men's version was covered with black felt. Mounted officers and men, regardless of branch, wore branch-colored plumes on the helmet tops; foot troops had spikes. Because a few infantry officers such as adjutants were mounted, they wore plumes instead of spikes. All regimental field-grade officers wore the mounted helmet, as did all Signal Corps officers. General Order 104 of 1885 allowed all bands, including those of foot units, to wear the mounted troops' plume.[3]

Initial regulations stated that officers were to wear large brass eagles and enlisted men were to wear forage cap insignia on helmets, but six months later, in June 1881, the army ordered all men to wear one of four eagles, although this had been the original intention. All enlisted soldiers except infantry, artillery, and cavalry wore a plain helmet plate with a small silver staff emblem on the shield, while the three arms had large crossed muskets, cannons, or sabers under the shield on the eagle's breast (Fig. 73-4). Enlisted men's and officers' plates used on these helmets are discussed in chapter 8, "Eagle Insignia." The sides of the 1881 helmets also carried brass buttons embossed with the branch insignia, providing still further distinction of a soldier's duty. In most cases troops replaced these dress helmets in 1903 and 1904 with the new visor cap.[4]

The design of the 1881 eagle plate differed extensively from the 1872 pattern. The

Fig. 73-3.

Fig. 73-3. *This cavalry band member holds an 1881 helmet. Generally mounted troops added a plume on the helmet top, while unmounted troops used a spike. Officers' helmets had buffalo-hair plumes, while enlisted men's had horsehair plumes.*

Fig. 73-4. *Helmet trimmings as shown in the 1881 report of the quartermaster general. The oak leaves and spike fit onto the helmet top for unmounted troops. The silver insignia were used by enlisted men of the Corps of Engineers, Ordnance Corps, Medical Department, commissary sergeants, and Signal Corps. Officers and regimental men applied silver numbers. Officers' eagles had the crossed arms and shield made of a separate piece of brass and applied to the eagle. The lower row shows side buttons.*

Fig. 73-4.

Fig. 73-5.

Fig. 73-6.

Fig. 73-7.

Fig. 73-8.

Fig. 73-5. *The medical detachment at Fort Gibson, Oklahoma, 1888, wearing white cloth-covered cork summer helmets. A few U.S. Army units wore experimental cork helmets in the late 1870s, and as a favorable result of that experiment the army adopted them universally in 1880. In the many years they were worn, several versions existed, including some with tan cloth. The helmets, both tan and white, could be worn with a wide range of uniforms and usually had the ventilator top, as worn by the men on the left. On the white version officers could wear a gilt spike, chain chin strap, and side buttons (right) when they wished, but in practice most officers wore either the enlisted men's model or removed the spike, leaving the decorative chain and side buttons. Cork summer helmets were not prescribed in uniform regulations after 1902, although a liberal wear-out period let them continue for over half a dozen years.*

Fig. 73-6. *An officers' cap of the type introduced in 1895. All officers wore the embroidered eagle, with generals distinguished by black velvet trim around the base instead of the black mohair worn by other officers, as shown in this example. A white version (without any insignia and with a variety of straps) came into use as the nineteenth century ended.*

Fig. 73-7. *Enlisted men of 1895–1902 wore this style of undress cap with appropriate metal branch insignia.*

Fig. 73-8. *The army bill cap worn today, with a flared crown, can be traced to this 1902 enlisted men's dress cap.*

1881 plate is easily recognized because the scroll bearing the motto *E Pluribus Unum* passes in front of the eagle's neck instead of forming an arc over the eagle's head, as in the earlier pattern (Fig. 73-2). German silver, or "white metal," regimental numbers 1/2 inch high went on the lower part of the shield.[5]

A turn-of-the-century provision, little noted today, was the modification of helmet ornaments for line officers detailed to the staff departments. These officers omitted the silver regimental helmet number and substituted an appropriate staff department metal insignia, the same color as for the shoulder knots, which in most cases would have been in silver.[6]

Besides the black helmets, the army had helmets in white and khaki for summer wear. Following experimental wear of the white helmet from 1875 to 1880, the quartermaster general finally authorized its wear for all troops serving in "extremely hot climates" (Fig. 73-5). A similar khaki helmet was authorized in 1882. Various cords and side buttons went on some of these helmets, but regulations never allowed any insignia on the front, although some men did add the eagles prescribed for the 1881 blue helmets. These tan and white helmets were phased out between 1905 and 1910.[7]

Historically the army changes headgear often, so it is interesting that European-style dress and service helmets lasted so long.

Introduced in 1872, they saw service for thirty-five years or more.

Visor Caps, 1895–Present

In 1895, new dark blue forage caps came into use. They were 3¼ inches high and cylindrically cut like a railroad conductor's cap. An officers' version with mohair braid around the base, an embroidered eagle, and a gold bullion cord ⅛ inch in diameter is shown in Fig. 73-6. The enlisted men's all-cloth counterpart (Fig. 73-7) had a metal branch insignia and a leather chin strap.[8]

The next version came with the 1902–1903 uniform. The cap exhibited a slightly flared crown and a removable branch-colored band near the base (Fig. 73-8).[9] Fig. 73-9 shows an artilleryman wearing this cap with the colored band removed for everyday wear. Subsequently, the caps became more flared every few years, with several minor but new versions introduced before World War I.

The quartermaster general introduced a screw-post fastening device for enlisted men's cap ornaments in 1896 (Fig. 73-10). These devices had a threaded post, which with a nut firmly held the ornament on the cap. To keep the insignia from rotating, one or more needle points were also fixed on the reverse. Men wore gilt or combined gilt and silver metal insignia on the various blue cloth bill caps. On the olive drab and khaki caps, which will be discussed below, men wore black-colored "bronze" insignia. Regimental numbers and company letters were brazed to the insignia, often with the aid of a small flat piece of brass. Generally, in 1905 smaller ornaments replaced the 1896 screw-post cap insignia.[10]

Olive drab and khaki caps, cut like the blue ones, were initially issued in 1905 for wear with the olive drab and khaki service uniforms on some occasions, the insignia being bronze and made with the 1896-style screw-post fasteners.[11] Several versions of these caps ensued, each with a slightly different crown, but generally with wider crowns over time. Examples are shown in Fig. 73-11.

In December 1917 the enlisted men's branch cap insignia changed to a universal device: a U.S. coat of arms on a 1½-inch disk.[12] The officers' eagle, taken from the Great Seal of the United States, became the insignia in 1902. It was worn in both gold and bronze until after World War I, when the bronze version was dropped. Although the design details of the cap and the insignia changed, the overall post–World War I form of both cap and insignia is still used today.

Several different minor changes were made to the service caps, including post–World War I changes of 1920, 1925, and the so-called Pershing model of 1930.[13] Until the 1950s men wore visor caps with the cloth in both olive drab and khaki to match the uniform coat, as shown in Fig. 73-12. Officers wore mohair or wool braid around the cap base, while enlisted men's caps omitted the braid and employed the same cloth as that of the rest of the cap.

Fig. 73-9.

Fig. 73-9. Men could use the 1902 dress cap for everyday wear without the removable, branch-colored band around the base.

Fig. 73-10.

Fig. 73-10. Screw-post fasteners for cap insignia were introduced by the quartermaster general in 1896. This allowed men to neatly and easily affix metal insignia to caps, the same concept used today.

Fig. 73-11. A farriers' class of 1911 included men from a variety of units wearing a wide spectrum of caps, both khaki cotton and olive drab wool. Two officers seated in the center of the front row have mohair braid around the base of their caps.

Fig. 73-12. Officers of 1947 wearing service caps. Those in the Army Air Force wore theirs without a stiffening wire.

Fig. 73-11.

Fig. 73-12.

To phase in the green uniform, the green visor cap was worn initially in the mid-1950s with the olive drab and khaki uniform and then with the green uniform. For field-grade and general officers, the visor was embroidered with gold oak leaves (Fig. 73-13).[14]

In the late nineteenth century, men at a few posts wore white caps because of the heat. Use of white caps expanded in 1900 to the army as a whole. Officers did not initially wear any ornaments on these caps, but cap cords came in three versions: for generals a 2/3-inch-wide gold lace strap, for staff officers a 1/8-inch-diameter gold bullion cord, and for line officers a 1/8-inch-diameter silk cord in the color of the arm. In November 1905 the army directed that eagles be applied to officers' white caps and that the various colored cords be eliminated. The form of these caps was the same as that of the dark blue ones: straight sides until 1902, then a flared crown. White caps returned with the white uniforms before World War I and again after World War II (Figs. 77-5, 77-6, and 77-7 in chapter 77, "White Uniforms").[15]

Officers wore blue caps with their dress and full dress uniform in the 1930s and after World War II. Generals adorned the sides of the cap with oak leaves, while company- and field-grade officers had branch-colored stripes trimmed with gold (Figs. 76-12, 76-13, and 76-14 in chapter 76, "Men's Twentieth-Century Dress Blue Uniforms").

Campaign Hats

A soft, wide-brimmed hat was introduced during 1872 in an attempt to provide protection on the frontier. It was a failure, and a new model with a stiffer brim was introduced four years later. Both were black and had crowns creased fore and aft. The real need was to protect the wearer from sun,

Fig. 73-13.

Fig. 73-13. Lieutenant Colonel Frank E. Storer wearing the service cap of the style introduced in the mid-1950s. Field grade and general officers wore gold-embroidered oak leaves on their cap bills.

Fig. 73-14.

Fig. 73-14. An 1872 black campaign hat. It had hooks and eyes that allowed men to fasten the brim up, but the soft, wide brim was unpopular and was replaced within four years by an improved hat.

Fig. 73-15.

Fig. 73-15. In 1876 the army introduced this black campaign hat, which was worn without insignia or cords. The cooler tan color replaced this black hat in 1883, and in 1899 hat cords were added. Only chaplains continued to wear black hats after 1883.

Fig. 73-16.

Fig. 73-16. This 1899 soldier wears a campaign hat to which are affixed the regimental number and company letter, just authorized that year.

wind, and rain, but the 1872 hat (Fig. 73-14) was too uncomfortable. The army finally corrected the hat's lack of ventilation and excess weight. The evolution continued when the campaign hat changed to tan in 1883. Materials, ventilators, and other changes continued throughout the campaign hat's life (Fig. 73-15).[16] During this late-nineteenth-century and early-twentieth-century period, chaplains' hats were black, without cords or other insignia.

In the late nineteenth century soldiers wore many unauthorized insignia on their campaign hats, such as forage cap insignia and the small metal corps badges introduced during the Spanish-American War. The army finally prescribed metal hat insignia between 1899 and 1907, and during that period enlisted men wore four different versions of regimental numbers and letters on their hat fronts (Fig. 73-16). In 1905 some noncommissioned officers were authorized to wear pin-back branch insignia on the hats, although there was, according to one 1899 commander, "the very common practice of wearing crossed sabers & c. on the hat."[17]

Both officers and enlisted men sewed various hat cords to the brim next to the crown, with the cord designs changing over time. Generals wore gold-colored cords, other commissioned officers had gold and black intermixed, and warrant officers used silver and black. Enlisted men's branch-colored cords had tassel ends until Civil War cords were used up in the 1870s and acorn-shaped ends when the army reintroduced hat cords in 1899 (Figs. 73-17, 73-18, and 73-19). In the twentieth century, branches with two colors had cords with intermixed colors until 1921–22, when the army switched to cords of one color and acorns of the other color. An exception was for machine-gun units, whose members introduced single-colored cords (light blue for infantry or yellow for cavalry) with red acorns during World War I.[18] Campaign hat cords are listed in Tables 73-1

Table 73-1. *Tassel-End Hat Cords.*

Color	Branch	Years of Authorization*
Light or Saxony blue	Infantry	1858–72
Scarlet	Artillery	1858–72
Yellow	Cavalry	1858–72
Yellow	Engineers	1858–72
Green	Riflemen	1858–61
Green and buff	Hospital stewards	1858–72
Orange	Dragoons	1858–61
Crimson	Ordnance	1858–72
Red and white	Indian Scouts	1890–1902

*Leftover Civil War stocks issued in 1887 and used until exhausted in the early 1890s.

Table 73-2. *One-Color Acorn-End Hat Cords.*

Color	Branch	Years of Authorization
Gold	Dragoon officers	1855–58
Gold	General officers	1858–WW II
Light blue	Infantry	1899, 1902–WW II
White	Infantry	1899–1902
Scarlet	Artillery	1899–WW II
Yellow	Cavalry	1855–58, 1899–WW II
Black	Signal Corps	1899–1902
Black	Support organizations	1917–20
Crimson	Ordnance	1899–1902
Buff	Post quartermaster sgt.	1899–1913
Buff	Quartermaster Corps	1913–WW II
Gray	Post commissary sergeant	1899–1913
Gray	Tank Service	1917–33
Green	Hospital Corps	1899–1902
Green	Army Service School Det.	1910–20
Green	Detached Enlisted Men's List	1921–WW II
Purple	Motor Transport Corps	1918–20
Olive drab	Student Army Training Corps	1919
Dark blue	Militia Bureau	1921–22, 1940

NOTE: World War II indicates the phase-out of the campaign hat, which continued until World War II.

Table 73-3. *Multicolored Intermixed Acorn-End Hat Cords.*

Color	Branch	Years of Authorization
Red and white	Engineers	1899–1921
Maroon and white	Hospital Corps	1902–21
Black and scarlet	Ordnance Corps	1902–21
Orange and white	Signal Corps	1902–21
Green and white	Army Service Det., USMA	1910–21
Green and white	Corps of Intelligence Police	1917–20
Green and white	Corps of Interpreters	1917–20
Red, white, and blue	Citizens Military Training Camps	1917–40
Black and white	Army field clerks	1917
Cobalt blue and yellow	Chemical Warfare Svce.	1918–21
Green and black	Air Service	1918–21
Green and yellow	Provost Marshal	1919–20
Green and red	Transportation Corps	1919–20
Gold and black	Commissioned officers	1858–WW II
Silver and black	Field clerks	1917–26
Silver and black	Warrant officers	1921–WW II

NOTE: World War II indicates the phase-out of the campaign hat, which continued into World War II.

through 73-5. Troops wore various campaign or service hats with some field uniforms until World War II.

The hat itself changed from being worn with a crease in the crown to four indentations made to form a "Montana peak" in 1911. Examples of the hat are shown in Figs. 67-2 and 67-3 of chapter 67, "Shirts," and a later version is shown in Figs. 73-20 and 73-21. After the World War I experience, several army factions attempted to do away with the campaign hat, citing its storage problems, procurement and maintenance costs, and other factors. Finally, in October 1941 the army made the campaign hat limited standard, although in 1939 the Quartermaster

Table 73-4. *Two-Color Hat Cords, Not Intermixed.*

Acorn Color	Cord Color	Branch	Years of Authorization
Red	Yellow	Cavalry (Machine-Gun Units)	1919–ca. 1924*
Red	Blue	Infantry (Machine-Gun Units)	1919–ca. 1924*
Red	Dark Blue	Militia Bureau	1922–40
White	Red	Engineers	1921–WW II
White	Maroon	Medical Dept.	1921–WW II
White	Orange	Signal Corps	1921–WW II
Yellow	Silver Gray	Finance Corps	1920–WW II
Yellow	Crimson	Ordnance Corps	1921–WW II
Orange	Blue	Air Corps	1921–30
Yellow	Cobalt Blue	Chemical Warfare Service	1921–WW II
Green	Yellow	Military Police	1922–WW II

NOTE: World War II indicates the phase-out of the campaign hat, which continued until World War II.
*Used by some machine-gun units depending upon stocks available from World War I.

Table 73-5. *Unofficial Hat Cords, ca. World War I.*

Organization	Colors
Civilian employees of the Signal Corps	Light orange/yellow and white
Volunteer Training Corps and reserve militia	Blue and white
YMCA	Steel blue*
Red Cross, Library Service, and similar organizations	Black†

*Used by some men before black was prescribed.
† Used before officially sanctioned near the end of the war.

Fig. 73-17.

Fig. 73-17. *Artillerymen in 1904 wearing a variety of hats and caps. The two men on the left wear the 1902-style blue cap, the next two wear the 1895-pattern cap, and the man on the right wears a tan campaign hat of the general style introduced in 1883. Branch-colored cords were reintroduced in 1899 to accompany company letters and regimental numbers which went on the front.*

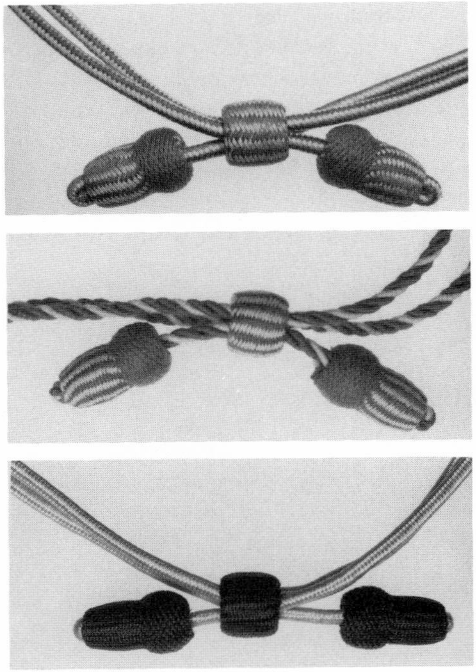

Fig. 73-18.

Corps had begun to limit its issue to mounted units, troops overseas, and other selected limited locations.[19]

The army revived the campaign hat, as a symbol of expertise and experience, in the mid-1960s for drill sergeants (Fig. 73-20).[20] These post–World War II personnel were not supposed to use a hat cord, and initially at some posts the insignia on the front was the distinctive insignia of the U.S. Army training centers. Even so, at some posts various colored hat cords came into use. Quickly in the mid-1960s the standard enlisted men's visored cap insignia became the prescribed insignia on the front of the drill instructors' campaign hats.

Campaign hats saw wide but unofficial use. After World War II some marksmanship teams adopted campaign hats because they were very functional on a rifle range. The U.S. Army marksmanship team from Fort Benning is shown in a photograph, Fig. 73-21, taken about 1960. More common than marksmanship team wear was the use of black campaign hats by cavalry units. In Vietnam many air cavalry officers wore black hats, as shown in Figs. 73-22 and 73-23. These hats usually carried hat cords and a wide range of other insignia, including rank insignia, cavalry or armor insignia, red and white cloth ovals, distinctive insignia, or aviators' wings. In the mid-1970s some units in the 1st Cavalry Division at Fort Hood, Texas, also adopted these "Cav hats."

Pillbox Caps

These unofficial headgear were primarily worn in the 1870s and early 1880s, most often by officers but occasionally by enlisted

Fig. 73-19.

Fig. 73-18. *Typical hat cords of the type used after 1899. While some cords were of a single color, others were of two colors. The patterns of these two-colored cords varied. Between 1899 and 1921 the two colors were intermixed in the cord, the acorn tips, and the keeper (slide). The post–World War I style had the cord of one color and the acorns and keeper of the second color. The cord at the top is the version that was prescribed by the U.S. Army; it has the two colors of the cord woven into a single strand. In the center is a privately made hat cord that has the two cord colors made from different color strands. The bottom cord is the post–World War I style with the cord of one color and the keeper and acorns of the other color.*

Fig. 73-19. *Enlisted men about 1906 wearing creased campaign hats.*

Fig. 73-20. *A drill sergeant instructs a basic trainee in rifle marksmanship at Fort Benning, Georgia, in 1984. Use of the campaign hat was reserved for qualified drill instructors after the mid-1960s, ending unofficial use of the hat by marksmanship teams.*

Fig. 73-21. *Members of the Army Marksmanship Unit about 1960. These men wear the campaign hat with the Montana peak, as adopted in 1911. A unique red, white, and blue hat cord with blue acorns was used by this unit, whose members wore campaign hats on the firing range. Officers wore the standard gold and black cord. When drill sergeants adopted campaign hats later in the 1960s, isolated wear of hats, like this, ceased.*

men. Because they were unofficial caps, no prescribed pattern existed, but photographic evidence shows that they had low-crowned, cylindrical bodies without any bill. Often pillbox caps were ornamented with some lace or cloth trim that did not appear on any other cap or hat, although frequently the soldier placed a cap insignia on the front of a pillbox cap. Two examples are shown in Figs. 73-24 and 73-25.

Fig. 73-21.

Fig. 73-22. *Two captains, members of A Troop, 3d Squadron, 17th Cavalry, at a unit party in Vietnam, 1970. They wear typical black hats used by many air cavalry units during the Vietnam War. Insignia on these hats were officers' gold and black hat cords, rank, and crossed sabers ordinarily worn as collar insignia.*

Fig. 73-23. *Chief Warrant Officers Stein and Nicholas of the Aeroweapons Platoon, B Troop, 1st Squadron, 9th Cavalry, 1st Cavalry Division, in Vietnam in December 1971. Besides the fire-resistant Nomex flight clothing adorned with unauthorized pocket patches, they wear "Cav hats" with silver and black cords, rank insignia, and bright metal cavalry insignia with unit numbers.*

Fig. 73-20.

Fig. 73-22.

Fig. 73-23.

Fig. 73-24. *A pillbox cap worn by a cavalry officer in the West after the Civil War. On the front of this nonregulation cap he wears crossed sabers.*

Fig. 73-25. *A first lieutenant of the New York National Guard. In his fatigue dress this officer wears his pillbox cap with embroidered rifles and regimental number. Pillbox caps began to appear at the close of the Civil War and were worn not only in militia units but also unofficially within the U.S. Regular Army during the 1870s and 1880s.*

Fig. 73-24.

Fig. 73-25.

Chapter Seventy-Four

Men's Headgear, World War I and Later

The garrison or overseas cap and the steel helmet are two pieces of headgear that the public usually associates with the U.S. Army. Both were introduced during World War I. In the more than seventy-five years since their introduction, several changes in design have taken place, and a wide range of other headgear has come into use. That unique French headwear, the beret, has been adopted by various armies, and since World War II the U.S. Army has joined in the worldwide rush of forces that allows special elite units to wear the beret.

Generally rank or unit insignia was worn on the headgear introduced during and after World War I. Some caps like the overseas cap during its first 40 years of existence also showed branch, while men's berets often showed both unit and rank. Besides rank or unit insignia, after World War II soldiers often added special badges usually worn on shirts, such as parachute or aviation badges, to the caps worn with fatigue uniforms.

Fig. 74-1.

Fig. 74-1. *A World War I major wearing an overseas cap. Officers' caps carried branch-colored braid around the edge of the curtain.*

Fig. 74-2.

Fig. 74-2. *World War I overseas caps were of olive drab wool and were to carry a branch insignia originally made for wear by enlisted men on the coat collar.*

Overseas Caps, 1917 to Present

In World War I trenches, soldiers found a need for new headgear. The helmet gave protection, but when the helmet was not needed—at staff meetings, in rest areas, and dozens of other times—some alternative cap was required. When the helmet was in use, the campaign hat and the service cap took too much storage room, and both were subject to being crushed. A small, soft headgear that retained its shape was needed. The overseas cap was the answer, because it could be folded up and put out of sight in pocket or pack. In was introduced to the American Expeditionary Forces by the French.

Officers wore rank insignia on the left side of the curtain, as the turned-up lower portion of the cap is called. Officers' branch was indicated by colored piping around the curtain edge (Fig. 74-1). A summary of these colors is in Table 74-1. Enlisted men were to wear a bronze collar disk on their cap, which had no piping (Fig. 74-2).[1] This cap came in many patterns based on national designs, and the cuts varied considerably (Figs. 74-3 and 74-4). Many of the early caps were made in Europe, so a wide range of quality and designs resulting. An unusual

Table 74-1. *World War I Officers' Overseas Cap Piping.*

Branch	Piping Color
Adjutant General's Department	Dark blue
Air Service	Green and black
Artillery	Scarlet
Cavalry	Yellow
Cavalry (machine-gun units)	Yellow and scarlet
Chaplains	Black
Chemical Warfare Service	Cobalt blue and yellow
Corps of Engineers	Scarlet and white
Corps of Interpreters	Green and white
Field clerks	Black and white
General officers	Gold
General Staff	Gold and black
Infantry	Light blue
Infantry (machine-gun units)	Light blue and scarlet
Inspector General's Department	Dark blue and white
Judge Advocate General's Department	Dark blue and light blue
Medical Department	Maroon
Motor Transport Corps	Purple
Ordnance Department	Black and scarlet
Provost Marshal General's Department	Yellow and green
Quartermaster Corps	Buff
Signal Corps	Orange and white
Tank Service	Gray
Transportation Corps	Scarlet and green

tank trooper is shown in Fig. 74-5 wearing an officers' collar insignia on his cap instead of the correct enlisted men's version; evidence shows that this was occasionally done after the close of the war.

After World War I the army discarded the overseas cap in favor of the campaign hat and the visor cap, and within the United States the overseas cap was not authorized or cited in regulations. The overseas cap, known as the field cap, was slowly revived for Air Corps officers, who wore it with branch-colored piping and an Air Corps insignia in 1925. Soon flying cadets adopted the cap, and in 1930 some aviation enlisted men began to wear overseas caps, but without piping or insignia. The Quartermaster Corps issued leftover World War I overseas caps initially to meet the need. The need for some type of headgear that could be folded up and that took only a small space remained among most army branches.[2]

Use of the overseas cap expanded to include members of tank or mechanized cavalry in April 1933 and was extended to mechanized Coast Artillery units seven months later. Initially, no insignia was to be placed on these field caps, but officers wore branch-colored piping on theirs. In 1937 mechanized and motorized units adopted the field cap, and in all units that had adopted distinctive insignia, the device was placed on the left of the cap, 1 inch from the front. In some units without distinctive insignia, men used a branch collar disk on the cap and officers wore rank insignia. In 1939 every driver and person assigned to a motorized vehicle was authorized the field cap, leaving the campaign hat only for horse-mounted men, the walking infantry, men in fixed emplacements, troops in Alaska, and the like. This same 1939 change called for the previous olive drab cap to be made in khaki for wear in the Philippines, Hawaii, Panama, and Puerto Rico. As will be seen, however, men at Fort Knox, the home of mechanized experimental units, wore various field caps apparently without regard for army-wide regulations.[3]

In practice the Quartermaster Corps continued to issue leftover World War I overseas caps until it was required to obtain new caps, which it finally did in 1938, when it issued the first specification for field caps.[4] Before that time many soldiers had purchased caps with their own money to improve their appearance. January 1933 saw the 1st Cavalry Regiment transferred to Fort Knox, Kentucky, with the mission of forming the

Fig. 74-3.

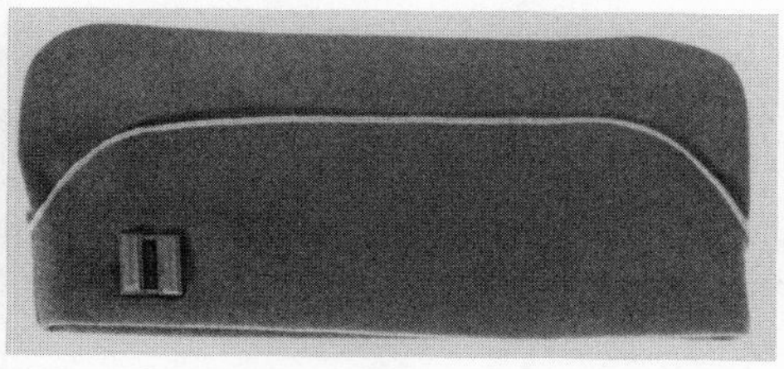

Fig. 74-4.

Fig. 74-5.

Fig. 74-3. Several countries had different patterns of overseas caps during World War I. The man on the left wears a British version, while the man on the right wears the American style.

Fig. 74-4. An officers' World War I overseas cap, with branch-colored trim. This style was known as the Belgian trench cap.

Fig. 74-5. This enlisted member of the Tank Corps wears an officers' branch insignia on his cap after the close of World War I. Upon their return to the United States, many army members switched to such unauthorized branch insignia.

army's first mechanized force. Three years later the 13th Cavalry jointed in the experiment. These units adopted a commercially made field cap that had a high crown and did not contain the internal fold like that of the official field cap. Enlisted men wore colored cords on these caps. In addition, these units and a few others wore khaki field caps during that time, despite the fact that the Quartermaster Corps stocked and issued only the olive drab wool version.

Photographs of these early mechanized cavalry units show that khaki field caps were worn with summer khaki uniforms, while nonregulation olive drab wool caps with the high crown and branch trim were also worn. Officers wore the gold and black braid, which corresponded to the colored trim used on the campaign cap. Branch-colored cloth disks went behind officers' metal rank insignia—again, despite army regulations (Fig. 74-6). Apparently the new forces at Fort Knox wrote their own rules. These changes did not preclude the wear of cotton khaki field caps before their official introduction in 1939, nor the early use of branch trim and metal rank insignia by officers.

Beginning in 1940, company- and field-grade officers officially switched to gold and black piping on the curtain, and enlisted men began to wear branch-colored trim, although, as noted, a few units already followed this practice.[5] Under these circumstances many officers in the late 1930s wore a branch-colored cloth disk under their rank insignia on the cap even though regulations called for distinctive insignia. Finally, change 2 to AR 600-40, 1942, called for officers to wear rank insignia on caps. A listing of the World War II cord-edge braid colors for garrison caps is in Table 74-2. Caps were issued by the Quartermaster Corps without any braid attached during World War II and the Korean War. The colored trim was issued separately. Many new soldiers, or those transferred from one branch to another, wore caps without any trim until the men sewed on the appropriate braid.

When the 1956 green uniform was introduced, enlisted troops' branch piping on the cap was eliminated, but generals continued to trim their cap in gold, company- and field-grade officers wore black and gold intermixed, and warrant officers had silver and black intermixed, following the World War II scheme.

The shape of the caps varied. The 1938 cap came with a huge internal fold, 5¾ inches wide, that caused the sides to stand nearly vertically when worn. This design was changed in 1940 to have a smaller internal fold, and the cap became known as the garrison cap.[6] Soldiers often pinned the pleat closed to improve the cap's appearance. During World War II commercial versions of the cap appeared without a pleat and became very popular. This demand resulted in the design, adopted in 1950, without the pleat.

Throughout the cap's life the cut varied, as did the manner of wear, although all of these caps conformed to the same general shape. Most men wore the garrison cap of World War II and shortly thereafter with the crown pushed down on top of the head, leaving small peaks in the front and back (Fig. 74-7). Armor units wore the cap stiff, and in the mid-1950s this style was adopted army-wide (Fig. 74-8).

FATIGUE CAPS

A wide assortment of work or fatigue caps and hats was introduced during and after World War I. Although only the Coast Artillery Corps had blue denim uniforms before the war, during the war virtually all

Table 74-2. *Cord-Edge Braid for World War II Garrison Caps.*

Branch	Colors
General officers	Gold
Other commissioned officers	Gold and black
Warrant officers	Silver and black
Flight officers	Silver and black
Adjutant General's Department	Dark blue and scarlet
Air Corps	Ultramarine blue and golden yellow
Armored Center and units	Green and white
Cavalry	Yellow
Chemical Warfare Service	Cobalt blue and golden yellow
Coast Artillery Corps	Scarlet
Corps of Engineers	Scarlet and white
Detached Enlisted Men's List	Green
Field Artillery	Scarlet
Finance Department	Silver gray and golden yellow
First Special Service Force	Red, white, and blue
Infantry	Light blue
Medical Department	Maroon and white
Military Police	Yellow and green
National Guard Bureau	Dark blue
Ordnance Department	Crimson and yellow
Quartermaster Corps	Buff
Signal Corps	Orange and white
Tank destroyer units	Golden orange and black
Transportation Corps	Brick red and golden yellow
Women's Army Corps	Old gold and moss-tone green

Fig. 74-6.

Fig. 74-6. *Just before World War II, use of the field cap became widespread, and it replaced the campaign hat. These officers assigned to a quartermaster regiment wear buff disks behind the rank on their caps; the doctor's white-edged maroon disk stands out in the second row. Braid was gold and black intermixed, corresponding to the color of campaign hat cords. Names of the cap changed with its design and use, evolving from overseas cap to field cap to garrison cap.*

Fig. 74-7.

Fig. 74-7. *Men of the Armored Force Replacement Training Center, 1942. The officer on the left wears his cap with the crown stiff and tipped on the left side of the head. Armored Force troops frequently wore their caps this way. The fourth officer from the left wears a soft-crowned issue cap. The officer fifth from the left wears the same type of soft-crowned cap, but with the crown pushed down. During World War II this style of wear became common, although often Armored Force members wore the crown stiff. The jackets and coats show the diversity of uniforms in use during World War II. The fifth officer from the left wears the winter Armored Force jacket, with the "shoulder" patch on the left chest, a common practice for tank troops.*

Fig. 74-8.

Fig. 74-8. *This ROTC cadet wears an olive drab 1950-style garrison cap with the crown stiff, the same style as that used by armor units starting in the 1930s and adopted army-wide in 1956.*

men began to wear them at different times. The denim hat was soft-crowned, made from eight sections, and sewn together with a soft brim. The army classified the denim hat as limited standard in 1940. The same design persisted when in 1941 the army introduced a cotton khaki field hat for use until a better cap or hat could be procured. This functional hat was very popular with the troops in the early days of the national emergency but was soon replaced by an olive drab herringbone twill version (Fig. 74-9).[7]

While the overseas cap and the various soft-brimmed hats filled part of soldiers' needs, there was still a need for a cap with a bill. The army issued a soft-billed olive drab herringbone twill cap for mechanics and others who wore the one-piece herringbone twill work uniforms.[8] This cap, along with the M-1943 field cap, became the model for subsequent billed caps worn with fatigue uniforms.

In 1951 the army brought out a field cap with a bill for use with fatigue clothing.[9] This soft-crowned cap was basically in the shape of a right circular cylinder, but because of the cloth sides, it did not hold its shape well. In Korea, General Matthew Ridgway popularized the practice of fixing the cap sides so they were stiff, presenting a neater appearance. Soon privately purchased caps made with stiff sides were in wide use, although regulations were silent on them. They were commonly called "spring-up caps" because they would spring back into shape after being crushed, or "coffee can caps" because their basic shape and size were similar to the common coffee cans then in use (Fig. 74-10).

In late 1963 the shape of the fatigue cap was modified to that of the popular baseball cap. As in the case of the previous various M-1951 field caps, commercial models were widely worn, and some of them strayed far from the official pattern. The 1951 field cap continued in limited use on ranger missions

Fig. 74-9.

Fig. 74-9. *In this 1941 field training setting men are wearing several different styles of headgear. The most popular are the cotton khaki field hat with the stitched cloth brim and the khaki overseas cap. In addition, a few others are worn. The man on the right end in the front row wears a herringbone twill field cap. The man on the right end in the third row (fourth from right, standing) wears a winter field cap.*

Fig. 74-10.

Fig. 74-10. *During the 1950s, the M-1951 field cap was worn with very straight, stiff sides, as shown in this photograph taken in Korea. The metal rank insignia worn by the sergeant was never sanctioned by regulations, but such metal and enamel chevrons were widely worn during the time of the Korean War.*

and in other special assignments. With the advent of the camouflage battle dress uniforms in the early 1980s the army reintroduced the 1951 field cap made in camouflage materials, and like the older official versions, it usually had ear flaps that tucked up inside the cap (Fig. 74-11).[10]

After World War II, when fatigue uniforms became common, officers placed rank insignia on their bill caps, while enlisted men used distinctive insignia (Fig. 74-12). In addition, special skill badges, such as parachute badges, were worn on the post–World War II bill caps.[11] The introduction of the camouflage M-1951 field cap, with its inherent emphasis on concealment, caused the army to revise its policy on insignia placed on the fatigue cap. Generally only metal rank insignia went on the cap, with everyone initially wearing subdued versions, but by the mid-1980s officers changed to bright metal so they could be distinguished from greater than the three or four feet required with the subdued insignia.[12]

Sun Helmets

Sun helmets, officially known as cloth-covered fiber helmets, were used in tropical climates before, during, and after World War II (Figs. 74-13 and 74-14). During World War II distinctive insignia were worn on the sun helmet, but after the war, on the few times it was worn, the sun helmet carried the standard cap eagle. Although authorization for its use was withdrawn in mid-1943, soldiers continued to wear the sun helmet, but later regulations usually failed to mention it. Even so, the front eyelet on sun helmets was still called a "distinctive insignia eyelet" into the 1970s. Authorized colors for sun helmets were white, khaki, and, after the introduction of the green uniform, olive green shade 107.[13]

Other Field Headgear

While older caps, hats, and helmets remained in use during and after World War II, newer, more diversified special headgear came into use concurrent with the adoption of new weapons and an increase in the size of the army. Aviation headgear, tank crewmen's helmets, and others all contributed to the large increase in styles of specialized headgear.

A popular World War II cap was the wool knit cap introduced in 1941. It had a short bill and a single flap that turned up around the outside or could be lowered to cover the ears in cold weather. It was worn in the field alone or under the helmet. Sometimes called a "jeep cap," it was worn without insignia. It was replaced by the pile field cap.

Designed for winter field use, the olive drab pile field cap, introduced in 1943, has undergone several revisions, and its descendant is still used today. It has wool or pile ear

Fig. 74-11.

Fig. 74-11. The field cap as modified in the early 1980s for wear with the battle dress uniform. Its design was basically unchanged from the original 1951 version, except for the patterned material. Once the camouflage battle dress uniform was introduced, only rank insignia went on the cap.

Fig. 74-12.

Fig. 74-12. This commander of one of the few National Guard units to serve in Vietnam wears the issue fatigue cap, commonly known as the baseball cap. Officers wore rank insignia on the front, while enlisted personnel wore distinctive unit insignia or rank insignia at differing dates. Frequently those who had earned special qualification badges such as parachute badges and aviation wings wore them on their fatigue caps in addition to the other insignia.

Fig. 74-13.

Fig. 74-13. General Jonathan Wainwright and some of his staff just a few days before the Japanese invaded the Philippine Islands. Their sun helmets carry distinctive unit insignia. Some soldiers wore the normal enlisted men's cap eagle on a 1½-inch disk on sun helmet before World War II.

Fig. 74-14.

Fig. 74-14. These noncommissioned officers were graduates of the pilot course to train drill sergeants in August 1964. Campaign hats were soon adopted as distinctive for drill sergeants.

Fig. 74-15.

Fig. 74-15. These soldiers wear both the camouflage and olive drab versions of the hot weather hat. The olive drab version was issued during the Vietnam War. Camouflage versions used in the 1960s were privately purchased, so their cut and camouflage patterns varied from the official versions.

Fig. 74-16.

Fig. 74-16. In the 1980s the hot weather sun hat was made in several materials, including the desert camouflage pattern shown here. Regardless of the material used, only subdued rank insignia were worn on the various sun hats.

flaps. The original version had a wool bill that was turned up in front, while the Korean War model had a plain turned-up visor. Later versions had hook-and-loop fasteners instead of strings to fasten the flaps, which rolled into multiple layers instead of simply being tied over the cap top when conditions did not warrant their use. On all of these caps officers usually wore rank insignia, while enlisted personnel wore the visor bare, with distinctive insignia, or with various sizes of cloth or metal chevrons.

The headgear that symbolized Vietnam was the hot-weather or tropical hat, which was worn in a wide range of official and unofficial patterns and cloth styles. These tropical hats generally had a soft crown and a semirigid stitched brim. Commonly called bush hats or boonie hats, these headgear were widely supplied to troops starting in 1967 and were used widely until after 1971,

Fig. 74-17.

Fig. 74-18.

Fig. 74-17. *The two U.S. Cavalry regiments in Europe wore black berets during the 1970s. These two officers of the 11th Armored Cavalry Regiment wear bright metal rank insignia in front of an oval red and white flash bearing the 11th Cavalry distinctive insignia. During the middle and late 1970s many units wore a wide range of berets, including tan, maroon, green, blue, and black ones.*

Fig. 74-18. *Worn at Fort Knox, Kentucky, in the late 1970s, this badge was planned to be the universal armor and cavalry beret badge for the U.S. Army.*

although some troops wore them both before and after these dates. After the Vietnam War the U.S. Army again issued the hot-weather sun hat, and it came in several materials and with various widths of brims. Examples are shown in Figs. 74-15 and 74-16.[14]

Berets

The U.S. Army's Special Forces first adopted the beret in 1955, and it was officially adopted in 1961. In Vietnam, U.S. advisors wore many of the various Vietnamese berets, and various U.S. units also started to wear berets. The U.S. units in Vietnam wore black, olive drab, camouflage, and various Vietnamese berets.[15] During the 1970s, ranger, airborne, some armor and cavalry, and a few other units began to wear berets. On most berets men wore unit-distinctive insignia, such as cloth flashes, accompanied by metal rank insignia. In some cases a few units adopted metal badges for the berets, but these badges designated a particular unit and not a branch. It is quite impossible to reach agreement in some cases as to what is a branch insignia and what is a unit insignia, but clearly company, battalion, or regimental distinctive insignia are not branch insignia in the context of this book.

Some armor and cavalry units adopted the black beret starting in the early 1970s. At different locations use of berets varied. In Europe, for example, the 2d and 11th Armored Cavalry Regiments were authorized black berets, the 1st Battalion of the 509th Airborne Infantry was authorized maroon berets in 1973, and in 1975 the 5th Quartermaster Detachment received maroon berets, but otherwise use of berets was restricted.[16]

Shortly after the introduction of the black armor beret, the Armor School at Fort Knox, Kentucky, attempted to formalize a beret badge for all armor and cavalry units. The original design, which I suggested, consisted of crossed sabers with World War II armored force insignia superimposed upon the upper part of the crossed sabers and a ribbon bearing *1776–1917* on the lower portion of the sabers. Because soldiers rolled up berets to stick them in their pockets, the original design also deliberately eliminated sharp points that might cause tears or might snag. The overall design underwent some modifications at Fort Knox, with several variations made, until the final armor beret badge (Fig. 74-18) was produced in quantity. The most essential elements had been retained, with a lightning bolt to show speed and armor striking power replacing the ribbon that had been originally suggested. With the army's elimination of berets for armor and cavalry units in 1979, the badge disappeared from headgear, although the "universal badge" had seen use only at Fort Knox.

In 1979 an army chief of staff policy of enforcing headgear regulations left the black beret for airborne and ranger units and a green beret for Special Forces. In December 1980 airborne units received maroon berets. All of these berets had cloth unit flashes (Fig. 74-19).[17]

Combat Helmets

During World War I the U.S. Army recognized that the British steel helmet did not offer adequate protection, but it could be made easily and quickly. It was adopted on the premise that an inadequate helmet was better than none.[18] It remained the standard combat helmet until just before the start of World War II, when a two-piece helmet set was adopted. The outer steel helmet provided better protection and was formed to fit the head better than the World War I helmet. Inside the steel helmet was a fiber and plastic helmet liner that contained adjustable webbing, allowing for a comfortable fit for any wearer. After World War II many units

Fig. 74-19.

Fig. 74-19. *Airborne units began to wear berets in the 1970s, and this practice was officially sanctioned army-wide in 1980.*

painted these helmet liners with various designs and insignia. Although the combat or protective helmet was originally to be used in field training or in war, the painted helmet liner was also worn with various service uniforms (Figs. 74-20 and 74-21).

In addition to these helmet liner markings, army-wide policy and regulations called for marking military police helmets with a variety of colored bands, numbers, and insignia that designated the wearer's unit. The colored bands on military police helmets indicated the higher headquarters to which the unit was assigned. A red band indicated a division unit, while blue and white bands showed a corps unit, for example.[19] The variety of helmet designs included painted designs or decals for unit-distinctive insignia, shoulder patches, rank device, and/or unit numbers. Very seldom were branch insignia used on combat helmets even officially.

Fig. 74-20.

Fig. 74-20. *A regimental commander and his orderly in 1955 wear painted helmet liners. The six-pointed star on the helmets is the shoulder patch of the 6th Division, also worn by the colonel on the shoulder of his long-sleeved khaki shirt. Decoration of helmet liners was unregulated by the Department of the Army, and thus many paint schemes were used.*

Fig. 74-21.

Fig. 74-21. *Infantry officer candidates, with a tactical officer, about 1965. The colored helmet liners with various shoulder patch designs worn by these candidates is typical of parade helmet liners used after the end of World War II.*

Chapter Seventy-Five

Women's Headgear

Army women have adopted many forms of headgear. During World War I, nurses, Red Cross workers, and telephone operators generally wore low-crowned, straight-brimmed hats or overseas caps. Examples of women's early-twentieth-century caps and hats are shown in Figs. 75-1 through 75-4.

World War II

There were several new caps and hats for women. These were made in various colors and materials to match the rest of the uniform, so a given style of hat may exist in several colors and materials. Members of the Women's Army Auxiliary Corps (WAAC) and later Women's Army Corps (WAC) used a so-called Hobby hat (Fig. 75-5), named for the corps director, Colonel Oveta Culp Hobby. This WAAC hat, developed by Knox Hats, was the same for both officers and enlisted women. Distinction was by the insignia placed on the front: small eagles on brass disks 1½ inches in diameter were used by enlisted women, while larger, silhouette brass eagles were used by officers. The stiff, visored caps were made in olive drab and in khaki to match the summer and winter uniforms. By 1945 women had quit wearing these caps.

For wear with work uniforms WAAC members received brimmed khaki twill hats

Fig. 75-1.

Fig. 75-2.

Fig. 75-1. *Nurses of the Spanish-American War period did not have prescribed outdoor uniforms, but that did not stop this nurse from wearing a uniform and insignia of the general type used by male medical personnel at the time. Use of military caps by women was not common; broad-brimmed caps were more stylish.*

Fig. 75-2. *Catherine Stimson, chief of American Expeditionary Forces nurses, in France, October 1918. Many women associated with the military, including American Red Cross workers, wore broad-brimmed hats of this style.*

Fig. 75-3. Telephone operators at First Army headquarters in France, November 1918. Women in World War I, including nurses, frequently wore overseas caps with their outdoor uniforms.

Fig. 75-4. Physical therapists at Walter Reed General Hospital, 1919. Female medical personnel, including nurses, dietitians, and therapists such as these, wore caps with ward uniforms. Nurses were required to wear white caps with ward uniforms into the late 1970s.

Fig. 75-3.

Fig. 75-4.

of the same general configuration as the cotton khaki field cap used by men early in World War II. A revised version, which appeared in 1943, was called the summer hat (Fig. 75-6).[1]

Women's garrison caps were longer than the men's versions and had a pronounced curve. Distinctive of the women's cap was a deep internal fold which allowed the cap top to open when the cap was worn. The cut allowed the cap to fit over women's longer hair. Braid and insignia on these caps were generally the same style as those on men's caps. No other style of headgear came in more colors. Enlisted WAC members wore cord edge braid of moss green and old gold. Nurses wore a blue cap with maroon cord braid; on it was worn the nurses' caduceus. In 1944 WAC members began to be issued overseas caps as replacements for the WAC Hobby hat, because Colonel Hobby finally decided in 1943 that a garrison cap could be worn by WAC members. The women's garrison (overseas) cap came

Fig. 75-5.

Fig. 75-6.

Fig. 75-5. *This cap, commonly called the Hobby hat after the corps director Colonel Oveta Culp Hobby, was worn by Women's Army Auxiliary Corps and Women's Army Corps members until it was replaced by field caps in 1944 and 1945. Visors and bodies of Hobby hats were either of olive drab wool for wear with winter uniforms or of khaki to match summer uniforms. Officers and enlisted women wore the same style caps, the distinction between the two being made by insignia.*

Fig. 75-6. *The women's summer hat for use with work uniforms.*

Fig. 75-7. *This WAC lieutenant is wearing a garrison cap of the type that came into wide use during 1944.*

in khaki, both tropical worsted and cotton; in olive drab wool; and in beige shantung and in darker wool crepe, the last two for wear with the summer and winter off-duty dresses. These popular caps were worn until 1954. An example of the garrison cap is shown in Fig. 75-7.[2]

The caps and hats worn by medical women initially were different from those used by WAAC and WAC members. Nurses, dietitians, and physical therapists, all officers, adopted a so-called nurses' service cap during World War II. Initially, the all-cloth cap had a very soft crown and an overly broad visor, above which was a 1-inch front strap ending in a bow. This old-fashioned model was quickly revised, and few, if any, of these caps saw service. The service cap, which was widely used, was revised in late 1942. It had a close-fitting body, a reinforced front to carry a standard officers' cap eagle, and a stitched semirigid bill. To match the various uniforms the nurses' service cap was in several cloths: beige, white, blue, and olive drab (Fig. 75-8).[3]

Fig. 75-7.

Hats and Caps after World War II

A unique women's hat came into use after World War II. The initial version, introduced in 1951, was worn with the brim turned up on the wearer's left and down on the right, with the insignia placed so that it was centered over the wearer's right eye (Fig. 75-9). It was made to go with the taupe and the dress white uniforms. The blue uniform, including a blue wool cap of the same general design, was added in 1957. Ornamentation on the blue caps consisted of two laurel leaf designs on the front brim for field-grade officers, and a 1/2-inch-wide gold or gold-colored strap across the front for company-grade and warrant officers.[4]

In July 1962 the army revised women's hats with the introduction of the army green

Fig. 75-8.

Fig. 75-8. *Surrounding a male physician, women medical officers of World War II wear their all-cloth service caps, known as the nurses' service cap by war's end. The two women in the light beige summer uniforms contrast with the others in the winter service uniforms. Taken in 1945 at Ashford General Hospital. The woman second from the right in the front row is Emma E. Vogel, who as a colonel later became the first chief of the Army Medical Service Corps.*

Fig. 75-9. *Commonly used women's headgear of the Korean War period. On the left is the white hat, which when properly worn had the insignia above the wearer's right eye. In the center is the taupe wool service cap. Although the service cap was cut generally similar to the World War II garrison cap, the Korean War taupe service cap did not have any braid around the curtain. The nurses' white cap, used on the wards, is on the right.*

Fig. 75-10. *The army green women's hat introduced in 1962. The gold strap at the base of the crown distinguished company-grade and warrant officers, while field-grade officers had gold-embroidered laurel leaves instead of the strap. Hats of this design replaced the earlier white and blue styles of the type shown in Fig. 75-9 (left).*

hat, which had the brim turned up in back and down in front and was much more fashionable than the earlier hats (Fig. 75-10). On this hat women wore eagles of a smaller size than those used by men, a change from the World War II practice. Several colors and variations of these special women's insignia exist, including that in post–World War II antique bronze. The hat was symmetrical with the brim rolled up in back, and the insignia was centered on the hat. There were three types of hatbands: enlisted women had a green hatband with an oval rise in the front to fit behind the insignia; company-grade and warrant officers added a ½-inch gold braid on the bottom of the band; and field-grade officers added gold bullion laurel leaves instead of the gold braid used by lower-ranking officers. The hat became optional instead of a required piece of clothing in late 1978.[5]

Similar blue and white hats were authorized at the same time for dress uniforms, although the previous styles with the brim turned up on one side could continue to be worn as long as they were serviceable. Even so, the July 1962 change required the hat insignia to be centered instead of worn over the wearer's right eye. At the same time, the older beige hat was declared obsolete effective July 1963, at which time the green hat would be worn with the beige uniform. Eventually the older blue hat, turned up on one side, became obsolete in mid-1969.[6]

Women's garrison caps of the 1950s and 1960s came without branch braid and with a

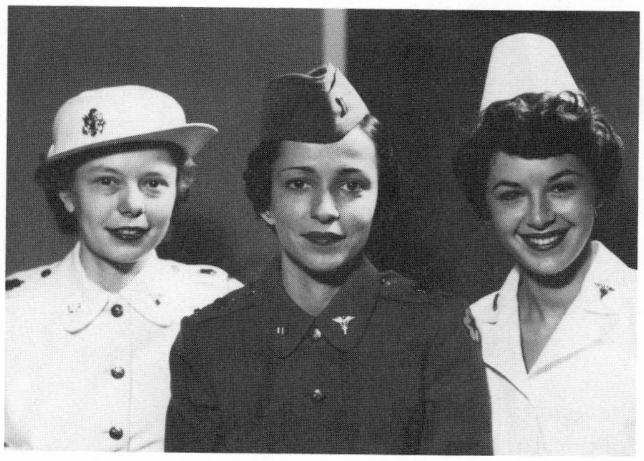

Fig. 75-9.

Fig. 75-10.

Fig. 75-11.

Fig. 75-12.

Fig. 75-11. *On the right, the light green cord uniform, which included dark green trim around the curtain of the matching cap. Between 1975 and 1980 the army green garrison cap could also be worn with the cord uniform.*

Fig. 75-12. *Captain Isabelle J. Smarts wears the new army green skirt, blouse, and garrison cap in 1962. Initially worn with only the green uniform, in the 1970s the dark green cap was also worn with other uniforms. This garrison cap became obsolete in 1980. When garrison caps returned to use in the early 1980s, the curtain was trimmed with cord: generals wore gold, field- and company-grade officers wore gold and black intermixed, warrant officers wore silver and black, and enlisted women wore dark green, the same color scheme as that used by men.*

higher curtain than that of the World War II version. The caps came in several colors. With the 1951 taupe uniform came a taupe cap that was ultimately made of several materials and that did not have special braid around the curtain. The taupe cap (Fig. 75-9) was used into the early 1960s until it was replaced by the army green cord uniform with garrison cap.[7]

The light green cord cap (Fig. 75-11) had dark green braid that presented an attractive appearance. It is interesting to note that the trim had no significance. This cap became obsolete on 30 September 1980. In 1975 the green garrison cap was authorized for wear with the cord uniform.[8]

With the beige uniform came a matching beige garrison cap, which was worn by officers and warrant officers of the WAC, nurses, and officers of the Army Medical Specialist Corps. It could be worn optionally by enlisted WAC members. This uniform became obsolete at the end of the 1960s.[9]

A widely worn green garrison cap was introduced with the women's green uniform. This cap, of the same general design as other women's caps, was also worn with the green cord uniform. This cap, Fig. 75-12, was declared obsolete effective in September 1980.[10]

Women also adopted a wool serge garrison cap in 1969 for wear with wool cold-weather field uniforms. This cap is especially interesting in that it functioned much like the cold-weather pile field cap and the utility (fatigue) cap. On the OG 108 (shade 108, olive green) garrison cap women wore the insignia of rank 1 inch back from the front edge. In addition, women could wear, equally vertically spaced with the rank insignia, one badge for a special skill such as aircrew member, diver, explosive ordnance disposal member, parachutist, and the like. This was the only case in which special badges could be worn on garrison caps by either men or women. The cap became obsolete in the early 1980s when the battle dress uniform cap became widely adopted.[11]

To replace the widely worn black beret, the army brought back the women's green garrison cap in September 1984. One change from the previous cap was the addition of braid like that for men: generals wore gold; commissioned officers, gold and black; warrant officers, silver and black; and enlisted women, green to match the cap.[12]

Berets

Berets were also worn by women. During World War II the Women's Airforce Service Pilots wore a beret with their uniforms, as

Fig. 75-13. *Women Airforce Service Pilots (WASP) of World War II were the first U.S. women in uniform to wear the beret.*

Fig. 75-14. *In 1975 the Army introduced a black beret for wear with several of the women's uniforms. By 1984 the revised garrison cap replaced the women's black beret.*

Fig. 75-15. *During World War II women wore many of the standard caps and helmets used by men. In addition, some special caps were used, as shown by this member of the WASP, who wore a bill cap when flying.*

Fig. 75-16. *The female drill instructors' hat had the left side of the brim snapped up. The army announced this hat in regulations of February 1979, although the army had authorized it several years earlier. This was in response to criticism that male drill instructors had distinctive headgear, but females did not.*

Fig. 75-13.

Fig. 75-14.

shown in Fig. 75-13. With the demise of the WASP, the beret died, but it was revived in the mid-1970s when a black beret was introduced for women. This 1975 beret was of a different form than that used by men at the same time.[13] The women's version carried the standard women's hat insignia then in use, which was placed to be centered on the wearer's head. The black, fur felt beret itself was worn centered on the head. An example is shown in Fig. 75-14.

The 1970s beret was worn with the green, green cord, blue, hospital white, and mint green uniforms as well as the exercise suit, then renamed the training duty uniform. The beret could be worn with fatigues in garrison, but not in the field. It ultimately replaced virtually all other headgear, and by October 1979 it was required for all women, replacing the garrison caps and the green hat. By 1983 a groundswell of complaints surfaced against the widespread wear of the beret. Women found it difficult to maintain and that it "unnecessarily set male and female soldiers apart." In response, the Army Clothing and Equipment Board decided in December 1983 to replace the beret with a green garrison cap.[14]

Other Headgear

Like the men, women adopted a great variety of uniforms during and after World War II, and these changes resulted in an extensive proliferation of specialized head-

Fig. 75-15.

Fig. 75-16.

gear. Medical women adopted unique hats or caps for hospital wear, use of field fatigue uniforms caused women to add men's caps to their wardrobe, and even bill caps were used during World War II by some WASP members when flying (Fig. 75-15).

Women drill sergeants received special hats with the left side of the brim snapped up and the right side parallel to the ground (Fig. 75-16). The standard enlisted women's hat insignia went on this headgear. During the winter of 1983–84, the army provided a cold-weather, black pile cap for winter wear with service uniforms. The so-called trooper cap carried standard service cap insignia and could be worn by both men and women.[15]

Section XXI

Men's White and Dress Uniforms

Chapter Seventy-Six

Men's Twentieth-Century Dress Blue Uniforms

As we have seen, until the last of the nineteenth century virtually all uniforms were made of dark blue wool. The uniform regulations of 1902 were very much an exercise of out with the old and in with the new, with both olive drab and new khaki uniforms coming into service. While the cut of uniforms also changed in 1902, one of the few constants was the retention of dark blue as the color of army clothing for dress occasions. The traditional use of blue, which stretches back to the Revolutionary War, has continued to today although during and after the two world wars the army suspended use of blue uniforms, threatening a severance of the historical connection today's soldier has with his or her forebears from Yorktown.

Standing-Collar Enlisted Men's Dress Coat, 1902

In 1902 the army brought out an enlisted men's dress coat that is easily separated from other uniforms. The coat had six bright brass buttons up the front and was without any outside pockets, while branch-colored piping edged the coat collar, cloth shoulder loops, and cuffs. For the first time, bright brass letters *US* went on the collar of all enlisted men's uniforms. Initially men also wore large brass collar ornaments (Fig. 76-1), but in 1905 the insignia were changed to the smaller size (Fig. 76-2). Soldiers added branch-colored breast cords (Fig. 76-3) to the coat and bands to the cap to change the dress uniform to full dress (Fig. 76-4).[1]

The coat's actual use varied over its life. The uniform lasted until the start of World War I, although during the last few years before the war its use became exceedingly scarce, and many regiments wore the dress or full dress uniform only two or three times a year. The War Department authorized its wear again in 1929, but temperaments had changed, and it was not worn by many soldiers, save some old-timers or men on special duties. When the coat was revived in 1929, men were to add brass hooks for the belt in the coat seams on each side, and officially it was always to be without a breast cord. This last provision was commonly disregarded. Thus modified, the standing-collar enlisted men's blue coat lasted until a more modern lapel coat became the accepted dress uniform in 1936 (Figs. 76-5 and 76-6).[2]

Officers' Dress Blue High-Collar Coats

Several twentieth-century dark blue full dress and dress coats exist. These are officer's "fancy" wear as often visualized by citizens.

Fig. 76-1.

Fig. 76-1. *Large enlisted men's branch insignia of this type were first issued in 1903 and were replaced by smaller pieces in 1905.*

Fig. 76-2.

Fig. 76-2. *Artillery staff noncommissioned officers before World War I in their blue dress uniforms. Several men wear insignia incorrectly. The master gunner, seated on the far right, should have small crossed cannons in a wreath on his cap, as does the master engineer seated next to him. The quartermaster sergeant, standing in the center, should have a US followed by a quartermaster insignia on each side of the collar. The two quartermaster sergeants both wear cap bands, which were a part of the full dress uniform.*

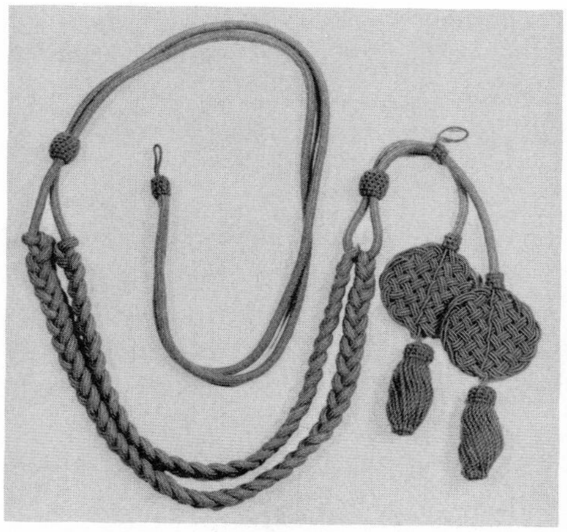

Fig. 76-3.

Fig. 76-3. *A 1902–17 enlisted men's breast cord. These were branch-colored and were added to the dress blue coat when the full dress uniform was prescribed. Enlisted men occasionally used them with the optional dress blue uniforms worn into World War II, but this practice was against regulations. For the U.S. Military Academy Band breast cords survived into the 1980s as part of the 1902-style high-collar full dress uniform. Some versions of the breast cords had the ends of the tassels free instead of constrained, as in this version.*

Fig. 76-4.

Fig. 76-4. *Colored cap bands and breast cords like the ones worn by this medical sergeant were added to the dress blue uniform to make it a full dress uniform.*

Even though dress uniforms are the most expensive of the uniforms, officers do not wear them frequently. In general, they are frock coats or uniform coats with square skirts extending more than sleeve length but ending well above the knee. Generals have dress coats with trim and other minor changes different from those of other officers, and all of these details are too minute for this overview. Common to dress blue uniforms, even today, is the use of branch colors to show arm or service.

The most elaborate twentieth-century coat was the 1902–17 full dress coat, which over time ultimately came in several versions. It was called full dress because coats of olive drab and of khaki were called service coats and because the 1895 sack coat already described became known as a dress coat in 1902. For all officers the full dress coat was double-breasted, thus allowing generals to

Fig. 76-5.

Fig. 76-5. A 1902 dress uniform worn in the 1930s, with distinctive insignia on the shoulder loops and an unauthorized shoulder cord, plus officer-style branch insignia.

have their traditional button groupings while field-grade officers had nine buttons in each of two rows. At the top the rows were 8–10 inches apart, narrowing to 4–5 inches at the waist. Captains and lieutenants had seven buttons in each row. Some officers, resplendent in their pre–Great War full dress uniforms, are shown in Figs. 76-7 through 76-10.[3]

Although details of the varieties of coats changed in the fifteen years the general style saw use before World War I, several points are worth noting. On the full dress coat generals wore epaulettes; other officers wore gold wire shoulder knots. Initially field-grade officers were to add a gold U.S. coat of arms to the shoulder knots, but this style never went into effect. Generals' standing collars were embroidered with oak leaves, while other officers had the collar trimmed top and bottom with 1/2-inch gold wire lace enclosing branch-colored material. On the sleeves, 2 1/2 inches from the end, went a band of 1/2-inch flat gold braid, surmounted by sleeve rank knots composed of 1/8-inch-wide gold lace and usually enclosing the branch insignia.[4]

Corps of Engineers officers wore similar coats, with scarlet and white piping added to the rear of the skirts. Quartermaster officers adopted still another variation of the full dress coat in 1911 when they added 2 1/2-inch buff cuffs and 1/8-inch-wide buff piping along the collar, left lapel, and left skirt. These full dress coats continued until they were suspended at the start of World War I, except that company-grade officers switched to nine buttons in a row in 1907, allowing all officers other than generals to wear the same coat.[5]

Corps of Engineers Officers' 1902 Uniform

One interesting forerunner to the twentieth-century general dress blue uniforms was the Corps of Engineers dress uniform first prescribed in March 1902 by adjutant general's General Orders 27. That order prescribed a short-lived coat of unique design and special trousers that varied depending on whether or not the officer was serving with the engineer battalions. The double-breasted coat had a scarlet collar carrying two stripes of gold lace edged with white braid, while the cuffs had three similarly constructed bands, as shown in Fig. 76-11.

Trousers were dark blue with 1 1/2 inches of scarlet piping edged with an additional 1/8 inch of white, except for those of officers attached to the battalion, who were to wear

Fig. 76-6.

Fig. 76-6. Enlisted members of the White House staff in the 1930s. All of the noncommissioned officers wear the 1902 dress blue uniform. The master sergeant in the back row on the right wears two small overseas chevrons, representing his World War I overseas service, over his large enlistment stripes.

Fig. 76-7. *Company-grade dress blue uniforms, 1902–1907, had two rows of seven buttons each. This second lieutenant's bottom buttons are covered by his belt.*

Fig. 76-8. *John J. Pershing as a captain in his 1902–1907 seven-button full dress coat.*

Fig. 76-9. *From 1902 until 1917 field-grade officers wore nine buttons in each row on the dress uniform, as did company-grade officers from 1907 to 1917. This officer is Captain Waterman, 7th Cavalry quartermaster, in 1907.*

Fig. 76-10. *After 1902 only generals continued to wear epaulettes with dress uniforms.*

Fig. 76-7.

Fig. 76-8.

Fig. 76-9.

Fig. 76-10.

the light blue trousers used by officers of the line, but with the engineers' scarlet and white stripes. These uniforms were replaced in 1903 by the dress blue uniform prescribed for other officers in mid- and late 1902.

Uniforms between the World Wars

In January 1929 the army revived the full dress coat for optional wear until a more modern version was prescribed in October 1936 (Figs. 76-12 and 76-13). This 1936 lapel coat had four brass buttons down the front and was without pockets. It was designed to be convertible to special full dress, full dress, and dress, the first two being the same except for the shirt and tie. The coat itself had branch indicated by stripes parallel to the sleeve ends: two 1/4-inch-wide gold lace stripes above and below a 1/4-inch silk stripe of the first color of the branch. Standard *US* letters and branch insignia went on the lapels.[6]

Some rather novel features, not seen before or since on U.S. Army uniforms, appeared on the 1936 coat, and these rather slight modifications were to change according to the category of dress. To adopt the uniform for dress wear, officers added stiffened, detachable shoulder loops about 2 1/4 inches wide. These loops were branch-colored, and if the branch had two colors, a 1/4-inch-wide edge in the second color went around the upper end. Rank went on the end of these shoulder loops. For full dress and special full dress, the shoulder loops were removed and replaced with shoulder knots, with rank insignia, of the style used previously. In addition, a special gold lace belt 1 5/8 inches wide, with three silk branch-colored stripes evenly spaced and 1/16 inch wide, was worn whenever the officer wore shoulder knots.[7]

The new uniform was altered in January 1937 by the addition of four inside hung pockets, each covered with a flap. The recently established shoulder loops disappeared, replaced by shoulder straps showing rank and branch, even though branch insignia remained on the lapel. This coat was prescribed for wear on social occasions until it became optional in July 1940 and was finally suspended from April 1943 until 1947. After World War II few officers bought the dress blue uniforms, and they were not widely used.[8]

Officers' Dress Uniforms after World War II

Officers' dress blue uniforms reappeared in a slightly different version in the mid-1950s (Fig. 76-14). While these coats carried branch and *US* insignia and shoulder straps

Fig. 76-11.

Fig. 76-12.

Fig. 76-11. *The dress blue uniform worn by Corps of Engineers officers, 1902–1903. Note the gold lace on the sleeves and on the collar.*

Fig. 76-12. *Major General G. O. Squier in a full dress uniform that was essentially the one prescribed before World War I. Branch insignia on the lower sleeve were used by branch chiefs and assistant branch chiefs only, while other generals wore only their rank.*

Fig. 76-13. A curious mix of pre–World War I and 1930s uniform ideas, combined with some personal concepts, resulted in this May 1931 blue dress uniform.

Fig. 76-14. The dress blue uniform introduced in the mid-1950s for officers. This captain, assigned to the 3d Infantry in the 1980s, also wears the old-style gilt belt with light blue stripes.

Fig. 76-15. Dress blue uniform of Chief of Staff General George Decker. The trouser and coat cuff stripes are gold. Collar insignia and shoulder straps have been removed to allow the basic coat to be seen clearly.

Fig. 76-16. When redesigned in the lapel version in the 1930s, the enlisted men's dress blue coat retained the branch trim around the collar. US and branch insignia went on the collar and distinctive insignia on the lapels. Chevrons were branch-colored.

Fig. 76-13.

Fig. 76-14.

Fig. 76-15.

Fig. 76-16.

Fig. 76-17.

Fig. 76-18.

Fig. 76-17. A dress blue enlisted men's uniform of the type introduced in the mid-1950s. Chevrons and other trim were yellow for all branches.

Fig. 76-18. U.S. Military Academy Band uniform, 1970s.

like those of the previous blue coat, the blouse itself changed. These new uniforms were made from new materials such as blends instead of pure wool, all trousers were decorated with gold stripes instead of branch colors, and patch pockets with pleats went on the chest. Generals wore a solid-colored gold lace stripe 1½ inches wide on the coat sleeve and dark blue trousers (instead of the sky blue used by other ranks) with two trousers stripes ½ inch apart (Fig. 76-15).[9] When this uniform was worn with a four-in-hand tie, it equaled a business suit, but with a bow tie it was considered more formal and the same as a tuxedo.

Enlisted Soldiers' Dress Blue Coats after 1936

With the revision of the officers' dress blue uniform in 1936, the Quartermaster Corps also prescribed an optional enlisted men's dress blue lapel coat (Fig. 76-16). Branch-colored piping trimmed the outer edge of the collar (but not the lapel), as well as shoulder loops and cuffs, a carryover from the older standing-collar style. Very little information survives about this coat because of the many changes in the officers' dress uniforms, which dominated the official documentation process. Photographs show that insignia varied, with some men wearing disks just like those on the service coat and others wearing pairs of officer-style collar and lapel insignia. The mix of insignia is understandable, given the lack of clear, published regulations and the history of previous enlisted men's blue uniforms carrying insignia not on disks, yet there is the contradictory evidence of all post-1917 enlisted men's coats that had only disk insignia. The army suspended use of this uniform in mid-1943.[10]

Like the officers' version, the enlisted men's dress uniform was changed when the army once again brought blue coats out of retirement in 1956. The new coat had the standard enlisted soldiers' disks for collar insignia and yellow nylon or rayon piping on shoulder loops and cuffs (Fig. 76-17).[11] The piping was no longer around the collar, and the 1956 coat had pleated upper patch pockets, with all pocket flaps scalloped instead of the older square pattern.

Some special organizations, including the U.S. Army Band, the U.S. Army Field Band, and the U.S. Military Academy Band, have had or continue to have dress blue uniforms, trim, or insignia unique to them (Figs. 76-18 and 76-19). As an addition to standard blue uniforms, 3d Infantry members wear a yellow-trimmed blue belt in a manner reminiscent of an earlier time (Fig. 76-20).

Fig. 76-19. *The U.S. Army Band special ceremonial uniform, 1970s.*

Fig. 76-20. *A member of the honor guard in Washington, D.C., wearing the standard dress blue uniform to which a special belt has been added. Selected ceremonial unit members wear this belt, but it is not worn by most soldiers.*

Fig. 76-19.

Fig. 76-20.

Chapter Seventy-Seven

White Uniforms

White uniforms meet several needs. They serve as summer dress clothing and as medical and food workers' clothing. Before World War I, the army made some stable and work garments in white. This chapter cursorily examines by date some of the common white uniforms. Besides these uniforms, pre-1832 band musicians frequently wore white coats, and white mess uniforms, introduced in 1902, exist. These are discussed elsewhere in this text.

Enlisted Men's Nineteenth-Century White Coats

In 1888 the army adopted a white cotton single-breasted sack coat with falling collar for enlisted men (Fig. 77-1). Coats were bleached for noncommissioned officers and bandsmen and unbleached for privates until 1899, when all coats became bleached. Five removable buttons, which could be "regulation gilt," white bone, or vegetable ivory, closed the front. Medical troops, cooks, and bakers commonly wore these coats on duty (Fig. 77-2). [1]

Enlisted Men's White Coats, 1900–14

No insignia went on the coat until 1900, when staff noncommissioned officers and soldiers added gilt insignia identical in design to their helmet overlays but with pin backs. Regimental men added similar brass unit numbers.[2] Because these 1900–1902 collar insignia were not identical in design and size to those gilt insignia that came into use on the 1902 dress blue uniform, they are often not familiar to collectors and historians today and are often misidentified. I believe the use of these particular small insignia paved the way for full-scale use of collar insignia by enlisted men in 1902.

Issue of the enlisted men's white coats was phased out in 1905 and 1906, and whites were replaced by summer khaki except for

Fig. 77-1. *Troops of the 2d Cavalry assigned to cooking duty in the field, 1897. Left: the white coat with five gilt buttons as introduced in 1888. Third from left: a blue shirt of the 1883 pattern. Right: the white trousers that were to accompany the 1888 coat.*

Fig. 77-1.

medical personnel. During the summers of 1907 and 1908 white uniforms reappeared for cooks and bakers (Fig. 77-3) and for summer wear by recruiting service members. Recruiting service personnel quit wearing the white uniform in March 1914.[3]

Officers' Dress Coats through World War II

Starting in 1895, "during the warm season" post commanders could authorize officers' white coats, similar to the 1895 undress coat, including white mohair braid but without shoulder straps or collar insignia. In 1897 the secretary of war approved the uniform for wear army-wide. Three years later the quartermaster general directed that cloth shoulder loops be added to the coat and that officers wear the collar and shoulder loop insignia as on the khaki blouse (Fig. 77-4). Insignia placement changed with the 1902 regulations so that either a new design of eagle from the Great Seal of the United States (1903–1905) or *US* (1905 and later) went on the collar near the front opening, with branch insignia spaced behind (Figs. 77-5 and 77-6). Rank insignia went on the shoulder loop near the shoulder seam. Fig. 77-7 shows a Doctor Baskette wearing a white uniform in 1923. Fig. 77-8 shows the 1934 Panama Canal Zone commander and his aide wearing the same 1900-style white coat, which was worn in tropical climates even during World War I.[4]

In July 1936 a white lapel coat replaced this standing-collar dress uniform. Until 1940, Regular Army officers in the tropics were required to have a white dress uniform, while reserve and National Guard officers were allowed, but not required, to wear them. After July 1940 the uniform was totally optional.[5]

Fig. 77-2. *Two dental assistants, 1905. Medical personnel were the only soldiers to wear white coats throughout the post-1902 period.*

Dress White Uniforms, 1956 and Later

In 1956 a new army philosophy was published to the troops. The optional white uniform, in use since World War II, was replaced by a white lapel coat uniform that was equated with dress blue clothing in tropical

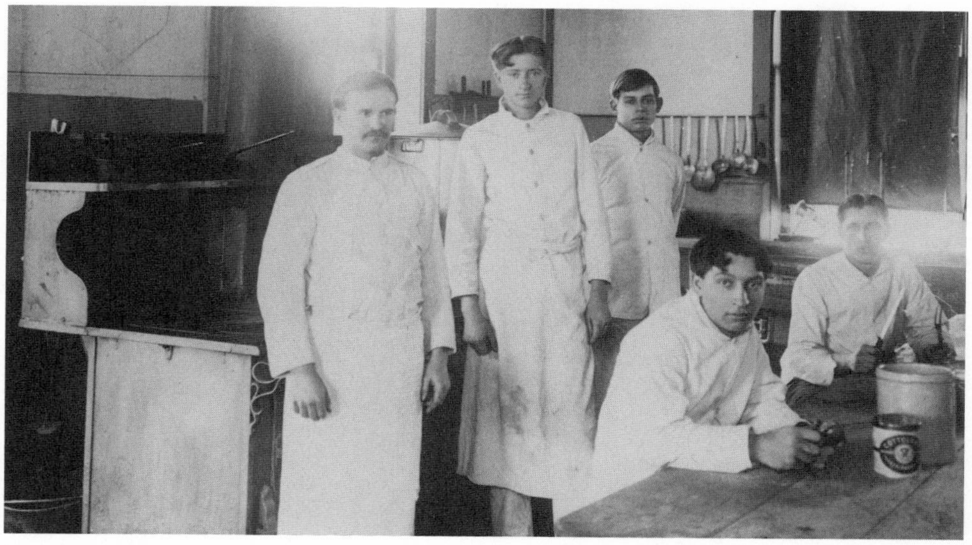

Fig. 77-3. *Cooks' white work uniforms. The army first recognized particular men as cooks in 1898, and within a very few years cooks and bakers had their own work uniforms. Officially, collar insignia and later special chevrons went on cooks' coats.*

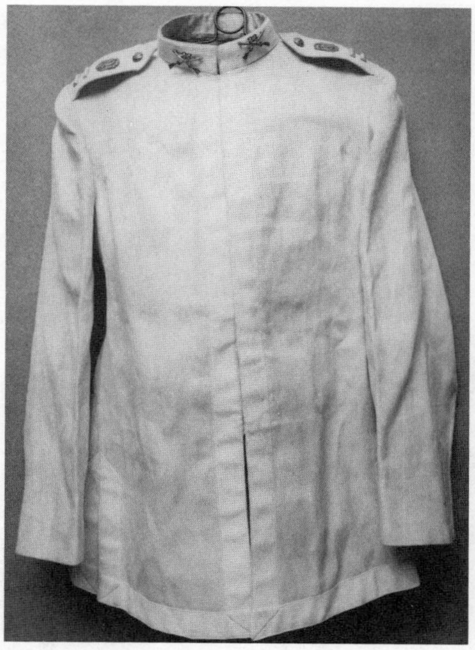

Fig. 77-4.

Fig. 77-5.

areas. For officers stationed in the tropics, the white uniform became mandatory. Shoes worn with the uniform went from white to black in 1956. Enlisted personnel were authorized optional dress white uniforms at the same time. Golden yellow chevrons were worn on the white coat (Fig. 77-9). Placement of *US* letters and branch insignia followed the same rules as for the olive drab and then the green uniforms.[6]

Medical and Food Services White Uniforms

Over the years, white has become established as the color of medical and food service personnel uniforms. Except for chevrons, these uniforms were usually without insignia. Fig. 77-2 shows an enlisted man in one of the few white, nondress coats that carried insignia until

Fig. 77-6.

Fig. 77-7.

Fig. 77-4. *An officers' 1900–1903 white coat. The same coat, but without the shoulder loops or insignia, had been introduced army-wide in 1897. The 1903 version was of the same design but with different ornaments on the collar and shoulder loops.*

Fig. 77-5. *The 7th Cavalry's regimental commissary officer and his young son, 1909. The officer wears the white uniform first described in 1902 regulations.*

Fig. 77-6. *Second Lieutenant George Patton and family, 1915. Patton wears the 1900-style white coat, with insignia as prescribed in 1902. Patton's rank was shown by the officers' uniform without any rank insignia, because second lieutenants' bars were not introduced until World War I. Patton is in his riding uniform with blue trousers instead of the normal white dress.*

Fig. 77-7. *This doctor wears the dress white uniform trimmed with white mohair on the collar and up the front. Besides the US and branch insignia on the collar, rank went on the shoulder loops. The photograph was taken in 1923.*

after World War II. Various white smocks worn by medical, veterinarian, and food services personnel between and during the world wars were without insignia.

Medical personnel in particular wore a range of specialized white apparel. In the 1950s these included long white cotton hospital coats worn over standard uniforms, and in the 1960s, short-sleeved, high-collar smocks with a maroon caduceus and *US* embroidered on the chest pocket. Officers wore branch and rank on the high-collar smocks, rank on the right, and branch insignia on the left. This high-collar smock was replaced in the early 1970s by white work uniforms that consisted of conventional trousers and open-collar lapel shirts. The shirts were really smocks with square

Fig. 77-8. *Center and right: The commanding general of the Panama Canal Zone and his aide in 1933 in their white dress uniforms. The coats were essentially those introduced in 1900, with the insignia first prescribed in 1905.*

Fig. 77-9. *White dress uniforms, 1970s.*

Fig. 77-8.

Fig. 77-9.

tails, worn outside the trousers. On these smocks dentists, nurses, dietitians, and therapists, all of whom were officers, wore branch and rank insignia on the collar, placed as on khaki shirts (Fig. 77-10). These white smocks were worn by those medical personnel who had contact with patients, while those engaged in administrative duties wore other uniforms. Enlisted personnel in these fields also wore the same uniforms without any insignia until the small metal chevrons were placed on the collar. Until the 1980s, these officers wore white shoes with their uniforms, while enlisted personnel wore black shoes. Unofficially, most locations allowed the use of permanent-press white uniforms from civilian sources as long as they generally conformed to the military appearance (that is, no cuffs on the trousers). Doctors usually wore white lab coats without any insignia over service uniforms.

Food service personnel after World War II wore plain white lapel-collar shirts and standard trousers, usually without any insignia. Some noncommissioned officers unofficially added chevrons. During the 1950s through the early 1970s use of shoulder patches and sleeve chevrons slowly spread to food service personnel in various units. With the advent of small metal collar chevrons, food service personnel officially began to wear them on the open collar of the white mess smocks and shirts (Fig. 77-11).

Fig. 77-10.

Fig. 77-10. *Army Medical Specialist Corps members, 1971. The captain standing wears the older style of medical smock with an embroidery caduceus and US on the pocket and with standard rank insignia on the right side of the standing collar. The caduceus bearing an S is on the left. The seated male officer wears the newer style of smock with a standard collar and insignia placed as on other lapel shirts. The female dietitians wear the standard hospital ward dress, with their insignia placed on the vertical axis of the collars.*

Fig. 77-11.

Fig. 77-11. *Food service personnel wore white uniforms, and when the army introduced small metal pin-on chevrons, those were worn on the white uniforms. The cap is made of paper.*

EVENING AND MESS UNIFORMS

Fig. 78-1. A 1902-pattern evening uniform. The long tails were approximately knee-length. Two buttons on each side of the coat front distinguish the 1902 style from that of 1948. Standard sleeve knots indicated rank, unlike later versions. This jacket had bare lapels, unlike the colored ones introduced on mess jackets in 1902.

ARMY UNIFORMS TODAY still bear witness to the dramatic revisions spelled out in 1902. Teddy Roosevelt and army commander Nelson Miles personally intervened in prescribing the officers' dress clothing. The first set of regulations, published in the summer, were suspended, and the final version, which came out on the last day of 1902, made several changes. Evening uniforms and mess jackets were prescribed in both regulations, but the December edition was more precise in describing the mess jackets.[1] These mess jackets are essentially the same cut and pattern as those worn today. The special evening uniform likewise remained in use with only minor changes until the 1970s. The evening and mess uniforms discussed include the long-tailed special evening coat; the blue mess uniforms, including the 1980s enlisted soldiers' version; and the white mess uniform.

Fig. 78-1.

EVENING UNIFORMS

Evening uniforms until 1975 were cut like a civilian formal tailed coat, and in fact regulations described them in such terms, although army buttons, sleeve ornamentation for grade, and gold shoulder knots or epaulettes were added. Lapels were bare, and the tails went to about the bend in the knee. Company- and field-grade officers wore the new pattern of 1902 gold wire shoulder knots, and generals wore either the knots or epaulettes. Rank was shown by sleeve knots that enclosed a branch insignia. The first pattern of coat is most easily distinguished by the two buttons on each side of the coat (Fig. 78-1).[2] Like many other uniforms, these were not worn during and after World War I.

The 1938 version was almost the same as the first type, except for generals of the Air Corps. While generals who were branch chiefs or assistant branch chiefs had their branch insignia on the sleeves below their stars, in the 1938 revision all generals of the General Headquarters of the Air Force also wore their branch insignia below their stars. Instead of epaulettes, generals wore only shoulder knots on the 1938 coat, as did all other officers.[3]

World War II interrupted use of evening uniforms again, and they were reinstituted with some modifications in December 1948 (Fig. 78-2). The 1938 coat could be worn until June 1955, at which time the 1948 style, with three buttons on each side, was

Fig. 78-2.

Fig. 78-2. *Evening uniform of the 1948 pattern (three buttons on each breast), worn by Chief of Staff General George Decker. Generals' sleeve ornamentation on all evening uniforms consisted of black velvet cuffs with gold-embroidered oak leaves and silver stars above the cuffs.*

required. The 1948 uniform differed from the 1938 version in that blue black or black trousers with 3/4-inch-wide gold stripes generally replaced the blue trousers with branch-colored stripes worn by many officers, and the sleeve insignia changed. The new sleeve knots were of the general trefoil shape but were made from a single 1/4-inch-wide piece of gold lace. All rank (including generals') went inside the knots, with captains' and lieutenants' bars horizontal and warrant officers' bars vertical (Figs. 78-3 and 78-4). Changes after 1948 were comparatively few until the tailed coat became obsolete in 1975. In March 1950 the sleeve ornamentation for generals changed back to the 1902 and 1938 style, except there was no branch insignia in any case.[4]

Evening uniforms changed in 1979 when the standard mess uniform, described below, became known as the army blue evening dress uniform when worn with a vest, a formal white dress shirt with wing collar, and a white bow tie.[5]

Blue Mess Uniforms

One distinctly military garb still worn today is the mess jacket. Blue mess jackets for the various staff corps and departments and the regiments could be adopted, starting in 1902, and while departments' and regiments' jackets could differ in detail, they were of the same cut. The army finally prescribed a standard design eleven years later, and this style is still generally used. After adoption of the 1913 standard design, branch was shown by appropriate colors on the lapels and by insignia contained in the rank knots worn on the lower sleeve.[6]

Only very minor changes have occurred since the jackets' reintroduction in 1938. While the 1913 jacket sleeve bands had 1/2-inch-wide gilt lace, the 1938 version changed the sleeve bands to consist of two 1/4-inch-wide gold stripes 1/4 inch apart, enclosing a branch-colored stripe. Rank

Fig. 78-3.

Fig. 78-3. *Field- and company-grade officers' sleeve ornamentation for post-1948 evening uniforms. These separately attached insignia had lace 1/4 inch wide except for the 1-inch-wide horizontal strip. Captains' and lieutenants' bars were to be horizontal. From 1948 until 1950, generals also used this device, with their stars in the same location as the bars shown.*

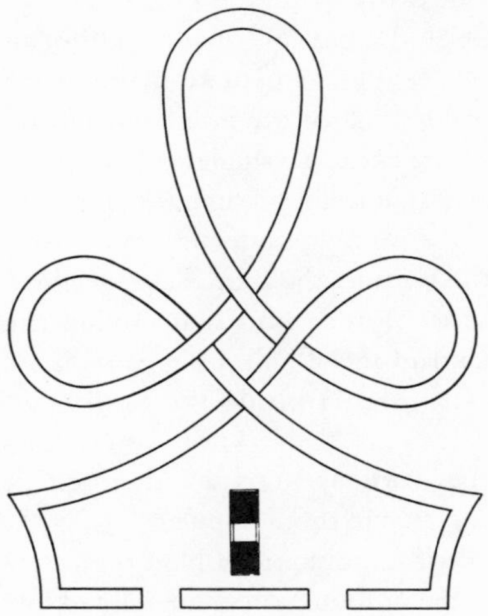

Fig. 78-4.

Fig. 78-4. *Warrant officers' evening dress sleeve insignia. The 1/4-inch-wide horizontal braid had 1/2-inch gaps 2 inches apart.*

Fig. 78-5. Mess uniform, 1938. Generals of the line had plain lapels, while generals of the support branches and all company- and field-grade officers wore branch-colored lapels. Sleeve ornamentation for generals who were chiefs of branches included their branch insignia. Generals' embroidered velvet cuffs had three buttons until the mess uniform was revived after World War II.

Fig. 78-6. A lieutenant colonel's blue mess jacket worn after World War II until the 1980s. The principal color associated with a branch went on the lapels of company- and field-grade officers' jackets, and the same color was displayed in the center of the cuff braid. Miniature medals and badges were optional with this post–World War II jacket, but full-sized awards could not be worn.

Fig. 78-7. Mess uniform sleeve knot, 1938–75, for a colonel of the Signal Corps. Before 1938 the band that went around the sleeve was simply a 1/2-inch-wide gold vellum, but after 1938 the top and bottom gold bands were 1/4 inch wide and enclosed a branch-colored 1/4-inch band. After 1975 this type of knot entered a wear-out phase and was optional, having been replaced by the single-strand trefoil shown in Fig. 78-8.

Fig. 78-5.

Fig. 78-6.

knots and metal branch insignia remained on the lower sleeve. When authorized again in 1952, the uniform was as before, except all staff generals wore branch insignia on their sleeves. Warrant officers wore only their insignia of grade on the sleeve, without any braid or knot, and thus their status was indicated by a lack of branch insignia and a sleeve knot (Figs. 78-5, 78-6, and 78-7).[7]

Mess Uniform, 1970s

In 1975 the army made the biggest change since the standardization of mess uniforms when the sleeve ornamentation was made somewhat like that of the evening uniform. The new knot became a single wide strip following the same trefoil design as before, but instead of the evening uniforms' wide sleeve band at the bottom, the mess jacket retained the branch-colored band that circled the sleeve. Standard metal rank insignia replaced the branch insignia inside the knot (Fig. 78-8). Older rank sleeve knots could continue to be worn, and this was done often, because these were more popular.[8]

The second innovation in blue mess uniforms was the introduction of an enlisted soldiers' mess jacket. The concept, presented to Department of the Army officials in the summer of 1979, was incorporated into regulations by 1981. Changes from the officers' uniforms were the use of dark blue lapels for all enlisted men regardless of branch, the omission of shoulder knots, and special sleeve ornamentation to show rank by small bright metal chevrons. The sleeve device was made from 3/4-inch gold braid and consisted of a stripe around the sleeve and of a "modified trefoil" that traced the inner shape of rank knot where branch insignia had been worn by officers (Fig. 78-9). At the same time, warrant officers were authorized the single sleeve knot and colored branch band previously used by commissioned officers, with a warrant officers' rank bar inside the knot.[9]

White Mess Uniforms

For a few years before 1911, when the War Department had encouraged regiments and staff departments to adopt their own mess uniforms, some organizations had taken white ones. In December 1911 and January 1912 officers throughout the army were advised of a standard white mess jacket that was optional in the United States but that could be required in the tropics. The waist-length jacket carried gold shoulder knots, but it was otherwise devoid of insignia except for the lower sleeve (Fig. 78-10).[10]

Sleeve markings varied more on the white mess uniform than on the blue version. Generals wore a 4-inch wide white

Fig. 78-7.

Fig. 78-8.

Fig. 78-8. *This design of sleeve knot was introduced in August 1975 for the mess jacket. It was made from 1/4-inch-wide material. Branch remained shown by the color of the 1/4-inch band that encircled the sleeve.*

Fig. 78-9. *This enlisted man models the 1979 mess uniform. On the lower sleeve is a so-called modified trefoil with brass chevron inside.*

Fig. 78-10. *An officers' white mess jacket with gold shoulder knots and white sleeve braid. This colonel shows his rank by the five strands that make up his trefoil on the lower sleeves, while his branch is shown by the crossed muskets on them. Black trousers went with the jacket.*

band with white stars above. Other officers wore a 1/2-inch-wide white band 2 1/2 inches from the end of the sleeve, with rank knots enclosing metal branch insignia. With the introduction of warrant officers after World War I came a series of two, three, or four sleeve bands instead of the knots used by commissioned personnel. The number of bands depended on the rank. Warrant officers removed all white sleeve braid in 1937 and were distinguished only by the metal warrant officers' insignia worn 4 inches above the sleeve bottom. In 1931 the white mess jacket, white cap, black dress trousers, and black silk evening tie comprised the tropical full dress uniform, when medals and decorations were worn. When the white mess jackets were revived after World War II, warrant officers' jackets carried metal rank insignia on lower sleeves that were otherwise without any braid. In December 1981 enlisted men were authorized white mess uniforms, with sleeve knots of the style worn on their blue mess uniforms.[11]

Waistcoats and Vests

Waistcoats and vests were often worn with mess and evening uniforms. The 1902 evening uniform included a "waistcoat of dark blue or white, cut low with full, open bosom, [with] three gilt regulation buttons." For mess jackets, the army called for vests of the color of the coat (either white or dark blue). By 1907 the vest for the dark blue mess jacket could be either white or dark blue, and by 1912 only a white vest was used with the evening uniform and the white mess uniform. On the last day of 1928, waistcoats worn with white mess jackets were to have three instead of the previous two gilt regulation buttons.[12]

When the mess and evening uniforms were revived in 1938, white vests with three small gilt buttons remained, and blue vests were not mentioned. The 1952 revision called for white vests, but of different patterns: with a rounded bottom without points for wear with the blue mess and with a pointed bottom for the evening uniform. By the 1960s the wearer could use either a black cummerbund, an option usually exercised, or a white

Fig. 78-10.

Fig. 78-9.

vest with a pointed bottom for the white mess uniforms and with a rounded bottom (without points) for the blue mess uniform. Later, with the white jacket the white vest with white buttons was prescribed when a formal shirt with wing collar was used, and a cummerbund remained optional with a standard shirt. Finally, when the blue mess jacket was accompanied by a cummerbund, it became known as the mess uniform, and when worn with a vest and white tie, it was the evening dress uniform. Thus vests were worn only with the white mess uniform and this version of the evening uniform.[13]

Initially trousers, socks, and shoes worn with the white mess jackets were white, but in mid-1928 local commanding officers could specify black in lieu of the standard white. In 1938 black became the prescribed color for these articles of clothing, and the black trousers were to have black silk or satin stripe. This practice continued after World War II.[14]

Section XXII

Women's Uniforms

Chapter Seventy-Nine

Women's Uniforms through World War II

Before World War II few women were formally associated with the army. To be sure, some seventeenth- and eighteenth-century women, such as, laundry women (some of whom were married to soldiers), accompanied the army. The army recognized some of these women at various times by mentioning them in orders or regulations, but women certainly were not considered part of the army or even a formal adjunct. During the Spanish-American War the army hired contract nurses, and some served in Cuba, marking the first time women were hired by the army and given an insignia to show their position. The Army Nurse Corps was formed in 1901, but these women were not members of the Regular Army until after World War II. Nurses had "relative rank" instead of actual rank, even though members of the Army Nurse Corps wore commissioned officers' insignia. The World War I navy included female yeomen, but the army never advanced to the point that women were on a par with men. On the whole, for the first forty years of the twentieth century, most women who were affiliated with the army were so because they were members of the medical profession.

Women's membership in the army exploded during World War II. In 1942, Congress allowed formation of the Women's Army Auxiliary Corps (WAAC), which was, as the name implies, an auxiliary or adjunct to the army instead of a full-fledged part of the service. But the WAAC women became part of the army in 1943 under the name Women's Army Corps (WAC), and women subsequently entered many diverse fields within the army.[1] These actions, coupled with the enormous expansion of the Medical Department, which also rapidly grew to include many new women, caused the army to create a series of uniforms that ultimately became more diverse than the men's clothing ensemble. Some of the medical uniforms worn before World War II are covered in chapter 11, leaving this overview to deal primarily with the period of World War II and later. Recall that women were either members of the WAC (or WAAC) or of the Medical Department until the 1970s.

Uniforms of Other Than Nurses and the WAC

Several groups of women were members of various quasi-military organizations and wore uniforms beginning during World War I. Perhaps the best-known uniformed nonmedical women of World War I were the "hello girls," telephone operators, of whom the general American public today is not aware. These women worked for the American Expeditionary Forces (AEF) in France and wore special uniforms that included distinctive chevrons. The chief operator even received the Distinguished Service Medal (Fig. 79-1).[2]

Other organizations that included women in uniform were the Quartermaster Corps in World War I, Women Airforce Service Pilots (WASP) in World War II (Fig. 79-2), and service clubs during and after World War II. A quarter of a century after their service, the women of the WASP finally received veterans' benefits, a tacit recognition of their service status, but generally speaking, most of the women just mentioned were not actually part of the army.

While the American Red Cross supplied army nurses with capes, the Red Cross also

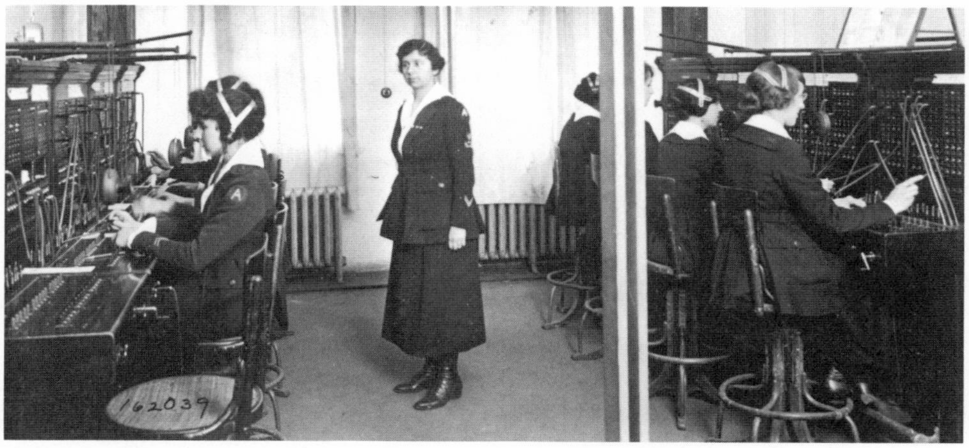

Fig. 79-1.

Fig. 79-1. *Grace D. Baker, chief telephone operator for the AEF, stands in the center of this room of operators in their uniforms. Miss Baker was awarded a Distinguished Service Medal in 1919 even though her service was with the army but not in it.*

Fig. 79-2. *During World War II Women Airforce Service Pilots (WASPs) wore uniforms and military insignia, yet until the 1970s they were not considered members of the military.*

put nurses, doctors, and others involved in foreign service work in uniform during World War I. The uniforms prescribed on 28 February 1918 were of gray whipcord made into a pleated skirt and a single-breasted, four-button sack coat tunic with lapels. Accoutrements included a gray cloth hat and the letters *US* on the shoulder straps. Red Cross sleeve markings indicated grade or rank are listed in chapter 11. In addition, distinctively colored ties, collar trim, and hatbands showed Red Cross workers' service, as shown in Table 11-2.[3] Uniforms prescribed for dietitians and physical therapists during and after World War I are shown in Figs. 11-122, 11-124, 11-127, and 11-130.

Fig. 79-2.

Nurses before 1920

Spanish-American War nurses wore standard civilian ward uniforms. By 1899 the War Department stated, "each nurse will provide herself with the prescribed nurses' uniforms of army blue and white." Only indoor (ward) uniforms were prescribed until World War I; nurses had no special outdoor clothing. When nurses received orders for Europe in 1917, the need for recognizable outdoor clothing arose. This resulted in a May 1917 approval of the blue serge outdoor uniform.[4]

World War I women's medical uniforms were relatively simple, but a brief overview of nurses' uniforms in that war may help show the problems of women's clothing in World War II. One outdoor uniform, a blue serge Norfolk suit, was the clothing selection for nurses in World War I, although minor variations did exist (Figs. 79-3 and 79-4). Another olive drab uniform was adopted in 1920 and remained the sole uniform pattern for nurses until 1940 (Fig. 79-5).[5]

World War II Medical Uniforms

Thus, with three basic uniforms: a white indoor uniform for ward use, a blue outdoor uniform created at the last minute in 1940 for women going overseas, and a twenty-year-old olive drab outdoor service uniform, the army was prepared to design and clothe women during the 1940s. This extremely

Fig. 79-3.

***Fig. 79-3.** Nurses were the only women really considered a part of the U.S. Army between the Spanish-American War and World War II. This World War I nurse wears one of several versions of a broad-brimmed hat and blue serge Norfolk jacket. The Norfolk jacket was originally a fashionable nineteenth-century leisure jacket worn by country gentlemen. The jacket remained popular until after World War I. When it was adopted as a nurses' outdoor coat, the pleats that started at each shoulder and extended straight down the front were sewn into the garment instead of being sewn in the original style of box pleats. The loose cloth belt with two buttons, typical of the civilian Norfolk jacket, transferred directly to the uniform. Bronze insignia went on the coat lapel. Note the gilt caduceus with white ANC monogram at the neck and the nonarmy buttons.*

Fig. 79-4.

***Fig. 79-4.** Wide variations existed in the World War I nurses' uniforms. This nurse from Kansas wears an overseas cap and army buttons on her uniform. Waists (shirts) and other uniform accessories came in different patterns and further proliferated clothing variations.*

Fig. 79-5.

***Fig. 79-5.** A 1920–40 U.S. Army nurses' olive drab uniform. Brass buttons and insignia replaced bronze ones in 1923. While the general cut remained conservative, changes such as the olive drab color and neckties pulled it closer to men's uniforms than the World War I version. This was the sole uniform worn outside of the hospital until 1940.*

limited need for women before 1941 was root cause of the diversity and conflicting direction seen during the creation and buildup of women's forces.

Women's World War II uniforms were a curious mixture of new ideas for women in the army and of concepts drawn from male uniforms. Insignia and insignia placement were generally the same as men's, although they were not always identical. Women officers were given assimilated ranks and generally treated as if they were commissioned.

After twenty years of service, the 1920 nurses' olive drab service uniform was no longer stylish. In the spring of 1940 the quartermaster general and the surgeon general adopted a two-piece wool outdoor uniform, although some nurses did not receive their initial distribution of the new clothes until 1942. The dark blue coat had shoulder loops trimmed with maroon cord edge braid and a 1/2-inch-wide maroon stripe around each sleeve end (Fig. 79-6). On the collar and lapels these medical women wore insignia much as male officers did. In a unique move women wore a standard caduceus on the accompanying garrison cap. A plain street-length skirt completed the uniform.[6]

The lengthy delay in issuing the blue uniform indicates the army's preparation to clothe the large number of women who joined the World War II Medical Department. As a result, the army created a great many new uniforms between 1942 and 1945

Fig. 79-6. The initial 1940 pattern of the nurses' outdoor uniform. The coat was dark blue with maroon trim on the shoulder loops and cuff braid. Unlike most other uniforms with four brass buttons, this one had three. The skirt was medium blue. Nurses usually wore a maroon-trimmed overseas cap with a caduceus insignia instead of this early cap. The belt carried over from the World War I Norfolk uniform and the olive drab 1920–40 coat.

Fig. 79-7. The World War II brown and white seersucker nurses' dress with matching jacket. The dress's collar carried US and nurse insignia; rank went on the jacket shoulder loops. The color and material were adopted so the uniform could be washed easily and cheaply compared to the white ward dress it replaced.

for medical women. Besides special versions of the fatigues similar to men's herringbone twill combat clothing, medical women received a white ward dress, a dark brown olive drab off-duty dress, a brown and white seersucker hospital dress, and a beige on-duty dress, besides a white summer uniform with maroon trim (Figs. 79-7 through 79-11). A variety of olive drab wool and khaki cotton shirts and slacks were introduced for nurses and women in transportation and for outdoor duties. In September 1942 olive drab became the preferred color for nurses' uniforms instead of the recently adopted blue.[7]

The actual switch to olive drab was from late 1943 to mid-1944, and olive drab colors lasted into the 1950s. By the time nurses' olive drab jackets were actually issued, the coat was the same pattern as the WAC jacket that will be discussed shortly. Nurses wore an olive drab six-gore skirt with the jacket, while WAAC and WAC officers wore "pink" skirts similar to male officers' "pink" trousers. In late 1942 the Nurse Corps adopted several WAAC uniform accessories to ease supply problems. Common articles included scarves, neckties, sweaters, cotton waists (shirts), stockings, shoes, gloves, and raincoats.[8]

White ward uniforms were approved in several versions from 1936 until late 1942, but the brown and white seersucker hospital uniform became the standard World War II garment for wear on ward duty. The army had experimented with several designs and

Fig. 79-8.

Fig. 79-6.

Fig. 79-7.

Fig. 79-9.

materials that would be practical on duty and be launderable under field conditions before settling on a wraparound one-piece dress. It was tied with a cloth belt at the left side and allowed easy fitting to individuals. A semifitted seersucker jacket without a collar and fastened with one button could be worn with the ward dress to provide a street outfit in warm weather (Fig. 79-7). In 1945 the dress was modified to a coat style instead of the wraparound, and the jacket was changed to a more attractive design. During 1943 brown and white seersucker shirts and slacks were adopted for nurses who needed to climb ladders to upper bunks on hospital ships and trains.[9]

Several other slacks were adopted during World War II by nurses. Woolen slacks were made for cold weather and for use in Europe. Both light and dark shirts were worn with these slacks at various times. For the Southwest Pacific, nurses were given khaki twill slacks, which offered more protection from mosquitoes than did the seersucker version.[10]

Several one-piece dresses were developed for women medical officers during World War II. These included an early 1942 dark blue dress for use at off-duty social occasions. In the summer of 1942 a lightweight beige dress with maroon trim was authorized for hot climates. In early 1943 the army introduced a similar olive drab dress, which replaced the 1942 blue one, as blue was being phased out as a color for medical uniforms.[11]

WAAC and WAC Uniforms, 1942–48

Members of the WAAC and the WAC assigned to medical duties often wore the same uniforms as those worn by women in the Medical Department, but in addition many other uniform were designed solely for

Fig. 79-11.

Fig. 79-10.

Fig. 79-8. *The wraparound seersucker dress could be worn without the jacket, but when nurses chose this option, the rank insignia went on the right collar, replacing the US insignia.*

Fig. 79-9. *The WAC beige hospital duty dress introduced for enlisted women in 1945. Collar insignia were worn with the axis vertical on this uniform.*

Fig. 79-10. *Nurses in Texas during World War II. Left to right: the first and fifth women wear the nurses' olive drab winter off-duty dress, the second woman wears the olive drab coat and skirt, the third wears the white ward uniform with the rank insignia placed vertically on the right collar, the fourth wears a beige summer coat with maroon trim and matching skirt, the sixth nurse has on the summer beige dress, and the last shows the 1940 dark blue nurses' uniform with maroon trim. Dietitians and physical therapists also wore these medical uniforms, which came in several types of materials and with both large and medium-sized brass buttons.*

Fig. 79-11. *This chief nurse is wearing a white waist (shirt) with insignia placed as on men's uniforms.*

Fig. 79-12.

Fig. 79-12. WAAC members, 1942. Officers' winter uniforms had dark olive drab jackets with light pinkish-gray skirts (left), while enlisted members' winter uniforms were medium olive drab (right). For summer wear both officers and enlisted women wore khaki jackets and skirts made of various materials, with the distinction between the classes made by insignia and the addition of cuff braid by officers.

Fig. 79-13.

Fig. 79-13. Colonel Oveta Culp Hobby, wearing her summer uniform as director of the WAAC. WAAC uniforms had dark plastic buttons, which were replaced by standard brass army buttons when the corps became the WAC. Instead of standard shoulder loops of the type used on men's uniforms, WAAC officers' jackets had sewn-down cloth strips which ran parallel to the shoulder seam to comply with the congressional requirement that the uniforms be different from those of the U.S. Army.

Fig. 79-14.

Fig. 79-14. WAC officers late in World War II wearing the dark olive drab jacket and pinkish-gray skirt (left) and the khaki tropical worsted summer uniform.

WAAC and WAC women. The WAAC, formed in the spring of 1942 so that its members could relieve men for combat duties, required new styles of uniforms. While female medical personnel had previously been associated with the army, as already noted, the concept of women who performed some of the same duties as men was totally new. Uniforms included skirt and jackets (equivalent to men's service coats) in several versions: khaki and olive drab, both with and without a cloth belt. Some of the original WAAC uniforms are shown in Fig. 79-12.[12]

The cloth belts worn with the winter and summer jackets were controversial from the outset. Although early WAAC members wore them, belts were eliminated in October 1942, primarily because the women pulled them too tight, spoiling the lines of the coats. Coats specifically made for wear without the belts also were made with dummy upper pocket flaps only; the original jackets had real, inside hung pockets.[13]

Note that the original WAAC jackets did not have conventional shoulder loops, but officers pinned their rank to a separately made cloth strip, pointed at each end and sewn to the shoulder with the long axis of the added strip perpendicular to the position of cloth shoulder loops on men's coats (Fig. 79-13). Standard cloth shoulder loops evidently came into use in 1943.

WAAC members wore olive drab plastic buttons bearing a walking eagle, but with the change to the WAC, the army switched to standard brass buttons. Officers wore "pinks and greens," while enlisted women's jackets were olive drab like the men's. Selection of colors was difficult, and throughout 1942 the WAAC considered various near-matching, matching, and contrasting colors. Various versions were obtained and issued, so a wide range of hues is found in 1942 and 1943 WAAC and WAC uniforms (Fig. 79-14). The 1943 WAC uniforms remained in use after the war (Fig. 79-15).[14]

Two common 1943 uniforms were beige off-duty dresses for WAC members—a light beige for summer wear (Fig. 79-16) and a darker version for the winter (Fig. 79-17). These dresses were developed in September 1943, when the WAAC was brought into the army, so that women would have appropriate clothing for unofficial social functions. WAAC members had been allowed to wear civilian clothes off-duty, but WAC members were not.[15]

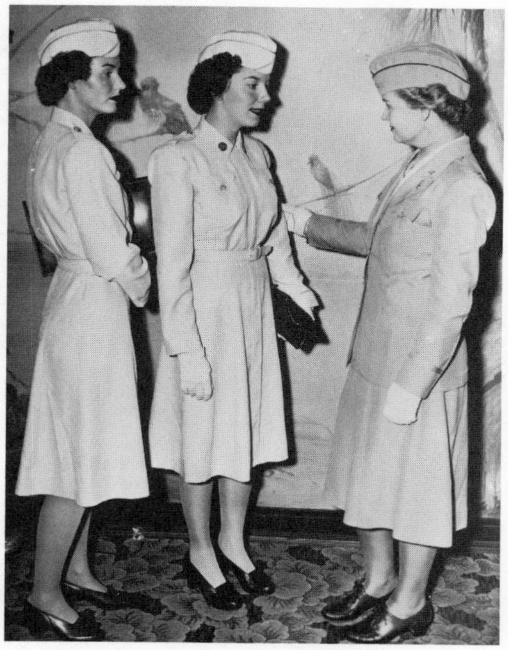

Fig. 79-16.

Fig. 79-15.

Fig. 79-17.

Fig. 79-15. *After World War II, enlisted members of the WAC switched to two pairs of disks on their jackets, just like those of enlisted men. The upper pair on the collar tips were the letters US, while the lower pair on the lapels were branch devices. The olive drab wool uniform was the same as that introduced for the WAAC, with only slight modifications.*

Fig. 79-16. *Two enlisted members of the WAC wearing the light beige summer off-duty dress, with Colonel Hobby, director of the WAC, on the right.*

Fig. 79-17. *This WAC wears a medium beige off-duty dress, which became very popular and was widely worn in 1944 and 1945.*

Women's Uniforms after 1948

Fig. 80-1. Taupe WAC uniforms of the early 1950s. Left to right: raincoat; the officers' jacket with skirt; the enlisted women's coat, which could be worn only with the skirt; the taupe dress worn by an enlisted woman; an enlisted women's white dress uniform; the enlisted women's version of the jacket and skirt; the same style of jacket worn with slacks; the officers' coat and dress; and the overcoat. Fashion designer Hattie Carnegie created these uniforms to be more fashionable than the World War II women's uniforms.

The multitude of uniforms used by Women's Army Corps (WAC) members and female medical officers clearly needed consolidation after World War II. Different offices within the army saw a variety of roles for women, and this inability to agree on women's places caused a struggle to dictate decisions about the female service members. One consequence was the lack of standardized uniforms and rules for wear of insignia during World War II. Following the declaration of peace and resolution of immediate issues within the army, the place of women in the army and, consequently, their uniforms came to the table for study.

In 1948 the new Department of the Army established a women's army uniform program that eliminated many of the World War II uniforms such as the specially colored summer and winter off-duty dresses. The new standard was similar to the men's uniforms and was basically the uniforms in use at the end of the war: olive drab shade 37 service coats or Eisenhower jackets for winter wear and khaki coats or khaki shirts for summer use.[1] These uniforms lasted only a short time until the army introduced a new color exclusively for women: taupe (shade 121).

Taupe remained distinctive of women into the 1950s, when the army began to wear other colors, including the green cord uniform. Uniform policies did not last long, at least for women, because the generals decided that women should wear the same color of

Fig. 80-1.

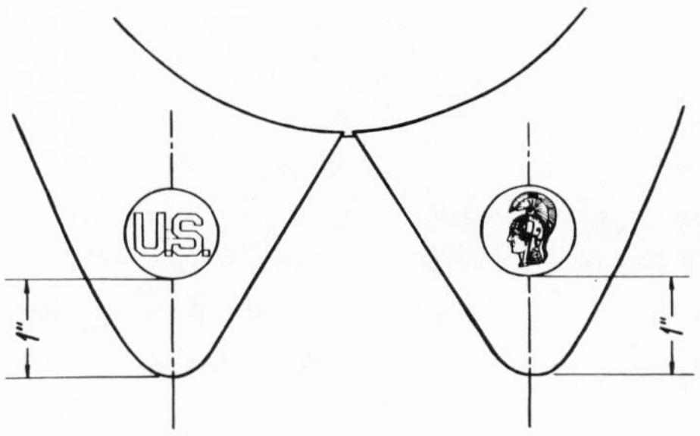

Fig. 80-2.

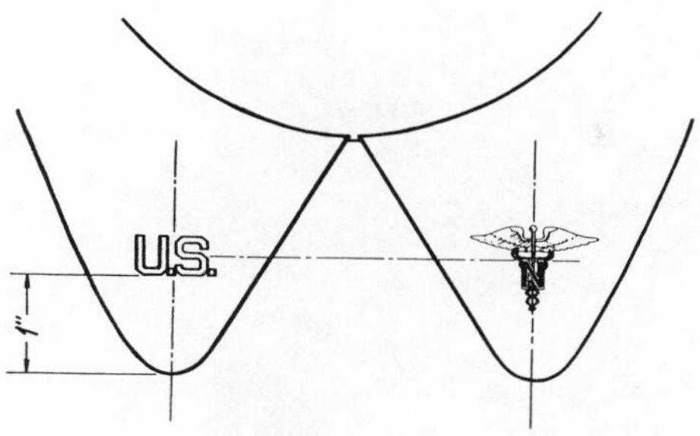

Fig. 80-3.

Figs. 80-2 and 80-3. *On the 1951 taupe uniform women wore insignia in a manner similar to their placement on the World War II WAC off-duty dress. These two figures show examples of insignia placement on the taupe uniforms.*

Fig. 80-4.

Fig. 80-4. *In 1954 the army introduced beige uniforms like this one. Officers added cuff braid on their coats.*

uniforms as men. With the standardization of army green, the army adopted it for women. This alleged exclusive use of army green soon was forgotten as new clothing color, such as mint green, was brought out.

Taupe and Beige Uniforms after World War II

Following the explosive growth in numbers of women in the army during World War II, with the subsequent 1948 consolidation of uniforms to the olive drab wool and the khaki the army decided that WAC and Medical Department women's uniforms would be the same. To fill this need the army introduced the taupe uniform set in 1951, along with a totally new color of hat insignia known as "antique bronze." The uniforms included a taupe wool coat and skirt that were primarily a winter uniform but that could be worn the year around and a taupe (shade 124) cotton dress as well as a taupe jacket that could be worn with either the winter skirt or with special-duty service uniform slacks (Fig. 80-1).[2]

The taupe jacket and coat buttoned to the neck and thus had collars but no lapels, which caused officers' branch insignia to go on the left collar tip and the *US* on the right. These insignia were worn with the horizontal axis perpendicular to the vertical, as shown in Figs. 80-2 and 80-3. The taupe dress was not worn with the top button closed, which allowed the collar to be open, but the insignia axis was vertical on this dress, too.[3]

The taupe uniform replaced all women's service uniforms except for the nurses' white ward uniform and a white dress uniform that was cut like the taupe service uniform. The taupe dress proved unsatisfactory, and in 1954 a beige uniform with a modified collar was prescribed (Fig. 80-4).[4]

The army beige uniform (shade 146), also called the light taupe uniform, consisted of a skirt and a fitted four-button coat that opened slightly at the top. Like the shade 121 coat, officers' and warrant officers' coats were trimmed on the lower sleeve with ½-inch-wide mohair braid. Insignia placement was similar to that on the taupe dress, with the *US* and branch ornaments' horizontal axes perpendicular to the vertical with the collar open. The popularity of this uniform led to the adoption in 1956 of a green and white striped two-piece summer uniform called the army cord uniform.[5]

Green Cord Uniform

In March 1956 the Army Uniform Board approved a green and whit hairline-striped (shade 160), two-piece uniform known as

Fig. 80-5.

Fig. 80-5. *The army green cord uniform, authorized for wear from 1959 through 1980. The material was green and white hairline striped, with cuffs and collar trimmed in a solid green cord.*

the army green cord uniform. The uniform (Fig. 80-5) was authorized for wear starting with the summer of 1959. The suit consisted of a four-button, short-sleeved coat and a skirt, both made from lightweight polyester, with the general cut similar to that of the beige uniform. False sleeve cuffs and the collar were trimmed in a solid green braid 1/8 inch in diameter. This popular uniform became obsolete on September 30, 1980.[6]

Green Uniforms

Army green uniforms were initially standardized for men and first issued in the mid-1950s. At that time the army agreed that women should have uniforms of the same color as men's to help identify service women as members of the army. Accordingly, in 1956 and 1957 the army considered and finally approved a specific decision to switch women to green uniforms, and the initial uniform, of shade 44 serge or gabardine, became available in 1960.[7]

The army green uniform was to play such a key part in the army's plans for women's clothing that a special regulation was published early in January 1960, spelling out how the clothing was to be integrated into the supply system. All commissioned and warrant officers and enlisted women were to have at least one green uniform by October 1962, with quartermaster stores to start sales on 1 July 1960. Use of the green uniform as winter wear was mandatory on 1 October 1964.[8] The uniform consisted of a fitted four-button coat with a V-necked open collar with rounded ends and a notched lapel with square corners. Women officers, like their male counterparts, wore a 1/2-inch-wide black mohair band on each sleeve, the lower edge 3 inches above the bottom of the sleeve (Fig. 80-6).

In October 1977 women were allowed a different type of green uniform after a 1975 army test of the pantsuit uniform, during which it had been worn by military policewomen at Fort Devens and Fort Dix and in the Washington, D.C. area. The new uniform, called the "army green pantsuit uniform," consisted of slacks and a five-button jacket. It was authorized for wear in several ways: for year-round wear with a gray-green (shade 413) turtleneck tunic or sweater (Fig. 80-7) under the coat, or with a tan or white shirt under the coat. For summer wear the uniform was just a tan or white shirt with either skirt or slacks. In 1979 another shade of green (shade 444) was also authorized, thus allowing two similarly cut uniforms, both green, to be worn concurrently.[9]

By 1981 army women were swamped with a multitude of uniforms, some from the

Fig. 80-6.

Fig. 80-6. *Left and right: The women's army green uniform, 1960.*

Fig. 80-7.

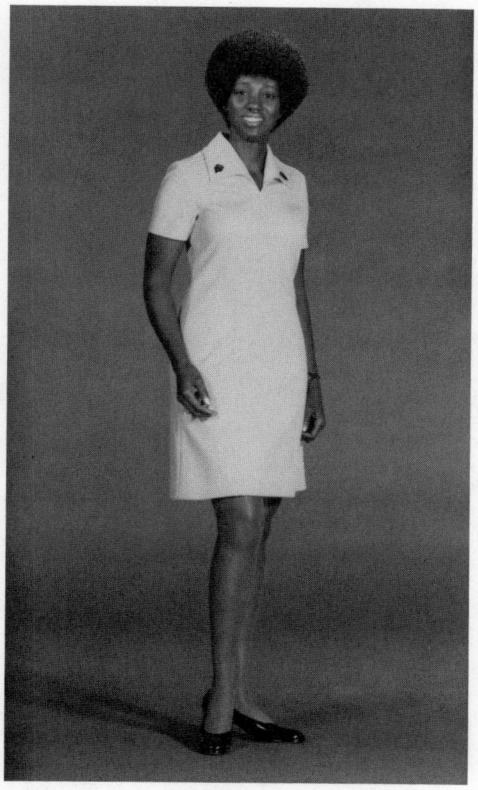

Fig. 80-8.

Fig. 80-7. *A 1976 model with the army green pantsuit with gray-green turtleneck tunic and black beret. This uniform could also be worn with tan or white shirts instead of the turtleneck sweater.*

Fig. 80-8. *The one-piece mint-colored dress, tested in 1973 and widely used later in the 1970s. The wide collar was an interesting variation influenced by civilian styles. A short, collarless jacket without insignia was optional with the uniform.*

1950s and others only two years old. Women had a much larger selection of military clothing than did male soldiers. As a result, in 1981 the army acted to consolidate women's uniforms by eliminating some and bringing out a new green uniform known as the green classic uniform. The coat had four buttons as before, but its pockets differed slightly from those of the earlier coat; still no upper pockets were used, but the two lower diagonal pockets had slanted flaps. Either a skirt or slacks could go with the coat to complete the classic uniform, which was to replace all other service uniforms (mint green, pantsuit, and original green) by September 1986.[10]

Mint Green Women's Uniforms

The first women's uniform of a bright, light green shade lasted only eleven years after its introduction in 1975. Officially called the "summer dress and jacket," this uniform was a 100 percent polyester, knit, shade 388 dress with an optional jacket. Branch insignia was placed on the dress's large collar as on a shirt. The jacket itself was different from any other uniform in that it depended upon the dress's large collar to carry insignia (Fig. 80-8). The uniform was the same for all officers and enlisted women, with distinction only by the insignia.[11]

In 1979 the army authorized two other shade 388 uniforms that later became available for general wear. These two-piece uniforms included a skirt and either a long-sleeved or short-sleeved jacket. Jackets were worn outside the skirt and had four-button fronts, with button-down shoulder loops (Fig. 80-9). The uniform became obsolete in September 1986.[12]

Women's White, Blue, and Black Dress, Mess, and Evening Uniforms

Female medical personnel have long worn various white dresses the year around as duty clothing, but in 1951 a new white summer uniform of the same design as the taupe uniform was introduced for dress wear. The optional uniform's coat had five buttons and closed from the waist to the coat collar (Fig. 80-10). By 1959 the uniform had evolved to a design similar to the popular light beige uniform with only four buttons and an open collar, apparently in response to the incongruity of wearing the earlier summer coat buttoned to the neck. The later style, which included an appropriate change in the placement of collar insignia, is shown in Fig. 80-11. Initially its buttons were of the antique bronze color, but in 1959 they were changed to gilt buttons. White cuff braid, 1/2 inch wide, distinguished officers.[13]

In June 1957 the army introduced an optional women's dress blue uniform, which the army soon directed as mandatory for most women officers. The blue uniform coat

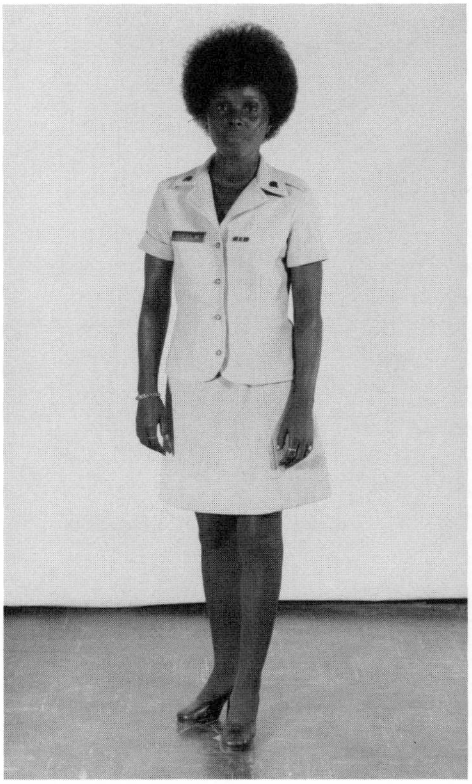

Fig. 80-9.

Fig. 80-10.

Fig. 80-11.

Fig. 80-12.

Fig. 80-9. *A skirt and jacket version of the women's mint green (shade 388) uniform. While civilian fashions obviously strongly influenced skirt length and material, the general cut of the new uniforms was also drawn from current styles. The two-piece uniform came with both long- and short-sleeved jackets.*

Fig. 80-10. *An officers' 1951 dress white uniform. This uniform hat was worn with the insignia centered above the right eye, in a stylish move. Buttons and cap insignia were "antique bronze" in color.*

Fig. 80-11. *By 1959 the dress white uniform had the jacket worn with the top button open and the collar and lapel pressed against the body front. Pocket placement and openings also changed with the uniform modifications.*

Fig. 80-12. *An enlisted women's dress blue uniform, introduced in 1957. Officers' uniforms carried shoulder straps that were 3 1/2 inches long instead of the 4-inch length specified for men.*

closed with four gilt buttons and was form-fitting, partially covering the wearer's hips, with the coat body about as long as the sleeves. The collar and lapels were of the design that was to become standard for women's uniforms: collars with rounded corners, *US* letters on the right and branch insignia on the left, with the small lapels bare. Commissioned and warrant officers had a sleeve band 3/4 inch wide like that of male officers, with the branch color in the center. Enlisted women had a 1/8-inch stripe of yellow braid. Officers' shoulder boards were worn like the men's, and the straps themselves were identical except that those for women were 3 1/2 inches long instead of the men's 4-inch length. A women's dress blue uniform is shown in Fig. 80-12.[14]

Fig. 80-13a.

Fig. 80-13b.

Fig. 80-13. *Women assigned to the U.S. Army Band wore special dress uniforms, including red caps and several combinations of white and dark blue coats and trousers. While women in the band essentially had the same uniforms as men, the women had an additional uniform that included long skirts (shown at the right) for use in concerts.*

In 1978 enlisted women assigned to selected army bands received special dress blue uniforms with floor-length skirts for concerts and slacks for marching performances. Also in the 1970s U.S. Army Band female members received other distinctive uniforms (Fig. 80-13). The tradition of special uniforms for band members continues even today.[15]

A blue evening jacket and floor-length skirt were the main components of the 1959 women's optional evening dress uniform for commissioned and warrant officers. The jacket was waist-length, without any buttons, and with a collar trimmed with gold bullion embroidery of a laurel leaf design. No branch insignia went on the uniform. The lower sleeves were decorated with the same type of modified sleeve knots as those used by male officers on their evening dress uniform (Fig. 80-14). The blue wool cape, which could be worn with the evening dress uniform, carried shoulder straps from the blue uniform, thus indicating both rank and branch (Fig. 80-15).[16]

A large number of new optional uniforms became available to women officers in 1969, replacing the previous evening dress uniform. The five new uniforms were based on two jackets of similar design, one white and one black. These jackets introduced new-style shoulder boards to indicate officers' rank and branch (Fig. 80-16), which had been the function of the shoulder straps on the blue uniform. The two jackets themselves were of identical design, differing only in material. Three gilt buttons decorated each side of the jacket front, which hung open. Lower sleeve knots were trimmed with mohair braid 1/2 inch wide and the same color as the jacket. No branch insignia appeared on the uniforms. The two jackets could be worn with skirts of various lengths and colors to make five uniforms, as listed in Table 80-1.[17]

In 1986 the army introduced additional dress and mess uniforms, which really consisted of a new jacket for wear as part of the white mess, all white mess, and evening white mess uniforms. It was cut similar to the 1969 style, and although some seams were different, the major change was in insignia. All female officers wore the same style of shoulder knot that male officers wore, and the sleeve ornaments also switched to the male design. Enlisted women could now wear these uniforms without shoulder ornaments and with the same cuff devices as those worn by male enlisted personnel: a "modified trefoil" containing small metal

Fig. 80-14. *Some women's uniforms of the late 1950s. The coat of the officer at the far left has cloth shoulder loops with metal rank insignia. This style was later changed so that women wore shoulder straps similar to those used by male officers. The center two women wear the then new green service uniforms. An enlisted women's dress blue uniform is on the right. The seated colonel has a midnight blue cape, which carried shoulder straps, as part of her evening dress uniform.*

Fig. 80-15. *An officers' evening dress uniform, authorized in 1959. The headband, jacket, five-gored skirt, and cummerbund were midnight blue.*

Fig. 80-14.

Fig. 80-15.

chevrons. Either this or the 1969 jacket could be worn with the 1969-pattern skirts.

The black mess and black evening mess uniforms remained, but introduced were new blue mess and blue evening mess uniforms for women. These were generally the same as the males' mess blue jacket designs except that the branch-colored lapels were curved and the jacket was cut for the female figure. Shoulder and sleeve devices were the same as those for the male counterpart. The dark blue dress worn with the jacket determined the uniform: with a skirt slightly past knee length the uniform was the blue mess uniform; with a floor-length skirt it was the blue evening mess uniform (Fig. 80-19). It is interesting to note that for men, only generals' trousers were dark blue, while others wore light blue. For the women, all skirts were dark blue, matching the jackets.[18]

Other Women's Uniforms

Other uniforms were required for field wear, hospital service, and other duties in which the various service coats, skirts, and dresses just described were inadequate. These include but are not limited to white hospital

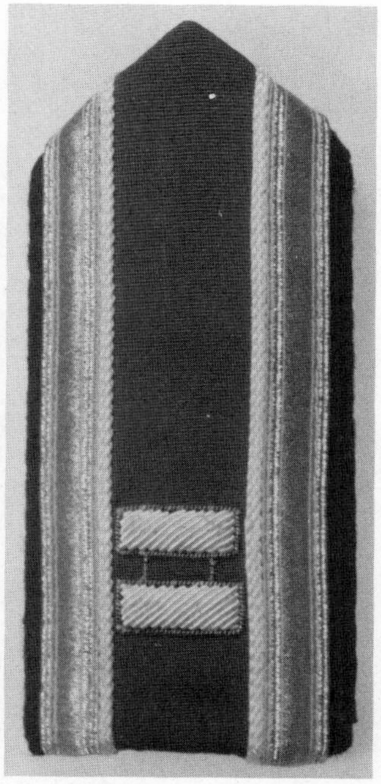

Fig. 80-16.

Fig. 80-17.

Fig. 80-16. *A shoulder board worn on women's mess and evening uniforms after 1969. The board was 4$\frac{11}{16}$ inches long at the outer edge. The gold borders were $\frac{3}{8}$ inch wide, and the background was in branch colors.*

Fig. 80-17. *A women's white mess uniform with black street-length skirt. A similar black jacket was authorized with this skirt.*

duty uniforms, special exercise suits (later called training duty uniforms), and field uniforms. In all cases, officers' and enlisted soldiers' clothing was identical, with only insignia distinguishing branches and grades.

In the cases of fatigue or field uniforms, the women's versions were different from men's until the late 1970s, when some women began limited wear of men's fatigues. Women's fatigues are most easily recognized by the placement of pockets on thigh fronts, by shirts worn outside the pants, and by field jackets that continued to be made only with buttons long after men's versions had switched to zippers and flaps (Figs. 80-20 and 80-21).[19]

Service women for many years were discharged for pregnancy, but eventually they were allowed to remain in the service during pregnancy, and in 1981 the army introduced a maternity uniform that consisted of an army green (shade 434) tunic, a skirt or slacks, and either a white or a green shirt. Officers wore branch and rank insignia on the shirt collar, while enlisted women wore bright brass chevrons on the collar. This practice was changed in 1983 so that officers wore only rank insignia on each collar.[20]

WOMEN'S INSIGNIA PLACEMENT AFTER 1951

On those women's uniforms that had no direct men's counterpart, such as the hospital dress and nursing uniforms, collar insignia were worn in a manner that was not like that of any other uniform. While the collar insignia were placed *similarly* to the style of other uni-

Table 80-1. *Women Officers' Formal Uniforms Components, 1969.*

	Black Mess	White Mess	All White Mess	Black Evening	White Evening
Black jacket	x			x	
White jacket		x	x		x
Black street-length skirt	x	x			
Black full-length skirt				x	x
White street-length skirt			x		

NOTE: An example of the white mess is shown in Fig. 80-17; an example of the all white mess is shown in Fig. 80-18.

Fig. 80-18.

Fig. 80-18. The women's all white mess uniform with short white skirt could be worn year-round by officers and warrant officers. Materials could be tropical-weight wool or tropical polyester wool. Female generals wore stars on the cuffs and gold cord knots on the shoulder.

Fig. 80-19.

Fig. 80-19. Not content with the five mess and evening uniforms introduced in 1969, in the 1980s the army authorized blue evening mess uniforms with floor-length skirts (shown) and blue mess uniforms with knee-length skirts.

forms, the *exact* placement varied. This practice continued with the introduction of new uniforms that had different collars.

White nurses' uniforms had insignia located much as they were worn on male officers' shirts, with rank on the right collar and branch insignia on the left collar. For this uniform, though, the insignia were placed vertically instead of being aligned parallel to the front collar edge. *US* and branch insignia combinations as worn in 1951 are described in Table 80-2. Placement is shown in Fig. 80-22.[21]

The proliferation of uniforms during the 1950s and through 1970 did not change the general concept of insignia placement, but specific placement changed with the new uniforms. The taupe coat had insignia placed perpendicular to the floor when the collar was closed, and the insignia were not repositioned when the collar was worn open. Newer uniforms such as the beige, blue,

Table 80-2. *Women's Collar Insignia Combinations, 1951.*

	Taupe and White Coats		**Taupe Summer Dress**		**Taupe Jacket**		**Hospital Dress**	
Insignia	**Right Collar**	**Left Collar**	**Right Collar**	**Left Collar**	**Right Collar**	**Left Collar**	**Right Collar**	**Left Collar**
US	B		B		B		E	
Branch		B		B		B		B
Rank							O	

LEGEND: R=Insignia worn on right collar
L=Insignia worn on left collar
B=Insignia used by both officers and enlisted women
E=Insignia used by enlisted women only
O=Insignia used by officers only

green, and cord uniforms had collars that were always worn open. In response to these new designs, the army specified that insignia were to be worn perpendicular to the ground with the collar in the open (normal) position. Shirt insignia for fatigue or field uniforms were worn like men's, with the central axis of officers' insignia parallel to the front collar edge, positioned as if the collar was worn closed. One exception was the wool serge coat, which was worn in the field during cold weather. This coat carried the *US* and branch insignia for officers, much like other women's uniforms. The result was that the subdued *US* insignia was made for the women. In 1975 officers' insignia on the cord uniform changed: while branch insignia remained on the left collar, a rank insignia replaced the previous *US* on the right collar. The rank was worn centered on the collar, parallel to the horizon.[22]

Various exercise suits had been authorized women since formation of the WACs in World War II, but for many years regulations were silent on the wear of insignia with those suits, simply pointing out that insignia went on the exercise uniform. The exact insignia were not described until 1969, when officers were explicitly told to wear rank and branch insignia on the collar in the same manner as on the hospital uniform. Enlisted women basic trainees were also told to wear the *US* and WAC insignia on their exercise suits at the same time, while other enlisted women wore metal chevrons on the collar.[23]

Several changes took place in the early 1980s when the mint-colored (shade 388) skirt and jacket uniforms replaced the cord uniform in 1979–80. The enlisted women's jackets carried small metal chevrons on the collar; no branch insignia or *US* letters were worn. Officers placed rank and branch insignia on the collar in a manner similar to their placement on men's shirts: parallel to the front edge of the collar. This was the same scheme followed on the 1975 mint green dress with optional jacket. This change came about simultaneously with the early-1975 introduction of small, bright brass enlisted grade insignia. As part of the pantsuit uniform, in the summer enlisted women could wear either a tan or a white shirt as an outer garment. When this was done, the bright brass chevrons went on both collars. Officers wore the rank on the right and branch on the left, as usual, with the insignia axis horizontal. No insignia went on the shirt when the jacket was worn.[24]

The 1970s saw a great increase in the number of women in the army, and there

Fig. 80-20. *Women's fatigue trousers, starting with the World War II version, had pockets on the front of the legs. They were further distinguished by exposed buttons on each side near the waist.*

Fig. 80-21. *Women's fatigue shirts buttoned opposite men's as did other women's shirts. Most noticeably, women wore their fatigue shirts outside the trousers, in contrast to the male soldiers.*

Fig. 80-20.

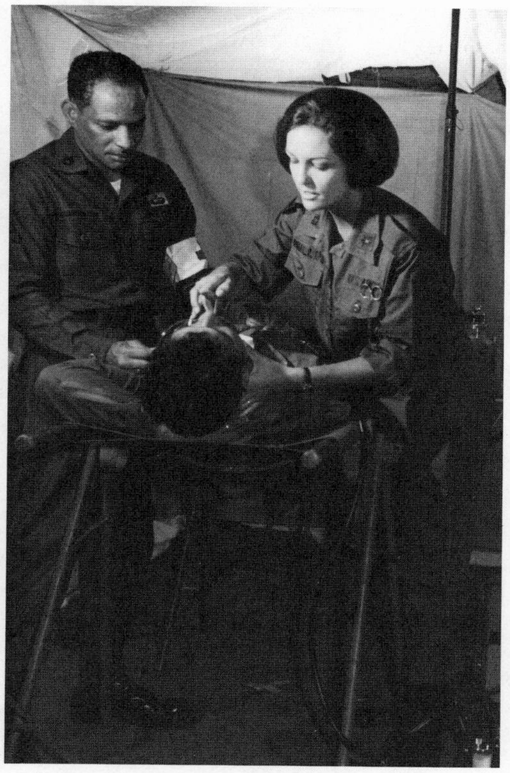

Fig. 80-21.

Fig. 80-22. Nurses wore rank and branch vertically on the hospital dress from World War II through the 1970s.

was a similar increase in the assignments available to women. Two indications of this change were the abolition of the WAC in November 1977 and the noted explosion in the styles of women's uniforms. As the various uniforms evolved, usually each one independently, the manner of insignia wear was haphazard. A 1977 survey of army commanders indicated that the many ways of insignia wear for both male and female personnel needed to be simplified. Between the two sexes and many uniforms, collar insignia were worn in seven different ways. In mid-1978 the Army Uniform Board changed the way branch, *US*, and grade insignia were worn: on all uniforms on which the branch of service and *US* letters were worn, the centerlines of the insignia were to be parallel to the inside edge of the collars and lapels, respectively. On all uniforms on which officers wore insignia of grade and branch of service, the insignia centerlines were to be parallel to the lower collar edge. On enlisted women's uniforms carrying small metal chevrons, the insignia centerline would bisect the angle of the collar point.[25]

Fig. 80-22.

Appendix

Insignia Fasteners

THE REVERSE of an insignia can often yield more information about its past than can the front. The means of fastening usually shows the insignia's purpose (whether it was worn on headgear or coat) and can frequently provide some indication of its age. Most early cross-belt plates, for example, were engraved by jewelers and silversmiths and had small round posts or hooks brazed or soldered onto the reverse. After 1800 some pieces had small wire loops on their reverse, indicating that they were ornaments only, because they lacked the heavy posts necessary to function as buckles. The earliest cross-belt plates are of cast brass, with three integral hooks on the reverse. The maker bent one hook and added two rivet-head posts to the other two after the plates were removed from the mold. The leather belt was permanently attached to the two rivet-head posts and adjusted for length by the hook. After 1815 many plates were die-struck in thin brass; a continuous three-pronged wire partially imbedded into the lead that filled the back fastened the plate to the belt.

The oldest known cap plates have small holes at the corner edges by which they were sewed or wired to caps (Fig. A-1). During the period 1813–21, wire loop fasteners, much like large button shanks, appeared. These were inserted through small holes or slots in the cap and held in place by leather strips or other pegs. These iron or wire loops lasted until after the Civil War because they allowed easy removal of the insignia for cleaning (Fig. A-2). Flexible wires replaced these loops for many militia insignia and for a few very late-nineteenth-century small Regular Army insignia (Fig. A-3). One end of a short wire was soldered to the insignia back, and the other end was worked through the fabric and then bent over. Many large Regular Army insignia of the late Indian War period had safety pin fasteners imbedded in the lead that filled the insignia back. On these ornaments unit numbers and letters were held in place with wires stuck into the same lead (Fig. A-4).

Fig. A-1.

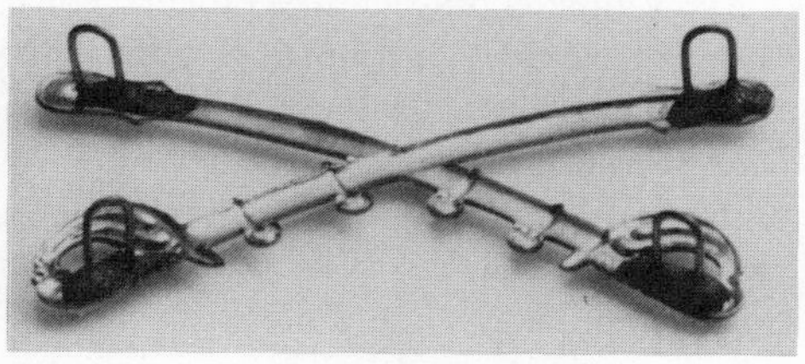

Fig. A-2.

Fig. A-3.

Fig. A-1. *Early U.S. Army soldiers sewed plates to their caps. Small holes were drilled near the edge of such insignia for that purpose.*

Fig. A-2. *During the middle decades of the nineteenth century, metal cap insignia had iron loops soldered to the reverse. Soldiers cut small slits in their caps, inserted the iron loops, and held the insignia in place with small pieces of leather or wood.*

Fig. A-3. *Many late-nineteenth-century militia insignia used wire fasteners. The Regular Army used this type of fastener only on a few selected insignia, such as small numbers and ornaments placed on helmet eagles and numbers and letters used on campaign hats.*

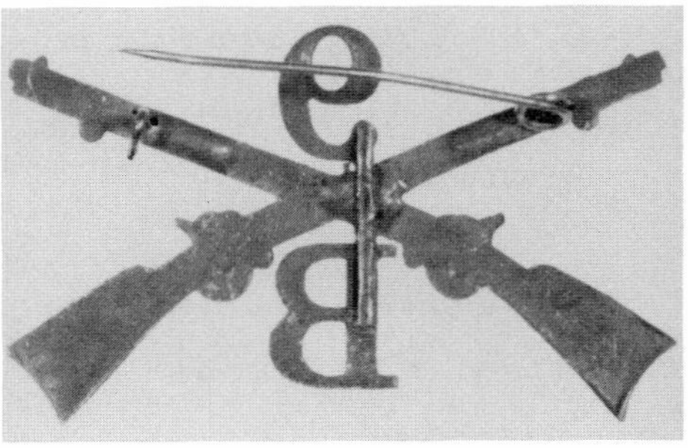

Fig. A-4.

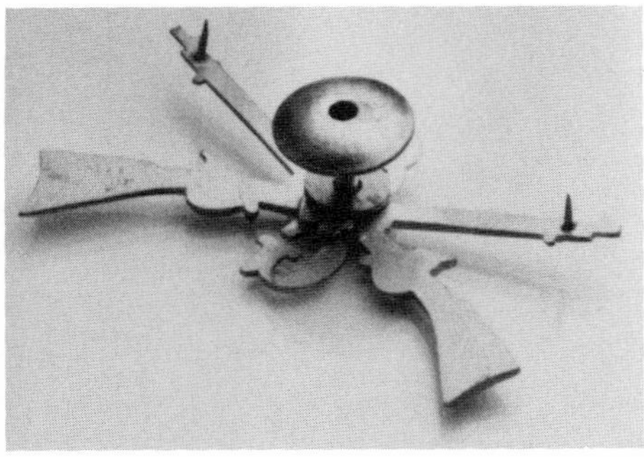

Fig. A-5.

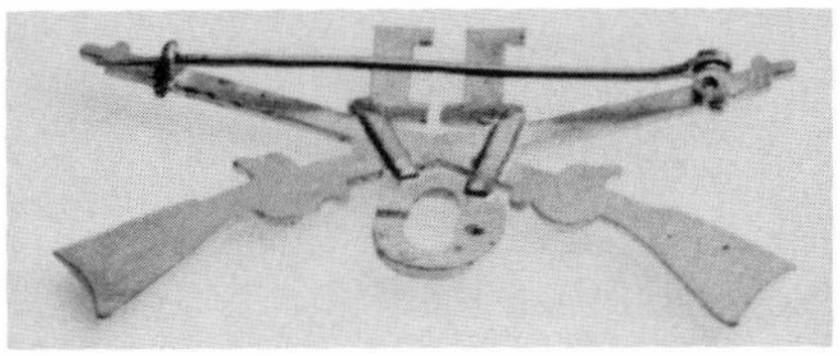

Fig. A-6.

Fig. A-7.

Fig. A-8.

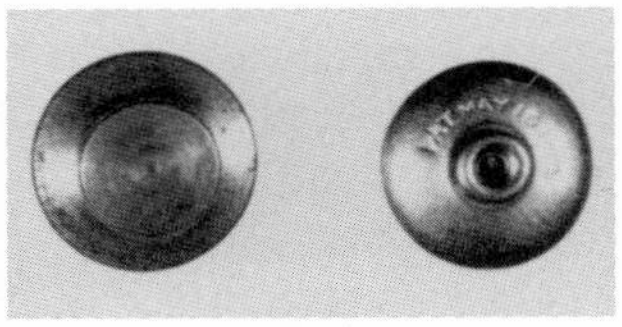

Fig. A-9.

Fig. A-10.

***Fig. A-4.** Late-nineteenth-century enlisted men's insignia on forage caps had lead-filled backs, and the lead held a safety pin fastener. Numbers and letters had small wires soldered to them and the other end of the wires inserted into the lead, making the entire insignia a single device.*

***Fig. A-5.** In 1896 the U.S. Army introduced screw-post cap insignia. A special round nut with a long shank went with the insignia. One or two small needle points were soldered to the back of the insignia to keep it from rotating. For some insignia, such as crossed cannons, identical designs were worn on both cap and collar between 1905 and 1918. The only difference between cap and collar ornaments was the use of a pin fastener for collar ornaments and a threaded screw post for cap insignia.*

***Fig. A-6.** The army used hinged pin fasteners on collar ornaments starting about 1902. This army-issued 1903–1905 infantry insignia has the catch made from wire and formed into a circular shape with a small cutout in one side to allow the end of the pin to slide into it.*

***Fig. A-7.** Officers' pin-back fasteners and those issued by the army starting about 1910 often had the catch made of a flat piece of bent metal. The U-shaped pivot, drift pin, and pointed fastening pin were generally the same design as those on the issued 1903–10 collar insignia.*

***Fig. A-8.** Officers' insignia introduced after 1892 often had small loops on the reverse to allow the metal piece to be sewn to the uniform. Insignia that fastened to the uniform in this manner generally were not used much after 1906, although in a few cases the practice continued past World War I.*

The army introduced threaded screw posts for caps in 1896.[1] These screw posts (Fig. A-5) are the only way one can tell if enlisted soldiers' insignia of the 1904–17 period were intended for caps, because many collar insignia were identical except for the fastener.

The longest-lived fastener is the pin. While safety pin fasteners of the type shown in Fig. A-4 were used on some early enlisted troops' insignia, hinged pin fasteners were the most common fasteners on collar insignia made from the late 1890s through World War II. Shown in Fig. A-6, these are still used today on some insignia. The hinged end of the fastening pin was usually made flat and drilled so that a small drift pin would serve as a pivot in a U-shaped piece of metal that was in turn soldered to the insignia back (Fig. A-7).

Many nineteenth-century officers' collar insignia have three or four small loops about 1/16 inch in diameter fixed to the insignia back so the insignia could be sewn to the uniform. Commonly used in the 1890s on etruscan insignia, this type of fastener was usually replaced by the more easily removable pin back during the early twentieth century, although a few World War I insignia were made with sew-on loops (Fig. A-8).

Fastening devices of both the removable button and the pin-back styles were widely used during the 1930s on officers' insignia. The removable button patent was requested in 1921 and granted in 1923. Today the device is commonly called a clutch, because the small metal button clutches or holds on to the tine (Fig. A-9). A thin tine soldered to the insignia reverse was inserted through the cloth. The removable button was then fastened to the tine on the opposite side of the material from the insignia. The clutch fastener was expensive to make, but officers could afford this extra cost of a few cents, so the clutch fastener came into wide use. By the close of World War II the clutch fastener was in nearly exclusive use by makers of collar insignia, in part because in 1943 a more cheaply made fastener was patented (Fig. A-10), although these simplified clutches were made before then and can be identified by the marking, "patent applied for."[2]

To compete with this patented device, insignia companies also introduced small threaded screw posts during the 1920s for officers' insignia. Three examples of various fasteners are shown in Fig. A-11 and A-12.

These fasteners caused minor damage to shirt and coat collars and were not widely accepted by soldiers, even though many insignia makers used them to compete with the clutch fastener. The simplicity of the clutch fastener and its easy attachment and removal account for its enduring popularity.

Enlisted soldiers' collar insignia worn on dress coats from 1902 through 1917 were generally similar to officers' devices, and in the federal establishment they came only with pin fasteners, except for campaign hat numbers and letters. Some states used staple-like prong fasteners (Fig. A-13).

The initial large size of the 1902 enlisted men's collar devices (Fig. A-14) caused the quartermaster general to reduce insignia size in early 1905, making enlisted men's and officers' insignia the same dimensions (Fig. A-15). Simultaneously, several minor design changes occurred, styled by the army as "modernization."[3] In enlisted men's insignia the size and design change provide an easy reference for dating. Mid- and late-nineteenth-century enlisted soldiers' collar devices initially were held by wires, just as cap insignia were.

Screw posts, first used on collar insignia in 1910, lasted well into World War II. The army began widespread use of enlisted troops' collar insignia with 1902 uniform regulations. Starting in 1910, the War Department placed insignia for enlisted men's field uniforms on 1-inch-diameter disks. The army made early disks with a background of fine lines or dots called "a matted field," which eventually became forty-eight lines per inch (Fig. A-16). In September 1921 the first backgrounds officially changed to crosshatched lines with small shields in the open areas (Fig. A-17). Gilt disks replaced the bronze ones in 1923, with the bronze disks reserved for wartime, although in practice nothing except bright metal insignia was subsequently used.[4]

Until World War II, U.S.-made enlisted soldiers' collar disk insignia were usually made with a short threaded screw post and round nut on the back. This allowed the insignia to be held close to the cloth yet not protrude into the wearer's neck, as shown in Fig. A-18. In a few cases pin backs were applied to enlisted men's disks, but for the high-collar coat the army issued disks with short screw posts.

In the 1920s and 1930s firms made disks with the insignia design brazed directly to the screw post. The post, with insignia attached, was then inserted through a small hole in the center of a 1-inch-diameter disk, and a thin nut with two pointed projections was then applied to hold the design tight to the background (Fig. A-19). The standard round fastening nut would then be applied to the post to keep the insignia on the coat collar. The thin nut's two projections faced away from the insignia, sticking into the coat's material to keep the disk from rotating.

The concept of making enlisted soldiers' collar disks with two pieces showing (the central design and the 1-inch-diameter back-

Fig. A-11.

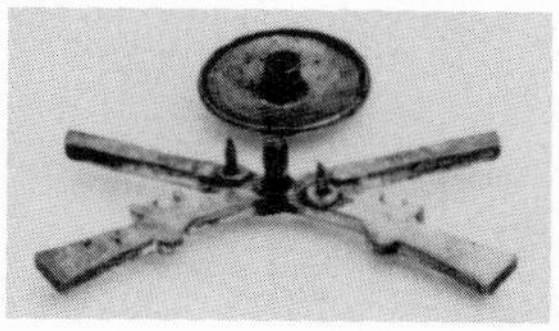

Fig. A-12.

Fig. A-14.

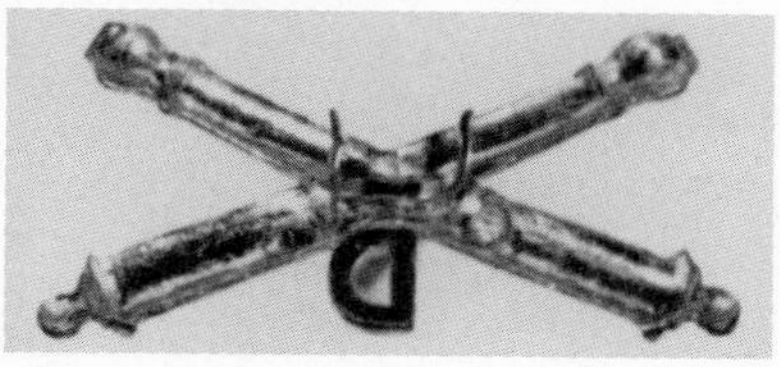

Fig. A-13.

Fig. A-15.

Fig. A-9. *The original clutch fastener, designed in 1921, was patented in 1923 as a removable button.*

Fig. A-10. *About the time of Pearl Harbor this style of simplified clutch fastener was first made, although the patent was not granted until 1943.*

Fig. A-11. *Very small threaded posts, pointed on the end and with round nuts, were used in the 1920s and 1930s. Fasteners of this type competed with the patented smooth post and clutch shown in Fig. A-9.*

Fig. A-12. *During the 1930s some collar and lapel insignia were made with a single threaded screw post and a large, flat, round nut. Two small pointed posts near the threaded post kept the insignia from rotating against the uniform cloth.*

Fig. A-13. *Many states issued insignia with these large staple fasteners. The two tines were stuck through the cloth and then bent over. The Regular Army did not use this type of fastener.*

Fig. A-14. *Between 1903 and 1905 enlisted men of the Regular Army wore large collar and cap insignia. These cavalry insignia were approximately 2½ inches wide.*

Fig. A-15. *In 1905 the quartermaster general reduced the size of enlisted men's collar and cap ornaments to the approximate size of those used by officers on their collars. These cavalry insignia were slightly less than 2 inches wide.*

Fig. A-16

Fig. A-17.

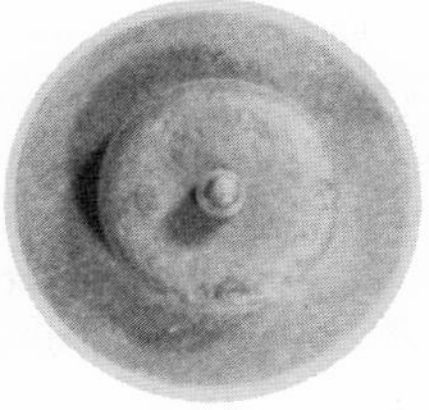

Fig. A-18.

Fig. A-16. When enlisted soldiers' service collar insignia were put onto a 1-inch disk, the background was "a matted field" consisting of very small dots. The background, also known as "stippled" or "pebbled," was later defined as consisting of forty-eight lines per inch, with sets of lines intersecting at 90 degrees.

Fig. A-17. A background of crossed lines with tiny shields in the open areas, as shown, was prescribed in September 1921 for enlisted men's collar insignia, although it took several years for the supply of existing men's disks with the matted field to be exhausted.

Fig. A-18. Enlisted men's disk collar insignia used between 1910 and the early 1940s were fastened to the coat with a threaded post and flat, round nut.

Fig. A-19. Privately made enlisted soldiers' insignia were manufactured starting in the late 1920s with the design soldered to a threaded screw post. This post was inserted through a 1-inch-diameter background disk, which was held in place by a thin nut. This assembly was then held to the uniform by a standard flat nut.

Fig. A-20. Near the end of World War II the previously used assembly and fastening device was modified so that the screw post was just long enough to hold a fastening nut that contained two tines. Soldiers then used clutches on the tines to hold the insignia to the uniform.

ground) resulted in many people calling this type of insignia the "two-piece" disk. In the 1920s and 1930s manufacturing companies changed from the regulation background of lines and shields to a smooth disk. This allowed the disk to be shined better. The army began to issue these disks, which were initially a private innovation, in 1937. Also in 1937, the army officially eliminated company letters, although in practice many soldiers wore privately purchased insignia, or stocks the army had on hand, that carried company designations.[5] Shortly after this change, several events occurred during World War II.

In January 1943, manufacturers began to make disks with two tines instead of a screw post in an effort to conserve metal and simplify construction. At the same time, the insignia went from a thick slug with a separate applied design to a thin, one-piece stamped insignia with the design and background made together.[6] Private industry con-

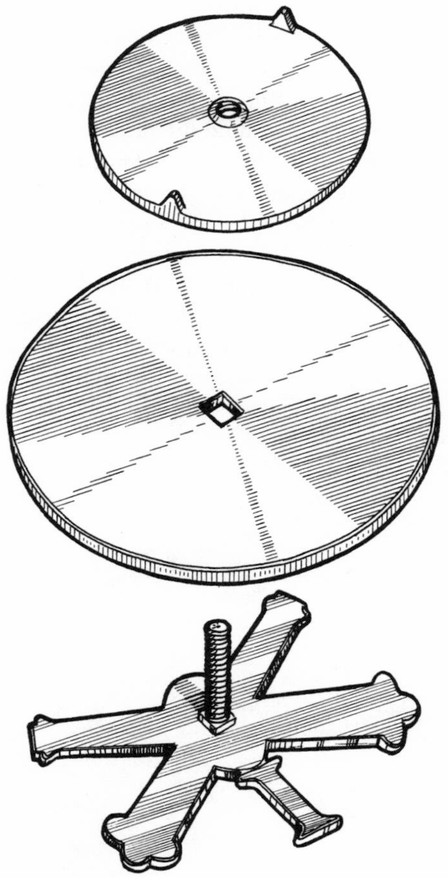

Fig. A-19.

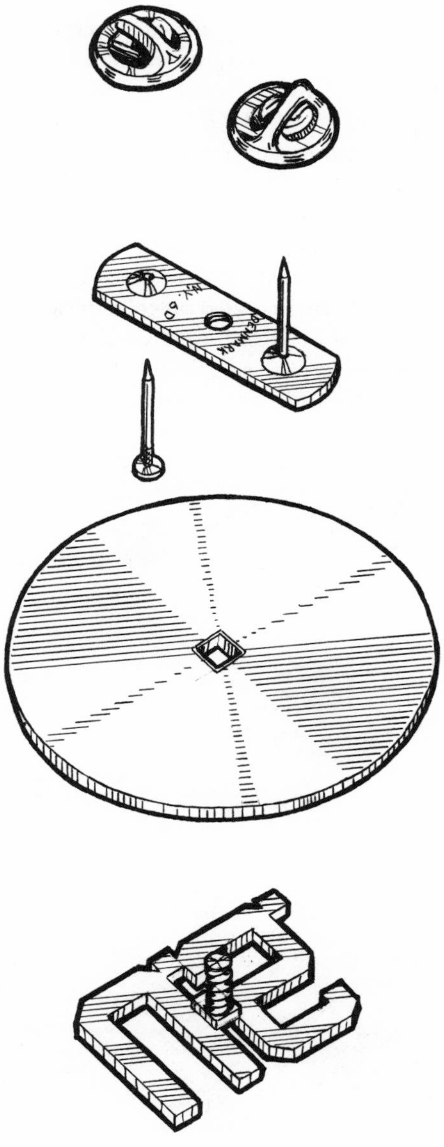

Fig. A-20.

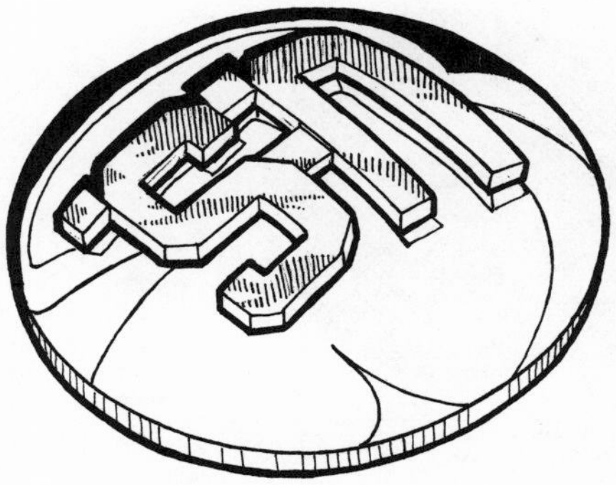

Fig. A-21.

tinued to manufacture disks with the design and the background separate but with the screw post short, just long enough to attach to a 3/4-inch-diameter disk that itself had two tines near the edge (Fig. A-20). Also, disks that had the background in a domed shape (Fig. A-21) began to appear, as well as disks with a silver finish. The "silver" disks were usually coated with white gold and required only a quick rub with a clean cloth to shine, as opposed to muscle and brass polish.

Metal insignia made outside the United States are rather common. During World War I, the American Expeditionary Forces (AEF) let a great many contracts with French manufacturers for purchase of officers' and enlisted troops' insignia. Both insignia can usually be identified by a finish of shiny enamel. The AEF purchased approximately 2.75 million French-made collar insignia.[7] Individual soldiers bought countless others directly from French makers. The two ways to most easily recognize French-made insignia are by the fastener and the finish.

Most French-made insignia, including some enlisted disks, are pin-backed. The long, pointed wire that holds the device to the uniform is usually wrapped around a short pivot pin so that the fastening wire has been bent 540 degrees (one and one-half turns), as shown in Fig. A-22. Where the loop makes more than one turn, it is laid flat so that one coil is next to the other instead of wrapping over itself. The blunt end of the fastening wire acts as a spring to maintain tension and keep the fastening pin in the catch. Catches are of a large open-loop shape and made from either wire or a narrow metal strip. The catch shape is generally like an oval bent open at one side. While U.S.-made insignia often exhibit wire catch loops, the domestic catches are smaller and usually round, like a circle with a portion cut out, instead of oval-shaped (Fig. A-23). The sharp pointed end of the French fastening wire typically extends 1/4 inch beyond the catch.

U.S. insignia makers chemically applied dark bronze-colored finishes, but the French often used a brown enamel or paint, each with a shiny finish. A few French insignia use a brown metal, although the fastener will identify the piece for what it is. Occasionally a French-made screw-post disk is found, but the post and fastening nut are noticeable different from those made in the United States.

During the U.S. Army's occupation of Germany following World War I, some German firms made collar insignia for U.S. troops. Construction of these enlisted soldiers' disks is similar to button construction, and it is probable that the disks were made at a button factory. The collar disks themselves are made from three pieces of thin metal, as is a modern military button. The gray-colored metal front piece was stamped with the insignia design and was then crimped over the back piece. This back part was made from either a shiny brass or grey metal like the front and usually had the legend *EXTRA FEIN*. The third piece of metal was the fastener, and these disks come with two types of fastening devices. The first is a screw post with two triangles on the button back cut and bent so that the points of the triangles penetrated the cloth and kept the

Fig. A-21. *Disks with a convex background were introduced by some manufacturers at the close of World War II.*

Fig. A-22. *U.S. insignia made in France during World War I can often be identified by the fastening pin wire that is wrapped one and one-half turns around the pivot pin. The second loop lies next to the first, and the short, nonpointed end acts to supply tension when the fastener is closed.*

Fig. A-23. *French-made insignia catches from the World War I era are usually made with large loops of either wire or a metal strap.*

Fig. A-24. *Some enlisted troops' disk collar insignia made in Germany after World War I for the occupation forces were constructed like a button. The fastener is either a button shank or, as shown in this case, a threaded screw post. These insignia are marked on the back EXTRA FEIN ("extra fine").*

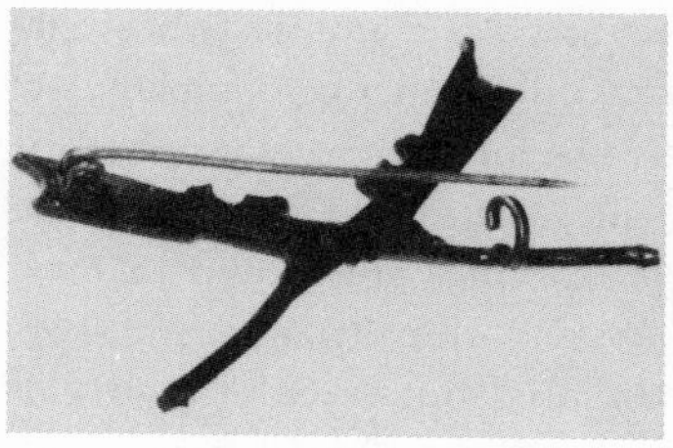

Fig. A-22.

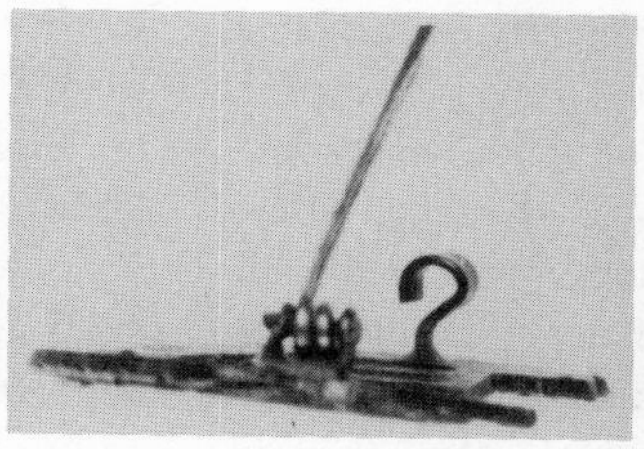

Fig. A-23.

Fig. A-24.

Fig. A-25.

Fig. A-26.

Fig. A-27.

Fig. A-28.

Fig. A-29.

Fig. A-25. *A few enlisted soldiers' collar insignia made in Germany immediately after World War II had safety pin fasteners held in place by a second piece of metal. This same type of fastener was occasionally used on post–World War I insignia made in Germany.*

Fig. A-26. *Screw-post backs continued to be used immediately after the end of World War II. Some German-made insignia for U.S. troops were constructed with screw posts. The front of the insignia was stamped from a single piece of metal.*

Fig. A-27. *Many U.S. insignia made in Germany in the late 1940s and the 1950s had smaller numbers and letters than did U.S.-made insignia. Distinguishing features of most German-made pieces are the neat letters and numbers added to the basic design.*

Fig. A-28. *Like enlisted soldiers' insignia, usually officers' German-made collar ornaments have small, neat numbers.*

Fig. A-29. *Occasionally German-made insignia have larger than normal letters and/or numbers. In addition, special abbreviations were used or unit designations were spelled out on some German-made collar ornaments.*

disk from rotating (Fig. A-24). The second fastening means is a button shank, which would have allowed the disk to be sewn to the collar or affixed with a ring or clip. These German-made insignia were usually finished with black paint, although this paint often flakes off, allowing the gray pot metal to show. Curious variations tend to occur, as in the case shown in chapter 42, "Transportation," which has Mercury's hat facing the wrong direction.

U.S. insignia made in Germany after World War II often exhibit interesting front designs and frequently have many numbers and letters added for a particular unit. Several examples are shown. The first disk is very unusual. The metal is a heavy slug, 0.070 inch thick at the center and evenly tapered to 0.050 inch at the edge, with the design stamped in relief. The reverse has a safety pin fastener, as illustrated in Fig. A-25. Embossed on one of the small disks that holds the pin to the insignia are the words *C. POELLATH SCHROBENHAUSEN.*

Another insignia made early in the occupation for the 18th Infantry is the piece shown in Fig. A-26. Construction is somewhat similar to that of the thin metal stamped disk made in the United States during World War II, the main difference being the fastener. The insignia is slightly convex. Made from 0.025-inch-thick metal, the edge is turned sharply to give the insignia an apparent thickness of 0.080 inch. A threaded screw post with a knurled nut fastens the disk to the garment.

One of the distinctive features that can identify insignia as German-made is the screw post. The German post is usually much thinner, with finer threads than that found on U.S. insignia. The thinner post and the tines are the only two ways to identify the common German pieces. American threaded screw posts are nominally 0.115 inch in diameter, while German posts are about 0.075 inch thick. The German posts appear to be about one-half the width of the American ones to many people. The thin posts are similar to those screw posts used on U.S.-made officers' insignia in the 1930s. Infrequently, some German-made insignia have the thicker 0.115 inch post, so the thicker post does not always indicate U.S. manufacture.

As previously mentioned, the German-made insignia often have added numbers and/or letters to show unit designations. These applications were most commonly made in the 1950s, a time when many units in the United States did not add the regimental or battalion number or company letter. Frequently the foreign-made numbers or letters are smaller than those on U.S.-made insignia. Two examples are shown in Figs. A-27 and A-28. Occasionally larger numbers and letters were used, but as with the smaller additions, their craftsmanship is very good. An example with a small number and large letter is shown in Fig. A-29. Special designa-

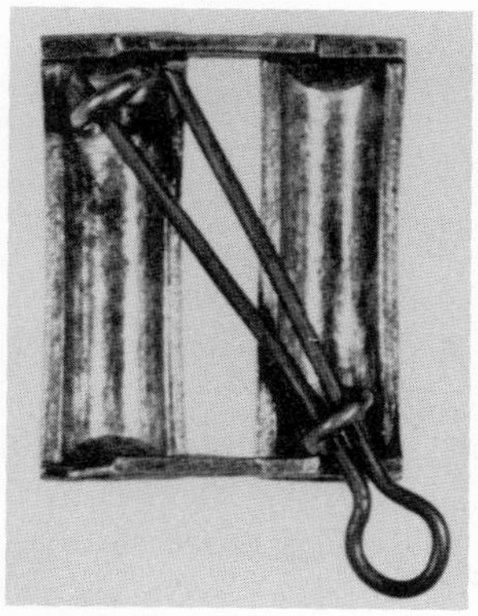

Fig. A-30.

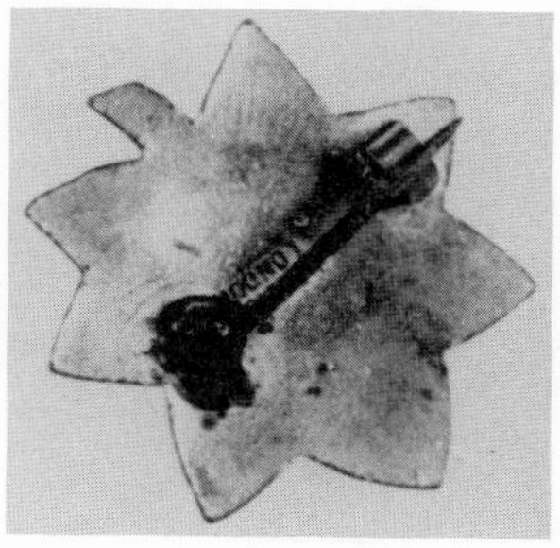

Fig. A-31.

tions or markings were often added to German-made insignia.

When U.S. forces arrived in Britain during World War II, English insignia manufacturers made devices for the soldiers, but in a few cases these had British fasteners, which required large grommet-reinforced holes in the uniform. An example typical of those made throughout the British Empire, as in India, is shown in Fig. A-30. More common is the British pin of the type shown in Fig. A-31, used on many insignia from 1917 through 1946, because between the wars the English exported some insignia to the United States. The hinge, when viewed from above, forms a triangle. This style also extends to some Australian and other British Commonwealth–made insignia, just as does the loop-type British fastener.

Longer, thicker foreign tines or prongs present on Far East– or German-made insignia also point to foreign manufacture. The clips or clutches are also of a poorer quality than the American clutches and since the 1970s have even been simply a piece of soft vinyl with a small hole in the center that holds to the tine by friction.

Fig. A-30. *A few U.S. insignia made in the British Empire have fasteners of the British style. These are loops affixed to the insignia reverse with a kind of cotter pin to hold the insignia to the uniform.*

Fig. A-31. *The most common British Empire insignia fastener used on U.S. insignia is this style of pin, easily recognized by the hinge end, which is formed into a triangular shape.*

NOTES

ABBREVIATIONS

AEF	American Expeditionary Forces
AGO	Adjutant General's Office
AR	Army Regulation
DA	Department of the Army
DF	Disposition Form
DOD	Department of Defense
GHQ	General Headquarters
GO	General Orders
HQ	Headquarters
HQA	Headquarters of the Army
MC&H	*Military Collector & Historian*
NA	National Archives
OQMG	Office of the Quartermaster General
QMC	Quartermaster Corps
QMG	Quartermaster General
RG	Record Group Number
SR	Special Regulation
TAG	The Adjutant General
TIOH	The Institute of Heraldry
WD	War Department

CHAPTER ONE

1. John Mollo, *Military Fashion,* pp. 36–37.
2. Geoffrey Parker, *The Thirty Years' War,* pp. 206–207.
3. Ibid., pp. 192–93.
4. Ibid., pp. 191–92.
5. John Hackett, *The Profession of Arms,* pp. 58, 59, 66–72.

CHAPTER TWO

1. Mendel L. Peterson, "American Army Epaulettes, 1814–1872," *MC&H,* Mar. 1951, p. 1.
2. Detmar H. Finke, "Insignia of the Continental Army, 1775–1783," *MC&H,* 1956, pp. 71–73; WD, AGO, GO 1, 20 Jan. 1854; WD, AGO, GO 92, 26 Oct. 1872, pp. 13–14; WD, GO 49, 28 Apr. 1917, sec. III.
3. WD, AGO, GO 92, 26 Oct. 1872, pp. 13–14; HQA, AGO, GO 132, 31 Dec. 1902, pp. 1, 15; WD, GO 47, 6 Apr. 1911; HQA, AGO, GO 20, Aug. 1860.
4. HQA, AGO, GO 104, 3 Oct. 1855; WD, *Annual Report of the Secretary of War, 1885,* p. 602; OQMG, Specification 185, 5 Apr. 1887.
5. Philadelphia inventories no. 153403, 1900 through 1902, list aiguillettes and shoulder knots of bandsmen by branch, RG 92, NA; HQA, AGO, GO 132, 31 Dec. 1902, par. 35. Officers' shoulder knots cloth centers were red for artillery, white for infantry, yellow for cavalry, and dark blue for all others until 1901, when the Corps of Engineers switched to red with white trim.
6. General observation. One example is in WD, AR 600-35, 31 Dec. 1926, par. 10a(1).
7. WD, AGO, GO 1, 20 Jan. 1854.
8. Alphaeus H. Albert, *Record of American Uniform and Historical Buttons,* pp. 18–80; HQA, AGO, GO 27, 17 Mar. 1902.
9. WD, AR 600-39, 4 Aug. 1944.
10. Raoul F. Camus, "The Military Band in the United States Army Prior to 1834" (Ph.D. thesis, New York University, 1969).
11. Francis B. Heitman, *Historical Register and Dictionary of the United States Army* 2: pp. 604–23; Camus, "Military Band"; WD, AGO, GO 31, 12 June 1851, par. 23: WD, *General Regulations for the Army* (1821), p. 159, par. 26; HQA, AGO, Order 38, 2 May 1833, p. 3; WD, AGO, GO 31, 12 June 1851, par. 23; WD, AGO, GO 92, 26 Oct. 1872, p. 7; HQA,

AGO, GO 120, 24 Oct. 1884; HQA, AGO, GO 132, 31 Dec. 1902, par. 74.

12. Camus, "Military Band." For later years, see a partial listing of general orders in *Subject Index to the General Orders and Circulars . . . 1881, to 1911,* p. 65; Philadelphia inventories no. 153403, 1900 through 1902, RG 92, NA.
13. Camus, "Military Band"; general observation of post-1832 regulations (often listed at the end of uniform regulations).
14. WD, *Regulations and Decisions Pertaining to the Uniform of the Army of the United States* (1901), par. 67.

Chapter Three

1. Francis P. Prucha, *The Sword of the Republic,* p. 6.
2. Ibid., p. 7; Maurice Matloff, ed., *American Military History,* pp. 101–104; William H. Guthman, *March to Massacre,* p. 27; *Journal of the Continental Congress, 1774–1789* 31:891–93.
3. Guthman, *March to Massacre,* pp. 26–27.
4. WD, *Legislative History of the General Staff of the United States . . . from 1775 to 1901,* p. 16; Guthman, *March to Massacre,* p. 25.
5. Guthman, *March to Massacre,* pp. 26–27.
6. Castle Island Orderly Book, vol. 8.
7. Harmar Papers, vol. 7, 21 April 1788, William L. Clemens Library, University of Michigan. My emphasis. The blending of utility and appearance was a new concept introduced by the United States.
8. Alphaeus H. Albert, *Record of American Uniform and Historical Buttons,* p. 44.
9. James B. Fry, *A Sketch of the Adjutant General's Department . . . ,* p. 13.
10. Guthman, *March to Massacre,* p. 26.
11. Albert, *Buttons,* p. 16.
12. Detmar H. Finke, "Collector's Field Book," *MC&H,* Dec. 1951, p. 87.
13. Guthman, *March to Massacre,* p. 27; Castle Island Orderly Book, vol. 8; Harmar Papers, vol. 7.
14. Heitman, *Historical Register* 2: p. 562.
15. "Waynes' Orderly Books," *Michigan Pioneer and Historical Society,* 24 (1905): p. 575.
16. William K. Emerson, "Cockades and Eagles," *MC&H,* 1983, pp. 104–12.
17. *The Writings of George Washington* 37: p. 11.
18. Detmar H. Finke, "Notes on Artillery Uniforms," *MC&H,* Mar. 1952, p. 15; Finke, "Collector's Field Book," *MC&H* Sept. 1951, p. 74.
19. Harmar Papers, vol. 7; Castle Island Orderly Book, 22 Sept. 1788; "Waynes' Orderly Books," p. 382.
20. "Wayne's Orderly Books," p. 622.
21. Ibid., p. 675.
22. Heitman, *Historical Register* 2: p. 563, Prucha, *Sword of the Republic,* p. 54; Albert, *Buttons,* pp. 17–18.
23. Heitman, *Historical Register* 1: p. 177.
24. WD, *Uniform of the Army of the United States, Illustrated, from 1774 to 1889,* p. 4; Finke, "Collector's Field Book," *MC&H,* Sept. 1951, p. 74.
25. Finke, "Collector's Field Book," *MC&H,* Sept. 1951, p. 74.

Chapter Four

1. Castle Island Orderly Book, vol. 8, 30 Jan. 1787; H. Charles McBarron and F. P. Todd, "Infantry of the Legion, 1794," *MC&H,* Sept. 1952, p. 65; "Wayne's Orderly Books," *Michigan Historical Society,* 24 (1905): pp. 413–14.
2. Heitman, *Historical Register,* 2: pp. 570–71.
3. Ibid., p. 577; J. Duncan Campbell, "Notes on the Insignia of the Riflemen, U.S. Army," *MC&H,* Apr. 1949, p. 8.
4. Heitman, *Historical Register* 2: pp. 578–81; Chambers to Irvine, letter in consolidated correspondence, box 1169, RG 92, NA. Campbell, "Notes on the Insignia," p. 8.
5. WD, *General Regulations for the Army* (1821), Article 65.
6. Heitman, *Historical Register* 2: pp. 592–93.

Chapter Five

1. John K. Mahon and Roman Danysh, *Infantry, Part I: Regular Army,* Army Lineage Series, pp. 11–14.
2. "Regulations for the Uniforms," in 1812 letter to Tench Coxe from Commissary General of Purchases; bill dated 24 Feb. 1812 from Crumpton to Coxe, letters received, Commissary General of Purchases; letter of 3 Nov. 1812 to Colonel Zebulon Pike and letter of 8 Nov. 1812 to Colonel Simonds, letters sent, Commissary General of Purchases, all in RG, 93, NA.
3. Letters received, Commissary General of Purchases, RG 93, NA.

4. Most cap plates were made in Philadelphia by either Armitage or Crumpton in 1813. The deputy commissary general of purchases in Boston contracted with Aaron Peasley for cap plates. These are the only known cap plate contractors during the period 1812–15.
5. Mahon and Danysh, *Infantry, Part I,* pp. 11–14.
6. Callendar Irvine to George Armitage, letters sent, Commissary General of Purchases, RG 93, NA.
7. Heitman, *Historical Register,* 2: p. 576.
8. J. Duncan Campbell and Edgar M. Howell, *American Military Insignia, 1800–1851,* pp. 14–15; Irvine to Secretary of War, letters sent, Commissary General of Purchases, RG 93, NA; Irvine to Military Storekeeper, Schuylkill Arsenal and Laboratory, RG 93, NA.
9. Campbell and Howell, *American Military Insignia,* illustration on p. 16.
10. Edgar M. Howell and Donald E. Kloster, *United States Army Headgear to 1854,* pp. 19–21; U.S. Senate, *Public Documents . . .*, 22d Cong., 1st sess., 1832, S. Doc. 1, 1:154; WD, *General Regulations for the Army* (1821), p. 155; 1825, pp. 157, 161.
11. Campbell and Howell, *American Military Insignia,* p. 42.
12. Howell and Kloster, *United States Army Headgear to 1854,* pp. 26–28.
13. *Regulations for the Uniform and Dress of the Army of the United States* (1851), pars. 13 and 31; Howell and Kloster, *United States Army Headgear to 1854,* pp. 59–67.
14. *Regulations for the Uniform and Dress* (1851), plate 14.
15. Edgar M. Howell, *United States Army Headgear, 1855–1902,* pp. 5–12; Heitman, *Historical Register* 2: pp. 602–609; WD, GO 3, 24 Mar. 1858.
16. WD, AGO, GO 6, 13 Mar. 1861, par. 45.
17. Howell, *United States Army Headgear, 1855–1902,* pp. 12–18.
18. WD, AGO, GO 67, 25 June 1872, par. XI.
19. AGO, GO 96, 14 Nov. 1875; AGO, GO 21, 20 Mar. 1876.
20. AGO, GO 96, 14 Nov. 1875.
21. WD, *Annual Report of the Quartermaster General, 1895,* pp. 32–33.
22. WD, *Annual Report of the Quartermaster General, 1896,* p. 5; WD, OQMG, Specifications 419, 13 Jan. 1897.
23. WD, OQMG, Specifications 754, 22 May 1905.
24. AGO, HQA, GO 4, 7 Jan. 1881; WD, *Annual Report of the Quartermaster General, 1881,* five unnumbered photographs; Gordon Chappell, *Brass Spikes & Horsehair Plumes: A Study of U.S. Army Dress Helmets, 1872–1903,* n. 64.
25. *Army and Navy Register,* 27 Apr. 1895; WD, *Regulations and Decisions* (1897), p. 9.
26. WD, AGO, Circular 25, 20 July 1898; WD, AGO, Circular 18, 15 June 1898.
27. Memo to the QMG from TAG, AG 421.7 (1-27-23), 2 Feb. 1923; sketch by A. DuBois of musket marked to be infantry insignia, on file, TIOH.
28. *Army and Navy Register,* 6 Dec. 1919, editorial, p. 715.
29. HQ, Hawaiian Department, Memo 1, 3 Jan. 1916; WD, *Regulations for the Uniform* (1912); WD, *Regulations for the Uniform* (1914).
30. WD, OQMG, Circular 23, 3 Oct. 1914.
31. WD, Change 2, 13 Mar. 1913, Uniform Regulations of 1912; WD, Changes 6, 28 Oct. 1918, Special Regulations 41.
32. WD, Changes 9, 16 Oct. 1923, AR 600-35; WD, Circular 15, 10 Mar. 1926.
33. HQA, AGO, GO 132, 31 Dec. 1902, pars. 67 and 69; WD, OQMG, Specifications 595, 22 Jan. 1903; *Army and Navy Register,* 11 Mar. 1905, p. 5.
34. WD, Circular 78, 17 Nov. 1909.
35. WD, Changes 1, 29 Dec. 1917, Special Regulations 42, par. 121.
36. *The Army Almanac,* pp. 632–33 and 650–81.
37. WD, Changes 1, 29 Dec. 1917, Special Regulations 42, par. 121(d); Mahon and Danysh, *Infantry, Part I,* pp. 44–45; WD, Changes 1, 29 Dec. 1917, Special Regulations 42, pars. 36(z) and 121(c); WD, Circular 72, 16 Mar. 1921, par. 11; HQ, Department of Puerto Rico, Circular 6, 24 Mar. 1899; HQ, Department of Puerto Rico, GO 65, 20 May 1899.
38. "The Insignia of the Uniformed Forces of the United States," *The National Geographic Magazine,* Oct. 1917, p. 414; WD, Circular 72, 16 Mar. 1921, par. 11.
39. James A. Sawicki, *Infantry Regiments of the U.S. Army,* p. 10; HQA, AGO, GO 113, 29 Oct. 1902; HQA, AGO, GO 132, 31 Dec. 1902, par. 106; WD, *Regulations and Decisions* (1901), par. 29.
40. HQA, AGO, GO 132, 31 Dec. 1902, par.

107; WD, OQMG Specifications 753, 22 May 1905, p. 4.

41. HQ, Philippine Department, GO 41, 10 July 1914.
42. WD, OQMG, Specifications 753, 22 May 1905, p. 4.
43. U.S. Congress, 66th Cong, 2d sess., H.R. 1920, ch. 227, p. 770; Sawicki, *Infantry Regiments of the U.S. Army,* p. 162.
44. U.S. Congress, 66th Cong. 2d sess., H.R. 1920, ch. 227, p. 770; HQ, Philippine Department, GO 41, 10 July 1914.
45. WD, GO 162, 22 Dec. 1917; WD, *Order of Battle of the United States Land Forces in the World War (1917–1919), Zone of the Interior* 3:pp. 313–14, 1566–70.
46. WD, Changes 3, 19 Feb. 1918, Special Regulations 42; WD, Memo for Director, Operations Division, General Staff, Aug. 1920, Subject: Collar Ornaments for Enlisted Men, TIOH files.
47. Mahon and Danysh, *Infantry, Part I,* p. 44; Sawicki, *Infantry Regiments of the U.S. Army,* p. 9.
48. Mahon and Danysh, *Infantry, Part I,* p. 44.
49. WD, Memo for Director, Operations Division, Aug. 1920, TIOH files.
50. WD, *Order of Battle of the United States Land Forces in the World War (1917–1919)* 3:pp. 224, 1277–1308, esp. pp. 1291 and 1305.
51. U.S. Congress, 66th Cong., 2d sess., H.R. 1920, ch. 227, p. 769; WD, Circular 72, 16 Mar. 1921, par. 12; first indorsement, 2 Sept. 1919, from TAG to Director, Purchase and Storage, to letter 421, 20 Aug. 1919, from Director, Purchase and Storage, to Col. Wyllie, Subject: Collar Ornaments and Insignia, TIOH files; memo for QMG from Chief, Equipment Branch, 28 Nov. 1921, Subject: Insignia for Tanks (Infantry), TIOH files; WD, Changes 2, 28 Mar. 1922, AR 600-35; WD, OQMG, Drawing CE-4-4-7, 16 Oct. 1921, rev. 3 Feb. 1923; WD, Memo from TAG to TQMG, 2 Feb. 1923, TIOH files.
52. WD, AGO, 421.7, Memo from TAG to TQMG, 2 Feb. 1923.
53. WD, AR 600-35, 25 Nov. 1927, par. 15b(2)(o); WD, AR 600-35, 31 Dec. 1926, par. 16b(2)(o)2.
54. WD, Circular 15, 10 Mar. 1926.
55. Sawicki, *Infantry Regiments of the U.S. Army,* pp. 13–14. A catalog from the Wolf-Appleton Company of New York City includes the "Tank-Infantry" insignia but not the Armored Force lapel device. Other insignia, especially shoulder patches, date the catalog as early 1942. Several photographs taken at Fort Knox and on display in the Armor School Weapons Department and in the Patton Museum also show this practice.
56. WD, AR 600-35, 31 Dec. 1926, par. 16b(2)(n).
57. WD, OQMG, Drawing CE-4-4-7, 16 Oct. 1921; WD, AG 421.7, memo from TAG to QMG, 2 Feb. 1923; memo of 2 Feb. 1923 with DuBois sketch, TIOH files; WD, AR 600-35, 14 Oct. 1921, par. 13b(2)(n).
58. Sawicki, *Infantry Regiments of the U.S. Army,* p. 112; WD, AR 600-35, 25 Nov. 1924, pars. 13b(1), 15b(2)(n); WD, Circular 15, 10 Mar. 1926.
59. WD, Changes 9, 16 Oct. 1923, AR 600-35, pars. 11a and 11c; Memo from TAG to Director, Purchase and Storage Division, 2 Sept. 1919; WD, AR 600-35, 14 Oct. 1921, par. 13c(4); WD, Circular 58, 19 Dec. 1927; WD, Circular 58, 31 Aug. 1937, sec. I, par. 1c; WD, AR 600-35, 25 Nov. 1924, par. 15c(4).
60. Dusenbury and Schwab, Inc., Catalog (1925); WD, Circular 58, 31 Aug. 1937; Mahon and Danysh, *Infantry, Part I,* pp. 53–54, 64.
61. WD, QMC Tentative Specification, PQD Number 189-A, 10 July 1942; WD, Circular 58, 31 Aug. 1937, sec. I, par. 1c.
62. DA, Changes 4, 27 Aug. 1952, SR 600-60-1.
63. Ibid.

Chapter Six

1. "Waynes' Orderly Books," *Michigan Pioneer and Historical Society Journal* 24 (1905), pp. 622–23, GO, Greenville, 26 June 1795.
2. *American State Papers, V, Military Affairs* 1:434; HQA, Order 50, 11 June 1832, p. 15.
3. Rene Chartrand, "The United States Forces of 1812–1816 . . . ," *MC&H,* Winter 1983, p. 144.
4. WD, *General Regulations for the Army* (1821), article 65, pars. 6–10; WD, *General Regulations for the Army* (1825), p. 157.
5. Edgar M. Howell and Donald E. Kloster, *United States Army Headgear to 1854,*

p. 3; James E. Hicks, *U.S. Ordnance* 2: p. 21; Howell and Kloster, *United States Army Headgear to 1854,* pp. 3 and 15; Heitman, *Historical Register* 2: pp. 570–73; Campbell and Howell, *American Military Insignia, 1800–1851,* p. 17.

6. Albert, *Buttons,* pp. 51–52.
7. Heitman, *Historical Register* 2:pp. 576–77; H. Charles McBarron, "Corps of Artillery, 1814–1821," *MC&H,* Dec. 1950, p. 55; Heitman, *Historical Register* 2: pp. 574–75; Campbell and Howell, *American Military Insignia, 1800–1851,* pp. 17–18.
8. Consolidated correspondence files, Box 1239, "Special Report of . . . Property . . . at Albany," Feb. 1818, RG 92, NA.
9. Heitman, *Historical Register* 2: pp. 570–80; Campbell and Howell, *American Military Insignia, 1800–1851,* pp. 7–8, 18.
10. J. Duncan Campbell, "Second Pattern Cap Plate U.S. Light Artillery, 1814," *MC&H,* Spring 1974, pp. 6–9.
11. Letters received, Secretary of War, RG 94, NA.
12. Letters sent, Commissary of Purchases, RG 92, NA.
13. Howell and Kloster, *United States Army Headgear to 1854,* p. 19; U.S. Senate, *Public Documents . . .* 22d Cong., 1st sess., 1832, S. Doc. 1, 1:154.
14. Howell and Kloster, *United States Army Headgear to 1854,* pp. 26–29; H. Charles McBarron, "1st U.S. Artillery Regiment, 1834–1851," *MC&H,* Dec. 1949, p. 2; HQA, AGO, Order 27, 2 Apr. 1834; *American State Papers, V, Military Affairs* 5:p. 235; Howell and Kloster, *United States Army Headgear to 1854,* pp. 59–67.
15. Howell, *United States Army Headgear, 1855–1902,* pp. 5–7.
16. Ibid., pp. 12–18.
17. James C. Frasca and John P. Gurnish, "Regulation Headgear," *North South Trader,* no. 6, 1979, p. 27.
18. Howell and Kloster, *United States Army Headgear to 1854,* pp. 26–29; WD, *General Regulations . . . , 1841,* p. 379; WD, *General Regulations . . . 1847,* p. 200.
19. *Regulations for the Uniform and Dress* (1851), p. 7 and plate 14.
20. WD, AGO, GO 3, 24 Mar. 1858.
21. WD, *Regulations for the Uniform and Dress . . . July 1872;* WD, *Annual Report of the Quartermaster General, 1881,* illustrations of helmet and trimmings; William K. Emerson, *Chevrons,* pp. 109–12; WD, *Regulations and Decisions* (1901), p. 37.
22. WD, QMG Specification 8, 17 June 1876; first indorsement from QMG to Philadelphia Depot, 20 Nov. 1872, box 1170, RG 92, NA; William K. Emerson, "U.S. Army Enlisted Cap Insignia, 1896–1905," *MC&H,* 1972, pp. 11–15; Heitman, *Historical Register* 1: pp. 61–62.
23. Heitman, *Historical Register* 1: pp. 61–62; WD, "Report of the Chief of Artillery," 2: *Annual Reports, 1907,* pp. 190–91.
24. Heitman, *Historical Register* 1: p. 52.
25. Emerson, "U.S. Army Enlisted Cap Insignia, 1896–1905," pp. 11–15; *Army and Navy Journal,* 11 Mar. 1905; William K. Emerson, "U.S. Army Enlisted Cap Insignia, 1905-1918," *MC&H,* 1977, pp. 29-39; WD, QMG, Specification 774, 20 Feb. 1905; WD, GO 197, 31 Dec. 1904, p. 33; WD, HQA, GO 132, 31 Dec. 1902, pp. 30–31.
26. Emerson, "U.S. Army Enlisted Cap Insignia, 1905–1918," pp. 29–39.
27. WD, GO 169, 14 Aug. 1907.
28. *Army and Navy Journal,* 23 Sept. 1916; WD, Changes 6, 12 Oct. 1916, *Specifications for the Uniforms (1915).*
29. Emerson, "U.S. Army Enlisted Campaign Hat Insignia, 1890–1907," *MC&H,* 1977, pp. 158–62.
30. WD, HQA, AGO, GO 68, 29 Sept. 1892; WD, *Annual Report of the Quartermaster General, 1901,* p. 68; WD, Circular 18, 15 June 1898.
31. WD, *Regulations and Decisions* (1901), p. 26.
32. HQA, AGO GO 132, 31 Dec. 1902, pp. 1, 25.
33. HQA, AGO, GO 81, 17 July 1902, p. 18.
34. HQA, AGO, GO 126, 4 Oct. 1900; *Army and Navy Journal,* 11 Mar. 1905.
35. WD, Changes 6, 28 Oct. 1918, Special Regulation 41; *Order of Battle of the United States Land Forces in the World War (1917–1919)* 3: p. 149.
36. Memo for the Secretary, Army War College, No. 8647–68, 6 Dec. 1917; WD, *Order of Battle of the United States Land Forces in the World War (1917–1919)* 3: pp. 149–50; WD, Changes 1, 29 Dec. 1917, par. 121, Special Regulation 42.
37. WD, Circular 25, 17 Jan. 1920; WD, Circular 384, 16 Nov. 1920.
38. WD, AR 600-40, 27 Sept. 1921, par. 38; WD, AR 600-35, 14 Oct. 1921, pars. 11b and 13b(2)(i).

39. WD, AR 600-35, 14 Oct. 1921, par. 13(b); WD, AR 600-35, 31 Dec. 1926, par. 16b(2)(k); WD, Changes 9, 16 Oct. 1923, AR 600-35; WD, Special Regulation 42, 15 Aug. 1917, par. 36(o); WD, AR 600-35, 31 Dec. 1926, par. 16b(2)(k).
40. WD, Changes 9, 5 May 1919, Special Regulation 42, par. 24(o); *Report on the Army: Report of General George C. Marshall to the Secretary of War,* p. 143.
41. DA, Circular 15, 1 Mar. 1951, sec. V.
42. WD, OQMG Drawing CE 4-4-31, 15 June 1936.
43. HQA, AGO, GO 81, 17 July 1902.
44. *Army and Navy Journal,* 11 Mar. 1905.
45. HQA, AGO, GO 132, 31 Dec. 1902, par. 60; WD, Changes 7, 30 Dec. 1916, *Specifications for the Uniforms . . . , 1915;* WD, OQMG, Circular 23, 3 October 1914; WD, Changes 6, 28 Oct. 1918, Special Regulation 41; WD, Changes 2, 13 Mar. 1913, *Regulations for the Uniform* (1912); OQMG, Circular 5, 9 Apr. 1914; WD, Changes 9, AR 600-35, 16 Oct. 1923.
46. WD, AR 600-35, 14 Oct. 1921, pars. 11b, 13b(2); WD, Circular 15, 10 Mar. 1926.
47. WD, AR 600-35, 10 Nov. 1941, p. 13; WD, OQMG Drawing CE 4-4-31, 15 June 1936.
48. DA, GO 23, 20 July 1950; HQ, DA, Change 13, 1 Feb. 1958, AR 670-5, pp. 61–62.
49. HQ, DA, GO 25, 14 June 1968; DA, AR 670-5, 1 May 1969, p. 14-8, par. 14-12i.
50. HQA, AGO, GO 81, 17 July 1902; WD, OQMG, Specification 595, 22 Jan. 1903; WD, OQMG, Specification 594, 22 Jan. 1903; WD, OQMG, Specification 742, 18 Feb. 1905; *Army and Navy Journal,* 11 Mar. 1905.
51. WD, OQMG, Specification 742, 18 Feb. 1905; *Army and Navy Journal,* 11 Mar. 1905; WD, OQMG, Specification 744, 20 Feb. 1905; WD, *Annual Report of the Secretary of War, 1907,* p. 177; WD, GO 169, 14 Aug. 1907.
52. WD, OQMG, Specification 1074, 12 Aug. 1910, p. 3.
53. WD, GO 182, 29 Sept. 1910; WD, Circular 72, 16 Mar. 1921, par. 11.
54. WD, Changes 1, 29 Dec. 1917, Special Regulation 42; AEF, GO 21, 5 Feb. 1918.
55. WD, Changes 1, 29 Dec. 1917, Special Regulation 42; WD, Circular 72, 16 Mar. 1921, par. 11; WD, Changes 9, 16 Oct. 1923, AR 600-35, par. 13c(3)(a).
56. WD, Circular 58, 19 Dec. 1927.
57. WD, Circular 25, 17 Jan. 1920.
58. Emanuel Raymond Lewis, *Seacoast Fortifications of the United States,* pp. 88–89; WD, Changes 9, 16 Oct. 1923, AR 600-35, par. 11a; WD, Circular 49, 21 Feb. 1947, sec. I, par. 26c(2).
59. Lewis, *Seacoast Fortifications,* p. 102.
60. WD, Circular 26, 1938.
61. DA, Changes 4, 27 Aug. 1952, SR 600-60-1.
62. DA, AR 670-5, 1 May 1969, par. 14-13i.
63. DA, GO 25, 14 June 1968; DA, AR 670-5, 1 May 1969, par. 14-13d.

Chapter Seven

1. Mary Lee Stubbs and Stanley Connor, *Armor-Cavalry, Part I: Regular Army and Reserve,* Army Lineage Series, pp. 3–8.
2. Ibid., p. 21.
3. Campbell and Howell, *American Military Insignia, 1800–1851,* pp. 7–8; Heitman, *Historical Register,* 2: pp. 568–69.
4. Campbell and Howell, *American Military Insignia, 1800–1851,* pp. 10–11; consolidated correspondence, H. Dearborn Notice of 21 May 1808, box 1169, RG 92, NA; John B. McMaster, *A History of the People of the United States* 6: p. 17.
5. Campbell and Howell, *American Military Insignia, 1800–1851,* p. 14; Heitman, *Historical Register* 2: pp. 570–79, 582–83, 584–85.
6. AGO, GO 38, 2 May 1833; Howell and Kloster, *United States Army Headgear to 1854,* pp. 41–44; James Frasca, "Regulation Headgear," *North South Trader,* Nov.–Dec. 1981, p. 29.
7. AGO, GO 38, 2 May 1833; Campbell and Howell, *American Military Insignia, 1800–1851,* p. 26; Heitman, *Historical Register* 2: pp. 586–87; *Regulations for the Uniform and Dress* (1851).
8. WD, AGO, GO 3, 24 Mar. 1858.
9. HQA, AGO, GO 18, 4 June 1846, sec. VI; AGO, GO 2, 13 Feb. 1850; AGO GO 25, 23 Aug. 1850; *Regulations for the Uniform and Dress* (1851); WD, AGO, GO 3, 24 Mar. 1858.
10. Samples in 3d Armored Cavalry Museum, Fort Bliss, Texas, 1976.
11. Heitman, *Historical Register* 2: pp. 586–87; AGO, GO 13, 15 Aug. 1855; WD, AGO, GO 3, 24 Mar. 1858; WD, AGO, GO 7, 24 June 1858, sec. II.

12. WD, AGO, GO 49, Act of Congress, 3 Aug. 1861; WD, *Revised Regulations, 1861,* pp. 12–13.
13. AGO, GO 2, 13 Feb. 1850; AGO, GO 25, 23 Aug. 1850; *Regulations for the Uniform and Dress* (1851); AGO, GO 13, 15 Aug. 1855; WD, AGO, GO 7, 24 June 1858.
14. Photograph B-2321, RG 111, NA.
15. WD, AGO, GO 9, 26 Oct. 1872; AGO, GO 67, 25 June 1873; Letter no. 3028, RG 92, NA; AGO, GO 8, 8 Feb. 1877; AGO, GO 21, 20 Mar. 1876, sec. II; WD, OQMG, Specification 8, 17 June 1876.
16. WD, OQMG, Specification 419, 13 Jan. 1879; Specification 754, 22 May 1905; WD, Changes 6, 12 Oct. 1916, *Specifications for the Uniforms . . . , 1915;* Emerson, "U.S. Army Enlisted Cap Insignia, 1905–1918," *MC&H,* 1977, pp. 29–39; WD, *Annual Report of the Secretary of War, 1897,* p. 336.
17. WD, OQMG, Specification 1231, 17 Sept. 1915; WD, Changes 1, 29 Dec. 1917, Special Regulation 42.
18. Howell, *United States Army Headgear, 1855–1902,* pp. 41–47; WD, *Annual Report of the Secretary of War, 1881* 1: plates 1 through 11 between pp. 304 and 307; letter to Asst. Secretary of War from QMG, 15 June 1904, TIOH files.
19. HQA, AGO, GO 22, 12 Apr. 1895.
20. HQA, AGO, GO 81, 17 July 1902, p. 8.
21. HQA, GO 63, 7 Apr. 1899; WD, AGO, Circular 18, 15 June 1898.
22. *Army and Navy Journal,* 11 Mar. 1905; WD, OQMG, Circular 23, 3 Oct. 1914; WD, Changes 6, 28 Oct. 1918, Special Regulation 41; WD, Changes 9, 16 Oct. 1923, AR 600-35.
23. WD, Changes 9, 16 Oct. 1923, AR 600-35, par. 11; WD, Changes 7, 8 Feb. 1919, Special Regulation 41, par. 93; WD, AR 600-35, 31 Dec. 1926, par. 14b.
24. WD, Changes 1, 29 Dec. 1917, Special Regulation 42, par. 36(z); WD, Changes 9, 16 Oct. 1923, AR 600-35, par. 13b(2); WD, AR 600-35, 25 Nov. 1924, pars. 15b(2)f) and 13a; WD, AR 600-35, 14 Oct. 1921, par. 13b(2)(f); WD, Changes 1, 1 Dec. 1928, AR 600-35, par. 16b(2)(f).
25. WD, AR 600-35, 31 Dec. 1926, par. 16a(2)(e); WD, AR 600-35, 25 Nov. 1924, par. 15b(2)(e); WD, AR 600-35, 31 Dec. 1926, par. 16b(2).
26. WD, Circular 15, 10 Mar. 1926; WD, AR 600-35, 31 Dec. 1926, par. 16b(2); WD, Changes 1, 1 Dec. 1928, AR 600-35, par. 16b(2)(f); WD, AR 600-35, 10 Nov. 1941; WD, Circular 15, 10 Mar. 1926; WD, AR 600-35, 31 Dec. 1926, par. 16b(7); WD, Changes 1, 1 Dec. 1928, AR 600-35, par. 16b(2)(f); WD, OQMG Drawing CE 4-4-30, 15 June 1936.
27. James A. Sawicki, *Tank Battalions of the U.S. Army,* p. 34.
28. *Army Times,* 17 May 1972, p. 10.
29. HQA, AGO, GO 132, 31 Dec. 1902, par. 69; OQMG, Specification 595, 22 Jan. 1903; WD, GO 197, 31 Dec. 1904, par. 70; OQMG, Specification 742, 20 Feb. 1905; WD, Circular 78, 17 Nov. 1909; WD, GO 63, 15 May 1917.
30. WD, Special Regulation 42, 15 Aug. 1917, par. 117(d); WD, Changes 1, 29 Dec. 1917, Special Regulation 42, par. 36(z); WD, Circular 72, 16 Mar. 1921.
31. Mary Lee Stubbs and Stanley R. Connor, *Armor-Cavalry, Part II, Army National Guard,* Army Lineage Series, pp. 53–54; WD, GO 5, 20 Feb. 1924; WD, Changes 1, 1 Dec. 1928, AR 600-35, par. 16c(4); WD, Circular 58, 19 Dec. 1927; WD, Circular 58, 31 Aug. 1937; WD, Changes 1, 1 Dec. 1928, AR 600-35, par. 16b(2)(f); WD, Changes 2, 22 Aug. 1933, AR 600-35.
32. WD, Circular 58, 31 Aug. 1937.
33. WD, QMG, Tentative Specification PQD, 189C, 5 Jan. 1943.

Chapter Eight

1. Phillip R. Smith, "Birds of Patriots," *Army Digest,* Mar. 1968, p. 34.
2. Richard H. Kohn, *Eagle and Sword,* p. 245; *The Writings of George Washington* 37: pp. 16–17.
3. *Writings of George Washington* 37: pp. 11, 53.
4. Campbell and Howell, *American Military Insignia, 1800–1851,* p. 9.
5. Detmar Finke, "Notes on Artillery Uniforms, 1801," *MC&H,* Mar. 1952, p. 15.
6. *American Daily Advertiser,* 11 June 1799, p. 3, col. 4.
7. *American State Papers, V, Military Affairs* 1: p. 434; 2: p. 239.
8. Ibid. 1: 856–58; Leonard F. Ball, "William F. Boyce, . . . , 1822–1836," *MC&H,* Summer 1972, p. 44.
9. *American State Papers, V, Military Affairs* 2: pp. 239–40; WD, *General Regulations for the Army* (1821), p. 154.

10. Howell and Kloster, *United States Army Headgear to 1854,* pp. 19–21, 26–29; *Regulations for the Uniform and Dress* (1851), plate 13.
11. Edgar M. Howell, *United States Army Headgear, 1855–1902,* pp. 22–28.
12. HQA, AGO, GO 50, 11 June 1832, p. 13; *Regulations for the Uniform and Dress* (1851), pp. 12–13.
13. *Regulations for the Uniform and Dress* (1851), pp. 6–7; HQA, AGO, GO 18, 4 June 1846, p. 2.
14. James C. Frasca, "Regulation Headgear, . . . , Part III, The Eagle Device," *North South Trader,* Jan.–Feb. 1980, p. 27.
15. Howell, *United States Army Headgear, 1855–1902,* pp. 35–41.
16. WD, *Dress of the General Staff* . . . , 31 May 1838, pp. 5, 8.
17. Howell and Kloster, *United States Army Headgear to 1854,* pp. 6–7.
18. HQA, AGO, GO 50, 11 June 1832, pp. 16–17; AGO, GO 30, 25 May 1829; WD, unnumbered announcement, 22 July 1829.
19. Howell, *United States Army Headgear, 1855–1902,* pp. 41–47.
20. WD, *Annual Report of the Quartermaster General, 1881,* illustrated plates.
21. WD, *Regulations and Decisions* (1901), par. 48; WD, *Annual Report of the Quartermaster General, 1912,* p. 18; Emerson, *Chevrons,* pp. 109–12.
22. WD, *Annual Report of the Quartermaster General, 1895,* p. 33 and illustration opposite.
23. HQA, AGO, GO 27, 17 Mar. 1902, p. 3; GO 132, 31 Dec. 1902, pp. 1, 14.
24. WD, GO 193, 15 Nov. 1905, sec. I; WD, OQMG Drawing CE 4-4-38, 15 June 1936.
25. Mattie E. Treadwell, *The Women's Army Corps,* p. 39; WD, AR 600-39, 5 Jan. 1944, p. 7.
26. DA, SR 600-37-2, 17 July 1951, par. 50a; DA, AR 670-32, 29 Jan. 1960, Table II; HQ DA, AR 670-32, 23 July 1962.
27. WD, Changes 1, 29 Dec. 1917, Special Regulation 42, par. 110; WD, Changes 9, 16 Oct. 1923, AR 600-35, par. 7a(3); WD, Specification 17-7, 13 Oct. 1919.
28. WD, OQMG Drawing CE 4-4-38, 15 June 1936.
29. DA, Changes 4, 27 Aug. 1952, SR 600-60-1.
30. WD, *Regulations and Decisions* (1899), par. 4a; *Regulations and Decisions* (1900), par. 26; letter no. 81606, 10th indorsement, 20 Feb. 1901, RG 92, NA.
31. HQA, AGO, GO 132, 31 Dec. 1902, par. 35; HQA, AGO, GO 36, 21 Mar. 1903, section II.
32. HQA, AGO, GO 132, 31 Dec. 1902, par. 53(a); WD, *Annual Report of Major General Davis, Commanding Division of the Philippines,* 1903, app. II, p. 66; WD, GO 197, 31 Dec. 1904, par. 56(a).
33. HQA, AGO, GO 132, 31 Dec. 1902, par. 34; WD, GO 47, 6 Apr. 1911, par. 8.

Chapter Nine

1. Albert, *Buttons,* pp. 7–12.
2. Ibid., 19–20.
3. Campbell and Howell, *American Military Insignia, 1800–1851,* p. 37; Letters sent, 11 Dec. 1819, RG 156, NA; Campbell and Howell, *American Military Insignia 1800–1851,* pp. 43, 44.
4. *Regulations for the Uniform and Dress* (1851), plate 14; WD, AGO, GO 6, 13 Mar. 1861, p. 7; Howell, *United States Army Headgear, 1855–1902,* pp. 5–12; WD, AGO, GO 247, 25 Aug. 1864.
5. The portraits in the Brady Collection (National Archives) offer many examples of generals' cap devices; some are B-60, B-2206, and B-2477. Photographs B-1912 and B-2530 show combined letters and stars. A wreathed volunteer unit device is shown in B-4262.
6. WD, *Revised Regulations 1861,* p. 13 and par. 1489; WD, AGO, GO 9, 27 Jan. 1882.
7. WD, *Annual Report of the Quartermaster General, 1895,* p. 33 and illustrations; WD, *Regulations and Decisions* (1898), par. 2b; WD, AGO, GO 53, 18 Apr. 1901.
8. The eagle from the Great Seal of the United States was prescribed in General Orders 82, HQA, AGO, 17 July 1902. The *US* letters returned by GO 197, WD 31 Dec. 1904. Also see *Army and Navy Register,* 12 Nov. 1904, p. 23.
9. WD, *Annual Report of the Quartermaster General, 1895,* p. 33 and illustrations.
10. WD, Changes 9, 1 May 1919, Special Regulation 41.
11. WD, AR 600-35, 14 Oct. 1921, par. 13b; WD, Changes 9, 16 Oct. 1923, AR 600-35, par. 11; WD, AR 600-35, 31 Dec. 1926, par. 16b(1); WD, AR 600-35, 14

Oct. 1921, par. 13b; WD, AR 600-35, 31 Dec. 1926, par. 16b(1).
12. WD, Circular 15, 10 Mar. 1926; WD, AR 600-35, 31 Dec. 1926, par. 14d; WD, Circular 14, 16 Mar. 1938; WD, Changes 1, 1 Dec. 1928, AR 600-35, par. 14d; WD, AR 600-35, 10 Nov. 1941, par. 24b.
13. DA, AR 670-30, 24 Oct. 1975, par. 17-6b(2).
14. Memo for the Chief of Staff, 4 Mar. 1926, no. 4-17102, from Major General Fox Connor, Assistant Chief of Staff, TIOH files.
15. WD, OQMG, Specification 595, 22 Jan. 1903; WD, OQMG, Specification 742, 18 Feb. 1905.
16. WD, Circular 68, 8 Oct. 1907; WD, Circular 78, 17 Nov. 1909; WD, *Regulations for the Uniform of the United States Army* (1911), par. 80(d).
17. WD, Changes 1, 29 Dec. 1917, Special Regulation 42, par. 121(a); *The National Geographic Magazine,* Oct. 1917, p. 414.
18. WD, Circular 15, 10 Mar. 1926, section II, par. 3b; Letter from P.S.D. to Colonel Wyllie, no. 421, 20 Aug. 1919, Subject: Collar Ornaments and Insignia, with 1st indorsement, 2 Sept. 1919, TIOH files.
19. WD, Circular 49, 21 Feb. 1947.
20. WD, Circular 329, 1 July 1919; WD, AR 600-35, 31 Mar. 1944, par. 26c(2)(o); WD, Circular 85, 29 Apr. 1941.
21. WD, Circular 13, 23 May 1898; WD, *Regulations and Decisions* (1901), p. 11; HQA, AGO, GO 132, 31 Dec. 1902, pp. 1, 20, 21; WD, GO 197, 31 Dec. 1904, pp. 1, 23, par. 56; WD, GO 49, 28 Apr. 1917.
22. WD, Changes 9, 1 May 1919, Special Regulation 41.
23. WD, Special Regulation 42, 15 Aug. 1917, par. 116(g).
24. WD, Changes 1, 29 Dec. 1917, Special Regulation 42, par. 121; WD, Changes 9, 1 May 1919, Special Regulation 42.
25. WD, Bulletin 16, 22 June 1916, pp. 39–40; WD, Changes 18, 30 Dec. 1916, *Regulations for the Uniform* (1914); WD, Changes 13, 14 Aug 1917, *Specifications for the Uniforms . . . ,* 1915; WD, Special Regulation 42, par. 35.
26. WD Changes 1, 29 Dec. 1917, Special Regulation 42, par. 121; Memo for the I.G., Office of the Inspector General, 333.9, 19 June 1918, TIOH files.
27. WD, Changes 9, 1 May 1919, Special Regulation 42; WD, AR 600-35, 14 Oct. 1921, par. 13.
28. WD, Circular 8, 16 Jan. 1922; WD, Changes 1, 6 Jan. 1922, AR 600-35.
29. WD, Changes 18, 30 Dec. 1916, *Regulations for the Uniform* (1914); WD, Changes 9, 1 May 1919, Special Regulation 42; WD, Changes 9, 16 Oct. 1923, AR 600-35, par. 11.
30. WD, Special Regulation 42, 15 Aug. 1917, pars. 34a, 35a, 36a; WD, GO 73, 7 Aug. 1918.
31. WD, Changes 21, 23 July 1917, *Regulations for the Uniform* (1914); *Army and Navy Register* 18 Aug. 1917, p. 206.
32. *The National Geographic Magazine,* Oct. 1917, p. 414.
33. L. Albert Scipio II with Buddy Patterson, *E.M. Collar Insignia (1907–1926),* p. 182, reference to *Army and Navy Register,* Mar. 1918; WD, Changes 1, 29 Dec. 1917, Special Regulation 41.
34. WD, Changes 4, 7 May 1918, Special Regulation 42, par. 121(a).
35. WD, "Report of the Chief of the Militia Bureau," *Annual Report of the Secretary of War, 1918,* 1: p. 1139.
36. WD, Changes 21, 23 July 1917, *Regulations for the Uniform* (1914); WD, Special Regulation 42, 15 Aug. 1917, pars. 34a and 35a; WD, GO 73, 7 Aug. 1918; WD, Changes 9, 1 May 1919, Special Regulation 41, par. 92.
37. WD, "Report of the Chief of the Militia Bureau," *Annual Report of the Secretary of War, 1918* 1: p. 1139.
38. WD, Changes 9, 1 May 1919, Special Regulation 41, par. 92; WD, AR 600-35, 14 Oct. 1921, par. 13(b)(1); WD, Changes 9, 16 Oct. 1923, AR 600-35, par. 11.
39. WD, AR 600-35, 31 Dec. 1926, par. 16b(1); WD, Circular 42, 5 Oct. 1925; WD, Circular 3, 1926; WD, Changes 1, 1 Dec. 1928, AR 600-35, pp. 3–4; WD, Circular 14, 1938; WD, Circular 58, 1 Mar. 1947, sec. III; WD, Circular 113, 11 Oct. 1940, sec. II.
40. WD, AR 600-35, 25 Nov. 1924, par. 49; WD, AR 600-35, 31 Dec. 1926, par. 26; WD, Circular 65, 12 Oct. 1936, sec. IV; WD, AR 600-35, 25 Nov. 1924, par. 49; WD, AR 600-35, 31 Dec. 1926, par. 26. WD, AR 600-35, 10 Nov. 1941, par. 64;

J. M. Nielson, "Alaska's Territorial Guard," *MC&H,* Summer 1978, p. 56.

41. WD, Changes 9, 1 May 1919, Special Regulation 42, par. 121(a).
42. WD, Circular 58, 31 Aug. 1937, sec. I, par. 1a; WD, Circular 113, 11 Oct. 1940; WD, Circular 58 1 Mar. 1947, sec. III.
43. WD, Memo for C/S, no. 8647-17, 24 Nov. 1916, TIOH files; WD, Changes 18, 30 Dec. 1916, *Regulations for the Uniform* (1914).
44. WD, "Report of the Chief of the Militia Bureau," *Annual Report of the Secretary of War, 1918* 1: pp. 1139, 1140.
45. WD, Militia Bureau, Circular 3, 14 May 1918.
46. WD, Bulletin 29, 28 May 1918, WD, Bulletin 47, 14 Aug. 1918.
47. *Army and Navy Register,* 26 Mar. 1905, p. 5.
48. TIOH sample with sample card.
49. *National Guard of the United States, State of New Jersey,* pp. xxxiii–xlvi, 325.

Chapter Ten

1. Fredrick P. Todd, "Notes on the Dress of the Regiment of Light Artillery, USA, 1808–1811," *MC&H,* Mar. 1950, pp. 10–11, and letter of 8 Oct. 1808.
2. Contract of 23 Mar. 1809, C/I, Box 57, RG 92, NA.
3. Howell and Kloster, *United States Army Headgear to 1854,* pp. 38, 40.
4. HQA, AGO, GO 10, 29 Feb. 1848, p. 2; Frank C. Townsend and Fredrick P. Todd, "Branch Insignia of Regular Cavalry, 1883–1872," *MC&H,* Spring 1956, p. 2.
5. *Regulations for the Uniform and Dress* (1851), plate 15; Howell, *United States Army Headgear, 1855–1902,* p. 67.
6. Howell, *United States Army Headgear; 1855–1902,* pp. 26–28*; United States Military Magazine*, pp. 80, 86.
7. WD, *Regulations for the Army of the United States, 1861,* par. 1426.
8. Consolidated correspondence, "Uniforms," Box 1170, letters from Colonel Easton, Philadelphia QM Depot, to QMG, with indorsements, 11 and 19 Sept. 1872, OQMG no. 1103, and Dec. 1872, no. 1601, RG 92, NA; WD, OQMG, Specification 419, 13 Jan. 1897, pp. 1, 4; WD, *Annual Report of the Quartermaster General, 1896,* p. 5; Consolidated correspondence, "Uniforms," Box 1170, letters from Colonel Easton, Dec. 1872 letter no. 1601, NA, RG 92; WD, OQMG, Specifications for Metallic Uniform—Coat, Helmet, Dress and Forage Cap Ornaments, 31 May 1876, pp. 3, 4. A possible explanation is that many early specifications are dated 31 May 1876, indicating the QMG office was taking the available articles and describing them as standard. Old numbers and letters could have been on hand in Washington at that time, although the Philadelphia Depot was issuing smaller numbers and letters.
9. WD, *Regulations for the Army of the United States, 1861,* par. 1426; Consolidated correspondence, "Uniforms," Box 1170, letter from Colonel Easton, Dec. 1872, no. 1601, RG 92, NA; AGO, GO 67, 25 June 1873, par. XI.
10. Howell, *United States Army Headgear, 1855–1902,* pp. 1–5.
11. Letter from Commander, 2d Cavalry, to AGO, 25 Jan. 1899, and 4th indorsement, 5 Apr. 1899, TIOH files; HQA, AGO, GO 128, 10 July 1899; Letters received, from Philadelphia Depot to OQMG, no. 153403, RG 92, NA.
12. HQA, AGO, GO 132, 31 Dec. 1902, par. 80; WD, OQMG, Specification 607, 2 Apr. 1903; Specification 635, 11 July 1903.
13. WD, OQMG, Specification 755, 22 May 1905.
14. Inventory of 15 Mar. 1901, no. 153403, p. 13, RG 92, NA.
15. General Staff Report 616, 18 May 1907, p. 7, TIOH files; WD, Circular 78, 17 Nov. 1909; Letter no. 233806, 8 Jan. 1907, with 13 indorsements, RG 92, NA; WD, GO 140, 23 June 1907; WD, GO 169, 14 Aug. 1907.
16. WD, OQMG, Specification 418, 13 Jan. 1897; WD, *Annual Report of the Quartermaster General, 1896,* p. 5; WD, OQMG, Specification 594, 22 Jan. 1903.
17. WD, OQMG, Specification 744, 20 Feb. 1905; WD, OQMG letter no. 246097 (AGO no. 1428357), Nov. 1908, with 32 indorsements, TIOH files; Letter 421.7-114-CE, 19 Apr. 1916, from Philadelphia Quartermaster to QMG, Subject: Ornaments, with 2 indorsements, TIOH files.
18. *Regulations for the Uniform and Dress* (1851), plate 15; WD, AGO, GO 3, 24 Mar. 1858, par. I, 4; WD, *Regulations for*

the Uniform and Dress . . . July 1872, p. 7; WD, *Annual Report of the Quartermaster General, 1883,* pp. 52, 56, 57; AGO, GO 120, 24 Oct. 1884; HQA, AGO, GO 2, 6 Jan. 1900, p. 4; Stock records of Philadelphia Depot, various dates, Fall 1900, OQMG no. 153403, RG 92, NA.

19. HQA, AGO, GO 50, 11 June 1832, p. 19; *United States Military Magazine* 2: pp. 80, 84; *Regulations for the Uniform and Dress* (1851), p. 9, plate 11.
20. WD, *Regulations for the Uniform and Dress . . . July 1872,* p. 13; HQA, AGO, GO 132, Dec. 1902, pp. 5, 15.
21. WD, Circular 68, 8 Oct. 1907; WD Circular 78, 17 Nov. 1909; *The Uniform of the Army of the United States,* 1 Oct. 1908; WD, Changes 1, 29 Dec. 1917, Special Regulation 42, par. 121; WD, Circular 58, 31 Aug. 1937, par. I.
22. WD, AR 600-35, 25 Nov. 1924, par. 15c(4); WD, Changes 1, 1 Dec. 1928, AR 600-35, par. 16c(4); WD, Changes 2, 22 Aug. 1933, AR 600-35, par. 16c(4); WD, AR 600-35, 25 Nov. 1924, par. 15c(4); WD, Changes 1, 1 Dec. 1928, AR 600-35, par. 16c(4).
23. Reference by date: 1847–WD, *General Regulations . . . , 1847,* pp. 194, 204, 205; 1863—See chapter on Corps of Engineers; 1872—WD, *Regulations for the Uniform and Dress . . . July 1872,* p. 20; WD, AGO, GO 107, 14 Dec. 1872; 1888—HQA, AGO, GO 29, 5 May 1888; 1890—HQA, AGO, GO 53, 23 May 1890; HQA, AGO, GO 130, 30 Oct. 1890.
24. WD, Circular 152, 13 Dec. 1940; WD, AR 600-40, 22 June 1931, par. 37c.
25. DA, SR 600-60-1, 26 Oct. 1951; DA, SR 600-60-1, 8 Apr. 1953; DA, AR 670-5, 20 Sept. 1956, par. 141; DA, AR 670-5, 23 Sept. 1966, par. 14-13; DA, "Wear of Unit Insignia under the Regimental System," Fact Sheet, Deputy Chief of Staff for Personnel, 20 Apr. 1983.
26. WD, Proceeding of the Equipment Board, 27 Oct. 1892; inclosure 3 to 3d indorsement to 1893 letter no. 3783, TIOH files; *Army and Navy Register,* 17 Apr. 1895; WD, *Annual Report of the Quartermaster General, 1895,* plate opposite p. 32.
27. AGO, GO 4, 7 Jan. 1881; WD, *Annual Report of the Quartermaster General, 1881,* photographic plates.
28. WD, Special Regulation 42, 15 Aug. 1917, par. 121(b); AEF, HQ Bulletin 20, 29 Dec. 1917, par. II; WD, Changes 9, 5 May 1919, Special Regulation 42, par. 121(c)(5); WD, Circular 72, 16 Mar. 1921, par. 11.
29. WD, OQMG, Memo for the Chief of Staff, 421 A-DS, 17 Sept. 1921, with drawing, TIOH files; WD, AR 600-35, 14 Oct. 1921, par. 13c(4).
30. WD, AR 600-35, 25 Nov. 1924, pars. 15c(3)(d) and 15d.
31. WD, Changes 9, 9 May 1919, Special Regulation 42, par. 121(c)(4); WD, Circular 72, 16 Mar. 1921, par. 11.
32. WD, Changes 3, 19 Feb. 1918, Special Regulation 42; Memo for Director of Operations Branch, WD, General Staff, 30 Aug. 1920, TIOH files; WD, Circular 72, 16 Mar. 1921; WD, *Order of Battle of the United States Land Forces in the World War (1917–1919)* 1: pp. 12–14.
33. Mahon and Daynsh, *Infantry,* Part I: Regular Army, Army Lineage Series, 53, 54; WD, Circular 72, 16 Mar. 1921; WD, OQMG Memo for the Chief of Staff 421 A-DS, 17 Sept. 1921, with drawing, TIOH files; WD, AR 600-35, 14 Oct. 1921, par. 13c(4).
34. HQ, DA, Changes 4, AR 670-5, 12 Oct. 1963, par. 129; DA, Drawing A-7-2, 20 Apr. 1964, TIOH files.
35. DA, AR 670-5, 23 Sept. 1966, par. 14-8; DA, Drawing A-7-3, 6 Apr. 1964, TIOH files; Michael A. Lattin, "Warrant Officer Course," *Ordnance Magazine,* Summer 1983, pp. 5–11.
36. WD, Changes 2, 22 Aug. 1933, par. 16d, AR 600-35.
37. Treadwell, *The Women's Army Corps,* App. D.

Chapter Eleven

1. L. D. Ingersoli, *A History of the War Department,* pp. 210–16; WD, *Order of Battle of the United States Land Forces in the World War, (1917–1919)* 3: p. 242; Heitman, *Historical Register,* 1: p. 41; WD, *Order of Battle of the United States Land Forces in the World War, (1917–1919),* 3: p. 242.
2. Rose C. Engelman, ed., *A Decade of Progress: The United States Army Medical Department, 1959–1969,* pp. 12–13.
3. *Military Laws and Rules and Regulations for the Armies of the United States,* 226; Mary C. Gillett, *The Army Medical Department,*

1775–1818, p. 150; WD, *General Regulations for the Army* (1821), article 65; (1825), par. 843.

4. HQA, AGO, GO 50, 11 June 1832, pp. 10, 11, 20.
5. HQA, AGO, GO 45, 3 Oct. 1840.
6. *Regulations for the Uniform and Dress* (1851).
7. WD, AGO, GO 92, 25 Oct. 1872, p. 20; HQA, AGO, GO 80, 18 Aug. 1896.
8. WD, *Regulations and Decisions* (1899), pp. 15, 17.
9. WD, *General Regulations for the Army* (1821), article 65; HQA, AGO, GO 45, 3 Oct. 1840.
10. *Regulations for the Uniform and Dress* (1851).
11. James C. Frasca and John P. Gurnish, "Regulation Headgear . . . Part IV," *North South Trader,* July–Aug. 1980, pp. 24–32.
12. WD, Circular 14, 12 Nov. 1892; *Army and Navy Register,* 13 Aug. 1892, p. 520; HQA, AGO, GO 39, 18 Aug. 1896.
13. HQA, AGO, GO 81, 17 July 1902, par. 55b.
14. WD, OQMG Drawing CE 4-4-32, 15 June 1936.
15. WD, *Annual Reports of the Secretary of War, 1909* 2: p. 174; WD, *Regulations for the Uniform of the United States Army* (1911), par. 1; WD, Changes 18, 30 Dec. 1916, *Regulations for the Uniform* (1914); DA, *The Department of the Army,* July 1972, p. 5-30.
16. WD, *Annual Report of the Secretary of War, 1891,* p. 16; HQA, AGO, GO 52, 24 May 1898, par. II; AGO, Circular 52, 20 July 1898; AGO, GO 127, 26 Aug. 1898, par. III.
17. HQA, AGO, GO 52, 24 May 1898; WD, *Annual Report of the Secretary of War, 1898,* pp. 180–81; HQA, AGO, GO 53, 18 Apr. 1901; HQA, AGO, GO 81, 17 July 1902, par. 85.
18. WD, *Order of Battle of the United States Land Forces in the World War (1917–1919)* 3: p. 255; WD, *Annual Report, 1909* 2: pp. 119–20; WD, Changes 5, 17 July 1918, Special Regulation 42, par. 36(ac).
19. WD, Circular 342, 15 Sept. 1920; John H. McMinn and Max Levin, *Personnel in World War II,* pp. 5, 6, 250; WD, Changes 5, 6 Nov. 1942, AR 600-35; DA, AR 670-5, Sept. 1956, par. 141; DA, SR 600-60-1, 8 Apr. 1953, par. 12ac(1)(a); DOD, *Federal Supply Catalog C2-14A, FSC Class 8455,* 8 June 1960, p. 41.
20. HQA, AGO, GO 9, 6 Feb. 1901, p. 8; WD, *Regulations and Decisions* (1901), p. 26; WD, AGO, GO 53, 18 Apr. 1901, par. II; WD, *Annual Reports, 1909* 2: p. 174.
21. WD, *Regulations for the Uniforms of the United States Army* (1911), par. 1; WD, Changes 18, 30 Dec. 1916, *Regulations for the Uniform* (1914), par. 1.
22. WD, Changes 1, 29 Dec. 1917, Special Regulation 42, par. 36; WD, Circular 342, 15 Sept. 1920.
23. HQA, AGO, Circular 55, 23 Nov. 1899; HQA, AGO, GO 53, 18 Apr. 1901, sec. I; HQA, AGO, GO 132, 31 Dec. 1902, par. 60.
24. WD, *Order of Battle of the United States Land Forces in the World War (1917–1919)* 3: p. 254; WD, Changes 18, 30 Dec. 1916, *Regulations for the Uniform (1914);* WD, Changes 7, 30 Dec. 1916, *Specifications for the Uniforms . . . ,* 1915; WD, Changes 1, 29 Dec. 1917, Special Regulation 42.
25. WD, Circular 342, 15 Sept. 1920.
26. *Historical Highlights of the Army Nurse Corps,* p. 2; WD, *Annual Reports, 1909* 2: p. 178.
27. WD, *The Medical Department . . . in the World War* 13: p. 301; WD, *Annual Report of the Secretary of War, 1899,* p. 380; WD, Surgeon General's Office, unnumbered circular, 20 June 1899, p. 8; *Historical Highlights of the Army Nurse Corps,* p. 2; AGO, GO 113, 22 Aug. 1901.
28. Leon W. Laframboise, *History of the Combat Support Branches,* p. 102.
29. WD, *Medical Department . . . in the World War* 13: pp. 302–303.
30. Photograph SC 35283, RG 111, NA; WD, Changes 7, 8 Feb. 1919, par. 28½, Special Regulation 41, lists the capes for the first time, although this change lists the articles as having been authorized by Changes 5, although that change did not include capes.
31. American Red Cross, *American Red Cross Uniforms.*
32. WD, Circular 342, 15 Sept. 1920; Letter, QM 421 S-Std, 31 Mar. 1942, "Insignia, Collar, Army Nurse Corps," from Lieutenant General Somervell to the Adjutant General, TIOH files; WD, OQMG Drawing CE 4-4-32, 15 June 1936.

33. Marlette Conde, *The Lamp and the Caduceus,* pp. 3–5, 7, 12–13, 14, 18, 51; WD, *Medical Department . . . in the World War* V, p. 124.
34. Conde, *Lamp and the Caduceus,* pp. 32–33; WD, Changes 6, 28 Oct. 1918, Special Regulation 41.
35. Conde, *Lamp and the Caduceus,* pp. 32–33, 78; *Army and Navy Journal,* 15 Mar. 1919, p. 989; WD, Changes 9, 16 Oct. 1923, AR 600-35, par. 11a(1); Conde, *Lamp and the Caduceus,* p. 77; Conde, *Lamp and the Caduceus,* pp. 33, 77; WD, AR 600-40, 25 Nov. 1924, par. 46.
36. Conde, *Lamp and the Caduceus,* p. 121.
37. WD, *Order of Battle of the United States Land Forces in the World War (1917–1919)* 3: p. 271.
38. Ibid., p. 255; Stanhope Bayne-Jones, *The Evolution of Preventive Medicine in the U.S. Army, 1607–1939,* pp. 156–57; *The National Geographic Magazine,* Oct. 1917, p. 414; E. E. Pearsons to M. G. Gorgas, OCE 203379, 1 Sept. 1917, TIOH files; WD, Changes 1, 29 Dec. 1917, Special Regulation 42.
39. Bayne-Jones, *Evolution of Preventive Medicine,* pp. 156–57; Blanche B. Armdield, *Organization and Administration in World War II,* pp. 1, 30, 97, 98, 115; McMinn and Levin, *Personnel in World War II,* pp. 7, 8.
40. McMinn and Levin, *Personnel in World War II,* p. 508; WD, Circular 67, 11 Dec. 1947; Anderson, *Army Medical Specialist Corps,* p. 402; DA, AR 670-5, 20 Sept. 1956, par. 141c.
41. *History of the American Field Service in France* 1: pp. 9, 10; WD, *Order of Battle of the United States Land Forces in the World War (1917–1919)* 3: pp. 252, 253, 256, 322.
42. Pearson to Gorgas, OCE 203379, 1 Sept. 1917, TIOH; *The National Geographic Magazine,* Oct. 1917, p. 414; WD, Changes 1, 29 Dec. 1917, Special Regulation 42.
43. WD AR 600-35, 14 Oct. 1921, par. 13b.
44. *The National Defense Act* (as amended by acts up to and including 7 June 1924), p. 3; McMinn and Levin, *Personnel in World War II,* pp. 7, 17, 508; DA, Circular 67, 11 Dec. 1947.
45. McMinn and Levin, *Personnel in World War II,* pp. 7, 17, 213, 214; WD, Changes 27, 2 Aug. 1943, AR 600-35; WD, Circular 67, 11 Dec. 1947. McMinn and Levin, *Personnel in World War II,* p. 508.
46. Anderson, *Army Medical Specialist Corps.* pp. 15–16, 17, 18; WD, *Medical Department . . . in the World War* V, p. 124.
47. Anderson, *Army Medical Specialist Corps,* pp. 25–26.
48. Ibid., pp. 29–32; WD, Office of the Surgeon General Circular Letter No. 7, 8 Feb. 1941.
49. WD, Office of the Surgeon General Circular Letter No. 51, 3 June 1942.
50. McMinn and Levin, *Personnel in World War II,* p. 17; WD, Changes 14, 6 Mar. 1943, AR 600-35; Anderson, *Army Medical Specialist Corps,* pp. 128–29; DA, Circular 67, 11 Dec. 1947.
51. Anderson, *Army Medical Specialist Corps,* pp. 46, 47; WD, *Medical Department . . . in the World War* XII, pp. 56, 57.
52. Anderson, *Army Medical Specialist Corps,* p. 47; WD, *Medical Department . . . in the World War* XII, p. 47; WD, Office of the Surgeon General Circular Letter No. 119, 8 Dec. 1941.
53. Beatrice Whitcomb to author, 29 Aug. 1983, and photograph enclosed with letter.
54. McMinn and Levin, *Personnel in World War II,* p. 17; WD, Changes 14, 6 Mar. 1943, AR 600-35; DA, Changes 8, AR 600-37, 27 May 1947; DA, Circular 67, 11 Dec. 1947.
55. McMinn and Levin, *Personnel in World War II,* p. 89; Anderson, *Army Medical Specialist Corps,* pp. 128, 129; WD, Office of the Surgeon General Circular Letter No. 51, 3 June 1942; WD, Circular 306, 22 Nov. 1943.
56. McMinn and Levin, *Personnel in World War II,* p. 508; DA, Circular 67, 11 Dec. 1947.
57. Anderson, *Army Medical Specialist Corps,* pp. 342, 402; DA, Circular 67, 11 Dec. 1947.
58. WD, Changes 9, 16 Oct. 1923, AR 600-35, par. 11a(2); WD, AR 600-35, 31 Dec. 1926, par. 14a(2)(a); DA, SR 600-60-1, 26 Oct. 1951, par. 12c.
59. WD, AGO, GO 53, 31 Oct. 1851; WD, AGO, GO 2, 28 Feb. 1857; WD, AGO, GO 6, 13 Mar. 1861; WD, OQMG, Specifications of 17 June 1876 for metallic uniform ornaments; WD, GO 9, 27 Jan. 1882; WD, *Annual Report of the*

Quartermaster General, 1882, p. 52.
60. WD, GO 56, 11 Aug. 1887; WD, GO 19, 21 Feb. 1901.
61. AGO, GO 81, 17 July 1902; WD, GO 197, 31 Dec. 1904; WD, Changes 1, 29 Dec. 1917, Special Regulation 42.
62. WD, *Revised Regulations, 1861,* 13; WD, OQMG Specification 130, 24 Feb. 1885; WD, OQMG Specification 200, 10 Mar. 1888; *MC&H,* 28: pp. 148–53, and 29: pp. 158–62.
63. WD, AGO, GO 52, 14 June 1881; WD, AGO, GO 56, 11 Aug. 1887; WD, AGO, GO 37, 13 Aug. 1896, par. II.
64. Both detailed price lists and inventories lists in *Annual Reports* 1880 and 1881 show coat insignia for staff except for hospital stewards. The 30 Nov. date is in WD, *Annual Report of the Quartermaster General,* 1882, p. 52.
65. WD, GO 56, 11 Aug. 1887; WD, *Annual Report of the War Department, 1897,* pp. 413, 414.
66. HQA, AGO, GO 56, 17 June 1902, p. 3, lists "Summer clothing, sack coats, collar devices for" at $.06 each. A National Archives memo, "Report of Unfilled Requisitions," 30 Apr. 1901, shows several unfilled orders for hospital corps "summer coat collar devices." Also see HQA, AGO, GO 2, 6 Jan. 1900, par. I, 36.
67. Inventories no. 153403, 1 Mar. and 16 Mar. 1901, RG 92, NA.
68. HQA, AGO, GO 19, 21 Feb. 1901; HQA, AGO, GO 81, 17 July 1902; HQA, AGO, GO 132, 31 Dec. 1902; HQA, AGO, GO 62, 28 Apr. 1903; WD, Circular 78, 17 Nov. 1909.
69. WD, Changes 9, 16 Oct. 1923, AR 600-35; WD, *Order of Battle of the United States Land Forces in the World War (1917–1919)* 3: pp. 255–56; WD, *Rewards for Service, United States Army,* p. 22.
70. WD, Memo 421A-DS, 17 Sept. 1921; WD, Circular 58, 19 Dec. 1927.

Chapter Twelve

1. *The Army Almanac,* p. 26; Albert, *Buttons,* p. 47.
2. *The Army Almanac,* p. 27.
3. Ralph Buzziard, "Insignia of the Corps of Engineers," *Military Engineer,* Jan.–Feb. 1958, pp. 26–27.
4. *American State Papers, V, Military Affairs* 1: p. 434, and 2: p. 240.
5. WD, *General Regulations for the Army* (1821), p. 157–58.
6. HQA, AGO, Order 50, 11 June 1832, p. 13.
7. "Corps of Engineers, Enlisted Men, 1803–1811," *MC&H,* Dec. 1951, pp. 81–83; Heitman, *Historical Register* 2: pp. 580–81.
8. Heitman, *Historical Register* 2:pp. 574–75; Prucha, *The Sword of the Republic,* p. 391; Albert, *Buttons,* pp. 80–81.
9. HQA, AGO, Order 50, 11 June 1832, p. 14; WD, *Regulations . . . , 1839,* pp. 12, 13.
10. U.S. House, 26th Cong., 2d sess., H. Rept. 125, serial 388; James C. Frasca, "Regulation Headgear . . . , Part VI, The Supporting Services," *North South Trader,* Nov.–Dec. 1981, pp. 24–33.
11. HQA, AGO, GO 36, 21 June 1839, p. 11.
12. Heitman, *Historical Register* 1: p. 43.
13. HQA, AGO, GO 36, 1839, p. 11; HQA, AGO, GO 7, 18 Feb. 1840.
14. WD, AGO, GO 92, 26 Oct. 1872, p. 20; WD, AGO, GO 107, 14 Dec. 1872; WD, AGO, GO 92, 26 Oct. 1872, p. 13; HQA, AGO, GO 27, 17 Mar. 1902, p. 3; HQA, AGO, GO 144, 7 Aug. 1899.
15. Frasca, "Regulation Headgear . . . Part VI," pp. 24–33; Buzziard, "Insignia of the Corps of Engineers," *Military Engineer,* Jan.–Feb. 1958, pp. 26–27; HQA, AGO, GO 7, 18 Feb. 1840.
16. Campbell and Howell, *American Military Insignia, 1800–1851,* pp. 27–28; WD, *General Regulations . . . , 1841,* p. 374.
17. WD, *General Regulations . . . , 1841,* p. 374; *Regulations for the Uniform and Dress* (1851), p. 9.
18. WD, *Revised Regulations, 1861,* p. 12.
19. WD, AGO, GO 92, 26 Oct. 1872, p. 10.
20. Campbell and Howell, *American Military Insignia, 1880–1851,* p. 28; Buzziard, "Insignia of the Corps of Engineers," pp. 26–27; HQA, AGO, GO 18, 4 June 1846, p. 4; HQA, AGO, GO 10, 29 Feb. 1848, p. 2.
21. *Regulations for the Uniform and Dress* (1851), p. 9.
22. WD, *Quartermaster Manual,* p. 16.
23. WD, AGO, GO 92, 26 Oct. 1872, p. 9; WD, AGO, GO 107, 14 Dec. 1872; WD, AGO, GO 67, 25 June 1873, par. IV; WD, OQMG, Specification 8, 17 June 1876, p. 1.
24. WD, OQMG, Specification 419, 13 Jan. 1897, pp. 2, 4; WD, OQMG, Specifica-

tion 744, 20 Feb. 1905, pp. 2, 4.

25. WD, OQMG, Specification 744, 20 Feb. 1905, pp. 2, 4; WD, OQMG, Specification 784, 14 Dec. 1905, p. 2; WD, OQMG, Specification 754, 22 May 1905; Letter no. 246097, 7 Nov. 1908, with indorsements, RG 92, NA; WD, OQMG, Specification 1075, 12 Apr. 1910.
26. WD, Changes 6, 12 Oct. 1916, *Specifications for the Uniforms . . . , 1915,* pars. 92(b), 94(b).
27. WD, OQMG, Specification 470, 13 July 1899.
28. HQA, Circular 14, 1892; WD, *Annual Report of the Quartermaster General, 1895,* plate "Insignias [*sic*] for Officers' Undress Coat"; HQA, AGO, GO 47, 30 July 1895.
29. WD, *Regulations and Decisions* (1901), p. 9; WD, OQMG, Circular 23, 3 Oct. 1914; WD, Changes 9, 16 Oct. 1923, AR 600-35.
30. HQA, GO 39, 3 May 1898, section II; WD, *Regulations and Decisions* (1898).
31. WD, Changes 9, 16 Oct. 1923, AR 600-35, p. 4; Letter, AG 300.35 (11-9-23), Subject: Collar Insignia for Engineers, 26 Feb. 1924; WD, AR 600-35, 25 Nov. 1924, par. 13(a)1; WD, AR 600-35, 31 Dec. 1926, par. 16b(2)(f).
32. WD, OQMG, Specification 80, 21 Apr. 1881.
33. *Regulations for the Uniform and Dress* (1851), plate 6; WD, AGO, GO 3, 14 Mar. 1858, p. 3; WD, OQMG, Specification 80, 21 Apr. 1881; HQA, AGO, GO 2, 6 Jan. 1900, p. 4.
34. WD, OQMG, Specification 595, 22 Jan. 1903, p. 2; Specification 742, 18 Feb. 1905, p. 2; Specification 1075, 12 Aug. 1910.
35. WD, Circular 72, 16 Mar. 1921, p. 3; WD, *Specifications for the Uniform of the United States Army, February 15, 1913,* pars. 98 and 102; WD, Changes 6, 12 Oct. 1916, *Specifications for the Uniforms . . . , 1915.*
36. WD, Circular 58, 19 Dec. 1907.

CHAPTER THIRTEEN

1. *Regulations for the Uniform and Dress* (1851), par. 219.
2. HQA, AGO, GO 17, 6 Mar. 1884; WD, AGO, GO 130, 1907, is an example.
3. WD, *Annual Report of the Secretary of War, 1885,* p. 602; HQA, AGO, GO 104, 3 Oct. 1885, sec. I; WD, OQMG, Specification 186, 5 Apr. 1887; WD, *Regulations for the Uniform of the United States Army, 1888,* illustrations; WD, OQMG, Specification 419, 13 Jan. 1897.
4. HQA, AGO, GO 23, 1885.
5. Dan Stanton, Division of Military History, Smithsonian Institution, conversation with author, 17 Apr. 1984.
6. WD, OQMG, Specification 594, 22 Jan. 1903; WD, Bulletin 16, 22 June 1916, p. 13, Memo report and attached correspondence forwarded to Chief of Staff from 1st Division General Staff, 8 Jan. 1904; WD, GO 197, 31 Dec. 1904, pars. 80, 81, 110, 111; WD, OQMG, Specification 838, 20 Oct. 1906; Letter 421.7, 30 Aug. 1916, from Philadelphia Depot Quartermaster to QMG, with 10 indorsements, Subject: Ornaments for Disciplinary Barracks Guards.
7. *Army and Navy Register,* 11 Mar. 1905, pp. 2, 3.
8. WD, GO 182, 29 Sept. 1910, par. 1.
9. John Elting, et al., "The U.S. Army Band," *MC&H* 19: p. 82; 24: p. 90; Letter 27-27, 1 Apr. 1927, from the U.S. Army Band to Commanding General, Military District of Washington, with 4 indorsements and memo; WD, Circular 58, 31 Aug. 1937, sec. I; Letter 27-27, 1 Apr. 1927, from the U.S. Army Band to Commanding General, Military District of Washington, with 4 indorsements and memo.
10. Elting et al., "The U.S. Army Band," 24: p. 90.
11. WD, AR 600-40, 31 Dec. 1926, par. 20.
12. HQA, AGO, GO 81, 17 July 1902, pars. 56, 67; Memo report and attached correspondence forwarded to Chief of Staff from 1st Division General Staff, 8 Jan. 1904; WD, GO 197, 31 Dec. 1904, pars. 80, 81, 110, 111; WD, OQMG Specification 753, 22 May 1905, p. 4; WD, OQMG, Specification 838, 20 Oct. 1906; Letter 421.7, 30 Aug. 1916, from Philadelphia Depot Quartermaster to QMG, with 10 indorsements, Subject: Ornaments for Disciplinary Barracks Guards; WD, GO 182, 29 Sept. 1910, par. 1.
13. WD, AR 600-35, 31 Dec. 1926, par. 16b(2)(ab); Elting et al., "The U.S. Army Band," 24: pp. 90–93.
14. WD, Circular 78, 17 Nov. 1909; WD, *Specifications for the Uniforms . . . ,* 1915,

pars. 91–102; WD, Circular 72, 16 Mar. 1921, par. 11.

15. WD, AR 600-40, 27 Sept. 1921, par. 19.
16. WD, Changes 6, 28 Oct. 1918, Special Regulation 41, par. 6½; WD, Changes 9, AR 600-35, 16 Oct. 1923; WD, Circular 58, 19 Dec. 1927.

Chapter Fourteen

1. HQA, GO 96, 14 Nov. 1875; WD, *Annual Report of the Quartermaster General, 1876,* p. 63; HQA, AGO, GO 8, 8 Feb. 1877. Cavalrymen with trumpets were known as trumpeters. These men wore cavalry sabers as insignia for several years (see HQA, GO 74, 20 Aug. 1891, par. 1817); WD, *Annual Report of the Secretary of the Army, 1885,* pp. 601, 602; *1886,* p. 239; WD, *Annual Report of the Quartermaster General, 1896,* p. 5; WD, OQMG, Specification 419, 13 Jan. 1897; *Army and Navy Register,* 13 Dec. 1902, p. 7; AGO, GO 81, 17 July 1902; HQA, AGO, GO 132, 31 Dec. 1902.
2. WD, OQMG, Specification 744, 20 Feb. 1905; *Army and Navy Register,* 11 Mar. 1905; WD, GO 118, 31 May 1907; WD, GO 169, 14 Aug. 1907; WD, Changes 6, 12 Oct. 1916, *Specifications for the Uniforms . . . , 1915,* par. 95; HQA, AGO, GO 132, 31 Dec. 1902, par. 106, 107; WD, OQMG, Specification 744, 20 Feb. 1905; WD, Changes 6, 12 Oct. 1916, *Specifications for the Uniforms . . . , 1915,* par. 95.
3. WD, OQMG, Specification 1075, 12 Aug. 1910, illustrations; WD, Changes 6, 12 Oct. 1916, *Specifications for the Uniforms . . . , 1915,* par. 95; WD, OQMG, Specification 838, 20 Oct. 1906; WD, OQMG, Specification 1075, 12 Aug. 1910.

Chapter Fifteen

1. James B. Fry, *A Sketch of the Adjutant General's Department . . . ,* pp. 11–13; Heitman, *Historical Register* 2: pp. 560–70; Fry, *A Sketch of the Adjutant General's Department . . . ,* pp. 18–19; DA, *Department of the Army,* pp. 5–13; DA, GO 23, 20 July 1950.
2. WD, *General Regulations for the Army* (1821), p. 156; HQA, AGO, GO 36, 21 June 1839; HQA, AGO, GO 50, 11 June 1832; *Regulations for the Uniforms and Dress* (1851), par. 55.
3. WD, *Regulations for the Uniform and Dress . . . July 1872,* pp. 13, 20; WD, AGO, GO 107, 14 Dec. 1872; WD, AGO, GO 67, 25 June 1873, par. XII.
4. WD, AGO, GO 67, 25 June 1873, par. XII; HQA, AGO, GO 144, 7 Aug. 1899.
5. WD, AGO, GO 107, 14 Dec. 1872.
6. HQA, Circular 14, 12 Nov. 1892; *Army and Navy Register,* 10 June 1893, p. 366; HQA, AGO, Circular 7, 15 May 1894; *Army and Navy Register,* 27 Apr. 1895, pp. 244–47; WD, *Annual Report of the Quartermaster General, 1895,* illustrated plate; HQA, AGO, GO 132, 31 Dec. 1902, par. 53; WD, Changes 9, 16 Oct. 1923, AR 600-35.
7. WD, AR 600-35, 25 Nov. 1924, pars. 13b(1), 15b(2)(a); WD, AR 600-35, 31 Dec. 1926, par. 16b(2); WD, Circular 15, 10 Mar. 1926; DA, AR 670-5, 23 Sept. 1966, par. 14-13a(1).
8. National Defense Act of 3 June 1920.
9. WD, *Monthly Strength of the Army,* 31 Dec. 1943.
10. "The Adjutant General, His Office and Department, 1775–1947," manuscript in Adjutant General's School Library, pp. 127–30.

Chapter Sixteen

1. Howell and Kloster, *United States Army Headgear to 1854,* pp. 26–30.
2. Heitman, *Historical Register,* 2: pp. 573; *American State Papers, V, Military Affairs* 1: p. 240; Heitman, *Historical Register* 2: pp. 580–83; WD, *General Regulations for the Army* (1821), p. 162, par. 47; WD, *General Regulations for the Army* (1825), p. 164, par. 658.
3. Heitman, *Historical Register* 2: p. 583; DA, GO 23, 20 July 1950.
4. HQA, AGO, Order 50, 1 June 1832, p. 17; HQA, AGO, Order 34, 25 Apr. 1833; HQA, AGO, Order 50, 1 June 1832, p. 17; HQA, AG0, Order 50, 21 May 1833, par. III; 26th Cong., 1st sess., H. Doc. 2, pp. 292–94.
5. *American State Papers, V, Military Affairs* 1: p. 430, HQA, AGO, Order 50, 1 June 1832, p. 17.
6. *Regulations for the Uniforms and Dress* (1851), plate 10; WD, *Regulations for the Uniform and Dress . . . July 1872,* p. 20; WD, AGO, GO 107, 14 Dec. 1872; HQA, AGO, GO 144, 7 Aug. 1899.
7. Howell and Kloster, *United States Army Headgear to 1854,* pp. 40–41; *Regulations*

for the Uniforms and Dress (1851), plates 14, 17; WD, AGO, GO 3, 24 Mar 1858; Howell, *United States Army Headgear, 1855–1902,* pp. 35–41.

8. WD, *Regulations . . .* (1839), p. 16.
9. *Regulations for the Uniforms and Dress* (1851), p. 7 and plate 15.
10. WD, AGO, GO 107, 14 Dec. 1872; Letter to Colonel Easton, 20 Nov. 1872, "Uniforms" box 1170, RG 92, NA; WD, AGO, GO 67, 25 June 1873, par. IV; WD, OQMG, Specification 8, 17 June 1876.
11. WD, OQMG, Specification 419, 13 Jan. 1897; WD, OQMG, Specification 594, 22 Jan. 1903; WD, OQMG, Specification 744, 20 Feb. 1905.
12. William K. Emerson, "U.S. Army Enlisted Campaign Hat Insignia, 1890–1907," *MC&H,* Winter 1977, pp. 158–62.
13. WD, *Regulations for the Uniform of the United States Army, 1888.*
14. *Army and Navy Register,* 10 June 1893, p. 366; HQA, AGO, GO 132, 31 Dec. 1902, par. 53; WD, Changes 9, 16 Oct. 1923, AR 600-35.
15. WD, Circular 15, 10 Mar. 1926; WD, AR 600-35, 31 Dec. 1926, par. 16b(2)(w).
16. WD, OQMG Drawing CE 4-4-33, 15 June 1936.
17. *Regulations for the Uniforms and Dress* (1851), p. 7 and plate 15; WD, OQMG Specification 8, 17 June 1876; WD, *Annual Report of the Secretary of War, 1885,* pp. 601–602.
18. HQA, AGO, GO 2, 6 Jan. 1900, par. I, 36; Letters and bids of 1 Mar. and 16 Mar. 1901, no. 153403, RG 92, NA; WD, OQMG, Specification 595, 22 Jan. 1903; WD, OQMG, Specification 742, 18 Feb. 1905.

Chapter Seventeen

1. DA, *The Department of the Army,* p. 5–33; Heitman, *Historical Register* 2: pp. 572, 574–81, *The Army Almanac,* p. 54; Heitman, *Historical Register* 2: pp. 596–97; *The Army Almanac,* pp. 54–55; WD, *Order of Battle of the United States Land Forces in the World War, (1917–1919)* 3: p. 231.
2. *American State Papers, V, Military Affairs* 2: p. 240; WD, *General Regulations for the Army* (1821), p. 162; *Regulations for the Uniforms and Dress* (1851), p. 7.
3. WD, AGO, GO 92, 11 Oct. 1872; p. 20; HQA, AGO, GO 53, 23 May 1890; WD, *Regulations and Decisions* (1901).
4. *Army and Navy Register,* 10 June 1890, p. 366; HQA, AGO, GO 132, 31 Dec. 1902, par. 53(b).
5. WD, AR 600-35, 31 Dec. 1926, par. 16b(2)(1).
6. Letter AG 421.7, Subject: Change of Insignia for the JAG Department, from TAG to QMG, 27 Dec. 1924; WD, AR 600-35, 25 Nov. 1924, pars. 15b(2)(g) and 13b(1); Letter AG 421.7, Subject: Change of Insignia for the JAG Department, from TAG to QMG, 27 Dec. 1924; WD, Circular 15, 10 Mar. 1926.
7. DA, *Department of the Army,* p. 5–33.
8. WD, GO 27, 22 Mar. 1918, par. XII; WD, *Order of Battle of the United States Land Forces in the World War, (1917–1919)* 3: p. 237; Memo 421, Insignia (CE-S), 10 Mar. 1920, Collar Ornaments for Enlisted Men, from Office Director of Purchase and Storage; National Defense Act of June 1920, 66th Cong., 2d sess., ch. 227, 1920, pp. 765–66.
9. DA, AR 670-5, 12 Feb. 1968, par. 14-13 (o)2.

Chapter Eighteen

1. Bill Mauldin, *The Brass Ring,* p. 94; Heitman, *Historical Register* 1: p. 1036; 2: pp. 560–63, 572–75.
2. Printed and signed copy of the act, dated 23 Aug. 1842, filed with General Orders for 1842, RG 92, NA; HQA, AGO, GO 65, 9 July 1884, p. 5; WD, *Annual Report of the Quartermaster General, 1909,* p. 42; *Annual Report of the Quartermaster General, 1891,* p. 5; Memo to Assistant Secretary of War, 9 Aug. 1909, TIOH files.
3. WD, GO 33, 23 Sept. 1912; WD, *Annual Report of the Quartermaster General, 1883,* p. 148; *1884,* pp. 12–17; WD, Technical Manual 10-380, QMG, 14 Feb. 1941, pp. 5–6; Card Catalog, Library of Congress.
4. AGO, GO 50, 11 June 1832, p. 9; AGO, GO 36, 21 June 1839; *Regulations for the Uniforms and Dress* (1851).
5. WD, AGO, GO 92, 26 Oct. 1872, p. 20; AGO, GO 74, 20 Aug. 1891; *Army and Navy Register,* 23 Nov. 1895, 29 Feb. 1896, and 6 June 1896; AGO, GO 40, 2 Sept. 1896.
6. Emerson, *Chevrons,* pp. 109–14.

7. HQA, AGO, GO 104, 3 Oct. 1885, section III; HQA, AGO, GO 6, 8 Feb. 1888, p. 7; William K. Emerson, "U.S. Army Enlisted Cap Insignia, 1896–1905," *MC&H,* Spring 1972, pp. 11–15; HQA, AGO, GO 132, 31 Dec. 1902, p. 30.
8. HQA, AGO, GO 132, 31 Dec. 1902, p. 30; WD, GO 39, 10 Mar. 1910, sec. IV; WD, *Specifications for the Uniform* (1913), par. 91.
9. William K. Emerson, "U.S. Army Enlisted Campaign Hat Insignia," *MC&H* 29, no. 4: pp. 158–62; WD, OQMG, Specification 470, 13 July 1899.
10. *Army and Navy Register,* 29 Feb. 1896.
11. HQA, AGO, GO 2, 6 Jan. 1900, p. 4; HQA, AGO, GO 132, 31 Dec. 1902, pars. 67, 69.
12. HQA, AGO, GO 132, 31 Dec. 1902, p. 29.
13. Letter from Center for Military History to author, 10 Sept. 1981.
14. WD, *Order of Battle of the United States Land Forces in the World War, (1917–1919)* 3: pp. 191, 1551–52; Letter for Director, Purchase and Storage, Clothing and Equipment Division, to Asst. Chief of Staff, Director of Purchases, 23 June 1919, TIOH Files.
15. Scipio, *E.M. Collar Insignia,* p. 107; WD, *Official National Guard Register for 1931,* p. 6; WD, *Official National Guard Register for 1938,* pp. 1365–67.
16. WD, *Official National Guard Register for 1931,* pp. 8; WD, *Official National Guard Register for 1926,* p. 38; WD, *Official National Guard Register for 1931,* p. 26.
17. WD, AR 600-35, 14 Oct. 1921, pars. 13b(2)(w), 13b(3)(f); WD, AR 600-35, 25 Nov. 1924, par. 16b(2)(y); WD, AR 600-35, 25 Nov. 1924, par. 15b(2)(y).
18. WD, Circular 15, 10 Mar. 1926; WD, AR 600-35, 31 Dec. 1926, par. 16b(2)(y).
19. WD, OQMG Drawing CE 4-4-33, 15 June 1936.

Chapter Nineteen

1. WD, *Legislative History of the General Staff . . . from 1775 to 1901,* p. 334; Heitman, *Historical Register* 1: pp. 40–41.
2. WD, GO 33, 23 Sept. 1912; WD, *Legislative History,* pp. 612–13; WD, *Annual Report of the Quartermaster General, 1868,* exhibit A.
3. *American State Papers, V, Military Affairs* 2: p. 240; HQA, AGO, GO 50, 11 June 1832, p. 12; AGO, GO 31, 1851, par. 59.
4. HQA, AGO, GO 4, 7 Jan. 1881; WD, *Legislative History,* pp. 612–25.
5. AGO, GO 38, 20 Mar. 1873; HQA, AGO, GO 113, 31 Oct. 1885; WD, *Uniform of the Army of the United States, 1882;* WD, OQMG, Specification 266, 9 July 1889; WD, OQMG, Specification 419, 13 Jan. 1897; WD, GO 33, 23 Sept. 1912; WD, Changes 2, 13 Mar. 1913, *Regulations for the Uniform* (1912); Emerson, "U.S. Army Enlisted Campaign Hat Insignia, 1890–1907," *MC&H,* Winter 1977, pp. 158–62.
6. WD, *Regulations for the Uniform and Dress . . . July 1872,* p. 20; HQA, AGO, GO 74, 20 Aug. 1891, pp. 4–5.
7. HQA, AGO, GO 39, 18 Aug. 1896.
8. Ibid.; *Army and Navy Register,* 22 Feb. 1896, p. 114; WD, Changes 2, 13 Mar. 1913, *Regulations for the Uniform* (1912).
9. WD, OQMG, Specifications for Metallic Uniform-Coat, Helmet, Dress and Forage Cap Ornaments, 31 May 1876; WD, *Annual Report of the Secretary of War, 1885,* pp. 601, 602; HQA, AGO, GO, 132, 31 Dec. 1902; WD, OQMG, Specification 1074, 12 Aug. 1910; WD, GO 33, 23 Sept. 1912.
10. WD, Circular 78, 17 Nov. 1909; WD, GO 33, 23 Sept. 1912; WD, Changes 2, 13 Mar. 1913, *Regulations for the Uniform* (1912).

Chapter Twenty

1. Earl F. Stover, *Up from Handyman: The United States Army Chaplaincy, 1895–1920; American State Papers, V, Military Affairs* 2: p. 240; WD, *General Regulations for the Army* (1821); WD, AGO, GO 36, 21 June 1839.
2. WD, AGO, GO 247, 25 Aug. 1864; HQA, AGO, Circular 1, 18 Feb. 1884; Michael J. Winey, "Clergy in Uniform," *Military Images* 4, no. 6: p. 12.
3. HQA, AGO, GO 10, 13 Feb. 1880; HQA, AGO, GO 29, 5 May 1888; HQA, AGO, GO 54, 1 May 1898.
4. WD, *Regulations and Decisions* (1900), p. 6; HQA, AGO, GO 132, 31 Dec. 1902.
5. HQA, AGO, GO 132, 31 Dec. 1902; WD, GO 197, 31 Dec. 1904; WD, GO 169, 14 Aug. 1907.
6. WD, QMG, Circular 5, 9 Apr. 1914.

7. WD, Changes 4, 22 May 1918, Special Regulation 41.
8. WD, AR 600-35, 25 Nov. 1924, par. 17a(3); WD, Circular 33, 2 June 1926, sec. III.
9. WD, Circular 19, 19 Mar. 1926; Robert L. Gushwa, *The Best and Worst of Times: The United States Chaplaincy, 1920–1945,* p. 19; WD, AR 30-3000, 2 June 1924, p. 8; WD, Special Regulations No. 40, revised 31 Dec. 1921, p. 6.
10. Roy J. Honeywell, *Chaplains of the United States Army,* p. 179.
11. Gushwa, *Best and Worst of Times,* pp. 40, 97; "New Branch Insignia, Jewish Chaplains, US Army," *The Trading Post,* Jan.–Mar. 1984, p.28.
12. Gushwa, *Best and Worst of Times,* p. 110; *Army Times,* 26 Nov. 1984, p. 27.
13. Stover, *Up From Handyman,* p. 151; WD, GO 79, 1904; WD, QMG, Circular 5, 9 Apr. 1914.
14. Gushwa, *Best and Worst of Times,* pp. 28–35.
15. Memo TAPC-PDH-Z, Subject: Buddhist Chaplain Insignia, 31 July 1990, and first endorsement, DAPE-MPH-S, 9 Aug. 1990; TIOH drawing B-2-62.
16. Memo for ADPE-HR-S from DACH-PPDT, Subject: Insignia for Muslim Chaplains, 14 Dec. 1992, and first endorsement, DAPE-HR-S, 8 Jan. 1993; TIOH drawing B-2-64.

Chapter Twenty-One

1. Fry, *Sketch of the Adjutant General's Department . . . ,* pp. 10–20; *The Army Almanac,* p. 52.
2. WD, *Dress of the General Staff and Regimental Officers,* p. 20; HQA, AGO, GO 36, 21 June 1839; HQA, AGO, GO 50, 11 June 1832; *Regulations for the Uniforms and Dress* (1851), par. 55; WD, *Regulations for the Uniform and Dress . . . July 1872,* p. 13; HQA, AGO, GO 29, 5 May 1888.
3. HQA, AGO, GO 53, 1880; WD, *Regulations and Decisions* (1901), pp. 15–16; IG Office memo, "Insignia, Inspector General's Department," 12 May 1893, TIOH files.
4. HQA, AGO, GO 132, 31 Dec. 1902, par. 53; WD, Change 6, 28 Oct. 1918, Special Regulation 42, par. 93.
5. WD, AR 600-35, 25 Nov. 1924, par. 15b(2)(p); WD, AR 600-35, 31 Dec. 1926, par. 16b(2)(p); WD, Circular 15, 10 Mar. 1926; WD, OQMG Drawing CE 4-4-32, 15 June 1936.
6. WD, Changes 9, 5 May 1919, Special Regulation 42; Memo for Director, Operations Division GS, Subject: Collar Insignia for Enlisted Men, 30 Aug. 1920, TIOH files; National Defense Act of June 1920, 66th Cong., 2d sess., ch. 227, 1920, p. 765.
7. DF from DAPE to DAAG-HD, 17 June 1976, Subject: Branch Insignia Wear Policy for Enlisted Personnel; Message from Commander, TRADOC, to AIG 7573, dated 18 1715 Z June 1976, Subject: AR 670-5.

Chapter Twenty-Two

1. *American State Papers, V, Military Affairs* 2: p. 240; P. M. Ashburn, *A History of the Medical Department of the United States Army,* p. 425; *Military Laws and Rules . . .* (1813), p. 226; WD, *General Regulations for the Army* (1821), article 65, par. 44; WD, *General Regulations for the Army* (1825), article 65, par. 864; HQA, AGO, GO 50, 11 June 1832, p. 10.
2. WD, *General Regulations . . . , 1841,* par. 1273; *Regulations for the Uniforms and Dress* (1851), par. 104; WD, *Regulations for the Uniform and Dress . . . July 1872,* p. 20; HQA, AGO, GO 74, 20 Aug. 1891, pp. 4, 5.
3. *Army and Navy Register,* 6 June 1896, p. 354; WD, *Regulations and Decisions* (1897), pp. 13, 15; HQA, AGO, GO 39, 18 Aug. 1896; WD, GO 33, 23 Sept. 1912, par. 1.
4. National Defense Act of June 1920, chap. I, sec. 9a; WD, AR 600-35, 14 Oct. 1921, par. 13b(2)(1); *The Army Almanac,* p. 44.
5. National Defense Act of June 1920, chap. I, sec. 9a.

Chapter Twenty-Three

1. *Legislation and Orders Relating to the Signal Service,* Myer Papers, Signal Corps Museum.
2. DA, *The Department of the Army,* pp. 5–32; WD, *Annual Report of the Chief Signal Officer,* 1889, p. 40; HQA, AGO, GO 74, 20 Aug. 1891, lists Signal Corps insignia with other branches for the first time.
3. Letters Sent, Office of the Chief Signal Officer, vol. 3, pp. 113–14, RG 111, NA.

4. Ibid., 161–62.
5. WD, AGO, GO 92, 26 Oct. 1872, p. 18; J. Willard Brown, *The Signal Corps in the War of the Rebellion,* opposite p. 384; Memorandum, Signal Office, WD, 9 May 1884, consolidated correspondence file, box 1171, RG 92, NA.
6. WD, AGO, GO 92, 26 Oct. 1872, pp. 9, 18; HQA, AGO, GO 52, 14 June 1881; HQA, AGO, GO 77, 13 July 1885.
7. Memorandum, Signal Office, WD, 9 May 1884, consolidated correspondence file, box 1171, RG 92, NA.
8. WD, AGO, GO 92, 26 Oct. 1872, p. 20; HQA, AGO, GO 86, 3 Dec. 1878; HQA, AGO, GO 30, 14 Apr. 1884; HQA, AGO, GO 53, 23 May 1890.
9. WD, *Regulations and Decisions* (1900), p. 9.
10. Letters Sent, Office of the Chief Signal Officer, vol. 3, pp. 113–14, RG 111, NA; Brown, *Signal Corps in the War of the Rebellion,* p. 444.
11. WD, *Annual Report of the Quartermaster General,* 1882, p. 52; HQA, AGO, GO 76, 16 Dec. 1887.
12. HQA, AGO, GO 18, 16 Feb. 1889, p. 1; HQA, AGO, GO 74, 20 Aug. 1891, p. 4; HQA, AGO, GO 52, 24 May 1898; HQA, AGO, GO 21, 25 Feb. 1901; HQA, AGO, GO 132, 31 Dec. 1902, par. 78.
13. WD, OQMG, Specification 744, 20 Feb. 1905.
14. Emerson, "U.S. Army Enlisted Campaign Hat Insignia, 1890–1907," *MC&H,* Winter 1977, pp. 158–62; WD, OQMG, Specifications 470, 13 July 1899; HQA, AGO, GO 132, 31 Dec. 1902.
15. *Army and Navy Register,* 10 June 1893, p. 366; WD, *Regulations and Decisions* (1898), par. 2; WD, *Regulations and Decisions* (1900), par. 2; WD, *Regulations for the Uniform* (1912), par. 26(k).
16. WD, Circular 15, 10 Mar. 1926, par. 5.
17. WD, AR 600-35, 14 Oct. 1921, para. 13b(29)(x) and 11; WD, Circular 15, 10 Mar. 1926, par. 5; WD, OQMG Drawing CE 4-4-33, 15 June 1936.
18. WD, *Annual Report of the Quartermaster General,* 1882, p. 52; WD, OQMG, Specification 595, 2 Jan. 1903.
19. HQA, AGO, GO 132, 31 Dec. 1902, par. 46.

Chapter Twenty-Four

1. Heitman, *Historical Register* 2: p. 605; WD, *Annual Report of the Secretary of War, 1897,* p. 218.
2. Letter from Lieutenant E. W. Casey to Secretary of War, 3 June 1890, TIOH files; HQA, AGO, Circular 10, 11 Aug. 1890, sec. VI.
3. HQA, AGO, Circular 10, 11 Aug. 1890, sec. VI.
4. Ibid.
5. Ibid.; WD, *Regulations and Decisions* (1899), par. 65; WD, AGO, GO 37, 12 June 1897, p. 4; HQA, AGO, GO 111, 16 Aug. 1900, p. 5.
6. Letter from Lieutenant E. W. Casey to Secretary of War, 3 June 1890, TIOH files; Letter no. 153403, 19 Nov. 1900, RG 92, NA; Inventory of 15 Mar. 1901, no. 153403, p. 13, RG 92, NA.
7. HQ, AGO, GO 132, 31 Dec. 1902, par. 105; WD, GO 140, 23 June 1907; WD, GO 169, 14 Aug. 1907.
8. WD, *Regulations for the Uniform* (1912), par. 44.
9. Letter no. 178141, 4 Aug. 1902, RG 92, NA; WD, OQMG, Specifications 1231, 17 Sept. 1915.
10. WD, Circular 72, 16 Mar. 1921, par. 11; WD, GO 33, 28 July 1922; WD, AR 600-35, 14 Oct. 1921, pars. 13c(1) and 13c(3)(d).
11. Tom Kiddoo," The Last Apache Scout," *Soldiers,* Sept. 1981, pp. 20–21.
12. Robert D. Burhans, *The First Special Service Force;* WD, Changes 4, 23 Oct. 1942, AR 600-35.
13. Burhans, *First Special Service Force,* pp. 298–99; John K. Mahon and Danysh, *Infantry, Part I; Regular Army,* Army Lineage Series, p. 887; WD, Circular 49, 21 Feb. 1947, sec. I; Charles M. Simpson, *Inside the Green Berets,* pp. 16, 19–21.
14. WD, Changes 4, 23 Oct. 1942, AR 600-35.
15. Burhans, *First Special Service Force,* p. 45.
16. Letter, ATSU-SP, Subject: Collar Insignia for Special Operations Enlisted Personnel, 23 Feb. 1984; *Army Times,* 17 Sept. 1964, p. 4; Memo, DAFE-HRP-U, Subject: Collar Insignia for Special Operations Enlisted Personnel, 26 June 1984, with "Approved" stamp dated 29 July 1984.

CHAPTER TWENTY-FIVE

1. WD, GO 56, 17 Sept. 1913, pars. 3, 4, 6, and 7.
2. WD, *Annual Report of the Quartermaster General, 1882,* p. 57; WD, *Annual Report of the Quartermaster General, 1893,* p. 68; WD, *Annual Report of the Quartermaster General, 1895,* pp. 27, 96.
3. WD, GO 26, 6 Feb. 1906; WD, GO 142, 14 Aug. 1906; WD, GO 154, 12 Sept. 1906, sec. II; Philadelphia Depot Quartermaster letter 421.7, 30 Aug. 1916, Subject: Ornaments for Disciplinary Barracks Guards, with 10 indorsements, TIOH files.
4. Emerson, "U.S. Army Campaign Hat Insignia, 1890–1907," *MC&H* 24, no. 4: pp. 158–62; WD, GO 183, 31 Oct. 1906.
5. WD, OQMG, Specifications 1231 and 1232, 17 Sept. 1915.
6. WD, OQMG, Specification 837, 20 Sept. 1906.
7. WD, Changes 9, 5 May 1919, Special Regulation 42, par. 121(c)(7); WD, Circular 72, 16 Mar. 1921.

CHAPTER TWENTY-SIX

1. Hewes, *From Root to McNamara,* p. 382; WD, *Order of Battle of the United States Land Forces in the World War (1917–1919)* 3: p. 229; HQA, AGO, GO 79, 15 July 1902, par. 87; WD, GO 48, 8 Mar. 1907, pp. 8, 9; National Defense Act of June 1920, 66th Cong., 2d sess., ch. 227, 1920, p. 769.
2. HQA, AGO, GO 132, 31 Dec. 1902, par. 53(b); Charles R. Steitz, "The Bureau of Insular Affairs," *Military Collectors Journal,* May–June 1983, pp. 2–3.
3. WD, GO 169, 14 Aug. 1907, par. 57(b).
4. WD, OQMG Drawing CE 4-4-30, 15 June 1936; Hewes, *From Root to McNamara,* p. 382.

CHAPTER TWENTY-SEVEN

1. Harold H. Elarth, *The Story of the Philippine Constabulary,* pp. 13, 14, 47–48, 60, 67; Dean C. Worchester, *The Philippines Past and Present,* p. 311.
2. Elarth, *Story of the Philippine Constabulary,* p. 13.
3. WD, GO 11, 19 July 1922; WD, GO 17, 19 Apr. 1921.
4. Vic Hurley, *Jungle Patrol,* pp. 48, 67, and picture following p. 78.
5. Letter no. 233554, 5th Indorsement, 25 Feb. 1908, and Letter no. 272035, 27 July 1910, both in RG 92, NA; *Manual for the Philippine Constabulary, 1911,* par. 691; HQ, Philippine Constabulary, GO 11, 19 July 1922, p. 81; HQ, Philippine Constabulary, Circular 21, 27 Aug. 1909.
6. HQ, Philippine Constabulary, GO 66, 27 Oct. 1903, p. 4; Bureau of the Constabulary, GO 16, 30 May 1908, par. 3; Philippine Constabulary, GO 29, 4 Nov. 1913, par. 4; *Manual for the Philippine Constabulary, 1918,* par. 343.
7. Hurley, *Jungle Patrol,* photograph after p. 78; Bureau of the Constabulary, GO 38, 17 Oct. 1907, par. 1; HQ, Philippine Constabulary, GO 11, 19 July 1922, p. 81; *Philippine Constabulary Regulations, 1930,* front color plate.
8. Hurley, *Jungle Patrol,* pp. 60, 110.
9. Bureau of the Constabulary, GO 2, 2 Jan. 1906, par. 6; Bureau of the Constabulary, GO 92, 1 Dec. 1905, par. 24; Bureau of the Constabulary, GO 37, 13 Sept. 1906; Bureau of the Constabulary, GO 4, 7 Jan. 1907.
10. Bureau of the Constabulary, GO 41, 26 Nov. 1907, par. 1; Bureau of the Constabulary, GO 3, 4 Jan. 1909, par. 1; HQ, Philippine Constabulary, GO 29, 20 Oct. 1911; HQ, Philippine Constabulary, Circular 17 (corrected copy), 19 May 1911.
11. John R. White, *Bullets and Bolos,* photograph, on unnumbered page, of Moro noncommissioned officer.
12. HQ, Philippine Constabulary, GO 103, 30 Aug. 1904; Bureau of Constabulary, GO 76, 5 Sept. 1905.
13. Ibid.
14. White, *Bullets and Bolos,* photograph, on unnumbered page, of Moro noncommissioned officer.

CHAPTER TWENTY-EIGHT

1. HQA, AGO, GO 30, 4 Mar. 1899, p. 3; HQA, AGO, GO 24, 1903, p. 6; HQA, AGO, GO 28, 17 Mar. 1902, sec. II.
2. WD, GO 76, 1904; HQA, AGO, GO 132, 31 Dec. 1902; WD, Specification 742, 18 Feb. 1905.
3. HQA, AGO, GO 132, 31 Dec. 1902, p. 30; WD, GO 197, 31 Dec. 1904, p. 32; WD, OQMG, Specification 742, 18 Feb. 1905.

4. HQA, AGO, GO 80, 24 April 1899, p. 6.
5. Emerson, "U.S. Army Enlisted Campaign Hat Insignia, 1890–1907," *MC&H,* 29, no. 4, pp. 158–62.
6. HQA, AGO GO 2, 6 Jan. 1900, p. 4; WD, OQMG, Specification 595, 22 Jan. 1903; Letter from Office of Clothing and Equipage Div. to Assistant Chief of Staff, Director of Purchase, 23 June 1919, and 1st indorsement, 14 June 1919, TIOH files.

Chapter Twenty-Nine

1. HQA, AGO, Order 50, 11 June 1832, p. 13.
2. HQA, AGO, GO 36, 21 June 1839, pp. 11, 12; WD, *General Regulations . . . , 1847,* p. 206.
3. HQA, AGO, GO 132, 31 Dec. 1902, par. 53(b); WD, AR 600-35, 14 Oct. 1921, par. 13b(2)(v); WD, Changes 9, 16 Oct. 1923, AR 600-36, par. 13b(2)(v).
4. WD, AR 600-35, 25 Nov. 1924, par. 15b(2)(x).
5. HQ, DA, Changes 27, 1 Aug. 1982, AR 635-100, par. 4-31a(2)(d).

Chapter Thirty

1. HQA, AGO, GO 15, 18 Feb. 1903, sec. 2.
2. *American State Papers, V, Military Affairs* 1: p. 434.
3. Ibid. 2: pp. 239–40; WD, *General Regulations for the Army* (1821), p. 158; WD, *General Regulations for the Army* (1825), pp. 160–62, 164; WD, *General Regulations for the Army* (1821), pp. 158–59, 160–61.
4. HQA, AGO, GO 50, 11 June 1832, pp. 8–9.
5. Ibid., p. 9.
6. Ibid., p. 12.
7. Ibid., p. 20.
8. HQA, AGO, GO 36, 21 June 1839, pp. 5, 8, 9.
9. Ibid., p. 19.
10. *Regulations for the Uniforms and Dress* (1851), p. 13; WD, *Annual Report of the Adjutant General, 1888,* table A, note c.
11. WD, *General Regulations . . . , 1847,* pp. 189, 215; *General Regulations . . . , 1841,* p. 386.
12. *Regulations for the Uniforms and Dress* (1851), p. 13.
13. WD, AGO, GO 27, 22 Dec. 1859.

Chapter Thirty-One

1. Hewes, *From Root to McNamara,* pp. 3–5.
2. Ibid., pp. 6–11; WD, GO 197, 31 Dec. 1904, par. 56(b); WD, GO 47, 6 Apr. 1911, par. 8.
3. U.S. Senate, *General Staff Corps and Medal of Honor,* 66th Cong., 1st sess., S. Doc. 58, 1919, p. 46; WD, *Order of Battle of the United States Land Forces in the World War (1917–1919)* 3: p. 29; National Defense Act, 7 June 1924, p. 7.
4. WD, GO 66, 12 July 1918, par. III; Hewes, *From Root to McNamara,* p. 41; WD, AR 600-35, 14 Oct. 1921, par. 11a(1)(b); WD, Changes 9, 16 Oct. 1923, AR 600-35, pars. 11a and 11b; WD, Circular 15, 10 Mar. 1926; WD, AR 600-35, 31 Dec. 1926, par. 16b(2)(m).
5. WD, GO 197, 31 Dec. 1904, par. 19; The National Defense Act 7 June 1924, p. 53; WD, AR 600-35, 10 Nov. 1941.
6. AEF, GO 134, 15 Aug. 1918; WD, AR 600-35, 10 Nov. 1941, par. 30a.
7. WD, Circular 45, 1933, sec. I; WD, Circular 1, 1937, sec. IV; DA, Chief of Staff Regulations No. 614-100, 9 Oct. 1979; *Army Times,* 8 July 1985, p. 16.

Chapter Thirty-Two

1. Fry, *Sketch of the Adjutant General's Department,* p. 29.
2. WD, *Legislative History of the General Staff,* p. 18; WD, *General Regulations for the Army* (1825), par. 864; (1821), article 65, par. 43; HQA, AGO, GO 50, 11 June 1832; HQA, AGO, GO 36, 21 June 1838; *Regulations for the Uniform and Dress* (1851); WD, AGO, GO 92, 26 Oct. 1872.
3. *Army and Navy Register,* 22 Mar. 1902; WD, AR 600-35, 25 Nov. 1924, par. 15b(2)(b); WD, AR 600-35, 31 Dec. 1926, par. 14a(3)(a); WD, AR 600-35, 10 Nov. 1941, par. 22d. The reference to pairs of insignia for blue uniforms is on WD, OQMG Drawing CE 4-4-30, dated 15 June 1936. AR 30-3000, June 1938, p. 17, lists aides' insignia in pairs.
4. Signal Corps no. 14028, RG 111, NA.
5. WD, AR 600-35, 14 Oct. 1921, par. 13b(3)(a); WD, Changes 9, 16 Oct. 1923, AR 600-35, par. 13b(2)(b); WD, AR 600-35, 14 Oct. 1921, par. 13b(3)(a); WD, AR 600-35, 31 Dec. 1926, par. 16b(2).
6. WD, Circular 15, 10 Mar. 1926; WD, AR 600-35, 31 Dec. 1926, par. 16b(2).
7. WD, OQMG drawing CE 4-4-30, dated 15 June 1936.
8. WD, Changes 3, 18 Apr. 1945, AR 600-35; Memo to Asst. Chief of Staff, G-1,

from the QMG, 5 Mar. 1946, Subject: Insignia for Military Aides to the President; letter from A. E. DuBois to Bailey, Banks and Biddle, 4 Apr. 1946; Memo for the Director of Personnel and Administration from office of the Secretary of the General Staff, 30 July 1946, Subject: Insignia for the Military Aide to the President; DA, Changes 1, 11 May 1953, SR 600-60-1; HQ, DA, AR 670-5, 8 Jan. 1971, par. 14-14a(2).

9. DA, SR 600-61, 26 Oct. 1951, par. 13; HQ, DA, Changes 3, 18 Feb. 1963, AR 670-5; Discussion with aides to the Assistant Secretary of the Army, June 1976, the Pentagon; DA, Changes 4, 12 Oct. 1963, AR 670-5, par. 135a(3.2).
10. Discussion with former aide to President Johnson, May 1976, Fort Belvoir, Va., and aides to secretary of the army, June 1976, the Pentagon; DA, AR 670-5, 8 Jan. 1971, par. 15-7b(3).
11. DA, Letter DALO-SMT-E, 12 Sept. 1972, subject, "Insignia, Branch of Service, Aide to General, Lieutenant, Major and Brigadier General"; DA, AR 670-5, 30 Jan. 1975, par. 14-14a(8).
12. DF, DAAG-HD, 4 May 1977, subject, "Insignia of Aides," with comment two, 20 May, from DAAG-HDZ-A and comment three from DAAG-ZA; DA, AR 670-1, 15 Feb. 1979, p. 26–27.
13. WD, AGO, GO 92, 26 Oct. 1872, pp. 13, 20; WD, *Regulations for the Uniform of the United States Army* (1911), par. 55(c).
14. Regulations do not mention aiguillettes, yet photographs show presidential aides wearing aiguillettes.
15. WD, Circular 66, 15 Oct. 1936, par. 2a; WD, Circular 92, 9 Apr. 1947, section I.
16. Memorandum for record, DAPC-PDH-Z, Subject: Insignia, Aide to VCSA, 10 June 1987; Memorandum for record, DAPC-PDH-Z, Subject: Presentation of Insignia, Aide, VCSA, 7 Oct. 1987.
17. TIOH Drawing B-2-44, 19 May 1969, revised 24 June 1987.
18. TIOH Drawing B-2-56, Aug. 1977, revised 26 June 1987.

Chapter Thirty-Three

1. WD, *Report of the Secretary of War, 1897,* p. 709; *Army and Navy Register* 13 Aug. 1892, p. 520; HQA, GO 36, 4 Mar. 1899; HQA, GO 45, 13 Mar. 1899.
2. HQA, GO 63, 7 Apr. 1899.
3. HQA, GO 76, 26 Apr. 1904; HQA, GO 88, 1904.

Chapter Thirty-Four

1. WD, GO 154, 12 Sept. 1906, sec. II; WD, OQMG, Specification 838, 20 Oct. 1906; Letter no. 236695, 24 Dec. 1907, RG 92, NA.
2. WD, OQMG, Specification 837, 20 Oct. 1906.
3. *The Uniform of the United States* (1908), plate 63.
4. Emerson, "U.S. Army Enlisted Campaign Hat Insignia, 1890–1907," *MC&H,* Winter 1977, pp. 158–62.
5. WD, Circular 72, 16 Mar. 1921, par. 11.

Chapter Thirty-Five

1. U.S. Senate, *General Staff Corps and Medal of Honor,* 66th Cong., 1st sess., S. Doc. 58, 1919, pp. 11–15, 45–53.
2. WD, memo for the Chief of Staff, 8647-17, 24 Nov. 1916, War College Division.
3. WD, Changes 7, 30 Dec. 1916, for the *Uniform Specifications* (1915), par. 25(t).
4. U.S. Senate, *General Staff Corps and Medal of Honor,* S. Doc. 58, 1919, p. 46; WD, Changes 1, 29 Dec. 1917, Special Regulation 42.

Chapter Thirty-Six

1. WD, TM 10-380, *Water Transportation,* 14 Feb. 1941, pp. 5, 6.
2. WD, *Marine Personnel Regulations,* Transportation Corps Pamphlet No. 4, "Regulation No. 23," Change 1, 1 Aug. 1945, sec. 2; Library of Congress card catalog; "Unified Sea Transportation," *Army Information Digest,* Nov. 1950, pp. 29–31; T. M. Knox, "The Work of the Army's Fleet," *The Quartermaster Review,* Mar.–Apr. 1930, p. 29; Chester Wardlow, *The Transportation Corps: Responsibilities, Organization, and Operations,* pp. 32–33.
3. WD, TM 10-380, 14 Feb. 1941, pp. 13–23; Wardlow, *Transportation Corps,* pp. 209, 229; Roland W. Charles, *Troop Ships of World War II,* p. 2.
4. Knox, "Work of the Army's Fleet," pp. 7, 23–27; WD, *Annual Report of the Quartermaster General, 1907,* p. 26; Quartermaster Department, *Regulations for Harbor Boat Service,* 15 Nov. 1904; Werner W. Moore, "Harbor Boats," *Quartermaster Review,* Sept.–Oct. 1938, p. 27; WD, *Annual Report of the Quartermaster General,* 1907, p. 25; Knox, "Work of the

Army's Fleet," pp. 7, 23–27; Wardlow, *Transportation Corps,* pp. 209, 229.

5. Wardlow, *Transportation Corps,* p. 109; "Unified Sea Transportation," *Army Information Digest,* Nov. 1950, pp. 29–31.
6. WD, *Regulations Prescribing Uniforms of the United States Army Transport Service,* 1899.
7. WD, *Regulations Prescribing Uniforms of the United States Army Transport Service,* Circular 7 (1912), p. 5, plates VI–VIII.
8. WD, AR 30-1180, 1 Oct. 1930, par. 1h.
9. Ibid., pp. 5, 6; National Geographic Society, *Insignia and Decorations of the Armed Forces,* p. 112.
10. Signal Corps 102615, RG 111, NA.
11. WD, *Marine Personnel Regulations,* Transportation Corps Pamphlet No. 4, "Regulation No. 23," Change 1, 1 Aug. 1945, sec. 2.
12. WD, *Annual Report of the Quartermaster General, 1904,* 31.
13. WD, OQMG, Specifications for . . . Harbor Boat Service Nos. 687 to 696, all dated 10 Sept. 1904; WD, *Regulations of the United States Army Transport Service,* 1912.
14. WD, AR 30-1180, 1 Oct. 1930.
15. WD, AR 30-1180, 22 May 1933, p. 3.
16. WD, *Regulations Prescribing Uniforms of the United States Army Transport Service* (1899), pp. 5, 6; WD, AR 30-1180, 1 Oct. 1930, pp. 5, 6.
17. WD, OQMG, Specifications for Caps for Harbor Boat Service, 687, 10 Sept. 1904; WD, AR 55-380, 31 Dec. 1942, par. 7f.
18. WD, *Marine Personnel Regulations,* Transportation Corps Pamphlet No. 4, Change 1, 1 Aug. 1945, par. 232.2c(1).
19. WD, *Regulations Prescribing Uniforms of the United States Army Transport Service* (1899); WD, *Regulations of the United States Army Transport Service,* 1912.
20. WD, *Marine Personnel Regulations,* Transportation Corps Pamphlet No. 4, "Regulation No. 23," Change 1, 1 Aug. 1945, sec. 232.2.
21. WD, AR 30-1180, 1 Oct. 1930, par. 3f(1).
22. AR 55-380, 31 Dec. 1942, par. 4c(4); Rudy Basurto, *Insignia of America's Little Known Seafarers,* p. 6; WD, *Marine Personnel Regulations,* Transportation Corps Pamphlet No. 4, "Regulation No. 23," Change 1, 1 Aug. 1945, pars. 234. 1d, e, f and 234.2a.
23. WD, *Regulations Prescribing Uniforms of the United States Army Transport Service* (1899); WD, AR 30-1180, 1 Oct. 1930, par. 4f(5); WD, OQMG, Specification 687, 10 Sept. 1904; Basurto, *Insignia of America's Little Known Seafarers;* WD, AR 30-1180, 1 Oct. 1930, par. 4f(5); WD, *Marine Personnel Regulations,* Transportation Corps Pamphlet No. 4, "Regulation No. 23," Change 1, 1 Aug. 1945, sec. 2.
24. WD, AR 600-40, 31 Dec. 1926, par. 20b(11).

Chapter Thirty-Seven

1. WD, *Annual Report of the Secretary of War, 1891,* pp. 343, 344; WD, Circular 54, 31 Aug. 1909; WD, GO 118, 15 June 1909; WD, GO 125, 25 June 1909.
2. HQA, AGO, GO 14, 12 Feb. 1900; Letter from Captain W. H. Miller, West Point Quartermaster, 25 Sept. 1894, to the QMG, TIOH files; Letter no. 153403 from OQMG to Philadelphia Depot, 9 Aug. 1900, box 2953, RG 92, NA; WD, *Annual Report of the Quartermaster General, 1902,* p. 26; Philadelphia inventories 153403, 15 Nov. 1900 and 15 Mar. 1901, RG 92, NA.
3. WD, *Annual Report of the Secretary of War, 1891,* pp. 343, 344; WD, GO 182, 29 Sept. 1910, sec. I; Letters and indorsements no. 246097, 1909 and 1910, RG 92, NA.
4. WD, *Specifications for the Uniform* (1913), par. 97(1); WD, Circular 72, 16 Mar. 1921, par. 11.

Chapter Thirty-Eight

1. National Defense Act of June 1920, sec. 13; Anne M. Boyd, *United States Government Publications,* p. 179; WD, Circular 130, 1942, par. I.
2. Letter for Chief, Air Service, to AEF Commander, 18 Apr. 1918, with 1st indorsement, 27 Apr. 1918, Organizational Records, Air Service, Historical Records, box 567, NA; 27 Apr. 1918 file "421-Insignia," TIOH files.
3. WD, *Order of Battle of the United States Land Forces in the World War (1917–1919)* 1: p. 21; WD, Changes 5, 17 July 1918, Special Regulation 42, par. 36(ad).

4. WD, AR 600-35, 14 Oct. 1921, par. 13c(3)(b).
5. Emerson, "U.S. Army Enlisted Cap Insignia, 1905–1918," *MC&H,* Spring 1977, pp. 22–30; J. Duncan Campbell, *Aviation Badges and Insignia of the United States Army, 1913–1946,* p. 39.
6. WD, AR 600-35, 25 Nov. 1924, par. 15c.
7. WD, AR 600-35, 14 Oct. 1921, pars. 11, 13b(2)(c), 13b(3)(b); WD, Circular 42, 5 Oct. 1925, par. 15b(2)(c); WD, AR 600-35, 31 Dec. 1926, par. 16b(2).
8. WD, Circular 42, 5 Oct. 1925; WD, AR 600-35, 22 June 1931, par. 39b(2)(b); WD, Changes 1, 1 Dec. 1928, AR 600-35, par. 14d.
9. WD, OQMG Drawing CE 4-4-30, 15 June 1936; WD, Circular 14, 16 Mar. 1938.
10. WD, OQMG Drawing CE 4-4-30, 15 June 1936; WD, Circular 130, 1942, par. I; WD, Circular 366, 1942, par. VI.
11. WD, Circular 42, 5 Oct. 1925, par. 8b; WD, AR 600-35, 31 Dec. 1926, par. 9b; WD, Changes 1, 1 Dec. 1928, AR 600-35, par. 13½; WD, AR 600-35, 22 June 1931, par. 38b; WD, Circular 87, 28 Dec. 1937, sec. II.
12. WD, Changes 1, 29 Dec. 1917, Special Regulation 41; WD, AR 600-40, 27 Sept. 1921, par. 18c.
13. Memo for the Chief of Staff from Major General Fox Connor, Asst. Chief of Staff, 4 Mar. 1926, TIOH files.
14. Campbell, *Aviation Badges and Insignia,* p. 49.
15. *Army Times,* 29 Aug. 1983, p. 2; HQ, DA, GO 6, 15 Feb. 1984.

Chapter Thirty-Nine

1. Stubbs and Connor, *Armor-Cavalry, Part II, Army National Guard,* Army Lineage Series, pp. 43–44, 46, 47, 49.
2. Ibid., p. 44; WD, "Report of the Director of Tanks Corps," *Annual Reports, 1918,* p. 1393; WD, *Order of Battle of the United States Land Forces in the World War (1917–1919)* 3: pp. 492, 493, 497, 1543, 1544; WD, *Order of Battle of the United States Land Forces in the World War, (1917–1917)* 3: p. 492.
3. WD, Changes 1, 29 Dec. 1917, Special Regulation 42, par. 36(2)(aa).
4. Memo for the Adjutant General, 19 Apr. 1918, WPD 3647-98; WD, Changes 4, 7 May 1918, Special Regulation 42, par. 36(2)(aa).
5. Dusenbury and Schwab, Inc., 1925 catalog, item 1972.
6. Stubbs and Connor, *Armor-Cavalry, Part II,* p. 58; WD, Circular 56, 25 Feb. 1942, sec. V; Letter AG 421.7 to Chief of Armored Force from the Adjutant General, 24 Apr. 1941, Subject: Distinctive Colors, Armored Force.
7. WD, Circular 49, 21 Feb. 1947, sec. I.
8. Stubbs and Connor, *Armor-Cavalry, Part II,* p. 75.
9. *The Ghosts of Patton's Third Army,* pp. 335–38.
10. Stubbs and Connor, *Armor-Cavalry, Part II,* p. 81.
11. Ibid., p. 68; WD, Changes 15, 13 Mar. 1943, AR 600-35.
12. WD, Circular 49, 21 Feb. 1947; Stubbs and Connor, *Armor-Cavalry, Part II,* p. 69.

Chapter Forty

1. WD, *Organization of the Services of Supply, AEF,* Monograph No. 7, p. 44; WD, *Order of Battle of the United States Land Forces in the World War (1917–1919)* 1: p. 13; Executive Order of 25 June 1918; WD, GO 62, 28 June 1918; WD, *Order of Battle of the United States Land Forces in the World War (1917–1919)* 3: p. 131.
2. WD, Changes 1, 29 Dec. 1917, Special Regulation 42, par. 36(ab); WD, *Order of Battle of the United States Land Forces in the World War (1917–1919)* 1: p. 25.
3. Fact Sheet TIOH, on Chemical Warfare Service Insignia, ca. 1965. AEF quartermaster price lists include officers' insignia for both the Chemical Service Section and Chemical Warfare Service on the same lists, with different prices.
4. Brooks E. Kleber and Dale Birdsell, *The Chemical Warfare Service: Chemicals in Combat,* US Army in World War II, pp. 24–25; WD, AR 600-35, 14 Oct. 1921, par. 13(b); WD, AR 600-35, 25 Nov. 1924, par. 15b(2)(h).
5. WD, Circular 15, 10 Mar. 1926; WD, AR 600-35, 31 Dec. 1926, par. 16b(2)(h).
6. WD, Circular 49, 21 Feb. 1947.
7. Unit members, *Gaz Alerte.*
8. QMG, Tentative Specification P.Q.D. 189c, 5 Jan. 1943.
9. U.S. Army Development and Readiness

Command, Fact Sheet 11-76, 10 Mar. 1976.

CHAPTER FORTY-ONE

1. *National Geographic Magazine,* Oct. 1917, p. 414; WD, Changes 1, 29 Dec. 1917, Special Regulation 42, par. 36.
2. WD, Circular 72, 16 Mar. 1921, par. 11.
3. WD, Changes 1, 29 Dec. 1917, Special Regulation 42, par. 121; Circular 72, 16 Mar. 1921, par. 11; WD, GO 33, 28 July 1922; WD, GO 26, 28 June 1923.
4. WD, AR 600-35, 25 Nov. 1924, par. 15b(2)(t).
5. WD, Circular 15, 10 Mar. 1926; WD, Circular 106, 10 Apr. 1942, sec. II; WD, Changes 10, 24 Aug. 1946, AR 600-40, par. 48e.
6. DA, AR 670-5, 28 Sept. 1959, pars. 132k and 134p.
7. DA, Changes 3, 18 Feb. 1963, AR 670-5, par. 134o; DA, Changes 13, 1 Feb. 1958, AR 670-5, par. 141p.
8. DA, Changes 13, 1 Feb. 1958, AR 670-5, par. 141p.

CHAPTER FORTY-TWO

1. WD, *Annual Report of the Chief of the Motor Transport Corps, 1919,* p. 4; WD, *Order of Battle of the United States Land Forces in the World War (1917–1919)* 3: pp. 315–16.
2. AEF, GO 37, 14 Sept. 1917; Wardlow, *The Transportation Corps,* pp. 30–32; WD, *Order of Battle of the United States Land Forces in the World War (1917–1919)* 3: p. 460; Wardlow, *The Transportation Corps,* pp. 28, 54, 55.
3. Memo for the Adjutant General from Chief of Staff, 23 Sept. 1918, Subject: Insignia of the Motor Transport Corps; WD, Changes 6, 15 Oct. 1918, Special Regulation 42; WD, *Organization of the Services of Supply, AEF,* Monograph No. 7, p. 67.
4. WD, Circular 72, 16 Mar. 1921.
5. WD, *Official Army Register,* Jan. 1938, p. 1365.
6. WD, Changes 7, 25 Jan. 1919, Special Regulation 42; Memo for Director, Operations Division, General Staff, 20 Aug. 1920, Subject: Collar Ornaments for Enlisted Men, TIOH files; WD, Changes 7, 25 Jan. 1919, Special Regulation 42; WD, *Organization of the Services of Supply, AEF,* Monograph No. 7, p. 89.
7. National Geographic Society, *Insignia and Decorations of the U.S. Armed Forces,* p. 75.
8. WD, Changes 12, 5 Feb. 1943, AR 600-35; DA, AR 670-5, Sept. 1966, par. 14-13.
9. OQMG, Tentative Specification P.Q.D. No. 189c, 5 January 1943.

CHAPTER FORTY-THREE

1. *Field Artillery Journal,* Sept.–Oct. 1976, pp. 35–36; WD, Bulletin 33, 9 Sept. 1916, pp. 9–10.
2. WD, Changes 21, 23 July 1917, WD, *Regulations for the Uniform* (1914), par. 4½.
3. WD, GO 36, 16 Apr. 1918, par. III.
4. HQ, AEF, GO 50, 27 Oct. 1917, par. 11; HQ, Philippine Department, GO 5, 4 Feb. 1918.
5. WD, AR 600-35, 14 Oct. 1921, pars. 13b(2)(aa) and (ab); WD, Changes 9, 16 Oct. 1923, AR 600-35; WD, Circular 15, 10 Mar. 1926.
6. National Defense Act of 30 June 1920, par. 4a; WD, *Order of Battle of the United States Land Forces in the World War (1917–1917)* 3: p. 79; WD, AR 600-35, 25 Nov. 1924, pars. 13a(3), 15b(2)(ab), 15b(2)(ac); WD, Circular 15, 10 Mar. 1926.
7. WD, Circular 72, 16 Mar. 1921, par. 12; WD, QMG Drawing CE-4-4-3, 27 May 1921; WD, Circular 72, 16 Mar. 1921; WD, AR 600-35, 14 Oct. 1921, par. 7b(2); WD, QMG Drawing CE-4-4-3, 27 May 1921.
8. *Army and Navy Register,* 24 Oct. 1925, p. 486, 5 Dec. 1925, p. 631, and 14 Aug. 1926, p. 151.
9. WD, Circular 384, 16 Nov. 1920; WD, Circular 72, 16 Mar. 1921; WD, Changes 9, 16 Oct. 1923, AR 600-35; WD, QMG Drawing, CE-4-4-3, 27 May 1921; WD, Circular 366, 1942, sec. VI, par. 4.
10. WD, AR 600-35, 25 Nov. 1924, par. 17a(4)–(6).
11. WD, AR 600-35, 14 Oct. 1921, pars. 15b(4), 15c; WD, Circular 98, 1941.
12. National Defense Act of 30 June 1922, par. 4a; WD, Bulletin 11, 1922, p. 69; WD, AR 600-40, 28 Aug. 1941, par. 46b(2) and figure 5.
13. WD, Circular 25, 17 Jan. 1920; WD, Circular 384, 16 Nov. 1920; WD, Circular 72, 16 Mar. 1921, par. 12.
14. WD, Changes 9, 16 Oct. 1923, AR 600-35; WD, AR 600-35, 25 Nov. 1924, par.

15b(2)(aa); WD, Circular 15, 10 Mar. 1926.

15. WD, AR 600-35, 31 Dec. 1926, par. 16b(2)(aa); WD, *Annual Report of the Chief of the Air Corps, 1931,* p. 10; *1934,* p. 7.

Chapter Forty-Four

1. *The Army Almanac,* p. 29; WD, *Order of Battle of the United States Land Forces in the World War (1917–1919)* 3: pp. 237, 368, 369, 374; WD, Changes 7, 25 Jan. 1919, Special Regulation 42; WD, *Order of Battle of the United States Land Forces in the World War (1917–1919)* 3: p. 409. WD, Circular 72, 16 Mar. 1921.
2. AEF, GO 8, 5 July 1917; AEF, GO 29, 31 Aug. 1917; AEF, GO 71, 10 Dec. 1917; WD, *American Expeditionary Forces, US Army Expeditionary Force, France, 1917, Report of the Provost Marshal General,* pp. 5–14.
3. WD, Memo for Director, Operations Division, GS, 30 Aug. 1920, Subject: Collar Ornaments for Enlisted Men, TIOH files; WD, Circular 72, 16 Mar. 1921, par. 11.
4. AEF, GO 17, 20 July 1917; WD, GO 29, 31 Aug. 1917; WD, GO 71, 10 Dec. 1917; WD, *Field Service Regulations, 1914, Corrected to January 15, 1918,* p. 180; AEF, GO 111, 8 July 1918, par. XI.
5. AEF, GO 152, 19 Sept. 1918, par. VI.
6. WD, Special Regulation 42, par. 121(b); WD, Changes 7, 23 Jan. 1919, Special Regulation 42, par. 121, WD, *Order of Battle of the United States Land Forces in the World War (1917–1919)* 2: pp. 25, 26.
7. WD, OQMG, Drawing CE-4-4-7, 16 Oct. 1921; WD, Changes 3, 20 Apr. 1922, AR 600-35; WD, AR 600-40, 27 Sept. 1921, par. 35b; WD, Circular 15, 10 Mar. 1926; WD, AR 600-35, 31 Dec. 1926, par. 16b(2)(u).
8. DA, GO 23, 20 July 1950.
9. Letter from the Center for Military History to the author, 9 July 1982.
10. Ibid.; WD, *Official National Guard Register for 1939,* p. 33.
11. DA, TIOH, Drawing No. B-2-7, 25 Feb. 1965; DA, AR 670-5, 8 Jan. 1971, pars. 14-13 and 14-13p.

Chapter Forty-Five

1. WD, Changes 5, 17 July 1917, Special Regulation 41; Memo for the Adjutant General, 28 Feb. 1918, TIOH files; Letter from Bailey, Banks and Biddle Co. to Colonel Lindsley, Philadelphia QM Depot, 23 Mar. 1918, TIOH files; WD, AR 600-35, 14 Oct. 1921, par. 13b(t); WD, AR 600-35, 25 Nov. 1924, par. 15b(2)(v); WD, Circular 15, 10 Mar. 1926.
2. WD, Changes 2, 22 Aug. 1933, AR 600-35, par. 16b(2)(v); WD, AR 600-35, 10 Nov. 1941, par. 24b(2)(s); WD, Changes 18, 29 Apr. 1943, AR 600-35; WD, Changes 25, 20 July 1943, AR 600-35; WD, Circular 49, 21 Feb. 1947.
3. WD, AR 600-40, 31 Mar. 1944, par. 49a.
4. WD, Changes 10, 1 June 1948, AR 600-35; DA, AR 670-5, 28 Sept. 1959, par. 132m; DA, Changes 1, 24 Nov. 1950, SR 140-5-3; DA, AR 670-1, Feb. 1979, par. 26-10a(27); DA, SR 140-5-3, 23 Sept. 1949.
5. National Defense Act of June 1920, chap. I, sec. 2; WD, Circular 72, 16 Mar. 1921, par. 11.
6. WD, Circlar 49, 21 Feb. 1947; DA, SR 600-60-1, 26 Oct. 1952, par. 12d; DA, SR 600-60-1, 8 Apr. 1953, pars. 10i and 12d; DA, AR 670-5, 20 Sept. 1956, pars. 141e and 139h(2).
7. DF, DAPE-HRP-P, 17 June 1976, Subject: Branch Insignia Wear Policy for Enlisted Personnel.

Chapter Forty-Six

1. WD, *Organization of the Service of Supply, AEF,* Monograph No. 2, pp. 37–39.
2. Sixth indorsement to letter from Director, ASC, APO 717, to CG, Services of Supply, 7 Dec. 1918, TIOH files; AEF, GO 198, 3 Nov. 1918; 6th indorsement to letter, from Director, ASC, APO 717, to CG, Service of Supply, 7 Dec. 1918.

Chapter Forty-Seven

1. C. Alison Scully, *The Course of the Silver Greyhound,* preface.
2. AEF, GO 199, 5 Nov. 1918, sec. V; AEF, GO 155, 13 Sept. 1918; PS&T Division memo, 311.4, 13 Dec. 1918, no subject, TIOH files.
3. Letter from Peaslee to Major James Waddell, 14 Jan. 1919, TIOH files; Memo from Lieutenant J. B. Fisher to Major Waddell, 9 Apr. 1919, and memo from George W. Burr to Colonel Wyllie, 9 Apr. 1919, TIOH files; WD, Circular 214, 10 June 1920, par. 3.

CHAPTER FORTY-EIGHT

1. Hewes, *From Root to McNamara,* p. 400; WD, *Order of Battle of the United States Land Forces in the World War (1917–1919)* 3: p. 284.
2. Captain Leonid Kondratiuk, "National Guard Insignia of Branch," *The Trading Post,* Oct–Dec. 1980; WD, AR 600-35, 25 Nov. 1924, pars. 13a(3), and 15b(2)(s); WD, AR 600-35, 14 Oct. 1921, par. 13b; WD, AR 600-35, 25 Nov. 1924, pars. 15b(2)(s) and 13b(1).
3. WD, AR 600-35, 31 Dec. 1926, pars. 14a(3) and 16b(2)(s); WD, Circular 15, 10 Mar. 1926; WD, AR 30-3000, 1 May 1933, p. 14; WD, OQMG Drawing CE 4-4-33, 15 June 1936.
4. WD, Changes 3, 10 May 1922, AR 600-35, par. 44c; WD, AR 600-40, Nov. 1924, par. 25c(3); WD, AR 600-40, Aug. 1941, par. 49c(3); WD, AR 600-40, Mar. 1944, par. 66b(3).
5. Kondratiuk, "National Guard Insignia of Branch."
6. Letter from Public Affairs Office, National Guard Bureau, 19 Dec. 1986, to the author; DF, NGB-ARP, 22 Oct. 1984, Subject: Wear of Insignia of Branch.
7. WD, AR 600-40, Sept. 1921, and regulations cited in note 4 above, this chapter; DA, SR 600-60-1, 26 Oct. 1951, par. 12p.

CHAPTER FORTY-NINE

1. WD, *Army Specialist Corps Regulations (Tentative),* 24 Mar. 1942.
2. Ibid.; WD, Changes 5, 17 July 1942, to *Army Specialist Corps Regulations (Tentative).*
3. WD, Changes 1, 15 Aug. 1942, AR 900-5; WD, Changes 5, 17 July 1942, to *Army Specialist Corps Regulations (Tentative).*
4. DF, 5 Sept. 1942, Subject: Suggested Design of Miniature Eagle Insignia, from William O. Hitchkiss to QMG, TIOH files; WD, Circulars 367 and 370, 1942.

CHAPTER FIFTY

1. Treadwell, *The Women's Army Corps,* pp. 6–10.
2. Ibid., pp. 6 and 221; HQ, DA, GO 20, 21 Nov. 1978, sec. I.
3. Risch, *A Wardrobe for the Women of the Army,* pp. 27–28.
4. Treadwell, *Women's Army Corps,* pp. 539–41; WD, AR 600-37, Apr. 1945; WD, AR 600-37, 3 Jan. 1944.

CHAPTER FIFTY-ONE

1. Memo for Commanding General, Strategic Services, SPQRD 421.4, 16 June 1943, Subject: Insignia Strategic Services, with study inclosures, from files of Charlie Edwards.

CHAPTER FIFTY-TWO

1. Hewes, *From Root to McNamara,* p. 405; WD, Circular 174, 3 July 1947; Undated fact sheet, TIOH, ca. 1963.

CHAPTER FIFTY-THREE

1. DA, AR 670-5, 20 Sept. 1956, par. 141d; DA, Changes 3, 18 Feb. 1963, AR 670-5.
2. DA, AR 670-5, 28 Sept. 1959, par. 131p.

CHAPTER FIFTY-FOUR

1. Hewes, *From Root to McNamara,* p. 402; DA, SR 140-5-3, 23 Sept. 1949.
2. DA, GO 51, 17 Aug. 1955, sec. I; Hewes, *From Root to McNamara,* pp. 224–25; DA, AR 670-5, 28 Sept. 1959, par. 131a.
3. DA, AR 670-5, 20 Sept. 1956, par. 141; DA, Changes 2, 9 Jan. 1957, AR 670-5; DA, AR 670-5, 28 Sept. 1959, par. 131a.
4. DA, AR 670-5, 8 Jan. 1971, par. 14-11n; DA, AR 670-1, 1 Nov. 1981, par. 26-9j.

CHAPTER FIFTY-FIVE

1. Fact sheet, "History and Duties of the Sergeant Major of the Army," 1 July 1983, Office of the Sergeant Major of the Army, pp. 1–2.
2. Emerson, *Chevrons,* pp. 199–202; *Army News Photo Features,* 19 July 1966, p. 1; DF, AGAH-C, 20 July 1966, Subject: Comments on the Insignia of the Sergeant Major of the Army.
3. DA, AR 670-1, 20 May 1987, par. 28-3.

CHAPTER FIFTY-SIX

1. DA, Memorandum for the Deputy Chief of Staff for Personnel, SAPA-SGM, Subject: Public Affairs Collar Insignia, 23 Jan. 1989.
2. DA, Memorandum for the Chief of Staff, Army, DAPE-MPH-S, Public Affairs Collar Insignia—Action Memorandum, 18 Oct. 1989; DA, Memorandum for Director, The Institute of Heraldry, SAPA-SGM, Subject: Public

Affairs Distinctive Collar Insignia, 5 Feb. 1990.

3. Letter AOJK-SP, Subject: Enlisted Collar Insignia for Career Management Field 37, Psychological Operations, 10 Sept. 1990, with 1st endorsement, DAPE-MPH-S, 10 Oct. 1990; TIOH drawing B-2-63, dated 19 Nov. 1990; 3d endorsement, DAPE-HR-S, 19 Dec. 1990, to letter AOJK-SP, Subject: Enlisted Collar Insignia for Career Management Field 37, Psychological Operations, 10 Sept. 1990.

Chapter Fifty-Seven

1. Conversations with Mr. A. E. Kauffman of Royal Oak, Mich., 1983. Mr. Kauffman has corresponded with num-erous 10th Mountain Division members concerning the division's World War II insignia.
2. DA, AR 670-340-8, 14 Aug. 1956; DA, AR 670-340-8, 3 Sept. 1959; DA, AR 670-10, 22 July 1969.
3. WD, GO 32, 28 July 1916; Act of Congress, 18 May 1918; WD, Changes 7, 8 Feb. 1919, Special Regulation 41, par. 49½.
4. DA, AR 145-2, 31 July 1970, pars. 2-7 and 4-2b.
5. Corps of Engineers Regulation 760-2-3, 30 Oct. 1969.
6. WD, Changes 1, 4 Sept. 1942, AR 600-35, par. 30½.
7. WD, AR 600-35, 31 Mar. 1944, par. 36; WD, AR 600-40, 31 Mar. 1944, par. 65; DA, AR 670-5, 23 Sept. 1966, par. 14-45.

Chapter Fifty-Eight

1. HQA, AGO, Order 50, 11 June 1832, p. 26.
2. *General Regulations for the Army,* 1825, pp. 158, 161; Ibid., pars. 839 and 847.
3. Greenville, 16 Feb. 1796, Michigan Historical Collections, General Wayne's Orderly Book, folio 2, vol. 34, copy in Military History Division, Smithsonian Institution; WD, *Military Laws and Rules and Regulations for the Armies of the United States,* 1 May 1813, p. 225.
4. WD, AGO, GO 36, 21 June 1839, pp. 5, 11.
5. WD, AGO, GO 50, 11 June 1832, pp. 1, 15, 26, 27.
6. Ibid.
7. HQA, AGO, GO 18, 4 June 1846, sec. VII.

Chapter Fifty-Nine

1. AGO, Order 36, 25 May 1829.
2. HQA, AGO, Order 50, 11 June 1832, pp. 5, 7–8, 13–18; WD, *Regulations for the Uniform and Dress . . .* (June 1839); HQA, AGO, GO 45, 3 October 1840.
3. WD, *General Regulations . . . 1847,* p. 215; HQA, AGO, GO 31, 12 June 1851, p. 2.
4. Ibid., pp. 8–9; WD, AGO, GO 286, 22 Nov. 1864; HQA, AGO, GO 31, 12 June 1851, pars. 2-4, 7.
5. HQA, AGO, GO 31, 12 June 1851, p. 5.
6. WD, AGO, GO 1, 20 Jan. 1854.
7. *Regulations for the Uniforms and Dress* (1851); WD, AGO, GO 1, 1854; WD, AGO, GO 3, 24 Mar. 1859, par. I,4.
8. WD, AGO, GO 92, 26 Oct. 1872, p. 7.
9. WD, *Annual Report of the Secretary of War, 1885,* plates 5 through 7; Memo for Acting Secretary of War, no. 1511986, 18 May 1909, RG 94, NA; Memo to Secretary of War, 29 Oct. 1909, TIOH files.
10. WD, AGO, GO 92, 26 Oct. 1872, pp. 13–14, 20; WD, *Regulations and Decisions* (1901), p. 19.
11. WD, AGO, GO 92, 26 Oct. 1872, p. 6; HQA, AGO, GO 76, 23 July 1879, p. 42.

Chapter Sixty

1. Fredrick P. Todd, *American Military Equippage,* 1: pp. 57–58; WD, AGO, GO 3, 24 Mar. 1858; *Military Images Magazine,* July–Aug. 1981, pp. 10–15; WD, AGO, GO 3, 24 Mar. 1858.
2. HQA, AGO, GO 45, 26 June 1883; WD, AGO, GO 92, 26 Oct. 1872; WD, GO 96, 19 Nov. 1875; HQA, AGO, GO 8, 21 Jan. 1885.
3. WD, Office of the Surgeon General, Circular 8, 1875; WD, QMGO, Specification 13, 12 Mar. 1879; HQA, AGO, GO 45, 26 June 1883.
4. Memo for the Assistant Secretary of War, 29 Jan. 1908, General Staff Report 1859, TIOH files; WD, *Annual Report of the Quartermaster General, 1912,* p. 18; U.S. Congress, *Report of the Quartermaster General,* HR Doc. 3, no. 2, vol. 2, 58th Cong., 3d sess., p. 5.
5. HQA, AGO, GO 22, 12 Apr. 1895; HQA, AGO, GO 68, 29 Sept. 1892; AGO, Circular 14, 12 Nov. 1892; *Army*

and Navy Register, 10 June 1893, p. 366; WD, *Annual Report of the Quartermaster General, 1895,* p. 33.

6. HQA, AGO, GO 76, 23 July 1879; Heitman, *Historical Register,* 1: pp. 17, 708.
7. HQA, AGO, GO 2, 6 Jan. 1900.
8. HQA, AGO, GO 132, 31 Dec. 1902, par. 18; WD, *Specifications for the Uniform . . . , 1913,* par. 14(b). Examples of use are in the Kentucky Military Museum, Frankfort, Ky. Provisions are in various editions of AR 600-40; one example is par. 1f, AR, 600-40, 31 Dec. 1926.
9. HQA, AGO, GOs 38 and 39, 7 and 9 May 1898; HQA, AGO, Circular 13, 23 May 1898.
10. HQA, AGO, GO 81, 17 July 1902, par. 20; HQA, AGO, GO 132, 31 Dec. 1902, par. 20; WD, GO 122, 13 July 1904; WD, *Annual Report of the War Department, 1905,* 2; pp. 45–46.

CHAPTER SIXTY-ONE

1. *American State Papers, V, Military Affairs* 2: p. 471; WD, *General Regulations for the Army* (1821), p. 289; Brown to Irvine, 16 Sept. 1819, Consolidated Correspondence file, box 1169, RG 92, NA.
2. WD, *General Regulations for the Army* (1821), p. 159; (1825), p. 161; (1821), p. 156; Heitman, *Historical Register* 2: pp. 578–81; WD, *General Regulations for the Army,* 1825, p. 161.
3. J. D uncan Campbell, "Notes on the Insignia of the Riflemen, U.S. Army," *MC&H,* Aug. 1949, p. 6; *American State Papers, V, Military Affairs* 3: pp. 214, 350; HQA, AGO, Order 50, 5 Apr. 1832, p. 21.
4. Discussions with Donald Kloster, Division of Military History, Smithsonian Institution; HQA, AGO, Order 100, 7 Nov. 1833; U.S. Congress. House 1834, *Report of the Commissary General of Purchases,* statements nos. 5 and 6, Doc. 2. 23d Cong., 2d sess., 1834.
5. HQA, AGO, Order 38, 2 May 1833, p. 2; HQA, AGO, GO 36, 21 June 1839, p. 24.
6. HQA, AGO, GO 18, 4 June 1846.
7. HQA, AGO, GO 31, 12 June 1851.
8. Michael J. McAfee, "U.S. Army Uniforms of the Civil War," *Military Images,* May–June 1982, pp. 10–15.
9. WD, AGO, GO 92, 26 Oct. 1872.
10. HQA, AGO, GO 31, 12 June 1851, par. 217.
11. WD, AGO, GO 124, 15 May 1863; WD, AGO, GO 111, 1864; *Smithsonian Federal Enlisted Uniforms of the Civil War,* videotape by Roberts Video Publishing Company, 1990.

CHAPTER SIXTY-TWO

1. WD, HQA, AGO, GO 31, 12 June 1851, par. 215.

CHAPTER SIXTY-THREE

1. HQA, AGO, Order 50, 11 June 1832.
2. HQA, AGO, GO 38, 2 May 1833; HQA, AGO, GO 18, 4 June 1846, pp. 2–3.
3. HQA, AGO, GO 31, 12 June 1851; WD, AGO, GO 1, 20 Jan. 1854; *Regulations for the Army of the United States, 1857,* pars. 1414, 1415; WD, AGO, GO 6, 13 Mar. 1861, p. 6.
4. WD, AGO, GO 132, 31 Dec. 1902, pars. 23, 74; WD, AR 600-38, 14 Aug. 1938, para. 40, 43.
5. WD, Circular 2, 7 Jan. 1938, sec. I.
6. DA, AR 670-5, 28 Sept. 1959, par. 27 b.

CHAPTER SIXTY-FOUR

1. Fatigue frocks are listed in tables of allowances. One example is WD, AGO, GO 64, 29 Nov. 1848, p. 2; WD, OQMG, Specification 19, 12 Mar. 1879.
2. WD, *Annual Report of the Quartermaster General, 1884,* p. 21; HQA, AGO, GO 32, 16 Apr. 1884; WD, OQMG, Specification 115, 31 May 1884; WD, OQMG, Specification 385, 9 Dec. 1895; WD, OQMG, Specification 676, 10 June 1904; WD, OQMG, Specification 116, 31 May 1884; WD, OQMG, Specification 677, 10 June 1904.
3. WD, Office Chief of QMC, Circular 11, 1 Apr. 1913, p. 6; WD, OQMG, Specification 676, 10 June 1904; WD, OQMG, Specifications 995 and 996, 24 Aug. 1908.
4. WD, OQMG, Specification 995, 24 Aug. 1908; WD, GO 37, 2 Mar. 1909; WD, Change 2, 13 Mar. 1913, Uniform Regulations of 1912; WD, Circular 37, 12 June 1909, par. II; WD, OQMG, Specifications 1273 and 1274, 20 Oct. 1917; WD, OQMG, Specification 1273A, 12 Apr. 1918; WD, OQMG, Specification 1347, 12 July 1918; WD, Specification 415-3-1346, 17 July 1919; WD, Specifi-

cation 415-3-18, 1 Aug. 1919; WD, Specification 6-124B, 22 Jan. 1937; WD, Specification 6-125A, 11 Mar. 1937.

5. WD, Specification 6-125A, 11 Mar. 1937; DA, AR 670-5, 8 Jan. 1971, chap. 4; WD, QMC Supply Catalog QM 3-1, May 1946, pp. 8, 14.
6. DA, SR 600-32-1, 30 Oct. 1952, par. 35; WD, Specification 6-125B, n.d., and Amendment 1; WD, Specification 6-124C, 31 Dec. 1940.
7. DA, Changes 3, 27 Oct. 1953, SR 600-60-1.
8. Erna Risch and Thomas Pitkin, *Clothing the Soldier of World War II,* pp. 64–67; WD, Circular 33, 28 July 1932, sec. IV; WD, Circular 96, 12 May 1941; WD, Circular 116, 12 June 1941.
9. Risch and Pitkin, *Clothing the Soldier of World War II,* p. 76.
10. WD, Changes 30, 14 Sept. 1943, AR 600-40.
11. Shelby Stanton, *U.S. Army Uniforms in the Vietnam War,* p. 113.
12. *Army Times,* 14 Oct. 1985, p. 10.
13. Stanton, *U.S. Army Uniforms in Vietnam,* pp. 9–10.
14. Risch and Pitkin, *Clothing the Soldier of World War II,* pp. 54–55; Stanton, *U.S. Army Uniforms in the Vietnam War,* pp. 225–26.

Chapter Sixty-Five

1. HQA, AGO, GO 18, 4 June 1846, p. 5; WD, *General Regulations . . . , 1847,* pp. 193, 198.
2. DA, SR 600-32-1, 30 Oct. 1952, pars. 14c, 15c.
3. *Regulations for the Uniforms and Dress* (1851), p. 10 and plate 20; WD, AGO, GO 6, 13 Mar. 1861, p. 15; M. J. McAfee, "U.S. Army Uniforms of the Civil War, Part V, The Overcoat," *Military Images,* Sept.–Oct. 1982.
4. HQA, AGO, Order 50, 11 June 1832, pp. 9–14, 16–18; HQA, AGO, GO 36, 21 June 1839, p. 18; WD, *General Regulations . . . , 1841,* pp. 380, 382; WD, *General Regulations . . . , 1847,* pp. 89, 192, 195, 201, 202, 205.
5. WD, GO 6, 13 Mar. 1861, p. 15; *Regulations for the Uniforms and Dress* (1851), p. 10 and plate 20; WD, *Regulations for the Uniform and Dress . . . July 1872,* p. 17; WD, OQMC Specifications 9 of 1880, 108 of 1884, 118 of 1884, 148 of 1885, 245 of 1889, 264 of 1889, 436 of 1897, 445 of 1897, and 448 of 1898.
6. Emerson, *Chevrons,* p. 60; WD, AGO, GO 92, 26 Oct. 1872, pp. 16–17; WD, *Uniform of the Army of the United States, 1882,* pars. 2703–2706; WD, *Regulations for the Uniform . . . , 1888,* pars. 2703–2706; HQA, AGO, GO 76, 23 July 1879, p. 36.
7. Letter, Alfred A. Woodhull to Surgeon General, printed by the Surgeon General, 31 Jan. 1868, (hereafter cited as Woodhull Report.) Gordon Chappell, *The Search for the Well-Dressed Soldier, 1865–1890,* pp. 27, 29, 32; WD, OQMG, Specification 6, 12 Mar. 1879; WD, OQMG, Specification 25, 12 Mar. 1879. Various annual reports of the quartermaster general list inventories of buffalo overshoes.
8. HQA, AGO, GO 76, 23 July 1879, p. 37; WD, *Annual Report of the Quartermaster General, 1884,* p. 308; WD, OQMG, Specification 95, 24 Oct. 1883.
9. HQA, AGO, GO 132, 31 Dec. 1902, pars. 21, 72; WD, OQMG Specification 629, 18 May 1903; WD, OQMG Specification 762, 26 Sept. 1904; WD, *Specifications for the Uniform . . . , 1913,* par. 38; WD, OQMC, Specifications 863 and 864, 15 May 1907; WD, GO 108, 29 June 1908, p. 4.
10. WD, GO 169, 14 Aug. 1907, par. 57(e); WD, *Regulations for the Uniform of the United States Army* (1911), par. 84(b); WD, Changes 1, 29 Dec. 1917, Special Regulation 42, p. 4; WD, Circular 8, 1 Feb. 1926, p. 6.
11. *Regulations for the Uniforms and Dress* (1851), p. 10; WD, *Uniform of the Army . . . 1882,* pars. 2703–2706; HQA, AGO, GO 132, 31 Dec. 1902, pars. 21, 72; WD, AR 600-35, 31 Mar. 1944, par. 16a(2); DA, SR 600-40-1, 22 June 1949; WD, *Regulations for the Uniform of the United States Army* (1911), n. 1 to par. 84; WD, Circular 60, 20 Oct. 1926; WD, AR 600-40, 31 Dec. 1926, pars. 41, 42a.
12. WD, AR 600-40, 27 Sept. 1921, par. 40c.
13. C. G. Sweeting, *Combat Flying Clothing,* pp. 1, 24, 56; WD, Special Regulation 41, 15 Aug. 1917; pars. 6, 9, 75(b), 83, 86, 99.
14. WD, Special Regulation 41, 15 Aug. 1917, par. 103(d); WD, Changes 1, 29 Dec. 1917, Special Regulation 41, par.

103(e).

15. WD, AR 600-35, 14 Oct. 1921, par. 5; WD, Circular 19, 19 Mar. 1926, sec. V; WD, Circular 8, 1 Feb. 1926, pp. 4, 5; WD, AR 600-35, 31 Dec. 1926, par. 5d(I)(d); WD, Changes 24, 25 June 1943, AR 600-35; Risch and Pitkin, *Clothing the Soldier of World War II,* p. 63; WD, Circular 1, 5 Jan. 1931, sec. I.
16. Risch and Pitkin, *Clothing the Soldier of World War II,* pp. 60–64; WD, Circular 64, 11 Feb. 1944; Risch and Pitkin, *Clothing the Soldier of World War II,* pp. 60–62; WD, Change 9, 26 Nov. 1942, AR 600-40.
17. Thomas M. Pitkin, *Quartermaster Equipment for Special Forces,* QMC Historical Studies No. 5, pp. 10–42.
18. WD, AR 600-35, 10 Nov. 1941, par. 9b(2) and fig. 7; WD, Changes 16, 3 Apr. 1943, AR 600-35; DA, SR 600-32-1, 11 Apr. 1951, par. 42; WD, Changes 21, 3 June 1943, AR 600-35.
19. DA, Circular 89, 1 Apr. 1948, n.3; DA, SR 600-40-1, 22 June 1949, par. 12.

Chapter Sixty-Six

1. WD, AGO, GO 13, 15 Aug. 1855, par. 15; WD, AGO, GO 6, 13 Mar. 1861, par. 123.
2. Annual clothing price lists show slickers for the first time in WD, GO 140, 25 June 1907; WD, GO 108, 29 June 1908, p. 1.
3. Paul J. Schultz, Hayes Otoupalik, and Dennis Gordon, *World War One Collectors Handbook,* pp. 2, 6; Risch and Pitkin, *Clothing the Soldier of World War II,* pp. 84–86.
4. WD, AR 600-40, 31 Mar. 1944, par. 33c; *The Officer's Guide* (1948), p. 81; DA, AR 670-5, 28 Sept. 1959, par. 110; Stephen J. Kennedy and Alice F. Park, *The Army Green Uniform,* pp. 19–20; DA, AR 670-5, 8 Jan. 1971, p. 13-4.
5. *Army Times,* 23 Oct. 1978, p. 8; DA, AR 670-5, 8 Jan. 1971, par. 14-10c and fig. 14-83; USA SPT ACTV PHILA PA message, STSAP-S, Subject: Interim Change to AR 670-5, 171000Z Nov. 1977.
6. WD, Changes 12, 15 June 1915, Uniforms Regulations, 1914; WD, AR 600-40, 31 Mar. 1944, par. 13.
7. Pitkin, *Quartermaster Equipment for Special Forces,* p. 15.
8. WD, AR 30-3000, 3 June 1940; WD, AR 30-3000, 4 Aug. 1941.
9. WD, GO 147, 3 Nov. 1911, sec. I, par. 2; WD, *Regulations for the Uniform of the United States Army* (1911), par. 84(c); WD, Special Regulation 42, pars. 58, 146; WD, Special Regulation 41, pars. 96, 123.
10. *Army Times,* 20 Apr. 1981; *Army Times,* 27 Oct. 1980; DARCOM message DRCPT-MT, 171630 Jun 81. *Army Times,* 19 Oct. 1981, p. 34.
11. Pitkin, *Quartermaster Equipment for Special Forces,* pp. 80–82.
12. DA, AR 670-5, 8 Jan. 1971, par. 13-20.
13. DA, AR 670-1, 1 Nov. 1981, par. 11-26; DA message DAPE-MPH-S, Subject: Black Windbreaker, 211000Z Nov. 1989.
14. DA message DAPE-MPH-S, Subject: Black Windbreaker, 211000Z Nov. 1989.

Chapter Sixty-Seven

1. WD, OQMG, Specification 76, 16 Feb. 1881; HQA, AGO, GO 4, 7 Jan. 1881; WD, OQMG Specification 79, 24 Feb. 1882; WD, *Annual Report of the Quartermaster General, 1883,* p. 57; HQA, AGO, GO 45, 26 June 1883; WD, OQMG, Specification 97, 26 Nov. 1883.
2. WD, AGO, Circular 26, 26 July 1898; WD, OQMG, Specification 502, 14 Feb. 1900; WD, OQMG, Specification 570, 25 Mar. 1902; WD, *Annual Report of the Quartermaster General to the Secretary of War, 1902,* pp. 6–7; WD, GO 169, 14 Aug. 1907, par. 100.
3. WD, AR 600-35, 25 Nov. 1924, pars. 9, 13b; Risch and Pitkin, *Clothing the Soldier of World War II,* p. 44.
4. Risch and Pitkin, *Clothing the Soldier of World War II,* pp. 31–32; WD, Circular 10, 19 Feb. 1935, sec. I.
5. DA, SR 600-40-1, 22 June 1949, par. 14b; DA, AR 670-5, 20 Sept. 1956, p. 25; HQ, DA, Circular 670-1, 7 Feb. 1966.
6. DA, AR 670-5, 30 Jan. 1975, par. 6-8; DA message DAPE-HCP-U, 151755 Z Mar. 1985, Subject: Uniform Phase Out and Possession Dates; DA, Interim Change 102, 20 July 1979, AR 670-1; *Army Times,* 23 Sept. 1985.
7. *Army Times,* 14 Aug. 1978; 2 Apr., 21 May, and 26 June 1979; DA, Interim Change 102, 20 July 1979, AR 670-1; DA message DAPE-MPM-S, 231630Z

Dec 88, Subject: Wear of Awards on the AG 415 Shirt; DA message DAPE-ZX, 131446Z Jan 89, Subject: Wear of Awards and Decorations on the Army Green 415 Shirt.

8. WD, *Regulations for the Uniform* (1914), par. 82; WD, Changes 18, 30 Dec. 1916, Uniform Regulations 1914, par. 82; Memo for the Chief of Staff, 8647-17, 24 Nov. 1916.
9. Memo for the Chief of Staff, Equip. 1265, 23 Aug. 1918; WD, Changes 6, 28 Oct. 1918, Special Regulation 41, par. 93.
10. WD, AR 600-35, 14 Oct. 1921, par. 11b; WD, AR 600-35, 31 Dec. 1926, par. 14b; WD, Changes 2, 25 Aug. 1942, AR 600-40.
11. WD, Changes 18, 30 Dec. 1916, *Regulations for the Uniform* (1914), par. 82b; WD, AR 600-40, 25 Nov. 1924, par. 39a(4); WD, AR 600-40, 31 Dec. 1926, par. 40.
12. DA, Changes 11, 24 Nov. 1947, AR 600-40, par. 52d; DA, AR 670-5, 23 Sept. 1966, pp. 5-1, 5-2, 14-8, 14-27; DA, Change 1, 11 Aug. 1975, AR 670-5, fig. 14-6.
13. WD, AR 600-40, 31 Dec. 1926, par. 11a(2)(a)6; WD, AR 600-40, 22 June 1931, par. 11a(2)(a)6; WD, Circular 3, 13 Jan. 1936, sec. I.
14. WD, AR 600-40, 31 Dec. 1926, par. 8a(2)(a)6.
15. DA, AR 670-5, 30 Jan. 1975, App. A.
16. DA, SR 600-32-1, 30 Oct. 1952, par. 36; DA, AR 670-5, 30 Jan. 1975, chap. 14, sec. II.

CHAPTER SIXTY-EIGHT

1. HQA, AGO, GO 39, 9 May 1898; *Army and Navy Register,* 2 July 1898, p. 11.
2. WD, AGO, GO 122, 6 Aug. 1898, sec. II; WD, *Annual Reports of the War Department, 1901,* vol. I, part 2: p. 318; WD, *Regulations and Decisions* (1899), p. 10; WD, AGO, Circular 15, 4 June 1898; HQA, AGO, GO 51, 23 May 1898; HQA, AGO, GO 97, 20 May 1899; WD, *Regulations and Decisions* (1901), p. 35; HQA, AGO, GO 39, 9 May 1898.
3. WD, *Regulations and Decisions* (1899), p. 10; WD, AGO, Circular 15, 4 June 1898; WD, OQMG, Specification 631, 6 June 1903.
4. WD, *Annual Report of the Quartermaster General, 1912,* p. 17; HQ, Philippine Division, GO 9, 2 Feb. 1912; HQ, Philippine Division, GO 46, 18 June 1912.
5. HQA, AGO, GO 39, 9 May 1898.
6. HQA, AGO, GO 132, 31 Dec. 1902, par. 69; WD, GO 197, 31 Dec. 1904, par. 70; *Army and Navy Register,* 11 Mar. 1905, p. 5; WD, Circular 78, 17 Nov. 1909; WD, *Regulations for the Uniform of the United States Army* (1911), par. 80(d).
7. HQA, AGO, GO 132, 31 Dec. 1902, par. 69.

CHAPTER SIXTY-NINE

1. WD, *Annual Report of the Secretary of War, 1902,* p. 29; HQA, AGO, GO 132, 31 Dec. 1902, p. 1, and par. 20; Letter to Assistant Secretary of War from QMG, 15 June 1904, TIOH files; WD, *Annual Report of the Quartermaster General, 1904,* pp. 6–7.
2. WD, OQMG, Specification 609, 14 Apr. 1903; WD, OQMG, Specification 1126, 15 Aug. 1911.
3. WD, GO 197, 31 Dec. 1904, pp. 1, 10; WD, GO 169, 14 Aug. 1907, p. 14.
4. GHQ, AEF, Bulletin 42, 29 June 1918, par. 1; WD, AR 600-40, 27 Sept. 1921, par. 55(a); WD, AR 600-35, 14 Oct. 1921, par. 5a; WD, Changes 9, 16 Oct. 1923, AR 600-35, par. 5a(1).
5. WD, *Annual Report of Major General George W. Davis . . . , Division of the Philippines* (1903), p. 66; Letter to QMG from TAG, 4 Jan. 1904, TIOH files; WD, GO 197, 31 Dec. 1904; WD, OQMG, Specification 742, 18 Feb. 1905.
6. Letter from assistant chief of staff, 22 Apr. 1907, TIOH files; WD, "Report of the Quartermaster General," *Report of the Secretary of War, 1907,* 2: p. 45; WD, Circular 78, 17 Nov. 1909; WD, *Regulations for the Uniform of the United States Army* (1911), par. 80(d).
7. HQA, AGO, GO 132, 31 Dec. 1902, pp. 1, 10, 53; WD, GO 197, 31 Dec. 1904, pp. 1, 23; WD, Circular 85, 19 Feb. 1919; WD, Changes 9, 16 Oct. 1923, AR 600-35.
8. WD, Circular 8, 1 Feb. 1926; *The Pennsylvanian Guardsman Monthly,* Jan. 1930, p. 5; author's general observation of photographs.
9. WD, *Annual Reports of the Secretary of War, 1909,* 2: p. 35; WD, OQMG, Specification 1059, 17 Mar. 1910.
10. WD, *Regulations for the Uniform of the*

United States Army (1911), par. 80c, and WD, Special Regulation 42, par. 121, are two examples.

11. WD, *Regulations for the Uniform* (1912), par. 71. Annual price lists indicated khaki chevrons would be issued until exhausted. For example, see GO 32, 24 Apr. 1914, p. 4; Emerson, *Chevrons,* pp. 184–86.

Chapter Seventy

1. WD, Special Regulation 105, 6 Dec. 1918.
2. WD, Circular 42, 5 Oct. 1925; WD, Circular 8, 1 Feb. 1926.
3. WD, AR 600-35, 31 Dec. 1926, par. 1c(1).
4. Ibid., par. 5a(1); WD, Circular 10, 22 Jan. 1940; Risch and Pitkin, *Clothing the Soldier of World War II,* pp. 36–39, 55–57.
5. The Lilley-Ames Co. catalog 362; WD, AR 600-40, 28 Aug. 1941, par. 2a(1)(a); DA, SR 600-32-1, 11 Apr. 1951, pars. 4a and 26b.
6. WD, Changes 6, 26 Nov. 1942, AR 600-35; DA, SR 600-40-1, June 1949, p. 5.
7. WD, AR 600-35, 25 Nov. 1924, par. 3b.
8. WD, AR 600-35, 31 Dec. 1926, par. 5a(1)(b); WD, Circular 8, 1 Feb. 1926; WD, AR 600-35, 14 Oct. 1921, par. 5a(4); WD, Changes 3, 18 Apr. 1945, AR 600-35; DA, SR 600-40-1, 22 June 1949, p. 6.
9. X. S. Barnes, "Uniforming the Army: A Study of Enlisted Men's Items," Philadelphia QM Depot, typed manuscript dated May 1945 in the Fort Benjamin Harrison Library; U.S. Army, Specification No. 6-66A, 2 Oct. 1936; Risch and Pitkin, *Clothing the Soldier of World War II,* p. 45.
10. WD, Circular 108, 12 Apr. 1942, sec. II; WD, AR 600-35, 31 Mar. 1944, par. 9b(2)(e); DA, SR 600-32-1, 11 Apr. 1951, pp. 6–7; DA, AR 670-5, 23 Sept. 1966, par. 6-1.
11. Risch and Pitkin, *Clothing the Soldier of World War II,* pp. 56–59.
12. Sweeting, *Combat Flying Clothing,* pp. 59–60.
13. WD, Circular 391, 30 Sept. 1944, sec. VII, par. 2b; WD, Circular 1, 1 Jan. 1945, sec. IV; WD Circular 294, 27 Sept. 1945; Jacket in collection of Paul F. Braddock bearing label, "Service coat officers, U.S.A.E.T.O. Specfn No. U/118500," shown in Fig. 70-19.
14. DA, Changes 4, Sept. 1950, SR 600-40-1, par. 3a.
15. WD, Circular 177, 15 June 1945, sec. VI; WD, Circular 294, 27 Sept. 1945, sec. XI; WD, Circular 100, 18 Apr. 1947; DA, Changes 3, 23 June 1950, SR 600-40-1, par. 3b.
16. DA, Mil-Specification J-1080(QMC).
17. Kennedy and Park, *The Army Green Uniform,* pp. 5, 8.
18. Ibid., p. 13.
19. *Army Times,* 30 Oct. 1989, p. 4.

Chapter Seventy-One

1. WD, Circular 244, 16 Sept. 1921.
2. WD, Circular 6, 2 Jan. 1943, sec. IV, par. 1; WD, Circular 83, 31 Mar. 1947, sec. I; WD, Circular 204, 2 Aug. 1947, sec. II.
3. WD, Circular 15, 10 Mar. 1926, sec. I, par. 3b(2); WD, Circular 16, 28 Mar. 1928, sec. II.
4. DA, Changes 11, 24 Nov. 1947, AR 600-40, pars. 51d, 67d(2)(b); WD, Circular 355, 3 Dec. 1946; DA, SR 600-40-1, 22 June 1949, par. 14b; DA, SR 600-60-1, 26 Oct. 1951, p. 46.
5. DA, AR 670-5, Changes 4, 12 Oct. 1963, par. 26c(1).
6. WD, AR 600-35, 31 Dec. 1926, pars. 5a(1)(c), 5a(2)(c).
7. DA, SR 600-60-1, 26 Oct. 1951, pp. 44–45; WD, AR 600-40, 31 Dec. 1926, par. 39b(2).
8. WD, Circular 294, 27 Sept. 1945, sec. XI; DA, SR 600-60-1, 26 Oct. 1951, pp. 44–45.

Chapter Seventy-Two

1. Howell and Kloster, *United States Army Headgear to 1854,* pp. 2–3.
2. Ibid.; WD, *Military Laws and Rules and Regulations for the Armies of the United States,* 1 May 1813, p. 225; WD, *Dress of the General Staff and Regimental Officers.*
3. Howell, *United States Army Headgear, 1855–1902,* pp. 80–83.
4. WD, *Uniform of the Army of the United States, Illustrated, from 1774 to 1889,* p. 3; Howell and Kloster, *United States Army Headgear to 1854,* p. 13.
5. Howell and Kloster, *United States Army Headgear to 1854,* 9; Notice signed by Secretary of War Henry Dearborn, 21 May 1808, Consolidated Correspon-

dence File, box 1169, RG 92, NA; Howell and Kloster, *United States Army Headgear to 1854,* pp. 10, 13.

6. Notice signed by Secretary of War Henry Dearborn, 21 May 1808, Consolidated Correspondence File, box 1169, RG 92, NA.
7. Adjutant and Inspector General's Office, *Military Laws, Rules and Regulations for the Army . . .* Sept. 1816, p. 131.
8. WD, *General Regulations for the Army* (1821), article 65.
9. Howell and Kloster, *United States Army Headgear to 1854,* pp. 26–30.
10. Ibid., pp. 31–35.
11. Howell, *United States Army Headgear, 1855–1902,* pp. 22–28.
12. Howell and Kloster, *United States Army Headgear to 1854,* pp. 22–25.
13. James C. Frasca, "Regulation Headgear," *North South Trader,* Nov.–Dec. 1981, pp. 26–29; WD, GO 18, AGO, 4 June 1846, sec. VI.
14. WD, GO 92, AGO, 26 Oct. 1872.
15. Howell, *United States Army Headgear, 1855–1902,* p. 20; Letter with three indorsements from Philadelphia Depot no. 3028 to WD, 14 Dec. 1872, RG 92, NA; AGO, GO 67, 25 June 1873; AGO, GO 8, 8 Feb. 1877.
16. Howell and Kloster, *United States Army Headgear to 1854,* pp. 56–58; WD, AGO, GO 25, 23 Aug. 1850.
17. Howell and Kloster, *United States Army Headgear to 1854,* pp. 59–68; Frasca, "Regulation Headgear," pp. 30–31; WD, AGO, GO 1, 20 Jan. 1854.
18. Howell, *United States Army Headgear, 1855–1902,* pp. 1–12.

Chapter Seventy-Three

1. Howell, *United States Army Headgear, 1855–1902,* pp. 35–36.
2. WD, GO 92, 11 Oct. 1872; Howell, *United States Army Headgear, 1855–1902,* pp. 62ff; WD, AGO, GO 92, 11 Oct. 1872.
3. HQA, GO 4, 7 Jan. 1881; HQA, AGO, GO 76, 23 July 1879, p. 38; WD, *Regulations of the Army of the United States,* [as Amended, to 1881]; HQA, GO 4, 7 Jan. 1881.
4. HQA, GO 4, 7 Jan. 1881; Howell, *United States Army Headgear, 1855–1902,* pp. 63–64; WD, *Annual Report Quartermaster General, 1881,* illustrations and specifications enclosed with report.
5. Gordon Chappell, *Brass Spikes and Horsehair Plumes.*
6. WD, *Regulations and Decisions* (1901), par. 3.
7. HQA, AGO, GO 72, 1880; Chappell, *Summer Helmets of the U.S. Army, 1875–1910,* p. 19.
8. Howell, *United States Army Headgear, 1855–1902,* pp. 83–88.
9. HQA, AGO, GO 132, 31 Dec. 1902, pp. 13–14.
10. WD, *Annual Report of the Quartermaster General, 1896,* p. 5; *Army and Navy Register,* 11 Mar. 1905, p. 5.
11. WD, GO 197, 31 Dec. 1904, pars. 80–81.
12. WD, Changes 1, 29 Dec. 1917, Special Regulation 42, par. 100.
13. WD, Circular 9, 20 Feb. 1930, sec. III.
14. DA, Changes 1, 17 Dec. 1956, AR 670-5, appendix notes.
15. Letter, L.S. 201, 1894, Fort Monroe, Virginia, to TAG, 10 July 1894, TIOH files; AGO, GO 39, 2 Apr. 1900; WD, GO 193, 15 Nov. 1905.
16. Howell, *United States Army Headgear, 1855–1902,* pp. 52–62.
17. Emerson, "U.S. Army Campaign Hat Insignia, 1890–1907," *MC&H* 29, no. 4: pp. 158–62.
18. Leroy Ross and William K. Emerson, "Hat Cords of the U.S. Army," *MC&H* 28, no. 4: pp. 148–53.
19. WD, *Report of the Quartermaster General, 1912,* p. 30; Risch and Pitkin, *Clothing the Soldier of World War II,* pp. 77–78.
20. DA, AR 670-5, 23 Sept. 1966, par. 13-8.

Chapter Seventy-Four

1. AEF, GO 64, 29 Apr. 1918, sec. IX; AEF, GO 149, 4 Sept. 1918.
2. WD, Circular 42, 5 Oct. 1925; WD, AR 600-35, 31 Dec. 1926, par. 9b; WD, Circular 11, 3 Mar. 1930; WD, *Annual Report of the Quartermaster General, FY 1930,* p. 36.
3. WD, Circular 19, 15 Apr. 1933; WD, Minutes of Quartermaster Technical Committee, 7 Oct. 1933; WD, Circular 57, 27 Nov. 1933; WD, Changes 2, 22 Aug. 1933, AR 600-35, par. 9b; WD, Circular 87, 28 Dec. 1937; WD, Circular 2, 6 Jan. 1939.
4. WD, Specification 8-114, 25 July 1938.
5. WD, Circular 157, 26 Dec. 1940.

6. WD, Specification 8-114A, 19 Feb. 1941.
7. Risch and Pitkin, *Clothing the Soldier of World War II,* pp. 78–80; WD, Circular 49, sec. II, 25 Mar. 1941.
8. Risch and Pitkin, *Clothing the Soldier of World War II,* pp. 77–78.
9. DOD, MIL-C-1911, 9 Jan. 1950, "Military Specification, Cap, Field, Cotton, OD with visor (Army)."
10. Stanton, *U.S. Army Uniforms of the Vietnam War,* p. 37; DOD, MIL-C-1911H, 26 Aug. 1982, "Military Specification, Cap Camouflage Pattern."
11. Numerous regulations list this requirement. One example is DA, AR 670-5, 8 Jan. 1971, par. 14-3e.
12. DA, AR 670-1, 20 May 1987, par. 3-5b.
13. WD, Changes 30, 14 Sept. 1943, AR 600-40; WD, AR 600-40, Changes 30, 14 Sept. 1943; Military Specification H 3364D, 13 Dec. 1978.
14. Stanton, *U.S. Army Uniforms of the Vietnam War,* pp. 41–46; DOD, MIL-H-43577 series, "Military Specification for Hats, Sun, Hot Weather."
15. Stanton, *U.S. Army Uniforms of the Vietnam War,* pp. 49–53.
16. HQ, U.S. Army, Europe, and Seventh Army, Letter, AWAGA-MM, Subject: Exceptions to Uniform Policy, 14 Mar. 1978.
17. *Army Times,* 3 July 1978, pp. 6, 36; DA Message DAPE-HPL, 251925 Z Aug. 1978; *Army Times,* 18 Sept. 1978, p. 3; 23 October 1978, p. 4; *Stars and Stripes* (European edition), Dec. 14, 1978, p. 1; *Army Times,* 25 Dec. 1978, p. 1; *Detroit Free Press,* 30 Nov. 1980, p. 4A; *Army Times,* 8 Dec. 1980, p. 1; DA Message, DRCPT-MT, 171630Z June 1981.
18. Benedict Crowell, *America's Munitions, 1917–1918,* pp. 222–24.
19. DA, AR 670-5, 28 Sept. 1959, pp. 52, 73.

Chapter Seventy-Five

1. Risch, *A Wardrobe for the Women of the Army,* pp. 22–24, 62, 64.
2. Treadwell, *The Women's Army Corps,* p. 530; WD, Circular 174, 4 May 1944; Treadwell, *The Women's Army Corps,* p. 158; DA, Changes 4, 12 Jan. 1953, SR 600-37-2.
3. Risch, *A Wardrobe for the Women of the Army,* pp. 99–100, 106–10.
4. DA, SR 600-37-2, 17 July 1951, pp. 9–10, 29; DA, Changes 7, 13 June 1957, SR 600-37-2.
5. DA, Changes 4, 5 July 1962, AR 670-30; *Army Times* (European edition), 14 Aug. 1978, p. 4.
6. DA, Changes 4, 5 July 1962, AR 670-30; DA, Changes 1, 14 Oct. 1969, AR 670-30.
7. DA, Change 6, 13 May 1954, SR 600-37-2; Changes 4, 12 Jan. 1953, SR 600-37-2; DA, AR 670-30, 20 Oct. 1959; DA, AR 670-32, 29 Jan. 1960; DA, Changes 4, 5 July 1962, AR 670-30.
8. DA Message DAPA-DW, Subject: Changes to AR 670-30, 201030 Z June 1975.
9. DA, Changes 6, 2 July 1963, AR 670-30; DA, AR 670-30, 25 Aug. 1966, par. 22.
10. DA, AR 670-1, 15 Feb. 1979, chaps. 12, 16.
11. DA, AR 670-30, 13 May 1969, par. 16-5a(1); DA, AR 670-1, 15 Feb. 1979, p. 26-6; DA, AR 670-1, 16 Jan. 1986, par. 7-2,c,(6).
12. *Army Times,* 16 Jan. 1984, pp. 1, 2; DA Message DAPE-HRP-U, Subject: Wear of the Female Garrison Cap, 122031 Z June 84; *Army Times,* 19 Nov. 1984, p. 51.
13. DA, AR 670-30, 24 Oct. 1975; *Army Times,* 4 Oct. 1976, p. 4.
14. DA, AR 670-30, 24 Oct. 1975, par. 1-3(c); *Army Times,* 4 June 1979, p. 4; U.S. Army, Europe, Message AEAPA-CI, Subject: Mandatory Uniform Wear Dates-Female Service Members, 052105 Z July 79; *Army Times,* 4 July 1983, p. 32; DA Message DALO-TST-B, Subject: Army Clothing and Equipment Board, 152053 Z Dec. 83.
15. *Army Times,* 9 Jan. 1984, pp. 1 and 2.

Chapter Seventy-Six

1. WD, OQMG, Specification 628, 6 May 1903; HQA, AGO, GO 132, 31 Dec. 1902, par. 67; *Army and Navy Register,* 11 Mar. 1903, p. 5; WD, GO 197, 31 Dec. 1904, p. 52.
2. WD, GO 49, 28 Mar. 1917; WD, Circular 5, 26 Jan. 1929, sec. III, par. 3; WD Specification 8-89, Dec. 1930, p. 3; WD press release dated 10 Oct. 1936. TIOH files contain copies of more than fifty letters dated during the period June through Sept. 1916, responding to a WD request

for information on use of the dress blue uniform. The vast majority of letters recommend discarding the uniform and cite infrequent use as the main reason.

3. HQA, AGO, GO 132, 31 Dec. 1902, pars. 18, 17.
4. Ibid., pars. 34, 35; HQA, AGO, GO 36, 21 Mar. 1903; HQA, AGO, GO 132, 31 Dec. 1902, par. 17; WD, GO 47, 6 Apr. 1911.
5. HQA, AGO, GO 27, 17 Mar. 1902; HQA, AGO, GO 132, 31 Dec. 1902, p. 7; WD, *Annual Report of the Quartermaster General, 1911,* p. 28; WD, *Regulations for the Uniform* (1912), par. 15(f); WD, GO 49, 28 Apr. 1917, sec. III; WD, GO 169, 14 Aug. 1907, p. 11.
6. WD, Circular 5, 26 Jan. 1929, sec. II; WD, Circular 66, 15 Oct. 1936.
7. WD, Circular 66, 15 Oct. 1936.
8. WD, Circular 7, 21 Jan. 1937; WD, Circular 75, 1940, sec. II; WD, Circular 90, 1 Apr. 1943, sec. III. Actual suspension of the blue uniform ended with WD Circular 274, 10 Sept. 1946, although wear did not really start until DA, Circular 31, 29 Oct. 1947, sec. IV.
9. DA, AR 670-5, 20 Sept. 1956, sec. VIII.
10. WD, Press release, 10 Oct. 1936. Suspension of the uniform is based on a general observation of photographs. One example is in National Geographic Society, *Insignia and Decorations of the U.S. Armed Forces,* p. 191; WD, Circular 101, 12 Apr. 1943, par. I.
11. DA, AR 670-5, 20 Sept. 1956, sec. VIII.

CHAPTER SEVENTY-SEVEN

1. WD, *Annual Report of the Quartermaster General, 1888,* p. 17; WD, QMGO, Specification 267, July 1889. WD, OQMG, Specification 368, 17 Oct. 1895; WD, OQMG, Specification 463, 28 Mar. 1899.
2. HQA, AGO, GO 2, 6 Jan. 1900.
3. WD, GO 169, 14 Aug. 1907, par. 101; WD, Circular 60, 29 Aug. 1907; WD, GO 93, 27 May 1908; WD, Changes 5, 12 Mar. 1914, Uniform Regulations of 1912.
4. WD, *Regulations and Decisions* (1897), p. 7; HQA, AGO, GO 22, 12 Apr. 1895; HQA, AGO, GO 2, 6 Jan. 1900, p. 1; HQA, AGO, GO 132, 31 Dec. 1902, par. 19; HQ, Philippine Department, GO 18, 27 Mar. 1918, p. 3.
5. WD, Circular 48, 25 July 1936; WD, Circular 75, 20 July 1940, sec. II.
6. DA, AR 670-5, 20 Sept. 1956, par. 116b; DA, Changes 4, SR 600-32-11, 16 Jan. 1956.

CHAPTER SEVENTY-EIGHT

1. HQA, AGO, GO 81, 17 July 1902, p. 35; HQA, AGO, GO 132, 31 Dec. 1902, pp. 23–24.
2. HQA, AGO, GO 132, 31 Dec. 1902, par. 54; WD, GO 169, 14 Aug. 1907, par. 58.
3. WD, AR 600-38, 17 Aug. 1938, pars. 10, 24.
4. DA, SR 600-38-1, 10 Dec. 1948, pars. 1, 2c, 2i, 2l; DA, AR 670-5, Jan. 1975, par. 12-2; DA, SR 600-38-1, 24 Mar. 1950, par. 2c(3).
5. DA, AR 670-1, 15 Feb. 1979, chap. 9.
6. HQA, AGO, GO 132, 31 Dec. 1902, par. 55; WD, *Specifications for the Uniform, 1913,* par. 35.
7. WD, AR 600-38, 17 Aug. 1938, par. 30; DA, SR 600-32-10, 5 Sept. 1952.
8. DA, AR 670-5, 30 Jan. 1975, pars. 10-5d(2), 11-5e(2) and (3), and fig. 11-3.
9. *Army Times,* 21 May 1979, p. 28; DA, AR 670-1, 1 Nov. 1981, chap. 8.
10. Proceeding of Equipment Board, 10 Oct. 1905, no. 221296, on file, TIOH; WD, *Regulations for the Uniform of the United States Army* (1911), par. 17.
11. WD, Circular 25, 17 Jan. 1920; WD, Circular 64, 25 Sept. 1937; WD, Circular 52, 17 Nov. 1931, sec. I; DA, SR 600-32-11, 5 Sept. 1952, par. 24c(3); DA, Interim Change Number 101, 1 Dec. 1981, to AR 670-1.
12. HQA, AGO, GO 132, 31 Dec. 1902, pars. 54, 55; WD, GO 169, 14 Aug. 1907, par. 59; WD, *Regulations for the Uniform of the United States Army* (1911), Part III, Special Evening Dress table, item 7; WD, Circular 59, 31 Dec. 1928.
13. WD, AR 600-38, 17 Aug. 1938, par. 45; DA, SR 600-32-10, 5 Sept. 1952, pars. 34, 49; DA, AR 670-5, 23 Sept. 1966, par. 10-7; DA, AR 670-1, 1 Nov. 1981, pars. 7-7 and 9-8.
14. WD, Circular 34, 10 July 1928, sec. I; WD, AR 600-38, 17 Aug. 1938, par. 42.

CHAPTER SEVENTY-NINE

1. *The Army Almanac,* p. 46.
2. WD, Changes 6, 28 Oct. 1918, Special

Regulation 41, par. 93(b).

3. American Red Cross, *American Red Cross Uniforms.*
4. WD, Surgeons General's Office, unnumbered circular, 20 June 1899, p. 8; WD, *The Medical Department . . . in the World War* 13: pp. 302–303.
5. Risch, *A Wardrobe for the Women of the Army,* pp. 98–99.
6. Ibid., pp. 99–106.
7. Ibid., pp. 104–105.
8. Ibid., pp. 106–108.
9. U.S. Army Specifications 6-15C, 17 Aug. 1936, and 6-15D, 19 July 1941; Risch, *A Wardrobe for the Women of the Army,* pp. 111–18.
10. Risch, *A Wardrobe for the Women of the Army,* p. 118.
11. Ibid., pp. 119–22.
12. Ibid., pp. 7–12, 50–53.
13. Ibid., pp. 37–38, 40–42.
14. Ibid., pp. 50–53.
15. Ibid., pp. 53–58.

Chapter Eighty

1. DA, Circular 94, 6 Apr. 1948; DA, Circular 377, 7 Dec. 1948, sec. III; DA, SR 600-37-1, 13 June 1949; DA, Change 1, 5 May 1950, SR 600-37-1; DA, Change 2, 15 Sept. 1950, SR 600-37-1.
2. Anderson, *Army Medical Specialist Corps,* pp. 359–62; DA, SR 600-32-2, 17 July 1951, sec. III.
3. DA, SR 600-32-2, 17 July 1951, sec. IV.
4. DA, SR 600-32-2, 17 July 1951, secs. I, II; Anderson, *Army Medical Specialist Corps,* pp. 389, 420.
5. Anderson, *Army Medical Specialist Corps,* pp. 420–24.
6. DA, AR 670-1, 15 Feb. 1979, par. 12-1; Anderson, *Army Medical Specialist Corps,* p. 421.
7. Anderson, *Army Medical Specialist Corps,* p. 422; DA, AR 670-32, 29 Jan. 1960, par. 6a.
8. Ibid.
9. DA message, DAPE-DW, Subject: Interim Change to AR 670-30 (Change 1), 041420Z Oct. 1977; *Army Times,* 30 Apr. 1975, p. 2; DA, AR 670-1, 15 Feb. 1979, chap. 15; *Army Times,* 3 Sept. 1979, p. 4.
10. DA, AR 670-1, 1 Nov. 1981, par. 14-1.
11. DA, AR 670-30, 24 Oct. 1975, sec. 6A.
12. *Army Times,* 30 Apr. 1975; DA, AR 670-1, 15 Feb. 1979, chap. 13; DA, AR 670-1, 16 Jan. 1986, par. 20-1.
13. DA, SR 600-37-2, 17 July 1951, par. 11; DA, SR 670-30, 20 Oct. 1959, sec. IX.
14. DA, Change 7, 13 June 1957, SR 600-37-2.
15. *Army Times,* 12 Dec. 1977, p. 6.
16. DA, AR 670-30, 20 Oct. 1959, sec. XI and par. 90.
17. DA, AR 670-30, 13 May 1969, chaps. 8 through 12.
18. DA, AR 670-1, 18 Feb. 1986, chaps. 26, 28.
19. Several publications show these fatigues. One example is AR 670-30, 13 May 1969, pp. 16-2 and 16-3.
20. DARCOM Message, DRCPT-MT, Subject: Revision of AR 670-1, 171630 Z June 1981; DA, AR 670-1, 1 Nov. 1981, chap. 24, sec. IV; DA Message, DAPE-HRL, 24 1830 Oct. 1983, Subject: Maternity Uniforms Wear Policies: Uniform Wear Out Dates.
21. DA, SR 600-37-2, 17 July 1951, sec. IV.
22. DA, AR 670-30, 24 Oct. 1975, pars. 17-6b(2), 17-2b(2).
23. DA, AR 670-30, 20 Oct. 1959; DA, AR 670-30, 13 May 1969, par. 17-1.
24. DA, AR 670-1, 1 Feb. 1979, par. 14-8; DA Message, DAPE-HPP, 212019 Feb. 1975, Subject: Enlisted Personnel Brass Insignia of Grade; DA Message DAPE-DW, 201030 June 1975, Subject: Change to AR 670-30, par. 5; DA, AR 670-1, 15 Feb. 1979, chap. 15.
25. HQ, DA, GO 20, 21 Nov. 1978; DA Letter, DAPE-HRL, 4 Oct. 1978, Subject: Remaining Recommendations of the 120th and 121st Army Uniform Board Proceedings.

Appendix

1. WD, *Annual Report of the Quartermaster General, 1896,* p. 5.
2. Patent 1,454,857, granted 15 May 1923, request filed Sept. 16, 1921; Patents 2,308,412 and 2,308,424, with additional patent 2,551,196.
3. *Army and Navy Register,* 11 Mar. 1905, p. 5.
4. WD, Circular 78, 17 Nov. 1909; WD, OQMG, Specification 1074, 12 Aug. 1910, sec. B; WD, Specification 17-7, 13 Oct. 1919; Memorandum for Chief of Staff, 421 A-DS, 17 Sept. 1921, Subject: Collar Ornaments, Service and Howitzer Companies; WD, Changes 9, 16

Oct. 1923, AR 600-35, par. 11; WD, AR 600-35, 31 Dec. 1926, par. 14c(2).

5. WD, OQMG Drawing CE 4-4-35, 1937; WD, Circular 58, 31 Aug. 1937, sec. I, par. 1a; WD, Circular 58, 31 Aug. 1937, sec. I, par. 1c.
6. Quartermaster Corps Tentative Specification, P.Q.D. 189c, 5 Jan. 1943.
7. General H. L. Rogers's private file, statement showing deliveries and cost of QMC-supplied disks purchased through 31 Dec. 1918, RG 92, NA.

Bibliography

Adjutant and Inspector General's Office. *Military Laws, Rules and Regulations for the Army of the United States.* E. de Krafft, Sept. 1816.

"The Adjutant General, His Office and Department, 1775–1947." Manuscript in Adjutant General's School Library.

Adjutant General's Department. *Subject Index to the General Orders and Circulars of the War Department and the Headquarters of the Army, Adjutant General's Office, from January 1, 1860, to December 31, 1880.* Washington, D.C.: GPO, 1913.

Adjutant General's Office. General Orders. Various dates.

The Adjutant General of the Army. *Music in Our Army: The Soul of the Service.* Washington: N.p., n.d.

Albert, Alphaeus H. *Record of American Uniform and Historical Buttons.* Boyertown, Pa.: Boyertown Publishing Company, 1977.

Allen, Jeremiah C. *Subject Index of the General Orders of the War Department, from January 1, 1809, to December 31, 1860.* Compiled under the direction of Brigadier General Richard C. Drum, Adjutant General's Department. Washington, D.C.: GPO, 1886.

American Daily Advertiser. Newspaper.

American Red Cross. *American Red Cross Uniforms.* Washington, D.C.: ARC, 1918.

American State Papers, V, Military Affairs.

Anderson, Robert S.; Harriet S. Lee; and Myra L. McDaniel, eds. *Army Medical Specialist Corps.* Washington, D.C.: Office of the Surgeon General, Department of the Army, 1968.

Armdield, Blanche B. *Organization and Administration in World War II.* Washington, D.C.: Office of the Surgeon General, 1963.

Army. Magazine published by the Association of the U.S. Army.

The Army Almanac: A Book of Facts Concerning the United States Army. Harrisburg, Pa.: The Stackpole Company, 1959.

Army Digest. Magazine published by the Department of the Army.

Army Information Digest. Later renamed *Army Digest.*

Army and Navy Journal.

Army and Navy Register. Newspaper.

Army Register. Published by the War Department each year or by the Department of the Army each year or every other year.

Army Times. Newspaper.

Ashburn, P. M. *A History of the Medical Department of the United States Army.* Boston: Houghton Mifflin Co., 1929.

Basurto, Rudy. *Insignia of America's Little Known Seafarers.* Privately printed, n.d.

Bayne-Jones, Stanhope. *The Evolution of Preventive Medicine in the U.S. Army, 1607–1939.* Washington, D.C.: Office of the Surgeon General, 1968.

Bazelon, Bruce S., and William F. McGuinn. *A Directory of American Military Goods Dealers and Makers, 1785–1885.* Privately printed, 1987.

Boyd, Anne M. *United States Government Publications.* New York: Wilson Co., 1941.

Brinkerhoff, Sidney B. *Boots and Shoes of the Frontier Soldier.* Tucson: Arizona Historical Society, 1976.

———. *Metal Uniform Insignia of the Frontier U.S. Army, 1846–1902.* 2d ed. Tucson: Arizona Historical Society, 1972.

———. *Metal Uniform Insignia of the U.S. Army in the Southwest, 1846–1902.* Tucson: Arizona Pioneers' Historical Society, 1965.

———. *Military Headgear in the Southwest, 1846–1890.* 2d ed. Tucson: Arizona Pioneers' Historical Society, 1967.

Brown, J. Willard. *The Signal Corps in the War of the Rebellion.* Boston: U.S. Veteran Signal Corps Association, 1896.

Bunkley, Joel W. *Military and Naval Recognition Book.* New York: Van Nostrand Company, 1917.

Burhans, Robert D. *The First Special Service Force.* Washington, D.C.: Infantry Journal Press, 1947.

Byrde, Penelope. *The Male Image: Men's Fashions in Britain, 1300–1970.* London: B. T. Batsford Ltd., 1979.

Campbell, J. Duncan. *Aviation Badges and Insignia*

of the United States Army, 1913–1946. Harrisburg, Pa.: Triangle Press, 1977.

———. "Notes on the Insignia of the Riflemen, U.S. Army," *MC&H,* (Apr. 49): p. 8.

———. and Edgar M. Howell, *American Military Insignia, 1800–1851.* Washington, D.C.: Smithsonian Institution, 1963.

Camus, Raoul F. "The Military Band in the United States Army Prior to 1834." Ph.D. thesis, New York University, 1969.

Castle Island Orderly Book, Vol. 8, Copy in Smithsonian Institution's Military History Division.

Catalogs of the following uniform and insignia dealers:
Army & Navy Store, 1919
Dusenbury & Schwab Incorporated, 1925
Fechmeimer Brothers, No. 190, 1914
Francis Bannerman, 1907
Francis Bannerman, 1927
Francis Bannerman, 1933
Henderson-Ames Company, List 49M, 1919
Lilley & Company, No. 49, 1914
Lilley & Company, Cadet No. 309, 1921
N. S. Meyer, 1930
N. S. Meyer, Change to 1930 catalog, 1932
Pettibone Brothers, Cadet No. 335, 1909
Ridabock & Company, 1878
Ridabock & Company, 1902
Russell's Incorporated, 1925
Smith Manufacturing Company, GAR Catalogue, 1880
Thomas Parry's Sons Co., 1905
W. A. Raymold, No. 300, 1895
W. A. Raymold, No. 300 Revised, 1896
W. A. Raymold, No. 302, 1899
W. A. Raymold, No. 315, 1900
Walter Reib, 1919
Warnock Uniform Company, 1900
William H. Horstmann, 1914
Wolf-Appleton, circa 1942

Chappell, Gordon. *Brass Spikes and Horsehair Plumes: A Study of U.S. Army Dress Helmets, 1872–1903.* Tucson: Arizona Pioneers' Historical Society, 1966.

———. *The Search for the Well Dressed Soldier, 1865–1890.* Tucson: Arizona Historical Society, 1972.

———. *Summer Helmets of the U.S. Army, 1875–1910.* Wyoming State Museum, 1976.

Charles, Roland W. *Troop Ships of World War II.* Washington, D.C.: Army Transportation Association, 1946.

Conde, Marlette. *The Lamp and the Caduceus.* Army School of Nursing Alumnae Association, 1975.

Copeland, Peter F. *American Military Uniforms, 1639–1968.* New York: Dover Publications, 1976.

Crowell, Benedict. *America's Munitions, 1917–1919.* Washington, D.C.: GPO, 1919.

Curtis, John O., and William H. Guthman. *New England Militia Uniforms and Accoutrements: A Pictorial Survey.* Sturbridge, Mass.: Old Sturbridge Village, 1971.

Department of the Army. Army Regulations. Various dates and numbers.

———. *The Department of the Army.* N.p., July 1972.

———. Special Regulations. Various dates and numbers.

———. *The Army Green Uniforms,* Pamphlet 355-10, September 1957.

Downey, Fairfax, and J. N. Jacobsen. *The Red Bluecoats.* Fort Collins, Colo.: The Old Army Press, 1973.

Elarth, Harold H. *The Story of the Philippine Constabulary.* Los Angeles: Philippine Constabulary Officers Association, Globe Printing Company, 1949.

Emerson, William K. *Chevrons: Illustrated History and Catalog of U.S. Army Insignia.* Washington, D.C.: Smithsonian Institution Press, 1983.

———. "Cockades and Eagles," *MC&H,* (1983): 104–12.

The Engineer. Magazine.

Engleman, Rose C., ed. *A Decade of Progress: The United States Army Medical Department, 1959–1969.* Office of the Surgeon General, 1975.

Faulk, Odie B. *The Geronimo Campaign.* New York: Oxford University Press, 1969.

Ferris, Robert G., ed. *Soldier and Brave.* Washington, D.C.: National Park Service, 1971.

Finke, Detmar H. "Insignia of the Continental Army, 1775–1783," *Military Collector & Historian* (1956): 71–73.

———. "Collector's Field Book," *MC&H* (1951): 74, 87.

———. "Notes on Artillery Uniforms," *MC&H* (1952): 15.

Foner, Jack D. *The United States Soldier between Two Wars: Army Life and Reforms, 1865–1898.* New York: Humanities Press, 1970.

Footlocker. Quarterly newsletter of the Association of American Military Uniform Collectors, published in Elyria, Ohio.

Fry, James B. *A Sketch of the Adjutant General's Department. . . .* New York: N.p., 1875.

General Regulations for the Army. Philadelphia: M. Carey and Sons, 1821.

General Regulations for the Army of the United States. Washington, D.C.: Davis and Force, 1825.

General Regulations for the Army of the United States, 1841. Washington, D.C.: J. and G. S. Gideon, 1841.

Geneal Regulations for the Army of the United States, 1847. Washington, D.C.: J. and G. S. Gideon, 1847.

The Ghosts of Patton's Third Army. Ed. Second Cavalry Association. Munich, Germany: Münchner Graphische, n.d. (ca. 1948).

Gillett, Mary C. *The Army Medical Department, 1775–1818.* Washington, D.C.: Center for Military History, 1981.

Gray, Andrew. "The American Field Service." *American Heritage Magazine,* Dec. 1974.

Grossman, John F. *Army Uniforms at Fort Snelling, 1821–1832.* Saint Paul: Minnesota Historical Society, 1974.

Gushwa, Robert L. *The Best and Worst of Times: The United States Army Chaplaincy, 1920–1945.* Washington, D.C.: Office of the Chief of Chaplains, 1977.

Guthman, William H. *March to Massacre.* New York: McGraw-Hill, 1970.

Hackett, John. *The Profession of Arms.* New York: Macmillan, 1983.

Harman Papers, Williams L. Clemens Library, University of Michigan.

Headquarters, American Expeditionary Forces. Various general orders, bulletins and circulars, 1917–19.

Headquarters of the Army. General Orders.Various dates.

Heitman, Francis B. *Historical Register and Dictionary of the United States Army, from its Organization, September 29, 1789, to March 1903.* 2 vols. Washington, D.C.: GPO, 1903; reprint, Urbana: University of Illinois Press, 1965.

Hewes, James E., Jr. *From Root to McNamara: Army Organization and Administration, 1900–1963.* Washington, D.C.: Center for Military History, United States Army, 1975.

Hicks, James E. *U.S. Ordnance.* Vol. II. Mount Vernon, N.Y.: Hicks, 1940.

Historical Highlights of the Army Nurse Corps. U.S. Army Health Service Command, n.d.

History of the American Field Service in France. 3 vols. Boston: Houghton Mifflin Company, 1920.

Honeywell, Roy J. *Chaplains of the United States Army.* Washington, D.C.: Office of the Chief of Chaplains, 1958.

Howell, Edgar M. *United States Army Headgear, 1855–1902,* vol. 2 in *Catalog of United States Uniforms in the Collections of the Smithsonian Institution.* Washington, D.C.: GPO, n.d.

———. and Donald E. Kloster. *United States Army Headgear to 1854,* vol. 1 in *Catalog of United States Army Uniforms in the Collection of the Smithsonian Institution.* Washington, D.C.: Smithsonian Institution Press, 1969.

Huntington, Robert T. *Accoutrements of the United States Infantry, Riflemen, and Dragoons, 1834–1839.* Alexandria Bay, N.Y.: Museum Restoration Service, 1987.

Hurley, Vic. *Jungle Patrol.* New York: E. P. Dutton and Company, 1938.

Index of General Orders and Circulars Affecting the Quartermaster's Department, U.S. Army, from 1865 to 1877, Inclusive. Comp. E. W. Hewitt and W. E. Coleman. Fort Leavenworth, Kans.: Chief Quartermaster's Office, Department of the Missouri, 1878.

Ingersoli, L. D. *A History of the War Department.* Washington, D.C.: Francis B. Mohun, 1880.

The Institute of Heraldry (TIOH) "Green Book," which is historical files, arranged chronologically, pertaining to uniform, insignia, and flags. This collection was assembled at the close of World War II and contains information copied from the National Archives as well as original files not easily found in other records centers.

Jacobsen, Jacques N., ed. *Regulations and Notes for the Uniform of the Army of the United States.* A series of reprints of U.S. Army uniform regulations supplemented by photographs. Staten Island, N.Y.: Manor Publishing, 1970s.

Jessup, John E., Jr., and Robert W. Coakley. *A Guide to the Study and Use of Military History.* Washington, D.C.: Center for Military History, 1979.

Johnson, Jesse J. *A Pictorial History of Black Soldiers in the United States (1619–1969) in Peace and War.* Hampton, Va.: Privately printed, 1970.

Journal of the Continental Congress, 1774–1789. Ed. Worthington C. Ford et al. 34 vols. Washington, D.C., 1904–37.

Katchner, Philip. *U.S. Cavalry on the Plains, 1850–90.* London: Osprey Publishing, 1985.

Kennedy, Stephen J., and Alice F. Park. *The Army Green Uniform.* U.S. Army Natick Laboratories Technical Report 68-41-CM, March 1968.

Kleber, Brooks E., and Dale Birdsell. *The Chemical Warfare Service: Chemicals in Combat. U.S. Army in World War II.* Washington D.C.: Office of the Chief of Military History, 1966.

Kohn, Richard H. *Eagle and Sword.* New York: The Free Press, 1975.

Kredel, Fritz, and Fredrick P. Todd. *Soldiers of the American Army, 1775–1954.* Chicago: Harry Regnery Company, n.d..

LaFramboise, Leon, W. *History of the Administrative and Technical Services Branch of Service Insignia.* Privately printed, 1986.

History of the Artillery, Cavalry, and Infantry Branch of Service Insignia. Steeleville, Mo.: Watson Publishing Company, 1976.

History of the Combat Support Branches, Branch of Service Insignia. Steeleville, Mo.: Watson Publishing Company, 1977.

Langellier, John P. *Parade Ground Soldiers.* Madison: Wisconsin Historical Society, 1978.

They Continually Wear the Blue. San Francisco: Barnes-McGee Historical Military Publications, 1974.

Legislation and Orders Relating to the Signal Service, U.S. Army, from 1860 to 1873. Myer Papers, Signal Corps Museum.

Lewis, Emanuel Raymond. *Seacoast Fortifications of the United States.* Annapolis, Md.: Leeward Publications, 1979.

Lewis, Waverly P. *U.S. Military Headgear, 1770–1880.* N.p., nd.

Lossing, B. H. *A History of the Civil War.* New York: The War Memorial Association, 1912.

McBarron, Charles. *The American Soldier.* Washington, D.C.: Office of the Chief of Military History, set 1, 1964; set 2, 1966; set 3, 1968.

———. and F. P. Todd, "Infantry of the Legion, 1794," *MC&H,* (Sept. 1952): p. 65

McMaster, John B. *A History of the People of the United States.* Vol. 6. New York: Appleton and Company, 1921.

McMinn, John H., and Max Levin. *Personnel in World War II.* Washington, D.C.: Office of the Surgeon General, 1963.

Mahon, John K., and Romana Danysh. *Infantry, Part I: Regular Army.* Army Lineage Series. Washington, D.C.: Office of the Chief of Military History, 1972.

Manual for the Philippine Constabulary, 1911. Manila: Bureau of Printing, 1911.

Manual for the Philippine Constabulary, 1918, Manila: Bureau of Printing, 1918.

Matloff, Maurice, ed. *American Military History.* Washington, D.C.: Office of the Chief of Military History, 1968.

Mauldin, Bill. *The Brass Ring.* New York: W. W. Norton & Co., 1971.

Military Collector & Historian. Journal of the Company of Military Historians, published quarterly since 1949.

Military Images. Magazine published in East Stroudsburg, Pa.

Military Laws and Rules and Regulations for the Armies of the United States. Washington, D.C.: Adjutant and Inspector General's Office, 1813.

Miller, Francis, ed. *The Photographic History of the Civil War in 10 Volumes.* New York: Review of Reviews Company, 1912.

Mollo, John. *Military Fashion.* New York: G. P. Putnam's Sons, 1972.

Moss, James A. *Combined Army Publications.* Menasha, Wis.: George Banta, 1917.

National Archives. Various files, especially in Record Group 92, Quartermaster General, and Record Group 94, Adjutant General.

National Geographic Society. *National Geographic Magazine.* Various issues, 1917–19 and 1942–45.

Insignia and Decorations of the U.S. Armed Forces. Rev. ed. Washington, D.C.: The Society, 1944.

National Guard of the United States, State of New Jersey. Baton Rouge, La.: Army and Navy Publishing Company, 1940.

North South Trader. Magazine.

Norton, Herman A. *Struggling for Recognition: The United States Army Chaplaincy.* Vol 2. Washington, D.C.: Office of the Chief of Chaplains, 1977.

Odgen, H. A., and Henry Loomis Nelson, *Uniforms of the United States Army.* Washington, D.C.: Quartermaster General; reprint, New York: Thomas Yossloff, 1959.

Ogden, Harry A., and Marvin Pakula. *Uniform of the United States Army.* Second Series. New York: Thomas Yoseloff.

The Officer's Guide. Various editions. Harrisburg: The Military Service Publishing Company, published from the 1930s through the 1960s.

Order of Battle of the United States Land Forces in the World War: American Expeditionary Forces. Vol. 1, Washington, D.C.: GPO, 1937.

Order of Battle of the United States Land Forces in the World War (1917–1919): Zone of the Interior. Vol. 3 in two parts. Washington, D.C.: GPO, 1949.

The Ordnance Magazine. Published by the Department of the Army.

Our Army and How to Know It. Scientific American Series. Munn and Company, n.d.

Parker, Geoffrey. *The Thirty Years' War.* London: Routledge, 1984.

Paulsen, Valdmar. *U.S. Army Facts and Insignia.* New York: Rand McNally & Company, 1918.

Peterson, Mendel L. "American Army Epaulettes, 1814–1872." *Military Collector and Historian* (Mar. 1951): 1.

Philippine Constabulary Regulations, 1930. Manila: Bureau of Printing, 1929.

Pitkin, Thomas M. *Quartermaster Equipment for Special Forces.* QMC Historical Studies No. 5. Washington, D.C.: Office of the Quartermaster General, 1944.

Prucha, Francis P. *The Sword of the Republic.* London: Macmillan, 1969.

Quartermaster Department. *Regulations for Harbor Boat Service,* 15 November 1904.

The Quartermaster Review. Magazine.

Regulations for the Uniform and Dress of the Army of the United States. Philadelphia: Horstmann, William H. and sons, 1851.

Regulations for the Uniform and Dress of the Army of the United States, . . . Boston: Robert Weir, 1857.

Report on the Army: Report of General George C. Marshall to the Secretary of War. Washington, D.C.: The Infantry Journal, 1943.

Rickey, Don. *Forty Miles a Day on Beans and Hay: Enlisted Soldier Fighting the Indian Wars.* Norman: University of Oklahoma Press, 1963.

Risch, Erna. *Quartermaster Support of the Army: A History of the Corps, 1775–1939.* Washington, D.C.: Office of the Quartermaster General, 1962.

———. *A Wardrobe for the Women of the Army.* QMC Historical Studies No. 12. Washington, D.C.: Historical Section, Office of the Quartermaster General, 1945; reprint, Springfield, Va.: George A. Petersen, n.d.

———. and Thomas Pitkin. *Clothing the Soldier of World War II.* Washington, D.C.: Office of the Quartermaster General, 1946.

Rodenbough, Theo. E. *From Everglade to Canon.* New York: Van Nostrand, 1875.

Sawicki, James A. *Cavalry Regiments of the U.S. Army.* Dumfries, Va.: Wyvern Publications, 1985.

———. *Field Artillery Battalions of the U.S. Army.* 2 vols. Dumfries, Va.: Centaur Publications, 1977.

———. *Infantry Regiments of the U.S. Army.* Dumfries, Va.: Wyvern Publications, 1981.

———. *Tank Battalions of the U.S. Army.* Dumfries, Va.: Wyvern Publications, 1983.

Schmitt, Martin F., and Dee Brown. *Fighting Indians of the West.* New York: Charles Scribner's Sons, 1948.

Schultz, Paul J.; Hayes Otoupalik; and Dennis Gordon. *World War One Collectors Handbook.* N.p., 1977.

Scipio, L. Albert, II, with Buddy D. Patterson. *E.M. Collar Insignia (1907–1926).* Silver Springs, Md.: Roman Publications, 1981.

Scully, C. Alison. *The Course of the Silver Greyhound.* New York: Putnam's Sons, 1936.

Simpson, Charles M. *Inside the Green Berets.* Navato, Calif.: Presidio Press, 1983.

Smithsonian Federal Enlisted Uniforms of the Civil War. Videotape. Roberts Video Publishing Company, 1990.

Soldiers. Official U.S. Army magazine.

Specifications. Various dates and numbering systems used for clothing and insignia from 1876 until the present. Usually published by the Quartermaster General's Office while it existed.

Specifications for the Uniform of the United States Army. Washington, D.C.: Office of the Quartermaster General, 15 February 1913.

Stanton, Shelby. *U.S. Army Uniforms in the Vietnam War.* Harrisburg, Pa.: Stackpole Books, 1989.

Stefen, Randy. *The Horse Soldiers, 1776–1943.* 4 vols. Norman: University of Oklahoma Press, 1977.

Stover, Earl F. *Up from Handymen: The United States Army Chaplaincy, 1865–1920,* Washington, D.C.: Office of the Chief of Chaplains, 1977.

Stubbs, Mary Lee, and Stanley R. Connor. *Armor-Cavalry, Part I: Regular Army and Reserve.* Army Lineage Series. Washington, D.C.: Office of the Chief of Military History, 1969.

———. *Armor-Cavalry, Part II: Army National Guard.* Army Lineage Series. Washington, D.C.: Office of the Chief of Military History, 1972.

Subject Index to the General Orders and Circulars of the War Department and the Headquarters of the Army, Adjutant General's Office, from January 1, 1881, to December 31, 1911. Washington, D.C.: GPO, 1912.

Sweeney, W. Allison. *History of the American Negro in the Great World War.* New York: Negro Universities Press, n.d.

Sweeting, C. G. *Combat Flying Clothing.* Washington, D.C.: Smithsonian Institution Press, 1984.

Todd, Fredrick P. *American Military Equipage.* Providence, R.I.: Company of Military Historians, 1974.

Trading Post. Magazine of the American Society of Military Insignia Collectors.

Treadwell, Mattie E. *The Women's Army Corps.* Washington, D.C.: Office of the Chief of Military History, 1954.

Unit Citation and Campaign Participation Credit Register. DA Pamphlet 672-1. Washington, D.C.: Headquarters, Department of the Army, 1961.

Unit members. *Gaz Alerte.* New York: A. E. Richardson Printing Company, 1919.

The Uniform of the Army of the United States. Compiled by the authority of the Secretary of War under the supervision of Brigadier General J. B. Aleshire, Quartermaster General, 1 October 1908.

Uniform or Dress of the Army of the United States. Philadelphia: William Horstmann, 1837.

U.S. Congress, Senate, 66th Cong., 1st sess. *General Staff Corps and Medal of Honor.* S. Doc. 58, 1919.

United States Military Magazine. Vol. 2. (1840–41). Philadelphia: Huddy and Duval; reprint, in one volume, York, Pa.: American History Publications, 1971.

Utley, Robert M. *Custer Battlefield.* Washington, D.C.: National Park Service, 1969.

War Department. *Annual Report of the Chief Signal Officer.* Washington, D.C.: GPO, 1889.

War Department, *Annual Report of the Quartermaster General.* Published each year in Washington, D.C., and usually containing details of work accomplished during the year by the department, especially from 1870 through World War I.

———. *Annual Report of the Secretary of War.* Published each year in Washington, D.C., and printed by the GPO, these contain reports of the quartermaster general, commissary general, and other senior army officials. Number of volumes and contents vary by year. Often appendices contained in the reports by department chiefs were omitted in secretary of war reports.

———. *Army Regulations.* Various years and subjects. After World War I these were numbered by subject with changes issued on an irregular basis. Most uniform and insignia regulations have been numbered in the 600s.

———. *Army Regulations.* Adjutant and Inspector General's Office, March 1819.

———. *Army Specialist Corps Regulations (Tentative).* Washington, D.C.: GPO, 1942.

———. *Dress of the General Staff . . . .* Washington, D.C.: Adjutant General's Office, 31 May 1838.

———. *Dress of the General Staff and Regimental Officers.* Washington, D.C.: Adjutant General's Office, 1832.

———. *Field Service Regulations.* Washington, D.C. Various dates and editions, with various corrections, were published.

———. General Orders and Circulars. These were published almost daily and were usually bound by year by the holders of the documents. The War Department published an index each year to be bound with these documents.

———. *General Regulations for the Army.* Philadelphia: M. Carey and Sons, 1821.

———. *General Regulations for the Army.* Washington, D.C.: Davis and Force, 1825.

———. *General Regulations for the Army of the United States, 1841.* Washington, D.C.: J. and G. S. Gideon, 1841.

———. *General Regulations for the Army of the United States, 1847.* Washington, D.C.: J. and G. S. Gideon, 1847.

———. *Illustrations of Chevrons.* Washington, D.C.: GPO, 2 February 1914.

———. *Legislative History of the General Staff of the United States . . . from 1775 to 1901.* Comp. Major General Harry Corbin. Washington, D.C.: GPO, 1901.

———. *List of War Department Documents Issued by the Adjutant General of the Army with Their Distribution.* Document 1008. Washington, D.C.: GPO, 1920.

———. *Marine Personnel Regulations,* Transportation Corps Pamphlet No. 4, "Regulation No. 23," Change 1, 1 Aug. 1945.

———. *The Medical Department . . . in the World War.* Washington, D.C.: GPO, vol. v, 1923; vol. xii, 1927; and vol. xiii, 1927.

———. *Official Army Register.* Washington, D.C.: GPO, The Adjutant General's Office, 1938.

———. *Official National Guard Register for 1926.* Washington, D.C.: GPO, Militia Bureau, 1926.

———. *Official National Guard Register for 1931.* Washington, D.C.: GPO, Militia Bureau, 1931.

———. *Official National Guard Register for 1938.* Washington, D.C.: GPO, Militia Bureau, 1938.

———. *Official National Guard Register for 1939.* Washington, D.C.: GPO, National Guard Bureau, 1940.

———. *Organization of the Services of Supply, AEF.* Monographs Nos. 2 and 7. Washington, D.C.: Historical Branch, War Plans Division, General Staff, 1921.

———. "QMG Drawings" of insignia from the 1920s and 1930s. On file at the Quartermaster Museum, Fort Lee, Va.

———. *Quartermaster Manual.* Printer's page proofs of 1865 manual from manuscript copy in Division of Military History, Smithsonian Institution.

———. *Regulations and Decisions Pertaining to the Uniform of the Army of the United States.* Washington, D.C.: GPO, 1897.

———. *Regulations and Decisions Pertaining to the Uniform of the Army of the United States.* 2d ed. Washington, D.C.: GPO, 1898.

———. *Regulations and Decisions Pertaining to the Uniform of the Army of the United States.* 3d ed. Washington, D.C.: GPO, 1899.

———. *Regulations and Decisions Pertaining to the Uniform of the Army of the United States.* 4th ed. Washington, D.C.: 1900.

———. *Regulations and Decisions Pertaining to the Uniform of the Army of the United States.* 5th ed. Washington, D.C.: GPO, 1901.

———. *Regulations for the Army of the United States, 1861.* New York: Harper & Brothers, 1861.

———. *Regulations for the Army of the United States, 1901 with . . . [Changes] to 30 June 1902.* Washington, D.C.: GPO, 1902.

———. *Regulations for the Uniform of the Army of the United States.* Philadelphia: Depot of the Quartermaster's Department, 1888.

———. *Regulations for the Uniform and Dress of the Army of the United States, July 1872.* Washington, D.C.: GPO, 1872.

———. *Regulations for the Uniform of the United States Army.* Document No. 405. Washington, D.C.: Office of the Chief of Staff, 26 December 1911.

———. *Regulations for the Uniform of the United States Army.* Washington, D.C.: GPO, 1912.

———. *Regulations for the Uniform of the United States Army, 1888.* Reprint, San Francisco: Barnes-McGee Historical Military Publications, n.d.

———. *Regulations for the Uniform of the United States Army (Revised Edition).* Washington, D.C.: GPO, 1914.

———. *Regulations Governing the Uniform in the Army Mine Planter Service.* N.p., 1919.

———. *Regulations of the Army of the United States, and General Orders in Force on the 17th of February 1881.* Washington, D.C.: GPO, 1881.

———. *Regulations Prescribing Flags, Signals, Funnel Marks, etc., Also Uniforms of the United States Army Transport Service.* Washington, D.C.: n.p., 1899.

———. *Regulations Prescribing Uniforms of the United States Army Transport Service.* Washington, D.C.: Quartermaster General's Office, 28 September 1899.

———. *Regulations Prescribing Uniforms of the United States Army Transport Service, Circular Number* 7. Washington, D.C.: Office of the Chief of the Quartermaster Corps, 1912.

———. *Revised Regulations for the Army of the United States, 1861.* Philadelphia: George W. Childs, 1862; reprint, Washington, D.C.: Smithsonian Institution, 1961.

———. *Rewards for Service, United States Army.* N.p., n.d. (ca. Dec. 1919).

———. *Special Regulations Number 41, Regulations for the Uniform of the United States Army.* Washington, D.C.: GPO, 1917.

———. *Special Regulations Number 42, Specifications for the Uniform of the United States Army.* Washington, D.C.: GPO, 1917.

———. *Specifications for Clothing, Camp and Garrison Equipage and Clothing and Equipage Materials.* Philadelphia: Quartermaster General, Philadelphia Depot, 1889.

———. *Specifications for the Uniform of the United States Army, February 15, 1913.* Washington, D.C.: Office of the Quartermaster General, 1913.

———. *Specifications for the Uniforms of the United States Army, 1915.* Washington, D.C.: GPO, 1915.

———. Training Manual 10-380, "Water Transportation." Office of the Quartermaster General, 14 Feb. 1941.

———. *Uniform of the Army of the United States, 1882.* Washington, D.C.: Office of the Quartermaster General, n.d.

———. *Uniform of the Army of the United States, Illustrated, from 1774 to 1889.* Washington, D.C.: Office of the Quartermaster General, n.d.

Wardlow, Chester. *The Transportation Corps: Responsibilities, Organization, and Operations.* Washington, D.C.: Office of the Chief of Military History, 1951.

The War of the Rebellion: A Compilation of the Official Records of the Union and Confederate Armies. Vols. 1 through 130. Washington, D.C.: GPO, 1874–1901.

"Wayne's Orderly Books." *Michigan Pioneer and Historical Society Journal* 24 (1905).

White, John R. *Bullets and Bolos.* New York: The Century Company, n.d.

Williams, Dion. *Army and Navy Uniforms and Insignia.* New York: Fredrick A. Stokes Company, 1918.

Woodhull, A. A. A letter printed by the Surgeon General's Office from Lieutenant Colonel A. A. Woodhull, 31 Jan. 1868, commonly known as the "Woodhull Report."

Worchester, Dean C. *The Philippines Past and Present.* New York: Macmillan Co., 1930.

The Writings of George Washington. 37 Vols. Ed. John C. Fitzpatrick. Washington, D.C.: GPO, 1931.

Wyllie, Robert E. *Orders, Decorations and Insignia: Military and Civil.* New York and London: G. P. Putnam's Sons, 1921.

Illustration Credits

Not only are photographs credited by source, but also where possible the photograph numbers are listed so that follow-on researchers may more easily locate the original illustrations. Within the federal government, historical photographs move from one depository to another. The sources listed are the sources from which the original photograph was obtained. In the late 1980s many military photographs were moved to the National Archives, and some former Air Force photographs were moved to the National Air and Space Museum of the Smithsonian Institution.

Many photographs are from a few central sources. These are abbreviated in the credits as follows:

DAVA—Defense Audio-Visual Agency

KU—The Pennell Collection in the Kansas Collection of the University of Kansas houses hundreds of glass negatives showing military activities at Fort Riley.

NA—Used for photographs from the National Archives. If a photograph is further identified only by a number, it comes from Record Group 111, Signal Corps photos. In a few cases other record groups have been used, and these are so noted.

S—Photographs taken by Frank Storer of the Storer-Spellman Studios in Detroit, Michigan. Mr. Storer, now retired in Madison Heights, Michigan, has retained the negatives of these pictures. Following the *S* is the serial number of the negative. Those that have the additional letter *C* are photographs taken of the J. Duncan Campbell collection.

SI—Photographs taken by the Smithsonian Institution. Numbering sequences vary depending upon when the original negative was taken.

Chapter One

1. NA 92-UF-3-6-13.

Chapter Two

1. KU 1570. **2.** KU 1395. **3.** SI 88990-D. **4.** S 5-7. **5.** S 17-8. **6.** Dr. Charles H. Cureton. **7.** U.S. Army Military History Institute, J. Craig Nannos Collection. **8.** S 13-5. **9.** S 33-16. **10.** Library of Congress. **11.** KU 2549. **12.** KU 516. **13.** NA B-3633. **14.** KU 236. **15.** KU 452. **16.** KU 2677.1. **17.** S 33-4. **18.** S 33-18. **19.** NA 91745. **20.** The White House, 11 Dec. 1989, P8758-09 CP. **21.** Office of the Chief of Staff. **22.** Courtesy Shelby L. Stanton. **23.** Massachusetts Commandery, Military Order of the Loyal Legion, and the U.S. Army Military History Institute. **24.** NA 83960. **25.** S 23-5-1. **26.** S 21-1-11. **27.** NA 83633. **28.** KU 2621. **29.** S 5-2-6. **30.** S 14-3-4. **31.** S 20-14-9. **32.** Courtesy Mike McAfee. **33.** KU 234. **34.** NA 114842. **35.** KU 525. **36.** U.S. Army photograph PC-188458. **37.** KU 38.1. **38.** KU 1166.

Chapter Threee

1. The West Point Museum Collections. **2.** Mackinac Island State Park Commission. **3.** S C-3-14. **4.** S C-3-12.

Chapter Four

1. S C-3-17. **2.** S C-3-19. **3.** S C-3-20. **4.** SI 38726-B. **5.** S C-3-15.

Chapter Five

1. S C-5-7. **2.** S C-4-18. **3.** S C-4-20. **4.** S C-5-14. **5.** S C-4-16. **6.** S C-5-10. **7.** J. Duncan Campbell. **8.** S C-3-10. **9.** S 5-15. **10.** S 5-3. **11.** S C-3-9. **12.** Author's drawing. **13.** J. Duncan Campbell. **14.** S C-5-18-1. **15.** S C-5-17-1. **16.** S C-5-17-2. **17.** S C-6-4. **18.** S C-5-20-1. **19.** S 16-10-4. **20.** S 6-8-4. **21.** S C-6-3-1. **22.** S C-6-3-2. **23.** S C-6-3-3. **24.** NA B-2524. **25.** S 18-2-1. **26.** S C-5-20-2. **27.** SI 73-6446. **28.** S 12-4-5. **29.** S 16-10-2. **31.** S 6-8-1. **32.** S 25-9-5. **33.** S 6-10-2. **34.** S 6-10-4. **35.** S 7-10-5. **36.** SI 73-2616. **37.** SI 73-6455. **38.** S S-2-7. **39.** S C-6-18-2. **40.** S 10-6-8. **41.** S 10-7-7. **42.** S 16-7-4. **43.** S 16-7-8. **44.** S 16-7-3. **45.** S 15-8-8. **46.** S 19-4. **47.** S 19-5. **48.** S 19-6. **49.** S S-3-20. **50.** S C-6-18-3. **51.** S C-6-18-1. **52.** S 10-6-3. **53.** S 5-1-1. **54.** NA 91775. **55.** S 9-10-1. **56.** S 5-1-6. **57.** S 5-2-6. **58.** S 4-10-6. **59.** S 5-1-8. **60.** S 5-1-5. **61.** S 16-7-11. **62.** S 25-6-5. **63.** S 5-4-3. **64.** S 5-4-1. **65.** S 5-2-8. **66.** S 16—9-3. **67.** S 5-3-3. **68.** S 5-2-1. **69.** S 5-5-1. **70.** S 5-5-4. **71.** S 5-2-4. **72.** S 5-3-6. **73.** S 5-3-5. **74.** S 5-3-10. **75.** S 4-10-2. **76.** S

5-3-8. **77.** S 10-9-6. **78.** S 5-6-7. **79.** NA 22361. **80.** S 4-9-1. **81.** S 11-9-3. **82.** S 5-2-3. **83.** S 5-1-2. **84.** S C-6-16-5. **85.** S 7-10-2. **86.** S 4-9-3. **87.** S 16-9-5. **88.** S 7-9-2. **89.** S 5-2-6. **90.** S 5-4-4. **91.** S 5-4-8. **92.** S C-16-6. **93.** S C-6-20-3. **94.** S 4-10-5. **95.** S 5-3-9. **96.** S 5-3-7. **97.** S 5-6-10. **98.** S 5-8-2. **99.** S 1-9-8. **100.** S S-1-20-1. **101.** S S-1-20-2. **102.** S 1-9-6. **103.** Buddy Patterson. **104.** KU PN 1082 I. **105.** Buddy Patterson. **106.** Buddy Patterson. **107.** Buddy Patterson. **108.** S 25-6-2. **109.** S 25-6-4. **110.** Buddy Patterson. **111.** Buddy Patterson. **112.** Buddy Patterson. **113.** Buddy Patterson. **114.** Buddy Patterson. **115.** Buddy Patterson. **116.** S 5-4-2. **117.** S 25-3-4. **118.** Buddy Patterson. **119.** S C-6-15-1. **120.** S 5-1-3. **121.** S 4-10-1. **122.** S C-20-1. **123.** Buddy Patterson. **124.** S 6-2-4. **125.** S 7-10-1. **126.** Mr. Richard T. Graney. **127.** S 15-8-4. **128.** S S-1-20-3. **129.** S S-1-20-5. **130.** S 6-2-6. **131.** S 6-2-8. **132.** Buddy Patterson. **133.** S 21-4-1. **134.** Buddy Patterson. **135.** Buddy Patterson. **136.** S 21-5-3. **137.** S 5-2-2. **138.** S 5-5-3. **139.** S 21-4-9. **140.** S 3-6-8. **141.** S C-1-9-1. **142.** S C-1-1-2. **143.** S 5-3-4. **144.** S 5-3-2. **145.** S C-6-15-4. **146.** S 11-9-9. **147.** NA 72447. **148.** Buddy Patterson. **149.** Buddy Patterson. **150.** S 21-4-6. **151.** S 5-3-1. **152.** S 5-4-5. **153.** S 25-3-3. **154.** Buddy Patterson. **155.** Buddy Patterson. **156.** S 25-3-2. **157.** S C-6-15-2. **158.** S C-6-15-3. **159.** S 4-9-7. **160.** S C-6-15-5. **161.** S 5-2-7. **162.** S 27-4-5. **163.** Courtesy Shelby Stanton. **164.** S 5-6-5. **165.** Buddy Patterson. **166.** S 27-7-2. **167.** S 5-8-11. **168.** S 13-2-2. **169.** S 5-6-11. **170.** S C-6-16-4. **171.** S 3-10-11. **172.** S 3-1-7. **173.** Buddy Patterson. **174.** S 25-11-1. **175.** S 2-10-4. **176.** S 2-7-4. **177.** S 2-4-6. **178.** S 2-7-1. **179.** S 1-8-8. **180.** S 25-1-1. **181.** S 25-1-5. **182.** S 25-9-4. **183.** The Institute of Heraldry. **184.** S 4-10-8. **185.** S 4-9-2. **186.** S 5-1-4. **187.** S C-6-16-3. **188.** S 10-10-9. **189.** S 8-8-9. **190.** S 3-6-10. **191.** S 3-6-1. **192.** S 3-2-1. **193.** S 3-6-6. **194.** S 3-6-7. **195.** S 8-8-3. **196.** S 3-10-9. **197.** S 3-8-11. **198.** S 3-8-9. **199.** S 3-8-1. **200.** S 2-3-11. **201.** S 4-2-3. **202.** S 4-2-7. **203.** S 3-9-4. **204.** S 3-3-10. **205.** S 25-2-2. **206.** S 3-10-2. **207.** S 3-1-2. **208.** S 3-3-3. **209.** S 3-2-8. **210.** S 3-1-4. **211.** S 3-3-7. **212.** S 3-3-8. **213.** S 2-10-10. **214.** S 8-2-2. **215.** S 1-2-3. **216.** S 1-2-4. **217.** S 1-2-2. **218.** S 1-7-5. **219.** S 2-10-5. **220.** S 1-5-7. **221.** S 1-2-6. **222.** S 8-3-5. **223.** S 3-1-5. **224.** S 1-8-1. **225.** S 25-7-2. **226.** S 25-7-3. **227.** S 25-1-4. **228.** Buddy Patterson. **229.** S 4-5-11. **230.** S 11-2-7. **231.** Buddy Patterson. **232.** S 25-11-3. **233.** Buddy Patterson. **234.** S 12-8-3. **235.** S 15-6-5. **236.** S 15-7-8. **237.** S 15-7-2. **238.** S 12-8-2. **239.** S 12-2-2. **240.** S 10-3-4. **241.** S 10-3-5. **242.** S 15-4-10. **243.** S 15-6-7. **244.** S 10-6-4. **245.** S 11-1-4. **246.** S 10-5-3. **247.** S 12-1-4. **248.** S 10-5-8. **249.** S 10-10-1. **250.** S 26-4.

Chapter Six

1. J. Duncan Campbell. **2.** S 25-2-4. **3.** J. Duncan Campbell. **4.** S C-7-10. **5.** S C-7-5. **6.** J. Duncan Campbell. **7.** S C-7-13. **8.** J. Duncan Campbell. **9.** SI 54121. **10.** S C-7-7. **11.** Sergeant H. H. Booker, 2d. **12.** J. Duncan Campbell. **13.** S C-7-2-1. **14.** S 6-10-1. **15.** S C-7-3-1. **16.** S 8-1-9. **17.** S 18-1-3. **18.** S C 7-2-2. **19.** NA B 2489. **20.** S S-3-13. **21.** S C-7-1-3. **22.** S S-2-5. **23.** SI 73-6397. **24.** S 17-2-2. **25.** S 19-3. **26.** SI 73-2608. **27.** S 8-7-5. **28.** S 8-7-3. **29.** S 10-7-2. **30.** S 8-5-7. **31.** S 10-7-6. **32.** S 16-4-1. **33.** S 8-5-4. **34.** S 15-10-4. **35.** S 14-5-4. **36.** S 7-4-5. **37.** S 11-7-3. **38.** S 11-7-2. **39.** S S-1-13-3. **40.** S 15-10-6. **41.** S 10-7-5. **42.** S 14-10-4. **43.** S C-1-12-1. **44.** S 7-5-6. **45.** S C-6-20-2. **46.** NA 94944. **47.** S C-7-3-2. **48.** S 7-8-8. **49.** S C-7-3-3. **50.** NA 90578. **51.** S C-7-3-4. **52.** S 3-5-10. **53.** S S-5-4. **54.** S S-4-5. **55.** S 7-9-4. **56.** S 7-6-7. **57.** KU 811. **58.** S C-1-5-5. **59.** S C-1-5-3. **60.** S C-1-5-2. **61.** S C1-5-4. **62.** S C-7-9-5. **63.** S 2-8-1. **64.** S S-2-10-2. **65.** S S-1-20-6. **66.** S C-1-6-1. **67.** S 7-7-2. **68.** S 15-10-1. **69.** S 7-7-4. **70.** S 7-6-8. **71.** S 7-7-6. **72.** S 7-6-5. **73.** S C-1-6-4. **74.** S 7-6-9. **75.** S 10-6-6. **76.** S 16-2-11. **77.** S 15-2-2. **78.** S 7-8-7. **79.** S 10-2-6. **80.** S 15-6-1. **81.** S 3-5-3. **82.** S 7-8-5. **83.** S 16-2-9. **84.** S 7-9-8. **85.** S 5-8-1. **86.** S 15-7-4. **87.** S 10-2-8. **88.** S 12-3-3. **89.** William Emerson. **90.** S 7-9-3. **91.** S 7-7-3. **92.** S 7-7-1. **93.** S 11-8-1. **94.** S C-1-4-1. **95.** S C-1-4-6. **96.** S C-1-4-2. **97.** S 7-9-1. **98.** S 7-7-5. **99.** S 3-5-2. **100.** S S-2-10-5. **101.** S 3-5-9. **102.** S 7-6-10. **103.** S 25-10-2. **104.** S 20-2-1. **105.** S 16-8-7. **106.** Buddy Patterson. **107.** S 7-6-6. **108.** S 7-5-3. **109.** S 27-12-2. **110.** S 27-12-1. **111.** S 10-8-3. **112.** S 7-5-4. **113.** S 7-5-9. **114.** S 10-2-9. **115.** S 16-3-1. **116.** S 15-7-9. **117.** S 7-9-6. **118.** S 10-2-11. **119.** S 10-2-12. **120.** S 25-10-1. **121.** S 14-4-9. **122.** S 11-10-7. **123.** S 10-2-10. **124.** S 11-1-1. **125.** S 10-3-6. **126.** S 20-4-10. **127.** S 11-5-9. **128.** S 11-1-5. **129.** S 16-2-6. **130.** Author's collection. **131.** S 16-5-7. **132.** S 15-4-5. **133.** S 16-2-5. **134.** S 16-2-7. **135.** S 15-7-6. **136.** S 10-5-6. **137.** S 12-4-3. **138.** S 2-2-5. **139.** S 7-5-5. **140.** KU 1618. **141.** S 14-6-9. **142.** Author's collection. **143.** S 1-9-2. **144.** KU PN 167G. **145.** Buddy Patterson. **146.** Buddy Patterson. **147.** Buddy Patterson. **148.** Buddy Patterson. **149.** Buddy Patterson. **150.** Buddy Patterson. **151.** Buddy Patterson. **152.** Buddy Patterson. **153.** S 1-8-11. **154.** Buddy Patterson. **155.** S S-2-11-1. **156.** Buddy Patterson. **157.** Buddy Patterson. **158.** S 22-3-6. **159.** Buddy Patterson. **160.** Buddy Patterson. **161.** Buddy Patterson. **162.** Buddy Patterson. **163.** Buddy Patterson. **164.** Buddy Patterson. **165.** Buddy Patterson. **166.** Buddy Patterson. **167.** Buddy Patterson. **168.** S 3-10-6. **169.** S 3-6-2. **170.** S 4-1-1. **171.** S 4-9-8.

172. S 3-2-5. **173.** Buddy Patterson. **174.** S 4-1-6. **175.** S 3-8-2. **176.** S 3-8-3. **177.** S 4-1-11. **178.** Buddy Patterson. **179.** S 4-2-11. **180.** S 3-8-5. **181.** S 3-9-7. **182.** S 3-10-8. **183.** Buddy Patterson. **184.** Buddy Patterson. **185.** Buddy Patterson. **186.** S 25-1-2. **187.** S 2-6-2. **188.** S 2-6-1. **189.** S 2-5-5. **190.** S 7-10-9. **191.** S 1-5-8. **192.** S 2-3-3. **193.** S 4-3-6. **194.** S 4-7-6. **195.** S 4-6-3. **196.** S 8-1-4. **197.** S 15-1-4. **198.** S 3-3-6. **199.** S 2-5-8. **200.** S 2-10-8. **201.** S 2-6-5. **202.** S 4-3-2. **203.** S 4-5-7. **204.** S 4-7-9. **205.** S 4-6-6. **206.** S 4-5-10. **207.** S 4-7-3. **208.** S 2-9-9. **209.** S 6-9-3. **210.** S 2-10-2. **211.** S 3-3-2. **212.** S 3-3-9. **213.** S 20-4-1. **214.** S 8-3-4. **215.** S 4-4-10. **216.** S 3-7-11. **217.** S 8-2-9. **218.** S 8-2-5.

Chapter Seven

1. S 21-2-1. **2.** S C-8-14. **3.** S C-2-15-1. **4.** SI AH 60778 B. **5.** S C-6-5-3. **6.** S 18-1-2. **7.** S 18-2-2. **8.** SI 73-6445. **9.** S C-2-16-3. **10.** Massachusetts Commandery, Military Order of the Loyal Legion, and the U.S. Army Military History Institute. **11.** S C-2-13-3. **12.** S C-6-5-1. **13.** S C-2-13-2. **14.** S C-2-13-1. **15.** S C-6-5-2. **16.** S 7-2-6. **17.** S 7-2-7. **18.** S C-2-15-2. **19.** Massachusetts Commandery, Military Order of the Loyal Legion, and the U.S. Army Military History Institute. **20.** S S-2-18. **21.** S C-2-11-2. **22.** S C-2-19-7. **23.** S C-2-11-3. **24.** S S-3-14-A. **25.** S C-2-11-1. **26.** SI 73-6518. **27.** S 16-10-1. **28.** S 6-10-3. **29.** NA B-2321. **30.** S 14-10-6. **31.** S 11-9-7. **32.** S 16-8-1. **33.** S 15-1-10. **34.** S 22-7-4. **35.** S C-6-7. **36.** S 19-2. **37.** S 9-10-2. **38.** S 6-2-3. **39.** NA RB-23 B. **40.** S C-1-1-1. **41.** S C-1-1-4. **42.** S C-1-1-3. **43.** S C-1-3-4. **44.** S 11-8-2. **45.** S 6-2-7. **46.** S 6-2-1. **47.** KU 2000I. **48.** S 10-9-5. **49.** S C-1-1-5. **50.** S C-1-3-5. **51.** S C-1-8-3. **52.** S 5-8-3. **53.** S 8-9-4. **54.** S 5-8-6. **55.** S 11-3-11. **56.** S 11-2-4. **57.** S 6-2-2. **58.** S 5-8-4. **59.** S C-18-6. **60.** S 11-1-9. **61.** S 15-6-6. **62.** S 14-7-5. **63.** S C-1-8-4. **64.** S 10-9-7. **65.** S 11-1-3. **66.** S 11-1-6. **67.** S 15-4-6. **68.** William Emerson. **69.** S 15-7-1. **70.** S 12-2-3. **71.** William Emerson. **72.** S 11-2-1. **73.** S 11-2-2. **74.** S 11-1-7. **75.** S 10-8-1. **76.** S 14-9-1. **77.** S 11-3-12. **78.** S 12-4-2. **79.** S 10-5-10. **80.** S 15-7-7. **81.** S 10-6-2. **82.** S 12-1-2. **83** S 12-2-1. **84.** S 13-3-7. **85.** S 10-8-2. **86.** S 11-2-3. **87.** S 1-9-7. **88.** S 21-3-5. **89.** Buddy Patterson. **90.** Buddy Patterson. **91.** Buddy Patterson. **92.** NA 44977. **93.** Buddy Patterson. **94.** S 21-3-6. **95.** Buddy Patterson. **96.** S 21-3-9. **97.** S 4-2-6. **98.** S 3-7-2. **99.** S 4-9-6. **100.** S 3-7-9. **101.** S 3-8-10. **102.** S 3-2-4. **103.** S 3-2-3. **104.** S 4-2-2. **105.** S 3-9-6. **106.** Buddy Patterson. **107.** S 1-3-8. **108.** S 1-4-11. **109.** S 1-4-3. **110.** S 2-10-7. **111.** S 15-1-3. **112.** S 2-9-4. **113.** S 2-6-11. **114.** S 8-8-5. **115.** S 2-5-6. **116.** S 4-4-5. **117.** S 1-3-7. **118.** S 4-6-11. **119.** S 2-6-6. **120.** S 1-5-4. **121.** S 2-6-3.

Chapter Eight

1. Courtesy Mount Vernon Ladies Association. **2.** Mackinac Island State Park Commission. **3.** S 25-14-2. **4.** S 25-4-4. **5.** S C-4-2-1. **6.** S C-4-2-2. **7.** S C-4-14. **8.** S C-4-2-5. **9.** S C-4-2-3. **10.** S C-4-2-4. **11.** U.S. Army Quartermaster Museum. **12.** SI 437 10. **13.** S 25-6-3. **14.** S 25-4-3. **15.** S 25-4-7. **16.** S S-3-15-2. **17.** S S-3-14B. **18.** S 33-6-4. **19.** S C-4-8. **20.** S C-4-5. **21.** S C-4-9. **22.** S C-7-20. **23.** S C-4-12-2. **24.** S C-4-12-1. **25.** S S-2-14-1. **26.** S C-5-18-2. **27.** S 18-1-1. **28.** S 10-9-8. **29.** S C-4-13. **30.** S C-6-13. **31.** S 19-1. **32.** S 17-4-2. **33.** S C-8-19. **34.** Courtesy Fred Gaede. **35.** *Annual Report of the Quartermaster General, 1881*; SI copy 86-11301. **36.** NA 92-UF-3-6-16. **37.** KU PN 1000. **38.** S 9-10-4. **39.** S 13-9-2. **40.** S 9-10-3. **41.** S 6-6-2. **42.** S 8-10-6. **43.** S 6-8-3. **44.** S 7-3-7. **45.** S 8-6-1. **46.** S 6-9-1. **47.** S 5-10-5. **48.** U.S. Army pho-tograph 139648. **49.** S 6-6-3. **50.** S 14-1-10. **51.** S 7-8-4. **52.** S 16-3-2. **53.** S 9-1-4. **54.** KU PN 6289i. **55.** S 7-9-7. **56.** S 6-2-5. **57.** S 6-1-4. **58.** S 9-1-1. **59.** S 5-10-2. **60.** S 8-5-5. **61.** S 9-1-2. **62.** S 7-3-8. **63.** S 5-10-4. **64.** Courtesy Association of the U.S. Army, from *AUSA News*. **65.** S 6-5-1. **66.** S 6-7-1. **67.** S 14-1-9. **68.** S 7-2-5. **69.** S 7-2-4. **70.** S 7-4-9. **71.** S 7-2-2. **72.** S 12-7-3. **73.** S 12-6-2. **74.** S 12-6-3. **75.** S 12-7-1. **76.** S 12-7-2. **77.** S 12-8-1. **78.** S 12-6-1. **79.** S 11-9-1. **80.** S 7-5-8. **81.** S 7-2-1. **82.** KU 1197. **83.** S 16-9-3. **84.** S S-5-18. **85.** S 7-3-6. **86.** S 6-8-2. **87.** S 16-3-3. **88.** S 7-9-9. **89.** S 23-9-4. **90.** S 7-9-9. **91.** S 23-15-1. **92.** S 23-5-6.

Chapter Nine

1. S C-2-6-1. **2.** S C-2-7-2. **3.** S C-2-7-1. **4.** S C-2-6-2. **5.** S S-3-5. **6.** S S-2-19. **7.** SI 73-6454. **8.** S C-2-6-4. **9.** S C-2-6-3. **10.** S C-2-7-3. **11.** NA B-1912. **12.** S C-6-8-1. **13.** S C-6-8-2. **14.** NA 90930. **15.** S 14-1-2. **16.** S 27-4-6. **17.** S 14-1-3. **18.** S 14-4-7. **19.** S 14-2-9. **20.** S 14-2-6. **21.** S 14-5-3. **22.** S 14-4-2. **23.** S 14-1-7. **24.** S 14-4-12. **25.** S 14-5-6. **26.** S 14-4-1. **27.** S 14-4-5. **28.** S 14-2-2. **29.** S 14-2-13. **30.** S 14-2-5. **31.** Author's collection. **32.** S 14-4-11. **33.** S 12-2-7. **34.** S 12-2-6. **35.** Author's collection. **36.** Buddy Patterson. **37.** 23-1-6. **38.** Buddy Patterson. **39.** Buddy Patterson. **40.** Buddy Patterson. **41.** S 23-1-9. **42.** S 3-7-1. **43.** S 3-7-9. **44.** S 4-9-5. **45.** S 1-4-6. **46.** S 2-9-10. **47.** S 1-5-5. **48.** S 1-5-1. **49.** S 2-4-2. **50.** S 2-5-1. **51.** S 13-3-5. **52.** S 1-8-3. **53.** S 6-9-4. **54.** S 4-8-3. **55.** S 4-4-7. **56.** S 4-4-6. **57.** S 4-6-8. **58.** S 2-5-11. **59.** Frank E. Storer. **60.** S 14-1-1. **61.** NA 89739. **62.** S 14-3-1. **63.** S 14-3-5. **64.** Buddy Patterson. **65.** Buddy Patterson. **66.** Buddy Patterson. **67.** S 14-2-1. **68.** S 14-1-5. **69.** NA 24312. **70.** S 15-3-13. **71.** S 14-5-7. **72.** S 14-3-8. **73.** S 14-3-13. **74.** S 14-1-6. **75.** S 14-4-6. **76.** S 14-

5-2. **77.** S 14-4-8. **78.** S 14-5-8. **79.** S 14-5-5. **80.** S 14-2-11. **81.** S 14-2-3. **82.** S 14-2-12. **83.** S 1-8-5. **84.** Buddy Patterson. **85.** Buddy Patterson. **86.** S 3-2-10. **87.** Buddy PatFterson. **88.** S 14-4-3. **89.** S 14-3-6. **90.** S 14-3-2. **91.** S 14-5-8. **92.** S 14-3-10. **93.** S 14-2-7. **94.** Buddy Patterson. **95.** Buddy Patterson. **96.** Buddy Patterson. **97.** Buddy Patterson. **98.** S 21-3-4. **99.** S 3-10-3. **100.** Buddy Patterson. **101.** S 14-3-7. **102.** S 14-3-11. **103.** S 14-3-12. **104.** S 14-4-4. **105.** S 14-1-4. **106.** S 14-3-3. **107.** S 21-1-9. **108.** S 21-1-10. **109.** Buddy Patterson. **110.** Buddy Patterson. **111.** Buddy Patterson. **112.** S 21-3-10. **113.** S 3-10-7. **114.** S 3-10-5. **115.** S 8-9-6. **116.** S 7-6-12. **117.** S 7-6-3. **118.** S 8-9-8. **119.** S 16-7-9. **120.** S 11-3-7. **121.** S 8-9-9. **122.** S 8-2-1. **123.** S 14-9-9. **124.** S 15-9-8. **125.** S 11-5-5. **126.** S 11-6-10. **127.** S 23-18-3. **128.** S 23-7-1. **129.** S 23-18-1. **130.** S 25-9-3. **131.** S 23-9-1. **132.** Buddy Patterson. **133.** S 4-1-2. **134.** Buddy Patterson. **135.** S 4-1-3. **136.** S 3-6-9. **137.** Buddy Patterson. **138.** Buddy Patterson. **139.** Buddy Patterson. **140.** S 3-2-7. **141.** S 8-2-4. **142.** S 8-5-3. **143.** S 3-5-6. **144.** S 2-10-6. **145.** S 2-4-5. **146.** S 8-3-8. **147.** S 4-8-1. **148.** Frank E. Storer. **149.** S 14-1-11. **150.** S 11-2-6. **151.** S 8-8-11. **152.** S 8-6-7. **153.** S 11-6-9. **154.** Courtesy Kevin Carroll. **155.** KU 2318. **156.** S 2-8-9. **157.** S 16-9-8. **158.** S 14-10-1. **159.** NA 93743. **160.** S 21-2-3. **161.** S 21-1-4. **162.** S 21-2-2. **163.** S 21-1-2. **164.** S 21-1-7. **165.** S 21-1-3. **166.** Buddy Patterson. **167.** Buddy Patterson. **168.** S 5-8-9. **169.** S 11-2-9. **170.** S 20-19-7. **171.** S 11-5-6. **172.** S 21-1-8. **173.** S 23-1-1. **174.** Buddy Patterson. **175.** S 21-1-1. **176.** Buddy Patterson. **177.** S 21-1-6. **178.** Buddy Patterson. **179.** Buddy Patterson. **180.** S S-1-14. **181.** S 27-4-4. **182.** S 5-8-8. **183.** S 5-8-5. **184.** S 8-7-8. **185.** S 8-7-9. **186.** S 14-7-11. **187.** S 10-10-11. **188.** Courtesy Gary Poppleton. **189.** S 11-10-15. **190.** S 23-1-5. **191.** S 23-3-4. **192.** S 3-1-3. **193.** S 8-2-3. **194.** S 23-3-6. **195.** S 23-7-2. **196.** S 3-7-6. **197.** Buddy Patterson. **198.** S 2-9-1. **199.** S 7-1-1. **200.** S 3-1-8. **201.** Buddy Patterson. **202.** S 33-1-6.

Chapter Ten

1. J. Duncan Campbell. **2.** J. Duncan Campbell. **3.** S 33-6-3. **4.** S 33-8-1. **5.** S 33-4-3. **6.** S 33-4-2. **7.** S 33-8-2. **8.** S 11-6-14. **9.** S 11-10-8. **10.** S 11-10-5. **11.** S 11-10-16 and S 11-10-4. **12.** KU 730. **13.** S 14-6-6. **14.** S 14-6-2. **15.** S 14-6-5. **16.** S 14-6-1. **17.** S 20-15-7. **18.** S 14-6-4. **19.** S 14-6-3. **20.** S 20-15-3. **21.** S 20-16-3. **22.** S 20-16-2. **23.** S 20-16-1. **24.** S 33-8-3. **25.** Regulations of 1851. **26.** S 14-6-8. **27.** S S-5-10. **28.** S 17-7. **29.** S 14-3. **30.** S 13-6. **31.** S 20-18-3. **32.** S 20-18-2. **33.** S 20-18-4. **34.** S 20-3-1. **35.** S 20-16-6. **36.** S 2-3-7. **37.** S 20-3-3. **38.** S 5-19. **39.** S S-4-14. **40.** S 10-5-2. **41.** S 15-9-4. **42.** S 14-10-2. **43.** S 20-4-5. **44.** Drawn by Terry Avery after original in the Institute of Heraldry. **45.** SI 60052. **46.** S 14-6-7. **47.** *Annual Report of the Quartermaster General, 1881,* copied by SI 86-11300. **48.** Buddy Patterson. **49.** Buddy Patterson. **50.** S 3-2-2. **51.** S 1-5-11. **52.** S 6-9-7. **53.** S 1-5-10. **54.** S 3-7-5. **55.** Buddy Patterson. **56.** S 1-4-9. **57.** S 2-5-2. **58.** S 2-9-7. **59.** S 1-4-2. **60.** S 1-7-10. **61.** S 8-9-2. **62.** Buddy Patterson. **63.** Buddy Patterson. **64.** KU PN 2366i. **65.** Buddy Patterson. **66.** Buddy Patterson. **67.** S 20-5-2. **68.** S 4-1-4. **69.** Buddy Patterson. **70.** S 3-9-10. **71.** S 8-9-1. **72.** S 23-16-2. **73.** S 20-5-7. **74.** S 23-13-2. **75.** S 20-8. **76.** S 20-7-1. **77.** S 22-5-7. **78.** S 22-4-2. **79.** S 20-5-6. **80.** S 20-7-2. **81.** S 14-9-8. **82.** NA 61198. **83.** S 11-6-11. **84.** NA 208-N-17827. **85.** S 20-4-4.

Chapter Eleven

1. U.S. Army Military History Institute. **2.** S S-5-9. **3.** S S-5-8. **4.** Courtesy Presidio of San Francisco Army Museum. **5.** S S-4-14. **6.** S S-1-11. **7.** S S-4-11. **8.** State Historical Society of Wisconsin. **9.** State Historical Society of Wisconsin. **10.** S S-3-7-1. **11.** KU 305. **12.** S 7-6-2. **13.** S 7-3-2. **14.** S 8-8-6. **15.** KU 1038. **16.** S 8-1-8. **17.** S 15-3-6. **18.** S 11-8-11. **19.** S 11-3-5. **20.** S 15-2-11. **21.** S 8-8-8. **22.** S 2-1-10. **23.** S 2-1-6. **24.** S 2-1-5. **25.** S 2-1-3. **26.** S 105. **27.** S 11-6-4. **28.** S 15-3-4. **29.** KU 2944.1. **30.** S 15-3-10. **31.** S 16-8-5. **32.** S C-6-11-5. **33.** S C-6-11-6. **34.** S 11-6-1. **35.** S 15-3-1. **36.** S 11-3-2. **37.** S C-6-11-1. **38.** S 2-1-7. **39.** S 14-9-4. **40.** S 16-2-4. **41.** S 2-1-1. **42.** S 8-8-4. **43.** S 16-8-3. **44.** KU 1322. **45.** S C-6-10-4. **46.** S C-6-10-3. **47.** S 8-7-1. **48.** S C-6-12-1. **49.** S 15-3-9. **50.** S 16-8-8. **51.** NA 42751. **52.** S 16-4-11. **53.** S 15-2-15. **54.** S 15-2-1. **55.** S 14-7-4. **56.** S 8-8-2. **57.** S 16-5-2. **58.** S 16-4-5. **59.** S C-1-3-3. **60.** KU 2357. **61.** KU 1089. **62.** Fort Leavenworth Army Museum. **63.** S C-6-10-2. **64.** S 11-3-3. **65.** S 15-3-2. **66.** S 15-3-8. **67.** S 15-3-3. **68.** S 16-9-9. **69.** S 11-3-4. **70.** S 16-1-6. **71.** S 12-3-1. **72.** S 16-1-1. **73.** S 16-5-4. **74.** S 16-1-2. **75.** Courtesy Fort Point and Army Museum Association. **76.** Buddy Patterson. **77.** S C-6-10-1. **78.** S C-16-1-4. **79.** S 16-9-7. **80.** S 16-9-2. **81.** KU 2998.1. **82.** Author's collection. **83.** S 16-2-12. **84.** S 16-1-12. **85.** S 16-5-3. **86.** S 16-1-11. **87.** S 12-4-1. **88.** S 15-1-6. **89.** S 11-6-3. **90.** S 16-9-6. **91.** S 16-4-10. **92.** S C-6-11-3. **93.** Buddy Patterson. **94.** S 15-2-12. **95.** S 15-2-7. **96.** S 15-3-11. **97.** S 11-6-2. **98.** S 10-5-9. **99.** Courtesy George Cress and *Military Images*. **100.** S 16-4-2. **101.** S 10-8-5. **102.** S 16-5-1. **103.** Shelby L. Stanton. **104.** S 10-10-7. **105.** S 16-8-10. **106.** S C-6-11-2. **107.** S 15-2-14. **108.** S 15-3-12. **109.** S 15-3-7. **110.** Terry Avery. **111.** Terry Avery. **112.** Terry Avery. **113.** S 15-2-3. **114.** S 10-10-6. **115.** Courtesy Shelby L. Stanton. **116.**

S 16-4-6. **117.** S 16-4-8. **118.** S 12-2-4. **119.** S 16-4-7. **120.** S 10-10-10. **121.** S 16-8-11. **122.** Office of the Surgeon General, Department of the Army. **123.** S 8-8-10. **124.** Office of the Surgeon General, Department of the Army. **125.** S 10-8-7. **126.** S 10-8-4. **127.** SI. **128.** S 8-7-4. **129.** S 22-3-5. **130.** NA 590881. **131.** S 16-4-3. **132.** S 10-8-6. **133.** S 16-1-1. **134.** Buddy Patterson. **135.** S 16-4-4. **136.** S 13-3-8. **137.** S 12-1-1. **138.** Buddy Patterson. **139.** S 2-1-8. **140.** S 16-4-9. **141.** S C-6-8-1. **142.** S C-6-8-2. **143.** S 13-1-2 and 11-10-10. **144.** S 13-1-2 and 11-10-2. **145.** S 8-4-4. **146.** S 14-10-9. **147.** S 15-1-8. **148.** S 8-5-1. **149.** KU 699.1. **150.** S 7-8-6. **151.** S C-6-12-4. **152.** S 16-3-5. **153.** S S-3-2-1. **154.** S C-6-12-3. **155.** S 16-7-7. **156.** KU 703. **157.** S 11-10-10. **158.** S 11-10-2. **159.** S 8-1-6. **160.** Buddy Patterson. **161.** Buddy Patterson. **162.** KU 2871.20. **163.** S C-6-12-2. **164.** S C-6-16-2. **165.** S 21-3-2. **166.** S 3-6-4. **167.** S 3-9-2. **168.** S 4-2-10. **169.** S C-6-11-7. **170.** S 1-4-5. **171.** S 1-8-6. **172.** S 4-5-2. **173.** S 7-10-6. **174.** S 11-5-7. **175.** S 4-7-5. **176.** S 2-4-10. **177.** S 1-4-10. **178.** S 4-8-4. **179.** S 2-7-7. **180.** S 13-3-4. **181.** S 20-2-3. **182.** S 16-1-10.

Chapter Twelve

1. S 23-7-4. **2.** The West Point Museum Collections. **3.** S S-2-13. **4.** 1851 regulations. **5.** The West Point Museum Collections. **6.** The West Point Museum Collections. **7.** S S-4-8. **8.** S S-5-1-2. **9.** S S-4-20. **10.** S S-2-14-1. **11** Custis Lee Mansion, National Park Service. **12.** NA B-5593. **13.** S C-2-2-2. **14.** S C 2-1-2. **15.** S S-2-20. **16.** S C-8-16. **17.** S 11-10-14. **18.** Library of Congress B 4171. **19.** NA 77-F-155-86-7. **20.** S 8-5-2. **21.** S 15-8-2. **22.** S 8-6-5. **23.** S 8-5-8. **24.** S 15-8-1. **25.** S 15-10-5. **26.** S 11-9-5. **27.** S C-2-1-4. **28.** S C-2-1-1. **29.** S C-1-16-3. **30.** Buddy Patterson. **31.** S 2-8-7. **32.** S C-2-4-1. **33.** S C-2-4-3. **34.** S C-2-2-4. **35.** S C-2-2-3. **36.** S 15-4-2. **37.** S 1-1-1. **38.** NA 35531. **39.** S 16-7-10. **40.** S 2-8-5. **41.** S 2-8-6. **42.** S 14-7-3. **43.** S 11-6-12. **44.** S 1-1-2. **45.** S 1-10-10. **46.** S 1-10-3. **47.** S 20-2-2. **48.** S 2-2-7. **49.** S 2-8-4. **50.** Buddy Patterson. **51.** S 3-1-1. **52.** S 1-10-6. **53.** S 20-6-1. **54.** S 10-6-5. **55.** S 7-6-1. **56.** Courtesy Shelby L. Stanton. **57.** S 11-10-1. **58.** 1851 regulations. **59.** U.S. Army Military History Institute. **60.** S 10-10-5. **61.** S 2-2-6. **62.** KU 1728. **63.** S 2-2-3. **64.** S 1-10-8. **65.** S 3-3-1. **66.** Buddy Patterson. **67.** S 21-3-11. **68.** S 21-4-8. **69.** S 21-4-3. **70.** Buddy Patterson. **71.** Buddy Patterson. **72.** S C-2-2-1. **73.** S 21-4-7. **74.** S S-1-12-2. **75.** S 3-7-8. **76.** Buddy Patterson. **77.** S 11-5-8. **78.** Buddy Patterson. **79.** Buddy Patterson. **80.** S 8-3-3. **81.** S 2-4-1. **82.** S 2-4-8. **83.** S 4-5-5. **84.** S 4-7-4. **85.** S 4-3-7. **86.** S 4-6-1. **87.** S 4-7-2. **88.** S 1-3-6. **89.** S 2-10-9. **90.** S 23-10-3. **91.** S 22-2-1.

Chapter Thirteen

1. S 14-7-7. **2.** S 15-1-5. **3.** S 11-10-13. **4.** S S-2-3-2. **5.** S 7-8-3. **6.** S 16-7-6. **7.** S 16-7-5. **8.** S 11-6-5. **9.** S 16-7-1. **10.** S S-1-13-4. **11.** S S-1-13-5. **12.** S 8-4-2. **13.** S 11-7-4. **14.** S 8-6-4. **15.** S 7-4-8. **16.** S 5-9-1. **17.** S 8-6-2. **18.** S 5-9-2. **19.** S S-2-3-1. **20.** S C-2-20-1. **21.** S 16-3-4. **22.** S 5-8-10. **23.** S 8-5-6. **24.** S 16-6-2. **25.** S 6-1-5. **26.** NA 461078. **27.** S 1-9-5. **28.** S 2-2-4. **29.** S 1-9-4. **30.** S 8-7-7. **31.** S 1-10-11. **32.** S S-2-11-2. **33.** S 10-9-9. **34.** U.S. Army, U.S. Military Academy 3378/AH68. **35.** S 15-4-8. **36.** S 15-4-9. **37.** Author's collection, courtesy Grace Sorel. **38.** Author's collection, courtesy Grace Sorel. **39.** NA 419024. **40.** S 15-4-7. **41.** U.S. Army Band, Master Sergeant Leroy Sundberg. **42.** S 14-1-8. **43.** Buddy Patterson. **44.** Buddy Patterson. **45.** Buddy Patterson. **46.** Buddy Patterson. **47.** Buddy Patterson. **48.** Buddy Patterson. **49.** Buddy Patterson. **50.** Buddy Patterson. **51.** S 4-1-5. **52.** S 4-2-8. **53.** S 15-1-2. **54.** S 3-10-4. **55.** S 10-9-10. **56.** S 1-7-4. **57.** S 2-3-5. **58.** S 2-3-10. **59.** S C-1-9-4.

Chapter Fourteen

1. S 11-5-3. **2.** S 10-3-9. **3.** S 15-10-8. **4.** S 11-8-10. **5.** S S-3-2-2. **6.** S 16-6-3. **7.** S 15-10-2. **8.** S 15-10-7. **9.** S S-2-12. **10.** S S-3-4. **11.** KU 1618. **12.** KU 1280.

Chapter Fifteen

1. S S-4-17. **2.** S 15-5-4. **3.** Buddy Patterson. **4.** S 23-3-8. **5.** S 23-3-1. **6.** S 10-1-11. **7.** S 23-10-6. **8.** S 23-11-2. **9.** S 23-6-3. **10.** S 15-4-1. **11.** S 20-4-9. **12.** S S-2-3-4. **13.** S 20-5-1. **14.** U.S. Army photograph, courtesy *Army* magazine. **15.** U.S. Army photograph, courtesy *Army* magazine. **16.** S 23-1-8. **17.** S 23-1-3. **18.** S 2-7-2. **19.** S 4-4-8. **20.** S 4-4-2. **21.** S 23-11-1. **22.** NA 90844.

Chapter Sixteen

1. From Scott's *Tactics*, published in 1840. **2.** S 25-2-3. **3.** From 1851 regulations. **4.** S S-4-7. **5.** S S-1-5. **6.** From 1851 regulations. **7.** U.S. Army Military History Institute. **8.** S S-3-18. **9.** S C-3-2-3. **10.** S 8-10-1. **11.** S 26-3-2. **12.** S 23-4-3. **13.** S C-3-2-1. **14.** S C-3-4-1. **15.** S 13-9-3. **16.** S 16-7-2. **17.** S 11-10-6. **18.** S 11-7-7. **19.** S 27-9-1. **20.** S 27-7-3. **21.** S 27-4-1. **22.** S 27-5-1. **23.** S 27-5-2. **24.** S 27-42. **25.** From 1851 regulations. **26.** S 14-7-9. **27.** S 16-2-3. **28.** Buddy Patterson. **29.** Buddy Patterson. **30.** S 3-6-11. **31.** S 11-6. **32.** S 3-9-5. **33.** S 3-3-5. **34.** S 2-4-3. **35.** S 13-3-3. **36.** S 1-5-3. **37.** S 2-3-4. **38.** S 1-7-8. **39.** S 2-6-7.

Chapter Seventeen

1. S S-4-3. **2.** S C-3-5-1. **3.** S 15-5-7. **4.** S C-3-6-5. **5.** S 20-10-7. **6.** S C-3-7-1. **7.** S 20-14-3.

8. S 20-14-1. **9.** S 20-14-2. **10.** Buddy Patterson. **11.** S 20-14-6. **12.** S 15-2-5. **13.** S 20-14-7. **14.** S C-3-7-3. **15.** S 20-10-8. **16.** S 2-1-4. **17.** S 20-10-3. **18.** S 20-11-2. **19.** S 20-11-1. **20.** S 20-11-3. **21.** Buddy Patterson. **22.** Buddy Patterson. **23.** S 10-4-8. **24.** S S-3-15-1. **25.** S 1-2-8.

CHAPTER EIGHTEEN

1. S C-1-10-2. **2.** S C-1-10-3. **3.** S 11-10-9. **4.** NA 92-UF-3-6-23. **5.** S 13-1-1. **6.** S 7-8-2. **7.** S C-1-9-5. **8.** S 7-4-7. **9.** S C-1-9-3. **10.** S 11-7-5. **11.** S C-1-12-4. **12.** S 15-8-7. **13.** S 15-10-3. **14.** S 15-8-3. **15.** S 11-9-6. **16.** S 20-11-5. **17.** S 20-11-6. **18.** S 2-1-23. **19.** S 23-4-4. **20.** S 20-12-4. **21.** S 20-14-8. **22.** S 20-14-9. **23.** S 20-15-4. **24.** S 20-15-5. **25.** S 20-14-4. **26.** S 20-14-5. **27.** S 20-15-1. **28.** S 20-15-2. **29.** S 20-14-10. **30.** S 16-9-1. **31.** S 15-2-10. **32.** S 16-2-10. **33.** S 20-12-5. **34.** S C-1-8-1. **35.** NA 38691. **36.** Buddy Patterson. **37.** Buddy Patterson. **38.** Buddy Patterson. **39.** S 3-2-6. **40.** S 3-6-5. **41.** S 3-5-5. **42.** S 7-10-7. **43.** S 4-2-9. **44.** S 4-2-1. **45.** S 2-9-3. **46.** S 1-4-8. **47.** S 2-4-4. **48.** S 2-7-10. **49.** S 1-8-3. **50.** S 4-7-8. **51.** S 7-1-9. **52.** S 4-3-10. **53.** S 20-2-6. **54.** S 20-11-4. **55.** S 20-11-7. **56.** S 20-12-7. **57.** S 20-12-3. **58.** S 20-12-2. **59.** S 23-11-4. **60.** S 22-2-2. **61.** S 23-12-1. **62.** S 23-13-3. **63.** S 23-13-1.

CHAPTER NINETEEN

1. S 11-10-11. **2.** S 7-3-3. **3.** S 11-10-11 and 13-1-2. **4.** S 8-4-1. **5.** S 16-5-5. **6.** S 10-5-4. **7.** S C-2-5-2. **8.** S 11-3-6. **9.** S S-5-15. **10.** SI 83-841. **11.** SI 83-841. **12.** S 11-3-9. **13.** S C-2-5-1. **14.** S C-2-16-2. **15.** S 10-9-1. **16.** S 16-8-12. **17.** Buddy Patterson. **18.** Buddy Patterson. **19.** S 4-1-10.

CHAPTER TWENTY

1. Bureau of Archives and History, New Jersey State Library. **2.** Author's collection. **3.** U.S. Army Chaplain School. **4.** Author's collection. **5.** KU 699. **6.** S C-1-6-5. **7.** S 6-6-4. **8.** S C-3-4-4. **9.** S 11-6-8. **10.** S 16-8-4. **11.** NA 13449. **12.** NA 35336. **13.** S 11-3-8. **14.** S C-3-5-3. **15.** S 15-2-13. **16.** S 14-9-5. **17.** S 8-6-3. **18.** S 8-6-6. **19.** S 23-5-4. **20.** S 10-4-7. **21.** S 1-2-7. **22.** S 1-7-7. **23.** Buddy Patterson.

CHAPTER TWENTY-ONE

1. S S-3-17. **2.** S S-4-12. **3.** S C-3-5-2. **4.** S 15-5-6. **5.** S C-3-6-1. **6.** S C-3-6-2. **7.** S C-3-6-4. **8.** NA 97393. **9.** S 20-5-3. **10.** S 23-3-6. **11.** S 20-5-4. **12.** S C-3-7-2. **13.** S 15-2-4. **14.** S 23-5-3. **15.** S 23-10-1. **16.** S 20-10-2. **17.** S 20-4-7. **18.** Courtesy *Army* magazine. **19.** S 23-3-9. **20.** S C-3-6-3.

CHAPTER TWENTY-TWO

1. S S-5-14. **2.** S S-5-13. **3.** S C-3-4-1. **4.** S C-3-5-5. **5.** S C-3-4-3. **6.** S C-3-4-7. **7.** S C-3-5-6. **8.** S C-3-4-2. **9.** S 3-2-9. **10.** S 3-7-3. **11.** S 21-4-4. **12.** S 21-4-2. **13.** S 4-2-4. **14.** S 8-3-1. **15.** S 11-5-2. **16.** S 4-6-10. **17.** S 1-7-3.

CHAPTER TWENTY-THREE

1. S S-3-11-3. **2.** S C-1-11. **3.** S 11-10-12. **4.** S 27-7-1. **5.** S C-1-10-1. **6.** S S-4-15. **7.** S S-1-2. **8.** From the collection of Dr. B. F. Cooling, photograph by Gordon Chappell, courtesy Dr. B. F. Cooling. **9.** S 10-7-1. **10.** S 15-8-5. **11.** S 2-2-1. **12.** S 14-5-10. **13.** S 1-1-3. **14.** S 11-9-2. **15.** S 8-9-7. **16.** S 16-8-9. **17.** NA 29643. **18.** Buddy Patterson. **19.** S 11-3-10. **20.** S 15-2-6. **21.** S 10-8-11. **22.** Buddy Patterson. **23.** S 15-9-10. **24.** S 19-9-11. **25.** S 15-9-3. **26.** S 14-9-6. **27.** S 15-4-4. **28.** S 15-9-6. **29.** S 11-9-10. **30.** S 12-1-8. **31.** S 15-9-1. **32.** S 3-5-4. **33.** Buddy Patterson. **34.** Buddy Patterson. **35.** S 3-10-1. **36.** S 4-9-4. **37.** S 2-6-9. **38.** S 2-9-11. **39.** S 3-3-4. **40.** S 1-8-9. **41.** S 4-3-8. **42.** S 4-4-4. **43.** S 4-5-4. **44.** S 2-5-9. **45.** S 8-3-2. **46.** S 8-1-5. **47.** NA.

CHAPTER TWENTY-FOUR

1. Denver Public Library, Western History Department. **2.** Courtesy Fort Sill Museum. **3.** S 11-10-3. **4.** Quartermaster Department. **5.** S 20-5-5. **6.** NA 81471. **7.** Buddy Patterson. **8.** Buddy Patterson. **9.** S 20-12-8. **10.** S 20-12-9. **11.** Author's collection. **12.** S 14-7-8. **13.** S 15-5-8. **14.** S 10-4-9. **15.** S 10-4-5. **16.** S 22-11.

CHAPTER TWENTY-FIVE

1. S 27-7-5. **2.** Buddy Patterson. **3.** Buddy Patterson. **4.** S 21-5-1. **5.** S 21-5-2. **6.** Buddy Patterson. **7.** Buddy Patterson. **8.** S 21-4-10. **9.** Buddy Patterson.

CHAPTER TWENTY-SIX

1. S C-1-14-3. **2.** S C-1-16-1. **3.** S 7-3-4. **4.** NA 7228. **5.** S 4-5-1.

CHAPTER TWENTY-SEVEN

1. Courtesy Presidio of San Francisco Army Museum. **2.** S 7-2-8. **3.** S C-1-3-2. **4.** S 23-5-5. **5.** S 4-9-9. **6.** NA 991497. **7.** NA 350-P-Qc 1-2. **8.** NA 99156. **9.** NA 350-P-Qc 2-2.

CHAPTER TWENTY-EIGHT

1. S C-1-14-2. **2.** S C-1-15-2. **3.** S C-1-16-2. **4.** S 8-7-2. **5.** S 1-1-5. **6.** S C-1-14-5. **7.** Buddy Patterson. **8.** S 3-5-7.

CHAPTER TWENTY-NINE

1. S 11-8-3. **2.** S C-1-9-2. **3.** S 4-9-10. **4.** S 5-8-7. **5.** S 5-6-3. **6.** NA 102216.

CHAPTER THIRTY

1. SI 61203. **2.** SI 605030. **3.** SI P65709.

CHAPTER THIRTY-ONE

1. S 3-5-8. **2.** S 2-8-10. **3.** S 10-5-7. **4.** S 4-10-9. **5.** S 4-10-4. **6.** S 5-6-6. **7.** S 8-8-7. **8.** S C-3-4-5. **9.** Courtesy Shelby L. Stanton. **10.** NA

98198. **11.** S S-6-9. **12.** S 17-1-1. **13.** NA 28335. **14.** S 13-2-13. **15.** S 13-3-1. **16.** S S-1-19. **17.** S S-1-15. **18.** S 20-6-2. **19.** S 12-1-5. **20.** S 27-7-4.

Chapter Thirty–Two

1. S 10-1-1. **2.** S 10-1-9. **3.** S 14-6-11. **4.** S 11-8-5. **5.** S 14-5-11. **6.** S 11-8-12. **7.** S 11-8-7. **8.** S 10-2-3. **9.** S 10-4-2. **10.** S 10-1-10. **11.** S 10-2-5. **12.** S 10-4-3. **13.** S 10-4-4. **14.** S 10-2-7. **15.** S 10-1-6. **16.** S 10-2-2. **17.** S 10-1-5. **18.** S 10-1-2. **19.** S 23-10-9. **20.** S 23-8-5. **21.** S 23-8-1. **22.** S 10 1-4. **23.** Official White House photograph, 13 Sept. 1989. **24.** S 23-7-7. **25.** S 10-2-1. **26.** S 10-1-12. **27.** S 10-4-1. **28.** S 23-8-3. **29.** S 23-8-4. **30.** S 23-10-10. **31.** S 23-8-6. **32.** S 12-4-4. **33.** S 23-15-2. **34.** S 23-1-3. **35.** S 23-12-3. **36.** S 22-1-2. **37.** S 23-14-3. **38.** S 23-14-2. **39.** S 10-1-7. **40.** S 23-7-6. **41.** S 14-5-9. **42.** S 14-6-10. **43.** S 14-2-4. **44.** S 15-5-1. **45.** S 15-5-2. **46.** S 10-1-8. **47.** NA 108884.

Chapter Thirty-Three

1. S C-1-15-3. **2.** S C-1-15-1. **3.** S 11-7-6.

Chapter Thirty-Four

1. S 13-9-1. **2.** S 11-8-4. **3.** S 7-3-5. **4.** S 2-2-2. **5.** Buddy Patterson. **6.** S 21-4-11. **7.** S 3-7-7. **8.** Courtesy Richard T. Graney.

Chapter Thirty-Five

1. S 14-5-12. **2.** S 14-5-13. **3.** S 10-6-7. **4.** S 11-8-6.

Chapter Thirty-Six

1. NA 14582. **2.** NA RB 1481. **3.** S 14-9-2. **4.** S 12-10-3. **5.** S 12-10-2. **6.** S 24-18-3. **7.** NA 96700. **8.** NA 96705. **9.** S 24-8. **10.** S 24-14-2. **11.** S 15-4-3. **12.** S 12-9-9. **13.** Courtesy Stefan Wesplowskie. **14.** NA 327555. **15.** NA 283977. **16.** NA 321707. **17.** S 12-10-4. **18.** S 14-9-3. **19.** S 15-7-3. **20.** U.S. Army Transportation Corps Museum. **21.** NA 96704. **22.** S 5-10-6. **23.** S 6-7-2. **24.** S S-1-8. **25.** S 12-5-2. **26.** S S-2-8. **27.** S 6-1-3. **28.** S 13-2-3. **29.** S 12-5-1. **30.** S 24-15. **31.** S S-2-3-3. **32.** S 7-10-3. **33.** S 14-10-7. **34.** S 6-5-4. **35.** S 11-7-1. **36.** S 12-10-5. **37.** SI. **38.** SI. **39.** SI. **40.** SI. **41.** SI. **42.** SI. **43.** SI. **44** . S C-306686. **45.** S 23-8-7. **46.** S 23-18-2. **47.** S 24-11-1. **48.** S 24-12-1. **49.** S 24-16-2. **50.** S 24-14-1. **51.** S 24-10-2. **52.** S 24-13-2. **53.** S 24-18-2. **54.** S 24-9. **55.** S 24-13-1. **56.** S 24-11-2. **57.** S 24-12-2. **58.** S 24-16-1. **59.** S 24-10-1. **60.** S 8-8-1. **61.** S 14-7-2. **62.** S 13-1-3. **63.** S 12-10-1. **64.** S 12-9-2. **65.** S 12-9-1. **66.** S 13-9-4. **67.** S S-4-19.

Chapter Thirty-Seven

1. S 8-4-3. **2.** S 20-15-6. **3.** S 6-9-2. **4.** S C-7-19-1. **5.** Buddy Patterson. **6.** S 7-2-3. **7.** Buddy Patterson. **8.** Buddy Patterson. **9.** U.S. Military Academy Archives. **10.** KU 1820. **11.** KU 2856.

Chapter Thirty-Eight

1. S C-7-14-5. **2.** S C-7-14-6. **3.** S C-7-17-1. **4.** NA 22393. **5.** NA 21333. **6.** S C-7-14-2. **7.** S C-7-14-1. **8.** S C-7-14-4. **9.** S C-7-17-2. **10.** S C-7-14-3. **11.** S C-7-15-2. **12.** S C-7-15-1. **13.** NA 51748. **14.** S C-7-15-3. **15.** S 23-3-7. **16.** S 23-3-2. **17.** Buddy Patterson. **18.** Buddy Patterson. **19.** Buddy Patterson. **20.** Buddy Patterson. **21.** Buddy Patterson. **22.** Buddy Patterson. **23.** Buddy Patterson. **24.** Buddy Patterson. **25.** Buddy Patterson. **26.** S C-7-15-4. **27.** S 23-3-5. **28.** S 3-10-10. **29.** S 3-9-3. **30.** S 22-6-2. **31.** S 8-1-2. **32.** S 2-7-5. **33.** S 1-5-3. **34.** S 1-8-4. **35.** S 1-8-7. **36.** S 4-8-9. **37.** S 2-7-8. **38.** S 4-3-1. **39.** S 23-3-4. **40.** S 23-7-5. **41.** S 22-6-1. **42.** S 7-7-7. **43.** S 12-3-4. **44.** NA 99339. **45.** U.S. Air Force, 20778. **46.** S 103. **47.** S 102. **48.** U.S. Air Force, 14128 AC. **49.** S 23-10-7. **50.** S 101. **51.** S 13-3-6. **52.** S 100. **53.** S 104. **54.** NA 29718. **55.** S 23-3-7. **56.** S 22-1-3. **57.** S 23-16-5. **58.** U.S. Air Force, 3029 AC. **59.** S 20-4-6.

Chapter Thirty-Nine

1. S 5-5-7. **2.** S 5-5-8. **3.** S 5-5-9. **4.** Buddy Patterson. **5.** S 5-5-5. **6.** S 5-5-6. **7.** S 5-4-6. **8.** S 5-6-8. **9.** S 6-6-5. **10.** S 6-6-7. **11.** S 6-6-6. **12.** S 15-2-9. **13.** Buddy Patterson. **14.** Buddy Patterson. **15.** S 3-6-3. **16.** Buddy Patterson. **17.** S 1-3-3. **18.** S 8-3-10. **19.** S 7-4-3. **20.** S 8-3-7. **21.** S 7-4-2. **22.** S 7-4-1. **23.** S 8-3-6. **24.** S 8-3-9. **25.** S 7-4-4. **26.** S 10-1-13. **27.** S 12-1-7. **28.** S 7-10-8. **29.** S 8-1-1. **30.** S 4-8-7. **31.** S 4-8-8. **32.** S 1-4-4. **33.** S 7-1-4. **34.** S 4-8-6. **35.** S 2-4-9. **36.** Author's collection, gift from Colonel Charles Gill, USA Ret. **37.** S 22-18-1. **38.** S 22-17-1. **39.** S 14-9-7. **40.** S 10-6-1. **41.** S 15-6-8. **42.** S 15-6-4. **43.** S 15-6-3. **44.** S 10-3-1. **45.** S 8-2-6. **46.** S 4-7-7. **47.** S 4-8-2. **48.** S 4-8-5. **49.** S 7-1-5. **50.** S 4-8-10. **51.** S 1-7-11. **52.** S 1-3-1. **53.** S 4-8-11. **54.** S 1-3-2. **55.** S 1-3-4. **56.** S 10-3-3. **57.** S 11-2-8. **58.** S 11-2-5. **59.** S 25-3-1. **60.** Buddy Patterson. **61.** Buddy Patterson. **62.** Buddy Patterson. **63.** S 10-9-3. **64.** Buddy Patterson. **65.** Buddy Patterson. **66.** Buddy Patterson. **67.** Buddy Patterson. **68.** S 12-3-6. **69.** S 2-5-3. **70.** S 2-5-10. **71.** S 2-3-2. **72.** S 2-3-8. **73.** Courtesy Donald Norton. **74.** S 6-9-6.

Chapter Forty

1. NA 90839. **2.** S C-2-19-5. **3.** S C-2-29-3. **4.** S C-2-19-6. **5.** NA 33172. **6.** NA 35533. **7.** S 22-3-1. **8.** S 22-3-2. **9.** Buddy Patterson. **10.** Buddy Patterson. **11.** S C-2-20-4. **12.** S C-2-20-2. **13.** S 22-7-1. **14.** S 23-16-3. **15.** Courtesy Shelby L. Stanton. **16.** S 22-7-2. **17.** S 23-13-4. **18.** S 23-12-5. **19.** S 25-6-1. **20.** Buddy Patterson. **21.** S 23-1-10. **22.** S 22-13. **23.** S 3-7-10. **24.** S 3-9-8. **25.** S 3-1-9. **26.** S 23-10-2. **27.** S 1-8-10. **28.** S 2-3-1. **29.** S 1-2-1.

Chapter Forty-One

1. S 23-1-4. **2.** S S-2-10-1. **3.** S S-1-20-4. **4.** S 14-7-10. **5.** S 23-1-2. **6.** Buddy Patterson. **7.** Buddy Patterson. **8.** Buddy Patterson. **9.** Buddy Patterson. **10.** Buddy Patterson. **11.** Buddy Patterson. **12.** Buddy Patterson. **13.** Buddy Patterson. **14.** S 1-10-1. **15.** S 1-10-2. **16.** Author's collection. **17.** S 15-9-5. **18.** Author's collection. **19.** S 12-1-3. **20.** S 4-3-4. **21.** S 6-9-9. **22.** S 2-3-10. **23.** S 7-1-8. **24.** S 2-10-3. **25.** S 2-3-9.

Chapter Forty-Two

1. S C-2-19-1. **2.** S C-2-19-2. **3.** S 11-6-6. **4.** S 11-6-7. **5.** S 16-8-2. **6.** S 8-7-6. **7.** S 5-6-9. **8.** S 5-8-12. **9.** Buddy Patterson. **10.** Buddy Patterson. **11.** Buddy Patterson. **12.** S 3-1-10. **13.** S 23-4-6. **14.** S 2-8-8. **15.** S 27-10-5. **16.** S C-2-19-4. **17.** S 3-1-6. **18.** S 7-8-1. **19.** S 5-6-4. **20.** S 5-6-2. **21.** S 12-3-5. **22.** Buddy Patterson. **23.** S 23-12-2. **24.** S 10-4-11. **25.** S 6-9-10. **26.** S 4-3-11.**27.** S 4-5-6. **28.** S 4-3-9. **29.** S 4-6-7. **30.** S 10-4-10.

Chapter Forty-Three

1. Buddy Patterson. **2.** Buddy Patterson. **3.** S 20-19-6. **4.** S 20-19-2. **5.** S 20-19-5. **6.** S 20-19-3. **7.** S 20-19-2. **8.** S 20-18-8. **9.** S 20-18-9. **10.** S 20-18-7. **11.** S 20-18-5. **12.** S 20-19-1. **13.** S 20-18-6. **14.** S 23-3-1. **15.** S 23-5-2. **16.** S 23-7-3. **17.** S C-1-14-4. **18.** S 23-3-8. **19.** S 23-3-9. **20.** S 23-4-7. **21.** S 23-4-5. **22.** S 16-5-6. **23.** S 10-6-9. **24.** S 10-5-5. **25.** S 7-7-8. **26.** S 6-1-2. **27.** S 6-7-3. **28.** S 6-5-3. **29.** Author's collection. **30.** S 27-9-1. **31.** S 22-4-1. **32.** S 20-18-1. **33.** S C-1-12-3. **34.** S 20-17-1. **35.** S 20-17-2. **36.** S 20-16-8. **37.** S 20-16-9. **38.** S 20-17-3. **39.** S 20-17-4. **40.** S 12-1-6. **41.** S 12-3-2.

Chapter Forty-Four

1. S C-1-3-1. **2.** Buddy Patterson. **3.** S 20-9. **4.** Buddy Patterson. **5.** S S-1-12-3. **6.** Buddy Patterson. **7.** Buddy Patterson. **8.** KU PN 2030I. **9.** S C-3-1-2. **10.** S C-3-2-2. **11.** S C-3-1-1. **12.** S C-3-2-4. **13.** S 23-14-1. **14.** S 3-2-11. **15.** S 23-9-2. **16.** S 23-10-4. **17.** S 23-16-1. **18.** S 23-12-4. **19.** S 3-8-6. **20.** S 3-1-11. **21.** S 2-4-7. **22.** S 7-1-7. **23.** S 2-9-2. **24.** S 3-3-1. **25.** S 11-5-4. **26.** S 1-3-5. **27.** S 23-3-3. **28.** S 2-3-6. **29.** S 11-5-1. **30.** S 4-5-8. **31.** S 4-7-1. **32.** S 2-6-10. **33.** S 1-5-9. **34.** S 1-4-7.

Chapter Forty-Five

1. S C-7-19-2. **2.** S C-3-1-3. **3.** S 14-7-6. **4.** S C-2-20-3. **5.** Courtesy Shelby L. Stanton. **6.** S 1-10-5. **7.** S 23-3-5. **8.** S 12-2-5. **9.** Buddy Patterson. **10.** Buddy Patterson. **11.** Buddy Patterson. **12.** S 3-8-8. **13.** S 3-9-1. **14.** S 1-5-2. **15.** S 2-7-9. **16.** S 2-7-11. **17.** S 6-9-8. **18.** S 4-7-10. **19.** S 4-5-9. **20.** S 13-3-2.

Chapter Forty-Six

1. S 32-6. **2.** Buddy Patterson.

Chapter Forty-Seven

1. S C-1-6-4. **2.** Buddy Patterson.

Chapter Forty-Eight

1. S 14-6-12. **2.** S 15-5-9. **3.** S 15-5-10. **4.** NA RG 168-G, folder H. **5.** S 23-4-2. **6.** S 23-10-8. **7.** S 23-7-8. **8.** S 23-7-9. **9.** S 23-3-2. **10.** S 11-8-8. **11.** S 11-8-9. **12.** U.S. Army photograph P-117342, courtesy *Army* magazine. **13.** Buddy Patterson. **14.** S 4-1-7. **15.** S 15-5-5. **16.** S 15-5-3. **17.** S 25-2-1.

Chapter Forty-Nine

1. S 6-5-2. **2.** S 14-5-1. **3.** S 14-7-1. **4.** NA 137865.

Chapter Fifty

1. S 15-1-1. **2.** S 2-10-1. **3.** S 11-3-1. **4.** S 4-6-5. **5.** S 2-6-8. **6.** U.S. Army photograph, courtesy *Army* magazine.

Chapter Fifty-One

1. S 4-7-11. **2.** S 10-4-13. **3.** S 20-2-9. **4.** S 20-2-8.

Chapter Fifty-Two

1. S 1-10-7. **2.** S 1-10-9. **3.** S 1-7-2. **4.** S 20-3-4.

Chapter Fifty-Three

1. S 15-9-7. **2.** S 2-10-11. **3.** S 2-6-4. **4.** S 4-4-1. **5.** S 1-7-1.

Chapter Fifty-Four

1. S 1-1-4. **2.** S 15-1-7. **3.** Author's collection. **4.** S 2-5-4. **5.** S 8-1-3. **6.** S 1-7-6.

Chapter Fifty-Five

1. U.S. Army Audiovisual Center. **2.** S 27-5-3.

Chapter Fifty-Six

1. Office of the Deputy Chief of Staff, Personnel.

Chapter Fifty-Seven

1. S 25-7-4. **2.** S 25-4-1. **3.** S 25-7-1. **4.** S 20-3-2. **5.** S 25-9-1. **6.** S 25-9-2. **7.** Courtesy A. E. Kauffman. **8.** Courtesy A. E. Kauffman. **9.** S 15-7-5. **10.** S 23-6-1. **11.** S 5-10-1. **12.** S 20-3-9. **13.** S 23-6-2. **14.** S 23-3-3. **15.** S 20-3-10. **16.** S 26-3-1. **17.** S 20-4-2. **18.** S 20-4-3. **19.** S 20-10-1. **20.** S 20-3-6. **21.** S 20-3-8. **22.** S 23-6-4. **23.** S 27-10-2. **24.** War Department. **25.** Department of the Army. **26.** NA 286023.

Chapter Fifty-Eight

1. Author's collection. **2.** Courtesy Rensselaer County Historical Society, photograph 69.217. **3.**

Washington/Custis/Lee Collection, Washington and Lee University, Virginia. **4.** Courtesy Stephen Osman. **5.** Massachusetts Commandery, Military Order of the Loyal Legion, and the U.S. Army Military History Institute. **6.** NA B 2717. **7.** S 117. **8.** Fort Leavenworth Museum. **9.** Division of Archives and Manuscripts, Pennsylvania Historical and Museum Commission, courtesy U.S. Army Military History Institute.

Chapter Fifty-Nine

1. Charles Cureton. **2.** Courtesy Amon Carter Museum, 81.65/3. **3.** Courtesy Amon Carter Museum, 81.65/14. **4.** Collection of Frank Storer. **5.** SI 41683. **6.** SI 50765. **7.** NA 92-UF-3-6-22. **8.** J. P. Langellier. **9.** S 29-2.

Chapter Sixty

1. SI 77-13392. **2.** J. P. Langellier. **3.** J. P. Langellier. **4.** NA 89532. **5.** Author's collection. **6.** U.S. Army Military History Institute. **7.** KU 440. **8.** KU 585.

Chapter Sixty-One

1. SI 65147-B. **2.** Collection of Michael F. Bremer. **3.** SI 59795-C.

Chapter Sixty-Two

1. Courtesy Mike McAfee. **2.** Courtesy Mike McAfee. **3.** Courtesy Mike McAfee.

Chapter Sixty-Three

1. Dr. Charles H. Cureton. **2.** NA 111-b-1191. **3.** KU 785. **4.** Author's collection. **5.** Author's collection, courtesy Redstone Arsenal Public Affairs Office.

Chapter Sixty-Four

1. KU 169. **2.** KU 716. **3.** KU 2650. **4.** NA 119676. **5.** Patton Museum of Cavalry and Armor. **6.** S 29-3. **7.** NA 192834. **8.** Courtesy R. T. Huntington. **9.** Courtesy 82d Airborne Division Museum. **10.** Courtesy National Infantry Museum. **11.** S 32-3. **12.** DAVA CC 102758. **13.** Courtesy Shelby L. Stanton. **14.** S 29-9. **15.** S 29-16. **16.** S 29-6. **17.** Courtesy Shelby L. Stanton. **18.** S 30-2. **19.** Author's collection. **20.** Author's collection.

Chapter Sixty-Five

1. Courtesy Ronn Palm and U.S. Army Military History Institute. **2.** NA RG 92-UF-3-1-2. **3.** NA RG 92-UF-3-6-12. **4.** Author's collection. **5.** Courtesy Sergeant H. H. Booker, 2d. **6.** Custer Battlefield National Monument. **7.** KU 1643. **8.** NA RB-2978. **9.** NA RG 92-UF-3-6-9. **10.** KU 2070. **11.** Fort Sill Museum. **12.** Fort Sill Museum. **13.** NA 49459. **14.** NA 27543. **15.** KU 2931. **16.** KU 2956. **17.** NA 32381. **18.** NA 51528. **19.** KU 3155. **20.** NA 128874, courtesy *Army* magazine. **21.** Author's collection, ETO photograph 45 7066. **22.** NA 223841, courtesy Stephen Henry. **23.** NA C 11533. **24.** NA CC 11534.

Chapter Sixty-Six

1. Department of the Army. **2.** U.S. Army Natick Labs, photograph 1150-4-89. **3.** NA 23893. **4.** U.S. Army Natick Labs, photograph 2345-5-81. **5.** Courtesy Patton Museum of Cavalry and Armor. **6.** Courtesy Patton Museum of Cavalry and Armor, Bk 5B-5. **7.** USAF photograph collection, National Air and Space Museum, 69128AC. **8.** Courtesy Eglin Air Force Base Museum and Ed Gliniecki. **9.** Courtesy Hank Johnson. **10.** U.S. Army Natick Labs, 1042-1761-3-77.

Chapter Sixty-Seven

1. KU 1869. **2.** NA 94-UM-204123. **3.** Courtesy R. T. Huntington. **4.** Gift from Charles A. Gill. **5.** U.S. Army, SC 222624. **6.** Department of the Army. **7.** Gift from Sergeant Major of the Army Connelly. **8.** S 27-3. **9.** S 27-2. **10.** S 27-1. **11.** Author's collection. **12.** NA 96053-85. **13.** Author's collection. **14.** Department of the Army. **15.** DAVA CC 102757.

Chapter Sixty-Eight

1. KU 722. **2.** NA 92-UF-3-10-2. **3.** NA 91865. **4.** KU 631. **5.** KU 1213. **6.** S 26-6. **7.** KU 866. **8.** KU 833. **9.** KU 2418.

Chapter Sixty-Nine

1. Author's collection. **2.** Courtesy M. C. Bruun. **3.** Courtesy Gil Sanow. **4.** KU 2596.1. **5.** KU 2714. **6.** KU 3184.5. **7.** KU 1957. **8.** KU 1983. **9.** S 29-10. **10.** KU 3362. **11.** KU 3177.9. **12.** S 29-12. **13.** KU 2435.4.

Chapter Seventy

1. NA B 1858. **2.** NA 21333. **3.** KU 3096. **4.** NA 102370. **5.** S 19-14. **6.** S 118. **7.** S 29-1. **8.** S 29-13. **9.** NA 115750 and 115762. **10.** Gift from C. A. Gill. **11.** NA 128861, courtesy Association of the U.S. Army. **12.** S 120. **13.** NA 102317. **14.** NA 102119. **15.** Pentagon photograph USAPA-62-A-717-1. **16.** Hank Johnson. **17.** NA 190720. **18.** S 28-1. **19.** Paul Braddock. **20.** K. C. Emerson. **21.** S 29-11. **22.** S 32-1. **23.** S 114.

Chapter Seventy-One

1. NA 92864. **2.** NA 99367. **3.** NA 129706. **4.** DA regulations. **5.** DAVA 339974-S. **6.** DA regulations. **7.** Author's collection. **8.** DA regulations. **9.** DA regulations. **10.** DA regulations.

Chapter Seventy-Two

1. Quartermaster Museum. **2.** National Library of Medicine, 81-150. **3.** SI 73-6442. **4.** SI 51671. **5.** J. Duncan Campbell. **6.** Courtesy Stephen Osman. **7.** SI 51668. **8.** SI 61122. **9.** SI 42260.

10. Courtesy Amon Carter Museum, 81.65/9. **12.** S S-6-7. **13.** S S-6-4. **14.** SI AH 51665. **15.** SI 73-2613.

Chapter Seventy-Three

1. NA 92-UF-2-11-6. **2.** NA 92-UF-2-11-7. **3.** KU 565. **4.** From *Report of the Quartermaster General, 1881,* courtesy Smithsonian Institution. **5.** National Library of Medicine, 79-369. **6.** SI 82-7802. **7.** SI 73-6440. **8.** S S-6-2. **9.** Author's collection. **10.** Courtesy Frank E. Storer. **11.** KU 2422. **12.** Dr. K. C. Emerson. **13.** Courtesy Frank E. Storer. **14.** SI 73-2592. **15.** Arizona Historical Society. **16.** KU 446. **17.** Buddy Patterson. **18.** KU 1384. **19.** Author's collection. **20.** U.S. Army, courtesy *Army* magazine. **21.** U.S. Army, courtesy Army Marksmanship Unit. **22.** Courtesy Lawrence Johnson. **23.** Courtesy George E. Nicholas, Jr., and Lawrence Johnson. **24.** Courtesy Lieutenant Colonel Frank Robertson. **25.** Collection of Anthony Gero.

Chapter Seventy-Four

1. KU 3071. **2.** S 30-6. **3.** Author's collection. **4.** S 30-4. **5.** Courtesy Frank E. Storer. **6.** Courtesy Kentucky Military Museum. **7.** U.S. Army pho-tograph, courtesy Patton Museum of Cavalry and Armor. **8.** Author's collection. **9.** NA 239816. **10.** NA 449851. **11.** U.S. Army, courtesy *Army* magazine. **12.** Department of Defense Still Media Depository, CC 058084. **13.** Author's collection. **14.** U.S. Army, courtesy *Army* magazine. **15.** Department of Defense Still Media Depository, DF-ST-86-07670. **16.** Department of Defense Still Media Depository, DF-ST-88-10384. **17.** Author's collection. **18.** Buddy Patterson. **19.** Author's collection. **20.** Author's collection. **21.** Courtesy National Infantry Museum.

Chapter Seventy-Five

1. Courtesy Richard T. Graney. **2.** NA 21356. **3.** NA 33116. **4.** Courtesy Armed Forces Institute of Pathology. **5.** NA 163521. **6.** NA 163524. **7.** DAVA C 2927. **8.** Author's collection (gift from Lt. Col. Beatrice Whitcomb, USA Ret.). **9.** Courtesy Center for Military History. **10.** Still Media Records Center CC-102761. **11.** Still Media Records Center CC-97549. **12.** Still Media Records Center CC-20639. **13.** Author's collection. **14.** Still Media Depository. **15.** Author's collection. **16.** Department of Defense Still Media Records Center.

Chapter Seventy-Six

1. KU 2256.1. **2.** Collection of Leonard F. Ball. **3.** S 26-5. **4.** KU 1414. **5.** Courtesy James Wilson. **6.** NA 96753. **7.** KU 2037. **8.** NA 90926. **9.** KU 1909. **10.** KU 2142. **11.** U.S. Army, Frontier Army Museum, Fort Leavenworth, Kansas. **12.** NA 96185. **13.** NA 96183. **14.** 1st Battalion (Reinforced), 3d Infantry. **15.** S 32-4. **16.** NA 115753. **17.** DAVA 461708. **18.** U.S. Military Academy. **19.** U.S. Army Band. **20.** 1st Battalion (Reinforced), 3d Infantry.

Chapter Seventy-Seven

1. KU 175. **2.** KU 1501. **3.** KU 1397. **4.** NA 92-UF-3-10-3. **5.** KU 2216. **6.** KU 2797. **7.** KU 3384.5. **8.** Author's collection. **9.** DAVA CC 099453. **10.** U.S. Army photograph, Fifth U.S. Army, 41-133-6793-1/AK-71, courtesy Lieutenant Colonel James B. Emerson. **11.** Courtesy Lieutenant Colonel James B. Emerson.

Chapter Seventy-Eight

1. Old Fort Niagara Association. **2.** S 32-5. **3.** Department of the Army. **4.** Department of the Army. **5.** NA 96184. **6.** S 29-7. **7.** Department of the Army. **8.** Department of the Army. **9.** DAVA SC 679265. **10.** S 113.

Chapter Seventy-Nine

1. NA 162039. **2.** Author's collection. **3.** NA 35283. **4.** KU 3031. **5.** NA 98326. **6.** NA 131554. **7.** NA 162514-B. **8.** Author's collection. **9.** DAVA C-2918. **10.** NA 368423. **11.** DAVA SC 220085. **12.** NA 133798. **13.** NA 1357 18. **14.** NA 320189. **15.** NA 320193. **16.** NA 208-N-27948. **17.** NA 186935.

Chapter Eighty

1. NA 388590. **2.** Courtesy Terry Avery. **3.** Courtesy Terry Avery. **4.** Still Media Records Center SC-60556 1. **5.** Still Media Records Center CC-25357. **6.** Still Media Records Center CC-17962. **7.** Still Media Records Center CC-102774. **8.** Still Media Records Center CC-90698. **9.** Still Media Records Center CC-95810. **10.** Courtesy U.S. Army Center for Military History. **11.** Still Media Records Center CC-102773. **12.** Still Media Records Center CC-16510. **13.** Courtesy U.S. Army Band. **14.** Still Media Records Center SC-545132. **15.** Still Media Records Center CC-12157. **16.** Department of the Army. **17.** Still Media Records Center CC-102764. **18.** Still Media Records Center CC-98923. **19.** Still Media Records Center SC-679265. **20.** Author's collection. **21.** Army Nurse Corps Historian, U.S. Army Center for Military History. **22.** Department of the Army.

Appendix

1. S C-4-20. **2.** S 26-1-7. **3.** S 26-1-2. **4.** S 20-15-3. **5.** S 26-1-8. **6.** S 26-1-5. **7.** S 22-9-1. **8.** S 26-2-1. **9.** S 22-19-1. **10.** S 22-14-4. **11.** S 26-1-6. **12.** S 26-1-4. **13.** S 25-9-6. **14.** S 14-10-6. **15.** S 15-1-10. **16.** S 21-3-8. **17.** S 20-6-7. **18.** S C-1-1. **19.** Courtesy Terry Avery. **20.** Courtesy Terry Avery. **21.** Courtesy Terry Avery. **22.** S 22-9-3. **23.** S 22-19-2. **24.** S 22-10-2. **25.** S 22-16-2. **26.** S 22-16-1. **27.** S 4-6-3. **28.** S 11-1-1. **29.** S 6-9-5. **30.** S 22-15-2. **31.**22-15-3.

Index

References to illustrations are printed in italics.